HISTORY IN DISPUTE

ADVISORY BOARD

HISTORY IN DISPUTE

Volume 20

Classical Antiquity and Classical Studies

Edited by **Paul Allen Miller and Charles Platter**

A MANLY, INC. BOOK

Detroit • New York • San Francisco • San Diego • New Haven, Conn. • Waterville, Maine • London • Munich

History in Dispute
Volume 20: Classical Antiquity and Classical Studies
Paul Allen Miller and Charles Platter

Editorial Directors
Matthew J. Bruccoli and Richard Layman

Series Editor
Anthony J. Scotti Jr.

For more information, contact
Thomson Gale
27500 Drake Rd.
Farmington Hills, MI 48331-3535
Or you can visit our Internet site at http://www.gale.com.

LIBRARY OF CONGRESS CONTROL NUMBER: 00-266495
1-55862-496-1

Printed in the United States of America
10 9 8 7 6 5 4 3 2

CONTENTS

About the Series xi

Acknowledgments xii

Permissions xiii

Preface by Paul Allen Miller and Charles Platter xiv

Chronology by Paul Allen Miller and Charles Platter xviii

Classical Studies: *Black Athena:* Does Martin Bernal's *Black Athena* make an important contribution to our understanding of the ancient world? 1

Yes. *Black Athena* makes a critical contribution to our understanding of the ancient world by significantly challenging the questions we ask of the past and our motivations for asking them. *(Patrice D. Rankine)* 2

No. *Black Athena* does not make a critical contribution to our understanding of the ancient world because Martin Bernal's study of the past, which includes his use of myth and source criticism, is fundamentally flawed. *(Patrice D. Rankine)* 6

Classical Studies: German Philological Tradition: Does the German philological tradition offer a superior knowledge of antiquity to that of British amateurism? 11

Yes. German philology far surpasses the British tradition in the production of useful knowledge about antiquity. *(William M. Calder III)* 12

No. British scholarship produces superior results in the long run, both in terms of a well-rounded knowledge of antiquity and of the resulting education offered to students. *(Ward W. Briggs Jr.)* 15

Classical Studies: Homosexuality: Did the concept of homosexuality exist in the ancient world? 19

Yes. Homosexuality was a meaningful concept in the ancient world, even if the word itself did not exist. *(Amy Richlin)* 20

No. While sexual acts between members of the same sex were common in antiquity, homosexuality did not exist as a category of personal identity. *(Jerise Fogel)* 23

Classical Studies: The Marxist Approach: Does Marxism remain a valid historical approach to the ancient world? 29

Yes. Marxist concepts have proven their worth in the understanding of ancient history and culture, even as Marxism continues to offer a coherent theoretical rationale for a holistic understanding of the ancient world. *(Peter W. Rose)* 30

No. The historical record does not permit a classical Marxist interpretation of history, and Marxism's heuristic value has been largely superceded by feminism, cultural studies, and other nontraditional approaches. *(Charles Platter)* 33

Classical Studies: Modern Critical Theory: Is modern critical theory a useful tool for understanding the ancient Mediterranean world? 38

Yes. Contemporary literary theory offers new insights into Greek and Roman literature and culture and provides a means for linking the ancient world to the world of today. *(Carl A. Rubino)* **39**

No. Critical theory is a form of obscurantist terrorism that is harmful to humanistic study as a whole and particularly deleterious to classics. *(Steven J. Willett)* **41**

Classical Studies: Translation: Does translation inevitably distort our engagement with the ancient world? **47**

Yes. Translation distorts our engagement with the ancient world because modern English does not offer the linguistic resources to convey classical culture. *(Elizabeth Vandiver)* **48**

No. Since ancient languages are no longer spoken, texts in those languages are fixed and more accessible through translation. *(Paul Allen Miller)* **52**

Greece: Aeschylus: Does democracy ensure the triumph of right over might as Aeschylus maintains in the *Eumenides?* **56**

Yes. In the *Eumenides,* Aeschylus presents the foundations of a concept of justice based on law and procedure. *(Yves Citton)* **57**

No. The institution of law and procedure is merely the formalization of power. *(Yves Citton)* **60**

Greece: Alcibiades: Was Alcibiades self-absorbed and irresponsible, caring little for the interests of Athens? **65**

Yes. Alcibiades was a megalomaniac who overturned the conservative policies of his protector, Pericles, in favor of reckless Athenian expansion. In the end, he was less Athens's savior than a cause of its downfall. *(Joel Allen)* **66**

No. Many of the stories told about Alcibiades are fictitious. In fact, his life was filled with many worthy achievements. *(Joel Allen)* **68**

Greece: Aristophanes: Was Aristophanes a reactionary? **72**

Yes. Behind the evident levity that pervades the work of Aristophanes lay the political attitudes of a man deeply suspicious of the Athenian democracy and with pronounced conservative politics. *(Charles Platter)* **73**

No. Although his comedies have a conservative side, Aristophanes faced many pressures in order to be a successful dramatist, and it would have been of only limited use for him to espouse one political position over another. His heavy use of allusion and parody combine to produce texts that are highly ironic with multiple meanings. *(Charles Platter)* **76**

Greece: Aristotle versus Plato: Did Aristotle make a more lasting contribution to philosophy than Plato? **81**

Yes. Aristotle has a more coherent theory of the good. *(Chad Wiener)* **82**

No. Plato is a greater philosopher than Aristotle because he demarcated the intellectual domain that philosophy occupied and in which Aristotle's own philosophic activity took place. Plato, moreover, created the conditions in which the mode of consciousness underlying Aristotle's work was able to crystallize and express itself. *(Matthew E. Kenney)* **85**

Greece: Demosthenes: Was Demosthenes' call to Athenian resistance against Philip II of Macedon doomed from the start? **89**

Yes. In spite of Demosthenes' best hopes, Athens's decline had been irreversible since losing the Peloponnesian War. It had neither the economic nor the political strength to mount a credible resistance to Macedonian hegemony. *(Joel Allen)* **90**

No. Demosthenes' resistance to Macedonian rule was not ill-conceived; his advice was heeded too late. *(Joel Allen)* **92**

Greece: Elgin Marbles: Should the Elgin Marbles be returned to Greece? 97

Yes. The Elgin Marbles should be returned to Greece because their illegitimate removal from the Parthenon compromised the integrity of the temple. Moreover, the Greeks have begun to implement the conditions set by the British government for the return of the marbles, most notably the restoration of the Acropolis and the building of a new museum. *(Nancy Sultan)* 98

No. The marbles should remain in the British Museum because Lord Elgin's legal removal saved them from destruction. They are available to a wider public than they would be in Athens, and their return to Greece would set a precedent that would empty many great museums of their collections. *(Nancy Sultan)* 101

Greece: Euripides: Was Euripides a misogynist? 106

Yes. Euripides' work demonstrates misogynistic tendencies. His plays portray women either as monsters who would disrupt the family or the state, or as models of self-sacrifice. Those few female characters who are empowered in his plays merely act like men. *(Paul D. Streufert)* 107

No. Euripides' plays demonstrate a sort of protofeminism rather than misogyny. The variety of strong and sympathetic women characters found in his plays demonstrates his commitment to critiquing patriarchal oppression in Athens. *(Paul D. Streufert)* 110

Greece: Herodotus: Was Herodotus the father of history? 114

Yes. Herodotus's attempt to describe fully events of the recent past and to explain the causes of those events marks the beginning of historiography in the Western European tradition. *(Elizabeth Vandiver)* 115

No. Although Herodotus's conception of the past as something susceptible to rational inquiry was groundbreaking, he did not provide a good example of how to put this concept into practice. *(William E. Hutton)* 118

Greece: Hesiod: Was Hesiod an oral poet? 123

Yes. Hesiod composed his songs without the use of writing. He did not inherit a written text, and he did not transmit one to others through writing. *(Apostolos N. Athanassakis)* 124

No. Hesiod composed his songs in writing; this non-oral method of composition might have included some written text inherited by him. *(Apostolos N. Athanassakis)* 126

Greece: Homer: Was Homer an oral poet? 130

Yes. The style of Homeric epic is not one of a poet who composed in writing, and comparative evidence from oral poetry in other cultures suggests traditional poetry is able to sustain large-scale compositions along the lines of the *Iliad* and the *Odyssey*. *(Robin Mitchell-Boyask)* 131

No. Homer's *Iliad* and *Odyssey* are longer than oral poems are likely to have been, and both show evidence of a thoughtful reworking of traditional material that is probably the product of written composition. *(Charles Platter)* 134

Greece: Library at Alexandria: Were there repositories other than the Ptolemies' Library at Alexandria of equal value in preserving Greek culture? 138

Yes. The existence of the Alexandrian Library was not a precondition for the production of standard texts of Greek authors or for the survival of Greek literature. Greek literary culture was widely diffused and practiced throughout the entire Mediterranean basin long before the conquests of Alexander and the beginning of the "Hellenistic" era. *(T. Keith Dix)* 139

No. The Ptolemies assembled the greatest collection of Greek literature from the classical period, during a time crucial for the transformation and transmission of the Greek cultural heritage, and they inspired imitators among the other Hellenistic dynasties and the Roman emperors. *(T. Keith Dix)* **141**

Greece: Literacy: Was literacy a sufficient force for producing the cultural revolution in Greece? **145**

Yes. The coming of literacy produced a cultural revolution in Greece by changing the structure of language. *(Paul Allen Miller)* **146**

No. Literacy did not produce a cultural revolution in Greece. Such assertions are based on oversimplified notions of what causes cultural change and the difference between oral and literate cultures. *(Paul Allen Miller)* **149**

Greece: Plato as an Aristocrat: Was Plato an aristocratic sympathizer with the oligarchic factions within the Athenian state?. . . . **154**

Yes. Plato was an aristocrat who favored rule by those with superior natures and thoroughly detested the democracy of his time. *(Charles Platter)* **155**

No. Plato, although an aristocrat of the highest pedigree, broke with his class when he met Socrates and developed a devastating critique of traditional aristocratic thinking about politics. *(Charles Platter)* **159**

Greece: Sappho: Does Sappho's poetry represent a departure from the traditional masculine view of love? **164**

Yes. Sappho's poetry departs from a traditional masculine view of love by presenting love relations as mutual and reciprocal, in contrast to the model of love relations found in Archaic Greek male poets. *(Ellen Greene)* **165**

No. Sappho depicts love relations as driven by domination and conquest. Her poems also treat typically male themes such as politics and philosophy. *(Ellen Greene)*. **167**

Greece: Sophists: Did the sophists exercise a pernicious influence on Greek culture? **172**

Yes. Some sophists, by cultivating a program of moral relativism, propounded teachings that had deleterious effects on Greek political and social life. *(Patrick O'Sullivan)* **173**

No. The sophists expounded richly diverse views on a range of issues, not necessarily renouncing ethical principles but rather opening up new areas for critical speculation and debate that enhanced the intellectual life of their own times and beyond. *(Patrick O'Sullivan)* **176**

Greece: Sports: Were ancient Greek sports amateur athletics? **181**

Yes. Ancient Greek athletes were not paid professionals, and the awards they received were usually honorary rather than financial. *(David H. J. Larmour)* **182**

No. Ancient Greek athletes frequently received monetary and material rewards, which effectively gave them a status similar to that of professionals. There is no ancient term that corresponds to the word *amateur. (David H. J. Larmour)*. **184**

Roman Period: the *Aeneid*: Was the *Aeneid* Augustan propaganda? **189**

Yes. The *Aeneid* was written in response to Augustus's deliberate and explicit cultural program. In spite of the immense subtlety of the poem, its fundamental endorsement of Roman and Augustan dominance cannot be avoided. *(Micaela Janan)*. **190**

No. Far from being a piece of propaganda, the *Aeneid* is a poem suffused with loss, suffering, and nostalgia. Virgil may well have "believed in Rome," but he was well aware of the immense costs involved in Rome's triumph. *(Carl A. Rubino)* 194

Roman Period: Cato: Were Cato's attacks on Hellenism pure political opportunism? 197

Yes. Cato's attacks on Greek culture at Rome were undertaken purely to advance his own position in the Roman ruling class. *(Philip Thibodeau)* 198

No. Cato's outbursts against Hellenism were based on a conviction that Greek culture had value but needed to be kept subordinate to Roman interests and customs. *(Philip Thibodeau)* 200

Roman Period: Christian Neoplatonism: Did Christian Neoplatonism evolve directly from the ancient philosophical tradition? 204

Yes. Christian Neoplatonists adhered to ancient philosophical traditions and gained enormous influence throughout the Christian world in the first millennium. *(Carlos Steel)* 205

No. Christian Neoplatonists rejected the tradition of open philosophical debate. *(Jan Opsomer)* 208

Roman Period: Cicero Versus Caesar: Were Cicero's contributions as a political figure ultimately more responsible and significant than Caesar's? 212

Yes. Cicero was a true statesman who dedicated himself to expanding the intellectual and moral frontiers of his compatriots. *(Carl A. Rubino)* 213

No. Cicero failed to recognize the fundamental currents of political change occurring around him. Caesar, by contrast, not only diagnosed the crisis correctly but was also able to act decisively to shape events. *(David H. J. Larmour)* 216

Roman Period: Donatist Controversy: Did Donatist bishops fail to offer a convincing defense of their beliefs at the Conference of 411 C.E. in Carthage? 221

Yes. The irrational and erratic behavior of the Donatist bishops during their debate with their Catholic antagonists in 411 C.E. clearly showed not only the bad faith in which they agreed to the proceedings but also the lack of a logical and legal argument that they could employ to defend their case. *(Erika T. Hermanowicz)* 222

No. The Donatists, who were faced with a hostile imperial court and bureaucratic overseers whose mission was to ensure their defeat, employed various strategies in order to fashion a transcript of the meeting that could be used to their benefit in subsequent legal appeals. *(Erika T. Hermanowicz)* 226

Roman Period: Elegists: Were the Roman elegists protofeminists? 231

Yes. The Roman elegists presented their *puellae* (beloveds) as powerful, autonomous women who refused to assume accepted roles of submission to men. *(Christel Johnson)* 232

No. The Roman elegists may have bent conventional male gender roles, but they did not offer women equality nor did their poetry seek to change the place of women in Roman society. *(Ellen Greene)* 234

Roman Period: Fall of the Republic: Was Roman decline inevitable with the fall of the republic? 238

Yes. The republican constitution was what made Rome great; without that structure, decline was inevitable. *(Mark A. Beck)* 239

No. The notion that the collapse of the republic led to the decline of Rome is a manifest ideological fiction that cannot withstand a rigorous examination in terms of chronology, the instability of the republic, the benefits of the imperial system,

and the class biases of the ancient commentators.
(Paul Allen Miller) 242

Roman Period: Gladiatorial Contests: Was the purpose of the gladiatorial contests to satisfy the blood lust of the Roman mob? 249

Yes. The gladiatorial games drew upon the bloodthirsty urges of a populace hardened by continual warfare and were used by the emperors as a means of keeping the mob entertained. *(David H. J. Larmour)* 250

No. Although they were spectacles of bloodshed, the gladiatorial games were designed as a manifestation of deeply rooted Roman values and aimed to display to the populace the power of their empire. *(David H. J. Larmour)* 253

Roman Period: Ovid: Does Ovid's exilic poetry represent a principled resistance to imperial tyranny? 257

Yes. In his exilic poetry Ovid subtly criticizes the ambitions of the emperor Augustus. *(Paul Allen Miller)* 258

No. Although his exilic poetry is full of ambiguities, Ovid acknowledges and accepts the power and authority of Rome. *(Paul Allen Miller)* 261

Roman Period: Ovid versus Virgil: Has Ovid's *Metamorphoses* had a greater influence than Virgil's *Aeneid* on postclassical literature? 265

Yes. Ovid's *Metamorphoses* has had a greater influence upon postclassical literature, as exemplified through its many translations and stage adaptations. *(Christel Johnson)* 266

No. Unlike Ovid's epic, whose main theme is indisputably metamorphosis, Virgil's *Aeneid* presents a nexus of themes that have supported a wide variety of interpretations. *(Sarah Spence)* 269

Roman Period: Pausanias: Is Pausanias a reliable source for the history of ancient Greece? 273

Yes. Pausanias was an honest and diligent researcher; his *Description of Greece* preserves much valuable information from antiquity that no other source provides. *(William E. Hutton)* 274

No. Pausanias wrote during an age when proper historical methodology was not observed or even recognized; the information in his *Description of Greece* is frequently inaccurate. *(William E. Hutton)* 278

Roman Period: Plutarch: Is Plutarch the founder of modern biography? 283

Yes. Plutarch is rightly considered the founder of modern biography because he had a profound influence upon later practitioners of the genre, especially Samuel Johnson and James Boswell. *(Mark A. Beck)* 284

No. Plutarch cannot be termed the founder of modern biography because his methods and concerns are not those of the biographer as the term is understood today. He wrote most of the *Lives* in pairs for the moral and philosophical instruction of his readers. *(David H. J. Larmour)* 287

Roman Period: Tiberius Gracchus: Was Tiberius Gracchus a honest champion of the Roman underclass? 292

Yes. Tiberius Gracchus was a determined champion of what he saw as the best interests of the Roman people. *(Joel Allen)* 293

No. Tiberius Gracchus was a failed aristocratic politician who manufactured a social crisis for his own political gain. *(Joel Allen)* 296

References 299

Contributors 311

Index 313

ABOUT THE SERIES

History in Dispute is an ongoing series designed to present, in an informative and lively pro-con format, different perspectives on major historical events drawn from all time periods and from all parts of the globe. The series was developed in response to requests from librarians and educators for a history-reference source that will help students hone essential critical-thinking skills while serving as a valuable research tool for class assignments.

Individual volumes in the series concentrate on specific themes, eras, or subjects intended to correspond to the way history is studied at the academic level. For example, early volumes cover such topics as the Cold War, American Social and Political Movements, and World War II. Volume subtitles make it easy for users to identify contents at a glance and facilitate searching for specific subjects in library catalogues.

Each volume of *History in Dispute* includes up to fifty entries, centered on the overall theme of that volume and chosen by an advisory board of historians for their relevance to the curriculum. Entries are arranged alphabetically by the name of the event or issue in its most common form. (Thus, in Volume 1, the issue "Was detente a success?" is presented under the chapter heading "Detente.")

Each entry begins with a brief statement of the opposing points of view on the topic, followed by a short essay summarizing the issue and outlining the controversy. At the heart of the entry, designed to engage students' interest while providing essential information, are the two or more lengthy essays, written specifically for this publication by experts in the field, each presenting one side of the dispute.

In addition to this substantial prose explication, entries also include excerpts from primary-source documents, other useful information typeset in easy-to-locate shaded boxes, detailed entry bibliographies, and photographs or illustrations appropriate to the issue.

Other features of *History in Dispute* volumes include: individual volume introductions by academic experts, tables of contents that identify both the issues and the controversies, chronologies of events, names and credentials of advisers, brief biographies of contributors, thorough volume bibliographies for more information on the topic, and a comprehensive subject index.

ACKNOWLEDGMENTS

Philip B. Dematteis, *Production manager.*

Kathy Lawler Merlette, *Office manager.*

Carol A. Cheschi, *Administrative support.*

Ann-Marie Holland, *Accounting.*

Sally R. Evans, *Copyediting supervisor.* Phyllis A. Avant, Caryl Brown, Melissa D. Hinton, Philip I. Jones, Rebecca Mayo, Nadirah Rahimah Shabazz, and Nancy E. Smith, *Copyediting staff.*

Zoe R. Cook, *Series team leader, layout and graphics.* Janet E. Hill, *Layout and graphics supervisor.* Sydney E. Hammock, *Graphics and prepress.*

Mark J. McEwan and Walter W. Ross, *Photography editors.*

Amber L. Coker, *Permissions editor.*

James F. Tidd Jr., *Database manager.*

Joseph M. Bruccoli, *Digital photographic copy work.*

Donald K. Starling, *Systems manager.*

Kathleen M. Flanagan, *Typesetting supervisor.* Patricia Marie Flanagan and Pamela D. Norton, *Typesetting staff.*

Walter W. Ross, *Library researcher.*

The staff of the Thomas Cooper Library, University of South Carolina are unfailingly helpful: Tucker Taylor, *Circulation department head, Thomas Cooper Library, University of South Carolina.* John Brunswick, *Interlibrary-loan department head.* Virginia W. Weathers, *Reference department head.* Brette Barclay, Marilee Birchfield, Paul Cammarata, Gary Geer, Michael Macan, Tom Marcil, and Sharon Verba, *Reference librarians.*

PERMISSIONS

ILLUSTRATIONS

P. 13 Mengs, Metropolitan Museum, New York

P. 42 ©Sophie Bassouls/CORBIS, 0000232075-008

P. 53 Lilly Library, Indiana University

P. 69 ©Bettmann/CORBIS, F9576

P. 87 ©Ted Spiegel/CORBIS, GL001738

P. 93 Ny Carlsberg Glyptothek, Copenhagen, I. N. 2782

P. 99 ©Reuters/CORBIS, UT0031451

P. 140 ©Bettmann/CORBIS, BE063187

P. 150 Egypt Exploration Society

P. 166 Manchester City Art Gallery, U.K.

P. 192 ©National Gallery Collection; by kind permission of the Trustees of the National Gallery, London/CORBIS, NG001700

P. 219 Robert Harding Picture Library, London

P. 228 ©Bettmann/CORBIS, PG3692

P. 235 British Museum

P. 240 ©Araldo de Luca/CORBIS, DE004671

P. 254 ©Alinari Archives/CORBIS, CAL-F-004237-0000

P. 262 ©Archivo Iconografico, S. A./CORBIS

P. 270 ©Roger Wood/CORBIS, RW005159

P. 276 ©age fotostock. All rights reserved

P. 289 Lilly Library, Indiana University

TEXT

P. 16 Roger Ascham, *The Schoolmaster,* edited by Lawrence V. Ryan (Ithaca, N.Y.: Cornell University Press, 1967), pp. 14–15. ©Cornell University Press

P. 43 Used by permission of Anne Mahoney, Lecturer in Classics, Tufts University

P. 75 *Wasps,* by Aristophanes, copyright 1938 by Random House, Inc., from *The Complete Greek Drama,* volume 2, edited and translated by Whitney J. Oates and Eugene O'Neill Jr. Used by permission of Lifetime Library, a division of Random House, Inc.

PREFACE

The time spanned by the essays in this volume amounts, with a few exceptions, to about one thousand years, beginning with the appearance of the Homeric poems in their present form, probably somewhere around 750 B.C.E., and ending with the controversies of the early Christian period in the fifth century C.E. Much of this span is often referred to as the "classical" period, a designation we owe to the Roman orator M. Cornelius Fronto, tutor of the emperor Marcus Aurelius (121–180 C.E.), who used the adjective *classici* ("of the highest citizen class") to refer to writers of the highest quality whose work was most worthy of emulation. This understanding of the literary and artistic production of Greece and Rome was enthusiastically adopted by Renaissance artists and intellectuals, who saw the classical tradition as a way of reinvigorating traditions that they had inherited from the Middle Ages. This classicism had a moral aspect as well. The works of the classical authors, many of which, especially those on the Greek side, had only become available in Western Europe within the last century through the sedulous endeavors of book hunters, exerted a powerful influence on education and moral reflection. Classical authors occupied a privileged place in the educational curricula, which led to the common practice among writers of using them as "authorities" to provide rhetorical support for a wide variety of positions. The great French essayist Michel de Montaigne (1533–1592) felt that this tendency led to abuse and mocked writers who quoted gratuitously from the classics. Yet, his own work is rich with quotation, showing that for him at least, and doubtless for many others in the sixteenth century, the authors of classical antiquity had an important moral-didactic role and could be used to organize moral reflection.

This interest in the classics as a source for ethical and moral reflection continued long after the Renaissance, as authors like Homer and Virgil provided readers with mythological models of virtue, while the essayist Plutarch and the historian Titus Livy singled out individuals who had led lives worthy of emulation, or whose vices had rendered them object lessons in what to avoid. Also important was the rich tradition of ancient philosophical works, beginning with those of Socrates, Plato, and Aristotle, which were read and synthesized by the Romans, adumbrated by the Stoics, Cynics, and Epicureans, then reinterpreted by Christian apologists such as St. Augustine, whose engagement with the classical tradition is especially profound. All of these authors continued to occupy important places in the educational systems of European countries and America as late as the end of the nineteenth century.

Much of this has changed today. The classics no longer occupy the same privileged position within the educational system that they once did. Latin in secondary schools, despite modest gains in the last two decades, must contend with more directly practical languages such as Spanish, and the teaching of ancient Greek has all but disappeared. The moral sensibilities of students are no longer typically formed by the examples drawn from Plutarch's *Parallel Lives,* in which the biographies of famous Greeks and Romans are compared. Some familiarity with Greek tragedy and epic, as well as Roman epic, is sometimes found, but the unquestioned supremacy of the classics has passed and will not come again in our time.

These developments say more about the changes that have taken place in Western society during the last century than they do about the classics. Internationalism and the development of new fields of knowledge have undermined the centrality of classics. Perhaps even more important has been the changing face of the student in postsecondary education. Once reliably male, white, and from privileged economic backgrounds, contemporary students are significantly more diverse. With this diversity have come interests and motivations that are not obviously best-fulfilled through the same curriculum that was appropriate for the largely homogeneous student body that attended the university in the nineteenth century and was preselected for a rather narrow range of postacademic careers. Thus, classics as a convenient system for instructing traditional elites about the ideological assumptions that undergird their way of life has largely faded from the scene. The passionate rhetoric that sometimes accompanies attempts to revive it is but a symptom of the fact that the cause is already lost.

If classics, however, is no longer regarded as the architectonic discipline—the one that organizes all the others, assigning to each its proper weight—and if our students are no longer encouraged to take the Greeks and Romans as their primary models for ethical behavior, it would nevertheless be rash to conclude that the justification for their serious study has likewise passed. The moralists, in fact, were not wrong. The authors of Greco-Roman antiquity were remarkable in their attention to philosophical and moral questions, the degree to which such questions were compatible with the requirements of citizenship, and how they might affect the structure of an ideal polity. From them, we may learn much that is relevant to understanding our own world.

In addition, by no longer looking at the ancient world with a view to justifying our own practices, we acquire a certain distance that allows us to attempt to see it as it was, with all its quirks, blemishes, and extraordinary accomplishments. This distance is an essential precondition for producing a volume such as the present one, predicated upon the idea that there is not a single, indisputable meaning to the facts of antiquity. Such an orientation would have been unthinkable for an age more heavily invested in the "rightness" of Greco-Roman culture, and where the classics were taught as unchanging monuments of the highest order—"classical" in the sense that Fronto intended it. Freed from the constrictions of this admittedly powerful and seductive vision, we can return to antiquity with the same questioning spirit that is in many ways its greatest legacy to us.

Classical culture presents us with an interesting problem that is encountered in many disciplines, to be sure, but usually not with the same systematic regularity. First, the student of antiquity is confronted with a paucity of data about the subject in question. On the surface such a claim seems far-fetched. Some of the greatest works of the ancient literary tradition—for example, Homer's *Iliad* and *Odyssey* or Hesiod's *Works and Days*—are quite long. To complain about gaps of information regarding texts such as these smacks of ingratitude. At the same time, despite the evident popularity of the *Iliad*, the *Odyssey*, and the *Works and Days* among readers in the fifth century, the poems, which appear to have reached their present form three centuries earlier, exist without any relevant *contemporary* cultural context that would explain how they came to be produced, who produced them, and how they survived. This information, to the degree that it can be said to be known at all, is not derived from the direct evidence we have at our disposal. There are no publisher contracts, reports of ticket sales, rough drafts, capsule reviews, or conversations with contemporaries—in short, the kind of data that a literary scholar would typically make use of for establishing the contemporary significance of a work is completely absent. Instead, researchers are compelled to proceed indirectly.

In the case of Homer, this has taken several directions, from attempting to make deductions based on what we know about the introduction of writing and literacy into Greece to detailed studies of Homeric dialect, classifications of the objects described by Homer (according to date, historical provenance, and types of technologies employed), and beyond. All of these approaches represent an attempt to grapple with the outstanding fact that the ancient world is silent about a great many questions that seem crucial to us for a proper understanding of the poems. What goes for the Homeric poems goes, to a greater or lesser degree, for all aspects of antiquity—literary or historical. Thus, the study of an ancient culture is a continual battle to find new ways to gather evidence from and about a stubbornly resistant past. This battle forces the researcher to develop new approaches and tactics not for the sheer pleasure of doing so, but because no better option exists for getting at the subjects in question.

Second, the issues under discussion here have maintained an unusual degree of public prominence in the nearly three thousand years that have intervened between their earliest expressions and the present day. It may be that phenomena of similar antiquity from many other cultures deserve to be studied with the same degree of assiduousness as those of classical antiquity. In point of fact, however, they have not received the same degree of loving, and occasionally hostile, attention in the West. This long familiarity means that for many classical texts and for many ancient historical problems there has already been an extended discussion, often going back a couple of millennia, as to the appropriate dispensation of the facts and their significance. The longevity of these disputes has important consequences for us here since it seriously restricts the range of historical issues that can truly be said to be "in dispute." Occasionally, a major archaeological discovery shakes up the field, or an important text thought to be lost is found in a library, or a papyrus scroll is unearthed. These events are exciting and produce lively disputes, but for most topics the sheer facts of the matter have been largely settled, often for centuries. Why is it, then, that these same topics continue to provoke the liveliest dispute among experts in the field? To answer this question, we must turn to the problem of the nature of "facts."

Methodology is crucial in evaluating data of all sorts. The truth of this statement is so obvious that, paradoxically, it is easy to neglect, especially when dealing with arguments about contemporary events or ideas about which we have strong intuitive feelings. In such cases, we are less attentive to the rhetoric that is being used to contextualize a problem, since we are already invested in what we have determined the solution must be. This sort of "refusal of thought" dominates public discourse at all levels, especially surrounding emotionally charged discourses like the contemporary American disputes over a woman's "right to choose" and the right to bear arms, among many others. It is also present in ways that are no less effective for their subtlety. Note that in the penultimate sentence, while maintaining the neutral tone of an academic essay, we adopted the rhetoric of the proponents of one side or another in the disputes mentioned. Anti-abortion activists do not, of course, describe their activity as taking away "the right to choose" but as *preserving* it—in this case "the right of the unborn." Nor do the advocates of gun control see themselves as taking away rights, but as asserting that there is a public good in restricting the sale of guns that outweighs the right of the individual.

This is not simply a question of "semantics," as is sometimes argued (although not by anyone who has ever sat in on a political strategy session), as if word choice were somehow separate from political intentions. If you accept that the abortion controversy is most accurately described as a debate about the right of a woman to personal choice, you will find it much more difficult to argue against abortion by appealing to the "right" of the unborn since the two rights may be incompatible. Similarly, if you accept that the debate on gun control is really about the individual choice, or "right," of a citizen to have guns, you will have difficulty arguing for a restriction of that right on the basis of what is good for society as a whole. Such rhetorical choices are ubiquitous, and the indirect ways in which they operate are in themselves a significant justification for an examination of how the "facts" of an historical situation are determined and how they should be organized and interpreted.

Classical civilization is well placed to be the focus of such an examination. As we have said, the basic historical facts have been in circulation for a long time. You would think that a consensus would have been reached long ago if the facts were able to be systematically presented. Instead, what we find are precisely the same sorts of disagreements that underpin the debates mentioned in the previous paragraph, along with many variations. These are not questions so much about what the facts are but about how they should be interpreted—how much a particular fact should be valued in the light of other facts that seem to point to a different conclusion, and, finally, what the total picture that emerges from the ensemble of facts should look like. It is therefore of the greatest possible value to study the essays that follow to see how in many cases the same basic set of facts allows the essays to draw conclusions that are antithetical to one another.

This aspect of the methodology is highlighted by the editorial decision to have the same author write both pro and con essays for many of the topics. This should not be viewed as inculcating a culture of insincerity by asking the authors to argue in favor of positions with which they themselves are not in agreement. Instead, it marks the explicit admission that shaping evidence in support of a particular conclusion is precisely what the historians and literary scholars do all the time. Thus, seeing what the same author does with essentially the same set of facts offers an extremely valuable look into the workshop where the ideas that drive historical inquiry are fashioned. What we find is that competent essays differ from one another, not in their ability to uncover facts, but in two interrelated choices they make. First, they differ in their determination of what facts are most relevant and what the relationship is of these to other facts deemed less relevant. From where does such a determination arise? The answer is not surprising: from previous determinations about what perspectives are valuable for historical research, what questions are in the greatest need of a solution, and, most generally, but also most crucially, what ideas about the world are most accurate, as judged by their ability to produce effective guides to the present and meaningful narratives about the past. If a writer does not think, for example, that feminism in any of its many versions has produced noteworthy positive outcomes in our society, then he or she will be unwilling to expect that a feminist look at antiquity will have anything to offer. If another admits that feminism has had positive effects on contemporary society, but also believes that historical issues can be evaluated accurately only in the exact terms in which they are proposed by contemporaries, he or she will find a panel on feminists' interpretations of antiquity full of anachronism and rather unhelpful. Most feminist interpretations of antiquity, therefore, will assume that the effect of feminism has been positive, and that feminist (or protofeminist) issues are often revealed by a close study of the evidence, even if they are not engaged explicitly. Such an argument will also choose to highlight different types of evidence than a traditional one and, unsurprisingly, will come to different conclusions. This is not a simple case of one writer being right and the other being wrong, but of two conclusions emerging from enquiries conducted under different ground rules. Yet, the differences between these sets of ground rules can easily be overstated. As we have already argued, much of the factual basis of classical studies is already accepted by all. Training in a particular discipline, in fact, largely presupposes that the would-be scholar has accepted a basic conception of what facts will be counted as evidence and how they may be used. For this reason, even arguments that are opposed often share much of the same material. Their conclusions, therefore, contain many concessions to opposing viewpoints and illustrate differences that result from differences in perspective.

In addition, the ancient Mediterranean world itself possessed a rich rhetorical tradition developed by men trained from boyhood to speak on a multitude of topics. It is no exaggeration to say that exercises of this sort formed the backbone of the training that produced not only the classic orators, from Pericles and Demosthenes to Cicero, but virtually all educated men from the fifth century B.C.E. to the fall of Rome.

This dispensation to argue both sides of the question is an important part of the legacy of the Greek sophists, as Patrick O'Sullivan notes elsewhere in this volume. It is present in the dictum attributed to Protagoras that "there are two opposite arguments on every subject" and is the justification for his famous rhetorical textbook, *Contrary Arguments,* as well as the anonymous *Dissoi logoi* (Double Arguments), which argues for and against a series of propositions on issues of contemporary interest. Likewise, dialectical and eristic exercises were an important part of philosophical training, and the ability to speak intelligently on any side of a question was highly valued. This type of education was later transported to Rome, where an indispensable part of the education of a young man would have included the composition of *suasoriae* on questions such as "Should Agamemnon sacrifice his daughter Iphigenia?" and *controversiae,* where legal cases were argued from the perspective of various imaginary characters.

Thus, in asking some of the writers to argue both sides of the issue, we have merely hewed to ancient tradition of rhetorical flexibility as a legitimate and sometimes necessary means of investigating a given topic. To our minds, however, this exercise is more than just a nostalgic evocation of the past. It is also a model for the improvement of rhetorical education in today's world: for by being compelled to advocate forcefully for a position with which one may not be in initial sympathy, and to understand it from the inside, we begin to appreciate its strengths and weaknesses with greater profundity and compassion. That has been our experience as writers, anyway, and we recommend the experiment to everyone.

This exposure to differences in perspective has the effect of opening up the classical world to us once again. Much of the best work done in classics recently attempts to incorporate multiple perspectives. This historical self-consciousness is not a postmodern aberration, but something that is intrinsic to the way in which classics has been constructed as a discipline: for the kind of historical distance mentioned above, which, we argued, allows us to look at classics from a certain remove, has been in place for a long time. Moreover, the fact that development in historical and literary research has taken place largely along the lines of national boundaries has tended to multiply rather than diminish the number of perspectives that compete for our attention. In the present volume the essays by Ward W. Briggs Jr. and William M. Calder III on the relative virtues of the British and Germanic approaches to classics illustrate this nationalistic dimension and show that this is not a recent development, but one going back at least two centuries. These essays also showcase the continued relevance of classics, no longer as a source of moral virtue to be accepted passively, nor only as a practical discourse capable of revealing much about the ancient world, but also as an exemplary discipline, with much material for *active* moral reflection, and much to contribute to a new century.

–PAUL ALLEN MILLER,
UNIVERSITY OF SOUTH CAROLINA
AND
–CHARLES PLATTER,
UNIVERSITY OF GEORGIA

CHRONOLOGY

2000–1900 B.C.E.

The Indo-European invasions of Greece occur. (*See* **Black Athena**)

1600 B.C.E.

The Minoan civilization, a Bronze Age culture, flourishes on Crete. The Minoans, renowned for their lavish palaces, clay writing tablets, paintings, pottery, and jewelry, influence the islands in the Aegean and the mainland of Greece.

1400–1200 B.C.E.

The Mycenaean civilization in Greece is at its height. A warlike people, the Mycenaeans build large cities and establish colonies in the East.

1250 B.C.E.

Troy, on the coast of northwestern Asia Minor, is sacked. This event gives rise to the epic poems of Homer, the *Iliad* and the *Odyssey*. (*See* **Homer**)

1100–1050 B.C.E.

The Dorians invade the southern Greek peninsula of Peloponnesus. This period is known as the Dark Ages of Greece, during which Mycenaean civilization collapses and linear B, the early Greek writing system, disappears.

776 B.C.E.

This year marks the traditional date for the founding of the Olympic Games. (*See* **Sports**)

753 B.C.E.

This year marks the traditional date for the founding of Rome.

750–700 B.C.E.

The Archaic period begins; Greek art becomes more naturalistic; and architecture is more harmonious and proportional.

The Phoenician alphabet is introduced. (*See* **Literacy**)

The Homeric poems as we know them begin to circulate. (*See* **Homer**)

The Greek poet Hesiod appears. His *Theogony* describes the origins of the world and the birth of the gods. A later didactic poem, *Works and Days,* recounts his daily experiences as well as precepts, fables, and allegories. (*See* **Hesiod**)

600–580 B.C.E.

The tyrant Pittacus rules at Mytilene; he voluntarily resigns power.

The lyric poets Sappho and Alcaeus are active on Lesbos. Sappho writes on love and personal relationships and is called the "tenth Muse" by Plato; Alcaeus writes on the same themes as well as hymns and political odes. (*See* **Sappho**)

594–593 B.C.E.

Solon is elected archon at Athens. Known as one of the Seven Wise Men of Greece, Solon initiates economic and constitutional reforms, including a more humane law code.

582 B.C.E.

The Pythian and Isthmian Games are founded. (*See* **Sports**)

573 B.C.E.

The Nemean Games achieve Pan-Hellenic status. (*See* **Sports**)

546–510 B.C.E.

The tyranny of the Peisistratids in Athens is marked by religious reforms, improved water supply and a major building program, expanded industry and commerce, and the promotion of internal order.

The last Etruscan king is expelled from Rome, and the republic is founded.

Circa 525 B.C.E.

Aeschylus is born. Ranked with Euripides and Sophocles as the greatest Greek tragic poets, Aeschylus is credited with writing some ninety plays, including *Persians, Seven Against Thebes, Suppliants,* the *Oresteia* trilogy, and *Prometheus Bound.* (*See* **Aeschylus**)

499–494 B.C.E.

The Ionians revolt against the Persian Empire.

496 B.C.E.

Sophocles is born; he writes more than 120 plays in his lifetime, including *Oedipus Rex, Oedipus at Colonus, Antigone, Electra, Philoctetes, Ajax,* and *Trachinian Women.*

490–479 B.C.E.

The Persian Wars occur, pitting the Greek city-states against the Persian Empire. The Greek historian Herodotus writes an account of the conflicts and earns the appellation *father of history.* (*See* **Herodotus**)

490 B.C.E.

At the Battle of Marathon, an Athenian army under Miltiades wins a decisive victory over a larger Persian force.

Circa 485 B.C.E.

Euripides is born; more than sixty plays are attributed to him, including *Alcestis, Medea, Hippolytus, Andromache, Madness of Heracles, Trojan Women, Iphigenia Among the Taurians,* and *Cyclops.* (*See* **Euripides**)

480 B.C.E.

A Greek naval force defeats a much larger Persian fleet in the straits of Salamis, near the Athenian port of Piraeus. This battle is followed by another important victory on land at Plataea in 479, thus effectively ending the Persian Wars.

478 B.C.E.

The Delian League is founded under Athenian leadership.

469 B.C.E.

The philosopher Socrates is born. He leaves no writings of his own, and his method of inquiry and instruction is known primarily through the writings of his pupil Plato. Along with Plato and Aristotle, Socrates establishes the philosophical foundations of Western culture. (*See* **Aristotle versus Plato**)

456 B.C.E.

Aeschylus dies. (*See* **Aeschylus**)

Circa 450 B.C.E.

The Classical period begins; Athens rises to preeminence in Greece; the Athenian enlightenment comes into its own. (*See* **Sophists**)

The playwright Aristophanes is born. He is the only extant representative of Athenian Old Comedy, which mocks social trends and prominent individuals of the community. Among his more than forty comedies are *Acharnians, The Clouds, The Wasps, The Peace, The Birds,* and *The Frogs.* (*See* **Aristophanes**)

432 B.C.E.

The Parthenon, a Doric temple of Athena located on the acropolis at Athens, is completed. (*See* **Elgin Marbles**)

431–404 B.C.E.

The Peloponnesian War is waged between Athens and Sparta and their respective allied city-states.

Circa 425 B.C.E.

Herodotus dies. (*See* **Herodotus**)

415–413 B.C.E.

At the urging of Alcibiades, the Athenians launch an unsuccessful expedition against Syracuse on Sicily. (*See* **Alcibiades**)

406–405 B.C.E.

Sophocles and Euripides die. (*See* **Euripides**)

399 B.C.E.

Socrates is put on trial for impiety and corruption of the youth of Athens. He is sentenced to death and dies surrounded by his disciples.

Circa 385 B.C.E.

Plato founds the Academy. (*See* **Aristotle versus Plato** and **Plato as an Aristocrat**)

Aristophanes dies. (*See* **Aristophanes**)

351 B.C.E.

The Athenian orator and statesman Demosthenes delivers his first *Phillipic* against

Macedonian hegemony in Greece. (*See* **Demosthenes**)

338 B.C.E.

Philip II of Macedon defeats the mainland Greeks at the Battle of Chaeronea, thus beginning direct Macedonian rule of Greece.

336 B.C.E.

Alexander the Great takes the throne after the assassination of his father, Philip II.

335 B.C.E.

Aristotle, a former student of Plato and the mentor of Alexander of Great, founds the Lyceum. (*See* **Aristotle versus Plato**)

334 B.C.E.

Alexander the Great crosses the Hellespont to begin the conquest of Asia.

331 B.C.E.

The port city of Alexandria is founded in Egypt.

323 B.C.E.

Alexander the Great dies in Babylon at the age of thirty-three. From this date is usually reckoned the beginning of the Hellenistic period, in which Greek culture spreads to Egypt and Asia.

322 B.C.E.

Aristotle and Demosthenes die. (*See* **Aristotle versus Plato** and **Demosthenes**)

305 B.C.E.

Ptolemey I Soter assumes the royal title in Egypt.

294–290 B.C.E.

Ptolemy I organizes the Museum and Library at Alexandria. (*See* **Library at Alexandria**)

Rome's victory over the Samnites completes Roman domination of central Italy.

280–275 B.C.E.

Pyrrhus, king of Epirus, invades Italy in order to aid Tarentum against the Romans.

264 B.C.E.

The funeral of Junius Brutus Pera marks the occasion of the first gladiatorial games in Rome. (*See* **Gladiatorial Contests**)

264–241 B.C.E.

The First Punic War is waged between Rome and the North African city-state of Carthage. The Carthaginian (Punic) Empire is forced to cede Sicily and the Lipari Islands and to pay an indemnity.

218–202 B.C.E.

The Second Punic War results in Roman hegemony over the western Mediterranean.

184 B.C.E.

Cato the Elder is elected censor in Rome. (*See* **Cato**)

164 B.C.E.

A priestly family known as the Maccabees leads a Jewish revolt, seizes Jerusalem, and purifies the temple.

149–146 B.C.E.

In the Third Punic War, Carthage is finally sacked by the Romans and its citizens enslaved.

146 B.C.E.

The Greeks revolt against Roman authority; Corinth is sacked.

133 B.C.E.

The tribune Tiberius Sempronius Gracchus promotes the redistribution of public land. (*See* **Tiberius Gracchus**)

123–121 B.C.E.

The tribune Gaius Sempronius Gracchus tries to enforce his brother's land reform and guarantee a fixed low price for grain for Roman citizens. (*See* **Tiberius Gracchus**)

107 B.C.E.

Marius, consul for the first of seven times, abolishes property qualifications for serving in the Roman army.

90–88 B.C.E.

During the Social War, Rome defeats rebellious Italian allies *(socii);* Roman citizenship is granted to all Italians.

88 B.C.E.

Mithridates II (the Great) of Parthia leads a major rebellion against Rome and invades Greece.

87–81 B.C.E.

The Roman Republic is rocked by civil wars.

81 B.C.E.
Sulla becomes dictator and posts proscription lists.

63 B.C.E.
The consul Cicero quells the conspiracy of Catiline and orders the execution of some of the conspirators. (*See* **Cicero versus Caesar**)

60 B.C.E.
Caesar, Pompey, and Crassus form the first triumvirate. (*See* **Cicero versus Caesar**)

58 B.C.E.
Caesar begins a military campaign in Gaul. (*See* **Cicero versus Caesar**)

53 B.C.E.
The Parthians defeat a Roman army under Crassus at Carrhae in present-day southeastern Turkey.

50 B.C.E.
The earliest mention of *lex Scantinia* (Cicero, *Ad Familiares* 8.12.3), barring pederasty with freeborn citizens, is made. (*See* **Homosexuality**)

49 B.C.E.
Caesar and his legions cross the Rubicon River and march on Rome.

48 B.C.E.
At the Battle of Pharsalus, Caesar defeats Pompey and is subsequently appointed dictator. (*See* **Fall of the Republic**)

44 B.C.E.
Caesar is assassinated, and the civil war resumes.

43 B.C.E.
Mark Antony, Octavian, and Lepidus form the second triumvirate; Cicero is proscribed and executed.

42 B.C.E.
At the Battle of Philippi in Macedonia, the triumvirate army defeats the republican forces led by Brutus and Cassius. (*See* **Fall of the Republic**)

40 B.C.E.
Octavian and Antony partition the empire; Octavian controls the west and Antony the east.

37 B.C.E.
Antony weds the Egyptian queen Cleopatra.

31 B.C.E.
Octavian defeats Antony and Cleopatra in a naval battle at Actium in western Greece.

27 B.C.E.
Octavian receives the title of *Augustus* from the Senate and begins the principate. (*See* **Fall of the Republic**)

19 B.C.E.
The poet Virgil dies; the *Aeneid,* a great epic of the founding of Rome, is published posthumously by his literary executors. (*See* ***The Aeneid***)

18 B.C.E.
The *Lex Iulia* regulating marriage and adultery is proclaimed. (*See* **Elegists**)

Circa 7 B.C.E.
Jesus of Nazareth is born.

8 C.E.
Augustus exiles the poet Ovid to Tomis near the Black Sea for promoting immorality and an unspecified error in *Ars amatoria.* (*See* **Ovid**)

14 C.E.
The emperor Augustus dies and is succeeded by his adopted son Tiberius.

14–37 C.E.
During the reign of Tiberius, the elections for Roman magistrates in popular assemblies end, and the imperial period begins.

Circa 30 C.E.
Jesus of Nazareth is crucified.

37–41 C.E.
The reign of the emperor Caligula is characterized by his erratic and cruel behavior.

41–54 C.E.
The emperor Claudius makes Britain a province and extends Roman rule in North Africa.

Circa 50 C.E.
The Greek biographer Plutarch is born. He will become famous for his *Parallel Lives,* in which he presents character studies of

famous Greeks and Romans in pairs. (*See* **Plutarch**)

54–68 C.E.
Nero, the last of the Julio-Claudian emperors, rules.

59 C.E.
Nero orders the death of his mother, Agrippina.

64 C.E.
A great fire sweeps through Rome; Christians are persecuted.

66 C.E.
A Roman army is defeated by insurgents in Palestine.

69–79 C.E.
During the reign of Vespasian, Jerusalem is captured and destroyed.

79–81 C.E.
Titus rules the Roman Empire. He completes construction of the Flavian amphitheater (Colosseum) in 80, opening it with a ceremony that includes one hundred days of games. (*See* **Gladiatorial Contests**)

81–96 C.E.
The reign of Domitian is characterized by the use of terror.

Circa 120 C.E.
Plutarch dies. (*See* **Plutarch**)

131–135 C.E.
The Jewish uprising in Palestine is suppressed; Emperor Hadrian expels the Jews from Jerusalem.

161–180 C.E.
Marcus Aurelius rules the empire; a dedicated Stoic philosopher, he is the author of *Meditations,* a collection of moral precepts.

Circa 170 C.E.
The Greek traveler and geographer Pausanias writes *Guide to Greece,* a valuable source of information on local history, topography, religious beliefs, and art. (*See* **Pausanias**)

201 C.E.
The empire passes legislation against Christians.

212 C.E.
Roman citizenship is extended to every free person within the borders of the empire.

244–270 C.E.
Plotinus, the chief proponent of Neoplatonism, lectures on philosophy in Rome. (*See* **Christian Neoplatonism**)

251 C.E.
The Goths and other barbarians begin to invade the empire.

251–260 C.E.
Periodic persecutions of Christians occur.

260–268 C.E.
During the rule of Gallienus, edicts against Christians are rescinded.

284–305 C.E.
The emperor Diocletian reorganizes the fiscal, administrative, and military infrastructure of the empire.

303 C.E.
A Roman imperial edict persecuting Christians is issued by Diocletian.

306 C.E.
Constantine becomes ruler of the western provinces of the Roman Empire.

311 C.E.
Galerius, ruler of the eastern provinces of the Roman Empire, issues an edict of toleration of Christianity.

312 C.E.
Constantine becomes sole emperor in the West after defeating Maxentius at the Battle of the Milvian Bridge. At this engagement legend states that a cross and the words *in hoc signo vinces* (by this sign thou shalt conquer) appeared in the sky. Constantine converts to Christianity.

330 C.E.
Constantine transfers the seat of the empire to Byzantium, which is renamed Constantinople.

354 C.E.
The great Christian theologian Saint Augustine is born.

361–363 C.E.
Emperor Julian (the Apostate) tries to revive paganism as the Roman state religion while maintaining toleration of Christianity.

395 C.E.
The Roman Empire is permanently divided into eastern and western halves.

410 C.E.
The Visigoths sack Rome.

Proclus, the last great Neoplatonic philosopher, is born. (*See* **Christian Neoplatonism**)

411 C.E.
The Council of Donatists and Catholics is held in Carthage at the behest of the emperor Honorius to determine which party holds the right, or orthodox, beliefs. Marcellinus, the emperor's representative at the meeting, declares for the Catholics after three days of deliberation. (*See* **Donatist Controversy**)

430 C.E.
Saint Augustine dies.

455 C.E.
The Vandals sack Rome.

476 C.E.
The last emperor of the western empire, Romulus Augustulus, is deposed by the barbarian Odoacer.

485 C.E.
Proclus dies. (*See* **Christian Neoplatonism**)

CLASSICAL STUDIES: *BLACK ATHENA*

Does Martin Bernal's *Black Athena* make an important contribution to our understanding of the ancient world?

Viewpoint: Yes. *Black Athena* makes a critical contribution to our understanding of the ancient world by significantly challenging the questions we ask of the past and our motivations for asking them.

Viewpoint: No. *Black Athena* does not make a critical contribution to our understanding of the ancient world because Martin Bernal's study of the past, which includes his use of myth and source criticism, is fundamentally flawed.

In 1987, Martin Bernal, a professor of government studies at Cornell University, wrote a 575-page monograph, *Black Athena: The Afroasiatic Roots of Classical Civilization.* The book, which was subtitled *Volume 1: The Fabrication of Ancient Greece 1785–1985,* set off an often-impassioned debate within and outside the field of classical studies (Berlinerblau 1999: 1–20). In it, Bernal argued that the view we currently hold of Greek history originated in late-eighteenth- and early-nineteenth-century Europe (Bernal 1987: 1–73). This "Aryan" Model of Greek culture, Bernal proffered, resulted from European racism and anti-Semitism—in sum, from a Eurocentric unwillingness to acknowledge the influence of non-Indo-European peoples on ancient Greece. The Greeks, according to the Aryan Model, which Bernal further divides between an initial "Broad" and a later "Extreme" version leading to the Jewish Holocaust of the twentieth century, were not significantly influenced by Egypt, Phoenicia, or any of the major civilizations of the ancient world.

While concentrating primarily on a discussion of modern Europe in the first volume, Bernal promised two additional volumes in the coming years. The second, subtitled *The Archaeological and Documentary Evidence,* was published in 1991. The third volume, which is as yet unpublished, would "use the Revised Ancient Model to throw some light on previously inexplicable aspects of Greek religion and mythology, and especially on the names of heroes or divine beings" (Bernal 1987: 63). In sum, Bernal would argue for (and propose a return to) the model of Greek civilization held before the nineteenth century, namely the Ancient Model. According to this model, the Greeks were well aware of the significant Near Eastern and African influences on their culture in every area, from art and architecture to mathematics and philosophy. Ancient writers openly acknowledged the impact of the Phoenicians and the Egyptians, the latter of whom Bernal characterizes as a people resembling modern Africans phenotypically, and African Americans even more so (Bernal 1987: 435–437).

To state that *Black Athena* stirred up controversy in the scholarly world and beyond would be an understatement. For classicists, the audacity of a professor of Chinese government fundamentally challenging what we know about the ancient world and purporting to do so with tools that the student of antiquity has painstakingly mastered (philology, art history, and archaeology) was unbearable. (For early discussion of the work, see Levine and Peradotto: 1989.) The classicist Mary R. Lefkowitz entered the fray with her 1992 article in *The New Republic,* titled "Not Out of Africa: The Origins of Greece and the Illusions of Afrocentrics." Many laypersons, from college students to scholars outside the professional fields of classical studies, welcomed the central theses of Bernal's corpus. Proponents of the Afrocentric movement, the academic subset to which Lefkowitz accused Bernal of belonging, were well acquainted with the sordid history of European and American race science and thinking, which extended to such academic fields as sociology and biology. They also knew that an alternate story of the past, one that celebrated the contributions of black Africans to world history, had existed since at least the eighteenth century (Berlinerblau: 133–161). Extreme or misguided Afrocentrists had argued for the essential African identity of such leading figures as Cleopatra, and Bernal now gave new credibility to their ideas. Given the great cultural and racial divide in American society, it is no wonder that the Black Athena debate played out, to a great extent, on American campuses and in the American media.

The core arguments against the Black Athena idea are laid out in Lefkowitz and Guy MacLean Rogers's 1996 collection of essays, *Black Athena Revisited.* The work brought together Egyptologists, philologists, and historiographers unanimously opposed to Bernal's theses. Other important responses include "Martin Bernal and His Critics," written by Suzanne Marchand and Anthony Grafton (1997: 1–35). The article visits the debate from the perspective of the intellectual historian and calls Bernal's critical flaws to the reader's attention. Jacques Berlinerblau's *Heresy in the University: The Black Athena Controversy and the Responsibilities of American Intellectuals* (1999), in addition to exploring the central theses in *Black Athena* and the opposition to them, raises the question of what the debate meant for the structure of knowledge and its dissemination, which are usually the province of institutions of higher education. The final word on Black Athena, despite arguments to the contrary, has not been spoken. Bernal's 2001 book, *Black Athena Writes Back: Martin Bernal Responds to His Critics,* shows that, contrary to what classicists might believe, we have not yet dealt Bernal's thesis its fatal blow.

—*Patrice D. Rankine*

Viewpoint: Yes. *Black Athena* makes a critical contribution to our understanding of the ancient world by significantly challenging the questions we ask of the past and our motivations for asking them.

The sociologist Maurice Halbwachs, like Paul Fussel and other scholars concerned with how societies recollect the past, offers a compelling study that has a significant bearing on the Black Athena debate. Halbwachs argues in *On Collective Memory* (1992) that the present is always shaped and reformed through the past. Conversely, our contemporary social and political concerns inform the questions that we ask of history and how we go about asking them. In his Ancient and Aryan Models, Martin Bernal proposed a distinct sociology of knowledge. Bernal was not primarily concerned with philology, art history, or archaeology, although he certainly realized that he would have to propose arguments within the frameworks of these disciplines. What concerned Bernal was the sociology of knowledge, that is, the question of how our understanding of the past came to be structured as it did (Berlinerblau: 77–129). On the particulars of the disciplines in question, Bernal is sometimes wrong, or he at times states his speculations in a heavy-handed way that no credible philologist, art historian, or archaeologist would. As Jacques Berlinerblau contends, Bernal's "big picturism," his need to propose broad schemas within which his general observations could fit, causes him to overstate his core theses (Berlinerblau: 15, 23). Nevertheless, there is no smoke without fire. Many of Bernal's more pivotal arguments are correct, such as the thesis that in modern times Europeans in general, and even some classical scholars in particular, were ethnocentric in fundamental and disturbing ways. Eurocentrism did underpin such modern blights as the slave trade and the Holocaust. While Ancient and Aryan Models as sweeping as the ones Bernal proposes are not likely to have existed, the particular social outlooks of modern Europe shape our view of the Greco-Roman world and the questions that we asked of it, as Berlinerblau argues in *Heresy in the University: The Black Athena Controversy and the Responsibilities of American Intellectuals* (1999).

Berlinerblau's book draws several highly suggestive conclusions about the importance of Bernal's work, and the pitfalls he faced. *Heresy in the University* argues that, although Bernal is sometimes blinded by his "big picturism" and the desire to fit his observation into neat and tidy models, he nevertheless raises critical questions about how modern, Western society views its past. There exists for every scholar a degree of what Berlinerblau calls "atmospheric determinism" (79–80), the influence of attendant ideological prisms such as Christianity, ethocentrism, or Romanticism. These ideological prisms no doubt influence readers of classical texts, and

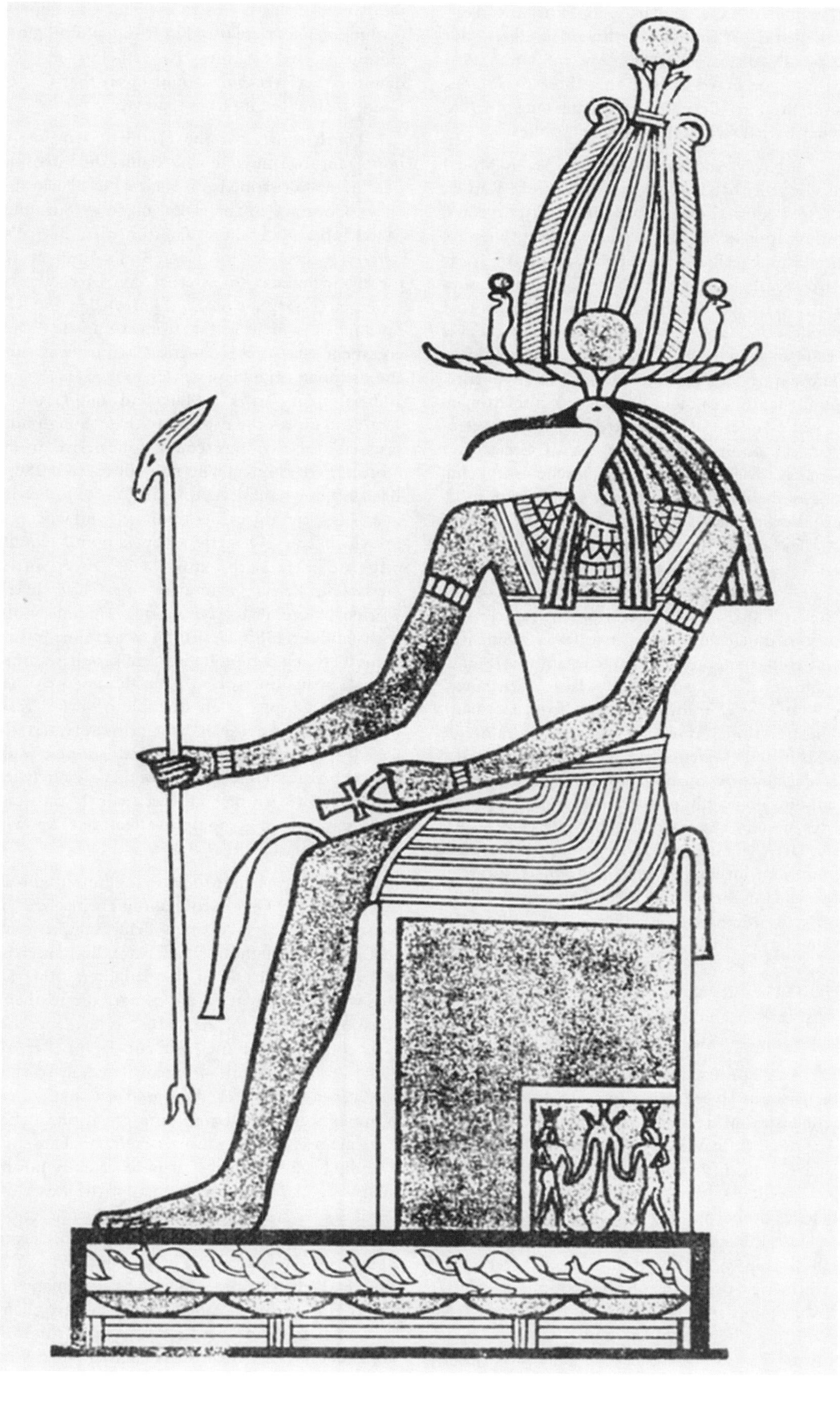

Drawing of Thoth Thrice Great, the Egyptian god of wisdom and purported author of the Hermetic Corpus, a collection of religious and philosophical writings

(from Patrick Boylan, Thoth, the Hermes of Egypt: A Study of Some Aspects of Theological Thought in Ancient Egypt, *1979)*

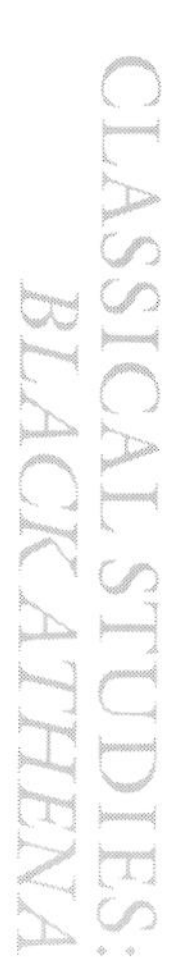

they inform how scholars reconstruct the classical world. Although Berlinerblau does not expressly dismiss Bernal's Ancient and Aryan Models, he makes it clear that these paradigms, so central to Bernal's study, are tangential to what Bernal really offers classical studies.

Bernal's Ancient Model and Aryan Model are not all that is at stake in his work. Rather, these models, though flawed in significant ways, refract approaches to the ancient world. They are useful in revealing the deeper issues in the study of classical civilization. Berlinerblau enumerates at least twelve variables in Bernal's study that would affect how the Greco-Roman world was reconstructed in the nineteenth century (82–92). These variables include racism, anti-Semitism, philhellenism, the idea of progress, and Romanticism. Modern ideas affected many branches of classical studies, the privileging of Greek over Roman society (a feature of philhellenism) being one of many examples. Bernal's critique of modern Europe has a bearing on areas of classical studies beyond his purview, such as Roman literature and drama. August Wilhelm Schlegel (1809), who praised "the poetic genius of the Greeks," also argued that Roman tragedy (the plays of Lucius Annaeus Seneca) was "bombastic and cold, unnatural in character and plot, [and] scandalous due to its absurd lack of elegance" (1966: 233–235, my translation from German). The traditional approach to Roman drama, its basis in actual phenomena (such as the influence of declamation on dramatic structure) notwithstanding, certainly played a role in shaping how later writers approached this material. Despite the fact that Seneca had been one of the most important influences on William Shakespeare at the end of the sixteenth century, critics of the early twentieth century, such as T. S. Eliot, continued to be influenced by the tastes of their predecessors. Bernal's position as an outsider to classical studies allows him to question how classicists approach the ancient world, and why, in a way that an insider might not.

The approach to Senecan tragedy in the early twentieth century is an example of how current tastes influence our evaluation of the past. Although Bernal does not mention this particular issue, his historiography could be applied to it as well. As it pertains to the Black Athena debate, Bernal wanted to demonstrate how the modern European mindset affected such areas of scholarship as the reception of the *Hermetica* (Hermetic Corpus), a collection of philosophical and religious writings attributed to Hermes Trismegistus, the Egyptian god "Thoth Thrice Great" (Bernal 2001: 385). Bernal argues that it was important to Isaac Casaubon to date the *Hermetica* to the second to third centuries C.E. because of his religious convictions (as a Christian writer). This is not to say that Casaubon's findings, which were based in strong philological arguments, were wrong. Nevertheless, a later date for the *Hermetica* would mean that Christianity influenced it rather than vice versa.

The late date for the Hermetic Corpus is important for someone who claims the integrity of Christian doctrine from ancient, secular influences. Contrary to the claim, made by Suzanne Marchand and Anthony Grafton, that Bernal's correct assessment of Casaubon's motives is merely incidental (6), Bernal consistently presents a necessary sociology of knowledge, the refutation of which is far from complete. The argument that the Hermetic Corpus "was not the Egyptian original which Plato read but a late and secondary work" (Marchand and Grafton 1997: 4) ignores the possibility that, though not original, the writings could still derive from more-ancient sources (Bernal 2001: 384–386). Bernal follows the Egyptologist W. M. F. Petrie in arguing that the earlier traditions and writings to which the Hermetic Corpus points could originate in the sixth century B.C.E. Parts of the *Hermetica,* Bernal maintains, could have been written before Plato, Casaubon's findings notwithstanding (385). Without a sustained dialogue between Egyptologists and classicists, the issues remain unresolved. The debate over the Hermetic Corpus is an example of how "real world" influences—such as Christianity, established traditions within classical studies, and entrenched academic disciplines that are rarely in conversation with one another (namely classical philology and Egyptology)—affect our knowledge of the past.

Bernal's Ancient Model relies in part on the myths that the Greeks told about themselves to reconstruct history. As one salient example (one that recurs throughout the debate), Bernal reads the mythological tale of the daughters of Danaus, who fled Egypt to avoid marriage to their cousins, the sons of Aegyptus, as evidence of early contact between Greece and Egypt (Bernal 1987: 76–120). While no reconstruction of the past can appropriately be based on myth, the arguments against Bernal's interpretation of the story are no more conclusive than the debate surrounding the Hermetic Corpus. Certainly Edith Hall is right in her assertion that the myth of Danaus's link to Egypt is in part the product of colonization in the classical period (which is too late to speak in terms of Egyptian influences on Greece). Nevertheless, as Bernal retorts, many of the myths retold in Athenian drama have their historical roots in the Bronze Age, a foundational period in Greek history (Bernal 2001: 90–101). In addition, Hall's observation that myths, including the story of Danaus, in the end serve a cultural purpose for the Greeks (allowing them to trace all peoples to Greece) has no bearing on the contact between Greece and Egypt that the myth suggests. While cultural crosscurrents such as trade do not have the same impact as colonization (O'Conner 1996: 49–61), the influence that trade can yield is certainly not negligible. Both Hall and Bernal are left to argue not from evidence as such but from what is plausible. This is what Bernal calls "competitive plausibility" (1986: 8, 9; for a discussion, see Berlinerblau: 71–74).

Where material evidence from the ancient world fails, classical philologists use language to argue the likelihood of their theses. The Homeric lexicon has long been an example of this approach. Our understanding of codes of honor and social institutions before the Archaic Period is almost completely derived from the epic poems. Along with the study of Indo-European, the Greek epic poems are our primary sources in the overwhelming absence of material evidence. Nevertheless, even in the area of language we are often forced to argue in terms of what is likely. The names of significant Greek cities such as Athens or Corinth, as well as gods like Athena and Apollo, are not Indo-European, and therefore there are gaps in our knowledge (Bernal 1986: 51–53; Lefkowitz 1996: 16). What language did the peoples that first inhabited these regions, named their cities, and instituted their religions, speak? Bernal steps precisely into this quagmire. While some of the solutions he offers might be untenable (such as his Egyptian etymology for Athena), he unearths some difficult problems in the study of the classics. In sum, Berlinerblau sees the idea of competitive plausibility as "one of *Black Athena*'s most timely theoretical contributions to the study of the ancient world" (71).

From this information it should be evident that Bernal's Ancient Model, while perhaps overstated, has bases both in historical fact and in what is plausible. We might correctly assert that it meant something different to Plato than it did to Casaubon whether the former borrowed from Eastern wisdom, such as it was. Because the ancients to some extent had different biases, values, and concerns from modern Europeans, their assumptions about the past followed other trajectories. One example is the modern preoccupation with race. As Frank M. Snowden Jr. asserts, the Greeks certainly did not approach black Africans in the same way that modern Europeans do. Bernal's attempt to find an Ancient Model is based on the realization that the past the Greeks constructed was, in important ways, different from the past we reconstruct. For the philhellenic, modern European, the purity of Greek culture from outside influences is of major importance. The Athenian preoccupation with autochthony (the idea that they had never been displaced from their land from the time they inhabited it) might seem similar to this, but the Greeks also had myths that linked them to Egypt and Phoenicia, and such stories aided their association to a greater past. Even Bernal's opponents admit that the ancient Greeks craved this connection to Egypt and the Eastern world at large. Modern Europeans of the nineteenth century, however, were less concerned with investigating these links, as Bernal claims, than they were with celebrating Greek civilization. Marchand and Grafton give a salient example of this in their discussion of F. A. Wolf. They claim that in 1795 Wolf "advocated the study of the transmission of the Hebrew text of the Old Testament as a means to better understand the history of the Homeric poems" (13). Nevertheless, by 1807 he had somehow decided that the study of the past "should restrict its purview to the Greeks and (rather grudgingly) the Romans." Bernal's Ancient Model distinguishes the way in which the Greeks viewed the past from the modern European reconstruction of the classical world.

Certainly Bernal's Models are crude, but even his opponents concede several central arguments, including the notion that classical scholars of the nineteenth century were essentially Eurocentric (Bernal's Aryan Model) and that this bias influenced the directions that their scholarship took. Hall sees little doubt "that Bernal is correct in arguing that modern racial prejudice has been one of the reasons why cultural contact between ancient Hellenophone communities and ancient Semitic and black peoples has been and is still being played down" (1996: 335). The modern field of classical studies has its basis in Eurocentric ideas. Wolf, as Marchand and Grafton concede, "regularly deprecated Jews in his university lectures" (16). One of the leading figures in the founding of the science of antiquity (Altertumswissenschaft), Wolf should not be taken to represent all European scholars, but neither were his ideas in any way unusual for his time.

Given that many eighteenth- and nineteenth-century intellectuals were unabashedly chauvinistic and that the classics were at the center of their cultural pride, the backlash among Afrocentric writers is not surprising. The skepticism with which these scholars approach the classics is in fact to some extent healthy. Berlinerblau argues, moreover, that Mary R. Lefkowitz's wholesale dismissal of Bernal on the issue of Afrocentrism is misinformed (Berlinerblau: 133–161). Bernal himself is not an Afrocentric scholar, but neither are his claims as marginal as Lefkowitz might have one believe. Bernal's arguments concerning the Greek indebtedness to Egypt and the primarily "African" nature of ancient Egyptian culture, like the arguments on the other side, had been proffered since at least the nineteenth century. While it is anachronistic to impose modern race thinking onto our view of the ancient world, writers like James W. C. Pennington (on the Afrocentric side) and Wolf (on the Eurocentric) have always viewed Greek civilization, to some extent, through the limitation of their own ethnic identity. Wolf, no less than the Afrocentric writer, should be approached from a critical distance.

Yet, Bernal's hypothesis is not without flaws. As has already been noted, he tends to paint his impressions in broad, sweeping strokes, at times misrepresenting important details. Bernal's misrepresentation of Johann Gottfried Herder, George Henry Grote, and Karl Otfried Müller is emblematic of the degree to which he overstates his schemas. While Bernal claims that Herder, for example, along with other Enlightenment thinkers, "provided a firm basis for the chauvinism and racism of the following two centuries" (Bernal 1986: 206), Robert Norton has argued to the contrary (Berlinerblau: 69). Similar corrections have been offered for several leading classical scholars (Marchand and Grafton; Berlinerblau: 68–74). When we check the evidence closely, we are led to the conclusion that there was perhaps no Aryan Model per se. An Aryan Model would imply some degree of conspiracy, since the contributions of non-European cultures would have to be repressed somewhat consciously. This does not seem to have been the case. Nevertheless, it is clear, as Bernal argues, that racism and anti-Semitism were strong ideologies in the nineteenth century, and we wonder to what extent these ways of thinking, as well as other peculiarities of the modern European imagination, have affected our view of the past.

Bernal's *Black Athena* makes a critical contribution to our understanding of the ancient world because, among other reasons, it lifts the veil of scholarly objectivity that often accompanies scientific inquiry. Bernal's work and the debate surrounding it help us to see that there is a great deal at stake in our study of the past. The more we are aware of our modern biases, including our need to erect and maintain the monument of a Western heritage, the better able we are to criticize ourselves and work against our preconceptions. In addition, Bernal reveals a bit of what can be lost when we close ourselves into academic silos. There is a wonderful and necessary conversation to be had between, among others, classicists and Egyptologists. The current configuration of academic disciplines to a great extent prevents us from using—or even knowing—findings from fields other than our own to help us to answer the questions that we raise about the past, as the example of the Hermetic Corpus demonstrates.

Black Athena Revisited (1996), although it is primarily an attempt to undermine Bernal's arguments, is one of the few mainstream volumes where Egyptologists are in conversation with classicists. (It might well be the first of its kind.) The Black Athena debate, therefore, occasions a fertile, ongoing discussion. Bernal's response reveals that many of the more important of his claims have not been refuted, although he himself admits to having made many errors in his work (2001: 1–20). Given the magnitude of the issues at stake, however, one is left to wonder if a subtler sociology of knowledge would even have been noticed. Societies, like people, fabricate their past to some extent unself-consciously. The processes of recollection and commemoration help us to navigate the world around us and to understand ourselves. Bernal's artificial and not-so-subtle reconstruction of the past will serve as both a roadmap and a caution sign to future students of the ancient world.

—PATRICE D. RANKINE,
PURDUE UNIVERSITY

Viewpoint:
No. *Black Athena* does not make a critical contribution to our understanding of the ancient world because Martin Bernal's study of the past, which includes his use of myth and source criticism, is fundamentally flawed.

According to the introduction to *The Oxford History of Greece and the Hellenistic World* (1988), "Mycenaean Greece was culturally dependent on the sophisticated arts of the Minoans, the non-Indo-European people flourishing on Crete and some of the Aegean islands. It was in contact also with other ancient cultures of the Near East: Hittites, Egyptians, Syrians." This statement is indicative of the general understanding among classical scholars regarding Greece's debt to non-Indo-European peoples. There is no denying that early Greeks were in contact with other civilizations, as the epigraph indicates. Martin Bernal's primary thesis, however, that the Ancient Greeks believed themselves to be culturally indebted to Egyptians (the Ancient Model) through colonization but that modern Europeans obscured this influence because of racism (the Aryan Model), is untenable. Bernal's fabrication of an Ancient Model is based in poor scholarly methods: a misuse of myth, faulty evaluation of sources, and unsound philology. As his many opponents have shown, there was no Ancient Model among the Greeks. Classical scholars by and large admit the influence of non-European peoples of the ancient world, such as the Egyptians or the Phoenicians, on Greek civilization. Nevertheless, Bernal wants to prove the existence of an Aryan Model, which, he argues, is a racist and anti-Semitic denial of aspects of the past, if he is to maintain the priority of an alternate view of history. What results from this need is the assertion that many of the leading nineteenth-century scholars of classical antiquity were racist. This attribution of racism, moreover, results from poor source-criticism, such as Bernal's reliance on secondary and tertiary sources rather than consulting the works of the scholars in question firsthand. If there is anything to be gained from Bernal's *Black Athena*, rather than a better understanding of the ancient world, it is a lesson in how not to conduct scholarly research.

Bernal's misappropriation of myth to argue historical claims is one of the fallacies evident early in the first volume of *Black Athena*. In order to support his argument that the Egyptians and Phoenicians had colonized the Peloponnese and central Greece from the second millennium B.C.E., Bernal reads the myths of Danaus and Cadmus historically. Regarding the former, we know from mythology that Danaus, the brother of Aegyptus, escaped to Argos with his fifty daughters, the Danaides, whom Aegyptus's sons were pursuing for marriage (Gantz 1993: 198–212). The Aegyptoi somehow force the Danaides into union, but the daughters of Danaus privately agree to murder their cousins on their wedding night. All but one girl, Hypermestra, carry out the plan. Her offspring with her cousin Lynkeus leads to a noble race including, most notably, Herakles. If the Danaides were kin to the Egyptians (as the myth suggests), then this would mean that Hypermestra's offspring, some of Greece's most celebrated stock, were of Egyptian descent. Herodotus, as Bernal argues, claims that the worship of the gods among the Pelasgians, the social group that supposedly inhabited the region at the time, derived from this union between Greece and Egypt (Bernal 1987: 75–120; 1991: 78–122). In a similar colonizing vein, Cadmus, the mythological founder of Thebes, brought the Phoenician alphabet to central Greece. Bernal argues that Cadmus's colonization of Thebes "was the stronghold of the Ancient Model because it was so vigorously and widely attested" (1987: 85).

Although Bernal establishes a distinction between myth and history, he argues (rightly) that legends, such as those of Danaus and Cadmus, contain seeds of truth. A widely known example of how legend functions is the saga of the Trojan War. The fact that Heinrich Schliemann, a wealthy philanthropist enamored of the classics, led an expedition at the end of the nineteenth century and uncovered the ancient city, proved that legends, such as those found in Homeric epic, had their basis in historical facts. In a similar vein, it is certainly possible for the story of Danaus's travel from Egypt to have some origin in actual events, but Bernal's reconstruction of these events, as we will see, is not plausible. He links the legends of the Danaides and of Cadmus to the arrival in Greece of a group called the Hyksos, attested in Herodotus, Hecataeus of Abdera, and Manetho. In Bernal's argument, the Hyksos, Indo-Aryan invaders from the north, had dominated Egypt between 1725 B.C.E. and 1575 B.C.E. During the same period, they invaded Crete, and Bernal attributes to them the importation of the sphinx and the griffin into that region (1991: 320–408). In Bernal's reconstruction, the historical presence of the Hyksos is linked to the arrival in Greece of the legendary daughters of Danaus, who came from Egypt as suppliants, *hiketides* (Lefkowitz 1996: 15–16).

The refutation of Bernal's reconstruction of history from myth is resounding. In the first place, although legends do contain remnants of history, it is often difficult, without the appropriate sources or artifacts, to uncover them. In addition to this, myths are a reflection of the sociopolitical concerns of the cultures that produce them (Hall 1996: 333–348). Edith Hall argues that the story of the Danaides, and its conspicuous presence in fifth-century tragedy, reflects Greek colonization during the seventh and sixth centuries B.C.E., and, more specifically, Athenian imperialism during the fifth century. Legends of earlier settlers justified the colonizing tendencies of their descendants. As Hall argues, myths such as that of Danaus are "profoundly ethnocentric from a *Hellenic* point of view, for they seek to trace the origins of all peoples back to Greek gods and heroes" (339). After all, Danaus's lineage is traceable to Greeks, not Egyptians: namely, Zeus and Io. It is unsound scholarship on Bernal's part to use the legend of Danaus to support the Hyksos' "colonization" of Greece.

Not only is Bernal's use of mythology misguided, but there is also no historical evidence for Egyptian colonization of Greece. The Egyptologist David O'Connor shows that, during the first half of the second millennium B.C.E., there was "no hint of contact with the Aegean" (1996: 53). After the Hyksos domination of Egypt (by the eighteenth dynasty, 1574–1293), there was contact between Aegean people and Egypt, but this exchange, according to O'Connor, marked a trade relationship and not colonization. In addi-

CADMUS

The following passage is from Pausanias's account of Cadmus, the legendary Phoenician founder of Thebes, whose origins are still disputed:

XII. [1] The Thebans in ancient days used to sacrifice bulls to Apollo of the Ashes. Once when the festival was being held, the hour of the sacrifice was near but those sent to fetch the bull had not arrived. And so, as a wagon happened to be near by, they sacrificed to the god one of the oxen, and ever since it has been the custom to sacrifice working oxen. The following story also is current among the Thebans. As Cadmus was leaving Delphi by the road to Phocis, a cow, it is said, guided him on his way. This cow was one bought from the herdsmen of Pelagon, and on each of her sides was a white mark like the orb of a full moon. [2] Now the oracle of the god had said that Cadmus and the host with him were to make their dwelling where the cow was going to sink down in weariness. So this is one of the places that they point out. Here there is in the open an altar and an image of Athena, said to have been dedicated by Cadmus. Those who think that the Cadmus who came to the Theban land was an Egyptian, and not a Phoenician, have their opinion contradicted by the name of this Athena, because she is called by the Phoenician name of Onga, and not by the Egyptian name of Sais. [3] The Thebans assert that on the part of their citadel, where today stands their market-place, was in ancient times the house of Cadmus. They point out the ruins of the bridal chamber of Harmonia, and of one which they say was Semele's into the latter they allow no man to step even now. Those Greeks who allow that the Muses sang at the wedding of Harmonia, can point to the spot in the market-place where it is said that the goddesses sang. [4] There is also a story that along with the thunderbolt hurled at the bridal chamber of Semele there fell a log from heaven. They say that Polydorus adorned this log with bronze and called it Dionysus Cadmus. Near is an image of Dionysus; Onasimedes made it of solid bronze. The altar was built by the sons of Praxiteles.

Source: *Pausanias,* Pausanias Description of Greece, with an English Translation by W. H. S. Jones, Litt.D., and H. A. Ormerod, *M.A., 4 volumes (Cambridge, Mass.: Harvard University Press; London: William Heinemann, 1918), Book 9: Boeotia, 9.12.1–4.*

tion, as Jacques Berlinerblau notes, the Hyksos themselves had invaded Egypt from northeastern Europe (1999: 51). The presence of the Hyksos in Greece marks a return. They might well have brought such symbols as the sphinx with them, but this fact would not alter our understanding of the past in any notable way (and certainly not in a way that would warrant a new model). Bernal's argument that "black" Egypt had a significant influence on ancient Greece, a touchstone of his Ancient Model, has no historical basis.

As Berlinerblau, Mary R. Lefkowitz, and Hall have argued, Bernal's reconstruction of the past is based, at least to some extent, on his unwillingness to work within the established traditions of source-criticism. (It is perhaps important to note, as Lefkowitz does, that Bernal had no formal training in classical philology or Egyptology.) As sources for the Minoan or Mycenaean periods in ancient Greece, Hecataeus of Abdera and Manetho, the sources from which Bernal collects his data, are more than one millennium removed. Their own sources are second- and thirdhand. Even Herodotus, whom Bernal seems to take at face value, has been subject, within the field of classical philology, to a long-standing critique of his historical methods (Lefkowitz 1996: 11–19). Bernal's poor evaluation leads him to one of his central theses, that the Greeks "stole" philosophy from Egypt (Berlinerblau 1999: 133–146; Bernal 2001: 384–386).

Poor methodology is apparent again in Bernal's analysis of the Hermetic Corpus. The corpus contains writings that Bernal argues were Egyptian in origin, and these writings were influential on Platonic philosophy, neo-Platonism, and early Christianity. The antiquity of the Hermetic Corpus, therefore, is important to Bernal's argument, as is the claim that it is Egyptian. Despite a tradition of source evaluation within the classics to the contrary, Bernal, citing the Egyptologist W. M. F. Petrie, dates the documents to the sixth or fifth centuries B.C.E.

Bernal's hypothesis concerning the Hermetic Corpus would certainly alter our understanding of the past, but long-established philological arguments counter his claims. In the first place, the Hermetic Corpus is a Gnostic document, written in Greek (Marchand and Grafton 1997: 3–6). Its authors attributed it to an Egyptian god, "Thoth Thrice Great," in keeping with a classical commonplace that held Eastern wisdom in high esteem. Isaac Casaubon, writing in 1614, proved that the work dates to the second and third centuries C.E., as Suzanne Marchand and Anthony Grafton argue. Casaubon showed, for example, that the abstract nouns found throughout the work do not occur in Greek until the first century C.E. (Marchand and Grafton 1997: 3). Bernal presents no refutation of Casaubon's philology. As in his use of ancient writers like Herodotus, Bernal fails to analyze the sources in a manner consistent with established practices within classical scholarship.

Rather than arguing on philological grounds or in source-critical terms, what Bernal does assert is that European scholars were racist and anti-Semitic. In the case of the Hermetic Corpus, Casaubon's work, according to Bernal, helped to lay the foundation for the reaction in Europe in the eighteenth century against the Ancient Model (Bernal 1987: 26–27). The shift toward an Aryan Model, which privileged Greece over Egypt, was concomitant with the rise of "racism based on skin colour in late-17th-century England, alongside the increasing importance of the American colonies, with their twin policies of extermination of the Native Americans and enslavement of African Blacks" (Bernal 1987: 27). Certainly racism is a significant blight on the history of modern Europe and America. Writers including Thomas Jefferson, Alexis de Tocqueville, and Abraham Lincoln held fast to the notion of the fundamental inferiority of blacks, even though each was, in his own way, sympathetic to the plight of Africans in the New World. Racism (or anti-Semitism) was not simply an offhanded opinion held in private. Rather, the modern mindset underpinned slavery, race science, and such twentieth-century nightmares as the Holocaust, segregation, and apartheid. These atrocities notwithstanding, Bernal has not proved his claim that racism and anti-Semitism in modern Europe caused the usurpation of a previously held view of the past.

In many cases, what Bernal has done is to accuse classical scholars in Europe of racism without the appropriate evidence, relying too often on secondary sources. Bernal builds his argument, which is that in the nineteenth century the Aryan Model replaced the Ancient Model, on sweeping accusations. Berlinerblau summarizes the controversy surrounding Johann Gottfried Herder, George Henry Grote, and Karl Otfried Müller, each of whom Bernal indicts with a form of Aryanism (Berlinerblau, 1999: 59–74). In none of these cases did the indiscretions of the scholars in question prove to have a significant effect on their scholarship. Marchand and Grafton have also debunked Bernal's broad claims concerning racist European scholars. In the case of Müller, they argue that the scholar, contrary to Bernal's indictment, "openly and willingly acknowledged Greece's (minor) debts to the cultures of the 'Orient'–by which some meant Ionia, some meant Persia, some meant Egypt, and some meant Mesopotamia" (1997: 15). Marchand and Grafton argue that, rather than an Aryan Model, there were in fact competing approaches to the past. While the classicist K. F. Hermann did not believe that myths linking Greece to Egypt were historically based, others, like Jacob Bernays, looked consistently to the ancient Near East for clues about Greek civilization. Bernal has presented nothing new in asserting that racism played a significant role in shaping the modern European imagination, and he adds little to our understanding of the past or classical philology.

As Bernal himself at points concedes, the idea of "Black" Athena, which is the culminating symbol of his arguments, is a product of late-twentieth-century American culture wars (Berlinerblau 1999: 133–146). At least the second portion of Bernal's argument, that Athena was in origin an Egyptian goddess, and that she, being Egyptian, was black, is based in a modern notion of race. Bernal's approach is anachronistic. Frank Snowden Jr., throughout his work, offers a more scholarly approach to classical philology (Snowden 1970; 1983). He shows, for example, that when Herodotus speaks of the blacks (the *aithiopes*) with whom the Greeks came into contact, we cannot impose our modern viewpoints onto the text. Although Hall is perhaps on the wrong track when she argues that Herodotus's *aithiopes* did not necessarily refer to Africans, the Greeks had no reason to hide any influence that black Africans might have had on their culture. The Greeks speak admiringly of black Africans (Ethiopians), and they made a clear distinction between this group and the Egyptians. What we find is that Bernal's reconstruction of the past serves misguided, modern needs.

There are clear, established scholarly methods in the study of the ancient world. Philologists approach texts based on a firm understanding of the classical languages (Greek, Latin, Hebrew, and others) and an historical awareness about the works and their interrelationships. The associated fields of art history and archaeology have their own established methods that can be used together with philology to better our understanding of the past. Arguments that oppose the authority of the established disciplines for the study of the past (namely, philology, art history, and archaeology) must be firmly rooted in material evidences, such as new findings in archaeology, art, or philology. Casaubon's study of the Hermetic Corpus is an example of how philological methods, when appropriately applied, can give us new insights. Bernal has not adhered to these scholarly methods, nor does he apply basic historical approaches of source-criticism. In the end, Bernal's assault on the professional fields of classical studies adds nothing to our understanding of the ancient world.

–PATRICE D. RANKINE,
PURDUE UNIVERSITY

References

Jacques Berlinerblau, *Heresy in the University: The Black Athena Controversy and the Responsibilities of American Intellectuals* (New Brunswick, N.J.: Rutgers University Press, 1999).

Martin Bernal, *Black Athena: The Afroasiatic Roots of Classical Civilization*, volume 1, *The Fabrication of Ancient Greece 1785–1985* (New Brunswick, N.J.: Rutgers University Press, 1987).

Bernal, *Black Athena: The Afroasiatic Roots of Classical Civilization*, volume 2, *The Archaeological and Documentary Evidence* (New Brunswick, N.J.: Rutgers University Press, 1991).

Bernal, *Black Athena Writes Back: Martin Bernal Responds to His Critics*, edited by David Chioni Moore (Durham, N.C.: Duke University Press, 2001).

John Boardman and others, eds., *The Oxford History of Greece and the Hellenistic World* (Oxford: Oxford University Press, 1988).

Timothy Gantz, *Early Greek Myth: A Guide to Literary and Artistic Sources* (Baltimore: Johns Hopkins University Press, 1993).

Maurice Halbwachs, *On Collective Memory*, translated by Lewis A. Coser (Chicago: University of Chicago Press, 1992).

Edith Hall, "When is a Myth not a Myth? Bernal's 'Ancient Model'," in Mary R. Lefkowitz and Guy MacLean Rogers, eds., *Black Athena Revisited* (Chapel Hill: University of North Carolina Press, 1996), pp. 333–348.

Stephen Howe, *Afrocentrism: Mythical Past and Imagined Homes* (London: Verso, 1998).

Mary R. Lefkowitz, *Not Out of Africa: How Afrocentrism Became an Excuse to Teach Myth as History* (New York: New Republic Books, 1997).

Lefkowitz, "Not Out of Africa: The Origins of Greece and the Illusions of Afrocentrics," *New Republic* (10 February 1992): 29–36.

Molly M. Levine, "The Marginalization of Martin Bernal: Review Essay on *Black Athena Revisited* by M. Lefkowitz and G. Rogers," *Classical Philology*, 98 (1998): 345–363.

Levine and John Peradotto, eds., *The Challenge of Black Athena*, special issue of *Arethusa*, volume 22 (Fall 1989).

Suzanne Marchand and Anthony Grafton, "Martin Bernal and His Critics," *Arion*, 5 (1997): 1–35.

David O'Connor, "Egypt and Greece: The Bronze Age Evidence," in Lefkowitz and Rogers, eds., *Black Athena Revisited* (Chapel Hill: University of North Carolina Press, 1996), pp. 49–61.

John D. Ray, "How Black Was Socrates? The Roots of European Civilization and the Dangers of Afrocentrism," *TLS: The Times Literary Supplement* (14 February 1997): 3–4.

August Wilhelm Schlegel, *Vorlesungen über dramatische Kunst und Litterature*, in Eckard Lefèvre, *Senecas Tragödien* (Darmstadt: Wissenschaftliche Buchgesellschaft, 1972).

Frank M. Snowden Jr., *Before Color Prejudice: The Ancient View of Blacks* (Cambridge, Mass.: Harvard University Press, 1983).

Snowden, *Blacks in Antiquity: Ethiopians in the Greco-Roman Experience* (Cambridge, Mass.: Harvard University Press, 1970).

CLASSICAL STUDIES: GERMAN PHILOLOGICAL TRADITION

Does the German philological tradition offer a superior knowledge of antiquity to that of British amateurism?

Viewpoint: Yes. German philology far surpasses the British tradition in the production of useful knowledge about antiquity.

Viewpoint: No. British scholarship produces superior results in the long run, both in terms of a well-rounded knowledge of antiquity and of the resulting education offered to students.

The second oldest literary profession is criticism. An illiterate Bronze-Age bard would scarcely have sung out his words before someone in the audience ventured an opinion. At some point, someone suggested that before venturing another opinion, it might be a good idea to get more information. Thus scholarship was born. To understand the two essays that follow, one must know that "scholarship" has since antiquity meant either something personal or published, specialized or broad, amateur or professional. Professional scholarship began with the introduction of formal education, and its earliest practitioners were schoolteachers or *grammatikoi.* In the sixth century B.C.E., philosophers such as Xenophanes looked for deeper meanings in the etymologies of words, and philology was born.

Professional philology with state support in the German manner began in the Museum at Alexandria, the Egyptian city founded by Alexander the Great in 331 B.C.E. as the capital of his empire. Alexandrian scholars began the work that defines classical scholarship to this day. They produced definitive editions of the great authors by systematically comparing manuscripts, and by using scientific methods, they discerned genuine from spurious works.

English amateurism has an ancient model in Rome's greatest scholar, Marcus Terentius Varro (116–27 B.C.E.). He was not a teacher but an independent man of means. His 490 books touched a multitude of subjects, including the Latin language, ancient culture, and literary history.

By the sixteenth century, the basic processes of modern textual criticism were so established that great French scholars like Guillaume Budé (1468–1540), Robert (1503–1559) and Henri Estienne (Stephanus) (1528–1598), Isaac Casaubon (1559–1614), and Joseph Justus Scaliger (1540–1609) were able to develop the fully annotated text and commentary we know today. The eighteenth century, however, is marked by English and Dutch contributions. Dutchmen like Pieter Burmann (1668–1741), Lodewijk Caspar Valckenaer (1715–1785), and Daniel Albert Wyttenbach (1746–1820) joined the great English figures: Richard Bentley (1662–1742), Edward Gibbon (1737–1794), and Richard Porson (1759–1808).

The modern philological revolution, however, began in Germany. The growth of knowledge, the refinement of method, and the challenge to the assumptions of previous generations came to full flower in the groundbreaking work of three great figures: J. J. Winckelmann (1717–1768), F. A. Wolf (1759–1824), and Barthold Georg Niebuhr (1776–1831). These towering figures inaugurated a new spirit of scientific inquiry and intellectual liberation. For them, the proper study of texts entailed an all-encompassing pursuit of all aspects of life in the author's era. Following the defeat of Napoleon, a sense of liberation further invigorated German scholarship so that it became the dominant force in classical philology until World War I.

England made its great contributions as well, from George Grote's (1794–1871) inimitable history of Greece (1846–1856) to the pioneering work of the "Cambridge Ritualists" in the new century. The British, however, became neither as specialized nor as productive as the Germans. Rather, as Sir John Edwin Sandys points out in his three-volume history of classical scholarship, "scholarship" was defined not as publication or simply learning but as "the sum of the mental attainments of a scholar." Breadth of understanding was valued above depth of investigation. English "scholarship" aims to ennoble personal character, while German "scholarship" aims to enlarge our common knowledge.

—*Ward W. Briggs Jr.*

Viewpoint:
Yes. German philology far surpasses the British tradition in the production of useful knowledge about antiquity.

The nineteenth and early twentieth centuries were the formative period for modern classical scholarship. The dates usually given are the matriculation of F. A. Wolf (1759–1824) at Göttingen on 8 April 1777 *(studiosus philologiae)* to the death of Ulrich von Wilamowitz-Moellendorff (1848–1931) on 25 September 1931. Except for new papyrological and archaeological discoveries, most of what is lasting in subsequent work simply repeats, refines, or imitates our superior predecessors. Modern classical scholarship easily becomes a Hesiodic progression from gold to iron. The Germans gave us fundamental editions of texts based on a scientific study of surviving manuscripts; examples include Immanuel Bekker's (1785–1871) *Corpus Aristotelicum* (Aristotle is still cited by the page numbers used in Bekker's edition), Theodor Bergk's (1812–1881) collection of the lyric poets, August Nauck's (1822–1892) collection of lost tragedies, Friedrich Meineke's (1790–1870) and Theodor Kock's (1820–1901) editions of the comic poets, Hermann Diels's (1848–1922) Presocratics, and Heinrich Stein's (1828–1917) Herodotus. Then we have the enormous undertakings begun at Berlin in the nineteenth century under August Boeckh (1785–1867) and Theodor Mommsen (1817–1903). Boeckh's *Inscriptiones Graecae* and Mommsen's *Corpus Inscriptionum Latinarum* are collections of all known Greek and Latin inscriptions preserved from antiquity. They were only possible because of the existence of academies of science that allowed the cooperation of international teams of scholars. The British Academy was a late and feeble imitation. Then came the some ninety volumes of Pauly-Wissowa's enormous encyclopedia of classical antiquity. The *Realencyclopädie* is repeatedly cited today by serious scholars. It even has an article on the kiss in antiquity, and the *Thesaurus Linguae Latinae,* detested by A. E. Housman because it made things too easy, is now on-line and repeatedly consulted.

How many permanent contributions to modern classical philology emerged from nineteenth- and early-twentieth-century Oxbridge? The answer is simple: several commentaries have become standard. Perhaps the greatest is Sir Richard Jebb's Sophocles. Anyone working on Sophocles must consult Jebb, but there is a revealing caveat. Jebb is cited for his translation or his elucidation of specific passages. No one ever bothers with Jebb's view of the *Philoctetes.* In short, Jebb saw the trees but not the forest *(Mikrophilologie).* One may add James Adam's *Republic,* Lewis Campbell's *Theaetetus,* W. H. Thompson's *Phaedrus,* John Conington's Virgil, and J. G. Frazer's Pausanias and Ovid's *Fasti;* and, a bit later, Cyril Bailey's Lucretius, A. W. Gomme's Thucydides, and F. H. Sandbach's Menander.

Apart from these works, there is one lasting contribution, but it is more American than British. The Loeb Library, now more than 450 volumes, was founded by a Jew of German origin and a Harvard graduate, James Loeb (1867–1933), who was driven back to Germany partly because of American anti-Semitism. Only after consultation with Wilamowitz, did he found what has become the standard collection of English translations from the Greek and Roman authors. For its first fifty years almost all the good editions were by Americans. Arthur Darby Nock (1902–1963) referred to "The Low-Ebb Library, good for the bad authors"—the only decent edition of a tragedian was Herbert Weir Smyth's Aeschylus. Moreover, Italian, French, or German scholars do not regularly use the facility. Thus, the case is proven: in comparison with the Germans the lasting British contribution to our modern knowledge of antiquity is minimal.

There are two principal reasons for this contrast: the ideology (what do we gain from studying ancient authors?) and the educational system. In reaction to Napoleon's wartime atrocities in Prussia, Germans gave up the French model of Frederick the Great (1712–1786) and replaced it with the Greek. Germans read ancient authors in order to improve themselves. Plato, Sophocles, Tacitus, and Virgil had something to say to a young reader that was crucial for the forming of his character. In his famous letter to a young man who wanted to study philology, Barthold Georg Niebuhr (1776–1831) wrote:

> Homer, Aeschylus, Sophocles, Pindar, these are the poets of the young man, these are those on whom great men nourished themselves and which, so long as literature enlightens the world, will ennoble for a lifetime the youthful souls inspired by them. . . . To those poets and among the prose writers to Herodotus, Thucydides, Demosthenes, Plutarch, to Cicero, Livy, Caesar, Sallust, Tacitus, to these I beg you urgently to devote yourself, to devote yourself exclusively to them. Don't read them in order to make aesthetic judgments about them; but to read yourself into them and to fill your soul with their thoughts in order to benefit through reading as you would benefit through the respectful hearing of speeches by great men.

When Wilamowitz was asked why one should learn Greek, his immediate answer was, "in order to read Greek books." In short, the ancient authors were not peripheral, an amusing waste of time, or an adornment of an upper class that had nothing else to do. They were central. This conviction added seriousness to the study of ancient authors. We have a valuable witness for the difference. Sir George Cornewall Lewis (1806–1863) wrote to K. O. Müller on 14 June 1831: "What is chiefly wanted in this country, is to make people consider Homer & Thucydides as something besides school-books. Every gentleman in this country (which I believe is nowhere else the case) learns Greek, more or less: but it is taught in so repulsive and imperfect a manner, that the moment a man has left the University, he throws away his Greek books for ever." This greater seriousness was encouraged by the fact that, unlike the English, many classical scholars such as Mommsen, Müller, Nauck, and Friedrich Nietzsche were the sons of strict Protestant pastors. They lost their faith but preserved Christian reverence for the written word. The Enlightenment had taught that Hellenism might replace Christianity. "Fidem Platonicam profiteor" (I profess the faith of Plato), declared Wilamowitz, at the same time holding that St. Paul was the man from whom he had learned least.

One should also look at the schools and universities. A boys' boarding school, such as Pforte, where Wilamowitz and Nietzsche learned Greek and Latin, was called an Internat. The more general term was gymnasium, quite different from an American gym. As in England, boys were taught at boys' schools. Senior proms, sex education, and sports did not exist. In fact, school and college athletics in the United States are a curse from our English forebears. Dr. Thomas Arnold (1795–1842), the headmaster of Rugby and editor of Thucydides, introduced school sports. His reason was simple: to reduce masturbation or worse among the boys, who slept unguarded in dorms at night. An exhaustive game of rugby would tire the boy sufficiently so that he would quickly fall asleep, unlike French boys, as Dr. Arnold reminds us. At Pforte, the hero was the best student, not a quarterback. From the start, boys learned that intellectual excellence was the first goal. No German school or university had a team that played against other schools or universities. If a Munich student wished to row, he would join a rowing club in town. No Munich team will ever play Berlin. The effect cannot be overestimated. A talented student was never dismissed as a failed athlete. Discipline was strict. Wilamowitz at Pforte was several times flogged before the other boys and placed in the *carcer,* a kind of brig for several days because he was caught smoking. The standards were high. At age fourteen, the classics master dictated Xenophon's *Anabasis* to the boys in Greek. They had to take it down in Latin. Wilamowitz learned to think and dream in Greek.

Boys normally graduated from the gymnasium at age twenty or twenty-one. Germans have

Eighteenth-century portrait of the German archaeologist J. J. Winckelmann, who was in charge of antiquities and the scriptor of the Vatican

(Mengs, Metropolitan Museum, New York)

never had the baccalaureate degree. The gymnasium provided the education of both prep school and liberal arts college. Entering the university was comparable to an American student entering graduate school. One specialized from the first semester. General education did not exist. The prolongation of adolescence that still characterizes American colleges and graduate schools was not there. Term papers and course examinations did not exist. After several years one took general exams that would entitle one to write a dissertation. One would have attended lectures of choice. Early on, German scholars, not least of whom was Friedrich Gottlieb Welcker (1784–1868), advocated the *Totalitätsideal,* the ideal of knowing everything that could then be known about antiquity. One must apply knowledge of the whole in order to interpret the specific. Welcker's reconstruction of lost tragedies was crucial here. One can annotate the *Philoctetes* competently if one knows tragic, especially Sophoclean, Greek well. To reconstruct Euripides' *Philoctetes,* one must know Euripidean Greek well but also be able to use the ancient lexicographers, scholia, Attic vase paintings, and Roman sarcophagi and deduce the original from comic parody. Jebb annotated preserved plays. He did not reconstruct lost ones. Such reconstructions resulted in the concept of *Altertumswissenschaft* in contrast to *Klassische Philologie,* that is, the science of classical antiquity, not simply an intensive study of preserved texts. Yet, separate departments for archaeology and ancient history did exist. A German archaeologist, unlike his American counterpart, has never been an illiterate among philologists or a digger of trenches amid explicators of beauty. Likewise, one could earn a doctorate in ancient history without wasting time preparing for examinations in British colonialism or the American Civil War. Specialization is the key to discovery. The German system encouraged this approach.

German universities, certainly since Wilhelm von Humboldt (1767–1835), perfected what we call the graduate program. Lectures, seminars, departments, and the Ph.D. degree were all German imports brought to the United States by American scholars who, because of their hatred of the English after two wars fought on U.S. soil, eagerly studied in Germany, especially Bonn and Göttingen, and until the *Lusitania* and Rhodes scholarships, not Oxbridge. A further German hurdle beyond American capacity existed–the *Habilitationsschrift.* This type of thesis was done several years after the doctorate on a subject chosen by its writer. Without it one could not hold a professorship. Oxbridge colleges in contrast were finishing schools for the sons of the rich and noble. Teaching was accomplished in tutorials, one or two students meeting weekly with a celibate divine who drilled them in grammar and had them translate Alfred Tennyson into Euripidean or indeed Pindaric Greek.

The American tag is "if you can't do it, teach it." A teacher is a loser looked upon with contempt and rightly paid an office boy's salary. Contrarily, German respect for a professor is enormous. It derives ultimately from the Platonic influence on men like Humboldt. A *philosophos* means one who is intellectually curious, always eager to learn. The conviction reached a high point with Werner Jaeger's (1888–1961) ideal of *paideia,* both culture and the transmission of culture to the young. Peter Corssen (1856–1928) wrote in a letter of 11 February 1902 to Wilamowitz that he was "a worm who lifelong crawls on his belly and eats filth" in contrast to the lion Wilamowitz. Jaeger called Wilamowitz a god, as Aristotle did Plato. Such adoration proves the influence that a teacher exerted on a student who would do his best to gain his master's approval. Excellence was encouraged.

Leopold von Ranke (1795–1886) early set the goal of historicism. It was to rediscover "wie es eigentlich gewesen [war]" ("how it really was"). One must use every available bit of evidence to re-create what happened. Wilamowitz wrote of Aristophanes' *Lysistrata:* "In the end the poem, meant for an hour, first has to be understood as what it intended to be on that occasion. Only then does one treat it for its absolute worth." Of the ancient writers he wrote: "The thinkers were men of flesh and blood with inner contradictions, such as we all have, with love and hate. The poets were that too. . . . If historicism means that one wants to grasp men as individuals in their time, then I confess that I belong to the allegedly *victa causa.*" At the end of his greatest work, *Herakles,* published in his fortieth year, he articulates the method that explains the enduring nature of the German contribution:

> It is far more to the point that the ancient poet speak, not some modern professor. We perform our task correctly only when we don't force our own mind into every ancient book that falls into our hands; but rather read out of it what is already there. That is precisely the specifically philological task of comprehending a different individual. It is a matter of one's sinking into another mind, whether that of an individual or of a people. In the self-sacrifice of our own individuality lies our strength. We philologists as such have nothing of the poet nor of the prophet, both of which to a certain degree the historian should have. On the other hand we ought to carry something of the actor in ourselves, not of the virtuoso who sets his own idiosyncratic touches onto the role; but of the true artist, who gives life to the dead words through his own heart's blood.

–WILLIAM M. CALDER III,
UNIVERSITY OF ILLINOIS

Viewpoint: No. British scholarship produces superior results in the long run, both in terms of a well-rounded knowledge of antiquity and of the resulting education offered to students.

According to Rudolf Pfeiffer in his *History of Classical Scholarship 1300–1850* (1976), "there is in England a long and continuous history of classical education, of humanistic ideas, and of the classical tradition in literature; but the chapter formed by the history of classical scholarship is relatively short." In terms of the publication of data and interpretations of the ancient world to scholars in the form of grammars, dictionaries, works of reference, *editiones maiores,* collections of inscriptions, archaeological discoveries, and so on, German superiority, at least for much of the nineteenth century, must be acknowledged. As Gilbert Murray (1866–1957), one of the few Englishmen of his time who knew German methods, characterized the German and English approaches: "The professional against the amateur; the specialist proper against the scholar and the gentleman." Yet, if one asks which system over the centuries has more consistently delivered to its future citizens a more useful mastery of the great authors of antiquity, set a higher premium on penetrating the thought rather than the life of the ancients, and more thoroughly permeated its society with the heritage of Greece and Rome, the answer would be England.

The basic English system, as M. L. Clarke points out, was the one imposed upon it in 78 C.E. by the Roman governor Agricola (40–93 C.E.). Boys around the age of twelve studied and imitated the greatest works of literature (usually Virgil, Terence, and Homer and the dramatists) under a *grammaticus* until they were turned over to a *rhetor* at fifteen for advanced exercises in rhetoric and composition. This system, run by teachers, not scholars, was intended to produce model citizens, not specialized researchers. The solid citizens produced by this system from the Middle Ages to the middle of the last century were deeply imbued with the ideals of classical society and perpetuated the intellectual and political vitality of the state along classical lines of courage, service, and moderation.

Most European systems hewed to the seven liberal arts of the *trivium* (grammar, dialectic, and rhetoric) and *quadrivium* (arithmetic, geometry, music, and astronomy) through the Renaissance. In England, not even the Reformation or Puritanism had much effect on the role of classics in the curriculum. When the Oxford Statutes of 1564–1565 added three branches of philosophy to the original seven arts, the role of classics was expanded from imitation of literature alone to include the intellectual history of the ancients. Roger Ascham (1515–1568) in *The Schoolmaster* (1571) tried to move away from original composition in Latin and Greek to translation into those languages as a means of understanding both languages, but this still meant a narrow scope for teachers. As A. E. Housman pointed out, the men such as Richard Bentley who made great discoveries in Latin meter in England (1662–1742) were not the ones who excelled at composing Latin and Greek verses. Yet, to judge by Alexander Pope's stinging portrait of Bentley in *The Dunciad* (1728), original scholarship was not itself so highly prized as was original Latin verse. John Milton (1608–1674), himself extraordinarily skilled at Latin composition, objected to the practice as "pure trifling in grammar and sophistry." Even the undeniably great scholars England produced in the next two centuries had little to do with the universities: Bentley, Edward Gibbon (1737–1794), Richard Porson (1759–1808), George Grote (1794–1871), the redoubtable Irish physician James Henry (1798–1876), Sir George Cornewall Lewis (1806–1863), W. R. Paton (1858–1921), and the Channel Islander Peter Paul Dobree (1782–1825).

If, by 1800, Latin was no longer the language of literature or commerce, the classics had still, in the words of the American classicist B. L. Gildersleeve (1831–1924), "penetrated English life, and proved themselves a working force." What exactly was the connection between knowing one's forms and becoming a pillar of English society? Clarke quotes an Eton master of the 1840s: "If you do not take more pains, how can you ever expect to write good longs and shorts? If you do not write good longs and shorts, how can you ever be a man of taste? If you are not a man of taste, how can you ever be of use in the world?" Intensive imitation of a few great authors gave the boys a deep and lifelong intimacy with their authors that Gildersleeve admired: "It is a great thing to breathe the same pellucid air with Vergil, to feel Horace playing about the heart-strings, to hear the music of the voiceful sea from which the Iliad and the Odyssey have risen." How does this communion compare with that of the German drudge measuring Athenian sewers or counting Romanian inscriptions? Gilbert Murray may have averred that "Iwan von Mueller's [1830–1917] Handbuch is by English standards an unapproachable marvel," but Porson's and Housman's seemingly effortless parodies of Greek tragedy are beyond the German's powers. Gildersleeve recognizes that the English familiarity with ancient authors made it virtually impossible that one of her scholars could fail to recognize a line of Virgil as did Lucian Mueller (1836–1898), or, like Theodor

TEACHING LATIN

Roger Ascham, humanist scholar, tutor, and later secretary to Queen Elizabeth of England, was best known for The Schoolmaster *(1571), a treatise on practical education. In the following excerpt from his posthumously published work, he recommends the "proper" way to teach Latin:*

There is a way, touched in the first book of Cicero *De oratore,* which, wisely brought into schools, truly taught, and constantly used, would not only take wholly away this butcherly fear in making of Latins but would also, with ease and pleasure and in short time, as I know by good experience, work a true choice and placing of words, a right ordering of sentences, an easy understanding of the tongue, a readiness to speak, a facility to write, a true judgment both of his own and other men's doings, what tongue soever he doth use.

The way is this. After the three concordances learned, as I touched before, let the master read unto him the epistles of Cicero gathered together and chosen out by Sturmius for the capacity of children.

First let him teach the child, cheerfully and plainly, the cause and matter of the letter; then, let him construe it into English so oft as the child may easily carry away the understanding of it; lastly, parse it over perfectly. This done thus, let the child, by and by, both construe and parse it over again so that it may appear that the child doubteth in nothing that his master taught him before. After this, the child must take a paper book and, sitting in some place where no man shall prompt him, by himself, let him translate into English his former lesson. Then, showing it to his master, let the master take from him his Latin book, and, pausing an hour at the least, then let the child translate his own English into Latin again in another paper book. When the child bringeth it turned into Latin, the master must compare it with Tully's book and lay them both together, and where the child doth well, either in choosing or true placing of Tully's words, let the master praise him and say, "Here ye do well." For I assure you, there is no such whetstone to sharpen a good wit and encourage a will to learning as is praise.

But if the child miss, either in forgetting a word, or in changing a good with a worse, or misordering the sentence, I would not have the master either frown or chide with him, if the child have done his dilligence and used no truantship therein. For I know by good experience that a child shall take more profit of two faults gently warned of than of four things rightly hit. For then the master shall have good occasion to say unto him:

N[omen], Tully would have used such a word, not this; Tully would have placed this word here, not there; would have used this case, this number, this person, this degree, this gender, he would have used this mood, this tense, this simple rather than this compound; this adverb here, not there; he would have ended the sentence with this verb, not with that noun or participle, etc.

Source: Roger Ascham, *The Schoolmaster,* edited by Lawrence V. Ryan (Ithaca, N.Y.: Cornell University Press, 1967), pp. 14–15.

Kock (1820–1891), could take a line of St. Paul to be a comic fragment.

While Britain produced some great classical scholars of drama after Porson—Peter Elmsley (1773–1825), Thomas Gaisford (1779–1855), and James Henry Monk (1784–1856), who edited Euripides while bishop of Gloucester and Bristol—there was no one near the stature of F. A. Wolf (1759–1824), August Boeckh (1785–1867), Barthold Georg Niebuhr (1776–1831), Friedrich Gottlieb Welcker (1784–1868), or Karl Otfried Müller (1797–1840), and Americans from Edward Everett to Gildersleeve knew it. The great schoolmasters like Thomas Arnold (1795–1842) of Rugby were sensitive to German activity and began moving the curriculum toward the Greek side, and pressing the study of "things rather than words" while adding prose authors to the reading lists and reducing verse composition.

With the coming of the *literae humaniores* in the 1840s, Oxford broadened the reach of classics. Ancient philosophy began to be taught with an eye to the works of moderns such as Immanuel Kant and Georg Wilhelm Friedrich Hegel. Again, this breadth explicitly did not encourage scholarship of the German kind, largely because troglodytes such as Benjamin Jowett (1817–1893), despised by true scholars, thought the university should prepare men for the world, not the ivory tower.

Where a German student concluded his doctoral studies with a publishable thesis on a scientific point of scholarly exactness, the British student took his Greats or sat for the Tripos and was examined on a wide range of learning, with an emphasis on philosophy or the mind of the Greek and Roman. When the German student sought a position, he was required to publish a book that was new and true, and once he became a professor, his contact with students was generally limited to prepared lectures. The British candidate would be required to show evidence of his "teaching capacity, intellect and general character" (Murray) and would be engaged in a tutorship that would cost him heavy draughts of time spent on tuition and personal supervision of the students. Which system is better for the student? Take the mediocrity in both systems: Do we prefer the Englishman who adds nothing to our knowledge but encourages by his humanity and culture generations of students to study his subject, or do we prefer Murray's "German who sets himself to some obscure piece of work as yet unattempted, which may yield valuable results, which can be achieved by industry without understanding"?

By the last quarter of the nineteenth century, German preeminence in the study of the ancient world had begun to slip away. The idealization of Greece as a perfect emblem of political and intellectual freedom by J. J. Winckelmann (1717–1768), endorsed and expanded by Johann Wolfgang von Goethe and the Romantics, was put into practice by Wilhelm von Humboldt (1767–1835) at the new University of Berlin and developed by Wolf into *Totalitätsideal,* the notion that in order to say *anything* about antiquity, one had to know *everything* about antiquity. As the ideal sought more knowledge, the knowledge paradoxically increased beyond the capacity of any one man to digest it, the last probably being Boeckh, though a case could also be made for Germany's greatest classicist, Ulrich von Wilamowitz-Moellendorff (1848–1931). Specialization, the natural result of such a system, narrowed student research at the same time that Oxbridge was enlarging it. The result was German students of narrower and thinner cultivation than the English. The system geared itself to cooperative projects such as Professor William M. Calder III has described above, but those projects required educated anonymous scientists content to carve such cathedrals of erudition. The system must adapt to produce this new kind of student. Thus the great failure of the German system came when the focus shifted from truly educating the students to fitting them out for the great academy projects that defined Germany's major contributions to classical learning toward the end of the century.

If the beginning of German superiority came with rejection of French culture at the defeat of Napoleon I in 1815, Housman is surely right to date the decline to the defeat of Napoleon III at Sedan in 1870. When Germany was fragmented and poor, it produced its best thought from Winckelmann through Wolf and Boeckh. After 1870, as Housman notes, when Germany's best brains recognized the great wealth that could accrue from business and politics, the pursuit of knowledge of the classical world took a backseat.

Some perspicacious Germans recognized that their system was failing them. Friedrich Nietzsche, with his unearned Ph.D. in classics from Leipzig, wrote that the system stifled creative thought and produced few men of letters. Wilamowitz in 1900 stated the ironic truth that *Wissenschaft* had destroyed antiquity as an ideal and a unity. It was left to the Americans and British prior to World War I to deliver the most telling offensives.

German limitations arising from emphasis on method rather than judgment were noted early by Matthew Arnold (1822–1888) in *God and the Bible* (1875): "Among German critics of the Bible, a sort of criticism which we may best, perhaps, describe as a *mechanical* criticism is very rife." Britain produced men with the skills of philologists who were also literary men, though they may have known no more German than their German counterparts knew English: Albert Jay Nock (1870–1945) cites Robert Yelverton Tyrrell (1844–1914) and Louis Claude Purser (1854–1932) in Ireland, Richard Claverhouse Jebb (1841–1905) and J. W. Mackail (1859–1945) in England, and Gildersleeve in America—"these had all the science there was, but they were primarily men of letters." Paul Shorey (1857–1934), an American man of letters with a German Ph.D., acknowledged "the debt of gratitude that we owe Germany" but felt the Germans were "blind to the crushing superiority of Jebb's Sophocles, Gaston Boissier's Cicero, or [Alfred (1845–1923) & Maurice (1846–1935)] Croiset's history of Greek literature and acquiesce in the judgment that dismisses [Walter] Pater's [1839–1894] *Plato and Platonism* 'as the trifling of an amateur.'" Nor, continues Shorey, was the German reputation for accuracy deserved: "the big ambitious books of the Nordens, the Heinzes, the Reitzensteins, the Joels, the Dümmlers, the Hirzels, the Wendlands, and even, alas! of the Wilamowitzes cannot be trusted. They cannot be used without laborious verification, and the verification too often reveals that the texts cited are mistranslated, misinterpreted, or, at any rate, do not prove the point." Housman decried "the disadvantage of employing slave-labour" in "the chain-gangs working in the ergastulum at Munich" on the first volume of the *Thesaurus Linguae Latinae,* which missed the occurrence in Juvenal of *aeluros,* the Greek word for *cat.*

As the British system linked modern with ancient literature in the translation exercises from English literature into Latin or Greek, and as the Greats exam relied on the connection between ancient and modern philosophy, so the true failure of German scholarship is the failure to acquaint the student with a breadth of knowledge, including knowledge of his own culture. According to Shorey:

> They do not know their own literature as Frenchmen and Englishmen know theirs, nor do they write with constant reference to it. And if they did it could supply them with no equivalent of the poetry of England, the drama and the prose of France. The consequent crudity and amateurishness of their criticism of life and letters is their misfortune and not their fault.

Nock describes his own schooling on the English model: "The ideal towards which we were steadily directed was that of a man of letters, not the man of science, the philologist, the grammarian, the textual critic." He also saw plainly the deficiencies of the German system reflected in his American students:

> I have seen many a graduate student who had gone to Germany to study under some great classicist, like a colour-blind botanist going to a flower-show with a bad cold in his head; he came back as a doctor of philosophy, knowing a great deal about his subject, I dare say, but not knowing how to appreciate or enjoy it.
>
> The services of German philological scholarship were inestimable, prodigious, the man of letters will always gratefully make use of them; he must then do so; but no amount of philology will of itself qualify a person as a man of letters.

The thrust of English education has been successful in implanting classical ideals in its future leaders. Gildersleeve observes, "Germany has no Gladstone, no Asquith, no Lord Bryce, no Lord Cromer." We may add in the twentieth century F. A. Hirtzel, editor of Virgil and diplomat in India, John Buchan, Snell Exhibitor and director of propaganda in World War I, or more recently Roy Jenkins and Michael Foote. Though Karl Marx, Nietzsche, and Sigmund Freud influenced the "Cambridge Ritualists" (Murray, Jane Harrison, A. B. Cook, and others), at the turn of the century, Germany had no classicists who were comparable revolutionary thinkers. "The German can neither compare with them nor appreciate them. And yet these writers are definitely technical and professional scholars," said Gildersleeve.

English academia has for millennia implanted not research methods but a superior culture in its citizens. Since the four-score years of German superiority in the 1800s, what young German with a Ph.D. is more likely than his English counterpart to be hired for a broad liberal arts curriculum in an American or British school? Many German classicists today, having survived pedantic dissertations, work increasingly in isolation not only from English and American classicists but from their own culture. Housman supposed that it may be another one thousand years before the next true critic of literature comes along, but given the virtues and vices of both approaches to "scholarship," is that true great critic more likely to be German or English?

–WARD W. BRIGGS JR.,
UNIVERSITY OF SOUTH CAROLINA

References

Ward W. Briggs Jr. and William M. Calder III, eds., *Classical Scholarship: A Biographical Encyclopedia* (New York: Garland, 1990).

C. O. Brink, *English Classical Scholarship* (Cambridge: Cambridge University Press, 1986).

Calder, *Men in Their Books: Studies in the Modern History of Classical Scholarship,* edited by John P. Harris and R. Scott Smith, *Spudasmata* 67 (Hildesheim, Germany & New York: G. Olms Verlag, 1998).

Calder and others, eds., "Teaching the English Wissenschaft: The Letters of Sir George Cornewall Lewis to Karl Otfried Müller (1828–1839)," *Spudasmata* 85 (Hildesheim, Germany & New York: G. Olms Verlag, 2002).

M. L. Clarke, *Classical Education in Britain 1500–1900* (Cambridge: Cambridge University Press, 1959).

B. L. Gildersleeve, "Brief Mention," *American Journal of Philology,* 37 (Winter 1916): 494–503; reprinted in *Selections from the Brief Mention of Basil Lanneau Gildersleeve,* edited by C. W. E. Miller (Baltimore: Johns Hopkins University Press, 1930), pp. 364–376.

A. E. Housman, *The Confines of Criticism: The Cambridge Inaugural 1911* (Cambridge: Cambridge University Press, 1969).

Gilbert Murray, "German Scholarship," *Quarterly Review,* 443 (April 1915): 330–339.

Albert Jay Nock, *Memoirs of a Superfluous Man* (New York: Harper, 1943).

Rudolf Pfeiffer, *History of Classical Scholarship 1300–1850* (Oxford: Clarendon Press, 1976).

John Edwin Sandys, *A History of Classical Scholarship,* 3 volumes, third edition (Cambridge: Cambridge University Press, 1921).

Paul Shorey, "American Scholarship," *Nation,* 92 (11 May 1911): 466–469; reprinted in *The Roosevelt Lectures of Paul Shorey (1913–1914),* edited by Briggs and E. C. Kopff (Hildesheim, Germany & New York: G. Olms Verlag, 1995), pp. 383–393.

Ulrich von Wilamowitz-Moellendorff, *History of Classical Scholarship* (Baltimore: Johns Hopkins University Press, 1982).

CLASSICAL STUDIES: HOMOSEXUALITY

Did the concept of homosexuality exist in the ancient world?

Viewpoint: Yes. Homosexuality was a meaningful concept in the ancient world, even if the word itself did not exist.

Viewpoint: No. While sexual acts between members of the same sex were common in antiquity, homosexuality did not exist as a category of personal identity.

Homosexuality is defined as the existence of a class of persons who engage individually in same-sex erotic behavior and, consequently, are viewed as a legal and/or social group. In the ancient Mediterranean, same-sex erotic behavior was widely attested from at least the seventh century B.C.E. through the fifth century C.E. (Celts: Aristotle, *Politics* 2.6.6; Athenaeus XIII 603a; Scythians, Persia: Herodotus 1.105, 135; Egypt and Near East: see the articles below). This chapter focuses primarily on Greece and Rome, and even in these places local and temporal differences were substantial.

Social norms shaped ancient sexuality in crucial ways. Athens and Rome were slave societies, and soldiers and slavers captured, kidnapped, and sold persons routinely. Slaves constituted one-fourth to one-third of the population in these cities. Slaveowners had unrestricted sexual access to slaves as well as freedmen/women.

Sexual acts were often framed in terms of penetration (see Catullus 16). The penetrator was seen as powerful/controlling (male/free/elite/conqueror), while the penetrated was viewed as powerless/controlled (female/slave/lower-class/conquered).

Women, even free adult property owners, lived under control of men. Marriage, dowry, and "tutelage" (*kuriate, tutela*) codified this social norm. Subordination of women was at the root of sexuality, creating tension around masculinity. With rare exceptions, women could not represent themselves or another in court; women who had sex with women were mocked; and citizen males were prosecuted for submitting to anal penetration.

Almost every person married, even day laborers and slaves. Women married at puberty; men first married as late as 30. While nonmarrying women appeared promiscuous or willful (uncontrolled), nonmarrying men appeared promiscuous or irresponsible/selfish/spendthrift (marriage was a wealth stabilizer).

Some groups were presumed sexually attractive: women aged 12 to 50; boys aged 12 to 18 (Stoics supposedly extended it to 28!); and "soft" (*malakos/mollis*) adult males. These included *kinaidoi/cinaedi,* male musician-dancers from Eastern traditions (Perdrizet XXIX–XXXI = Antiquarium Berlin 8451) with a reputation for "passive" sex (Herondas 2.74; Strabo 14.648; Martial 2.43.13, 10.98.2; Juvenal 14.30). For Romans the term *malakos/mollis* was an insult (compare Plato, *Gorgias* 494e; Aeschines 2.99). Lust toward *molles* was socially problematic, and accusations of such lust were used in verbal attacks, rape threats, and jokes.

We have practically no information on the sexual tastes of women that does not come through upper-class men. The only female-authored writings that remain are: Sappho, Nossis (if she existed), the two Sulpicias, a possible Pompeiian graffito, and scattered letters and love spells on papyri. Sappho dwells on youth, softness of skin and hair, and grace of clothing and movement as attractive qualities in both women and men. The remains of the others are too slight to allow firm generalizations.

—Jerise Fogel and Amy Richlin

Viewpoint: Yes. Homosexuality was a meaningful concept in the ancient world, even if the word itself did not exist.

Scholars are divided on the existence of the idea of "homosexuality" in antiquity, perhaps because the twentieth-century term *homosexuality,* which includes all same-sex desire, has denoted a stigmatized category. The idea that social categories persist across time and cultures is now often said to be "essentializing" (usually a derogatory term), while the idea that social categories are always in process, ever created anew, is known as "social constructionism." Often the idea that "homosexuality" did not exist as a category before the modern period is felt to be liberating, the idea being that without the category there was no stigma, or at least there was no stereotyping of behavior or individuals.

However, there are problems with this reasoning. Models that are depressing are not therefore wrong. Conflicting elements can coexist, and, different as the ancient sex/gender systems may be from ours, they may share important features. Premodern terminology does not have to map onto modern terminology in order for the same ideas to be present. In addition, while not all members of the set (same-sex lovers) were stigmatized, some of its subsets were: we need to keep track of them.

One current popular idea of sexual categories holds that this is a matter of "orientation": each person will consistently want to be one way or the other, "heterosexual" people desiring only people of the opposite sex, "homosexual" people desiring only people of the *same* (Gr. "homo-"). This notion does not correspond exactly with general ancient ones; many ancient texts attest that the same adult male might desire both women and adolescent males (pederasty). Yet, the approval rating of pederasty varied locally and temporally, and by class—for example, in Rome it was considered wrong for any male but a slave or prostitute to be penetrated, all penetrated male bodies being tainted. In addition, adult males clearly held the adolescent male body to be strongly differentiated from their own—not exactly "homo." Moreover, other types of same-sex desire were decidedly nonnormative, and two main groups suffered: men who let other men penetrate them, and women who had sex with women.

Writers did occasionally discuss same-sex lovers as a class of persons (note that close to 100 percent of all extant texts were written by adult males). The famous (comic) speech attributed to Aristophanes in Plato's *Symposium* (fifth century B.C.E., 189d–193e) divides lovers into male-female, male-male, and female-female. Some lump together both kinds of nonnormative sex: the Roman freed slave Phaedrus (first century C.E., *Fables* 4.12), the Jewish moralist pseudo-Phocylides (first century C.E., *Sentences* 175–227; Brooten 1996: 62–63), and the Roman satirist Juvenal (second century C.E., *Satire* 2.47–49). Some writers express desire only for their own sex: Sappho's love poems address women; Plato and his followers (400 B.C.E. onward) and the Stoics (300 B.C.E. onward) markedly prefer young men and scorn women, as seen most famously in Plato's *Symposium* and *Phaedrus.* Change was thought possible; Pliny's *Natural History* includes a prescription for use on husbands who "hate sex with women," so "the harmony of the whole house is preserved" (first century C.E., 28.99).

Both popular and scientific texts distinguish nonnormative sexual types and search for causes. Greek life science concerns itself with this issue going back to some of the earliest texts; Parmenides (early fifth century B.C.E.) is quoted as saying "effeminate or sexually passive men were sometimes generated in the act of conception" (in Caelius Aurelianus *On Chronic Disorders* 4.9.133, fifth century C.E.; = Hubbard 2003: 10.5). Aristotle gives the cause as either "natural deformity" or "habituation," comparing such men with the mentally ill, nail-biters, and those who like to eat dirt (*Nicomachean Ethics* 7.5.3–5; = Hubbard 2003: 5.13). Caelius Aurelianus says men who desire to be penetrated, like women who desire women, have a mental illness and not a physical abnormality (*On Chronic Diseases* 4.9.132–133; compare Brooten 1996: 143–162). Physiognomists hold that a skilled practitioner can recognize such men by their physical traits, no matter how much they might try to suppress them (Gleason 1995: 77; compare Hubbard 2003: 10.6, 7). Astrological writers argue that sexual orientation is caused by the position of the stars at a person's birth—for nonnormative males, the conjunction of Venus, Mars, the Sun, and the Moon in a feminine sign (Firmicus Maternus Mathesis 6.31.4, fourth century C.E.; Masterson 2001: 65–66; compare Hubbard 2003: 10.38–41). These scientific opinions have a popular correlative in texts that refer to nonnormative sexuality as a *nosema* or *morbus* (disease). The implications of such beliefs are important; some ancient doctors recommend clitoridectomy for women with inordinate, possibly same-sex, desires (Brooten 1996: 162–171). Short of surgery, Pliny's *Natural History* includes a prescription for curing men of *probrosa mollitia*, "reprehensible softness" (28.106).

The long list of insulting terms applied to persons with nonnormative sexual desires similarly indicates that some people in antiquity were imagined to be exclusively interested in partners of the same sex: terms include, for men, Gr. *malakos*/Lat. *mollis* (soft), Gr. *kinaidos*/Lat. *cinaedus* (one who shakes his shameful parts); for women, *tribas* (rubster). There are no statements of desire for such a person (thus their partners remain invisible). We also have almost no first-person statements by such persons, the major exception being the poetry of Sappho and some of her successors, especially Nossis. There are a few papyri from Roman Egypt with magical spells expressing the desire of a woman for a woman (Brooten 1996: 73–113), and perhaps a graffito from Pompeii. As for pederasty, there are some Greek graffiti from boys about men (especially IG 1.924; see Hubbard 2003: 2.22–27); some cryptic lines in the satires of the Roman poet Persius (5.21–51); and, startling, the love letters between the young Marcus Aurelius and his teacher Cornelius Fronto. In general, the penetrated position seems to be also the written, rather than writing, position. Did *molles* men have a conscious group identity? One cannot know, but many observers so claim (see especially Juvenal *Satire* 2 = Hubbard 2003: 9.38).

Indeed, many texts in both Greek and Latin talk about nonnormative sexuality and the persons who practice it. The function of these texts for social control is clear: at all levels of sophistication, these words act to enforce social norms. Literary invective starts in archaic Greece with the poetry of Archilochus (seventh century B.C.E., Hubbard 2003: 1.3) and continues strongly in the comedies of Aristophanes (fifth century B.C.E.), in which accusations of a liking for being penetrated anally are often used to insult specific Athenians, characters onstage, or even members of the audience in general (Henderson 1992: 209–215). The fourth-century B.C.E. Athenian court speeches are full of ruinous gossip (Hunter 1994: 96–119). The conventional nature of insults and jokes should not blind us to their social function; when, during the Hellenistic period, comic drama starts to turn Sappho and Nossis into comic figures, that situation tells one something (but what?) about both the visibility and the danger of sex between women at that time.

Jokes about the body of the male slave as object for his master's use are fairly common in Plautus's comedies (circa 200 B.C.E.) and in the fragments of the plays written by his contempo-

SOLON'S LOVE

Plutarch made these observations about the distinguished Athenian politician and poet Solon:

I. Didymus the grammarian, in his reply to Asclepiades on Solon's tables of law, mentions a remark of one Philocles, in which it is stated that Solon's father was Euphorion, contrary to the opinion of all others who have written about Solon. For they all unite in saying that he was a son of Execestides, a man of moderate wealth and influence in the city, but a member of its foremost family, being descended from Codrus. [2] Solon's mother, according to Heracleides Ponticus, was a cousin of the mother of Peisistratus. And the two men were at first great friends, largely because of their kinship, and largely because of the youthful beauty of Peisistratus, with whom, as some say, Solon was passionately in love. And this may be the reason why, in later years, when they were at variance about matters of state, their enmity did not bring with it any harsh or savage feelings, but their former amenities lingered in their spirits, and preserved there, *smouldering with a lingering flame of Zeus-sent fire,* the grateful memory of their love. [3] And that Solon was not proof against beauty in a youth, and made not so bold with Love as "to confront him like a boxer, hand to hand," may be inferred from his poems. He also wrote a law forbidding a slave to practice gymnastics or have a boy lover, thus putting the matter in the category of honorable and dignified practices, and in a way inciting the worthy to that which he forbade the unworthy. [4] And it is said that Peisistratus also had a boy lover, Charmus, and that he dedicated the statue of Love in the Academy, where the runners in the sacred torch race light their torches.

Source: *Plutarch,* Plutarch's Lives, *with an English translation by Bernadotte Perrin, 11 volumes (Cambridge, Mass.: Harvard University Press / London: Heinemann, 1914–1926).*

raries. By the mid second century B.C.E., the satirist Lucilius is already mocking the *cinaedus* (Richlin 1992: 169), and similar jokes would form a staple of the satirist's art, especially for Persius in the reign of Nero and for Juvenal in the reign of Trajan; likewise for the epigrammatist Martial, Juvenal's friend, and for the Syrian/Greek comic writer Lucian, their contemporary. The same kinds of jokes permeate Roman texts from the subliterary (graffiti, political lampoons, and the songs the soldiers sang at the triumphs of Roman generals), to the gossip fossilized in letters and life writing from various periods, to rhetorical invective (Richlin 1992: 105–143). Pejorative lists of the physical traits of *molles* men are common: they curl their hair, wear makeup, lisp or warble, scratch their head with one finger, depilate their bodies, put one hand on their hip, sway when they walk, wear fancy clothes, and wear "unbelted" togas. Similarly pejorative lists show up in the few texts on *tribades* (see Hubbard 2003: 9.26; 10.9).

Invective was used in contest situations, where the truth value of the claim must be suspect: in public insult matches in Athens and Rome; in accusations about insufficiently manly style in rhetorical competitions; and, in court, with the common insinuation that a man's opponent had let his body be used sexually in his youth. Indeed, the mode of education favored by most cultures in the ancient Mediterranean, in which elite males were intensively schooled together, provided a logical setting for such discourse. It is important to realize that these contestatory and social forms of stigma—essentially name-calling—were matched by more material forms—sticks and stones. At the family level, the Greek *kyrios* and the Roman *paterfamilias* were entitled to discipline those in their power, and Valerius Maximus writes approvingly of a Roman father who killed his adult son for "dubious chastity" (first century C.E., 6.1.5); such behavior would be seen as bringing shame on the family. At the public level, Aiskhines in "Against Timarkhos" (fourth century B.C.E.) accuses his opponent of having prostituted himself in order to debar him from public speaking, through the process of the *dokimasia rhetoron* (scrutiny of speakers; Winkler 1990: 54–64). Similarly, a whole complex of Roman legal practices inflicted civil disabilities on males who allowed their bodies to be "used womanishly" (Richlin 1993): the status of *infamia* could be inflicted on a citizen via statute (the *lex Julia municipalis,* first century B.C.E.), the censors' mark, or the praetor's edict. *Infamia* seems to have been widely applied within Roman culture of the late Republic and empire, and probably would have affected more people than the mysterious *lex Scantinia,* a statute that seems to have aimed at regulating male sexual behavior. Moreover, at some point in the empire a penalty was formulated for a man who "allowed impure sexual use of his body": he is fined half his assets and debarred from making a will, a significant deprivation in a culture greatly concerned with inheritance (Paulus *Sententiae* 2.26.12–13). The one positive thing about these penalties is that they suggest invective is directed at real-life sexual subcultures, probably centered in the big cities (Rome, Alexandria, or Antioch).

Legal penalties and statuses should be seen in the context of negative reactions to the whole sex/gender system described here as normative. Jewish observers from the first century C.E. onward seem both confused and repelled by this system; Philo of Alexandria, in a well-known observation, decries pederasty and merges it with sex between adult males (*On the Special Laws* 3.37–42). One talmudic commentator says, "Is it not enough that we are subjugated to the seventy nations, but even to this one [that is, Rome], who is penetrated like women?" (*Genesis Rabah* 63: 10 p. 693, compare Satlow 1995: 213). St. Paul includes effeminates and "those [men] who have sex with men" among those excluded from the kingdom of God (*Corinthians* 6: 9–10; Brooten 1996: 215–302). The subliterary and probably nonurban apocalyptic texts, starting from the second century C.E., consistently lump all sexual transgressors together into the same pits of hellfire (Brooten 1996: 305–314), suggesting that sexual experimentation in the ancient Mediterranean was something one would need to search for in the big city, and with care even there.

Erotic pederastic literature all but disappears by the third century C.E. as urban culture diminishes with the empire under attack, and, with the rise of Christianity, does not return, though pederastic desire itself continues to be attested in the form of tirades, satires, and rules against it. Laws grew harsh (Masterson 2001: 47–52): in 342 C.E. "choice punishments" were decreed for men who "wed like women" (probably death by torture, *Codex Theodosianus* 9.7.3). In 390, Theodosius I called for death by burning as a punishment for male prostitutes (*Codex Theodosianus* 9.7.6; compare *Collatio* 5.1.1). The emperor Justinian probably made sex between men a capital offense for both partners (*Institutiones* 4.18.4). There is, however, no evidence on the actual frequency of such executions. Also, late antiquity has no monopoly on cruelty; one should not forget that clitoridectomies were being prescribed in the second century C.E. and might keep in mind the Roman treatment of androgynous children in the Republic, known from the prodigy lists of Julius Obsequens: they were put out to sea on rafts and left to die (Butler 1998).

Some scholars claim that it was not same-sex object choice that bothered people in antiquity but the breaking of gender-role norms. Yet, it is not possible to separate these two elements in the ancient sources. Thus, Scipio Aemilianus, perhaps in a speech he gave as censor in 142–141 B.C.E., attacks one Sulpicius Galus (Gellius 6.12.4–5): "A man who daily is adorned before his mirror, covered with perfumes, whose eyebrows are shaven, who walks around with his beard plucked out and his thighs depilated, who as a very young man at dinner parties lay curled up against his lover dressed in a leotard, who is not only a wine fancier but a man fancier—does anyone doubt about him, that he did the same thing that *cinaedi* do?"

Overall, it is not just important to know that people in antiquity did have sexual categories. What matters is what they did with them. One owes a duty to the past to remember and beware.

—AMY RICHLIN,
UNIVERSITY OF SOUTHERN CALIFORNIA

Viewpoint:
No. While sexual acts between members of the same sex were common in antiquity, homosexuality did not exist as a category of personal identity.

The norms outlined in the introduction to this chapter had a great impact on the expression of same-sex eroticism in the ancient world. Yet, they did not have the effect of creating a social or legal class of "homosexuals." First, homoerotic activity was already part of ancient sexual norms in some ways. It was thought "normal" in all periods, for instance, for an adult man to express sexual attraction to an adolescent boy. Even "soft" adult male slaves were often socially acceptable lust objects for free men, so long as those slaves played the "passive" role in bed. The extreme legal emphasis on the rape of young citizen men is very revealing: present-day U.S. rape laws almost universally assume male-on-female rape; Greek and Roman laws were concerned with rape of young men by older men.

A Greek or Roman male's socially prescribed sexual role changed with age, however, in a way that is unfamiliar to most of us. In Greece, particularly Sparta, Crete and seventh to fifth century B.C.E. Athens, a "pederastic" model existed, especially among the upper class in Athens, that divided men into younger, desirable *eromenoi* (beloved boys) and older, desiring (ideally, also mentoring) *erastai* (lovers). Intercourse with a free boy was against the law, but pederastic romance thrived. In Rome a similar timescale applied. Cicero could damage Clodius's reputation by accusing him of fraternizing with "gigolos, full-grown male prostitutes, and female prostitutes" (*For T. Annius Milo* 55). Full-grown male sexual partners were a possible source of shame to a man because their age suggested they might be penetrators (Suetonius: *Caligula* 24.3; *Galba* 21). Lucian (*True Story,* second century C.E.) pictures his fanciful Moon-Men (among whom there are no women) changing gender roles as they grow, beginning as wives and ending as husbands—an extension *ad absurdum* of the idea that young boys were sexually like girls/women.

In short, ancient Greeks and Romans took it for granted that gender status changed with age, class, nationality, slavery/freedom, and other factors: most people seem not to have believed that humans are born with one, unchanging sexual orientation. Nevertheless, those with desires unsuitable for their gender status were considered abnormal. Ancient medical treatises discuss why some grown men prefer penetration by other men, behaving like women—but no medical authors find male attraction to adolescent boys problematic. Seneca quotes a quip (*Controversiae* IV pr. 10) spoken in defense of a man accused of having been his patron's passive lover: "Inchastity is a genuine accusation for a freeborn man; for a slave a necessity; for a freedman a duty." Not all gender roles were flexible: women were not imagined to pass through a stage of sexual passivity into adulthood: their "passive/pursued" status was unchanging. This gender flexibility of course had its limits—antiquity was not a utopia for same-sex lovers. Men who desired grown male partners beyond the age of puberty ran the risk of being classified as "effeminate" unless they expressed their lust in such aggressive ways as made clear that they were not "passive." Yet again, these expressions of male lust toward men and boys were socially acceptable.

How were men supposed to feel about women, then? Homosexuality implies heterosexuality; it comes into use as a concept in a society where an adult male is expected to be attracted by women exclusively. Often, the sources seem to find something almost nerdy about a man attracted only to women (note Plato's admittedly biased comments, in Aristophanes' speech in *Symposium,* on the "manly" nature of male-male partners). Several self-defenses of men whose affections were primarily directed toward women exist, including that of the love poet Ovid. Amid a series of embarrassing quirks of the Emperor Claudius (gorging himself then sleeping in a convenient position to vomit, falling asleep in court, being obsessed with dice playing, and so forth), Suetonius adds that he was attracted passionately to women while "boys and men left him cold" (*Claudius* 33). Many playful Hellenistic comparisons of the differing attractions of women and boys for men exist (Plutarch, *Erotikos,* 4.23; ps.-Lucian, *Erotes* 13f.; Propertius 2.4; Achilles Tatius, *Leucippe and Clitophon* 2.35–38; cf. Lucretius 4.1053–1054): they imply a rational choice of lover based on generalized gender characteristics and personal preferences (boys were less artful but sweeter, while women were more skilled and responsive). Catullus writes love poetry to both "Lesbia" and "Juventius" (compare especially "kiss" poems 5, 7, 48). These texts imply a certain parity of desire: "real" men might reasonably be attracted to either grown women or boys, and probably to both. (There are few poems written by men to young girls, in fact, although Longus's *Daphnis and Chloe* tells a story of young heterosexual lovers who are age-mates.)

Homoerotic activity also came within societal norms in the strong literary and social traditions, somewhat foreign to modern Western tastes, about heroic same-sex couples. Stories of archaic Sparta, and Homer's *Iliad* (in later eras Patroclus and Achilles were read as a love pair), glamorized same-sex attachments between noble warriors. Plutarch's *Life of Lycurgus* (although late: first century C.E.) describes the customs of Sparta, including institutionalized male and female homoeroticism, as strange but admirable; likewise, stories concerning Spartan, Cretan, Chalkidian (Plutarch, *Erotikos* 17; also Athenaeus XIII 601e), and other pederastic traditions (seventh century Thera: IG XII 3.536–601, 1410–1493). The Theban "Sacred Band" of warriors, however fictional, was widely believed in antiquity to be composed of pairs of devoted male lovers (Plutarch, *Pelopidas* 18-20; Athenaeus 13.561E; Polyaenus 2.5.1; the actuality is doubtful: see Leitao, in Nussbaum and Sihvola). Harmodios and Aristogeiton, the "Tyrant-Killers," were immortalized in Athenian art, storytelling, and oratory (Plato, *Symposium* 182B–D; Plutarch, *Moralia* 760C; other tyrant-killing pairs: Athenaeus 602a). Romantic friendships between males strongly influenced the literary tradition. Cicero as a young man wrote love poetry to his slave Tiro (Pliny, *Letters* 7.4; Carcopino). Roman literature celebrated heroic friendships: Orestes and Pylades, Nisus and Euryalus, and Theseus and Pirithous, sometimes implicitly sexualized through the casting of one of the two in the pair as younger. When Hadrian publicized his love for Antinous, he was acting within a well-known literary tradition of honorable love norms, not "coming out of the closet" (Spartianus, *Life of Hadrian* 14.5; Cassius Dio 69.11; Ammianus Marcellinus 22.16.2.)

In ancient Greek novels, male same-sex desire is presented without comment alongside male-female desire (Xenophon of Ephesus's *Ephesiaca,* Nonnos's *Dionysiaca,* Achilles Tatius, Longus's *Daphnis and Chloe*). No doubt the strength of the pederastic model influences presentation (Konstan 1994, 10, 35; although he comments also "no polarity here of homosexuality and heterosexuality . . . ," 120, citing Halperin 1990); but male-male relationships, even prospectively long-term, are ubiquitous. In Xenophon's *Ephesian Tale,* Hippothous, one of the main characters, is a freelance bandit portrayed as intensely attracted and loyal to the young male hero of the story. Hippothous was once the lover of a "boy-love" (who was, however, explicitly his age-mate), who died tragically, according to the pederastic romantic paradigm. At the end of the story, he winds up the partner of an "attractive young Sicilian man" with whom he "shares all his possessions" (5.9) and who follows him to Italy (5.13); in order to make their life-partnership possible, Hippothous formally adopts his lover (5.15), and they settle down in Ephesus (after erecting a monumental tomb for Hippothous's dead "boy-love" on nearby Lesbos), next door to the happy heterosexual protagonist- couple. Hippothous's clear sexual preferences give his overriding love for the male hero Habrocomes, whom he briefly takes on as a companion in his daredevil life as a robber-pirate, overtones of heroic companionship. Xenophon presents two male protagonists (who participate in the heroic friendship paradigm) and a female protagonist (who winds up romantically attached to one male protagonist).

The traditions around women are not similarly well developed but sometimes echo the heroic friendship ideal. The existence and occasional expression of female-female passion is vouched for by traditionally phrased lesbian love spells that have survived on lead tablets and papyri (for example Rowlandson #286; Brooten 73–113; Hallett 1998). Lesbian girlhoods and ideals are not visible outside Sappho's poems. Amazons are not generally portrayed as lovers of other women (although note the red-figure vase of Andokides, Paris, Louvre F 203, discussed by Rabinowitz 2002: 137); they do, however, indicate fascination with the idea of same-sex military companionship—a group of mixed female and male fighters seems not to have occurred to Greek writers. In Sappho some see a feminine challenge to the pederastic model (Greene 82–105); certainly present is the idea of devoted female compan-

Detail on a vase of two males embracing and preparing to kiss, circa 510 B.C.E.

(J. Paul Getty Museum, Malibu, California)

ions joining in song and dance. Plutarch (*Life of Lycurgus*) admires Spartan women's quasi-pederastic system. Iamblichus's *Babylonian Tale* (second century C.E.) contained a "subplot about the queen of Egypt, Berenice, and her passion for the beautiful Mesopotamia" containing heroic overtones (Photius, *Bibliotheca* 94; Boswell 84). Such traditions about female-female pairs call to mind Lillian Faderman's "romantic friendships."

In many places social conventions and laws respected same-sex love between men and boys. The Athenian democracy's legal tradition included Solon's poems and laws (fr. 25; slaves were prohibited from the *palaistra* and from pederastic relations: Plutarch, *Solon* 1). Aeschines claims in a public suit against a citizen man accused of prostituting himself to men as a youth that he himself was the (chaste) lover of many boys in the *gymnasia:* a good relationship brings shame on neither lover nor beloved (*Timarkhos* 135, 137, 156f.). Married men's boy sexual companions, generally prepubescent or pubescent slaves (Richlin 1992a: chapter 2 and *Appendix*), were so common that some women negotiated to exclude them in Hellenistic marriage documents (Cantarella 171–172; *Papyrus Tebtynis* 1.104.18–20, 92 B.C.E.; Rowlandson #126, 173 B.C.E.; Brooten 109). Quintus Catulus's poem to his *puer* (boy-love) is quoted by Aulus Gellius (*Attic Nights* 19.9). Catullus (the "Juventius Cycle," including 48, 99 and other poems), Martial (for example 12.75, 12.96), and Juvenal (Sixth Satire) write in praise of boys. The *Greek Anthology* is full of epigrams that celebrate them. For Catullus, teasing the bridegroom's uppity concubine about his coming fall from grace is a humorous part of the marriage celebration (61.126–140).

Some Romans frown on male concubines, but in so doing prove that they were commonplace; they certainly were not illegal. Columella warns landowners not to make former male concubines into farm managers (1.8.1), presumably because of the continuing stigma of passivity/effeminacy. In Petronius's *Satyrica,* Encolpius is the former concubine of Lichas, who recognizes him by his penis (a joke on Lichas as well). Sallust remarks about supposed Roman cultural decline in the late second century B.C.E.: "men suffered themselves to be used as women, women put their modesty up for sale" (*Catiline,*

13.3). The criticism falls on free men's taking the passive role, and not on male lust toward boys or concubines: that was human nature.

Jewish culture and laws, which prohibited same-sex relations of all kinds (ps.-Phocylides, *Sentences* 213–16), were thought eccentric by Greeks and Romans, Egyptians and Canaanites. Jews in turn found pagan customs abhorrent, especially (under the same classification in Jewish texts) same-sex marriage, eunuchs, and female performers (Brooten 64–66). The last two were widespread: note the international phenomenon of educated *hetairai* (educated female performers and prostitutes; compare in Mesopotamia the well-known pre-Islamic *qīyan* culture; Cadiz's famous female exotic dancers [Pliny, *Letters* 1.15; Martial 14.203, 5.78, 6.71, 11.16]; and Egyptian female dancers and singers [Gardner 246]). Writing in the same era as Paul of Tarsus, Philostratus implies (*Epistles* 5; second century C.E.) to a young male correspondent that noninterest in male lovers indicates that he is not civilized; Basil and Libanius continue the pederastic ideal amid the late antique Christian/pagan mix.

This is not to say that there were not people oppressed on account of nonnormative sexuality. *Cinaedi* may designate a group (Richlin 1993); independent Roman matrons, actually adulterous or not, were another, enduring moral and legal strictures meant to rein in their influence—note the hostile view of Baiae's woman-friendly salon culture in Cicero's *For Caelius*. Bad sexual practice (whether adultery, permission of anal penetration, some kinds of prostitution, or being a woman who "acted like a man") was an accusation used to control: laws, fines, corporal punishment, and public mockery were tools of this control. Yet, in popular perception, family/household structures were not threatened by "homosexual" impulses or pursuits on the part of the male head of household, which thanks to the sexual double standard were an expected part of married life, unwanted as they might be by wives. Lesbian impulses of *matronae* were assimilated to heterosexual adultery, and prosecuted accordingly.

In Rome, a man found guilty of "passive" sex suffered the stigma of *infamia*. This lowered status prohibited both men and women from being legal advocates, sitting on juries, bringing some criminal accusations, joining the army (OCD[2], *infamia*); one also sacrificed immunity from corporal assault by authorities. To put this term in perspective, however, *all* gladiators, trainers of gladiators, actors, singers, dancers, prostitutes, and brothel owners were by definition *infames;* and women generally already suffered from many of the restrictions imposed by *infamia* (Edwards 69–76). The professions subject to *infamia* were also vaguely and broadly defined: tavern waitresses were automatically counted as prostitutes (Gaius 4.56.3; Gardner 249).

Immunity from corporal assault by authorities, in theory the right of all Roman citizens, had, in fact, never been extended to poorer citizens, who relied upon a parallel legal system of special magistrates with the right to use bodily force; later laws codified the differing legal treatment of the upper (*honestiores*) and lower (*humiliores*) classes (Crook 69). Given this situation, some found it advantageous to incur *infamia* deliberately; some women even registered as prostitutes to evade adultery laws (Gardner 247–248).

Men and women who simply desired other men and women of their age as life partners had few options. As in Xenophon's *Ephesian Tale,* Roman law allowed the formal adoption of one citizen man by another. Alternatively, life as a free man under *infamia* meant living under the radar to some extent, and possibly made some kind of "gay marriage" a reality (compare the milieu of Petronius's satire). Courtesans might live with one another similarly because of class and gender segregation, but these people do not seem to constitute a self-conscious legal or social category.

One inference from Michel Foucault's research is that gender-specific object choice was not a crucial category of sexuality for the ancient world (Foucault 1986; Halperin 1989; Halperin, Winkler, Zeitlin eds. 1990; Larmour, Miller, Platter eds. 1998; Boswell 1980, 58–59; Parker 1997, 60–62, citing Wiseman 1985, 10). In nineteenth- century Germany and Europe, heterosexual relations had become so rigidly normative that gender identity began to depend upon them and rigidify—that is, if one is attracted to women, one must therefore be "masculine," and vice versa (compare the oldest novels on the subject such as Radclyffe Hall's *Well of Loneliness*). What we call "homosexuality" was defined as a firm social and legal identity, regardless of status, citizenship, and age, against this backdrop. The making of "homosexuality" as we know it, as the basis for formation of social and legal identity, is relatively recent and was not part of the belief system of the Romans and Greeks.

—JERISE FOGEL,
MARSHALL UNIVERSITY

References

John Boswell, *Christianity, Social Tolerance, and Homosexuality: Gay People in Western Europe from the Beginning of the Christian Era to the Fourteenth Century* (Chicago: University of Chicago Press, 1980).

Bernadette J. Brooten, *Love Between Women: Early Christian Responses to Female Homoeroticism* (Chicago: University of Chicago Press, 1996).

Shane Butler, "Notes on a Membrum Disiectum," in *Women and Slaves in Greco-Roman Culture,* edited by Sandra R. Joshel and Sheila Murnaghan (London: Routledge, 1998), pp. 236–255.

Eva Cantarella, *Bisexuality in the Ancient World,* translated by C. Ó. Cuilleanáin (New Haven: Yale University Press, 1992).

Jérôme Carcopino, *Daily Life in Ancient Rome: The People and the City at the Height of the Empire,* edited by Henry T. Rowell, second edition (New Haven: Yale University Press, 2003).

John R. Clarke, *Looking at Lovemaking: Constructions of Sexuality in Roman Art 100 B.C.–A.D. 250* (Berkeley: University of California Press, 1998).

David Cohen, *Law, Sexuality, and Society* (Cambridge: Cambridge University Press, 1991).

Cohen and Richard Saller, "Foucault on Sexuality in Greco-Roman Antiquity," in *Foucault and the Writing of History,* edited by Jan Goldstein (Oxford: Blackwell, 1994), pp. 35–59, 262–266.

J. A. Crook, *Law and Life of Rome, 90 B.C.–A.D. 212* (Ithaca, N.Y.: Cornell University Press, 1967).

James Davidson, "Dover, Foucault and Greek Homosexuality: Penetration and the Truth of Sex," *Past and Present,* 170 (2001): 3–51.

K. J. Dover, *Greek Popular Morality in the Time of Plato and Aristotle,* revised edition (Indianapolis: Hackett, 1994).

Catharine Edwards, "Unspeakable Professions: Public Performance and Prostitution in Ancient Rome," in *Roman Sexualities,* edited by Judith Hallett and Marilyn B. Skinner (Princeton: Princeton University Press, 1997), pp. 66–95.

Lillian Faderman, *Surpassing the Love of Men: Romantic Friendships and Love Between Women from the Renaissance to the Present* (New York: Morrow, 1981).

Michel Foucault, *The History of Sexuality,* Volume 3: *The Care of the Self,* translated by Robert Hurley (New York: Random House, 1986).

Jane F. Gardner, *Women in Roman Law and Society* (Bloomington: Indiana University Press, 1986).

Maud W. Gleason, *Making Men: Sophists and Self-Presentation in Ancient Rome* (Princeton: Princeton University Press, 1995).

Ellen Greene, "Subjects, Objects, and Erotic Symmetry in Sappho's Fragments," in *Among Women: From the Homosocial to the Homoerotic in the Ancient World,* edited by Nancy Rabinowitz and Lisa Auanger (Austin: University of Texas Press, 2002), pp. 82–105.

Jasper Griffin, "Augustan Poetry and the Life of Luxury," *Journal of Roman Studies,* 66 (1976): 87–105.

David M. Halperin, *One Hundred Years of Homosexuality and Other Essays on Greek Love* (New York: Routledge, 1990).

Halperin, "Why is Diotima a Woman? Platonic *Erôs* and the Figuration of Pleasure," in *Before Sexuality: The Construction of Erotic Experience in the Ancient Greek World,* edited by Halperin and others (Princeton: Princeton University Press, 1990), pp. 257–308.

Jeffrey Henderson, *The Maculate Muse,* revised edition (Oxford: Oxford University Press, 1992).

Thomas K. Hubbard, ed., *Homosexuality in Greece and Rome: A Sourcebook of Basic Documents* (Berkeley: University of California Press, 2003).

Virginia J. Hunter, *Policing Athens: Social Control in the Attic Lawsuits, 420–320 B.C.* (Princeton: Princeton University Press, 1994).

David H. J. Larmour and others, eds., *Rethinking Sexuality: Foucault and Classical Antiquity* (Princeton: Princeton University Press, 1998).

Mark Anthony Masterson, "Roman Manhood at the End of the Ancient World," dissertation, University of Southern California, 2001.

Dominic Montserrat, *Sex and Society in Graeco-Roman Egypt* (London: Kegan Paul, 1996).

Holt N. Parker, "The Teratogenic Grid," in *Roman Sexualities,* edited by Hallett and Skinner (Princeton: Princeton University Press, 1997), pp. 47–65.

William Armstrong Percy III, *Pederasty and Pedagogy in Archaic Greece* (Urbana: University of Illinois Press, 1996).

Nancy Rabinowitz, "Excavating Women's Homoeroticism in Ancient Greece: The Evidence from Attic Vase Painting," in *Among Women: From the Homosocial to the Homoerotic in the Ancient World,* edited by Rabinowitz and Auanger (Austin: University of Texas Press, 2002), pp. 106–166.

Amy Richlin, *The Garden of Priapus: Sexuality and Aggression in Roman Humor* (New York: Oxford University Press, 1992).

Richlin, "Not before Homosexuality: The Materiality of the Cinaedus and the Roman Law against Love between Men," *Journal of the History of Sexuality,* 3 (1993): 523–573.

Michael L. Satlow, *Tasting the Dish: Rabbinic Rhetorics of Sexuality,* Brown Judaic Studies 303 (Atlanta: Scholars Press, 1995).

Paul Veyne, "L'Homesexualité à Rome," *Communications,* 35 (1982): 26–33.

Craig Williams, *Homosexuality and the Roman Man* (Oxford: Oxford University Press, 1999).

Williams, *Roman Homosexuality: Ideologies of Masculinity in Classical Antiquity* (Oxford: Oxford University Press, 1999).

John J. Winkler, *Constraints of Desire: The Anthropology of Sex and Gender in Ancient Greece* (New York: Routledge, 1989).

Winkler, "Laying Down the Law: The Oversight of Men's Sexual Behavior in Classical Athens," in *Before Sexuality: The Construction of Erotic Experience in the Ancient Greek World,* edited by Halperin and others (Princeton: Princeton University Press, 1990), pp. 171–209.

T. P. Wiseman, *Catullus and His World: A Reappraisal* (Cambridge: Cambridge University Press, 1985).

CLASSICAL STUDIES: THE MARXIST APPROACH

Does Marxism remain a valid historical approach to the ancient world?

Viewpoint: Yes. Marxist concepts have proven their worth in the understanding of ancient history and culture, even as Marxism continues to offer a coherent theoretical rationale for a holistic understanding of the ancient world.

Viewpoint: No. The historical record does not permit a classical Marxist interpretation of history, and Marxism's heuristic value has been largely superceded by feminism, cultural studies, and other nontraditional approaches.

Karl Marx's love of the ancient world cannot be contested. He wrote his dissertation in Latin on Greek atomist philosophy. Legend has it that once a year he sat down and reread in Greek the whole of Aeschylus's *Oresteia.* He is also on the record as considering Aristotle the West's greatest philosopher. Nonetheless, somewhat surprisingly, Marxism has not been a major force in the scholarly study of the ancient world. There have been relatively few orthodox Marxists in classics in the West. Nor did researchers in the former Soviet Union and its allies produce a significant body of publications on the ancient world that differed substantially from that published by even the most conservative positivist philologists in the United States and Western Europe. Soviet philology largely confined itself to technical linguistic and historical problems, with the occasional nod to the inexorable march of history. With a few notable exceptions, then,—for example, the works of Peter Rose and G. E. M. de Ste. Croix—there has been a dearth of important, explicitly Marxist studies of the ancient world.

There are several explanations for this fact. First, the Cold War hardly fostered an intellectual environment where Marxists in the West were likely to be welcomed with open arms in the halls of academe, especially in such a traditionally conservative discipline as classics. While there were few explicit bans, the adoption of a suspect method and an unpopular political position was, and still is, not the best way to insure publication and promotion. Second, the repressive environment of the Soviet Union was not conducive either to producing significant theoretical innovations or to any other form of scholarly risk taking. The results were drearily predictable: philology and boilerplate historical materialism. There is, however, a third possibility: Marxism itself may simply be an incoherent or ill-founded theory.

Peter W. Rose in his essay for Marxism concedes the first two points and chooses to make his stand on the third. He offers a powerful and persuasive argument for the continued value of Marxism based on its theoretical coherence and its explanatory power. He notes that while there has been a paucity of major Marxist studies on the ancient world, those that do exist have been significant contributions to the field and offer the promise of even more such holistic analyses of ancient social and economic structures to come.

Charles Platter in his opposing essay suggests that there may be a subtler, but also, ultimately more powerful reason for the relative lack of significant Marxist studies of the ancient world. He contends that the kind of documentary evidence necessary to perform a properly Marxist analysis of ancient society is simply not available. Consequently, Marxism as a systematic theory of history and society is doomed to remain an unfalsifiable proposition in classics. Platter does not deny Marxist theory's ability to open new perspectives on ancient society, but he notes that its heuristic value long since has been appropriated and surpassed by feminism, cultural studies, and other nontraditional methods of study.

—Paul Allen Miller

Viewpoint: Yes. Marxist concepts have proven their worth in the understanding of ancient history and culture, even as Marxism continues to offer a coherent theoretical rationale for a holistic understanding of the ancient world.

In view of the militant polarization of the Cold War and the chilling effect of McCarthyite Red-hunting in the 1950s, it is not surprising that little openly Marxist work on the ancient world has appeared in English, and what did appear (for example, Thomson, Wason) was not always of the highest quality. At the same time, the historian described in 1975 as "the best living social historian of Greece and the one most prepared to face the methodological problems which social history implies" (Finley 1981, ix) was heavily influenced by Karl Marx and Marxist thinkers at the outset of his career. As Moses I. Finley himself described it, "Marxism is . . . built into my intellectual experience . . . Marx . . . put an end to any idea that the study of history is an autonomous activity and to the corollary that the various aspects of human behaviour–economic, political, intellectual, religious–can be seriously treated in isolation" (Finley 1981, xi). After Finley was hounded out of this country in 1954 by the House Committee on Un-American Activities, his outlook shifted in several ways, but his rigorously holistic approach to all issues and his abiding concerns with slavery, ideology, politics, and economics owe much to his early immersion in Marx–"not even primarily *Das Kapital*, but also Marxist historical and theoretical works," as he put it (Finley 1981, xi).

The upheavals of the late 1960s produced a promising glimmer of interest in openly Marxist approaches to classical antiquity, but the Cold War mentality largely reasserted itself. Nonetheless, the terms in which a question is posed tend to set the parameters within which any answer may be formulated. The chapter question suggests there is a legitimate doubt about Marxism in temporal terms: either it is pronounced obsolete because it was formulated so long ago, and more-adequate critical approaches have rendered it irrelevant, or more-immediate historical changes have demonstrated its invalidity. While in Western Europe and the United States there has long been a virtual cottage industry devoted to demonstrating the alleged irrelevance of Marxism, it is the collapse of the Soviet Union that has especially empowered liberals and conservatives alike to dismiss it. Yet, Marxism is like a cork that keeps popping back up just when its detractors are convinced that they have safely consigned it to the depths. The worldwide anti-globalization movement, for example, which at the level of tactics and strategy has been at pains to distance itself from both the "Old Left" and the "New Left," has felt compelled to turn to Marxism for an adequate theory and critique of capitalism even if the "M-word" is studiously avoided (for example, O'Connor in Yuen, and others).

No methodology in itself offers a magic key to truth. As G. E. M. de Ste. Croix, the greatest Marxist historian of antiquity, has rightly said:

> Even mediocre work produced by the purely fact-grubbing historian may at least, if his facts are accurate and fairly presented, be of use to others capable of a higher degree of synthesis, whereas the would-be sociologist having insufficient knowledge of the specific historical evidence for a particular period of history is unlikely in the extreme to say anything about it that will be of use to anyone else. (Ste. Croix 34)

This caution is particularly relevant to the issue of Marxism as a methodology. The intellectual and physical horrors perpetrated in the name of Marxism in the former Soviet Union alone–not to mention many other horrors justified in the name of Marxist orthodoxy–must inspire in any would-be defender the deepest doubts. Not only were millions of human beings persecuted, tortured, and executed for alleged crimes against Marxist "truth" (for example, Medvedev, Franklin, especially 242–344), contemporary history was shamelessly distorted and all cultural production subjected to deadening constraints in the service of a murderously paranoid regime that called itself "Marxist" (Wilson 246). Even if one is willing to entertain the belief that the Soviet experience entailed massively grotesque distortions of the thought of Marx and Friedrich Engels, one still has to pose the question: what was it about Marx's thought that lent itself to such an appropriation?

Perhaps the most succinct statement of what sets Marxism apart from other methodologies is the eleventh of Marx's "Theses on Feuerbach," written in 1845 when Marx was twenty-six: "The philosophers have only *interpreted* the world, in various ways; the point, however, is to *change* it" (Tucker 145). While it can be argued that all methodologies entail ideological commitments, most commonly to the perpetuation of the status quo, Marxism is uniquely threatening and potentially dangerous in its explicit commitment to changing the world. It is dangerous because not all changes, whatever the intentions, turn out to be better for humankind and because the struggle to bring about meaningful change usually provokes deadly conflicts. It is threatening because it challenges us to take sides consciously or at the very least to become self-reflecting about commitments that most of us prefer leaving unconscious.

For Marx, taking sides most often took the form of making a rigorous critique of the status quo rather than offering formulas for preferable alternatives. An early programmatic declaration of his represents a lifelong commitment: "We do not attempt dogmatically to prefigure the future, but want to find the new world only through criticism of the old. . . . If the designing of the future and the proclamation of ready-made solutions for all time is not our affair, then we realize all the more clearly what we have to accomplish in the present—I am speaking of a *ruthless criticism of everything existing*" (Tucker 13). Vladimir Lenin, Leon Trotsky, and Joseph Stalin were able to appropriate the element of critique of the status quo as justification for their own alternatives that increasingly moved toward the opposite of the scattered hints in Marx of a desirable alternative future. For example, from his early "Contribution to the Critique of Hegel's *Philosophy of Right*" (1843, Tucker 16–25, especially 19–21) to his late text on the Paris Commune ("The Civil War in France" 1871, Tucker 618–652), Marx remained committed to radical participatory democracy. Lenin's most inspiring text, *State and Revolution* (1917), quotes heavily from Marx's discussion of democracy and lays out a programmatic sketch of what a genuinely democratic society would look like. Yet, Lenin himself could not have been further from a sincere commitment to democracy and used all his power to establish a system where practical participation in the decisions affecting the lives of citizens was systematically excluded and where a real, thoroughgoing critique of the type so characteristic of Marx at his greatest became fatal. The collapse of the Soviet Union, rather than sinking Marxism, liberated it from its most unwelcome encumbrance. The French philosopher Jacques Derrida, who for so many years had nothing to say of Marx, declared in 1993, "it will always be a fault not to read and reread and discuss Marx. . . . It will be more and more a fault, a failing of theoretical, philosophical, political responsibility. When the dogma machine and the 'Marxist' ideological apparatuses (States, parties, cells, unions, and other places of doctrinal production) are in the process of disappearing, we no longer have any excuse, only alibis, for turning away from this responsibility" (Derrida 13).

Photograph of the nineteenth-century German political philosopher Karl Marx, who demonstrated a profound interest in classical studies throughout his life

(Library of Congress)

Closely related to Marx's notion of "taking sides" is perhaps the most central feature of Marx's analysis of societies in history, his focus on "class struggle." After a brief preface, *The Communist Manifesto* (1848) begins with a programmatic declaration:

> The history of all hitherto existing society is the history of class struggles. Freeman and slave, patrician and plebeian, lord and serf, guild-master and journeyman, in a word, oppressor and oppressed, stood in constant opposition to one another, carried on an uninterrupted, now hidden, now open fight, a fight that each time ended, either in a revolutionary re-constitution of society at large, or in the common ruin of the contending classes. (Tucker 473–474)

A few elements in this statement require comment. Marx's claim applies to "all hitherto existing society"—not just to capitalism. Criticism that dismisses Marx as only relevant, if at all, to nineteenth-century developments implicitly ignores this claim. Marx's contention that class struggle is not only "uninterrupted" but also sometimes "hidden" and sometimes "open" calls for an historical mode of analysis that goes well beyond an exclusive focus on bloody insurrections in which issues of class are explicit, though such events, relatively rare as they are, also merit the closest inspection. The final phase, "ended, *either* in a *revolutionary* re-constitution of society at large, *or* in the common ruin of the contending classes," offers a salutary, realistic corrective to those more optimistic and polemical passages in Marx in which a better future seems inevitable. Whatever his passionate hopes, Marx had read too much history to believe that the side representing humanity's best interests always triumphed. So too his use of "revolutionary" should not be read exclusively in terms of the model of the French Revolution (Furet and Althusser 77) but rather the emphasis is on the "re-constitution of society at large," a process that could, he was well aware, take several centuries in some cases. Finally, the specific examples he offers ("freeman and slave, patrician and plebeian, lord and serf, guild-master and journeyman, in a word, oppressor and oppressed") point toward what he means by "class" and the decisive levels on which he conceived of society being "constituted."

Central to Marx's analysis of society are the concepts of "mode of production" and "relations of production." In his preface to a book characteristically titled *A Contribution to the Critique of Political Economy* (1859), Marx attempted to summarize what he called "the guiding thread for my studies":

> In the social production of their life, men enter into definite relations that are indispensable and independent of their will, relations of production which correspond to a definite stage of development of their material productive forces. The sum total of these relations of production constitutes the economic structure of society, the real foundation on which rises a legal and political superstructure and to which correspond definite forms of social consciousness. The mode of production of material life conditions the social, political and intellectual life process in general. It is not the consciousness of men that determines their being, but, on the contrary, their social being that determines their consciousness. (Tucker 4)

One feature of this formulation that should make it especially congenial to historians weary of the endless fragmentation and explanatory vacuums of the traditional empiricist historians (White 163–190, compare Jameson 1988: 2.148–177) is its implicit will to describe a social totality, to account not only for how a society meets its most essential needs for material survival but also its social, political, and intellectual life process in general. Georg Lukács, one of Marx's greatest followers in the twentieth century, has especially elaborated and developed this concept of the social totality (for example, Lukács 145, 151–154).

Like all attempts to summarize concisely a complex and constantly evolving system of thought, this passage of Marx is open to interpretations that can be used to discredit the system as a whole. The final chiastically arranged antithesis with the repeated term *determines* has been used along with several other polemically stated arguments in Marx to pin him with the label of *determinist.* This elegant but troubling dictum is aimed above all at Georg Wilhelm Friedrich Hegel. This philosopher's account of history as a sequence of great *ideas* that emerge, generate their antithesis, engage in conflict, and thus produce a new idea that is the synthesis of the two earlier, conflicting concepts both provoked and inspired Marx's emphasis on *material* production. The preceding sentence ("The mode of production of material life *conditions* the social, political and intellectual life process in general") far more accurately reflects Marx's predominant emphasis. As he put it in another text, "Men make their own history, but they do not make it just as they please; they do not make it under circumstances chosen by themselves, but under circumstances directly found, given and transmitted from the past. The tradition of all the dead generations weighs like a nightmare on the brain of the living" (Tucker 595). At the same time Marx attacks the illusion of complete free will. From his doctoral dissertation on the difference between Democritus and Epicurus to his "Critique of the Gotha Program," Marx consistently defended the idea that individuals have real choices that have major consequences.

The mode of production, he insists, however, is inherently "social," a collective, structural aspect of society into which individuals are born and over which as individuals they have no control. Individuals may conceivably withdraw from society and sustain their material existence in a manner at odds with the mode of production into which they are born, but precisely to the extent they do this, they cease to be part of society. If one is born into a slave-owning society, one may be free to struggle against that mode, but almost every aspect of one's daily relations will be conditioned by the reality of slavery. Marx's first two examples in the *Communist Manifesto* ("freeman and slave, patrician and plebeian") obviously speak to the world of classical antiquity, an area he studied extensively both as a young man, when he seriously considered an academic career, and throughout his life. The pairing points to a decisive aspect of his conception of class: class is always *relational;* no class exists independent of the class to which it is opposed. It is precisely in the mode of production that this opposition emerges: in all known societies, at least since the agricultural revolution, one class oppresses another by extracting from it a surplus of value that is appropriated for the benefit of the oppressing class to the detriment of the oppressed class. This relationship colors—"conditions" in Marx's term—all other relations in society.

At the same time that Marx's first two examples point to the centrality of relationship and exploitation in his conception of class, they introduce a complexity that the sequence of binary oppositions tends to obscure: the Roman patrician was simultaneously an owner-oppressor of slaves and pitted against the legally free plebs—even as the Athenian aristocratic landowner tended to perceive the demos, the free smallholders and landless citizens, as his natural opponent in the political arena. Moreover, the sense in which the rich landowner "oppressed" his slaves and oppressed the free masses is significantly different. This is precisely the issue—different class positions simultaneously occupied by the same individuals and different levels of class struggle—that Ste. Croix sets out to analyze in his magisterial, seven-hundred-page study, *The Class Struggle in the Ancient Greek World* (1981), a work that in itself constitutes the best positive response to the question posed for this essay. The word *Greek* in the title is rather misleading since this text covers the whole span of the ancient world from the Archaic period in Greece to the fall of the Roman Empire, an issue for which he offers a complex and compelling argument. There is no space here to enter into the passionate debates inspired by this book, but even its most ferocious detractors have acknowledged its theoretical sophistication and massive learning. Non- Marxist historians cannot afford to ignore its powerfully argued conclusions. Moreover, his influence as a teacher has had a profound impact on distinguished younger historians (for example, Paul Cartledge, Anton Powell, and contributors to *Crux*) who, while not declaring themselves "Marxists," show the impact of his work on every page.

To sum up, the greatest contributions of Marx to the study of the ancient history are his insistence that the technological and human means by which a society produces its basic necessities and its surplus wealth and that the inherently conflictual human relations associated with this production process profoundly condition all other aspects of social and intellectual life. His approach is uniquely holistic in its quest for the specific forms in which the different aspects of a society—its economic, political, and intellectual life—impinge upon each other.

—PETER W. ROSE,
MIAMI UNIVERSITY, OHIO

Viewpoint:
No. The historical record does not permit a classical Marxist interpretation of history, and Marxism's heuristic value has been largely superceded by feminism, cultural studies, and other nontraditional approaches.

The history of the ancient Mediterranean world would appear to be an excellent proving ground for a Marxist approach to history. The period seems well supplied with the raw materials. We have traditional aristocracies intent upon reserving their privileges as well as economic developments in highly organized city-states such as Athens that allow for new, speculative use of capital in workshops, factories, mining, and trade. Furthermore, much of this intense economic activity is made possible by the exercise of slave labor, a practice for which we have the traces of a polemic concerning its nature in Aristotle (*Politics, Book One*) and Aristophanes (*Wealth* 6–7). Despite this apparent *embarras de richesses,* Marxist historical analysis has remained of limited value for the study of the period, with occasional powerful examples to the contrary. Some of the hostility to Marxist history could no doubt be described as an outgrowth of Cold War politics. In this context, "non-ideological" approaches to historical subjects could be understood as offering tacit support for the institutions of Western liberal democracy, which, incidentally, were their chief sponsors. How these analyses would have looked in a century when they would not be dominated by the fear of Bolshevism's totalizing vision and the horrors of European fascism is anyone's guess. Nevertheless, the recent demise of the Soviet Union and the disappearance of Marxism as a credible political threat allow us to consider, perhaps for the first time, the question as to the utility of a Marxist analysis in the understanding of the ancient world. It is particularly striking, then, that even in a relatively neutral political climate, Marxism has relatively little to offer students of the classical world.

Karl Marx was not unfamiliar with the world of Greece and Rome. In fact, his doctoral dissertation was on classical philosophy, and his writing shows that his understanding of classical antiquity helped shape his thought throughout his life. Despite this considerable interest in the period, it is significant that Marx never produced a full-scale, detailed analysis of the conditions of class, labor, and capital in the ancient world, and that his full attention was instead directed to the appearance of these phenomena under industrial

DEMOCRITUS AND EPICURUS

Karl Marx's doctoral dissertation, submitted in early 1841 at the University of Jena, examined the atomistic theories of two natural philosophers:

Greek philosophy seems to have met with something with which a good tragedy is not supposed to meet, namely, a dull ending. The objective history of philosophy in Greece seems to come to an end with Aristotle, Greek philosophy's Alexander of Macedon, and even the manly-strong Stoics did not succeed in what the Spartans did accomplish in their temples, the chaining of Athena to Heracles so that she could not flee.

Epicureans, Stoics and Sceptics are regarded as an almost improper addition bearing no relation to its powerful premises. Epicurean philosophy is taken as a syncretic combination of Democritean physics and Cyrenaic morality; Stoicism as a compound of Heraclitean speculation on nature and the Cynical-ethical view of the world, together with some Aristotelean logic; and finally Scepticism as the necessary evil confronting these dogmatisms. These philosophies are thus unconsciously linked to the Alexandrian philosophy by being made into a one-sided and tendentious eclecticism. The Alexandrian philosophy is finally regarded entirely as exaltation and derangement—a confusion in which at most the universality of the intention can be recognised.

To be sure, it is a commonplace that birth, flowering and decline constitute the iron circle in which everything human is enclosed, through which it must pass. Thus it would not have been surprising if Greek philosophy, after having reached its zenith in Aristotle, should then have withered. But the death of the hero resembles the setting of the sun, not the bursting of an inflated frog.

And then: birth, flowering and decline are very general, very vague notions under which, to be sure, everything can be arranged, but through which nothing can be understood. Decay itself is prefigured in the living; its shape should therefore be just as much grasped in its specific characteristic as the shape of life. Finally, when we glance at history, are Epicureanism, Stoicism and Scepticism particular phenomena? Are they not the prototypes of the Roman mind, the shape in which Greece wandered to Rome? Is not their essence so full of character, so intense and eternal that the modern world itself has to admit them to full spiritual citizenship?

I lay stress on this only in order to call to mind the historical importance of these systems. Here, however, we are not at all concerned with their significance for culture in general, but with their connection with the older Greek philosophy.

Should not this relationship urge us at least to an inquiry, to see Greek philosophy ending up with two different groups of eclectic systems, one of them the cycle of Epicurean, Stoic and Sceptic philosophy, the other being classified under the collective name of Alexandrian speculation? Furthermore, is it not remarkable that after the Platonic and Aristotelean philosophies, which are universal in range, there appear new systems which do not lean on these rich intellectual forms, but look farther back and have recourse to the simplest schools—to the philosophers of nature in regard to physics, to the Socratic school in regard to ethics? Moreover, what is the reason why the systems that follow after Aristotle find their foundations as it were ready made in the past, why Democritus is linked to the Cyrenaics and Heraclitus to the Cynics? Is it an accident that with the Epicureans, Stoics and Sceptics all moments of self-consciousness are represented completely, but every moment as a particular existence? Is it an accident that these systems in their totality form the complete structure of self-consciousness? And finally, the character with which Greek philosophy mythically begins in the seven wise men, and which is, so to say as its central point, embodied in Socrates as its *demiurge*—I mean the character of the wise man, of the *sophos*—is it an accident that it is asserted in those systems as the reality of true science?

It seems to me that though the earlier systems are more significant and interesting for the content, the post-Aristotelean ones, and primarily the cycle of the Epicurean, Stoic and Sceptic schools, are more significant and interesting for the subjective form, the character of Greek philosophy. But it is precisely the subjective form, the spiritual carrier of the philosophical systems, which has until now been almost entirely ignored in favour of their metaphysical characteristics.

I shall save for a more extensive discussion the presentation of the Epicurean, Stoic and Sceptic philosophies as a whole and in their total relationship to earlier and later Greek speculation.

Let it suffice here to develop this relationship as it were by an example, and only in one aspect, namely, their relationship to earlier speculation.

As such an example I select the relationship between the Epicurean and the Democritean philosophy of nature. I do not believe that it is the most convenient point of contact. Indeed, on the one hand it is an old and entrenched prejudice to identify Democritean and Epicurean physics, so that Epicurus' modifications are seen as only arbitrary vagaries. On the other hand I am forced to go into what seem to be microscopic examinations as far as details are concerned. But precisely because this prejudice is as old as the history of philosophy, because the differences are so concealed that they can be discovered as it were only with a microscope, it will be all the more important if, despite the interdependence of Democritean and Epicurean physics, an essential difference extending to the smallest details can be demonstrated. What can be demonstrated in the small can even more easily be shown where the relations are considered in larger dimensions, while conversely very general considerations leave doubt whether the result will hold when applied to details.

Source: *Karl Marx, "Difference Between the Democritean and Epicurean Philosophy of Nature in General," in "The Difference Between the Democritean and Epicurean Philosophy of Nature. With an Appendix"* (1902).

capitalism. In fact, to judge from his remarks in various places, Marx seems to have been undecided himself on how to understand many of the crucial aspects of antiquity necessary for such an analysis, from the significance of slavery in the ancient economy to the precise constitution of the "classes" that made up those societies (Cartledge and Konstan).

The argument is not being made that Marx subscribed to a kind of historical exceptionalism, by which the authors of what has sometimes been called "the Greek miracle" are thought of as having somehow escaped the limited opportunities and constraints on historical and cultural development felt and exploited by other societies. That he believed that the experience of Greek and Roman societies corresponded to his overall historical vision seems too obvious to entertain serious reservations. The difficulties lie in discerning whether and how the ruling class produced its surplus value through slave labor, given the fragmentary state of the historical evidence upon which scholars must base their interpretations. Chapter 1 of *Das Kapital* (1867) offers a detailed theorization of commodity exchange and surplus value, but how did the expropriation of surplus value occur in a precapitalist economy (that is, before the commodification of labor itself and the institution of a strict division between use and exchange value)? It is beyond question that the aristocratic and oligarchic elements dominated society, but to what degree? What percentage occurred as a result of slave labor? What percent through other exchanges, such as those with small landholders and day laborers (*thetai* in Greece)? To what degree did the fact that the holdings of large Athenian landholders were typically not contiguous–and so required highly decentralized management–limit their opportunities for exploiting the labor of dependents, free or slave? How did this situation differ from the Italian estates of the Roman period (*latifundia*)? To these questions, and many more, the evidence available to historians provides unsatisfactory answers, owing in part to the accidental destruction of texts and artifacts during the last two millennia, in part to the lack of centralized record keeping in Greco-Roman society, and in part to the almost total lack of interest in the type of macroeconomic data, without which an attempt to write the history of labor and value is like painting from memory. Historians such as G. E. M. de Ste. Croix have made brave efforts to view ancient history in terms of class struggle, but finally the material basis for such an analysis is simply not at hand.

In the face of the paucity of economic data from which to draw, historians can hardly be faulted for paying less attention to global patterns in history than to the details of social and political life, of which there is at least a fragmentary historical record that provides some check upon what can be asserted and denied. This position entails no necessary claims about the merits of so-called nonideological approaches to history, if such a thing were to be discovered. Nevertheless, anyone who is seriously interested in the ancient world per se, as opposed to those who might wish to see in it either the beginnings of class society or a lost Eden from which we have been cast, inherits an ethical duty to pay attention to and to analyze first and foremost what is actually there. What we have is a largely aristocratic tradition, preserved in a wide variety of forms: annalistic, poetic, didactic, and occasionally documentary (in the form of public inscriptions describing expenses, contributions, and expropriations). Archaeology adds to this picture, although its findings are often circumscribed by the fragmentation of the remains and the difficulty in generalizing from the evidence. The picture that emerges from that body of evidence, despite its overall aristocratic orientation, is likewise heterogeneous, a mixture of self-justification, artistic exploration, and philosophical critique–much of it is of the highest quality and of great intrinsic interest. It is also, unfortunately, a collection of data resistant to classical Marxist analysis.

Classical Marxism styles itself not only as a way of looking at history but a metahistorical discourse capable of producing a history of history itself. The present state of historical evidence for the ancient Mediterranean world is insufficient to support Marxism's claim in any way that would rise above the level of unsubstantiated generalization. Nor are future discoveries likely to be sufficiently momentous to change a situation in which a priori deduction must supply what the historical record lacks. Yet, even if the critics of classical Marxist analysis are justified, might Marxism nevertheless prove its utility for investigating the conditions of life in the ancient world? After all, has not one of the most significant results of Marxist analysis been its ability to remove the gaze of historians from the motives and abilities of kings and generals, to the lived existence of ordinary men and women? Could the most legitimate contribution of Marxism to historical research be decidedly un-Marxist?

There is something to be said for the hypothesis that Marxism has had a strong heuristic role to play in the development of contemporary decentralized historical studies. Changing the exclusive focus from political history *tout court* has opened the field of investigation to new subjects of analysis and individuals whose history has until recently gone unexamined. Scholars of feminism, psychoanalysis, and sexuality arguably owe to Marxism the intellectual labor that has allowed their research interests to prosper and helped to make them part of the interpretative community that decides what constitutes historical discourse in the future.

Particularly valuable in this respect has been the concept of the "double hermeneutic," elaborated by the Marxist critic Frederic Jameson, a style of interpretation that allows for the copresence of elements within a body of evidence that work both for and against the overall ideological assumptions of the author's class or the genre in which she is writing. Yet, despite the convergence of Marxism with new theoretical methodologies, the result has not been a plethora of differently focused analyses that nevertheless in some larger sense confirms the outlines of Marx's theory of history. Scholars have seen within classical texts the traces of dissident voices. Those voices are often contextualized in such a way that issues of great political and ideological moment are transposed into the realm of mythic history (such as the anger of Demeter at the rape of Persephone in the *Homeric Hymn to Demeter* and the anger of Juno at the prospect of Trojan victory in Virgil's *Aeneid*). Thus, even voices of resistance are often co-opted by the dominant literary and political culture and represented not as ongoing challenges to the established order but as crises *already* surmounted in the mythic past. Similarly, much attention has been given to Sappho's poetry, in which feminine culture is valorized and allowed to stand in contrast to the masculine values of Homeric poetry, even as it affirms a place for itself within the male-dominated society of sixth-century B.C.E. Lesbos. By means of Jameson's "double hermeneutic," these multiple perspectives are recuperable for feminist, sexuality, or cultural studies. The arguments of scholars so engaged can reveal much about the ideological background of the texts in question, but the implication of their conclusions for classical Marxist questions concerning class struggle, surplus value, and historical materialism remain vague, giving the impression that the Marxist elements that helped give rise to these new critical traditions have been left behind and are no longer considered necessary by their practitioners.

Although Marxism's heuristic value in enabling other critical methodologies seems well established, it has not yet fulfilled its promise as either an independent historical methodology or a verifiable theory of history. Nor in the absence of the discovery of significant new historical sources is the situation likely to change. Within that context, however, there continues to be a place for contributions that are contiguous with Marx's vision. Even the new methodologies can occasionally be found entering by the back door. Sandra R. Joshel attempted to reconstruct the lives of Roman women in the service of a feminist project but came to see that, in this case anyway, a projected study of lost feminine culture turned out to reveal far more when cast as a chapter in the lost history of working-class culture. Still, these advances have been modest, and it may be that the collapse of the Soviet Union will turn out to be a major benefactor in the development of Marxist analysis, not as a totalizing vision of inexorable progress but as a set of interpretive tactics to open up important aspects of antiquity.

–CHARLES PLATTER,
UNIVERSITY OF GEORGIA

References

Louis Althusser, *For Marx* (New York: Random House, 1969).

P. A. Cartledge and F. D. Harvey, eds., *Crux: Essays in Greek History Presented to G. E. M. de Ste. Croix on His Seventy-Fifth Birthday* (London: Duckworth, 1985).

Cartledge and David Konstan, "Marxism and Classical Antiquity, " in *The Oxford Classical Dictionary,* edited by Simon Hornblower and Antony Sprawforth, third edition (Oxford: Oxford University Press, 1996), pp. 933–934.

Jacques Derrida, *Specters of Marx: The State of the Debt, the Work of Mourning, and the New International* (New York: Routledge, 1994).

Moses I. Finley, *The Ancient Economy* (Berkeley: University of California Press, 1973).

Finley, *Ancient Slavery and Modern Ideology* (New York: Viking, 1980).

Finley, *Democracy Ancient and Modern* (New Brunswick, N.J.: Rutgers University Press, 1973).

Finley, *Economy and Society in Ancient Greece* (New York: Viking, 1981).

W. Bruce Franklin, *Sunlight at Midnight: St. Petersburg and the Rise of Modern Russia* (New York: Basic Books, 2001).

François Furet, *Marx and the French Revolution* (Chicago: University of Chicago Press, 1988).

Frederic Jameson, *The Ideologies of Theory: Essays 1971–1986,* volume 2: *The Syntax of History* (Minneapolis: University of Minnesota Press, 1988).

Jameson, *The Political Unconscious: Narrative as a Socially Symbolic Act* (Ithaca, N.Y.: Cornell University Press, 1981).

Sandra R. Joshel, *Work, Identity and Legal Status at Rome: A Study of the Occupational Inscriptions* (Norman: University of Oklahoma Press, 1992).

Georg Lukács, *History and Class Consciousness: Studies in Marxist Dialectics* (Cambridge, Mass.: MIT Press, 1971).

Roy A. Medvedev, *Let History Judge: The Origins and Consequences of Stalinism* (New York: Knopf, 1972).

S. S. Prawer, *Karl Marx and World Literature* (Oxford: Oxford University Press, 1978).

Peter W. Rose, "The Case for Not Ignoring Marx in the Study of Women in Antiquity," in *Feminist Theory and the Classics,* edited by Nancy Sorkin Rabinowitz and Amy Richlin (New York: Routledge, 1993).

Rose, "Ideology in the *Iliad:* Polis, *Basileus, theoi,*" *Arethusa,* 30 (1997): 151–199.

Rose, *Sons of the Gods, Children of Earth: Ideology and Literary Form in Ancient Greece* (Ithaca, N.Y.: Cornell University Press, 1992).

G. E. M. de Ste. Croix, *The Class Struggle in the Ancient Greek World* (Ithaca, N.Y.: Cornell University Press, 1981).

George Thomson, *Aeschylus and Athens* (London: Lawrence & Wishart, 1940).

Thomson, *Studies in Ancient Greek Society,* volume 1: *The Prehistoric Aegean* (New York: Citadel, 1965).

Robert C. Tucker, ed., *The Marx-Engels Reader,* second edition (New York: Norton, 1978).

Margaret O. Wason, *Class Struggles in Ancient Greece* (London: Gollancz, 1947).

Hayden White, *Metahistory: The Historical Imagination of Nineteenth-Century Europe* (Baltimore: Johns Hopkins University Press, 1973).

Edmund Wilson, "Marxism and Literature," in *20th Century Literary Criticism: A Reader,* edited by David Lodge (London: Longman, 1972), pp. 241–252.

Eddie Yuen and others, eds., *The Battle of Seattle: The New Challenges to Capitalist Globalization* (New York: Soft Skull, 2001).

CLASSICAL STUDIES: MODERN CRITICAL THEORY

Is modern critical theory a useful tool for understanding the ancient Mediterranean world?

Viewpoint: Yes. Contemporary literary theory offers new insights into Greek and Roman literature and culture and provides a means for linking the ancient world to the world of today.

Viewpoint: No. Critical theory is a form of obscurantist terrorism that is harmful to humanistic study as a whole and particularly deleterious to classics.

The theory wars that roiled through departments of English and comparative literature during the 1980s came late to classics. The philological model of German *Altertumswissenschaft* and the English tradition of classical humanism remained the dominant paradigms for studying the ancient world throughout the 1970s and 1980s. By the 1990s, however, that trend had begun to change. Scholarly journals that once held it as a point of pride to publish only the most scientific, historically grounded work began to accept articles using Marxist, structuralist, poststructuralist, and psychoanalytic methods.

Many reasons exist for this shift. First, classicists may be primarily interested in ancient Greece and Rome, but they are scholars living in the contemporary world, and it is only natural that they should be curious about and experiment with approaches gaining credence in neighboring disciplines. Second, the present generation of classicists is fundamentally different from that which came to maturity in the late 1960s and early 1970s. It is more demographically diverse. Classicists today are much more likely to be women, nonwhite, and from middle-class or even lower-class backgrounds than was once the case. It is only natural that this more diverse professoriat would reflect a wider range of approaches to the texts and contexts that constitute the classical tradition. Moreover, many of today's classicists went to public high schools where Latin and Greek were not available. Consequently, they come to the study of the ancient world relatively late in their academic careers, often after having begun as scholars of English, history, or philosophy. Thus, they bring with them a variety of disciplinary approaches that reflect their broader, although rarely deeper, scholarly interests and experiences.

Finally, there is a growing sense that much of the basic philological spadework has been done for the major texts of the classical period. Some scholars react to this perception by applying their skills to new kinds of texts. Thus, there has been a growing group of trained classicists who have turned their attention to editing, commenting upon, and producing editions of neglected neo-Latin authors from the Medieval and the Renaissance periods. Others have turned their attention to the study of classical scholarship per se, producing histories of the discipline and biographies of its leading exponents. Lastly, some have decided to return to the traditional texts armed with a new theoretical scholarly apparatus.

There are, then, structural, intellectual, and demographic reasons for the increased prominence of theory in studying the ancient world. It seems unlikely that this situation will change anytime soon. The question is whether this is a desirable situation or a symptom of intellectual decline. Both cases can and have been made. As the two essays that follow make clear, the partisans of theory and its opponents are articulate and passionate advocates. It is hard, however, to see how such interchanges do anything but attest to the continuing intellectual vitality of classics as a humanistic discipline.

—Paul Allen Miller

Viewpoint: Yes. Contemporary literary theory offers new insights into Greek and Roman literature and culture and provides a means for linking the ancient world to the world of today.

An assumption exists, all too common among classicists, that the so-called traditional way of doing classics does not involve any theoretical or ideological underpinnings. There are people who still think of classical studies as "the science of antiquity" (after the German *Altertumswissenschaft*), and many classicists continue to speak as if they occupied a privileged space, free from ideology, above the fray, capable of deciphering the unalloyed truth about the ancient world. There is also the harmful tendency of classicists to idealize the ancient world—particularly the world of the "ancient Greeks"—as a special place imagined to be far superior to the contemporary world in which we live, free from all its conflicts and uncertainties.

Both of these lamentable tendencies are on display in the desperate and sometimes intellectually dishonest attempts of some classicists to discredit the work of Martin Bernal, who has invited us to rethink, and thus to demystify, our manner of looking at ancient Greece. One of Bernal's most significant accomplishments has been to uncover the connections that link the "traditional" way of doing classics to several misguided and outmoded nineteenth-century notions, including ethnocentrism and outright racism (Bernal, *Black Athena*, Vol. 1, pp. 3–120, and Vol. 2, pp. 1–12 and 27).

The truth is that, despite the strident claims of many classicists, there is far more to classical studies than the mere collection of facts about the ancient world (see Peradotto, "Texts and Unrefracted Facts"). The "traditional" way of doing classics, which remains committed to an ideology of the "original" and of "what really happened," and which is given to such odd metaphors as "staying close to the text" and even "sticking to the text," was not handed down from on high, but developed historically, in the intellectual currents of the nineteenth century. Furthermore, as Bernal and Friedrich Nietzsche before him have taught us, the romanticization and idealization of the ancient world is in fact a distortion of and disservice to the classical past.

It is interesting to note how many of the French "founders" of contemporary theory are solidly grounded in classics and history. Roland Barthes, for example, received a degree in classics from the Sorbonne, went on to get an advanced degree for work on Greek tragedy, and was one of the founders of a group devoted to the performance of ancient drama. Jacques Derrida is a favorite target for many conservatives, classicists and otherwise, but the briefest look at such writings as "Plato's Pharmacy" (*Dissemination*, pp. 61–171) leaves no doubt as to his classical learning and ease with ancient Greek (how many of his detractors have troubled to take that look?). René Girard began his career as a medievalist, having studied in Paris at the Ecole des Chartes, an institution devoted to the training of archivists and historians. The wide-ranging Italian writer Umberto Eco remains a medievalist: his *Tesi di Laurea* at the University of Turin, which became his first book, dealt with the aesthetics of St. Thomas Aquinas, and the Middle Ages figure prominently in his subsequent work—not least in his novel *The Name of the Rose,* a worldwide best-seller. And who could seriously question the classical learning of such writers as Michel Foucault or Mikhail Bakhtin? Indeed, some of those original theorists—for example, Paul Veyne and Jean-Pierre Vernant—remained practicing classicists.

What today's classicists call literary theory began with the arrival of two French intellectual movements—structuralism and poststructuralism—in America and later in England (see Macksey and Donato, *The Languages of Criticism*). Beyond the strident debate and the often tortured language, and setting aside the undoubted excesses that have been perpetrated in their name (see Eco, *The Limits of Interpretation* and *Interpretation and Overinterpretation*), what are structuralism and poststructuralism really all about? That question need not be so difficult as it sometimes seems, as the following synopsis of some of their fundamental ideas will show:

• Language, according to the Swiss linguist Ferdinand de Saussure, is a system of signs. Different sounds—or different combinations of letters—produce different meanings: difference engenders meaning. A sign is a combination of a signifier (an "acoustic image") and a signified (a concept). Signifiers thus refer to other signifiers, signs to other signs, and words to other words (Saussure, *Course in General Linguistics,* pp. 65–81.) Dictionaries, for example, typically tell us what words mean by referring us to other words, not by presenting real examples or physical models of what words are supposed to represent.

• It follows that the complex systems of words called texts do not capture things or "reality" but refer to other texts. Texts evoke and are evoked by other texts. This assumption addresses the motivation and significance of both reading and writing. Readers and writers bring to the texts they confront and produce complex and multiple systems of codes that are in constant flux—that is, they bring their own texts. That is how reading and writing involve the phenomenon of "intertextuality" (Barthes, "From Work to Text," in Harari, *Textual Strategies,* pp. 73–81).

• Since texts evoke and are evoked by a virtual infinity of other texts, any truly authoritative reading of a text is impossible—as is a truly authoritative "canon" of privileged texts. The deaths of authors, for example, come to signify the limitations of their authority over their texts—limitations clearly perceived by Plato in the *Phaedrus* and *Letter 7* (assuming we are willing to accept Plato's authorship of this last work). Attempts to use history, philology, cultural norms, and the like to determine the "correct" meaning of a text or to establish a truly authoritative canon of texts are in reality attempts to limit the meaning of texts, to control the power of language to "disseminate" meaning (Barthes, *Criticism and Truth,* pp. 63–94; Foucault, "What is An Author?," *Language, Counter-Memory, Practice,* pp. 114–138; Eco, *Postscript to The Name of the Rose,* pp. 1–7).

• Insofar as they are of necessity provisional, all readings are misreadings. No reading can encompass the totality of meaning inherent in a text and its interactions with all its possible readers. Texts remain inexhaustibly and irreducibly rich.

According to Derrida (*Of Grammatology;* "Différence," *Margins of Philosophy,* pp. 1–27; and throughout his early work), Western philosophy has distorted the meaning of the sign by attempting to unify the signified and make it the origin of the signifier, naming it as the "presence" behind the signifier and thus creating a transcendental absolute. Yet, the sign is an irreducible structure that points to an ever-absent presence, one that is interminably deferred, marked only by its "trace."

Western philosophy, Derrida continues, also has concentrated on binary oppositions, setting concepts against their opposites and then establishing a hierarchy by valorizing one term and giving it absolute authority over the other. Yet, when one sees a binary opposition as a trace structure, it is possible to undermine the hierarchy—to "deconstruct" it—by placing the valorized term "under erasure," denying its absolute nature while conserving it as a trace. Neither term of a binary opposition can stand on its own. It is always marked by a radical alterity, by the presence of its other, its opposite. In this way a concept can be said to carry within itself the principle of its own death.

Derrida maintains that we must seek a more comprehensive approach to knowledge, one that goes beyond the either/or thinking associated with binary oppositions, one that will generate meaning in a playful way, going in both directions at once, totalizing without ever arriving at an absolute totality.

Whether one chooses to agree with all of this, there can be no question that we are faced with arguable positions, far from nonsense. It is true that the arguments have often been couched in difficult and abstruse language, perhaps, at times, unnecessarily. We must remember, however, that some difficult and subtle concepts are involved here, and that such concepts are not easily expressed in clear and transparent language (see Rubino, *"Lectio difficilior praeferenda est"*). It is also true that those classicists who love to accuse literary theory of being mired in unintelligible jargon ought to take a look at their own idiolect, which bristles with formidably abstruse technical language. So abstruse, in fact, that first-year graduate students in classics must endure one or two semesters of something called "proseminar" just to learn the jargon! Like the critics mentioned by Catullus in Poem 22, many conservative classicists never seem to notice the heavy sack of jargon hanging from their own backs.

Not only do the principles upon which literary theory rests make sense in themselves, but they also enable us to make a real engagement with ancient authors. Plato, for example, was himself a literary theorist (see above on the *Phaedrus* and *Letter 7;* see also the *Ion* and *Republic* [Books 3 and 10] among other dialogues). Literary theory, with its emphasis on the nature and power of language, has given us some new tools with which to confront Plato's attempts to control language and restrict its capacity for generating meaning. In a well-known line from his *Ars Poetica,* Horace, yet another theorist, tells us that poems are like paintings ("ut pictura poesis," 361), but contemporary literary theory questions the nature of representation in ways that add new dimensions to the complexities of Horace's seemingly simple statement. Contemporary theory has also given us new ways to examine the question of genre (see, for example, Miller, *Lyric Texts and Lyric Consciousness*) and to probe the meanings of the desire that is on display in a genre such as lyric (see Janan, *When the Lamp is*

Shattered). Theory has also enabled us to view Greek and Roman plays as real performance pieces (remember Barthes's commitment to performance), not mere museum pieces or stages in the history of theater.

The plain fact is that literary theory supplies a means for giving the classics a way to speak to us today, to make them far more than idealized artifacts to be constantly polished up. This has been made abundantly clear in the work of many classicists, much of which has appeared, over the years, in the journals *Arethusa, Helios,* and *Ramus.* In the end, the fundamental question about the performance of a Greek play or an analysis of a Latin poem is not "How did they really do it back then?" or "How faithful is it to the original?" The fundamental question is "How well do such things enable the classics to speak to us today?" Literary theory has given the classics a new voice, a vibrant and resonant voice that says a great deal indeed.

–CARL A. RUBINO,
HAMILTON COLLEGE

Viewpoint:
No. Critical theory is a form of obscurantist terrorism that is harmful to humanistic study as a whole and particularly deleterious to classics.

Since the rise of postmodernism as a recognized discipline in the 1980s, the partisans of critical theory inside classics have repeatedly charged it with "a resistance to theory" in the words of Paul de Man. This resistance has sometimes been portrayed as a continuation of the quarrel over the proper goal of classical scholarship, hermeneutics or philology, which split the German academy in the late eighteenth and early nineteenth centuries. August Boeckh, advancing the theories of his teachers Friedrich August Wolf and Friedrich Schleiermacher, argued that the focus of the new discipline should be on interpreting ideas and developing a systematic science of hermeneutics, while Gottfried Hermann held that its proper object was the increase of philological knowledge and the practice of restoring literary texts through textual criticism. Philology won the debate through the nineteenth and most of the twentieth centuries. If one replaces hermeneutics with modern critical theory, the quarrel and the resistance continue today. There is, however, one crucial difference between classics today and classics two hundred years ago: the profession has advanced decisively in Boeckh's direction by making the critical interpretation of texts a central activity pursued with a pragmatic, if not systematic, mix of historical, formal, and philological techniques.

The continuing defiance of critical theory is often dramatized as a kind of neo-Luddite opposition to a new cognitive science that has in just two or three decades swept away so-called *belle tristic* criticism. Indeed, some proponents of theory try to foreclose all debate about it with a neat rhetorical ploy: they assert that any attempt to contain theory by making it into a topic of study like others is a form of resistance to theory and then seal off all further rational analysis by claiming that even resistance to theory is a part of theory. Like a vast dilating anaconda, theory devours the basis for its external appraisal. Because of theory's airtight resistance to analysis, it is necessary first to expose some of its basic premises and procedural tactics before showing how useless it is for our understanding of the ancient Mediterranean world.

Postmodernism derives from a mix of poststructuralism and deconstructionism, both of which were initially movements to criticize the tenets of 1960s structuralism. Modern critical theory, by contrast, developed from neo-Marxist and feminist theory with the addition of postcolonial, gender, and queer theory (the argument that sexual and gender identities are not fixed and do not therefore determine who we are). Perhaps the most salient feature of both postmodern and critical theory is the rejection of all thinking that combines knowledge with empirical experience to seek universal truths or, as they are called pejoratively, "meta-narratives." Jean-Françoise Lyotard said it nicely: "I define postmodernism as incredulity toward meta-narratives" (xxiv). This means that everything European philosophy and science have held to be fundamentally true at an abstract level is in fact contingent, fragmented, historically constructed, and culturally dependent. More sinisterly, however, this Eurocentric conception of knowledge has advanced a covert agenda to empower members of one dominant social caste by suppressing all the others. In overthrowing the foundational assumptions and procedures on which prior European philosophy has attempted to ground truth, critical theory is at heart a revolutionary political movement disguised behind the facade of historicist relativism. Postmodern critics who take up cultural studies follow a procedural recipe with blind obedience. When confronting a philosophical, social, political, or psychological theory, they make no attempt to determine its inherent truth-value, but immediately and drearily proceed to uncover its hidden patriarchal, logocentric, or identitarian bias. Slavoj Zizek rightly considers the abandonment of any con-

Jacques Derrida, the influential French philosopher and founder of the International College of Philosophy, in Paris, December 1987

(© Sophie Bassouls/CORBIS)

cern for the truth-value of a theory, which he calls "cognitive suspension," a common feature of historicist relativism. "The problem with such a procedure of historicist relativism," he notes, "is that it continues to rely on a set of silent (non-thematized) ontological and epistemological presuppositions on the nature of human knowledge and reality–usually a proto-Nietzschean notion that knowledge is not only embedded in but also generated by a complex set of discursive strategies of power (re)production" (500). For both Zizek and his mentor Jacques Lacan, modern science is not one of the meta-narratives subject to ideological cognitive mapping.

Aside from its denial of any foundational truth or reality in the universe, an absurd claim that the sciences and most humanistic disciplines blithely ignore in their acquisition of new knowledge, critical theory holds several other assumed but completely unsupported positions: the autonomous subject of our consciousness is a mere linguistic convention; language is not an instrument for conveying fixed meaning or describing reality because humans are equivalent to symbol systems and those systems with their associated meanings are contingent, relational, and dynamic; every text is a tissue woven from many former texts and can never be reified as a single, integral object of study because of the complex indeterminacy of the tissue; the objective interpretation of the past is impossible; and disinterested scholarship is a myth. All of these assertions have been subjected to massive and repeated falsifications (see the bibliography). They constitute an epistemological nihilism that ought to stifle writing and theorizing; they do not because theorists modestly relativize their own position by placing its claims *sous rature* ("under erasure") in order to do the opposite: to privilege that position so it can mount an effective attack on the rhetoric of power and the stability of meaning. "We don't write *theory,*" they imply, "we write *texts* which, because they are subject to erasure, merely play with theory. After all, only texts exist." Deconstructors relish this sort of self-referential paradox, oblivious to its frivolity and falsity.

So many new vogues of theory have swept into literary criticism since the 1980s that it has burst from lack of coherence and left behind a vast eclectic detritus of splintered movements. With the possible exception of the neo-Marxists, who think they have a set way to read literature, no one really knows what the designated object of criticism may be (see Egginton and Gilgen). The critics are in a postunitary stage: they cannot agree on what literature means; they cannot assume that what they write about the literature they do read is comprehensible to other critics; and they cannot even hope that they have some books in common. That explains why literary criticism is slowly being absorbed by cultural studies.

The loss of conceptual unity in criticism seems to have opened the dam of *theorrhaea* ("theory flow"), a portmanteau word coined by J. G. Merquior (189–260) to parody the deconstructionist research program. The stylistic consequence of *theorrhaea,* freed from any core of settled principles, is convoluted syntax, chaotic organization, and pretentious jargon. The surge of eclectic *theorrhaea* guarantees unreadable English. Critics have rushed to the defense of their style by proclaiming the jargon fallacy: complex thought requires a complex style. The claim is patently false and has been repeatedly disproved, but the unbearable heaviness of obscurity continues to narrow the readership of theory.

The proclaimed triumph of critical theory was, therefore, as premature as it was hubristic. Its epistemic nihilism has been thoroughly discredited. Deconstruction proper is largely extinct in U.S. universities, where its domestication at the hands of critical theorists has led to what we might call "soft core" deconstruction, "a technique for unreading texts" that shirks Jacques Derrida's ontological daring (Merquior, 228). It is a fairly simple technique of applying extreme polysemy to hunt out apparently irreconcilable meanings that undercut any literary coherence or intention.

Modern critical theory is, as we have seen, a revolutionary political movement based on feminist, gender, neo-Marxist, postcolonial, and queer ideologies. Each of its constituents is fractured along dozens of different approaches, biases, philosophies, and activist agendas. Collectively, they are mostly performative, not constative, and characterized by cognitive suspension in Zizek's sense. They do not seek to produce evidence-based knowledge but to prosecute radical change in our perception of history and in the structure of the sociopolitical world. They are, in short, an oppositional social and political praxis. Their anachronistic application to the ancient Greco-Roman world can only result in error, misunderstanding, and distortion. We simply do not have enough broad, factual, impartial information about the social, political, religious, and cultural life of that world, particularly the Greek world from the eighth to the third centuries B.C.E., on which to base theories that were designed originally for analysis of contemporary cultures where source material is rich. We are somewhat better off in the case of Rome, particularly from the Augustan period down to the death of Commodus in 192 C.E., but even here almost all the documentary evidence comes from a narrow social and educational spectrum, all male and full of gaps. In the absence of so much hard evidence, at a distance of nearly three thousand years from the ancient world, theorists must extort conclusions from oblique sources–iconography, literature, philosophical treatises, forensic speeches (the favorite hunting ground these days), urban planning, and even residential design. Absent strict factual controls, the potential for embroidery and misrepresentation is immense.

The case of Sappho is instructive. We know virtually nothing about aristocratic Mytilenean society in seventh-century B.C.E. Lesbos, but because Sappho has become the paradigmatic lesbian poet, the "tenth Muse" as Plato never called her, fabrication and wild speculation supplant ignorance. She and her poetry, of which only one complete poem (Fr. 1) survives, must be sited in a modern feminist and queer landscape as an inspirational model, the *fons et origo* of gay poetry. We know nothing about the performance conditions for Sappho's verse and cannot even pronounce definitively on her sexual orientation, yet the critics continue to advance pure conjecture as probable fact. Perhaps the most ludicrous of all these inventions is "Sappho schoolmistress": the proprietor of a finishing school for the island's aristocratic daughters, who studied poetry and explored the finer points of sensual and erotic awareness with her.

The same treatment is given Sulpicia, the only Roman poetess whose work has survived from antiquity. She lived in the first century B.C.E. and has left us six short elegiac epigrams included in the manuscripts of Tibullus (4.7–12). Other than that, all is guesswork. Her poetry is mediocre, but once again she must be "reclaimed" as a key feminist poet and subjected to enhancive hermeneutics. The ceaseless reanimation of Sappho and Sulpicia is symptomatic of reanimators' desire to perform the past with a new script.

SULPICIA

The short elegies by the unmarried Roman aristocrat Sulpicia record her love affair with a young man in the first century B.C.E. Such a display of sexual independence ran counter to the mores of the day. Below is the first of her six poems:

At last the love I've waited for has come.
(No shame to say so: more to cover up).
My Camenae called on her in prayer,
and Cytherea brought him to my heart.
Venus kept her promise: now she can tell
my tale of joy to those who don't believe.
I hardly want to give this letter up
so no one else sees it before he does.
I'm glad I did it—why wear a prudish mask,
as if he wasn't good enough for me!

Source: *Sulpicia,* Six Poems, *edited and translated by Anne Mahoney, Lecturer in Classics at Tufts University.*

Perhaps the worst consequence of the revolutionary bent in theory is the wholesale indictment of the Greco-Roman world for its sexism, imperialism, slavery, and tyranny at the expense of all its other accomplishments. The quest to indict Eurocentrism, phallogocentrism, and patriarchy in the ancient world turns Greco-Roman culture into a grotesque parody that lacks any redeeming value. It can conveniently be discarded as the foundation of Western culture. Current notions of identity politics make the deracination of the West a highly desirable goal, one that critical theorists have largely abetted in this phase of antifoundationalism.

Even if critical theory eventually sheds some of its revolutionary praxis, its goal will always be to uncover *what* a text–which is everything–really means, not *how* it means. Yet, the ancient world, which has given us all our principal literary genres, viewed poetry, history, and philosophy as creative endeavors governed by traditions in which the *how*–the poetics, the rhetorical models, the stylistic techniques, the tropes, the myths, and the thematizations–played the paramount role. To be creative for a Greek or Roman historian, for example, meant to align oneself with a tradition and continue it in modified form, as the long line of Greek historians running from Herodotus through Thucydides and Polybius to Procopius shows. One sees the same in Roman historians from Caesar through Sallust, Livy, and Tacitus to Ammianus Marcellinus. The same is true in drama and poetry. Tradition is absolutely essential to any humanistic work, explaining why theory has tried so consistently to destroy it. Scholarship in Greek and Latin cannot sever itself from these living traditions without becoming solipsistic.

The humanities, whose core lies in Greece and Rome, are based on the preservation and transmission of the cumulative heritage of the past. That is only possible by hewing to a communal form of research that does not permit individual license, exemption from logical scrutiny, or appeal to special epistemological status. Every critical obscurity and every political allegation must be confronted with a demand for evidence. Yet, "the most enduring fault of literary criticism as a field," John M. Ellis writes, "has been its readiness to abandon the communal sense of a shared inquiry, in which individual perceptions are expected to be tested and sifted by others. A shared inquiry means a commitment to argument and dialogue, while a criticism that insists on the value of each individual critic's perspective . . . refuses to make that commitment" (159). Within the study of English and the narrow domain of classics into which theory has penetrated, a muddled pluralism now reigns because objectivity, truth, and factuality are assumed to be nonexistent. Pluralism rests on what the philosopher John Searle has called "perspectivism," the notion that we never have unmediated access to reality because it is always mediated by our perspectives. Knowledge, therefore, is perspectival and not objective, so the perspective of any critic is just as valid as that of any other.

No field, however, is more dependent on communal scholarship than classics. Its core disciplines–languages, linguistics, history, textual criticism, commentary, and archaeology–are only possible through shared inquiry, respect for evidence, and logical scrutiny. These disciplines will never be displaced by any extensive training in or application of critical theory as a proof of professional competence, though a nodding acquaintance with the main lines of its thought might be a helpful prophylactic to students. Hermann was, after all, fundamentally right about the goal of classics.

In their groundbreaking paper "Against Theory," Steven Knapp and Walter Benn Michaels argue for the "fundamental inseparability" of the three main conditions for interpretation: authorial intention, text, and reader. Against this unity they pose "theory," which privileges one or another of the three conditions (hermeneutics the intention, deconstruction the text, and relativism the reader). Theory attempts to take a position outside this interpretive practice by first creating problems and then proposing hypotheses to answer the questions about the problems. Since it is impossible to reach a valid position outside practice, theorists should stop trying, and the whole theoretical enterprise should cease. It will not of course, but in the case of classics, which must deal with canonical texts running from the eighth century B.C.E. to the third century C.E., disarticulating the interpretive concord between authorial intention, text, and reader adds to the existing difficulties of temporal distance, textual lacunae, and historical ignorance: hermeneutics abolishes the reader's responsibility to make his own interpretation; it dehumanizes the text as a disembodied other; and it alienates intention into an infinite regression. This threefold process has been most destructive on interpretations of ancient drama, especially the comedy of Aristophanes and Menander, whose plays are taken as mirrors of society with the proper hermeneutical polishing.

Searle, an inveterate opponent of postmodern relativism and textual metaphysics, reports a conversation he once had in French with Michel Foucault in a February 2000 Reason Online interview (available at http://reason.com/0002/fe.ef.reality.shtml). Foucault, who was even more opposed to Derrida than Searle, stated that Derrida practiced the method of "obscurantisme terroriste." When Searle asked, "What the hell does that mean?" Foucault explained that Derrida writes so obscurely you cannot tell what he is saying–that is the obscurantism–and then when someone criticizes him, he can always say, "You didn't understand me. You're an idiot!"–that is the terrorism. Although the *morbus Gallicus* in its severest form is dead in France and on its last breath in the United States, with only a few fishy deconstructors now active, modern critical theory continues to mount a massive assault on the humanities and indeed on the notion of humane studies. There is no better characterization of the strategy its partisans follow than "obscurantisme terroriste."

–STEVEN J. WILLETT,
SHIZUOKA UNIVERSITY OF ART
AND CULTURE

References

M. M. Bakhtin, *The Dialogic Imagination: Four Essays,* edited by Michael Holquist, translated by Caryl Emerson (Austin: University of Texas Press, 1981).

Roland Barthes, *Critical Essays,* translated by Richard Howard (Evanston, Ill.: Northwestern University Press, 1972).

Barthes, *The Pleasure of the Text,* translated by Richard Miller, with a note on the text by Howard (New York: Hill & Wang, 1975).

Martin Bernal, *Black Athena: The Afroasiatic Roots of Classical Civilization,* volume 1, *The Fabrication of Ancient Greece 1785–1985* (New Brunswick, N.J.: Rutgers University Press, 1987).

Bernal, *Black Athena: The Afroasiatic Roots of Classical Civilization,* volume 2, *Archaeological and Documentary Evidence* (New Brunswick, N.J.: Rutgers University Press, 1991).

Frederick C. Crews, *The Pooh Perplex* (Chicago: University of Chicago Press, 2003).

Crews, *Postmodern Pooh* (New York: North Point, 2002).

Jacques Derrida, *Dissemination,* translated, with an introduction and additional notes, by Barbara Johnson (Chicago: University of Chicago Press, 1981).

Derrida, *Margins of Philosophy,* translated, with additional notes, by Alan Bass (Chicago: University of Chicago Press, 1982).

Derrida, *Of Grammatology,* translated by Gayatri Chakravorty Spivak (Baltimore: Johns Hopkins University Press, 1976).

Derrida, *Writing and Difference,* translated, with an introduction and additional notes, by Alan Bass (Chicago: University of Chicago Press, 1978).

M. J. Devaney, *"Since at Least Plato" and Other Postmodern Myths* (New York: St. Martin's Press, 1997).

Terry Eagleton, *After Theory* (New York: Basic Books, 2003).

Umberto Eco, *The Aesthetics of Thomas Aquinas,* translated by Hugh Bredin (Cambridge, Mass.: Harvard University Press, 1988).

Eco, *The Limits of Interpretation* (Bloomington: Indiana University Press, 1990).

Eco, *The Name of the Rose,* translated by William Weaver (San Diego: Harcourt Brace Jovanovich, 1983).

Eco, *The Open Work,* translated by Anna Cancogni, with an introduction by David Robey (Cambridge, Mass.: Harvard University Press, 1989).

Editors of Lingua Franca, *The Sokal Hoax: The Sham that Shook the Academy* (Lincoln: University of Nebraska Press, 2000).

William Egginton and Peter Gilgen, "Disciplining Literature in the Age of Postdisciplinarity: An Introduction," *Stanford Humanities Review,* 6 (Winter–Spring 1998) <http://www.stanford.edu/group/SHR/6-1/html/intro.html>.

John M. Ellis, *Against Deconstruction* (Princeton: Princeton University Press, 1989).

Ellis, *Language, Thought, and Logic* (Evanston, Ill.: Northwestern University Press, 1997).

Ellis, *Literature Lost: Social Agendas and the Corruption of the Humanities* (New Haven: Yale University Press, 1999).

Michel Foucault, *Language, Counter-Memory, Practice: Selected Essays and Interviews,* edited, with an introduction, by Donald F. Bouchard, translated by Bouchard and Sherry Simon (Ithaca, N.Y.: Cornell University Press, 1977).

René Girard, *Deceit, Desire, and the Novel,* translated by Yvonne Freccero (Baltimore: Johns Hopkins University Press, 1965).

Girard, *Violence and the Sacred,* translated by Patrick Gregory (Baltimore: Johns Hopkins University Press, 1977).

Paul R. Gross and Norman Levitt, *Higher Superstition: The Academic Left and Its Quarrels with Science* (Baltimore: Johns Hopkins University Press, 1997).

Josué Harari, ed., *Textual Strategies: Perspectives in Post-Structuralist Criticism* (Ithaca, N.Y.: Cornell University Press, 1979).

Micaela Janan, *"When the Lamp is Shattered": Desire and Narrative in Catullus* (Carbondale & Edwardsville: Southern Illinois University Press, 1994).

Steven Knapp and Walter Benn Michaels, "Against Theory," *Critical Inquiry,* 8 (Summer 1982): 723–742.

Jean-François Lyotard, *The Postmodern Condition: A Report on Knowledge,* translated by Geoff Bennington and Brian Massumi (Minneapolis: University of Minnesota Press, 1984).

Richard Macksey and Eugenio Donato, eds., *The Languages of Criticism and the Sciences of Man* (Baltimore: Johns Hopkins University Press, 1970).

J. G. Merquior, *From Prague to Paris: A Critique of Structuralist and Post-Structuralist Thought* (London: Verso, 1986).

Paul Allen Miller, *Lyric Texts and Lyric Consciousness: The Birth of a Genre from Archaic Greece to Augustan Rome* (London: Routledge, 1994).

Christopher Norris, *Against Relativism: Philosophy of Science, Deconstruction, and Critical Theory* (Oxford: Blackwell, 1997).

John Peradotto, "Texts and Unrefracted Facts: Philology, Hermeneutics, and Semiotics," *Arethusa,* 16 (Fall–Spring 1983): 15–33.

Carl A. Rubino, *"Lectio difficilior praeferenda est:* Some Reflections on Contemporary French Thought and the Study of Classical Literature," *Arethusa,* 10 (Spring 1977): 63–83.

Rubino, "Opening Up the Classical Past: Bakhtin, Aristotle, Literature, Life," *Arethusa,* 26 (Spring 1993): 141–157.

Rubino, "Umberto Eco," in *Italian Novelists Since World War II, 1965–1995,* volume 196, *Dictionary of Literary Biography,* edited by Augustus Pallotta (Columbia, S.C.: Bruccoli Clark Layman / Detroit: Gale Research, 1999), pp. 132–144.

Ferdinand de Saussure, *Course in General Linguistics,* edited by Charles Bally and Albert Sechehaye in collaboration with Albert Reidlinger, translated by Wade Baskin (New York: Philosophical Library, 1959).

Alan D. Sokal and Jean Bricmont, *Fashionable Nonsense: Postmodern Intellectuals' Abuse of Science* (New York: Picador, 1999).

David C. Stove, *Scientific Irrationalism: Origins of a Postmodern Cult* (New Brunswick, N.J.: Transaction, 2000).

Raymond Tallis, *Enemies of Hope: A Critique of Contemporary Pessimism* (New York: St. Martin's Press, 1997).

Tallis, *In Defence of Realism* (Lincoln: University of Nebraska Press, 1998).

Tallis, *Not Saussure: A Critique of Post-Saussurean Critical Theory* (New York: St. Martin's Press, 1995).

Tallis, *Theorrhoea and After* (New York: St. Martin's Press, 1998).

Roger Trigg, *Reality at Risk: A Defence of Realism in Philosophy and the Sciences* (Totowa, N.J.: Barnes & Noble, 1980).

Paul Veyne, *Writing History: Essay on Epistemology,* translated by Mina Moore-Rinvolucri (Middletown, Conn.: Wesleyan University Press, 1984).

Keith Windshuttle, *The Killing of History: How Literary Critics and Social Theorists Are Murdering Our Past* (New York: Free Press, 2000).

Slavoj Zizek, "A Symptom–of What?" *Critical Inquiry,* 29 (Spring 2003): 486–503.

CLASSICAL STUDIES: TRANSLATION

Does translation inevitably distort our engagement with the ancient world?

Viewpoint: Yes. Translation distorts our engagement with the ancient world because modern English does not offer the linguistic resources to convey classical culture.

Viewpoint: No. Since ancient languages are no longer spoken, texts in those languages are fixed and more accessible through translation.

The problem of translation faces any nonnative student of any culture from any epoch. No modern scholar, surely, would argue that translation does not "distort" the reader's impression of the original, whatever the source and target languages of the text to be translated. Yet, a translator whose source texts are in a modern language is able to turn to native speakers of the source language for elucidation of difficult or ambiguous passages. Even so, there can never be complete transparency or equivalency from one language to another. Beyond the most basic level ("Where is the train station?"), the "same" sentences do not and cannot mean exactly the "same" thing in two different languages, not even in two living languages spoken in similar cultures. Our question here really becomes, "does translation distort our engagement with the ancient world *more* than it would distort our engagement with a modern culture"? We can never recover a full understanding of the day-to-day lives, beliefs, and aspirations of ancient peoples, but does *translation itself* hamper our understanding more than would be the case were we dealing with a living culture? Is it accurate to say that *translation itself* "distorts our engagement with the ancient world"?

One school of thought answers these questions "yes"; the necessity of accessing ancient cultures' own belief systems wholly through translation of languages no longer spoken exacerbates the difficulties presented by the temporal remoteness of those cultures. In this view, the transposition of an ancient Greek or Latin text's ideas into a modern language gravely distorts and misrepresents that text's content. Lacking the ability to interact directly with native speakers of these languages and limited by the survival of some texts but not others, we are inevitably doomed to an engagement with the ancient world that is both less complete and more misleading than our translation-based engagement with contemporaneous cultures.

Another view, however, holds that translation of ancient texts is no more "distorting" than translation of any other work. Indeed, it can be argued that since the ancient languages are no longer spoken, their words' meanings are fixed in a way that the words of a living language cannot be and are therefore more, not less, accessible through translation. Furthermore, any interpretation of any text is a kind of "translation," and in any act of reading the goal of transparency of meaning is illusory. A good translation of an ancient text, then, is no more deceptive than any other translation of any other text; and the choices the translator makes are themselves a kind of interpretation or commentary on the source text, whether that text is ancient or modern.

Those, then, are the two main positions on the question of translation's distortion of our engagement with the ancient world; the first, that translation does indeed cause even greater distortion when we deal with the ancient world than when we face a text from a modern, living culture; the second, that all interpretation is a form of distortion and that the fixed nature of ancient languages makes texts in those languages, if anything, more accessible to comprehension through translation than texts in a living, changing language.

—Elizabeth Vandiver

Viewpoint: Yes. Translation distorts our engagement with the ancient world because modern English does not offer the linguistic resources to convey classical culture.

Writing of "the belief that real translation is impossible," George Steiner says that the best one can hope for in translation is "a convention of approximate analogies, a rough-cast similitude, just tolerable when the two relevant languages or cultures are cognate, but altogether spurious when remote tongues and far-removed sensibilities are in question" (Steiner, 1998, 77). When we approach the ancient world, we are dealing precisely with "remote tongues and far-removed sensibilities" and are thus attempting not only to engage with and understand, on their own terms, cultures that no longer exist, but to do so through reading documents in languages that are no longer spoken.

The words of any language carry with them shades of meaning, which align themselves differently even in closely related languages. Furthermore, the traces of words' histories, their use in idioms and catchphrases, and the whole range of associations that accrue around any given word can never be "carried across" (the basic sense of "trans-late") into any other language. Yet, all these problems are exacerbated enormously when the source language belongs to the ancient world. Unable to ask a native speaker for assistance, the translator of ancient texts confronts a host of difficulties that lead to inevitable distortions. The most obvious stumbling block, a word of completely unknown meaning, is a rarity; instead, the translator of Greek and Latin must deal with words whose meanings are only too well known.

This apparent paradox manifests itself at two opposite poles. Some words seem to have one "transparent" meaning, easily transferred from source to target language; others have several meanings, and require a choice among various different possible translations. To illustrate the first of these problems, let us consider the classical Greek word *theos.* Any lexicon of classical Greek will say that *theos* "means" god. Yet, if a translator translates *theos* as "god"—or worse still, God with a capital G—the modern English word triggers in the reader an array of unexamined assumptions: that the entity described by this term is omniscient, omnipotent, transcendental, merciful, righteous, the creator of the universe, and loving toward humankind. However, none of these attributes can be accurately ascribed to the Greek *theoi.* Does *theos,* then, "mean" god? It is hardly an exaggeration to say that it does not, that it means something different for which we have no exact English equivalent. The "easy" translation here masks a profound cultural and conceptual gulf.

On the opposite pole, consider *logos.* This term's most basic translation is "word," but it also means, among other things, story; speech; and reason or rational faculty. In some contexts, including its famous appearance in the opening chapters of St. John's Gospel, "word" does not appropriately represent *logos.* "In the beginning was the Word" is without question a distorting translation of *en archêi ên ho logos.* "In the beginning was the rational faculty" or "in the beginning was reasoned argument" might come closer to catching the full semantic field of *logos.*

Words that appear simple, then, can lead to distortions of understanding, both through a reader's unconscious assumptions about a concept's meaning or through the different groupings of associations and resonances in the ancient language and the modern. Those are among the difficulties the translator faces in an ancient text. Even more formidable are those words whose English descendants are in common usage, but with quite different meanings from their parent words. To illustrate all these points, let us look at a specific fifth-century B.C.E. Greek text: the opening sentence of Herodotus's account of the Persian Wars.

We shall pass over the impossibility of reproducing an author's style in a second language; as important as style is from the literary point of view, here we are concerned with the accessibility of historical information, not with the beauty and characteristic "feel" of an original text. What interests us as students of history is the *content* of the ancient work; cannot a competent translator simply tell us what an ancient author really said?

The separation of style and content is not a simple matter; but assuming, for the sake of argument, that it can be achieved, translation nevertheless distorts our understanding and interpretation of the content of ancient works. The six translations included as a sidebar give some sense of the complexity and difficulty involved in rendering the programmatic sentence of Herodotus's great work into English, and illustrate the types of choices the translator must make and their implications.

The sentence's third word, *historiê,* is the ancestor of our word *history,* but to translate it thus is to invite misunderstanding. A modern author who opens a work by saying "I am writing history" immediately sets himself or herself in the framework of a recognizable tradition; indeed, such an author has to specify which of several theoretical and methodological frameworks he or she intends to follow. But although there are many different modern approaches to the practice of history, readers and writers alike recognize that there is an intellectual discipline called "history" and share at least broad assumptions about what that discipline entails. Yet, when Herodotus wrote, the Greek language had no word for history. However Herodotus conceptualized his purpose, he cannot have thought that he was "writing history" as a later historian could, and a translation should not imply that he did make any such claim for himself. Instead, the term Herodotus uses in his opening sentence to describe the nature of his work, *historiê,* means "inquiry" or "research," which is in fact how most of our sample translations choose to render it.

Here, at least, the difficulty is fairly easily overcome; while the translator may be sorely tempted to render *historiê* as "history," if that temptation can be resisted, there is nothing opaque or confusing to the reader about the terms "inquiry" and "research." But in the next word, we face a more difficult problem. This, Herodotus says, is the *apodexis* of his *historiê. Apodexis* means "showing forth," but this translation would not convey much to the reader. Two of our sample translations translate *apodexis* as publication, but this term is strongly anachronistic. Herodotus did not "publish" his work in any modern sense; he did not send a manuscript to a publisher who oversaw the editing and distribution of the work. Rather, Herodotus most likely "showed forth" the results of his inquiry by reading it aloud. Should *apodexis,* then, be translated as "performance"? But would a modern reader understand what is meant by "This is the performance of the inquiry of Herodotus of Halicarnassus"? The statement "This is the publication of the *History* of Herodotus" is immediately intelligible, but falsifies the original. The statement "This is the performance of the inquiry of Herodotus" is accurate, but can only be understood through the medium of extensive footnotes.

Four of our translators attempt a middle ground between the literal "showing forth" and the anachronistic "publication." A. D. Godley and David Grene opt for "set[ting] forth"; Aubrey de Sélincourt says that Herodotus "displays his inquiry," and Robin Waterfield adds a noun to give "Here are presented the results of the enquiry." Among these attempts, "display" perhaps best captures the sense of *apodexis.* But even that fails to convey the likely circumstances of Herodotus's "display" of his research. "Presentation," "display," and even "setting forth" all imply the visual more than the aural, a presentation to the reader's view rather than to the listener's ear. This shift in the mechanics of "publication" is not the immediate province of the translator; and yet, to ignore or elide it distorts what Herodotus is "really saying."

Herodotus next tells us that his purpose is to keep *ta genomena ex anthrôpôn* from becoming faded or forgotten through time. *Ta genomena ex anthrôpôn* means "the things that have come about from human beings," a crucial delineation of Herodotus's subject matter. The main difficulty posed by the phrase is how exactly to render *genomena,* especially in conjunction with the preposition *ex. Genomena* is a participle, literally meaning "the having-become-things"–the things which have come into being. But the preposition *ex,* which means "out of" or "from," affects our choice of translation. The question arises, should we render *ex anthrôpôn* as "among human beings," so that Herodotus is referring to events that have happened to people; or should we render it more strongly as "from," so that Herodotus is talking about events that have arisen from human agency? Again, our sample translations diverge. Henry Cary and Walter Blanco both render *ta genomena* as "actions"; Grene and Sélincourt place a similar stress on the implied human agency in their renderings–"what man has brought into being" and "human achievements." But Waterfield's "human events" downplays the agency of *ex,* and implies that the *genomena* are simply things that have happened *among* humans rather than *because of* humans. Finally, Godley takes *ex anthrôpôn* not with *ta genomena* at all, but with the next phrase, and renders *ta genomena* loosely as "the memory of the past."

Herodotus narrows *ta genomena* down by specifying that he is concerned in particular with *erga megala te kai thômasta*. The adjectives *megala* and *thômasta* mean "great" and "astonishing," respectively; the difficulty here lies in the noun *erga*, which means both works *and* deeds. Herodotus thus allows himself scope to recount noteworthy human productions, such as the pyramids of Egypt, and noteworthy human actions, such as the Persian Wars. It is no simple matter to find one English word that emphasizes both these senses; the necessity to choose between "works" and "deeds" means that, again, each translator inevitably distorts the Greekless reader's understanding of Herodotus's statement. If one must choose, "deeds" (as Cary, Godley, Grene, and Sélincourt all choose to render *erga*) is probably better, since Herodotus's narrative does, after all, recount the Persian Wars. But Blanco is a dissenter, with his choice of the term "monuments"; and Waterfield perhaps tries to preserve a hint of both senses in "important and remarkable achievements."

Herodotus says, in the next phrase, that he is concerned with the *erga* of both Greeks and *barbaroi*. This last term is an example of a treacherous pitfall for the translator; as we have already discussed with the term *historiê*, when an English word is directly derived from a Greek one, it is tempting to use the English term to translate the Greek. But when the word in question has accrued meanings not present in the original, that is a mistake; *barbaroi* does not mean "barbarians" in the sense that word would later acquire. Rather, this word simply meant "foreigner" in Greek. And yet Cary, Grene, Blanco, and Sélincourt all yield to the temptation and render *barbaroi* as "barbarians."

Barbaroi is not the only term in this phrase to challenge the translator. Herodotus says that the *erga* were *apodechthenta*–shown forth–by both Greeks and *barbaroi*. *Apodechthenta* is directly related to the noun *apodexis;* thus, Herodotus uses the same term for the manifestation of the *erga* as he used for his own presentation of his research. But only one of our samples, Sélincourt, preserves this verbal connection by using the English verb "display" in both instances. English style tends to avoid repetition; but it is surely not without importance that Herodotus chooses to use cognate terms for the manifestation, in the past, of those *erga* that he hopes that his own work's manifestation, in the present, will preserve.

At this point in the sentence, we reach one of the most subtle, and most intractable, problems for the translator–the problem not of the basic dictionary meanings of a word in the source language, but rather of its associations and resonances. It is impossible to recapture or preserve in the target language the rich network of associations that accrue around certain words in the source language, and yet those associations are without question part of the overall "meaning" of the source text. Herodotus tells us that his motivation for recording *erga megala te kai thômasta* is to keep them from becoming *aklea*–"without glory." *Aklea* is not in itself difficult to translate; it is a negative built from *kleos,* which means "glory" or "renown." Three of our translators use forms of "renown" to render *aklea;* the others use "report," "fame," and "glory." Those are all perfectly adequate translations of the basic meaning of *aklea,* but they give the English-speaking reader no hint of the rich and powerful associations attached to the Greek word, which directly reflects the terminology and ethos of Homeric epic. An epic confers *kleos* upon those whose deeds it recounts. When Herodotus says that he wants to prevent the wondrous achievements of the past from becoming *aklea,* he is arrogating to himself a role similar to that of the epic bard, and this association is present in the word itself. But the English word "glory" raises very different associations–among them echoes of religious language–and does not immediately bring up the worldview of Homeric epic in the mind of the modern reader.

Finally, Herodotus ends his programmatic sentence by saying he wants in particular to explore the question of why–*di' hên aitiên*–Greeks and foreigners warred with one another. Three of our six translators render *aitiê* as "reason"; two give "cause," and one says simply "why." Again, as with *erga,* the translator's choice of one term excludes other important senses. *Aitiê* means not only "cause" or "reason," but also "legal charge," "responsibility," and "blame." Herodotus is asking not only "Why did Greeks and non-Greeks fight with one another?" but also, more specifically, "Who was at fault, whose responsibility was it, who should take the blame?" In the sentence that immediately follows, he says that Persian *logioi*–those skilled in *logos*–counted the Phoenicians as originally *aitioi;* that is, carrying the *aitiê* for the enmity between Asia and Greece. A translation that omits the sense of guilt or blame from *aitiê* thus leaves out an important element of the connection between Herodotus's opening sentence and what follows immediately after it; and yet each of our representative translations *does* omit this sense.

At every juncture, the translator's choice steers the reader down one path of associations, semantic fields, and emphases, and cuts off the others that are equally present in the Greek. And as with this sentence, so with the rest of Herodotus's text and with all texts: at every step, the translator must force interpretative decisions

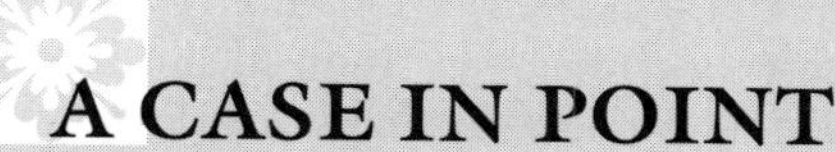

A CASE IN POINT

Below are six modern translations of the same passage from Herodotus:

Hêrodotou Halikarnêsseos historiês apodexis hêde, hôs mête ta genomena ex anthrôpôn tôi chronôi exitêla genêtai, mête erga megala te kai thômasta, ta men Hêllesi ta de barbaroisi apodechthenta, aklea genêtai, ta te alla kai di' hên aitiên epolemêsan allêloisi.

Translation

This is a publication of the researches of Herodotus of Halicarnassus, in order that the actions of men may not be effaced by time, nor the great and wondrous deeds displayed both by Greeks and barbarians deprived of renown; and among the rest, for what cause they waged war upon each other.

Source: *Henry Cary,* Herodotus: A New and Literal Version *(New York: Harper, 1854), p. 1.*

Translation

What Herodotus the Halicarnassian has learnt by inquiry is here set forth: in order that so the memory of the past may not be blotted out from among men by time, and that great and marvellous deeds done by Greeks and foreigners and especially the reason why they warred against each other may not lack renown.

Source: *A. D. Godley,* Herodotus, *Loeb Classical Library, Volume 1 (Cambridge, Mass.: Harvard University Press, 1960), p. 3.*

Translation

I, Herodotus of Halicarnassus, am here setting forth my history, that time may not draw the color from what man has brought into being, nor those great and wonderful deeds, manifested by both Greeks and barbarians, fail of their report, and, together with all this, the reason why they fought one another.

Source: *David Grene,* The History: Herodotus *(Chicago: University of Chicago Press, 1988), p. 33.*

Translation

This is the publication of the research of Herodotus of Halicarnassus, so that the actions of people shall not fade with time, so that the great and admirable monuments produced by both Greeks and barbarians shall not go unrenowned, and, among other things, to set forth the reasons why they waged war on each other.

Source: *Walter Blanco,* Herodotus: The Histories, *Norton Critical Edition, edited by Blanco and Jennifer Tolbert Roberts (New York & London: Norton, 1992), p. 3–4.*

Translation

Herodotus of Halicarnassus here displays his inquiry, so that human achievements may not become forgotten in time, and great and marvellous deeds—some displayed by Greeks, some by barbarians—may not be without their glory; and especially to show why the two peoples fought with one another.

Source: *Aubrey de Sélincourt,* Herodotus: The Histories *(London: Penguin, 1996), p. 1.*

Translation

Here are presented the results of the enquiry carried out by Herodotus of Halicarnassus. The purpose is to prevent the traces of human events from being erased by time, and to preserve the fame of the important and remarkable achievements produced by both Greeks and non-Greeks; among the matters covered is, in particular, the cause of the hostilities between Greeks and non-Greeks.

Source: *Robin Waterfield,* Herodotus: The Histories *(Oxford & New York: Oxford University Press, 1998), p. 3.*

upon readers who are unaware of alternative interpretations. That is, of course, true of any and all translation; there is never a possibility of one-to-one correspondence between languages, and any translation of any text will distort to a greater or lesser degree. Yet, when we are translating not only across languages but across epochs, and translating the texts of cultures whose vocabularies have formed the basis of so many of our own different cultural assumptions, the problems are multiplied. The apparent closeness and familiarity of terms such as *historiê* or *barbaroi,* the apparent one-to-one correspondence between words such as *theos* and "god," make the distance between source and target languages even wider and more treacherous to navigate. Apparent transparency hides a dense cloud of misinterpretation and distortion.

"As every generation retranslates the classics out of a vital compulsion for immediacy and precise echo, so every generation uses language to build its own resonant past" (Steiner, 1998, 30). We do indeed "build our own resonant past" in our reading of the ancient world through translation; but the more resonant it is with our own language, our own cultural assumptions, and our own modes of thinking, the less ancient and the more modern it becomes.

–ELIZABETH VANDIVER,
WHITMAN COLLEGE

Viewpoint:
No. Since ancient languages are no longer spoken, texts in those languages are fixed and more accessible through translation.

There is something perverse in a professor of classics and comparative literature arguing against the concept that translation distorts our engagement with the ancient world. I have spent the majority of my adult life teaching and studying Latin, Greek, and French texts in the languages in which they were written. I am a strong believer in learning as many languages as well as one possibly can. Thus, I am certainly not going to advocate anything so absurd as that there is no need to study ancient languages and that one can simply rely on whatever English version happens to be handy for access to an ancient work and the world that made it possible.

Nonetheless, I do want to challenge some of the assumptions that underlie our professional disdain for translation. There is a certain philological presumption that, if only we could know the original languages well enough, we could reconstruct exactly what Homer, Virgil, or Herodotus meant. This notion makes certain assumptions about the nature of meaning, and consequently of translation, that are fundamentally untenable. It assumes that the meaning of a text is a stable unified entity that can at least theoretically come into the reader's immediate possession. In short, it presumes that there is *an* "original" text and that access to it can be acquired through the accumulation of sufficient expertise. That is precisely the notion that I wish to call into question.

My argument will have three major points. First, I would argue that anytime we read or think about texts that are not written in our birth language, we are engaged in translation, even if we read the text in the language in which it was written. Thus, there is no study of the ancient world that is not an exercise in translation. Second, interpretation itself must be understood as a form of translation, as an exercise in transposing a word or words into their sets of possible substitutions, or of transposing one code into another code or set of codes. Thus, there is no escaping the problematic of translation, even in our mother tongue. It is meaningless to speak of its "inevitable distortion" since that distortion is the condition of possibility for meaning per se. Third, translation reveals new possibilities of meaning. As such, it does not distort the original, but makes it possible for the text to remain a living document. It is not a necessary evil but the very medium through which texts come alive.

My first point, then, is that the philological ideal is a mirage. Anytime we encounter texts not written in our birth language, that encounter takes place within a frame of reference. My primary frame of reference is necessarily the language in which I normally write, speak, and think. Indeed, I can only note the discrepancies between the language that is the object of my study and that which limns my primary frame of reference to the extent that I experience the difficulty of translating one into the other. Consequently, there is never an encounter with an ancient text–since none of us grew up speaking and writing ancient Greek or Latin with other native speakers–that is not always an exercise in translation. That is not to say that picking up the Penguin version of Virgil will give me the same experience as reading the Latin, especially after I have read a lot of other texts in the language and have developed a feel for the ways in which certain words and phrases are commonly used. It is, however, important to note that the difference between those two experiences only becomes perceptible in relation to the primary frame of reference that makes them possible. I can only note that *pietas* in Latin has a fundamentally dif-

ΗΡΟΔΟΤΟΥ ΑΛΙΚΑΡΝΑΣΣΕΩΣ ΙΣΤΟΡΙΑ ΕΝ ΕΝΝΕΑ ΤΜΗΜΑΣΙΝ, ΑΚΑΙ ΜΟΥΣΑΣ ΚΑΛΕΙ. ΙΣΤΟΡΙΩΝ ΠΡΩΤΗ. ΚΛΕΙΩ.

First page of the first edition in Greek (1502) of Herodotus's *History of the Persian Wars*

(courtesy of The Lilly Library, Indiana University)

ferent set of connotations than *piety* does in English if I am referring to English. *Canus* does not mean both "gray" and "white" in Latin, but in English. *Historiê,* as used by Herodotus, only has a problematic relation to "history" in English. The whole problem of the multiple layers of meaning and the possibility of distortion cannot occur in a monologuic environment. Only in dialogue with other languages, dialects, and codes does our mother tongue open up to us. Our encounter with the specificity of the ancient target language is only made possible in terms of the tongue through which we first sought to taste the world. Translation makes the original possible as the original.

This does not mean that *pietas, canus,* or *historiê* were ever self-identical in their original language. A given word only has meaning in relation to other words in the same linguistic system. That is true for two reasons. First, as the great Swiss linguist Ferdinand de Saussure discovered, the relation between any given sign and its meaning is ontologically (but not historically) arbitrary. That is to say, there is no necessary relation between a given set of sounds and a specific meaning or signification. The sounds that make up *dog* have no relation to man's best friend, and there is no reason per se why we should associate the four-legged beast with this particular set of phonemes, other than the fact that *dog* is not *hog*, *dig*, or *dot*. This doctrine, known as the arbitrariness of the sign, ultimately demonstrates that language is a function of difference. A word means what it means not in itself but because it is not another word. Consequently, meaning is not a stable substance but a potentially fluid set of relations between signs.

That brings us to our second point. If a given word in a given language only has meaning in relation to other words, then its meaning would be a function of its ability to be "translated" into those other words. Take an example: what does *gray* mean? If we have abandoned the idealist notion of specific words and concepts being inherently tied to specific abstract meanings or forms, as modern linguistics forces us to, then there is no such thing as an inherent "grayness" to which the word makes reference. Its meaning is its usage. Look at any standard dictionary. What you will find as a definition is a string of synonymous words and phrases. *Gray: a blend of black and white; dreary, dismal; having gray hair, old; ambiguous, as in a gray area of the law.* The result on a pragmatic level is that a word means the words or combinations of words that can be substituted for it in a sentence. A word does not possess a "meaning" per se; it possesses relations to other words.

Thus, even within our own language, we are always translating, and those translations are never exact. *Gray* and *dismal* are substitutable for one another in certain contexts: "it's a gray day"; "it's a dismal day." They are not interchangeable. I can paint my room "gray," but I cannot paint it "dismal"–though many might find "gray" a "dismal" color for my room. *Gray* and *dismal*, then, do not possess the exact same set of denotations and connotations. Their potential substitutability does not render them identical to one another. Yet, I cannot understand what *gray* means except in terms of its possible substitutions. Indeed, it has no concrete meaning outside of that set of substitutions. Likewise, when we say that *canus* in Latin does not mean the same thing as *gray* in English, but that *gray* is one of the possible translations of *canus*, we are saying that *gray* is a possible substitution for *canus* in certain contexts, that is, when one is rendering into English certain restricted uses. In other contexts, a possible substitution for *canus* might be either *albus* or *white*. The structure of the process is, thus, the same whether we are translating inter- or intralinguistically. Meaning is fundamentally a process of translation.

One further consequence of this fundamental insight that meaning is relational and differential rather than substantive and self-identical is that there is in fact no original meaning to be recovered. If a word only means what it means in relation to other words and not because it contains some necessary and fixed identity, then the philological dream of recovering exactly what Herodotus understood by *historiê* or Virgil by *pietas* is fundamentally misguided. Each of those words only has meaning to the extent that certain nonidentical substitutions can be made for them in certain contextually specific usages. That was as true for Herodotus and Virgil as it is for us. It is a fact of language, not history. Those substitutions, be they in the original or another language, will always necessarily have connotations and usage patterns that differ from the words themselves. Interpretation, then, is never identical to the thing interpreted. Moreover, inasmuch as *historiê* and *pietas* only have meaning to the extent that they enter into these relations of substitution, then their meanings are always something other than themselves. The object of interpretation, therefore, can never be to recover the pristine unity of what an author or text originally meant but to encounter a fundamental otherness. It is the way this otherness is shaped and structured in unique but never stable and self-identical ways that is the ultimate object of interpretation. All interpretation, then, is in essence a form of translation, a transposition of one set of terms into another, which is not identical to the first. That is what we call reading.

If, then, the only way we ever encounter texts not written in our native tongue is through translation, and if the process of interpretation within a language is fundamentally indistinguishable from that of translation, then translation ceases to be the distorting mirror through which antiquity is hidden from us. It renders possible an authentic encounter with the ancient world. Differences between translations do not reveal the distortion produced by the interlinguistic passage but become the possible interpretations that open the original to us. To say that *historiê* in Herodotus neither means merely "research," nor "inquiry," nor "history," and that English, therefore, denies us access to the unsullied Greek original is to fail to realize that *historiê* means "research," "inquiry," and "history" only because of the attempt to translate it. On a broader plane, while Alexander Pope's *Iliad* may contain many anachronisms, who would deny that Homer's poem enjoys the status it does in Anglo-American culture and has attracted the scholarly study that it has in part because of Pope's great poem? By the same token, even so idiosyncratic a text as Ezra Pound's famous "mistranslation," "Homage to Sextus Propertius," opened up the possibility of fundamentally new forms of meaning in the text of the Roman elegist, forms that dramatically increased the poet's stature in modern scholarship.

What should be deplored, then, is not the necessity of translation but the assumption that any translation could ever get it right and that there is *a* "right" to get. There is no one right interpretation because texts by definition have no one meaning. What is needed are more translations into more languages and more codes of explanation so that the possibilities of meaning that exist within the texts and that are the legacy of the ancient world become as fully and variously realized as possible. Translation does not inevitably distort our engagement with the ancient world: it is its condition of possibility.

—PAUL ALLEN MILLER,
UNIVERSITY OF SOUTH CAROLINA

References

M. M. Bakhtin, *The Dialogic Imagination: Four Essays,* edited by Michael Holquist, translated by Caryl Emerson (Austin: University of Texas Press, 1981).

D. Thomas Benediktson, *Propertius: Modernist Poet of Antiquity* (Carbondale: Southern Illinois University Press, 1989).

Walter Blanco, *Herodotus: The Histories,* Norton Critical Edition, edited by Blanco and Jennifer Tolbert Roberts (New York & London: Norton, 1992).

Reuben A. Brower, ed., *On Translation* (Cambridge, Mass.: Harvard University Press, 1959).

Henry Cary, *Herodotus: A New and Literal Version* (New York: Harper, 1854).

Jacques Derrida, *Of Grammatology,* translated by Gayatri Chakravorty Spivak (Baltimore: Johns Hopkins University Press, 1976).

A. D. Godley, *Herodotus,* Loeb Classical Library (Cambridge, Mass.: Harvard University Press, 1920).

David Grene, *The History: Herodotus* (Chicago: University of Chicago Press, 1988).

Basil Hatim and Ian Mason, *The Translator as Communicator* (London & New York: Routledge, 1997).

Ferdinand de Saussure, *Course in General Linguistics,* edited by Charles Bally and Albert Sechehaye in collaboration with Albert Riedlinger, translated by Wade Baskin (New York: McGraw-Hill, 1966).

Aubrey de Sélincourt, *Herodotus: The Histories* (London: Penguin, 1996).

George Steiner, *After Babel: Aspects of Language and Translation,* third edition (Oxford & New York: Oxford University Press, 1998).

J. P. Sullivan, *Ezra Pound and Sextus Propertius: A Study in Creative Translation* (Austin: University of Texas Press, 1964).

Lawrence Venuti, ed., *Translation Studies Reader* (London & New York: Routledge, 2000).

V. N. Voloshinov, *Marxism and the Philosophy of Language,* translated by Ladislav Matejka and I. R. Titunik (Cambridge, Mass.: Harvard University Press, 1986).

Robin Waterfield, *Herodotus: The Histories* (Oxford & New York: Oxford University Press, 1998).

GREECE: AESCHYLUS

Does democracy ensure the triumph of right over might as Aeschylus maintains in the *Eumenides?*

Viewpoint: Yes. In the *Eumenides,* Aeschylus presents the foundations of a concept of justice based on law and procedure.

Viewpoint: No. The institution of law and procedure is merely the formalization of power.

Nothing seems more opposed to our civilized sense of justice than the following summary of the law(lessness) of the jungle: *might makes right.* Throughout history, philosophers have debated about the possibility for human institutions to open a space where the weak would be protected from the oppression of the strong. Does force prevail in the human world as it permeates all of nature? Can we ever be equal toward the law, in spite of our uneven actual strengths? Can the definition and enforcement of rights successfully keep force at bay? And if we do believe that justice is indeed possible, what is the best way to administer it? Is retaliation (an eye for an eye) a valid principle of equity, or is it a denial of justice? How should an institution be structured in order to make justice real?

Aeschylus's tragedy the *Eumenides* (performed in 458 B.C.E.) provides a remarkably rich kaleidoscope where one can catch a glimpse of the main arguments developed on these issues over the last four hundred years of Western philosophy. Set against this background, the play seems to stage both the *necessity* and the *impossibility* of providing justice though the mediation of democratic institutions.

On the one hand, the *Eumenides* appears to be a celebration of Athenian democracy: after generations of murders and revenge, the play ends with the pacifying foundation of a tribunal, the Areopagus, which was a central feature of the city's legislative and political life. The spectators of 458 B.C.E. were therefore shown the origins of the human institution that was making justice real in their world. Moreover, the plot puts a spectacular emphasis on some procedures (open debate of ideas, casting of votes equal in value in spite of the inequality of the voters) that confirm and strengthen the democratic principles on which the city's constitution was built. On the face of it, the play ends on a triumph of right and reason over might and fury.

At the same time, however, Aeschylus made several narrative and poetic choices, which reveal the highly problematic nature of these democratic institutions. Instead of showing the voting process and the adversarial legal system under their most convincing light, he seems to have undermined the foundation on which a tribunal like the Areopagus can claim to stand: in a subtle and roundabout way that anticipates much of what has been recently (re)asserted by postmodern philosophers, Aeschylus depicts justice more as a veil for power than as a measure of right. Rhetoric, arbitrariness, and bad faith play a bigger role in the solution of the conflict than rational arguments and honesty: under its self-congratulating surface, the ending's "triumph" appears rather as a fragile victory in a hard-fought power struggle.

Can justice be grounded on anything else than might? Aeschylus raises the question without solving it. Yet, as he explores it, he maps a territory on which later philosophers will endlessly tread.

—*Yves Citton*

Viewpoint: Yes. In the *Eumenides,* Aeschylus presents the foundations of a concept of justice based on law and procedure.

As the overall plot of Aeschylus's trilogy clearly suggests, questions of justice arise only after one has overcome the mechanical and self-destructing logic of retaliation, displayed in *Agamemnon* and the *Libation-Bearers,* the first and the second parts of the *Oresteia.* In the first tragedy, King Agamemnon, who led the Greeks to their victory against the Trojans, comes back home to his palace only to be slain by his wife, Clytaemnestra, and her lover, Aegisthus. Clytaemnestra cannot forgive Agamemnon for the murder of their daughter Iphigenia, sacrificed to bring good winds to the Greek fleet on its way to war, while Aegisthus pursues a family vendetta that goes back to crimes committed between their fathers. The endless cycle of vengeance continues into the next generation when, in the second play, Agamemnon's son, Orestes, returns from exile to exact revenge on his mother and her accomplice. So far, justice is conceived merely under its primitive form of an eye for an eye: the victim's blood can only be expiated by the perpetrator's murder; his relatives then call for more blood, with the extinction of each clan as the only end in sight.

The third play of the trilogy, the *Eumenides,* stages a successful attempt to break this circle, and sets in place a new approach to justice. During its first half, Orestes is chased by the Erinyes (also known as the Furies), bloodthirsty deities in charge of avenging Clytaemnestra's murder. A personification of retaliation, the Erinyes look no further than to Orestes' objective deeds: thou killed (thine mother), therefore thou shalt be killed. After having placed himself under the protection of Apollo and Athena, Orestes arrives in Athens, where his "case" gives rise to the constitution of a tribunal, the Areopagus. In accepting this "institutionalization," the furious and savage Erinyes are eventually transmuted into the gentle and civilized Eumenides.

What is this new conception of justice set up in the last scenes of the *Oresteia*? As the first exchange between Orestes and Athena clearly shows, we turn away from the mechanical application of a simple rule (retaliation, blood for blood), enforced by the victim's clan. Instead, we now face a question identified as too complex and inextricable to be resolved according to preexisting rules. When Athena is called to judge whether Orestes acted righteously or not (v.468), her first reaction is to suspend her personal judgment on the case and use instead her discrimination to institute a collective body, a tribunal made up of Athenian citizens in charge of seeking the truth and of avoiding injustice (v.484). We, therefore, trade the lethal fascination of dual relations (between the perpetrator and the victim, caught in endless reversals) for a triadic structure mediating the conflictual claims of the accuser (the Erinyes) and the defendant (Orestes, and his advocate-inspirer Apollo) with the addition of a third, exterior, and superior party (Athena and the Areopagus).

We should briefly pause on the modern echoes of this constitutional moment depicted in the play. In the move from Argos (the scene of the crimes) to Athens (the place of judgment), one can already foresee David Hume's and Adam Smith's insistence on approaching justice as a matter of *distance:* if my sense of what is right depends on a moral sentiment, as such authors claim, my judgment will constantly be swayed by the propensity we all have to prefer the near over the remote (my son over my cousin, my relative over a stranger, my neighbor over a person living on another continent). In order to be just, and to allow one's moral sense to express itself without distortion, one must therefore take the point of view of an "impartial spectator"—a point of view embodied in the play by the Athenian citizens (who represent onstage the actual spectators sitting in the theater), or, in today's trials, by a jury of peers.

In the conflicting parties' agreeing to recognize Athena as their superior arbiter, one can already recognize Thomas Hobbes's theoretical gesture of founding the possibility of justice on an original *contract:* I renounce my universal (natural) right to do whatever I see fit for my purpose if you vow to do the same and agree with me to transfer our faculty of judgment to a third party (the Sovereign, the State) in charge of propounding and enforcing laws. We will then call "just" the actions that respect these laws and "unjust" those that transgress them. The benefits of such an agreement are not only peace, the possibility of economic cooperation and development, but also justice itself, conceived as a political equalization of our unequal natural

ATHENA IS CALLED TO JUDGE

The matter is too great, if any mortal thinks to pass judgment on it; [470] no, it is not lawful even for me to decide on cases of murder that are followed by the quick anger of the Furies, especially since you, by rites fully performed, have come a pure and harmless suppliant to my house; and so I respect you, since you do not bring harm to my city. [475] Yet these women have an office that does not permit them to be dismissed lightly; and if they fail to win their cause, the venom from their resentment will fall upon the ground, an intolerable, perpetual plague afterwards in the land.

So stands the case: [480] either course—to let them stay, to drive them out—brings disaster and perplexity to me. But since this matter has fallen here, I will select judges of homicide bound by oath, and I will establish this tribunal for all time. Summon your witnesses and proofs, [485] sworn evidence to support your case; and I will return when I have chosen the best of my citizens, for them to decide this matter truly, after they take an oath that they will pronounce no judgment contrary to justice.

Source: *Aeschylus,* Aeschylus, *volume 2:* Eumenides, *translated by Herbert Weir Smyth (Cambridge, Mass.: Harvard University Press, 1926).*

endowments: in Jean-Jacques Rousseau's words, the social contract "substitutes for such physical inequality as nature may have set up between men, an equality that is moral and legitimate, [so] that men, who may be unequal in strength or intelligence, become every one equal by convention and legal right" (*The Social Contract,* Book I, Chapter 9).

With this new structure come several basic rules of conduct, starting with one recently presented by Stuart Hampshire as the only remaining universal definition of justice still acceptable in our multicultural societies: "Hear the other party!" To be just in one's deeds and not only in one's words, as Athena tells the Erinyes, one must hear both sides when they disagree (v.428). Justice appears therefore to consist less in a substantial definition of what is fair than in a *procedure:* the result of the process will be deemed "just" or "fair," independently of its concrete outcome, as long as the formal rules of procedure specified to adjudicate the matter have been respected.

Such a formalist approach is deeply ingrained in all modern conceptions of justice. It seems obvious to all of us that, in order for an arbitration between conflictual claims to be receivable as just, formal, written laws and guidelines must spell out beforehand the ways in which the investigation and the sentence will be carried out. The discretionary power of the judge, entrusted to see the singular substance of each case beyond the formal category of the law, is only acceptable within the narrow margins left by the tightly knit fabric of a code, jurisprudence, and overlayering of precedents. The original position of Apollo (before the translocation to Athens), exonerating Orestes without being accountable for his decision, seems to us today as incompatible with justice as that of the Erinyes, in their mechanical application of a blind and inflexible law. Justice has to be located somewhere in the middle: constrained in its application by a framework of formally spelled-out procedures, while remaining adaptable to the specificity of each singular case–in a constant tension where Aristotle has located the essence of "equity," defined as a correction of the law where it is defective owing to its necessary universality.

On top of the inherent instability of a "just" (formal) law in constant need of "adjustments" in the name of equity, the increasingly multicultural nature of our societies brings another set of fundamental problems. If Hampshire considers the "Hear the other side" principle as the only satisfactory foundation to postmodern justice, it is because any substantial definition of the just relies on basic assumptions about values that often differ from one culture to the next: within many communities, today as well as in the past, it is "unjust" not to acknowledge the gifts of God and not to thank Him for them; within others, it is unjust to slaughter animals for the mere pleasure of our human palates. How is one to define "The Just" in a society where all these contradictory systems of belief must somehow coexist in peace? It is no coincidence if over the last thirty years theories of justice have tended to give an increasing weight to procedural approaches, since it allows them to specify what is right without having to define what is good. Plus, Hampshire adds, it seems that all societies do integrate, at one level or another, basic institutions allowing for conflicting claims to be expressed and taken into consideration–which gives to the "Hear the other side" principle a de facto universal value.

It appears, therefore, that the grounding of the notion of right in our societies rests on the process staged by Aeschylus in the *Eumenides.* In conformity with Athena's opening statements, our basic collective position is to say that we do not know beforehand who is right and who is wrong. Some social groups call for harsh punishments, for mandatory sentences, for the death penalty, and for retaliatory military expeditions; others believe that people trapped in poverty deserve help and education rather than prison sentences and bombs. Like Athena's, our solution consists in suspending our judgment and in delegating our power to judge the outcome of a debate. The "good" way to deal with urban crime or foreign aggression is trusted to come out of the "right" procedure: democracy. Let us hear each party's arguments in their conflictual claims, and let us allow the rule of sheer numbers to settle the issue. It is striking that in the play Athena's vote is only one among many, with the sole marginal privilege of being that of a tie-breaker: in a spectacular homage to the egalitarian principle of Athenian democracy, the goddess Athena puts herself on par with mere humans. This rule of sheer numbers can seem counterintuitive: a god knows more and better than a human being, a philosopher knows more and better than a shoemaker, and it would make sense to give their voice more power in the decision-making process. The play seems to overcome such objections, and presents directly the "right" procedure as that where the best solution will emerge from a mechanism that equalizes the differences in power (physical strength, skills, knowledge, and wisdom).

We seem thus projected into the (neo)Kantian universe of our early-twenty-first-century Western democracies. Laws and political institutions must consider all human beings as formally equal. Their differences, in terms of power and capacities, can have bearings on their status within the economic sphere, but are denied to have any consequence in the abstract sphere of their political and legal rights: everybody is allowed to receive a fair trial, to vote, to meet with others and publicize their views. For most of us, justice in a society consists precisely in the fact that this sphere of legal and political rights is protected from the pressures of (physical, financial, and economic) might: if you can kill me, ruin me, fire me, jail me because I do not think, speak, or vote in a manner that pleases you, my "basic human rights" are deemed violated. The too many countries in which such abuses of power commonly take place are reputed not to be democratic: they are not "just" societies because they fail to open this protected space of debate, which is the essence of our "public sphere."

If Athena may appear as the inventor of modern justice, it is, therefore, less because she tames the savage beasts of blind retaliation than because she manages to stage their bloodthirsty doctrine as one voice among others, within a rational debate on crimes and punishments. Through the Kantian project of Enlightenment (give every human being the freedom to exchange ideas, and, as a consequence, mankind will collectively rise toward higher levels of truth and happiness), we reach the model of open democracy articulated by Jürgen Habermas, centered on the public sphere conceived as a space where a rational debate on collective means and ends is trusted to guide our sociopolitical development. Athena here represents this form of reason conceived as a process rather than as a fixed faculty: "rational" is whatever decision may come out of a debate where everybody respects the basic rules of polite and serious discussions (let the other party speak, pay full attention to its views, allow yourself to modify your opinion in light of convincing arguments, and so forth). In this sense, it is precisely because human beings are *not* fully rational that we need a democratic debate: rationality is not located in any of the participants, but in their interaction, that is, in the compromises reached through the confrontation of their imperfect reasons.

This debate is analytical in nature: Orestes must explain his motivations; the Erinyes must spell out the consequences of letting such criminals go free; and Apollo must build theories about the relative importance of husbands and wives, mothers and fathers. The adversarial procedure allows for the uncovering of logical inconsistencies in each party's discourse: the Erinyes are quick to point out that Zeus, whom Apollo invoked to vindicate fathers' rights, bears little authority on the issue, since he chained and suppressed his own father Cronos (v.641). Yet, this process of counterargumentation is precisely what allows for collective rationality to grow and improve. Had Athena (or Apollo, or any other character) known beforehand how to solve the issue between Orestes and the Erinyes, the play would have had nothing to represent. The debate generated by Athena produced a solution, and a rationality, which did not preexist.

One might think that the basic issue of justice has not yet been addressed: is it "just" that Orestes be allowed to walk free after having killed his own mother? We can argue ad infinitum about his claim to have been purified by slaughtering a few animals as expiatory victims, or about the type of punishment that would "compensate" for the murder of a mother, or about the punishment deserved by Clytaemnestra herself, or about Apollo's responsibility in the whole course of events–and countless other substantial issues of the same type. The function of the trial is precisely to close such an endless discussion (and allow us to move forward, and to free the living from the weight of the dead). What makes the sentence "just" is the procedural fact that Orestes' and the Erinyes' "rights" during the trial were respected by the due process it followed.

Now, if one were to ask what guarantees that these procedures themselves were "just" or "fair," one would have to return to the notion of contract, seen above through its Hobbesian echo: both Orestes and the Erinyes formally agreed to accept Athena's decision (whatever it might be). The ultimate foundation for the rights enjoyed by individuals consists in contracts to which they have willingly subscribed: only on this basis can institutions of justice be constructed. Contracts always involve risks and trade-offs (the Erinyes may have been better off, had they refused Athena's arbitration), but the benefits to be expected from the institutions of justice greatly outweigh these risks, and fully justify the trust put into them.

In summary, the second half of the *Eumenides* remarkably illustrates what has come to be accepted as the essence of justice in our modern Western democracies. To keep at bay both the self-destructive logic of mechanical retaliation and the oppressive logic of force, justice requires the constitution of a space devoted to adversarial and rational debates, where reason has a chance to emerge from the collective act of voting. This artificial space, resulting from a human process of "institution" depicted in the play, goes *against* the laws of nature, insofar as it overcomes both the "law of the jungle" and the natural drives of our (revengeful) passions. This space is necessary and sufficient to endow each individual with a number of "rights," independently of that individual's actual strengths and weaknesses. Athena's gesture illustrates the only way we humans can build a social space free from the two symmetrical evils she evokes in establishing the Areopagus, anarchy and tyranny (v.696). Twenty-five centuries later, this assertion of rights against the pressure of might remains the best way for us to work toward a more just world.

–YVES CITTON,
UNIVERSITY OF PITTSBURGH

Viewpoint: No. The institution of law and procedure is merely the formalization of power.

Aeschylus's *Eumenides* does indeed offer a remarkable model to illustrate the notion of justice in our Western tradition, but far from providing us with its foundations, it radically undermines its credibility. Under the surface of a patriotic celebration of Athens's democratic institutions, the play invites us to reflect about the trappings of judicial procedures and, ultimately, about the fragility of democracy. As much as it anticipates certain central tenets of modern liberalism, the tragedy is to be located in a long and strong tradition that—from Carneades to Blaise Pascal, Benedict de Spinoza, Karl Marx, Friedrich Nietzsche, and more recently Michel Foucault, Gilles Deleuze, or Alain Badiou—denounces the delusions of a faith in "justice" and of any approach based on the notion of "rights." Let us take the main articulations of the "liberal" reading and see how the play systematically undermines the principles it appears to establish.

The institution of a space of rights protected from the pressures of might. On the face of it, with the constitution of the tribunal of the Areopagus, Athena neutralizes both the state of war originally prevailing between Orestes and the Erinyes, and the unequal relation of power tilted in favor of a troop of goddesses against a mere human. The question is: what made this neutralization possible? The answer is clear: it is only a particular *relation of power* that has allowed for this space of "right" to be implemented. It is because Orestes secured the support of a god, Apollo, that he found himself in a position to resist the goddesses. The Areopagus is not a place where the state of war is suspended or neutralized: the ongoing rivalry between the old earthly deities represented by the Erinyes and the new Olympian gods permeates the proceedings through and through. Athena and her Athenians, the supposedly "third" party in charge of being the "impartial spectator" ideally positioned to arbitrate the conflict in a fair (since distant and disinterested) manner, are in fact bound to side with the goddess's fellow Olympians. The fact that the tribunal's location and name refer to Ares, the god of war, is no coincidence: judiciary and political proceedings are merely "war by other means."

Under the surface of *legal* arguments about the murder of Clytaemnestra, the background of *political* power struggles infiltrates virtually every turn of the plot. Behind countless pompous evocations of justice and righteousness, Aeschylus insists on revealing the complex negotiations, trade-offs, and dirty deals that—much more than issues of guilt or fairness—will settle the outcome of the trial. Athena's first words on stage (v.397) tell us that she was just given new land around Troy by the leaders of the victorious Greek army (led by Agamemnon)—a way for Aeschylus to justify Athens's claims on its colony of Sigeum, which will start paying tributes to the metropolis eight years after the performance of the play. Orestes' last words echo the goddess's opening statements, since he leaves the stage promising an everlasting alliance between Argos and Athens (vv.762–774). While the jurors are casting their votes, Apollo and the Erinyes exchange threats of reprisals against the city, in case the decision would stand with the other party (vv.711–730). As for the whole last quarter of the play (vv.778–1047), it is entirely devoted to buying off the Erinyes' alliance: for the price of a temple and a few processions, the Furies will not carry out their threat to poison and ravage the city. What is so openly displayed in this particular case by Aeschylus remains true (but more or less successfully hidden) in any legal and political settlement: conflicts of interests and thirst for revenge are not put to rest by abstract appeals to justice, but by the concrete push and shove of complex power struggles.

Right equals might. Is it possible, though, to abandon all illusions about rights, and build a political philosophy based on the sole reality of might? That is precisely the challenge faced by the Spinozist tradition. For Spinoza, nothing is beyond the basic laws of nature according to which might (and only might) makes right. The human, social, political world is not an independent island, isolated from the rest of the universe, but a part of nature where all the laws of natural necessity apply. The traditional foundations for notions like justice, responsibility, merit, desert, or free will are radically undermined by the acknowledgment of the fact that humans, like wolves, are constrained by physical causes to do, think, or will, this rather than that. Our only specificity, as humans, is to be located in our brain's capacity to reason, that is, in our capacity to understand things by their causes. Thanks to this capacity, two processes of empowerment can go hand in hand: the one that allows us to be less easily carried away by our irrational affects and the one that gives us a better grasp on the causal relations that determine our behavior. It is here that Spinoza encounters the eponymous stake of Aeschylus's play, the transformation of the furious Erinyes into the peaceful Eumenides: their name (<Gr. *eumenes,* "kindly") announces Spinoza's program of pacifying, improving, and bettering a mind conceived both as a principle of life and as the source of our passions. The domestication of the affects (vengeance, resentment, and hate) that permeated the first parts of the trilogy requires compromises, negotiations, pressures, and lures, which are not a matter of justice, but of intelligence. Athena knows well that she owes her final victory over the Erinyes, not to her righteousness, but to her expertise in persuasion (v.970): she knows better than anyone that intelligence requires flexibility as well as cunning, and that it excludes the obsessive rigidity on procedural matters that characterizes those who put excessive emphasis on the notion of right.

Justice as a formal procedure. On the face of it, within the protected space of the newly instituted tribunal, due process is followed: the conflicting parties are indeed allowed to present their rationale, to bring and cross-examine witnesses, to hear and counter the rhetorical moves of the opposite side. Nobody draws a sword during the proceedings, which remain on the whole a civilized exchange of arguments with only minor slips into invectives and insults. After having listened to both parties, the jurors cast their vote in what appears to be a remarkably proper secret ballot. Let us even give Athena the benefit of the doubt regarding the composition of the Areopagus: she genuinely chose the "best" among her citizens (487), without discreetly preselecting or programming the jury to agree with her views. Does it mean that, since the procedure (accepted without qualm by both parties) was respected to the letter, the result was *by the sole fact of this formal respect* in conformity with justice?

We could first stress the striking fact that, in this celebration of Athenian democracy, Aeschylus decided to present a case of democratic *gridlock:* in a remarkably dramatic (and puzzling) move, he had the ballot result in a split vote, so that the opinion of the goddess, after having been spectacularly equalized to that of a mere human, ends up counting double (in view of her superior nature). Apart from this last-minute procedural twist, which tilts the case in favor of Orestes, the main question raised by this split vote is that of the law of sheer numbers as a source of legitimacy in democracy. When the electors are split almost evenly between two positions (as it is the case in most modern Western democracies), does the marginal difference of a few percent really allow us to believe that the winners carry a more "rational" proposal than the losing side?

Rationality and the democratic debate. This idea leads to a more fundamental, and yet more concrete, problem: how "rational" was the exchange of arguments that resulted in Orestes' exoneration? Here again, Aeschylus seems to do all he can to prevent us from being fooled by the mirage of justice. Apart from Orestes and the Erinyes, who present their version of the case in rather simple and direct one-liners, most of the argumentative action is provided by Apollo. After the opening gesticulations, where he pompously invokes truth, justice, and Zeus's authority, he spends most of his time splitting hairs about the differences between Agamemnon's murder and Clytaemnestra's: the institutional bond of marriage should be stronger than the natural bond of blood (vv.213–223); a king, killed by deceit upon his return from a victorious war, cannot be compared with a mere woman, lecherous and deceitful, whose reign raised the indignation of her people (vv.625–639); anyway,

Detail from a fourth-century B.C.E. vase depicting a performance of Aeschylus's *Eumenides*

(from J. M. Roberts, The Illustrated History of the World, *Volume 2:* Eastern Asia and Classical Greece, *1999)*

science amply demonstrates that the mother is not really the parent, but only the indifferent vessel to which the father lends his precious seed for a temporary period of primitive development (vv.657–663); if a living proof of this biological theory was needed, Apollo concludes, it would be standing right in front of everyone in this tribunal, since Athena herself was born without a mother (vv.663–666).

It is clearly more as the leader of the Muses, and as an expert rhetorician, than as the god of light that Apollo intervenes in the trial: Reason has little to do with his train of thought. It is highly significant that Aeschylus should use the two same words of "witness" (*martys*) and "proof" (*tekmêrion*) both to have Athena devise the formal procedure in charge of guaranteeing the justice of the outcome (v.485) and to have Apollo abuse such terms in his moment of most outrageous sophistry (v.662–664). As Stanley Fish suggested, the institutional space of legal argumentation is protected from the force and violence of the outside world only to see force reappear in its most intimate core: rhetoric. Even if we were to admit that Apollo's recourse to biology was credible, and "rational," within the theories in favor in 458 B.C.E., that would only make it clearer that the force of a logical argument, the force of Reason itself, is no guarantee of any "absolute" epistemic validity: it only means that this argument happens to be dominant within this cultural context. If gender biases are prevalent in a society, no tribunal and no formal rules of procedure about proofs and witnesses can prevent the violence of sexist prejudices from permeating the reasoning of the most "scrupulous" and most "objective" jurors, since their definition of reason will be structured along such prejudices: in Fish's words, "force turns out to be the content of the mechanism designed to control it" (p. 516).

For those who would still see the adversarial-democratic procedure as a mediation of rationality, Aeschylus took the trouble to have Athena "justify" her vote in favor of Orestes. And what is striking in her "final judgment" is that her opinion in no way considers the objective merits of each party's argument, but openly presents itself as a pure expression of idiosyncratic prejudice: "my vote I shall add to Orestes' side. For mother have I none that gave me birth, and in all things, save wedlock, I am for the male with all my soul, and am entirely on the father's side" (vv.735–738).

Were we to push our reading (anachronistically) of the play one notch further, we could describe Clytaemnestra, and her (female) representatives, the Erinyes, as *victims,* in the manner Jean-François Lyotard contrasts this term with that of *plaintiff.* In a sexist society, a woman is a victim because the wrong that is inflicted upon her (killing, forced sex, harassment, explicit or hidden barriers to education and employment) cannot be proven in front of any court of law because this wrong is not receivable nor even visible from the point of view of the dominant ideology (for which it is only natural, reasonable, and "just" to have women submit to their husband's sexual drives and do housework instead of writing philosophy). In any society, says Lyotard, "hard" issues of justice always elude the institutional frame of tribunals and parliaments: they cannot be reduced to mere *litigations,* where an impartial judge can settle a case along standards and value systems shared by both parties; they rather take the form of a *differend,* where each party carries standards and value systems that are incompatible, and between which the judge will have to take sides, losing therefore his position of superior arbiter. It is a telling symptom that in Aeschylus's play Athena should end up explicitly casting her vote as a daughter of Zeus: she has always-already taken a side in the conflict by the sole fact that her worldview is that of an Olympian, as opposed to that of the old earthly deities represented by the Erinyes. Similarly, a "secular" judge has always-already taken sides, even before a religious "fanatic" is presented to his court, because he can only judge him in accordance with his secular conception of the rule of law: in such *differends,* the institutional space of the tribunal imposes by force its dominant values on its victim. When one is faced with a *differend,* justice simply *cannot* be done.

Here again, as our societies become increasingly multicultural, it would be foolish to trust the formal apparatuses of tribunals and the rational debates taking place in the public sphere fairly to arbitrate the countless *differends* to come. The main case made by Lyotard or Fish against Habermas's views is that the definition of what is "rational" and of what should be the basic rules of a debate excludes and represses beforehand several opinions and worldviews (in spite of the tolerance claimed by our enlightened rationality). This rather academic discussion leads to diverging practical strategies in the struggle for justice: while, in the eyes of the liberal tradition, the action should take place within the frame of the current institutions and amend them from the inside, for the more radical thinkers of postmodernity, the fight for justice requires one to challenge the outside boundaries that limit any existing institution. In their view, justice will not be made by tribunals or in parliaments, but in the streets, through extralegal actions putting pressure on the media and on the dominant ideology.

The delusion of justice. The most subversive vistas of postmodernism may in fact take us back to the essence of the Greek tragedy: what indeed is a tragedy, if not a *differend* in its Lyotardian definition, that is, a conflict in which both parties carry standards and justifications that are equally valid but incompatible, and between which any choice is bound to be unjust? This leads us to consider an option spelled out by the ancients themselves, most (in)famously by Carneades: there simply is no justice in this world—and anybody who keeps looking for it not only wastes his time but is a fool likely to be taken advantage of.

While Blaise Pascal refused to go that far, he articulated on three levels this position of radical skepticism, which still inspires many thinkers. The *average man* believes that there is, "out there," an objective (divine, transcendent, or natural) model of justice, which the laws and customs of his country more or less approach. The *half-wise* knows that customs, laws, and definitions of the just vary from culture to culture, and he realizes "there is no justice per se," but only agreements and "shared understandings" within given communities to consider this or that as good or evil, holy or taboo: this half-wisdom is factually correct but socially dangerous, since its advocates tend to go around denouncing the arbitrariness of existing laws, and therefore undermine the social order. The (really) *wise man,* for his part, realizes both that there is no objective standard of justice *and* that it is necessary for humans to be fooled into believing in the existence of such a standard: the faith in justice is not founded in reason, but it nevertheless has desirable social and moral effects, and it would be more foolish not to be fooled by it than to give into its delusion. The fact that *this* law is "the" law is always a result of power struggles and not a consequence of its conformity with eternal justice—but the law should be obeyed, nevertheless, because it is the law, not because it is just. Force and justice are inextricably linked to each other: we can try to use force justly or to give power to justice, but those who pretend to separate them, or to isolate one from the other, may as well try to live without breathing.

From this perspective, the ambiguities of Aeschylus's play make it a perfect illustration of Pascal's views. To the average Athenian citizen, it confirmed and strengthened the foundation of his faith in the city's judicial and political system as a celebration of Athenian self-instituting democracy. To the half-wise postmodern critic, it simultaneously reveals the highly fragile and problematic nature of democratic institutions. To the true deconstructionist, the tragedy offers a powerful illustration of the necessary delusions of justice: it shows *both* the emancipatory power inherent in the constitution of a space for adversarial, rational, and democratic debate, *and* the radical insufficiency of approaching justice only in terms of contracts, procedure, and formal rights.

–YVES CITTON,
UNIVERSITY OF PITTSBURGH

References

Aeschylus, *The Oresteia,* translated by Herbert Weir Smyth (Cambridge, Mass.: Harvard University Press, 1926).

Aristotle, *Nichomachean Ethics,* translated by H. Rackham (Cambridge, Mass.: Harvard University Press, 1926).

Alain Badiou, *Ethics. Essay on the Understanding of Evil,* translated by Peter Hallward (New York: Verso, 2000).

Jacques Derrida, "Force of Law: The Mystical Foundation of Authority," *Cardozo Law Review,* 11 (July–August 1990): 919–1046.

Stanley Fish, *Doing What Comes Naturally* (Durham, N.C.: Duke University Press, 1989).

Jürgen Habermas, *Between Facts and Norms: Contribution to a Discourse Theory of Law and Democracy,* translated by William Rehg (Cambridge, Mass.: MIT Press, 1998).

Habermas, *Moral Consciousness and Communicative Action,* translated by Christian Lenhardt and Shierry Weber Nicholsen (Cambridge, Mass.: MIT Press, 1990).

Stuart Hampshire, *Justice Is Conflict* (Princeton: Princeton University Press, 1989).

Thomas Hobbes, *Leviathan* (Harmondsworth, U.K.: Penguin, 1985).

David Hume, *A Treatise of Human Nature* (Oxford: Clarendon Press, 1974).

Immanuel Kant, *Grounding for the Metaphysics of Morals,* translated by James W. Ellington (Indianapolis: Hackett, 1983).

Kant, *Perpetual Peace and Other Essays,* translated by Ted Humphrey (Indianapolis: Hackett, 1983).

Jean-François Lyotard, *The Differend: Phrases in Dispute,* translated by Georges Van Den Abbeele (Minneapolis: University of Minnesota Press, 1988).

Baise Pascal, *Pensées,* translated by W. F. Trotter (New York: Modern Library, 1941).

Jean-Jacques Rousseau, *The Social Contract and Discourses,* translated by G. D. H. Cole (New York: Dutton, 1950).

Adam Smith, *The Theory of Moral Sentiments* (Indianapolis: Liberty Fund, 1984).

Benedict de Spinoza, *A Theologico-political Treatise and a Political Treatise,* translated by R. H. M. Elwes (New York: Dover, 1951).

GREECE: ALCIBIADES

Was Alcibiades self-absorbed and irresponsible, caring little for the interests of Athens?

Viewpoint: Yes. Alcibiades was a megalomaniac who overturned the conservative policies of his protector, Pericles, in favor of reckless Athenian expansion. In the end, he was less Athens's savior than a cause of its downfall.

Viewpoint: No. Many of the stories told about Alcibiades are fictitious. In fact, his life was filled with many worthy achievements.

One might classify the second half of the Peloponnesian War as a struggle among four independent superpowers: Athens, Sparta, Persia, and Alcibiades. The last merits comparison with the other major political entities of the war because he was both a man without a country and a man of all countries, commanding respect wherever he traveled by means of irresistible charisma and fearless, creative policies that were independent, some would argue, of any national sentiment. Chosen as one of the leaders of the Athenian expedition against Sicily in 415 B.C.E., he was abruptly removed in the fallout from the religious scandal concerning the desecration of the herms and the profanation of the Mysteries. He sought refuge among Athens's archenemy, Sparta, and then moved on to Persia, the past enemy of all Hellenes yet an indispensable ally in the current pan-Hellenic conflict. In 411 he was invited back to Athens, only to be forced to flee again in 406, following the defeat of one of his lieutenants at the Battle of Notium. As a final testament to what might be called his flexibility in patriotism, he died among the Persians shortly thereafter.

Alcibiades' ability to survive as he hopscotched around the Mediterranean and his skill as a diplomat at a time when information traveled slowly and was incomplete are easy to acknowledge. The issue in dispute in this chapter is the question of what caused the extreme vicissitudes in Alcibiades' career. Was Alcibiades as careless and reckless as many literary sources imply, with little feeling for his home polis? The record is full of Alcibiades's bold maneuvers, which could easily be construed as self-serving. Or was he a victim of a mercurial democratic assembly, which forced him to fend for himself in spite of his devotion to Athens? Proponents of this argument could point to other disastrous decisions made by the democracy and to the tendency for hostile sources to distort the character of their enemies. In either case, the debate should offer new insights into the nature of total democracy and the role and status of individual leaders therein.

—Joel Allen

Viewpoint:
Yes. Alcibiades was a megalomaniac who overturned the conservative policies of his protector, Pericles, in favor of reckless Athenian expansion. In the end, he was less Athens's savior than a cause of its downfall.

After his father was killed in battle, Alcibiades was taken in, at five years old, by his mother's first cousin, Pericles, who was then the most powerful political figure in Athens. He was raised in Pericles' house and, we are told, was cherished by him as a surrogate for his own sons, who had proven to be disappointing. Pericles clearly was a strong influence in Alcibiades' early development. It perhaps comes as a surprise, then, to learn that Alcibiades, having grown to adulthood and having achieved a high rank within the democracy for his daring and eloquence, pursued a personal philosophy and foreign policy that were completely at odds with those of his former protector, who had died of the plague in 429. Whereas Pericles had a reputation for restraint and circumspection, Alcibiades was a notorious drunkard, philanderer, liar, and daredevil. Whereas, according to Thucydides, Pericles had advocated a conservative strategy of nonexpansion and retrenchment for the duration of the war with Sparta, Alcibiades argued for aggressive military campaigns and for conquest on an unprecedented scale, looking west toward Sicily and the North African holdings of Phoenician Carthage. It is in the motivations for Alcibiades' imperial aspiration and in the conduct of his policies where one begins to formulate a case against him as a cause of the failure of Athens in the Peloponnesian War. His megalomania, greater than any sense of loyalty to home and friends, drove him to play fast and loose with Athenian resources at just the wrong time, when Athens was locked in an arduous struggle with Sparta. He was portrayed in several sources as an equal-opportunity traitor, having betrayed, two times each, the three great powers of the war: Athens, Sparta, and Persia.

Alcibiades' first significant activity as a public figure had to do with overturning the Peace of Nicias, which had been struck with Sparta in 421, and antagonizing Sparta to the point of reinvigorating the war. Believing that matters were unsettled regardless of the word of the treaty, and desiring to strike while Athens was strongest, Alcibiades went about forging new alliances with Sparta's enemies: Argos, the second-strongest polis in the Peloponnese, and Elis and Mantinea, all located along Sparta's northern perimeter. Thucydides says that the reason for Alcibiades' plot was twofold and personal. First, he was jealous of Nicias, who had led the diplomatic effort. Second, he sought revenge against the Spartans who had shown him disrespect on account of his youth when he had tried to intervene on their behalf concerning Spartan prisoners of war. Thucydides thus implies that Alcibiades was acting out of spite, regardless of the strategic reasons he gave in public for the alliance with Argos. The new ties to Argos and the others did not break the word of the treaty—Argos was free to ally with Athens if it wanted—but Alcibiades' actions certainly violated the spirit of the peace; the Spartans could not be expected to sit idly while a network of their rivals cornered them in the lower Peloponnese. Spartan envoys accordingly came to Athens to try to salvage the peace and defuse the Argive alliance. Alcibiades sabotaged their efforts, however, by first promising to support them in the negotiations—one of the envoys, Endius, had ties to Alcibiades' extended family—but then openly deriding them as illegitimate and insincere ambassadors once the assembly was under way. His confrontational attitude completely caught them off guard; it was his first betrayal of Sparta.

In making the Argive alliance, Alcibiades was gambling on a strategy that Pericles had rejected as imprudent years earlier. At the outset of the war, Pericles planned to stick to the sea, avoid land-based confrontations, and demonstrate to the Spartans that naval power was the untouchable sphere of influence of the Athenians. The principal gain for Athens was to be primarily on the seas, not the utter defeat of the Spartans. By embarking on an essentially land-based experiment, Alcibiades hoped for a quick victory, but ultimately failed. His combined forces were defeated by the Spartans at the Battle of Mantinea in 418, and the war was back on. Alcibiades' risky and hawkish machinations were parodied on the contemporary stage: in Aristophanes' metaphorical comedy *The Peace* of 421, a personification of War does everything he can to thwart the hero Trygaeus's attempts to recover the lost peace and thereby return Athens to its former prosperity. The character of War, speaking with a pronounced lisp, is a thinly disguised stand-in for Alcibiades, who was famous—and famously charming—for a similar speech impediment. As the audience cheered Trygaeus on against War/Alcibiades, they implicitly judged the latter's policies as destructive to their way of life (Moorton, 1988).

In 415 Alcibiades again went against Pericles' conventions when he proposed leading an expedition to Sicily. Rather than focusing on maintaining Athens's current empire, he sought to add a large, distant island, known for its wealth. Thucydides identified greed as a principal motivation for Alcibiades' plan, noting that he had run an unprecedented seven chariots in the Olympic Games of 416 at great expense and sought the spoils of a new war in order to maintain his extravagant lifestyle. Once again, it was Nicias who was Alcibiades' chief rival in the debate. The assembly, however, was enamored of Alcibiades and sided with him against Nicias. They voted to increase the size of the fleet for the new war and appointed him leader, along with Nicias and Lamachus. The expedition is commonly cited as the beginning of the end for Athens in the war, in that it resulted in the annihilation of much of Athens's fleet in 413. Opening up a second front in the midst of a war was a mistake that the Athenians had evidently failed to learn in the wars of the previous generation: in 459 they had sent an armada to fight the Persians in Egypt even as they were engaged in a war with the Peloponnesians, and after five years of maintaining such a distant navy, their fleet was routed by the Persians in 454. So now in Sicily, forty years later, a similar fate befell the expedition, as it was wiped out in the harbor of Syracuse. Although the Athenians managed to hold on for another decade after the Sicilian disaster, they never achieved the aura of invincibility that they had in the early years of the war.

When the Sicilian expedition had barely begun, Alcibiades abandoned it and defected to Sparta as he fled a summons from the assembly to stand trial for a sacrilege. On the morning of the scheduled departure of the fleet for Sicily, it was discovered that the herms of Athens had been defaced. These sacred, abstract statues of Hermes, god of travel, were the guardians of entryways and crossroads, and their mutilation was seen as both an ill omen for such a distant journey and a profound lack of respect on the part of the perpetrators. It was never discovered who had ruined the herms, but the sacrilege ignited a fervor for religious scruples that eventually implicated Alcibiades. In the spirit of strengthening Athens's religious foundations, an investigation suggested that several Athenians, including Alcibiades, had made a mockery of rituals associated with the Eleusinian Mysteries in a private, drunken party. Although Alcibiades wanted to clear his name immediately, he set sail for Sicily regardless, fearing that his expedition would otherwise lose momentum. Alcibiades' rivals seized the opportunity to bring him down; when he was absent and therefore unable to use his legendary charm to sway the jury, they succeeded in charging him with crimes against the gods. The summons drove him to switch sides to Sparta, at which point he was convicted in absentia. Whether or not Alcibiades was guilty of the crime, he had long cultivated a reputation as a bon vivant, which made him a viable suspect for such dangerous disrespect of public institutions. In this respect his political downfall was a product of his own personality. His literary contemporaries, including Aristophanes, Thucydides, and Socrates (via Plato), all alluded to his profligate behavior. In general, Alcibiades did not comport himself as a leader and so should share blame for his disgrace even if he was the target of an opposing faction.

Away from Athens, Alcibiades acted as the enemy of his former polis. While in Sparta he gave two pieces of advice that severely compromised Athenian security. First, he suggested that the Spartans blockade the Athenians at Syracuse and fight a decisive battle confined in that harbor, where the size of the Athenian fleet would work against itself. Second, he recommended that the Spartans establish a fort at Deceleia north of Athens, which would deny the Athenians access to their valuable silver mines. Alcibiades' assistance to the Spartans was, at worst, blatantly treasonous, and at best, spiteful and petty. Even as a fugitive, he could have acted with more restraint. Nevertheless, he continued to

ALCIBIADES: MEGALOMANIAC?

Aristophanes, in his play The Frogs, *has two characters debate the merits of Alcibiades; on balance, the judgment is ambiguous. Dionysus, visiting the Underworld, is trying to decide which tragedian to bring back with him, Euripides or Aeschylus:*

DIONYSUS: Now, whichever of you can think of the best piece of advice to give the Athenians at this juncture, he's the one I shall take back with me. Now, here's my first question: what should be done about Alcibiades? Athens is in a very tricky situation, you know.

EURIPIDES: What do the Athenians think about it, themselves?

DIONYSUS: Ah. You may well ask. They love him. But then again they hate him. And then again, they want him back. But you tell me what you think, both of you.

EURIPIDES: Quickness and brains are what we seek, I know / He's quick—to harm, but when we need him, slow / Brilliant enough to plan his own escape / But useless when the City's in a scrape.

DIONYSUS: That's neat. I like that. Very good. And Aeschylus, what's your opinion?

AESCHYLUS: It is not very wise for city states / To rear a lion's whelp within their gates / But should they do so, they will find it pays / To learn to tolerate its little ways.

Source: *Aristophanes,* The Frogs, and Other Plays, *translated by David Barrett (Baltimore: Penguin, 1971).*

GREECE: ALCIBIADES

provide Athens's enemies with insider information when he moved to Persia in 412, ostensibly as a negotiator for the Spartans. Alcibiades' advice to Tissaphernes, the Persian satrap, was that the Persians play each Greek side against the other so that the weakening of both Athens and Sparta could create a vacuum that Persia could fill. On the surface, he was still acting for Sparta, but behind the scenes he was now favoring Persia.

Alcibiades' ultimate effort to return to Athens in 411 had less to do with desiring to help his homeland than with extricating himself from his latest precarious position. Certain that Spartan envoys to Persia would discover his double game, he approached leaders of the Athenian fleet at Samos with the promise that he could provide them with Tissaphernes as an ally if they accepted him back, and that he would only return if the democracy in Athens were moderated by a more oligarchic presence. The oligarchic revolution of 411 B.C.E. was the result, and although it lasted only four months, it disrupted Athens at a time of great distress. Alcibiades was able to rejoin the Athenian fleet even though his promise of bringing Tissaphernes with him proved to be empty. Although he headed the fleet, he prudently did not return to his polis in person until four years later in 407. Opinions vary concerning his behavior during this period. On behalf of Athens he won several key battles over the Spartans, most notably at Cyzicus. Yet, one scholar's close reading of Xenophon suggests that, in between the flashes of brilliance, Alcibiades dragged his feet and focused more on building up a cushion of finances for his personal career and return to Athens (Robertson, 1980). It would seem that Alcibiades' renewed devotion to Athens was incomplete, for he abandoned Athens for a second time in 406, after one of his lieutenants was defeated at Notium. Fearing that the people of Athens would hold him responsible, he fled for an independent fortress on the Hellespont. Once again, he tried to return to Athens's side in 405, when he approached the fleet at Aegospotami, warning them of their exposed position and the proximity of the Spartan fleet. When his fellow Athenians (if he can now be considered an Athenian) were finally defeated at Aegospotami, he turned once again to Persia. According to Diodorus Siculus, his plan to gain acceptance there was to betray Cyrus, the younger brother of the current king, Artaxerxes, by revealing Cyrus's plot to seize the throne (Ellis, 1989). However, Alcibaides' luck had run out, and, to cite one of the several recorded scenarios for his death, the Spartan Lysander, as part of a diplomatic deal with Persia, demanded that he be killed once and for all.

Anecdotes about Alcibiades often portray him as a reprobate. In Plato's *Symposium*, he shows up to the banquet drunk, late, and uninvited. In the comedies of Aristophanes, he appears or is alluded to repeatedly as a warmonger or a lush. According to Plutarch, Alcibiades once bit his opponent when he was losing in a wrestling match, and when he was teased for fighting like a woman, Alcibiades claimed that he bit like a lion. Plutarch also says that when Alcibiades' guardian Pericles asked to be left alone so that he could prepare his accounts for inspection by the democracy, the young Alcibiades suggested that his time would be better spent in figuring out how not to render his accounts and to dominate the people instead. Even if some of these stories are overblown, they imply at least a critical mass of outrageous behavior and a lack of self-control that conspired to fail Athens in its time of need. On balance, in spite of the several victories Alcibiades won for Athens, his conduct must be judged as a detriment to any side that, for the moment, he had joined.

–JOEL ALLEN,
QUEENS COLLEGE,
CITY UNIVERSITY OF NEW YORK

Viewpoint: No. Many of the stories told about Alcibiades are fictitious. In fact, his life was filled with many worthy achievements.

According to Plutarch's biography, Alcibiades cut off the tail of his dog because he thought it was funny. It is hard to imagine a charge that is nastier, or more of a cliché, than hurting puppies. If the stories of Alcibiades' bizarre and immoral behavior, especially in Plutarch, seem overly sensational and fantastic, it is most likely because they were inventions or exaggerations, which snowballed in their preposterousness during the five hundred years that separated Alcibiades' death from Plutarch's career as a biographer during the Roman Empire. When thinking about Alcibiades, the modern reader tends to get caught up in the sex and violence that was reported of his personal life. Ancient biography, as a genre, was a clearinghouse of rumor and innuendo, pitched low as light entertainment, almost novelistic. Some of these stories are obviously impossible: when Plutarch says that the Athenian priestess Theano refused to curse Alcibiades even though she had been ordered to do so, one modern scholar has shown that official curses were common and not shunned in classical Athens, that women were in no position to express dissent in matters of religion, and that Plutarch borrowed the text for the anecdote from Sophocles' *Antigone* (Sourvinou-Inwood, 1988). Inasmuch as many other anecdotes are no doubt fictional, it is important to approach the melodramatic elements of Alcibiades' life story with caution and to judge him through a focus on historical events. Moreover, his career included many services to the state worthy of note.

If one considers Alcibiades' two principal contributions to the Peloponnesian War as an Athenian–his sabotage of the Peace of Nicias and his proposal of the Sicilian expedition–there are grounds to deny the charge of undue aggression. Nicias's peace treaty with Sparta, while in keeping with Pericles' original objectives in the war, was arguably naive and ill conceived, and many of the issues that sparked the war to begin with were still not resolved. Sparta still felt threatened by Athens's brash, imperial behavior; Sparta's allies, especially Corinth, still despised Athens's control of the sea; and the Athenians still refused to give up Pylos, their fortress on the Spartan coast. It was only a matter of time before tensions would flare anew, and Alcibiades' decision to line up Argos and other Peloponnesians in anticipation of a renewed conflict put Athens in a more comfortable situation. Also Pericles' strategy of prudence had several flaws that would have been obvious to Athenians by 421: it was expensive to rely on a navy (the Athenian treasury became depleted in the first several years of the war); it was unhealthy to remain cooped up behind the city walls (a devastating plague struck Athens in 430); and any rebellion of Athens's naval allies could potentially undermine the whole effort (as did the rebellion of Lesbos in 428). Taking the war to Sparta's backyard, and doing so on land, held the element of surprise, and it can be considered a mark of Alcibiades' genius. Moreover, relying on Peloponnesian allies, such as Argos, risked little for the Athenians themselves in the event of failure, yet promised huge rewards in the event of success. Alcibiades, though departing from Pericles' strategy of patience, kept to his basic principle of never risking too much at once. One could argue that Alcibiades' plans for the Argive alliance were exactly what Athens needed at this time.

The same kind of low-risk, high-payoff quality characterized Alcibiades' original plans for the Sicilian expedition, as well. According to Thucydides, he initially requested fewer ships for the enterprise than ultimately sailed. The reason for the increase in the size of the fleet was that Nicias, in his attempt to dissuade the assembly from the expedition, argued that the island was bigger than most Athenians realized and that more manpower was required: in addition to ships and troops, they would need horses, archers, even bakers, to survive so far from home. This was reverse psychology: Nicias expected the Athenians to call off the expedition once they understood the full expense. Yet, for Nicias the plan backfired, and the assembly only assigned more and more ships to conquer the island outright. Alcibiades, however, had planned to do much less than overrun the island with force. According to Thucydides, his intention was to circumnavigate the island and stop at the major harbors, building alliances through persuasion and diplomacy. Persuasion was Alcibiades' forte, and there was every reason to respect such a plan as wise and–what is especially Periclean–safe. It was Nicias who mistakenly favored outright attack, and it was Nicias who carried it out once Alcibiades was forced to flee.

Bust of the Athenian general and politician Alcibiades, who served with the philosopher Socrates during the Peloponnesian War

(© Bettmann/CORBIS)

Thucydides allows room for Alcibiades to be relieved of the charge of greed or personal ambition as the motivations for embarking on the expedition. While he does say that Alcibiades was eager for money and glory following his spendthrift ways at the 416 Olympics, he ultimately faults the malice of Alcibiades' rivals as the true problem: "Although publicly his conduct of the war was as good as could be desired, individually, his habits gave offense to everyone,

ALCIBIADES: MISUNDERSTOOD HERO?

In this passage, Thucydides delivers an ambiguous judgment of the role of Alcibiades in the failure of the Sicilian expedition. Readers may find reasons both to blame and exonerate him:

By far the warmest advocate of the expedition was . . . Alcibiades, son of Clinias, who wished to thwart Nicias both as his political opponent and also because of the attack he had made upon him in his speech, and who was, besides, exceedingly ambitious of a command by which he hoped to reduce Sicily and Carthage, and personally to gain in wealth and reputation by means of his successes. For the position he held among the citizens led him to indulge his tastes beyond what his real means would bear, both in keeping horses and in the rest of his expenditure; and this later on had not a little to do with the ruin of the Athenian state. Alarmed at the greatness of his license in his own life and habits, and of the ambition which he showed in all things soever that he undertook, the mass of the people set him down as a pretender to the tyranny, and became his enemies; and although publicly his conduct of the war was as good as could be desired, individually, his habits gave offense to everyone, and caused them to commit affairs to other hands, and thus before long to ruin the city.

Source: *Thucydides,* History of the Peloponnesian War, *6.15, translated by Richard Crawley, edited by W. Robert Connor (London: Everyman's Library, 1993).*

and caused them to commit affairs to other hands, and thus before long, to ruin the city" (6.15: trans. Crawley, 1993). By inverting the terms of Thucydides' appraisal, an argument emerges that is similar to one at play in American business and government relations in the 1970s: if "what is good for General Motors is good for the United States," then what happens to be good for Alcibiades' wealth and position can also be seen as a benefit to the empire as a whole. So long as Alcibiades was free to pursue his own personal fortune through a tactical venture in Sicily, Athens would have grown stronger as well. In Thucydides' eyes, it was the check on Alcibiades leveled by the dissatisfied and envious democracy that was the mistake, and not his greed.

Alcibiades' chameleon-like changes of polis and state have been interpreted as self-serving when in reality circumstances gave him no alternative short of suicide. His first shift, from Sicily to Sparta, was prompted by a witch-hunt back in Athens concerning a religious infraction. As judgments based on religion often do, the trial in which he was convicted in absentia relied on hearsay and was predicated on an irrational fear of the supernatural. It is unfair to allege that Alcibiades brought on the charges that he profaned the Eleusinian Mysteries, whether true or false, through a profligate lifestyle. On this issue, Thucydides again sides with Alcibiades in subtle ways, giving him a speech before the Spartans where he says, in essence, that the Athens that exiled him is not the Athens he knows, nor the one for which he fights: "I do not feel that I am attacking my country. Rather I am trying to recover it. The true patriot is not he who prefers to love his country rather than attack it, but he who loves it so much that he will stop at nothing to recover it" (6.92: trans. Crawley, 1993). According to Thucydides, Alcibiades believed that the democracy was destroying his polis.

There is no doubting that Alcibiades was a thoughtful tactician. He seems to have had Athenian interests at heart when he left Sparta for Persia. In Persia he advised Tissaphernes to let Sparta and Athens wear each other down in their war. This apparently treasonable suggestion was in fact a boon for the Athenians: the Persians thus decreased their support to Sparta and effectively removed Athens from the crosshairs of their army. When Alcibiades rejoined the Athenian navy in 411 after his exile, he led the fleet in a string of successes in the Aegean, most notably at Cyzicus where the Athenians succeeded in killing a Spartan admiral and sinking sixty of their ships. When he left Athens for the second time, after the defeat at Notium in 406, he was simply avoiding, for the second time, the irrational fury of the assembly. Alcibiades believed the assembly would not forgive a military loss, even if it was preceded by repeated success and even if it had been caused by a careless underling and not by himself. In such a move he proved to be prescient: in the following year the assembly voted to execute generals who had been victorious at the battle of Arginusae because they had failed to retrieve the corpses of Athenian sailors in the face of an oncoming storm. The moment when a polis executes its generals even after they had won a battle is the moment when Alcibiades receives justification for his flight. In any case, from this semi-self-imposed retirement, he still followed the progress of the war and still offered Athens his assistance. He warned the Athenians stationed at Aegospotami that their position on an open beach was unsafe. To their peril, the Athenians ignored the advice; their navy was soon wiped out in the final battle of the war. The charge that Alcibiades was reckless and irresponsible thus begins to falter.

The anecdotes of Alcibiades' life paint a picture of occasional carelessness, occasional malice, and perpetual self-interest. In Plutarch, they can be chalked up to the irresponsible nature of

Roman biography, but one must also consider the comments of his contemporaries, who either knew him personally or were absent by just one or two degrees of separation. In Aristophanes, we find an attitude that evolved over time. In the *Peace* (421), Alcibiades is the personification of war itself. In Aristophanes' *Birds* (414), which was produced just after Alcibiades was recalled from Sicily, one character fears that he will be recalled by the assembly from the Red Sea; the expectation is that the audience will find amusement in Alcibiades' plight. In the *Thesmophoriazusae* (411), when Alcibiades was in Persia, a character expresses outrage at all men who contemplate tyranny and negotiate with Persians—the reference to Alcibiades is unmistakable. Yet, all of these are comedies, and the jokes are lighthearted. Moreover, they are not all consistent in their orientation. One could interpret them in an opposite way: the expectations that the audience will laugh at Alcibiades might be seen as a sign that they partly felt solidarity with him. In one of Aristophanes' later plays, *The Frogs* of 405, the god Dionysus tells the shade of the tragedian Euripides that the city of Athens wants to bring back Alcibiades, because the city "loves him, hates him, and yet wishes to have him all the same." In short, the comedic references of Aristophanes are open to interpretation; they might be thought of as gestures of support.

Aristophanes may be taking his lead in this ambiguous portrayal from the historian Thucydides, who also seems to defend Alcibiades as much as he criticizes him. Thucydides' narrative often speaks of Alcibiades in juxtaposition to the Athenian democracy as a collective, and careful reading by one scholar shows that Thucydides used the person of Alcibiades as a distillation of the Athenian people (Forde, 1989). According to Thucydides, both are brash, greedy, vain, hubristic, and most importantly, both are self-destructive. Both tend to arrive at sophistic justifications for their actions, just as Alcibiades had to betray Athens in order to survive, and just as the Athenians practiced genocide on the island of Melos when the Melians preferred neutrality to Athenian subjugation. In both cases, the justification for crucial decisions involved a retooling of what was considered moral. There is a paradox in Alcibiades in that the qualities that made him valuable to the Athenian war effort are the qualities that unleashed a backlash against him—his ambition, cleverness, and courage. The same paradox holds true for the polis in general: the creativity and ruthlessness of the Athenian democracy both made it the "School of Hellas" (according to Thucydides' Pericles) and Hellas's unbearable overlord. In thinking about Alcibiades, replace the words reckless and deceitful with bold and innovative, and he suddenly becomes a hero, misunderstood.

—JOEL ALLEN,
QUEENS COLLEGE,
CITY UNIVERSITY OF NEW YORK

References

Aristophanes, *Peace*.

Walter M. Ellis, *Alcibiades* (London & New York: Routledge, 1989).

Steven Forde, *The Ambition to Rule: Alcibiades and the Politics of Imperialism in Thucydides* (Ithaca, N.Y. & London: Cornell University Press, 1989).

David Gribble, *Alcibiades and Athens: A Study in Literary Presentation* (Oxford: Clarendon Press, 1999).

Lisa Kallet, *Money and the Corrosion of Power in Thucydides: The Sicilian Expedition and Its Aftermath* (Berkeley: University of California Press, 2001).

Richard F. Moorton Jr., "Aristophanes on Alcibiades," *Greek, Roman, and Byzantine Studies,* 29 (1988): 345–359.

Robin Osborne, "The Erection and Mutilation of the Hermai," *Proceedings of the Cambridge Philological Society,* 31 (1985): 45–73.

Plutarch, *Alcibiades*.

Noel Robertson, "The Sequence of Events in the Aegean in 408 and 407 B.C.," *Historia,* 29 (1980): 282–301.

Christiane Sourvinou-Inwood, "The Priestess in the Text," *Greece and Rome,* 35 (1988): 28–39.

Thucydides, *History of the Peloponnesian War,* translated by Richard Crawley, edited by W. Robert Connor (London: Everyman's Library, 1993).

GREECE: ARISTOPHANES

Was Aristophanes a reactionary?

Viewpoint: Yes. Behind the evident levity that pervades the work of Aristophanes lay the political attitudes of a man deeply suspicious of the Athenian democracy and with pronounced conservative politics.

Viewpoint: No. Although his comedies have a conservative side, Aristophanes faced many pressures in order to be a successful dramatist, and it would have been of only limited use for him to espouse one political position over another. His heavy use of allusion and parody combine to produce texts that are highly ironic with multiple meanings.

Greek tragedy had its roots in the sixth century B.C.E. when Athens was governed by the tyrant Pisistratus, who sponsored the genre by making it part of the City Dionysia, a yearly festival in honor of the god Dionysus. Comedy, by contrast, developed much later. The first publicly sponsored comic performances took place in 470 B.C.E., forty years after the fall of the Pisistratid dynasty and the installation of a democratic system of government in Athens.

The type of comedies performed at this time may well have been quite different from the comedies of Aristophanes. They were loosely structured, and many contained send-ups of scenes from mythology, in the manner of Euripides' satyr-play *Cyclops.* Within a generation of its inclusion within the festival calendar, however, "Old Comedy" had evolved, its changes derived in part from the abusive poetry of poets such as Archilochus and Hipponax. These plays, in contrast to those that featured the burlesque of mythology, were oriented toward current events and featured the mockery of prominent individuals as well as the parody of tragedy and other popular literary forms.

History has not been kind to the practitioners of Old Comedy. Except for the eleven complete plays of Aristophanes, no other comedies of the period have survived. On the other hand, we have about a quarter of Aristophanes' plays. So what is lacking in breadth for Old Comedy is compensated for to a degree by the depth in which we can study the work of the man generally acknowledged as its greatest practitioner.

The large amount of literary evidence available allows us to ask questions about Aristophanes' comic techniques and political beliefs that are often impossible for authors whose work is much less well preserved. The data are not altogether consistent, however, and some plays are difficult to interpret. Aristophanes in places seems to be a reactionary thinker, with little sympathy for the democratic institutions that sponsor his productions. In other places his sophisticated literary practices and his unenthusiastic support for bringing back "the good old days" cast his conservatism in an ironic light. The issue at hand, however, is an important one, and one wonders whether a synthesis of the two views might not be possible. At any rate, the reputation of Aristophanes is only enhanced by this debate. Brilliant, complex, and innovative, he seems to exceed the reach of theses that seek to reduce his efforts to a formula or political slogan.

—Charles Platter

Viewpoint:
Yes. Behind the evident levity that pervades the work of Aristophanes lay the political attitudes of a man deeply suspicious of the Athenian democracy and with pronounced conservative politics.

Despite the sheer volume of comic wit produced in the service of the Athenian democracy over the course of a forty-year career in the theater, Aristophanes' true political loyalties lay not with the democratic politician Pericles and his successors, but with their adversaries, whose preferences tended toward oligarchy. G. E. M. de Ste. Croix (1972) characterizes Aristophanes as hostile to the developments within the Athenian imperial state and describes the dramatist's political views as "of a conservative, Cimonian variety (371)," a judgment for which the evidence is plentiful and convincing. This essay will attempt to defend Ste. Croix's position by discussing four of the many areas where Aristophanes' antidemocratic bias can be seen clearly: 1) his evident coziness with aristocratic elites composed of men "whose names it is pleasant to mention" (*Clouds* 528) and whom he further gratifies by failing to subject them to the same withering scorn that is deployed against Cleon and the other democratic politicians; 2) his virulent opposition to the Peloponnesian War, which he shared with other dissident conservatives, whose income was based on their large holdings of land; 3) his hatred of contemporary artistic and literary developments, expressed most forcefully in the oft-repeated praise of Aeschylus and ridicule of Euripides; and 4) his bitter and protracted criticism of the citizen *demos,* the ultimate source of authority in the Athenian state. In the end, although much of what we see in Aristophanes can be understood as simply for laughter's sake, the volume of material, together with its consistent antidemocratic tone, is surely no accident and reflects the sentiments of the author, even after allowances have been made for comic distortion.

Old Comedy, the name given to the style of aggressive humor practiced by Aristophanes and his contemporaries, never wearied of ridiculing individuals by name *(onomasti komoidein).* Particularly prominent are politicians: Cleon, Cleonymous, Hyperides, and Lysistratus. All are frequently the butt of Aristophanic jokes, as might be expected for prominent public figures in the hands of a satirist. Yet, Aristophanes is largely silent about their opponents, extremely prominent men themselves. Cimon, the son of Miltiades, is mentioned only once, in the *Lysistrata* (1144), and there fondly. The same thing is true with Thucydides (not the historian) son of Melesias, a rival of Pericles, ostracized in 443. He is only mentioned once in *Acharnians* (702–712) by a sympathetic chorus that speaks of his mistreatment at the hand of the younger generation. Similarly, important contemporary figures like the aristocratic Alcibiades and the conservative politician and general Nicias are mentioned far less frequently than their overall prominence would lead one to expect, and references to them are far less hostile than those directed at the democratic politicians. Compare this situation with the torrent of insults directed against Cleon in *Knights* alone, and Aristophanes' sensibilities are not hard to divine. Further, Aristophanes shows his sympathy for the conservatives by making frequent use of buzzwords that the aristocratic factions used to describe themselves, like *chrestoi* ("useful men") and *kaloikagathoi* ("fine and noble men"), as well as the words they used for the democratic politicians and their supporters (for example, *poneroi,* "worthless men").

Aristophanes also takes up causes that should be associated with the so-called *chrestoi,* and it is within this context that his well-known opposition to the Peloponnesian War (441–404) should be viewed. Three plays, *Acharnians, Peace* (421), and *Lysistrata* (411), take up this topic. Modern readers of Aristophanes typically imagine him a pacifist on this basis, but, from a contemporary perspective, this attitude toward the war clearly aligns him with the aristocratic *apragmon* (quietist), typically a large landholder who respected the orderliness of Spartan society and had no personal interest in acquiring new territory or in opening new markets (Carter 1986). Obviously, men of such a temper were already well-off and wanted to avoid any disruption of the status quo. The supporters of war were the democratic leaders, who built support for their positions by pointing to the opportunities for advancement that conquest brought with it. Pericles' Funeral Oration, as described by Thucydides (2. 34–46), praises the *polupragmosyne* ("busyness") of these men who in his view make Athens "the school of Greece," in contrast to the quietists whom Pericles pointedly calls "useless." Aristophanes did not see it that way. In at least three plays spanning fifteen years (*Acharnians, Peace,* and *Lysistrata*) he championed the antiwar cause of the quietists, explicitly defended Sparta in two plays (*Acharnians* and *Lysistrata*), and did everything in his power to discredit the motives of the democrats who supported the war on strategic grounds and prosecuted it to the best of their abilities.

In reading the entire corpus of Aristophanes, one is struck by the consistent attitude toward artistic issues expressed over the course of his career. Culture that harks back to the Marathon generation is good while contemporary culture is both denatured and emasculated. This polarity is played out most prominently by Aristophanes' obvious preference for Aeschylus, a veteran of the Battle of Salamis in 481 and the greatest tragedian of his day, over Euripides, whose work regularly tests the traditional justifications that undergird Athenian society. Aristophanic comedy regularly juxtaposed the two writers, most famously in *Frogs* (405), where the god Dionysus despairs of tragedy's future in Athens after the deaths of both Sophocles and Euripides within a year. So he resolves to go to Hades himself to bring back Euripides to the Athenian stage. This plan goes somewhat awry, however. The poetry chair in Hades, previously occupied by Aeschylus, is now being contested by the newly arrived Euripides, and Dionysus is called upon to judge between them. Throughout all of this chaos Euripides is relentlessly skewered as a vulgar, popular poet whose work undermines the traditional beliefs (like the innate superiority of the upper classes) upon which Athenian society rests. Aeschylus may be bombastic but he does not buck tradition. Further, Euripides' work is represented as being full of sophistic argumentation that also undermines tradition and, in the words of fifth-century Athenian critics, "makes the weaker argument stronger." Those are the same rhetorical tactics that have allowed the *poneroi* to rise to positions of (undue) influence within the courts and the assembly, to judge from Aristophanes' negative portrayals in *Knights* and *Wasps* particularly. As a result, these parvenus have displaced the traditional aristocracy who is better positioned to work for the *true* interests of the city (that is, *their own*). In the end, despite his original intention to bring back Euripides, Dionysus cannot even bring himself to declare his favorite poet the victor. Not only does Dionysus award the victory to Aeschylus, but he also resolves to bring him back to Athens in place of Euripides, while Euripides is left in Hades. In this most public of confrontations between the democratic Euripides, with his emphasis on rhetorical virtuosity over the advantages of birth, and Aeschylus, the upholder of traditional morality, Aristophanes' *Frogs* clearly comes down on the side of the latter.

This negative characterization of Euripidean tragedy in *Frogs* is not an accident. Anti-Euripidean passages are found from the beginning of Aristophanes' career to the death of Euripides and beyond. Aristophanes' first extant play, *Acharnians,* opens with Dikaiopolis, its hero, recalling how his mouth hung open expectantly as he waited for a tragedy by Aeschylus to begin (10). The play continues with a hilarious visit to the house of Euripides to see the poet's storeroom of ridiculous costumes and contains a sustained parody of his play *Telephus,* featuring a king disguised as a beggar. The incongruity of the king in rags appears to have symbolized for Aristophanes what democracy had done to the city that produced the Marathon-fighters, the generation that saved Greece by driving off the Persian invasions of 490 and 481–479. Aeschylean tragedy had built a monument to the deeds of this generation by means of an elegant and stately dramatic form. In Aristophanes' view, however, Euripides had taken that form and perversely trivialized it. This attitude to Euripides is shown even more clearly by Aristophanes in *Thesmophoriazusae* (*Women Celebrating the Festival of the Thesmophoria,* 414), in which he again brings Euripides onstage, first to recruit a male relative to infiltrate the women's festival on his behalf, then, after the relative has been captured, to impersonate his own characters in a series of ridiculous, unsuccessful attempts at rescue. The relative eventually gets away, no thanks to Euripides, and throughout the play the tragedian is represented as a foolish figure, trivializing, and therefore trivialized by Aristophanes.

One of the most extraordinary aspects of Aristophanes' comedy is the strong hatred his characters show for the democratic institutions of Athens and the individuals that are associated with them. In three plays, *Acharnians* (425), *Birds* (414), and *Ecclesiazusae* (*Women Running the Assembly,* 393) the Athenian government is replaced with a comic version of the city. In *Acharnians,* Dikaiopolis concludes a separate peace with the Spartans when the Athenians are unwilling to do so and builds his own marketplace to trade with foreigners. In *Birds* two Athenians, tired of the interference at home on the part of their fellow citizens, build a city among the birds in the sky. In *Ecclesiazusae* the women, appalled at the lack of ability displayed habitually by their husbands, sneak into the Assembly disguised as men, and vote to turn power over to the women. They then institute a system of rule so ridiculously communistic that it (but only it) makes Athenian democracy look good by comparison.

All of these plays clearly show Aristophanes' lack of confidence in the democratic government. His most sustained attacks on the system, and the men who ran it, are found in two early plays, *Knights* (424) and *Wasps* (422). *Knights* is Aristophanes' most abrasive play, no small claim for an author whose use of obscenity alone has spawned a 228-page book (Henderson 1975). The play consists of unrelieved attacks on a vulgar slave named Paphlagon, a thinly disguised portrayal of the politician Cleon, who has bamboozled his senile old master Demus (the personified city of Athens) and who now tyrannizes over the other slaves, including the upright Nicias. He is only displaced in the end by the appearance of a sausage seller, a character even more vulgar and

LABES THE DOG

In Wasps Aristophanes uses the trial of a dog named Labes to satirize the litigiousness of the Athenians. The dog was accused of stealing a cheese:

Philocleon: He is a thief and a conspirator.

Bdelycleon: No, he is the best of all our dogs; he is capable of guarding a whole flock.

Philocleon: And what good is that, if he eats the cheese?

Bdelycleon: What? He fights for you, he guards your door; he is an excellent dog in every respect. Forgive him his larceny! He is wretchedly ignorant, he cannot play the lyre.

Philocleon: I wish he did not know how to write either; then the rascal would not have drawn up his pleadings.

Bdelycleon: Witnesses, I pray you, listen. Come forward, grating-knife, and speak up; answer me clearly. You were paymaster at the time. Did you grate out to the soldiers what was given you? —He says he did so.

Philocleon: But, by Zeus! He lies.

Bdelycleon: Oh! Have patience. Take pity on the unfortunate. Labes feeds only on fish-bones and fishes' heads and has not an instant of peace. The other is good only to guard the house; he never moves from here, but demands his share of all that is brought in and bites those who refuse.

Philocleon: (Aside) Oh! Heaven! Have I fallen ill? I feel my anger cooling! Woe to me! I am softening!

Bdelycleon: Have pity, father, pity, I adjure you; you would not have him dead. Where are his puppies? *(A group of children costumed as puppies comes out)* Come, poor little beasties, yap, up on your haunches, beg and whine!

Philocleon: Descend, descend, descend, descend!

Bdelycleon: I will descend, although that word, "descend," has too often raised false hope. None the less, I will descend.

Philocleon: Plague seize it! Have I then done wrong to eat! What! I, crying! Ah! I certainly should not be weeping, if I were not stuffed with lentils.

Bdelycleon: Then he is acquitted?

Philocleon: It is difficult to tell.

Bdelycleon: Ah! My dear father, be good! Be humane! Take this voting pebble and rush with your eyes closed to that second urn and, father, acquit him.

Philocleon: No, I know no more how to acquit than to play the lyre.

Bdelycleon: Come quickly, I will show you the way. *(He takes his father by the hand and leads him to the second urn)*

Philocleon: Is this the first urn?

Bdelycleon: Yes.

Philocleon: (Dropping in his vote) Then I have voted.

Bdelycleon: (Aside) I have fooled him and he has acquitted in spite of himself. *(To Philocleon)* Come, I will turn out the urns.

Philocleon: What is the result?

Bdelycleon: We shall see. *(He examines both urns)* Labes, you stand acquitted. *(Philocleon faints)* Eh! Father, what's the matter, what is it? *(To slaves)* Water! Water! *(To Philocleon)* Pull yourself together, sir!

Philocleon: (Weakly) Tell me! Is he really acquitted?

Bdelycleon: Yes, certainly.

Philocleon: (Falling back) Then it's all over with me!

Bdelycleon: Courage, dear father, don't let this afflict you so terribly.

Philocleon: (Dolefully) And so I have charged my conscience with the acquittal of an accused being! What will become of me? Sacred gods! Forgive me. I did it despite myself; it is not in my character.

Bdelycleon: Do not vex yourself, father; I will feed you well, will take you everywhere to eat and drink with me; you shall go to every feast; henceforth your life shall be nothing but pleasure, and Hyperbolus shall no longer have you for a tool. But come, let us go in.

Philocleon: (Resignedly) So be it; if you will, let us go in.

Source: *Aristophanes,* Wasps, *in The Complete Greek Drama, volume 2, edited and translated by Whitney J. Oates and Eugene O'Neill Jr. (New York: Random House, 1938), pp. 641–643.*

foul-mouthed than Paphlagon himself, who somehow brings about the rejuvenation of old Demus and the shameful defeat of Paphlagon. In *Wasps* Aristophanes' target is the citizen juries that were one of the most important tools in eroding the monopoly on power previously enjoyed by the aristocratic classes with whom Aristophanes evidently sympathized. The juries, Aristophanes suggests, are a farce. Filled with ineffectual old men, and manipulated by opportunists like Cleon, the version of justice they uphold is practically criminal in itself. The central scene of the play is a parody of a trial, at which Labes the dog is judged by the leader of the jurors, Philocleon ("Cleon-lover"). In addition, contributing spectacularly to the diminution of the respect and honor due to the court, this scene ends with Philocleon expertly bamboozled by his son, Bdelycleon ("Cleon-hater") into mistakenly acquitting the dog and failing to live up to his proverbial harshness as a juror. Like *Knights, Wasps* has few kind words for the Athenian democracy, satirizing its leaders, their speaking habits and ways of life, and ridiculing its attempts to administer justice as the poor efforts of ridiculous, deluded old men.

The playwrights of Old Comedy were under tremendous pressure to appeal to the broadest circle of spectators. Their jokes, therefore, do not have an absolutely consistent political orientation. Aristocrats are also attacked, although infrequently. Nevertheless, the general political cast of Aristophanes is overwhelmingly biased against the democratic faction that dominated the Athenian government, and supportive—sometimes explicitly, at other times only tacitly—of the upper classes whose prerogatives had been usurped by their social inferiors.

–CHARLES PLATTER,
UNIVERSITY OF GEORGIA

Viewpoint:
No. Although his comedies have a conservative side, Aristophanes faced many pressures in order to be a successful dramatist, and it would have been of only limited use for him to espouse one political position over another. His heavy use of allusion and parody combine to produce texts that are highly ironic with multiple meanings.

Aristophanic comedy is without a doubt one of the most complex literary genres of ancient Greece. In the space of a few lines Aristophanes regularly moves us out of a conversation drawn from everyday life to a piece of political satire, up to the elevated diction of serious poetry, then down again along a byway through surprisingly varied scatological humor, and on to sustained parody, both high and low, of Euripidean tragedy. It is a mixture of serious and laughable things, then, as the frog-chorus sings in the play of the same name (389–390). But how is this mixture to be judged? Moreover, is it absolutely obvious which are laughable and which serious? Lamachus in *Acharnians,* who eventually is carried onstage after unheroically stepping on a vine-prop, is certainly a serious *acting* character, but his seriousness leaves him open for comic exploitation. An inflexible figure, he represents a type that is inevitably funny, as the philosopher Henri Bergson remarks.

Despite such problems, and other similar ones too numerous to mention, it has been a regular practice of scholars and historians to attempt to mine Aristophanes for historical information. This practice is not objectionable in itself, but given the literary complexity of "Old Comedy," it has to be done with the greatest possible care, as Christopher Pelling (2000) has argued convincingly. Further, these mining operations have the unintended effect of drawing the attention of readers away from the rollicking comedy built out of the frequent juxtapositions of incongruous material alluded to above and concentrating it on questions of history and political attitudes; that is, serious things, not laughable ones. As a result, serious scholars maintain that Aristophanes is a political reactionary who, despite his presence at the heart of the Athenian democratic institution of the theater for some forty years, longed for the days before this newfangled Euripidean rhetoric was on the lips of every young man, when the lower classes knew their place, and the serious business of politics was left to the *kaloikagathoi* ("fine and noble men").

Now, it seems quite likely that Aristophanes had political views of some kind. All of us do, even if we are blithely unaware of them. The question before us here, however, is a different one: can Aristophanes' political views be derived from the ensemble of jokes, parodies, boasts, ironic insinuations, and so on, that constitute Aristophanic comedy? To this the answer is an emphatic "No." This essay will argue that the ironic structure of the comedies, as well as their complex multigeneric makeup, prevents them from advocating particular political positions. In so doing, the essay will consider four topics: 1) that a preponderance of material critical of the ruling regime is inevitable within a genre where satire is a major contributor to the comic action, and such a critical orientation need not be taken literally; 2) that the critics of democratic rule are often themselves presented as ridiculous figures; 3) that the many parallels between Euripides and Aristophanes himself attest to a greater harmony between the two than is often acknowledged; and 4) that Aristophanes' comic utopias, his replacements for the democratic city, are presented as flawed and do not represent partisan critiques of the ruling regime.

Democratic rule and contemporary Athenian culture admittedly receive much criticism in Aristophanes, while figures from past generations and their sympathizers get off rather lightly by comparison. The generation of the Marathon fighters is openly lauded at the expense of the contemporary present, and the notorious *Übermensch* Alcibiades is subjected to little more than some mild wisecracks about his lisp (*Wasps* 44–46). On the surface, this adversarial position with respect to the present would seem to argue for an oligarchic or aristocratic bias on the part of the poet. That is indeed the conclusion reached by those who wish to characterize Aristophanes' efforts as part of an attempt to undermine the democratic government and the culture it helped to produce. Yet, such a conclusion goes far beyond the evidence at our hands. Further, it is in direct contradiction to the methodology laid out in *Clouds* by the chorus. In surveying Aristophanes' innovative spirit, they mention his treatment of political figures:

> But always I display my craft, bringing on new ideas
> Completely different from the others, and all clever,
> I who punched Cleon in the stomach when he was great,
> And didn't dare to trample him again when he was down.
> But my rivals, once Hyperbolus gave them an opening,
> They squashed him on every occasion, and his mother, too. (547–552)

The above passage comes from the *parabasis,* a type of scene in which the chorus "steps aside" (hence, the name *para-basis*) from its role as old men, clouds, frogs, birds, or gnats and speaks directly to the audience either about the poet, or in his name. In this case, they first mention his commitment to innovation, an aspect of Aristophanic comedy mentioned repeatedly throughout his work. Second, they apply that observation to his treatment of public figures. Aristophanes' treatment of Cleon, taken by defenders of the hypothesis that Aristophanes is the enemy of democracy as damning evidence of his contempt for democratic leaders, is here illustrated by the poet's representatives as an example of literary opportunism that Aristophanes abandoned as soon as it became passé. Further, according to the passage, it is just this lack of unrelieved, vitriolic opposition that distinguishes Aristophanes from his rather less distinguished rivals. All the comic poets, it seems, attack the government in power, but Aristophanes moves on to something else while the others are still piling on. This highly literary and aesthetic approach to invective is not the sort of behavior we ought to expect of a man committed to a political cause. Indeed, it suggests that the "cause" is primarily a vehicle for generating laughter.

This conclusion is further corroborated if we pay attention to details surrounding much of the criticism in Aristophanes. In *Acharnians* Dikaiopolis ridicules modern art, drives Euripides to distraction, and gapes in anticipation of a play by Aeschylus. On the surface, he appears to express the personal feelings of Aristophanes. Yet, if he does, it is only accidentally, for Dikaiopolis, too, is a ridiculous comic figure. Even in the prologue (1–42), where he polemicizes so effectively for the old days, Dikaiopolis shows a distinct lack of urbanity. His ignorance of the performance schedule shows him to be an outsider in the art world. Further, after his disquisition on aesthetics, his considerations are far less lofty. As he waits for the assembly to begin, he catalogues his activities with bathetic specificity: "I moan, I yawn, I stretch, I fart, I'm confused, I write, I pull hairs, I do sums" (30–31). This banality contrasts strikingly with the judgmental tone Dikaiopolis uses at the beginning of the play, and its effect is to undermine his credibility and create doubt about how seriously we can take the criticisms he levels at contemporary Athens.

This tactic of pulling the rug out from under the messenger is common throughout the Aristophanic corpus. Defenders of the old days are routinely infirm and ridiculous, like the chorus of old men in *Wasps.* In *Acharnians,* again, the old chorus sharply criticizes the predatory rhetorical practices of the young, but in doing so it presents the older generation as so doddering and inept as to be unworthy of any defense at all (676–691). So, also in *Frogs* the criticisms of Euripides leveled by Aeschylus are undermined not only by Aeschylus's evident partisanship but also by the obscurity and pompousness that are shown to characterize his own work. In short, then, Aristophanes goes out of his way to avoid allowing his characters to assume a serious position that is not itself ridiculous. In so doing, he renders them unable to communicate his own serious political doubts about the Athenian democracy, if he indeed had them.

From *Acharnians* (425 B.C.E.) to *Frogs* (405 B.C.E.), written immediately after Euripides' death, Euripides is one of Aristophanes' favor-

ἈΡΙΣΤΟΦΆΝΟΥΣ ΚΩΜΩΔΊΑΙ ἘΝΝΈΑ

ARISTOPHANIS COMOEDIAE NOVEM.

Πλοῦτος	Plutus.
Νεφέλαι	Nebulæ
Βάτραχοι	Ranæ
Ἱππεῖς.	Equites
Ἀχαρνεῖς.	Acharnes
Σφῆκες.	Vespæ
Ὄρνιθες.	Aues
Εἰρήνη.	Pax
Ἐκκλησιάζουσαι.	Contionantes

I Ἐπίγραμμα εἰς Ἀριστοφάνη. THIBALLIER

Βίβλοι Ἀριστοφάνευς θεῖος πόνος αἷσιν Ἀχαρνεὺς
Κισσὸς ἐπὶ χλοερὴν πουλὺς ἔσεισε κόμην.
Ἠνὶδ᾽ ὅσον Διόνυσον ἔχει σελίς. οἷα δὲ μῦθοι
Ἠχεῦσι, φοβερῶν πληθόμενοι χαρίτων.
Ὦ καὶ θυμὸν ἄριστε καὶ Ἑλλάδος ἤθεσιν ἶσε
Κωμικέ, καὶ στύξας ἄξια καὶ γελάσας.

Frontispiece and title page for the editio princeps (1498) of Aristophanes' works

(courtesy of The Lilly Library, Indiana University)

ite comic targets. He is regularly ridiculed for having popularized tragedy, and for having deprived it of its dignity, through his use of sophistic argument, immoral plots, his emphasis on female sexuality, and his disregard of tradition. This last aspect does not always receive the attention it deserves in determining the precise relationship of Euripides to Aristophanes, for instead of marking the lines that separate them, Euripides' commitment to novelty joins him to the innovative Aristophanes and helps explain why he appears so frequently in his plays.

This emphasis on novelty is plainly visible in the passage quoted above, where Aristophanes asserts his unwillingness to be content with old targets like Cleon, but its presence is ubiquitous in his work. Both *Clouds* and *Wasps* comment conspicuously on Aristophanes' commitment to "new ideas" (*Clouds* 547), both in the self-conscious *parabases* and in the dramatic action itself with its elaborate parodies of tragedy and current speculation. The *parabasis* of *Acharnians* shows Aristophanes bragging to the spectators that his comedy has taught them to be distrustful of foreign rhetoric in creating a critical spirit among the audience (634). Yet, in all of these attempts at self-characterization, the image that is represented is similar to the negative one Aristophanes constructs for Euripides: innovative, untraditional, critical. As Aristophanes makes Euripides say in his own defense in *Frogs:*

I led them to think such things
Inserting logic with skill
And critical thought so they could think and discover everything
Now people are better at running their households than before,
And at everything else, investigating with a "How can this be?" "Where is it?"
And "Who took that?" (971–979)

Thus, Euripides and Aristophanes can be shown to share many characteristics. That is perhaps unsurprising for contemporary dramatists who were supremely talented and truly innovative. Their similarity is detrimental, however, to the argument that Aristophanes hated Euripides for his commitment to the spread of rhetorical education among the populace at large. It has been argued that Aristophanes perceived in Euripidean tragedy a growing tendency to adopt comic practices and so viewed Euripides as a literary rival (Bowie 1993). If that is true, then there might have been some animosity between them, but not for the reasons that are most often stated: that Euripides' relentless updating of Athenian tragedy and his interest in rhetoric and critical thinking made him anathema to Aristophanes. The reverse is really the case. In adopting comic practices, Euripides developed a dramaturgy that encroached progressively further on comic territory and established himself as a whole new kind of rival to Aristophanes.

Aristophanic comedy has no shortage of alternate worlds. In *Birds,* two Athenians abandon the *polupragmosyne* ("busy-ness") of Athens and found a new city with the birds in the sky. In *Ecclesiazusae,* women dissatisfied with the men who run the city disguise themselves in male clothing and vote to hand the city over to the women, which is to be run in the future on the basis of pure communism, and in *Plutus* the blind god of wealth has his sight restored and bestows his blessings upon only the just. These utopias are often understood as political critiques of Athens since utopian fiction is inevitably political, depending as it does upon the creation of parallel worlds, which stand in critical contrast to the real world either explicitly or implicitly. This same logic can be applied to Aristophanes' fantastic creations, and it can be argued that in setting up a competing polis, he discredits Athens in its present form and holds out the prospect of a better regime.

This conclusion, however, is more apparent than real in the case of Aristophanes, for his utopian constructions seem to be presented in such a way as to display their fatal flaws. The communistic state of the *Ecclesiazusae* is revealed as a sham in the final lines of the play when the chorus invites the audience to a banquet featuring a dish with a name eleven lines long (unsurprisingly, the longest word in Greek) but advises them to grab an omelet so that they will have something to eat (1175–1178). The naturally just state of universal wealth in *Plutus* turns out to be still dependent on the unnatural situation of slave labor, and the creation of a "quietist" state in *Birds,* presumably the goal of many real-world Athenian oligarchs, leads to a universal tyranny, in which even the Olympian gods are displaced by the "busy" Athenians and their bird allies. Thus, in all of these cases, what begins as a criticism of the Athenian state turns out to have problems of its own that prevent it from critiquing Athens without qualification. Like Aristophanes' self-descriptions, like his apparent dismissal of Euripides, and like the critics of democracy discussed above, so too the flawed utopias are more ambiguous in their implications than meet the eye. They show Aristophanes as a comic writer of great power and complexity, but one whose political opinions cannot be deduced from his comedies with any great confidence.

–CHARLES PLATTER,
UNIVERSITY OF GEORGIA

References

Henri Bergson, *Le rire: essai sur la signification du comique* (Paris: Presses Universitaires de France, 1940).

A. M. Bowie, *Aristophanes: Myth, Ritual, and Comedy* (Cambridge: Cambridge University Press, 1993).

Eric Csapo and William J. Slater, *The Context of Attic Drama* (Ann Arbor: University of Michigan Press, 1995).

James Davidson, "Fish, Sex, and Revolution in Athens," *Classical Quarterly,* 43 (1993): 53–66.

Kenneth J. Dover, *Aristophanic Comedy* (Berkeley & Los Angeles: University of California Press, 1972).

Anthony Edwards, "Historicizing the Popular Grotesque: Bakhtin's Rabelais and Attic Old Comedy," in *Theater and Society in the Classical World,* edited by Ruth Scodel (Ann Arbor: University of Michigan Press, 1993), pp. 89–118.

Simon Goldhill, *The Poet's Voice: Essays on Poetics and Greek Literature* (Cambridge: Cambridge University Press, 1991).

Malcom Heath, *Political Comedy in Aristophanes* (Göttingen: Vandenhoeck & Ruprecht, 1987).

Jeffrey Henderson, *The Maculate Muse: The Use of Obscenity in Greek Comedy* (New Haven: Yale University Press, 1975).

David Konstan, *Greek Comedy and Ideology* (Oxford: Oxford University Press, 1995).

Mary Lefkowitz, *Lives of the Greek Poets* (London: Duckworth, 1981).

Douglas M. MacDowell, *Aristophanes and Athens: An Introduction to the Plays* (Oxford & New York: Oxford University Press, 1995).

Christopher Pelling, *Literary Texts and the Greek Historian* (London & New York: Routledge, 2000).

Ralph Rosen, *Old Comedy and the Iambographic Tradition* (Atlanta: Scholars' Press, 1988).

G. E. M. de Ste. Croix, *The Origins of the Peloponnesian War* (Ithaca, N.Y.: Cornell University Press, 1972).

Alan H. Sommerstein, *Acharnians, Edited with Translation and Notes* (Warminster, U.K.: Aris & Phillips, 1980).

Sommerstein, *Birds, Edited with Translation and Notes* (Warminster, U.K.: Aris & Phillips, 1987).

Sommerstein, *Clouds, Edited with Translation and Notes* (Warminster, U.K.: Aris & Phillips, 1982).

Sommerstein, *Ecclesiazusae, Edited with Translation and Notes* (Warminster, U.K.: Aris & Phillips, 1999).

Sommerstein, *Frogs, Edited with Translation and Notes* (Warminster, U.K.: Aris & Phillips, 1996).

Sommerstein, *Knights, Edited with Translation and Notes* (Warminster, U.K.: Aris & Phillips, 1981).

Sommerstein, *Lysistrata, Edited with Translation and Notes* (Warminster, U.K.: Aris & Phillips, 1990).

Sommerstein, *Peace, Edited with Translation and Notes* (Warminster, U.K.: Aris & Phillips, 1985).

Sommerstein, *Plutus, Edited with Translation and Notes* (Warminster, U.K.: Aris & Phillips, 2001).

Sommerstein, *Thesmophoriazusae, Edited with Translation and Notes* (Warminster, U.K.: Aris & Phillips, 1994).

Sommerstein, *Wasps, Edited with Translation and Notes* (Warminster, U.K.: Aris & Phillips, 1983).

GREECE: ARISTOTLE VERSUS PLATO

Did Aristotle make a more lasting contribution to philosophy than Plato?

Viewpoint: Yes. Aristotle has a more coherent theory of the good.

Viewpoint: No. Plato is a greater philosopher than Aristotle because he demarcated the intellectual domain that philosophy occupied and in which Aristotle's own philosophic activity took place. Plato, moreover, created the conditions in which the mode of consciousness underlying Aristotle's work was able to crystallize and express itself.

The question of whether Aristotle is a better philosopher than Plato is not merely about which of these two philosophers should be placed more prominently in the pantheon celebrating Greek genius. It is more a question of whether Aristotle is of greater value than Plato. Determining a person's worth is not easy. One must first decide by which criteria value and worth should be judged. With regard to the content of their philosophies, one may judge Aristotle and Plato in terms of which of the two offers a more coherent and true account of human life and the world. One may, alternatively, judge them in terms of which has had the greatest or widest influence upon the history of philosophy, specifically, and the history of thought, generally. Regardless of the criteria one chooses to employ, one cannot escape the conclusion that both Aristotle and Plato remain relevant to who we are. We are asking, after all, whether Aristotle is more valuable than Plato *to us.* Our answer to this question is a reflection of what *we* value, and that, in turn, is a reflection of our understanding of the world and our place in it. The arguments that follow, then, should not be understood as definitive answers that can be either accepted or rejected, but as invitations to consider what it means to be human.

Chad Wiener argues that Aristotle is a greater philosopher than Plato because Aristotle's conceptions of the good and the good life are more coherent than those of Plato. Wiener contends, furthermore, that the Aristotelian conception of the good life is viable, whereas the Platonic conception is not. Plato conceives of the good as a nonmaterial unity that exists separate from the physical and sensible world. However, it cannot be perfectly instantiated in the world. Consequently, a perfectly good life is not possible. Aristotle understands the good of any particular thing as the complete realization or actualization of its potency. The good, then, may be perfectly realized in the physical world. Thus, the good life is a viable life for human beings. In a Platonic world, a human being strives to be good but never is good. In an Aristotelian world, a human being may be good.

Matthew E. Kenney contends that Plato is philosophically superior to Aristotle in that Plato not only established the domain of discourse in which Aristotle's philosophic activity occurred, but also engendered the conditions in which the mode of consciousness underlying Aristotle's work was able to come to fruition. Plato, he argues, was the first person to provide a coherent and detailed account of what constitutes philosophy. Aristotle practiced the philosophy Plato created, and, thus, Plato made Aristotle's work possible. More importantly, however, Plato's efforts to establish philosophy as a unique discipline engendered an environment in which a new mode of consciousness crystallized and asserted itself. This new mode of consciousness is defined by a distinction between the knowing subject and the object known. Aristotle's philosophic activity presupposes this distinction and, therefore, is dependent upon Plato's accomplishments.

—Matthew E. Kenney

Viewpoint: Yes. Aristotle has a more coherent theory of the good.

To illustrate the significance of the good life, an issue of paramount importance to both Plato and Aristotle, one may profitably examine motion, as it was understood in ancient philosophy. Such an approach may seem at first arduous and off the topic, but this examination is absolutely relevant to the idea of the good life in Plato and to the evident superiority of Aristotle's approach to the question.

For Aristotle and Plato, philosophy raises questions about the basic truths of reality, but it also involves asking about the worth of human actions and what kind of life is worth living. But if we are to engage in answering these kinds of questions, then we must be conscious of the ignorance with which we begin. For if we already knew their answers, we would not have asked the questions at all. For Plato and Aristotle, philosophy begins with a similar admission. We begin in ignorance or in a dark cave where all we have are reflections of what might be true ideas. The philosopher's task is to see that these shadows only point us out of the cave and away from the flux of the sensible world toward the light of the truth or the good itself.

This similar approach to philosophy and the good in Plato and Aristotle conceals an important difference, however. Although both agree that philosophy is the pursuit of the good, they differ as to what, specifically, the good is. Moreover, they differ profoundly regarding the possibility of attaining the good life in this world. Their answers are complex, but to summarize briefly, for Plato the good can only be experienced outside of the world of ceaseless change in the world of the forms, while for "solider Aristotle" human happiness is the activity, specifically, of doing moral actions that exist within the wider context of the political art that makes such questioning possible.

The problem of motion is central to ancient Greek philosophy. Why it is a problem at all can be understood by investigating one of the paradoxes of Zeno of Elea (early fifth century B.C.E.). According to him, the assumptions that account for an arrow in flight are contradictory. Motion entails material changing from one position to another over time. Yet, anything material has a determinate position at any given time, and being in a determinate position is the same as being at rest. From this observation, Zeno concludes that motion must be the aggregate of discrete positions occupied by the arrow over time, each of which, paradoxically, is not in motion. In other words, motion is composed of instances of nonmotion. Since this definition of motion is contradictory, Zeno's paradox implies that motion is not possible, and the ancient evidence suggests that he regarded it rather as an illusion we experience.

Zeno's paradoxes have fascinated philosophers for centuries, although they have persuaded few. Yet, the premises of his argument seem intuitively true. Clearly, a moving object must occupy a succession of states. But if something *occupies* a state, it can hardly be *in motion.* So in order to solve the problem of motion, it was thought necessary to show how any plurality of successive states can be *known* in the strict sense of having a fixed and definite characteristic. For Plato and Aristotle this meant attempting to grasp the plurality by means of some unity.

Both Plato's and Aristotle's solutions entail positing a nonmaterial intellectual structure *(eidos)* underlying reality, but the status of these forms differs. As we will see, for Plato the idea of transcendent forms means there is one form of the good that accounts for the plurality of good things. Aristotle's forms will be functional unities that relate to particular things. So, to anticipate our conclusions regarding the good life, the good for Aristotle will be relative to each function, and not some universal good. We will now move to consider which set of arguments best resolves the problem of motion.

A form for Plato is a nonmaterial unity, that is, the idea of a concept, separate from, and prior to, the examples of it that exist in the physical world. In contrast to physical objects, which are subject to constant change, and for this reason always in a state of "becoming" something else, forms can be said to "be," that is, to exist without reference to the possibility of change. But the sensible world, by contrast, is intrinsically plural. For example, in the physical world the form of the good does not exist, only good actions, which are themselves mixed with other things (secondary motivations, accidents of color, size, and taste) that are neither necessarily good or bad. Consequently, if Plato's forms are unified and immaterial, they must also exist outside of, or transcend, this world. This model provides a solution to Zeno's paradox by understanding the arrow in two separate ways. Understood in this way the object that flies, changing its position through a succession of moments, and thus largely unknowable, is equivalent to the life of ceaseless change in the world, while the arrow as an object outside of time with a known position and characteristics is analogous to the relationship of the forms to the physical world.

Yet, this solution to the problem of plurality and flux of the world produces another, equally grave, problem. If forms are absolutely nonmaterial, how can it be that they account for the unifying characteristics of sensible objects (the resemblance in all physical chairs that allows us to infer the existence of a "form of the chair")? If, on the other hand, the forms can be said to influence, or alter, the structure of the material world, there must be some material quality that allows them to do so. But by "doing so," and by producing changes in other things, they inevitably change themselves and so are not outside of the realm of becoming at all. At best, sensible objects could be images or copies of the forms, and our evidence suggests that Plato himself was not fully satisfied with this solution. In the *Parmenides* he imagines Socrates' great predecessor Parmenides leveling a devastating critique of the idea that sensible objects somehow "participate" in the forms. Since the sensibles must have some likeness to a form, and a form is the unifying principle behind many similar objects, then it follows that there must be another form to account for the likeness of the form to the sensibles. But this leads into an infinite regress and a plurality of forms that have no explanatory power at all. So the problem of participation shows that the forms cannot relate, or even explain, the objects in the sensible realm.

This conclusion regarding the forms has profound consequences for the idea of the good life in Plato. If the form of justice, or of the good, does not exist in the phenomenal world, then it is clear that human beings can never be entirely just or happy while they are alive. At best, they can strive for the good life without ever obtaining it. By arguing in this way, Plato preserves the realm of the forms as a separate entity, intelligible and eternal, but at a high cost, for it means relegating the good life to the status of a defective, or impossible, pursuit, instead of being the entire raison d'être for the existence of philosophy.

For Aristotle the problem of participation as construed by Plato is unsolvable. His first move is to define the form as an actuality *(energeia).* That means it has an essence, or a kind of specific work that it does. But for Aristotle, the work of any sensible being requires a certain kind of material, which he calls potency *(dynamis).* Now, since the potency is necessary to do the work that makes the thing what it is, it does not change when the thing is at work. Rather, the potency and the actuality are one when the thing is performing its unique job, whether that means running a state, if you are a political leader, or producing acorns, if you are an oak tree. In other words, in contrast to Plato, where the forms needed to be apart from the sensible world in order to remain unities, Aristotle here locates the unity in the structure that unites a sensible being with its potency. He refers to this unity as *entelecheia,* a concept notoriously difficult to render into English, but translated accurately, if laboriously, as "being-at-work-staying-itself" (Sachs, pp. li–liii). So, for Aristotle, form and matter can be unified *in the sensible realm* when the work is present in the material. If that is true, then sensible objects can be said to have being, not just becoming, as in Plato. Further, if human beings have access to being, then Aristotle can explain how the good life is possible in the sensible realm, for the good of a thing will be expressed in the *entelecheia* of the event that occurs when its form and matter are one. It is an answer much more simple and matter-of-fact than Plato's, but it has a decided advantage in its ability to preserve the idea of the good life as a goal that is intelligible for humans.

But how does Aristotle's concept of being solve the problem of motion? The unity of an entity is expressed through a kind of function it can perform. But this function, which is a kind of complex motion, is done for its own sake. Living beings, for example, engage in two kinds of movements: development from embryo to adult and the work their function enables them to perform. So Aristotle concludes that there are two kinds of motions, each of which is a whole, rather than composed of discrete parts, as Zeno assumed. What is the difference between these two motions and why is each a whole? The development of a living being is like a trip from Athens to Sparta. Once one has arrived at Sparta, then the motion is complete since it has reached its end. This motion is not a discrete collection of moments as Zeno assumed, for the motion is only understood as a whole in relation to its end. Once the whole motion exists (or any one part of it), only then can we then divide it into discrete parts. Motion, thus, is prior to its divisions. So, a living being develops in such a way that its material becomes organized in order for it to perform its function or work. But this motion ceases to be when the organism is complete, that is to say, when it can perform its work. Actually doing the work is like the motion of sightseeing. This kind of motion does not have a discrete beginning and end. Rather, each moment one is sightseeing the action is complete. In this way, then, Aristotle rejects Plato's absolutist account of motion, replacing it with a more flexible model based firmly in our lived experience.

Aristotle's correction of Plato has important ethical consequences. In the *Nicomachean Ethics* he attempts to determine what material aspects of our soul are relevant to a discussion of ethics and the good life. Aristotle argues that our function is acting according to a rational principle, and the end it will obtain is happiness. For Aristotle, however, acting according to a rational principle is based on an understanding of habits or character *(ethos)*, which are the material aspects of the soul pertinent to moral action, and which are in our soul only through repetitive action. Moral behavior for Aristotle is thus the habitual action guided by a rational principle. The rational principle decides which habits are most appropriate to cultivate, and the character thus produced occupies a mean between two extremes.

How does knowing the mean and developing the character appropriate to the mean allow the form and material of our soul to be unified, and so, happy? The soul's end is acting ratio-

THE SOUL

[1098b] (1) [20] Nor again must we in all matters alike demand an explanation of the reason why things are what they are; in some cases it is enough if the fact that they are so is satisfactorily established. This is the case with first principles; and the fact is the primary thing—it *is* a first principle. [21] And principles are studied—some by induction, others by perception, others by some form of habituation, and also others otherwise; [22] so we must endeavor to arrive at the principles of each kind in their natural manner, and must also be careful to define them correctly, [23] since they are of great importance for the subsequent course of the enquiry. The beginning is admittedly more than half of the whole, and throws light at once on many of the questions under investigation.

VIII. Accordingly we must examine our first principle not only as a logical conclusion deduced from certain premises but also in the light of the current opinions on the subject. For if a proposition be true, all the facts harmonize with it, but if it is false, it is quickly seen to be discordant with them.

[2] Now things good have been divided into three classes, external goods on the one hand, and goods of the soul and of the body on the other; and of these three kinds of goods, those of the soul we commonly pronounce good in the fullest sense and the highest degree. But it is our actions and the soul's active exercise of its functions that we posit (as being Happiness); hence so far as this opinion goes—and it is of long standing, and generally accepted by students of philosophy—it supports the correctness of our definition of Happiness.

[3] It also shows it to be right in declaring the End to consist in certain actions or activities, for thus the End is included among goods of the soul, (20) and not among external goods.

[4] Again, our definition accords with the description of the happy man as one who "lives well" or "does well"; for it has virtually identified happiness with a form of good life or doing well.

[5] And moreover all the various characteristics that are looked for in happiness are found to belong to the Good as we define it. [6] Some people think happiness is goodness or virtue, others prudence, others a form of wisdom; others again say it is all of these things, or one of them, in combination with pleasure, or accompanied by pleasure as an indispensable adjunct; another school includes external prosperity as a concomitant factor. [7] Some of these views have been held by many people and from ancient times, others by a few distinguished men, and neither class is likely to be altogether mistaken; the probability is that their beliefs are at least partly, or indeed mainly, correct.

[8] Now with those who pronounce happiness to be virtue, or some particular virtue, our definition is in agreement; for "activity in conformity with virtue" involves virtue. [9] But no doubt it makes a great difference whether we conceive the Supreme Good to depend on possessing virtue or on displaying it—on disposition, or on the manifestation of a disposition in action. For a man may possess the disposition without it producing any good results. . . .

Source: *Aristotle,* Nicomachean Ethics, *in* Aristotle in Twenty-three Volumes, *translated by Harris Rackham, volume 19 (Cambridge, Mass.: Harvard University Press / London: Heinemann, 1934).*

nally. The material necessary to act is the sum of its habits, or character. When one's soul has a moral character, then the action committed will be in accord with one's own passions. But to have a moral character is to use your rational faculty to determine the mean. So, not only does the action develop and sustain your rational faculty, it also produces in the soul a harmony or unity of desired result and outcome. There is no other end or reward of a moral action than the action itself since the soul's function or end is to do just these actions. As a result, individuals in Aristotle are fully capable of moral action, the result of which is a happy or good life, unlike in Plato, where the good can only exist in some separate nonmaterial world.

Aristotle's understanding of happiness as the complete life, in which one's actions are in accord with one's moral character, points to a final point, his superior conception of politics. Unlike for Plato, whose perfect city retains the same otherworldliness as his metaphysics, Aristotle's conception of political life cannot be regulated within a monolithic design with a lonely philosopher-king at the apex. For him the life of moral activity on the part of an *isolated* individual is not self-sufficient since such activity requires a community in which one can interact with other moral agents. Only in the city, which instills moral habits in us from birth, can a human being, the *zoon politikon,* or "animal disposed to city-living," as he so famously expressed it, truly engage in moral action. Hence, Aristotle concludes that political science is the master science since it determines all aspects of our lives. The just city then is no phantom, or mere heavenly idea, but an integral part of the good life of any moral agent.

So why conclude that Aristotle is a better philosopher than Plato? We have seen that Aristotle solves the problem of motion more satisfactorily than Plato since he avoids the problem of participation: the form and material can be one if we conceive of the form as a functional unity—having a certain kind of work as its end. This conclusion leads Aristotle to determine that the good life is possible in this world as opposed to a perpetual striving in Plato. Finally, Aristotle's conception of the just city is constitutive of the good life, whereas Plato in the *Republic* sees the just city as merely necessary for the pursuit of philosophy, but the philosopher must actually leave the city, the darkness of the cave, to pursue knowledge and the good itself. Aristotle, on the other hand, shows that the cave itself can be lit up and the truth revealed by our own activity within it.

—CHAD WIENER,
UNIVERSITY OF GEORGIA

Viewpoint:
No. Plato is a greater philosopher than Aristotle because he demarcated the intellectual domain that philosophy occupied and in which Aristotle's own philosophic activity took place. Plato, moreover, created the conditions in which the mode of consciousness underlying Aristotle's work was able to crystallize and express itself.

Determining whether Plato is a greater philosopher than Aristotle is not possible if one does not possess an understanding of what constitutes philosophy. A difficulty exists, however, in that there is no suitably articulated conception of philosophy that could accommodate the greatest achievements of each thinker. Aristotle practiced a philosophy that was already an organized discipline in which one could receive formal training. His greatest achievements occurred within the domain of that discipline, as he contributed greatly to the methodological and theoretical development of regions within the domain of the philosophic discipline. Plato also contributed greatly to methodological and theoretical concerns, but those contributions are less significant than those he made in attempting to establish philosophy as a legitimate and privileged discipline. Indeed, he was the individual principally responsible for establishing philosophy as a discipline distinct from and (supposedly) superior to poetry, tragedy, oratory, and sophistry. If one conceives of philosophy as a discipline in which one investigates questions in the realms of, for example, physics, metaphysics, ethics, and the human soul, a conception that accounts for Aristotle's activity, then Plato's greatest achievements are not philosophical. One would be forced to compare a weakened Plato with Aristotle at his strongest.

Plato is the greater philosopher precisely because he was the first person to articulate a coherent and detailed description of what constitutes philosophy. Plato invented philosophy, in that he defined a particular intellectual and ethical life and named it the philosophic life. He demarcated the boundaries of the philosophic domain. Aristotle worked within that domain, thus his achievements were made possible by Plato's accomplishments. Yet, they were not made possible only in the sense that Aristotle practiced certain activities that Plato identified as philosophic. They were also made possible in the sense that Plato engendered the epistemic conditions under which a new mode of human consciousness was able to crystallize and assert itself. In other words, in attempting to establish philosophy as a legitimate discipline, Plato pushed human consciousness to a point at which a new mode became not only a viable possibility, but also an inevitable occurrence. This new mode of human consciousness underlies and makes possible the type of philosophic activity in which Aristotle was engaged.

Plato conceived of philosophic activity as a preferable alternative to the traditional means of *paideia*. The word *paideia* denotes the process by which wisdom, moral excellence, political acumen, and military prowess were engendered in those adolescent men who were eligible to become citizens in a Greek polity. This broad and predominately informal process of education also ensured the continued good health of the polity itself: good citizens make good polities. In order to supplant the traditional means of effecting *paideia* with philosophy, Plato needed not only to articulate what constitutes philosophy but also to distinguish philosophy from those other disciplines and to explain why philosophy was preferable to them. Andrea Wilson Nightingale observes, "It is for this reason that, in dialogue after dialogue, Plato deliberately set out to define and defend a new and quite peculiar mode of living and of thinking. This alone, he claimed, deserved the title of 'philosophy'" (Nightingale 1995, 11). Thus, the Platonic dialogues provide the reader an aperture through which the creation of philosophy may be observed.

Traditionally, there were two principal means of effecting *paideia:* poetry (particularly epic poetry) and the practice of *sunousia* (literally "being together"). According to Eric Havelock, epic poetry served as a type of encyclopedia or repository for the moral, political, and technical knowledge that Greek society valued, and poetry in general addressed and preserved *nomoi* and *ethea,* the traditional, informal laws and customs of Greek society (Havelock 1963, chapter 4). When a young man learned the Homeric epics or Hesiod's *Theogony* or *Works and Days,* he acquired a body of knowledge to which he could appeal should he ever have a question about how to behave in a given circumstance, or how to perform a particular activity. *Sunousia* involved a relationship, usually but not necessarily erotic, between an adolescent who would be eligible for citizenship and an adult citizen. The older man functioned as a mentor for the adolescent and educated him in the business of a citizen. However, during the fifth century, Greek *paideia* began to change. The predominance of poetry and traditional *sunousia* was challenged by the rise of *sophoi,* who were itinerant teachers offering instruction (for a fee) in oratory, and *arête,* "excellence" (Beck and Thomas 1996, 507). The *sophoi* were a challenge to poetry because they threatened to supplant it as the source of knowledge pertaining to moral, technical, and political wisdom; they posed a threat to traditional *sunousia* because adolescents were abandoning relationships with the older citizens of their polities and seeking out, indeed paying for, the company of *sophoi.*

Within this intellectual environment, the verb *philosophein* ("to philosophize") and its cognates did not carry any special connotation; nor were they used often (Nightingale 1995, 14; Havelock 1983, 56–57). When they were used, rather, they denoted an "'intellectual cultivation' in a broad and unspecified sense," which was pursued by "a smaller group of individuals, namely, people who have the time and the inclination to engage in intellectual pursuits as young men and adults" (Nightingale 1995, 15). During the fifth century, then, the philosopher was an individual who pursued education broadly, studying whatever might enrich him intellectually. *Philosophia* ("philosophy"), consequently, was the activity of strengthening one's intellect through activity in a broad spectrum of "fields" or studies (for example, mathematics, poetry, rhetoric, and grammar).

In the Platonic dialogues, there are many attacks against both the *sophoi* and the poets, as well as the type of education each offered. By defining sophistry and poetry, and by identifying their shortcomings, Plato was able to give definition to his conception of philosophy. Nightingale notes, "It is precisely by designating certain modes of discourse and spheres of activity as 'anti-philosophical' that Plato was able to create a separate identity for 'philosophy'" (Nightingale 1995, 11). Plato's critiques of poetry and of sophistry are epistemically oriented; he critiques those activities because they instill a semblance of wisdom, rather than true wisdom, in the human soul. For Plato, moral excellence and the ability to govern justly are both dependent upon knowledge. In other words, his ethics and his politics are epistemically grounded. If one lacks knowledge of what courage is or of what justice is, then one cannot truly be courageous or just. On occasion one may accidentally act courageously or justly, but one cannot do so intentionally. In order to be truly courageous or just, one must be able to identify which action in a given situation is the courageous or just action, and to perform it. One must know with certainty that what one is doing is the morally excellent act. Neither the poet nor the sophist possesses knowledge of moral excellence, so neither can impart such knowledge. Consequently, neither the poet nor the sophist can engender moral excellence in the soul of another human being.

According to Plato, philosophy is the only intellectual pursuit by which one may acquire the knowledge necessary for moral, political, and military excellence. Through philosophy, one may come to possess knowledge of the *forms.*

Detail of Plato and Aristotle from *The School of Athens;* fresco by Raphael in the Vatican, Stanza della Segnatura, Rome, 1510–1511

(© Ted Spiegel/CORBIS)

Although the status of the *forms* in the Platonic dialogues is problematic (Kahn 1996, 329–330), there is no doubt that they are presented as the ontological basis for the epistemology in which Plato's ethical and political theories are grounded. The *forms* are immutable and eternal essences. There are, for example, many beautiful things, but these particular objects are also large or small, of a particular shape and color, and so forth. Particular beautiful things, moreover, are perishable. Helen, wife to Menelaus and principal cause of the Trojan War, is beautiful, but she is also a female human being, a Greek, treacherous, lustful, and so forth. The *form* of beauty, by contrast, is beauty, pure and simple. It is, moreover, the cause of particular beautiful things. It does not become ugly; it does not perish. Thus, beauty itself is more real than particular beautiful things. True knowledge, that is, knowledge that is certain and immutable, is knowledge of the *forms.* If a person knows what justice itself is, then he or she will be able to identify correctly and with certainty which actions are just and which unjust. Such a person, moreover, would act justly without fail. Thus, in order to be truly excellent and wise, a person must possess knowledge of the *forms.* True reality is the basis for true knowledge, and true knowledge is the basis for true excellence.

The *paideia* Plato offers in place of poetry and sophistry is ontologically based. It is grounded upon those essences, the *forms,* that are the immutable and eternal reality of the world in which we live. Philosophy is that activity by which one progresses toward and finally attains knowledge of the *forms.* In the *Republic,* Plato even proposes a moderately detailed program of study for aspiring philosophers, beginning with a general conditioning of the soul so that it desires what is beautiful and good and ending with an intense and protracted study of the *forms.* Only after completing this program, at the age of fifty, would a person be capable of governing others. In addition to such explicit discussions of what constitutes philosophy, one may also consider the dialogues themselves as discussions of what philosophy is. Domains of inquiry such as epistemology, metaphysics, morals and ethics, education, politics, and social order are investigated in the dialogues, and one may conclude that these are areas that the philosopher studies. Thus, Plato provides an account not only of what the philosopher should study, but also for what the philosopher is looking. Ultimately, this account of the philosopher and his activity is an account of a new type of *paideia,* of a new and comprehensive discipline by which wisdom and moral excellence may be engendered in the human soul.

Underlying the philosophic *paideia* Plato proposes is a new mode of human consciousness in which the object known is recognized as distinct from the knowing subject. Plato is not the sole creator of this new mode of consciousness, but, rather, he is the person in whom it crystallized and asserted itself. In the Platonic dialogues, one finds the victory speech made after a long and difficult battle. Considering the details of that battle is not necessary here; a discussion of the mode of consciousness supplanted and of that which replaced it will suffice. Havelock denotes the mode of consciousness supplanted as the "Homeric state of mind" and attributes its downfall to the introduction of writing into Greek society. In an oral society, information is preserved through memorization, and poetic verse is easier to memorize than prose statements, because it employs psychic or mental energy more efficiently. Nonetheless, memorization of poetic verse is demanding and consumes most, if not all, of a person's psychic energy. There is no opportunity for the individual who must memorize to create a distance between himself and what is memorized, and to consider what is memorized critically. What is memorized is part of who one is. The individual identifies himself with what is memorized (Havelock 1963, chapters 8, 9).

The written word removes the need for memorization. What had been memorized may be written down, set aside, and referred to when necessary. Moreover, one's psychic energy is freed from the duty of memorization. According to Havelock, two things followed from the introduction of writing and the freeing of psychic energy from the duty of memorization. The information written down eventually became something *other,* something different from the person who had memorized. It became, in other words, a distinct object available for epistemic consideration by the knower. The objectification of what is known corresponded to the person who knows separating himself from what is known, to the creation of a critical distance between the knower and what is known. It corresponded, in other words, to the emergence of the subject-object distinction (Havelock 1963, chapters 11, 12). This separation of the knower from the known and the recognition of the known as a distinct object occurred simultaneously.

This new mode of consciousness crystallized in the thought of Plato and is a direct result of his attempt to establish philosophy as a discipline distinct from poetry, sophistry, rhetoric, and the like. It is, moreover, a mode of consciousness that underlies the philosophic activity of Aristotle. Plato's inquiry into *being,* for example, takes *being* as an object to be studied, an object that is something distinct from human beings (at least in the sense that a human being cannot be identified with *being qua being*). Aristotle's contributions to philosophy would not have been possible were it not for this mode of consciousness, and, so, his work is dependent upon Plato's own work. Plato is indeed the greater philosopher.

–MATTHEW E. KENNEY,
UNIVERSITY OF SOUTH CAROLINA

References

J. L. Ackrill, *Aristotle the Philosopher* (Oxford: Oxford University Press, 1981).

F. A. G. Beck and Rosalind Thomas, "Education, Greek," in *The Oxford Classical Dictionary,* edited by Simon Hornblower and Antony Spawforth (Oxford: Oxford University Press, 1996), pp. 506–509.

R. G. Collingwood, "Aristotle," in *The Idea of Nature* (Oxford: Oxford University Press, 1945), pp. 80–92.

Edward Halper, "Aristotle on Knowledge of Nature," in *Form and Reason: Essays in Metaphysics* (Albany: State University of New York Press, 1993), pp. 93–116.

Eric A. Havelock, "The Linguistic Task of the Presocratics," in *Language and Thought in Early Greek Philosophy,* edited by Kevin Robb (La Salle, Ill.: Hegeler Institute, 1983), pp. 7–82.

Havelock, *Preface to Plato* (Cambridge, Mass.: Harvard University Press, 1963).

Charles H. Kahn, *Plato and the Socratic Dialogue: The Philosophical Use of a Literary Form* (Cambridge: Cambridge University Press, 1996).

Jacob Klein, "Aristotle, An Introduction," in *Ancients and Moderns,* edited by Joseph Cropsey (New York: Basic Books, 1964), pp. 50–69.

Alasdair MacIntyre, "Aristotle's Account of the Virtues," in *After Virtue: A Study in Moral Theory,* second edition (Notre Dame, Ind.: University of Notre Dame Press, 1984), pp. 146–164.

Andrea Wilson Nightingale, *Genres in Dialogue: Plato and the Construct of Philosophy* (Cambridge: Cambridge University Press, 1995).

Timothy A. Robinson, *Aristotle in Outline* (Indianapolis: Hackett, 1995).

Joseph Sachs, *Aristotle's Metaphysics* (Santa Fe, N.Mex.: Green Lion, 1999).

GREECE: DEMOSTHENES

Was Demosthenes' call to Athenian resistance against Philip II of Macedon doomed from the start?

Viewpoint: Yes. In spite of Demosthenes' best hopes, Athens's decline had been irreversible since losing the Peloponnesian War. It had neither the economic nor the political strength to mount a credible resistance to Macedonian hegemony.

Viewpoint: No. Demosthenes' resistance to Macedonian rule was not ill-conceived; his advice was heeded too late.

In 338 B.C.E. at the Battle of Chaeronea, a combined force of Athenians, Thebans, and other, smaller Greek poleis lost to the superior forces of Philip II of Macedon. In the two decades leading up to the battle, the Athenians had been divided over the question of how fierce a resistance they should offer Philip as he gradually moved southward, or if they should resist him at all. Demosthenes, a powerful orator and statesman, was the famous proponent of challenging Philip before he grew too strong, while others pursued more-accommodating responses, ranging from keeping Philip at bay through diplomacy to welcoming him outright as a new overlord for Athens. In evaluating the wisdom of Demosthenes' policies, three questions dominate the debate in this chapter. First, one must assess the strength of Athens and its Greek coalition in the face of the new Macedonian phalanx. Did the southern Greeks even stand a chance? Second, Philip, on the surface at least, claimed that he was a friend of the Greeks and that he wanted to be the protector of their interests rather than their prison guard. One must decide the sincerity of such assertions. And finally, the quality of life in Athens and in Greece generally, as it was in the fourth century, needs to be considered. Could the Greeks achieve stability and prosperity on their own, as independent states, in the new state of affairs following the devastation of the Peloponnesian War? In short, was Athens worth saving?

One could restate the problem confronting Athens in its relationship with Philip in the mid fourth century as a conflict between national freedom and personal security. To benefit from the safety and wealth of Philip's kingdom, Athens would have to relinquish its autonomy, while to remain free, the Athenians would have difficulty in maintaining an acceptable quality of life. However, it is important throughout this chapter to disregard what is known about events following Chaeronea; Demosthenes and his contemporaries, obviously, could not have predicted the future. To the Athenians of the mid fourth century, autonomy and security were not necessarily mutually exclusive.

—Joel Allen

Viewpoint: Yes. In spite of Demosthenes' best hopes, Athens's decline had been irreversible since losing the Peloponnesian War. It had neither the economic nor the political strength to mount a credible resistance to Macedonian hegemony.

In the mid fourth century B.C.E., around the time Philip II was emerging as a powerful king in northern Greece, the polis of Athens was a shadow of its former self. Not only had it lost the great empire of the years before the Peloponnesian War, but also having gone through a minor resurgence in the early 370s B.C.E., it had lost those gains as well. Destructive bickering both within Athens and on the Pan-hellenic scene made it impossible to present a united front in foreign policy. The economy of the region was disrupted and unpredictable. What might be described as a general complacency, or even malaise, had settled among the Greeks of the south, keeping them from taking risks or devoting sufficient resources to matters of national security. All in all, Athens was in a slow steady descent from its heights during the mid fifth century.

Such a climate can maintain a precarious equilibrium only if there are no deviations from the expected course of events, or in other words, if there are no surprises. But a surprise is exactly what Philip II of Macedon was, coming out of a land that had historically been, to the southern Greek mind, disorganized and barbaric. The scene of constant internecine warfare and violent butchery within the ruling dynasties, Macedon was thought to have little respect for any civilized rule of law, and thus not to be a threat to Greek freedom. During this period of neglect, Philip II was able to dominate his unruly neighbors, prey upon the misconceptions of the south, move quickly, and insinuate himself into Greek domestic political disputes of the day so that resistance to him not only became futile, but, even further, never had a chance to germinate as a political idea in the first place.

The prestige of Athens as a naval power, and consequently its ability to hold on to an empire, had seriously deteriorated in the years following the Peloponnesian War. In 357 the three large islands of Chios, Rhodes, and Cos, along with the important coastal town of Byzantium on the Hellespont, defected from the Athenian League. Mausolus, a nearby Persian satrap, had successfully goaded these cities into making a bid for freedom in order to form a new, separate sphere of influence in the eastern Aegean. The Athenian navy, the jewel of the sea in past generations, lost two naval battles in trying to keep them in check, first at Chios's harbor and then at Embata. Athenian naval strategy appears to have lost its edge: at Embata the Athenian admiral, Chares, had carelessly decided to engage the enemy in spite of a storm and paid for the mistake with defeat. Moreover, the Athenian assembly still exhibited a mercurial nature when it came to handling its military leaders. In response to the loss at Embata, the Athenian assembly recalled one of Chares' coleaders, Timotheus, in spite of his impressive record of accomplishment. In 365 Timotheus had led the Athenians in a conquest of Samos, and in 362 he had laid siege to Amphipolis. In 355, however, he was forced into exile. Without this capable leader, any war effort on the part of the Athenians must have been compromised. With the Athenian fleet in the hands of lesser men, they experienced more losses than were typical of their history. When Diopeithes attempted to establish *cleruchs,* or citizen settlers, in Philip's Thracian territory in 342, for example, he had to raise funds for the navy in part by levying taxes on merchant ships. His makeshift force was easily defeated and driven off. The navy would have been hard-pressed to sustain a long war with Philip.

One reason for the overall Athenian weakness in the fourth century was the internal divisions and the nature of the debate on the question of how to treat Philip. Rather than reasoned discussion, leading statesmen within Athens took cheap personal shots at one another and thus trivialized matters of importance. The rivalry between Chares and Timotheus was replaced in the younger generation by a rivalry between Demosthenes and Aeschines. Both were envoys in the two embassies to Philip, which arranged the Peace of Philocrates following the fall of Olynthus and Philip's victory in the Sacred War, but they developed opposing points of view on the Macedonian question. In the second embassy, Aeschines carried an effort to grant exceedingly generous concessions to Philip, which Demosthenes later criticized. Shortly after they returned, Demosthenes and one of his associates, Timarchus, prepared to accuse Aeschines of taking bribes from Philip. Aeschines countered by dredging up rumors of homosexual escapades and prostitution from Timarchus's youth. Although he had no evidence, he succeeded in having Timarchus convicted of immorality, with the result that Timarchus lost his citizenship and no longer had the right to bring suit in a court of law. Aeschines' case was built on salacious gossip and innuendo that had little to do with current events, and it lowered Athenian politics to new depths. Three years later in 343, Demosthenes finally brought his case against Aeschines to trial, but Aeschines was narrowly acquitted. Both rivals were compelling orators, and their contentious debate ruined Athenian chances, which were slight already.

A lack of cooperation also characterized the Greek states at large in matters of international relations. The old alliances of the Peloponnesian War had crumbled, and the new ones that replaced them were weak by comparison. Powerful cities had competed with each other for a generation, and the consequent bad blood among states produced a "save-yourself" mentality. In 342 Philip marched south from Epirus in western Greece, where he had earlier married Olympias and installed her brother as king. He entered Ambracia, just across the Corinthian Gulf from the Peloponnese, and from there he threatened the free Greek states. Demosthenes and others hastily organized a stopgap coalition of Peloponnesian allies, including Argos, Megalopolis, Mantinea, and the Achaean League. Philip backed down for the moment, and the emergency passed, but in a final, more forceful push south in 338, he directed his efforts at Boeotia and Attica. In this conflict, however, the Peloponnesian allies, so recently acquired, declared neutrality and left Athens to fend for itself. There was little esprit de corps among the Greeks, and they were willing to join with others only when their own security was in jeopardy.

Rather than make the hard decision of going to war in order to confront Philip, the southern Greeks were more concerned with avoiding conflict. Their relationship with Philip might be called one of appeasement. Philip was effective at diplomacy and managed to convince the Greeks time and time again that he had their best interests at heart. In 357 when Philip laid siege to Amphipolis in the north, the Athenians failed to respond to the inhabitants' call for help, instead believing Philip's false promise that he would turn it over to them in the future. In 352 when Philip was moving against Heraion Teichos in Thrace, the Athenians could have sent help, but quickly embraced a rumor that Philip was ill (he was not) and did not send the necessary aid. In 350 when Olynthus needed help in resisting Philip, the Athenians sent mercenaries to help twice, but did not commit with citizen troops until late in the conflict, and even then, they did not set sail because of unfavorable winds. In 346 at the instigation of Eubulus, the Athenians swore an oath to enter the so-called Peace of Philocrates with Philip even though Philip had not yet agreed to the treaty, and the status of key border states, notably Phocis, had not been covered. At times when military action clearly would have been a better policy, the Athenians appeared not to have had the heart for battle. As Raphael Sealey points out, the loss for Athens in the fall of Olynthus was not so much to its material wealth or strength as to its symbolic position as hegemon over other Greek states: from the example of Olynthus, allies of Athens must have realized that their protector would not come to their rescue when they were threatened.

Changes in the conduct of public finance also reflect the Athenians' general aversion to war. In 354 Eubulus took over the theoric fund, which paid for several public works including festivals. As director of the fund, he successfully lobbied for more revenues of the empire to be directed to his jurisdiction and away from military expenditures. The money paid for improvements in infrastructure and provided for disbursements to the Athenian poor at festivals. It has been argued that Eubulus's management of public finance contributed to the apathy of the people of Athens in matters of international significance. Now that citizens received payments from the theoric fund, they had less incentive to serve as rowers in the navy, a traditional source of income for the landless. It was not a time for money to be spent on festivals, however, and Demosthenes was only able to intervene and redirect the funds to military campaigns in 340 just before Chaeronea. In the meantime, the Athenians had repeatedly avoided war.

Unfortunately for Athens, Philip was as adept at military planning as he was at diplomacy. He was unlike his fellow Macedonians in that he spent three years of his adolescence in southern Greece, detained in Thebes as a hostage against his family. While there, he is said to have learned new military tactics from Epaminondas, who had led the Thebans in filling the power vacuum left by the fall of Sparta in 371. Philip's military innovations include forming his battle line into a wedge, rather than a straight line, introducing the *sarissa,* or long pike, to the arsenal of the hoplite phalanx, using his cavalry more freely, paying more attention to his navy, and augmenting an elite corps of fighters called the "Companions" of the king. He was also revolutionary for Macedon in that he considered the long-term consequences of military decisions. In 355, for example, he strategically planted a colony near the gold mines at Crenides and renamed the town Philippi. And in order to shore up his own base, he broke up Thessaly into four districts (tetrarchies) and replaced their indigenous leaders with Macedonian governors loyal to him, thus eliminating potential rivals. This forward thinking and organization marked a departure from the past, ad hoc nature of Macedonian warfare.

With all his military advances and clever strategizing, Philip knew when to proceed with restraint, and he pulled back his forces when it was prudent. On several occasions, he waited until the

PHILIP MARCHES WHERE HE PLEASES

In this passage from the Third Philippic, Demosthenes describes how difficult it would be to fight Philip, comparing the Macedonians with the Spartans of old:

I am told that in former times the Lacedaemonians and all the other Greeks would invade and ravage the enemy's land with hoplites and citizen armies for four or five months only during the campaigning season, and then return home. They were so old-fashioned in outlook . . . that they would not purchase any service from anyone, but war was waged according to rules and openly. But now you see the greatest damage has been done by traitors, and not as a result of regular pitched battles. You hear of Philip marching where he pleases followed not by a phalanx of hoplites, but by light-armed troops, cavalry, archers and mercenaries—this is the kind of army he has around him. When, further, he falls upon a people torn by internal strife and no one marches out to defend the land, so suspicious are they of one another, he brings up his engines and lays siege to the city. I pass over the fact that he draws no distinction between summer and winter, and that he has no season set apart for suspending operations.

Source: *M. M. Austin,* Economic and Social History of Ancient Greece *(London: B.T. Botsford, 1977), pp. 337–338.*

Greeks themselves came to him. In 356 he answered the call for support from Olynthus and helped them conquer their neighbor, Potidaea. In 353 the Thessalians asked him to drive the Phocians out of their territory, and he was happy to comply. Seven years later, however, it was the Phocians, under the leadership of a new, pro-Macedonian faction, who sought his aid, and he gladly switched sides. In 342 factions in Eretria and Oreus, two important towns on the strategically important island of Euboea, asked him to help defeat their domestic rivals, and he accordingly established them in power. In these last two cases–Phocis and Euboea–Philip was able to occupy the moral high ground of a just war (he had been asked to intervene, after all) even while improving his position for a war with larger powers. From Phocis, he acquired Thermopylae, the narrow pass that protected southern Greece from advances from the north, and once in Euboea, he was practically in Athens's backyard.

As a result of a multifaceted weakness on the part of the Greeks–economic, diplomatic, political, and psychological–Philip II's ultimate conquest was inevitable. No amount of stumping on the part of Demosthenes, the great rabble-rouser of the Athenians, could have stirred them to appropriate action. Demosthenes himself had departed from his anti-Macedonian policies at Olynthus to support the Peace of Philocrates for a time, abandoning Amphipolis, which in turn damaged Athenian freedom. Later, of course, he retracted his support and called for war, but if even Philip's staunchest foe had moments of doubt, the Macedonians all but faced an open door. By such tactics, he was also able to undermine the influence of Demosthenes and his allies by making them out to be alarmists and in this way render their attempts to oppose him largely ineffective.

–JOEL ALLEN,
QUEENS COLLEGE,
CITY UNIVERSITY OF NEW YORK

Viewpoint:
No. Demosthenes' resistance to Macedonian rule was not ill-conceived; his advice was heeded too late.

Resistance to Philip II was a viable option for the Athenians for much of their relations with Macedon in the fourth century, on up to the Battle of Chaeronea in 338 B.C.E. Many of the obstacles that confronted the Athenians were equally vexing for Macedon, including recalcitrant allies, economic hardship, and internal division at home. While strong on land, Philip still was not adept at seafaring, giving the Athenians a distinct advantage in some conflicts, including control of the strategically and economically important Hellespont. Even on land, the Athenian will to resist Philip, while flagging in some key moments, could be ignited by vigorous oratory. Their record in battle against Philip was far from dismal, and included enough successes to demonstrate that the outcome of Chaeronea was not preordained. And when they set their minds to it, the Athenians could still command respect in international relations. If Demosthenes' advice had been followed sooner, the Athenians could certainly have suppressed the Macedonian threat.

Philip was not at all invincible on the battlefield; he clearly understood this fact and never pushed a situation that was not in his favor. In 352 he withdrew from Thermopylae rather than face a combined force of Athenians, Spartans, and Achaeans, and in 342 he withdrew from Ambracia when the Athenians met him again with their (admittedly short-lived) Peloponnesian alliance of Argos, Megalopolis, Mantinea, and the Achaean League. As innovative as his military tactics were, they were derived in large part from the examples

Statue of the Athenian statesman Demosthenes, regarded as the greatest of Greek orators

(Ny Carlsberg Glyptothek, Copenhagen, I.N. 2782)

he witnessed during his boyhood in Thebes; the Greeks might thus have easily anticipated his maneuvers. Onomarchus of Phocis, for example, was able to defeat Philip twice in Thessaly. Philip eventually managed to rally and overcome Onomarchus, but the short war showed that he could be defeated. At sea his weaknesses were repeatedly exposed. The year 340 was particularly rough for him: he was driven away from both the coastal towns of Perinthus and Byzantium. Having spread himself too thinly by dividing his army between the two, he could not prevent Athenian ships and their allies from provisioning those trapped behind the walls. Indeed, Philip's single greatest success in his mounting struggle with the Greeks, apart from Chaeronea, was his seizure of three forts at Thermopylae, but they had been all but turned over to him because of factional strife in Phocis, which controlled them. In short, when the Greeks bothered to resist, Philip was often checked.

At home, Philip faced a more dangerous kind of political division than what characterized the tawdry debates in Athens between Demosthenes and Aeschines. In Macedon, assassination was the preferred form of rebuttal. The court was infamous for its deadly internal squabbles; Philip, in order to take the throne in the first place, had to kill his young nephew for whom he was regent. The Athenians deftly manipulated this fact to their advantage. In 342 when Philip entered Epirus and drove out Arrybas in order to marry the king's niece, Olympias, and place her brother, Alexander, on the throne, Arrybas promptly fled to Athens, where he sought asylum. The Athenians received him warmly, and they set up an inscribed decree in his honor, which still exists today. The assembly made it known that it would work to put Arrybas back on the throne. It was a provocative call for neighbors of Epirus to help them against Philip, in spite of his new marriage connection, and it distracted him from his efforts against Athens. To pursue this strategy further, Demosthenes went on an embassy to Thessaly in 342 to pull the rug out from under Philip by undermining his base of support. He would not have made such a move without some suspicion that Philip was weak among his own constituents. The embassy gets only slight attention in the sources; it would be good to know more about Demosthenes' specific objectives and his contacts with Philip's domestic rivals. In any case, Philip clearly was alarmed: he responded by planting new garrisons in the region and reinforcing existing ones (Sealey, 1976). Philip's own demise demonstrates how much the Athenians could legitimately hope for as a consequence of internal strife in Macedon. He was killed less than two years after Chaeronea, stabbed to death at his daughter's wedding by an assassin who was believed to be working in the employ of his wife Olympias, from whom he had by then become estranged. Dynastic rivalries, therefore, always had to be taken into consideration in the decision making of Macedon's opponents and always contributed to a measure of unpredictability in political events.

The Athenians were impressive in their efforts to hold on to their empire. As proven by Demosthenes' backdoor negotiations in Thessaly, Athenian diplomacy was still bold, effective, and a threat to Philip. In 357 even as they lost several large islands from their alliance, they were able to add Euboea, their wealthy neighbor. The Euboeans had sent out embassies to both Thebes and Athens, offering their support, essentially, to the highest bidder. Timotheus, ever looking for easy ways to maintain Athens's prominence, argued for prompt action, and a relatively small force was thus able to secure the island from Thebes. Also in 357 Chares established a treaty with the successors of Cotys in Thrace, which was in place in its final form by 356–355. In the following year, the Athenians continued to shore up their presence on Amorgos and Andros, on the former, with a full garrison, and on the latter, with a citizen governor. Moreover, the losses of Chios, Cos, and Rhodes as allies at the Battle of Embata in that same year should not weigh heavily against Athens, given the role of nature (a storm) and a single reckless admiral (Chares) in the failure. Under more capable hands, especially at sea, Philip and others could be kept in line.

Late in the game when hostilities between Athens and Macedon were no longer concealed and Demosthenes' suspicions of Philip's imperial ambitions had been confirmed, the Athenians were still able to rally support among their allies. As Philip laid siege simultaneously to Perinthus and Byzantium, both on the Hellespont, a combined fleet of ships from Chios, Rhodes, and Cos, the original rebellious allies of 357, joined the Athenian effort. The Athenians also won assistance in the form of troops and other supplies from Persia by informing them of Philip's eastward progress in their direction. It is further testimony to Philip's vulnerability that in his exit raids across the Chersonese after giving up the Hellespont, he is said to have accomplished little. Keeping in mind the Athenians' adroitness at arranging last-minute alliances, one understands that the tardiness of Demosthenes' final alliance to resist Philip hardly guaranteed failure. Famously, many large Greek poleis sat it out, but even so, the Athenians were joined not only by Thebes but also by Corinth, Euboea, Megara, Corcyra, and the Achaean League. They were defeated, but one cannot legitimately call the defense foolhardy.

Critics of Demosthenes' resistance of Philip as a doomed enterprise might point to the failure of Athens to defend adequately its ally Olynthus, which fell to Macedon in 348 after the Athenians dragged their feet in sending sufficient aid. But one scholar has argued that Athens had a strategic incentive in forsaking Olynthus, given that it had formed a sensible strategy around defending two other, more tactically important sites: Thermopylae and the Hellespont (Sealey, 1976). The former, located on a narrow pass further south from Olynthus, was easier to fortify, and an army there could halt Philip's southern advance. The poleis on the Hellespont provided the Athenians with an outlet for sea-based trade, and so in 353–352 they planted *cleruchies,* or governing colonies made of Athenian citizens, in Byzantium. Olynthus did not hold as much value for Athenian security as did these other sites, and its fall should not be counted as a failure of Athenian will; on the contrary, the Athenians still exhibited, occasionally, a proactive diplomacy. In 342 Athens engineered two unlikely networks to form an effective buffer zone against Philip: they united several cities to stop Philip from advancing southward in the Peloponnese, and they forged a league of the three principal towns in Euboea. Both coalitions were short-lived: in later years the Peloponnesians did not come to Athens's aid at Chaeronea, and a faction of Euboans actually welcomed Philip into their walls. Nevertheless, the alliances distracted Philip for the time being and showed that the Athenians were willing and able to stand against Philip when they saw that doing so was in their strategic interests. Appeasement is the wrong word to describe Athens's and their allies' aggressive efforts at diplomacy when war was an option.

Oratory had a profound effect on mobilizing resistance and inspiring courage in the face of adversity. In this sense, Demosthenes himself was something of a secret weapon and a constant threat to Philip. He spoke out for the first time against Macedon in 351 in the so-called *First Philippic,* when he called upon the Athenians to fight Philip for control of Amphipolis. In 349 he delivered three speeches called the *Olynthiacs,* where he beseeched his countrymen to deflect Philip from Olynthus. He was a gadfly to the peace party and was particularly critical of the diversion of public revenues to the theoric fund for festivals, which he successfully halted in 339. His momentary support of the Peace of Philocrates in 346 came at a time when he was cornered in policy debates, both foreign and domestic, and opposition would have been politically suicidal. When the circumstances allowed he quickly shifted back to his stance of resistance. In the *Second Philippic,* delivered in 344–343, Demosthenes warned the Athenians that Philip was sending money and troops to Messene and Argos in order to help defeat the Spartans. The exposé did the trick of forcing Philip to abandon the project. In other speeches, including two more *Philippics,* Demosthenes outlined specific actions that needed to be taken, made forceful recommendations, and hammered away at any argument that Philip would some day simply go away. The orator who supposedly honed his diction by rehearsing his speeches with rocks in his mouth was a formidable foe. It is perhaps a small triumph that he outlived Philip for twelve years.

Acquiescence to Philip simply was not an acceptable solution. He had proven to be less than a friend to the southern Greeks, and the

PRIZES OF WAR

In this passage, Didymus points out the cruelty that Philip was capable of, and thus, how necessary it was to fight him:

According to Philorchus (the ships) were 230 in number, according to Theopompus, 180, and from these he gathered 700 talents. Those things were done the year before in the archonship of Theophrastus who was archon after Nikomachus, as Philochorus in particular recounts in the following words: 'Chares sailed away to a gathering of the royal generals, leaving warships at Hieron to see to the marshalling of the vessels from the Pontus. And Philip, observing that Chares was not present, at first attempted to send his warships to seize the transports, but, being unable to capture (them), he shipped his soldiers over to the other side against Hieron and became master of the transports. In total there were not less than 230 vessels. And judging these to be prizes of war he broke them up and used the timbers for his siege-engines. In addition he came into possession of grain and hides and a great amount of money'.

Source: *Phillip Harding, ed. and trans.,* From the End of the Peloponnesian War to the Battle of Ipsus *(Cambridge: Cambridge University Press, 1985), pp. 119–120.*

Athenians were not blind to his potential abuses of power. In 357, when he was still in the process of laying siege to Amphipolis, Philip promised that he would turn the town over to Athens as their rightful, historic possession but then reneged and kept it for himself. After both sides had agreed to the Peace of Philocrates in 346, the Athenians swore their oaths not to try to conquer more territory, but Philip deliberately stalled the Athenian ambassadors at Pella and did not take the oath himself until after he had acquired more of Thrace on the sly. Moreover, when Philip took charge of Thermopylae from Phalaecus of Phocis, he imposed unduly harsh terms on the Phocians, surprising his allies in the Peace of Philocrates. And when Philip used his newfound position to exercise influence over Cersobleptes, the heir of Cotys of Thrace and an Athenian ally, the Athenians, in keeping with the spirit of the treaty, asked him to desist but were denied. Finally, in 340 when Athens and Macedon were all but openly at war, he showed how cruel he could be when he captured and sacked an entire merchant fleet of at least 180 ships. Too much was at stake when Philip began to encroach on Athens's near neighbors. The essence of Athenian identity–its democracy–was irrelevant under a tyranny, and there was no other option but resistance. Moreover, the future of Athens and its allies as well as that of Philip himself often hung on a thread. While the contest was uneven from a military perspective, the outcome was uncertain until the end, sufficiently so to give the Athenians and their allies every hope for a final reversal of fortune.

–JOEL ALLEN,
QUEENS COLLEGE,
CITY UNIVERSITY OF NEW YORK

References

Aeschines, *Against Ctesiphon.*

Aeschines, *Against Timarchos.*

Demosthenes, *Olynthiacs.*

Demosthenes, *On the Chersonese.*

Demosthenes, *On the False Embassy.*

Demosthenes, *On the Peace.*

Demosthenes, *Philippics.*

J. R. Ellis, *Philip II and Macedonian Imperialism* (Princeton: Princeton University Press, 1976).

Nick Fisher, *Aeschines: Against Timarchos* (Oxford: Oxford University Press, 2001).

N. G. L. Hammond, *Philip of Macedon* (Baltimore: Johns Hopkins University Press, 1994).

Mogens Hansen, *The Athenian Assembly in the Age of Demosthenes* (Oxford: Oxford University Press, 1987).

Edward M. Harris, *Aeschines and Athenian Politics* (Oxford: Oxford University Press, 1995).

Julia Heskel, "The Political Background of the Arrybas Decree," *Greek, Roman, and Byzantine Studies,* 29 (1983): 185–196.

Isocrates, *Panegyricus.*

Isocrates, *Philippus.*

Samuel Perlman, ed., *Philip and Athens* (New York: Barnes & Noble, 1973).

Plutarch, *Demosthenes.*

Raphael Sealey, *A History of the Greek City-States, ca. 700 to 338 B.C.* (Berkeley: University of California Press, 1976).

GREECE: ELGIN MARBLES

Should the Elgin Marbles be returned to Greece?

Viewpoint: Yes. The Elgin Marbles should be returned to Greece because their illegitimate removal from the Parthenon compromised the integrity of the temple. Moreover, the Greeks have begun to implement the conditions set by the British government for the return of the marbles, most notably the restoration of the Acropolis and the building of a new museum.

Viewpoint: No. The marbles should remain in the British Museum because Lord Elgin's legal removal saved them from destruction. They are available to a wider public than they would be in Athens, and their return to Greece would set a precedent that would empty many great museums of their collections.

The Greek temple to the goddess Athena, *Parthenos* (Maiden)—the Parthenon—is one of the most revered historic monuments in the world. It was built between 447–432 B.C.E. on the rock of the Acropolis in Athens, where it still stands, a holy ruin. For nearly 2,500 years the Parthenon has embodied the ancient Greek ideas of justice, freedom, and intellectual and artistic excellence that marked the height of the political power of Athens in the fifth century. It has endured centuries of earthquakes, military operations, weather, pollution, and looting. Fragments of monumental sculpture from the Parthenon and other buildings on the Acropolis can be found in museums around the world, but the largest collection outside Greece—and the most hotly debated—are the so-called Elgin Marbles, housed in the British Museum in London.

In 1801, Thomas Bruce, seventh Earl of Elgin, the British ambassador to the Ottoman Empire in Greece, obtained a permit from the occupying Turkish government in Athens that he used to remove and carry away half of the surviving sculptures from the Parthenon. In 1816 the sculptures were acquired by the British government and presented to the British Museum, where they remain to this day, housed in the Duveen Gallery. The Elgin Marbles properly include architectural sculpture from four monuments on the Acropolis in Athens, but the objects of greatest dispute in the collection are the fifty-six blocks of the frieze, fifteen metopes, and seventeen pedimental figures that belong to the Parthenon proper. For two hundred years, from the moment that Lord Elgin's Italian overseer Giovanni Battista Lusieri removed the sculptures from the building using saws, ropes, and pulleys, the Greeks and their friends in Britain have been lobbying for their return. The British government has consistently rejected requests for restitution.

Both the Greeks and the British agree that the Parthenon marbles must remain in a museum, for their safety, preservation, and for the enrichment and education of the widest possible audience. The current retentionists argue their case on several points, most strongly on precedent: that Elgin's legal removal saved the marbles from probable destruction at the hands of the Turks or their successors, and that the artifacts were, and are, much better off in the British Museum than they would have been, or would be, in

Athens. Further, the retentionists argue, returning the marbles to Greece would open an alarming "floodgate" of return that would divest museums of their collections.

The restitutionists reject these arguments; they argue most emphatically that the Parthenon metopes and frieze are not freestanding sculptures that can be appreciated on their own, but are structurally part of a building, and can only be understood in that context. For this reason, they argue exclusively for restitution of the Parthenon marbles and are willing to give up their right to claim any other pieces in the museum. Moreover, Greece has accepted and implemented all of the conditions that the British people have set for the return of the marbles. Supporters of restitution believe that the ethics of the case, and the global goodwill that the return would foster, should be the final motivation for making Greece a "gift of their marbles."

The issue of who owns cultural property is complex; all passion and politics aside, the most important issue is how to best preserve archaeological context and cultural heritage for present and future generations.

—Nancy Sultan

Viewpoint: Yes. The Elgin Marbles should be returned to Greece because their illegitimate removal from the Parthenon compromised the integrity of the temple. Moreover, the Greeks have begun to implement the conditions set by the British government for the return of the marbles, most notably the restoration of the Acropolis and the building of a new museum.

In a 1986 speech to the Oxford Union, Melina Mercouri, former Greek minister of culture, pleaded for the return of the "Elgin Marbles" to Greece, declaring: "There is a Michelangelo 'David'. There is a da Vinci 'Venus'. There is a Praxiteles 'Hermes'. There is a Turner 'Fishermen at Sea'. *There are no Elgin Marbles*!" Who has the right to the sculptures from the Parthenon–Greece or Britain? How do we define "ownership" of archaeological artifacts? This question is a complex one that affects all objects in museums and at excavation sites around the globe. How have museums acquired the best examples of ancient art, and has the acquisition of antiquities over the centuries been legal and ethical?

The Parthenon temple was commissioned by the Greek general Pericles after Greece defeated the Persians in 480 B.C.E. The temple, dedicated to Athena, patron deity of Athens, replaced the old temple to the goddess on the Acropolis, which had been destroyed by the Persians. Conceived by Pericles as a symbol of "the adventurous spirit" of Athens that had "forced an entry into every sea and into every land," the Parthenon embodies the ancient Greek ideas of justice, freedom, and intellectual and artistic excellence that marked the height of the political power of Athens in the fifth century. "Mighty indeed are the signs of our power which we have left. Future ages will wonder at us, as the present age wonders at us now," Pericles boasted some time after the completion of the temple. Clearly, he envisioned the monument as the embodiment of the confidence and pride of democratic Athens, whose people paid for its construction.

The Parthenon held panhellenic importance in antiquity, and later became the visible symbol of Greece's legacy to Western European culture, ideas, and values. Designed by architects Iktinus and Kallikrates under the watchful eye of Phidias, the sculptor who acted as general director for Pericles' building program on the Acropolis, the temple represents a culmination of Greek artistic expression. A model for future ages, the Parthenon is unique, both in conception and construction. The building and its sculptures were conceived and executed as part of a plan to construct a larger temple than the norm, which called not only for a Doric style peripteral temple measuring 69.51 x 30.86 meters with 46 columns on the exterior (with others inside) and two pediments on the gable ends with freestanding sculptures depicting the birth of Athena and her contest with Poseidon for supremacy in Attica, but also, uniquely, for 92 metopes in high relief narrating Greek myths of special interest to Athens, and a low relief frieze of 111 panels depicting the Panathenaia–the great civic festival honoring Athena. Inside the temple stood a colossal gold and ivory statue of the goddess herself, designed and executed by Phidias. The temple was executed in nine years (although work continued on the pedimental sculptures until 432 B.C.E.) and dedicated at the Panathenaic festival in 438 B.C.E.

The Parthenon stood almost intact for more than two thousand years. During the Byzantine period, it was transformed into a church, and between 1208 and 1458 it served as the church of the Frankish dukes; later it became a Turkish

Visitors viewing some of the Elgin Marbles on display at the British Museum

(© Reuters/CORBIS)

mosque, complete with minaret. Despite a good deal of remodeling and transformation of purpose, the building remained holy, revered, and well preserved. The first great destruction of the temple occurred on 26 September 1687, when the Franks attacked the Turks and bombarded the Parthenon, exploding a powder magazine that had been stored inside. Fourteen columns of the peristyle were destroyed and nearly all of the interior building. The building stood in this general condition throughout the Turkish occupation of Athens, until the arrival in 1799 of the new British ambassador to Ottoman Turkey—Thomas Bruce, seventh Earl of Elgin.

Lord Elgin was a product of a generation of Europeans captivated by classical Greek culture, art, and architecture—a revival of interest that began in the eighteenth century. Aware of the drawings of the Acropolis published by Stewart and Rivett twelve years before, Elgin was well informed about architectural sculpture, but also knew that the Europeans were more interested in sculpture than architecture and valued it more. In his desire to help reposition England as the cultural center of Europe, Elgin decided that he would have drawings and casts made of the antiquities in Athens, especially the sculptures on the Acropolis. He would send them back to England and make them available to British artists in order to improve the modern art of Great Britain. For two years Elgin's workmen and subordinates, under the direction of Italian painter Giovanni Battista Lusieri, made copies and drawings of the ruins. Then, in the middle of 1801, Elgin changed his plan. Why settle for drawings and casts, when he could obtain the real thing? At this time Greece was part of the Ottoman Empire, ruled from Constantinople, and Elgin took advantage of his political position to obtain a *firman,* or permit, from the Turkish government that he used to remove the sculptures from the building and ship them to England.

Elgin later explained to the British House of Commons that he took down the sculptures from the Parthenon in order to "save them" from probable destruction at the hands of the Turks. The truth is rather different. The removal of the marbles was neither legal nor moral. Eyewitness accounts and correspondence, especially Elgin's own letters written between 1801 and 1816, along with Parliament records previously unused and unpublished, are the primary source of the facts in the case. The legitimacy and propriety of the removal of the marbles was disputed immediately, first by Constantinople and the Greeks themselves, a subjugated and impoverished people under Ottoman rule, and by philhellenes like George Gordon, Lord Byron, who spoke out on behalf of the Greeks who, he knew, were outraged by the acts but helpless to stop them; other Britons at the time and thereafter joined the protest. Elgin was obliged to defend his actions from the start.

In his letters, Elgin's "altruism" is proven false, for he intended not so much to "save" the marbles from the Turks as to "collect as much marble as possible" to decorate his own home, "Broomhall," in Scotland. "You do not need any prompting from me," he exclaimed in a letter to Lusieri in 1801, "to know the value that is attached to a sculptured marble, or historic piece. Look out for . . . fine marble . . . that could decorate the hall . . . ," he requested. Sadly for Elgin, a series of unfortunate circumstances short-circuited this new plan. The cost of removing the marbles, shipping them, rescuing them when his cargo ship *Mentor* sank off Kythera, and storing them for years broke him financially. In the end, as we learn from Elgin's correspondence with his colleague William Hamilton, a trustee of the British Museum in 1815, Elgin was forced to sell the marbles to the British government to pay off his debts.

As allies with the British against the French, the Ottoman Turks at this time were especially indebted to the British for Admiral Horatio Nelson's victories over Napoleon Bonaparte in Egypt. As Elgin himself and his chaplain Philip Hunt admit in correspondence and recently published documents from the Select Committee of the House of Commons, this political situation cleared the way for him to make deals; the *firman* itself, which is in fact a second permit granted to Elgin, was identified by William St. Clair and published in full for the first time by him in 1998. The only existing copy of the permit is what may be an official Italian translation of the original Turkish document.

The wording of the *firman* clearly grants Elgin access to the Acropolis and permission to make drawings, to cast molds, and to "dig," and then, in ambiguous language, he is allowed to "take away any pieces of stone with inscriptions or figures." Nowhere does the Italian document explicitly give Elgin permission to dismantle the building of the Parthenon. Hunt admitted to the Select Committee in 1816 that the ambiguous terms of the *firman* had been exceeded; it was he, a self-described "fortune-hunter," who had arranged for the removal of the sculptures. Furthermore, the amount of money exchanged between Elgin and the Turkish officials exceeds any tradition of gift-exchange that existed at the time, and amounts rather to bribes and pay-offs to secure that Elgin's workmen would not be disturbed. In 1810, when Elgin pressured another British ambassador, Robert Adair, to help him get the marbles away, Adair was told by the Turks that Elgin had never had permission to carry off any Parthenon marbles, and that all of Elgin's actions on the Acropolis had been illegal from the start. One year later Elgin himself admitted as much in a letter to the prime minister. Shifts in politics alone eventually enabled Adair and others to help Elgin.

Therefore, though Hunt had obtained for Elgin a *firman* from Turkish authorities, the published evidence proves that by removing the architectural marbles Elgin exceeded the terms even of a loosely written document; he paid large bribes to corrupt officials and took immoral advantage of his position as ambassador and relied on the political clout of British friends such as Adair and Hunt to remove and ship away the sculptures of the Parthenon. Further, he misled the Select Committee about his motives, which were not to "save" the marbles from destruction, but to decorate his house and to make him and his colleagues rich.

The actual removal of the marble metope and frieze sculptures was difficult, for these panels, unlike the pedimental sculptures, are not freestanding decoration added to the building, but are built *into* the structure. Lusieri and the workmen used saws and chisels to quite literally hack the panels of the metopes and frieze off the building, damaging both the sculptures and the monument in the process; several of the panels were irreparably harmed, and some destroyed utterly during removal. The destruction of the architectural elements caused by the saws and accidents could not be duplicated by any fate under normal circumstances. It is impossible to say whether the remaining sculptures would have suffered a "worse fate" if left on the building. Further, we must consider the negative impact of transportation and improper storage during thirty-three missions and seventeen trips to England, not to mention an eighteen-month salvage operation to recover sculptures from the bottom of the sea after Elgin's ship *Mentor* sank.

After much debate over the authenticity and acquisition of the marbles, the British Parliament finally purchased Elgin's lot of Parthenon sculptures in 1816 and presented them to the British Museum to be "held in perpetuity." Thereafter, they became known as the "Elgin Marbles," and were moved around in the museum until Joseph Duveen, first Baron Duveen, funded a new building for them in 1938. Were the sculptures "safe" once they were finally installed in the British museum? Indeed not. "In her sooty vitals, London stores these marble monuments of the gods, just as some unsmiling Puritan might store in the depth of his memory some past erotic moment, blissful and ecstatic sin," complained Nikos Kazantzakis in his poem *England* in 1939.

As investigating scholars have proven, the sculptures were damaged when molded for plaster casts, which removed all the surviving polychromy and some of the patina; by pollution in London, as Duveen admitted in 1939; by undesirable climatic conditions in the museum; and worst of all by several "cleanings," the most serious of which, in 1937–1938, employed abrasives and copper chisels to remove "London grime" and to satisfy the erroneous perception that the marbles should be white (they had in fact been painted, perhaps by the famous ancient Greek artist Polygnotus). The cleaning scandal was covered up by the museum for sixty years. Art historians, archaeologists, museum curators, and scholars who have studied the pieces and continue to study them have shown that the marbles have been divested of their surviving paint and luster, their color, and their surface texture since being installed in the British Museum. Further, they are devoid of all context. What worse fate would they have suffered if left on the building? The Parthenon marbles are sacred images inextricable from the temple monument itself. Only when viewed together with the monument do they explain the religion and culture of the ancient Athenians.

The 1970 UNESCO Convention on the transfer of cultural property made it a crime to acquire smuggled objects, and the large collections of ancient art purchased by museums from private individuals in the late nineteenth and first half of the twentieth century, such as the Cessnola Collection of Cypriot Art in the Metropolitan Museum in New York or the Elgin Marbles, would not be acquired today. Although the trustees of museums have created acquisition guidelines that are in full compliance with the UNESCO Convention, the traffic in stolen antiquities remains a multi-billion-dollar international business.

This being said, over the years museums around the world, responding to legal pressures, have returned objects after convincing claims were made. No "floodgate" of return has occurred. These restitutions have been handled on a case-by-case basis and kept as quiet as possible. In 1982 Melina Mercouri, the minister of culture for Greece, urged England to return the Parthenon marbles to Greece. Her request was denied; however, in response, the British Committee for the Restitution of the Parthenon Marbles was formed and has been lobbying actively. Recent polls show that the British people support 3-1 the return of the marbles as a gesture of international goodwill and friendship toward a country whose culture has so influenced Europe and the world. Polls in the House of Commons find that 66 percent of the M.P.s (84 percent of Labour) support restitution of the marbles to Greece as long as three conditions are met: 1) Greece pays for the cost of return, and for the creation of a complete set of copies; 2) Greece makes no further claims on the museum for restitution; and 3) Greece develops a complete restoration project of the Acropolis and builds a new Acropolis museum to house the collection.

These conditions have been accepted gladly by the Greek government, and are being implemented. In 1983 the Greeks began a set of twelve restoration programs that included securing the rock of the Acropolis, reducing pollution in Athens and dealing with its effects, archival research, construction restoration, inventory, and the relaying of ancient paths leading to the Acropolis. In the summer of 2000 Athens began a two-stage tender process for their new Acropolis Museum. The chosen architect, Bernard Tschumi, in collaboration with Athens-based architect Micael Photiadis, created a 210,000-square-foot space with the capacity for visitors to simultaneously view the Parthenon sculptures, the Parthenon building, and the Acropolis. In November 2004, Deputy Culture Minister Petros Tatoulis announced that the construction contract has been signed, and the New Acropolis Museum is scheduled for completion in 2006.

At least ten thousand visitors per day would experience the marbles in their homeland, in an Athenian museum facing the Parthenon where they can be understood and appreciated as architectural elements of a sacred building. In January 1999, a majority of members of the European Parliament (339 of 626) signed a petition urging the British Museum to return the Parthenon marbles to Greece, and the EU supplied funds for the construction of the new Acropolis Museum. Therefore, the return of the Parthenon marbles to Greece is not simply a matter of dispute between Greece and Britain but holds much wider significance. Restitution would be just and generous, beneficial not only to Greece and Britain but also to the world.

—NANCY SULTAN,
ILLINOIS WESLEYAN UNIVERSITY

Viewpoint:
No. The marbles should remain in the British Museum because Lord Elgin's legal removal saved them from destruction. They are available to a wider public than they would be in Athens, and their return to Greece would set a precedent that would empty many great museums of their collections.

There is no doubt that Thomas Bruce, seventh Earl of Elgin, revered ancient Greek art and wanted it preserved for posterity. Like many educated upper-class Britons of his day, Lord Elgin was a philhellene, captivated by the form and design of classical Greek artistry. In 1799 he realized that his new appointment as ambassador to Ottoman Turkey would afford him an opportunity to improve the arts of Great Britain by making available to artists and writers casts and drawings of the great Greek monuments. He employed architects, draftsmen, and craftsmen to execute this plan on the Acropolis, working under the direction of Italian painter Giovanni Battista Lusieri; work began on this ambitious project with a legal *firman* (permit) from the ruling Turkish government in 1800.

By this period in history, Greece had been under the rule of the Ottoman Turks for more than three hundred years. The ancient Acropolis had been converted into a garrison, and the Parthenon, into a mosque. The Greeks were a subjugated people, with no power to protect or preserve their antiquities; the situation was not a healthy one for the surviving monuments and artifacts. Lusieri reported to Elgin that "the Turks continually defaced the statues and pounded them down to make mortar." Hearing constant news of the destruction of the artifacts on the Acropolis, Elgin determined that the marbles must be removed for their safety; as he stated before the House of Commons, Elgin believed that if he did not remove the best examples of ancient Greek art, they would be lost to the civilized world.

Knowing that the Ottomans were indebted to the British for their alliance against the French, he requested, and obtained, a second *firman* to allow removal of the sculptures to England, with language allowing the workmen to "take away any pieces of stone with inscriptions or figures." Collection continued from 1801 to 1804 with additional *firmans;* when the political climate was again favorable for Britain in 1810, Sir Robert Adair, British ambassador in Constantinople, acquired for Elgin a final *firman* allowing him to ship all the remaining antiquities in his collection program to England. Had he the financial resources, Lord Elgin would likely have established his own private museum for the collection, which he would have made available to artists and scholars. He was certainly not trying to "get rich" from the Parthenon marbles, as his detractors have implied. In fact, the expense involved in his collection program ruined Elgin financially. Having spent all his energy and resources for the better part of twenty years striving to enrich the culture of his country and preserve classical Greek art for posterity, he died in poverty in 1841; it took his family thirty-four years to pay off all his debts.

Lord Elgin's reputation has been unfairly damaged by Romantic poets whose passionate adoration for all things Greek skewed the facts of the matter. Soon after he heard of the removal of the marbles, the Romantic poet George Gordon, Lord Byron wrote two poems criticizing Elgin: *Childe Harold's Pilgrimage* (1812) and *The Curse of Minerva* (1812). These poems, which became widely popular, amount to character assassination and are responsible, in large part, for the exaggerated and unfairly negative opinion of Elgin held by people today. Furthermore, the nineteenth-century passion and admiration for classical Greek art and culture espoused in popular poetry as well as classical scholarship helped to fuel the international trade in antiquities by increasing the value of Greek art around the world. (The market value of a cultural artifact rises in direct proportion to the amount of admiration and importance placed on it by respected individuals and leading authorities.) In short, those who loved Greece unwittingly aided and abetted the looting of her antiquities. The Greeks themselves at the time were not entirely blameless in this regard. They, too, recognized the value of their legacy to the international market, and contributed to the trade in antiquities both before and after Greece became independent in 1829.

The Acropolis of Athens had been looted by treasure hunters since antiquity, but in the nineteenth and early twentieth centuries major European powers, motivated by this period's romantic passion and enthusiasm for classical antiquities, were eager to fill their museums. If Elgin had not removed the marbles, someone else certainly would have. The French, the British, and the Americans at the time of Elgin were engaged in "museum wars," on behalf of the Louvre, the British Museum, and the Metropolitan Museum of Art, respectively; trustees never met without acquiring a work of classical art for their great collections. Such practices are characteristic of the morality of the time and cannot be judged by contemporary mores or laws.

In the unlikely event that no one removed the Parthenon marbles, they would most likely have been destroyed by earthquake, weather, conversion, or war. The Parthenon had suffered through earthquakes, a ruinous fire in the second century B.C.E., and a series of renovations since it was built, but conversions–the most severe of which occurred around 450 C.E., when the temple was converted into a church for the first time–caused the most damage. The Byzantine Christians constructed an apse on the east end of the building and dismantled, destroyed, and/or defaced the sculptures of the east pediment, frieze, and metopes; the remaining metopes on the other three sides were also deliberately defaced. In the following centuries the

Parthenon suffered from further conversions, renovations, and pilfering.

In the mid fifteenth century, the Ottoman Turks defeated their Frankish predecessors in Athens and set up their stronghold on the Acropolis. They stored their artillery and powder magazines in the ancient monuments; the Propylaia, the Temple of Athena Nike, and the Parthenon were all destroyed by accidental or war-related explosions and conversions by the Turks. The greatest overall damage to the Parthenon came not from the removal of the marbles but from an artillery projectile, fired by the besieging Venetians on 26 September 1687, which exploded one of the powder magazines stored inside the temple. Two centuries later, during the Greek War of Independence, the Turks happily destroyed the columns of the Parthenon to get at the lead clamps inside, which they used for bullets.

Clearly, the monuments of the ancient Greeks held no cultural interest for the occupying Turks, but, recognizing the value of Greek art, they were ready to sell (or gift) artifacts to whomever they courted as an ally at the moment. Elgin did not steal the marbles. The legal status of the collection is established beyond a doubt; any argument against the legality of removal of the Parthenon marbles is a boondoggle. The *firmans* (permits) acquired by Lord Elgin between 1801 and 1810 were absolutely legal according to the international law at the time, as the Ottoman government in Greece was recognized both *de jure* and *de facto;* the Ottoman Turks had absolute legal authority over the Parthenon. Although the language of the *firman* is ambiguous, the document was twice ratified by the Turkish government to allow the removal of the Parthenon marbles.

In 1816, after determining that Elgin had the legal authority as a private individual to remove the marbles and that the marbles were authentic fifth-century Greek artifacts, the Select Committee of the House of Commons bought Elgin's collection and donated it to the British Museum to be held "in perpetuity." The marbles were housed in a permanent "Elgin Room," which was constructed for them in 1832 on the west side of the museum, and, as it was quite common at that time to name a collection after its donor, the antiquities became known by the public as the "Elgin Marbles." The entire collection comprises architectural sculpture from four monuments on the Acropolis in Athens, including the fifty-six blocks of the Parthenon frieze, fifteen metopes, and seventeen pedimental figures. Shortly before World War II, a new gallery funded by another philhellene, Joseph Duveen, first Baron Duveen, was built especially for the collection. It is in the Duveen Gallery, renovated and reopened in 1962, where the Parthenon marbles are installed today, officially labeled "The Sculptures of the Parthenon."

From the moment that the British Museum acquired the Parthenon marbles, the curators have done everything in their power to preserve, protect, and display the artifacts in the context that will allow for the greatest safety, accessibility, and understanding by the widest possible audience. To this end, the curators of the collection have worked continually with their Greek colleagues, and over the decades the British Museum has supplied many casts of the sculptures to Athens. Six million visitors from the far corners of the world visit the British Museum annually–twice as many as would visit them in Athens. The British Museum–free and open seven days a week to the world–holds international status as a center for Parthenon studies. It offers conferences, seminars, scholarly and general publications; it maintains a state-of-the-art web interface and facilitates learning through close links with the Center for Acropolis Studies in Athens.

Could Athens better provide for the marbles? Would the marbles be safer? Would they be more available in Athens to educate the public? The answer to all three of these questions is "No." Over the centuries since Greek independence, the Greek archaeological service has been working hard to preserve the Acropolis, but a deteriorated environment has ravaged the monuments. Political instability and a lack of sufficient

SHRINKING GODS

George Gordon, Lord Byron's narrative poem Childe Harold's Pilgrimage. A Romaunt *(1812) recounts the journey of an imaginary pilgrim through the Mediterranean region. This excerpt from Canto II makes an obvious reference to the Elgin Marbles:*

XV

Cold is the heart, fair Greece! that looks on thee,
Nor feels as lovers o'er the dust they loved;
Dull is the eye that will not weep to see
Thy walls defaced, thy mouldering shrines removed
By British hands, which it had best behoved
To guard those relics ne'er to be restored.
Curst be the hour when from their isle they roved,
And once again thy hapless bosom gored,
And snatch'd thy shrinking Gods to northern climes abhorr'd!

Source: *George Gordon, Lord Byron,* Childe Harold's Pilgrimage. A Romaunt *[Cantos I and II] (London: Printed for John Murray, William Blackwood, Edinburgh, and John Cumming, Dublin, by Thomas Davison, 1812).*

resources impede progress toward restoration. Mistakes were made in past restoration projects, which caused much more harm than good. The iron clamps are a case in point. The Greek Archaeological Service has spent years replacing the oxidized iron clamps with titanium.

The original jointing of the monuments was close-cut and fitted without cement or mortar, but accomplished with wooden dowels or iron clamps made rustproof with a sheathing of lead, which sealed the clamp and provided a cushion. So tight and solid were these joints that Lord Charlemont, visiting the Acropolis in 1749, could not fit a penknife between them. This ancient technique was not studied thoroughly and carefully by modern archaeologists and engineers who, beginning in the 1830s, attempted to restore blocks and columns damaged by violence or earthquake; the modern use of iron clamps and dowels sheathed in lead or mortar, repeated for decades culminating with the damaging work of N. Balanos in the 1920s and 1930s, proved disastrous for the structures. Oxidation of the iron caused by sea air, pollution, and acid rain have caused the clamps to rust, swell, and split, shattering the marble. As Graham Binns, chairman of the British Committee for the Restitution of the Parthenon Marbles, remarked in 1997, the columns "look like patients in a hospital, draped in drip-tubes."

The structural integrity of the monuments is dangerously undermined, and the surface of the surviving marbles has been worn away. Pollution in Athens has done irreparable damage to all the surviving surfaces of ancient buildings and artifacts on the Acropolis, and continues to threaten their existence, despite Athenian attempts to improve conditions. The Greeks are painfully aware of this, and have removed most—but not all—of the architectural sculptures on the Parthenon. Despite a plan announced in 1983 by the Committee for the Preservation of the Acropolis Monuments to remove all surviving sculptures to the museum in Athens, some sculptures even now remain on the building, where they are covered by carbon and sulfur dioxides from automobiles and factories.

It has been more than a decade since former minister of culture Melina Mercouri announced the third of four international competitions for a new Acropolis museum, but it has yet to be built. At this writing, the winners of the most recent competition, Bernard Tschumi Architects, have broken ground; construction may be delayed, however, because the museum is being built on top of an archaeological site. Furthermore, it is unclear how long it will take for the installation of the artifacts that are currently housed in Athenian museums, many of which must be repaired and restored. The fact is that though their intentions are good, the Greeks have yet to fulfill their commitments on behalf of the marbles.

The rich cultural heritage of ancient Greece is, in the words of the ancient Greek general Pericles, "an education," not only for Greece itself, but the world. The Parthenon marbles are a source of national pride in Britain, where they have been enriching the artistic and cultural life for more than two hundred years, inspiring generations of writers, poets, artists, architects, and scholars. As the English poet Percy Bysshe Shelley so eloquently wrote: "We are all Greeks." The British have long-standing cultural, emotional, and political ties to Greece—ancient and modern. Indeed, it was the philhellenism of the British, fueled in great part by the installation of the Parthenon marbles in 1816, that facilitated the freeing of Greece from Turkish rule and the creation in 1833 of the modern Greek state.

Those who insist that the British government should return the marbles in order to "restore the integrity" of the Parthenon by "uniting it with its sculptures" are romantics who deny the hard fact that for the sake of their conservation and preservation the Parthenon marbles must be housed in a museum—they will not go back on the monument. Experts on all sides agree on this point. Furthermore, the British Museum is only one of many institutions to hold artifacts from the Parthenon. Pieces of the monument can be found in France, Germany, Italy, the Vatican, Denmark, and Austria. Should all these museums return these objects? What would happen to world culture if museums were entitled only to display objects from their own countries? The whole notion of a museum as a center of world cultural and historical education would be called into question.

Political nationalists who claim that no one but the Greeks themselves are entitled to the Parthenon marbles have less of an interest in preservation, conservation, and education than they do in power and prestige. This attitude, when taken too far, is dangerous and goes against the UNESCO Convention of 1970, which encourages the interchange of cultural property among nations to "increase knowledge of the civilization of Man, enrich the cultural life of all peoples, and inspire mutual respect and appreciation among nations."

Even if every museum sent their collections back to Greece, there would be no restitution of the Parthenon to its original glory. The best way to ensure proper contextual viewing of the entire monument of the Parthenon is to place plaster casts of the sculptures on the building. This is achievable, and by far the best solution. Legislation enacted in 1963 prohibits the British Museum from deaccessioning its collection, though it may loan objects: it will take an Act of Parliament, therefore, to change the permanent status of the Parthenon marbles. The most important concern should be how to best preserve archaeological context and cultural heritage for present and future generations; at the time of this writing, Greece is not yet prepared to do right by the marbles, and they should remain in the British Museum. The British government legitimately owns them, and is morally committed to conserving the artifacts and making them available for the world to appreciate and admire.

–NANCY SULTAN,
ILLINOIS WESLEYAN UNIVERSITY

References

John Boardman, *The Parthenon and its Sculptures* (London: Thames & Hudson, 1985).

British Museum: Department of Greek & Roman Antiquities: Parthenon <http://www.thebritishmuseum.ac.uk/gr/grparth.html>.

Vincent J. Bruno, ed., *The Parthenon* (New York & London: Norton, 1974).

Joan B. Connelly, "Parthenon and Parthenoi: A Mythological Interpretation of the Parthenon Frieze," *Journal of the Archaeological Institute of America,* 100 (1996).

B. F. Cook, *The Elgin Marbles,* revised edition (London: British Museum Press, 1997).

Christopher Hitchens, *The Elgin Marbles: Should They be Returned to Greece?* (London & New York: Verso, 1997).

R. H. Howland, ed., *The Destiny of the Parthenon Marbles* (Washington, D.C.: Society for the Preservation of the Greek Heritage, 2000).

Ian Jenkins, *Archaeologists and Aesthetes: In the Sculpture Galleries of the British Museum 1800–1939* (London: British Museum Press, 1992).

Jenkins, *The Parthenon Frieze* (London: British Museum Press, 1994).

McDonald Institute for Archaeological Research <http:/www.mcdonald.cam.ac.uk/index.htm>.

John H. Merryman, *Thinking about the Elgin Marbles: Critical Essays on Cultural Property, Art, and Law* (The Hague & Boston: Kluwer Law International, 2000).

Karl Meyer, *The Plundered Past* (New York: Atheneum, 1973).

Jenifer Neils, *Worshipping Athena: Panathenaia and Parthenon* (Madison: University of Wisconsin Press, 1996).

Neils, ed., *The Parthenon Frieze* (Cambridge: Cambridge University Press, 2001).

Olga Palagia, *The Pediments of the Parthenon* (Leiden: Brill, 1993).

A. H. Smith, "Lord Elgin and his Collection," *Journal of Hellenic Studies,* 36 (1916).

William St. Clair, *Lord Elgin and the Marbles: The Controversial History of the Parthenon Sculptures* (Oxford: Oxford University Press, 1998).

Kathryn Tubb, ed., *Antiquities: Legal, Ethical and Conservation Issues Trade or Betrayed* (London: Archetype, 1995).

GREECE: EURIPIDES

Was Euripides a misogynist?

Viewpoint: Yes. Euripides' work demonstrates misogynistic tendencies. His plays portray women either as monsters who would disrupt the family or the state, or as models of self-sacrifice. Those few female characters who are empowered in his plays merely act like men.

Viewpoint: No. Euripides' plays demonstrate a sort of protofeminism rather than misogyny. The variety of strong and sympathetic women characters found in his plays demonstrates his commitment to critiquing patriarchal oppression in Athens.

Few discussions of Euripides' life and career can avoid the question of the playwright's understanding of women. Certainly there is no debating the frequency with which women appear in Euripides' nineteen extant plays. Twelve are named for women characters or choruses, and all but two (*Rhesus* and *Cyclops,* both oddities in the Euripidean corpus) feature prominent female roles. The question then arises whether Euripides championed women and their social plight in fifth-century Athens or merely played the opportunist, exploiting issues of gender on the Athenian stage and ultimately reinforcing patriarchal values. Regardless, he developed some of the most memorable and disturbing characters in all of Western theater. One need look no further than Medea, an infamously assertive and violent character, or Phaedra in *Hippolytus,* to find characters who make startling choices yet still command a surprising degree of sympathy from audiences. *Trojan Women,* one of his most powerful portrayals of gender politics, stages not only younger women (Cassandra and Andromache) but also Hecuba, the matriarch of the Trojan royal family. This fascination with marginal characters in terms of gender and race defined Euripides as a bold experimentalist.

Charges of misogyny have dogged the playwright since at least 411 B.C.E. when Aristophanes, an accomplished comic playwright, produced *Thesmophoriazusae.* This comedy, named after the participants in a religious festival exclusive to women, gives voice to the anger of Athenian women toward Euripides. One such character says of him, "But there is he, calling us double-dealers, / False, faithless, tippling, mischief-making gossips, / A rotten set, a misery to men" (392–394). Though Aristophanes' play may well have identified a contemporary bias against Euripides, the vehemence of these charges, as well as their context, indicates that the comic playwright was probably exaggerating popular reception of the tragic playwright's female characters.

Twentieth-century critics have debated the issue thoroughly, some agreeing with Aristophanes' assessment, others reading Euripides as a sort of early feminist. As early as 1913, Gilbert Murray passionately defended Euripides' intentions, noting that characters like Medea influenced the suffragette movement. In recent years several full-length studies of the problem have appeared, including Nancy Sorkin Rabinowitz's *Anxiety Veiled: Euripides and the Traffic in Women* (1993).

A satisfying answer to this question will require reflection upon the degree to which any artist can transcend the prevailing attitudes of his or her culture toward gender. The question of Euripides' and his fellow Athenians' misogyny is of growing importance for those interested both in classical studies and issues of gender and feminism as scholars and students continue to assess the value of Greece and Rome as a defining source for contemporary culture.

—*Paul D. Streufert*

Viewpoint:
Yes. Euripides' work demonstrates misogynistic tendencies. His plays portray women either as monsters who would disrupt the family or the state, or as models of self-sacrifice. Those few female characters who are empowered in his plays merely act like men.

The parameters of this question—was Euripides a misogynist?—need clarification. Rather than ask if the historical figure himself was a misogynist, we should ask if Euripides' work demonstrates misogynistic tendencies. Writers as early as the Roman poet Catullus (circa 84–54 B.C.E.) have correctly chastised readers who would infer biographical information from an artist's work. Given the nature of Greek tragedy and drama in general, it comes as little surprise that the plays of Euripides include a significant number of opposed characters. He wrote both strong and passive women, both helpful and brutal men, and even gods of varied moral character, none of whom define Euripides' own political and social views with absolute certainty. During the period of Euripides' career (455–407/6 B.C.E.), Athens undeniably oppressed and ignored women to the advantage of men. Men controlled the government, the courts, the arts, and every means of power and representation. Social customs imposed severe restrictions on the freedoms of married Athenian women, and Athenian literature contains numerous examples of men instructing or managing women with regard to their behavior. In light of this cultural milieu, we must also ask whether Euripides' writing demonstrates a significant degree of resistance to these sexist attitudes or merely reinforces the agenda of the patriarchy.

Though Euripides did challenge the polis on several issues, most notably Athenian policy during the Peloponnesian War, his work demonstrates a conservative tendency toward female characters. Rather than subvert the predominant understanding of gender roles in his city, Euripides reinforced them by staging a number of monstrous women. He exploited the fears of his audience, and, as Sarah Pomeroy notes, fear often plays a major role in the generation and perpetuation of misogyny (1975, 97). Additionally, Euripides' work exhibits a didactic approach. Aristotle in *Poetics* (60b33–35) and Aristophanes in his play *Frogs* (1053–1056) have misled us into thinking that Euripides' tendency toward realistic speech and action excludes instruction on behavior. Sophocles and Aeschylus are thought to have been the teachers of the Greek theater, but in fact Euripides too served as pedagogue in his presentations at the City Dionysia. He taught men to fear women with power and women to sacrifice themselves for the good of the patriarchal state.

Greek tragedy, like the city that produced it at its annual spring festival, offers little of actual consequence to women. Many feminist critics have noted its artificial nature, arguing that despite the high number of significant women characters found in the extant tragic texts, the means of representation firmly rested in male hands. Nancy Sorkin Rabinowitz rightly points out that all writers, producers, and performers of these texts were men (1993, 2). Helene Foley goes even further by arguing that Greek tragedy sought to privilege Athenian males not only vis-à-vis women, but also by exploiting dichotomies of class and nationality (2001, 12). Even in Euripides, who was known for writing with greater realism than either Sophocles or Aeschylus, we observe few things that go unexaggerated. All of the characters of Greek tragedy, both male and female, were created by a poet seeking to win a prize at a dramatic contest. Even if he composed strong, empowered women, such characters were less likely to inspire liberation for the women in his audience than fear in the men. When one examines the evidence from his plays closely, the highest aspiration for an Athenian woman was noble self-sacrifice for her family and country.

Euripides demonizes women principally through issues of fertility and childbearing. Women's control over this aspect of Athenian life evidently concerned the men of his audience, and women who would subvert or interfere with fertility or the family appear monstrous in his plays. Athenian husbands went to great lengths to regulate their wives' bodies, but these women ultimately controlled the production of heirs, the sign of a successful and healthy polis. This lack of control produced a sort of "womb envy" on the part of the husbands, as evidenced by

A TERRIBLE TEMPER

In the opening scene of Medea, *a nurse describes the tension in the household of her mistress:*

But now all is enmity, and love's bonds are diseased. For Jason, abandoning his own children and my mistress, is bedding down in a royal match, having married the daughter of Creon, ruler of this land. Poor Medea, finding herself thus cast aside, calls loudly on his oaths, invokes the mighty assurance of his sworn right hand, and calls the gods to witness the unjust return she is getting from Jason. She lies fasting, giving her body up to pain, wasting away in tears all the time ever since she learned that she was wronged by her husband, neither lifting her face nor taking her eyes from the ground. She is as deaf to the advice of her friends as a stone or a wave of the sea: she is silent unless perchance to turn her snow-white neck and weep to herself for her dear father and her country and her ancestral house. All these she abandoned when she came here with a man who has now cast her aside. The poor woman has learned at misfortune's hand what a good thing it is not to be cut off from one's native land.

She loathes the children and takes no joy in looking at them. And I am afraid that she will hatch some sinister plan. For she has a terrible temper and will not put up with bad treatment (I know her), and I fear she may thrust a whetted sword through her vitals, [slipping quietly into the house where the bed is spread,] or kill the royal family and the bride-groom and then win some greater calamity. For she is dangerous. I tell you, no man who clashes with her will find it easy to crow in victory.

Source: *Euripides,* The Medea of Euripides, *translated by Gilbert Murray (New York: Oxford University Press, 1906), Episode 1.*

mythological figures like Zeus, who usurped the role of the mother and birthed two of his children, Athena and Dionysus. In this case, Zeus represents a desire on the part of the Greek male to dispense with the role of the woman in childbearing. Two of Euripides' most well-known male characters express this same idea: Hippolytus rants, "Why, why, Lord Zeus, did you put [women] in the world, / in the light of the sun? If you were so determined / to breed the race of man, the source of it / should not have been women" (617–619). Jason too expresses a similar desire to Medea (573–575).

Though Medea is often remembered for the murder of her children, a monstrous and terrifying act with clear ramifications for Jason and his line, perhaps one of Euripides' more subtle devices in the text is the control that Medea wields over fertility. In a variety of ways, Medea plays the monstrous woman who decides the fate of three males—Jason, Aegeus, and Creon—through their children. Obviously, Jason's fertility has been cut off directly, as Medea murdered his sons as well as his new wife, the young princess of Corinth, who surely would have given him further heirs and cemented his place in the city. Medea controls Aegeus with the promise of fertility, assuring him that her drugs will produce an heir for him and Athens. Her manipulation of fertility ensures her safe haven at the end of the play, and Aegeus's willingness to extend guest-host friendship to Medea in exchange for fertility drugs reveals the high degree of anxiety men at this time felt concerning women's control over reproduction. Medea destroys Creon's line as well as the stability of Corinth, as the king dies with his daughter—presumably his only child—a clear indication of the link between family and the state. Though Medea offers an example of an empowered woman full of justified rage, her steady control over reproduction and fertility most likely inspired fear in the men of Euripides' audience. Far from being a cry for equality or social change, *Medea* warns and teaches its audience the dangers of losing control over women.

Other female characters in Euripides' plays control fertility after the fact by threatening or destroying a family's children. Though not as menacing as Medea, women who would cause the death of children, particularly those that would come between a patriarch and his sons, likely caused anxiety in the playwright's original audience. Euripides' misogynistic tendencies appear in *Hippolytus* as three characters—Aphrodite, Phaedra, and the Nurse—conspire against the young title character. Like Medea, Phaedra can be read as a sympathetic character to a point. Through no fault of her own, her sexual desire for her stepson has been kindled by the goddess Aphrodite, and the Nurse betrays her trust by revealing the secret to Hippolytus. The young man delivers a misogynist diatribe (616–668), an unjustified attack on Phaedra in absentia. Phaedra's subsequent actions, suicide and a false accusation of rape against Hippolytus, reverse audience sympathies. Though she first played the innocent victim, her false testimony against Hippolytus, which leads to his death at his father's hands, strips her of any sympathy the audience may have felt for her. Conversely, Hippolytus, who may have alienated some of the audience with the vehemence of his reaction against Phaedra, may regain their sympathy with his pathetic and unjustified death. Through the action of women, Theseus has been symbolically castrated by the death of his son. The family and perhaps the state have been destroyed. Again, women who would wield power appear as monstrous in Euripides' plays, and the playwright, rather than questioning or subverting the patriarchy of Athens, merely encourages its need for control.

While women like Phaedra and Medea provide negative models of feminine behavior, Creusa in *Ion* instructs more subtly, as she initially threatens the family and state but ultimately compromises in order to help them. When Creusa unknowingly meets her lost son Ion, the product of Apollo's rape, and hears that her husband Xuthus plans on adopting him, she attempts to poison the boy. The plot is thwarted, and soon after, son and mother discover each other and reconcile. At the conclusion of the play, Athena, that most androgynous of Greek goddesses and Athens's own special protector, requests Creusa's silence on the truth, implying that Xuthus's ignorance on the matter will benefit the family and state. Athena promises that Creusa, who once posed a threat to the patriarchal order, shall be rewarded and glorified for her sacrifices. Creusa avoids the label of monstrous woman because her plot to murder her child fails. In this text Euripides reveals the subservient and passive role women are to play in a successful civilization.

As Rabinowitz points out in her critique of Euripides, female characters in his plays who are not monsters often behave in such a way as to support the patriarchal order, some going so far as to sacrifice their lives (1993, 14). These idealized women, both young and old, appear in a number of his plays, and their presence suggests that Euripides encouraged such self-sacrifice. The playwright offers women a chance to participate in the glorification of the state or family in response to male oppression, giving them an alternative to Medea's path. The young title character of *Iphigenia at Aulis,* who willingly accepts her role as an offering on behalf of Agamemnon and the Greek army, provides a clear behavioral paradigm. Though mistreated by her father, who lies to her concerning a marriage to Achilles, the child ultimately chooses to offer herself as a sacrifice. When she speaks of accepting this burden (1375–1403), Achilles praises her in no uncertain terms, noting her bravery and patriotism. In a sense the girl takes on an androgynous or even masculine role, even while avoiding battle by dying for the noble sake of war. She expresses the misogynistic sentiment "in war [it is] far better that / Many women go to their death, if this / Keep one man . . . alive" (1392–1394). If Euripides wrote this line without irony, the character clearly implies an appropriate political role for women in fifth-century Athens. Polyxena, in the play *Hecuba,* provides a Trojan parallel to Iphigenia. This virgin also willingly accepts her role as a sacrificial victim to the Greek army. Like Iphigenia, she protects her family by comforting her mother and wins the respect of the observing men. In his messenger speech, the Greek herald Talthybius praises Polyxena and tells of her modesty in death (518–582). Though Euripides may have subverted ideas of race and nationality by glorifying the barbarian Trojan, he reinforced the notion that young women can gain glory with such an act. The idealized virgin is valued for nothing other than her potential for protecting male institutions.

The sacrificial paradigm extends beyond virgins to matrons in two of Euripides' other plays. While *Iphigenia at Aulis* and *Hecuba* explore matters of political concern, *Alcestis* shows a wife willing to sacrifice herself for her husband. Through Apollo's help, Admetus, Alcestis's husband, has been allowed to cheat death by finding a substitute. After pursuing a number of options, Admetus asks his wife to take his place in Hades, and, like a noble Euripidean woman, she accepts, thus saving her family and her husband's more valuable life. Soon after her death, the hero Heracles, a family friend, journeys to the underworld and rescues her. The play ends with reconciliation and marriage typical of many ancient comedies. Admittedly, Euripides draws Admetus as a foolish and selfish character, and in writing him may have been commenting on such traits in Athenian males. Nonetheless, the message of the play is clear: women who support their husbands shall be honored and rewarded. Any suffering that they may endure may be corrected by divine intervention. As in many European folktales, "happily ever after" implies restoration of the patriarchal order by way of marriage and family. *Helen,* one of his later (412 B.C.E.) and less popular plays, also investigates the idea of sacrifice, but in less concrete terms. Rather than show Helen as a monstrous character, worthy of blame for having deserted her family, Euripides treats her as one wrongfully accused. As explained in the prologue to the play, contrary to legend, Helen did not betray her family or state by running off with the Trojan Paris. Rather she was transported to Egypt, leaving Paris to kidnap a phantom in her form, thus setting off the Trojan War. By the end of the play, the gods have sorted out the mess and promised to restore Helen to a place of honor. Euripides thus saves Helen, whose name and reputation have been sacrificed, from charges of promiscuity. As in *Alcestis,* women play the sacrificial victim, but earn honor and reward. As in other Greek texts, Helen remains an object fit only for rescue and possession.

One may argue that Euripides advocates empowering women, citing his many characters that act aggressively in response to male oppression. While his women rarely accept their situations passively—to do so would rob the drama of its intensity—too often the women merely become masculine, trading the behavior of women for that of men. Euripides in doing so reinforces the misogyny of his audience by making women work within the patriarchal system. To be empowered in Euripides' dramatic world, women must engage in male discourse and behave like men. Rarely does he make any attempt to understand or show women in their own communities or on their own terms. Medea, before turning monstrous and murdering her children, speaks like a warrior in telling the Chorus, "What [men] say of us is that we have a peaceful time / Living at home, while they do the fighting in war. / How wrong they are! I would very much rather stand / Three times in the front of battle than bear one child" (248–251). In like manner, the title character in *Hecuba* plays the part of the warrior, murdering and blinding the men responsible for her suffering. In *Trojan Women* Hecuba resorts to words, debating a case much like a man. Her performance persuades her male audience, Menelaus, and attacks a woman, Helen. Her mastery of rhetoric, while it does show agency, reveals that for women to be empowered in Euripides, they must act and speak like men.

Euripides' writing, then, exhibits not a feminist call for the liberation and empowerment of Athenian women, but rather an anxiety over such things. The extant plays offer encouragement and instruction on behavior to both men and women. Additionally, they demonstrate misogyny in their willingness to exploit the plight of the women of fifth-century Athens for their own dramatic ends. There exists no proof that his plays encouraged social reform. After all, the playwright's goal in that most competitive of ancient Greek city-states was not the liberation of women but the winning of a dramatic contest.

—PAUL D. STREUFERT,
UNIVERSITY OF TEXAS AT TYLER

Viewpoint:
No. Euripides' plays demonstrate a sort of protofeminism rather than misogyny. The variety of strong and sympathetic women characters found in his plays demonstrates his commitment to critiquing patriarchal oppression in Athens.

It is difficult to assess the damage Aristophanes did to Euripides' reputation concerning the women of his day. In the passage cited in the introduction, we see an Athenian woman lambasting the Greek tragedian for his poor treatment of her colleagues, and, ever since, Euripides' reputation has been tarnished with the charge of misogyny. At the same time, both ancient and modern readers surely are aware of the exaggerations common to the comedy of Aristophanes. Athenians of the late fifth century expected to see the lampooning of public figures like Euripides in the *Thesmophoriazusae* or Socrates in the *Clouds,* and Aristophanes would have been foolish to ignore these men, obvious targets for parody given their innovative views on religion and politics. True, the comic playwright's critique of Euripides may contain a kernel of truth, but after surveying Aristophanes' extant plays, one could just as easily make the argument that Euripides gave a rare voice to the women of his day. For example, in the *Frogs,* a comedy that includes a contest between Euripides and his more conservative predecessor Aeschylus, Euripides points out that in his plays "The men, the slaves, the women, all made speeches / The kings, the little girls, the hags. . . ." Aeschylus snidely retorts, "Just see the things he teaches! / And shouldn't you be hanged for that?" to which Euripides responds, "No, by the Lord Apollo! / It's democratic!" (949–952a).

There can be little doubt that men dominated Athens in the late fifth century at the expense of women. Marriage was an institution whose sole raison d'être was the production of heirs. Even in terms of physical space, Athenian women were constantly subordinated to men. With the exception of attendance at religious festivals, married Athenian women were generally restricted to their husbands' homes (Pomeroy, 1975, 79). In direct contrast, the tragedies of Euripides reveal an author deeply concerned with subverting and critiquing this situation. Many of his women characters refuse to play the subordinate to men, choosing instead either aggressive or passive resistance. Close reading of his plays reveals not a misogynist or patriarch, but the opposite. Modern audiences should read Euripides as a sort of protofeminist, one troubled by the inequity he saw between the genders and anxious about its ramifications for his city. His plays, as they criticize the patriarchy of Athens, demonstrate resistance and a subtle call for social reform.

To begin this brief exploration of the question, let us examine first, not Euripides' female characters, but rather his male characters. Few of his men demonstrate the positive qualities valued by fifth-century Athenians. There are but a few examples of honest, resourceful, or insightful men in Euripides' nineteen extant plays. His most memorable characters act foolishly, display weakness, or at best, behave with startling naiveté. The men in his popular and controversial play *Medea* prove weak foils to the domineering title character. Jason, who knows better than anyone Medea's history of child murder, allows her unchallenged custody of their children. Additionally, he attempts to counsel Medea, chastising her for her poor understanding of politics. He says condescendingly, "I, for my part, have always tried to calm down / The anger of the king, and wished you to remain. / But you will not give up your folly, continually / speaking ill of him, and so you are going to be banished" (455–458). Jason's assertion of Medea's failure in handling Creon marks him as a political sycophant, an unappealing character to an Athenian democrat. His explanation of the new marriage as a means of cementing his family's happiness and success in Corinth demonstrates near comic fatuousness. Aegeus, who at first glance appears to be the only positive male character in the play, offers Medea Athens's protection, unaware that she has planned to murder Jason's young bride and her own children. Granted, Aegeus's actions may be read as noble, since Athens enjoyed celebrating its role as protector of the disenfranchised (see Sophocles' *Oedipus at Colonus*), yet one wonders how willingly he would have promised sanctuary to Medea had he inquired into her murderous plot. His desire to have children and Medea's promise to provide him with fertility drugs persuaded him to make a potentially dangerous decision for his city. Creon, like Jason and Aegeus, acts with startling recklessness by granting Medea's wish to remain in Corinth an additional day. Rather than allowing these characters to behave in their traditional roles as noble heroes and kings, Euripides subverts audience expectation and elevates Medea, a woman and a foreigner.

Though Aristotle credits Sophocles with being the most Homeric of the Greek tragedians, Euripides too staged the heroes of Homer's *Iliad,* yet not without a critique of the heroic ideal. *Iphigenia at Aulis* tells an early chapter of the Trojan War story, portraying two important heroes, Agamemnon and Achilles, as weaklings. In the course of the play, they both vacillate and ultimately prove ineffective against the mob and political necessity, allowing the young Iphigenia to be sacrificed to allow the Greek forces to leave Aulis for Troy. Agamemnon, the central character of the play, first writes a false letter, deceiving his wife into bringing their daughter to Aulis. He then chooses to rescind it for an honest course. Soon after, he changes his mind again, deciding that Iphigenia must die to safeguard her family against the throng of angry Greek soldiers. Achilles, likewise, speaks like a hero in the play, promising to protect the young Iphigenia against the Greeks, yet his threats of force ultimately prove empty. In the end the women of the play, Iphigenia and Clytemnestra, act more nobly than their male counterparts.

Youths comprise an additional and perhaps more forgivable set of weak Euripidean men. In characters like Pentheus (*Bacchae*) or the title character of *Hippolytus,* Euripides reveals an impatience with the arrogance of young men. Both Pentheus and Hippolytus misunderstand and ultimately blaspheme religious cults tied directly to women, and both die at the hands of family members. The former, whom Jennifer March rightly reminds us must be read as immature (1990, 58), in his vehement condemnation of the Dionysian cult, displays the lack of sophistication and inflexibility of a new ruler. Other tyrants in Greek tragedy, Sophocles' Creon for example, act in similar fashion, yet demonstrate a more savvy understanding of political matters. Hippolytus, like Pentheus, reads the world and his relationships with the gods as a series of simple dichotomies. In the prologue to the play we learn from Aphrodite that he has ignored her, choosing instead to worship Artemis (1–17). His simplistic understanding of the gods, coupled with his misogynistic tirade later in the play (616–668), clearly mark him as another of the playwright's foolish men, all of whom offer indirect proof of Euripides' sympathy toward Athenian women.

Unlike these foolish or cowardly men, many of Euripides' women prove their worth by demonstrating skills or attitudes highly valued by the men of his audience. One unusual and common trait demonstrated by Euripides' women characters is extreme ability in argumentation and rhetoric, a highly valued skill among Athenians of the late fifth century. Though actual women of Euripides' time would have had little or no exposure to methods of argumentation to the Pnyx, the meeting place of the assembly, Euripides' women characters argue passionately, adroitly, and most often convincingly. Indeed, Euripides may be using these characters as a mouthpiece, speaking through them directly to the audience, and if this is so is it not significant that he often chose women, those categorically denied a voice in the democracy of Athens, to speak his mind?

Medea ranks as one of Euripides' most convincing rhetoricians in her debate with Jason (446–626). Though she begins with an ad hominem attack (465), she wisely invokes the Greek ethical code of helping friends and harming enemies (Blundell, 1989, 1), asserting that Jason has violated this code and treated his friend, Medea, like an enemy (469–472). While returning to that point several more times, she also claims responsibility for saving Jason's life (476–482) and reminds him of her sacrifice in betraying her own country and people (483). After asserting his betrayal of wife and children in seeking marriage with Creon's daughter (488–491), she cleverly stresses that Jason has broken a sacred oath.

Amphora painting of Euripides' Medea murdering her child, circa 330–320 B.C.E.

(Louvre)

As all Athenians knew, Zeus protected vows, and Medea, a foreigner, here invokes the religious system of Euripides' audience. Continuing with this device, Medea concludes her speech with a dramatic appeal and an analogy: "O God, you have given to mortals a sure method / Of telling the gold that is pure from the counterfeit; / Why is there no such mark engraved upon men's bodies, / By which we could know the true ones from the false ones?" (516–519).

Jason, on the other hand, relies on bravado and condescension to carry his speech. He begins, "As for me, it seems I must be no bad speaker. / But, like a man who has a good grip of the tiller, / Reef up his sail, and so run away from under / This mouthing tempest, woman, of your bitter tongue" (522–525). He dismisses Medea's role in saving his life during the quest for the Golden Fleece, conveniently ascribing it instead to Aphrodite (527–528). After an attack on Medea's "barbarian" heritage (536–541), Jason states an obvious falsehood: he claims to be marrying Creon's daughter in the best interests of Medea and their children (548–550). Considering that any sons born to Jason and his new Greek wife would have been heirs to the Corinthian throne vis-à-vis their mother and maternal grandfather, Jason's assertion is probably untrue. In such a case, the sons of Medea and Jason would likely receive little political power or attention, at least to judge from the situation in Hippolytus, which suggests that fathers eventually mistreat sons from prior, less noble marriages.

Many other plays of Euripides use this device. Other talented women speakers include both Greek women and those most obviously "other" to a fifth-century Athenian male. Clytemnestra delivers a devastating and poignant speech to her husband in *Iphigenia at Aulis* (1146–1208). In both *Hecuba* and *Trojan Women* the downtrodden yet tenacious Hecuba demonstrates remarkable rhetorical skill. In these plays, the audience watched a foreigner, a Trojan, convince two of the most important representatives of the Greek forces (Menelaus and Agamemnon, respectively) to follow her advice. Euripides insisted that his audiences see Greek males obviously defeated or persuaded by women's rhetoric, a fact that displays the playwright's assertion of the value of women.

Admittedly, not all of Euripides' women characters act with absolute integrity. Medea, Phaedra, Hermione (in *Andromache*), and Agave (in *Bacchae*), to name a few, make destructive choices in their dealings with the gods or family. Rather than reinforcing his culture's misogynist tendencies, these artistic choices on the playwright's part prove his commitment to dramatic equity. His feminism becomes apparent in his refusal to idealize or romanticize female characters. In the face of oppression, women, like men, may act wisely or foolishly. However, Euripides demonstrates a significant degree of compassion for the difficult circumstances Athenian culture created for women.

Creusa, the central figure in *Ion,* offers a prime example of Euripides' complicated female characters. There is little doubt that Creusa's actions nearly produce tragic results. Fearing her husband's newly adopted son Ion, who in reality is her own by the god Apollo, Creusa attempts to poison the young man. The plot is discovered, and, through a clever deus ex machina, Athena reunites Ion and his mother. As Sue Blundell observes, Euripides treats this rape survivor with fairness and compassion (1995, 126). In doing so, he critiques the common treatment of actual survivors of rape; in most cases Athenian women were immediately divorced by their husbands.

Compared to other women of Greek tragedy, Euripides' female characters typically demonstrate more complexity and likely generated more interest for audiences. Compare his Medea with Sophocles' resolved yet foolhardy Antigone or Aeschylus's single-mindedly evil Clytemnestra. In Medea we find a negotiation of the good/evil dichotomy, a character who combines the most dramatic characteristics of both. Like other dramatists charged with misogyny—Eugene O'Neill or David Mamet for example—Euripides' refusal to demonize or glorify women outright belies his commitment to dramatic realism.

A valid question that may be raised in conclusion concerns the matter of exploitation. In delving so often into the circumstances and troubles with the women of his day, could one charge the playwright of merely being an opportunist, an artist who used the oppression of Athenian women to his own advantage? Though no line of reasoning may answer this question definitively, anecdotal evidence of Euripides' life may provide a speculative response. If the ancient biographies of Greek writers contain even a portion of the historical facts, Euripides clearly was fascinated by and even belonged to a philosophical community in Athens. He reputedly was friends with Socrates, with whom, as Diogenes Laertius reports, he read the work of Heraclitus (Barnes, 1987, 100). Diogenes also identifies Euripides as a student of Anaxagoras, another of the so-called pre-Socratic philosophers (Barnes, 1987, 237). His link to these thinkers suggests that, like his philosopher colleagues, Euripides was interested in challenging the social, religious, scientific, and political beliefs of his fellow citizens. As argued above, the patriarchal system of Athens oppressed women in a variety of ways, denying them citizenship, education, justice, and even the freedom of movement in their husbands' democratic city. Undoubtedly, Euripides noticed and addressed this inequity, wisely refusing to simplify matters by making all of his women characters virtuous and all of his male characters malicious. His mere association with Socrates does not prove this point, yet it reveals Euripides' membership in a specific community that valued critical thinking, social activism, and the careful evaluation of Athenian culture. Historically, readers of classical literature have privileged Socrates in this matter, most likely because his mode of inquiry seems more serious and truthful than drama. We must not, however, underestimate Euripides' own contributions to social reform in late-fifth-century Athens.

—PAUL D. STREUFERT,
UNIVERSITY OF TEXAS AT TYLER

References

Aristophanes, *Frogs,* translated by Gilbert Murray (New York: Random House, 1938).

Aristophanes, *Thesmophoriazusae,* translated by Benjamin Bickley Rogers (Cambridge, Mass.: Harvard University Press, 1955).

Aristotle, *Poetics,* translated by Richard Janko (Indianapolis: Hackett, 1987).

Jonathan Barnes, *Early Greek Philosophy* (New York: Penguin, 1987).

Mary Whitlock Blundell, *Helping Friends and Harming Enemies: A Study in Sophocles and Greek Ethics* (Cambridge: Cambridge University Press, 1989).

Sue Blundell, *Women in Ancient Greece* (Cambridge, Mass.: Harvard University Press, 1995).

Euripides, *Alcestis,* translated by Richmond Lattimore (Chicago: University of Chicago Press, 1955).

Euripides, *Hecuba,* translated by William Arrowsmith (Chicago: University of Chicago Press, 1958).

Euripides, *Helen,* translated by Lattimore (Chicago: University of Chicago Press, 1956).

Euripides, *Hippolytus,* translated by David Grene (Chicago: University of Chicago Press, 1942).

Euripides, *Ion,* translated by Ronald Frederick Willetts (Chicago: University of Chicago Press, 1958).

Euripides, *Iphigenia at Aulis,* translated by Charles R. Walker (Chicago: University of Chicago Press, 1958).

Euripides, *Medea,* translated by Rex Warner (Chicago: University of Chicago Press, 1944).

Helene P. Foley, *Female Acts in Greek Tragedy* (Princeton: Princeton University Press, 2001).

Judith P. Hallett, "Feminist Theory, Historical Periods, Literary Canons, and the Study of Greco-Roman Antiquity," in *Feminist Theory and the Classics,* edited by Nancy Sorkin Rabinowitz and Amy Richlin (New York: Routledge, 1993), pp. 44–72.

Jennifer March, "Euripides the Misogynist?" in *Euripides, Women, and Sexuality,* edited by Anton Powell (London: Routledge, 1990), pp. 32–75.

Gilbert Murray, *Euripides and His Age* (New York: Holt, 1913).

Sarah B. Pomeroy, *Goddesses, Whores, Wives, and Slaves: Women in Classical Antiquity* (New York: Schocken, 1975).

Rabinowitz, *Anxiety Veiled: Euripides and the Traffic in Women* (Ithaca, N.Y.: Cornell University Press, 1993).

Froma I. Zeitlin, "Playing the Other: Theater, Theatricality, and the Feminine in Greek Drama," in *Nothing to Do with Dionysus? Athenian Drama in its Social Context,* edited by John J. Winkler and Zeitlin (Princeton: Princeton University Press, 1990), pp. 63–96.

GREECE: HERODOTUS

Was Herodotus the father of history?

Viewpoint: Yes. Herodotus's attempt to describe fully events of the recent past and to explain the causes of those events marks the beginning of historiography in the Western European tradition.

Viewpoint: No. Although Herodotus's conception of the past as something susceptible to rational inquiry was groundbreaking, he did not provide a good example of how to put this concept into practice.

"Herodotus of Halicarnassus here displays his inquiry. . . ." These words are the opening of an extraordinary and rich prose work written around 425 B.C.E., which is usually called *The Histories* of Herodotus. The narrative ranges widely over time and place and through different forms of explanation; it not only includes descriptions of far-flung peoples and long-ago cultures and recounts strange myths and stories of fabulous creatures, but it also describes the events of a great war between Greece and Persia that had happened some sixty years before Herodotus wrote. Modern scholars call this book *The Histories,* but Herodotus himself merely said that he was displaying his "inquiry"; there was no Greek word meaning "history" when Herodotus wrote. In fact the modern term *history* is derived from *historiê,* the Greek word for "inquiry" that Herodotus uses in his opening sentence.

Herodotus, then, probably did not think that he was writing history, since history was a conceptual category that did not yet exist. Yet, his work is often identified as the first history in the European tradition, and since antiquity he has been called the "father of history." The reason for this lies in Herodotus's own statement about what he was inquiring into; he says in his opening sentence that he wants to memorialize the great deeds of Greeks and foreigners and that in particular he wants "to show why the two peoples fought with one another." This declaration, that Herodotus's purpose is to undertake rational inquiry into the causes of events, contains the seeds of the later historiographical tradition. Yet, is the concept of rational inquiry into causation enough, in and of itself, to qualify a work as history? Was Herodotus the father of history, or is his work too far removed from rational historical analysis, too filled with marvels, myths, and good storytelling in the place of logical analysis, to merit the description *history*?

Answers to these questions fall into two main camps. While there is no doubt that Herodotus's stated attempt to discover the causes of events gives him a place of crucial importance at the beginning of the European historiographical tradition, there is likewise no doubt that his work does not meet the standards of modern historical writing. He includes a great deal of material that is, from the modern historian's viewpoint, irrelevant to his topic; more importantly still, he includes forms of explanation such as divine causation and types of writing such as dramatic storytelling that have no place in the modern historian's repertoire. Thus, although almost all scholars recognize the importance of Herodotus's focus on causation, some think that while he may have laid the groundwork for historiography, he is too rooted in mythical forms of explanation, and too credulous and lacking in critical method, to be considered an historian himself. Others hold that Herodotus's contribution to the beginnings of historiography was so crucially important that it is valid to recognize him as the first historian, even though his method leaves much to be developed later.

—*Elizabeth Vandiver*

Viewpoint: Yes. Herodotus's attempt to describe fully events of the recent past and to explain the causes of those events marks the beginning of historiography in the Western European tradition.

Herodotus has been called the "father of history" ever since Cicero coined the phrase in 52 B.C.E. Of the ancient Greek writers whose work has come down to us, Herodotus was the first to take the events of the recent past as his main subject and, most crucially, to try to identify, through rational inquiry, the *causes* of those events. The germ of true historiography lies in this attempt, not just to describe events but to explain *why* things happened as and when they did. To say that Herodotus was the "father of history" does not mean that his writing displays all the techniques of documentation, verification, and source citation that modern historiographical method requires; but it does mean that his approach to narrating the past provided a crucial foundation on which later historians could build their discipline.

Herodotus's interest in the causes of events is clearly shown in his programmatic opening sentence. He says that he is recounting the results of his "inquiry" (*historiê*) "so that human achievements may not become forgotten in time, and great and marvellous deeds—some displayed by Greeks, some by barbarians—may not be without their glory; and especially to show why the two peoples warred with one another" (Book 1, Prologue). As has often been noted, this sentence displays Herodotus's debt to Homeric epic in many ways, but it also makes very clear his distance from epic. As does Homer, Herodotus wants to celebrate the glories of the past; but unlike the bard whose subject is the mythical heroes of the remote past, Herodotus's goal is to record and explain the achievements and conflicts of human beings in the recent past. Furthermore, while Homer, at the beginning of the *Iliad*, says that events fell out because of the "will of Zeus," Herodotus focuses on human actions and human responsibility. Even when he cites a divinity as the cause of an event, Herodotus normally includes a purely human cause for that event as well.

Herodotus is interested in human achievements in general, and in the causes of East-West conflict in particular. Most especially, his work is concerned with the Greco-Persian war of 490 and 480–479 B.C.E. One criticism often leveled against Herodotus is that he includes much that modern scholars would exclude from the realm of historiography, such as accounts of marvels and curiosities, geographical details, and ethnographical descriptions of various different cultures. From the modern historian's viewpoint, none of these are directly related to his topic, the war between Greeks and Persians. Some readers find Herodotus's "digressions" charming, while others find them distracting or annoying; but it is undeniable that they break the thread of the narrative in ways that are at times puzzling to the modern reader.

We should remember, however, that *digression* is a modern term for these passages; Herodotus himself did not necessarily consider these descriptions of peoples and places irrelevant to his primary topic. Herodotus was inventing, "from the ground up," a methodology of rational explanation for the causes of human events; it is unreasonable to expect him to have the modern historian's finely honed sense of what is directly relevant to the point at issue. Furthermore, to explain the nature of the Persian threat to Greece, Herodotus needed to look at other empires that had existed throughout the Mediterranean region. In his view, the conflict between Persians and Greeks was the latest example of a continuing conflict between East and West, which encompassed the Trojan War of legend as well as the Persian War of recent memory. Thus, examining the customs and governments of other cultures and their interactions with both Persians and Greeks was indeed pertinent to Herodotus's topic: the continuing conflict of East and West.

While Herodotus's work is far from being a neatly organized, purely historical account of the events and causes of the Greco-Persian War, its overall narrative shape leads directly and clearly to its culmination in the description of that conflict. The *Histories* consists of nine "books," or papyrus rolls. In Book 1, Herodotus outlines the beginnings of the conflict between East and West. Here he touches on the realm of myth by recounting legendary kidnappings and counterkidnappings of women, including the abduction of Helen by Paris, which caused the Trojan War. Book 1 also looks at the more recent past,

ANTS AS BIG AS FOXES

Below is Herodotus's description of a gold-gathering technique in the wilds of India:

CII. Other Indians dwell near the town of Caspatyrus and the Pactyic country, north of the rest of India; these live like the Bactrians; they are of all Indians the most warlike, and it is they who are sent for the gold; for in these parts all is desolate because of the sand. [2] In this sandy desert are ants, not as big as dogs but bigger than foxes; the Persian king has some of these, which have been caught there. These ants live underground, digging out the sand in the same way as the ants in Greece, to which they are very similar in shape, and the sand which they carry from the holes is full of gold. [3] It is for this sand that the Indians set forth into the desert. They harness three camels apiece, males on either side sharing the drawing, and a female in the middle: the man himself rides on the female, that when harnessed has been taken away from as young an offspring as may be. Their camels are as swift as horses, and much better able to bear burdens besides.

CIII. I do not describe the camel's appearance to Greeks, for they know it; but I shall tell them something that they do not know concerning it: the hindlegs of the camel have four thighbones and four knee-joints; its genitals are turned towards the tail between the hindlegs.

CIV. Thus and with teams so harnessed the Indians ride after the gold, being careful to be engaged in taking it when the heat is greatest; for the ants are then out of sight underground. [2] Now in these parts the sun is hottest in the morning, not at midday as elsewhere, but from sunrise to the hour of market-closing. Through these hours it is much hotter than in Hellas at noon, so that men are said to sprinkle themselves with water at this time. [3] At midday the sun's heat is nearly the same in India as elsewhere. As it goes to afternoon, the sun of India has the power of the morning sun in other lands; as day declines it becomes ever cooler, until at sunset it is exceedingly cold.

CV. So when the Indians come to the place with their sacks, they fill these with the sand and drive back as fast as possible; for the ants at once scent them out, the Persians say, and give chase. They say nothing is equal to them for speed, so that unless the Indians have a headstart while the ants were gathering, not one of them would get away. [2] They cut loose the male trace-camels, which are slower than the females, as they begin to lag, one at a time; the mares never tire, for they remember the young that they have left. Such is the tale. Most of the gold (say the Persians) is got in this way by the Indians; they dig some from mines in their country, too, but it is less abundant.

Source: Herodotus, *translated by A. D. Godley (Cambridge, Mass.: Harvard University Press, 1920), 3.102–105.*

describing the subjugation of the culturally Greek region of Ionia by Croesus, king of Lydia (ruled circa 560–546 B.C.E.), and the rise of Cyrus the Great (died 530 B.C.E.) and the Persian empire. Thus, the opening book of Herodotus's work sets the stage for the development of the narrative.

Books 2 and 3 continue the description of the Persian Empire and its conquests. Book 2 is entirely taken up with a discussion of Egypt's geography, culture, and history, but that is not entirely extraneous to Herodotus's overall theme, since one of the most important campaigns waged by a Persian emperor before the war against Greece was the conquest of Egypt by Cyrus's son Cambyses (died 522 B.C.E.). Book 3 concentrates on the accession and rule of Cambyses' successor Darius (died 486 B.C.E.). In Book 4, Herodotus recounts Darius's campaigns against Scythia and Libya. Again, we should not let Herodotus's rich ethnographical accounts of these two nations blind us to the forward movement of his narrative as a whole. Herodotus's opening sentence said that the work would not only explain why Greeks and Persians went to war with one another, but would also memorialize great and astonishing achievements of both Greeks and foreigners. Given this double purpose, the degree to which Herodotus follows a "through-line" of historical explanation is remarkable as he incorporates descriptions of foreign nations' topography and strange peoples' customs into the overarching design of his work.

In Book 5, Herodotus begins to focus his narrative more closely on events leading up to the Greco-Persian War. He describes the revolt of Ionian city-states against their Persian overlords (in 499–494 B.C.E.), when the Athenians sent aid to the Ionians and so attracted the enmity of the Persian emperor Darius. With this preparation, Herodotus moves into his account of the Persian War itself, beginning in Book 6 with a description of Darius's invasion of Greece in 490 and his defeat by the Athenians at Marathon. Books 7 through 9, the capstone of the work, focus on the second invasion of Greece by Darius's son Xerxes in 480–479. These books include Herodotus's accounts of the battles of Thermopylae, Artemisium, Salamis, Plataea, and Mycale and narrate the Persians' eventual retreat from Greece. Thus, *The Histories* moves from remote antiquity to the recent past, from a sweeping portrait of foreign lands and peoples to specific spots in Greece, and from broad ethnographical and cultural descriptions to fine details of battle. The overall pattern is clear: a narrowing down into a detailed and vivid description of the Persian War.

Far from being a hodgepodge of disconnected anecdotes, then, Herodotus's work does exactly what he says it will do in his opening sentence: it describes the great achievements and marvelous artifacts of both Greeks and barbarians, and considers in particular why and how those two groups came to war with one another. It is true that Herodotus does not write in the same style as a modern historian; but it is worth considering some of the reasons why his style contains elements that seem, to modern readers, more suited to heroic epic or to fiction than to history. Herodotus set out to write the narrative of a war that had occurred some sixty years before he wrote (we do not know the exact dates of the composition of *The Histories,* but the work was probably completed around 425 B.C.E.). This means that Herodotus had to depend, as sources, on the memories of very old eyewitnesses or else on the secondhand accounts given by those eyewitnesses' children and grandchildren. And when he wanted to recount events leading up to the Persian War, his sources became even more problematic.

The modern historian, writing about events of 100 or 150 years ago, can turn to newspaper archives, to contemporaneous books, and to other written sources. While Herodotus probably had access to some written source material (perhaps including some official Persian records), for the most part he must have relied on oral tradition, on the accounts handed down for several generations in families and communities. Given this limitation on his source material, it is no surprise that Herodotus casts many of his accounts in the form of stories that seem to the modern reader more akin to myth or to folktale than to "history." To take a famous example, Herodotus quotes conversations between Croesus, king of Lydia, and the Athenian sage Solon (1.30–32). Of course, Herodotus could not possibly know, in circa 430 B.C.E., what Croesus said or thought in circa 560 B.C.E. Yet, oral tradition preserves the memory of the past in the form of stories, and we cannot fault Herodotus for working within the tradition available to him. Rather, we should give him credit for what stands out about his work: the attempt to organize, sift, and evaluate different traditions in order to discover how one event led to another, and how apparently unconnected occurrences have bearing upon one another. When we consider Herodotus as the founder of European historiography, it does not matter that he includes fictional conversations between Croesus and Solon; what matters is that he recognized that the defeat of Croesus by Cyrus, king of Persia, was a crucial step in the development of the Persian empire and that the Persians would not have been in a position to attack Greece some sixty years later had not Cyrus and Croesus gone to war with one another. This use of rational analysis to discover a chain of causation is the crucial aspect in Herodotus's contribution to historiography.

Next in importance to Herodotus's recognition that causation is discoverable by rational inquiry, we should place his attempt to compare different sources with one another. Again, while he falls short of the standards of modern historians, the important point is that he made the attempt at all. Herodotus repeatedly tells us where he got his information and who his informants were, and cites different explanations of the same events when he has heard different versions. Perhaps most notably, Herodotus several times cites explanations that he himself finds unbelievable. The importance of this methodological decision on Herodotus's part can scarcely be overestimated; he has recognized the importance of preserving the evidence, of recording what he has heard and presenting it for his readers (and for future historians) to evaluate on their own. Unlike the Homeric bard, Herodotus does not claim divine inspiration; unlike the omniscient narrator of a novel, he does not in effect say to his readers "take my word for it." Instead, he cites his sources, even when he disagrees with them: "These men made a statement which I myself do not believe, though others may. . . ." (4.42). This is an extremely important step in the development of historiography and is also a strong guarantee of Herodotus's trustworthiness.

The question of Herodotus's reliability has been raised since antiquity. He includes many details, especially of "natural history," that are not believable–for instance, that there are fox-sized ants in India that gather gold (3.102–105)–and modern archaeology has shown that even some of his less far-fetched statements are incorrect. Yet, we must be careful here not to import anachronistic standards of the historian's task into our evaluation of Herodotus's accomplishment. Herodotus reports what his sources told him, and we should not fault him if, when he was given false information and had no means of checking its accuracy, he relies upon that evidence. In his account of Egypt, for instance, his interpretation of a supposed inscription on the pyramid of Cheops is ludicrously inaccurate (2.125). But there is no reason to think that the inaccuracy was Herodotus's own rather than his interpreter's; Herodotus does not claim to have read hieroglyphics himself, and so he had to rely on what he was told. Again, the modern historian has a whole panoply of resources for cross-checking and verifying facts, and we correctly fault a modern historian who does not do so. But Herodotus would not have had such resources available to him. The fact that he cites differing accounts *when he can* indicates that he recognized the importance of verification by more than one source; he cannot be held responsible for mistakes in sources that he was unable to verify.

While archaeology may have pointed out some of Herodotus's mistakes, it has also verified his status as an "honest reporter" in some very surprising ways. Space requires us to consider only two of these: the Bisitun Inscription and Scythian royal burials.

In Book 3 (61–88), Herodotus relates the story of the death of Cyrus's son Cambyses and the accession of Darius to the throne of Persia. Herodotus tells us that Cambyses had killed his own brother Smerdis, but that after Cambyses' death an imposter pretending to be Smerdis usurped the throne. This imposter was exposed and overthrown by seven conspirators, and one of these, Darius, became king after the false Smerdis's death. Herodotus's version of these events finds remarkable verification in the "Bisitun Inscription," a trilingual carving set up by Darius himself and rediscovered in 1836. This inscription gives an account of the conspiracy against Smerdis and the accession of Darius. Though there are some important differences from Herodotus's version, the inscription agrees in many of its details with Herodotus's account: for instance, that Smerdis was an imposter and that Cambyses had killed his real brother (points that modern historians find unlikely). Furthermore, the names of six of the seven conspirators correspond to the names Herodotus gives.

We cannot know if the Bisitun Inscription is independent verification of Herodotus's account, or if it was Herodotus's source; copies of this inscription existed elsewhere in the Persian empire, and it is possible that Herodotus used one such copy. But whether he drew upon this inscription itself or upon other sources, the Bisitun Inscription argues forcefully for Herodotus's accuracy. He did not simply invent his version of Darius's accession; he based it upon Persian sources, whether documentary or oral, and he reproduced those sources with a remarkable degree of accuracy.

The Bisitun Inscription is not the only instance in which archaeology supports Herodotus. Twentieth-century archaeology has confirmed many points that were once assumed to be impossible in Herodotus's description of Scythia and the Scythians. For example, in his description of Scythian royal burial customs (4.71–72), Herodotus says that horses and attendants were buried along with the king. The discovery of Scythian royal burial mounds has proven that Herodotus's description is remarkably accurate. Details that used to be seen as evidence of Herodotus's overcredulity or even of his dishonesty now offer the best proof of his fidelity to his sources.

To sum up, Herodotus was not a modern historian. His work includes as much ethnography, geography, and folktale as it does history. But the kernel of historical writing and historical method is without question there; in his attempt to sort and weigh evidence, to recount accurately what his informants told him, to report different explanations of the same events, and, first and foremost, to describe "why they went to war with one another," Herodotus does indeed deserve to be called the "father of history."

–ELIZABETH VANDIVER,
WHITMAN COLLEGE

Viewpoint:
No. Although Herodotus's conception of the past as something susceptible to rational inquiry was groundbreaking, he did not provide a good example of how to put this concept into practice.

Herodotus is the first author known to have applied the term *history* to a narrative of past events. For that reason alone he deserves the title he is often given, the "father of history." Yet, as a model for future historians to follow in the gathering of evidence and the composing of historical accounts, Herodotus comes up short in many respects. *History (historiê)* is a word of Greek origin meaning "inquiry" or "adjudication." By using this term Herodotus advertises his account as the result of rational processes. Just as a judge gathers evidence, listens to different sides of an issue, and tries to come to a fair and impartial decision about the truth of a matter, so Herodotus portrays himself as a seeker of truth, hunting down the best sources of information, seeing things for himself wherever possible, and solving discrepancies between sources using the power of reason.

Applying rational methods to the study of the past, or even the notion of doing so, was an important innovation in thinking about the past. Before Herodotus's time, the past was not generally considered a subject to be investigated critically. What people knew of the past was enshrined in poetic sagas such as Homer's *Iliad* and *Odyssey,* recited by bards who claimed the inspiration of the gods as their source of knowledge. In addition, governments, powerful families, and religious authorities manufactured and maintained accounts of past events, either in oral or written form, which invariably justified and helped to support their powerful positions in society. None of these sources of knowledge about the past was open to question. Like the accounts of past events in the Bible, no contrary versions of events were recorded, and no possibility that the version of the past on offer might be incorrect or incomplete was ever admitted.

Herodotus, who hailed from the city of Halicarnassus in western Anatolia, was influenced by the successes of early Greek scientists and philosophers, many of whom also lived and wrote in the Greek cities of the western Anatolian coast. Herodotus believed that techniques of observation and calculation employed by these early thinkers could also be applied to the realm of past human events. Though he stood at the threshold of a new way of looking at the past, however, Herodotus could not completely divorce himself from old ways of thinking. Herodotus's uncle, Panyassis, was, like Homer, an epic poet who wrote stirring lays about the great deeds of the Greek heroes. From Panyassis, Herodotus seems to have acquired not only a flair for storytelling but also an appetite for the marvelous and the fantastic. He also seems to have inherited the notion that the purpose of telling tales about the past was not to record the truth or to examine the way that human societies function but to glorify the great deeds of national heroes. This attitude is evident in the very first sentence of his *Histories:* "Herodotus of Halicarnassus here displays his inquiry *[historiê],* so that human achievements may not become forgotten in time, and great and marvellous deeds – some displayed by Greeks, some by barbarians, may not be without their glory" (Book 1, prologue). In many respects, though he calls his work a history, a better way to think about it might be as an epic poem written in prose.

In point of fact, a good deal of the material in Herodotus's account is thinly disguised myth. Herodotus begins his *Histories* with an explanation of why the East and the West (and, ultimately, the Persians and the Greeks) first came into conflict. He launches into a string of stories, which he ascribes to "learned Persians" (1.1) and "the Phoenicians" (1.5), about a series of abductions of women that people from either side of the East-West divide perpetrated on each other: first the Phoenicians kidnap the Greek princess Io; the Greeks in retribution kidnap the Phoenician princess Europa and the Colchian princess Medea, and so on (1.1–5). In reality these are not Persian or Phoenician stories at all but transparently adulterated Greek myth. In the traditional versions of these myths, Io was not kidnapped by Phoenician pirates but was instead transformed into a cow by her lover, the god Zeus, and driven from Greece in bovine form by Zeus's jealous wife Hera. Europa was not kidnapped by Greeks but by Zeus himself, who took the form of a bull and carried her over the waters on his back from her home to the island of Crete. Herodotus has rationalized these myths: he has removed the gods and the magical metamorphoses, but myths they remain.

The opposite process is visible even more frequently in Herodotus: he often takes real historical events and narrates them in a way that is clearly fictional and mythologizing. For instance, after telling the tales of the kidnapped women, Herodotus embarks on the story of King Croesus of Lydia. Croesus appears to have been a real king who ruled a wealthy empire in western Anatolia only fifty years or so before Herodotus was born. Some of the events that Herodotus associated with Croesus may have actually happened, but the way Herodotus tells his story is obviously fictionalized. He reports in detail a meeting Croesus had with a famous visitor, Solon, the great lawgiver of Athens (1.29–33). After showing Solon all the riches in his palace, Croesus asks Solon to name the man he thought was the most fortunate human being ever. Croesus expects the answer to be himself. Yet, Solon responds with the name of an obscure Athenian who died bravely in battle. Croesus, incredulous, asks the question again, but again Solon disappoints him in his response. Finally, in exasperation, Croesus asks Solon why he, Croesus, should not be considered the most fortunate. Solon responds with a lengthy sermon, which Herodotus reports verbatim, to the effect that no man should be called fortunate until he has ended his life fortunate. The lesson for Croesus is that his current good fortune is no guarantee of future good fortune. Croesus dismisses Solon as a fool, but the future course of Croesus's life proves the wisdom of Solon's remarks. Soon afterward, Croesus consults the oracle of

Bust of the Greek historian Herodotus, author of a systematic study of the Greco-Persian wars from 500 to 479 B.C.E.

(National Museum, Naples)

Apollo at Delphi, asking whether he should wage war on the mighty Persian empire. The god responds that if Croesus attacks the Persians he will destroy a great empire. With supreme confidence Croesus leads his armies against the Persians and does end up destroying a great empire: his own. Croesus ends his days as a captive of the Persian king, finally realizing–too late–the truth in Solon's warning.

In addition to being full of implausible dramatic detail, the entire tenor of the Croesus story betrays a very traditional and moralizing strain of thought that pervades Herodotus's histories. The moral of Croesus's story, that success breeds arrogance, arrogance breeds recklessness, and recklessness inevitably brings on disaster, is a traditional lesson that can be found in the earliest Greek poetry, and this same lesson is preached by Herodotus again and again in the way he casts his narrative of historical events. In fact, one of the evident motives Herodotus has in telling the Croesus story is to foreshadow the stories of even weightier figures to come. The culmination of Herodotus's account is the narrative of the second Persian invasion of Greece, led by the mighty Persian king Xerxes. Xerxes is the most powerful man in the world, the lord of a vast and wealthy empire that stretches from the Indus valley to the Mediterranean, from the Danube to the Nile. Like Croesus he is very conscious of his exalted position. Like Croesus he imagines that no force on earth, to say nothing of the tiny Greek cities, could stand up to him. Like Croesus his arrogance leads him to disaster when his huge army and navy are crushed by the plucky, tenacious, and god-fearing Greeks. Xerxes' story is Croesus's story writ large, and the moral is the same. Moralizing and foreshadowing are acceptable elements of epic poetry and novels, but not rational historiography.

The stories of both Croesus and Xerxes display another nonhistorical feature of Herodotus' account, the intervention of the supernatural. Herodotus's tales are full of oracles, portents, future-telling dreams, and visitations of gods and heroes. As in the story of Croesus, Herodotus frequently quotes prophecies from the shrine of Apollo at Delphi. Indeed, it is thought that one of Herodotus's chief sources of information was the official accounts of the priests at Delphi. As one might suspect with such a source, the prophecies Herodotus reports always turn out to be true. To Herodotus's traditional way of thinking, the defeat of Persia was the result of divine vengeance against Persian arrogance and excess, and the signs of this divine partisanship are frequently put on display. At one point in Xerxes' invasion a storm catches a portion of the Persians' enormous fleet and destroys it, leveling the odds somewhat for the vastly outnumbered Greeks. Herodotus's opinion on this is that "God was indeed doing everything possible to reduce the size of the Persian fleet and bring it down to the size of the Greek" (8.13). A true historian exhausts all natural explanations before resorting to the supernatural. Herodotus shows no such compunction.

Another flaw in Herodotus's methods is his low standard of pertinence. Like his uncle, Herodotus is a storyteller, a garrulous raconteur, and he often diverges from the main thread of his narrative to engage in long-winded digressions, seemingly for no reason aside from the pleasure of telling the story. Examples of this are almost too numerous to choose from, and would stretch the scope of this article to relate in detail, but to mention just a few, there is the interesting way that the Athenian tyrant Peisistratus reached the throne (1.59–64), the madness and gruesome death of king Cleomenes of Sparta (6.74–84), and the lengthy discussion of the causes of the yearly flooding of the Nile (2.19.32). If any of the information in these digressions is pertinent to the main topic of the work, Herodotus does not bother to point out the significance. This digressive tendency is even more importantly on view in the structure of the history as a whole. The ostensible subject of his work, the war with Persia, occupies only the last four of the nine books of the *Histories.* The rest is devoted to a rambling panorama of topics in which, apparently, anything having to do with the Mediterranean world and the Near East is fair game. He devotes an entire book (Book 2) to the history and geography of Egypt. The topic is marginally pertinent since Egypt was an important part of the Persian empire, but nothing justifies the great detail and breadth of Herodotus's exposition of nearly every aspect of Egyptian culture and history. Apparently, the urge to share his unique knowledge with his audience overcame any sense of historical relevance.

One of the things that Herodotus is often praised for are these travels, as well as his general desire to see firsthand the things that he is writing about. Unfortunately, Herodotus seems to have brought to these ethnographic parts of his work the same tendency toward mythologizing that is evident elsewhere. His descriptions of foreign peoples tend toward caricatures, with their customs and practices drawn in a way to exaggerate the contrast between them and the Greeks. Perhaps the best example of this is what he says about the Egyptians (2.35):

> The Egyptians themselves in their manners and customs seem to have reversed the ordinary practices of mankind. For instance, women attend market and are employed in trade, while men stay at home and do the weaving. In weaving the normal way is to work the threads of the weft upwards, but the Egyptians work them downwards. Men in Egypt carry loads on their heads, women on their shoulders; women urinate standing up, men sitting down. . . .

All of this, together with similar passages detailing the customs of other peoples, serves to emphasize the idea that the Greeks represent the norm in human affairs as opposed to the deviations and distortions of their neighbors. As such, Herodotus's ethnography must be counted as part of his ahistorical bias rather than as evidence of his historical acumen.

On this subject, it is also worth noting that some scholars, citing discrepancies between Herodotus's accounts of these foreign places and the archaeological findings, have argued that Herodotus did not actually visit many of the places, including Egypt, that he claimed to have visited. If that is true, then Herodotus's accounts of these regions are not only biased but fraudulent. Herodotus would be convicted of playacting the role of an honest researcher in order to increase the immediacy and believability of his account. In the same vein, one prominent scholar, Detlev Fehling, has argued that one of Herodotus's practices for which he is often compared to modern historians, the frequent citing and comparing of differing accounts for events, is likewise fictitious. Fehling believes that Herodotus manufactures these accounts himself in order to add interest and to portray himself as the impartial adjudicator of past events. An example would be the passage already cited from the beginning of the work dealing with the kidnapped women. As we have seen, Herodotus ascribes these stories to Persian and Phoenician sources, when clearly the stories are Greek in origin.

Some scholars believe that it is possible to strip away all that is mythical, fictional, biased, and exaggerated from Herodotus's narratives to find a kernel of well-researched and reliable historical material. But that is wishful thinking. Herodotus is our earliest surviving historical text. There is much in his account for which he is our only source; thus there is no way to check the veracity of the bulk of what he claims. Even for historical events within his own lifetime, however, Herodotus can be shown to be careless with the facts. For instance, in discussing Xerxes' invasion, Herodotus places the total number of Persian military forces, both naval and infantry, at an incredible 2,317,610. Estimates of modern historians are that Herodotus inflated the number of Persian troops by a factor of ten or more in an effort to make the Greek victory seem all the more glorious. What trust can we put in a researcher who would invent such a number?

In sum, while Herodotus's *Histories* is endlessly entertaining and stands as an unparalleled monument of Greek thinking about the place of Greece in the world at the start of the golden age of classical Greece, it is difficult to hold up his methods as models of historical research. While he can be given credit for introducing, or at least popularizing, important ideas about how to approach the past on a rational basis, he cannot be said to have provided a good example of how to put those ideas into practice.

–WILLIAM E. HUTTON,
COLLEGE OF WILLIAM AND MARY

References

Detlev Fehling, *Herodotus and his "Sources": Citation, Invention, and Narrative Art,* translated by J. G. Howie (Leeds: Francis Cairns, 1989).

Charles W. Fornara, *Herodotus: An Interpretative Essay* (Oxford: Clarendon Press, 1971).

Thomas Harrison, *Divinity and History: The Religion of Herodotus* (Oxford: Clarendon Press, 2000).

François Hartog, *The Mirror of Herodotus,* translated by Janet Lloyd (Berkeley: University of California Press, 1988).

Herodotus, *The Histories,* translated by Aubrey de Sélincourt (London: Penguin, 2003).

Donald Lateiner, *The Historical Method of Herodotus* (Toronto: University of Toronto Press, 1989).

Arnaldo Momigliano, "The Place of Herodotus in the History of Historiography," in *Studies in Historiography* (New York: Harper & Row, 1966), pp. 127–142.

James S. Romm, *Herodotus* (New Haven: Yale University Press, 1998).

Rosalind Thomas, *Herodotus in Context: Ethnography, Science and the Art of Persuasion* (Cambridge: Cambridge University Press, 2000).

K. H. Waters, *Herodotos the Historian: His Problems, Methods and Originality* (London & Sydney: Croom Helm, 1985).

GREECE: HESIOD

Was Hesiod an oral poet?

Viewpoint: Yes. Hesiod composed his songs without the use of writing. He did not inherit a written text, and he did not transmit one to others through writing.

Viewpoint: No. Hesiod composed his songs in writing; this non-oral method of composition might have included the use of some written text inherited by him.

There is no strict agreement among scholars as to what oral poetry is. On the whole, hardly anyone denies that at various periods of history there were, and in some places there still are, singers or simply poets who can compose lengthy poems without the aid of writing and then perform them either as fixed oral narratives or as oral narratives that dwell on the key elements of a story but may differ significantly and creatively from one performance to the next. However, the moment these ideas are applied in a more specific, philological way, to the poetry of Homer and Hesiod, swords are drawn, and words take wing and combative aim.

Milman Parry did the most influential research on oral poetry in the early part of the twentieth century. He studied the heroic songs of Serbo-Croatian singers in a systematic way, combining meticulous fieldwork with rigorous linguistic study of the texts he recorded. Parry came to several conclusions about the nature of true oral poetry. Only the briefest reference can be made to them here. One of the main features of oral composition is the use of formulaic expressions. Readers may recall Homer's "white-armed Hera," "unharvested sea," "cloud-gathering Zeus," and "So he spoke. . . ." Similar formulas and even more complex ones are the distinguishing feature of both Serbo-Croatian and Homeric poetry. Parry discovered that the singers he studied did not perform a text they had memorized, a fixed text, that is. Instead they employed traditional language and traditional formulaic devices to create a new song each time. It has been said that the illiterate bards of Serbo-Croatia did not have a concept of a fixed text for epic song. In addition to formulaic phrases or formulaic clusters of expressions, the singer had inherited and also developed a thematic technique of construction of oral narrative. Preparing a feast, celebrating a victory, burying a warrior, and putting on one's armor are good examples of thematic usage.

To Herodotus, Hesiod and Homer were the two oldest poets of Greece. Herodotus speaks twice of Hesiod and Homer as the two greatest and oldest (2.53, 3.32). He seems to follow a definite chronology, perhaps one of his own, and he places both poets four hundred years before his time (885 B.C.E. counting from his own birth; 845 B.C.E. counting from his floruit, according to the *Marmor Parium*). Many modern scholars, mostly following the tradition created by Aristarchus, give Homer a place of greater antiquity, and, especially in recent years, they assign to Hesiod the date of 700 B.C.E. as a sort of median number for his presumed life span.

—Apostolos N. Athanassakis

Viewpoint:
Yes. Hesiod composed his songs without the use of writing. He did not inherit a written text, and he did not transmit one to others through writing.

Ever since Milman Parry conducted his researches in the oral poetry of the South Slavic bards of former Yugoslavia, all early epic has come under new and powerful reexamination. Many fascinating and compelling arguments have been put forth to show that the Homeric epics were composed and transmitted orally, that is, without the help of writing. What about Hesiod? In his case, the enormously important dynamics of the heroic society are lacking. There are no great feasts and no honorific portions of choice meat for the singer. There are, in fact, no heroes, and *kleos* (glory) as well as *timê* (honor), the two most pivotal imperatives of the heroic way of life, register negatively on Hesiod's scale of social values. Indeed, violence, which is inherent to the notion of heroic warfare, is the principal cause of ruin and even decadence in Hesiod's story of man as mirrored in the myth of the five generations (*Works and Days,* 109–196).

In many ways, Hesiod was an oral poet, but not entirely the oral poet who could fit into the model that walks out of the instructive researches of Parry, A. B. Lord, and so many other investigators of twentieth-century oral poetry. To begin with, the realities of twentieth-century Yugoslavia may echo, but not necessarily reproduce, the realities within which the singers of Archaic Greece practiced their highly appreciated profession. Hesiod's encounter with the Muses, his empowering vision, fits much more into the beliefs of polytheistic ancient Greece and saint-filled Christian Greece than into the beliefs and ways of a mostly Muslim Serbo-Croatian society. The Muses told Hesiod to go forth and sing the gods and sing the truth. The Muses gave Hesiod no written text, no tablets. That is a powerful argument for the oral character of Hesiod's poetry, for the living word and not the written one being passed on to audiences of his own age and, through them, to their inheritors of subsequent ages. The fact that Hesiod was born in Askra, Boeotia, a village so close to Thebes, the mythic and near-historical center for the importation of the Phoenician alphabet into Greece, may not have been a decisive factor in the way Hesiod learned and practiced his poetry. In our own age, there clearly exist practitioners of classical music within a stone's throw from rockers, rap virtuosos, synthesizers, inventive blues singers, and even outmoded country-western lyricists. Hesiod may have chosen to tell the story of how he met the Muses in order to signal to his listeners that he was a traditional oral singer, and not one of the new converts to a foreign importation.

It is clear that Hesiod inherited a great deal of mythology about the universe, the gods, the powers, and the hierarchies of powers. In his *Theogony,* however, he sings of the cosmos and of the generations of the gods in ways that bespeak a theorist and a driven proponent of a new and revolutionary ideology: a whole system of materialist theology founded on traditional lore. His descriptions of Hecate's jurisdiction, of the battle of Zeus against the Titans, as well as of the battle of Zeus against the monstrous Typhoeus, are products of his own imagination. Hesiod must have rehearsed these themes and memorized them many times before he performed them for his audiences. Mnemosyne, Memory, is the mother of all transmission and delivery, including transmission and delivery that is of the creative and innovative kind. Hesiod's underworld (*Theogony,* 721–814) contains traditional fundamental concepts and entities and serves as a jail for the defeated enemies of Zeus. The murky Tartaros, where the roots of the earth and the sea lie, Hades and Persephone, and the awesome river Styx were not invented by Hesiod. However, the tripartite model of the world, the spatial accommodations for Atlas, Day, Night, Sleep, and for the Titans themselves, all seem to originate with the poet and to be ideal for dynamic oral composition and performance. As in Homer so, too, in Hesiod, the merciless arrays of names and lengthy catalogues deserve special attention. Of the many daughters of Nereus, the Old Man of the Sea, Homer names thirty-four (*Iliad,* 18.37–51). In the *Theogony,* Hesiod names fifty-two daughters of Nereus (240–264) and, before his listeners have a chance to recover from this mnemonic feat, he proceeds, in a more charitable and playful mood, to introduce by name only forty-two of the three thousand daughters of Okeanos. With a small leap of the imagination we can recover the tension, the suspense, and the humor this great singer created with his well-calculated tactics. Here the use of the alphabet, welcome perhaps before performance and, from our usual point of view, essential during it, could be debated. The preacher's or the professor's small index card with acronyms and other reminders might have easily had its analogue in Hesiod's day. Every profession has its secrets, its tricks. Yet, it is highly unlikely that Hesiod did any such thing. The lists fit into the performative dynamics and techniques of oral composition perfectly. The skilled and highly gifted poet deployed them to provoke, scare, and defeat his competitors and also to score major points among his audience. At such moments in a given performance, listeners no doubt became more interactive with the poet and cheered him on to surpass ordinary expectations.

In the *Works and Days,* Hesiod refers to his concept of Eris (Strife) as he expressed it in his earlier poem, the *Theogony,* and he clearly returns to his account of the creation of the first woman, again in the *Theogony* (570–616), to revise significant details. One usually revises a written text. His method here is almost scholarly. Is it possible that, by the time Hesiod composed the *Works and Days,* his *Theogony* had been written down? Be that as it may, the orality of the two poems differs almost as much as their subject matter. What Hesiod himself did not invent in the *Works and Days* must have come to him not only from other oral poems but also from the traditional wisdom lore of his native Boeotia as well as from the lore of other parts of Greece. Wisdom literature on a great variety of agricultural tasks and related skills, equipment and tools, of course, antedates Hesiod. Instruction in such matters as well as use of astronomical information for the construction of a timetable of the farmer's activities may have been observed and verified and even catalogued more poetically by Hesiod, but these topics belong to his cultural inheritance. The instructions are not thorough, but they are useful, pithy, and easy to memorize.

Hesiod knew stretches of set text of oral literature. His main theme of the interdependence of work and justice was persistent, yet allusive and digressive enough to allow him to pack much ready-made folk wisdom into the body of his fervid and rigid social, economic, and legal thought. Here the poet made free use of oral lore and oral song that may not have been affected by the improvisational and performative dynamics of Parry's model. He took pieces of oral text that he arranged and presented orally. He may have even introduced variations for each performance, but these variations would, most likely, represent small omissions, small additions, and changes in the order of presentation.

Hesiod's much-admired descriptions of winter and summer have the ring of the folk song or, at least, owe much to the tradition of widely known folk songs. Here, too, most of the oral text adopted by Hesiod was set, and it must have been largely set for his performances. Would song contests allow this practice? The slight variations and the skilled arrangement, as well as the almost obsessively recurring sermon on work, justice, and shame, might indeed win the admiration of audiences.

By the late Archaic Age, Greeks must have had the ability to appreciate the articulation of shared traditional values, familiar to them from song, yet now reinvigorated and given coherence by a powerful new singer. They had heard expressions such as "Give to those who give to you, never to those who do not" or even "No shame in work but plenty of it in sloth." A taboo such as "Never piss into springs" was probably something that Hesiod's compatriots had heard many times, perhaps in the infamous smithy of Askra where men thronged for idle talk. Such phrases are usually whole lines or couplets. To change them is to rob them of their power and their universal acceptance. Hesiod took as many of these as he could fit into his poem. He took them orally, and gave them orally.

Hesiod won a great prize, an eared tripod, in the song contest in honor of Amphidamas of Chalkis, Euboea. He brought it back to Askra and dedicated it to the Muses of Helicon on the very spot where they taught him "flowing song." Hesiod does not mention writing anywhere. Even if he was familiar with the new revolutionary art, he stayed away from it, and he made no use of it in the composition of his songs.

The journey to Chalkis took Hesiod over sixty feet of water, which he claims is the extent of all the sailing he had done. There is humor in

Bust of Hesiod, often called the "father of Greek didactic poetry"

(National Museum, Naples)

this statement because the poet delivers it in the middle of that section of the *Works and Days* in which he gives advice on ships, sea trade, and seasonal navigation (618–694). This sort of contextualization of Hesiod's ignorance of the sea must not mislead us into believing that the poet was disavowing his limited knowledge of the sea. Hesiod's father came to Askra, Boeotia, on a black ship, fleeing grim poverty. The poetry of this passage is not what the young men of Askra were likely to sing or to have learned from their fathers. Common sense here would dictate that much of the poetry of this passage, hence much of the song, Hesiod learned from his father. The section on navigation (618–694) contains the information about Hesiod's father. It also mentions the poet's journey to Chalkis, Euboea. Awareness of the heroic age is compressed into a terse reference to the gathering of the Greek forces at Aulis, the port from which Hesiod sailed to Euboea (650–653). If we set aside Hesiod's autobiographical lines (633–640 and 650–661), the first part of the section on navigation consists of forty-three lines, while the second part (663–694) amounts to a not disproportionate thirty-one lines. The beginning lines of the section, "And if longing seizes you for sailing the stormy seas / when the Pleiades flee mighty Orion . . . ," sound like the beginning of a folk song. In fact, lines 618–645 may represent a song inherited from Hesiod's immigrant father as well as a few reflections and sentiments of his talented son, Hesiod.

The second part of the discourse on navigation consists mostly of wisdom lore: do this, don't do that! Yet, no one who knows Greek poetics and song, ancient and not so ancient, can fail to see how lines 686–694 must have touched and instructed the hearts of Hesiod's listeners everywhere in Greece:

> Man is a fool, his soul's his purse
> dying in the waves is harsh death
> hear advice well-given, friend
> don't load all your goods on hollow ships
> leave more behind than you load on your boat.
>
> (*Works and Days,* 686–690)

In the section on navigation, we have a perfect example of tradition carried on and reinvigorated. Father sings, son learns, and son integrates into song his own experiences and his own talent. That is what oral singing is all about. Yes, there is meter, and there are formulaic expressions, but, more than that, there is integration of the old with the new, memory and experience alive in the presence of people who share, applaud, and reward.

–APOSTOLOS N. ATHANASSAKIS,
UNIVERSITY OF CALIFORNIA,
SANTA BARBARA

Viewpoint:
No. Hesiod composed his songs in writing; this non-oral method of composition might have included the use of some written text inherited by him.

The *Theogony* and the *Works and Days* were composed at different periods during Hesiod's life. The alphabet existed, and Hesiod could not have been ignorant of it. His *Theogony* is orally robust. His *Works and Days* may have benefited more from the threat of the new invention. He may have even had strong feelings about recording and performing orally what the new technocrats were threatening to monopolize. These questions cannot be settled. One thing is certain, Hesiod inherited oral poetry and proceeded to produce more of it in a more self-conscious and deliberate way than his teachers and ancestors.

According to mythic tradition, it was Kadmos, the Phoenician founder of Thebes, who brought the alphabet to Greece. Hesiod mentions Kadmos (*Theogony,* 975) and his daughter, Semele (940). From scholiasts' references to his works, we know that the story of Phoinix and Europa appeared in one of his works (fragment 140 in Merkelbach/West). He also tells us that some of the great men of the heroic age met their death "fighting over the flocks of Oedipus, at Seven-gated Thebes, in the land of Kadmos" (*Works and Days,* 163–164). Unlike Herodotus who, centuries later, shows knowledge of the "Phoenician letters" as the models of the Greek letters (5.38), Hesiod does not mention writing anywhere. In view of a famous passage in Homer that clearly refers to the writing of a letter (*Iliad,* 6.166ff.), all this is rather astonishing. On the other hand, nowhere in the *Works and Days* does the poet mention cheese or olives, so familiar to him and so important to the local economy. Sometime in the early part of the eighth century B.C.E., young Dorian recruits were using the young Greek alphabet to carve obscenities into the rocks of the acropolis of Thera (I G XII.iii. 536, Buck, *Dialects,* p. 305). There is no compelling evidence whatever that the alphabet had not reached Boeotia by this time and that Hesiod did not know it. Quite the contrary, a man of Hesiod's intelligence, born to an immigrant Ionian family of some modest substance, may have applied himself industriously to the learning of the new skill, a skill that clearly offered new possibilities to those who could produce text for songs, traditionally oral text, of course. Yet, the question is not whether the alphabet was known or available to Hesiod, but, rather, whether he made use of it to compose his poetry.

The strongest arguments for the assertion that Hesiod made use of writing may be inferred not so much from the way his poetry compares with that of Homer with regard to percentage, distribution, and deployment of the formulaic material of traditional oral poetry—which is indeed embedded in his work—but rather from the progression of his *arguments,* from their ideological *orientation,* from the absence of similes, and so forth, from his omission of the *psychai* (souls) in his elaborate underworld, from his purposeful elevation of Hecate, and from his persistently didactic intent. He begins his *Theogony* with an invocation of the Muses and the story of how he met them. He explains how they empowered him to be a singer. Then he tells of their birth and of their names not to glorify them but to show how singers are related to kings in more ways than one. In the myth of the succession of the divine generations he methodically promotes the argument that cunning/intelligence is a more powerful weapon than physical might. Zeus combines both and thus he comes to be the supreme god. The argument is further elaborated in the myth of Prometheus, whose overreaching intelligence is not matched by the might necessary to unseat Zeus. Homer does not build this sort of argument, certainly not in Hesiod's systematic, philosophical way. In the *Works and Days,* Hesiod suddenly recalls that he had mentioned Eris (Strife) in the *Theogony,* and he then proceeds to demonstrate its duality: destructive Eris as opposed to competitive and productive Eris. Hesiod couches his argument for the interdependence of work and justice in a way that reverberates throughout the major parts of his poem. This threading through, this weaving of an argument, and this navigation of complexities does not suggest a preliterate manner of composition.

The idea that there is a good and a bad Eris, a good and a bad hope, and a good and a bad woman, that is, the duality of entities, seems to foreshadow the more-daring speculations of the natural philosophers of Ionia. Such a way of thinking seems more proximate to the time when great thinkers made use of writing. From Hesiod's *Theogony,* we learn that Erebos (Darkness) and Night, both the offspring of Chaos, mated to produce luminous Ether and Day (123–125). Further on in the *Theogony,* we read that Night gave birth to Death, to Sleep, to Dreams, as well as to a host of ills, including Old Age and Strife (211–225). We have a complex strain of thought here, a keen desire to produce a generative chart of various powers, various physical and social realities that confront man. The chances that this sort of poetic narrative was composed orally are slim. The question also arises as to what audience would be amused or captivated by the contortions, the omissions, and, in general, by the abstruse leaps of the singer's imagination in a narrative of this kind. The use of writing and reading (recitation) cannot be excluded here.

Awareness of the connection between some words and of their derivation even at the level of folk etymology does not presuppose literacy. The best example in Homer has to do with the origin of the name of Odysseus (*Odyssey,* 19.405–412). Hesiod, however, uses both etymology and folk etymology in subtler and more imaginative ways. So it is with his use of *aêdôn* (nightingale/singer) and *aoidos* (singer) in his story of the hawk and the nightingale (*Works and Days,* 202–211). His explanation of the names of the Titans (*Theogony,* 207–210) and of the Cyclopes (*Theogony,* 144–146) shows not only skill but also insightful and didactic preoccupation with language. In his account of the birth of Aphrodite, Hesiod weaves his views of the origin of the name of the goddess and of two key epithets applied to her into a new story (*Theogony,* 190–200). In this case, folk etymology becomes part of the creative forces that shape the poem. All this has the makings of deliberate literate composition.

Hesiod employs the traditional language of archaic poetry. In details, such as meter and its effect on the various phonemic concessions words make when they are made subject to metrical necessity, Hesiod's poetry does not differ in any significant way from Homer's heroic epics. Yet, once a poet adopts a particular language as his medium of expression, the poet will, if anything, strive to be true to the conventions of the medium, to speak, as it were, the language as perfectly as possible. Hesiod did not imitate Homer because he was part of the early Archaic Age, and he inherited the common poetic language, which cannot have been too different from the dialect his own father spoke when he sang to his son about the sea and the perils of the sea trade. The fact that Hesiod employs the traditional language of epic poetry does not in any way prove that he was an oral poet who did not make use of writing.

Hesiod's poetry is not heroic poetry. It has little in common with the songs of the Serbo-Croatian bards of the earlier part of the twentieth century. So, to take the norms of their songs and apply them to the songs of Hesiod is to commit an understandable and pardonable methodological error. They performed their long and impressive songs in ways that made literacy unnecessary or even destructive to their spontaneous and entirely oral method of composition. Content matters; subject matter is paramount. Hesiod's *Theogony* and *Works and Days* are poetic compositions that bear no substantial or ideological relationship with the Serbo-Croatian songs Milman Parry and A. B. Lord studied.

FIFTY-TWO DAUGHTERS

[240] And of Nereus and rich-haired Doris, daughter of Ocean the perfect river, were born children, passing lovely amongst goddesses, Ploto, Eucrante, Sao, and Amphitrite, and Eudora, and Thetis, Galene and Glauce, [245] Cymothoe, Speo, Thoe and lovely Halie, and Pasithea, and Erato, and rosy-armed Eunice, and gracious Melite, and Eulimene, and Agaue, Doto, Proto, Pherusa, and Dynamene, and Nisaea, and Actaea, and Protomedea, [250] Doris, Panopea, and comely Galatea, and lovely Hippothoe, and rosy-armed Hipponoe, and Cymodoce who with Cymatolege and Amphitrite easily calms the waves upon the misty sea and the blasts of raging winds, [255] and Cymo, and Eione, and rich-crowned Alimede, and Glauconome, fond of laughter, and Pontoporea, Leagore, Euagore, and Laomedea, and Polynoe, and Autonoe, and Lysianassa, and Euarne, lovely of shape and without blemish of form, [260] and Psamathe of charming figure and divine Menippe, Neso, Eupompe, Themisto, Pronoe, and Nemertes who has the nature of her deathless father. These fifty daughters sprang from blameless Nereus, skilled in excellent crafts.

Source: *Hesiod,* Theogony, *240–264, in* The Homeric Hymns and Homerica, *translated by Hugh G. Evelyn-White (Cambridge, Mass.: Harvard University Press; London: Heinemann, 1914).*

Catalogues are important. The catalogue of ships in the second book of the *Iliad* is not only a superb register, a *Who's Who,* of the warriors that sailed to Troy, but also an astonishing feat of memory preceded by a prayer, an emotional invocation to the Muses. Homer's invocation to the Muses in *Iliad* 2.484–493 has the emotional intensity and commitment of soul found only in such rare passages as St. Paul's immortal words on love in 1 Corinthians 13. Without the gift of memory, which only the Muses can bestow, Homer can only in vain try to remember the names and relevant military and genealogical details of a vast host of men and ships. Likewise, in an almost formulaic analogue, St. Paul cannot do anything truly outstanding without love, which is the gift of God. St. Paul was a highly literate and highly educated orator. He preached the word and then wrote down much of what he presented orally to various Christian communities. He moved from spontaneous orality to literary composition, and he probably felt no tension between the two. Hesiod too may have performed first in the old oral style to local Boeotian audiences, and then written down more polished and artfully composed versions of his performances. When Hesiod speaks of the daughters of Nereus, he introduces us to a bevy of fifty-two women (*Theogony,* 240–264). Fifteen epithets are lavished on some of the most memorable of them. Homer names only thirty-three of the daughters of Nereus, thirty-four, in fact, with Thetis included. Okeanos, says Hesiod, has three thousand slender-ankled daughters. Of them he names forty-two. Of these forty-two, seven receive the distinction that comes with an epithet describing beauty or any other significant attribute. Hesiod mentions more names and uses more epithets than Homer. That in itself does not prove anything. Yet, whereas oral poetry can achieve spectacular feats of memory, literate poetry can always outdo oral poetry in recording more names, epithets, and details. One can remember ten names, but with the help of writing, one can record twenty or fifty names far more easily. Hesiod's catalogues of the Nereids and of the Okeaninai may be more ambitious because Hesiod could read and write. To the proponents of the untainted theory of oral composition and oral performance, that may be anathema. They have adopted a rigid position. If you can read and write, you cannot be an oral poet. If you are an oral poet then, ipso facto, you cannot read and write. Those are extreme positions.

The truth is somewhere in between. Hesiod knew the alphabet, and he knew how to write. Hesiod inherited oral poetry and the new skill, knowledge of the alphabet, to produce the kind of poetry that his Boeotian compatriots could understand, but his broader and panhellenic audiences could appreciate even more. Hesiod may be like another distinguished Greek, General Makryyannis, one of the greatest and most inspiring figures of the Greek War of Independence, contemplating a life rich in adventures and suffering: "All these things provided me, in my old age, with the incentive to learn how to write in my old age, to record everything. Let others write about me what they know. I shall speak the naked truth" (Vlachoyannis 2000: 108). Is this, the truth of an illiterate man who learns how to write at the age of fifty-one, similar to the truth of the Muses of Hesiod's *Theogony* 28: "we know, when we wish, to proclaim the truth"? Hesiod may have been another Makryyannis, a remarkable man, a singer, by the way, who learned how to write when he was well past his encounter with the Muses? Hesiod spans the oral and the written tradition, but the poetry that we possess of him is far from innocent of the alphabet and its distinct advantages.

–APOSTOLOS N. ATHANASSAKIS,
UNIVERSITY OF CALIFORNIA,
SANTA BARBARA

References

Egbert J. Bakker, *Linguistics and Formulas in Homer* (Amsterdam: J. Benjamin, 1988).

Ruth Finnegan, "What is Oral Literature Anyway? Comments in the Light of Some African and Other Comparative Material," in *Oral Literature and the Formula,* edited by Benjamin Stolz (Ann Arbor: University of Michigan Press, 1976).

John Miles Foley, *Oral-Formulaic Theory and Research* (New York: Garland, 1985).

A. B. Lord, *The Singer of Tales* (Cambridge, Mass.: Harvard University Press, 1960).

Gregory Nagy, "Hesiod," in *Ancient Writers I,* edited by T. J. Luce (New York: Scribners, 1982).

Nagy, *Homeric Questions* (Austin: University of Texas Press, 1996).

Milman Parry, *The Making of Homeric Verse,* edited by Adam Parry (New York: Oxford University Press, 1987).

I. Vlachoyannis, ed., *Stratêegou Makrygiannêe apomnêemoneumata [The Memoirs of General Markiyannis]* (Athens, 1964).

William Whallon, *Formula, Character, and Context: Studies in Homeric and Old Testament Poetry* (Cambridge, Mass.: Harvard University Press, 1969).

GREECE: HOMER

Was Homer an oral poet?

Viewpoint: Yes. The style of Homeric epic is not one of a poet who composed in writing, and comparative evidence from oral poetry in other cultures suggests traditional poetry is able to sustain large-scale compositions along the lines of the *Iliad* and the *Odyssey.*

Viewpoint: No. Homer's *Iliad* and *Odyssey* are longer than oral poems are likely to have been, and both show evidence of a thoughtful reworking of traditional material that is probably the product of written composition.

In "The Immortal," his secular retelling of the medieval folktale of "The Wandering Jew," Jorge Luis Borges imagines a Homer who acquires physical immortality and spends interminable centuries living and reading, acts that for him grow progressively more difficult to distinguish, until at last he feels that he has become "everyone and no one." Borges's decision to treat the identity of Homer as an important aesthetic issue is significant on an historical level as well, for no poet except Shakespeare rivals him in being so central to the Western literary tradition, while being at the same time so mysterious as a biographical subject. This understanding is not a unique modernist insight but one felt acutely by the ancient Greeks as well, who developed a variety of theories of who Homer was and where he came from to compensate for the fact that he had already become an obscure figure. This aspect of Homer itself could be mocked. In the *True History,* written by the satirist Lucian of Samosata in the second century C.E., the narrator of the fabulous journey tells of a visit to the Islands of the Blessed, which turn out to be populated by historical and mythological figures alike. There he meets Homer himself, who delights in exploding the many lies that have been told about him and his poetry, and offers the ultimate indignity for admirers of the Hellenic national poet—that he was not Greek at all, but a Babylonian!

The two essays that follow take up an important aspect of Homer's elusive presence by addressing the question of orality and how it may have affected the composition of the Homeric poems. For some time now the dominant mode of thought has been that the poems were not the composition of a single artist (Homer) but the result of a long tradition of oral-formulaic poetry by which poets learned a repertoire of metrical formulas and contributed to it, if need arose, to improvise stories whose length would be determined only by the singer's skill and the attentiveness of his audience. Basing his argument upon the hypothesis first proposed by Milman Parry and taken up by his student Albert Lord and others, Robin Mitchell-Boyask develops the thesis of Homer as an oral poet, whose works everywhere show the effect of a style that is oral, not written. Charles Platter concedes that many features of orality can be seen in Homeric epic but points to many aspects in the poems that a theory of oral-formulaic composition cannot explain and draws attention to the tremendous size of the poems, completely without parallel in the performance culture that can be derived from the *Iliad* and the *Odyssey.*

In both essays the figure of the historical Homer lurks but remains undiscovered and undiscoverable. Tantalizing as the prospect of finding him may be, to be denied it is not such a hard fate; after nearly three millennia, we are used to disappointment, and we have the poems (a pretty nice compensation) into which the ghost of Homer has fled. As Borges's Homer puts it, "When the end draws near, there no longer remain any remembered images; only words remain."

—*Charles Platter*

Viewpoint:
Yes. The style of Homeric epic is not one of a poet who composed in writing, and comparative evidence from oral poetry in other cultures suggests traditional poetry is able to sustain large-scale compositions along the lines of the *Iliad* and the *Odyssey.*

The question posed in this chapter immediately creates two further ones whose answers are necessary to address the larger problem: What do we mean by "Homer," and what is an oral poet? Greek tradition early on ascribed to Homer both the *Iliad* and *Odyssey,* as well as a series of songs about the Olympian gods that came to be known as the Homeric Hymns because their style, content, and atmosphere all matched those of the longer heroic epics. These works depict the activities of oral poets and, some have thought, maybe even Homer himself. In one of the longest songs, the *Hymn to Apollo,* its singer breaks off and identifies himself as "the sweetest of singers . . . a blind man who dwells in rocky Chios" (169–172). The bard is a singer who carries his lyre, like Apollo himself, with him. This image, complete with blindness, is repeated in book 8 of the *Odyssey,* where the Phaeacians' local bard Demodocus sings a series of three songs to the disguised Odysseus and his hosts. Demodocus seems to be represented as composing in his performance his songs from traditional materials for his immediate audience but begins with the story of the quarrel between Odysseus and Achilles, which is thematically significant for Homeric epic as a whole and might offer a glimpse at an alternative tradition to the *Iliad* as we have it (Nagy 1979.42–58). Then Demodocus hears the growing tension between Odysseus and the young men of Ithaca, threatened in their courtship of Princess Nausicaa by this handsome, charismatic, but older stranger, a tension that results in mutual rebukes and that is closed by Odysseus's claim to bodily excellence, save for his legs, still wobbly from his time at sea. Demodocus, taking that cue, composes a song on the defeat of Ares by the lame Hephaestus, a song that, naturally, delights Odysseus since it, like the others, is really about him. Last, Odysseus himself requests to hear Demodocus's song about the Trojan Horse, and, judging from Homer's description, this one is considerable in length and composed during the performance. Now, while many used to believe that these blind bards are in fact Homer, these portraits seem more useful as accounts of the nature of oral poetry and its composition. The first bard's location in Chios is tempting because the language of Homeric poetry does suggest an origin in the Greek islands off the coast of Asia Minor. The blindness of both singers is likely generated by the tradition in Greek myth that connects blindness with divine knowledge. In other words, the bards are not Homer, but they may have been something like Homer.

Yet, who was Homer? Was there "a" Homer? The ancient Greek tradition believes there was but disagrees over what it was, exactly, that Homer composed and often attributes to Homer the entire Epic Cycle, which was a series of heroic epics depicting the entire Trojan War from its origins until the returns home of all its heroes. The *Iliad* and *Odyssey* are the only surviving components of the larger Cycle. Aeschylus is said to have called his tragedies "slices from the banquet of Homer," implying a reliance on Homeric epic for plot material; yet, what we know of Aeschylean drama and the Epic Cycle suggests that the tragedian drew on more than the *Iliad* and the *Odyssey* for his dramas. Herodotus is the earliest extant Greek author to distinguish Homer from the composer of the *Cypria* (another part of the Epic Cycle) on the basis of the different legends concerning Helen in Egypt. Aristotle then, just over a century later, differentiates between the *Iliad* and the *Odyssey* and the rest of the Epic Cycle on the basis of the greater unity in the former. Plato refers to "Homer" repeatedly and without complication, most infamously in the *Republic.* The Roman critic Longinus could write that the *Odyssey* was the product of Homer in his old age, with the intensity of the *Iliad* mellowed and loosened, like the glow of a setting sun. Thus, while there was debate in antiquity concerning what Homer composed, the ancient world had little doubt that there was indeed a Homer, even if that Homer was capable, to paraphrase Horace in the *Ars Poetica,* of nodding.

Those nods, when Homer seems to err and contradict himself, formed part of the stimulus for the German scholar Friedrich A. Wolf's *Prolegomena to Homer* (1795), which gave birth to

DEMODOCUS THE BARD

This song the famous minstrel sang; but Odysseus grasped his great purple cloak with his stout hands, and drew it down over his head, and hid his comely face; for he had shame of the Phaeacians as he let fall tears from beneath his eyebrows. Yea, and as often as the divine minstrel ceased his singing, Odysseus would wipe away his tears and draw the cloak from off his head, and taking the two-handled cup would pour libations to the gods. But as often as he began again, and the nobles of the Phaeacians bade him sing, because they took pleasure in his lay, Odysseus would again cover his head and moan. Now from all the rest he concealed the tears that he shed, but Alcinous alone marked him and took heed, for he sat by him, and heard him groaning heavily. And straightway he spoke among the Phaeacians, lovers of the oar: "Hear me, ye leaders and counsellors of the Phaeacians, already have we satisfied our hearts with the equal banquet and with the lyre, which is the companion of the rich feast. But now let us go forth, and make trial of all manner of games, that yon stranger may tell his friends, when he returns home, how far we excel other men in boxing and wrestling and leaping and in speed of foot." So saying, he led the way, and they followed him. From the peg the herald hung the clear-toned lyre, and took Demodocus by the hand, and led him forth from the hall, guiding him by the self-same road by which the others, the nobles of the Phaeacians, had gone to gaze upon the games. They went their way to the place of assembly, and with them went a great throng, past counting; and up rose many noble youths. There rose Acroneus, and Ocyalus, and Elatreus, and Nauteus, and Prymneus, and Anchialus, and Eretmeus, and Ponteus, and Proreus, Thoon and Anabesineus, and Amphialus, son of Polyneus, son of Tecton; and up rose also Euryalus, the peer of man-destroying Ares, the son of Naubolus, who in comeliness and form was the best of all the Phaeacians after peerless Laodamas; and up rose the three sons of noble Alcinous, Laodamas, and Halius, and godlike Clytoneus. These then first made trial in the foot-race.

***Source:** Homer,* The Odyssey, *2 volumes, translated by A. T. Murray (Cambridge, Mass.: Harvard University Press, 1919), book 8, sections 83–120.*

"the Homeric question." Wolf, having noticed that there are narrative inconsistencies in Homer (which some since have insisted are not actual inconsistencies) and that writing and reading do not exist in Homeric epic (aside from a brief reference in *Iliad* 6. 168–169), argued that what we call "Homer" is in fact the product of a compilation, or series of compilations, over a long period of time that were stitched together, and, because there was no single artistic hand, sometimes the seams of those stitches are visible; thus, the Greek term for the professional Homer singer, rhapsode, was returned to its original meaning of "song-stitcher." Thus arose the long battle, still continuing today, between the "analysts," who follow Wolf's lead, and the "unitarians," who believe in a single "monumental composer" (Whitman, Kirk) who shaped each epic, or even both, based on the traditions of oral epic.

The bridge to the concept of the monumental, but traditional, composer was the publications, in middle of the twentieth century, of Milman Parry and Albert Lord on the nature of oral poetry and its implications for the study of Homeric epic. On the basis of extensive fieldwork on oral poets in Yugoslavia, Parry articulated a theory that traditional language and themes could enable a poet to compose large-scale poems without the aid of writing. Thus, while the Homeric epics ultimately survived to our era because of the invention of writing, they were composed and transmitted orally. Parry demonstrated that Homer's repertoire consisted of a stock of traditional fixed phrases, which he called "formulas," that could describe most of the typical situations in a heroic poem; these are the memorable noun-epithet combinations such as "swift-footed Achilles" and "cloud-gathering Zeus" that could occupy a given place or places in the traditional hexameter lines of Greek poetry, sometimes even filling the entire line. While these phrases were limited in number (at least in the texts we have), they were sufficient enough in quantity and flexibility to enable a poet to shape his performance according to the needs of the situation. Parry thus demonstrated that the formulaic system in Homeric epic was so intricate and logical that it could only have arisen from many generations of refinement in performance. When a poet reaches a certain point in the hexameter line, he has at his disposal a range of formulas that can fit the metrical space; so, often his choice of formula can be as individually expressive as a completely original phrase. What is especially striking in Parry's discoveries is the sheer *economy* (to use Parry's term) of the formula systems. For example, for eleven significant gods and heroes in the *Iliad* and *Odyssey* there are 824 uses of 55 different formulas. Yet, these formulas also cover a large scope, as 88 percent of the formulas cover the four main parts of the hexameter line. Parry thus concluded that the scope and economy found in Homeric poetry are so rich and intricate that they cannot be the work of a single poet, especially one who wrote. The formulaic system is the pen and paper of the oral poet, the aid to memory that liberates him while composing in performance. The contribution of Lord, Parry's student, was to show how traditional themes were as integral as traditional language in the composition of heroic poetry. Broad themes and story motifs enabled a poet to compose, during performance, intricately structured works on the scale of the *Iliad* and the *Odyssey.* Certain types of scenes, such as ones of hospitality or arming, could be extended as needed and alternated with one another in an effective and recognizably structured sequence. When the generic aspects of certain scenes are violated, such as when Patroclus leaves Achilles' spear behind during his arming scene, we are directed to pay attention by the poet's decision not to exploit fully the recognizable themes of his craft.

Now, at this point, one might object that the sheer, simple existence of the texts of Homeric epic argues against Homer's being an oral poet. If Homer was an oral poet, then why did his art not die with him? And since the epics were in fact written down, how could their oral nature not be affected—or, perhaps, infected—by writing? Indeed, after the initial florescence of the Parry-Lord theories, a scholarly backlash resurrected an old concept in a revised form: that, while Homeric epics may have had their origins in oral performance, their length required the assistance of writing in their composition. While this is an attractive hypothesis, it does not in itself refute the work of Parry and Lord, which showed that large-scale oral poems are indeed possible. Moreover, such arguments seriously underestimate the powers of human memory, especially when aided by the techniques of traditional oral poetry. One possible escape from this conundrum is through the theory that Homer, or at least an authoritative performer of Homer, dictated his poems to a literate scribe, and the process of dictation and transcription may have affected the final product. Parry and Lord themselves transcribed performances of Yugoslavian bards. However, we lack evidence that such dictation ever took place in ancient Greece. Moreover, it is unclear how the Homeric epics could be performed regularly and transmitted essentially verbatim by purely oral means until they could be transcribed. It now seems likely that, as Homeric epic evolved toward what we would now recognize, it became increasingly traditional and conservative, even if not entirely fixed.

A major, crucial component in the transmission of the oral Homer to us appears to have been the institution of the performance of Homer at the Panathenaic Festival in Athens during the sixth century B.C.E. Two fourth-century texts, Lycurgus's *Against Leocrates* (102) and the pseudo-Platonic *Hipparchus* (228b), report that during that time Athens had initiated public performances of Homeric epic, and only Homeric epic, at the quadrennial Panathenaea. Of particular note is the claim in the latter that Hipparchus (one of the last tyrants in Athens) "first brought the epics of Homer into this land, and compelled the rhapsodes to go through them, one taking over from the other, in sequence, just as they do now still" (Nagy 1996.80–81). Already in *Iliad* 9 (188–191) we see a description of Achilles himself singing the "fames of men" (*klea andrôn*—a periphrasis for heroic poetry) accompanied by his lyre with Patroclus waiting for his great friend to finish, presumably, Gregory Nagy suggests (2003.43–44), so he himself might take up the next part of the song in turn. The notion of an edict requiring the poems to be performed in order, however, suggests that during the reign of Hipparchus or his father Pisistratus, rhapsodes were thought to have strayed too far from some Homeric ideal, and thus the institutions of the Panathenaea would somehow regularize them into something more canonical. This stabilization has come to be known as the "Peisistratean recension." Yet, even this stabilization does not imply the aid of writing, for a group of master rhapsodes, even if illiterate, could have collectively guided the process. Presumably, as literacy increased in Athens during the fifth century, there began to emerge transcripts of these performances, even as the oral performance tradition continued unabated, so the transcripts themselves did not become authoritative master copies for those performers.

Yet, if "Homer" develops through oral tradition and is finalized by a collective, is it still "Homer"? What does it mean to be Homer then? Nagy (1996.90–91) argues that the etymology of the name of Homer as the primordial mythic originator of epic poetry can be explained as "he who joins together," as a carpenter does a wheel, the Greek for which, *kuklos,* generates the word "cycle": "If this etymology is correct, then the making of the Cycle, the total sum of epic, by the master poet Homer is a metaphor that pictures the crafting of the ultimate chariot-wheel by the ultimate carpenter or 'joiner'." Homer is thus the name of the performance tradition of these epics that evolved into the texts that we have now. Homer is not just a poet but the "culture hero" (to continue to use Nagy's terminology) of epic poetry; indeed, Homer thus becomes oral epic poetry itself. Homer perhaps signals this with an epic poet inside the *Odyssey* whom we discussed before, whose name, Demodocus, means "received by the people" (Nagy 1979.17–19). The names of these bards are generated by their functions in the epic tradition, just as the names of the heroes of these epics are generated by their stories. The name of Akhilleus (to return to a more Hellenic form for the purposes of etymological clarity) means something like "he who brings pain *(akhos)* to the people *(laos)*" (Nagy 1979.69–83), while the name of Odysseus Homer twice links to the effect he has on others and the gods on him; first, Athena asks her father Zeus (1.62) "why are you so angry *(odusao)* at [Odysseus]?" and, second, when Odysseus recalls how his grandfather Autolycus named Odysseus because "I have aroused anger *(odussamenos)* in many" (19.407). Like hero and like poet, names are generated by their functions in the traditions of heroic poetry. Let us then conclude by changing our thesis, that Homer was not just an oral poet but oral epic poetry itself.

–ROBIN MITCHELL-BOYASK,
TEMPLE UNIVERSITY

Viewpoint:
No. Homer's *Iliad* and *Odyssey* are longer than oral poems are likely to have been, and both show evidence of a thoughtful reworking of traditional material that is probably the product of written composition.

The major event in twentieth-century Homeric scholarship was the development of the Milman Parry–Albert Lord hypothesis, which argued that the *Iliad* and the *Odyssey* were hugely indebted to a preliterate, oral tradition of composition through which poets composed extemporaneously through the manipulation of fixed metrical phrases also known as formulas. This hypothesis was particularly influential because it appeared to offer a way around the impasse that at the time of Parry's earliest works was more than a century old. In 1795 Friedrich A. Wolf had drawn attention to the fact that the Homeric poems had been produced in an age before literacy was widespread in the Greek world. Indeed, beyond a single obscure reference in the *Iliad* (6.168–170) the poems do not refer to writing at all. Moreover, the length of the poems, some 15,693 lines in the case of the *Iliad* and only a slightly more economical 12,109 for the *Odyssey,* meant that we were left with the paradox of poems of monumental length composed without the aid of writing. Wolf's observations set off a flurry of activity among scholars who tended to argue for one of two basic positions: 1) the *Iliad* and the *Odyssey* were composed of shorter (and therefore more easily memorizable) poems that had later been more or less clumsily edited into a coherent whole by a literate scribe; 2) the *Iliad* and the *Odyssey* are the work of a single author whom the ancients knew as Homer. Adherents of the first view became known as analysts for their tendency to "analyze" the text of the poems so as to detect the various strata out of which they were composed. Those who remained committed to the second opinion, in turn, were known as unitarians for their belief in the essential "unity" of the poems.

After a century of argument, much fine observation of the *Iliad* and the *Odyssey* had taken place. Yet, little had been concluded. Unitarians were not able to surmount the Wolfian paradox to explain how such monumental texts could be composed without writing and had offered adequate explanations neither for the fact that the poems are so repetitive nor for the abrupt transitions that characterize them throughout. Analysts, on the other hand, despite having the advantage of a single, elegant hypothesis to explain all of these features–they are the residue of incomplete compiling by the editor and, indeed, are themselves strong evidence for the validity of the analysts' claims–had not been able to achieve consensus about the various layers that made up the poems. If the supposed strata from which the *Iliad* and the *Odyssey* were composed were not self-evident, perhaps the analytical method was flawed in principle and the schemata it produced arbitrary fictions. It was within the context of this debate, which had grown gradually less productive, that Parry's hypothesis became so influential.

Yet, the model of Homeric epic as simply oral is inherently flawed: for neither the *Iliad* nor the *Odyssey* has reached us or any other scholar, whether ancient or modern, via the oral tradition. They have only been studied as texts copied and recopied over time until the invention of movable type in the fifteenth century C.E. As Barry Powell points out: "We may take it for granted that our literary artifacts, Homer and Hesiod, reflect orality, but the only evidence for their living song nevertheless comes from written texts" (Powell 2002, p. 13). What if it turned out, as Powell suggests, that "the qualities of great oral poetry are those of great literate poetry: strong characters, vivid language, compelling narrative, ethical conflict, and satisfying resolution"? In that case, the Homeric poems might not even represent a written tradition just a step removed from its oral source–and so preserving most of the features of the older, preliterate tradition–but two more or less distinct traditions that draw independently on the same aesthetic principles for similar artistic effects.

Yet, this is certainly taking things too far. If the Parry-Lord hypothesis does nothing else it certainly accounts for many of the repetitive aspects of Homeric verse in a convincing way. Surely, after all, the epithet-noun combinations, like "swift-footed Achilles" and "Zeus, father of gods and men," are more persuasively explained as compositional devices than as examples of unusually repetitive poetry. Nevertheless, saying that the Homeric poems make use of, or are derived from, oral poetry is not the same thing as saying that the poems are oral, in the same sense that the Serbo-Croatian songs transcribed by Parry and Lord are oral, that is, composed without the aid of writing by means of a traditional poetic vocabulary *and* possessing a plausible performance context.

If the Homeric poems are oral we should expect to find signs of the performance context for which they were produced. We are immediately struck, however, by the already-noted length of the poems. The recitation, or better, re-creation (if the oral-formulaic theory is correct) of the *Iliad* and the *Odyssey* would have taken days, far longer than what even the most avid audience could, let alone would, sit through. Nor is there any hint that such constraints affected the shape of the two poems. For there are no clear internal breaks at regular intervals that would have been convenient stopping points. Note that the conventional division of each poem into twenty-four books proves nothing. Such divisions are the result of Hellenistic scholarship that was produced centuries after the Homeric poems reached their final form, and there is no reason to assume that they reflect anything about performance history.

The Homeric poems speak loudly to this issue, for there are several apparently programmatic passages where the performance of poetry is discussed. Most significant is the fact that in these examples the chosen story is always a short episode, like the punishment of Ares and Aphrodite (*Odyssey* 8.266–366), and not something "to be continued" in the manner of any book of Homer. The closest thing to a counterexample would be the "performance" of Odysseus, who narrates his own story to the Phaeaceans in books 9–12 of the *Odyssey*. Yet, the circumstances here are clearly special. There is ample evidence to suggest that the Phaeacean love for poetry is unusually intense, and, in the end, Odysseus is not a traveling poet but a hero who has experienced the events he narrates. Therefore, without strong corroborating evidence his bardic practice and its reception cannot be taken to reflect the norms in Homer's time. Thus, there is a crucial difference between the society described by the Homeric poems and the society necessary for the consumption of "Homeric" poems as we know them.

If Homer is oral, that should presumably mean something such as that his poetry comes out of a tradition that has developed over generations, incorporating and assimilating new material as it became useful to do so. Yet, there is a surprising degree of discontinuity here (Page 1963). Homeric heroes are aware of the existence of "bright iron," for example, but it is not clear that they have any use for it except as a means of exchange. Their weapons instead are of bronze, showing that the technology of war comes from linguistic strata developed prior to the use of iron in weapon making. Other archaeological inconsistencies can be found. The shield of Ajax dates from a different period than the shields of the other Homeric warriors, and the famous boar's-head helmet of Dolon in book 10 of the *Iliad* is far out-of-step with the more substantial headgear of Achilles, Hector, and the rest. This sort of inconsistency, of which further examples could be given, gives more the impression of a heterogeneous mass of material worked into shape by a later compiler than of a homogenizing oral tradition made smooth by frequent telling and retelling of the same stories.

Nowhere is the type of incongruity felt more strongly than in the preparations for the famous embassy scene in book 9 of the *Iliad* when an embassy of Odysseus, Diomedes, and Phoenix goes to visit Achilles, who has withdrawn from the battle with the offer of reparations made by Agamemnon to induce him to return. The preparations for the mission are elaborate as Agamemnon enumerates the gifts he will provide, after which the heroes depart for Achilles' camp. The sequence of events here is unproblematic, but small discrepancies point to a more complex narrative past to this scene. Unlike in English, where nouns and verbs appear only in the singular and the plural, Greek distinguishes between singular, plural, and "dual" for things that appear in pairs. This fact is significant for the present discussion because as Agamemnon's three ambassadors walk along the beach "they" become "both" (9.182–185). That is to say, the third-person plural verbs disappear and are replaced by "duals." That is unlikely to be the result of a copying error, which tends to result in the production of simpler texts, not the introduction of exotic grammatical forms. Instead, it seems likely that the story of the embassy to Achilles that appears in the *Iliad* was once two stories, one which had a cast of two and the other with a cast of three (Page 1963). It is not possible to reconstruct these stories in detail, but there are parallels that suggest ways the two-man narrative might have been shaped. For example, the pairing of the wily Odysseus and the plain-spoken Diomedes recalls the embassy of Odysseus with Menelaus to request the return of Helen, which is described by the Trojan prince Antenor in book 6. Whatever the precise content of the story, however, this incident from book 10 shows that the poem as we now have it did not spring straight from the illiterate genius of an anonymous representative of the oral tradition but represents a subsequent stage of organization where the poet (or editor) has attempted, either without sufficient skill or interest, to

Vase painting of Homer's hero Odysseus gouging out the eye of the cyclops Polyphemus

(from William Harlan Hale, The Horizon Book of Ancient Greece, *1965)*

incorporate two similar but not identical versions of the same story. It is not, therefore, the work of an "oral poet" in any sense that the term gives us insight into the composition of the poem as we have it. Instead, we have poems that bear the imprint of an original consciousness operating on traditional material and developing it in new ways, occasionally without sufficient attention to details (Heubeck, Fowler).

Scholars have seen more positive effects of this reshaping of the oral tradition in many other places in the poems. Alfred Heubeck, for example, emphasizes this aspect of Homeric composition in his discussion of Telemachus's search for his father, which occupies books 1–4 of the *Odyssey,* and books 9–12 of the same poem, in which Odysseus narrates his adventures to the Phaeaceans. Both passages have been targets of analytic criticism, which has seen them as separate poems. While not contesting this claim, Heubeck stresses instead the degree to which both stories are artistically integrated into the overarching story told by the poems. Thus, at practically the same moment that Telemachus embarks on the journey to search for news of his father, Calypso reluctantly agrees to send Odysseus homeward with the result that father and son return to Ithaca in close succession (books 14–16). This neat blending of the two stories has a variety of artistic effects, in addition to setting up the plot for the destruction of the suitors, which is necessary for Odysseus if he is to reclaim his wife and property. Both father and son end up at the cottage of the swineherd Eumaeus, yet the reception they receive from the herdsman's dogs is quite different and illustrates graphically the cost of Odysseus's absence. The dogs immediately challenge him (14.29–36), and he is only saved from being mauled by the intervention of Eumaeus, in stark contrast to the fawning reception they give Telemachus when he arrives a little later (16.4–6). The presence of father and son in the same place at this point also allows for significant attention to be paid to the recognition of Odysseus, who is disguised as an old man, and for a bond to be forged between them that will be crucial if the restoration is to take place. Clearly, then, the Telemachus story is not an incidental part of the *Odyssey* grafted on indifferently but the product of great care given by a masterful storyteller.

Further, the *Odyssey* seems to possess a strong awareness of the *Iliad* not as a fluid structure but as a text with a definite shape. It "sequelizes" the *Iliad* in a number of passages to offer a retrospective view of the Trojan War and the values that sustained it. Most famous in this respect is the famous conversation with Achilles in Hades that Odysseus narrates to his Phaeacean hosts, in which Achilles responds to Odysseus's observation that he is supreme in Hades just as he was in life with the assertion that he "would rather slave on earth for another man . . . than rule down here over all the breathless dead" (11.489–491, trans. Fagles). In speaking that way Achilles reprises the theme of heroic virtue and its limits, which is important for understanding his behavior in the *Iliad.* There he recalls his mother Thetis's description of the prophecy that offers him the choice of a brief spectacular life and a long one without glory (book 9). Despite his difficulties with Agamemnon, however, Achilles never wavers long about what his choice will be. When he first speaks to the ambassadors from the Greek army, Achilles tells them that he will sail for Greece the next day. By the end of the book, however, he has definitely forgotten that threat, and before long he, too, will return to the fighting. In the *Odyssey,* however, he has had time to reflect on that decision, and his comment to Odysseus, with its reflection on his own fate, points to an author who had the other poem before him and took pains to juxtapose the two texts carefully.

No one doubts that Homeric poetry derived from an oral tradition. It surpassed that tradition in so many ways, however, that it can scarcely be called oral itself. Heubeck imagines the creative consciousness behind the *Odyssey* as "the spirit of a young poet who has himself become conscious of the questionable and limited validity of those aristocratic values which for earlier heroic poetry had been the props of an idealized view of the world and the pillars of a healthy society" (Heubeck, p. 21). Robert Fowler is more circumspect, reckoning this issue as one of the "unknowables," but maintains, nevertheless, that the poems were conceived as new kinds of texts "lovingly revised" with the aid of writing. Yet, Fowler ultimately rejects the simple dichotomy between oral and written: he describes the literate author(s) of the *Iliad* and the *Odyssey* as "oral poets" (Fowler, p. 230). We may accept this view, but to do so we will have to abandon the understanding of orality as preliterate in favor of a more nuanced view that includes Homer, or even Homers, with pens in hand.

–CHARLES PLATTER,
UNIVERSITY OF GEORGIA

References

John M. Foley, ed., *Oral-Formulaic Theory: A Folklore Casebook* (New York: Garland, 1990).

Robert Fowler, "The Homeric Question," in *The Cambridge Companion to Homer,* edited by Fowler (Cambridge: Cambridge University Press, 2004), pp. 220–232.

Jasper Griffin, "The Epic Cycle and the Uniqueness of Homer," *Journal of Hellenic Studies,* 97 (1977): 39–53.

Alfred Heubeck and others, *A Commentary on Homer's Odyssey,* volume 1 (Oxford: Clarendon Press, 1988).

Ralph Hexter, *A Guide to the Odyssey* (New York: Vintage, 1993).

Richard Janko, "The *Iliad* and Its Editors: Dictation and Redaction," *Classical Antiquity,* 9 (1990): 326–334.

Minna Skafte Jensen, *The Homeric Question and the Oral-Formulaic Theory* (Copenhagen: Museum Tusculanum, 1980).

Geoffrey S. Kirk, *Homer and the Epic* (Cambridge: Cambridge University Press, 1965).

Kirk, *The Songs of Homer* (Cambridge: Cambridge University Press, 1962).

Albert Lord, *The Singer of Tales* (Cambridge, Mass.: Harvard University Press, 1960).

Richard Martin, *The Language of Heroes: Speech and Performance in the Iliad* (Ithaca, N.Y.: Cornell University Press, 1989).

Gregory Nagy, *The Best of the Achaeans: Concepts of the Hero in Archaic Greek Poetry* (Baltimore: Johns Hopkins University Press, 1979).

Nagy, *Homeric Questions* (Austin: University of Texas Press, 1996).

Nagy, *Homeric Responses* (Austin: University of Texas Press, 2003).

Denys Page, *History and the Homeric Iliad* (Berkeley & Los Angeles: University of California Press, 1963).

Milman Parry, *The Making of Homeric Verse: The Collected Papers of Milman Parry,* edited by Adam Parry (Oxford: Clarendon Press, 1971).

Barry Powell, *Homer and the Origin of the Greek Alphabet* (Cambridge: Cambridge University Press, 1991).

Powell, *Writing and the Origins of Greek Literature* (Cambridge: Cambridge University Press, 2002).

M. L. West, "The Rise of the Greek Epic," *Journal of Hellenic Studies,* 108 (1988): 151–172.

Cedric H. Whitman, *Homer and the Heroic Tradition* (Cambridge, Mass.: Harvard University Press, 1958).

Friedrich A. Wolf, *Prolegomena to Homer,* translated by Anthony Grafton and others (Princeton: Princeton University Press, 1985).

GREECE: LIBRARY AT ALEXANDRIA

Were there repositories other than the Ptolemies' Library at Alexandria of equal value in preserving Greek culture?

Viewpoint: Yes. The existence of the Alexandrian Library was not a precondition for the production of standard texts of Greek authors or for the survival of Greek literature. Greek literary culture was widely diffused and practiced throughout the entire Mediterranean basin long before the conquests of Alexander and the beginning of the "Hellenistic" era.

Viewpoint: No. The Ptolemies assembled the greatest collection of Greek literature from the classical period, during a time crucial for the transformation and transmission of the Greek cultural heritage, and they inspired imitators among the other Hellenistic dynasties and the Roman emperors.

Alexander the Great founded Alexandria in 331 B.C.E., but the city was really the creation of Ptolemy I Soter and Ptolemy II Philadelphus, the first two members of the Macedonian dynasty that succeeded to the rule of Egypt. From the outset of their regime, the Ptolemies promoted intellectual, artistic, and cultural activity in their capital. Their policy has been described as an attempt on the part of Alexander's successors "to validate themselves by portraying themselves . . . as the sole legitimate heirs to the value and the values of their great cultural predecessors" (Most, 1990). Those cultural predecessors were the Greek city-states of the classical age (the fifth and fourth centuries B.C.E.), Athens in particular. The Macedonian successors of Alexander had something else to prove: Macedonians had been trying to convince the Greeks that they, too, were Greeks, since the beginning of the fifth century, through their participation in panhellenic games, patronage of Greek poets, and adoption of other Greek customs. The Athenian playwright Euripides spent his final years at the court of King Archelaus in Macedonia, and the philosopher Aristotle served as tutor to the young Alexander. The Ptolemies were continuing this tradition when they established institutions such as the Library in Alexandria.

The Ptolemies amassed undoubtedly the greatest collection of Greek literature in the ancient world, and their Library appears to have played a crucial role in preserving Greek culture for future generations. Yet, not all ancient evaluations of the Library were positive. The Roman philosopher Seneca, writing in the first century C.E., has this to say:

> Forty thousand books burned at Alexandria [a reference to the story that the Library was burned when Julius Caesar attacked the city in 48 B.C.E.]; let another praise "the most beautiful monument of royal opulence," as did Titus Livy [the Roman historian], who says that it was the outstanding accomplishment of the elegance and care of kings. That was not "elegance" or "care," but "studious luxury"—no, not even "studious," because they had collected not for study but for show . . . (*de tranquilitate animi* 9.4–5).

Before we assess the Library's role, some cautions about the evidence are in order. First, the Library finds only rare mentions in Greek and Latin authors, and epigraphy and archaeology have added little to our knowledge. Second, much of our information about the Library dates from the first century B.C.E. or later, by which time the Library may have become a monument, rather than a living and growing institution. Most of our evidence for Alexandrian collecting practices comes from the physician Galen, writing in the second half of the second century C.E.; the most detailed account of the Library's foundation comes from the Byzantine historian John Tzetzes, writing in the twelfth century C.E. Third, Greek authors are infected by nostalgia for the literature, culture, and cultural institutions of classical Greece and the Hellenistic kingdoms, when Greek culture reigned supreme in the Mediterranean, before the coming of the Romans; while Roman authors are infected by national antipathy toward the Hellenistic kingdoms, especially for Egypt, the last to oppose Roman domination.

—*T. Keith Dix*

Viewpoint:
Yes. The existence of the Alexandrian Library was not a precondition for the production of standard texts of Greek authors or for the survival of Greek literature. Greek literary culture was widely diffused and practiced throughout the entire Mediterranean basin long before the conquests of Alexander and the beginning of the "Hellenistic" era.

John Tzetzes' account of the foundation of the Ptolemies' Library at Alexandria suggests that its initial mission was the "correction" of the texts of Greek poets. This interest in establishing fixed texts for Greek authors is part of the ongoing shift in Greek creative practice and consciousness from orality to literacy, a shift well under way by the last quarter of the fifth century B.C.E. The comic playwright Aristophanes had already realized that written texts could ensure the survival of the author's memory and works beyond his own lifetime: in Aristophanes' comedy *Frogs* (produced in 405 B.C.E.) the god Dionysus recalls how he read (rather than saw and heard performed) a tragedy by the recently deceased Euripides. In the next century, as Aeschylus, Sophocles, and Euripides came to be recognized as the "classics" of Athenian tragedy, the Athenian statesman Lycurgus (circa 325 B.C.E.) proposed that the city preserve texts of their tragedies and use them to assure that actors did not depart from the texts; presumably these are the texts that one of the Ptolemies "borrowed" and declined to return. These anecdotes suggest that the existence of the Alexandrian Library (or another such collection) was probably not a precondition for the production of standard texts of Greek authors.

That the Ptolemies did assemble the greatest collection of Greek literature from the classical period seems assured; but what we do not have evidence for is how the treasures of the library might have been shared with a larger public. We do not hear of the copying of texts from the Library; nor do we hear of scholars wandering through the Library, finding unexpected treasures, and holding discussions within the Library, as we occasionally do for Roman imperial libraries. Nor do we hear contemporary poets such as Callimachus or Theocritus, both of whom lived in Alexandria and wrote about other Ptolemaic institutions, praise the Ptolemies for the foundation of the library, as we hear Roman poets praise the foundation of imperial libraries in the age of Augustus. There seems to be only one story in ancient literature that involves the consultation of the Alexandrian Library, and it nicely illustrates the quality of our evidence.

The story comes from the Roman architect Vitruvius, writing a manual on architecture in the first century B.C.E. Vitruvius begins this anecdote by asserting that the Attalid kings of Pergamum, a Hellenistic kingdom in western Asia Minor, founded their library even before the Ptolemies founded the Alexandrian Library and that the Pergamene example inspired the Ptolemies to build a library. This assertion is clearly wrong: while we cannot give a certain date for the foundation of the Alexandrian Library, it belongs at the latest in the reign of Ptolemy II Philadelphus, so before 246 B.C.E.; the library at Pergamum, on the other hand, belongs to the period between 197 and 160 B.C.E. Here, as at other times in Roman history, the Pergamene propaganda machine seems to have been much more effective in Rome than the Alexandrian one. Vitruvius claims that the Attalids established their library "for common delectation," a claim made by no other author about any of the Hellenistic royal libraries and one that does not seem to accord with the available evidence; but his claim that Ptolemy was moved by unbounded jealousy and avarice to establish his library does accord with the legendary rivalry over libraries between the Ptolemies and the Attalids.

Vitruvius reports that Ptolemy wished to take measures for the future growth of the library and so established public literary contests; again, Vitruvius seems to make a claim

Undated illustration of scholars in the Library of Alexandria

(© Bettmann/CORBIS)

not made elsewhere that Hellenistic rulers conceived of their libraries as spurs to literature. Ptolemy selected six literary men to judge the literary contests, then turned to "those who were in charge of the library" for help in finding another judge (thus bringing the number of judges up to seven, a "canonical" number in the ancient world). They suggested one Aristophanes, who spent his days reading all the books in the library "in order." Poets were first to compete (in accordance with the higher valuation of poetry over prose throughout Greek history). The other six judges voted to award the first prize to the poet who had received the most applause from the audience. Aristophanes, however, said that the prize should go to the poet who had least pleased the audience. In response to the indignation of the king and the audience, Aristophanes said that the only true poet was the man he had chosen, that the rest had recited things not their own, and that judges ought to approve original compositions, not thefts. Relying upon his memory, Aristophanes brought out texts from certain bookcases and forced the poets to confess their borrowings. The king had the poets tried for theft, then sent them off in disgrace; and he rewarded Aristophanes with gifts and made him head of the Library. In its outcome the contest of the poets becomes a contest for the librarianship, and Aristophanes must be Aristophanes of Byzantium, literary scholar and librarian at Alexandria around 200 B.C.E. For Vitruvius, the point of his story is that Aristophanes valued originality over what Vitruvius calls theft and what we might identify as borrowing or slavish imitation. Vitruvius's story accords with the report in Porphyry (circa 300 C.E.) that Aristophanes drew up a list of parallel passages from the comic playwright Menander and from Menander's models and "gently" proved (in Porphyry's words) that Menander had borrowed from others. A reasonable inference from this anecdote in Vitruvius is that the Alexandrian Library was much more important for scholarship than for either wider dissemination of Greek literary culture or encouragement of literary production.

The idea that the Alexandrian Library was necessary for the survival of Greek literature seems to rest on a fundamental misunderstanding of the nature of cultural life in the ancient Mediterranean world. Greek literary culture lived not only in the several hundred Greek city-states, and not only in the new cities founded by Alexander and his Hellenistic successors, but also among many "barbarian" peoples, for example, in Rome and other towns throughout the Italian peninsula. An elementary education in Greek literature consisted of memorization and explication of passages from certain basic authors, such as Homer. In a world where general illiteracy must always have been the norm rather than the exception, there was still something like a mass audience for literature, through the medium of public performance (for drama and choral poetry) and of individual recitation (the usual mode of initial "publication" of a new literary work throughout antiquity). Perhaps more important than the circulation of texts was the circulation of the producers, performers, and pedagogues of Greek literature: itinerant poets like Archias, whose "lecture tour" of Greek cities brought him from his native town of Antioch to the Greek cities of southern Italy and finally to Rome, where he instructed and entertained Cicero and other Roman aristocrats with his poetry; and the "Artists of Dionysus," the guilds of Greek actors and musicians who brought drama to cities throughout the Mediterranean. The first formal production of drama on a Roman stage took place in 240 B.C.E., with a comedy and a tragedy written by Livius Andronicus, who probably came to Rome as a prisoner of war from the Greek city of Tarentum in southern Italy; his Latin adaptation of the *Odyssey* became a textbook for Roman schoolboys for generations. From that point on, there was certainly both Greek literature in Rome and Greek influence on Latin literature, and Hellenistic Greek literature, produced by Theocritus, Callimachus, and Apollonius in Alexandria and elsewhere, was particularly influential; but there is no evidence that the treasures of the Alexandrian Library played any meaningful role in that phenomenon, or even that the Romans were aware of the existence of the Library before the end of the first century B.C.E. To believe otherwise is to mistake a symbol of Greek cultural life for the instrument of that life.

The Ptolemies may have intended no more than what they did accomplish, which was to build a monument to high culture, or at least to high cultural aspirations, and to memorialize the literature and literary culture of the bygone age of classical Greece. Perhaps the best epitaph for the Alexandrian Library is the phrase that Seneca seems to have found in Livy but that he rejected, *pulcherrimum regiae opulentiae monimentum*, "the most beautiful monument of royal opulence." We should remember that the Latin word *monimentum* often signified a tomb; perhaps it is fitting that Egypt, the land admired by the Greeks for the invention of embalming, served as the final resting place for so much of Greek literature.

–T. KEITH DIX,
UNIVERSITY OF GEORGIA

Viewpoint: No. The Ptolemies assembled the greatest collection of Greek literature from the classical period, during a time crucial for the transformation and transmission of the Greek cultural heritage, and they inspired imitators among the other Hellenistic dynasties and the Roman emperors.

What the Ptolemies intended to accomplish by founding the Library at Alexandria, we do not know, but we can get some hint of both their intentions and their accomplishments from what ancient authors say about the Library. The Greek geographer Strabo, writing in the time of Augustus, asserts that it was Aristotle who "taught the Ptolemies the arrangement of a library." Presumably he meant that Aristotle was responsible for the arrangement of the Alexandrian Library. This assertion is doubtful on chronological grounds: Aristotle left Athens in 323 B.C.E. and died in Chalcis in 322; there is no ancient report that Aristotle visited Egypt after his departure from Athens. Furthermore, Ptolemy I Soter, who became satrap (governor) of Egypt in 323, is unlikely to have devoted himself to the establishment of a library during the troubles of the next year after the death of Alexander.

While Aristotle himself probably did not take in hand the arrangement of the Library, a pupil from his Peripatetic school may have done so. According to the biographer Diogenes Laer-

FULFILLING A ROYAL WISH

The following is an excerpt from the Letter of Aristeas, an account of the production of the Greek translation of the Jewish Scriptures for the library of Ptolemy II Philadelphus. In 1684 C.E., the English monk Humphrey Hody determined that the document was a forgery, probably written by a Hellenized Jew in Alexandria in the mid second century B.C.E.:

The Memorial of Demetrius to the great king. "Since you have given me instructions, O king, that the books which are needed to complete your library should be collected together, and that those which are defective should be repaired, I have devoted myself with the utmost care to the fulfilment of your wishes, [30] and I now have the following proposal to lay before you. The books of the law of the Jews (with some few others) are absent from the library. They are written in the Hebrew characters and language and have been carelessly interpreted, and do not represent the original text as I am [31] informed by those who know; for they have never had a king's care to protect them. It is necessary that these should be made accurate for your library since the law which they contain, in as much as it is of divine origin, is full of wisdom and free from all blemish. For this reason literary men and poets and the mass of historical writers have held aloof from referring to these books and the men who have lived and are living in accordance with them, because their [32] conception of life is so sacred and religious, as Hecataeus of Abdera says. If it please you, O king, a letter shall be written to the High Priest in Jerusalem, asking him to send six elders out of every tribe—men who have lived the noblest life and are most skilled in their law—that we may find out the points in which the majority of them are in agreement, and so having obtained an accurate translation may place it in a conspicuous place in a manner worthy of the work itself and your purpose. May continual prosperity be yours!"

[33] When this memorial had been presented, the king ordered a letter to be written to Eleazar on the matter, giving also an account of the emancipation of the Jewish captives. And he gave fifty talents weight of gold and seventy talents of silver and a large quantity of precious stones to make bowls and vials and a table and libation cups. He also gave orders to those who had the custody of his coffers to allow the artificers to make a selection of any materials they might require for the purpose, and that a hundred talents in money should be sent to provide sacrifices for the temple and [34] for other needs. I shall give you a full account of the workmanship after I have set before you copies of the letters. The letter of the king ran as follows:

[35] "King Ptolemy sends greeting and salutation to the High Priest Eleazar. Since there are many Jews settled in our realm who were carried off from Jerusalem by the Persians at the time of their [36] power and many more who came with my father into Egypt as captives—large numbers of these he placed in the army and paid them higher wages than usual, and when he had proved the loyalty of their leaders he built fortresses and placed them in their charge that the native Egyptians might be intimidated by them. And I, when I ascended the throne, adopted a kindly attitude towards all [37] my subjects, and more particularly to those who were citizens of yours—I have set at liberty more than a hundred thousand captives, paying their owners the appropriate market price for them, and if ever evil has been done to your people through the passions of the mob, I have made them reparation. The motive which prompted my action has been the desire to act piously and render unto the supreme God a thank offering for maintaining my kingdom in peace and great glory in all the world. Moreover those of your people who were in the prime of life I have drafted into my army, and those who were fit to be attached to my person and worthy of the confidence of the [38] court, I have established in official positions. Now since I am anxious to show my gratitude to these men and to the Jews throughout the world and to the generations yet to come, I have determined that your law shall be translated from the Hebrew tongue which is in use amongst you [39] into the Greek language, that these books may be added to the other royal books in my library. It will be a kindness on your part and a regard for my zeal if you will select six elders from each of your tribes, men of noble life and skilled in your law and able to interpret it, that in questions of dispute we may be able to discover the verdict in which the majority agree, for the investigation is of the highest possible importance. I hope to win great renown by the accomplishment of this [40] work. I have sent Andreas, the chief of my bodyguard, and Aristeas—men whom I hold in high esteem—to lay the matter before you and present you with a hundred talents of silver, the first fruits of my offering for the temple and the sacrifices and other religious rites. If you will write to me concerning your wishes in these matters, you will confer a great favor upon me and afford me a new pledge of friendship, for all your wishes shall be carried out as speedily as possible. Farewell."

Source: *R. H. Charles, ed. and trans.,* The Letter of Aristeas *(Oxford: Clarendon Press, 1913).*

tius, the Athenian philosopher and statesman Demetrius of Phalerum heard the lectures of Theophrastus, Aristotle's successor as head of the Peripatetic school, and Demetrius gained for Theophrastus, who was not an Athenian citizen, the right to acquire property in Athens, which put the "school of Aristotle" on a firmer legal footing. In the upheavals that followed the death of Alexander in 323 B.C.E., Demetrius became governor of Athens at the instigation of Cassander, who then controlled Macedonia; when a rival Macedonian dynast, Demetrius Poliorcetes, captured Athens in 307, Demetrius of Phalerum fled from Athens and eventually came to the court of Ptolemy I Soter in Egypt. Peripatetic influence seems to have been strong at the court of Soter: in addition to the presence of Demetrius, Soter made overtures to Theophrastus; and Straton of Lampsacus, Theophrastus's successor as head of the school, served as tutor to Ptolemy's son Ptolemy II Philadelphus. After Soter's death around 283, Philadelphus banished Demetrius to the Egyptian countryside because Demetrius had advised Soter to make another son his heir, and Demetrius died soon thereafter.

Modern scholars have asserted that Demetrius inspired the foundation of the Library; our only ancient evidence for his role comes from the so-called Letter of Aristeas, which relates the story of the Septuagint, the translation of the Old Testament from Hebrew into Greek undertaken at Alexandria. The letter purports to be written by one Aristeas, commander of the bodyguard of Philadelphus, to his brother Philocrates. Aristeas says that Philadelphus ordered Demetrius, who was in charge of the king's library, to collect all the books in the inhabited world; through purchase and copying, Demetrius had already collected two hundred thousand scrolls and hoped to bring the number to five hundred thousand (the Greek word *biblia* refers to individual papyrus rolls, "scrolls," and since many individual works of literature would have required more than one scroll, we cannot say how many "books" these numbers represent; in any case, ancient estimates of library size tend to be multiples of ten thousand). Demetrius suggested to Philadelphus that he ask for a translation of the Jewish law. In response to the request of Philadelphus, seventy-two learned Jews (or seventy, according to other sources, hence the name *Septuagint*) were sent from Jerusalem. Taking up residence on the island of Pharos, these scholars produced a Greek translation of the Law in seventy days. One obvious problem with this story is the role of Philadelphus, who is supposed to have banished Demetrius as soon as he became king; and the Letter of Aristeas is now considered an ancient forgery, written not at the time of the events it purports to record but a century later. While many aspects of the story of the Septuagint are incredible, nevertheless it is hard to see how Demetrius became part of the story unless he was in fact associated with the Alexandrian Library; and while the claim that Philadelphus intended to collect all the books in the world is necessary to the development of the story, nevertheless it suggests that the Library could be seen as a storehouse of all knowledge.

Aristotle's library might well have provided an organizational model for the Alexandrian Library. Strabo also describes Aristotle as "the first we know of to have collected books"; while this cannot be literally true, since the book collector was already a recognized type in Athens by the end of the fifth century B.C.E., books do seem to have been particularly important to Aristotle and his school. Aristotle recommended the consultation of written works as a first step in the process of dialectic, and he began the type of literature known as *doxography,* that is, the collection and discussion of the views of earlier philosophers; his work in this area must have required a collection of books. The school's research activities, such as collecting constitutions and official records, would also have added to the school's store of texts. The possession of a library seems to have played a much more critical role in the development of the Peripatetic school than it did in the development of any other philosophical school. Aristotle's library may have aimed to be a systematic one–indeed, Strabo's claim that Aristotle taught the Ptolemies the arrangement of a library suggests the systematic nature of the library–and the library was a distinctive feature of the Peripatetic school. So the Alexandrian Library may have a claim on Aristotle as an ideological founder, if not an actual founder.

Putting aside the claim that the Ptolemies intended to collect all the books in the world, we can consider two questions central to our understanding of the importance of the Library: did the Library constitute a comprehensive collection of Greek literature, and did it further the growth of Greek literature and learning? A look at some of the anecdotes about Ptolemaic collection practices provides some interesting evidence.

The Byzantine scholar John Tzetzes, writing in the twelfth century C.E., says that Ptolemy II Philadelphus commissioned the tragic playwright Alexander of Aetolia to correct the texts of tragedies and satyr plays, the tragic playwright Lycophron of Chalcis to correct comedies, and the scholar Zenodotus of Ephesus to correct the other poets, especially Homer. We know that Zenodotus, who seems to have been the first official librarian of the Alexandrian Library, produced texts of Homer and other Greek poets, as did two of his successors as librarian, Aristophanes of Byzantium and Aristarchus of Samothrace. Tzetzes' account suggests that the scholarly activities of the Alexandrian Library were encouraged by, or perhaps even suggested by, their royal patrons; and we can assume at the least that the collection of texts for the Library facilitated the editorial work of Zenodotus and his successors.

Two incidents reported by the physician Galen, writing in the second century C.E., highlight two aspects of Ptolemaic bibliomania, desire for rarities and desire for as many books as possible. One of the Ptolemies borrowed from Athens the texts of Aeschylus, Sophocles, and Euripides, presumably the city's official copies, and gave the Athenians a security deposit of fifteen talents, an enormous sum, for their return. The king had the highest quality copies made, which he gave to the Athenians; he kept the Athenian originals for Alexandria and forfeited the fifteen talents. It seems that the Ptolemies wanted to possess not just the complete works of the three great Athenian tragedians but also the best possible copies: Athenian origin assured their authenticity, and the price proved their value. Another anecdote in Galen points to indiscriminate collecting: every ship unloading at Alexandria was supposed to be searched for books; the books would be seized and copied, and the copies given to the original owners. Galen adds that these books were labeled "from ships" and did not go immediately into the Library but instead were stored "in certain rooms"; so perhaps some of the confiscated books were eventually found wanting and were not admitted to the Library. This anecdote provides a nice counterpart to the story of the Athenian tragedians: on the one hand, it recalls the claim of "Aristeas" that Ptolemy Philadelphus intended to collect all the books in the world, as it suggests that the Ptolemies kept collecting even after they had the "classics" in hand, and on the other hand, even though the books confiscated by the customs service might prove unworthy of the Library, the Ptolemies still wanted the "originals."

In addition to assembling the greatest collection of Greek literature from the classical period, during a period crucial for the transformation and transmission of the Greek cultural heritage, the Ptolemies helped to save Greek culture in another way–by inspiring imitators among the other dynasties that succeeded to Alexander's empire. In Macedonia, the Antigonids had a library at Pella, from which the Roman conqueror of Macedonia, Lucius Aemilius Paullus, allowed his sons to select books as their share of the spoils in 168 B.C.E.; and the Seleucids had a library in their capital at Seleucia. The most famous library after Alexandria was the library of Pergamum, founded between 197 and 160 B.C.E.; the rivalry over libraries between the Ptolemies of Alexandria and the Attalids of Pergamum was legendary, ending only with the extinction of both dynasties. The Alexandrian Library continued to exist during the period of Roman control of Egypt; and with the example of Alexandria before them, Roman emperors endowed their own capital city of Rome with a series of great libraries.

–T. KEITH DIX,
UNIVERSITY OF GEORGIA

References

Ernst Badian, "Greeks and Macedonians," in *Macedonia and Greece in Late Classical and Early Hellenistic Times,* Studies in the History of Art, Volume 10, edited by Beryl Barr-Sharrar and Eugene N. Borza (Washington, D.C.: National Gallery of Art, 1982), pp. 22–51.

Luciano Canfora, *The Vanished Library* (Berkeley: University of California Press, 1990).

T. Keith Dix, "Aristotle's 'Peripatetic' Library," in *Lost Libraries: The Destruction of Great Book Collections Since Antiquity,* edited by James Raven (New York: Macmillan, 2004), pp. 58–74.

Mostafa El-Abbadi, *The Life and Fate of the Ancient Library of Alexandria* (Paris: UNESCO, 1990).

Peter M. Frazer, *Ptolemaic Alexandria* (Oxford: Clarendon Press, 1972).

Karen H. Jobes and Moises Silva, *Invitation to the Septuagint* (Grand Rapids, Mich.: Baker Academic, 2000).

John P. Lynch, *Aristotle's School* (Berkeley: University of California Press, 1972).

Roy MacLeod, ed., *The Library of Alexandria* (London & New York: I. B. Tauris, 2000).

Glenn W. Most, "Canon Fathers: Literacy, Morality, Power," *Arion,* 1 (1990): 35–60.

Gregory Nagy, *Poetry as Performance: Homer and Beyond* (Cambridge: Cambridge University Press, 1996).

Kevin Robb, *Literacy and Paideia in Ancient Greece* (Oxford: Oxford University Press, 1994).

GREECE: LITERACY

Was literacy a sufficient force for producing the cultural revolution in Greece?

Viewpoint: Yes. The coming of literacy produced a cultural revolution in Greece by changing the structure of language.

Viewpoint: No. Literacy did not produce a cultural revolution in Greece. Such assertions are based on oversimplified notions of what causes cultural change and the difference between oral and literate cultures.

In 1928, Milman Parry defended his doctoral dissertation at the Sorbonne, *L'epithète traditionelle dans Homère.* Beneath the innocuous, philological title lurked a radical thesis that would eventually rewrite not only our study of Homer but would also create an entire scholarly discipline, the study of orality. Every reader of Homer, whether in translation or the original Greek, remarks upon Homer's repetitive diction. This facet of the Homeric poems is most evident in what are known as noun-epithet clusters. Why is dawn always rosy-fingered, Achilles always swift-footed, and Menelaus always of the loud war cry? Parry set out to answer just these questions. The result he came up with was startling: the noun-epithet clusters were evidence that the Homeric poems were orally composed.

The audacity of the claim is breathtaking, and Parry's work did not receive immediate acceptance. How could these poems of twelve thousand lines apiece and astonishing narrative complexity be composed without the aid of writing? The answer lay in a system of formulas that extended beyond the basic noun-epithet clusters that lay at the foundation of Parry's thesis. Formulas were set groups of words that always appeared at the same place in the metrical line and served the same function. The study of the Homeric corpus revealed literally thousands of these formulas. The theory was thus advanced that formulas allowed oral poets to string together traditional stories by deploying a prefabricated diction that allowed their attention to be focused on narrative development rather than linguistic invention.

In the 1930s Parry began fieldwork with his graduate student at Harvard, Alfred Lord. Together they traveled to Serbia where they interviewed and recorded many traditional bards. These poets, like the Homeric poets, recounted tales of martial valor in the distant past, such as the battle of Kosovo against the invading Turks, without the aid of writing. Their method of composition was precisely what Parry and Lord predicted based on their study of Homeric formulas.

By the 1950s, when the theory of oral composition in the Homeric poems had begun to gain broader currency in the scholarly community, another set of questions began to be asked. If Homeric culture was the product of a long tradition of oral bards retelling the tales sanctified by tradition, whereas the later tragedians, Plato, the sophists, Herodotus, and Thucydides were all authors of written texts, in what sense can the latter culture, that of fifth-century Athens, be called a culture of writing? How precisely does literate culture differ from oral culture? To what extent did alphabetic writing produce the miracle that is Greece? These questions are still hotly debated today. It is not clear that there are any easy or unambiguous answers.

—Paul Allen Miller

Viewpoint: Yes. The coming of literacy produced a cultural revolution in Greece by changing the structure of language.

Literacy matters. We all know that. That is why we want people to learn to read. On one level, it is for pragmatic reasons: to be functional in modern society, a person must read. Nonetheless, most of us also think literacy important for other reasons. We believe that reading is important as an experience. There is a pragmatic basis for it as well: you cannot encounter the great ideas of world culture if you cannot read. However, our commitment to reading goes even deeper. Perform a thought experiment. Assume that all the content, all the ideas, had been miraculously abstracted from Homer, Plato, Virgil, and Augustine. Now imagine electrodes planted in your brain that would transmit those "ideas" to you directly with perfect comprehension and retention. Would the experience be the same as reading the texts? Would it have the same effect?

Literacy matters because the abstraction of content from form just proposed is impossible. Ideas never exist outside a mode of inscription, outside a physical embodiment, and that embodiment affects how we experience those ideas and thus the nature of meaning itself. In the terms of linguistics, there are no signifieds without signifiers, and those signifiers only exist to the extent they are joined together in different sorts of syntaxes and styles. As Marshall McLuhan said in one of scholarship's great oversimplifications, "the medium is the message."

Indeed, it is only because of such oversimplifications that controversies over the effect of literacy arose in the first place. Media do deliver messages, but messages can never be reduced to media–otherwise, translation would be impossible. Ever since Milman Parry's discovery of oral composition in the Homeric epics and the subsequent realization that civilization and culture do not depend on writing, scholars have debated exactly what difference the introduction of literacy made in both ancient Greece and beyond. There have been overgeneralizations as well as assertions of technological determinism, and those should be avoided. Writing in a vacuum never produced anything, but in determined cultural contexts it has been of great moment. In the ancient Mediterranean, writing and literacy made possible three fundamental changes in the way we think about, and therefore experience, the world. First, the syntax of literacy, and thus its mode of linguistically representing the world, possess different potentials from that of orality. Second, graphic systems of representation permit greater distance and abstraction from experience than do purely oral forms. Third, writing makes the book possible and consequently creates new structural possibilities for representing experience.

Anyone who has read Homeric Greek immediately notices two qualities: the repetitive nature of the diction and the simplicity of the syntax. This repetitiveness first led Parry to posit his theory of oral-formulaic composition. Parry and his associate Albert Lord, using comparative data gathered from fieldwork with Serbo-Croatian bards, definitively established that the Homeric poems were composed using a set of traditional formulas. A formula is a group of words that always appears in the same order in the same place in the metrical line, as in the famous "rosy-fingered dawn" of the *Odyssey.* Oral bards are able to compose long and complex narratives on traditional themes by stringing together these formulas. The nature of such composition is additive, which accounts for the simplicity of the syntax. The narrative moves forward through the addition of discrete units, seldom more than a line in length. The unit of thought is the phrase, not the complex periodic sentence familiar to readers of Virgil. Oral syntax by nature, then, tends to be paratactic rather than hypotactic. That is to say, it favors loose coordination over the tight subordination characteristic of rhetorical prose. Such changes, from an oral, predominantly paratactic, to a literate, predominantly hypotactic style, do not happen overnight. They are part of a larger, more complex cultural process. Thus, in Herodotus, the first extended prose author we possess from antiquity, and the first writer of history, the syntax remains largely paratactic. However, when his successor Thucydides writes a generation later, a distinctively complex prose style and syntax has evolved.

These findings on oral syntax and style are confirmed by comparative data from a variety of sources. If one looks at *Beowulf* or other Old English poems that were orally composed or produced under the influence of a still active oral tradition, one finds the same type of syntactical parataxis. Wlad Godzich and Jeffrey Kittay in

ROSY-FINGERED DAWN

The following are just some of the references to the "rosy-fingered dawn" in Homer's The Odyssey:

Book 2, Line 1

Soon as early Dawn appeared, the rosy-fingered, up from his bed arose the dear son of Odysseus and put on his clothing.

Book 3, Line 490

So soon as early Dawn appeared, the rosy-fingered, they yoked the horses and mounted the inlaid car, and drove forth from the gateway and the echoing portico.

Book 5, Line 120

Thus, when rosy-fingered Dawn took to herself Orion, ye gods that live at ease begrudged her, till in Ortygia chaste Artemis of the golden throne assailed him with her gentle shafts and slew him.

Book 9, Line 150

As soon as early Dawn appeared, the rosy-fingered, we roamed throughout the isle marveling at it; and the nymphs, the daughters of Zeus who bears the aegis, roused the mountain goats, that my comrades might have whereof to make their meal.

Book 12, Line 5

As soon as early Dawn appeared, the rosy-fingered, then I sent forth my comrades to the house of Circeto to fetch the body of the dead Elpenor.

Book 13, Line 15

They then went, each man to his house, to take their rest; but as soon as early Dawn appeared, the rosy-fingered, they hastened to the ship and brought the bronze, that gives strength to men.

Book 17, Line 1

As soon as early Dawn appeared, the rosy-fingered, Telemachus, the dear son of divine Odysseus, bound beneath his feet his fair sandals and took his mighty spear, that fitted his grasp, hasting to the city.

Book 19, Line 425

But as soon as early Dawn appeared, the rosy-fingered, they went forth to the hunt, the hounds and the sons of Autolycus too, and with them went goodly Odysseus.

Book 23, Line 240

And now would the rosy-fingered Dawn have arisen upon their weeping, had not the goddess, flashing-eyed Athena, taken other counsel.

***Source:** Homer,* The Odyssey, *2 volumes, translated by A. T. Murray (Cambridge, Mass.: Harvard University Press / London: Heinemann, 1919).*

The Emergence of Prose trace a similar pattern in the evolution of medieval French romances from an oral poetic style, through the first "unrhymed" versions, then to the fully developed prose narratives of the late Middle Ages.

A skeptic might say, "fine, but these are merely superficial differences of style–not substantive differences in meaning." However, to argue that changes in syntactical organization do not produce effects on the level of meaning is to argue for the idleness of philology and literary study. It is to accept the position of the freshman in his first English class, who, after his professor has carefully explicated Yeats's "Leda and Swan," replies, "why didn't he just say that?" The answer of course is: he did. If we concede that word choice and syntactical organization are integral to meaning and its reception, as every teacher of poetry must, then we will also concede that the new modes of complex hypotaxis and subordination made possible by writing produced new possibilities of meaning.

Among these possibilities is an increased level of abstraction. Take mathematics, often considered the closest we can come to a pure system of abstract relational meaning. No system of mathematics, beyond elementary arithmetic, has ever been devised without an agreed-upon system of graphic representation. Algebra only came into being with the advent of the Arabic numerical system, not only because of its greater ease of calculation, but also because of the discovery of zero as a number, that is to say as a graphic representation that can enter equations. It is precisely for this reason that the early Pythagoreans believed in the substantive nature of concepts such as numbers–represented as a series of points drawn in the sand and later on paper–because they could not conceive of them apart from their system of representation.

Thought does not exist outside of meaning, and meaning only occurs within a system of regulated signifiers that makes the joining and production of discrete signifieds possible. Inscription fixes the flux of experience and allows it to become a direct object of reflection in a way that is inconceivable in the relentlessly linear progression of oral recitation and reception. It thus allows the number four to be thought as opposed to four apples, four shields, or four bronze tripods. It allows the concept itself to emerge as an independent reality separate from any concrete narrative.

Similarly, Achilles and Agamemnon do not argue about the nature of justice in the *Iliad,* but over who has done the other wrong according to the rules of the heroic code. Likewise, Hesiod in the *Works and Days,* a poem rooted in the oral tradition, does not debate the definitions of proper conduct, but prescribes rules of behavior. In *The Republic,* however, the question is not who is the just man or what are just actions, but what is justice. The answer demanded cannot be a narrative drawn from the storehouse of the formulaic bard, but must be a logical demonstration. This form of abstract conceptual thought is not found in the oral tradition. As Eric A. Havelock famously argues in *A Preface to Plato* (1963), writing is what makes philosophy as an organized system of concepts possible. It creates a new temporality of experience that allows for an increased distance between it and its mental representation. Thus, Plato's Socrates seeks the form of justice–as a series of abstract relations akin to the harmonic ratios of music or the formal relations of geometry–not a list of approved behaviors. Nor is it accidental that Plato prescribes pure mathematics as the primary discipline of his philosopher kings (*Republic,* 7). Plato's own famously conflicted sentiments about writing do not contradict Havelock's arguments, but merely locate Plato at the threshold between two modes of reflection. The Platonic corpus marks the liminal space where narrative thought, which predominates in the oral tradition, definitively crosses over to the world of abstract reason in the shape of a conscious split between the flux of experience and the timelessness of the ideal forms.

Havelock's insight, his deduction of the cultural and experiential consequences of Parry's discovery of oral composition, has received confirmation from a variety of corners. Media theorists from McLuhan to Friedrich Kittler have offered corroboration through their investigations of the relations between information systems and cognition. Likewise, Paul Zumthor has shown that many of the same processes are recapitulated in the reemergence of the oral poetic tradition during the Middle Ages. Less well known, but more rigorous, is the work of the Russian cognitive scientist Alexander R. Luria, who did fieldwork in Soviet Central Asia during the 1920s and 1930s when mass literacy campaigns were being launched. By comparing the results of tests given in villages where literacy had been achieved against those the campaign had yet to reach, Luria demonstrated that villagers who had received instruction in literacy exhibited substantially different cognitive structures from those of their peers. In the villagers whose culture remained largely oral, objects were commonly classified in terms of a narrative of their utility as opposed to abstract logical categories. The predominantly oral mode of thought, Luria is careful to note, is no less sophisticated, and in some ways more useful for the villager's daily life, than the rule-based modes of thinking that predominated in the literate peasantry. It is, however, different.

The last way in which literacy changed the way in which the ancients (and thus we) experience the world is by making possible a fundamentally new discursive structure: the book as a compositional whole. Texts, unlike oral performances, are subject to rereading. One can take up a book of poems and read them straight through, but one can also read the second in terms of the first and then reread the first in terms of the second, and skip to the fourth, checking the third at one's leisure. It is more difficult to do on a papyrus scroll than in modern books but hardly impossible. Often, more than one poem was written in a column, and two to three columns could be held open to inspection at a time. Moreover, rerolling is no more difficult than unrolling, allowing the reader to move backward and forward through the scroll.

All of this seems commonsense, but the possibilities it opens in poetic composition and the representation of experience are no less radical than those of hypertext in the age of the Internet. A singer like Sappho would have sung to her community, and her song would have been judged worthy of remembering depending on whether it represented an experience or desire with which the audience could immediately identify. Readers, however, encountered Sappho's songs three centuries later as collected and arranged by her Alexandrian editors. They compared them to one another, following themes, metrical patterns, and recurring phrasings that would not have been as apparent to an audience hearing these same poems days, months, and even years apart. Soon, the ability to collect and arrange preexisting poems into books suggested the idea of composing poetry books directly. Poets began to explore the multiple levels of meaning created by pairing poems on similar and contrasting subjects, by creating metrical and thematic symmetries, and by producing fragmented narratives that could be recombined in more than one fashion.

Thus, when Catullus in his poem 51 translates Sappho 31, a poem about being struck dumb by the sight of one's beloved, it becomes a fundamentally different poem. First, it is a *translation:* a bookish exercise bringing linguistic structures from one context to another separated by five hundred years and hundreds of miles. It is self-consciously literary in a way that would be inconceivable to a singer of the oral tradition. Second, it inserts that poem in an immediate poetic context. Although there is debate over exactly what form Catullus's corpus took in antiquity, it is generally conceded that poems 50 and 51, owing to certain resemblances in diction, are a pair, even though the topic of the first is poetic composition and the second love. Again, outside the context of a collection, this kind of pairing would be very difficult to achieve, being contingent upon the listener's ability to recall subtle similarities of vocabulary even as he or she listened to the next poem. Moreover, it would depend upon these two poems always being performed together. Third, Sappho's poem in Catullus's translation becomes part of the larger narrative of Catullus's relationship with his beloved, Lesbia. Poems chronicling their stormy affair are scattered throughout the corpus and invite comparison to one another. One poem in particular, number 11, is the only other poem in the corpus in Sapphic stanzas. In it, Catullus asks two companions to bid his lady adieu on account of her monstrous infidelity. The tone is in such contrast to 51 that to many these poems represent the beginning and end of the affair, respectively.

The result is that where Sappho's poem 31 was directly addressed to her community of listeners, Catullus with the same material creates a multilayered aesthetic object that represents a fundamentally different type of experience. While Sappho's is communal and linear in orientation, Catullus's presents at least three different narrative temporalities simultaneously: the learned poet who translates a recherché text from a distant but esteemed culture; the sequential juxtaposition of poem 50's story of poetic composition, with 51's declaration of love; and poem 51's recontextualization within the larger story of the Lesbia affair and specifically with poem 11. The result is the creation of a speaking subject that is not only more distanced from his or her experience, and hence capable of abstract artistic reflection on it, but also one who is not so much defined by his or her relation to the immediate community as by a complex internal narrative in which poetic composition, literary learning, and profound emotion all play a role. It is thus not only poetry that has changed, but also our capacity to represent, and so to have, certain forms of experience.

In sum, literacy matters because it changes the structure of language. A change in language that allows new structures of meaning to appear and new stylizations of experience to evolve cannot but have a revolutionary effect on cultural institutions and the individuals who inhabit them. That such changes do not happen in a vacuum goes without saying. Nonetheless, to argue that one can change the nature of the way meaning is experienced, without changing its nature and our own, is a non sequitur. Writing made such changes possible, even if it did not fully control them.

–PAUL ALLEN MILLER,
UNIVERSITY OF SOUTH CAROLINA

Viewpoint:
No. Literacy did not produce a cultural revolution in Greece. Such assertions are based on oversimplified notions of what causes cultural change and the difference between oral and literate cultures.

Since the time of the Romantics, there has been a fascination with preliterate, folk cultures. Whether in the lays of Ossian or Jean-Jacques Rousseau's noble savage, the desire to hearken to a simpler, more direct voice of experience has been all but irresistible to modern Western man (Nagy, 1990: 1). The corollary of this fetishization of the unlettered folk has been a corresponding elevation in importance of that which marks the rupture between preliterate natural man and his civilized cousin: the advent of writing. Thus, on one side, there is the spontaneous voice of the people embodied in a poetry that arises directly from the collective will, on the other there are the deliberate products of reflection and hard-won erudition. Writing is either the culprit or the savior, depending on the view adopted, but the scenario remains roughly the same. The notion of a literate revolution in Greece is nothing more than a late reflex of this most basic Romantic impulse to create an absolute opposition between nature and culture.

None of this is to say that writing and the demise of oral formulaic composition had no effect on Greek culture. Rather, what must be recognized is that the existence of these two technical systems for storing and retrieving cultural information, writing and the oral poetic tradi-

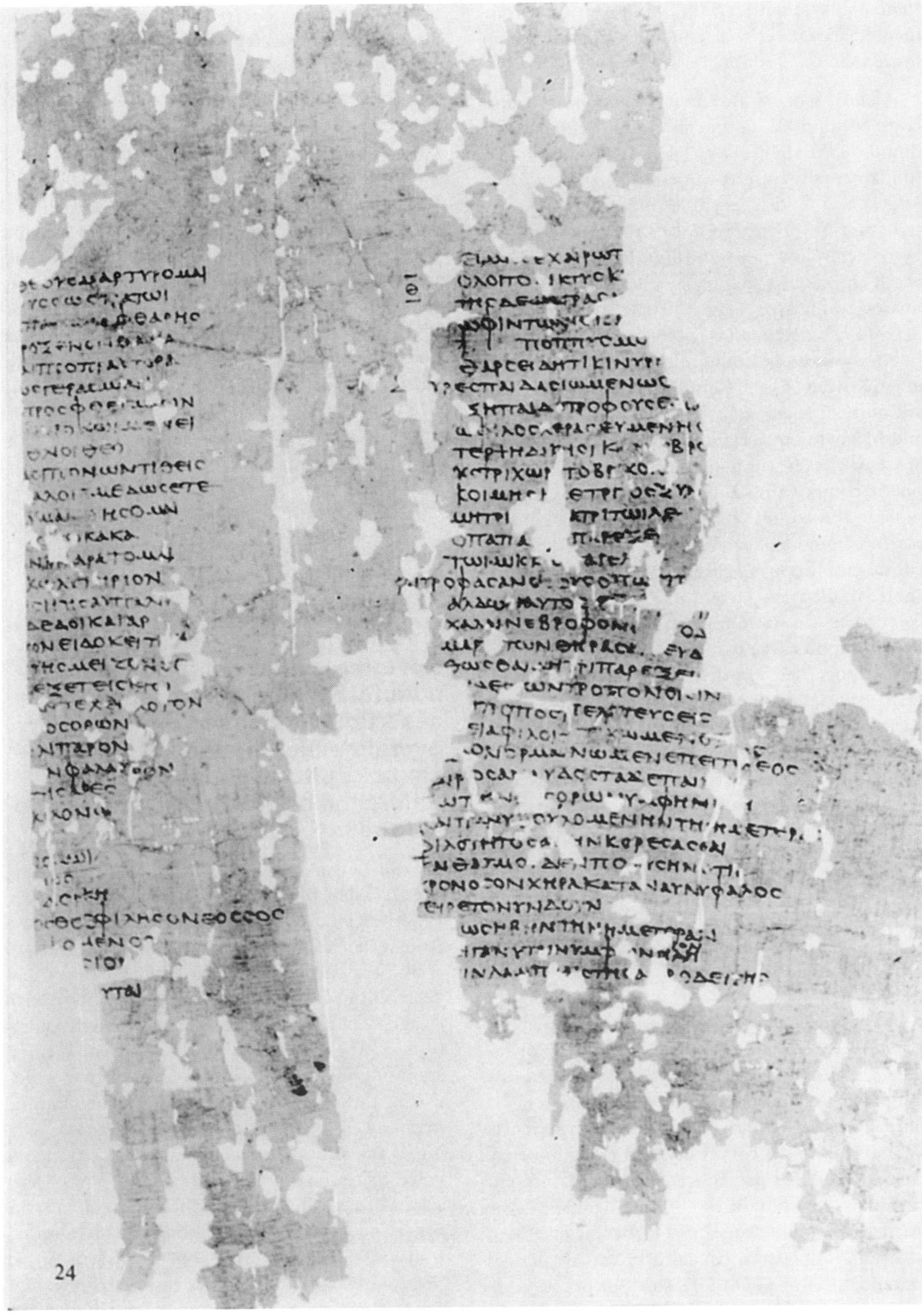

Fragment of a second-century C.E. papyrus with the text of Aeschylus's *Net Fishers*

(Egypt Exploration Society)

tion, were but two factors in a much more complicated equation that would seek to account for the cultural revolution that swept Greece in the period from the end of the sixth to the early part of the fourth centuries B.C.E. In this period we see the formalization of geometry, the invention of history as a genre of scholarly writing, the beginning of the formal study of rhetoric, the invention of democracy, and the transformation of philosophy from a set of speculations on the nature of the physical realm into a systematic inquiry into the nature of the good, the true, and the beautiful. In addition to an increase in literacy and an increase in the availability and use of books during this period (Lowenstam, 1997: 45, 64; Graff, 1987: 21–24), equally or more decisive were the class conflicts that drove the political innovations, increases in trade and colonization that spread information, and traditions of conflict resolution that placed a premium on persuasion and public speaking that can be seen as early as the council scenes in the *Iliad*. To grant a decisive causal agency to any one factor necessarily leads to a distorted and oversimplified theory of cultural change. Moreover, the terms orality and literacy are often poorly defined, so that they are treated as absolute states, rather than complex conditions existing in a wide variety of gradations. Thus, while the speculations of Eric A. Havelock and others on the effects of a "literate revolution" in Greece have been stimulating and led to useful investigations into the oral aspects of Greek culture, most of the general theories about "oral culture" and "oral mentalities" on which they are based do not stand up to rigorous logical and empirical scrutiny.

One of the primary problems with most of the assertions about the nature of oral culture and oral poetry is that they deploy overly narrow definitions of orality that do not do justice to the full diversity of the phenomenon. As Gregory Nagy, one of the foremost scholars of the Homeric poems and of oral composition has observed, "The descriptive term *oral* in *oral poetry* has come to have an overly narrow meaning, restricted by our own cultural preconceptions about writing and reading. We feel the need to define oral in terms of the *written:* if something is *oral,* we tend to assume a conflict with the notion of the *written*" (1990: 8, emphasis in the original). Thus, on the one hand, some scholars only define poetry as oral if it was improvised extemporaneously in the manner of the Serbian bards studied by Milman Parry and Albert Lord. Poems committed to memory and repeated verbatim by this definition are not oral, regardless of their means of diffusion. From this perspective, all extant versions or mentions of Homeric poetry were in fact not strictly oral, since as soon as there became an *Iliad* or an *Odyssey* to be repeated, the poems became the fossilized records of a once vital tradition of immediate composition. The rhapsodes through whom the Homeric poems spread through Greece clearly memorized texts and did not spontaneously recompose the *Iliad* and *Odyssey* with every recitation even if they did edit depending on the audience and occasion. Moreover, the rhapsodes were anything but spontaneous. They reflected on what they recited and their roles in that recitation. They were expected to interpret the poems as well as simply repeat them, even if those interpretations, as ridiculed in Plato's caricature of Ion, may not have always withstood the glare of later philosophical scrutiny (Thomas, 1992). Moreover, we know that other written texts were often memorized and transmitted orally. Did those texts somehow mysteriously become "oralized" in the process? If not, then what is the difference in kind between memorizing and repeating a text learned by ear, as in the case of most rhapsodes, and those learned initially by sight and spread only secondarily by ear (Finnigan, 1977: 21)? Where exactly does orality end and literacy begin? The mistake of course is to treat these states as monolithic conditions with uniform qualities and predictable effects.

Writing of course does have certain advantages. It generally makes it possible to store and retrieve an increased volume of detailed information, preserving it over a longer period of time, and with potentially greater accuracy. Although even that is hardly without question. The oral transmission of the Vedas over 2,500 years makes a good counterargument, and the notorious corruption of some medieval manuscripts should make us wary of granting these advantages to writing automatically. But even if these points are conceded, the question is whether they provide sufficient grounds to produce a cultural revolution per se.

Havelock, Walter Ong, and others have argued that there is a direct causal relationship between literacy and the rise of abstract rationality in the West. But such bald assertions do not hold water (Thomas, 1989: 25–26). First, as every reader of their newspaper's "Letters to the Editor" page is painfully aware, the ability to write and the ability to reason have no necessary relation. The world is filled with literate fools. Second, if we accept their thesis, we are faced with the problem of accounting for Socrates: he is often given credit for the birth of Western philosophy as a reasoned inquiry into values and behaviors. Yet, as we know from Xenophon, Socrates did not write. Was he, therefore, devoid of the ability to reason abstractly?

Moreover, his lack of writing seems not to be a mere accident of history. Rather, the oral nature of his inquiries was integral to their self-conception. The entire practice of Socratic *elenchus*–the procedure of question and answer through which an interlocutor's beliefs are tested and found wanting and from which the desire for philosophy arises as we come to recognize our own ignorance–is dependent upon the face-to-face interaction of the dialogic form. It is for this reason that Plato rejects writing in the *Phaedrus* as a means of inquiry into the nature of the truth, rather than a mere prompt to memory:

> You might say that [written words] understand what they are saying, but if you ask them what they mean by anything they simply return the same answer over and over again. Besides once a thing is committed to writing, it circulates equally among those who understand the subject and those who have no business with it; a writing cannot distinguish between suitable and unsuitable readers. And if it is ill-treated or unfairly abused it always

needs its parent to come to its rescue; it is quite incapable of defending or helping itself. (Hamilton, 1973: 97)

Writing, rather than being the foundation of Socratic dialectic, at least insofar as Plato understands it, is its antithesis. The written text can neither ask nor answer questions, nor address itself to specific interlocutors. It is not subject to the practice of *elenchus* on which Socratic inquiry rests.

Finally, the Greek Enlightenment of the fifth century certainly had the effect of applying reason's corrosive gaze to the traditional structures of Greek, and especially Athenian, life. That is true whether we are speaking of Socrates or the sophists and the teachers of rhetoric. But there is no good reason to attribute these developments to a rise in literacy per se, since it is unclear that literacy was ever widespread or a decisive factor in ancient social history. It would be worth our while to linger over this last point for a moment. The basic facts of Greek literacy need to be reviewed. The Greek alphabet was invented in the eighth century sometime before 750 B.C.E. Its use was initially limited in part because papyrus and other suitable writing materials were rare and expensive. The result is that during the first 250 years of writing's use in Greece, its impact was very limited (Harris, 1989: 45–47; Thomas, 1989: 23). By the time of the Persian Wars, some reading instruction was available in Athenian schools, and by the beginning of the fourth century (Harris, 1989: 57–59), Plato finds it perfectly reasonable to portray the young aristocrat Lysis as able to read and write even though his parents cannot (*Lysis,* 209 B-C). Yet, this same passage, far from demonstrating any intellectual prestige or acumen acquired by the young man, treats this ability as a simple skill no different from chariot racing, horse breeding, or other kinds of expertise a young man from a wealthy family might pursue. The fact is that our best estimates for literacy rates in classical Athens do not exceed 5 to 10 percent (Harris, 1989: 114). If the introduction of writing per se were the primary causal factor behind the Greek Enlightenment, it seems strange that it should take two and a half centuries for its effects to be felt and stranger still that it should turn out to be a phenomenon of such limited scope. Thus, Havelock's claim that the alphabetic book produces "literate consciousness" is at best an oversimplification and at worst a meaningless tautology (1982: 11).

Of course, it would be ridiculous and reductive to claim that literacy has no effect, but it would not be too much to say that literacy has no *one* effect. Its impact is context dependent. As William Harris wittily observes, the consequences of literacy can be compared to those of consuming a bottle of wine: "the effects may be dramatic or insignificant, according to circumstances and the physiology and psychology of the individual. Anyway bottles of wine do sometimes have effects" (1989: 41). Literacy and orality are not monolithic phenomena that produce uniform effects, but rather multiform phenomena that maintain complex and overdetermined relations with the societies in which they are found. The impact of writing on a given culture is ultimately dependent upon the "values, beliefs, and customs already there" (Thomas, 1989: 33–34).

One of the less fortunate corollaries of the cultural relativity of the effects of literacy is that the tendency to universalize and idealize those effects often produces theories with a pronounced ethnocentric bias. Literacy, in most studies, is defined as alphabetic literacy, and the effects it produces are generally assumed to be those produced in the Greece of the fifth-century Enlightenment. Comparative data from other cultures with different writing systems or where the introduction of writing produced different effects are almost never included. Thus, as Rosalind Thomas notes, alphabetic writing in the works of Havelock stands as the sine qua non for the development of abstract reason per se. Yet, the case of the modern Chinese engineer who learns one of the most difficult scripts in the world, whose pictographic nature is the antithesis of the analytical qualities supposedly embodied in alphabetic writing, is never considered. But who would want to claim that such a person lacks reason (Thomas, 1992: 54–55)? In fact, what is most frequently offered is a circular argument. Alphabetic writing is said to have produced the birth of Western reason because when the occidental *logos* assumed its codified form in the texts of Plato, Aristotle, and the sophists, it did so in alphabetic writing. This syllogism is not sound. The material relation between the conditions in which the phenomenon occurred and those that were necessary for it to occur is never demonstrated.

In summation, literacy did not produce a cultural revolution. The opposition between written and oral culture is a product of a facile Romantic dichotomy between nature and culture. The thesis of a cultural revolution is founded on monolithic definitions of literacy and orality, an oversimplified history of literacy in Greece, and often harbors implicit ethnocentric assumptions that identify reason with the West and its alphabetic writing.

–PAUL ALLEN MILLER,
UNIVERSITY OF SOUTH CAROLINA

References

Ruth Finnigan, *Oral Poetry: Its Nature, Significance, and Social Context* (Cambridge: Cambridge University Press, 1977).

Harvey J. Graff, *The Legacies of Literacy: Continuities and Contradictions in Western Culture and Society* (Bloomington: Indiana University Press, 1987).

William V. Harris, *Ancient Literacy* (Cambridge, Mass.: Harvard University Press, 1989).

Eric A. Havelock, *The Literate Revolution in Greece and Its Cultural Consequences* (Princeton: Princeton University Press, 1982).

Havelock, *A Preface to Plato* (Cambridge, Mass.: Harvard University Press, 1963).

Jeffrey Kittay and Wlad Godzich, *The Emergence of Prose: An Essay in Prosaics* (Minneapolis: University of Minnesota Press, 1987).

Friedrich A. Kittler, *Gramophone, Film, Typewriter,* translated by Geoffrey Winthrop-Young and Michael Wutz (Stanford, Cal.: Stanford University Press, 1999).

Albert Lord, *The Singer of Tales* (Cambridge, Mass.: Harvard University Press, 1960).

Steven Lowenstam, "Talking Vases: The Relationship Between the Homeric Poems and Archaic Representations of Epic Myth," *Transactions of the American Philological Association,* 127 (1997): 21–76.

Alexander R. Luria, *Cognitive Development: Its Cultural and Social Foundations,* translated by Martin Lopez-Morillas and Lynn Solotaroff, edited by Michael Cole (Cambridge, Mass.: Harvard University Press, 1976).

Marshall McLuhan, *The Gutenberg Galaxy: The Making of Typographic Man* (Toronto: University of Toronto Press, 1962).

Paul Allen Miller, *Lyric Texts and Lyric Consciousness: The Birth of a Genre from Archaic Greece to Augustan Rome* (London: Routledge, 1994).

Gregory Nagy, *Pindar's Homer: The Lyric Possession of an Epic Past* (Baltimore: Johns Hopkins University Press, 1990).

Walter J. Ong, *Orality and Literacy: The Technologizing of the Word* (London: Methuen, 1982).

Jeff Opland, *Anglo-Saxon Oral Poetry: A Study of Traditions* (New Haven: Yale University Press, 1980).

Adam Parry, ed., *The Making of Homeric Verse: The Collected Papers of Milman Parry* (Oxford: Oxford University Press, 1971).

Milman Parry, *L'epithète traditionelle dans Homère: Essai sur un problème de style homérique* (Paris: Société Editrice "Les Belles Lettres," 1928).

Rosalind Thomas, *Literacy and Orality in Ancient Greece* (Cambridge: Cambridge University Press, 1992).

Thomas, *Oral Tradition and Written Record in Classical Athens* (Cambridge: Cambridge University Press, 1989).

Paul Zumthor, *Introduction à la poésie orale* (Paris: Seuil, 1983).

GREECE: PLATO AS AN ARISTOCRAT

Was Plato an aristocratic sympathizer with the oligarchic factions within the Athenian state?

Viewpoint: Yes. Plato was an aristocrat who favored rule by those with superior natures and thoroughly detested the democracy of his time.

Viewpoint: No. Plato, although an aristocrat of the highest pedigree, broke with his class when he met Socrates and developed a devastating critique of traditional aristocratic thinking about politics.

Socrates was a poor man, famous for his extraordinary personality and eccentric habits, as well as his execution by the Athenian democracy as an enemy of the city. We have an abundance of information about him from the people who knew him. With Plato, however, we are much less well served. He is absent from the dialogues and extremely reticent about himself. He is not unknown to us entirely, however. His upbringing was aristocratic, as were his associates (many of whom were also associated with Socrates), and the dialogues themselves, with their emphasis on the superior knowledge of the expert, bear frequent testimony to a man whose spirit was not egalitarian in any way. To some, as a result, he has seemed a man deeply hostile to the values that help determine the ideologies of Western liberal democracies. If the philosopher of science Karl Popper were alive today, he might well see Plato as a friend of terrorism. At any rate, Plato's relationship with the democracy is complex, at best, and one is tempted to suspect that he, like Aristotle, saw democracy only as the best of the possible regimes.

Yet, there are many interpretative difficulties in Plato, not the least of which is the determination of just what it is the dialogues represent. In a letter Plato dismisses a handbook of his teaching supposedly composed by Dionysus of Syracuse, the dissolute tyrant who studied under Plato during several brief, tumultuous periods. "Such writers," Plato says, "can in my opinion have no real acquaintance with the subject. I certainly have composed no work in regard to it, *nor shall I ever do so in the future, for there is no way of putting it in words like other studies*" (341c). Plato's statement here is remarkable, for it brings into question the significance of his extraordinary literary output, which amounts to more than forty dialogues, occupying five large volumes in Greek. If that is not Plato's "teaching," then what is it? Of course, by debunking the pretensions of Dionysus in this way, Plato attempts to protect his dialogues from misappropriation by a man unfit for philosophical activity. Yet, by putting into question the ability of his writing to produce wisdom, he problematizes the nature of the dialogues themselves, with profound implications for our understanding of Plato's political thought, particularly as expressed in his most famous work, the *Republic.*

In the end we are left with a paradox that is perhaps inevitable. Plato was a writer of vast talent and a thinker of great power. His relationship with his aristocratic upbringing was ambivalent, for he perceived its assumptions about the importance of tradition and the unchanging superiority of the upper classes as an impediment to real progress in wisdom and political life. At the same time, it was this class that not only produced him but also helped produce a culture that made possible and even encouraged the activities of people such as Socrates, whom Plato adopted as an icon for the life spent in philosophic pursuits.

—*Charles Platter*

Viewpoint:
Yes. Plato was an aristocrat who favored rule by those with superior natures and thoroughly detested the democracy of his time.

Karl Popper described Western society as still laboring under the "stupefying" effects of "the spell of Plato" and saw the philosopher as an enemy of the egalitarian trends in post-Enlightenment societies that he referred to as "the open society." Despite Plato's deserved reputation as a stylist and the popularity of the Socrates whom he sought to vindicate and preserve, Plato was seen by Popper as the direct ancestor of modern totalitarianism. In this assessment he was largely correct. Throughout the Platonic dialogues there is a strong strain of antidemocratic thought, from the choice of Socrates as Plato's philosophic hero, to his attempts to create a rigid and unchanging political system in the *Republic* and the *Laws.*

Plato's antidemocratic bias, however justified philosophically, is a logical consequence of his birth and upbringing. Tradition says that his mother Perictione was a descendent of Solon, who in 594 B.C.E. was called upon to reform the laws of Athens to deal with the socio-economic crisis that threatened the stability of the Athenian polis. On the side of his father, Ariston, political authority was even more ingrained, for the family traced its lineage back even further to Codrus, one of the early kings of the city and a son of Poseidon (Diogenes Laertius 3.1).

Aristocratic sympathies were not just a feature of decayed gentility. The family was extremely prominent in Athens. His uncles, Critias and Charmides, were well known for their oligarchic sympathies, as were many other relatives and acquaintances, a fact that Plato himself admits in one of his letters. Further, despite the fact that Plato might be excused from our consideration because he never undertook a traditional political career, his work shows no real attempt to disassociate himself from the attitudes of his family. In fact, the *Republic* (or, perhaps more accurately, the *Constitution*), unapologetically creates a blueprint for a society based on the aristocratic ideal that power and authority are given to those "best by nature." We are not encountering an obscure part of Platonic thought here. The *Republic* is, after all, the centerpiece of Plato's work. Yet, it is a work that runs counter to much of the thought that made Greek culture possible. For example, the aristocratic Pericles, leader of Athens for many years until his death in 429 B.C.E., describes Athenian political life in a manner almost diametrically opposed to that of Socrates in the *Republic:* "Although only a few may originate a policy, we are all able to judge it" (Thuc. 2.40.2). In Pericles' Athens there are no permanent citizen classes and no philosopher-kings, only an ongoing attempt to develop the capacities of the city to its utmost and to recruit from the citizen body those most qualified to create policy and implement its decisions.

In contrast, the dialogues can be read virtually as an extended tribute to the family of Plato. The most striking example of this is in *Charmides,* in which Socrates converses with Plato's uncle Critias, later to achieve infamy as one of the sacrilegious revelers who participated in the Mutilation of the Herms, and then again as one of the Thirty Tyrants who ruled Athens during the short-lived oligarchic revolution at the close of the Peloponnesian War (404–403 B.C.E.). The bulk of the conversation, however, is with another of Plato's uncles, Charmides himself, who, like his cousin, was implicated in the Mutilation of the Herms, became a member of the Thirty, and died fighting for the oligarchic cause. In *Charmides,* Socrates extols the lineage of Critias's (that is, Plato's) family. Likewise prominent in the dialogues are Plato's brothers, Adeimantus and Glaucon, the principal interlocutors of Socrates in the *Republic,* and Critias, the grandfather of Critias the Tyrant, who participates in the conversation of *Timaeus,* and after whom an incomplete dialogue on the early history of Athens is named. It is thus no exaggeration to say that Plato's aristocratic connections leave unmistakable traces upon the dialogue to which his philosophical fame is indebted. In the *Republic,* by contrast, Socrates envisions that the establishment of the perfect city will require the expulsion of all citizens over the age of ten (540e), so that the "tablet" of the old city may be wiped "clean" (500d–501a).

Plato's association with Socrates is so much a part of our philosophical folklore that it is difficult not to think of them together. But there was certainly no necessity that they should come together simply because they lived

DUTIES OF A MIDWIFE

[149a] Socrates

Have you then not heard, you absurd boy, that I am the son of a noble and burly midwife, Phaenarete?

Theatetus

Yes, I have heard that.

Socrates

And have you also heard that I practice the same art?

Theatetus

No, never.

Socrates

But I assure you it is true; only do not tell on me to the others; for it is not known that I possess this art. But other people, since they do not know it, do not say this of me, but say that I am a most eccentric person and drive men to distraction. Have you heard that also?

[149b] Theatetus

Yes, I have.

Socrates

Shall I tell you the reason then?

Theatetus

Oh yes, do.

Socrates

Just take into consideration the whole business of the midwives, and you will understand more easily what I mean. For you know, I suppose, that no one of them attends other women while she is still capable of conceiving and bearing but only those do so who have become too old to bear.

Theatetus

Yes, certainly.

Socrates

They say the cause of this is Artemis, because she, a childless goddess, has had childbirth allotted to her as her special province. Now it would seem she did not allow [149c] barren women to be midwives, because human nature is too weak to acquire an art which deals with matters of which it has no experience, but she gave the office to those who on account of age were not bearing children, honoring them for their likeness to herself.

Theatetus

Very likely.

Socrates

Is it not, then, also likely and even necessary, that midwives should know better than anyone else who are pregnant and who are not?

Theatetus

Certainly.

Socrates

And furthermore, the midwives, by means of drugs [149d] and incantations, are able to arouse the pangs of labor and, if they wish, to make them milder, and to cause those to bear who have difficulty in bearing; and they cause miscarriages if they think them desirable.

Theatetus

That is true.

Socrates

Well, have you noticed this also about them, that they are the most skillful of matchmakers, since they are very wise in knowing what union of man and woman will produce the best possible children?

Theatetus

I do not know that at all.

Socrates

But be assured that they are prouder of this [149e] than of their skill in cutting the umbilical cord. Just consider. Do you think the knowledge of what soil is best for each plant or seed belongs to the same art as the tending and harvesting of the fruits of the earth, or to another?

Theatetus

To the same art.

Socrates

And in the case of a woman, do you think, my friend, that there is one art for the sowing and another for the harvesting?

Theatetus

It is not likely.

[150a] Socrates

No; but because there is a wrongful and unscientific way of bringing men and women together, which is called pandering, the midwives, since they are women of dignity and worth, avoid matchmaking, through fear of falling under the charge of pandering. And yet the true midwife is the only proper matchmaker.

Theatetus

It seems so.

Socrates

So great, then, is the importance of midwives; but their function is less important than mine. For women do not, like my patients, bring forth [150b] at one time real children and at another mere images which it is difficult to distinguish from the real. For if they did, the greatest and noblest part of the work of the midwives would be in distinguishing between the real and the false. Do you not think so?

Theatetus

Yes, I do.

Socrates

All that is true of their art of midwifery is true also of mine, but mine differs from theirs in being practiced upon men, not women, and in tending their souls in labor, not their bodies. But the greatest thing about my art is this, [150c] that it can test in every way whether the mind of the young man is bringing forth a mere image, an imposture, or a real and genuine offspring. For I have this in common with the midwives: I am sterile in point of wisdom, and the reproach which has often been brought against me, that I question others but make no reply myself about anything, because I have no wisdom in me, is a true reproach; and the reason of it is this: the god compels me to act as midwife, but has never allowed me to bring forth. I am, then, not at all a wise person myself, [150d] nor have I any wise invention, the offspring born of my own soul; but those who associate with me, although at first some of them seem very ignorant, yet, as our acquaintance advances, all of them to whom the god is gracious make wonderful progress, not only in their own opinion, but in that of others as well. And it is clear that they do this, not because they have ever learned anything from me, but because they have found in themselves many fair things and have brought them forth. But the delivery is due to the god and me. And the proof of it is this: many before now, [150e] being ignorant of this fact and thinking that they were themselves the cause of their success, but despising me, have gone away from me sooner than they ought, whether of their own accord or because others persuaded them to do so. Then, after they have gone away, they have miscarried thenceforth on account of evil companionship, and the offspring which they had brought forth through my assistance they have reared so badly that they have lost it; they have considered impostures and images of more importance than the truth, and at last it was evident to themselves, as well as to others, that they were ignorant.

Source: *Plato,* Theatetus, *in* Plato in Twelve Volumes, *translated by Harold N. Fowler (Cambridge, Mass.: Harvard University Press; London: Heinemann, 1921).*

in Athens, and we should be extremely cautious about importing into the fifth century modern notions about students who go off to college and stumble into a class taught brilliantly by a charismatic professor. In Athens, by contrast, there were no universities, only lessons taught to children by a tutor, and, beginning in the fifth century, courses of lectures taught by itinerant teachers known pejoratively as sophists. In addition, the world of Athenian society was a small one, especially at the upper echelons of society, and associations typically came about through the web of family connections rather than through chance meetings. This fact is particularly significant for the relationship between Plato and Socrates because they share considerably more than meets the eye. Otherwise, we can assert with some conviction that they would never have met, let alone become close associates.

Socrates was well known in Athens for more than his wisdom. He was famously poor, although this poverty was no doubt relative (he did, after all, support a wife and three sons). It is beyond question, however, that he disdained the signs of status pursued by many prominent

Athenians, believed in a "divine sign" that forbade him to do certain things, and had a propensity for falling into speculative reveries that caused him to stand motionless and silent for long periods of time (for example, *Symposium*). Yet, even with these eccentricities and his lack of a political career, Socrates has many of the same aristocratic associations, as does Plato. Despite his assertion in the *Apology* that he conversed with craftsmen, the dialogues themselves show that his interlocutors are with few exceptions the jeunesse dorée, their fathers and relatives, as well as visiting sophists. Critias, Charmides, and the brothers of Plato have been mentioned. This is well illustrated in *Laches,* a dialogue about courage between two groups of elites and Socrates. Two aristocratic but otherwise undistinguished Athenians, Lysimachus and Melesias, have prevailed upon two prominent public figures, the urbane general Nicias and his colleague Laches, to advise them on the appropriate type of education for their sons. Nicias suggests that they consult Socrates, with whom he seems to be quite familiar, and Laches, who has witnessed the personal courage of Socrates firsthand, is quick to add his assent. Lysimachus, who does not know Socrates personally, is hesitant at first but then realizes that he has heard the young men talking about Socrates and singing his praises and, what is more, that this Socrates is the son of his old associate Sophroniscus (181a). What is significant about all of this, of course, is that not only is Socrates well known to the present generation of aristocratic leaders–which could, after all, be because of his own outstanding abilities–but that his father was as well, suggesting that the two families frequent the same social milieu. Moreover, there is some suggestion in the dialogues that Socrates' wife, Xanthippe, was related to the family of Pericles and that the brother of Socrates may well have occupied the office of archon under the Thirty (Nails).

The most important of all of these associations is Socrates' relationship with the Alcibiades, whom he repeatedly attempted to convert to philosophy. This relationship is the basis for Plato's *Alcibiades,* forms an important digression in the *Symposium* (212c–213a), and is the point of the programmatic allusion in the *Theatetus,* in which Socrates disclaims responsibility for the notorious careers of many of his associates, comparing his own activity to that of a midwife unable to bear children herself, who is nevertheless capable of assisting in the delivery of others (149a–150e). According to that analogy, Socrates claims that he never attempted to teach anyone anything, being himself "barren," but only attempted to help them give birth to their own wisdom. It is hardly his fault, he argues, if leaving his side prematurely, they had the misfortune to "miscarry" and become oligarchic revolutionaries. Such passages show not only how persistent were the antidemocratic sympathies among Socrates' associates but also how eager Plato was to give them a spin favorable to the memory of his friend.

Plato's *Republic* is a founding document for the haters of democracy. Yet, it is hardly the only work of Plato to exemplify this spirit. The antidemocratic tone of the dialogues rings loudly in *Crito,* for example, a dialogue between Socrates and his oldest friend, situated in prison, soon after the condemnation of Socrates. Here the personalities of Plato and Socrates are fused but point to the same conclusion. Crito has visited the prison to urge Socrates to take his advice, as well as his money, and escape to Thessaly, a course of action that is justified in his view on the grounds that the decision of the court to condemn Socrates is unjust. Crito also expresses concern for his own reputation, since if Socrates dies many will think that he did nothing to help his friend. Socrates wonders why it is of any interest to Crito and himself what "the many" believe since those who are "most reasonable" will believe that things turned out just as they did (44c). Crito objects that the present circumstances show quite clearly how important it is to take into account the opinions of "the many," since they have the power to do great damage if one runs afoul of them (44d). Socrates' reply here is telling: "If only, Crito, the many could do the greatest evils, so that they could also do the greatest good. That would be fine. As it is, they can do neither; for they are not able to make a man wise or foolish, but they act at random" (44e). To understand Socrates' point accurately, it is useful here to recall the assertion of Pericles quoted above, that in Athens all men are capable of judging. For Socrates, however, such men, "the many," cannot be said truly to judge, for their perception of their own desires and the significance of whatever situation confronts them is so confused and underanalyzed that the gulf between their intentions and the consequences of their actions renders "judging" the least appropriate verb to describe their actions. Thus, in *Crito,* even in the face of death, Socrates maintains his philosophic allegiance to the antiegalitarian message of his life's work.

Nor is this attitude confined to the *Crito.* We see contempt for the principles of democratic government abundantly in the *Apology of Socrates,* which gives Plato's version of the speech Socrates gave at his trial (his contemporary Xenophon published another) in 399 B.C.E. after he had been accused of corrupting the youth and of introducing the worship of new gods into the city. In this work Plato makes Socrates antagonize the Athenian jurors persistently by calling them "O Athenians," in place of the conventional form of address, "O judges." It is only at the end of the speech, in his address to those who have voted to acquit him, that he utters the technical term and addresses the right-thinking minority as "true judges" (40a).

Contempt for Athenian judicial process runs throughout the dialogue. A single example will have to stand for many. Early in the speech he proclaims himself to have been engaged in his work by Apollo himself, who declared through his oracle at Delphi that no one in Greece was wiser than Socrates. After proclaiming his philosophical activity as a service to Apollo, he declares it to have been a great public service to Athens as well, which he says is like a large noble horse that needs to be stung by a fly to avoid dozing its life away. Moreover, he is the fly, or gadfly, to use the archaic expression that has been handed down. He asserts that the unexamined life is not worth living, and after his condemnation, when called upon to propose a penalty for himself *in accordance with the law,* he suggests that he ought to receive a life of free dinners in the Prytaneum at the expense of the city. This last detail is omitted from the defense speech written by Socrates' friend Xenophon, and so, incidentally, may give some insight into Plato's own feelings. At any rate, although the defense speech preserved by Xenophon includes an account of Apollo's oracle (14–15), more or less consistent with that of Plato, Xenophon merely states that Socrates refused to name a penalty after his conviction and forbade his friends to do so as well (23). Thus, it appears that Plato takes Socrates' antagonistic bearing before the Athenian judges and raises his ironic attitude toward his accusers and judges to a new level. As in his behavior toward the "judges" discussed above, and toward "the many" in the *Crito,* Socrates, with what certainly looks like the tacit approval of Plato, maintains a finely developed sense of superiority and does not recognize the right of common citizens to judge him in any but the most legalistic sense of the term.

Plato was not a fascist. His association with the eccentric Socrates, the profundity of his philosophic thought, and the superior literary artistry with which he expressed them evidently drew him further and further away from the manor in which he was born. There is no reason to suspect that he was not appalled at the crimes of his relatives and friends during the brief reign of the Thirty, nor that he did not breathe a sigh of relief with the restoration of the democracy. Nevertheless, his political and social allegiances remained in place, no doubt in part out of allegiance to his mentor, Socrates, who seems to have cultivated similar ones. They are much in evidence in the works of political theory like the *Republic* and the *Laws,* which provide much of the philosophical armature for authoritarian regimes to come, but they are present throughout his work, and the subtle charm with which he weaves them into his thought probably constitutes the greatest danger of all to the champions of egalitarian rule.

–CHARLES PLATTER,
UNIVERSITY OF GEORGIA

Viewpoint:
No. Plato, although an aristocrat of the highest pedigree, broke with his class when he met Socrates and developed a devastating critique of traditional aristocratic thinking about politics.

Although born to one of the more aristocratic families in Athens, Plato followed Socrates in advocating a profoundly critical spirit regarding received wisdom and tradition. This attitude made him many enemies within the democracy, but like his mentor he was a loyal citizen and turned his back on family members who attempted to recruit him in the service of oligarchy. Moreover, the entire tendency of philosophical life, as portrayed in the dialogues, is to move as far away from political life as possible. It will be recalled that even the best city described in the *Republic* is predicated on the idea that philosophers will reluctantly agree to be kings, a possibility that gains no more likelihood from Socrates' formulation in the *Phaedo* that philosophy consists of "the art of dying and being dead." Finally, while the emphasis on personal behavior that permeates the dialogues leads Plato to make use of the traditional vocabulary of ethical action that he inherited from Homer and the aristocratic tradition, the definitions he comes up with for ideas like courage, excellence, moderation, and piety are so far from what traditional aristocrats meant by them that they amount to a scathing indictment of the social structure that produced them. By comparison, democracy, with its many defects, from a Platonic perspective looks like the best regime of the possible forms of government and the one most conducive to authentic philosophic thought.

We must begin with an important methodological consideration and attempt to correct a habit of misstatement that appears frequently even in scholarly writing about the Platonic dialogues, wherever we find sentences with the words "according to Plato . . ." or "Plato's view is . . ." or "Plato says that . . ." and the like. On the surface, this kind of language seems innocuous, no different than the kind of thing we see in any essay about Aristotle, Georg Wilhelm Friedrich Hegel, the president of the United States, or the commissioner of Major League Baseball–anyone with a body of thought, or opinion, from which we can derive relatively noncontroversial inferences about the individual's views. In the case of Plato, however, this type of statement seriously misleads the reader and has important ramifications for the proposition in question here.

Plato did not write in the first person, except in the *Letters,* whose authenticity will probably never be established beyond doubt. There are no Platonic lectures, treatises, diaries, talking points, or position papers. Plato instead composed dialogues, minidramas in which no one character's perspective is allowed to dominate absolutely. To complicate the issue further, Plato himself does not appear in the dialogues, eliminating him in advance as his own interpreter. Nor is this absence accidental, for Plato draws our attention to the two exceptions, first in the *Apology* where Socrates is made to propose a fine as punishment after his conviction (in place of his original request for free dinners) on the pledge of Plato and some others (38b). Second, in the *Phaedo,* the dialogue in which the final conversation and death of Socrates are portrayed, the narrator Phaedo lists the people present in the prison and explains the absence of Plato by adding that he was sick (59b). The absence of the author from the scene of the dialogues means, of course, that in the Platonic dialogue there is no Platonic character to indicate reliably the position of the author vis-à-vis the arguments of the dialogue and makes it impossible for readers to appeal to "what we know Plato thought" in determining their significance. Moreover, by alluding directly to his absence, and to his lack of direct participation in the conversations, Plato warns us in advance against treating him as the ultimate authority and ceding our own interpretative faculties to his.

It can be argued that in the problem of Plato's absence there is less than meets the eye, for although Plato is a nonfactor in the dialogues, his absence is compensated for by the presence of Socrates, his philosophic double. Admittedly, Socrates' character is dominant in many of the dialogues, and he would certainly be unfit as a philosophical hero for Plato if he did not share important areas of belief with the disciple who chose to devote his powerful abilities as a thinker and as a writer to memorialize him. Yet, when we look at the dialogues as a whole, the relation of Socrates to Plato is unclear. Does Socrates always speak for Plato? Or, as many think, is there a progression in the dialogues from direct recollection of Socratic views to later Platonic ones? And how are we to interpret the dialogues in which Socrates' position cannot be equivalent to the "meaning" of the dialogue in any straightforward sense?

In *Parmenides,* for example, the young Socrates is subjected to a withering critique of the doctrine of the forms by the elder philosopher Parmenides. As a result, not only do we have a dialogue in which the center of authority is not Socrates but we also have a powerful and unrebutted critique of what is often taken to be a central piece of Platonic theory. In other words, not only is Socrates wrong in his conversation with Parmenides but he is also wrong wherever else he successfully promotes the forms or "ideas" as a way of getting around the thorny issue of timeless being in a world characterized by unceasing change.

The case of the *Parmenides* is not an isolated instance of the authority of Socrates being undermined by the dialogic situation. In the *Sophist* and the *Statesman,* Socrates gives way to a stranger from Elea, and in the *Laws,* Plato's longest dialogue, Socrates is nowhere to be found. The result of this situation is that we must agree that if Socrates' view and Plato's view are supposed to be identical, then these dialogues are surprisingly empty of both. If, on the other hand, the view of Plato comes from somewhere else than the mask of Socrates, then we will be in need of a methodology to extract it differently from the one that has been proposed. Finally, if the perspectives of Socrates and Plato are shown not to be identical in these dialogues, what hope do we have, besides that provided by unsupported speculation, that they are in, say, the *Republic,* or in any of the other dialogues?

For reasons that cannot be completely known, Plato thought that the dialogue was the best vehicle for his philosophical message and constructed it in such a way that the sentiments expressed could not be reduced simply to the authority of Plato or the charisma of Socrates. We must respect the methodological implications of his decision, however, for if the spirit of the dialogue does not lie in the literary representation of the author, or in his favorite character, then it must lie in the ensemble of the dialogue itself (Strauss). Yet, this admission is crippling for the assertion that Plato is a hater of democracy, whose true allegiance is to the aristocratic world of his upbringing, for in making it we concede in advance that Plato never says anything directly and therefore will be an ineffective spokesman for any social attitude or class identity, a conclusion that will surprise no one who has read the *Seventh Letter,* in which Plato (if the letter is genuine) expresses his great ambivalence about the political activities of his relatives and acquaintances and attempts to justify his refusal to join them.

The magnitude of the change wrought by Plato's dialogues is impossible to overstate, least of all in his approach to ethics, where he appropriated the traditional terms he inherited from Homer and the aristocratic tradition and developed a superior understanding of them that completely contradicted aristocratic assumptions. An essay of this length cannot hope to do justice to the breadth of this endeavor. Still, it is possible to give some sense of Plato's revolutionary thought in the context from which it arose. The elite fighters immortalized in Homeric poetry are often styled "the best of the Achaeans." The word for "best," *aristoi,* connotes a degree of excellence deriving from the superior nature of these men, who trace their ancestry from aristocratic forebears often back to the Olympian gods themselves. The sense of absolute certainty about this status of such a nature is intrinsic to the concept in Greek, where *physis* (nature) is derived from the verb *phyein,* "to grow." Thus, according to this way of thinking, our nature represents the "natural" culmination of our growth. According to the same logic, the upper classes are superior to the lower ones because of their superior natures, which, in turn, justify their authority over lesser citizens. In short, *arête* (excellence) is no accident.

The dialogues of Plato challenge the assumptions of this idea at every turn, especially in the aporetic dialogues, whose participants begin the conversation assuming that the inherited ideas about behavior that guide their actions are well thought out and worthy of veneration but end up in confusion *(aporia)* after the ideas are shown to be dubious and largely incoherent. Traditional notions of piety *(Euthyphro),* friendship *(Lysis),* courage *(Laches),* beauty *(Hippias Major),* and moderation *(Charmides),* as well as *arête* itself *(Meno, Protagoras),* all turn out to be far more ambiguous creatures under the examination of Socrates than they were ever assumed to be in aristocratic society. Further, it is suggested that none of these terms might be explained successfully except in the context of a general account of the Good. This last point is particularly important, for according to the traditional aristocratic view of life, nature was unproblematic; *arête* and its attendant virtues followed *naturally* from the expression of superior *natures,* as adornments to it. In the dialogues, however, the situation is precisely opposite, for instead of having a soul that expresses the virtues to adorn its nature, we have exercises like philosophy that help to shape the soul in such a way that it may become more virtuous (Hadot). Yet, even that is not the extent of the shift. For by suggesting that adequate answers to the questions about virtue are attainable only through an understanding of the abstract idea of the Good, the dialogue implies that a person will not be truly virtuous until that understanding has been attained. No idea could be more unacceptable to a concept of inherited virtue than this one.

Plato's apparent lack of sympathy for aristocratic ideas did not make him a sentimental champion of the lower classes, however. In fact, he saw in them the same vice that affected the upper classes–the tendency to defer to received opinions on important topics, together with the unwillingness or inability to attempt to think clearly and precisely about what they were saying. It is in this context that Plato develops *doxa* (opinion) as a word with especially pejora-

Bust of Plato, disciple of Socrates and founder of the Academy

(Sala delle Muse, Vatican)

tive connotations, suggesting an idea that does not have an argument to back it up, and juxtaposes it with the truth, which is the goal of philosophy. Both upper and lower classes are rendered equally insensible by their attachment to *doxa,* a spurious knowledge that must be recognized as such before progress in ethics and philosophy can begin. Until they do so, however, both classes represent a reconstituted version of "the many," the traditional euphemism used to describe the lower classes (at the time the adherents of democracy), and who stand in contrast to the legitimate aristocracy of "the few" who have been persuaded of the superiority of the philosophical way of life.

The reuse of traditional expressions can cause confusion, just as we saw earlier in Plato's reinterpretation of *arête* and the other virtues. This irony, a hallmark of Socrates, is no less present for the subtlety with which it is deployed. Thus, when Socrates replies to Crito's assertion that "the many" have the power to do great harm by countering that they merely act at random (and so do harm only accidentally), he uses the traditional ethical vocabulary that separates "the few" wealthy aristocrats from "the many" who are supposed to look up to them (44d). In fact, however, "the many" to whom he refers are not democrats who fail to defer to their betters but all who are under the mistaken impression that wealth, power, rank, and ancestry are more important for a person than the state of her/his soul (29d–30b). That is the same message that Plato has Socrates convey in the *Apology,* and like the comment in *Crito,* it applies to all, regardless of class, who fail to grasp the unique importance and unceasing demands of the Socratic way of life.

It is necessary to make a final point about how Plato portrays the relationship of Socrates to the democratic regime of Athens. Whatever his political sympathies, Socrates was a loyal citizen of Athens who, as the testimony of Xenophon confirms, fulfilled his civic duties with striking success (Nails). In *Laches* we hear of his bravery from the commanding general himself, and in the *Symposium* Alcibiades offers a panegyric on how Socrates saved his life while they were on campaign. Socrates alludes to this service as well in the *Apology* (28e) and describes his fidelity to the law the only time he was called upon to play a public role in the administration of the state. He also mentions how he personally risked death to avoid collaborating with the Thirty, who attempted to implicate as many citizens as possible in their crimes (32a–d). Perhaps even more telling is his attachment to the city, which is well attested to in the dialogues. In *Phaedrus,* Phaedrus makes fun of Socrates for his lack of familiarity with the countryside, to which Socrates replies with the famous dictum that trees and country places are unwilling to teach him but that men in the city are (230d). This focus on the city in general, however, can be narrowed. Socrates justifies his unwillingness to flee execution in the *Crito* by appealing just to this fact that he has never sought to leave Athens, even for a festival (52b). So how strange it would be for him at his age to wander through Greece in search of an alternate place to live! What would he look for? An area more hospitable to philosophy than Athens? Would the horse-loving rulers of Thessaly with their dissolute ways and autocratic inclinations offer greater freedom of expression than Athens, where he had been left to do as he chose for seventy years (53a–d)? This argument shows that Socrates' criticism of Athenian democracy, even filtered through the lens of Plato, for whom the execution of Socrates showed the democracy in its absolutely worst light, must be seen against the backdrop of fidelity to the government of Athens.

This conclusion holds for Plato, too. After all, he did not look back, except into the mythical past of the city *(Timaeus)* to find a city of greater virtue than the present one. Indeed, in *Gorgias,* he has Socrates criticize in no uncertain terms the great men of the fifth century: Miltiades, Themistocles, Cimon, and Pericles, for leaving the city in worse shape than they found it (503d). He dreamed of a city that could improve the conditions of contemporary life, but as Cicero was to say, the *Republic* is a paradigm that shows the limits of politics rather than a plan for political revolution. Plato was more concerned by far to foment revolutions in the soul, as his own lack of involvement in politics indicates clearly. Even in Sicily he represents himself as acting more out of fidelity to his friend Dion than out of conviction that a philosophical regime under the tyrant Dionysus was possible. For the most part, however, he lived and died, as his mentor Socrates did, within the walls of Athens, critical but apparently satisfied that no other place offered greater prospects for the practice of philosophy.

–CHARLES PLATTER,
UNIVERSITY OF GEORGIA

References

Julia Annas, *An Introduction to Plato's* Republic (New York & Oxford: Clarendon Press, 1981).

Annas and Christopher Rowe, eds., *New Perspectives on Plato, Modern and Ancient* (Cambridge, Mass.: Harvard University Press, 2002).

Ernest Barker, *Greek Political Theory: Plato and His Predecessors* (London: Methuen / New York: Barnes & Noble, 1960).

Seth Benardete, *The Argument of the Action: Essays on Greek Poetry and Philosophy* (Chicago: University of Chicago Press, 2000).

Ruby Blondell, *The Play of Character in Plato's Dialogues* (Cambridge: Cambridge University Press, 2002).

Guy Cromwell Field, *Plato and His Contemporaries: A Study in Fourth-Century Life and Thought* (London: Methuen, 1967).

Hans Georg Gadamer, *Dialogue and Dialectic: Eight Hermeneutical Studies on Plato,* translated by P. Christopher Smith (New Haven: Yale University Press, 1980).

W. K. C. Guthrie, *A History of Greek Philosophy,* 6 volumes (Cambridge: Cambridge University Press, 1962–1981).

Richard Kraut, ed., *The Cambridge Companion to Plato* (Cambridge & New York: Cambridge University Press, 1992).

Diogenes Laertius, *Lives of Eminent Philosophers,* translated by R. D. Hicks (London: Heinemann; New York: Putnam, 1925).

Debra Nails, *The People of Plato: A Prosopography of Plato and Other Socratics* (Indianapolis & Cambridge: Hackett, 2002).

Plato, *The Collected Dialogues of Plato, Including the Letters,* edited by Edith Hamilton and Huntington Cairns (New York: Pantheon, 1961).

Karl Popper, *The Open Society and Its Enemies,* volume 1: *Plato* (London: Routledge, 1945).

Alice Swift Riginos, *Platonica: The Anecdotes Concerning the Life and Writings of Plato* (Leiden: Brill, 1976).

Leo Strauss, *The City and Man* (Chicago: University of Chicago Press, 1964).

Alfred Edward Taylor, *Plato: The Man and His Work* (New York: Dial, 1929).

Eugène Napoleon Tigerstedt, *Interpreting Plato* (Stockholm: Almqvist & Wiksell International, 1977).

Gregory Vlastos, *Socrates: Ironist and Moral Philosopher* (Ithaca, N.Y.: Cornell University Press, 1991).

Catherine Zuckert, *Postmodern Plato: Nietzsche, Heidigger, Strauss, Derrida* (Chicago: University of Chicago Press, 1996).

GREECE: SAPPHO

Does Sappho's poetry represent a departure from the traditional masculine view of love?

Viewpoint: Yes. Sappho's poetry departs from a traditional masculine view of love by presenting love relations as mutual and reciprocal, in contrast to the model of love relations found in Archaic Greek male poets.

Viewpoint: No. Sappho depicts love relations as driven by domination and conquest. Her poems also treat typically male themes such as politics and philosophy.

As a poet and as an influential literary figure, Sappho has had great appeal over the ages. Since she first wrote her poems on the Greek island of Lesbos at the end of the seventh century B.C.E., she has been considered one of the most important poets in the Western tradition. From antiquity to the modern era, Sappho has prompted centuries of speculation about her life and admiration for her powerful lyrics. Plato's fifth-century B.C.E. reference to Sappho as the "tenth Muse" is one of the many indications we have for the high esteem in which she was held even in ancient Greece. While she remains an iconic and influential figure throughout much of the lyric tradition in the West, her poetry has clearly provoked a good deal of curiosity and criticism as well.

Indeed, the origins of the modern meaning of "lesbian" most likely can be traced to Sappho. Many of Sappho's poems evoke a community of women whose relationship to one another is undeniably homoerotic. In some of her poems, Sappho herself, or at least a female speaker named "Sappho," expresses passionate, erotic feelings toward another woman. Even in poems that do not deal explicitly with love, Sappho often depicts herself as part of a world in which the emotional and/or erotic bonds between women take center stage. Because ancient Greek society was largely male-dominated, Sappho's focus on a "woman-centered" world in her poetry has, at least in part, made her a fascinating yet vexing subject of speculation and fantasy.

Speculation about Sappho has also been fueled by the fact that Sappho's poetry survives mostly in fragments. Although her poems were collected into nine books by scholars in Alexandria a few centuries after Sappho wrote them, only forty fragments long enough to be intelligible survive. While approximately two hundred fragments have been attributed to Sappho, many of those fragments contain only one or two words. Thus, a great deal of the scholarship on Sappho during the twentieth century dealt either with attempts to reconstruct her poetic texts or to construct her biography, despite the fact that there is no solid evidence for knowing anything concrete about her life. A dominant feature of twentieth-century scholarship on Sappho, particularly up until the 1960s, is an attempt to explain away the homoerotic elements in her poetry by turning her into either the head of a religious cult for young girls or a teacher in a kind of finishing school for young aristocratic women. Yet, in the last few decades, scholars have tended to focus on the literary content of Sappho's poems and its relationship to literary and cultural traditions. More recently, the increasing influence of gender studies within classics has had a significant impact on Sappho scholarship. Indeed, critical debates on her often focus on the extent to which her poetry may be considered "feminine" or, to borrow a phrase from Diane Rayor, "woman-specific." The following opposing viewpoints reflect these critical debates, focusing on how Sappho's gender is or is not a defining feature of her poetic discourse.

—Ellen Greene

Viewpoint: Yes. Sappho's poetry departs from a traditional masculine view of love by presenting love relations as mutual and reciprocal, in contrast to the model of love relations found in Archaic Greek male poets.

One of the most pressing issues in Sappho criticism during the last two decades has concerned questions about the extent to which Sappho's gender shapes the nature of her poetic discourse. Recent scholars have provided persuasive arguments for showing how Sappho's poetry ought not to be interpreted as merely the emotional outpourings of a passionate woman. These scholars have shown the artistry at work in Sappho's lyrics, pointing out the various ways her poems employ many of the literary conventions and themes used by Archaic Greek male poets. While I agree that it is important to acknowledge Sappho's indebtedness to Homer and to the traditions of Archaic poetry, I contend that Sappho's poetry presents a woman-specific discourse that differs perceptibly from male patterns of erotic poetry.

For the Greeks, erotic relationships were essentially hierarchical and defined in terms of the opposition between active and passive. One was either in the active position of a lover or in the passive position of a beloved. In the works of male Archaic poets, erotic desire is typically presented in accordance with the active/passive model, with the male in the active role and the woman in the passive position. In contrast, Sappho's poems express the active erotic desire of the female speaker in the poems and, at the same time, present a pattern of mutuality and reciprocity between two female lovers. Neither of the female lovers is presented as an object; Sappho portrays both as subjects engaged in a relationship of mutual erotic fulfillment. Through a brief examination of two of Sappho's poems that best illustrate this pattern of mutuality, I will show how Sappho's poetic texts offer an erotic practice and discourse outside of male assumptions of dominance and submission.

I begin with a discussion of the last two stanzas of Sappho's fragment 1, often called the "Hymn to Aphrodite." Not only does this poem use the relationship between the female narrator and the goddess to represent a nonhierarchical ideal for relationships between women, but it is also the poem sometimes employed by scholars to illustrate how Sappho, like her male contemporaries, offers a vision of eros as an expression of the desire for domination. My reading of this poem will refute this view. In this poem, Sappho calls on Aphrodite, the goddess of love, to help Sappho regain the affections of her lover. The poem makes it clear that in the past Aphrodite has aided Sappho in the fulfillment of her desires. In the next to last stanza of the poem, Aphrodite "answers" Sappho's call, telling her that soon the woman who now rejects her will love her once again. The last stanza is, presumably, Sappho's own voice, expressing confidence that Aphrodite will help her fulfill her desires:

> Richly-enthroned, immortal Aphrodite,
> daughter of
> Zeus, weaver of wiles, I beseech you,
> do not subdue me with pain and anguish.
>
> But come to me, if ever in the past you heard my
> cries from afar, and leaving the house
> of your father, you came,
>
> Your golden chariot yoked. Beautiful sparrows
> brought you swiftly over the black earth,
> their wings fluttering from heaven through
> mid-air,
>
> And quickly they came. But you, Blessed One,
> with a smile on your immortal face,
> asked what did I suffer, this time again,
> and why, again, I called,
>
> And what I most want in my frenzied heart,
> Whom, again, am I to persuade back to your
> heart?
> Who, O Sappho, does you wrong?
>
> For if she flees, soon she will pursue; and if she
> does not receive gifts, soon she will give them.
> And if she loves not, soon she will love even
> against her will.
>
> Come to me even now, and release me from
> cruel
> anxieties; and fulfill all that my heart desires,
> you yourself be my ally.

The next to last stanza of this poem appears to portray erotic desire as an endless game of flight and pursuit, a game that might suggest a model of erotic relations based on conquest and domination. Some have read Aphrodite's reassurance to the speaker in this stanza as confirma-

that, according to the grammar of the poem, involves only subjects.

Sappho's use of military terminology in the speaker's request to Aphrodite to be her ally in the last line of the poem may seem to identify Sappho with masculine values of conquest and militarism. In asking Aphrodite to be her cofighter or fellow soldier in the "battle" of love, the speaker asks Aphrodite to come into an alliance of mutuality with her. The speaker's use of the word *ally* to describe her relationship with the goddess suggests that she is imagining a relationship based on equality and reciprocity. Further, the word *ally* can also refer to an alliance between states, thus heightening the sense in which the speaker envisions herself in an equal partnership with Aphrodite based not on a model of dominance and aggression but on affiliations between equals. Moreover, in light of Aphrodite's (Homeric) reputation for ineffectual, obstructive conduct in martial affairs and her clearly inappropriate presence in the exclusively male world of the battlefield, it would seem that Aphrodite's role as the speaker's ally would not follow the male model for battle partners. Thus, we cannot assume that an alliance between the speaker and Aphrodite involves the attempt to conquer an adversary at all. Rather, Sappho negates the values associated with martial conquest and substitutes in its place an alliance with Aphrodite that turns the domination of one over the other into *persuasion*—the power to seduce another into a relationship of mutual desire. The speaker asks Aphrodite to be her ally not in order to conquer or dominate the beloved, and certainly *not* to make the beloved passively accept her affections. Rather, the speaker calls on Aphrodite to help stir the beloved from passive indifference into *active* affection. The speaker imagines a situation where her beloved actively pursues. Also we should not assume that the speaker has to become passive if her beloved is to become active; that would be simply to assume the male model of dominance and submission. The poem itself in no way makes this suggestion. On the contrary, the purpose of the speaker's alliance with Aphrodite is to rouse her beloved, so that *each* is to be both lover and beloved, each of them active, desiring subjects.

Fragment 94 is the only surviving poem of Sappho's that explicitly dramatizes an erotic encounter between two women. The poem thus illustrates clearly how Sappho envisions love relations as reciprocal. In this poem Sappho never describes the beauty of the beloved as static, nor does she portray the beloved as a passive object of desire. Rather, she describes her exclusively in terms of her *effect* on the speaker herself and on their surroundings:

Sappho; oil painting by Charles-August Mengin, 1877

(Manchester City Art Gallery, U.K.)

tion of the view that the roles of lover and beloved eventually will be reversed. Such a view is based on the idea that in the relationship between the two lovers, there has to be a subject and an object at all times. In other words, one of the lovers has to be dominant and the other submissive. This argument rests on the observation that Aphrodite's statements to Sappho contain no direct object. I agree that the lack of a direct object in Aphrodite's consolation of the speaker is important. But the real significance of the lack of direct objects (of fleeing, pursuing, and loving) in those lines is that the speaker is suggesting that neither she nor her beloved are characterized as *objects* of each other's love. The speaker does not imagine that the consummation of (her) love involves *either* domination or submission. The beloved is portrayed as a subject whether she is fleeing or pursuing, giving or receiving. Indeed, the subject *she* in these lines can be either the speaker *or* her beloved. The speaker is describing, in general terms, the reciprocal movements of desire in which she and her beloved both participate in the process of giving and receiving, loving and being loved—a process

Honestly, I wish I were dead.
Weeping she left with many tears,

And said; "Oh what terrible things
we endured. Sappho, truly,
against my will I leave you."

And I answered: "Go, be
happy, and remember me;
For you know how we cared for you.

And if not, then I want
to remind you . . . of the wonderful
things we shared.

For many wreaths of violets and
roses . . .
you put on by my side,

And many woven garlands
fashioned of flowers,
you tied round your soft neck,

And with rich myrrh,
fit for a queen,
you anointed . . .

And on a soft bed,
tenderly,
you satisfied (your) desire.

And there was
no sacred place
from which we were absent,

no grove,
no dance,
no sound. . . ."

Like the "Hymn to Aphrodite," fragment 94 begins in a mood of helpless despair. Like the speaker in fragment 1, the speaker here is able to raise herself out of her distressed state of mind by remembering past erotic fulfillment. Through a merging of the voices of lover and beloved, Sappho dramatizes the shift from the sad circumstances of separation to an idyllic world of memory and imagination.

At the beginning of the poem, we hear the distinct voices of the speaker and her departing lover shift back and forth in response to one another. This has the effect of emphasizing their separation, the fact that they are both subject to circumstances they cannot control. The speaker's direct recollection of the time of departure locates both the narrator and the woman who is leaving in a temporal sequence of events in which they are each distinct characters within the narrative reported by the speaker. The predominantly descriptive mode of discourse here preserves the sense of separateness between the two lovers. However, Sappho's response to the departing woman begins to remove us from the immediate moment of departure to the experience of love in the past. Sappho's request in line 8 that the woman remember draws the poem away from the dramatic portrayal of the woman leaving to the more inward situation of remembering.

From stanza 5 until the end of the poem Sappho describes a scene of idyllic beauty and erotic fulfillment. The speaker, her beloved, and the community of women evoked in the poem are all connected in the aura of sensations and erotic stimulation. Yet, Sappho does not describe her beloved in a way that presents her as static, as something that can be possessed. Rather, Sappho focuses on the "total affect" of the beloved that arouses desire–the movement of the beloved's body, the flow of her garments, the smells and textures that surround her. Here, in what is perhaps the best example of Sappho's portrayal of the beloved woman, the speaker does not depict the beloved as a passive object of desire, nor does she present the beauty of the beloved as something satisfying in itself. Rather, the speaker presents the body of the beloved as a site of erotic agency. The dynamic actions associated with the beloved (putting around, putting on, anointing, and satisfying) emphasize the active desire of the beloved woman. She is not merely a static entity to be gazed upon with pleasure; she is presented, instead, through a series of actions that involve both her and the speaker. The speaker celebrates their shared experiences by calling to mind images of the beloved woman as the subject of her own desires, as one who acts rather than as one who is acted upon. The description of the beloved's actions (putting on, anointing, and satisfying) in stanzas 5 through 8 flow into the actions the two lovers undertake together in the ninth stanza of the poem. In line 11, the return to "we" as the subject reminds us that the fulfillment of desire depends on a symmetrical arrangement between lover and beloved–an arrangement in which they are both actively engaged in the pursuit of erotic fulfillment.

–ELLEN GREENE,
UNIVERSITY OF OKLAHOMA

Viewpoint: No. Sappho depicts love relations as driven by domination and conquest. Her poems also treat typically male themes such as politics and philosophy.

Sappho addresses many of her poems to other women and seems to evoke an all-female world apart from the typical male concerns of war and politics. It would be a mistake, however, to assume that Sappho's literary voice and her poetic discourse can be simply categorized as "feminine." Sappho's use of military terminology and her allusions to Homeric heroes in the context of characterizing love relations imply that Sappho often attempts to show a commonality between love and war, between the masculine drive to dominate and conquer and so-called feminine desire. Thus, like her male counterparts, Sappho often presents erotic relations as defined by a dynamic of power, in which one is either in the active or passive position. Moreover, throughout her corpus Sappho makes abundant use of Homeric references, thus reflecting an awareness of epic, its militarism and atmosphere of masculine combat and struggle. Although Sappho's love poems usually focus on homoerotic relations between women, they nonetheless suggest that violence and aggression are often integral parts of love in general.

One of the ways Sappho utilizes Homeric language and thus brings into focus the menacing world of the battlefield is her insertion of Homeric similes into the celebratory world of the wedding song. Two such examples are fragments, believed to be parts of marriage songs, that compare the bride to fruit either about to be plucked by gatherers or trampled by shepherds.

105a
[the bride]
just like a sweet apple which turns red on the
uppermost branch,
on the top of the top-most; but the apple-
gatherers forgot it,
or rather, they didn't forget it, but they could
not reach it . . .

105c
Like the hyacinth in the hills
which the shepherds step on,
trampling into the ground the flower in its
purple . . .

In the first simile, the image of the reddening fruit is associated semantically with the blood spilled on the battlefield. In Homer's *Iliad,* similes are often used to provide a respite from war, bringing into focus the natural world in contrast to the scenes of violence in war and the assertion of masculine military might. Sappho's use of Homeric similes in the context of a wedding song suggests the potential violence implicit in the impending marriage. While Sappho depicts the unattainability of the apple, that is, the intact innocence of the bride, the gatherers' eventual possession of the fruit is implied. The apple ripens for the gatherers who will ultimately pluck and consume it. In fragment 105c the flower has already fallen. The indifference of the shepherds to the flower's beauty emphasizes the tragic pathos in the flower's destruction. The image of the purple flower recalls the purple blood described in Homer's scenes of death and destruction on the battlefields of Troy. While some of Sappho's poems evoke the idyllic world of female affiliation, a world segregated from the violence and strife of masculine concerns, other poems suggest an ominousness that haunts the pristine, insular feminine sphere. The epic context of Sappho's similes—in particular, the sense of aggression suggested by those similes—points to violence as an integral part of erotic experience.

Not only do Sappho's poems often evoke the masculine world of the battlefield, but also her characterizations of eros can be compared to those in the poetry of male Archaic poets. Ibycus, for example, portrays the lover as subject to a violent force. He characterizes eros as a "dark, pitiless wind" that "rocks and tosses" his heart. Archilochus describes his experience of love in a similar way: "I lie here miserable and broken with desire, pierced through to the bones by the bitterness of this god-given painful love. O comrade, this passion makes my limbs limp and tramples over me." Likewise, in fragments 47 and 130 Sappho describes herself as violently shaken by love. Moreover, in fragment 130 Sappho's characterization of Eros as the "loosener of limbs" is also applied to descriptions of death in Homer:

47
Love shook my heart, like the wind
assailing the oaks on a mountain.

130
Eros the loosener of limbs shakes me again–
bitter-sweet, untamable, crawling creature.

Also, in one of Sappho's most famous poems, fragment 31, Sappho describes herself in a state of physical and mental collapse at the sight of her beloved:

31 (lines 7–16)
For whenever I see you, I cannot speak,
my tongue is broken and a thin flame runs
under my skin.

With my eyes I see nothing, my ears buzz,
and cold sweat covers me.
Trembling seizes my whole body.
I am greener than grass; at such times
death isn't far from me.

Sappho's depiction of herself in this poem mirrors her characterizations of eros as a violent force that renders her powerless. Several scholars have pointed out that in fragment 31 Sappho applies Homeric battle terminology to the sphere of love. The catalogue of Sappho's reactions to the presence of her beloved may be compared to Homeric catalogues of the coward's "response to the stress of ambush." Sappho's depiction of the breakdown of her body in fragment 31 alludes to Homeric descriptions of the body as an assembly of parts. As the noted scholar Page du Bois argues, "Sappho adopts here (in fragment 31) a traditional, conventional, epic description of the body, familiar to her and her audience from the traditional poetry, to express what appears to be a disintegration of her own body." In addition, Sappho's image of her broken tongue recalls Homer's request for help from the Muses, goddesses of song, before he embarks on his catalogue of ships: "I could not recount the multitude of them, nor name them, not if I had ten tongues and ten mouths, not if I had a voice never to be broken" (*Iliad,* 2.488–490). Thus, the view that Sappho's poetic discourse reflects a separate woman-centered world, apart from men, war, and politics, cannot be supported when we consider the extent to which her poems show similarities to those of male Archaic poets and also utilize Homeric material. Clearly, Sappho's discourse reflects a profound engagement with a male literary tradition. The fact that, for example, Sappho uses the image of the Homeric body to depict love suggests that Sappho envisions the (female) lover much like a wounded soldier on the battlefield.

Moreover, the next to last stanza of Sappho's "Hymn to Aphrodite," which pictures love in terms of dominance and submission, echoes the ways in which male Archaic poets typically envision love relations. In response to Sappho's request that the goddess of love help Sappho win back her beloved's affections, Aphrodite offers Sappho the consolation of knowing that soon the positions of lover and beloved, pursuer and pursued, will be reversed:

For if she flees, soon she will pursue; and if she
does not receive gifts, soon she will give them.
And if she loves not, soon she will love even
against her will.

In this stanza Sappho pictures love relations as a game of flight and pursuit. The lovers are depicted in the positions of either active or passive, dominant or submissive. The one who receives gifts is in the passive position, while the one who gives them is active. Sappho suggests that the relationship between the two lovers is based on the fact that each of them at any given time has to be in the active or passive role, that the relationship is thus essentially hierarchical. We can see a similar view of erotic relations in the poetry of Sappho's male counterparts. Anacreon, for example, characterizes love as a game of conquest; in one of his most famous poems he expresses confidence that he will be able to "tame" his object of affection:

My Thracian foal, why do you glare with disdain
and then shun me absolutely as if I knew
nothing of this art?

I tell you I could bridle you with tight straps,
seize the reins and gallop you around the posts
of the pleasant course.

But you prefer to graze on the calm meadow,
or frisk and play, lightly prancing–having no
manly
rider to break you in.

Like Sappho, Anacreon portrays the erotic relationship in terms of a dynamic of power. Both poets depict themselves in a position of mastery over a helpless, vulnerable object of desire. Although Sappho explores the dynamics of a love relationship between women, her poetry shows how she envisions erotic desire in

IN LOVE AND WAR

Sappho's use of Homeric battle terminology in fragment 31 is readily apparent when compared to the following excerpt from the Iliad:

Then to him the wise Meriones made answer: "Aye, in mine own hut also and my black ship are many spoils of the Trojans, but I have them not at hand to take thereof. For I deem that I too am not forgetful of valor, [270] but I take my stand amid the foremost in battle, where men win glory, when so the strife of war ariseth. Some other of the brazen-coated Achaeans might sooner be unaware of my fighting, but thou methinks of thine own self knowest it well."

And to him Idomeneus, leader of the Cretans, made answer: [275] "I know what manner of man thou art in valor; what need hast thou to tell the tale thereof? For if now all the best of us were being told off besides the ships for an ambush, wherein the valor of men is best discerned—there the coward cometh to light and the man of valor; for the color of the coward changeth ever to another hue, [280] nor is the spirit in his breast stayed that he should abide steadfast, but he shifteth from knee to knee and resteth on either foot, and his heart beats loudly in his breast as he bodeth death, and the teeth chatter in his mouth; but the color of the brave man changeth not, [285] neither feareth he overmuch when once he taketh his place in the ambush of warriors, but he prayeth to mingle forthwith in woeful war—not even in such case, I say, would any man make light of thy courage or the strength of thy hands. For if so be thou wert stricken by a dart in the toil of battle, or smitten with a thrust, not from behind in neck or back would the missile fall; [290] nay, but on thy breast would it light or on thy belly, as thou wert pressing on into the dalliance of the foremost fighters. But come, no longer let us loiter here and talk thus like children, lest haply some man wax wroth beyond measure; nay, but go thou to the hut, and get thee a mighty spear."

Source: The Iliad of Homer: Done into English Prose, *translated by Andrew Lang and others (London: Macmillan, 1903).*

much the same way as her male counterparts. The masculine model of desire, based on the drive of one to dominate the other, finds expression in Sappho's poetry, despite the fact that the atmosphere of Sapphic verse is primarily female.

Further, the idea of a Sappho exclusively focused on feminine concerns ignores the evidence for Sappho's involvement and interest in the traditionally masculine sphere of politics. We know from the poetry of Sappho's contemporary Alcaeus that the politics of Lesbos was often violent and tumultuous. Although Sappho's surviving fragments do not show as much interest in the political situation on Lesbos as Alcaeus's poetry, they do nonetheless reveal that Sappho was at least somewhat involved in political affairs. In one of her fragments, Sappho attacks a woman named Mica whom she calls an "evil-doer" because she chose the friendship of the women associated with the royal family of Mytilene, Lesbos's capital. In other fragments Sappho attacks a number of other powerful families on Lesbos through insults to the women of those families. In fragment 57, Sappho berates Andromeda for falling in love with a "country woman":

> What country woman bewitches your mind . . . dressed
> in a rustic dress . . . not knowing how to draw the rags over her ankles?

Sappho's concern about social class in the example above is indicative of the ways in which her poetry in general champions aristocratic values. Like Alcaeus, Sappho clearly reveals herself to be an aristocrat, waging war against powerful rival clans. Although Sappho's attacks on the women of those clans might be construed as having an erotic cast to them, in keeping with the homoerotic character of her verse, Sappho's invectives are consistent with the politics of Archaic Greece in general. Women of aristocratic families were typically used as a means of social control by many of the tyrants. Attacks on women of noble clans were often the means by which rival families competed against one another.

Moreover, in some of her surviving verse, as in the poetry of Theognis, Archolochus, Anacreon, and Alcaeus for example, Sappho attempts to define what it means to be a noble man, that is, a man who supports the old aristocratic values in the face of the new wealth. Fragment 148, for instance, could easily have been written by a male poet:

> Wealth without virtue is not a harmless neighbor.
> The mixing of them both is the height of good fortune.

Likewise, fragment 50 shows Sappho's concern for ethics and aristocratic social relations—concerns we tend to associate with male writers:

> For the beautiful man is beautiful only to look at,
> but the good man will become instantly beautiful as well.

These two fragments clearly demonstrate that Sappho is not merely interested in the private and domestic concerns typically associated with women in Archaic Greek culture. They show Sappho's interests in declaring what she considers important and in defining abstract notions of beauty and goodness.

In one of her most famous poems, fragment 16, Sappho uses the myth of Helen to explore the meaning of both beauty and desire. The first stanza of the poem makes a general assertion about the interconnectedness of beauty and desire. Beauty, Sappho tells us, is "whatever anyone loves." Sappho's approach in this poem may be considered philosophical in the broad sense, in that Sappho subordinates the specific examples of Helen and Sappho's own object of desire, Anaktoria, to the more general definition of beauty put forth in the opening stanza. Sappho goes on in the second stanza to declare that this definition is "completely intelligible to all." The Greek word for "intelligible" is *suneton,* a word that often has philosophical implications. Sappho makes it clear from the beginning of the poem that, like the philosophers, she attempts to find a unifying principle that will help make sense of the diversity of human experience. At the end of the poem, Sappho draws a parallel between the desire she has for Anaktoria and the desire soldiers have for the glory of war. Sappho thus suggests a continuity of desire that governs both female and male worlds, the worlds of love and war. In so doing, Sappho recognizes the philosophical endeavor of discovering a concept, or set of concepts, that explains human identity and experience.

Clearly, some aspects of Sappho's verse may be considered "feminine." Yet, the political and philosophical content in Sappho's poetry as well as her depiction of the love relationship in terms of a dynamic of power make it impossible to characterize Sappho's poetic language as merely, or even predominantly, feminine. We have also seen how Sappho's poems have a great deal in common with the poetry of male Archaic writers, especially those whose poems are particularly concerned with erotic desire.

—ELLEN GREENE,
UNIVERSITY OF OKLAHOMA

References

Anne Burnett, *Three Archaic Poets: Archilochus, Alcaeus, Sappho* (Cambridge, Mass.: Harvard University Press, 1983).

Claude Calame, "Sappho's Group: An Initiation into Womanhood," in *Reading Sappho: Contemporary Approaches,* edited by Ellen Greene (Berkeley: University of California Press, 1997), pp. 113–124.

Anne Carson, "The Justice of Aphrodite in Sappho Fr. 1," *Transactions of the American Philological Association,* 110 (1980): 135–142.

Page du Bois, "Sappho and Helen," *Arethusa,* 11 (1978): 89–99.

Du Bois, *Sappho Is Burning* (Chicago: University of Chicago Press, 1995).

Ellen Greene, "Apostrophe and Women's Erotics in the Poetry of Sappho," *Transactions of the American Philological Association,* 124 (1994): 41–56.

Greene, ed., *Re-Reading Sappho: Reception and Transmission* (Berkeley: University of California Press, 1997).

Judith Hallett, "Sappho and Her Social Context: Sense and Sensuality," *Signs,* 4 (1979): 447–464.

André Lardinois, "Subject and Circumstance in Sappho's Poetry," *Transactions of the American Philological Association,* 124 (1994): 57–84.

Mary Lefkowitz, "Critical Stereotypes and the Poetry of Sappho," *Greek, Roman, and Byzantine Studies,* 14 (1973): 113–123.

Paul Allen Miller, *Lyric Texts and Lyric Consciousness* (New York & London: Routledge, 1994).

Holt Parker, "Sappho Schoolmistress," *Transactions of the American Philological Association,* 123 (1993): 309–351.

Charles Segal, "Eros and Incantation: Sappho and Oral Poetry," *Arethusa,* 7 (1974): 139–160.

Marilyn Skinner, "Woman and Language in Archaic Greece, or, Why is Sappho a Woman?" in *Feminist Theory and the Classics,* edited by Nancy S. Rabinowitz and Amy Richlin (New York: Routledge, 1993), pp. 125–144.

Jane McIntosh Snyder, *Lesbian Desire in the Lyrics of Sappho* (New York: Columbia University Press, 1997).

Eva Stehle, "Sappho's Private World," in *Reflections of Women in Antiquity,* edited by Helene Foley (New York: Gordon & Breach, 1981), pp. 45–61.

Ulrich von Wilamowitz, *Sappho und Simonides: Untersuchungen uber griechische Lyriker* (Berlin, 1913).

Margaret Williamson, *Sappho's Immortal Daughters* (Cambridge, Mass.: Harvard University Press, 1995).

Lyn Hatherly Wilson, *Sappho's Sweetbitter Songs* (New York & London: Routledge, 1996).

John J. Winkler, "Double Consciousness in Sappho's Lyrics," in *Constraints of Desire: The Anthropology of Sex and Gender in Ancient Greece* (New York & London: Routledge, 1990).

GREECE: SOPHISTS

Did the sophists exercise a pernicious influence on Greek culture?

Viewpoint: Yes. Some sophists, by cultivating a program of moral relativism, propounded teachings that had deleterious effects on Greek political and social life.

Viewpoint: No. The sophists expounded richly diverse views on a range of issues, not necessarily renouncing ethical principles but rather opening up new areas for critical speculation and debate that enhanced the intellectual life of their own times and beyond.

It is particularly appropriate that a book whose premise is that there are (at least) two sides to every story should have a discussion of the sophists of classical Greece. For the realization that the world of experience is open to varying interpretations remains one of the greatest and most characteristic legacies of these thinkers. The term *sophist* will here denote one of those intellectuals active in the Greek world from around the mid fifth century into the fourth century B.C.E. as public teachers and/or speechwriters on a wide range of subjects. The most notable names are Protagoras, Gorgias, Hippias, Prodicus, Antiphon, Thrasymachus, Antisthenes, Isocrates, and Alcidamas—we could plausibly add the names Socrates and Democritus—most of whom came as foreigners to Athens to ply their trade there and elsewhere. The sophists never comprised any school, yet were the inheritors of the intellectual tradition of the pre-Socratic philosophers and earlier poets, whose works they engage with, challenge, and develop on many levels. What differentiates the sophists is their role as paid or publicly recognized teachers and instigators of "advanced education" often guided toward practical ends. Much of what the sophists taught or speculated on involved one or more of the following: rhetoric, linguistics, grammar, ethics, epistemology, political theorizing, ethnicity, religion, literary criticism, psychology, and aesthetics (in addition to mathematics and physical speculations). Their students tended to be wealthy men who realized that superior oratorical skills could enhance their political prospects in democratic cities such as Athens, which were dominated by law courts and public assemblies. What sophists could offer by way of rhetorical training and a more sophisticated understanding of social and political issues became marketable in such an environment. Sometimes this public dialogue led to a profound rethinking of accepted cultural norms, so that conventional religious, ethical, and political ideas were now subject to the scrutiny of many citizens, including the nouveaux riches who could afford to pay.

It has been unfortunate that most of the sophists' writings have disappeared, not least because our main ancient sources tend to be rather hostile to them. Any account of the first sophist must acknowledge this attitude. Certainly, negative connotations of the term *sophist* were current by Plato's time (*Prot.* 312a); and Aristophanes in his *Clouds* (first performed 423 B.C.E.) had famously parodied elements of sophistic education, with Socrates as his prime target. Yet, many sophists were spectacularly successful in their lifetime, and being called a "sophist" did not always imply censure (cf. Pindar, *Isthm.* 5.28; Cratinus fr. 2 K-A; Hdt. 1.29, 4.95, etc.). Protagoras moved within the exalted circle of Pericles, and Gorgias, Prodicus, and Hippias, who not only attained wealth by teaching in many regions of Greece but also performed at panhellenic festivals and were official ambassadors for their own poleis. Some may not always provide satisfying answers to the problems they raise (at least in their extant writings), and others may have exploited their teaching and rhetorical abilities to accrue large amounts of money. Yet, the impact of the sophists on their own day was profound, and their legacy a rich and varied one. Beyond ushering in relativism and skepticism, it also led to the promulgation of ideas important in their own right that were to influence subsequent thinkers, ancient and modern, especially in the development of humanistic thought.

—*Patrick O'Sullivan*

Viewpoint: Yes. Some sophists, by cultivating a program of moral relativism, propounded teachings that had deleterious effects on Greek political and social life.

In assessing the validity of charges of corruption aimed at the sophists, it is crucial to understand where such charges come from. For the often polemical nature of many of our sources against the sophists warns us against too readily assuming that such hostility was always justified. Ever since Plato, the overwhelming view has been that Socrates at least in no way deserved his fate (although some contemporaries, such as Polycrates, felt otherwise). In addition, caution is warranted before too readily pointing an accusing finger at those sophists not so fortunate to have as magnificent a writer as Plato to defend them. That said, a polemical stance in itself does not necessarily invalidate a particular point of view, and the extent of the negative reactions aroused by the sophists and Socrates indicates that they presented a problem for some contemporaries. The charges against the sophists vary in their scope and nature, and their sources are extensive, including, most famously, Plato and Xenophon, who attempt to divorce Socrates from the sophists generally. Another famous detractor is Aristotle, and we find attacks on sophists among some comic poets, and even other sophists themselves.

Accusations of sophistic corruption are found in fifth-century comic poets such as Aristophanes (especially the *Clouds*) and Eupolis (*Flatterers* frr. 156–190 K-A). Aristophanes makes Socrates the head of a sophistic "thinkery" that not only engages in inane physical speculation but also encourages an amoral outlook by teaching a kind of rhetoric designed to distort the truth and convince anybody of anything. The conflict between older morality and the new is played out most explicitly in the famous *agon* (debating scene) where the "Weaker Argument," embodying sophism, takes on and gets the better of the old-fashioned "Stronger Argument," who also receives comic treatment at the hands of the poet (889–1112). By using such names for these figures, Aristophanes may well be referring to Protagoras's rhetorical training, which, according to Aristotle (*Rhet.* 1402a 24), involved making the weaker argument stronger (Protagoras B 6b). Eupolis's play survives only in fragments but seems to have depicted certain sophists as shamelessly sponging off rich young men who played host to them and were their students. These plays cannot, of course, be read as historically accurate documents since they inevitably involve the gross absurdities and distortions essential to Old Comedy. Yet, for the jokes to work they must at least correspond, or play up to, some aspect of popular perception of the sophists.

Elsewhere the perceived damaging influence of certain sophists occurs in the comparatively more sober texts of some Attic orators of the fourth century B.C.E. Aeschines in his speech *Against Timarchus* (173) notes that the Athenians put "Socrates the Sophist" to death because he taught Critias. And we learn from Xenophon that Socrates' association with Critias and Alicibiades similarly came back to haunt him (*Mem.* 1.2.12). Alcibiades had a love-hate relationship with his fellow citizens, at one point siding with Sparta during the war, then making his way back to Athens where he was welcomed for his undeniable talent, only to fall out with them again. After the war the dictatorship of the Thirty was imposed on Athens, becoming ever more brutal and oppressive with Critias as its most murderous and ruthless member (Xenophon *Hellenica* 2.3–4). The view that Socrates as their teacher was somehow responsible for their acts seems to have been held by some of his contemporaries and introduces a political element to the hostility sophists could arouse. The trial of Socrates, for allegedly corrupting the youth and refusing to acknowledge the gods of the city, provides the most telling evidence that sophists, or people perceived as such, could attract the hostility of the citizenry on religious grounds, too. Later stories of the public burning of books written by certain sophists also revolved around charges of impiety. The works of Protagoras (A 4; cf. A 12) are said to have suffered such a fate

PLATO, GORGIAS

[456d] For other exercises are not to be used against all and sundry, just because one has learnt boxing or wrestling or fighting in armor so well as to vanquish friend and foe alike: this gives one no right to strike one's friends, or stab them to death. Nor, in all conscience, if a man took lessons at a wrestling-school, and having got himself into good condition and learnt boxing he proceeded to strike his father and mother, or some other of his relations or friends, should that be a reason for [456e] hating athletic trainers and teachers of fighting in armor, and expelling them from our cities. For they imparted their skill with a view to its rightful use against enemies and wrongdoers, [457a] in self-defense, not provocation; whereas the others have perverted their strength and art to an improper use. So it is not the teachers who are wicked, nor is the art either guilty or wicked on this account, but rather, to my thinking, those who do not use it properly. Now the same argument applies also to rhetoric: for the orator is able, indeed, to speak against every one and on every question in such a way as to win over the votes of the multitude, practically in any matter he may choose to take up: [457b] but he is no whit the more entitled to deprive the doctors of their credit, just because he could do so, or other professionals of theirs; he must use his rhetoric fairly, as in the case of athletic exercise. And, in my opinion, if a man becomes a rhetorician and then uses this power and this art unfairly, we ought not to hate his teacher and cast him out of our cities. For he imparted [457c] that skill to be used in all fairness, whilst this man puts it to an opposite use. Thus it is the man who does not use it aright who deserves to be hated and expelled and put to death, and not his teacher.

Source: The Gorgias of Plato, *edited and translated by W. H. Thompson (London: Whittaker, 1871).*

because of his pronouncement that he could not be sure about the existence of the gods because of the obscure subject matter and the shortness of human life (B 4). Prodicus also speculated on the divine, seeing the gods as really deifications of benign elements such as the sun, moon, and so on (B 5); and a dramatic fragment sometimes assigned to Critias (B 25) sees the gods as a human fabrication designed to ensure good behavior in mortals. The historicity of the book-burning episodes has in recent times been doubted by many scholars (cf. also *Meno* 91d–e). Yet, the fact that such stories could gain currency in the first place again indicates at least a climate of resentment directed at some sophists for the challenges they posed to conventional religion.

It is noteworthy that the sophists exhibit a considerable spirit of competition, if not mutual disdain, among themselves. Plato gives us a glimpse of the, at times, agonistic relations among the sophists in his *Protagoras.* The great sophist and subject of the dialogue, outlining his area of expertise, pointedly looks in the direction of the polymath Hippias when announcing that he himself does not waste young men's time with poetry, numbers, astronomy, and geometry—the subjects Hippias was known to teach (*Prot.* 318e). Rather, Protagoras aims to teach them *euboulia* (good management of their own affairs) and *arete,* which for him means civic excellence and success both in word and action (Prot. 319a). The great speechwriter, Isocrates, does his best to differentiate himself from those sophists who engage in trivial topics and quibbling and make personal attacks on him (*Antidosis* 2-3; cf. also *Against the Sophists, passim*). Likewise his opponent Alcidamas, who champions extemporaneous oral speechmaking, attacks those sophists who restrict their rhetorical abilities to written speeches and who have neglected education and research (*On Sophists,* especially 1–2, etc.). Such objections coming from these sources tend to give credence to some critiques about certain sophists as pedants and quibblers made by Plato and Aristotle.

By offering education to members of the public willing to pay, the sophists opened up the possibility of social and political advancement to those outside the old aristocracy, whose values came under scrutiny as a result. This conflict is particularly pertinent to the great *nomos-phusis* (culture-nature) debate that preoccupied so much sophistic thought. By positing that laws, religion, and traditional ethical precepts were relative to the cultures that lived by them and not the inevitable products of nature, some sophists threw down a powerful challenge to the old order whose tenets had largely been constructed by and for the aristocratic classes. Not surprisingly, many in the upper classes, including Plato and Xenophon, saw major problems in what the sophists had to offer and attempted to counter their influence in various ways. Xenophon's Socrates scathingly sees the sophists as prostitutes who sell their wisdom to anyone willing to pay (*Mem.* 1.6.13). Plato played no small role in disseminating the notion of "the sophist" in his dialogue of the same name as a purveyor of false, yet deceptively plausible ideas, which exploit the opinions of a susceptible public. Similarly, Aristotle generalized that the sophists made money through apparent, not real, wisdom (*Soph. Elench.* 1.165a 21–23).

Plato also suggests that what the sophists really do is pander to what the "many"—whose views he objected to on many levels—already believe (*Rep.* 493a). Plato therefore argues that the sophists focus not on abstract concepts of truth, beauty, and goodness that inform so much of his own philosophical outlook within the context of his doctrine of the ideal Forms but rather on what will appeal to their paying public. If Plato has correctly grasped the situation, some consequences of this sophistic outlook will be a skepticism about the purported universals of goodness, knowledge, justice, and the divine, which will be replaced by an emphasis on what is useful, advantageous, and beneficial in the here and now. This willingness to see important issues in relative, pragmatic, and subjectivist terms is conceivably detectable in the evident outlook of a number of sophists. Certainly Plato (*Tht.* 152a, etc.) and Aristotle (*Metaph.* 1062b 13–15) viewed Protagoras's famous "man-measure" dictum that way. In other sophistic views on ethics, epistemology, and rhetoric, it is possible to see a similar relativism and skepticism. Certain instances of *Realpolitik* in the speeches and actions of the combatants described by Thucydides in his history of the Peloponnesian War, as well as the views maintained by various characters in Platonic dialogues, would seem to be extensions of some sophistic attitudes. Through them we may gauge something of the influence of some sophistic thought.

The opening statement of Protagoras's book, *On Truth,* or *Knock-Down Arguments,* which is the most famous of all sophistic utterances, runs thus (B 1): "Of all things man is the measure; of things that are that (or how) they are; of things that are not that (or how) they are not." Ever since Plato's *Theaetetus,* this has been taken as espousing a moral and intellectual relativism, so that each individual person is the sole arbiter of his or her own reality. On this reading, Socrates asks how Protagoras can justify taking fees for teaching if each man is the measure of his own wisdom, and attempts to show that the statement is self-refuting. There are other ways to view this statement, but it has been linked to Protagoras's rhetorical teaching that there are two contrasting arguments on any subject (B 6a), the use of which could enable a speaker to make the weaker argument stronger (B 6b). The usual view, then, is that Protagoras's teaching will focus on what is most advantageous for his student, so that the most persuasive case can be put from any vantage point, regardless of its morality or truth. Protagoras himself was no amoralist, as his avowal of the importance of justice and respect for civic life shows (*Prot.* 322d–324d; cf. *Meno* 91d–e). Yet, some ancient observers evidently felt that the kind of rhetorical training he evinced could undermine traditional morality, if Aristophanes' *Clouds* is anything to go by.

Plato further objected (*Phdr.* 267a) that Gorgias and the orator Tisias privileged probability over truth. Indeed, the cleavage between the word and any reality is a characteristic feature of much of Gorgias's extant writings, some of which take skepticism to its extremes. One of his works, *On Not Being* (B 3), made three bold assertions: nothing exists, even if it did it is incomprehensible, and even if comprehended it remains incommunicable. The last point rests on the inability of language to refer to anything beyond itself. Thus language, for Gorgias here, involves an endless cycle of specious representation. Yet, for all the limits of language's referential capacity, Gorgias acknowledges its persuasive power, which he sees as working deceptively on our emotions like a drug on the body or a form of witchcraft. These points he makes in his *Encomium of Helen* (especially 8–14), a speech ostensibly designed to exculpate her from any blame associated with the Trojan War, but more a celebration of the psychological powers of logos or speech/language in any form. Gorgias apparently sees such powers as morally neutral (apart from one reference to "evil persuasion" [*Hel.* 14]), and in the Platonic dialogue named after him is presented as imparting them to such unscrupulous figures as Callicles. This figure, found only in Plato's *Gorgias,* renounces laws as burdens imposed by an inferior majority to be rejected by the naturally superior man whose gifts permit him to satisfy his desires at others' expense and aspire to tyranny (*Gorg.* 483b–d, 492b–d). Gorgias himself claims that rhetoric should be used for good and honorable ends and plausibly suggests that a teacher cannot be held responsible if a student abuses what he has been taught (*Gorg.* 456d–457c). Also, Callicles is not a sophist, or teacher of any kind, and in fact openly expresses hostility toward them (*Gorg.* 520a). Yet, Callicles' invocation of the *nomos-phusis* antithesis may be read as a distortion of the sometimes more enlightened and penetrating criticisms of *nomos* we find in Antiphon (B 44) or Hippias (C 1). Similarly, Callicles' view of justice bears some superficial resemblance to the claim made by Thrasymachus in the *Republic* (337c) that what passes for justice is merely what serves the interests of the stronger party. Thrasymachus cannot be said to endorse this state of affairs, but it is the kind of sophistic observation that would nonetheless appeal to someone like Callicles. His interest in rhetoric gleaned from Gorgias is the surest sign of sophistic influence on him, whatever he may think of the teachers of *arete.*

Callicles may well be a Platonic invention, but his ethical precept asserting the right of the stronger to rule the weak with more regard for self-interest than justice finds chilling parallels in the speeches and attitudes of certain figures in

Thucydides' history. Pericles tells the Athenians their empire is "like a tyranny," which would be dangerous for them to let go even if it was wrong of them to have acquired it (2.63.2). Cleon in the Mytilenean debate makes the same point more brutally in urging the Athenians to mete out collective punishment to the formerly rebellious island for the sake of empire, even if such action defies what is fair (3.37–40). Interestingly, he shows contempt for public debate (3.38), yet demonstrates a command of oratory to rival any sophistically trained demagogue. His opponent in the debate, Diodotus, wins his case, but the appeal is solely to Athenian self-interest, rather than any claim about the injustice of slaughtering and enslaving the island's citizens (3.41–48). In the Melian dialogue (5.84–111), the Athenians, who want to fortify the island of Melos against the inhabitants' wishes, show a cold disdain for older notions of justice, which they now see as simply about equality of power. In all other situations, the weak submit to the strong. When the Melians attempt to bring in moral issues and invoke divine favor, the Athenians dismiss this tactic as unrealistic, saying among men the superior always prevail through "natural necessity," which they also see as a "law" (5.105). True to their word, the Athenians put the Melians to the sword when these "negotiations" break down, unaware that disaster will soon strike them in the wake of the Sicilian expedition and the end of the war itself.

Are we to blame the sophists for such developments? No sophistic text remotely endorses the kinds of atrocities Thucydides describes or the attitude of a Callicles. Critias himself is sometimes numbered among the sophists because of his extensive writings, which included dramas, poems, and prose political treatises; but he never taught, and in fact banned that most sophistic activity, teaching the art of logos (Xen. *Mem.* 1.2.31). Yet, some ruthless figures may have felt themselves given a free rein to act shamelessly in the wake of certain iconoclastic sophistic pronouncements and speculations. Traditional ideas about the existence of the gods had been challenged on various levels, albeit not for the first time (cf. Xenophanes B 15, 16, 23-26). The rule of law, concept of justice, and ethical standards had in some quarters also been incisively questioned, which conceivably allowed demagogues to abuse the powers of rhetoric acquired by sophistic training for their own self-seeking ends. That the majority of sophists intended this result is extremely unlikely, as Socrates' defense of them suggests (*Meno* 91d-e), to say nothing of their own writings. However, their influence on Greek culture was not always a happy one.

–PATRICK O'SULLIVAN,
UNIVERSITY OF CANTERBURY,
NEW ZEALAND

Viewpoint:
No. The sophists expounded richly diverse views on a range of issues, not necessarily renouncing ethical principles but rather opening up new areas for critical speculation and debate that enhanced the intellectual life of their own times and beyond.

It begs several questions to speak of the sophists as having a "program of moral relativism" at all. Firstly, their role as paid teachers with a focus on attaining success within the competitive world of the polis left plenty of room for dissent among them, and they comprised no unified body of thought or "program." Secondly, the charge of relativism is not easy to uphold against them, given that many did have strongly articulated notions of truth, especially when engaging in the *nomos-phusis* (culture-nature) debate controversy. Even the views of Protagoras, whose "man-measure" dictum has, for many, become synonymous with epistemological and ethical individualism, need not be seen as embodying total moral relativism. At the same time the question of the sophists' influence is a complex one. In some instances, the direction of influence is not always so easy to detect, so conceivably, at least as far as epic poetry and tragedy are concerned, some sophists may be allowing themselves to be influenced by these media. We know Gorgias spoke favorably of tragedy (B 23; cf. B 24); Hippias wrote elegies (B1) as well as studying tragedies and epic (A 12); and Protagoras saw the analysis of poetry as the most important part of a man's education (*Prot.* 338e–339a). It would be naive and simplistic, then, to see the sophists as producing a series of destructive one-way effects on their social and intellectual milieu.

In dealing with "relativism" we again confront Protagoras's great "man-measure" dictum, worth quoting once more (B 1): "Of all things man is the measure; of things that are that (or how) they are; of things that are not that (or how) they are not." Did Protagoras mean it as Socrates interprets it, that is, as an individualistic or subjectivist credo? Some alternative readings suggest themselves, and they go straight to the heart of the problems of translation. It is not clear whether the word for "things" *(chremata)* signifies ethical as well as physical objects. Does "man" *(anthropos)* refer to an individual or humankind in general? Also, it is not clear whether the word *estin* (are) is existential or predicative in Greek, that is, does it merely refer to a statement of existence or to a quality of existence? Perhaps the statement is intentionally ambiguous and may well have existed as a discrete pithy pronouncement, like an oracular utterance or the maxims of Heraclitus. It is conceivable that Protagoras is speaking about an ethical-epistemological situation that applies to the human race as a whole. He would not be the first to make such "relativistic" pronouncements that apply to whole cultures or species, as certain remarks by Xenophanes (B 14, 15, 16) and Heraclitus (B 37, 61) show. That may still make his statement express a relativistic view, but one that still allows for appeal to external and communal values as a criterion beyond an individual's perceptions. Protagoras's avowed "agnosticism" (B 4) stresses the difficulties of ascertaining the existence of the gods from the point of view of humanity generally: the subject is obscure and human life short. We know from other references to Protagoras's life and work that he appears to have upheld the importance of communal, democratic values. A close associate of Pericles, he drafted the democratic constitution of the Athenian colony of Thurii (fr. A 1); in Plato's dialogue the *Protagoras,* the Sophist tells his myth of the origins of communal life in the polis (*Prot.* 322d–324d). Here the need for political excellence (*arete*) is to be shared among all and can be taught, and justice, moderation, and respect for law are emphasized as essential to the functioning of the city-state. In this dialogue Protagoras's stated goal of teaching good citizenship and management of one's affairs (*euboulia*) indicates he had a clear idea of what was desirable for others who needed to have it taught to them. His views on education seem to tally with this principle: that it involves natural talent and training (B 3; cf. B 10). A title of a lost Protagorean work, *On Human Error* (fr. B 8e), suggests that within Protagoras's worldview there are definitely right and wrong ways for humans to behave.

Protagoras's interest in *Orthoepeia,* or Correct Use of Language (fr. A 26), was something he apparently shared with other intellectuals such as Prodicus (A 19) and Democritus (B 20a), and suggests that for him language had some referential capacity to a reality beyond itself, which needed proper articulation. In the *Theaetetus* (167a7), Plato ascribes to him the view that it is impossible to think "what is not." That would seem to fly in the face of Protagoras's supposed relativism and works such as *Contradictory Arguments* (B 5) and *Art of Debating* (B 6), and his view that there are contrasting arguments or *logoi* on every subject (B 6a). One attempt at reconciling these apparently disparate pieces of evidence has been for some to claim that for Protagoras two opposing views do not so much contradict each other as talk about different aspects of the same thing. This theory has implications for another charge brought against him, namely that he taught people to make the weaker argument stronger (B 6b). While often interpreted as a technique of spurious rhetoric and verbal trickery (Aristophanes' *Clouds* 112–115; cf. Arist. *Rhet.* 1402a 24–28), this need not always have such negative overtones. Protagoras's rhetorical teaching seems to assume, reasonably, that there are varying degrees of validity to any number of points of view and that speakers need to make their own case as clear and persuasive as possible. If Protagoras's aim is to inculcate political excellence in his students, then he could focus on teaching them to identify what is most advantageous for the polis, beyond what may be obvious to their fellow citizens and then persuading them of this view. This type of rhetoric may thus be directed toward a communal good, rather than simply encouraging a moral vacuum. An example may be found in Thrasymachus's *Politeia* or *Constitution* speech (B1). Here the speaker makes an incisive, paradoxical point that various power-hungry factions in the polis are really arguing the same cause as their opponents, unbeknownst to themselves, and that they should lay aside this destructive in-fighting.

If "moral relativism" should not be too glibly applied to Protagorean ethics and epistemology, the same holds a fortiori for many other sophists, particularly in the context of the *nomos-phusis* debate. This important aspect of sophistic speculation raised profound questions about human behavior, institutions, and beliefs and was paralleled in a number of Greek writings during the Classical period—for example, Herodotus 3.38.4, or Sophocles' *Antigone* (esp. 450ff). Many questions related to this issue still resound today: Are cultural norms natural or man-made? How do we judge which is a better way of life among differing cultures or in our own? Is law a fundamentally repressive concept, or does it ensure the existence of civilised communities? What are the origins of religion? Is justice about moderation and respect or merely another name for the exercise of power by the strong over the weak? Is human excellence (*arete*) innate, or can it be taught? A related series of sophistic questions also focused on language, rhetoric, and persuasion. To what degree could they convey truth? Are they inherently deceptive, manipulative, even seductive media? How do they affect us? Should we welcome or distance ourselves from such effects? The sophists' discussion of such issues was one of the most fertile areas of their thought, in which some thinkers championed *nomos* over *phusis,* or vice versa, in several strongly worded views that are often anything but relativistic.

In the political sphere, *nomos* is promoted by certain sophists with the firm idea of a communal good in mind, rather than with the aim of

Bust of Socrates, considered by many to be a member of the sophist movement

(Museo Nazionale, Naples).

pointing out the arbitrary nature of human institutions. This concept becomes clear in the text of the Anonymus Iamblichi. This text extends Protagorean ideas of the importance of harnessing and training natural talent from an early age (1.2–3), so that qualities of eloquence, wisdom, and strength are directed toward good and lawful ends (3.1). Indeed, the importance of upholding law is a recurrent idea in the text, and we are told that one should exercise self-control (4.1), avoid pursuing money for its own sake (4.2-6), and, most crucially, obey communal laws and resist the desire to rule over others in defiance of law (6.1). Lawlessness *(anomia)* is held up as the greatest evil that results in tyranny and lawfulness *(eunomia)* as the greatest good whose benefits for the community are outlined (7.1, 7.12). There is not much grist for Callicles' mill here. Interestingly, law *(nomos)* is not only seen as essential to human life and inseparable from justice, but is alluded to as a king *(basileus),* ingrained in our very nature along with necessity and justice (6.1). Here, then, *nomos* and *phusis* are combined. In linking law, justice, and nature in this way, the Anonymus Iamblichi stresses, in ways that develop evidently Protagorean thought, an ethics based on a communal, as opposed to a selfishly individual, good.

Other takes on the *nomos-phusis* issue seem more adventurous and perhaps hold more appeal to post-Romantic sensibilities. Those who upheld *phusis* over *nomos* often saw the latter as oppressive, some even calling it a "tyrant" that forces many things on us against our nature. Hippias says so in the *Protagoras* (337d–338b) when intervening in the dispute between Socrates and the great sophist and trying to make the point that those present at the discussion are akin by nature, even though not by *nomos.* How far beyond this select gathering Hippias would take this idea is uncertain, but a striking papyrus fragment of Antiphon's *On Truth* (B 44) outlines the superiority of *phusis* over *nomos* in all instances and advocates, not anarchy, but a kind of enlightened self-interest. In the most famous portion of the papyrus, Antiphon postulates a concept of the equality of all humans. He denounces conventional Greek snobbery and xenophobia, stating that "we all have the same nature in all respects, both barbarians and Greeks" (fr. B44B, col. 2; 266–299) and outlines physical characteristics shared by all. Such a statement would be particularly bold in the climate of mid-late fifth-century Athens when Persian-barbarian-bashing was a stock-in-trade of orators and dramatists of the day. This challenging of conventional prejudice along egalitarian lines manifested itself elsewhere among the sophists. Lycophron, while upholding *nomos* as a guarantor of justice (B 3), elsewhere challenged the custom of distinguishing between low- and highborn (B 4). Alcidamas in his speech to the Spartans to liberate Messene circa 360 B.C.E. (Schol. on Arist. *Rhet.* 1376b6) takes the egalitarian line further: "God has made all people free; nature has made no-one a slave." In certain tragedies by Euripides the unnaturalness of slavery is alluded to (*Melanippe* 511, *Ion* 854–856, etc.), as it is in a Sophoclean fragment (591 Radt), but Alcidamas's pronouncement condemns the institution more forcefully in terms invoking "God," "nature," and "all people." Indeed, it strikes a more humane note than anything Plato, Aristotle, or the authors of the Old or New Testaments had to say on the ubiquitous institution of slavery.

A final few points can be made about the sophists' contribution to rhetoric, aesthetics, and the development of prose. It is easy to see how Protagoras's interest in exploring two or more sides of an issue manifests itself in the histories of Herodotus (3.80–82, etc.) and Thucydides (e.g., 3.37–50, 6.9–23, etc.), who both place considerable importance on public debate where argument and counterargument are played out. Likewise, in Euripides' dramas the *agon,* or debating scene, is a notable feature of many of his plays–for instance, *Hecuba, Trojan Women,* and *Supplices*–in which issues of justice, responsibility, and politics are debated. Another key figure here is Gorgias, whose arrival in Athens in 427 B.C.E. marks a watershed in the history of rhetoric when he by all accounts astonished his hearers with his grand, poetic style. His use of antithesis, balance, alliteration, and assonance has been detected in the writing of Thucydides, among others. It is interesting that a reexamination of Helen's role in the Trojan War appears both in Gorgias's work and Euripides' *Trojan Women* (415 B.C.E.) and *Helen* (412 B.C.E.); but the question of influence between dramatist and orator remains open. Gorgias's *Encomium of Helen* (B 11) stresses the psychological, emotional, and deceptive elements of *logos* in all its forms—poetry, debate, and philosophy—as well as the beguiling effects of vision and visual art on the onlooker. With some justification he has been called the founder of Western aesthetics, and much in Plato's famous attack on poetry and painting in *Republic* 10 draws on Gorgias, albeit for rather different purposes and conclusions. At the same time sophistic literary criticism can be clearly detected in Aristophanes' dramas. For instance, the *Frogs,* with its great discussion of tragedy—at once learned, sophisticated, and hilarious—shows clear indebtedness to the semantics of Protagoras (A 26), Prodicus (A 13, A 19; cf. *Frogs* 1119–1197) and Gorgias (B 24; cf. *Frogs* 1021, etc.). How seriously Aristophanes' attack on the "new intellectualism" in the *Clouds* was meant is hard to say since he was certainly open to the insights of sophistic analysis of poetry.

One of the most interesting elements of Gorgias's *On Not Being* (B 3) is its challenge to the nature of language (in addition to ontology and epistemology), which for him can never truly convey information about anything outside itself. Here we may detect not only a reaction to the Eleatic monism of Parmenides, who postulated the unity of thought, language, and being, but also the ancient roots of postmodernism. The intellectual implications of this Gorgianic skepticism can be found in Thucydides' focus on the distortions of language in his account of the stasis in Corcyra (3.81–84). In that bloody episode, people attempted to conceal the horrific reality and usurpation of values around them by using specious terminology to describe their actions and attitudes. Thucydides does not posit an unbridgeable gulf between language and referent per se. But he is certainly alive to possible instances of such a gulf as outlined by Gorgias, which gives his account of this event real intellectual acumen. Appropriately enough, Gorgias as teacher of rhetoric emerges as something of a paradox. By drawing our attention to the power and limitations of language, he thus increases our awareness of its potential to hold us in its thrall, and so he paves the way for greater critical scrutiny of the uses and abuses of this all-pervasive medium.

The sophists cannot be held accountable for the cataclysmic events that beset the Greek world in the late fifth century. Their speculations were too wide-ranging, and they were too often at variance with each other for them to be reduced to some sort of school of pernicious "moral relativism." Even the supposed "relativism" of thinkers like Protagoras does not abandon ideas of communal law *(nomos)* and justice. For many who uphold the supremacy of *phusis* over *nomos,* relativism has little or no place in their ethical or behavioral theories. The challenge that some laid down to the arbitrariness of *nomos,* such as the institutions of slavery, racial prejudice, or class snobbery, could lead to liberating and humane ideas, rather than pandering to certain would-be tyrants, such as Callicles. The view ascribed to Thrasymachus in book 1 of Plato's *Republic* that justice is whatever serves the stronger party's interests should not be assumed to have his endorsement. Elsewhere, Thrasymachus had described justice as the greatest good for mortals (B 8), rather than as a weapon for the strong, and his *Politeia* outlines the pitfalls of power-hungry faction fighting. He seems, rather, to be playing devil's advocate to Plato's Socrates (see esp. *Rep.* 1.349a–b), and may well be making a point about specious terminology, like others of his day, such as Thucydides. It is clear, then, that the sophists' challenging insights, questions, and iconoclastic pronouncements enriched the thinking of dramatists, statesmen, orators, and historians of their age, with whom there is likely to have been reciprocal engagement. In raising the questions they did, the sophists were not necessarily attacking traditional concepts but working toward a fuller, more articulated understanding of what these concepts involved. The stimulus to further great thought induced by the sophists is evident not least in the fact that their two most eloquent and influential critics, Plato and Aristotle, invariably take up issues traceable to this group of thinkers.

—PATRICK O'SULLIVAN,
UNIVERSITY OF CANTERBURY,
NEW ZEALAND

References

Richard Bett, "The Sophists and Relativism," *Phronesis,* 34 (1989): 139–169.

Frederick Copleston, *A History of Philosophy,* volume 1: *Greece and Rome* (New York: Image Doubleday, 1962).

Hermann Diels and Walther Kranz, *Die Fragmente der Vorsokratiker,* 3 volumes, sixth edition (Berlin: Weidmann, 1951).

Michael Gagarin and Paul Woodruff, eds., *Early Greek Political Thought from Homer to the Sophists* (Cambridge: Cambridge University Press, 1995).

Gorgias, *Encomium of Helen,* edited by Douglas MacDowell (Bristol, U.K.: Bristol Classical, 1982).

George Grote, *A History of Greece,* 12 volumes, second edition (London: Everyman, 1906).

William Keith Chambers Guthrie, *The Sophists* (Cambridge: Cambridge University Press, 1971).

Terence Irwin, "Plato's Objections to the Sophists," in *The Greek World,* edited by Anton Powell (London & New York: Routledge, 1995), pp. 568–590.

George Kerferd, *The Sophistic Movement* (Cambridge: Cambridge University Press, 1981).

Kerferd, ed., *The Sophists and Their Legacy* (Wiesbaden: Steiner, 1981).

Sir Geoffrey Lloyd, *The Revolutions of Wisdom: Studies in the Claims and Practice of Ancient Greek Science* (Berkeley: University of California Press, 1987).

Michael Lloyd, *The Agon in Euripides* (Oxford: Clarendon Press, 1992).

Anthony Long, *The Cambridge Companion to Early Greek Philosophy* (Cambridge: Cambridge University Press, 1999).

Ludwig Radermacher, *Artium Scriptores. Reste der voraristotelischen Rhetorik* (Vienna: Rudolf M. Rohrer, 1951).

Herbert Rankin, *Sophists, Socratics, and Cynics* (London & Canberra: Croom Helm, 1983).

Jacqueline de Romilly, *The Great Sophists of Periclean Athens,* translated by Janet Lloyd (Oxford: Clarendon Press, 1992).

Charles Segal, "Gorgias and the Psychology of the Logos," *Harvard Studies in Classical Philology,* 66 (1962): 99–155.

Friederich Solmsen, *Intellectual Experiments of the Greek Enlightenment* (Princeton: Princeton University Press, 1975).

Rosamund Sprague, ed., *The Older Sophists: A Complete Translation of the Fragments in* Die Fragmente der Vorsokratiker, *edited by Diels-Kranz. With a New Edition of Antiphon and Euthydemus* (Columbia: University of South Carolina Press, 1972).

Edmund Zeller, *Outlines of the History of Greek Philosophy,* translated by L. R. Palmer, thirteenth edition (London: Routledge & Kegan Paul, 1931).

GREECE: SPORTS

Were ancient Greek sports amateur athletics?

Viewpoint: Yes. Ancient Greek athletes were not paid professionals, and the awards they received were usually honorary rather than financial.

Viewpoint: No. Ancient Greek athletes frequently received monetary and material rewards, which effectively gave them a status similar to that of professionals. There is no ancient term that corresponds to the word *amateur.*

The question of whether Greek athletes were "amateurs" or "professionals" is an issue of considerable importance for scholars of ancient sport and for the organizers of the modern Olympic Games. The terms *amateur* and *professional* do not exist in ancient Greek vocabulary, but the issue can be approached by analyzing such matters as: What were the athletes' training arrangements? Was there any state funding of athletes? What kind of prizes and rewards did athletic victors receive? The question is complicated by the fact that our evidence for ancient Greek sports comes from sources spanning a thousand years, from Homer to the Roman Empire, during which time practices may have changed.

The debate centers on several pieces of evidence from ancient writers and inscriptions. These are, however, open to varying interpretations, so that often the same piece of evidence is cited in support of each claim. It is agreed upon that athletes at the Olympia and the other major panhellenic festivals received symbolic crowns of vegetation as markers of their victory: those who argue for amateur status maintain that this is of pivotal importance for it shows that victors did not compete for material or monetary prizes; on the other side, it is argued that athletic victors subsequently received material and monetary rewards from their home cities. Information available from Athens complicates the picture, since an inscription records that jars of olive oil and other valuable prizes were awarded to victors in the Panathenaea. Is this an isolated case, to be explained by the democratic politics of Athens, or does it indicate that different practices prevailed at local festivals from those at the panhellenic "crown games"?

The case for amateur athletics is anchored in the archaic and classical periods of Greek history. Evidence of valuable prizes in Homer's account of the funeral games held for Patroclus in book 23 of the *Iliad* is dismissed as irrelevant because it comes from an early and poetic source. Similarly, the development of athletics into an organized career, complete with "guilds" of athletes and a year-round cycle of competitions, which occurs in the Hellenistic and Roman periods, is regarded as a "corruption" of the original Greek ideal. The argument against amateur status is undoubtedly strengthened by both the Homeric account and the later developments, for they show a continuum, in which athletes received, one way or another, payment for their skills.

Attention has recently focused on the origins of the term *amateur* and the whole notion of amateur athletics. In a polemical reexamination of both ancient and modern evidence, David C. Young contends that Greek amateur athletics is a myth, a systematic distortion of the ancient source material that has its origins in the class struggles of nineteenth-century England. Since the publication of this study, the term *amateur* has generally ceased to be used by Greek scholars; it lives on, however, in many documents relating to the Olympic Games and in the popular imagination.

—David H. J. Larmour

Viewpoint:
Yes. Ancient Greek athletes were not paid professionals, and the awards they received were usually honorary rather than financial.

The most important athletic festival held by the ancient Greeks was the Olympia, which was established in honor of Zeus at least by the year 776 B.C.E. and had probably been in operation long before then. This was the oldest and most prestigious of all the athletic festivals in the so-called panhellenic circuit of four major festivals, and, even as the number of athletic gatherings increased over the centuries, the Olympia retained its status as "first and foremost" among them all. The practices that were followed at the Olympia, therefore, served as a model for many other athletic festivals, and this is especially true in the matter of the prizes awarded to victorious athletes. Although the picture becomes more complicated in the Hellenistic and Roman periods, when Greek athletics became subsumed into larger cultural trends, if we want to characterize the Greek athletic ideal accurately, we must base our conception on how the Olympia was run in the period when Greece was free from outside influences. Much of the evidence comes from nonspecialist literary sources, but when this is combined with information preserved on inscriptions, we get a fairly clear idea of the basic principles upon which athletic competition was established.

The second-century C.E. writer Lucian of Samosata makes the athletic competitions and the prizes at the Olympia the subject of an imaginary dialogue between the Greek sage Solon and a Persian visitor, Anacharsis, set around the year 590 B.C.E. Lucian consciously strove to imitate classical Greek writers, and, although he often writes in a satirical vein, his understanding of athletic practices both in his own time and earlier is probably accurate. When Anacharsis, the perplexed Persian visitor, comments sarcastically on the fact that competitors are willing to suffer severe bodily pain for crowns that are made of mere laurel, pine, or celery leaves, Solon responds that the crowns handed out are "tokens" or "symbols" of victory and that their main purpose is to recognize the victors. When they wear these crowns, he continues, the athletes are considered "equal to the gods." It is clear from this passage that the awarding of these crowns was the central moment in the celebration of an athlete's victory. Whether that was still true in Lucian's day–although it probably was at the Olympia, at least–he is describing something that would have been familiar to his listeners. It is possible too that Lucian wanted to hold up the "purity" of the Olympia in the archaic and classical periods as a counterexample to what went on in many festivals during his day; this would fit in with his generally nostalgic approach to Greek culture, which is evident in his other writings about literature and philosophy. The Olympia festival was well known as a bastion of conservative practices and values and was especially resistant to change.

The crowns that Anacharsis and Solon refer to were garlands of plant material, sacred to the particular deity in whose honor the contests were held, given to victors at the Olympia (where the crown was made from an olive tree sacred to Zeus) and the three other panhellenic gatherings: the Isthmia (made from pine); the Nemea (made from celery); and the Pythia (made from laurel). These festivals consequently became known as the "crown games." The Olympia and Nemea were held in honor of Zeus, the Isthmia to worship Poseidon, and the Pythia to glorify Apollo. These festivals were, in fact, the only major gatherings of the Greeks as a single people that occurred in the classical era. They were a unique experience of a "national" consciousness and were held on regular cycles, each covering four years. Hence, they were incredibly significant cultural events. The greatest glory that an ancient athlete could aspire to was to be crowned victor in an event at a panhellenic festival, and if he won crowns at all four festivals in one four-year circuit, he achieved a kind of "superstar" status as a "circuit victor" (the equivalent of the "grand slam" today). Because of the cultural prestige of these crown games, most other Greek festivals followed similar practices, although some may have supplemented crowns with other forms of prizes. At the great Athenian festival of the Panathenaea, held in honor of the city's patron goddess Athena, victors received amphoras of olive oil, which probably had similar symbolic value to the plant crowns distributed at the panhellenic festivals. They may also have been designed to promote the export of one of the city's most important products. Some have speculated that the amphoras of oil were intended as the equivalent of money and that, therefore, they indicate a trend toward the professionalization of athletic competition. While this is possible, it has to be remembered that Athens is a special case and that the prize arrangements at the Panathenaea were heavily influenced by the political and social policies, first of the reforming leader Pisistratus and later of the radical Athenian democracy. It is the only place, for instance, where we hear of prizes for second and third place in athletic contests. The distribution of material prizes may have had much more to do with the political policies of democracy, which would have promoted the redistribution of wealth and the breaking down of the traditional aristocratic ethos surrounding athletics. In other words, the Athenian preference for a democratic group consciousness, as opposed to the highly individualistic and competitive ideology of the aristocratic elite, may have had peculiar ramifications in the traditionally aristocratic area of athletic competition.

It is clear from the available sources from across the Greek world, however, that ancient athletes were generally accustomed to receiving prizes that were honorary and symbolic, rather than monetary, in nature. This is entirely appropriate in view of the fact that athletic competitions, or *agones,* were held in a highly religious setting. That is an aspect of ancient athletics that often gets overlooked in modern accounts. The purpose of the *agon* was emphatically to glorify the god, not to reward the athlete with material goods. Confirmation of this is provided by another source, namely the Victory Odes, or *epinikia,* composed by the lyric poet Pindar to honor victorious athletes at the four panhellenic festivals. Commissioned by the athlete's family or native city, these poems devote little attention to the athlete himself or how he achieved his victory, concentrating instead on his lineage, his links with the realm of the divine, and the moral obligations that the victory has laid upon the athlete as an ideal specimen of the Greek male citizen. We get no physical description of the athlete and are constantly directed away from the present to the past. The whole aura surrounding athletic victory suggests an intense preoccupation with a realm beyond the material, a realm where the reputation and standing of the athlete has everything to do with his connections with the gods and his control of destructive human emotions, like arrogance, pride, and greed. To exhibit concern with material or monetary benefits would be a sign of falling short of this ideal and would be seen as evidence of moral corruption.

Another important matter, which tends to support the thesis of amateur status, is the training that an athlete underwent before participating in a major athletic competition. At the Olympia we know that all competitors were required to be in training for a full ten months before they could compete, including a month just before the festival itself under the direct supervision of local officials at the host city of Elis. It is generally assumed from this that most athletes came from relatively wealthy backgrounds, as they would have been required to support themselves financially throughout these mandatory training periods. Unless he was independently wealthy, it would have been difficult for an athlete to spend that much time away from earning his living. Hence, the argument can plausibly be made that these athletes were wealthy amateurs rather than paid professionals. A good case in point would be the Athenian politician Alcibiades, who came from an aristocratic background and entered the chariot-racing contest at Olympia, paying for the expenses himself. Many of the athletes honored by Pindar in his *epinikia* clearly come from aristocratic families. There were, of course, exceptions to this, but the sources suggest that athletes from poor backgrounds were a rarity.

Were these victory crowns then really the only prizes that athletes received? There is some evidence that athletes were rewarded materially by their home cities when they returned as victors from the panhellenic competitions; for example, we know that some received free meals at public expense. Others may have been given statues commemorating their achievements or even amounts of money. It would be a mistake, however, to regard this as evidence of a professional status: it is likely that such rewards came after an athlete had won a victory, or several victories, rather than that he was somehow supported during the period of his training or that he was sent to compete with funds from the public purse. It is possible that famous athletes like Milo of Croton or Theagenes of Thasos became wealthy because of their athletic prowess, but they were exceptions to the norm and hence occasion comment in the ancient sources. There is often the suggestion in such accounts that athletes who became wealthy or arrogant as a result of capitalizing on their achievements have abandoned the modesty and moderation expected of victors. Both Milo and Theagenes, for instance, are said to have met with unfortunate deaths, and their lives are narrated by the sources in the language of fables illustrating the maxim that "pride goes before a fall." This is a maxim that can be heard in many of Pindar's Victory Odes. In any case, we have to be careful to distinguish between the awards presented by the festival officials managing the competitions and what was given to the athlete by his fellow citizens when he returned to his native city. It is also important to remember that these benefits were confined

Sculpture of athletes exercising; the absence of beards corresponds with ancient Greek athletic practices

(Athens Museum)

to victors who made up a small proportion of the contingent of athletes that would travel to take part in the contests. There is no suggestion in any of the ancient sources that nonvictors received any kind of reward. Indeed, within the extremely competitive and individualistic ideology of Greek athletics there was no glory or recognition whatsoever attached to athletes who lost or even those who came in second; the presence of prizes for second- and even third- and fourth-place competitors in the Athenian Panathenaea is an anomaly, which, as mentioned earlier, should be attributed to the uniquely "democratic" concerns of the Athenian festival authorities.

All of the evidence cited so far reflects the situation in the archaic and classical periods of Greek history, that is, down to about the end of the fourth century B.C.E. In the subsequent Hellenistic and Roman periods, the training of athletes becomes more organized by the authorities of the city-state, and it is here that the arguments for something approaching the modern professional status might appear to be stronger. We know, for instance, that athletes were organized into guilds and that their training and preparation for contests became much more systematic. As far as we can tell, however, these guilds, or *sunodoi,* were not primarily concerned with guaranteeing payments for athletes on a professional basis. Evidence from the Roman era does suggest that some kind of remuneration was involved: athletes training for the Augustan Games in Naples, for example, were paid a drachma a day. These games were known as "Greek-style" but were fundamentally Roman in their management and operations. It is probable that such practices came to Greece during the Roman era and might lie behind the criticisms made by the Greek-speaking doctor Galen in the second century C.E.: he attacks the extreme nature of athletic training methods and disapproves of the fact that athletes collect larger sums of money than anyone else. These trends, however, represent a corruption of the original ideal of Greek athletics and cannot be taken as evidence for anything like professional status in the modern sense.

—DAVID H. J. LARMOUR,
TEXAS TECH UNIVERSITY

Viewpoint: No. Ancient Greek athletes frequently received monetary and material rewards, which effectively gave them a status similar to that of professionals. There is no ancient term that corresponds to the word *amateur.*

Before we start investigating the athletic practices of the Greeks with reference to their supposedly amateur or professional features, it is necessary to clarify the terminology we are going to employ. The term *amateur* in the context of athletics refers to a sportsman who is not paid to practice and perform his sporting activities but who does so largely for the pleasure of participating. In amateur athletics there are no prizes as such, only tokens or symbols of victory, the most familiar example of which is the medal given out at the Olympic Games today. This concept is quintessentially modern and has its roots in the social changes brought about by capitalism in the social fabric of nineteenth-century European and American society. The category of the amateur athlete was established, one might say invented, in England in the nineteenth century and, subsequently, gave rise to the division between amateur and professional status that became a source of much dispute during the twentieth century. Attempts to sustain the idea of an amateur status in the face of the increasingly important role of money in popular sports have frequently involved an emotional or moral appeal to the traditions of the ancient Greeks. The question of whether ancient Greek sports were amateur athletics is thus really not so much about athletic practices in Greece as it is about a modern debate over how sports should be managed.

The question of whether amateur status, or at least something recognizably akin to it, ever existed among the ancient Greeks is relatively simple to answer: the Greeks did not have a word for "amateur" and consequently acknowledged no such category. The evidence goes all the way back to Homer: in the account of the funeral games held in honor of the slain hero Patroclus in book 23 of the *Iliad,* the poet describes several athletic events and lists the prizes that Achilles set out for the winners; these include tripods, bowls, livestock, clothing, women, axes, and iron. It is only reasonable to assume that this account reflects the customs operating in the era when Homer was composing (circa 750 B.C.E.) as well as in much earlier times, and it shows that giving valuable prizes for athletic competitions was a practice of long standing. Of course, it is possible to argue that impromptu funeral games (described by a poet after all)–held to honor a dead hero–are not the same as organized athletic contests, but the two are in fact connected through such fundamental elements as sacrifice and the celebration of the life force in nature. Both of these elements can be discerned in the rituals of the Olympia, for instance, which began and concluded with elaborate sacrificial ceremonies.

The argument in favor of a kind of ancient amateurism depends, when all is said and done, on just one particular detail concerning athletic rewards: the prizes handed out at the major panhellenic festivals–the Olympia, Pythia, Isthmia, and Nemea–had no monetary value; they were simple crowns of foliage made from a plant sacred to the god in whose honor the competitions were being held. The notion that these were the only prizes that a victor received, however, in turn relies heavily upon remarks made in a dialogue written by Lucian of Samosata in the second century C.E. Lucian was primarily a satirical writer, and his imaginary conversation between Solon and the visiting Persian Anacharsis has to be read in the light of his generally playful and ironic attitude. Nonetheless, the crown of vegetation does appear to have been a defining feature of athletic ritual, signifying the important link between the athletic victor and the divinity for whom the contests were performed. Like an Olympic gold medal today, it doubtless held much greater symbolic value and emotional worth than a large sum of money.

Even if a symbolic crown was the only reward handed out at the Olympia and the other panhellenic contests, it was a token of victory that could certainly be used for revenue generation outside the confines of the festival itself. It was a symbol of currency. The standing of an athlete who had won a victory at a panhellenic festival, against competitors from all over the Greek world, was astoundingly high, and it is no exaggeration to say that it was the equivalent of "superstar" status today. When a victorious athlete returned to his home city, it was the custom for him to be rewarded with accolades, which were material and monetary in character, including room and board at public expense and statues commissioned from renowned sculptors. The poet Xenophanes, who wrote in the last half of the sixth century B.C.E., forcefully criticizes the honors heaped upon athletic victors by cities. There would be no reason for this outburst if such criticisms were unfounded. We know from various sources that money was circulating in various ways at the Olympia festival, for there are references to the problem of bribery, and the officials in charge, the Hellanodikai (judges of the Greeks), took stern measures to discourage corruption. Athletes and money were clearly no strangers to each other. Fines were levied on those who broke the festival rules. Some might argue that it was the absence of monetary prizes that led to bribes being used, since athletes could be lured by the extra reward of money; others would counter that bribery and corruption exist separately from the prizes and cannot be taken as evidence for their nature.

As early as 600 B.C.E., we have an inscription stating that an athlete called Cleombratos, having won a victory at the Olympia, dedicated a tithe (a tenth) of the prize to the goddess Athena. Since it is obviously impossible to dedicate a tenth of a crown of leaves, we must assume that Cleombratos had also received a monetary reward, either from his home city of Sybaris or (less likely) from the officials of the Olympia festival itself. Sybaris was a famously wealthy city in ancient Greece, so it is possible that this was a local anomaly. There is, however, other evidence that tends in the same direction. In Athens, for example, the reforming politician Solon, who was entrusted with the task of changing laws in order to promote commercial prosperity and social harmony (achieved largely by curtailing the dominance of the landed aristocracy), made an important provision concerning the payments given to athletic victors around this same time: he says that a winner at the Isthmia is to receive a hundred drachmas, a winner at the Olympia five hundred. This meant that an Olympic victor

CELEBRATING AN OLYMPIC VICTORY

[1] Water is best, and gold, like a blazing fire in the night, stands out supreme of all lordly wealth. But if, my heart, you wish to sing of contests, [5] look no further for any star warmer than the sun, shining by day through the lonely sky, and let us not proclaim any contest greater than Olympia. From there glorious song enfolds the wisdom of poets, so that they loudly sing [10] the song of Cronus, when they arrive at the rich and blessed hearth of Hieron, [12] who wields the scepter of law in Sicily of many flocks, reaping every excellence at its peak, and is glorified [15] by the choicest music, which we men often play around his hospitable table. Come, take the Dorian lyre down from its peg, if the splendor of Pisa and of Pherenicus placed your mind under the influence of sweetest thoughts, [20] when that horse ran swiftly beside the Alpheus, not needing to be spurred on in the race, and brought victory to his master, [23] the king of Syracuse who delights in horses. His glory shines in the settlement of fine men founded by Lydian Pelops, [25] with whom the mighty holder of the earth Poseidon fell in love, when Clotho took him out of the pure cauldron, furnished with a gleaming ivory shoulder. Yes, there are many marvels, and yet I suppose the speech of mortals beyond the true account can be deceptive, stories adorned with embroidered lies; [30] and Grace, who fashions all gentle things for men, confers esteem and often contrives to make believable the unbelievable. But the days to come are the wisest witnesses. [35] It is seemly for a man to speak well of the gods; for the blame is less that way. Son of Tantalus, I will speak of you, contrary to earlier stories. When your father invited the gods to a very well-ordered banquet at his own dear Sipylus, in return for the meals he had enjoyed, [40] then it was that the god of the splendid trident seized you, [41] his mind overcome with desire, and carried you away on his team of golden horses to the highest home of widely-honored Zeus, to which at a later time Ganymede came also, [45] to perform the same service for Zeus. But when you disappeared, and people did not bring you back to your mother, for all their searching, right away some envious neighbor whispered that they cut you limb from limb with a knife into the water's rolling boil over the fire, [50] and among the tables at the last course they divided and ate your flesh. [52] For me it is impossible to call one of the blessed gods a glutton. I stand back from it. Often the lot of evil-speakers is profitlessness. If indeed the watchers of Olympus ever honored a mortal man, [55] that man was Tantalus. But he was not able to digest his great prosperity, and for his greed he gained overpowering ruin, which the Father hung over him: a mighty stone. Always longing to cast it away from his head, he wanders far from the joy of festivity. [59] He has this helpless life of never-ending labor, [60] a fourth toil after three others, because he stole from the gods nectar and ambrosia, with which they had made him immortal, and gave them to his drinking companions. If any man expects that what he does escapes the notice of a god, he is wrong. [65] Because of that the immortals sent the son of Tantalus back again to the swift-doomed race of men. And when he blossomed with the stature of fair youth, and down darkened his cheek, he turned his thoughts to an available marriage, [70] to win glorious Hippodameia from her father, the lord of Pisa. He drew near to the gray sea, alone in the darkness, and called aloud on the deep-roaring god, skilled with the trident; and the god appeared to him, close at hand. [75] Pelops said to the god, "If the loving gifts of Cyprian Aphrodite result in any gratitude, Poseidon, then restrain the bronze spear of Oenomaus, and speed me in the swiftest chariot to Elis, and bring me to victory. For he has killed thirteen [80] suitors, and postpones the marriage [81] of his daughter. Great danger does not take hold of a coward. Since all men are compelled to die, why should anyone sit stewing an inglorious old age in the darkness, with no share of any fine deeds? As for me, on this contest [85] I will take my stand. May you grant a welcome achievement." So he spoke, and he did not touch on words that were unaccomplished. Honoring him, the god gave him a golden chariot, and horses with untiring wings.

[88] He overcame the might of Oenomaus, and took the girl as his bride. She bore six sons, leaders of the people eager for excellence. [90] Now he has a share in splendid blood-sacrifices, resting beside the ford of the Alpheus, where he has his attendant tomb beside the altar that is thronged with many visitors. The fame of Pelops shines from afar in the races of the Olympic festivals, [95] where there are contests for swiftness of foot, and the bold heights of toiling strength. A victor throughout the rest of his life enjoys honeyed calm, [99] so far as contests can bestow it. But at any given time the glory of the present day [100] is the highest one that comes to every mortal man. I must crown that man with the horse-song in the Aeolian strain. I am convinced that there is no host in the world today who is both knowledgeable about fine things and more sovereign in power, [105] whom we shall adorn with the glorious folds of song. A god is set over your ambitions as a guardian, Hieron, and he devises with this as his concern. If he does not desert you soon, I hope that I will celebrate an even greater sweetness, [110] sped by a swift chariot, finding a helpful path of song when I come to the sunny hill of Cronus. For me the Muse tends her mightiest shaft of courage. Some men are great in one thing, others in another; but the peak of the farthest limit is for kings. Do not look beyond that! [115] May it be yours to walk on high throughout your life, and mine to associate with victors as long as I live, distinguished for my skill among Greeks everywhere.

Source: *Pindar, Olympian 1 for Hieron of Syracuse, Single Horse Race, 476* B.C.E., *in* The Odes of Pindar: Including the Principal Fragments, *translated by John Sandys, second revised edition (London: Heinemann / New York: Putnam, 1919).*

would be able to purchase five hundred bushels of grain and could thereby enter the top class in the new system of financial rankings he instituted. It is generally assumed that these payments to victors were new and designed to widen the participation in athletic contests to include individuals who were not wealthy enough to devote themselves to full-time training in preparation for competition at the panhellenic festivals. Before Solon's reforms, it is likely that the training requirements—especially the Olympic stipulation that an athlete had to have been in full-time training for ten months before competing—strongly favored members of the aristocratic and wealthy elite. Thus, although it is possible that before 600 B.C.E. most athletes could be styled as "amateur" in the sense that they relied upon their own wealth to cover all the expenses involved in training and competition, it is apparent that early on, in Athens at least, the principle of paying athletes was established. Later, at the end of the fifth century, a character in a play by the tragedian Euripides delivers a sustained denunciation of athletes, primarily for their accumulation of undeserved wealth.

Athens also provides evidence for the distribution of valuable prizes to athletes by the organizers of a festival: in the inscription that records part of the arrangements for the great Panthenaea held in honor of the city's patron goddess Athena. This was a major festival in the classical era, and, even if it did not have official panhellenic status, it certainly aspired to it. Competitors came not only from Athens itself but from other cities. Just as Athens set the trend in so many cultural matters—like drama and philosophy—so its practices in the realm of athletics can hardly have gone unnoticed by other Greek city-states. The inscription in question, often called the "Prize List," details an elaborate system of rewards for victorious athletes, ranging from varying numbers of amphora of olive oil to bulls and payments of one hundred or two hundred drachmas. It is striking that no crowns are mentioned: scholars speculate that the jars of olive oil somehow replaced these, but these vessels had definite material, and probably also monetary, value. Athens is not the only location where we hear of such prizes. The poet Pindar, who composed Victory Odes to celebrate winners at panhellenic contests, mentions in his tenth *Nemean Ode* that the city of Argos gave out vases of oil, silver cups, woolen cloaks, and bronzes as prizes. There may be evidence here of a distinction between the four panhellenic festivals and smaller, local gatherings: the normal practice at the latter was likely to hand out prizes of tangible value. Perhaps this was a way to induce competitors to attend. It is also likely that local festivals were more open to changing their practices over time since the panhellenic organizers, especially at the Olympia, were famously conservative in their adherence to tradition.

In postclassical times, that is to say in the Hellenistic and Roman eras, there is plenty of evidence for payment of athletes and financial support of their training. The fact that athletic competitors were organized into "guilds" suggests that there was a professional structure developing. We have evidence for the guild at Ephesus, in existence probably about 200 B.C.E., and for the Heracles guild in Rome in the second century C.E. We should see these guilds as natural developments of long-standing habits among the Greeks. Athletics was by this stage organized as a profession much like any other and was regarded as a suitable career for a young man with the necessary talent and application. Many athletes now competed in festivals that were new, often established by kings and emperors in order to project their power and reputation. There was a substantial increase in the number of athletic festivals after the death of Alexander the Great in 323 B.C.E., as Hellenistic kings sought to glorify their achievements with public spectacles. This trend became even more marked among the Roman emperors: Augustus established a festival to celebrate his victory over Mark Antony and Cleopatra at Actium in 31 B.C.E., and later emperors established games named after themselves, such as Nero did with the Neronia. These events did not have the religious underpinning of the venerable old panhellenic gatherings and may, therefore, have been more flexible in their arrangements. That could have extended to the nature of the prizes, which probably included amounts of money. There was, moreover, a need to ensure a supply of well-trained athletes, and this need encouraged the development of an organized class of professional athletes, trainers, and managers.

Thus, we can discern a continuum in the practices of Greek athletics, beginning with Homer and ending in the Roman period, and in the rewarding of athletes with prizes that were valuable in the material or monetary sense. It is possible that there was an interlude, in the archaic era, when a kind of aristocratic exclusivity went hand in hand with the distribution of purely symbolic victory crowns, but we have to be careful about extending this to a general concept of amateurism on the modern model. In his groundbreaking study, *The Olympic Myth of Greek Amateur Athletics* (1985), David C. Young systematically destroys the "amateur myth," first by locating its origins in nineteenth-century English class warfare and the rebirth of the Olympics in 1896, and second by demonstrating that the ancient evidence simply does not support the idea (or rather ideal) of ancient Greek amateurism. He argues that the whole notion of amateurism was imposed upon the ancient sources, which were systematically misread and sometimes blatantly distorted in order to preserve it as the dominating ethos of the modern Olympic Games. This study has shifted the ground of the debate about amateur status: in the face of Young's impressive marshaling of all the available evidence, ancient and modern, it has become increasingly difficult to maintain the position that ancient Greek sports were amateur athletics in anything like the modern sense.

–DAVID H. J. LARMOUR,
TEXAS TECH UNIVERSITY

References

E. Norman Gardiner, *Athletics of the Ancient World* (Chicago: Ares, 1980).

H. A. Harris, *Greek Athletes and Athletics* (London: Hutchinson, 1964).

David H. J. Larmour, *Stage and Stadium* (Hildesheim: Weidmann, 1999).

Stephen G. Miller, *Arete: Greek Sports from Ancient Sources* (Berkeley: University of California Press, 1991).

H. W. Pleket, "Games, Prizes, Athletes and Ideology," *Arena,* 1 (1976): 49–89.

Rachel S. Robinson, *Sources for the History of Greek Athletics* (Chicago: Ares, 1981).

David C. Young, *The Olympic Myth of Greek Amateur Athletics* (Chicago: Ares, 1985).

ROMAN PERIOD: THE *AENEID*

Was the *Aeneid* Augustan propaganda?

Viewpoint: Yes. The *Aeneid* was written in response to Augustus's deliberate and explicit cultural program. In spite of the immense subtlety of the poem, its fundamental endorsement of Roman and Augustan dominance cannot be avoided.

Viewpoint: No. Far from being a piece of propaganda, the *Aeneid* is a poem suffused with loss, suffering, and nostalgia. Virgil may well have "believed in Rome," but he was well aware of the immense costs involved in Rome's triumph.

Publius Vergilius Maro, widely regarded as the greatest Latin poet, was born in northern Italy, near the city of Mantua, in 70 B.C.E. According to the ancient biographical tradition, Virgil (or Vergil) was educated in Cremona and Milan. Later, he established himself at Rome and began to compose poetry. His first work was a group of ten pastoral poems, known as the *Eclogues,* published around 39 B.C.E., followed by the *Georgics* (29 B.C.E.), didactic poetry on the subject of farming, and finally, Rome's great national epic, the *Aeneid,* which was left incomplete at Virgil's death in 19 B.C.E.

Sometime after the publication of the *Eclogues,* Virgil became associated with the circle of poets around Maecenas, the trusted friend of Octavian, the future emperor. At this time, however, the future of Rome was still much in doubt. Civil war had begun when Julius Caesar invaded Italy at the head of an army and continued after his assassination. Octavian, styling himself as the avenger of his adopted father, organized armies and came to a temporary accord with his primary rivals, Marcus Antonius and Marcus Aemelius Lepidus. The coalition did not last. The triumvirs became enemies, and hostilities ensued until 31 B.C.E., when the fleet of Octavian routed that of Antonius at the Battle of Actium.

Virgil prospered during the civil wars. He had chosen the winning side, and, as a result of the Battle of Actium and Octavian's ascendancy to a position of absolute authority, he came to be associated with the ruling regime. His final work, the *Aeneid,* offers a lavish foundation myth for the Romans, as it traces the struggles of the refugees from burning Troy, led by "dutiful Aeneas," and as they seek the glorious future prophesied for their descendants in Italy. Their journey is hampered, however, by Hera, who resents the fact that the Trojans/Romans will displace the city of Carthage from its position of preeminence. She causes further obstacles even after the Trojans' arrival in Italy, helping to rouse the native tribes against Aeneas. Jupiter finally persuades her to relent, and she agrees, on the condition that the Trojans give up their Trojan ways and become Italians. The scene is then set for a conclusion that will affirm the lasting presence of Aeneas and his men in Italy. In the final scene of the poem, Aeneas defeats Turnus in single combat.

On the surface it would seem perverse to suggest that a poem so manifestly patriotic could be anything other than propaganda for the regime of Augustus, Virgil's indirect patron. Indeed, in Book 6, Aeneas's father

Anchises gives him a long prophecy of Rome's future that is especially favorable to the emperor. Nonetheless, much recent scholarship has detected a less optimistic side of the poem, as well. The two essays that follow offer strong arguments for their respective positions, thus showing how the richness of Virgil's achievement resists all attempts to confine it to a single meaning.

—Charles Platter

Viewpoint: Yes. The *Aeneid* was written in response to Augustus's deliberate and explicit cultural program. In spite of the immense subtlety of the poem, its fundamental endorsement of Roman and Augustan dominance cannot be avoided.

Virgil's epic poem, the *Aeneid,* chronicles the mythical founding of Rome. It was written during a time when what it meant to be Roman was a field of contestation—the last decades of the first century B.C.E. Augustus Caesar had angled for supremacy at Rome since the assassination of his uncle and adoptive father Julius Caesar in 44 B.C.E. He effectively won supremacy when he defeated his last serious rival, Mark Antony, at the Battle of Actium in 31 B.C.E. The Roman Republic's change to the rule of one man entailed radical revision of its sociopolitical order. Such upheaval sharpened the need to coax a totality from the division and incoherence of Roman cultural identity. The contradictory forces traversing that identity were not only Rome's status as nominal republic yet de facto monarchy, but also its increasing Hellenization, and the heterogeny of peoples and cultures the expanded empire encompassed.

One of Augustus's responses to that need was a cultural program that marshaled both the visual and the verbal arts to portray a blessed world centered on Rome, where a great ruler wielded dominion over an empire at peace. As Paul Zanker has noted, Augustan art and architecture emphasize the city-state's centrality, its status as a unifying reference point: Rome stretches the pacifying aegis of her divine mandate to govern over the world's belligerent chaos. In the service of this vision, Augustus placed the *Milliarium aureum* (gilded milestone) near the venerable monuments of the Forum Romanum in 20 B.C.E., while his powerful deputy Agrippa commissioned the *Mappa Mundi* (map of the world) displayed publicly in the Porticus Vipsaniae. Both artifacts symbolized Rome's control of space, as both the political and geographical center of the world. Even the city's commonest commercial transactions conveyed the same message: the magnificent decoration of the granaries built by Agrippa (the *Horrea Agrippiana*) reminded both the Romans and the world who came to supply them with its grain and who exactly was the "foremost nation in the world," in the historian Livy's phrase *(princeps terrarum populus).*

Virgil's *Aeneid* is the era's definitive poetic answer to the challenge of articulating a coherent national identity, an answer conceived under Augustus's pressure and patronage. The epic projects a unifying conceptualization of *Romanitas* back to a time before either Rome or Romans. Aeneas and his followers sail toward Italy from the eastern Mediterranean as relics of a Troy recently destroyed by the Greeks. They must found a new nation by settling in the new, western land. Latium's King Latinus initially welcomes them; however, the king's former prospective son-in-law, Rutulian prince Turnus, begins a war in order to lay claim to the Latin princess Lavinia and to the Latin throne. The ensuing conflict pits native Italians against Trojans—that is, one ancestral half of the Romans-to-be battles the other half in a quasi-civil war. In order for the proto-nation-state of Rome to be forged from a heterogenous mixture of foreigners and Italian natives, Eastern and Western cultures, enemies and allies in internecine strife, Aeneas must win decisively. And he does: in the climactic final moments of the poem, he runs his sword through the now utterly defeated and suppliant Turnus.

That moment epitomizes the value of the poem to advancing the Augustan vision of Rome. As much as Augustus's architectural monuments, the *Aeneid* returns to the Romans an image of themselves as history's "winners" and as providentially so: their mandate bids them redeem the world, to order and pacify it by ruling it. David Quint argues that the *Aeneid* represents a turning point early in the history of epic that tied the genre to "a specific national history, to the idea of world domination, to a monarchical system, even to a particular dynasty" (Quint, 1993: 8). Virgil's own poetic successors anticipate this argument, given that they respond to the poem as a definitive apology for imperialism—an apology to which some, such as Ovid and Lucan, take vigorous exception.

Ovid's epic poem the *Metamorphoses* mocks the representation of imperialism as essentially self-sacrificing. Ovid exaggerates the Virgilian Aeneas's self-abnegation, his sacrifice of personal desires to the promotion of the collective Roman future, into colorlessness and insipidity. In the *Metamorphoses,* Aeneas and his followers become little more than a plot device for eliciting stories, as they listen attentively but passively to other characters tell fables: how Anius's daughters become doves or how the witch Circe changed Picus into a woodpecker. Yet, Ovid's more pointed response is his one great foundation tale, the mythical history of Thebes. Ovid's gods grant Thebes nothing but waves of homicidal impulses, a legacy of internecine strife that eventually destroys the city. By making Thebes' demonic "divine mandate" darkly mirror Rome's long history of civil wars, Ovid opposes a deeply skeptical sense of Roman destiny's true nature to Virgil's hopeful vision.

Lucan dissented more pointedly from that vision by shifting the historical grounds of contention from distant myth to latter-day memories. Writing in the middle of the first century C.E., he composed the *Bellum Civile,* also known as the *Pharsalia.* His epic narrates the struggle between the Roman generals Pompey the Great and Julius Caesar during the final decades of the Roman republic and of the last century B.C.E. Where Virgil portrays Augustus Caesar as the divinely ordained culmination of all Rome's hopes for peace, unity, and prosperity, Lucan concentrates on the problematic figure of Julius Caesar. Lucan's Caesar is a cold-blooded megalomaniac, for whose unbounded ambitions his soldiers are inexplicably willing to die wholesale. The Roman general inverts the controlling dictum in the *Aeneid* of heroic self-abnegation, whereby the individual and his interests must be sacrificed to the commonweal. In the *Bellum Civile,* the Many (Caesar's soldiers) sacrifice themselves for the One (Caesar). As the prototype of Caesarism and of the Caesars' dynastic ambitions, Lucan's Julius Caesar throws into relief the outlines of the tyrant in Virgil's Augustus.

Recent generations of classical scholars have fought against the distasteful idea of the *Aeneid* as imperial propaganda. Most influential among these has been the group of scholars known as the "Harvard School," whose ideas emerged in the 1950s in the United States and gained traction in the 1960s from discontent with America's own disastrous entanglement with imperialism during the Vietnam War. Representative voices from this group include Adam Parry, Wendell Clausen, and Michael Putnam. These readers see the famous "melancholy" that the Victorian Matthew Arnold believed characterized the poem as indicating Virgil's skepticism and interrogation of the imperial project. They read in Virgil bitter regret for the costs to the conquered of nation- and empire-building, costs such as the Italian

MASTERS OF THE WORLD

In the following excerpt from the Aeneid, *the god Jupiter tells his daughter Venus about the mighty city of Rome:*

Smiling reply, the Sire of gods and men, with such a look as clears the skies of storm chastely his daughter kissed, and thus spake on: "Let Cytherea cast her fears away! Irrevocably blest the fortunes be of thee and thine. Nor shalt thou fail to see that City, and the proud predestined wall encompassing Lavinium. Thyself shall starward to the heights of heaven bear Aeneas the great-hearted. Nothing swerves my will once uttered. Since such carking cares consume thee, I this hour speak freely forth, and leaf by leaf the book of fate unfold. Thy son in Italy shall wage vast war and quell its nations wild; his city-wall and sacred laws shall be a mighty bond about his gathered people. Summers three shall Latium call him king; and three times pass the winter o'er Rutulia's vanquished hills. His heir, Ascanius, now Iulus called (Ilus it was while Ilium's kingdom stood), full thirty months shall reign, then move the throne from the Lavinian citadel, and build for Alba Longa its well-bastioned wall.

"Here three full centuries shall Hector's race have kingly power; till a priestess queen, by Mars conceiving, her twin offspring bear; then Romulus, wolf-nursed and proudly clad in tawny wolf-skin mantle, shall receive the sceptre of his race. He shall uprear and on his Romans his own name bestow. To these I give no bounded times or power, but empire without end. Yea, even my Queen, Juno, who now chastiseth land and sea with her dread frown, will find a wiser way, and at my sovereign side protect and bless the Romans, masters of the whole round world, who, clad in peaceful toga, judge mankind. Such my decree! In lapse of seasons due, the heirs of Ilium's kings shall bind in chains Mycenae's glory and Achilles' towers, and over prostrate Argos sit supreme. Of Trojan stock illustriously sprung, lo, Caesar comes! whose power the ocean bounds, whose fame, the skies. He shall receive the name Iulus nobly bore, great Julius, he. Him to the skies, in Orient trophies dress, thou shalt with smiles receive; and he, like us, shall hear at his own shrines the suppliant vow. Then will the world grow mild; the battle-sound will be forgot; for olden Honor then, with spotless Vesta, and the brothers twain, Remus and Romulus, at strife no more, will publish sacred laws."

Source: *Vergil,* Aeneid, *1.254–292, translated by Theodore C. Williams (Boston: Houghton Mifflin, 1910).*

Virgil reading the *Aeneid* to Emperor Augustus and Octavia; painting by Jean-Joseph Taillasson, 1787

(© National Gallery Collection; by kind permission of the Trustees of the National Gallery, London/ CORBIS)

tribes shedding their blood in futilely opposing the Trojans' incursion into Italy. However, Charles Martindale has shrewdly pointed out that such bittersweet compunction typifies the "White Man's Burden" perspective of most empires. This viewpoint construes empire as the weight of civilizing the world pressing upon the shoulders of the governors. The imperialists' nostalgic solicitousness for the inevitable extinction of the governed's pristine state is not at all incompatible with energetically pursuing domination. To the contrary, the victors can see the civilizing force of imperialism as costly but ultimately eudaemonic, even for the conquered.

The *Aeneid* captures just this vision of the world as needing the Romans to set it right when (for example) Virgil describes the wondrous Shield that Vulcan fashions for Aeneas, whereon the god depicts dramatic scenes from Roman history. Roman contempt for the non-Roman components of the empire emerges plainly from this description. The Shield's portrayal of the Battle of Actium shows Augustus leading a strong, disciplined, homogenous army of Italians into battle, unified as though the Social Wars (the conflict between Rome and its Italian allies, 91–87 B.C.E.) had never taken place. By contrast, the enemy is portrayed as Eastern, heterogeneous, easily disunited, and easily routed. The tableau displaces Augustus's actual foe at Actium, the Roman Mark Antony, in favor of Egyptian Cleopatra. A (mere) woman leads into battle a motley assemblage of various Eastern tribes and nations. Egypt's strange beast-like gods fight alongside them, but get much the worst of it from the magnificent Olympian gods shown aiding Augustus's forces. The Shield's last-described tableau shows Augustus celebrating his triple triumph, which commemorated his victories at Actium, Alexandria, and in Dalmatia (29 B.C.E.). These are again represented as victories over foreign tribes, though Actium and Alexandria were instead key conflicts in Augustus's and Mark Antony's contest for supreme power in Rome. The triumphal parade shows various peoples—Germans, Africans, and so forth—marching down the streets of Rome, as though foreign peoples' natural place in the world were to parade in chains for the entertainment of Romans and their emperor.

One of Parry's most influential essays speaks of a counterweight to such triumphalism in the "other voice" of the *Aeneid* plaintively lamenting the human costs of empire. Yet, Virgil shows unambiguously how criticisms of the imperial project will fare. The poem regularly silences those who bear the unwelcome message of what has been sacrificed to founding this new nation, a price reckoned in blood, exile, and sheer fatigue. For instance, when the Trojans reach Sicily in Book 5, the men enthusiastically celebrate funeral games for Anchises, Aeneas's father, but the Trojan women sit apart, exhausted, despondent, and wishing desperately to be done with journeying. They try to burn the ships that keep carrying them ever onward. Aeneas responds by jettisoning them completely, leaving them with his kinsman Acestes to found a colony on Sicily. One woman, Euryalus's mother, travels onward with Aeneas. Yet, when in Book 9 she loses her young son to the war between Turnus and Aeneas, her heartfelt lament begins to unnerve the soldiery; Trojan soldiers carry her quickly out of hearing. The Trojans silence criticisms from outside their tribe no less efficiently. Shortly after Euryalus's mother is carried offstage, from the battlefield the Trojans hear the Italian Numanus Remulus taunting them as luxurious effeminates, in contrast to the impoverished but hardy native Italians. Aeneas's son Ascanius silences Numanus's objurgations by shooting an arrow through his throat. Only the disempowered and the doomed complain of the project of founding Rome, or of the worthiness of its founders. The poem quickly hushes these detractors—sometimes compassionately and tenderly, sometimes brutally, but always efficiently.

The *Aeneid* implicitly but routinely justifies such ruthlessness by linking such suppression to the always-superior force exerted by "reasons of state." When in the closing moments of the poem Turnus concedes victory to Aeneas, but asks with quiet dignity to be spared his life, Aeneas hesitates. He decides to finish Turnus only after he has seen the baldric Turnus wears. This artifact had belonged to the young Arcadian prince Pallas, Aeneas's ally, whom Turnus had killed in battle. The baldrick portrays a war between brothers—another version of civil war—that obliquely comments on Aeneas's Italian war. Because of enmity between the brothers Danaus and Aegyptus, Danaus instructs his fifty daughters to marry Aegyptus's fifty sons, but to murder their husbands on the wedding night. Forty-nine dutifully obey their father; one, Hypermnestra, spares her husband, Lynceus.

Those who wish to read the *Aeneid* as criticizing Augustan imperialism regularly turn to Aeneas's interpretation of the baldrick as a proof text (for example, Putnam 1994 and 1998). They point out that in killing a suppliant, Aeneas acts directly counter to the directive Anchises' ghost gave him in Book 6, when dead father and living son met in the Underworld. Anchises formulated the imperial mandate for Aeneas and for all future Romans as the necessity to "war down the proud and spare the conquered" *(debellare superbos et parcere subiectis).* They claim further that, in not sparing the conquered Turnus, Aeneas has misread the baldrick's message. He ignores Hypermnestra's example as the one Danaid who spared her husband, a shining instance of the virtue of mercy toward enemies *(clementia)* celebrated by such poets as Horace.

Yet, this reading needs to be tested against the message conveyed by the most public representation of the Danaids contemporary to the *Aeneid.* The subject matter of Pallas's baldrick reproduces one of the portraits of just vengeance within the splendid temple Augustus erected on the Palatine to his patron god, Apollo. In the intercolumniations of its colonnades stood fifty statues of the Danaids; equestrian statues of the fifty sons of Aegyptus faced them from the open space of the temple. These shared the sacred site with two other depictions of the god's reprisals against hubris: the slaughter of Niobe's children, whom he and his sister Diana killed because Niobe had insulted their mother, Leto, and the crushing of the Celtic assault on the god's island, Delphi. Yet, the Danaids link Aeneas's killing Turnus not only to Apollo righteously quashing his enemies, but to the battle of Actium on the Shield. Their unwanted husbands are the sons of Aegyptus—the eponymous forebears of Egypt, the nominal foe at Actium. The fifty brides' tale metaphorically recounts the civilizing West's vengeance against the degenerate East. Further, Virgil assimilates Antony to Egypt by emphasizing the presence at Actium of Cleopatra, his "Egyptian wife" *(Aegyptia coniunx).* Antony becomes thereby a (dis)honorary Egyptian, another son of Aegyptus. Virgil also aligns Antony with Turnus, insofar as love of a woman—Cleopatra and Lavinia, respectively—inspires each to go to war, each to lose his life. Aeneas's being inspired to kill Turnus by a representation of the fifty brides aligns the Trojan leader with the *princeps'* own architectural homage to Nemesis. Aeneas eliminates Turnus as Octavian eliminated Antony: better that one man die than that a nation should perish before it were (re)born.

The *Aeneid* is a complex work, more intricate by far than the label *Augustan propaganda* can fully encompass. Yet, therein lies the power of its persuasion. As an elegant, nuanced, thoughtful reflection on the Roman past and anticipation of the Roman future, its captivating intelligence convinces more easily than would a cruder brief for the Augustan program. It was Virgil's fortune—or misfortune—to have written the definitive version of Roman imperialism as Manifest Destiny, and of Augustus Caesar as its divinely appointed Generalissimo. Modern sentiment may regret that fact, but we ignore it at our peril.

–MICAELA JANAN,
DUKE UNIVERSITY

Viewpoint: No. Far from being a piece of propaganda, the *Aeneid* is a poem suffused with loss, suffering, and nostalgia. Virgil may well have "believed in Rome," but he was well aware of the immense costs involved in Rome's triumph.

In the first book of Virgil's epic, we find Aeneas, a refugee from Troy, in the temple of Juno at Carthage, looking at some opulent wall paintings displaying the great events of the Trojan War. Aeneas himself, of course, had been a participant in that war; and, indeed, he is one of those depicted in the paintings. Aeneas finds the pictures consoling. "Here too," he says to his comrade Achates, "people weep at the way the world goes, and things that pass away leave an impression on their hearts" (*Sunt lacrimae rerum et mentem mortalia tangunt,* 1.461–462, my translation). It is difficult to understand how anyone reading that episode, and that line, in particular, can argue that Virgil's poem is a work of propaganda, Augustan or otherwise.

Those who find "Augustan propaganda" in the poem refer, of course, to passages such as 1.254–296, where Jupiter tells Venus of the eventual and inevitable founding and triumph of Rome. There is also the much-discussed scene in the Underworld, where his father Anchises shows Aeneas the glorious pageant of Roman heroes lined up to take their place on the world stage (6.756–891). Yet, both those passages end on an ambiguous note. Jupiter ends his prophecy not on a simple congratulatory note but with a striking picture of the violence that Roman hegemony is meant to contain:

> And grim with iron frames, the Gates of War
> Will then be shut: inside, unholy Furor,
> Squatting on cruel weapons, hands enchained
> Behind him by a hundred links of bronze,
> Will grind his teeth and howl with bloodied
>   mouth.
>
> 1.293–296

As for the triumphal pageant, it ends not with one of the great personages of victory but on a note of ineffable sadness, with the picture of Marcellus, a young man full of promise but destined to die before that promise could be fulfilled. Seeing the noble youth, who walks with "clouded brow and downcast eyes," Aeneas wants to know who he is. His father answers, with tears welling up in his eyes:

>   Oh, do not ask
> About this huge grief of your people, son.
> Fate will give earth only a glimpse of him,
> Not let the boy live on.
>
> 6.868–870

Anchises ends by addressing Marcellus himself:

> Child of our mourning, if only in some way
> You could break through your bitter fate. For you
> Will be Marcellus. Let me scatter lilies,
> All I can hold, and scarlet flowers as well,
> To heap these for my grandson's shade at least,
> Frail gifts and ritual of no avail.
>
> 6.882–886

Those are the closing words of the great pageant, and they are also the last words Anchises speaks in the *Aeneid.* According to the ancient commentators Servius and Donatus, Augustus's sister Octavia, who was Marcellus's mother, burst into tears when Virgil recited this passage to the two of them.

The endings of both passages should cause considerable discomfort for those who contend that the poem is a work of propaganda. They ought not to go on overlooking the obvious pathos of such passages. The plain fact is that there is far too much complexity and sadness in Virgil's poem to support a triumphalist and propagandistic reading.

Perceptive readers have always been quick to sense this. The Anglo-American poet T. S. Eliot is one of them. Writing only six years after the end of World War II, which filled the world with so many refugees, Eliot calls Aeneas the "original Displaced Person, the fugitive from a ruined city and an obliterated society, of which the few other survivors except his own band languish as slaves of the Greeks." Aeneas's end, Eliot concludes, "is only a new beginning; and the whole point of the pilgrimage is something that will come to pass for future generations. His nearest likeness is Job, but his reward is not what Job's was, but is only in the accomplishment of his destiny" ("Virgil and the Christian World," p. 143). Those who see the poem as a piece of propaganda like to place a lot of emphasis on fate and destiny, but Virgil, as Eliot notes, is only too aware of the loss, suffering, and sadness that destiny can bring.

In an address given close to the end of the war, Eliot offers a perceptive reading of the encounter between Dido and Aeneas in the Underworld. Dido, of course, snubs Aeneas, refusing to speak to him. According to Eliot, "Dido's behaviour appears almost as a projection of Aeneas' own conscience." Dido will not forgive Aeneas, but "most important is that Aeneas does not forgive himself" ("What is a Classic?," pp. 63–64). Aeneas may serve his destiny, which will lead to the founding and triumph of Rome, but he cannot forgive himself for doing so.

Many classical scholars, especially in America and Britain (see Schmidt, "The Meaning of Vergil's *Aeneid:* American and German Approaches"), have taken Eliot's path. Adam Parry, for example, begins his pioneering essay on "The Two Voices of Virgil's *Aeneid*" with a discussion of a brief passage from Virgil's version of the Homeric Catalogue of Ships. The passage tells the story of Umbro, a priest destined to die at the hands of the Trojans in the Italian war:

> the priestly Umbro,
> Sent from Marruvium by King Archippus,
> Came with his helm in olive neatly bound,
> A man of power, who had a gift of soothing
> Vipers and vile-breathing water snakes
> By a sung rune or stroking into sleep:
> He calmed their rabidness and by his skill
> Relieved men bitten by them. Yet his lore
> Would not enable him to heal the blow
> He took from a Dardan spear; no sleepy charms
> Or mild herbs gathered in the Marsian hills
> Availed against his wounds. Umbro, the wood
> Of Angitia mourned you, and Fucinus'
> Mirrors mourned you, the clear quiet lakes.
>
> 7.750–760

Here, as in many other passages, says Parry, we find the mournful voice of the *Aeneid.* In this supremely poignant passage, the landscape of old Italy, destined to be changed forever by the coming of Rome, laments the loss of one of its dearest sons. Parry moves from this passage to argue that a simple triumphalist reading of the *Aeneid* is a false reading, ignoring, as it must, all the loss, sadness, and frustration conveyed by the poem. The closing words of his essay are notable: "The *Aeneid* enforces the fine paradox that all the wonders of the most powerful institution the world has ever known are not necessarily of greater importance than the emptiness of human suffering" ("The Two Voices of Virgil's *Aeneid,*" 80, reprinted in Commager, p. 125).

It must also be noted that classicists, more than most other scholars who deal with literary texts, have an unfortunate tendency to simplify. This tendency would force us into a world of simple dichotomies: Virgil was either pro-Augustan or anti-Augustan, the *Aeneid* is either a piece of propaganda or an effort at debunking, and the like. Yet, as Parry and others have shown, the poem speaks with several voices. It is obvious that Virgil "believes in Rome," but it is equally obvious that he is aware of the enormous costs involved in Rome's triumph.

Some years ago I taught at St. John's College, where the curriculum relied on primary sources, not on commentaries or textbooks. Once, while we were discussing a passage from Homer in the seminar, a student said that knowing "the Greek view" on an issue raised there would help us to understand the meaning of the passage. Knowing that I was a classicist, he asked me what "the Greek view" was. Looking at the text, I suddenly realized that what scholars present as "the Greek view" on the issue in question was nothing more than an interpretation of the passage under discussion. Thus, using "the Greek view" to interpret the passage would have constituted a textbook example of circular argumentation. It has long seemed to me that importing baggage like "Augustan culture" or "Augustan propaganda" to explain the *Aeneid* is to indulge in the same interpretive fallacy. What scholars have defined as "the Augustan view" is often simply an interpretation of the writings of Virgil or his contemporaries Horace and Livy. In the case of the *Aeneid,* a narrow and one-sided reading of the poem has been used to construct a house of cards called the "Augustan value system," which is then invoked in support of an equally one-dimensional and false view of the poem. This, it seems to me, is exactly what those who argue that the *Aeneid* is Augustan propaganda have done.

Let my take my final cue from T. S. Eliot, who ends both his essays on Virgil by alluding to Dante, one of our greatest poets. Dante lived and wrote in the thirteenth and fourteenth centuries of our era, after the end of the Roman Empire and the coming of Christianity, long after the passing of Virgil and Augustus. What interest could a piece of Augustan propaganda have possibly held for him? Yet, Dante chose the author of the *Aeneid* as his "leader, lord, and master," the one who would guide him through the mysteries of the *Inferno* and *Purgatorio* (*Inferno* 2.140). That he did so speaks volumes about the true meaning of Virgil's poem.

–CARL A. RUBINO,
HAMILTON COLLEGE

References

John D. Bernard, ed., *Vergil at 2000: Commemorative Essays on the Poet and His Influence* (New York: AMS, 1986).

Wendell Clausen, "An Interpretation of the *Aeneid,*" *Harvard Studies in Classical Philology,* 68 (1964): 139–147.

Clausen, *Vergil's Aeneid and the Tradition of Hellenistic Poetry* (Berkeley: University of California Press, 1984).

Steele Commager, ed., *Virgil: A Collection of Critical Essays* (Englewood Cliffs, N.J.: Prentice-Hall, 1966).

D. R. Dudley, ed., *Virgil* (London: Routledge & Kegan Paul, 1969).

T. S. Eliot, "Vergil and the Christian World," in *On Poetry and Poets* (New York: Noonday, 1961), pp. 135–148.

Eliot, "What is a Classic?" in *On Poetry and Poets* (New York: Noonday, 1961), pp. 52–74.

Don Fowler, *Roman Constructions: Readings in Postmodern Latin* (Oxford: Oxford University Press, 2000).

S. J. Harrison, ed., *Oxford Readings in Vergil's Aeneid* (Oxford: Oxford University Press, 1990).

W. R. Johnson, *Darkness Visible: A Study of Vergil's Aeneid* (Berkeley: University of California Press, 1976).

C. S. Lewis, "Vergil and the Subject of Secondary Epic," in *A Preface to Paradise Lost* (Oxford: Oxford University Press, 1942), pp. 33-39.

Charles Martindale, *Redeeming the Text: Latin Poetry and the Hermeneutics of Reception* (Cambridge: Cambridge University Press, 1993).

Adam Parry, "The Two Voices of Vergil's *Aeneid,*" *Arion,* 2.4 (Winter 1963): 66–80.

Christine Perkell, ed., *Reading Vergil's Aeneid: An Interpretative Guide* (Norman: University of Oklahoma Press, 1999).

Michael C. J. Putnam, "Two Ways of Looking at the *Aeneid,*" *Classical World,* 96 (Winter 2003): 177–184.

Putnam, *Virgil's Aeneid: Interpretation and Influence* (Chapel Hill: University of North Carolina Press, 1995).

Putnam, "Virgil's Danaid Ekphrasis," *Illinois Classical Studies,* 19 (1994): 171–189.

Putnam, *Virgil's Epic Designs: Ekphrasis in the Aeneid* (New Haven: Yale University Press, 1998).

Stephanie Quinn, ed., *Why Vergil?: A Collection of Interpretations* (Wauconda, Ill.: Bolchazy-Carducci, 2000).

David Quint, *Epic and Empire: Politics and Generic Form from Vergil to Milton* (Princeton: Princeton University Press, 1993).

Carl A. Rubino, "Le Clin d'oeil échangé avec un chat: Some Literary Presentations of the Problem of Self and Other," *MLN,* 88 (December 1973): 1238–1261.

Rubino, "'Smitten by a Desire to See Again What I Had Once Loved': Homecomings in Homer, Virgil, and Proust," *MLN,* 99 (September 1984): 941–950.

Ernst A. Schmidt, "The Meaning of Vergil's *Aeneid:* American and German Approaches," *Classical World,* 94 (Winter 2001): 145–171.

Sarah Spence, "Cinching the Text: The Danaids and the End of the *Aeneid,*" *Vergilius,* 37 (1991): 11–19.

Spence, ed., *Poets and Critics Read Vergil* (New Haven: Yale University Press, 2001).

Susan Ford Wiltshire, *Public and Private in Vergil's Aeneid* (Amherst: University of Massachusetts Press, 1989).

Paul Zanker, *The Power of Images in the Age of Augustus* (Ann Arbor: University of Michigan Press, 1988).

ROMAN PERIOD: CATO

Were Cato's attacks on Hellenism pure political opportunism?

Viewpoint: Yes. Cato's attacks on Greek culture at Rome were undertaken purely to advance his own position in the Roman ruling class.

Viewpoint: No. Cato's outbursts against Hellenism were based on a conviction that Greek culture had value but needed to be kept subordinate to Roman interests and customs.

The period in Rome's history which saw Cato the Elder or Cato the Censor (234–149 B.C.E.) become its foremost speaker, writer, and politician overlapped with one of the most tumultuous and exciting events in ancient history—the decisive encounter between the Greeks and Romans. What took place between these two peoples was a sort of mutual invasion. On the one hand, Roman control over the affairs of the Greek city-states grew by leaps and bounds. Following what had long been standard practice with regard to its neighbors, Rome passed rapidly from ally to defender to liberator of various Greek states, inevitably turning each into a Roman protectorate, with Roman garrisons to enforce the peace and Roman administrators to manage it. In this way, Greece came to join the many other great nations already absorbed into the empire.

Yet, even as generals were sending home loot and prisoners captured in their Greek conquests, a Hellenistic revival of sorts was taking place, not at Athens or Rhodes but in Rome itself. Many of those same Greek prisoners, along with Greeks sent to Rome on diplomatic missions and those who were simply curious about the world's most powerful city, settled there and began introducing their new masters to centuries' worth of Greek achievement in literature, art, oratory, and philosophy. The Romans, citizens of an old but not particularly sophisticated nation, could not help but be dazzled, and a mania for all things Greek swept through the city.

It was a confusing time to be Roman. Assumptions of cultural superiority were being challenged at precisely the same time military and even political supremacy had been proven beyond all doubt. The Roman poet Horace would later give the paradox expression: "Captured Greece took the barbarous victor captive."

In Scipio Africanus we find an individual who tried to live this paradox, accepting both the Roman military and the Greek cultural conquest as good things. In Cato the Elder, by contrast, we see someone who wanted to resolve the paradox in a way that would leave Rome on top. Cato's career was marked by frequent attacks on Hellenism and its spread within Rome. Yet, oddly enough, Cato also did much to promote elements of Greek culture, especially Greek literature, among his contemporaries. What to make of this fact—whether it can best be explained by Cato's political aims, or by a distinction he drew between the good and bad aspects of Hellenism—is the matter at issue in the essays that follow.

—Philip Thibodeau

Viewpoint: Yes. Cato's attacks on Greek culture at Rome were undertaken purely to advance his own position in the Roman ruling class.

In 205 B.C.E., in the waning years of the Second Punic War, Cato's career took a new, more political direction as he began serving in the first of the sequence of magisterial offices known as the *cursus honorum.* He had recently been elected quaestor, an official charged with overseeing the distribution of state funds, and was to carry out his duties under the consul Publius Cornelius Scipio. At the time, Scipio was in Sicily busily preparing the force that was to invade the African mainland and bring the war home to Carthage; within a few years the Second Punic War would come to a conclusion, with Scipio having earned the title *Africanus* for his successful campaign. Cato joined the staff at army headquarters in Syracuse, a large and luxurious Greek-speaking city on the east coast of Sicily. After a quick look around, the quaestor professed outrage at what he found: the general, his consul, was spoiling the soldiers with liberties, not just allowing them to wander the city but actively sponsoring attendance at Greek-style gymnasiums and outdoor theaters. When Scipio waved off his complaints, Cato immediately returned to Rome to denounce his laxness before the Senate. His hope apparently was that the tribunes sent to investigate would remove Scipio from his position as commander. In the event, Scipio was able to convince the officials that his acquiescence to Greek ways was doing nothing to hinder his or his troops' preparations for war, and he retained his post. The invasion went ahead, and Scipio was not to miss his chance at coming glory. Yet, Cato was not at all discouraged; in the following years he kept up his attacks on Scipio and his circle, finding ever more subtle ways to charge him with Hellenization. When one of his charges finally did stick, the aftermath saw Cato elected censor—the highest office in the *cursus honorum*—and Scipio left a broken, disheartened old man.

Was Cato's indignation at the Hellenizing of his rival sincere, either on this or on later occasions? His attacks are often taken at face value by scholars who see in him the principled crusader, fighting an often losing battle against the tide of Greek influence and its corrupting effects on the Roman psyche. Yet, a closer look at the record of this forceful, yet intensely shrewd, politician shows his anti-Hellenism to be a means, not an end. Cato's real target was not Greek culture per se, but those of his aristocratic opponents who betrayed an enthusiasm for it.

To be sure, it is not hard to find instances of Cato engaging in open and often highly vituperative attacks on Hellenism, especially those components of it that we now associate with the liberal arts. Start with oratory. Cato, who was himself a public speaker of considerable gifts, once maintained that the difference between Greek and Roman orators lay in the fact that the former spoke from their lips, the latter from their hearts. The Greek rhetoricians were, in his characterization, as impractical as they were insincere: the course in rhetoric taught by men like Isocrates was so long and complicated that by the time their pupils graduated, they were fit only to plead their cases before the judges of the underworld. Philosophy fared little better: he described Socrates as a babbling idiot who undermined traditional values, taught his students to disobey the law, and laid the foundations for tyranny; Greek philosophers as a group reminded him of the songs sung at funerals. Those who followed the new vogue for high poetry (another Greek-inspired art) he referred to derisively as "punks." Finally, Cato targeted the Greek art of medicine for special abuse, warning his son that Greek doctors regarded all Romans as barbarians, whom they were bound by oath to poison. When Cato predicted that the acceptance of Greek learning by the Romans would ruin them and lead to the end of their status as a dominant world power, he was merely drawing out his position to its logical conclusion.

That is, if hostility to things Greek *was* his position. For despite his many attacks on Hellenism, a substantial body of evidence points in the opposite direction, toward Cato's intimate familiarity with and even acceptance of Greek culture. It is quite certain that Cato knew the Greek language from fairly early on in his career and throughout his adult life was familiar enough with its literature to be able to make subtle allusions to Homer, Demosthenes, and Xenophon, among others. Several anecdotes betray a grasp of Greek history that one could only pick up from reading the historians, and Plutarch noticed that many of Cato's favorite sayings were in fact Latin versions of Greek originals. Cato also did much to advance the cause of literature at Rome—so much so that he could be said to have invented Latin prose as a major art form. And as it happens, the genres he chose to write in all had firm Greek roots. The first history of Rome written in Latin was by Cato; his *Origins* traced the history of the city from its foundation (by Greek settlers, in fact) down to his own time. He was also the first to compose a Greek-style technical treatise (his manual *On Agriculture*) and was apparently the earliest Roman orator to follow Greek custom and publish written versions of his own speeches. Furthermore, despite his professed contempt for it, Cato gave a major boost to the art of poetry when he brought Ennius to Rome, who would go on to become Rome's premier epic poet, doing pioneering work in the translation of Greek poetic genres into Latin. Cato even kept a learned Greek slave named Chilon in his house to tutor members of his family—all save for his son, whom he taught himself.

Such acts are hard to square with the public facade of hostility to Greek culture and its pernicious influences. While railing publicly against the effects of Hellenism, Cato was clearly doing much to promote the acceptance of Greek learning among his contemporaries. The inconsistency is glaring and evidence enough that his attacks on Hellenism were not founded on a principled opposition. Yet, that does not mean they lacked purpose. For a man in Cato's shoes, eager to become an important player in Roman politics yet lacking the normal qualifications of family and clan, challenges to the Hellenism of his blue-blooded opponents proved to be the perfect tool.

For all the much-heralded balance of the Republican constitution, with its dynamic interplay between the Senate, the magistrates, and the people, Rome was essentially ruled by an aristocratic clique. Six or seven patrician families supplied the lion's share of magistrates, and the heads of those families were generally considered the most powerful men at Rome. While there were no political parties in the modern sense—the positions families adopted on various issues were more often than not based on tactical considerations rather than adherence to ideological principle—alliances between powerful families were party-like in the way they monopolized power and defined the rules of the game. Plebeian families might enter the fray, too, by siding with families who would advance their interests—but there was a catch: when it came to membership in the political club, only families who previously had had members elected to office need apply.

Cato came from a plebeian family with no such qualifications. His clan, the *gens Porcia,* hailed from rural Tusculum; it had produced several decorated soldiers but no elected officials. Yet, despite this handicap, Cato flourished politically. In fact, he did more than flourish: he rose rapidly through the ranks of the *cursus honorum,* even winning the office of censor, the most prestigious of them all. This constituted an incredible achievement made all the more impressive when one considers how few compromises he made with the ruling clans along the way. His success was something that the many Romans who voted for him clearly admired.

Yet, the reaction of most aristocrats could hardly have been more different. From their perspective, Cato was an upstart, pure and simple. Alluding dismissively to his lack of noble blood, they would have called him a *novus homo,* a "new man." It was a slur that followed the logic of much Roman thinking: what was good was old. The aristocrats were good because their families had served Rome for generation after generation, in some cases with records of service going all the way back to the foundation of the city itself. Cato by contrast was new and thus no good; at any time his aristocratic opponents could tar him with the brush of "novelty."

To combat such fantastic and deeply entrenched prejudice and to counter the aristocracy's identification of itself with authentic Roman-ness, Cato needed an argument of equal simplicity and power. And he found it, once he recognized how vulnerable his opponents' enthusiasm for all things Greek had made them.

It was not a matter simply of stating the charge and laying out the evidence. A skilled opponent—and Scipio was nothing if not a skilled opponent—could easily lay on the charm, point proudly to his record of achievements, and leave Cato looking mean-spirited and jealous. The incident in Syracuse in 205 showed clearly enough that a direct assault would come to nothing. What Cato planned instead was to create a systematic portrait of the Greek as a subtle, dissembling, talkative, good-for-nothing, luxury-loving, antisocial menace, and to lodge it firmly in everyone's mind. Most Romans, out of a deep sense of moral superiority, were ready enough to regard this caricature as true; and nothing any Greek

THOSE GREEKS

In a treatise of moral exhortation that was addressed to his son but that seems to have been intended first and foremost for public consumption, Cato outlined the sort of rules a good Roman ought to live by. While the bulk of the treatise is lost, the following fragment gives a good sense of the work's overall tone—and outlines the kind of attitude toward Greeks that Cato thought his Roman audience should have:

I shall speak about those Greeks in their proper place, Marcus my son, as to what I know as a result of my inquiries at Athens, and I shall demonstrate what benefit there is in looking into their literature, but not in studying it thoroughly. Theirs is an utterly vile and unruly race; and consider that this is said by a prophet: when that race gives us its literature it will corrupt everything, and all the more so if it sends here its doctors. They have taken an oath among themselves to kill all barbarians by their medicine, and this very thing they do for a fee, so that they should be trusted and many destroy with ease. They constantly speak of us too as barbarians, and they insult us more filthily than others by calling us Opici. I have forbidden you to have dealings with doctors.

Source: *Cato the Elder, "To his Son," fragment 1, in Alan E. Astin,* Cato the Censor *(Oxford: Clarendon Press, 1978).*

could say would serve to refute it. Cato's slurs on Greek culture were all part of an effort to create a general atmosphere of prejudice and suspicion; once it was in place, like a carefully hung net, all he had to do was wait for his opponents to make a misstep and reveal by their own deeds the degree of their corruption by Hellenism.

The mistake Cato had been waiting for came in two parts. The first involved the brother of Scipio Africanus, Lucius. In 189 B.C.E., at the battle of Magnesia, Lucius had led a Roman army to a crushing victory over the forces of the Greek king Antiochus the Great. As part of the settlement, Antiochus agreed to pay an indemnity of 500 talents, which Lucius promptly distributed among his troops. Two years later, once the good feeling generated by the victory had dissipated somewhat, a pair of tribunes known as the Petilii came before the Senate and formally asked it to investigate the matter of the 500 talents. Their argument was this: in distributing the money to his soldiers, Lucius had treated it as war loot, that is, as his own property—yet if it was an indemnity, it belonged to the state, and that made Lucius's action something akin to embezzlement. It should be pointed out that questions like this did not normally arise; it was perfectly acceptable for generals to fudge such distinctions in order that they might reward their victorious troops as quickly as possible. That such charges could be raised and then taken seriously can be explained only by the fact that they played on a new suspicion—for the matter hinged on the question, what *had* Lucius, who was as much a philhellene as his brother, said to the Greek king Antiochus during negotiations? That was the question, or at any rate the suspicion, that Cato's constant anti-Hellenic propagandizing had made possible. In fact, Cato had left nothing to chance: he was the one who instructed the Petilii to raise the charge in the first place.

Scipio recognized Cato's authorship of this political maneuver and saw as well that he, rather than his brother, was the real object of attack. In a dramatic countermove, Scipio appeared before the Senate and tore up the record books relating to the payment, in effect daring the senators to disregard his record of loyal service and well-known personal integrity in preference to rumors and baseless charges. While this action seems to have quieted the Senate, another tribune of the people pressed the matter further and threatened Lucius with a choice between prison or a huge fine. Since his brother's destruction of the books had made it impossible for him to defend himself properly, Lucius chose the fine. Thus, the climate of anti-Hellenistic prejudice paid Cato its first dividend, as it enabled him to turn a normally empty accusation into something with much more bite.

The second act was a close replay of the first, only this time with Scipio himself the direct target of attack. In 184 a tribune named Marcus Naevius charged Scipio with treason before a popular assembly. Once again the issue was Scipionic dealings with Antiochus, and once again the charge was based on rumor, yet gained strength from its consistency with the kind of popular prejudice Cato was spreading. The upshot was that before the battle of Magnesia, Scipio had come to an understanding with Antiochus that might (the sources, tellingly, are not clear on the exact issue) have spared his life. Once again Scipio reacted by storming out of the meeting; proof enough, in the minds of the suspicious, that he had something to hide. Nothing came of the matter formally, but Scipio was so discouraged by his countrymen's fickleness that he retired from politics; within the year he passed away. Cato, by contrast, went on to defeat a slate of candidates sponsored by the Scipios' allies in an election for censor; he was about to begin his now famous censorship.

When we consider Cato's conflict with the Scipios and his career as a whole, we can see that his anti-Hellenism was neither a matter of principle nor a personal quirk. It was instead a weapon, one Cato used to stave off the aristocratic prejudice against a "new man" like himself. By imprinting memorable images of the sneaky Greek and the corrupt philhellene in people's minds, Cato was laying the groundwork for a more subtle and powerful attack on his enemies. Cato, in short, had no intellectual argument against Hellenism; his was a rhetorical argument deployed to meet political ends, pure and simple.

—PHILIP THIBODEAU,
BROOKLYN COLLEGE

Viewpoint:
No. Cato's outbursts against Hellenism were based on a conviction that Greek culture had value but needed to be kept subordinate to Roman interests and customs.

Students of Cato's attitude toward Hellenism have tended to see the issue in a strictly political light, at times ascribing to Cato a rather Machiavellian outlook on affairs. While it cannot be denied that Cato's public actions were played out within the hurly-burly of Roman politics, an account that focuses only on the political aspects of his crusade will leave many important questions unanswered. Perhaps the most significant of these is why Cato had such a mixed record, excoriating Greek culture at certain times and welcoming it at others, when a consistent stance would presumably have been easier to hold and defend. In particular, how did he decide when a given piece of Hellenism was unworthy of Rome, and when it was so valuable that it should be promoted among his countrymen? To suggest that Cato resisted Hellenism from calculations of political expediency alone leaves us incapable of understanding why he welcomed it on some occasions. A second look at the evidence reveals the basis for Cato's distinction: in his eyes, elements of Greek culture were tolerable and even welcome, provided that their acceptance posed no threat to Rome's culture and customs.

It is worth emphasizing from the start that Cato was capable of holding a position for reasons that transcended political expediency. No one can seriously doubt, for example, that Cato was a devotee of the rigorous and, as he saw it, old-fashioned cult of personal discipline. The image of Cato as a zealous and rather puritanical reformer, righteous and severe in his principles, is more than an image; it is a fact. During the notorious contest for the censorship in 184 B.C.E., for example, Cato presented himself as the reform candidate, who would root out deeply entrenched corruption. Nor was he practicing class warfare or engaging in a crusade against his opponents in the nobility; Cato promised to correct abuses of state privileges no matter where he encountered them, however great or small the abuser. As Plutarch tells us, this was the riskier course, since he was going up against a slate of opponents who clearly intended to promise the electorate what it wanted to hear. Yet, Cato stuck to his position and won. Once elected, he made good on his promises, often carrying his program further than his mandate might have allowed. Mere political expediency is insufficient to explain actions of this sort: the censorship was the most prestigious of all civil offices, and Cato valued it for what it enabled him to accomplish in the way of reform, rather than for the status it conferred. His behavior during his censorship is consistent with that during other phases of his career: with his governorship of Sardinia, for example, when he is said to have made his tour of the province on foot, with an escort consisting of nothing more than a single servant. Examples like this could be multiplied almost indefinitely, but the point is clear: if Cato's devotion to a severe and disciplined life, and his consequent hostility to corruption, were matters of conviction, then it is plausible that his attitude toward Hellenism might also be grounded in principle.

The nature of that principle becomes clearer if we take a second look at cases where Cato introduced Greek culture to his fellow Romans. Literary examples loom large here. Cato essentially invented Latin prose as a significant art form, with the first important works of history, oratory, and instruction written in Latin, all products of his pen. To be sure, Cato did not invent these genres: libraries full of Greek history, oratory, and technical writing were already in existence. Cato knew this material and followed its conventions as he wrote. Yet, in the finished works the Greek influence is almost completely invisible; only someone already familiar with the Greek background would have been likely to note the affinities and the borrowings.

Bust of Cato the Elder, the Roman statesman who advocated the high morals and simple life of the early republic and opposed Hellenism

(from Elizabeth Rawson, Cicero: A Portrait, *1975)*

Take for example his history of Rome, the *Origins.* The opening paragraph of the work contains an allusion to the Greek writer Xenophon: compare Cato's phrase—"men of standing and importance ought to be able to account for their leisure as well as their business-time"—with this quote from Xenophon's *Symposium:* "I believe that good, noble men are obliged to accomplish noteworthy things both at work and at play." Cato carried the Greek sentiment over into his own language but did nothing to advertise its Greekness, simply appropriating the quote without attributing it. Plutarch himself noticed that many of the famous "sayings" attributed to Cato were nothing more than Latin translations of preexisting Greek aphorisms. Yet, it took a scholar of Plutarch's caliber to notice this. For the large majority of Romans, Cato's expressions must have come across as products of his own wit.

What is true of individual phrases and sayings is likewise true of the writings considered as a whole. The *Origins* seems to have been a history in the Greek sense of the term, with a narrative focused on prominent men that used prior social, political, and military accomplishments to explain those that came later. Yet, in certain respects the *Origins* seems to have been un-Greek. Perhaps the best illustration of this is the fact that Cato left out all the names of the Roman generals and leaders! His was a history of a people rather than of persons; of the character of a community rather than of individual characters. In short, it was history in a Roman rather than a Greek key—or so Cato must have seen it. In the same way, Cato's treatise on agriculture extended the tradition of various Greek writings on the topic yet did much to disguise the fact; read in isolation, the work appears to be the first *ever* written on the subject. He also gave it a Roman stamp: where most Greek writings tackled both the theory and the practice of farming, Cato's sole concern was with practice: for most of its length the treatise consists of nothing but instructions and lists.

In short, Cato was happy to appropriate elements of Greek high culture whenever he felt that there was something useful to be gained from it. Yet, crucially, (1) he always took care to Romanize his borrowings; and (2) he never attempted to publicize his learning or to identify himself with the Greek writers who were his inspiration. This approach may raise questions about Cato's originality, but it at least helps us understand why Cato felt justified assuming a double attitude toward Hellenism: in his work, the Greek elements were always properly subordinated to the Roman. Appropriating Greek learning in this way left him free to criticize without risk of hypocrisy those individuals who adopted Greek learning *and* were eager to advertise their association with it.

What was wrong with such advertisement? In Cato's eyes, such behavior was demeaning for Romans—and what is more, it constituted a tacit admission that their own, native learning and culture were inferior to the Greek. Recent work by the historian Erich S. Gruen has done much to explain how this attitude informed Cato's attacks on Hellenism. In one speech, for example, Cato criticized the tribune Marcus Caelius for, among other things, singing, dancing, doing imitations, and "performing Greek verses." Presumably, it was not the quality of Marcus's performance that Cato objected to, nor the fact that he was a person who happened to appreciate the arts. Rather, it was the sight of Caelius, an elected Roman official, publicly lowering himself to such Greek-style behavior that prompted Cato to speak out.

Cato's rebuke of the Roman senator A. Postumius Albinus offers an even more vivid illustration of the values Cato wished to uphold. Albinus had written a history in Greek. In the preface to the work he apparently asked his readers to forgive any infelicities or mistakes in usage, presumably on the grounds that he was not a native speaker of the language. Cato publicly took him to task for this, emphasizing that he had undertaken the work of his own free will; it was, he said, as if a boxer were to enter the ring, then ask the audience before the fight to pardon him in case he was too slow and ended up getting punched! It was not choosing to write in Greek that rankled with Cato—there was nothing wrong with the boxer agreeing to the fight; rather, it was the humiliating spectacle of Albinus begging the Greeks' pardon. For Cato, the cultural contest between Greek and Roman was a true contest, one in which there could only be a single winner, and in which every Roman defeat brought the entire culture one step closer to elimination.

An incident from earlier in his career shows how Cato thought such situations should be handled. As a military officer on a diplomatic mission to Athens in 191 B.C.E., Cato was required to deliver a speech before the assembly. Plutarch tells us that he could readily have delivered the speech in Greek, had he so chosen; instead he gave it in Latin and had it translated. His aim was surely to create the effect Plutarch says was created: even though they could not understand it, the Athenians marveled at the Latin, whose speed and brevity stood in marked contrast to the long-winded Greek translation. Cato was wholly intent on his status as a Roman addressing Greeks; his language was not just adequate to the task of international communication, it was in certain respects superior to Greek. When it came to language, a good Roman did not stoop; and what was true of language went doubly for culture.

Cato's consistent aim was to keep Greek culture subordinate to Rome's. Hellenic customs were acceptable only so long as they did not disrupt customary Roman hierarchies. This distinction extended to the private as well as the public realm. It was an old Roman tradition (at least as Cato understood it) that Roman fathers and sons should avoid and be ashamed to see each other naked. This taboo was clearly a side effect of the intense subordination of son to father in Roman culture: fathers had such sweeping authority and power over their sons' lives that it was even within their rights to punish a disobedient son with death. Since viewing one another naked would tend to make their common humanity uncomfortably clear, the practice had for a long time been taboo. Cato reported that in his own day imitation of Greek practice had spread, leading fathers and sons to break with tradition and bathe together. By contrast his family stuck to the old custom. He rejected the new not because it was Greek per se, but because of the threat it potentially posed to traditional values and hierarchies.

Cato's unqualified hostility to Greek doctors may be regarded in the same light. It should be noted that unlike other artisans, Greek medical practitioners never received any support from Cato, whether explicit or tacit. The crucial difference between a doctor and, say, a poet or historian is that a doctor must see and touch his patrons, oftentimes when they are naked and debilitated. The idea of a Roman of any rank interacting with a Greek in this way was apparently too much for Cato. Even if the treatment were for the Roman's personal benefit, the reversal of status could not be tolerated. While Cato justified his advice to his son to "have no dealings with doctors" as the only way to save him from a large-scale Greek conspiracy to poison all Romans, one may infer that the humiliation involved in the treatments was the true source of his anxiety.

Shame, status, prestige, tradition, and hierarchy—these were the factors that shaped Cato's attitude toward Hellenism, much more so than considerations of political expediency. The contrast is most vividly illustrated from a famous incident that took place in 155 B.C.E., six years before Cato's death. By this time, Scipio Africanus was but a fading memory; Cato had achieved almost every distinction that a Roman politician could receive, and possessed a huge and unshakable personal authority. Destroying his opponents was no longer the concern it might have been earlier in his career; keeping Rome on the straight and narrow was. In that year the city of Athens sent an embassy to Rome consisting of three philosophers, Carneades the Academic, Diogenes the Stoic, and Critolaus the Peripatetic. Athens had been engaged in a dispute with the nearby town of Oropus; dissatisfied with a ruling handed down by arbitrators, the city decided to make a direct appeal to Rome itself. After arriving in the city, the three ambassadors, who were all gifted speakers, began giving a series of public lectures on philosophical topics. Carneades, most notoriously, argued in defense of the notion of "natural justice" on one day; then, on the next, sought to demonstrate that there was no such thing.

The lectures caused a sensation, and crowds flocked to hear both the radical new ideas and the eloquent manner of their presentation. Even staid Roman senators got caught up in the excitement: a certain Gaius Acilius eagerly put himself forward to be the ambassadors' interpreter when they spoke before the Senate, presumably because he saw the role as something prestigious.

This state of affairs was too much for Cato, who urged the Senate to hear the ambassadors' case as soon as possible, in order that they might go home and save the youth of Rome from corruption. When the ambassadors were gone, he said, young men would once again be able to turn their attention to "their laws and their magistrates." Cato bore no ill will to Carneades and the others, Plutarch tells us; he was simply opposed to Greek philosophy. To which we may add that he desired to bring to a swift conclusion the sad spectacle of Romans nearly throwing themselves at the feet of the Greeks.

–PHILIP THIBODEAU,
BROOKLYN COLLEGE

References

Alan E. Astin, *Cato the Censor* (Oxford: Clarendon Press, 1978).

Erich S. Gruen, *Culture and National Identity in Republican Rome* (Ithaca, N.Y.: Cornell University Press, 1992).

Livy, *The Dawn of the Roman Empire, Books 31–40,* translated by J. C. Yardley (Oxford: Oxford University Press, 2000).

C. B. R. Pelling, "Plutarch: Roman Heroes and Greek Culture," in *Philosophia Togata: Essays on Philosophy and Roman Society,* edited by M. Griffin and J. Barnes (Oxford: Clarendon Press, 1989), pp. 199–232.

Plutarch, *Roman Lives,* translated by Robin Waterfield (Oxford: Oxford University Press, 1999).

David Sansone, *Plutarch: The Lives of Aristides and Cato* (Warminster, U.K.: Aris & Phillips, 1989).

Howard H. Scullard, *Roman Politics 220–150 BC,* second edition (Oxford: Oxford University Press, 1973).

S. C. R. Swain, "Hellenic Culture and the Roman Lives of Plutarch," *Journal of Hellenic Studies,* 110 (1990): 126–145.

ROMAN PERIOD: CHRISTIAN NEOPLATONISM

Did Christian Neoplatonism evolve directly from the ancient philosophical tradition?

Viewpoint: Yes. Christian Neoplatonists adhered to ancient philosophical traditions and gained enormous influence throughout the Christian world in the first millennium.

Viewpoint: No. Christian Neoplatonists rejected the tradition of open philosophical debate.

Neoplatonism was the last great philosophical system of the ancient world. It originated with Plotinus (circa 205–270 C.E.)—or rather with his teacher Ammonius Sakkas, about whom little is known—and soon wiped out all other philosophical schools. Its most outstanding representatives, after Plotinus, included Porphyry (circa 232–circa 303), Iamblichus (circa 245–circa 326), Proclus (412–485), Damascius (born circa 480; head of the Academy when it was closed in 529), John Philoponus (circa 490–circa 570; as a Christian, he turned against his pagan teachers), and Simplicius (contemporary and opponent of Philoponus). The Neoplatonists thought of themselves as the true followers of Plato (427–347 B.C.E.), but their philosophy was much more systematic than Plato's and tried to harmonize the thought of Plato and Aristotle.

Christian thinkers naturally felt attracted to the deeply religious Neoplatonic way of thinking, to its stress on the immortality of the soul and its affinity with the divine, to its depreciation of the body and the material world, to its postulation of an eternal and divine reality, and to its transcendentalist view of the divine. Although the hard-core adherents of Neoplatonism were rather hostile to the Christians, Neoplatonism influenced Christian theology up to the point that scholars speak of a Christian Neoplatonism.

The influence of Neoplatonism can be felt especially in the writings of St. Augustine (354–430 C.E.), Synesius (circa 370–circa 413), the Cappadocian Fathers (St. Basil of Caesarea, circa 330–379; St. Gregory Nazianzen, 329/330–389/390; and St. Gregory of Nyssa, circa 330–395), Pseudo-Dionysius the Areopagite (circa 500; an author who managed to let people believe that he was the person who had heard St. Paul preach in Athens but in fact copied whole passages from Proclus's works and presented them as ancient Christian doctrine), and Boethius (circa 480–circa 524). Among the Christians some wanted to see their "wisdom" as the continuation of ancient philosophy. They called Christianity the new philosophy; they claimed that "pagan" philosophers such as Socrates and Plato had a soul that was "Christian by nature" (Tertullian, *Apol.* 17), or indeed that Plato had learned the philosophy of Moses from Jeremiah in Egypt (Eusebius of Caesarea, *Praep. ev.* 11.10.14; 12.12; 13.12.1; Clement of Alexandria, *Strom.* 1.22.150). Whereas fanciful notions like these today only make us smile, the underlying idea, that the Christian Neoplatonists were indeed the true heirs of the ancient philosophic tradition, is as hard to discard as it is to prove.

The question of whether Christian Neoplatonism is the true heir of the ancient philosophical tradition cannot be answered simply yes or no. For one thing, it is not at all clear what it would mean to be a "true heir." The relationship between Christians and non-Christians in late antiquity is extremely complex. What we witness is a convergence of major cultural changes taking place over several centuries and pertaining to different aspects of life, changes that involved both continuity and innovation but in the end would lead to a truly different civilization, that of the Middle Ages. Neither the ancient philosophical tradition nor early Christianity should be thought of as unitary and monolithic. For the sake of this debate, however, positions have to be drawn in a more clear-cut way than would be the scholarly norm. Both authors are aware that the complexity of the situation does not allow straightforward answers. The positions that they defend are not necessarily their own (Jan Opsomer confesses to have adopted, for the sake of the argument, a more "rationalistic" position than would normally be his).

—Jan Opsomer

Viewpoint: Yes. Christian Neoplatonists adhered to ancient philosophical traditions and gained enormous influence throughout the Christian world in the first millennium.

What does the word *betrayal* mean? A son is undoubtedly the heir of his father, but he does not necessarily adopt his ideas. Plato himself said he had had to commit intellectual "parricide" since he had been forced to "murder" his "father" Parmenides in order to develop his own philosophy on being and non-being. Still, I would claim that Plato's philosophy is a true "heir" of Eleatic philosophy, although others may call it a betrayal.

Turning to the Neoplatonists, again one may raise the question, are they faithful interpreters of Plato, or are they using and manipulating Plato to construe their own system of thought? To be sure, many elements of Plato's philosophy reappear in Plotinus and Proclus: the immortality of the soul, the desire to become similar to the gods, the distinction between the sensible and the intelligible realm. Yet, how much of the political and ethical dimension of Plato's philosophy is left in Neoplatonism? It has been said, correctly, that Plato as read by the Neoplatonists is a "Plato dimidiatus": a Plato cut in half, with excessive emphasis on the otherworldliness of his philosophical project. Does this, however, constitute a betrayal of Plato, or is it a creative development of a tendency already present in his work?

Similar questions may be raised when comparing Christian Neoplatonism with its pagan counterpart. Of course, on many points there is great antipathy between the two schools, as is evident from their countless polemical writings. Nevertheless, as I shall argue, the transformation of Neoplatonic philosophy, as it became integrated in Christian wisdom, was not a betrayal but a creative and most valuable modification, which, moreover, guaranteed Neoplatonism a continuing and expanding spiritual influence. If Christian intellectuals, such as Augustine, had not adopted and adapted Neoplatonism, the influence of the solitary philosopher Plotinus would have been marginal: only a few devotees and disciples would have been inspired by him. This, however, is not what happened: in its Christian form Neoplatonism became the major current of philosophy for the first millennium. Similarly, the substantial influence of Proclus is primarily due to the Christian and Arabic adaptation of his thought (by Pseudo-Dionysius and in the so-called *Liber de causis,* which in the Middle Ages was believed to be a work by Aristotle).

Already, before Justinian decided to close the school of Athens, the non-Christian philosophical tradition had become a rather marginal phenomenon in late antique civilization. Its sole practitioners were an esoteric group of intellectuals, nostalgic for the past glories of Hellenic culture, practicing magical rituals, and praying to the old gods. Pagan Neoplatonism was an ideology at the service of a culture in decay.

When ancient civilization entered into crisis and, as a result of the invasions of the Germanic and Arabic tribes, all but collapsed in the fifth through seventh centuries C.E., its philosophical tradition could well have disappeared along with its educational and social structures. This did not happen. On the contrary, philosophy, once it became integrated in the Christian (and later the Jewish and the Islamic) culture, gained a new importance and was disseminated across new countries and cultures. In his *De doctrina christiana,* Augustine uses the story of the plundering of Egypt by the Israelites to justify the use Christians make of pagan culture. The moral is clear: take without reservation whatever is good, useful, and true in a civilization, but abandon its immoral aspects (such as idolatry, slavery, and the cruel circus)! The most precious thing one can take is philosophy. Christians can make a better use of the moral and philosophical doctrines than the inventors of those doctrines because Christians practice them in the worship of the true god.

WHATEVER HAS BEEN RIGHTLY SAID BY THE HEATHEN, WE MUST APPROPRIATE TO OUR USES

60. Moreover, if those who are called philosophers, and especially the Platonists, have said aught that is true and in harmony with our faith, we are not only not to shrink from it, but to claim it for our own use from those who have unlawful possession of it. For, as the Egyptians had not only the idols and heavy burdens which the people of Israel hated and fled from, but also vessels and ornaments of gold and silver, and garments, which the same people when going out of Egypt appropriated to themselves, designing them for a better use, not doing this on their own authority, but by the command of God, the Egyptians themselves, in their ignorance, providing them with things which they themselves were not making a good use of; in the same way all branches of heathen learning have not only false and superstitious fancies and heavy burdens of unnecessary toil, which every one of us, when going out under the leadership of Christ from the fellowship of the heathen, ought to abhor and avoid; but they contain also liberal instruction which is better adapted to the use of the truth, and some most excellent precepts of morality; and some truths in regard even to the worship of the One God are found among them. Now these are, so to speak, their gold and silver, which they did not create themselves, but dug out of the mines of God's providence which are everywhere scattered abroad, and are perversely and unlawfully prostituting to the worship of devils. These, therefore, the Christian, when he separates himself in spirit from the miserable fellowship of these men, ought to take away from them, and to devote to their proper use in preaching the gospel. Their garments, also,—that is, human institutions such as are adapted to that intercourse with men which is indispensable in this life,—we must take and turn to a Christian use.

Source: *St. Augustine,* De doctrina christiana *(On Christian Doctrine), Book II, Chapter 40, Christian Classics Ethereal Library <http://www.ccel.org/a/augustine/doctrine/doctrine.html>.*

Augustine's view could be considered a dreadful narrowing of the practice of philosophy since philosophy is now being forced to serve at the behest of faith. Yet, historically, the takeover turned out to be a liberation of Neoplatonism, cutting it off from its connections with the old religion and rituals, which were themselves doomed to disappear. That the Neoplatonic philosophy did not disappear together with the civilization that spawned it can only be explained by its integration within a new spiritual and intellectual project in which it could flourish once again.

One could object that the price of this liberation was to become enslaved in a much deeper way than ever before. Philosophy now became the handmaiden of theology. Despite the close ties between late Neoplatonism and pagan Hellenic religion, ancient philosophy had always kept an intellectual distance and was never subservient to a dogmatic orthodoxy. It cannot be denied that the Christian religion, once it had secured a dominant position, became intolerant toward nonbelievers. This fact, however, should not be blamed on the Christian integration of Neoplatonism, but should rather be explained by the sociological situation of a dominant faith. Would the Neoplatonic religion have been more tolerant if it had been the state religion that the emperor Julian hoped it would become? One should not too quickly project modern ideas of tolerance onto antiquity (where even Socrates was condemned for not accepting the traditional gods).

A similar comment can be made about the way Jan Opsomer introduces the problem of the relation of faith to reason in the essay below. That the Christian thinkers advanced the position "credo quia absurdum" is a view defended in all antireligious polemics since the Enlightenment. Yet, no patristic author defended such a view, not even Tertullian (who was himself not a Christian Platonist), who is often credited with it. In the treatise quoted by Opsomer (*De incarnatione Christi*), Tertullian points to the fact that many central articles of the Christian creed, such as the incarnation or death of God, seem to be absurd and foolish to the wise men. Yet, as St. Paul said, what is foolish for the world is wisdom for those who believe: "After all, you will not be 'wise' unless you become a 'fool' to the world, by believing the foolish things of God." And in the section of the *Confessions* to which Opsomer refers, Augustine is not defending the idea that we must believe something "because it is absurd." On the contrary, Augustine is, as always, intent on investigating the reasonability of belief. "In the case of the Manicheans," he writes, "our credulity was mocked by the audacious promise of knowledge, and then so many most fabulous and absurd things were forced upon belief because they were not capable of demonstration." As he discovered, the act of faith is not something absurd, but the necessary condition of understanding. Take the whole account of history:

> what a multiplicity of things which I had never seen, nor was present when they were enacted, and so many accounts of places and cities which I had not seen; so many of friends, so many of physicians, so many now of these men, now of those, of which unless we should believe, we should do nothing at all in this life; lastly, with how unalterable an assurance I believed of what parents I was born, which it would have been impossible for me to know otherwise than by hearsay. (*Confessions* 6.5 [7])

In all these matters we must rely on what other people have seen and believe what they say on their authority. Taking all this into consideration, there are many good reasons, Augustine claims, to believe the revelation of the prophets and Jesus, who have an even greater authority than the persons I rely on in daily life.

I think, therefore, it is false to use the modern conflict between faith and reason to try to understand the difference between Christian and non-Christian forms of Neoplatonism. After all, even the Neoplatonist Proclus defended the view that toward the divine an attitude of faith surpasses rational science:

> What is it that unites us to the good? What is it that causes in us a cessation of activity and motion? [. . .] It is the faith of the gods that ineffably unites all to the Good. For we should not search for the Good in a cognitive imperfect manner, but, by giving ourselves up to the divine light and closing our eyes, we should after this manner become established in the unknown and occult unity of beings. For such a kind of faith as this is superior to the cognitive activity. (*Platonic Theology*, I, ch. 25).

In my view the "faith vs. reason" issue did not play an important role in the conflict between Christian and non-Christian Neoplatonists. At stake were other issues such as the desacralization of the world (pagans considered the world divine), the idea that the world was created in time and doomed to disappear at the end of time, the views on redemption and election of individual humans, the divine creator entering into the world, and his resurrection. Christian Neoplatonists went to a lot of trouble to show that none of these doctrines was "absurd." On the contrary, they argue there are good reasons for accepting them. In short, they understood Christianity not as a contradiction to philosophy, but as its realization. Christian Neoplatonism brings to fulfillment what only had been a vain attempt by many conflicting sects to determine the nature of, and ultimately attain, happiness. I would claim that the continuity of the philosophical tradition from antiquity to the early Middle Ages is much greater than the discontinuity in religious beliefs may suggest. This does not mean that I deny that Neoplatonism underwent a radical transformation once it entered the Christian faith, but those changes constitute a wonderful testimony to the creativity of philosophy.

Let me mention two further examples to strengthen my point. It has been noted that the Neoplatonists discovered the concept of the "self," which gained a much greater richness than ever before in the history of philosophy. Neoplatonic philosophy exhorts us to return to ourselves and find in ourselves the whole of reality, even the divine principle. Augustine adopted this theme of self-reflexivity from Plotinus and Porphyry but gave it such an incredible concrete existential richness, bringing the whole experience of his life to it, that his "confessions" would become the model for autobiographical writing. The *Confessions* are indeed—seen in the context of ancient philosophy—the most incredible document about the self (not to mention the discovery of the will associated with it) that antiquity produced.

My second example pertains to eschatology. According to the Neoplatonic view, the movement of procession and return is an eternal cycle that constitutes each being in its relation to its causes. Christian thinkers historicized this process. All things "proceed" from God when they are "created" at the beginning of time; they will return to God at the end of time, when the sensible world will disappear. This may be a distortion of the Neoplatonic doctrine. However, this interpretation made it possible to give a real meaning to history and the contingent events of human life within a metaphysical perspective.

For all these reasons I have no problem considering Augustine, Gregory of Nyssa, Pseudo-Dionysius, Maximus Confessor, Eriugena, Bonaventure, Thomas Aquinas, Meister Eckhardt, Cusanus, Ficino, and the Cambridge Platonists all as true heirs of the Neoplatonic tradition. In their many different positions they represent a wonderful kaleidoscope of ideas—something that would never have been possible if Platonism had remained confined to the esoteric circles of Athens and Alexandria.

—CARLOS STEEL,
K. U. LEUVEN

Viewpoint: No. Christian Neoplatonists rejected the tradition of open philosophical debate.

After fierce resistance and a prolonged death struggle, ancient philosophy passed away in the sixth century C.E. In the preceding centuries, it had ceased to play a significant role in both the east and the west of the Roman Empire. The Neoplatonic schools in Athens and Alexandria survived the longest, but they too were doomed. Emperor Justinian closed the school at Athens in 529, a date that has come to symbolize the end of ancient philosophy, and, in a way, of philosophy itself, at least for some time.

The closing of the school was an act of violence. It was not, however, a single decision that finished off the philosophical schools. Justinian's diktat brought to its close a sad historic process in which the ancient philosophic tradition had slowly been strangled. The reason for the persecution of the philosophers was none other than Christian intolerance: Christians were unable to stomach the mere existence of an intellectual tradition that did not accept the premises by which they themselves were bound. From a strategic point of view the Christians made the correct decision: they rightly sensed that the presence, within what was now their society, of an independent body of intellectual thought was dangerous, and potentially fatal, to the new order of things. Living together in peace was possible only with those who blindly accepted their creed. Dissent was not tolerated.

At the same time the Church more or less successfully incorporated the prestige of the tradition it had vanquished by adopting the name *philosophy* for its own intellectual efforts. Thereby it claimed to be the heir to that tradition. In order to make that claim credible, the Fathers had to develop some strange strategies and arguments. The oddest was probably the idea that the best of "pagan" philosophy had really been Christian all along, since some heathens too had received the Revelation and came therefore close to being, unbeknownst to themselves, Christians. It is true that Christians were not the only ones to have adopted this strategy: "pagan" Neoplatonists claimed to belong to a tradition that was older than Plato and had roots in ancient wisdom. Their claim, however, is not completely unjustified. After all, Plato's thought undeniably shows the influence of religious traditions such as Pythagoreanism and Orphism, and was deeply rooted in traditional Greek religious beliefs. Plato moreover openly declared his admiration for the ancient culture of Egypt and suggested, like others before him, that Greek learning owed a debt to that part of the Mediterranean world. Compared to the historical constructs of Plato and his followers, fancy as they may be, the Christian attempt to enlist Plato as one of their own is simply ludicrous: Plato never heard of Moses. More importantly, the intellectual culture to which he belonged was fundamentally different from that of the Jews and from what the Christian world would turn out to be.

Of all the philosophical sects and schools that flourished in the first centuries C.E., Christians felt most attracted to Platonism. The more intellectually minded among them massively borrowed (Neo-)Platonic ideas in order to develop a comprehensive theory of the world and god. Early Christian views on eternity, for instance, were Platonic in essence (and continued to be so for a long time) and not biblical at all. Later these thinkers would be called Christian Neoplatonists. When this term was first used, it was not meant as a compliment. Especially since the end of the seventeenth century, purists referred to the "Christian Neoplatonists" as those who had strayed from the path of orthodoxy when they imported a foreign body of thought into Christian religion. Christian Neoplatonists were, then, people who distorted the true nature of Christianity. That claim, however, is matter for another debate.

For the current discussion it is more important to see what the Christians did to ancient Platonism when it fell into their hands. It has already been said that they ultimately abolished the schools that were non-Christian–"heathen" or "pagan," as they called them derogatorily (there is no reason, from the perspective of ancient philosophy, why one would accept these appellations). Defenders of the Christians could, however, retort that despite this historical fact Christianity saved ancient philosophy by incorporating it. Now it cannot be denied that the large majority of ancient philosophic works owe their material survival to the work of Christian monks, who industriously copied by hand texts they found interesting–but that is not the issue. The question is, rather: did ancient philosophy live on within the Christian tradition? My answer would be a qualified "no."

The Christian Neoplatonists stripped ancient Platonism of some of its essential features. What they retained can only be called a travesty of ancient philosophy, since what was truly philosophical about it was discarded. Only in the later Middle Ages did philosophy manage to establish a status that was somewhat independent from theology, although it remained its *ancilla* (maidservant). That the Church Fathers denatured ancient philosophy should be no cause for surprise, for one of the reasons why they wanted to assimilate it in the first place, was exactly to take the sting out of it, to make it harmless. If they somehow incorporated it, then maybe they could keep out the real Platonism. So perhaps it would be better to call their philosophy a Christian anti-Platonism.

Why do I claim that the Platonism they espoused in fact represents a break with the ancient philosophic tradition (for I think that the Christian Neoplatonists did not only betray Platonism, but ancient philosophy in general)? What makes the surrogate so different from the original, that it should not be allowed to pass for the true heir of that tradition? Let us look more closely.

When the Epicureans said that death really is the end, or that the gods lead a life of leisure without caring for the well-being of humans, most other philosophers strongly disagreed. They attacked the Epicureans and tried to prove that they were wrong. Ancient philosophers were not always polite and respectful when making their points. Of course, everyone thought their position was the correct one—even if that meant only, as was the case for the skeptics, that they were right in not making strong truth claims. Nonetheless, although ancient philosophers fought for their own causes, they did not prevent their opponents from stating their points of view and bringing forward their arguments. No ancient philosopher was afraid of a debate. And although the Platonists or Stoics disliked the views of the Epicureans, they had nothing against their being their neighbors. Philosophers of different schools tolerated each other's existence.

This situation changed with the Christians. Not only did they say there is only one way to the truth—in this they were no different from the others—they would also get rid of their competitors as soon as they got the chance. They thereby betrayed the tradition of free philosophical debate.

One could object that this was merely a matter of power, which should be distinguished from the *intellectual* positions of the Christian Platonists: we should rather look at their views about ethics, logic, metaphysics, and so on, and at how those ideas relate to the philosophical views that were current prior to the Christian monopoly. Such an approach would miss the most crucial point, however. Whoever wants to determine whether the Christians betrayed the ancient philosophical tradition or not, should not confine her- or himself to mere doctrinal points. It is more important to look at philosophy as a practice. Philosophy is not just a set of doctrines, it is fundamentally a type of activity and a specific attitude toward inquiry. My claim is that the fact that the Christians finally chased the philosophers out of their empire and threatened the physical well-being of anyone who tried to propagate non-Christian views about God or the world was not incidental. It was rather the consequence of a more fundamental attitude that is incompatible with that of a true philosopher. That is why their sort of "philosophy," Christian Neoplatonism, is no philosophy at all. It does its best to pass for one, but we should not be deceived by the disguise.

A philosopher puts his trust in reason as the only criterion of philosophical truth. Arguments alone decide what will be accepted as true. The Christians use reason, too; it would be foolish to deny that, but their ultimate criterion is the Revelation. When necessary, its authority defeats all reasonable arguments. They are even proud of that: *credo quia absurdum* ("I believe [it] because it is absurd"), a statement that goes back to Tertullian (circa 160–circa 225) (*De carn. Christi* 5.2; also Augustine, *Confessions* 6.5), catches an essential aspect of the early Christian mind-set. To a real ancient philosopher that statement is nonsense. Of course, there is nothing wrong with accepting something that seems unlikely at first sight but turns out to have the better argument going for it. But how can one accept something merely *because* it is absurd?

Let us, however, try to understand why anyone would say such a thing. The underlying reasoning may be the following: "I hear or read something that strikes me as absurd. That it is absurd should also be clear to its author. Yet this idea is asserted without hesitation. Whoever said this must have had a good reason for it, a reason that I do not understand. My source must be wiser than I, or have access to information that I do not have, so I must believe it." That is indeed what it means to believe a source for the sole reason that it is considered an authority. By accepting the authority, one implicitly acknowledges one's own inferiority to one's source. When this source is moreover believed to be divine revelation, it becomes immune to any form of criticism based on reason. In other words, whereas the philosopher has confidence in the human rational abilities, the believer is at heart distrustful of human reason. This contrast should be qualified. On the one hand, the confidence of the philosopher is not absolute: a real ancient philosopher tries to determine the limits of what s/he can know, explores the domain that belongs to the realm of reason, and refrains from pressing any truth claims beyond the limits of reason. The Christian Neoplatonists, on the other hand, did not completely distrust their own intellect. They would tend to believe, however, that whatever the intellect knows, it knows by the grace of God, and would accept that its efforts can in principle always be overruled by the authority of the Revelation. What set the Christian Neopla-

Bust of the Roman philosopher Plotinus, founder of the Neoplatonic school of thought

(from Pierre Hadot, Plotinus, or the Simplicity of Vision, *translated by Michael Chase [1993]; frontispiece)*

tonists apart from the philosophers they called "pagan" is essentially their radically different intellectual attitude, which made argument subservient to authority.

Another important difference consists in the related fact that the Jewish God of the Christians abhorred competition: according to Scripture, he had declared himself unique and had issued the commandment that only he should be worshiped. As a consequence, existing local religious traditions could only survive if they disguised themselves as aspects of his cult. In stark contrast to this, the traditional Greek and Roman religions had always been open to other religions and had never excluded foreign gods. The philosophers had granted them a place in their system or had looked for truths contained in all kinds of traditions. It is not so much the case that Christians were monotheists, and pagans polytheists: after all, did not the Christians believe that their God formed a trinity, being one and three at the same time? "The one God exists in three persons and one substance" was the consensus, inspired by pagan Neoplatonism, that would be enforced upon the believers. The last "pagan" Neoplatonists were in a sense the truer monotheists, as they insisted much more strongly on the absolute unity and transcendence of the first principle. Even so, they were polytheists in that they accommodated a plurality of heterogeneous deities at lower levels of their metaphysical hierarchy.

Apart from the general difference in intellectual outlook, there were of course also *doctrinal* points that were specific for the Christians, but which the ancient philosophers rejected. One could say that these doctrinal differences are less decisive for the debate at hand: after all, doctrinal differences had always set the various philosophical schools apart from each other. Moreover, Christian dogmas received their definitive form only after many centuries of harsh internal controversies, and many of the views of the early Christians became heretical in retrospect and retroactively. Nonetheless, one may point to some doctrines that defined the essence of early Christendom but would have been rejected unanimously by the ancient philosophers. Either they would have found these Christian views nonsensical or they would have seen no reason why one should accept them.

The most important of the "absurd" beliefs is the idea of the Incarnation and the Resurrection, that is, the belief that the Son of God took flesh and was killed, and later resurrected. As a result of the Christological controversies of the fourth and fifth centuries settled at the Council of Chalcedon of 451, it was decided that the historical Christ was at once both fully God and fully man and formed a mysterious unity with his Father (and the Holy Ghost). The unity of Godhead and manhood was moreover assigned to a definite date in history: the life and death of Christ could be dated and located. The idea that God himself did not just manifest himself, but somehow became flesh, and this only once and in one place, at a defining moment of human history, was too far-fetched for the philosophers–not to mention the belief that this incarnated God let himself be slaughtered by humans. This was the view that St. Augustine considered unique to Christianity: he had discovered that many other Christian ideas were also current in the philosophical schools, in particular, among the Platonists, but this one view he had found nowhere else. No wonder: it was too ridiculous for words, the philosophers thought.

The historicity of God's relation to the world included the view that the sacrifice of Christ was intended to save the world and the human race at this one point in its history. Furthermore, this act was thought to have been both necessary and urgent, for the early Christians believed that it would soon have been too late: the world was going to end any day now. This conviction constitutes another major difference: the apocalyptic perspective was alien to ancient philosophers.

Whereas Christians believed that the world had a beginning and an end, most non-Christians were convinced the world was everlasting (in both directions). In the early days of philosophy, the view that the world had been created in time was not uncommon. This was after all the idea expressed in the ancient cosmogonical narratives that were part of the common stock of the Mediterranean cultures. The biblical Book of Genesis tells one variation (or rather two) of this myth. Plato presents a similar story in his *Timaeus,* but most of his interpreters believed that this should not be taken literally. By the end of antiquity, all non-Christian philosophers accepted the arguments against a temporal beginning of the world. Equally strong were their arguments against the idea that time would end. They did not reject the view that the universe could be destroyed. In fact, many thought it would be, in the sense that the well-ordered cosmos that we know would return to chaos. These people actually held the view that chaos and order succeed one another in an unceasing series of cycles. What all philosophers rejected was the view that the world was created *out of nothing* and would be resolved *into nothing.* They had arguments showing that being cannot originate from, and cannot disappear into, absolute nonbeing. For the Christians these arguments were overruled by the authority of Genesis, which most of them interpreted literally. With such people, one cannot discuss.

–JAN OPSOMER,
UNIVERSITY OF COLOGNE

References

A. H. Armstrong, ed., *The Cambridge History of Later Greek and Early Medieval Philosophy* (Cambridge: Cambridge University Press, 1967).

H. J. Blumenthal and R. A. Markus, eds., *Neoplatonism and Early Christian Thought: Essays in Honour of A. H. Armstrong* (London: Variorum, 1981).

John M. Dillon, *The Golden Chain: Studies in the Development of Platonism and Christianity* (Aldershot, Hampshire, U.K.: Variorum / Brookfield, Vt.: Gower, 1990).

Dillon, *The Great Tradition: Further Studies in the Development of Platonism and Early Christianity* (Aldershot, Hampshire, U.K. & Brookfield, Vt.: Ashgate, 1997).

Dominic J. O'Meara, *The Structure of Being and the Search for the Good: Essays on Ancient and Early Medieval Platonism* (Aldershot, Hampshire, U.K.: Variorum / Brookfield, Vt.: Ashgate, 1998).

O'Meara, ed., *Neoplatonism and Christian Thought* (Norfolk, Va.: International Society for Neoplatonic Studies, 1982).

Jaroslav Pelikan, *The Christian Tradition: A History of the Development of Doctrine,* volume 1, *The Emergence of the Catholic Tradition (100–600)* (Chicago: University of Chicago Press, 1971).

John M. Rist, *Augustine: Ancient Thought Baptized* (Cambridge: Cambridge University Press, 1994).

Rist, "Plotinus and Christian Philosophy," in *The Cambridge Companion to Plotinus,* edited by Lloyd P. Gerson (Cambridge: Cambridge University Press, 1996), pp. 386–413.

Paul Shorey, *Platonism: Ancient and Modern* (Berkeley: University of California Press, 1938).

ROMAN PERIOD: CICERO VERSUS CAESAR

Were Cicero's contributions as a political figure ultimately more responsible and significant than Caesar's?

Viewpoint: Yes. Cicero was a true statesman who dedicated himself to expanding the intellectual and moral frontiers of his compatriots.

Viewpoint: No. Cicero failed to recognize the fundamental currents of political change occurring around him. Caesar, by contrast, not only diagnosed the crisis correctly but was also able to act decisively to shape events.

Two writers and politicians of genius loom large over the last century of the Roman Republic. In many ways Gaius Julius Caesar (100–44 B.C.E.) and Marcus Tullius Cicero (106–43 B.C.E.) are mirror images. Both were masters of the Latin language; both were interested in the theory as well as the practice of rhetoric; and both were adept at navigating the shifting alliances and factional infighting that characterized the final decades of the Republic. For all their similarities, however, two more dissimilar characters can hardly be imagined.

Caesar was born into a patrician family, which though it had not been of the highest political prominence in recent generations, nevertheless had genuine claims to grandeur. In politics, Caesar was generally a supporter of the *populares,* or those who allied themselves with the people, as opposed to the traditional oligarchic elite. Caesar also proved to be a military man of genius and, with the campaign in Gaul, was able to establish an independent power base outside the shifting sands of Roman political alliances. This would prove decisive when his final break with Pompey came.

In literary matters Caesar was an advocate of the plain style. His prose is restrained and a model of Latinity. The stylistic tic for which he is best known is in many ways symptomatic of his political acuity: his *Commentaries* on the Gallic and Civil Wars are written in the third person. The effect is one of distance and objectivity. In fact, the *Commentaries* are elaborately staged pieces of propaganda that inevitably show Caesar to his best advantage. Nonetheless, the touch is light and often goes unnoticed.

Caesar was an impatient innovator who, in his attempt to reform the Roman Republic, destroyed it. His assassination, however, did not restore the old order but sealed its doom. Cicero was fundamentally a conservative who looked back to a perceived Golden Age of republican rule. His ideal was the *concordia ordinum,* or consensus of the orders, which was a compact between Roman society's two top echelons: the senatorial and equestrian orders.

Cicero's nostalgia is ironic because he, unlike Caesar, was an outsider to the Roman political system. A *novus homo* from a prominent family in Arpinum, Cicero entered Roman politics without an established base. He rose to the rank of consul on the powers of his oratorical brilliance. Consequently, however, he was always dependent upon other, more powerful men from traditional aristocratic families, chief among them Pompey. These were men who not only brought with them established political alliances but also considerable military experience. They did not hesitate to abandon the brilliant Cicero when political expediency demanded it.

Cicero was an advocate of the middle style. His prose is more elaborate than Caesar's and more explicitly self-congratulatory, but he also left a body of rhetorical theory, as well as political and moral philosophy, that is unrivaled in classical Latin. His *Philippics* against Marc Antony are not only rhetorical masterpieces but also examples of true political courage in the resistance to incipient tyranny. He was willing to die for his principles. Caesar more often killed for his.

—Paul Allen Miller

Viewpoint: Yes. Cicero was a true statesman who dedicated himself to expanding the intellectual and moral frontiers of his compatriots.

Who was the greater statesman, Cicero or Caesar? The answer to that question, of course, largely depends on how we define the word *statesman,* which is surely a word laden with heavy baggage. Would anyone, for example, refer to a woman—even Catherine the Great, to take a notable example—as a statesman? Imagine trying to feminize the word by changing it to *stateswoman,* or trying to render it neutral by saying *statesperson.* The fact is that the word remains inextricably tied to the male gender and can really be applied only to men. In trying to decide whether Cicero or Caesar was the greater statesman, then, we must take care to keep all the baggage firmly in mind.

According to Caesar's biographer, Matthias Gelzer, there are two qualities that characterize a statesman:

> One is a quick grasp of and prompt reaction to the circumstances with which he is faced: this can save the needs of the moment by allowing him to take account of existing trends with a clear head. The second, and nobler, is creative political ability, which can lead the statesman's contemporaries in new directions and itself create new circumstances. (*Caesar,* p. 1)

Gelzer's definition, of course, requires that we tip the scales in favor of Caesar, who is known for his legendary swiftness and the cataclysmic changes he brought to the Roman political order. Caesar had, as Michael Grant says, "an abnormally energetic ability to get things done," and he also had the ability to get them done with extraordinary speed (*The Twelve Caesars,* pp. 31–33, cited by Barbara McManus, www.vroma.org/~bmcmanus/caesar.html). Cicero, on the other hand, took time—sometimes, perhaps, too much time—mulling over difficult issues and proper courses of action, and thus he is often accused of weakness and vacillation. If the race goes to the swift, we must suppose that Caesar would clearly take the prize.

Caesar's opponents, several of whom would eventually become his assassins, were quick to note that he could be ruthless in the pursuit of his goals. Yet, this ruthlessness is a characteristic often admired, and even required, in politicians. Thus, Niccolò Machiavelli, who based much of his political theory upon a careful study of the ancient Romans, argued that a leader must be ruthless and unyielding if he is to succeed in effecting real and lasting change. Cicero, on the other hand, was deficient in ruthlessness and possessed an abundance of the warmth and humanity that Caesar seemed to lack. Did this make Cicero less of a statesman? Perhaps so, in the brutal world of realpolitik inhabited by strongmen like Alexander the Great, whom Caesar sought to emulate (Suetonius, *Julius Caesar* 7, in *The Twelve Caesars,* p. 16), Napoleon, who sought to emulate Caesar, and, of course, Caesar himself. Not so, however, in the eyes of countless others—among them the eminently realistic Voltaire, who says that Cicero "taught us how to think" (cited by Grant in his introduction to Cicero, *Selected Works,* p. 30), and the founders of the United States of America, who revered Cicero for his courageous and eloquent stand against tyranny.

Unlike the patrician Gaius Julius Caesar, who came from one of Rome's oldest and most noble families, Marcus Tullius Cicero was not born to the purple. Indeed, he was not even born in Rome. He came from the small town of Arpinum, which was also the hometown of the upstart general Gaius Marius. Cicero's family was not a poor one. He received the best education his father's money could buy, and there were powerful connections that made it possible for him to contemplate a bright future in Rome. He made the most of those advantages, quickly establishing himself as the preeminent lawyer in Rome and reaching the successive levels of the senatorial ladder, normally reserved for members of the Roman aristocracy, at the earliest eligible age. Although he made the compromises that then and now seem necessary for establishing a career in law and politics, his rise to eminence was marked by an abiding concern for justice and decency. In the case that carried him to the top of the Roman legal pyramid, for example, he

PLUTARCH ON CICERO

For Cicero, it may be said, was the one man, above all others, who made the Romans feel how great a charm eloquence lends to what is good, and how invincible justice is, if it be well spoken; and that it is necessary for him who would dexterously govern a commonwealth, in action, always to prefer that which is honest before that which is popular, and in speaking, to free the right and useful measure from everything that may occasion offence. An incident occurred in the theater, during his consulship, which showed what his speaking could do. For whereas formerly the knights of Rome were mingled in the theater with the common people, and took their places among them as it happened, Marcus Otho, when he was praetor, was the first who distinguished them from the other citizens and appointed them a proper seat, which they still enjoy as their special place in the theater. This the common people took as an indignity done to them, and, therefore, when Otho appeared in the theater they hissed him; the knights, on the contrary, received him with loud clapping. The people repeated and increased their hissing; the knights continued their clapping. Upon this, turning upon one another, they broke out into insulting words, so that the theater was in great disorder. Cicero being informed of it, came himself to the theater, and summoning the people into the temple of Bellona, he so effectually chid and chastised them for it, that again returning into the theater they received Otho with loud applause, contending with the knights who should give him the greatest demonstrations of honor and respect.

Source: *Plutarch,* The Lives of the Noble Grecians and Romans, *translated by John Dryden (Chicago: Encyclopedia Britannica, 1952), p. 709.*

offered a passionate and supremely effective prosecution of the corrupt Gaius Verres, who had committed frightful abuses while he was governor of Sicily, where Cicero himself had once held public office, serving as quaestor.

By 63 B.C.E., when he was forty-three years old, this small-town boy had climbed to the highest rung of the Roman political ladder, the consulship. The major event of his term was the suppression of an attempted coup d'état by Lucius Sergius Catiline, a frustrated radical of noble birth whose supporters were rumored to include not only the immensely wealthy Marcus Licinius Crassus but also Julius Caesar himself, ambitious as always but cash starved at this stage of his career. Cicero reckoned that he had saved Rome and its republic by defeating Catiline, but he also felt that the Roman establishment never gave him the credit he deserved for doing so. Indeed, his insistence on receiving due recognition for his accomplishments sometimes comes to resemble an obsession, giving fuel to his detractors, who accuse him of vanity, weakness, and insecurity.

The defeat of Catiline did not put an end to the crisis plaguing the Roman political order, and three years later the three most powerful figures of the time–Caesar, Crassus, and the preeminent general Gnaeus Pompeius–made an illegal backroom agreement to divide the power of the state among themselves. Cicero was asked to join the deal but refused to do so, on the grounds that it posed a mortal threat to the Roman constitution. The result was that Cicero went into political eclipse. Only a few years later he was condemned to endure a year of exile, and the confiscation of his property, for his role in executing some of Catiline's accomplices.

In the meantime, Caesar's star was rising. After serving as consul in 59, he was awarded the governorship of Gaul, where his phenomenal success as a military commander gave him an army on whose loyalty he could count and where he made himself a wealthy man, all the while extending the sphere of Roman power. While Caesar was in Gaul, however, his opponents back in Rome worked against him, eventually winning his one-time ally Pompey to their cause. In 49 the Senate ordered Caesar to give up his command and return to Rome. Return he did, but he brought his army along with him, thus fomenting the civil war that put a definitive end to the tottering Roman Republic. Pompey and his allies abandoned Rome for Greece, where they were pursued by Caesar, who defeated them in 48. Pompey fled to Egypt, where he was murdered, leaving Caesar in sole control of the Roman world. He continued to exercise and augment this power until 44, the year of his assassination.

Cicero's detractors, taking full advantage of our access to his private correspondence, which is often unflattering, are fond of claiming that these years did not comprise his finest hour. Yet, what could he do? Returning from exile, he remained on the sidelines, watching the Republic spin toward its eventual destruction. Both sides courted him, but he kept his distance, fearing that, no matter which side won, the result would be tyranny. Writing to his friend Atticus in the month following the outbreak of the civil war (*Selected Works,* p. 80), Cicero poses a series of questions that should haunt any thoughtful and decent person caught in his dilemma:

> Should one stay in one's country even if it is under totalitarian rule?
>
> Is it justifiable to use any means to get rid of such rule, even if they endanger the whole fabric of the state? Secondly, do precautions have

> to be taken to prevent the liberator from becoming an autocrat himself?
>
> If one's country is being tyrannized, what are the arguments in favour of helping it by verbal means and when occasion arises, rather than by war?
>
> Is it statesmanlike, when one's country is under a tyranny, to retire to some other place and remain inactive there, or ought one to brave any danger in order to liberate it?
>
> If one's country is under a tyranny, is it right to proceed to its invasion and blockade?
>
> Ought one, even if not approving war as a means of abolishing tyranny, to join up with the right-minded party in the struggle against it?
>
> Ought one in matters of patriotic concern to share the dangers of one's benefactors and friends, even if their general policy seems to be unwise? (*Letters to Atticus* 9.4, in *Selected Works,* p. 80)

Cicero's final question is deeply personal: if someone has done great services for his country and been treated shamefully on that account, should he voluntarily endanger himself on behalf of his country, or is he permitted to think of himself and his family, and refrain from fighting against those in power? Face-to-face with a world of violence and chaos, Cicero asks the questions we all ought to ask–and they are surely questions eminently befitting a true statesman.

His detractors also tend to gloss over the fact that during his years of political marginalization Cicero, like Winston Churchill, closer to our own time and also a powerful orator, produced a torrent of writing. The list is astounding, covering the entire gamut of humanistic learning–and, indeed, giving the humanities their name. The years running from 55 to 44, the penultimate year of his life, witnessed the appearance of a series of works whose influence on subsequent ages, from Rome right up to our own time, is incalculable. Those works include *On the Orator, On the State, On Laws,* the *Hortensius,* the *Academic Treatises, On the Highest Degrees of Good and Evil,* the *Tusculan Disputations, On Divination, On Destiny, On Duties, On Old Age, On Friendship,* and *On the Nature of the Gods.* All the while, of course, Cicero continued to pursue his legal career and even served an obligatory but unwelcome year as governor of Cicilia.

In the tumultuous months following the assassination of Caesar, Cicero, who was now sixty-two years old, was once again drawn into the center of political life. The vacuum left by Caesar's death was being quickly filled by Marc Antony, but Cicero felt that Antony's power could be checked and some semblance of republican order restored. On 31 August 44, nearly twenty years after he had taken decisive action against the threat posed by Catiline, he took another courageous and fateful step, delivering a speech against Antony in the Senate. This was the first in a series of fourteen *Philippics,* which took their title from the speeches the great Athenian orator Demosthenes had delivered against Philip of Macedon, the father of Alexander the Great. Although Cicero's speech was somewhat moderate, Antony's reaction was not. Cicero responded by writing and circulating his *Second Philippic,* which Grant aptly describes as "the most famous and effective of all political pamphlets" (in his introduction to the *Second Philippic,* in Cicero, *Selected Works,* p. 101). Though never actually delivered as a speech, the *Second Philippic* remains a work of unparalleled eloquence, an impassioned defense of liberty and a profound expression of genuine patriotism. After beseeching Antony to think of his country, Cicero concludes with a look back at his own career:

> if, nearly twenty years ago, I declared in this very temple that death could not come prematurely to a man who had been consul, how much greater will be my reason to say this again now that I am old. After the honors that I have been awarded, Senators, after the deeds that I have done, death actually seems to me desirable. Two things only I pray for. One,

Modern bust of the Roman orator, statesman, and philosopher Cicero, who favored a return to republican order following the assassination of Julius Caesar in 44 B.C.E.

(Museum of the Capitol, Rome)

> that in dying I may leave the Roman people free—the immortal gods could grant me no greater gift. My other prayer is this: that no man's fortunes may fail to correspond with his service to our country! (*Second Philippic* 119, in *Selected Works,* pp. 152–153)

His words make it plain that Cicero felt he was risking his life in coming out against Antony.

He was. It would not be long before the young Octavian, declared in Caesar's will to be his adopted son and heir, decided to throw in his lot with Antony, thus dashing Cicero's last hopes for the life of the republic—and for his own. When the list of losers and potential threats, all marked for death, was drawn up, Cicero's name, along with the names of his brother and nephew, was on it. On 7 December 43, after a halfhearted attempt at escaping to Greece, Cicero was killed.

Many years later, Octavian, who had long since disposed of Antony and was now known as Caesar Augustus, came upon one of his nephews reading a book by Cicero. The boy was terrified, but the great Augustus merely took the book from him and stood there reading it. He handed it back with the following words: "A learned man, my child, a learned man and a lover of his country" (Plutarch, *Cicero* 49, in *Fall of the Roman Republic,* pp. 360–361). At this point in his life, perhaps, even the mighty Augustus might have come to suspect that Cicero was more worthy than his own foster father.

Who was the greater of the two? Gelzer, cited at the beginning of this essay, says that the noblest characteristic of a statesman is "creative political ability," which can lead people in new directions and create new circumstances. For all his failings, Cicero possessed this quality in abundance. In a life marked by tireless and ultimately courageous work, he gave his fellow Romans a clear vision of what their political life could—and should—be. Cicero, like the rest of us, could not break free of cultural constraints (he was, for example, a staunch believer in Rome's right to subdue and rule "inferior" peoples), yet he managed to reach beyond his culture and his contemporaries, bequeathing to the generations to come, including our own, some of their noblest ideals.

Perhaps the final answer should be left to Caesar himself, who, we should remember, would have delivered his assessment while Cicero was still alive. Cicero, according to Caesar, had reached greater heights than any victorious general. "It is more important," Caesar said, "to have greatly extended the frontiers of the Roman spirit than the frontiers of the Roman empire" (Pliny, *Natural History* 7.117). Caesar, of all people, would have known the truth; his judgment should therefore be our own.

—CARL A. RUBINO,
HAMILTON COLLEGE

Viewpoint:
No. Cicero failed to recognize the fundamental currents of political change occurring around him. Caesar, by contrast, not only diagnosed the crisis correctly but was also able to act decisively to shape events.

In his pairs of *Parallel Lives,* the Greek author Plutarch, who surveys several centuries of Greek and Roman history from the vantage point of the second century of the Roman Empire, compares many Greek and Roman statesmen with each other. The choice of whom to pair with whom is not undertaken lightly, and so we should take due note of the fact that Plutarch links Cicero with Demosthenes, and Caesar with Alexander. His rationale appears to be the following: Cicero and Demosthenes were great orators, whose "cause" was ultimately lost—in Cicero's case preserving the Roman Republic; in Demosthenes' case staving off Macedonian dominance of Greece—while Caesar and Alexander were political and military prodigies (flawed, certainly) who changed the world and the course of history. In one sense, Plutarch has it right: just as he would never have dreamed of putting Cicero and Caesar in the same category, so it is Caesar's political genius that makes him not only a greater statesman than Cicero, but also perhaps the greatest of all Roman statesmen.

The question as to whether Cicero or Caesar was the greater statesman has its origin in the work of the German historian Theodor Mommsen, who praised Caesar as the ideal statesman and criticized Cicero as a political trimmer who stood in the way of his progress. Since Mommsen, various others have taken up the issue, and a range of opinions has resulted, some championing Caesar, some Cicero, and some attempting to steer a middle course. The question has rarely been pursued without drawing parallels with recent history and contemporary political leaders, which is what makes the debate especially fraught. It has proved virtually impossible to speak of Caesar, for instance, without making references to such figures as Napoleon, Adolf Hitler, Franklin D. Roosevelt, and Winston Churchill. There is no agreement as to what constitutes a statesman either: a general notion of three qualities—an ability to respond to a crisis, a creative political vision, and a lasting impact on future development—seems to be about as close as one can get to anything like consensus.

Caesar and Cicero were born roughly contemporaneously into different family circumstances—the former into a venerable clan of politically savvy nobles, the latter into a respectable provincial family without a political pedigree—but into the same, crisis-ridden political circumstances. It has been speculated that they both might have witnessed young Pompey's Triumph in 81 B.C.E., sanctioned by the Senate in contravention of the rules, and the political careers of these three men were to become intricately bound up with each other. The last century of the Roman Republic was marked by continual struggle between forces that would eventually tear it apart: between the Senate and other classes that sought power, between civilian authority and the implicit power of large armies, and between powerful individuals jockeying for position as supreme man in the state. The underlying factor was the reluctance of the Senate to share what had hitherto been its exclusive right to rule with the various groups that had newly arrived on the political scene: the business classes, urban masses, Italian allies, and the army as it had been reformed by Marius. Consequently, the last century of the Republic has frequently been characterized by the terms *crisis* and *revolution*. Personal ties and obligations, money and bribery, violence and military force were the means by which this cataclysmic political struggle was played out.

Contrary to some claims, the interweaving of politics, money, and the military was not something invented by Caesar. He simply proved far more effective at exploiting it than his rivals. Much has been made of Caesar's "ruthlessness" and "unscrupulousness" in pursuit of power and his own interests, the ultimate proof of which is his fateful decision to make war on his own country by crossing the Rubicon in 49 B.C.E. Yet, it must be remembered that Cicero, who is often hailed as the great champion of the laws and certainly presented himself as such, on more than one occasion went beyond what was legal in the cause of defending the Republic, as he saw it. Having already skirted the edges of legality in his punishment of the leaders of Catiline's "conspiracy" in the late 60s, he was considerably bolder in his final struggle with Antony after Caesar's death in seeking to deny him his lawful authority as a consul. He also argued in one of his series of outspoken speeches against Antony (*Philippic* 11.27) that Brutus and Cassius should wage war against Dolabella on behalf of the Republic, even though they held no legal command, giving as justification the fact that they had already constituted "their own Senate" on occasion. One can imagine that he made many remarks of this ilk in his later, admittedly extreme, circumstances. In defense of the Senatorial elite, then, Cicero was willing to adopt tactics that were not so different from Caesar's when it suited him. The notion that Cicero heroically strove to uphold the laws while Caesar simply overrode them to get his way is, therefore, a vast oversimplification. In connection with this, we should also consign the pejorative term *Caesarism* to the cultural history of the nineteenth century, where it was coined and where it belongs. Used to describe a form of rule based on military power, disguised under the cloak of a legitimate monarchy, and accompanied by the preservation of Republican institutions in name but not in reality, Caesarism was rightly dismissed by Marx as a "schoolboy expression" that was of no value in understanding either Caesar or history. It also serves little to ruminate too much on whether or not Caesar wanted to be made "king" of Rome: the evidence is too contradictory and vague to allow us to reach a firm conclusion on this matter. It is clear that he sought and accepted unprecedented individual power as *dictator perpetuus,* but what the future extent and direction of this would have been had he not been assassinated remains an area for speculation and argument. We cannot assume that all of Cicero's fears would have been realized, nor that they were reasonable: one historian, Andreas Alföldi, regarded the regime that Cicero fought to preserve as "a collective monarchy of nobles who were sucking the blood from the Empire like leeches." In Cicero's treatise on political theory, *On the Republic,* moreover, he actually promotes the idea of a "leader" or "director" of the state *(rector* or *moderator rei publicae),* which may not have been all that different from Caesar's vision of his own role.

If we are to assess who was the greater statesman, then, we must evaluate both men in the context of the political circumstances of the late Republic, rather than through the lenses of later history, and we should try to do so according to as neutral and basic a definition of a statesman as possible: (1) one who takes a leading role in the affairs of the body politic, (2) one who is skilled in managing political affairs for the common good, and (3) one who shows political vision in responding to a crisis.

With regard to involvement in politics, it is generally agreed that from 59 until 44 Cicero was basically impotent in the face of more powerful individuals to effect policy. He presents himself in his triumph of putting down the Catilinarian conspiracy as the savior of Rome and the Republic, but he indicates that the Senatorial elite was never sufficiently grateful to him for this. Sallust's monograph about the conspiracy tells a more complex story than Cicero's own words: in it the debate between Cato and Caesar, between the forces of reaction and change, is central, while the role of Cicero the consul is peripheral. Caesar's speech, moreover, exhibits a political sophistication and rhetorical skill far beyond that we find in Cicero's Catilinarian speeches. Three years later Cicero found himself

PLUTARCH ON CAESAR

This love of honor and passion for distinction were inspired into them and cherished in them by Caesar himself, who, by his unsparing distribution of money and honors, showed them that he did not heap up wealth from the wars for his own luxury, or the gratifying of his private pleasures, but that all he received was but a public fund laid by the reward and encouragement of valor, and that he looked upon all he gave to deserving soldiers as so much increase to his own riches. Added to this also, there was no danger to which he did not willingly expose himself, no labor from which he pleaded an exemption. His contempt of danger was not so much wondered at by his soldiers because they knew how much he coveted honor. But his enduring so much hardship, which he did to all appearance beyond his natural strength, very much astonished them. For he was a spare man, had a soft and white skin, was distempered in the head and subject to an epilepsy, which, it is said, first seized him at Corduba. But he did not make the weakness of his constitution a pretext for his ease, but rather used war as the best physic against his indispositions; whilst, by indefatigable journeys, coarse diet, frequent lodging in the field, and continual laborious exercise, he struggled with his diseases and fortified his body against all attacks. He slept generally in his chariots or litters, employing even his rest in pursuit of action. In the day he was thus carried to the forts, garrisons, and camps, one servant sitting with him, who used to write down what he dictated as he went, and a soldier attending behind him with his sword drawn. He drove so rapidly that when he first left Rome he arrived at the river Rhone within eight days. He had been an expert rider from his childhood; for it was usual with him to sit with his hands joined together behind his back, and so to put his horse to its full speed. And in this war he disciplined himself so far as to be able to dictate letters from on horseback, and to give directions to two who took notes at the same time or, as Oppius says, to more. And it is thought that he was the first who contrived means for communicating with friends by cipher, when either press of business, or the large extent of the city, left him no time for a personal conference about matters that required despatch. How little nice he was in his diet may be seen in the following instance. When at the table of Valerius Leo, who entertained him at supper at Milan, a dish of asparagus was put before him on which his host instead of oil had poured sweet ointment, Caesar partook of it without any disgust, and reprimanded his friends for finding fault with it. "For it was enough," said he, "not to eat what you did not like; but he who reflects on another man's want of breeding, shows he wants it as much himself." Another time upon the road he was driven by a storm into a poor man's cottage, where he found but one room, and that such as would afford but a mean reception to a single person, and therefore told his companions places of honor should be given up to the greater men, and necessary accommodations to the weaker, and accordingly ordered that Oppius, who was in bad health, should lodge within, whilst he and the rest slept under a shed at the door.

Source: *Plutarch,* The Lives of the Noble Grecians and Romans, *translated by John Dryden (Chicago: Encyclopedia Britannica, 1952), pp. 583–584.*

excluded from political influence when he refused to join the triumvirate of Caesar, Crassus, and Pompey and even was exiled from the city for a year. There is no doubt that Cicero was a man of importance–and even more of moral stature–in Republican politics, and that is why both Caesar and Pompey assiduously courted him before the Civil War began, but he should be seen more as a kind of "elder statesman" figure or, in modern American terms, more like a venerable senator than a statesmanlike president. When we compare his record with Caesar's, who managed to direct affairs at Rome even when he was absent on military campaigns in Gaul, and who was almost always at the center of things, it is clear that Cicero was much more successful in the realm of the philosophical and moral discussion of political affairs than he was in the real political arena. When he did end up in the center of things, opposing Antony in a last-ditch attempt to save the system he valued, Cicero showed personal courage and some quick thinking, but, however much he is to be praised for his stand, it remains true that he was simply overwhelmed by historical forces.

As far as concerns managing affairs for the common good–and, after all, what use is a statesman if he does not have the common good in mind?—Caesar deserves credit for his practice of treating neutrals as friends and his famous clemency *(clementia)* toward his former enemies. Although this clemency was a powerful political and ideological weapon, often deployed with the most cynical motives, and although his opponents saw it—correctly—as pardoning those over whom he had no legal authority, it does indicate an "inclusive" and pragmatic perspective befitting a true statesman. Beyond this, we may consider Caesar's legislation, on which one expert, Zvi Yavetz, comments as follows, after surveying the 38 laws associated with him: "Caesar was a popular leader because the basic needs of the people were his primary consideration. He distributed land in Italy and in the colonies, provided for the corn supply, for the relief of debts, and took care of rent problems. For the masses, he organized entertainments, distributed gifts and benefits, provided conditions to ensure an increase in the birth-rate and his huge development projects produced an income for thousands" (211–212). There is, moreover, a discernible thread of rational reorganization running through Caesar's legislative program, typified by his reformation of the Roman calendar. Bringing the calendar year into harmony with the astronomical year was a long overdue reform, and removing from priests the power to insert days and months at will was an entirely sensible step. Although they were clearly not designed to strengthen the role of the Senate, the Caesarian laws are not those of an extremist or a revolutionary; rather, they constitute a moderate effort to extend the base of the government in a way that Rome had often done before. This was appropriate and indeed necessary, given the fact that it was now responsible for the administration of a large empire.

Statue of Julius Caesar, conqueror of Gaul and victor in the Roman civil war, first century B.C.E.

(Robert Harding Picture Library, London)

This brings us to the third criterion for statesmanship: political vision in response to a crisis. Cicero tended to see the crisis in the Republic in moral terms, as a struggle between the good men *(boni)*—those for the most part like himself—and the bad *(improbi)*—those who threatened the Senatorial order. Because his thinking was in this and in so many other ways "unpolitical," he was unable to recognize the impossibility of governing a huge empire with the institutions of a city-state, whereas Caesar diagnosed the problem and came up with one solution, namely his appointment as *dictator* for life. Exactly how much "vision" this shows has been hotly debated: some argue that he set in motion the process that resulted in Augustus's final constitutional settlement later, but others would say that he cannot be credited with this. It has been suggested that Caesar knew how to get monarchical power, but not what to do with it. In fact, if anyone, it is Cicero who is to be credited with Augustus's much more tentative Principate and for his making at least the pretense that the Republic had been "restored." It was Cicero's legacy, says Christian Habicht (99), "more than anything else, that made it virtually impossible for Augustus to follow in Caesar's footsteps. Cicero, therefore, was responsible for the concessions which the new monarchic system made to republican tradition." Of course, these concessions did not last much beyond Augustus himself, so one might conclude that Caesar's vision—albeit one based on personal ambition—proved the more accurate in the long run. Indeed, according to the philosopher Georg Wilhelm Friedrich Hegel, Caesar's monarchy was historically and objectively "necessary," demanded by the circumstances since "the democratic constitution could no longer be really maintained."

In conclusion, we can say that both Caesar and Cicero wanted to be leaders of the Roman state—and perhaps to be the most important individual in the political landscape—but, while Caesar for the most part succeeded in achieving this goal, Cicero's efforts more often than not ended in failure. In assessing the "statesmanship" of each, it is vital to separate Cicero the man, with all his outstanding intellectual talents and contributions to Roman culture (in rhetoric, philosophy, theology and so on), from Cicero the politician. Likewise, we must distinguish between Caesar the politician and Caesar the brilliant general, captivating writer, and charismatic individual. Caesar's aristocratic background gave him the skills and resources that he needed to manipulate both friends and enemies; Cicero's status as an outsider never allowed him full access to the web of power. Caesar's charismatic personality, imbued as it was with decisiveness, quickness, and flexibility, proved to be an effective asset in the turbulent and unpredictable world of Roman politics; Cicero's more cautious and reflective personality, accompanied by what even his admirers admit was a certain injudiciousness of speech and a tendency to push himself forward when it might have been wiser to stay in the background, did not serve him so well in these conditions. Although neither man lacked courage and determination, Caesar has to be reckoned the greater statesman of the two.

–DAVID H. J. LARMOUR,
TEXAS TECH UNIVERSITY

References

Caesar, *The Civil War,* translated by Jane F. Gardner (Harmondsworth, U.K.: Penguin, 1967).

Caesar, *The Conquest of Gaul,* translated by S. A. Handford (London: Penguin, 1982).

Cicero, *Letters to Atticus,* translated by D. R. Shackleton Bailey (Harmondsworth, U.K.: Penguin, 1978).

Cicero, *Letters to His Friends,* 2 volumes, translated by Bailey (Harmondsworth, U.K.: Penguin, 1978).

Cicero, *On the Good Life,* translated by Michael Grant (Harmondsworth, U.K.: Penguin, 1971).

Cicero, *Selected Political Speeches,* translated by Grant (London: Penguin, 1989).

Cicero, *Selected Works,* translated by Grant (Harmondsworth, U.K.: Penguin, 1971).

Anthony Everitt, *Cicero: The Life and Times of Rome's Greatest Politician* (New York: Random House, 2002).

Matthias Gelzer, *Caesar: Politician and Statesman,* sixth edition, translated by Peter Needham (Cambridge, Mass.: Harvard University Press, 1968).

Michael Grant, *The Twelve Caesars* (New York: Scribners, 1975).

Christian Habicht, *Cicero the Politician* (Baltimore: Johns Hopkins University Press, 1990).

Barbara McManus, "Rome: Republic to Empire" <www.vroma.org/~bmcmanus/romanpages.html>.

Christian Meier, *Caesar,* translated by David McLintock (New York: Basic Books/HarperCollins, 1995).

T. N. Mitchell, *Cicero: The Ascending Years* (New Haven: Yale University Press, 1979).

Mitchell, *Cicero: The Senior Statesman* (New Haven: Yale University Press, 1991).

Pliny, *Natural History,* volume 2, translated by H. Rackham (Cambridge, Mass.: Harvard University Press, 1942).

Plutarch, *Marius, Sulla, Crassus, Pompey, Caesar, Cicero, in Fall of the Roman Republic, Six Lives by Plutarch,* translated by Rex Warner (Harmondsworth, U.K.: Penguin, 1972).

Elizabeth Rawson, *Cicero: A Portrait* (London: Allen Lane, 1975).

Andrew M. Riggsby, "The Cicero Homepage" <www.utexas.edu/depts/classics/documents/Cic.html>.

R. E. Smith, *Cicero the Statesman* (Cambridge: Cambridge University Press, 1966).

C. E. W. Steel, *Cicero, Rhetoric, and Empire* (Oxford: Oxford University Press, 2001).

Suetonius, *Julius Caesar,* in *The Twelve Caesars,* translated by Robert Graves (London: Penguin, 1989), pp. 13–53.

Ronald Syme, *The Roman Revolution* (Oxford: Oxford University Press, 1939).

The VRoma Project <www.vroma.org>.

Zvi Yavetz, *Julius Caesar and His Public Image* (Ithaca, N.Y.: Cornell University Press, 1983).

ROMAN PERIOD: DONATIST CONTROVERSY

Did Donatist bishops fail to offer a convincing defense of their beliefs at the Conference of 411 C.E. in Carthage?

Viewpoint: Yes. The irrational and erratic behavior of the Donatist bishops during their debate with their Catholic antagonists in 411 C.E. clearly showed not only the bad faith in which they agreed to the proceedings but also the lack of a logical and legal argument that they could employ to defend their case.

Viewpoint: No. The Donatists, who were faced with a hostile imperial court and bureaucratic overseers whose mission was to ensure their defeat, employed various strategies in order to fashion a transcript of the meeting that could be used to their benefit in subsequent legal appeals.

The Donatists were Christians from Roman North Africa whose origins can be traced to the great persecution of the emperor Diocletian (284–305 C.E.), a devout polytheist who believed that the Christians were seditious revolutionaries. In 303 Diocletian ordered all those living in Roman territory to perform sacrifice (something Christians refused to do) and commanded his administrators to confiscate from Christian establishments the Scriptures as well as liturgical accoutrements used during services. Those priests and Church officials who did not comply with the emperor's order were arrested. Some were tortured and executed. Faced with the horrible prospect of Roman prison—torture of prisoners not of high social status constituted routine judicial procedure—some bishops and priests obeyed and handed over Church Bibles to imperial agents. The persecution itself, which was not implemented with equal severity throughout Rome's administrative territories, was ended by imperial decree in April 311 C.E.

The Christian communities began to recover and rebuild under the supporting hand of Diocletian's successor, Constantine (305–337 C.E.), who was the first Christian emperor, but fierce disagreements arose among African Christians regarding the spiritual and administrative consequences of having complied with Diocletian's orders. Many people believed that bishops who handed over the Scriptures (called in Latin *traditores,* "handers-over") were no longer capable of administering the sacraments because they had "broken" the connection between their office and the power that informed that office—the Holy Spirit. The sacraments the *traditores* now performed had no connection to divine power. Thus, those they baptized were not, in fact, baptized (baptism was necessary for salvation), and the men they ordained as priests were not, in fact, priests. These Christians, known to us as the Donatists, insisted that for the Church to maintain its purity, those whom the *traditores* had baptized required rebaptism by a bishop whose purity assured him connection to the Holy Spirit and, consequently, efficacy in performing the sacrament.

By the late 300s C.E. the Donatists constituted the majority of Christians in North Africa. They were sharply at odds with Catholic (that is, non-Donatist) Christians, and the two sides continually tangled with one another for a century, even to the point of bloodshed and murder. In 410 the Roman emperor of the West, Honorius, ordered Catholics and Donatists to meet in the city of Carthage (just north of present-day Tunis in Tunisia) to discuss their differences. An imperial agent by the name of Marcellinus was commissioned by the emperor to judge the proceedings. Marcellinus was to determine, once and for all, which Christian faction held the orthodox or "right-thinking" position. What makes this meeting so notable for ancient historians as well as for readers of this book, whose essays explore the tremendous flexibility inherent in historical interpretation, is the fact that a partial transcript of this meeting, signed and authenticated by both Donatist and Catholic representatives, survives. Despite the ability of modern historians to read a verbatim report of the proceedings of 411, they still disagree as to how to interpret just what happened between the Donatists and Catholics that summer in Carthage.

—Erika T. Hermanowicz

Viewpoint: Yes. The irrational and erratic behavior of the Donatist bishops during their debate with their Catholic antagonists in 411 C.E. clearly showed not only the bad faith in which they agreed to the proceedings but also the lack of a logical and legal argument that they could employ to defend their case.

For the Catholics of North Africa, the convening of the Conference of 411 was the culmination of almost a century of intense diplomacy with local and imperial authorities. The Catholics had compiled their arguments against the Donatists years before and had employed them with consistency and perseverance. They planned to use them again in 411. This particular conference was to settle theological differences among warring Christian factions, but the Donatists themselves were almost secondary characters in this drama; the religious and historical arguments they employed were so weak and halfhearted that the meeting in 411 merely served to underscore for imperial authorities what had long been suspected: the Donatists were a belligerent and violent faction that had no interest in repairing relations or enjoying a religiously unified Africa. For the salvation of souls and for the social stability of Africa, the Donatists had to be brought to heel.

It is difficult to present the Conference of 411 from the Catholic point of view, since all the careful planning and well-arranged arguments that they intended to use were undercut by the Donatists in bizarre, time-wasting tactics consisting largely of intrusive non sequiturs. The Catholics had to wait for the illogical, frenetic outbursts made by the opposing side to subside before discussing any point of substance.

The best way to approach the Catholic side of the argument is to delineate the arguments the Catholics had been using against the Donatists since the early 300s C.E. (but were largely submerged in the delaying tactics of the Donatists) and then address the events of the Conference of 411 itself.

The Catholic argument against Donatism as presented since the initial rift after 311 C.E. consisted of three broad points. First, the Donatists terrorized African towns and cities; their violent attacks on farmers, estate owners, and Catholic clergy had claimed limbs and lives. Second, the Donatists had always avoided direct negotiations with their Catholic counterparts. This indicated that their entrenched isolation took precedence, in their minds, over the unity of the Church. Third, the Catholics and Donatists differed on what constituted the Church of Christ on earth in terms of its composition: who should be in it and how it was to maintain its purity. We will take these points in order.

In October 410 C.E. a group of Catholic bishops gained audience with the emperor Honorius. They presented him with a letter of request regarding the Donatists and religious factionalism in Africa. We are not exactly sure what the document said, for it was never released to the public. We do know, however, how Honorius responded. He wrote a direct letter to his imperial administrator, Marcellinus, ordering the Catholic and Donatist sides to meet, with clear indications that the Donatists must abandon their heresy and reconcile with the Catholics. Honorius himself was a Catholic, and, while personal predilections may have introduced some prejudice, his attitude was also informed by decidedly unsavory encounters with the Donatists in the past. In 404 a Donatist embassy arrived at the imperial court with petition in hand requesting that legislation recently promulgated against them in Africa be repealed; whatever chances the Donatist embassy had of convincing the emperor were lost when Honorius learned of the increasing attacks being mounted against Catholics at the instigation of Donatist clergy. St. Augustine had barely escaped an ambush in the summer or autumn of 403. Other Catholic bishops had been kidnapped, rolled in mud, rolled in dung, undressed and publicly paraded, and beaten with fists and wooden bats. Several Catholic sources note that

Donatist bands blinded victims with a brew of homemade acid. One bishop had been stabbed and then thrown off the top of a tower; fortunately, he recovered sufficiently to show the emperor his scars. From the surviving evidence, it appears that Honorius's denial of the Donatist appeal can be traced in large part to his anger at their resorting to brutal violence to cow the Catholics. The Donatists had argued from the beginning of their disagreement with the Catholics that they were persecuted; they were the true heirs of the Christian martyrs who had died brave deaths in the arena. That argument rings hollow when one reads of these attacks against Catholic clergy.

Catholics again turned to the emperor for help against Donatist violence in 408 when Catholics bishops were waylaid and murdered in the streets. An embassy traveled to Ravenna, the emperor's current residence, at a difficult time. Italy was under siege from the Goths, and travel on the peninsula was almost impossible. Catholic reward for several months' efforts was an outraged letter from Honorius that reiterated Donatists were heretics and liable to heavy monetary fines. Local judges were to do their utmost to protect Catholic clergy; attacks were to be prosecuted to the full extent of the law: exile or execution. This particular Catholic embassy did not return to Africa until 409, and they were, not surprisingly, shocked to discover just a few months after coming home that Honorius had issued a law suspending the antiheresy laws he had recently passed. Donatists were no longer considered heretics: all property was to be returned to them; they were not subject to fines. Two of the bishops who had just returned to Africa boarded another ship bound for Italy to meet with the emperor again. Historians assume that Honorius made this seemingly illogical reversal at a moment of desperation. The Goths were tightening their grip on Italy, and Honorius was frantic about many things, one in particular being the continued support of Africa, as that territory fed Rome's poor citizens for more than half of every year. Along with massive tax breaks to wealthy farmers, Honorius also lifted restrictions against the Donatists, who comprised about half the population of North Africa—a sure way to garner an upsurge in popularity.

The secret embassy of 410 convinced Honorius that legislation against the Donatists must be reactivated; they probably argued that the best way to clarify and publicize the emperor's decision was for the Donatists and the Catholics to debate face to face, with adjudication provided by imperial representatives: thus, the birth of the 411 Conference.

Second, we turn to the question of the unity of the Church. The indivisible nature of the Church universal was a concept that stretched back to the apostles and St. Paul, but fractioning and splits had been a common occurrence since the Church's infancy. According to many Catholic thinkers, those who "broke" with the Church along theological lines (regarding the nature and purpose of God) were called "heretics"; those who "broke" along procedural lines, that is, they maintained the same fundamental beliefs regarding the nature of God and Christology (the nature of Christ), but believed differently in terms of administrative and earthly Church matters, were called "schismatics." The accusation of heresy was much more serious. These two categories could, however, merge. St. Augustine argued that a schism could become heresy if the schism's adherents demonstrated no interest in resolving differences. Years of resistance and generations of self-imposed isolation meant that schismatics, in this case the Donatists, had no real devotion to the idea of the Church universal.

In opposition to Donatist aloofness, the Catholics were always eager to meet their opponents in public debate. A rift in the Church was dangerous for the many souls the Church succored. That thought is fundamental to understanding the Catholic hierarchy in North Africa and should not be glossed over. The Catholics were also confident of their debating skills and their method of argument; they were not afraid of bitter confrontation. Debates in the ancient world—among philosophers and theologians—were dramatic and exuberant, and the debaters used every rhetorical weapon at their disposal, including insulting personal attacks. St. Augustine and his episcopal colleagues tried several times to arrange public discussions with Donatist bishops, all to no avail. The first attempts consisted of very polite invitations by letter; some Donatist bishops initially accepted, but then later declined. Frustrated, the Catholic bishops in 401 and 403 again invited the Donatists to debate, but this time they requested that African imperial administrators lend their support by forcing the Donatists to comply. The Donatists still managed to avoid the meetings. When the emperor Honorius promulgated legislation against them in the year 405, the Donatist bishops responded by sending an embassy to Italy in 406. They told the emperor they were willing to talk, but by then it was too late; the Catholics had what they wanted. The Donatists had been told to return to the Catholic fold. Why would the Catholics want a debate then? The emperor had settled the question.

Donatist resistance to open discussion constituted the second argument in demonstrating that the Donatists were clearly wrong in their beliefs. Their recalcitrance in the face of constant invitation amply proved that the Donatists not only were heretics, but they were also clearly aware of their own fallibility, as they did not want public debate to expose the inherent weakness of their beliefs.

Third, the Catholics objected to Donatist claims of legitimacy as an institution. The two groups had not differed on theological issues; they shared common ground regarding the nature of God and Christ. What separated them was their understanding of the constitution and character of the Church itself. The Donatists believed in the purity of the Church on earth. To remain pure, and thus to ensure the help and cooperation of the Holy Spirit in ecclesiastical matters, especially the sacraments, the Donatists insisted that those who were found to be "impure"–and in that category they placed all Catholics, but they focused attention upon clergy who had handed over the Scriptures during the imperial persecution and those whom the *traditores* had ordained–were to be denied communion with the Church unless they were rebaptized: the baptism they previously received, according to the Donatists, being of no effect.

The Catholic (specifically Augustinian) response to this bid for purity within an earthly institution was outright rejection. As Augustine repeated in many treatises, human beings do not have the capacity to determine who is "pure" and who is not. That is God's concern exclusively. Augustine employed several metaphorical images found in Scripture to prove his point: when casting a net, one brings up all sorts of fishes, good and bad; on the threshing floor, the wheat and the chaff are indiscriminately mixed. It is for God at judgment to separate the worthy and unworthy. Augustine, an astute student of the human heart, believed there were many people who *seemed* good and holy; on the other hand, there were many people who were publicly reviled and detested. But who knew? The first may secretly do evil in act and secretly think evil in heart. The reviled, for all their rejection by humans, may be truly beloved of God. Who are we and who are the clergy that they can make the decision who is blessed by God and who is not? For Augustine, people live as best they can; they should forgive others and hope that they themselves are forgiven. To judge more severely, to the extent of denying sacrament, succor, and salvation, is simply wrong.

Penetrating deeper into the theology proper, the Catholics determined that the Donatist attitude regarding baptism (or rebaptism), when brought to its logical conclusion, meant that human beings, not God, were responsible for the efficacy of the sacrament. To assert that an impure bishop can "infect" and "destroy" the sacraments means that God's work is subject to reversal by man, an impossible statement. Bishops ordain and baptize not of their own power, but through God. The sacrament retains its power, its validity, no matter who the bishop is, or what he has done.

As to the Conference of 411, the Catholics arrived aggressively confident; they knew they could outmaneuver the Donatist argument at any time, but now they had the chance to do so in front of the emperor's representatives. They were, therefore, upset to encounter, from the first moment, Donatists' attempts to derail the proceedings. The Catholics had been clear in their correspondence to Marcellinus as to the approach they would take and their order of argumentation. The Donatists, however, tried to overturn the process by avoiding the issues altogether. They first insisted on a head count of all Catholic bishops present at the Conference in order to detect "padding" of numbers by the Catholics, but it was evidently a move to avoid addressing the substantive issues. The next day's scheme was vociferously denounced by all Catholic bishops: a Donatist demand to review all of the minutes of the previous meeting–not just notes made by the stenographers in shorthand, but the actual completed and published minutes–before proceeding. This was another pointless delaying tactic: their concern about collusion and forgery is nonsense as the Donatists had four of their own stenographers present who both wrote and verified the minutes.

As to the third and final day, the Donatists made some points from Scripture that Marcellinus found pertinent enough to demand a response from the Catholics, but the majority of the day concerned Donatist demands to have various documents reread, which had already been inserted into the proceedings. They also spent a great amount of time arguing that they should be privy to the Catholic letter presented to the emperor Honorius in 410. The Catholics explained that the document addressed several issues, some of which were private, and that for the Donatists and the public at large to see them was inappropriate. Marcellinus concurred, saying that it was not a part of his express written instructions to release a copy of any material not specifically referred to by the emperor.

The demand to see this letter formed part of a larger Donatist attempt to identify who was the plaintiff at the 411 Conference. They wanted the record to show which party had demanded that the meeting be convened. To place responsibility on the Catholics squarely situated them in the role of accuser or persecutor; the Donatists, as persecuted, were the true heirs of the martyrs who had died in the arena and in the prisons during the reign of Diocletian. The persecuted were

ON THE THRESHING FLOOR

But he urges that "we find that the apostles, in all their epistles, execrated and abhorred the sacrilegious wickedness of heretics, so as to say that 'their word does spread as a canker.'" What then? Does not Paul also show that those who said, "Let us eat and drink, for to-morrow we die," were corrupters of good manners by their evil communications, adding immediately afterwards, "Evil communications corrupt good manners;" and yet he intimated that these were within the Church when he says, "How say some among you that there is no resurrection of the dead?" But when does he fail to express his abhorrence of the covetous? Or could anything be said in stronger terms, than that covetousness should be called idolatry, as the same apostle declared? Nor did Cyprian understand his language otherwise, inserting it when need required in his letters; though he confesses that in his time there were in the Church not covetous men of an ordinary type, but robbers and usurers, and these found not among the masses, but among the bishops. And yet I should be willing to understand that those of whom the apostle says, "Their word does spread as a canker," were without the Church, but Cyprian himself will not allow me. For, when showing, in his letter to Antonianus, that no man ought to sever himself from the unity of the Church before the time of the final separation of the just and unjust, merely because of the admixture of evil men in the Church, when he makes it manifest how holy he was, and deserving of the illustrious martyrdom which he won, he says, "What swelling of arrogance it is, what forgetfulness of humility and gentleness, that any one should dare or believe that he can do what the Lord did not grant even to the apostles,—to think that he can distinguish the tares from the wheat, or, as if it were granted to him to carry the fan and purge the floor, to endeavor to separate the chaff from the grain! And whereas the apostle says, 'But in a great house there are not only vessels of gold and of silver, but also of wood and of earth,' that he should seem to choose those of gold and of silver, and despise and cast away and condemn those of wood and of earth, when really the vessels of wood are only to be burned in the day of the Lord by the burning of the divine conflagration, and those of earth are to be broken by Him to whom the 'rod of iron has been given.'" By this argument, therefore, against those who, under the pretext of avoiding the society of wicked men, had severed themselves from the unity of the Church, Cyprian shows that by the great house of which the apostle spoke, in which there were not only vessels of gold and of silver, but also of wood and of earth, he understood nothing else but the Church, in which there should be good and bad, till at the last day it should be cleansed as a threshing-floor by the winnowing-fan. And if this be so, in the Church herself, that is, in the great house itself, there were vessels to dishonor, whose word did spread like a canker. For the apostle, speaking of them, taught as follows: "And their word," he says, "will spread as doth a canker; of whom is Hymenaeus and Philetus; who concerning the truth have erred, saying that the resurrection is past already; and overthrow the faith of some. Nevertheless the foundation of God standeth sure. Having this seal, the Lord knoweth them that are His. And, let every one that nameth the name of Christ depart from iniquity. But in a great house there are not only vessels of gold and of silver, but also of wood and of earth." If, therefore, they whose words did spread as doth a canker were as it were vessels to dishonor in the great house, and by that "great house" Cyprian understands the unity of the Church itself, surely it cannot be that their canker polluted the baptism of Christ. Accordingly, neither without, any more than within, can any one who is of the devil's party, either in himself or in any other person, stain the sacrament which is of Christ. It is not, therefore, the case that "the word which spreads as a canker to the ears of those who hear it gives remission of sins;" but when baptism is given in the words of the gospel, however great be the perverseness of understanding on the part either of him through whom, or of him to whom it is given, the sacrament itself is holy in itself on account of Him whose sacrament it is. And if any one, receiving it at the hands of a misguided man, yet does not receive the perversity of the minister, but only the holiness of the mystery, being closely bound to the unity of the Church in good faith and hope and charity, he receives remission of his sins,—not by the words which do eat as doth a canker, but by the sacraments of the gospel flowing from a heavenly source. But if the recipient himself be misguided, on the one hand, what is given is of no avail for the salvation of the misguided man; and yet, on the other hand, that which is received remains holy in the recipient, and is not renewed to him if he be brought to the right way.

Source: *"In Which He Treats of What Follows in the Same Epistle of Cyprian to Jubaianus," Chapter 12, Book IV, in The Seven Books of Augustine, Bishop of Hippo, On Baptism, Against the Donatists <http://www.newadvent.org/fathers/14084.htm>.*

the pure; they were the righteous. The Catholics were not particularly eager to address the question of plaintiff, but they used its introduction to their advantage. The Donatists were preoccupied with who convened the 411 meeting, but all the Catholics had to do was remind the opposing party that they were the ones who petitioned the emperor Constantine in the early 300s. The Donatists had also requested, in 406, that the emperor call a meeting like the one being held. The Donatists were the party who first took the dispute to a secular forum; they were the first to break rank with fellow Christians. In sum, there was no moral issue at stake here. Clearly, the Donatists welcomed meetings and imperial interference if they were of profit. The argument about identifying the plaintiff was nothing more than special pleading.

Despite attempts to derail the proceedings, the Donatists were not successful in winning the sympathy, or the vote, of Marcellinus. The evidence underscoring the inherent failings—theological and institutional—of Donatism was ample. The Catholics may have been prevented from arguing their points according to plan, but in the end all they had to do was watch the Donatists bury themselves in their hopelessly tangled and circular rhetoric.

—ERIKA T. HERMANOWICZ,
UNIVERSITY OF GEORGIA

Viewpoint: No. The Donatists, who were faced with a hostile imperial court and bureaucratic overseers whose mission was to ensure their defeat, employed various strategies in order to fashion a transcript of the meeting that could be used to their benefit in subsequent legal appeals.

Roman North Africa (comprising present-day Morocco, Algeria, Tunisia, and Libya) was fertile and prosperous territory. Aristocrats tended olive groves on their massive estates and sold the lucrative crop's oil throughout the Mediterranean. African farms exported to Rome enough grain to feed that city's urban poor for more than half of every year. You still find African red slipware, the popular ceramic Romans used for their dishes, in farmers' fields and archaeological sites as far away as central Turkey. North Africa was full of beautiful cities adorned with all the amenities of cultured life: baths, amphitheaters, temples, and theaters. In the *fora,* or central squares, where law cases were heard and teachers instructed their pupils, the magnificent public buildings were decorated with paintings and Latin inscriptions. Famous writers and intellects, like the biographer Suetonius, the novelist Apuleius, and the theologian St. Augustine, went to school in Africa's cities, places like Carthage, which was a huge sprawling city, one of the four largest in the empire, bested in size and population only by Rome herself. North Africa was a strenuously intellectual land, sophisticated and serious; its residents had earned early on a reputation for religious devotion well before people began hearing about Christianity.

This preface provides some necessary background frequently overlooked by modern scholars who find it difficult to approach the conflict between the Donatists and Catholics with any kind of historical objectivity. The vast majority of evidence that we have about the Donatists was generated and preserved by the Catholics, who eventually solicited decrees from the emperor outlawing Donatism. The exception to this, of course, is the transcript of the 411 Conference, where we hear Donatist bishops speaking on their own behalf. Catholic manipulation and control of the evidence results in a skewed historical picture that belies what we know of life in Roman North Africa. For example, Donatists have the reputation of being a bunch of rustics, stupid and backward. Contrary to Catholic propaganda, however, Donatist bishops living in towns and cities were accomplished professionals: writers, lawyers, and rhetoricians. St. Augustine, Catholicism's strongest opponent of Donatism, borrowed many of the ideas found in his *City of God* from Donatist intellectuals. The Donatist bishops who presented their case at the 411 Conference were highly accomplished lawyers and orators who had just a few years earlier conversed with the Roman emperor himself.

Another reason why historians approach this era of Roman history with predetermined and inevitable bias is found in the name *Donatist.* It is a misnomer. The Donatists squarely rejected this appellation given to them by the Catholics because it implied that they had "broken off" from the universal Catholic Church and had formed their own idiosyncratic sect. "Donatist" comes from the name Donatus, a member of the clergy who in the early 300s C.E. was elected bishop of Carthage by protest vote against the man who already held that office, Caecilian. Caecilian was the bishop of Carthage, but as he had been ordained by a *traditor*—at least that is what the Donatists claimed—he was considered by many to be spiritually and sacramentally ineffective. The Donatists protested the election of Caecilian to the emperor Constantine the Great, but after some debate and hesitation, Constantine decided that it was counterproductive to penalize clergy who had cooperated with imperial authorities during Diocletian's persecution. Caecilian maintained his office. The point is that the Donatists continued to be called Donatists, but the supporters of Caecilian, who, according to the Donatists, should have been called the "Caecilianists," maintained the name *Catholic*. "Catholic" means universal or liberally encompassing, and indicates not only that the Catholics constituted the majority of Christians, but also that they were the true representatives of the world Church. It is salutary to remember, however, that the Donatists constituted the majority Christian group in North Africa. They too believed that they were the true and universal church; it was the Catholics (or Caecilianists) who had broken away.

Keeping these points in mind, we turn to the Conference of 411. Catholic and Donatist bishops, close to 600 in number, gathered at Carthage in late May. At odds and at close quarters for a century–most of the larger African towns had both Donatist and Catholic bishops–the sides had traded accusations, threats, blows, and kidnappings for generations. These people did not like each other, and the transcript of the 411 Conference reveals a lifetime of frustration and impatience. The debaters shouted, interrupted, accused, and insulted. Both sides were excited and on edge, that is clear, but many modern historians believe that the Donatists engaged in bizarre tactics in a misdirected effort to harass, if not defeat, their opponents. Historians assert that the Donatists were not intelligent or savvy enough to argue effectively in court: they talked too much, they spoke off the point, they switched lines of argumentation in mid speech and spent the first two days of the three-day debate trying to derail discussion. They refused to address substantive theological issues with the Catholics and resorted instead to useless nitpicking. Whenever St. Augustine later wrote about this conference, he remarked that the Donatists deliberately eluded direct confrontation in order to irritate their opponents. They had no solid, legitimate means to defend their position. They were wrong, they knew it, and they were hoping to collapse the Conference in a heap of cross-purposed rhetoric. Historians overall have been sympathetic to Augustine's view.

If we attune ourselves to the legal and forensic strategies employed by learned men in the Roman Empire, however, we can see that there was a logical method behind Donatist actions. We turn to specific events of the three-day conference. Initially, Donatist actions may appear strange, but we will see that they were done with purpose. For example, on the first day (1 June 411), the Donatists insisted that all signatures of attending Catholic bishops (all 286 of them) be verified in person to prevent fraud on the Catholic side. When all had been counted, the day was long over and the proceedings suspended until 3 June.

On the morning of the 3 June, the Donatists informed Marcellinus, the imperial agent in charge of the proceedings, that they refused to continue until they had in hand a complete and verified transcript of the previous day's meeting. They wanted to be sure that the minutes had not been altered by Catholic or imperial personnel. The request was met with strenuous resistance, but when the Catholics saw that the Donatists were going to press this point until this day too was over, they capitulated, exasperated that the Donatists had managed, again, to waste time. The meeting was suspended from 3 June until 8 June, when a full transcript could be rendered, submitted to both parties for approval, and then distributed to the public.

When the two parties finally met for the third time, the Donatists were ready to speak. They did so at length, and their expansiveness was sharply criticized. We read the reactions of the Catholic bishops: *"In multiloquio numquam fuit sapientia"* (There has never been wisdom in speaking too much! [*Gesta* II.31]) and *"O breve responsum! Quam multum dicitur, ubi inveniri non potest quid dicatur"* (What a succinct answer! You've talked so much I don't know what it is you've said [*Gesta* III. 201]). The Donatists loquaciously insisted that certain proclamations and mandates previously issued by the emperor Honorius as well as by the supervising agent Marcellinus and the Catholics be read and reread; they were again accused of wasting time.

Another tactic the Donatists employed: they repeatedly asked St. Augustine, who was one of the seven designated orators on the Catholic side, to tell the assembled bishops who had ordained him. The Catholic representatives violently protested the validity and appropriateness of such a question. What was the point? What did this have to do with anything? But the Donatists kept repeating: *"Unde coepisti? Quem habes patrem?"* (Who ordained you? Who is your father? [*Gesta* III.299 ff.]).

Finally, the Catholics grew impatient with the Donatists' method of arguing points. The parties had tentatively negotiated an agreement previous to the meeting that stipulated the debate would either be grounded exclusively in Scripture–that is, bishops would make, defend, and refute points using only biblical citation–or they would argue adhering strictly to historical documentation. Argument from history, which would include the evidence from judicial cases, proconsular and imperial letters, and the contents of church archives, was designed to prove

Bust of the emperor Diocletian, who persecuted Christians in the early fourth century C.E.

(© Bettmann/CORBIS)

which of the parties–Catholic or Donatist–was responsible for the rift between African Christians. The agreement immediately collapsed, in part because of Donatist determination to have it both ways, that is, to argue from history when it seemed advantageous and from Scripture when the opportunity presented itself. Marcellinus, the agent in charge, felt obligated to halt the proceedings to reorient discussion.

The Donatist bishops did not act from naiveté, cowardice, or belligerence. Nor were they wasting time. Justifiable suspicions of this conference determined Donatist behavior. From the beginning, the meeting of 411 was designed to give the Catholics the clear advantage. The Roman emperor in the West, Honorius, was a Catholic and thus inclined to sympathize with his coreligionists. Imperial prejudice against the Donatists had been mounting since the early 400s when several Catholic delegations traveled to court to speak with the emperor Honorius. The Catholics pressed their case using two successful strategies: first, they claimed that Donatists continually committed acts of violence against them. Donatist bands did occasionally attack Catholics, but what the Catholics did not say about themselves is that they aggressively entered Donatist territory on preaching missions, kidnapped Donatists, and held them until they agreed to convert. Second, the Catholics manipulated imperial directives that legislated against heretics and criminals by attempting to stretch existing laws to include Donatists within the definition of heretics. They began pursuing test cases in the 390s and continued to press, unsuccessfully, until they finally won on a local appeal in 404.

The Donatists had visited the emperor as well, but they were not inclined toward the same intense level of legal and political lobbying pursued by the Catholics. Resorting to external mediation and courting imperial power was not as imperative for the Donatists because they constituted the majority of Christians in North Africa and did not need the help. They were, however, highly disturbed at what the Catholics were doing. Catholic actions, in Donatist minds, constituted nothing less than unholy persecution. Catholic attacks against the Donatists were akin to pagan persecution of Christians in the days of Diocletian. That sentiment must not be underestimated.

Donatist belief regarding persecution at the hands of Catholics seemed vindicated when they received news that a secret delegation of Catholic bishops had approached the Roman emperor Honorius to ask him to force the Donatists to meet with the Catholics in a conference. The emperor issued a brutal letter in October 410 stating that the heresy of Donatism was to be thoroughly refuted. The Donatists recognized from this letter that this was not going to be a conference where opponents argued and debated on equal footing, but a predetermined show trial that would only embarrass and humiliate the Donatist side. Their options were limited. They could not ignore the summons, for the emperor also decreed that if the Donatists did not accept the invitation, they would automatically be declared the losers: all their churches and property would cede to Catholic ownership and the Donatist bishops would be declared heretics. Faced with this impossible alternative, the Donatists decided to appear at the trial in full force.

They arrived in town quite aware that they were probably going to lose; the emperor emphatically favored their capitulation. The Donatists thus adopted a multifaceted strategy that was designed to facilitate the use of transcripts of the Conference for later appeals. The Donatists knew they were facing impending defeat, so they pitched their presentation toward a postconference reevaluation and retrial. The emperor had vacillated on this issue previously and had once even repealed his own antiheresy legislation; perhaps he would do so again. If not, an emperor only lives so long; his successor might be more sympathetic.

Let us return to the Conference and take another look at what really informed Donatist actions. Almost six hundred Donatist and Catholic bishops arrived in Carthage. It had been previously negotiated that in order to facilitate orderly and substantive debate, only thirty-six clerics were to participate in the proceedings (for each side: seven speakers, seven legal advisers, and four stenographers responsible for recording and proofing the transcripts). On the first morning, eighteen Catholics in attendance of Marcellinus were much surprised to see *all* the Donatist bishops enter the hall. This constituted a breach in conference protocol, but the Donatists gained their point and forced the Catholics to recall their bishops for an official head count. By the tabulation, everyone–the public at large, Marcellinus, the Catholics, and the emperor–would know that the Donatists were not a renegade group of isolated radicals, but the majority Church in Africa.

As to the second day when the Donatists refused to begin until they had read a copy of the transcribed minutes from the previous session, delay tactics may indeed have been at work: they needed more time to coordinate their responses. Yet, it is also true that the Donatists were legitimately concerned about collusion between their opponents and Marcellinus. After all, the Catholics had elicited support from the emperor to call this conference by means of an official letter that the Donatists were forbidden to read. In other words, the Catholics had made accusations that may have been total fabrications. The Donatists knew their accusers, but they were not exactly sure of what they were being accused. Hence, the suspicion. That secret letter is also probably why they forced the court stenographers to read and reread public letters relating to the Conference. If they gained access to this secret correspondence with the emperor at a later date and found that it contradicted the letters publicly circulated, the Donatists could charge that they had been brought to Carthage on false pretenses.

The questions posed of Augustine: "Who is your father? Who ordained you?" may not have garnered the Donatists any immediate theological triumphs, but they were also playing the character issue. The public would read these transcripts; if the Donatists could color Augustine's reputation with allegations of episcopal illegitimacy and ties to *traditores,* it might deflate Catholic respectability.

Finally, it was important to the Donatists that they appear to be the persecuted party. Christian martyrs thrown to the wild beasts in past imperial persecutions were considered the true heroes of the Church. The Donatists strove to associate themselves with this model: the persecuted were the righteous. As such, they wanted to emphasize the fact they had been forced to attend this meeting. The previous appeal by the Catholics to Honorius offered proof positive that the Donatists were the defendants, not the accusers; however, when the Catholics began to refer to old documents from the time of Constantine wherein the Donatists protested the election of Caecilian, the Donatists found themselves being called the instigators or plaintiffs regarding the split in the Church itself. They, not the Catholics, had been the first to seek external support from secular power. When the Donatists realized that they could not focus attention on the subpoena of 410 but had to answer for every contact they had enjoyed with the court, they did what any good legal team would do: switch tactics. They abandoned their historical approach and proceeded to argue from Scripture. After they gained ground, they reverted to historical documentation and the issue of persecution. They were poking and prodding the legal case constructed by the Catholics. If Marcellinus had accepted just one objection, if he had agreed, even to a limited extent, that the Catholics were indeed the plaintiffs, the Donatists just might have been able to exploit the weakness to bring down the entire Catholic edifice. If not, they would use the transcript to fight another day.

–ERIKA T. HERMANOWICZ,
UNIVERSITY OF GEORGIA

References

Actes de la Conférence de Carthage en 411, edited and translated by Serge Lancel (Paris: Les Editions du Cerf, 1972–1991).

St. Augustine, *Letters,* translated by Sister Wilfrid Parsons, S.N.D. (New York: Fathers of the Church, 1951–1956).

St. Augustine, *Writings Against the Manichaeans and the Donatists,* in *The Nicene and Post-Nicene Fathers of the Christian Church,* First Series, volume 4 (Grand Rapids, Mich.: Eerdmans, 1989).

Peter Brown, *Augustine of Hippo* (Berkeley: University of California Press, 1967).

Robert B. Eno, "Some Nuances in the Ecclesiology of the Donatists," *Revue des Etudes Augustiniennes,* 18 (1972): 46–50.

William Frend, *The Donatist Church: A Movement of Protest in Roman North Africa* (Oxford: Clarendon Press, 1952).

Emilien Lamirande, "Augustine and the Discussion of Sinners in the Church at the Conference of Carthage (411)," *Augustinian Studies,* 3 (1972): 97–112.

Serge Lancel, *Saint Augustine,* translated by Antonia Nevill (London: SCM Press, 2002).

Claude Lepelley, "The Survival and Fall of the Classical City in Late Roman Africa," in *The City in Late Antiquity,* edited by J. Rich (London: Routledge, 1992), pp. 50–76.

Optatus of Milevis, *Against the Donatists,* translated by Mark Edwards (Liverpool: Liverpool University Press, 1997).

The Theodosian Code and Novels and the Sirmondian Constitutions, edited and translated by Clyde Pharr (Princeton: Princeton University Press, 1952).

Maureen A. Tilley, "Dilatory Donatists or Procrastinating Catholics: The Trial at the Conference of Carthage," *Church History,* 60 (1991): 7–19.

ROMAN PERIOD: ELEGISTS

Were the Roman elegists protofeminists?

Viewpoint: Yes. The Roman elegists presented their *puellae* (beloveds) as powerful, autonomous women who refused to assume accepted roles of submission to men.

Viewpoint: No. The Roman elegists may have bent conventional male gender roles, but they did not offer women equality nor did their poetry seek to change the place of women in Roman society.

In 1973 the scholar Judith Hallett started a debate that continues to this day: were the Roman elegists protofeminists? Before her article, "The Role of Women in Roman Elegy: Counter-Cultural Feminism" (1973), the study of Latin erotic elegy was a relatively staid and decorous affair. Certainly, it had long since been conceded that in the poetry of Catullus, Gallus, Tibullus, Propertius, and Ovid (all active in the first century B.C.E.), there was plenty of sex—or at least plenty of talk about sex. Erotic elegy is defined by the poet's devotion to his beloved *(puella)*. Certainly, it was also clear that politics played an important role in these same poets' poetry. Augustan policies were praised and blamed (sometimes simultaneously), campaigns against the Parthians were anticipated, and imperial building projects were celebrated and ridiculed. Nonetheless, before Hallett's incendiary piece, few suspected the presence of a properly sexual politics in these poems. The gender roles of the poets and their *puellae* were largely taken for granted.

In many ways, the rhetoric of Hallett's article is now quite dated. Thirty years later, terms such as *counter-culture* are much more suspect than they were in the heady days of the early 1970s. By the same token, feminism itself has become a much more complicated affair. Who is a feminist and what is feminism are topics of hot debate in many circles. Nonetheless, what every serious scholar of Latin elegy would concede today is that sexual politics forms one of the central topics of these complex and multifaceted poems, and this concession was not widely made before Hallett's article. The elegists are in fact obsessed with power relations between the sexes and the ways in which those power relations intersect with, influence, and are influenced by the larger political structures of Roman society at this time.

The fact that those larger political structures were in a state of flux during this period is surely not incidental to the elegists' concern with sexual politics. The period between Catullus's death (circa 54 B.C.E.) and the end of Ovid's erotic elegiac production (circa 1 C.E.) witnesses the rise of Julius Caesar as dictator (48 B.C.E.), his assassination (44 B.C.E.), the ensuing civil wars, and the inauguration of the Augustan principate, as well as its successor, the empire (29 B.C.E.). This was a time in which many of the basic verities of Roman political and personal ideology were being renegotiated. It would be shocking if sexual relations were not an integral part of that matrix. The following essays present two different views of elegy's role in that fundamental renegotiation.

—*Paul Allen Miller*

Viewpoint:
Yes. The Roman elegists presented their *puellae* (beloveds) as powerful, autonomous women who refused to assume accepted roles of submission to men.

The Roman elegists composed and published poetry for approximately fifty years. In his book *The Latin Love Elegy* (1969) Georg Luck notes that the Roman elegiac tradition was born of Greek elegy whose themes included "war, politics, the pleasures and pains of life in general, love, friendship, [and] death." Unlike their Greek predecessors, the Roman elegists developed these same themes into verse that reads as if it is born of personal experience. Gallus, Catullus, Tibullus, Propertius, and Ovid wrote collections of poetry that dealt with their relationships with lovers who were most often of the opposite sex.

The Roman erotic elegists wrote collections of poetry that may be considered radical. Their works contain characters that do not fit within the normal gender roles of typical Roman men and women. Each poet presents a narrator who is in love with an unyielding mistress, a *domina*. This woman is tough and seemingly unattainable; she demands total devotion from the poet. Rather than behave as a traditional woman, she independently rules her life. The *domina* is an unmovable, harsh woman beneath whom the poet assumes the role of *servus amoris* (the slave of love); this relationship represents a possible departure from the behavior expected of a Roman woman. She is portrayed as a strong, independent person who decides her own fate and demands unwavering dedication from her lover, the poet. Throughout the entire first book of Propertius's poetry, Cynthia is portrayed as the dominant figure who is free to commit infidelities while the poet is expected to remain faithful. According to tradition, Roman women were expected to maintain constant devotion to their husbands, who were free to enjoy other women.

Even though the Roman woman enjoyed more freedoms than most women of ancient cultures, her livelihood and status were still determined by the dominant male figure in her life. The Roman woman was free only so far as the man in her life would allow. Therefore, the introduction of women who refused traditional female roles of subordination to men demonstrates the tendency of Roman elegy to unsettle the expected relationships between man and woman. The *domina* is a single woman living on her own who resists submission to men. Because these writers dared to present women who behaved differently than expected, the Roman erotic elegists have been thought of as early feminists. One of Tibullus's lovers, Nemesis, behaves as if she is a *meretrix* (Greek courtesan) who is only concerned with money. She is free to dump Tibullus in exchange for someone wealthy enough to provide her with luxuries; Tibullus, however, remains faithful to his love and is even willing to become a field slave in order to be with her.

The image of a powerful *domina* extends beyond the love affair. By writing about women who were independent, the elegists offered society a written text that could serve as an inspiration to actual Roman women. It is difficult to establish the precise identity or to label the type of women the elegists were writing about. Scholars have attempted to identify the real women and men behind the works of the Roman elegists. It has been proposed that Catullus's "Lesbia" was Clodia Metelli, a woman from a prominent Roman family, and that Gallus's "Lycoris" was the actress Cytheris. Some believe these women were based solely upon Greek courtesans who immigrated to Rome. Others argue that they are Roman *matronae* (matrons) who, having grown weary of being submissive to men, took up the lifestyle of a *meretrix*. No matter the inspiration, the *dominae* of Roman erotic elegy had the potential to encourage a more liberal attitude toward the freedoms extended to women. The actual identities of these poets' lovers, while interesting, are not pivotal to a discussion of the manner in which the texts inspired by these women both reflected and possibly initiated changes in gender roles within the Roman empire.

Although these characters may not have been crafted to resemble any single woman, the elegists made them seem real by writing about them in such a way as to conjure the image of an actual love affair. Terminology appropriated from marriage and business agreements was often incorporated into the vocabulary the elegists used to describe their engagements with the *domina*. Therefore, by first introducing women who were not submissive and then discussing them with the same language used to engage wives and business partners, the elegists, in a feminist manner, extended a particular type of equality to their mistresses. Catullus tells Lesbia in poem 72.3–4 that he loves her as a father loves his sons and sons-in-law—not in the manner that most men love their girlfriends. Paul Allen Miller notes in the introduction of *Latin Erotic Elegy: An Anthology and Critical Reader* (2002) that this sort of "relation of mutual respect and affection between a man and a woman" was not usual in the ancient world. In fact, Augustus was so concerned with the movement away from traditional customs of courtship and marriage within the upper class that he enacted laws against adultery and attempted to force young bachelors to marry. In poem 2.7, a poem concerning the repeal of one such law, Propertius is pleased because he will not have to marry a traditional Roman woman and may continue his affair with Cynthia. He calls her both mistress and wife (2.6), proclaiming that not even Jove can part lovers and that Caesar, though skilled in battle, cannot dissolve their love with laws (2.7). This ideology is common among the elegists. They are more inclined to serve their *dominae* than to serve the state.

The adjective *mollis* (soft) is frequently used to describe the elegists. In-depth analysis of this adjective is not necessary in order to realize the sexual implications of this term. The adjective *durus* (hard) is a regular characteristic of the *domina.* The language of the elegists positions the women as more masculine than men. These sorts of literary tools enabled women to be placed, if only in the literature, in a position of equality or superiority to their male counterparts.

By taking a traditionally feminine position, the elegists functioned as sexual agitators. Judith Hallett, a feminist classical scholar, notes in her essay, "The Role of Women in Roman Elegy: Counter-Cultural Feminism" (1973), that elegists, "like other counter-culturists of today, tried to forge a new, more meaningful set of values, embody them in actions which substituted for conventional social practices, and glorify them through art, the most exalted and effective means of human communication." One measure of the elegists' potential threat to traditional Roman values is Ovid's exile to the Black Sea. Ovid called himself the *praeceptor amoris* (teacher of love). The forum for his teaching was erotic elegy. He says in *Tristia* 2.207 that the cause of his exile was "carmen et error" (poetry and mistake). Following the tradition of his predecessors, Ovid was attempting the "conversion of others to their beliefs and behavior" (Hallett 1973, 115), and he paid for it dearly.

Ovid's work, in the eyes of Augustus, was threatening enough to warrant stern action. The *Amores, Ars Amatoria,* and the *Heroides* all represent a conscious continuation of the former elegists' themes. In the *Amores,* Ovid begins by pointing out that being an elegist requires the poet to shun traditional obligations. He tells his girlfriend, Corinna, how to keep her husband from finding out about them so they can have sex. The image of poet as the *praeceptor amoris* blossoms in the *Ars,* where Ovid's poetry teaches young men how to pick up women. The *Heroides* are letters written in first person that give voice to women of classical myth. Here, Ovid attempts to present the often neglected feminine side of myths traditionally dominated by the masculine point of view. The letter, for example, of Dido to Aeneas presents the legendary founder of Rome as her lover; Dido sees him not as Virgil's hero but as an unfaithful cad. The *Heroides* gives voice to characters who were often marginalized. By presenting alternate versions of mythical situations filtered through fresh, female voices, he drives home his desire to stand outside the accepted norms of political and literary circles in Rome.

LESBIA

Once you used to say you knew only Catullus, Lesbia, that you would not hold Jove before me. I loved you then, not only as a fellow his mistress, but as a father loves his own sons and sons-in-law. Now I do know you: so if I burn at greater cost, you are nevertheless to me far viler and of lighter thought. How can this be? you ask. Because such wrongs drive a lover to love the more, but less to respect.

Source: *Catullus,* The Carmina of Gaius Valerius Catullus, *Poem 72, edited and translated by Leonard C. Smithers (London: Smithers, 1894).*

The work of one female Roman elegist, Sulpicia, remains. The niece of an influential patron of the arts, Messalla, Sulpicia must have received a complete and progressive education. Her work survives within a collection of the works of Tibullus. Thus, we can infer that her contemporaries knew both Sulpicia and her work. Her poetry discusses her own love affair with Cerinthus. Although her poems are emotionally charged and offer insight into her amorous affair, Sulpicia's narrator is not a *domina.* She is an unmarried woman of the nobility who is involved in an affair and who expects the same steadfast dedication from her lover as do the *dominae* of her contemporaries' poetry. She does, however, point out that her social status warrants the respect of her lover, so despite their gender differences, it is he, not she, who owes submission in the game of love.

The works of the Roman erotic elegists are varied, but their desire to exact and demonstrate changes in trends relative to masculine and feminine relationships is constant through all their texts. Roman erotic elegy was at times blatantly opposed to traditional Roman subjection of women to men while at other times subversively opposed. Although their innovation with the genre ended with the exile and death of Ovid, the texts have been preserved and continue to influence literature and art.

–CHRISTEL JOHNSON,
FRIENDS SEMINARY, NEW YORK

Viewpoint: No. The Roman elegists may have bent conventional male gender roles, but they did not offer women equality nor did their poetry seek to change the place of women in Roman society.

During the last two centuries B.C.E., the legal and social regulations placed on women in Roman society became less restrictive, especially compared with ancient Greek women who were largely confined to the private spaces of their homes. Nonetheless, there is substantial evidence within the surviving texts of Roman literature that women continued to be regarded as inferior to men, as ungovernable creatures whose inherent irrationality and dangerous sexuality required them to be under the constant guardianship of males. The Roman elegists, however, appear to elevate women to a singularly exalted stature—a stature women did not enjoy in real life.

Roman elegy is predicated on clearly defined roles for the elegist and his female mistress. The elegist, typically, portrays the male in the traditionally subservient role of the female and, at the same time, depicts the female beloved as masterful, active, and dominant. The elegists often refer to their mistresses as *dominae* (female rulers) who subject their lovers to the torments of abandonment and betrayal. The elegist's apparent servitude to his mistress, at least nominally, accords his mistress complete domination and control over him. Several scholars, including some noted feminists, have thus taken the position that the women featured in elegy are appreciated as people in their own right and that the Roman elegists indicated their noncompliance with traditional gender norms by deliberately inverting sex roles in their poetry—depicting women as dominant and men as subservient.

However, a close examination of how the elegists portray women and amatory relations in general clearly shows that the elegists' portrayal of their mistresses as dominant allows them to reinforce stereotypical views of women as sexually and morally wanton, as figures who ultimately need men to keep their unbounded sexual impulses in check. Despite the gender inversion portrayed in Roman elegy, the elegists do not elaborate a role for the female mistress that grants her an elevated social status. Rather, the nontraditional role of the male narrator in elegy serves to emphasize the elegist's alienation from traditional male pursuits, such as law, politics, and the military. In fact, the passive position of the elegiac lover and the representation of his mistress as correspondingly active affords elegists the opportunity to explore alternative models of male sexuality while at the same time elaborating ingenious ways to relegate women to subordinate roles.

Most obviously, elegists often associate the elegiac mistress with nature, with the "uncivilized" urges and passions regarded as disruptive of the social and political order. In addition, throughout elegy we see the male narrator identify his mistress as matter for poetic composition. Propertius, for example, portrays his beloved Cynthia as a pictorial object that both arouses his erotic fantasies and serves as a vehicle for his artistic fame. By identifying the elegiac mistress with matter, with nonrational nature, the elegist emphasizes women's object status and thus structures ideal amatory relations from a traditionally masculine perspective, that is, a perspective based on male fantasies of control over women's sexuality and autonomy. The Roman elegists are thus by no means feminists. While they certainly explore in various ways unconventional forms of masculinity, their portrayals of women, for the most part, reinforce traditional notions of them as mere objects of male desire.

A prime example of this can be seen in Propertius's elegies. In poem 3 of book 1, Propertius compares his sleeping mistress to famed mythological heroines, while implicitly comparing himself to the corresponding male heroes. In all three of the poet's mythological representations of his mistress, he links her position of helplessness with his own heightened sexual arousal. The elegist makes it clear that Cynthia is most desirable to him as long as she remains a fantasy—a static projection of his own desires. Moreover, he describes himself arranging garlands on her head, rearranging her hair, and trying to place apples in her lap. This serves to create an image of Cynthia as a statue-like figure, a mannequin the poet may arrange to serve his own fantasies and desires. The poem emphasizes how the elegist's sexual arousal depends on turning his mistress into a static, pictorial object he can gaze at without any interference from a real-life mistress. The comparisons in the poem between Propertius's mistress and mythological heroines envision the female beloved as defenseless, lacking in agency of her own, and most attractive to the poet when he can completely control her sexuality and autonomy. Similarly, in poem 1 of Propertius's second book, he describes himself as most inspired to write poetry when his mistress is either asleep or naked. Not only is the female mistress most desirable to the elegist when she is in a position of helplessness and vulnerability but he also explicitly links his poetic creativity to a position of dominance over his beloved. He claims that it is his mistress who inspires his verse, yet avows

Undated painting inspired by Catullus's poem *The Desertion of Ariadne;* the maiden watches as her faithless lover abandons her on the island of Dia

(British Museum)

that "a great story is born out of nothing" (Elegy 2.1). The logic of the poet's argument leads us to infer that the "nothing" that generates elegy is the mistress herself.

Throughout his collection of elegies, Propertius emphasizes the moral degeneracy of his mistress and of women in general. Not only does he often describe his mistress as faithless and sexually unrestrained but he also vilifies women in general for lapsing into depravity if they are not under the control and watchful eye of a man. In Elegy 1.11, Propertius claims, "As is the rule: once the guardian is removed, the girl lapses, and faithlessly, no longer remembers mutual gods" (lines 15–16). Likewise, Tibullus often casts his mistress Delia, and women in general, in the stereotypical role of the sexually unrestrained female who needs to be monitored and controlled. In his Elegy 1.6, Tibullus expresses the wish that Delia be trusted to *his* keeping, as the only remedy for her wantonness.

One of the chief ways the elegist objectifies his mistress is by linking her with poetic production, characterizing her, implicitly or explicitly, as fertile material for his verse. In Propertius 1.11, for example, the poet makes clear to Cynthia that her fame depends on the continuation of her position as his mistress. In other words, the poet suggests that Cynthia offer herself to him as material for his poetic practice. Only if Cynthia remains the subject of his poems, the poet argues, will her name be remembered for eternity. Propertius encloses Cynthia's name within a reference to his own poems, implying that the figure of the elegiac mistress is less a woman he is wooing than a subject for his writing. Even more explicitly, in his collection of elegiac poems, the *Amores,* Ovid blatantly dehumanizes his mistress by openly asking her to offer herself to him as fertile material for his elegies. Like Propertius, Ovid's paradigm of amatory relations is often predicated on an image of the woman as a defenseless captive deprived of humanity and autonomy. In his *Amores* 1.3, Ovid tries to seduce his recalcitrant mistress by promising that he will bring her the same immortality accorded to mythological heroines. Yet, the heroines Ovid chooses as examples (Io, Leda, and Europa) are mythological figures who, in various ways, have all been victims of male deceit and aggression. Moreover, the fame these heroines received came about as a result of their status as sexualized objects, as captives whose immortality arose at the cost of their autonomy and humanity. Ovid claims that his mistress will also be immortalized if only she agrees to a similar kind of captivity. By demanding that the mistress offer herself to him as "fertile material" for his poems, Ovid equates the woman's identity with materiality and thus implicitly turns her into a dehumanized commodity he may use in service to his own poetic accomplishments.

Moreover, like Propertius, Ovid also depicts his female beloved more as an art object than as a living mistress. In *Amores* 1.7, Ovid compares his mistress to blocks of white marble, thus explicitly emphasizing that his "ideal" woman is an inanimate, voiceless object he may "mold" in accordance with his own literary and erotic aims. In the same poem, Ovid goes on to compare his mistress to objects in nature that are all subject to forces that control their movement: poplar leaves, a slender reed, the surface of a wave, and water distilled from snow. These images all underscore Ovid's portrayal of his mistress as lacking in agency, as the passive recipient of the poet's erotic and literary manipulations. Ovid's dehumanization of the elegiac mistress also takes the form of justifying acts of violence against her and emphasizing that he derives erotic pleasure from controlling his mistress through aggression. In *Amores* 1.7, after describing a physical assault on his mistress, Ovid admits that she looks more attractive to him: "Therefore, was I able to tear her arranged coiffure? Her hair in disarray looked beautiful." Further, in *Amores* 1.5, Ovid narrates an erotic encounter with his mistress, describing it in terms of his domination and conquest of her. Not only does he describe her as the loser in the battle of love but he also presumes that her efforts to "fight him off" are a charade used to arouse him even more. Further, Ovid describes his mistress's naked body as a series of dismembered images. He praises her shoulders, arms, flank, and thigh in a way that fetishizes her. He never mentions her head, face, or eyes–parts of the body most associated with a person's humanity. Ovid thus dehumanizes his mistress not only through his dismemberment of her but also through a kind of decapitation that renders her voiceless and deprived of individuality.

Another, perhaps more subtle, manner in which the elegists objectify and dehumanize their mistresses is by emphasizing how they serve as a vehicle of the elegists' own poetic fame. In Propertius's Elegy 2.8 he identifies himself with the hero Achilles and implicitly links his mistress with Achilles' captive Briseis. These mythological comparisons serve to accentuate the close association between the activation of male heroism and the mistress's subordinate position. In Elegy 2.1, Propertius makes it clear that the epic ideal of glory in death achieves greater renown for him than possessing the elegiac mistress. He asserts that for him "to die in love is glory." While Cynthia supposedly inspires him to write verse, he clearly identifies her with the story he will tell about their affair and thus links his posterity to the "great story" for which he will remembered.

In 2.8 Propertius envisions his faithless mistress as an enemy he must fight to the death; he characterizes her as *ferrea* (iron), an image that recalls the masculine world of weaponry and war. Setting his mistress up as his enemy in the war of love allows Propertius to imagine a glory for himself that arises out of the dishonorable death of the elegiac mistress; the moral degeneracy Propertius associates with Cynthia makes his imagined slaughter of her seem noble. Moreover, in elegy 2.9 Propertius again invokes the image of his perfidious mistress, comparing the faithless vows made by women to the trustworthy pledges among male friends. Although Propertius again identifies his mistress as his enemy, he characterizes himself as a warrior primarily in relation to his male rival. The elegiac mistress is thus configured as the medium of exchange between men, offering the possibility of heroic action for the male lovers competing for the woman's attentions. At the end of 2.9 Propertius imagines himself fighting his rival to the death. Again, Propertius compares himself to Achilles, this time, however, emphasizing how Achilles' ability to wreak vengeance on his rival wins him glory and demonstrates his superiority in the male arena. The woman merely facilitates reciprocity between male rivals; Propertius makes it quite clear that the amatory relationship is subordinated to the network of male social relations that constitutes the fabric of Roman society.

Ovid also emphasizes in his elegies the ways in which women are little more than commodities of exchange between men. In his collection of love poems, the *Amores,* Ovid attempts to make deals with the husband of his mistress so that she will become more desirable. In one poem (*Amores* 2.19) Ovid admonishes the husband for being too permissive with his wife, and in the other poem (*Amores* 3.4) Ovid encourages him to loosen his restrictions on her. While Ovid's positions toward his mistress in the two poems seem contradictory, they are alike in that they both presume the woman's lack of autonomy and control over her own sexuality. Ovid openly admits that whether the husband is permissive or vigilant with his wife, he is trying to manipulate the husband in order to make his own amatory pursuit more challenging and thus more exciting. Although Ovid appears to engage the husband of his mistress in order to have a relationship with her, the arguments Ovid uses to convince the husband emphasize how both men will ultimately benefit from controlling the woman's sexuality. In *Amores* 3.4, Ovid compares his mistress to a spirited horse that needs to be controlled whether through permissiveness or discipline. Ovid implies that in order for the husband and the lover to maintain their dominance over the woman, they must conspire to tame the female's inherently unruly nature.

Despite the elegists' depiction of themselves as subservient, their portrayal of their mistresses as objects of desire and exchange suggests that they cannot be considered "proto-feminists," if by "proto-feminists" we mean people who espouse and practice the treatment of women as autonomous beings. Both Propertius and Ovid often use well-known myths depicting female captivity and powerlessness to dramatize their ideal woman. This suggests a paradigm for love relations in which male dominance over women is inevitable. In *Amores* 2.19, for example, Ovid compares his ideal mistress to the mythical women Io and Danae, women whose abuse at the hands of their male lovers renders them as silent captives. We could trace many such examples in which the elegists use myth to characterize their mistresses as either helpless creatures in need of rescue or as sexually wanton witches requiring a master to tame them.

–ELLEN GREENE,
UNIVERSITY OF OKLAHOMA

References

Leslie Cahoon, "The Bed as Battlefield: Erotic Conquest and Military Metaphor in Ovid's *Amores*," *Transactions of the American Philological Association,* 118 (1988): 293–307.

Cahoon, "Let the Muse Sing On: Poetry, Criticism, Feminism, and the Case of Ovid," *Helios,* 17 (1990): 197–211.

Frank Copley, "*Servitium Amoris* in the Roman Elegists," *Transactions of the American Philological Association,* 78 (1947): 285–300.

A. A. Day, *The Origins of Latin Love Elegy* (Oxford: Oxford University Press, 1938).

Mary-Kay Gamel, "*Non Sine Caede:* Abortion Politics and Poetics in Ovid's *Amores,*" *Helios,* 16 (1989): 183–206.

Barbara Gold, "'But Ariadne Was Never There in the First Place': Finding the Female in Roman Poetry," in *Feminist Theory and the Classics,* edited by N. S. Rabinowitz and A. Richlin (New York: Routledge, 1993), pp. 75–101.

Ellen Greene, "Elegiac Woman: Fantasy, *Materia,* and Male Desire in Propertius 1.3 and 1.11," *American Journal of Philology,* 116 (1995): 303–318.

Greene, "Sexual Politics in Ovid's *Amores:* 3.4, 3.8, and 3.12," *Classical Philology,* 89 (1994): 344–351.

Judith Hallett, "The Role of Women in Roman Elegy: Counter-Cultural Feminism," *Arethusa,* 6 (Spring 1973): 103–124.

Alison Keith, "*Corpus Eroticum:* Elegiac Poetics and Elegiac *Puellae* in Ovid's *Amores,*" *Classical World,* 88 (1994): 27–40.

Duncan F. Kennedy, *The Arts of Love: Five Studies in the Discourse of Roman Love Elegy* (Cambridge: Cambridge University Press, 1993).

Georg Luck, *The Latin Love Elegy* (Edinburgh: R. & R. Clark, 1969).

R. O. A. M. Lyne, *The Latin Love Poets* (Oxford: Oxford University Press, 1980).

Lyne, "*Servitium Amoris,*" *Classical Quarterly,* 29 (1979): 117–130.

Paul Allen Miller, *Latin Erotic Elegy: An Anthology and Critical Reader* (New York: Routledge, 2002).

Miller, *Lyric Texts and Lyric Consciousness: The Birth of a Genre from Archaic Greece to Augustan Rome* (New York: Routledge, 1994).

Amy Richlin, "Reading Ovid's Rapes," in *Pornography and Representation in Greece and Rome,* edited by Richlin (Oxford: Oxford University Press, 1992), pp. 158–179.

A. R. Sharrock, "Womanufacture," *Journal of Roman Studies,* 81 (1991): 36–49.

Maria Wyke, "Mistress and Metaphor in Augustan Elegy," *Helios,* 16 (1989): 25–47.

Wyke, "Written Women: Propertius' *Scripta Puella,*" *Journal of Roman Studies* (1987): 47–61.

ROMAN PERIOD: FALL OF THE REPUBLIC

Was Roman decline inevitable with the fall of the republic?

Viewpoint: Yes. The republican constitution was what made Rome great; without that structure, decline was inevitable.

Viewpoint: No. The notion that the collapse of the republic led to the decline of Rome is a manifest ideological fiction that cannot withstand a rigorous examination in terms of chronology, the instability of the republic, the benefits of the imperial system, and the class biases of the ancient commentators.

The number of significant contributing causes to the civil wars and, consequently, to the collapse of the Roman Republic, presents a problem to the historian. Do we begin our story with the professionalization of the armies by Gaius Marius at the end of the second century B.C.E., which hastened the development of largely private armies, like those who followed Julius Caesar and his rivals? Or do we choose the dictatorship of Sulla in 81 B.C.E., which undermined the separation of functions in the Roman constitution so praised by Polybius? Or perhaps the start should be the creation in 59 B.C.E. of the First Triumvirate, the coalition between Caesar, Gaius Pompeius, and Marcus Licinius Crassus to work collectively for their common ends. It is even possible to begin as late as the fateful decision of Caesar to cross the Rubicon with his army in defiance of the Senate (49 B.C.E.), effectively invading Italy and forcing the state to respond in kind. At whatever point we choose to begin, however, we shall proceed to trace a story that absolutely transformed the Roman state, with important consequences for centuries to come.

But did these changes cause Rome to decline? Can we already see in the civil wars the origins of the "decline and fall" chronicled by Edward Gibbon? Or did the empire create its own possibilities for virtue, as Tacitus suggests in the biography of his father-in-law, Agricola? For Gaius Julius Caesar Octavianus, later known as the emperor Augustus, it is inappropriate to speak of either change or decline. He wanted to be remembered not for having created the Roman imperial state, but for having restored the republic after a generation of civil wars. In the record of accomplishments he composed later in his life, he claims to have transferred the republic "from my power to the authority of the senate and people of Rome" (*Res gestae* 34). From this statement it appears that Augustus was convinced about two things: 1) that the republic still existed and 2) that it was both possible and desirable to hand it back to the Senate and people of Rome in the same form. As will be seen in the essays that follow, much of our evaluation of the present viewpoint will be determined by the manner in which we understand the terms of the emperor's statement and how we evaluate it within the context of the turbulent first century. For Mark A. Beck the limitation of political freedom and the restrictions on aristocratic competition led to stagnation within the senatorial class and eventual decline, while Paul Allen Miller chooses to emphasize the relative ease with which the upper classes were able to accommodate themselves to the new regime.

—Charles Platter

Viewpoint: Yes. The republican constitution was what made Rome great; without that structure, decline was inevitable.

The earliest Greek historians, Herodotus and Thucydides, perceived that history is "dominated by the two antithetical desires for liberty and power" (Raaflaub 2002, p. 184). This maxim certainly finds exemplification in the history of the rise and fall of Rome. Many power struggles, both internal and external, resulted collectively in the gradual expansion of Roman hegemony to include much of Europe, the Near East, and North Africa. Rome's greatest era of expansion took place during the second phase of its historical development under the republic. Traditionally dated to 509 B.C.E., the Roman Republic supplanted the early monarchy, founded in 753 B.C.E., with an oligarchic (Syme) or democratic form of government, as more recent research has indicated (Brunt, Millar 1998, 2002). These circumstances, the rapidity and scope of Rome's expansion and impact of the change in her form of government, require explanation and are of crucial importance for understanding the consequences of the fall of the Roman Republic.

The precise reasons for the gradual decline of the Roman Empire, as I will argue, are localized in the transformation of Roman government from what we may term a democracy to a legitimized dictatorship. The Roman Republic breathed its last gasp when Octavian, the future emperor Augustus, seized sole control of the state after the Battle of Actium in 31 B.C.E. and succeeded in reestablishing an autocratic form of government. This transformation had such deleterious consequences on the political and ideological vigor of the Romans that subsequent decline was inevitable. I will briefly trace the factors involved in Rome's ascent to dominance in order to explain how, with the inception of the principate, the loss of the liberty that had been guaranteed by their democratic constitution could have such a long-term, adverse impact on Rome's fortunes.

This constitution, much admired and imitated from antiquity to modern times, was perhaps the single most impressive element of the Roman Republic serving to guarantee the health and stability of the state. The first historian to appreciate this fully was Polybius (circa 200–circa 118 B.C.E.), a Greek who was taken to Rome as a captive. Polybius marveled at Rome's sustained expansion and thought that an investigation of the reasons for its success would be a rewarding and instructive enterprise:

> There can surely be nobody so petty or apathetic in his outlook that he has no desire to discover by what means and under what system of government the Romans succeeded in less than fifty-three years [from 220–167 B.C.E.] in bringing under their rule almost the whole of the inhabited world, an achievement which is without parallel in human history. (Polybius, 1. 1. 5; this and all other translations of Polybius by Ian Scott-Kilvert.)

In the historian's opinion the true virtue of the Roman constitution and the factor responsible for its stability was its mixed nature. Beginning his analysis with Aristotle's three simple forms of government–kingship, aristocracy, democracy and their degenerate forms, monarchy (or tyranny), oligarchy, and mob-rule (or ochlocracy)–he then traces the cycle of corruption in which the three good forms are alternately followed by the three bad forms, with the natural progression being monarchy to kingship to tyranny to aristocracy to oligarchy to democracy to ochlocracy and finally monarchy again (6. 3. 8–5. 9, Walbank 1972). It was the Spartan lawgiver Lycurgus, Polybius says, who first recognized that "every type of constitution which is simple and founded on a single principle is unstable, because it quickly degenerates into that form of corruption which is peculiar to and inherent in it" (6. 10. 1–2). With the mixed constitution, the Romans were able to break out of this cycle since, as Lycurgus foresaw and the Romans discovered through experience, the powers of each element of the constitution are counterbalanced by the others, and this uniform reciprocity or counteraction results in a persistent state of equilibrium (6. 10. 6–14). Polybius thought that the Roman constitution had reached its most perfect state at the time of the Second Punic War (218–201 B.C.E.) when they fought against the forces under the command of the great Carthaginian general Hannibal (6. 11. 1). The elements of the Roman constitution, as Polybius notes, were three in number, with the monarchic element represented by the power of the consuls, the aristocratic element by the Senate, and the democratic element by the power of the people to elect officeholders and by their important role in the law courts as jurors (6. 11. 11–14. 12). He goes on to explain in detail how the system of checks and balances, as we would term it, was operative in the Roman state at that time, but we do not need to go into detail on this matter (6. 15. 1–17. 9; Lintott). It is sufficient for our purposes to note that, for Polybius, the true litmus test of the strength and vitality of a constitution is its ability to withstand emergencies, as when some grave external threat compels all three branches to work together in unison, thus allowing the state to achieve its intended goals in a timely and prompt way (6. 18. 1–8). Hannibal's invasion of Italy represented just such a test, which the Romans were able to negotiate with great success despite several critical setbacks. Machiavelli,

Statue of Octavian, who received the title *Augustus* (exalted or sacred) and became the first Roman emperor, circa 20–17 B.C.E.

(© Araldo de Luca/CORBIS)

Montesquieu, and the principal authors of the U.S. Constitution also came to recognize the strength and resiliency conferred on a state by virtue of its having a mixed constitution (Lintott; Millar 2002).

Their constitution is surely not, however, alone responsible for Rome's expansion and world domination. Polybius's analysis of the causes of Rome's success did not cease with his analysis of the Roman constitution. He also recognized that Rome's success was contingent on the military capabilities of her well-disciplined citizen army (as opposed, for instance, to the Carthaginians who relied on mercenaries) and the ability the Romans in general displayed to adapt and learn from her adversaries (6. 25. 11; 6. 52. 4–11). Modern historians have elaborated on Polybius's observations. Kurt Raaflaub (1996) has undertaken to elucidate the precise reasons for Roman expansion, by tracing its early origins, in an article bearing the allusive title, "Born to Be Wolves? Origins of Roman Imperialism." He notes that Roman expansion in the Mediterranean world was dictated by the competitive ideology of the aristocracy and popular pressure. The chronic shortage of sufficient land for agricultural use, a common problem confronting the poorer classes in early agrarian societies, placed pressure on their leaders to acquire more territory by warfare. As Raaflaub (1996, 296f.) explains:

> War was necessary to satisfy the material and "ideological" needs of the aristocracy that had adapted its social structures and value system to the demands of a warring community, needed recurring opportunities to prove its leadership and valor, and was involved in an intense internal competition that increased even further when plebeian families were integrated into the elite. And war became necessary to resolve social and economic problems of the citizen community and maintain domestic balance and peace.

Nearly continuous external threats served to intensify Rome's state of militarism. A further aspect of Roman policy worth mentioning was their consistent assimilation of a considerable number of people through the bestowal of citizenship, thus increasing the manpower available for military service. This may have caused a population influx from the poorer outlying regions of Italy toward Rome, which would have helped to maintain the pressure applied on the Roman leadership to engage in further conquests (Raaflaub 1996).

The social and political prestige accorded to successful Roman leaders should not be underestimated as a driving force in traditional republican ideology. One of the most illustrative examples of the social ramifications of superlative achievement is the ceremony surrounding the funeral procession, so well described by Polybius (6. 53. 1–54. 6). In this procession the body of the deceased is carried into the Forum, where his son or another close relative delivers the eulogy from the speaker's platform *(rostra)*. Men wearing wax masks *(imagines)* modeled after the features of the illustrious members of the dead man's family also took part in the procession and seated themselves on ivory curule chairs before the *rostra*, each one accompanied with the insignia of the highest office he occupied. Polybius perceptively draws attention to the psychological impact of this spectacle on the audience:

> By these means the whole populace–not only those who played some part in these exploits, but those who did not–are involved in the ceremony, so that when the facts of the dead man's career are recalled to their minds and brought before their eyes, their sympathies are so deeply engaged that the loss seems not to be confined to the mourners but to be a public one which affects the whole people (6. 53. 3).

Polybius is clear about the most significant impact this immortalization of glory has on Roman society, "But the most important consequence of the ceremony is that it inspires young men to endure the extremes of suffering for the common good in the hope of winning the glory that waits upon the brave" (6. 54. 3).

Harriet Flower in her comprehensive study of Roman ancestor masks stresses the uniqueness of this Roman custom and its civic/secular quality:

> No other ancient culture we know of made realistic wax masks of office-holding family members and kept them in the home, or used them for actors to wear at funerals. . . . The *imagines* have no connections with the magic or spirit world, and they were not used to conjure up the spirits of ancestors from the dead. Their secular and civic character can, therefore, be used to reveal the particular culture created by Rome's leading families. (2)

The masks were symbols of political power; power acquired by victories and achievements. Only through a continuous renewal of this political power through election to prestigious offices could a Roman family maintain its high social status. The social structure of the system incessantly propelled its most prominent members ever onward to new realms of achievement. The rapid growth and expansion of Rome's dominion that took place during the republican period was symptomatic of this ideology of competition and conquest.

The principate of Augustus induced a notable transformation in this fundamental ideology of the ruling elite that had long-term consequences for the viability of the Roman Empire. The consolidation of power in the person of the emperor led to a reduction of incentives for others. Under this new, more passive and reactive form of Roman government, the competitive proactive ethos of the republican era became obsolete, especially in those instances where the emperor's power might in some way be, or seem to be, infringed upon or even challenged (Millar 1977). The preponderance of power in the hands of one nonelected ruler disrupted the balance and stability of the republican constitution. The holding of high offices *(cursus honorum)* lost its former allure and gradually became a ceremonial affair rarely based on martial glory or oratorical ability but usually based instead on the emperor's prerogative. The glory of military achievement was virtually restricted to one man, the emperor. No Roman senator could seriously question the emperor's status without running a grave risk. The severe turnover of senators in the imperial period is likely attributable to the demoralizing and, at times, lethal impact of the principate on Rome's leading families (Talbert). Freedom of speech was restricted (Mayer). Fear and dissimulation prevailed (Rudich). Corruption increased (Macmullen). Traditional symbols of power such as the *imagines* were appropriated by Augustus and his successors in propagandistic displays (Flower). The celebration of triumphs by Roman generals (more than 230 were celebrated in the republican era) fell to the emperor and his family alone during the Roman Empire (Badian). By contrast the change in importance of election to higher office led to a decrease in the significance of the *imagines* for the aristocracy, accompanied by a loss of civic pride (Flower).

In conclusion, the fall of the republic led to a new, intrinsically flawed form of government, the principate. The sources of the flaws are: the succession of the emperor was determined by birth and not merit; the emperor was subject to no constraints and was not compelled to wield his absolute power responsibly; and incentives and opportunities for personal achievement, so important for the growth and expansion of the Roman Republic (the quest for military command, glory, and public office among the aristocracy) were curtailed. Whereas the proactive form of republican government, supported by a superior constitution, had fostered greater security as the Roman elite jostled for the opportunity to win glory through military exploits, the principate, by evoking jealousy, nepotism, and corruption, eroded the fabric of Roman society and caused the ideological evisceration of the ruling elite. The stagnation and decline of the Roman Empire ultimately ensued. The fall of the republic, therefore, necessarily rendered Roman decline inevitable.

–MARK A. BECK,
UNIVERSITY OF SOUTH CAROLINA

Viewpoint:
No. The notion that the collapse of the republic led to the decline of Rome is a manifest ideological fiction that cannot withstand a rigorous examination in terms of chronology, the instability of the republic, the benefits of the imperial system, and the class biases of the ancient commentators.

Tacitus, near the beginning of his *Annales,* writes that Augustus through fear and patronage was able to convince the senatorial elite to accept a form of servitude and domination (1.2). This passage is often cited as evidence that the advent of the empire produced an irreparable loss of liberty on the part of the Roman populace and thus represented the first step down a slippery slope of decline that eventually resulted in the collapse of the empire. Such a reading, however, is tendentious in the extreme. It is generally deployed by apologists for a certain vision of liberalism that equates the writer's definition of freedom with a vision of Golden Age republican virtue that manifestly never existed. It then argues that because present society has lost "freedom" (capitalism, property rights, local control of schools, traditional morality, and so on), we too are on the slippery slope of decline and will end up like the decadent Romans of ancient lore. The rhetoric of decline and decadence is always suspect and is inevitably weighed down with strong ideological value judgments. In point of fact, this understanding of Roman history is supported neither by the passage from Tacitus in question, nor by elementary chronology, a critical understanding of republican history, or a concrete analysis of the effects of empire.

The first thing to recognize is that while Tacitus does use the terms *servitium* (slavery) for Augustus's relation to the senate, he also manifestly says that the senatorial elite preferred the new situation because of the increased safety and stability offered by the Augustan settlement. He is both unsentimental about the republican past and realistic about the motives of the *princeps* and the senatorial order. The passage deserves to be read in full. It makes clear that in the wake of constant civil war, from the time of the assassination of Julius Caesar (44 B.C.E.) to the Battle of Actium (31 B.C.E.), the promise of peace and prosperity offered under the rule of Augustus was preferable to continued bloodshed and danger. In short, even for many in the senatorial elite, the republic had long since ceased to be a desirable commodity well before the date of its formal demise:

> After the death of Brutus and Cassius, there was no longer a military that belonged to the people. Sextus Pompeius was defeated in Sicily. And with Lepidus out of the way and Marcus Antonius killed, lest there be any commander of the Julian faction left besides Caesar, [Octavian] put aside the name *triumvir.* Styling himself *consul* and saying he was content to protect the people with the power of the tribune, while he enticed the soldiery with gifts, the people with provisions, and the rest with the sweetness of calm idleness, he gradually increased his power and gathered into himself the duties of the senate and the legal magistrates with no one opposing him, since those who were the most warlike *[ferocissimi]* had fallen in battle or during the proscriptions. The rest of the nobles were brought along by being offered high office and great wealth, which made them all the

GIBBON

The History of the Decline and Fall of the Roman Empire, a massive study of six volumes and 1.5 million words, was written by the English historian Edward Gibbon between 1776 and 1788. In the following excerpt, Gibbon offers an explanation for the fall of the Roman Empire in the West:

The rise of a city, which swelled into an empire, may deserve, as a singular prodigy, the reflection of a philosophic mind. But the decline of Rome was the natural and inevitable effect of immoderate greatness. Prosperity ripened the principle of decay; the causes of destruction multiplied with the extent of conquest; and as soon as time or accident had removed the artificial supports, the stupendous fabric yielded to the pressure of its own weight. The story of its ruin is simple and obvious; and instead of inquiring *why* the Roman empire was destroyed, we should rather be surprised that it had subsisted so long. The victorious legions, who, in distant wars, acquired the vices of strangers and mercenaries, first oppressed the freedom of the republic, and afterwards violated the majesty of the purple. The emperors, anxious for their personal safety and the public peace, were reduced to the base expedient of corrupting the discipline which rendered them alike formidable to their sovereign and to the enemy; the vigour of the military government was relaxed and finally dissolved by the partial institutions of Constantine; and the Roman world was overwhelmed by a deluge of barbarians.

The decay of Rome has been frequently ascribed to the translation of the seat of empire but this history has already shown that the powers of Government were *divided* rather than *removed.* The throne of Constantinople was erected in the East; while the West was still possessed by a series of emperors who held their residence in Italy, and claimed their equal inheritance of the legions and provinces. This dangerous novelty impaired the strength and fomented the vices of a double reign: the instruments of an oppressive and arbitrary system were multiplied; and a vain emulation of luxury, not of merit, was introduced and supported between the degenerate successors of Theodosius. Extreme distress, which unites the virtue of a free people, embitters the factions of a declining monarchy. The hostile favourites of Arcadius and Honorius betrayed the republic to its common enemies; and the Byzantine court beheld with indifference, perhaps with pleasure, the disgrace of Rome, the misfortunes of Italy, and the loss of the West. Under the succeeding reigns the alliance of the two empires was restored; but the aid of the Oriental Romans was tardy, doubtful, and ineffectual; and the national schism of the Greeks and Latins was enlarged by the perpetual difference of language and manners, of interests, and even of religion. Yet the salutary event approved in some measure the judgment of Constantine. During a long period of decay his impregnable city repelled the victorious armies of barbarians, protected the wealth of Asia, and commanded, both in peace and war, the important straits which connect the Euxine and Mediterranean seas. The foundation of Constantinople more essentially contributed to the preservation of the East than to the ruin of the West.

As the happiness of a *future* life is the great object of religion, we may hear without surprise or scandal that the introduction, or at least the abuse of Christianity, had some influence on the decline and fall of the Roman empire. The clergy successfully preached the doctrines of patience and pusillanimity; the active virtues of society were discouraged; and the last remains of military spirit were buried in the cloister: a large portion of public and private wealth was consecrated to the specious demands of charity and devotion; and the soldiers' pay was lavished on the useless multitudes of both sexes who could only plead the merits of abstinence and chastity. Faith, zeal, curiosity, and more earthly passions of malice and ambition, kindled the flame of theological discord; the church, and even the state, were distracted by religious factions, whose conflicts were sometimes bloody and always implacable; the attention of the emperors was diverted from camps to synods; the Roman world was oppressed by a new species of tyranny; and the persecuted sects became the secret enemies of their country. Yet party-spirit, however pernicious or absurd, is a principle of union as well as of dissension. The bishops, from eighteen hundred pulpits, inculcated the duty of passive obedience to a lawful and orthodox sovereign; their frequent assemblies and perpetual correspondence maintained the communion of distant churches; and the benevolent temper of the Gospel was strengthened, though confirmed, by the spiritual alliance of the Catholics.

The sacred indolence of the monks was devoutly embraced by a servile and effeminate age; but if superstition had not afforded a decent retreat, the same vices would have tempted the unworthy Romans to desert, from baser motives, the standard of the republic. Religious precepts are easily obeyed which indulge and sanctify the natural inclinations of their votaries; but the pure and genuine influence of Christianity may be traced in its beneficial, though imperfect, effects on the barbarian proselytes of the North. If the decline of the Roman empire was hastened by the conversion of Constantine, his victorious religion broke the violence of the fall, and mollified the ferocious temper of the conquerors.

This awful revolution may be usefully applied to the instruction of the present age. It is the duty of a patriot to prefer and promote the exclusive interest and glory of his native country: but a philosopher may be permitted to enlarge his views, and to consider Europe as one great republic, whose various inhabitants have attained almost the same level of politeness and cultivation. The balance of power will continue to fluctuate, and the prosperity of our own or the neighbouring kingdoms may be alternately exalted or depressed; but these partial events cannot essentially injure our general state of happiness, the system of arts, and laws, and manners, which so advantageously distinguish, above the rest of mankind, the Europeans and their colonies. The savage nations of the globe are the common enemies of civilised society; and we may inquire, with anxious curiosity, whether Europe is still threatened with a repetition of those calamities which formerly oppressed the arms and institutions of Rome. Perhaps the same reflections will illustrate the fall of that mighty empire, and explain the probable causes of our actual security.

I. The Romans were ignorant of the extent of their dangers and the number of their enemies. Beyond the Rhine and Danube the northern countries of Europe and Asia were filled with innumerable tribes of hunters and shepherds, poor, voracious, and turbulent; bold in arms, and impatient to ravish the fruits of industry. The barbarian world was agitated by the rapid impulse of war; and the peace of Gaul or Italy was shaken by the distant revolutions of China. The Huns, who fled before a victorious enemy, directed their march towards the West; and the torrent was swelled by the gradual accession of captives and allies. The flying tribes who yielded to the Huns assumed in *their* turn the spirit of conquest; the endless column of barbarians pressed on the Roman empire with accumulated weight; and, if the foremost were destroyed, the vacant space was instantly replenished by new assailants. Such formidable emigrations no longer issue from the North; and the long repose, which has been imputed to the decrease of population, is the happy consequence of the progress of arts and agriculture. Instead of some rude villages thinly scattered among its woods and morasses, Germany now produces a list of two thousand three hundred walled towns: the Christian kingdoms of Denmark, Sweden, and Poland have been successively established; and the Hanse merchants, with the Teutonic knights, have extended their colonies along the coast of the Baltic as far as the Gulf of Finland. From the Gulf of Finland to the Eastern Ocean, Russia now assumes the form of a powerful and civilised empire. The plough, the loom, and the forge are introduced on the banks of the Volga, the Oby, and the Lena; and the fiercest of the Tartar hordes have been taught to tremble and obey. The reign of independent barbarism is now contracted to a narrow span; and the remnant of Calmucks or Uzbecks, whose forces may be almost numbered, cannot seriously excite the apprehensions of the great republic of Europe. Yet this apparent security should not tempt us to forget that new enemies and unknown dangers may *possibly* arise from some obscure people, scarcely visible in the map of the world. The Arabs or Saracens, who spread their conquests from India to Spain, had languished in poverty and contempt till Mahomet breathed into those savage bodies the soul of enthusiasm.

II. The empire of Rome was firmly established by the singular and perfect coalition of its members. The subject nations, resigning the hope and even the wish of independence, embraced the character of Roman citizens; and the provinces of the West were reluctantly torn by the barbarians from the bosom of their mother country. But this union was purchased by the loss of national freedom and military spirit; and the servile provinces, destitute of life and motion, expected their safety from the mercenary troops and governors who were directed by the orders of a distant court. The happiness of an hundred millions depended on the personal merit of one or two men, perhaps children, whose minds were corrupted by education, luxury, and despotic power. The deepest wounds were inflicted on the empire during the minorities of the sons and grandsons of Theodosius; and, after those incapable princes seemed to attain the age of manhood, they abandoned the church to the bishops, the state to the eunuchs, and the provinces to the barbarians. Europe is now divided into twelve powerful, though unequal kingdoms, three respectable commonwealths, and a variety of smaller, though independent states: the chances of royal and ministerial talent are multiplied, at least, with the number of its rulers; and a Julian, or Semiramis, may reign in the North, while Arcadius and Honorius again slumber on the thrones of the South. The abuses of tyranny are restrained by the mutual influence of fear and shame; republics have acquired order and stability; monarchies have imbibed the principles of freedom, or, at least, of moderation; and some sense of honour and justice is introduced into the most defective constitutions by the general manner of the times. In peace, the progress of knowledge and industry is accelerated by the emulation of so many active rivals: in war, the European forces are exercised by temperate and indecisive contests. If a savage conqueror should issue from the deserts of Tartary, he must repeatedly vanquish the robust peasants of Russia, the numerous armies of Germany, the gallant nobles of France, and the intrepid freemen of Britain; who, perhaps, might confederate for their common defence. Should the victorious barbarians carry slavery and desolation as far as the Atlantic Ocean, ten thousand vessels would transport beyond their pursuit the remains of civilised society; and Europe would revive and flourish in the American world, which is already filled with her colonies and institutions.

III. Cold, poverty, and a life of danger and fatigue fortify the strength and courage of barbarians. In every age they have oppressed the polite and peaceful nations of China, India, and Persia, who neglected, and still neglect, to counter-balance these natural powers by the resources of military art. The warlike states of antiquity, Greece, Macedonia, and Rome, educated a race of soldiers; exercised their bodies, disciplined their courage, multiplied their forces by regular evolutions, and converted the iron which they possessed into strong and serviceable weapons. But this superiority insensibly declined with their laws and manners: and the feeble policy of Constantine and his successors armed and instructed, for the ruin of the empire, the rude valour of the barbarian mercenaries. The military art has been changed by the invention of gunpowder; which enables man to command the two most powerful agents of nature, air and fire. Mathematics, chemistry, mechanics, architecture, have been applied to the service of war; and the adverse parties oppose to each other the most elaborate modes of attack and of defence. Historians may indignantly observe that the preparations of a siege would found and maintain a flourishing colony; yet we cannot be displeased that the subversion of a city should be a work of cost and difficulty; or that an industrious people should be protected by those arts which survive and supply the decay of military virtue. Cannon and fortifications now form an impregnable barrier against the Tartar horse; and Europe is secure from any future irruption of barbarians; since, before they can conquer, they must cease to be barbarous. Their gradual advances in the science of war would always be accompanied, as we may learn from the example of Russia, with a proportionable improvement in the arts of peace and civil policy; and they themselves must deserve a place among the polished nations whom they subdue.

Source: *Edward Gibbon, "General Observations on the Fall of the Roman Empire in the West," Chapter 39, in* The History of the Decline and Fall of the Roman Empire, *volume 1 (London: W. Strahan & T. Cadell, 1776), Christian Classics Ethereal Library Website <http://www.ccel.org/g/gibbon/decline/volume1/chap39.htm>.*

> more ready for *servitude,* so that becoming enriched under the new state of affairs they preferred the safe world of the present to the dangerous world of the past.

Clearly, Tacitus is out of sympathy with the decision made by the elites under Augustus. But what does he actually say? First, after a period of political violence, Octavian (later Augustus) became the leader of the Julian faction, upon the death of Antony. Second, in this role he assumed the titles of consul and tribune. These were traditional offices, hence Augustus's claim that he restored the republic. Third, he convinced the public to accept this through insuring that the troops were rewarded, the people were fed, and a period of calm reigned after nonstop civil war and bloodshed. Fourth, having won the assent of the vast majority of the population, he was not opposed by the senatorial elite. In part that is because those who were most likely to take up arms against him *(ferocissimi)* had already perished, and in part because he offered the rest tangible, and not negligible, benefits if they accepted the new regime. Given the choice between wealth, office, and peace on the one hand, and renewed civil war on the other, with no promise that anything better would emerge, most members of the elite made the rational calculation.

It is hard to see in what sense any of this represents decline unless you have already conceded the notion that rule by the senatorial elite was inherently superior to other forms of governance and was therefore to be identified with freedom and the health of the state. Nor, it should be remembered, are we talking about the whole of the senatorial order, but only those elements that most jealously guarded their own privileges *(ferocissimi),* which, it should also be remembered, were no less arbitrary in relation to the vast majority of the population than those Caesar arrogated to himself. The republican senatorial elite was a closed circle of wealth and aristocratic privilege into which only the rarest *novus homo* ("new man") was able to penetrate. The republican constitution, as Ronald Syme points out, was a sham and in fact was nothing more than a loose consensus among the leading families of Rome that allowed them to compete for power to the exclusion of the vast majority of the population. From the time of the end of the Second Punic War (218–201 B.C.E.), there was greater and greater social instability in Rome. Citizen soldiers away on campaign had their property seized by greedy creditors. Public lands were expropriated by already-wealthy magnates who worked their estates with slave gangs, and the population was forced off the land into the city where a large unemployed urban proletariat was created. When the Gracchi at the end of the second century proposed land reform as a method of addressing these manifest social ills, even if at times they resorted to extraconstitutional means to get their legislation passed and enacted, they were beaten to death by gangs of outraged senators. The next hundred years was one of almost nonstop civil conflict culminating in Julius Caesar's being declared dictator for life, his subsequent assassination, and ensuing civil war. The result of this conflict was the loss of hundreds of thousands of lives through war, proscription, starvation, and disease. When Augustus was proclaimed first citizen by the Senate *(princeps),* who could see this as the beginning of decline rather than the end of headlong collapse, except a rump faction of the senatorial elite who nostalgically dreamed of the privilege of competing for supreme power with others of their kind?

Nonetheless, if the republic was hardly the Golden Age, the empire had more than its share of horror stories that have often been used to point a moral treatise or illustrate a sermon. Did not Caligula make his horse a senator, force senator's wives to work in a brothel, and force bad poets to lick the ink off their scrolls? Did not Nero poison his own mother and use Christians as torches for his garden parties? Did not Vespasian encourage the growth of a network of informers while forcing his daughter to abort a child that he himself fathered? The answer to all of these questions is "yes." The republic, however, was a brutal place too. One need only read Cicero's *Verrines* to see the kind of depredations visited on the populace by a cruel and corrupt provincial governor, or recall the slaughter of eighty thousand Roman citizens in Asia Minor in the course of a revolt against corrupt tax farmers at the beginning of the First Mithridatic War (89–85 B.C.E.) to realize that cruelty and arbitrary behavior were common features of the ancient world, and emperors had no monopoly on them (nor are they as uncommon in the modern world as we might wish to believe).

The fact of the matter, however, is that most of the cruelties of the emperors were not visited on the general population but on the senatorial elite, and not all emperors were cruel. For the average peasant in Gaul, Spain, or the Italian countryside, the empire was a Golden Age of peace, prosperity, good roads, reliable courts, and educational improvement. It was a time of increased social mobility. Emperors came not just from a few inbred Roman families, as was the case with the republican consulate, but from Spain, Ilyria, and other provinces. Freedmen rose to positions of economic power and prominence (witness Juvenal and Petronius's satires of them). Poets and philosophers traveled in a cosmopolitan world that allowed for a constant movement between the center and the periphery as testified to by the cases of Martial, both Senecas, Apuleius, and St. Augustine. The fact is that

Roman citizenship was widely disseminated and presented real legal guarantees that, while not the equivalent of the Bill of Rights or the Rights of Man, were genuinely respected, as testified to by St. Paul's ability to appeal directly to the emperor. Local control remained strong, and many citizens were able to satisfy their political ambitions by attaining municipal magistracies.

Indeed, even the worst emperors, from the point of view of the senatorial elite, were often widely popular among the urban masses and their provincial confreres. Striking evidence of this is found in the fact that Nero's resurrection was regularly reported for hundreds of years after his death, and his return to Rome was often rumored. Perhaps the most persuasive evidence of the stability and fundamental prosperity of the imperial system throughout most of its existence, however, is that with the exception of the religiously inspired revolt of the Jews in Palestine, the empire suffered not a single political uprising during its existence. The revolt of Spartacus at the beginning of the last century of the republic was the final real challenge to the hegemony of Roman rule and the sociopolitical order that undergirded it. When Rome eventually fell, it was not because of civil war or the revolt of imperial provinces but repeated external invasions.

Of course, as the ultimate fate of St. Paul, some Christians under Nero and Diocletian, and the Jews at Massada indicates, the empire was not an ideal political order and could perpetrate horrific abuses. Several things, however, need to be borne in mind before we rush to moral and political judgment. First, persecutions of Christians were sporadic and not systematic. Many emperors took the point of view that as long as the congregations did not become obstreperous they should be left in peace. Second, from the Roman point of view, Jewish nationalism and the concomitant refusal to recognize the statutory divinity of the emperor were political, not religious, acts. It was of no importance to the Roman authorities what people believed, but the refusal to make a public gesture of obeisance to the emperor was the equivalent of a declaration of revolt. There was never a systematic attempt to root out Judaism or to persecute Jews, as is testified to by the large Jewish population in the city of Rome itself. Third, the norm in the ancient Mediterranean was religious syncretism. If you worship a different set of gods than I do, then I either assimilate your gods to mine or adopt your gods wholesale into my pantheon. You in turn are expected to do the same. The Christian and Jewish refusal to recognize any god but their own was, therefore, widely perceived as not only a rejection of the political order but also a rejection of civilization per se. Christians were thus often rumored to be cannibals, with the ceremony of the Eucharist cited as evidence. In short, while the early sporadic persecutions of Judaeo-Christian monotheists demonstrate the limits of imperial tolerance and respect for individual rights, they hardly constitute decisive evidence that the fall of the republic necessarily led to Rome's decline. Indeed, the main reason the Jewish revolt was crushed and Christians were persecuted under the empire rather than under the republic is that there were no such revolts and no Christians during the republic.

This issue brings us to our final line of argument: chronology. To say that the fall of the republic inevitably led to the decline of Rome is absurd on its face. The end of the republic is typically dated to Octavian's defeat of Antony at Actium in 31 B.C.E., although the republican constitution had been a dead letter for almost a hundred years prior to that. Rome was not sacked by the Visigoths until 410 C.E., and the last Western emperor, Romulus Augustulus, was not deposed till 476. The empire thus presented a by-and-large stable order for more than four hundred years and lasted for more than five hundred. The eastern empire continued at Byzantium until the fall of Constantinople in 1490. When one realizes that the founding of the republic is traditionally dated to the expulsion of the last king, Tarquinius Superbus, in 508 B.C.E., it becomes clear that the empire as a political entity was in no way inferior to the republic and in fact safeguarded the interests of most of its citizens far better than the republic. If this was decline, it was one that would be the envy of many states' ascents. The big losers in the fall of the Roman Republic were not the Roman people, but the wealthy and powerful senatorial elite.

In summary, the fall of the republic did not inevitably lead to decline because most people were better off under the empire than the republic, and the Roman state was an empire for at least as long as it was a republic. The rhetoric of decline in the ancient sources is the product of a senatorial elite nostalgic for its lost arbitrary privileges, and, in modern writers, it is the product of ideology. Even the passages in Tacitus, often cited to prove imperial decline, do not support that thesis if read with a critical eye.

–PAUL ALLEN MILLER,
UNIVERSITY OF SOUTH CAROLINA

References

Ernst Badian, "Triumph," in *The Oxford Classical Dictionary,* third edition, edited by Simon Hornblower and Anthony Spawforth (Oxford: Oxford University Press, 1996).

P. A. Brunt, *The Fall of the Roman Republic and Related Essays* (Oxford: Oxford University Press, 1988).

Brunt, *Social Conflicts in the Roman Republic* (New York: Norton, 1971).

Werner Eck, "Senatorial Self-Representation: Developments in the Augustan Period," in *Caesar Augustus: Seven Aspects,* edited by Fergus Millar and Erich Segal (Oxford: Clarendon Press, 1984), pp. 129–168.

Harriet I. Flower, *Ancestor Masks and Aristocratic Power in Roman Culture* (Oxford: Oxford University Press, 1996).

Karl Galinsky, *Augustan Culture: An Interpretive Introduction* (Princeton: Princeton University Press, 1996).

William V. Harris, *War and Imperialism in the Late Republic* (Oxford: Oxford University Press, 1979).

Andrew Lintott, *The Constitution of the Roman Republic* (Oxford: Clarendon Press, 1999).

Ramsay Macmullen, *Corruption and the Decline of Rome* (New Haven & London: Yale University Press, 1988).

Roland Mayer, ed., *Tacitus: Dialogus De Oratoribus* (Cambridge: Cambridge University Press, 2001).

Fergus Millar, *The Crowd in Rome in the Late Republic,* Jerome Lectures 22 (Ann Arbor: University of Michigan Press, 1998).

Millar, *The Emperor in the Roman World (31 BC – AD 337)* (London: Duckworth, 1977).

Millar, *The Roman Republic in Political Thought: The Menahem Stern Jerusalem Lectures* (Hanover, N.H. & London: University Press of New England, 2002).

Wilfried Nippel, *Public Order in Ancient Rome* (Cambridge: Cambridge University Press, 1995).

Polybius, *The Rise of the Roman Empire,* translated by Ian Scott-Kilvert (Harmondsworth, U.K.: Penguin, 1979).

Kurt Raaflaub, "Born to Be Wolves? Origins of Roman Imperialism," in *Transitions to Empire: Essays in Greco-Roman History, 360–146 B.C., in Honor of E. Badian,* edited by Robert W. Wallace and Edward M. Harris (Norman: University of Oklahoma Press, 1996), pp. 273–314.

Raaflaub, "Philosophy, Science, Politics: Herodotus and the Intellectual Trends of his Time," in *Brill's Companion to Herodotus,* edited by Egbert J Bakker and others (Leiden & Boston: Brill, 2002), pp. 149–186.

Vasily Rudich, *Political Dissidence under Nero: The Price of Dissimulation* (London & New York: Routledge, 1993).

G. E. M. de Ste. Croix, *The Class Struggle in the Ancient Greek World: From the Archaic Age to the Arab Conquests* (Ithaca, N.Y.: Cornell University Press, 1981).

H. H. Scullard, *From the Gracchi to Nero: A History of Rome from 133 BC to AD 68* (London: Methuen, 1963).

Jo-Ann Shelton, *As the Romans Did: A Sourcebook in Roman Social History,* second edition (Oxford: Oxford University Press 1998).

Ronald Syme, *The Roman Revolution* (Oxford: Clarendon Press, 1939).

Richard J. A. Talbert, *The Senate of Imperial Rome* (Princeton: Princeton University Press, 1984).

F. W. Walbank, *Polybius* (Berkeley: University of California Press, 1972).

L. P. Wilkinson, *The Roman Experience* (Lanham, Md.: University Press of America, 1974).

T. P. Wiseman, *Catullus and His World: A Reappraisal* (Cambridge: Cambridge University Press, 1985).

ROMAN PERIOD: GLADIATORIAL CONTESTS

Was the purpose of the gladiatorial contests to satisfy the blood lust of the Roman mob?

Viewpoint: Yes. The gladiatorial games drew upon the bloodthirsty urges of a populace hardened by continual warfare and were used by the emperors as a means of keeping the mob entertained.

Viewpoint: No. Although they were spectacles of bloodshed, the gladiatorial games were designed as a manifestation of deeply rooted Roman values and aimed to display to the populace the power of their empire.

The popular image of the gladiatorial games is one of extreme violence and cruelty perpetrated upon human and animal victims for the simple entertainment of the Roman masses. The huge arena known as the Colosseum, built in the middle of downtown Rome, testifies to the central importance of these bloodthirsty spectacles in Roman life, especially during the period of the empire. Documentary evidence provides ample proof of the elaborate organization that was required for the presentation of these spectacles of death in Rome and in every major town throughout the empire. Three main categories of combatants or victims can be identified: prisoners of war and condemned criminals; exotic and dangerous animals from Africa and elsewhere; and the highly trained fighters known as gladiators. In all cases, the people seated in the arena watched one act of killing after another, frequently for days on end. In the imperial era, at least, it is fair to say that the arena was a significant, if not the major, form of public entertainment in the typical Roman city. These details are generally agreed upon, but the interpretation of them leads to two differing views of how we should regard what went on in the arena.

Drawing upon the famous formulation by the Roman satirist Juvenal of "bread and circuses," some have argued that these spectacles were cynically developed by emperors into a means of social control through mass entertainment. The killings in the arena took place during festivals that became increasingly lengthy and that served as a public display of munificence by the emperor to his subjects. Ever greater numbers of combatants and victims were procured, and the organizers were always on the lookout for novelties and refinements of cruelty to hold the interest of what must have been a fairly jaded audience. The total lack of any sympathy on the part of the viewers toward the humans and animals in the arena indicates that they came simply to watch them being killed, preferably in as entertaining a manner as possible. The games probably exploited the lack of sensitivity to killing that was a result of the more or less continual warfare upon which the Roman Empire was built and maintained. This is the traditional view.

More recently, some have argued that the spectacles in the arena were in fact laden with symbolic value and ideological messages that were far more powerful than simple bloodlust on the part of the viewers. The killing of prisoners and criminals depicted Roman justice in action, while the slaughter of animals demonstrated Roman power over nature. Gladiators, moreover, are a complex phenomenon in Roman culture: they were trained to fight in the true Roman manner, to face death without flinching, and to die or be spared according to a strict code of military and moral conduct. The fact that many gladiators survived to fight another day suggests that they were not simply there to be killed. The arena was a mirror in which the Roman populace could view its empire in microcosm and watch the defining characteristics of Romanness (*Romanitas*) being acted out before their eyes. It is still true that these spectacles served the interests of the imperial state, but they did so more through their symbolism than through entertainment.

—David H. J. Larmour

Viewpoint: Yes. The gladiatorial games drew upon the bloodthirsty urges of a populace hardened by continual warfare and were used by the emperors as a means of keeping the mob entertained.

The popular image of the Roman arena is deeply rooted: a place constructed for the sole purpose of presenting spectacles of torture and murder for the entertainment of the Roman masses, who viewed the suffering and death that occurred in the sand below with a lack of empathy matched only by the emperor's cynical exploitation of the lowest popular taste for his own popularity and security. The available evidence offers much to confirm the essential components of this popular image, even if it has sometimes been exaggerated. To understand the gladiatorial games and the arena, we have to understand how Rome was established as an imperial power over the inhabitants of the entire Mediterranean basin. The Roman state was built upon the brutal subjugation of neighboring peoples and the forceful incorporation of their territory into the realm of Roman authority. Any resistance was met with severe measures, designed to intimidate enemies and demonstrate the inevitability of Roman power. Early on, the practice of first humiliating and then executing prisoners of war in the ceremonial procession known as the Triumph seems to have developed into the practice of making them fight to the death in front of their captors. It is as if someone suddenly thought up this way of having prisoners make themselves useful as entertainment before they were killed, and the idea immediately caught on. The first gladiatorial fight that we know of took place in the year 264 B.C.E. The ritual or religious associations of the gladiatorial games and other spectacles of killing in Roman culture are shrouded in mystery, and it is difficult to say anything precise about them. It is possible that the Romans inherited some of these practices from the Etruscans. They certainly did not learn them from the Greeks. The appeal of the spectacles of killing in the arena depends on the transformation of victims—animals, prisoners of war, and criminals—into entertainers, and this was a link that, once made, Roman society developed to its limits using all of its genuinely remarkable skills in organization and commerce.

The practice of having people and animals kill each other for the entertainment of Roman citizens needs to be viewed within the wider context of the brutality and violence that pervades Roman culture. This cannot be underestimated. It ranges from the corporal punishment that was meted out on a regular basis to Roman schoolboys, through the abuse and torture of slaves, to the rigid discipline operating within the Roman army on all levels. Violence, indeed, appears to have been inseparable from such cultural virtues as courage, truthfulness, honor, and justice. The evidence from slaves in court cases, for instance, was thought to be reliable only if they had been tortured in order to extract it. The Roman religious system was based on the performance of animal sacrifice, which meant that the public slaughtering of animals was regular and commonplace. There is little in Roman cultural documents to suggest that animals—rather like slaves and territories—were viewed as anything other than resources to be used and consumed. It is no exaggeration to say, therefore, that a Roman grew up amid acts of violence and hence came to regard it as a normal part of life. This impression was no doubt intensified by experiences on the battlefield and the campaigns of military conquest prosecuted against neighboring peoples as the empire was expanded to cover the entire Mediterranean area. In the traumatic final years of the Roman Republic, which came to an end with the triumph of Octavian over Mark Antony and Cleopatra in 31 B.C.E. at Actium, the whole population was caught up in a succession of civil wars. These caused great suffering to the average Roman citizen and were accompanied by acts of extreme violence and cruelty. It is only reasonable to expect that these events left their mark on the Roman psyche, and it comes as no surprise, therefore, that in the imperial era that followed, amid the great material prosperity and the welcome absence of warfare close to home, these violent urges should have found an outlet in the spectacles of the arena.

It is also important to recognize that these spectacles early on became bound up with the realm of politics. By the year 122 B.C.E., we find

DRINKING IN THE MADNESS

In the following account, St. Augustine describes his friend Alypius's reaction to viewing a gladiatorial combat for the first time:

He had gone on to Rome before me to study law—which was the worldly way which his parents were forever urging him to pursue—and there he was carried away again with an incredible passion for the gladiatorial shows. For, although he had been utterly opposed to such spectacles and detested them, one day he met by chance a company of his acquaintances and fellow students returning from dinner; and, with a friendly violence, they drew him, resisting and objecting vehemently, into the amphitheater, on a day of those cruel and murderous shows. He protested to them: "Though you drag my body to that place and set me down there, you cannot force me to give my mind or lend my eyes to these shows. Thus I will be absent while present, and so overcome both you and them." When they heard this, they dragged him on in, probably interested to see whether he could do as he said. When they got to the arena, and had taken what seats they could get, the whole place became a tumult of inhuman frenzy. But Alypius kept his eyes closed and forbade his mind to roam abroad after such wickedness. Would that he had shut his ears also! For when one of the combatants fell in the fight, a mighty cry from the whole audience stirred him so strongly that, overcome by curiosity and still prepared (as he thought) to despise and rise superior to it no matter what it was, he opened his eyes and was struck with a deeper wound in his soul than the victim whom he desired to see had been in his body. Thus he fell more miserably than the one whose fall had raised that mighty clamor which had entered through his ears and unlocked his eyes to make way for the wounding and beating down of his soul, which was more audacious than truly valiant—also it was weaker because it presumed on its own strength when it ought to have depended on Thee. For, as soon as he saw the blood, he drank in with it a savage temper, and he did not turn away, but fixed his eyes on the bloody pastime, unwittingly drinking in the madness—delighted with the wicked contest and drunk with blood lust. He was now no longer the same man who came in, but was one of the mob he came into, a true companion of those who had brought him thither. Why need I say more? He looked, he shouted, he was excited, and he took away with him the madness that would stimulate him to come again: not only with those who first enticed him, but even without them; indeed, dragging in others besides. And yet from all this, with a most powerful and most merciful hand, thou didst pluck him and taught him not to rest his confidence in himself but in thee—but not till long after.

Source: *St. Augustine,* Confessions *(circa 400), Book 6, Chapter 8, Christian Classics Ethereal Library <http://www.ccel.org/a/augustine/confessions/confessions.html>.*

the reformist political leader Gracchus–whose program was basically aimed at improving the lot of the poor and dispossessed among the citizenry–using the public exhibition of combatants in order to win supporters to his cause. In the first century B.C.E., Julius Caesar showed that he understood clearly the political value of public spectacles in terms of getting votes, and in 46 he produced the first mock naval battle. As in much else, Caesar was an innovator, both in the content and the scale of his entertainments, and he established a trend of ostentation that was followed by all the emperors who came after him, as each tried to outdo his predecessor in the lavishness and novelty of the spectacles that he generously "gave" to the populace. In the imperial era, many new and improved arenas were erected in Rome and throughout the empire, the most astounding of which was the Flavian amphitheater, or Colosseum, right in the center of the capital. With its vast seating capacity of perhaps 80,000 and its elaborate production devices, as well as its many amenities for the audience's comfort, the Colosseum was the ultimate in spectacular and bloody entertainment. Humans and animals were held in cells under the floor, ready to be sent up to their deaths in an efficient process of slaughter that could go on for days or weeks. The Colosseum was also the ultimate device of political control, for it was to a substantial extent through the distractions provided by the arena that the imperial government was able to keep the huge, and potentially unruly, mass of the Roman population quiescent. The emperor appeared in the Colosseum in the capacity of Producer of the Show, and hence was the recipient of the crowd's approval, even gratitude. Emperors kept order through "bread and circuses," to borrow a famous phrase from the satirist Juvenal: as long as the Roman mob was well fed and well entertained, it was unlikely to involve itself in political activities or to seek a radical change in the imperial system of government. Emperors usually arranged for snacks and treats to be distributed to the crowd during the spectacles, which confirms the close connection between the "bread" and the "circuses" made by the satirist. It is not an exaggeration to say that the emperor both created and "fed" the appetite of the crowd for blood with ever more elaborate menus of death and destruction.

It is striking that no Roman author makes any criticism of the arena on the basis of its cruelty or inhumanity. Even the philosophers, whom we might expect to have the most substantive objections, confine their lukewarm reproaches to deviations from the norm and to examples of imperial injustice, and, in particular, to the effects on the passions that the arena arouses on educated people like themselves. Seneca, the main spokesman for the Stoic school, goes so far as to cite the gladiator as a model for the philosophy student, who should imitate his detached courage in the face of danger or death and who should train himself every bit as rigorously as the gladiator preparing for the fights in the arena. There is ample evidence to prove that all segments of Roman society both attended and approved of the gladiatorial games and the other spectacles of death. The complex seating arrangements of the Colosseum, in fact, are thought to have mirrored the structures of the Roman state itself, with men separated from women and the various classes sitting in different parts of the amphitheater. When the citizenry went to the arena, then, they had a good view of themselves and the whole body politic, as well as of the mangled bodies of their enemies and subjects in the sand below. There was no real sense of shame in being seen at the games and certainly no sense of shame about the public and open performance of death and destruction. Indeed, all of the killing that went on in the arena had the stamp of official approval firmly planted upon it. Gladiatorial mosaics, moreover, decorated the floors of many private homes, indicating that the arena and its killing were regarded as acceptable subjects of artistic decoration by the wealthy and educated elite.

The spectacles in the arena can be divided into three categories and were generally presented in the same order. In the morning, there were wild-beast fights, with exotic animals encouraged to attack and kill each other. There was a whole industry devoted to procuring wild animals mainly from Africa to feed the demands of the arena. At midday, the executions of condemned criminals and other "non-persons" took place: these sometimes took the form of mock hunts, in which victims took on ravenous animals, or mythological reenactments of such stories as the death of Orpheus, with the unfortunate actor being eaten by bears. Sometimes the condemned were burned alive. In the afternoon, everyone settled down for the highlight of the day, the gladiatorial combats. These attracted the greatest enthusiasm from the crowd, many of whom were truly fanatical in their devotion. Every move by a gladiator was intently watched and evaluated by the connoisseurs of death, and, at the end, the viewers would shout out instructions to the victor, to the effect that he should either "finish off" his opponent or "spare him." Emotions sometimes ran high, which was all part of the thrill of the afternoon. Thus, watching the gladiatorial combat gave the crowd a temporary sensation of total power, the power to kill or reprieve an individual. Some gladiators became cult figures, admired for their skill or courage or even their supposed sexual prowess. It has been surmised that the display of half-naked gladiators constituted a kind of psychosexual spectacle, designed to titillate and excite the viewers through its heady mixture of desire, danger, and death. Much of the excitement of the arena can be attributed to its voyeuristic panderings. The gladiator is a fantasy figure in the imperial consciousness, the object of simultaneous disgust and desire. Such was his allure that even some freeborn Roman citizens, and perhaps even some emperors, felt an uncontrollable urge to enter the arena themselves.

Roman imperial society was characterized by material prosperity, but it is clear from all sorts of sources that along with this went a deep-seated psychological anxiety. The freedoms enjoyed in earlier days by the citizens of the republic—to speak openly, to discuss matters of public policy in the Assembly or the Senate, and to elect their leaders—no longer existed in reality, even though the political apparatus of the republic was retained for the sake of appearances by the emperors, many of whom were regarded with suspicion and sometimes outright fear by the population. The emperors themselves were constantly anxious about the precariousness of their power base and the threat of conspiracies against them. The arena became the place where all of these anxieties were contained and diverted into other outlets: the emperor sought to placate and control the crowd by appearing as the benefactor who gave them entertainments; the crowd displaced its fears onto the action in the sand and experienced a feeling of power over the non-Roman, a power that it "shared" with its fellow citizen, the emperor. The animals and individuals who fought and died in the arena did so, then, to relieve the spectators of their anxieties, which brought about a sensation of catharsis and pleasure. As Tertullian, admittedly a hostile Christian witness but nonetheless a perceptive one, puts it: "in this way they found comfort for death in murder." The spectacle was repeated over and over in a futile attempt to lay these anxieties to rest. The number of days in the Roman calendar devoted to such events was already at 66 in the reign of the first—and relatively restrained—Emperor Augustus, who also offered "extraordinary" games in honor of members of the imperial family. The number of holidays continued to increase throughout the empire, so that it had reached 135 by the time of Marcus Aurelius, and had grown to over 175 by the fourth century C.E. Special shows were held to celebrate military victories, such as Trajan's conquest of the Dacians, marked by four months of animal and gladiatorial combat, involving 10,000 beasts and 10,000 fighters.

Thus, while elaborate and inventive arguments have been made that the spectacles of the arena may have had "deeper" significance and been the bearers of important messages of cultural meaning, it is clear from the organization behind them, the care with which the emperors oversaw them, and the enthusiasm with which they were received, over and over again, day after day, year after year, that they were primarily entertainment for the Roman masses. The violence and brutality at their core cannot be explained away; indeed, it was their main attraction. As such, the arena games were the most striking public manifestation of the central role of domination and killing in Roman imperialist culture.

—DAVID H. J. LARMOUR,
TEXAS TECH UNIVERSITY

Viewpoint:
No. Although they were spectacles of bloodshed, the gladiatorial games were designed as a manifestation of deeply rooted Roman values and aimed to display to the populace the power of their empire.

There is no denying the violent and bloody nature of the spectacles of the Roman arena, which has been thoroughly documented, but it is a mistake to approach these performances through the lens of modern Western sensibility. The practices of the arena have to be understood in their broader cultural context, one that is far removed, and in all sorts of ways strikingly different, from twentieth-century Western norms or, perhaps one should more accurately say, ideals of behavior. We also have to be careful to distinguish among the different types of spectacle that were presented in the arena since people attended them for various reasons—to watch the punishment of criminals, to marvel at exotic animals from far-flung regions of the empire, or to study the courage and fighting skills of the highly trained gladiators. Each type of spectacle communicated something different to the viewers about what it meant to be Roman and about the phenomenon of Roman power in the world. The arena served as a kind of mirror in which the citizens of the empire could see how it functioned: the spectacles involving animals demonstrated the control exercised by Rome over the natural world and the consumption of resources from faraway places; the executions of criminals were a powerful illustration of the power of the law, upon which the whole empire rested; finally, the fights between gladiators showed the traditional Roman virtues of bravery and military prowess in action, and once again demonstrated the state's control over life and death. Sometimes the spectacles had a specific historical reference—for instance, when Julius Caesar had a section of the Campus Martius dug out and filled with water and 6,000 participants re-created a battle between the Tyrians and the Egyptians—but most often they were more universal in their messages. When the Roman citizen went to the games, he saw his own identity being constructed and validated before his eyes. The arena showed the world and the empire in microcosm to its viewers.

Arena spectacles did not arise suddenly. They most probably had their origins in sacrificial rites that were performed to appease the spirits of the dead and to guarantee the continuation of life and were perhaps learned by the Romans from the older civilization of their neighbors, the Etruscans. These rites are ancient fertility practices, reflecting the agricultural basis of civilization. The essence of sacrifice is that by giving up something valuable and alive, the individual or community gains something more precious, namely the preservation of its own existence. In a setting where death and the threat of annihilation through famine, warfare, disease, or natural disaster were very much present, and at the front of people's consciousness in a manner we often find it hard to relate to today in the modern Western world, it is no surprise that sacrifice occupied a central role in social ritual. This may well lie behind the presentation of wild-beast fights and the mass killing of animals in the arena. By extension, the killing of human beings can also be seen in terms of sacrificial offerings. It is something of a misnomer to refer to these events as "games" although that is the most widely used term in popular parlance. The Latin word used for a gladiatorial spectacle is *munus* (plural *munera*), which has the basic meaning of

Deatail in a mosaic of gladiatorial combat from Torre Nuova

(© Alinari Archives/CORBIS)

service or duty with particular reference to rites of sacrifice associated with funerals or tributes to the dead. These *munera* were originally organized on a private and individual basis, usually by wealthy individuals who could afford to pay for trained fighters, but they were later taken over by the state as they grew in importance and their political value was realized. The sacrificial elements were not forgotten, however, even during the height of the empire. One indication of this is the way gladiators were treated just before their appointment with death. On the night before the spectacles were to be held, gladiators were taken to a lavish banquet where they were put on display to members of the public. This detail suggests that the victims were presented as "scapegoats," who were treated to a "last supper" before their coming sacrifice. The fact that gladiators were expected to be "willing" to die also has unmistakable analogies with sacrificial animals, for it was a bad omen if such victims did not approach the altar willingly.

Just as they were associated with the preservation of life and fertility, so the arena spectacles are also linked with the preservation of social order within the community. The arena was a place where the basic structures of Roman/non-Roman, justice/crime, and self/other were displayed without shadows or "gray areas." Some would argue that all social order is ultimately based on violence, either actual or threatened, and one important feature of this violence is that it must be seen to be done. The Roman state depended for its stability upon the functioning of a rigid system of discipline, involving manifest penalties and punishments, that was performed in public. This was especially true of capital punishment. Severe crimes had to receive severe punishment, if only to deter others from attempting similar acts. Thus, the executions of criminals in the arena were only partly punitive and were designed primarily as a deterrent: they were a means of demonstrating to the populace that breaking the law would inevitably result in harsh punishment. Scholars have discovered that the deity Nemesis, who is a spirit of justified vengeance and retribution for crimes, was closely associated with the Roman arena. This suggests that the killing of the criminals at least was viewed as the enactment of appropriate retributive justice against those who threatened the social order. Originally, such executions were held in the Forum, the center of commercial, political, and legal activity in Rome; the transposition to the arena signifies, on one level at any rate, a desire to make the executions visible to larger groups of witnesses. It also removed the condemned individuals to a separate space of containment, cleansing the public space of undesirable criminal elements. That these executions could be entertaining was probably an unexpected "bonus"; once that was discovered, however, Roman political leaders and ambitious politicians were happy to exploit its potential for winning popular support. It was more the Roman genius for organization and commercial exploitation that turned these events into entertainment, then, than an innate desire to watch acts of cruelty and bloodshed for their own sake.

What about the gladiators? Although perhaps the best known of all participants in arena events, and undoubtedly the ones to whom the most mystique is attached, the gladiators really constitute a different class altogether. The term *gladiator* is often used without much discrimination to refer to anyone who fought or died in the arena, but it actually refers to a specific kind of combatant: one who was trained in a special school to the point where his fighting skills were honed to the highest level of military readiness. Discipline was harsh, and the training was brutal in the extreme, but the trainees were well fed and received excellent medical care. The echoes of Roman military training are obvious. In fact, it is likely that there would not have been gladiators in ancient Rome at all without the Roman military tradition. The Roman state was built up and held together through military conquest, and this was achieved through armies of conscripted citizen soldiers. Training for battle and learning to handle weapons in offensive and defensive moves were considered necessary skills for the Roman male: his family, property, community, and life depended on these skills. It is notable that many of the arena spectacles had strong military connections; for instance, games were often held in conjunction with Triumphs to celebrate significant victories in the field. The mock battles we hear about were probably performed to mark the end of a successful campaign, and maybe to "narrate" it, as well as to prepare the onlookers for the next one that would inevitably follow on its heels. In an era when the means of mass communication were extremely limited, the public spectacle took on enormous significance as the bearer of information about battles and victories, conquered peoples and territories, and the meaning of imperial power. It is in this context, then, that we should consider the figure of the gladiator and his central importance in Roman culture.

The gladiator, unlike the animals or the criminals that were ruthlessly cut down or tortured to death, occupied an ambiguous position in the eyes of spectators. On the one hand, since many gladiators were prisoners of war or criminals who had been condemned to the arena as punishment, they were viewed as outcasts, as vivid manifestations of the despised "other" against which the Roman state defined itself. The gladiator was an "infamous" figure, little more than human refuse, deserving nothing better than complete dehumanization and death in full view of his betters. On the other hand, because they had been trained in what was to all intents and purposes a Roman military school, and had acquired the skills and, more importantly, the courage of the ideal Roman soldier, they were simultaneously regarded as manifestations of the virtuous warrior. The gladiators embodied spectacularly, on one level, the discipline and virtue that characterized the Roman citizen soldier. Hence, their actions in the arena were watched with an eye to detail that bordered on obsession among the spectators. Every move was scrutinized and particular attention was paid to whether the gladiator flinched or blinked at any point in the action: he was trained not to show any fear or hesitation in the face of danger. The gladiator was, then, both something closely related to the self and something at the same time radically other. The fascination he exerted upon the spectators depended upon this ambiguity, which was not present in the case of the animals or the condemned criminals.

Gladiators became increasingly specialized over time, and varieties of fighters proliferated: Samnites, Thracians, Gauls, "net-men" *(retiarii)*, and many others. Some categories appear to have been derived from the fighting methods or armor used by particular tribes against whom the Romans had fought. Great care was taken to match combatants with appropriate adversaries, so as to guarantee a spectacular fight. Thus, for example, a lightly clad net-man would never fight another net-man; he would face a heavily armed, but less mobile, Samnite. The arrangements were far from haphazard: everything had to be thoroughly planned and thought out in advance. It was also important for the trainer and the producer to get their money's worth, and not simply squander valuable resources. We know that gladiators did not always die in the arena. It has been estimated that anywhere from one in five, to one in two, was likely to die on any given day. There was a brand of fight called "without any survivor" *(sine missione)*, but this was rather rare, and the Emperor Augustus, in fact, banned such events (although they were later reintroduced and offered as an especially lavish gift on a special occasion). The relatively good survival rate, at least in the short term, may have had something to do with the high monetary value of a good gladiator in whom much time and training had been invested by his owner. It was not sensible to waste the best fighters, and their popularity with the crowds could be exploited for profit. We also hear of several gladiators who stayed alive long enough to reach retirement status, and were discharged with a ceremonial wooden sword. Some gladiators are even said to have earned sufficient funds to purchase their freedom and leave the arena. Thus, a gladiator could, by manifesting exceptional courage and skill, change his status from despised outcast to popular hero and return from "social death" to be reintegrated into the citizen body. Excellence in this case brought a tangible reward, and was interpreted as a symbolic triumph over death, recalling the sacrificial elements mentioned above. The thrill of seeing such exceptional cases may have been an important element in the popularity of the games with the audience. It added to the excitement of the unexpected, upon which the success of the spectacle depended.

The gladiator embodied, or had the potential to embody, the cardinal Roman virtue of courage in the face of danger and death, as well as a form of noble self-mastery, that harked back to what were remembered as the glorious days of the republic. The gladiator's willingness to die recalled the heroic self-sacrifice, or *devotio,* of the best republican generals, who died with their honor intact. Thus, the spectators were gazing nostalgically upon an idealized version of their history as well as an entertaining spectacle in the present. This may explain why some freeborn citizens or freedmen voluntarily enlisted as gladiators, although more were probably driven to do so because of bad debts or poverty. They "contracted" or "conscripted" themselves for a set period of time, assuming the servile status of gladiators. Ancient authors rarely praise these volunteers, but the existence of the practice does demonstrate that the arena was more than a pit of certain death. Legal measures prohibiting such contracts suggest, moreover, that they were not uncommon. Thus, we can see that in the case of the gladiators, the rigid border between the viewers in the seats and the combatants in the sand became permeable. For all these reasons, then, the picture of the Roman arena is a complex one, and it is too simplistic to conclude that it was "pure pandering" to the blood lust of the mob.

–DAVID H. J. LARMOUR,
TEXAS TECH UNIVERSITY

References

Roland Auguet, *Cruelty and Civilization: The Roman Games* (New York: Routledge, 1994).

Carlin Barton, *The Sorrows of the Ancient Romans: The Gladiator and the Monster* (Princeton: Princeton University Press, 1993).

Richard C. Beacham, *Spectacle Entertainments of Early Imperial Rome* (New Haven: Yale University Press, 1999).

Michael B. Hornum, *Nemesis, the Roman State, and the Games* (Leiden: Brill, 1993).

Donald G. Kyle, *Spectacles of Death in Ancient Rome* (New York: Routledge, 1998).

John Pearson, *Arena: The Story of the Colosseum* (New York: McGraw-Hill, 1973).

Paul Veyne, *Bread and Circuses: Historical Sociology and Political Pluralism,* translated by B. Pearce (London: Allen Lane, 1990).

Thomas Wiedemann, *Emperors and Gladiators* (New York: Routledge, 1992).

ROMAN PERIOD: OVID

Does Ovid's exilic poetry represent a principled resistance to imperial tyranny?

Viewpoint: Yes. In his exilic poetry Ovid subtly criticizes the ambitions of the emperor Augustus.

Viewpoint: No. Although his exilic poetry is full of ambiguities, Ovid acknowledges and accepts the power and authority of Rome.

In 7 C.E., Ovid was summoned to Augustus and sent into exile at Tomis on the Black Sea. The causes of his banishment are shrouded in mystery. He lists two: "carmen et error" (poetry and a mistake, *Tristia* 2.207). The "mistake" was something he was not permitted to discuss. He tells us he saw something that he should have reported but did not. It is generally believed that either he witnessed one of the sexual indiscretions for which Augustus's granddaughter, Julia, was exiled, or had knowledge of the intrigues surrounding the imperial succession at the end of Augustus's reign. Beyond that, nothing can be said. The "poetry" in question, however, can be clearly identified as the *Ars Amatoria,* Ovid's humorous manual of seduction.

The exilic poetry consists of two primary collections, the *Tristia* and the *Epistulae ex Ponto.* The *Tristia* presents a speaker who is at times reminiscent of Ovid's earlier poetry. In the first two books, he is witty and urbane. He recognizes Augustus's authority but is not above deflating it with a double entendre. The last three books of the *Tristia* and the four books of the *Epistulae ex Ponto* are progressively more somber.

This poetry has not been widely read in the twentieth century. The complaints of exile, however moving, become tedious after a time. Ovid's wheedling before Augustus can be unseemly. Recently, however, several scholars have argued that there is more to these poems than meets the eye. The poet's compliments to Augustus can be read as thinly disguised barbs and his apologies as indictments.

Augustus, of course, need not have ever read Ovid's exilic poetry at all. Augustus can refuse to play Ovid's rhetorical game and simply leave him in Tomis until his death in 17 C.E. The years go by, and every year Ovid writes another volume of verse. Each is met with stony silence on the part of both the emperor and his successor, Tiberius. Yet, not one of those volumes is suppressed. Ovid is still allowed to write and publish. In fact, he was exiled to Tomis under the terms of what was called a *relegatio* rather than *exilium,* which meant that he kept his citizen's rights and property. He simply was not allowed to leave Tomis. As such, he was able to serve simultaneously as an example of Augustus's clemency toward his enemies and his implacable anger. Thus, even those passages where the poet seems to resist imperial dominance can also be read as underwriting the emerging absolutist system. As such, this poetry is now the subject of some controversy. While some wish to rehabilitate these poems as a noble act of covert resistance to tyranny through the poet's sheer rhetorical brilliance, others see in these same poems a willingness to accede to the demands of empire and abject capitulation before the seats of power.

—*Paul Allen Miller*

Viewpoint:
Yes. In his exilic poetry Ovid subtly criticizes the ambitions of the emperor Augustus.

Ovid's exilic poetry, far from representing a capitulation to Augustan imperial ambition, is a vast hall of mirrors in which every statement turns into its opposite. Each moment of seeming flattery is instantly undercut by a vicious satirical jibe. Each moment of abject sycophancy becomes an accusation of tyranny and a sly assault on imperial absolutism. This can perhaps best be seen in *Tristia* 2, Ovid's book-length defense of his life and art from the charges *(carmen et error)* that had led to his *relegatio.*

In this poem, perhaps more than any other, Ovid chooses to speak the truth to power (Williams 1994: 161–162). In what pretends to be both an act of contrition and an *apologia pro vita,* the poet launches into something closer to a satirical diatribe (Kenney 1983: 150). Thus, while the poem's speaker superficially seems not to be attacking but praising the emperor, nonetheless, as Jo-Marie Claassen notes, "excessive adulation and lip-service to the emperor's ideal of national poetry, and also many examples of *praeteritio* create an atmosphere of criticism" (1989: 265).

Ovid's exilic poetry in general, and *Tristia* 2 in particular, are constructed through a series of complex intertextual appropriations that allude not only to his own earlier offending works, particularly the *Ars Amatoria* (Art of Love), but also to Horace and the Callimachean tradition of the *recusatio,* or "poem of refusal." This latter form, as perfected by the Augustan elegists and Horace, entails the poet's claim to have been invited to write an epic poem in praise of a given patron or the *princeps* (first citizen, Augustus's euphemistic title). The poet politely declines, alleging a lack of ability in the epic genre. At the same time, he normally gives specimens of precisely the kind of verse he claims not to have been able to produce.

This is exactly what Ovid does when he argues that he had tried to write an epic in praise of Augustus but was unable:

> But if you were to order me to tell how the Giants were tamed
> By Jove's fire, the burden would be too great.
> To raise up the great acts of Caesar requires a rich vein
> Of genius, or the work will be conquered by its matter.
> And even so I tried. But I seemed to detract from,
> and what is worse, be a positive blemish to your virtues. (*Tristia* 2.332–338)

This passage nicely captures the double meanings intrinsic to the form. The *recusatio* is a peculiarly double-voiced kind of poem that simultaneously articulates resistance to the demands of a powerful patron, deference to those demands, and a subtle demonstration that that deference is feigned. Thus, in the passage just cited, Ovid first gives us a taste of traditional panegyric epic. Augustus is implicitly pictured as Jupiter smiting the rebellious Giants with his thunderbolt, an image the poet often uses for the *princeps's* wrath toward himself. At the same time, Ovid also claims to have been unable to produce a poem that would have been worthy of its subject. Yet, the real reason for Ovid's failure may be less a lack of innate ability–difficult to believe in one of antiquity's most gifted versifiers–than an incapacity to praise what is unworthy.

This way of reading these lines becomes more persuasive when we recognize that the whole passage consists of an elaborate series of puns. Thus, the middle couplet, while certainly able to bear the laudatory construction presented in the translation above, could equally well be translated: "to bury the monstrous acts of Caesar requires a rich vein of genius, or the work will be conquered by its matter." In this case, the latter part of the last line means not so much that Augustus's greatness will overwhelm Ovid's meager talent, as that if Ovid's epic voice is not able to hide the monstrosity of Augustan rule, his work will be crushed by Augustus. In short, how do you write the praises of a despot without showing him to be a despot? By the same token, the last couplet could just as easily be read to say: "no matter how hard I try, whenever I try to praise you it sounds like blame" as "I seemed to detract from, and what is worse, be a positive blemish to your virtues."

The use of the *recusatio* thus implicates the poet in a tradition in which poets never quite say what they mean when addressing the seat of power. The intertextual precedent of that tradition and the frequent allusions to other poems throughout the exilic corpus invite us to perceive precisely such ambiguities and ironies. Ovid in this poem is most himself when he appears to means the opposite of what he says. He is most authentic when he dresses his thought in the words of others. The Ovidian voice constructed by and through the *Tristia* thus becomes the perfect metaphor for the subjection of and resistance to empire.

Indeed, as the poet himself notes throughout these poems, he is in a real sense dead (Williams 1994: 12–13; Claassen 1988: 168). The question of sincerity, on this level, is beside the point. The poet here can only mean what he says on one level on the condition that on another he does not. Thus, at *Tristia* 2.287 the poet argues that the *Ars Amatoria* is no more to blame for vice than other Roman institutions that are equally susceptible of misuse. These institutions include temples themselves, and he says with a wink, "quis locus est templis augustior?" (What place is more august than temples). The passage is susceptible to two logically–but not rhetorically–mutually exclusive readings. The first, which I would label the literal, reads the statement as being essentially tautological, "what place is more holy than temples." This would have been the only interpretation of *augustior* prior to Octavian receiving his honorific cognomen, *Augustus,* from the Senate in 27 B.C.E.

The second or ironic reading sees a pun on Augustus's name and notes the wit of associating the emperor with places of possible seduction, particularly in a poem that seeks to defend its author against charges of corrupting the morals of young women. According to this interpretation, Ovid is no more to blame for the misuse of the *Ars Amatoria* than Augustus is for the seductions that occur in august temples. This reading gains in depth when we realize that the temples the poet names were all constructed or reconstructed by the *princeps* and noted in the *Res Gestae* (an official list of accomplishments) as among his proudest achievements in rebuilding the city and reestablishing traditional religion (Williams 1994: 202). Thus, what could be more like Augustus, *augustior,* than these temples that he himself caused to be built or refurbished? And it is precisely this play on words that also allows the line to be read as a form of flattery that provides the poet with a much-needed plausible deniability should he be charged with insulting Augustus. Ovid, according to this flattering reading, merely defends the *Ars Amatoria* in its own terms and says even the holiest of places, those most associated with the *princeps,* are subject to misuse and misinterpretation (Evans 1983: 16–17).

The key thing to recognize is not that we must choose between these last two readings, as the vast majority of criticism of the exilic poetry has done (Evans 1983: 10–11), but that on the most basic level they are the same. They are both fundamentally ironic insofar as they directly undermine the literal reading. This undercutting reading gains in cogency when the reader recognizes that the temples and porticoes mentioned in the passage are precisely those listed in the *Ars Amatoria* as ideal places to pick up girls (*A.A.* 1.67–262; Williams 1994: 202–203). In the *Ars Amatoria,* the entire Augustan building plan is appropriated for erotic purposes (Edwards 1996: 24). Indeed, critics have in the past interpreted this passage in the *Tristia* as a covert attack on "Augustus' well-known sensuality" (Holleman 1969: 54), for Suetonius notes that not only was Augustus known as a practiced adulterer, but his wife Livia often played the procurer for him.

Moreover, the whole point of *Tristia* 2's defense of the *Ars Amatoria* is that works "rarely succeed in having only the consequences their creators intended. . . . The readings of a poem . . . cannot be controlled by the author; the interpretations of a monument cannot be controlled by the builder" (Edwards 1996: 25). The same kind of "misreading" that sees the *Ars Amatoria* as a source of vice would also claim that the temples themselves cause the seductions that take place within their precincts. Ovid is no more to blame for corrupting the morals of Rome's women than Augustus himself! This is hardly an innocent statement. To "misread" Ovid's recollection of the *Ars Amatoria* in *Tristia* 2's catalogue of temples as anti-Augustan is to perform the same "misreading" as those who would accuse Augustus of promoting seduction by building the temples in which it occurs.

Ovid is even so generous as to provide exemplary misreadings of the temples by an imaginary perverse *matrona.* Thus in *Tristia* 2.295–296 we find "venerit in magni templum, tua munera, Martis, / stat Venus Ultori iuncta, vir ante fores" (she will have come into the temple of great Mars, your gift, Venus stands joined to the avenger, her husband before the door). The temple of *Mars Ultor,* dedicated in 2 B.C.E., was vowed by Augustus in return for his victory over the assassins of Julius Caesar. It featured a statue of Venus, the patron deity of the Julian clan, joined with that of Mars in an allegorical representation of the alliance of the power of war to the imperial clan's patron goddess. This would be the literal reading and its flattering gloss. *Iuncta,* however, can have sexual connotations, being from the same root as the English "conjugal." The ironic reading, thus, has Venus and Mars engaged in an act of sexual congress (Traill 1992: 505–506). *Vir,* moreover, refers to Vulcan, a representation of whom was placed outside the temple. Venus's husband is here reduced to the figure of the "locked-out lover," a traditional character in the kind of erotic poetry the writing of which got Ovid in trouble in the first place. Nonetheless, what we have here is also an accurate description of a perfectly pious temple, erected for the glory of Augustus and his clan (Traill 1992: 506–507). The ironic vision of Venus and Mars engaged in sexual intercourse before the helpless eyes of Venus's rightful husband, however, makes the literal reading a dead letter and cannot have been meant to please a ruler who prided himself on the moral restoration of Rome.

Tristia 2, however, is not the only poem in the exilic works to feature such damning double

ARS AMATORIA

You, who in Cupid's roll inscribe your name,
First seek an object worthy of your flame;
Then strive, with art, your lady's mind to gain;
And last, provide your love may long remain.
On these three precepts all my work shall move:
These are the rules and principles of love.
Before your youth with marriage is oppress't,
Make choice of one who suits your humour best
And such a damsel drops not from the sky;
She must be sought for with a curious eye.
The wary angler, in the winding brook,
Knows what the fish, and where to bait his hook.
The fowler and the huntsman know by name
The certain haunts and harbour of their game.
So must the lover beat the likeliest grounds;
Th' Assemblies where his quarries most abound:
Nor shall my novice wander far astray;
These rules shall put him in the ready way.
Thou shalt not fail around the continent,
As far as Perseus or as Paris went:
For Rome alone affords thee such a store,
As all the world can hardly shew thee more.
The face of heav'n with fewer stars is crown'd,
Than beauties in the Roman sphere are found.
Whether thy love is bent on blooming youth,
On dawning sweetness, in unartful truth;
Or courts the juicy joys of riper growth;
Here may'st thou find thy full desires in both:
Or if autumnal beauties please thy sight
(An age that knows to give and take delight;)
Millions of matrons, of the graver sort,
In common prudence, will not balk the sport.
In summer's heats thou need'st but only go
To Pompey's cool and shady portico;
Or Concord's fane; or that proud edifice
Whose turrets near the bawdy suburbs rise;
Or to that other portico, where stands
The cruel father urging his commands.
And fifty daughters wait the time of rest,
To plunge their poniards in the bridegroom's
breast.
Or Venus' temple; where, on annual nights,
They mourn Adonis with Assyrian rites.
Nor shun the Jewish walk, where the foul drove
On sabbaths rest from everything but love.
Nor Isis' temple; for that sacred whore
Makes others, what to Jove she was before;
And if the hall itself be not belied,
E'en there the cause of love is often tried;
Near it at least, or in the palace yard,
From whence the noisy combatants are heard.
The crafty counsellors, in formal gown,
There gain another's cause, but lose their own.
Their eloquence is nonpluss'd in the suit;
And lawyers, who had words at will, are mute.
Venus from her adjoining temple smiles
To see them caught in their litigious wiles;
Grave senators lead home the youthful dame,
Returning clients when they patrons came.
But above all, the Playhouse is the place;
There's choice of quarry in that narrow chace:
There take thy stand, and sharply looking out,
Soon may'st thou find a mistress in the rout,
For length of time or for a single bout.
The Theatres are berries for the fair;
Like ants or mole-hills thither they repair;
Like bees to hives so numerously they throng,
It may be said they to that place belong:
Thither they swarm who have the public voice;
There choose, if plenty not distracts thy choice.
To see, and to be seen, in heaps they run;
Some to undo, and some to be undone.

Source: *Ars Amatoria 1.40–110, in* Ovid's Art of Love, in Three Books, *translated by John Dryden and others (London: Printed for Jacob and Richard Tonson, 1764).*

meanings. Another example can be found at *Tristia* 4.4.13–16:

> ipse pater patriae (quid enim est civilius illo?)
> sustinet in nostro carmine saepe legi,
> nec prohibere potest, quia res est publica Caesar,
> et de communi pars quoque nostra bono est.
>
> [The father of our country himself (for what is more public/civil/like a citizen than that?) allows himself often to be read in our poetry, nor is he able to prohibit it, because Caesar is public property and part of our common wealth.]

The pun on *civilius* ("more public / more civil / more like a citizen") in the context of the initial rhetorical question possesses the exact same structure as that on *augustior*. The literal reading would be essentially tautological: what could be more characteristic of the Roman *civitas* or "community," and hence of civic identity, than the *pater patriae* or "father of the country," another honorific title bestowed upon Augustus? The ironic reading would be the acknowledgment of the tautology and the recognition that the city is now being defined as much in terms of Augustus as vice versa. The flattering reading would then attribute the virtues of civility and civilization to the *princeps* who is the *pater patriae* and therefore both the reflection of the city and the source of that reflection's meaning. The ironic and the flattering reading thus fold into one another so that each only makes sense in terms of the other. There is no reading here that even momentarily pictures Caesar as anything other than an absolute ruler, and there is more than a passing flirtation with an accusation of despotism. Augustus is the source from which the meaning of being a *civis,* or "citizen," derives. This same reading is confirmed in the next couplet, where the clause "res est publica Caesar" can be translated in three different fashions: the literal, "Caesar is public property"; the ironic, "Caesar is the republic"; and the flattering, "Caesar is the public sphere." This couplet clearly gives the lie to one of Caesar's favorite notions, that he had "restored the republic." He did not restore the traditional constitution but rather made the republic his own.

In short, then, while certain passages in the exilic poetry can be read as flattering, or even sycophantic, in every case those same passages can be read as ironic. Ovid, then, far from capitulating to Augustus's imperial ambitions, becomes one of his sharpest critics. The exilic poetry is a hall of mirrors in which every piece of flattery instantly is transformed into its opposite.

—PAUL ALLEN MILLER,
UNIVERSITY OF SOUTH CAROLINA

Viewpoint:
No. Although his exilic poetry is full of ambiguities, Ovid acknowledges and accepts the power and authority of Rome.

Many readers have been troubled by the seeming artificiality of Ovid's poetry. It is with audible relief then that many critics turn from this artificial world to the exilic poetry. Yes, it can be repetitive, and even whining, but here readers since Aleksandr Pushkin claim to hear the accents of authenticity. Here poet and persona coincide as never before. Here we have a truly personal poetry (Dickinson 1973: 158). Here the poet at last is forced to address the objective circumstances of his actual life, cast alone upon the shores of the Black Sea, the victim of his own genius and imperial fury. Here he is forced to recognize that there is only one person who can save him from his fate, the *princeps,* or "first citizen," a traditional title appropriated by Augustus to mask the extraconstitutional nature of his power. If Ovid quakes before Augustus as a god, although we may detect at times a wry smile, Ovid nonetheless recognizes and proclaims in a direct and unmistakable way the reality of imperial power. In so doing, he effectively underwrites it.

Ovid in his exilic poetry, as in his earlier amorous verse, is once again a jilted lover. Ovid in exile is longing for Rome: the cultural, literary, and political capital where his star had once brightly shone. He is an unhappy lover singing before the locked door that stands between him and the object of his desire. Now, however, what the poet seeks is not the charms of a *docta puella* (learned girl), as was the case in his previous works, the *Amores* and the *Ars Amatoria,* but Rome and Augustus (Claassen 1999: 89; Edwards 1996: 118). At *Epistulae ex Ponto* 2.7.38, the poet shows himself standing before the "closed door" of Rome, while in *Epistulae ex Ponto* 1.7.35–38 he fears that the house of Messalinus, the son of his former patron, has become closed to him through a "misplaced" fear of Caesar's wrath. Finally, at *Tristia* 3.2.21–24 we find the distraught poet tormented by his desire for Rome and for his home, while locked out before the door of death that would provide the ultimate respite from his pain.

There is then a certain cogency to the naive representational reading. The "Ovid" who stands plaintively before the door of death (*Tristia* 3.2.21–24) does represent the persona of the unhappy lover, so familiar from Ovid's earlier erotic verse. Only the object of desire has changed from an imaginary literary object, the conventional beloved of erotic elegy, to Rome itself. Yet, this coincidence of the poet and his previous persona cannot be taken at face value as the index of an unambiguous sincerity. Rather, it is the traumatic trace of Ovid's death to the civic community of Rome (Claassen 1999: 239–240). In these poems the subject of Latin love elegy has been exiled to a world beyond the living. He has been cast into limbo. His existence now is spectral. He no longer prowls the streets of Rome as a poet and lover but lives on in the realm of the dead (*Tristia* 3.11.25–26), or, more properly, in the world of those who cannot die (*Epistulae ex Ponto* 1.2.37–38). He is neither of our world, nor the next. In Tomis he lives the life of one who has become an emblem of absolute subjection to imperial power (*Tristia* 4.1.41–44). He is excluded from Rome and the publicly recognized system of cultural and political honors and hence from what defines life for the glitterati of this first generation of empire. From this otherworldly state only a god could save him: Augustus.

Yet, his death-like existence is also what makes his salvation at the hands of the *princeps* possible. The realm conjured by the *Tristia* and the *Epistulae ex Ponto* is one in which Augustus is both the poet's only savior and the true cause of his damnation. He must, therefore, be approached with care. The *princeps* is at the center of a new cultural universe. He occupies the apex of a pyramid of interlocking ties in which individuals are recognized as subjects only to the extent that

***Portrait of Ovid;* painting by Luca Signorelli, circa 1475–1523**

(© Archivo Iconografico, S.A./ CORBIS)

they are subordinated to his authority. The *princeps* comes to define the very meaning of the phrase, "sum civis Romanus" (I am a Roman citizen). Citizenship has become synonymous with subjection.

The omnipresence of the *princeps* in the *Tristia* and *Epistulae ex Ponto* is almost suffocating, even as he is simultaneously half a world away. He is present and absent, inside and outside, the cause and cure of Ovid's plight. Augustus in the exilic poetry is called the *pater patriae,* or "father of the country" (*Tristia* 2.39, 2.181, 2.574, 4.4.13), and in this apotheosis of the paternal function he leaves no place for his would-be heirs, except that of imaginary identification with the community of which the *princeps* has become the image (Videau-Delibes 1991: 250). Ovid and his peers can never aspire to assuming a position of independent communal symbolic recognition that is not simultaneously one of recognized submission to the center of authority. To the extent that Ovid has any remaining cultural capital, it is because Augustus allows him to have it.

Augustan political culture, as portrayed in the exilic poetry, is a series of concentric circles orbiting around a single center. The principate, as the early empire is known, had abolished the complex world of late republican factional politics, with its competing loyalties, shifting alliances, and space for individual maneuver. Thus, in *Epistulae ex Ponto* 1.7.21–22, addressed to the son of the poet's former patron Messalla Corvinus, M. Valerius Messalla Messalinus, Ovid asks, "What person of any note does not *fashion* himself to be a friend to the Caesars? Have pity on one who is weary. You were my Caesar." This seemingly innocuous bit of flattery to a potential patron is revealing. The self of the principate is one that must be produced. You must fashion yourself into one of Caesar's friends. No one assumes such a process to be natural, nor is sincerity a prerequisite. Rather, the adoption of a determined-subject position by members of the aristocracy is the mark by which Caesar's power is affirmed. The factitious nature of this process of subjectivation and subjection is manifest to all. That, in fact, is the strongest proof of its efficacy. In the republican period, the institution of aristocratic *amicitia* (friendship) had been founded on an ideology of reciprocity that served to smooth over status differences and reinforce a feeling of mutual obligation. Yet, there could be no reciprocity in this world in which the *princeps'* friends must refashion themselves to accept imperial subjection. Messalinus must *make* himself into Caesar's friend, and in so doing he explicitly subjects himself to the latter's power. The mask of mutual service and reciprocity has been removed. Ovid, in turn, must do the same in relation to Messalinus.

An analogous picture of multiple levels of personal subordination gathered round a single center is painted in *Epistulae ex Ponto* 1.9 addressed to Cotta Maximus, Messalinus's brother. A poem on the death of the poet Albinovanus Celsus, *epistle* 1.9 asks Cotta to show the same care for Ovid that he has for Celsus (1.9.55–56). The most important image for us, however, comes early in the poem (1.9.35–36). There, while telling how Celsus sought Cotta's patronage, Ovid calls Cotta's home a temple where Celsus practiced certain rites. These are the same rites that Cotta observes in the imperial household. This depiction, even if undercut by Ovid's subtle wit, both alludes to the cult of emperor worship and casts Celsus and Ovid in relation to Cotta in the same roles as Cotta assumes in relation to Augustus. Ovid therefore submits himself to Cotta, as *dominus,* or "lord," just as Cotta subjects himself to the "lord of the earth." The empire is a world in which everyone must know his place. Ovid will assume his, and, through the example of his poetry, he will teach others to do the same.

In *Epistulae ex Ponto* 2.2.121–124, Ovid paints his most explicit portrait of this new model of the individual's relation to imperial power. This letter is addressed to Messalinus. Ovid hopes the son of Messalla Corvinus will now become his patron, too. He portrays the young aristocrat as a priest who has the power to transmit the poet's prayers to Augustus, the living god. This is a model of patronage as divine intercession. Its import is made clear in *epistle* 2.3's reference to Cotta as the *princeps* of the poet's friends (*Epistulae ex Ponto* 2.3.31–32). Ovid's relation to the brothers, Cotta and Messallinus, is thus analogous to their relationship to Caesar. As he is a god to them so they embody and mediate the divine for him:

> Since we are removed a world away from the fatherland, we are not allowed to prostrate ourselves before the gods themselves, whom you worship. As a priest bear these requests to the immortals, but add also your own prayers to my words. (*Epistulae ex Ponto* 2.2.121–124).

In exile, Ovid is twice removed from the divine presence that offers legal and symbolic legitimation. He can only approach it indirectly. At the center of the vast web of social, political, and personal relations that constitutes Roman imperial society is Augustus, who has been transformed into a living god (Claassen 1999: 227).

We should, of course, not lose our sense of humor. From a traditional republican perspective, there is no small irony in Ovid's depiction of the imperial family as the gods of the earth. Nor can the implicit accusation that the *princeps* has transformed the rest of Rome, including the noble sons of Messalla, into virtual slaves be disregarded (Williams 1994: 158; Videau-Delibes 1991: 233–234). *Servus,* or "slave," is the ideological corollary to *dominus,* or "lord." One cannot say the one without implying the other. Nonetheless, the question must be posed: how is that irony functionally distinguishable from flattering acceptance? For the poet, far from proposing an alternative, accepts the Augustan settlement as, if not inherently right, then at least necessary.

Indeed, at *Epistulae ex Ponto* 2.1.17–18, a poem on Tiberius's triumph over the Dalmatians in 12 C.E., Ovid observes that "the joys of Caesar's mind are my own to the utmost of my ability: that house has nothing private." The flattering intent of the couplet cannot be denied. Yet, it also possesses subtler implications. Let us concentrate on the final clause. Two additional layers of meaning have a claim on our attention here. On one level this statement means that Caesar's *domus* (house) is the public face of Rome. It is not the mere household of a private citizen occupying a political office in the polity. It is the embodiment of the new Roman order. The *pater patriae* is the ground of our imaginary identity. On another level, if Caesar's *domus* has nothing private, if it is completely public and constitutes the totality of what is defined as public, then the rest of the population no longer has any share in the *res publica* (the republic but also, literally, the common-wealth). Caesar has become the state. "As the poet says in *Tristia* 4.4.15, 'res est publica Caesar' ('Caesar is the republic'). He is the state. To the extent that public life continues to have meaning in Rome, it does so only through Caesar. Caesar has nothing private because the *res publica* is Caesar" (Miller 2004: 217).

What the exilic poetry reveals, therefore, in spite of Ovid's irony and rhetorical dexterity, is that what it means to be a Roman citizen has inalterably changed. Ovid does not so much resist this new concept and practice of *Romanitas* as he codifies it. At *Epistulae ex Ponto* 2.8.19–20, Ovid celebrates receiving from Cotta two pictures of the imperial family (Claassen 1999: 285n.99). He sets them up as images to be worshiped and declares, "as long as I look at this man (i.e., Augustus), I seem to make out Rome, for he maintains the appearance of his fatherland." Once again, the *princeps* is the living image of the *res publica.* The whole scene possesses an element of the comic and the absurd, with Ovid worshiping the pictures of people whom he has known personally as all-too-flawed humans.

Nonetheless, as Peter Green notes, the equation of Caesar with Rome was hardly an aberration. Rather, it directly invokes one of the tenets of imperial Stoicism, "which virtually equated the Roman Empire (symbolized in the person of the Princeps) with the eternal divine cosmos controlling the world" (1994: 326). The later Stoics may have resisted Nero and Domitian, but their simultaneous equation of the state with the cosmic order, and their nurturing of a realm of personal freedom apart from the uncertainties of political engagement, made them the perfect model for a new conception of what it means to be a Roman citizen. It is this model whose first exemplar can be glimpsed in the exilic poetry. Ovid may suggest that the new face of Rome is founded on absolutist subjection and even depict the absurdity of worshiping one's masters as idols, but he also maintains that these new masters *are* the face of Rome and these *are* the gods we will now worship. No alternative model proposed. None is even conceivable. In the end, Julio-Claudian supremacy is accepted at "face" value (Green 1994: 325; Evans 1983: 25).

–PAUL ALLEN MILLER,
UNIVERSITY OF SOUTH CAROLINA

References

Jo-Marie Claassen, "Carmen and Poetics: Poetry as Enemy and Friend," in *Studies in Latin Literature and Roman History,* volume 5, edited by Carl Deroux (Brussels: Collection Latomus, 1989), pp. 252–266.

Claassen, *Displaced Persons: The Literature of Exile from Cicero to Boethius* (Madison: University of Wisconsin Press, 1999).

Claassen, "Ovid's Poems from Exile: The Creation of a Myth and the Triumph of Poetry," *Antike und Abendland,* 34 (1988): 158–169.

R. J. Dickinson, "The *Tristia:* Poetry in Exile," in *Ovid,* edited by J. W. Binns (London: Routledge & Kegan Paul, 1973), pp. 154–190.

Catherine Edwards, *Writing Rome: Textual Approaches to the City* (Cambridge: Cambridge University Press, 1996).

Harry B. Evans, *Carmina Publica: Ovid's Books from Exile* (Lincoln: University of Nebraska Press, 1983).

Peter Green, *Ovid: The Poems of Exile* (London: Penguin, 1994).

A. W. J. Holleman, "Ovidii Metamophoseon liber XV 622-870 *(Carmen et error),*" *Latomus,* 28 (1969): 42–59.

E. J. Kenney, "Ovid," in *The Cambridge History of Classical Literature,* volume 2, part 3, edited by Kenney and W. V. Clausen (Cambridge: Cambridge University Press, 1983), pp. 124–161.

Paul Allen Miller, *Subjecting Verses: Latin Love Elegy and the Emergence of the Real* (Princeton: Princeton University Press, 2004).

David A. Traill, "Ovid, *Tristia* 2.8, 296, and 507: Happier Solutions," *Hermes,* 120 (1992): 504–507.

Anne Videau-Delibes, *Les* Tristes *d'Ovide et l'élégie romaine: Une poétique de la rupture* (Paris: Klincksieck, 1991).

Gareth D. Williams, *Banished Voices: Readings in Ovid's Exile Poetry* (Cambridge: Cambridge University Press, 1994).

ROMAN PERIOD: OVID VERSUS VIRGIL

Has Ovid's *Metamorphoses* had a greater influence than Virgil's *Aeneid* on postclassical literature?

Viewpoint: Yes. Ovid's *Metamorphoses* has had a greater influence upon postclassical literature, as exemplified through its many translations and stage adaptations.

Viewpoint: No. Unlike Ovid's epic, whose main theme is indisputably metamorphosis, Virgil's *Aeneid* presents a nexus of themes that have supported a wide variety of interpretations.

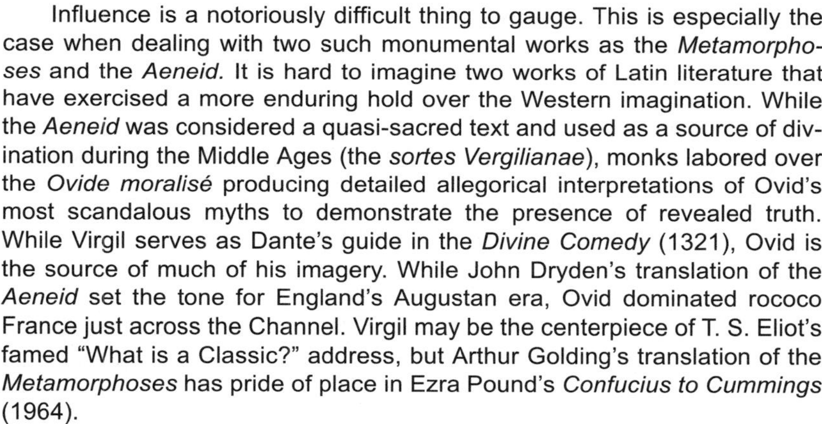

Influence is a notoriously difficult thing to gauge. This is especially the case when dealing with two such monumental works as the *Metamorphoses* and the *Aeneid.* It is hard to imagine two works of Latin literature that have exercised a more enduring hold over the Western imagination. While the *Aeneid* was considered a quasi-sacred text and used as a source of divination during the Middle Ages (the *sortes Vergilianae*), monks labored over the *Ovide moralisé* producing detailed allegorical interpretations of Ovid's most scandalous myths to demonstrate the presence of revealed truth. While Virgil serves as Dante's guide in the *Divine Comedy* (1321), Ovid is the source of much of his imagery. While John Dryden's translation of the *Aeneid* set the tone for England's Augustan era, Ovid dominated rococo France just across the Channel. Virgil may be the centerpiece of T. S. Eliot's famed "What is a Classic?" address, but Arthur Golding's translation of the *Metamorphoses* has pride of place in Ezra Pound's *Confucius to Cummings* (1964).

It is also hard to imagine two more different works. Although both texts lay claim to the title of *epic poetry,* the *Aeneid* is the original document of manifest destiny. It is a grand mythological synthesis, combining the stories and structure of the *Iliad* and the *Odyssey* into a single unified narrative designed to demonstrate both the costs and the necessity of the rise of Roman rule. The *Metamorphoses* in contrast is a great baroque cento of stories within stories. Claiming to present the entire history of the universe as a tale of change and transformation, it is filled with rapes, grotesque shape shifting, and restless wit both in and out of season.

The following two contributors in turn take different tacks in demonstrating their respective theses. Christel Johnson, arguing after the fashion of the 1980s pop song "Elvis Is Everywhere," demonstrates that Ovid is ubiquitous. In translation, on the stage, in the schools, in poetry and prose, the *Metamorphoses* and its author are an unfailing source of fascination from the Middle Ages to the present. Sarah Spence does not attempt to match Johnson citation for citation but rather argues that the *Metamorphoses* has a parasitic relation to the *Aeneid.* It assumes and is structured around the *Aeneid,* and thus wherever Ovid is, Virgil was always there first. Spence then provides a reading of William Shakespeare's most Ovidian piece, *A Midsummer Night's Dream* (circa 1595–1596), to document her case. She closes with a subtle disquisition on why Sigmund Freud cites Virgil, rather than Ovid, at the beginning of *The Interpretation of Dreams*

(1900). In the end, both Johnson and Spence may be right. Ovid is everywhere, and Virgil got there first.

—Paul Allen Miller

Viewpoint: Yes. Ovid's *Metamorphoses* has had a greater influence upon postclassical literature, as exemplified through its many translations and stage adaptations.

Ovid was already skilled in erotic elegiac verse when he composed the *Metamorphoses* in hexameters (the meter of epic) at the end of his career. In it, he offers the reader more than a traditional epic along the lines of the *Aeneid.* Ovid presents known myths through the lens of erotic exchange. In the *Metamorphoses,* humans are transformed into animals, minerals, and vegetables as the result of a struggle, either physical or emotional, relative to either their own or a god's passions. This monumental work, which speaks to us on an emotional and visceral as well as intellectual level, has exercised an unparalleled influence on postclassical literature for these reasons: its treatment of myth; the audience's fascination with the author himself; and the study and practice of translation.

Though Ovid was extremely popular throughout the Middle Ages, it was during the Renaissance that Ovidian translation came into its own. Thomas Howell (1560) and Thomas Peend (1565) both translated excerpts of the *Metamorphoses* into Elizabethan English. Yet, beyond doubt, the most influential, complete translation from this period was that of Arthur Golding; his complete edition was first published in 1567 and commanded four more printings. As Raphael Lyne observes,

> His translation is undoubtedly a monument: read by Shakespeare and Spenser, it conveys a spirited Ovid with all his range of emotion and diversity of plot. It is a monument which may well have amused Ovid greatly. The urbanity which suffuses Ovid's work is sometimes accompanied by a kind of detachment: not a cool lack of emotion, but rather an enigmatic distancing of feeling which is the consequence of consummately witty artistry. Golding encounters stories in a very different way, delivering every twist and turn in as whole-hearted a manner as possible. (2002, 252).

Golding's translation served as an inspiration for others who were interested in more creative appropriations of Ovid's epic such as William Shakespeare and Edmund Spenser. His text also proved that a classical work could be translated in such a way as to speak to a contemporary audience while maintaining the spirit of the original.

George Sandys' *Ovid's Metamorphosis Englished, Mythologiz'd, and Represented in Figures* (1632) was impressive in its own right. A more formal work, this text was accompanied by full illustrations. Sandys, unlike Golding, produced a translation that did not indulge in contemporary colloquialism. Following both Golding and Sandys, Samuel Garth printed a translation in the eighteenth century. This version is a compilation of several poets' texts: the most famous contributor was John Dryden. Garth's version lacks the continuity and focus of previous translations. Still, Lyne (2002, 256) describes this text as "grandiose" and claims Garth's greatest ingenuity was "in deploying the efforts of Dryden, Addison, Tate, Gay, Pope, Congreve, and Rowe, as well as those of eleven others including himself."

The early-modern period was not the end of translation for the *Metamorphoses.* In 1994 David Slavitt completed *The Metamorphoses of Ovid, Translated Freely into Verse.* His primary goal, reminiscent of Golding, is to appeal to a contemporary audience. As Lyne notes (2002, 259):

> His anachronisms do not come across as punch lines partly because they are neatly contained within a generally successful attempt at English hexameters, but mostly because they have an Ovidian ability to supply vividness and ironic alienation at the same time. The features for which Slavitt is best known are his added notes of internal commentary, attacking or defending or categorizing what is being done, in some ways responding expansively to things which in the Latin poem are implied by negotiation with well-worn convention.

Slavitt engages the text on his own terms, unlike Allen Mandelbaum's translation (1995), which is truer to the original. The Loeb edition, born out of the use of Ovidian texts in grammar schools, remains indispensable for those who enjoy the benefit of both Latin and English text (Miller, 1984).

Ovid, however, was known not only through the reading of translations into English but also through the practice of translation in schools and universities. Young boys were introduced to Latin verse through Ovid in grammar school (Maslen 2000, 17). Students were expected to translate the text into English and render a Latin prose summary. This practice certainly pressed Ovid's tales of change upon the minds of young scholars. In order to seduce students, "biographies of Ovid, prefixed to editions of his poems from the 1490s, frequently relate that the poet himself was a reluctant pupil, who rebelled against his training in the law. Many of his readers and imitators presented Ovid as someone who you would want to read under the desk in the back row of the classroom" (Burrow 2002, 304). Naturally, this encouraged young men to get to know both author and text. Scholarly and popular translation of Ovid declined after the Renaissance, but Ovid's presence continued to be felt in classrooms. Throughout the nineteenth century, "translations of all Ovid's works appear in such exotically named series as Kelly's Classical Keys, Bohn's Classical Library, the Tutorial Series, Aids to the Classics, Gibson's Interlinear Translations, and the Hamiltonian System. The most successful series to emerge from these, the Loeb Classical Library, is still a staple" (Lyne 252). By interacting with Ovid's *Metamorphoses* as a means of mastering Latin grammar, students continued to be influenced by Ovid. Translations of the *Metamorphoses* ranged from the poetic and the scholarly to mere lessons in grammar.

The tales in the *Metamorphoses* of erotic transformation are centered around struggles and conflicts that interest every man. Writers from a wide variety of genres have gleaned inspiration from its pages. English poet John Gower's *Confessio amantis* (circa 1390–1392) is a moralizing text inspired by the *Metamorphoses'* account of Pyramus and Thisbe. According to Jeremy Dimmick in *The Cambridge Companion to Ovid* (2002, 281), this text represents more than simple mimicry and moralization. "The stories adapted from the *Metamorphoses,* unvarnished and often bleak accounts of sexual obsession and violence, constitute a demonic world within Gower's poem, whose challenge to its rationalist leanings must be accommodated as well as resisted." Gower, like Ovid, created a text inspired by the work of his predecessors, and like Ovid his text stretches and expands upon what came before. Ovid's tales of change were adaptations of known myths, but by putting his own twist on these stories, he brought them to a wider audience and gave them new life.

Dante too was influenced by Ovid, and although Virgil certainly reigns supreme in his works, "there are about 100 references to Ovid" (Highet 1970, 79). Similarly, Boccaccio's *Fiammetta amorosa* (1343–1344) found inspiration in the *Metamorphoses.* For example, the stories of Leander and Achimenedes, Io, Pyramus and Thisbe, and Dido all appear in this text (Highet 1970, 91); the versions, in some instances, are not identical to Ovid's renditions. Still, it is clear that in this work Ovid was the source for most of Boccaccio's classical references. Geoffrey Chaucer found inspiration for several works in the *Metamorphoses; The Book of the Duchess* (circa 1368–1369) contains the story of Ceyx and Alcone (book 2), but in his version the lovers are not changed. Arguably, Ovid's house of Fame (book 12) was in Chaucer's mind when he wrote his own *House of Fama* (circa 1378–1381). He also included the story of Pyramus and Thisbe in his *Legend of Good Women* (circa 1386). Spenser's *Faerie Queene* (1590) regularly presents grotesque creatures and landscapes gleaned from the *Metamorphoses.* In book I, Errour is described in terms that resemble those used to characterize Ovid's Scylla. "Ovidian locales are repeatedly associated with sinister revivals of the dead and with a temptation to wander endlessly away from moral obligations" (Burrow 2002, 313). Spenser also borrowed more-positive themes from Ovid, particularly the idea of continual transformation and renewals.

INVOCATION

My soul is wrought to sing of forms transformed to bodies new and strange! Immortal Gods inspire my heart, for ye have changed yourselves and all things you have changed! Oh lead my song in smooth and measured strains, from olden days when earth began to this completed time!

Source: *Ovid,* Metamorphoses, *book 1, Invocation, edited and translated by Brookes More (Boston: Cornhill, 1922).*

The known facts of Ovid's life created intrigue. Ovid says in *Tristia* 2.207 that he was exiled for *carmen et error* (poetry and mistake). Naturally, readers turned to his works in their quest for more-intimate details. Ben Jonson's *The Poetaster* (1601) thus offers a fictive vision of Ovid's life and even mentions his fellow elegists Propertius and Tibullus. Yet, Ovid's life exercised a fascination on more authors than Jonson alone. The story of Ovid's exile comes to function as an allegory for poetry's place in early-modern society, and the *Metamorphoses* plays the master trope in this reading. Thus, in his discussion of *The Steele Glas* (1576) by George Gascoigne, R. W. Maslen (2000, 20) points out that the author begins the text "with an application of the story of Philomela to the censorship of poetry." The mythological heroine whose tongue is cut out figures the poet as exile, silenced in his own land. He further argues:

> building on foundations laid by its Elizabethan precursors, *The Steele Glas* introduces us

> to a world where the *Metamorphoses* has subtly changed its status since the days of the early humanists. It is no longer a text to be read and commented on in an effort to recover its perennial moral secrets. Instead it serves as a tool whereby the secrets of contemporary culture—and especially the ruling classes—may be subjected to close reading and critical commentary by the knowing poet. (2000, 20)

The Steele Glas not only offers an example of the manner in which Gascoigne benefited from the knowledge of both Ovid's life and texts, it also shows how he transmuted that knowledge into a biting commentary on current social conditions.

The examples of Ovid's influence upon Shakespeare are numerous. Colin Burrow (2002, 206) notes, "Shakespeare is the most famous Elizabethan re-embodiment of Ovid." The *Metamorphoses* certainly inspired Shakespeare's *Venus and Adonis* (1593), and although the narrative is not exactly the same, the theme of a manly woman in pursuit of a frail man is constant (book 10). The story of Philomela (book 6) can be seen through the dramatic violence in *Titus Andronicus* (1594). As Gilbert Highet summarizes in *The Classical Tradition* (1970, 61): "There Lavinia, like Philomela, is ravished and has her tongue cut out, but her hands are cut off too, so that she may not write." Again, the story is slightly different, but the thematic foundation of the helpless girl who is brutalized and silenced remains. The troupe of hapless performers in *A Midsummer Night's Dream* (circa 1595–1596) enact their own version of the Pyramus and Thisbe myth (book 4). The love affair of *Romeo and Juliet* (circa 1595–1596) is another embodiment of the fruitless affair of Pyramus and Thisbe. *The Winter's Tale* (1611) envelops the story of Pygmalion and his lovely ivory statue (book 10).

Modern literature has also been marked by Ovid's influence. Franz Kafka was of course inspired to write his own *Metamorphosis* (1915). More recently Michael Hofmann has edited a text titled *After Ovid: New Metamorphoses* (1997). In his introduction Hofmann (1997, xi) discusses the reasons for a renewed interest in Ovid: "Such qualities as his mischief and cleverness, his deliberate use of shock—not always relished in the past—are contemporary values. Then, too, the stories have direct, obvious and powerful affinities with contemporary reality." He points out that suffering and emotional issues relative to "holocaust, plague, sexual harassment, rape, incest, seduction, pollution, sex-change, suicide, hetero- and homosexual love," all contained within Ovid's classical text, are modern concerns. I would also note that these same issues most assuredly figured into Ovid's popularity with Renaissance scholars and laymen. Hofmann's wholly contemporary work consists of poems by a variety of authors all rooted in Ovid's versions of myth; these poems, however, take the struggles embedded at the core of each myth and spin them in modern directions. Alice Fulton's refashioning of the Daphne and Apollo myth (Hofmann, 46–47) contains the following image of Apollo as a hunter preparing to stalk his virgin prey:

> Though she expected him / to wear blaze orange, supernatural / as the sun, he tracked her down in camo- / skin, which 'disappears in a wide variety of terrains'. / He owns every pattern in the catalogue. / After considering *Hollywood Treestand* / ('all a nymph sees is limbs') / and *Universal Bark,* ('a look most guys relate to') / he chose a suit of *Laurel Ghost,* / printed with a 3-D photo of the forest, / which 'makes you so invisible / only the oaks will know you're there' / Even his arrow's shaft is camo. / Only his ammo jackets gleam / like lipstick tubes.

In order to grasp fully this meticulously crafted passage, readers must know Ovid's original account of Apollo's pursuit of Daphne. Presenting him as a hunter in "camo" who is equally concerned with looking good and being prepared for the hunt captures the classical image of beautiful Apollo. Additionally, his choice print, *Laurel Ghost,* is a sad portent of Daphne's fate. Other selections in the book, such as Fred D'Aguiar's *Pyramus and Thisbe,* offer a twist to the original. Pyramus says to Thisbe (111): "I am black and you're white: / What's the day without night / To measure it by and give / It definition; life. / We'll go where love's colour- / Blind and therefore colured." D'Aguiar uses the familiar story of separated lovers to examine the barriers some interracial couples face. It is certainly a timely discussion.

Early translations, biographies, mimicry, and refashionings of Ovid are equal testaments to the relevance of Ovid's work across genres and history. Virgil's *Aeneid* was also translated and mimicked; the author was Christianized and honored by clerics. Despite Virgil's popularity, I contend Ovid's *Metamorphoses* bested the *Aeneid.* Authors such as Golding, Sandys, and Slavitt have been able to render unique translations owing to the *Metamorphoses'* extraordinary pliability. Ovid's text centers around change, instability, and the hope for renewal. Hofmann's assessment of Ovid's appeal for the contemporary audience holds true for Ovid's reception by all postclassical readers. The *Metamorphoses'* portrayal of the frail human condition with an emphasis upon constant rebirth speaks to all generations.

Boccaccio's *Fiammetta amorosa* presents an abandoned heroine who finds solace in the stories of change taken from the *Metamorphoses.* This image of one who looks outside herself for evidence of others' suffering and triumph is possible in part because the *Metamorphoses* continually offers unexpected outcomes (admittedly grotesque at times) in the lives of humans. Scholars still struggle with these basic conflicts. Ovid's *Metamorphoses,* unlike traditional epics (Homer, Ennius, and Virgil), provides twists and alternate, sometimes comical, outcomes for serious moral dilemmas. Virgil's *Aeneid* could not embody such contradictory refashionings, and yet the human condition is one of constant change and uncertainty. Even though Ovid has often been criticized as flippant, this sense of play with language has actually served the author well. His work is approachable and susceptible to various interpretations; its openness offers authors greater freedom of inspiration. The examples above all provide proof of Ovid's immeasurable malleability.

–CHRISTEL JOHNSON,
FRIENDS SEMINARY, NEW YORK

Viewpoint:
No. Unlike Ovid's epic, whose main theme is indisputably metamorphosis, Virgil's *Aeneid* presents a nexus of themes that have supported a wide variety of interpretations.

There can be little doubt that Ovid's epic has reached deeply into both the literary tradition and the popular imagination. Mary Zimmerman's Broadway production of the *Metamorphoses* (2002) is but the latest in a long line of adaptations of the imaginative stories that make up the epic and include such diverse reworkings as the medieval *Ovide moralisé*–metamorphosis as Christian allegory–*West Side Story* (1961), and *The Fantasticks.* Yet, as influential as these stories have been–and as compelling as the theme of metamorphosis is that links them together and provides their unifying thread–the influence of the epic qua epic cannot compare to that of Virgil's *Aeneid.* To begin with, Ovid's epic cannot be considered apart from Virgil's. It is the classicizing stability of the *Aeneid* that, in part, enables Ovid's epic to cohere: it is around the stable core of Virgil's poem that Ovid's dances and flirts, abbreviating where Virgil goes on at length, expatiating where Virgil is silent. So instead of Virgil's fourth book on Dido, Ovid gives us four lines:

> . . . Libycas vento referuntur ad oras.
> Excipit Aenean illic animoque domoque
> Non bene discidium Phrygii latura mariti
> Sidonis inque pyra sacri sub imagine facta
> Incubuit ferro deceptaque decipit omnes.
> (*Met.* 14.77–81)

> (When headwinds drove them to the Libyan coast.
> There Dido made Aeneas welcome to
> Her home and heart, her heart too ill-inured
> To bear the parting from her Trojan spouse.
> Feigning a holy rite, she built a pyre
> And fell upon his sword and, duped herself,
> Duped all. (Melville, p. 327)

But where Virgil fails to tell the story of Arethusa, Ovid tells tale within tale, all prefaced by a clear allusion to the opening of the *Aeneid:* Virgil's "arma virumque cano" becoming Ovid's "arma manusque meae." Ovid bounces off Virgil and in so doing points up the earlier poem's centrality.

It is, in fact, the near compulsion for authors after Virgil to acknowledge him as a predecessor that suggests that the *Aeneid* is the greater poem. Ovid is the first to respond in kind to the epic, and in so responding he serves to establish Virgil's canonicity and influence. Yet, Virgilian reception begins in his own time–contemporaries Horace and Propertius are among those who comment specifically on his works–and the commentary tradition begins shortly after, whereas Ovidian commentary does not start until the ninth century C.E. It is to Virgil's Aeneas as hero of the pagan world that Augustine reacts in his *Confessions* (circa 400), and, more strikingly perhaps, it is the structure of the *Aeneid* as a whole that guides Augustine's choices in the telling of his own epic journey.

Moreover, Ovid's tales fall in and out of fashion, whereas it is the interpretations of Virgil's story, not the story itself, that change with time. That is, because Ovid's epic has been received by literary history as a series of tales that demonstrate transformation, its popularity waxes and wanes with the aesthetic mores of an era: when transformation is useful to the literary and popular imagination, Ovid's tales are popular; when not, they are ignored in favor of tales of stability and order. Yet, Virgil's epic remains central to the literary imagination of every era, even though its message is variously interpreted. It is for this reason that T. S. Eliot proclaims in "What is a Classic?": "Whatever definition we arrive at, it cannot be one that excludes [Virgil]–we may say confidently that it must be one which will expressly reckon with him." That is, all literature considered canonical after Virgil must make reference to Virgil, even if the understanding of the message of the *Aeneid* changes with time: at some times he is the voice of order; at others, his poem undermines the stultifying authority of empire. The ability of the poem to speak to many audiences has broadened not only its appeal but

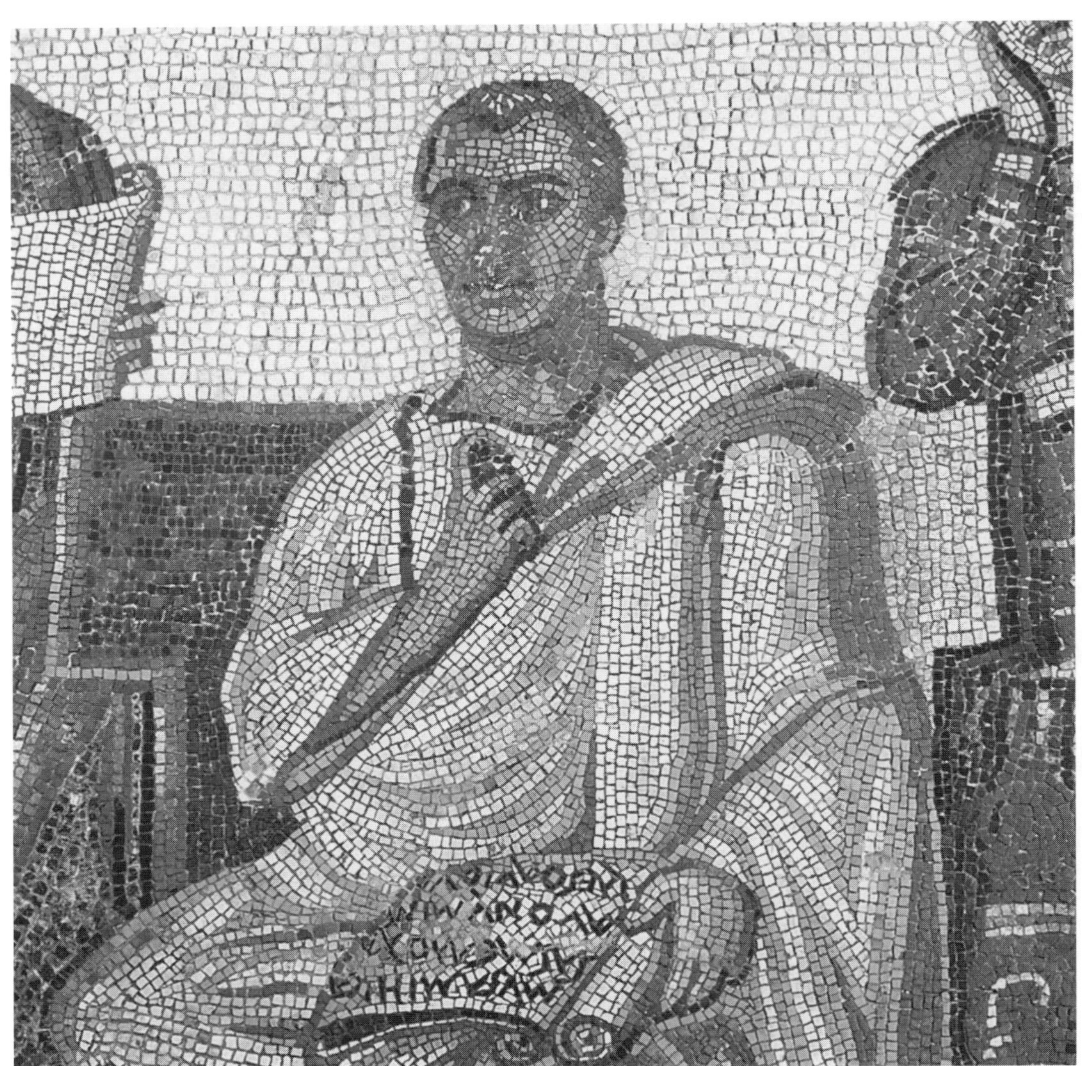

Detail of a mosaic of Virgil from Sousse, Tunisia

(© Roger Wood/CORBIS)

also its influence. As Gian Biagio Conte has argued: "Virgil's *Nachleben* is Western literature."

Perhaps the best example of this point is to be found in works by William Shakespeare, where both Ovid's and Virgil's influence is strong. Rather than analyzing a play that is avowedly Virgilian, such as *The Tempest* (1611), one can take as test case the one play that is arguably most Ovidian: *A Midsummer Night's Dream* (circa 1595–1596). Here Ovid's influence is undeniable. Not only do the "rude mechanicals" perform a version of "Pyramus and Thisbe" that is derived from Arthur Golding's translation of the *Metamorphoses,* but that same tale also provides the structuring motivation for the main events of the play: the escapades of the four lovers in the woods outside of Athens. The interplay between the rustics rehearsing the story of Pyramus and Thisbe and the lovers who are enacting it–and, in the process, undergoing a transformation informed by the metamorphic force that pervades the play–is only enhanced by the use of language that continually draws the theme of metamorphosis to the fore. The influence of the *Metamorphoses* also on the subplot of the fairies and their marital spat is made clear when the lead rustic, Bottom, is transformed into a donkey by the mischievous sprite, Puck. "Bless thee, Bottom, bless thee! thou art translated," says Quince the carpenter: while *translatio* is the Latin form of metaphor, not metamorphosis, the root sense of "carrying over" is shared by both: Bottom is transformed or metamorphosed. That these metamorphoses are particularly Ovidian is suggested by the fact that the source of the love potion, the flower "love-in-idleness," turned from white to red with a shot from Cupid's arrow, just as the fruit of the mulberry tree, which marks the place of Thisbe's death in Ovid's tale, is first stained by her blood and then changed permanently to a dark-red fruit ("nam color in pomo est, ubi permaturuit, ater").

Yet, there is a key moment even in *A Midsummer Night's Dream* that is pure Virgil: at the end of act 3, the king fairy, Oberon, commands his ally, Puck, to put everything right with the lovers, so that "when next they wake, all this derision / shall seem a dream and fruitless vision." The erotic chaos that has preceded this moment, both for the fairies and the lovers, will become more chaotic before it is over; yet, the urge to right the wrongs of the night, to instill order even in the forest outside of Athens and resolve the chaos of the play, is expressed through a striking Virgilian allusion. Oberon instructs Puck to "overcast the night . . . with drooping fog as black as Acheron." This descent into the underworld is given a "local habitation and a name," to borrow from elsewhere in the play, as Puck links the eventual emergence from the depths of Acheron with the dawning of the new day:

> My fairy lord, this must be done with haste,
> For night's swift dragons cut the clouds full fast;
> And yonder shines Aurora's harbinger,
> At whose approach ghosts wand'ring here and there,
> Troop home to churchyards.

To which Oberon replies:

> But we are spirits of another sort.
> I with the morning's love have oft made sport,
> And like a forester the groves may tread,
> Even till the eastern gate, all fiery-red,
> Opening on Neptune with fair blessed beams,
> Turns into yellow gold his salt green streams.

The order promised by the new day that will end the play, enabling the metamorphic reorganization of the night to be resolved in the comic stability of the marriages of the lovers and their duke and duchess, here echoes the emergence of Aeneas from the underworld and his arrival at the mouth of the Tiber, signaling the end of his journey and the birth of Rome:

> Iamque rubescebat radiis mare et aethere ab alto
> Aurora in roseis fulgebat lutea bigis,
> cum uenti posuere omnisque repente resedit
> flatus, et in lento luctantur marmore tonsae.
> Atque hic Aeneas ingentem ex aequore lucum
> prospicit. hunc inter fluuio Tiberinus amoeno
> uerticibus rapidis et multa flauus harena
> in mare prorumpit. (*Aen.*7. 25–32)

> (And now the waves were beginning to be tinged with red from the rays of the sun and Aurora on her rosy chariot glowed in gold from the heights of heaven, when of a sudden the wind fell, every breath was still and the oars toiled in a sluggish sea. Here it was that Aeneas, still well off shore, sighted a great forest and the river Tiber in all its beauty bursting through it into the sea with its racing waves and their burden of yellow sand.) (West, p. 163)

Gavin Douglas's translation of this passage highlights the redness of the dawn ("walxin red," "brown sanguine"), but what is most striking is how both the Latin and the contemporary translations emphasize the yellow color of the Tiber as it spills into the ocean. Douglas speaks of the "Tybir flowand soft and esely, / With sworland welis, and mekill yallow sand," translating the "multa flavus harena" of the Latin. Shakespeare's temporal threshold between night and morning is a transformation of Virgil's spatial boundary drawn at the mouth of the Tiber. For Shakespeare it is the movement from night to day that makes the sea yellow gold; for Virgil it is the meeting of sea and land as the Tiber pours into the Tyrrhenian Sea. Shakespeare skillfully deploys Virgilian allusion here to end the chaos associated with the Ovidian forces of the forest and the night and enable reentry into the ordered society of Athens.

There is no doubt of Ovid's permeating influence on *A Midsummer Night's Dream.* Metamorphosis drives the entire play; all plots and subplots are influenced by Ovid. And yet, by bringing Virgil in at the denouement, Shakespeare seems to be drawing a clear distinction between Ovid's and Virgil's roles. While Ovid drives the plot and subplots, it is Virgil who enables the play to end with comic stability. It is precisely for this reason that the interpretation of Virgil's work has often been restricted to a pro-Augustan propagandistic text: Virgil, above all, seems ready to stand for order and authority. The fact that we measure every classic against his argues as much for this as the fact that Shakespeare brings him in to end *A Midsummer Night's Dream.* Because his epic is nationalistic and imperial and its overt plot seems to uphold order, the poem as a whole is seen as embodying the ordering principle for Western literature: we rely on the *Aeneid* to assert the principles of canonic stability.

If that were the extent of it, I think we would have to acknowledge a tie in the contest between Ovid and Virgil. As their use by Shakespeare might suggest, Ovid infuses the postclassical tradition with transformative energy while Virgil often represents the sanity of order. Yet, Virgil's influence transcends this easy dichotomy and, as a result, suggests a wider-reaching influence. For when Sigmund Freud wrote his seminal text, *The Interpretation of Dreams* (1900), on the working of that transformative land of the subconscious, he cites not Ovid but Virgil as his epigraph: "Flectere si nequeo superos, Acheronta movebo" (If I cannot prevail upon the gods above, I shall move hell; Juno's call to arms in the seventh book of the *Aeneid*). As James Strachey records, Freud notes in *Gesammelte Schreiben* 3 (1925) 169 that "this line of Virgil [*Aeneid* VII, 312] is intended to picture the efforts of the repressed instinctual impulses" (*Interpretation of Dreams,* p. 647, n. 1). Virgil's text here serves the function we might expect of Ovid's. The fact that Freud quotes Virgil, not Ovid, as the voice of the repressed is echoed in much recent scholarship on the poem—

starting with the groundbreaking work of Michael C. J. Putnam–and suggests a level of influence that extends beyond order, ideology, and even literature. In the larger project of writing about civilization and its discontents, it is Virgil's epic, not Ovid's, whose influence is most far-reaching. Virgil's association with authority and order is tempered by a complexity of vision that enables his exploration of ideology in the *Aeneid* to have an influence that outmatches the reach of Ovid's *Metamorphoses.*

–SARAH SPENCE,
UNIVERSITY OF GEORGIA

References

Christopher Baswell, *Virgil in Medieval England: Figuring the* Aeneid *from the Twelfth Century to Chaucer,* Cambridge Studies in Medieval Literature, 24 (Cambridge: Cambridge University Press, 1995).

Barbara Boyd, ed., *Brill's Companion to Ovid* (Leiden & Boston: Brill, 2002).

Sarah Annes Brown, *The Metamorphosis of Ovid From Chaucer to Ted Hughes* (London: Duckworth, 1999).

Colin Burrow, "Re-embodying Ovid: Renaissance Afterlives," in *The Cambridge Companion to Ovid,* edited by Philip Hardie (Cambridge: Cambridge University Press, 2002), pp. 301–319.

David F. C. Coldwell, ed., *Selections from Gavin Douglas* (Oxford: Clarendon Press, 1964).

Gian Biagio Conte, *Latin Literature: A History,* translated by Joseph B. Solodow (Baltimore: Johns Hopkins University Press, 1994).

Jeremy Dimmick, "Ovid in the Middle Ages: Authority and Poetry," in *The Cambridge Companion to Ovid,* edited by Hardie (Cambridge: Cambridge University Press, 2002), pp. 264–287.

T. S. Eliot, *What is a Classic?: An Address Delivered Before the Virgil Society on 16 October 1944* (London: Faber & Faber, 1945).

Joseph Farrell, "Ovid's Virgilian Career," *MD,* 52 (2004): 41–56.

Sigmund Freud, *The Interpretation of Dreams,* edited and translated by James Strachey (London & New York: Penguin, 1976).

Philip Hardie, *Ovid's Poetics of Illusion* (Cambridge & New York: Cambridge University Press, 2002).

Hardie and others, eds., *Ovidian Transformations: Essays on the Metamorphoses and Its Reception* (Cambridge: Cambridge Philological Society, 1999).

Ralph J. Hexter, *Ovid and Medieval Schooling. Studies in Medieval School Commentaries on Ovid's Ars Amatoria, Epistulae ex Ponto, and Epistulae Heroidum* (Munich: Bei der Arbeo-Gesellschaft, 1986).

Gilbert Highet, *The Classical Tradition Greek and Roman Influences on Western Literature* (Oxford: Oxford University Press, 1970).

Michael Hofmann, *After Ovid: New Metamorphoses* (New York: Noon Day, 1997).

Craig Kallendorf, *In Praise of Aeneas: Virgil and Epideictic Rhetoric in the Early Italian Renaissance* (Hanover, N.H.: University Press of New England, 1989).

Raphael Lyne, "Ovid in English Translation," in *The Cambridge Companion to Ovid,* edited by Hardie (Cambridge: Cambridge University Press, 2002), pp. 249–263.

Lyne, *Ovid's Changing Worlds: English* Metamorphoses, *1567–1632* (Oxford & New York: Oxford University Press, 2001).

Allen Mandelbaum, *The Metamorphoses of Ovid* (New York: Harvest, 1995).

R. W. Maslen, "Myths Exploited: The Metamorphoses of Ovid in Early Elizabethan England," in *Shakespeare's Ovid: The* Metamorphoses *in the Plays and Poems,* edited by A. B. Taylor (Cambridge: Cambridge University Press, 2000), pp. 15–30.

Frank Justus Miller, *Metamorphoses,* edited by J. P. Goold, Loeb Classical Library, third edition (Cambridge, Mass.: Harvard University Press, 1984).

Michael C. J. Putnam, *The Poetry of the* Aeneid (Cambridge, Mass.: Harvard University Press, 1965).

L. D. Reynolds, ed., *Texts and Transmission: A Survey of the Latin Classics* (Oxford: Clarendon Press, 1983).

David Slavitt, *The Metamorphoses of Ovid, Translated Freely into Verse* (Baltimore: Johns Hopkins University Press, 1994).

Sarah Spence, ed., *Poets and Critics Read Vergil* (New Haven, Conn.: Yale University Press, 2001).

Richard Thomas, *Virgil and the Augustan Reception* (Cambridge & New York: Cambridge University Press, 2001).

Margaret Tudeau-Clayton, *Jonson, Shakespeare and Early Modern Virgil* (Cambridge & New York: Cambridge University Press, 1998).

ROMAN PERIOD: PAUSANIAS

Is Pausanias a reliable source for the history of ancient Greece?

Viewpoint: Yes. Pausanias was an honest and diligent researcher; his *Description of Greece* preserves much valuable information from antiquity that no other source provides.

Viewpoint: No. Pausanias wrote during an age when proper historical methodology was not observed or even recognized; the information in his *Description of Greece* is frequently inaccurate.

Little is known about Pausanias aside from what can be learned in the pages of the single work that survives under his name, the *Description of Greece.* He seems to have come from the vicinity of Magnesia on Sipylus, a Greek city in western Anatolia. His dates of birth and death are unknown, but he was alive during the time of the Roman emperors Hadrian, Antoninus Pius, and Marcus Aurelius, whose combined reigns stretched from 117 to 180 C.E. During this period Greece and the rest of the Greek-speaking world had been part of the Roman Empire for roughly three centuries.

Pausanias's *Description of Greece* is unique among surviving works in Greek literature: a ten-volume account of the southern part of the Greek mainland based on the author's own travels and research. Much of what was considered Greece at the time was omitted by Pausanias, but his account does cover the area that was home to the most famous cities and shrines from the glory days of Greek civilization, including Athens, Sparta, Corinth, Thebes, Delphi, and Olympia. Pausanias arranges his account as a series of itineraries from place to place. Along these itineraries, he describes punctiliously and, in the eyes of many, somewhat dryly and tediously what there is to see in the way of statues, temples, tombs, and other structures that were reminiscent of Greece's days of independence. As an eyewitness account of the state of Greece in the second century C.E., Pausanias's work has proved to be an invaluable source of information for modern scholars. His text has been used by archaeologists as a guide for where to excavate and by art historians who rely heavily on his descriptions of artworks and his attribution of them to individual artists.

The following debate, however, will focus not on his descriptions of sites and monuments but on another aspect of his work that is equally important: the historical material that he includes in his account. Pausanias did not confine himself to listing what he saw on his travels; he also recorded the history and mythology associated with each locality and monument that he visited. About half of the text in the *Description of Greece* is taken up by such myths, folktales, and histories. Much of the historical information Pausanias records is not found in any other ancient source. Evaluating the reliability of his assertions is, therefore, a major concern for historians of ancient Greece.

—William E. Hutton

Viewpoint: Yes. Pausanias was an honest and diligent researcher; his *Description of Greece* preserves much valuable information from antiquity that no other source provides.

While few would rank Pausanias among the greatest historians of antiquity, the valuable evidence that he gives us on many topics in ancient Greek and Roman civilization cannot be ignored. The standards by which we judge Pausanias must be stringent but realistic. Not even the most highly regarded ancient historians, such as Herodotus, Thucydides, or Polybius, would live up to twenty-first-century standards of historical methodology. All historians, moreover, must set limits to the chronological scope that they cover and make choices about what types of facts and events they will include in their accounts. Finally, mistakes are endemic to the process of creating an historical account of any length, and no historian, ancient or modern, is free from them. To condemn Pausanias for shortcomings that all practitioners of the historian's craft are prey to, especially historians in antiquity, would oblige us to condemn as unreliable the vast majority of historical information that survives from the ancient world. Every historical source, including Pausanias, must be evaluated carefully, and an attempt must be made to identify as far as possible their weaknesses, biases, and omissions. Yet, in most cases Pausanias, even though he was not exclusively, or even primarily, devoted to historical research, can be shown to be a reliable reporter.

First, it would be good to remind ourselves just how important a source Pausanias is. Pick up any dozen or so modern works on ancient Greek or Roman history, culture, religion, art, or archaeology, and you will be hard pressed to find one that doesn't refer to Pausanias in the index, so plentiful is the information he provides and on such a broad range of topics. An extraordinary amount of the material he writes on is treated by no other ancient author, a fact that should be put down to his credit rather than held against him. While he definitely shared his contemporaries' reverence for Greece's classical heyday, when it comes to historical matters, he takes pains to steer clear of well-worn paths. He does not ape his classical masters by retelling the Battle of Salamis or by dilating on the outbreak of the Peloponnesian War; he instead exerts his most intense historiographical efforts on stories with which the people of his time would not be thoroughly familiar. In general, this means that it is not the classical period at all (480–323 B.C.E.) but the preceding Archaic period (700–480 B.C.E.) and the subsequent Hellenistic period (323–31 B.C.E.) that most attract his attention. Here are some of the major events and movements for which Pausanias produces extended treatments and for which he is either the only source or almost the only source: the migration of the Greeks to the coast of Ionia in the period following the end of the Bronze Age (7.1.1–5.13); the history of the Messenian Wars (eighth and seventh centuries B.C.E.), of which Pausanias gives by far the most complete and detailed account (4.4.1–4.27.8); the invasion of Greece by the Gauls in 279 B.C.E. (1.3.5–4.6; 10.19.4–23.3); the reigns of the Hellenistic kings of Egypt and Pergamum (1.6.1–8.1); the history of Sardinia (10.17.1–18.1); the history of the wars between Rome and the Achaean League, which led to the destruction of Corinth in 146 B.C.E.; and the complete subjugation of Greece to Rome (7.7.1–17.4). There are also many shorter passages in which Pausanias gives us unique information about historical events.

Of course, Pausanias himself did not live at the time of these events, so his use of earlier sources needs to be scrutinized. Some have criticized him in this regard, calling into question his judgment for using, for instance, the poet Rhianos as a major source for his history of the Messenian Wars. It is true that Rhianos's poetry, as far as we can reconstruct it from Pausanias's text, was full of the imaginative and fantastic touches typical of epic poetry, and it is also true that some of these elements make their way into Pausanias's account. Yet, Rhianos was a scholar in addition to a poet. Aside from his poetry he also produced editions of Homer and other works of criticism. If he is typical of poets in the Hellenistic period, he prided himself on writing poetry that was well researched. Hence, once we isolate those parts of Pausanias's account that seem aggrandized or mythologized, what is left over once we discount such accretions has a good chance of being based on solid information.

It is also true that, like all writers of the period, Pausanias strove to emulate classical models, but the notion that he distorted his accounts of certain events to make them resemble passages in Herodotus and other writers does not have much evidence to support it. To take the example of the Gallic invasion of 279 B.C.E., the points of similarity between Pausanias's account and Herodotus's account of the Persian invasion of 480 B.C.E. can be summarized as follows: like Herodotus's Persians, the Gauls of Pausanias's account enter central Greece through the pass at Thermopylae, where the Greeks in both cases mount a defense. The Gauls and the Persians both discover a path by which the defending forces can be flanked. After the

Persians and the Gauls break through Thermopylae, they proceed to the oracle of Apollo at Delphi, where they are assailed by violent signs and portents sent by the god. One possible explanation for these similarities could be that Pausanias was trying to evoke the spirit of Herodotus for his readers, but an equally possible explanation is that the two invasions actually were similar. The most practical route for an invading army to take through the mountainous terrain of central Greece goes by way of Thermopylae, and the narrow pass at Thermopylae is also the most advantageous spot on that route for defenders to try to stop an invasion. Thermopylae was the site of many other battles in antiquity, and even in World War II, British forces chose Thermopylae as the best place to set up a defense against the German invasion of Greece. Once south of the pass, a visit to the wealthy and relatively undefended shrine of the god at Delphi would hardly be a surprising step for either the Persian or Gallic army to take. The likeliest explanation for the resemblance between Pausanias and Herodotus in these accounts, therefore, is not that Pausanias was copying Herodotus, but rather that Pausanias saw in the similarities between the two invasions an opportunity to serve both the cause of truth and the memory of the Father of History at the same time.

In all, there is no compelling evidence to say that Pausanias chose his sources carelessly, used them uncritically, or distorted their testimony irresponsibly. In the case of Hieronymos of Kardia, he is only one of several sources, both written and oral, that Pausanias criticizes explicitly. The fact that Pausanias lambastes Hieronymos at one point for his favoritism toward King Antigonos (1.9.8) yet seems to follow Hieronymos elsewhere is not necessarily an inconsistency. More likely, Pausanias is simply doing what all modern historians do when dealing with an ancient source: assessing his biases and using that assessment to determine what is reliable and what is suspect in his testimony. Although Pausanias does not name his sources as a matter of course, he still cites an impressive array of respectable historians, including Herodotus, Thucydides, Hellanicus, Xenophon, Theopompus, Philistus, and Polybius. Some have suggested that Pausanias did not actually read the works of all these historians or that he read only secondhand summaries and collections of excerpts, but here again, there is no firm evidence to which one can point to prove this hypothesis. In part, such assertions come from a general prejudice against Greek writers of the Roman period, a prejudice that arises from a certain infatuation with the classical period of Greek civilization even among scholars of modern times.

In at least one respect Pausanias must be considered superior to other historians of ancient Greece: his extensive travels in Greece brought him into direct contact with sources of historical information to which no other historian had access. Though their careers doubtlessly led them to visit many places in the Greek world, not even Herodotus and Thucydides are known to have traveled as extensively in mainland Greece or to have visited many of the remote places that Pausanias sought out. In these places Pausanias was exposed to local traditions, both written and oral, that no other historian records. On his travels Pausanias was also able to consult hundreds of rock-cut inscriptions that Greeks habitually set up in public places to record governmental decisions or to commemorate important persons and events. One of Pausanias's modern champions, Christian Habicht, has made a special study of Pausanias's use of inscriptions and has shown that he used inscriptions to add great depth to the historical accounts in many parts of his work. In some cases Pausanias was able to glean from inscriptions facts about important episodes in history that otherwise would have gone unrecorded. For instance, Pausanias saw a *tropaion* (victory monument) near the Athenian agora and, by reading the dedicatory inscription, learned that it commemorated an Athenian victory in a cavalry battle against the Macedonian troops of Cassander in the late fourth century B.C.E. No other source mentions this battle, which, from the site of the victory monument, must have occurred within the walls of Athens. From other inscriptions in Athens and elsewhere, Pausanias was also able to record several details of the careers of two Athenian statesmen, Olympiodoros and Kephisodoros. The former was apparently the leading figure in Athens for several decades after the death of Alexander the Great. He was instrumental in resisting Macedonian attempts to subdue Athens and, by the time of his death in circa 280 B.C.E., had rendered Athens (temporarily) free from foreign control (Paus. 1.26.3; 10.18.7; 34.3). Kephisodoros was likewise a leading figure in Athens, but from a later period (late third to early second century B.C.E.). He led the Athenian resistance against another ambitious Macedonian king, Philip V, and engineered alliances against him with several foreign powers including Rome (Paus. 1.36.5–6). From the spotty references to these men in other sources, no one could have guessed their prominence and importance in these crucial phases of Athenian history. Pausanias literally saved these two men from oblivion.

All available evidence points to the conclusion that when Pausanias consulted inscriptions and incorporated information from them in his account, he did so with a high degree of care and accuracy. This is all the more remarkable in light

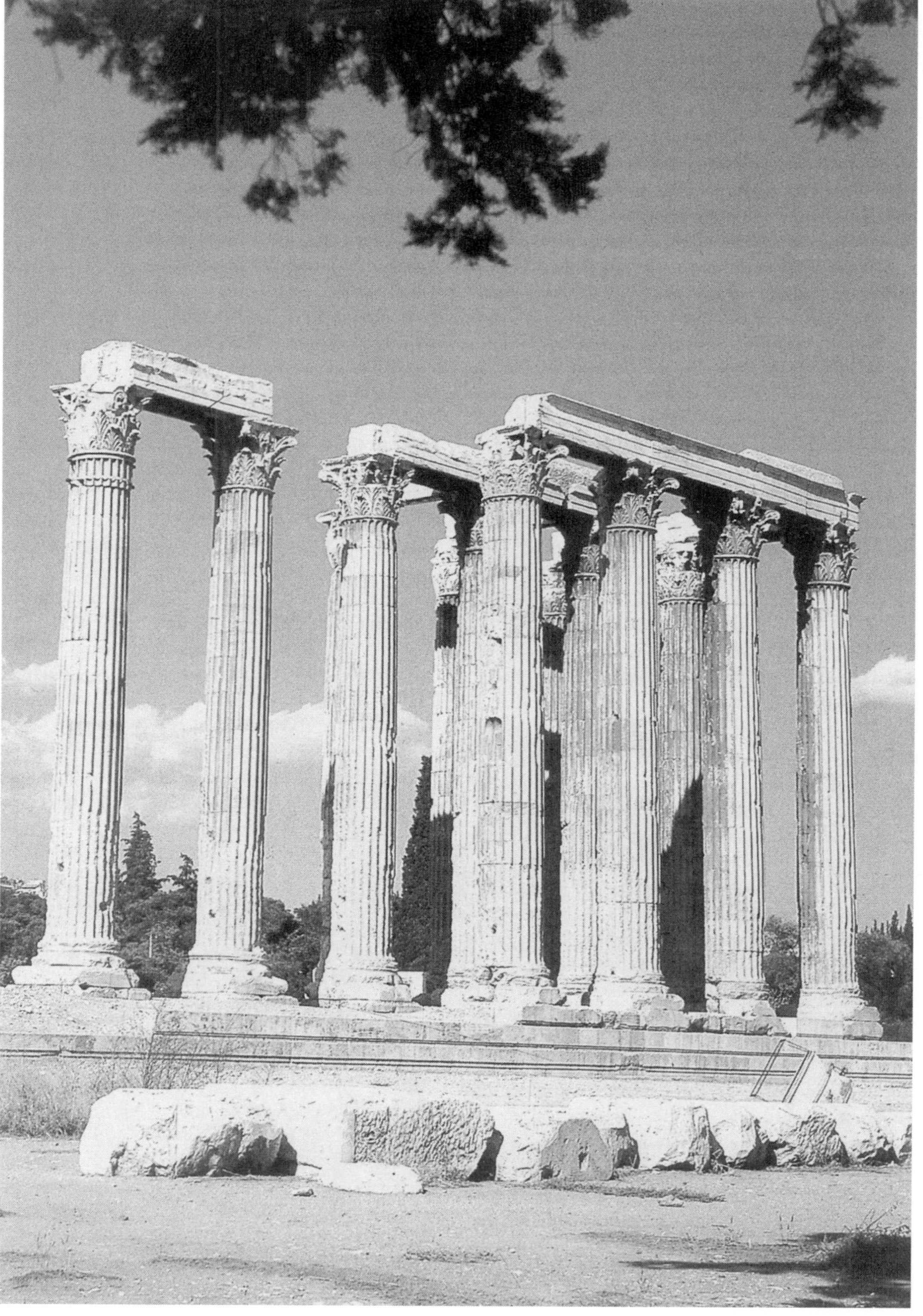

Temple of Zeus, southeast of the Athenian Acropolis

(age fotostock)

of the fact that many of these inscriptions were written in local dialects of Greek that differed substantially both from Pausanias's native dialect and from the literary dialect in which he wrote. While Pausanias, like all historians, makes mistakes from time to time, the general trend in recent decades has been to discover that what was previously thought to be an error on the part of Pausanias is in fact no error at all. Near the entrance to the famous shrine of Apollo at Delphi, for instance, Pausanias reports a monument dedicated by the people of Tegea, a city in the territory of Arcadia (10.9.5). Archaeologists discovered a monument near the spot that Pausanias describes, but the inscriptions on that monument identified it as an offering of the Arcadian cities in common rather than a sole offering of the Tegeans. This was classified as one of Pausanias's errors until recently, when it was discovered that a monumental colonnade behind the Arcadian dedication was in fact built by the Tegeans alone. Clearly, it was this structure, and not the Arcadian monument, to which Pausanias was referring.

Also, on the subject of things about which Pausanias gives us unique information, his portrait of Greece in the second century C.E. must also be considered as one of the greatest legacies he bequeaths to modern historians. In recent decades historians have come to realize that in investigating the past it is not only battles and political changes and famous men that are important. Everything about a culture, its economy, social structure, and the religious and moral ideals of its people, provides the context from which important trends develop and important individuals emerge. No single historian can give a complete picture of all the potentially important facets of a culture, even for a limited period of time, but Pausanias's unparalleled efforts in documenting the contemporary state of Greece provide us a glimpse of aspects of the history of the Greek people that no other author comes close to dealing with. While it is true that his direct statements on subjects like the economy and society of second-century Greece are rare, they are not totally absent: he tells us, for instance, that flax was an important commodity produced in the territory of Elis (5.5.2) and that harvesting the mollusk that was used for purple dye was practiced off the coast of southern Lakonia (3.21.6). He tells us that the women of Patrai, one of the chief cities of Roman Greece, outnumbered men two to one, that they were employed in the weaving of flax from Elis, and that they "had as much of a share of Aphrodite's charms as any other women" (7.21.14). In the course of his travels he notes many instances of shrunken cities, deserted villages, abandoned and dilapidated shrines, and other effects of three centuries of Roman rule on the Greek landscape. What Pausanias has to say on political and military issues of the Roman era is relatively meager in comparison to the attention he lavishes on earlier eras; but he does discuss the depredations of the Roman consul Sulla in Greece (for example, 1.20.4–7), the founding of Roman colonies on Greek soil and the effects of that on the local population (for example, 2.1.2; 7.18.7; 10.38.4), and, on a more positive note, the benefactions of Greek-friendly emperors such as Nero (for example, 10.12.8) and, especially, Hadrian (for example, 1.18.6–9), and of prominent Roman citizens such as the senator Antoninus (2.27.6) and Herodes Atticus (for example, 2.1.7).

More important than these scattered remarks, however, is the copious information he provides on the local traditions preserved by the various communities in Greece and on the religious beliefs and practices within these communities. He describes a strange ritual he found being practiced by the people of Hermion, for instance (2.35.7): a series of four young cows, one after the other, are led into the temple of Demeter. The doors on the temple are closed, and the cows are killed by a group of four old women left behind inside and furnished with sickles for the purposes of the sacrifice. It is considered a bad omen if all four cows do not fall on the same side. In Patrai he observed another unusual ritual in honor of the goddess Artemis (7.18.11–13): the first day of the celebration is marked by a grand procession with the priestess of Artemis being carried in a chariot drawn by deer. The second day culminates with an enormous bonfire into which people throw a great variety of fruits and animals, including live birds, boars, deer, gazelles, wolves, and bears (both cubs and adults). Pausanias claims to have witnessed occasions on which a bear or other animal tried to escape from the fire, but the people always managed to catch them and drag them back. The countryside of second-century Greece was alive with all sorts of interesting practices of this sort, and Pausanias provides us vastly more information about them than any other source. In doing so, he gives us indispensable testimony concerning what it meant to be Greek at this point in history.

In sum, Pausanias was in many ways a product of his age. The things he chose to write about were determined in no small part by a typical Greek sense of nostalgia for the days when Greece, not Rome, was the leading civilization in the Mediterranean world. Yet, Pausanias was no simple-minded imitator, engaged in re-creating some classical model in a debased and derivative fashion. He set himself a unique task and pursued that task with great perseverance and consistency. Instead of rehashing classical themes that had been treated by dozens of authors before him, he deliberately sought out the unusual and the little-known, both in terms of the places he visited and in terms of the portions of Greece's pre-Roman history that he chose to focus on in his research efforts. From what we can tell, he recorded what he discovered, both in the field and in the library, with care, honesty, prudence, and—in most cases—accuracy. The more archaeologists have excavated in Greece, and the more that has been uncovered that pertains to Pausanias's account, the greater the appreciation has become for just how reliable Pausanias was as a reporter. There is no reason to think that that trend will not continue.

—WILLIAM E. HUTTON,
COLLEGE OF WILLIAM AND MARY

Viewpoint: No. Pausanias wrote during an age when proper historical methodology was not observed or even recognized; the information in his *Description of Greece* is frequently inaccurate.

To understand the case against Pausanias, one must first understand something of the time in which he lived. The second century C.E. was a period when the past was important to the Greeks. The respect they received from the rest of the Roman Empire depended not on their economic prowess or their military might but on their ability to claim a connection to the long-lost world of their revered classical ancestors. As a result, the Greeks were avidly interested in their past—one might even say that they to a large extent lived in the past. Yet, the psychological and political stake they had in the past as a source of status and self-esteem made it difficult for them to have the critical perspective to examine it the way historians must. To educated Greeks of the time, history consisted of tales of triumph and disaster, object lessons in the perils of pride and the vicissitudes of fortune that one imbibed from an early age and memorized by rote along with chunks of Homeric poetry. The issues and controversies of the past had all been solved, or at least reduced to a manageable number of stock problems that young men would learn to debate in the role-playing exercises that were part of their oratorical training: Should the three hundred Spartans retreat from Thermopylae? What would Alexander the Great say to the Persian king? To a large extent the Greeks viewed the past as a static monument toward which one gazed with reverence and awe, rather than as a real period of human history susceptible to rational scrutiny.

Even among highly educated intellectuals of the period, this abstract, monumental view of history predominated. While certain areas of study produced important and original work, such as the fields of medicine and philosophy, the most visible and influential practitioners of high culture at the time were public performers referred to as "sophists," traveling "wise-men" who built highly popular and well-remunerated careers for themselves in the practice of declamation (quasi-impromptu oratory). The surviving orations of these sophists, men such as Dion of Prusa and Aelius Aristides, are textbook examples of style over substance; displays of hackneyed themes and commonplaces dressed up in a carefully studied imitation of classical oratorical prose. Imitation would be a good word to choose if one wanted to characterize the entire cultural output of the imperial period of Greek literature in a single term. In a real sense this was a time when culture was a matter of impersonation, as people continued into adulthood the role-playing exercises they were subjected to in school. The sophists, for instance, through their language, the topics of their orations, the examples they chose to illustrate their points, and even the way they lived their lives strove not just to emulate but to *be* great classical rhetoricians like Demosthenes or Isocrates. Sometimes this impulse toward living in the past produced a queer time-warp effect, as when Dion of Prusa, addressing an audience around 100 C.E., referred to the constant trouble that the Spartans have in keeping the population of Helot serfs under control. Helot rebellion was something the classical Spartans had to worry about, but it had ceased to be much of an issue some centuries before Dion brought it up. Similarly, Pausanias himself refers to it as if it were a currently raging controversy over the dispute between the Egyptians and the Phrygians on who had the oldest language. This controversy, if it ever existed, had probably faded from the forefront of people's attention even before Herodotus mentioned it in the fifth century B.C.E., some six hundred years earlier than Pausanias.

We can see the effects of this culture of playacting on the art of writing history. Perhaps the best of a small group of historians worth mentioning from this period is Arrian of Nikomedia, a slightly older contemporary of Pausanias. Arrian patterned his writings and, indeed, his life after the classical Athenian historian Xenophon. Like Xenophon, Arrian was a military man and a statesman in addition to being a man of letters. Arrian gave his most important work, a history of the campaigns of Alexander the Great against Persia, the title *Anabasis* (Inland March), paying homage to Xenophon, who also wrote an *Anabasis* recording his own experiences as a mercenary soldier in Asia. Arrian even went so far as to promote himself as the "New Xenophon." As an historian, Arrian is far from incompetent, and his *Anabasis* is one of the few records of Alexander's career that is in any way reliable. Yet, we can get a sense of how far the standards for critical historical research had slipped in this period when we read the preface to his *Anabasis.* There, Arrian tells us that he followed primarily the accounts written by Aristoboulos and King Ptolemy I of Egypt. His choice of Ptolemy as a source was based on his opinion that it "would be more shameful for a king to lie" (Arrian, *Anabasis,* prologue). Since most of the work of the lesser historians of this era has been lost, we can only imagine how much more naive their critical standards were.

Such was the level of historical scholarship during the time that Pausanias undertook his work. It would be generous to say that Pausanias did no worse than was typical for the period, but that would be stretching the truth. To begin with, one thing that must be acknowledged when one considers Pausanias's contribution to historical literature is that he was not primarily an historian. The majority of his effort went not into historical research but into traveling and compiling a topographical account of the sights and monuments he found in his tours around Greece. Even in this, the one area in which he can truly be said to have made an original contribution to Greek letters, his record is far from perfect. The first page of his work contains a particularly egregious error: on approaching by sea the headland of Sounion at the eastern tip of Athenian territory, he states that there is a temple to Athena on the top of the promontory (Pausanias, *Description of Greece* 1.1.1). There was a temple of Athena on the cliffs of Sounion, but the most significant temple on the spot in his time, and at any time as far back as the late fifth century B.C.E., was instead the temple of the sea god Poseidon, several columns of which still stand as a spectacular landmark for the seaborne traveler. Pausanias either ignores this conspicuous temple or misidentifies it. Scholars of the late nineteenth and early twentieth centuries found so many apparent errors of this sort that they even suggested that Pausanias had not actually visited many of the places he describes. Admittedly, subsequent archaeological investigation has resolved several of these difficulties in Pausanias's favor, to the extent that Pausanias's status as a genuine eyewitness to the things he describes is no longer seriously in question. That is all the more reason, however, to be troubled by the number of errors that remain in his account. It seems only prudent to assume that Pausanias would have been at least as careless and imperceptive in his historical researches as he was in the process of describing what there was to see right in front of him.

Even where Pausanias is at his best, his account of both topography and history is severely limited in scope. Sharing his contemporaries' fixation on the classical past of Greece, he mentions few buildings, few works of art, and few historical events that postdate the absorption of Greece into the Roman Empire in the middle second century B.C.E. Pausanias could have been a valuable reporter in a time for which there are relatively few contemporary accounts, but about events of his own times, Pausanias is almost silent. He could have told us much that we do not know about the functioning of a Roman province in his era, and about the adaptations that Greek communities made to the governmental structure of the empire, but concerning contemporary politics and governmental affairs, he displays a supreme indifference. Pausanias could have illuminated subjects on which we are almost completely in the dark, such as the social structures and the economies of Greek communities of the time, but on these topics as well, Pausanias has little to say. He rarely mentions the inhabitants of the places he visits, except as sources of information about the monuments in their territory; nor does he pay much attention to landforms, natural resources, agricultural practices, or settlement patterns.

Pausanias does not make a habit of naming the sources for the historical material he records, so there is not a large amount of evidence to go on in determining how critical he is in handling his sources. Occasionally, though, one finds indications that his critical standards are no better than what was typical of the period, which is to say regrettably low. For instance, his longest single historical account consumes most of book 4 and chronicles the wars fought by Sparta in the eighth and seventh centuries B.C.E., first to conquer the neighboring territory of Messenia, then to quell a Messenian revolt (4.4.1–4.27.8). A little way into the story, he discusses a discrepancy in his sources, and we learn through this inadvertent process which sources he is following: Myron of Priene and Rhianos of Bene. Both were writers of the Hellenistic period about which little else is known, but one thing we know about Rhianos's Messenian history is that it was in verse and took the form of a heroic epic in the tradition of Homer. Predictably, Pausanias comes to the conclusion that Rhianos is more accurate on the point in question, and Rhianos's poem is, apparently, the source that Pausanias used for much of what turned out to be his greatest historiographical effort. To the influence of Rhianos we can probably attribute some of the more fabulous and romanticized episodes in Pausanias's Messenian account, such as frequent oracles and portents, and episodes in which the rebel leader is released from captivity by a Spartan priestess who has fallen in love with him (4.17.1) and is saved after being tossed into a chasm by an eagle that swoops down under him and carries him to a soft landing (4.18.5–7).

The fact that Pausanias mentions a discrepancy in his sources and bothers to explain his reasons for choosing one over the other might be taken as a sign of at least a minimal interest in historical method, but here we need to refer once again to the issue of playacting. Pausanias is a full participant in his era's passion for imitation: his style is a curious and idiosyncratic pastiche of the styles of several classical authors, chief among which is Herodotus. Pausanias does not go so far as did certain other authors of the period and write his narrative in Herodotus's distinctive Ionic dialect (as Arrian did in his *Indica* and as Lucian did in his essay *On the Syrian Goddess*). Yet, apparently he did see some affinity between his project and the work of Herodotus, especially, perhaps, in the ethnographic sections of Herodotus's *Histories* where he visits and describes foreign countries such as Egypt. Pausanias borrows several phrasings and figures of speech that are typical of Herodotus's easily recognizable style. He even adapts entire sentences from Herodotus and puts them to what is usually a more banal use. For instance, a phrase near the beginning of Herodotus's *Histories* announces the scope of the historian's work: "I shall proceed further in my account, treating in like fashion both small and great cities of men" (Herodotus, *Histories* 1.5.3). Pausanias adapts this sentence and uses it as a transition from a minor digression back to the main course of his account: "I must go further in my account, treating in like fashion all things Greek" (1.26.4). On the subject of source criticism, Pausanias says at one point, "it is necessary for me to say the things that are said by the Greeks, but it is not necessary for me to believe them all" (6.3.8), closely echoing another declaration of Herodotus: "I have to say the things that are said, but I do not have to believe in them in all ways" (Herodotus 7.152). Given this penchant for imitation, the question arises as to whether passages in which Pausanias refers to his sources express skepticism in one account or another, or seem to deliberate between two or more accounts, reflect his efforts as an historian or his efforts to *resemble* an historian. At one point, he delivers a harsh criticism of the third-century B.C.E. historian Hieronymos of Kardia: "Hieronymos . . . has a reputation for writing with malice against the [Hellenistic] kings except for Antigonos, and of giving unjust favor to Antigonos" (1.9.8), but this criticism seems to have been one that not even Pausanias himself took seriously since he apparently follows Hieronymos for his account of much of the early Hellenistic period.

The impulse to imitate extends even into the reporting of historical events: his narration of an invasion of Greece by the Gauls in the early third century B.C.E., which involved a valiant but unsuccessful defense by the Greeks at the pass of Thermopylae and a subsequent attack by the invaders on the shrine at Delphi (10.19.4–23.4, and more briefly, 1.3.5–4.6), is clearly patterned after Herodotus's account of the Persian invasion of 480 B.C.E. His account of the death of Hannibal (8.11.10) differs significantly from other sources, but bears a striking resemblance to that of Herodotus on the death of the Persian king Kambyses (Herodotus 3.64–66). In passages such as these, Pausanias comes dangerously close to the line between history and fiction, and perhaps even crosses over that line.

Finally, there are several cases where Pausanias is simply in error. Despite his apparent fondness for Herodotus, he states that the city of Haliartos in Boiotia was sacked by the Persians who invaded in 480 B.C.E. In fact, it was sacked by the Romans who were fighting against King Perseus of Macedon some three hundred years later (9.32.5; 10.35.2). Pausanias obviously misunderstood his sources and thought they were talking of Persia when they referred to Perseus. At Olympia he attributes to Miltiades, the hero of Marathon, an offering that was actually dedicated by his grandfather, Miltiades son of Kypselos (6.19.6), a mistake he could have avoided by reading Herodotus more carefully (6.36). He says the long walls that ran between Athens and its port were built by Themistokles, but they were not actually built until long after Themistokles had ended his days in exile (1.2.2). He places the famous tyrant Anaxilas of Rhegion in the mid seventh century B.C.E., when in fact Anaxilas flourished in the early fifth century (4.23.6). He says that the Sicilian tyrant Hiero I was assassinated by a man named Deinomenes, when in reality it was Hiero's grandson Hieronymos who suffered that fate (6.12.4). On two occasions (4.29.1; 4.32.2), he confuses the Macedonian general Demetrius, who captured the city of Messene in the late third century B.C.E., with the contemporary Macedonian prince Demetrius, son of Philip V.

THERMOPYLAE AGAIN

Anyone who so wishes can compare the number of those who mustered to meet king Xerxes at Thermopylae with those who now mustered to oppose the Gauls. To meet the Persians there came Greek contingents of the following strength: Lacedaemonians with Leonidas not more than three hundred; Tegeans five hundred, and five hundred from Mantineia; from Orchomenus in Arcadia a hundred and twenty; from the other cities in Arcadia one thousand; from Mycenae eighty; from Phlius two hundred, and from Corinth twice this number; of the Boeotians there mustered seven hundred from Thespiae and four hundred from Thebes. A thousand Phocians guarded the path on Mount Oeta, and the number of these should be added to the Greek total.

[2] Herodotus does not give the number of the Locrians under Mount Cnemis, but he does say that each of their cities sent a contingent. It is possible, however, to make an estimate of these also that comes very near to the truth. For not more than nine thousand Athenians marched to Marathon, even if we include those who were too old for active service and slaves; so the number of Locrian fighting men who marched to Thermopylae cannot have exceeded six thousand. So the whole army would amount to eleven thousand two hundred. But it is well known that not even these remained all the time guarding the pass; for if we except the Lacedaemonians, Thespians and Mycenaeans, the rest left the field before the conclusion of the fighting.

[3] To meet the barbarians who came from the Ocean the following Greek forces came to Thermopylae. Of the Boeotians ten thousand hoplites and five hundred cavalry, the Boeotarchs being Cephisodotus, Thearidas, Diogenes and Lysander. From Phocis came five hundred cavalry with footmen three thousand in number. The generals of the Phocians were Critobulus and Antiochus.

[4] The Locrians over against the island of Atalanta were under the command of Meidias; they numbered seven hundred, and no cavalry was with them. Of the Megarians came four hundred hoplites commanded by Hipponicus of Megara. The Aetolians sent a large contingent, including every class of fighting men; the number of cavalry is not given, but the light-armed were seven hundred and ninety, and their hoplites numbered more than seven thousand. Their leaders were Polyarchus, Polyphron and Lacrates.

[5] The Athenian general was Callippus, the son of Moerocles, as I have said in an earlier part of my work, and their forces consisted of all their seaworthy triremes, five hundred horse and one thousand foot. Because of their ancient reputation the Athenians held the chief command. The king of Macedonia sent five hundred mercenaries, and the king of Asia a like number; the leader of those sent by Antigonus was Aristodemus, a Macedonian, and Telesarchus, one of the Syrians on the Orontes, commanded the forces that Antiochus sent from Asia.

[6] When the Greeks assembled at Thermopylae learned that the army of the Gauls was already in the neighborhood of Magnesia and Phthiotis, they resolved to detach the cavalry and a thousand light armed troops and to send them to the Spercheius, so that even the crossing of the river could not be effected by the barbarians without a struggle and risks. On their arrival these forces broke down the bridges and by themselves encamped along the bank. But Brennus himself was not utterly stupid, nor inexperienced, for a barbarian, in devising tricks of strategy.

[7] So on that very night he despatched some troops to the Spercheius, not to the places where the old bridges had stood, but lower down, where the Greeks would not notice the crossing, and just where the river spread over the plain and made a marsh and lake instead of a narrow, violent stream. Hither Brennus sent some ten thousand Gauls, picking out the swimmers and the tallest men; and the Celts as a race are far taller than any other people.

[8] So these crossed in the night, swimming over the river where it expands into a lake; each man used his shield, his national buckler, as a raft, and the tallest of them were able to cross the water by wading. The Greeks on the Spercheius, as soon as they learned that a detachment of the barbarians had crossed by the marsh, forthwith retreated to the main army. Brennus ordered the dwellers round the Malian gulf to build bridges across the Spercheius, and they proceeded to accomplish their task with a will, for they were frightened of Brennus, and anxious for the barbarians to go away out of their country instead of staying to devastate it further.

[9] Brennus brought his army across over the bridges and proceeded to Heracleia. The Gauls plundered the country, and massacred those whom they caught in the fields, but did not capture the city. For a year previous to this the Aetolians had forced Heracleia to join the Aetolian League; so now they defended a city which they considered to belong to them just as much as to the Heracleots. Brennus did not trouble himself much about Heracleia, but directed his efforts to driving away those opposed to him at the pass, in order to invade Greece south of Thermopylae.

Source: *Book 10, chapter 20, in* Pausanias: Description of Greece, *5 volumes, translated by W. H. S. Jones and others (Cambridge, Mass.: Harvard University Press / London: Heinemann, 1918–1935).*

Even where the evidence is right before his eyes, Pausanias often makes errors. We are lucky enough to have found some inscriptions that Pausanias apparently saw and recorded information from. Unfortunately, his record of reporting such information correctly leaves something to be desired. A milestone found in Olympia proclaims that Sparta is 630 stadia (about 75 miles) from Olympia; Pausanias, who apparently saw the same stone, reports the figure as 660 stadia (6.18.6). At the entrance to the Athenian Acropolis, Pausanias speculates that a pair of statues of horsemen might depict the sons of Xenophon the historian (1.22.4), an idea he apparently gets from an inscription on the base naming a different Xenophon as one of the dedicators of the statues. At the city of Megara, Pausanias misreads a tomb inscription and gives credit to a Megarian leader Orsippos for conquering land from Megara's neighbors. The inscription actually celebrates Orsippos for gaining back land that Megara's neighbors had conquered (1.44.1).

This list might be extended if we had other reliable sources with which to check the majority of things that Pausanias says. Unfortunately, much of the historical material he includes in his account occurs nowhere else. Where we can verify his testimony with independent information, his record does not inspire confidence. Pausanias is undoubtedly an important writer. His attempt to provide a detailed, eyewitness description of Greece is something that no other ancient writer attempted, and for that reason alone he deserves credit. Yet, however well he performed that task, and however useful his *Description of Greece* may be to archaeologists and art historians, in the matter of writing history he must be considered something of an amateur. While modern historians can scarcely avoid consulting his text and considering the information he has to give, utmost caution is in order when doing so.

–WILLIAM E. HUTTON,
COLLEGE OF WILLIAM AND MARY

References

Susan E. Alcock, *Graecia Capta: The Landscapes of Roman Greece* (Cambridge: Cambridge University Press, 1993).

Alcock and others, eds., *Pausanias: Travel and Memory in Roman Greece* (Oxford: Oxford University Press, 2001).

Graham Anderson, *The Second Sophistic: A Cultural Phenomenon in the Roman Empire* (London: Routledge, 1993).

K. W. Arafat, *Pausanias' Greece: Ancient Artists and Roman Rulers* (Cambridge: Cambridge University Press, 1996).

Jaś Elsner, *Art and the Roman Viewer: The Transformation of Art from the Pagan World to Christianity* (Cambridge: Cambridge University Press, 1995).

J. G. Frazer, *Pausanias' Description of Greece,* 6 volumes (London: Biblo & Tannen, 1897).

Christian Habicht, *Pausanias' Guide to Ancient Greece,* second edition (Berkeley: University of California Press, 1998).

W. H. S. Jones and others, trans., *Pausanias: Description of Greece,* 5 volumes (Cambridge, Mass.: Harvard University Press, 1971–1978).

Peter Levi, trans., *Pausanias, Guide to Greece* (Harmondsworth, U.K.: Penguin, 1971).

W. Kendrick Pritchett, *Pausanias Periegetes I* (Amsterdam: Gieben, 1998).

Pritchett, *Pausanias Periegetes II* (Amsterdam: Gieben, 1999).

Simon Swain, *Hellenism and Empire: Language, Classicism, and Power in the Greek World,* AD *50–250* (Oxford: Oxford University Press, 1996).

ROMAN PERIOD: PLUTARCH

Is Plutarch the founder of modern biography?

Viewpoint: Yes. Plutarch is rightly considered the founder of modern biography because he had a profound influence upon later practitioners of the genre, especially Samuel Johnson and James Boswell.

Viewpoint: No. Plutarch cannot be termed the founder of modern biography because his methods and concerns are not those of the biographer as the term is understood today. He wrote most of the *Lives* in pairs for the moral and philosophical instruction of his readers.

If Plutarch is to be styled the founder of modern biography, then we should expect to see his influence clearly in the works of the most important modern practitioners of the form. And indeed, a study of content and structure shows that both Samuel Johnson and James Boswell exhibit their debt to Plutarch throughout their work. Johnson's emphasis on the valuable insight to be gained by the average person through reading biographies and on the psychological closeness it engenders reflects a quintessentially Plutarchan conception of biography. Boswell, following the same path, explicitly cites Plutarch as a primary influence on his biographical art. Both Johnson's and Boswell's biographies depend upon creating an empathetic understanding for their subject by the judicious use of significant details and by the selective use of telling anecdotes, two strategies of which Plutarch is an admitted master. The presentation of events in a basically chronological order, so that the narrative moves along with the life of the subject, is also an inheritance from Plutarch's *Lives.* This reflects a clear preference for Plutarch's methodology over that of his main ancient rival, the Roman biographer Suetonius: he uses a nonchronological structure, grouping material together under various themes and topics, which robs many of the particular details and anecdotes of their wider significance. In the light of the decisive and unmistakable influence that Plutarch exerts on the first modern writers of biographies, then, it can be argued that he is the founder of modern biography.

The argument against crowning Plutarch as the founder of modern biography, while not disputing his influence on such writers as Johnson, Boswell, and many others, rests on the claim that Plutarch himself did not write biographies in the modern sense of the word. There is no ancient Greek term for "biography" or "biographer," and Plutarch makes clear that his *Lives* are primarily ethical in their purpose, designed to instigate processes of self-evaluation and self-formation in his readers. The elaborate structure of the *Parallel Lives*—a Greek *Life,* followed by a Roman *Life,* and ending with a formal *Comparison* of the two—indicates that Plutarch had a much broader purpose in mind than simply recording historical and biographical material. The *Parallel Lives* are an attempt to bring the Greek and Roman worlds into closer association, with particular reference to how educated Greeks, now living under the rule of imperial Rome, should come to terms with the historical forces they had experienced. Consequently, close examination of the *Lives* reveals that some of the most definitive techniques of modern biography—such as the unbiased selection of the most important details in an individual's life and the presentation of a character in all its often contradictory complexity—are subordinated to the programmatic demands of Plutarch's unique project. Although many later biographers certainly demonstrate indebtedness to Plutarch in various ways—including his mastery of the revealing anecdote and the slight, but telling, detail—the purpose and nature of his *Parallel Lives* are fundamentally different from those of modern biography.

—David H. J. Larmour

Viewpoint: Yes. Plutarch is rightly considered the founder of modern biography because he had a profound influence upon later practitioners of the genre, especially Samuel Johnson and James Boswell.

The phrase "founder of modern biography," if it may be accurately applied to Plutarch, implies that his contribution to the development of biographical literature exerted a direct and profound influence on later biographers at a stage when the genre had achieved its modern form. This stage is dated uniformly in historical descriptions of the genre to eighteenth-century England and the person of Samuel Johnson (1709–1784). To affirmatively adduce Plutarch, therefore, as the founder of modern biography requires that we trace his influence to Johnson and establish its efficacy in Johnson's biographical productions or statements he made pertaining to biography. It also requires that we comprehend the essential nature of Plutarch's biographical works so as to properly identify and distinguish his influence in the writings of Johnson and others. In the background lurks the question as to why a literary genre that purports to describe the life of an individual should need an exemplary founder-figure, since its structure–tracing a life from the cradle to the grave–is dictated by the circumstances of the human condition.

Despite having been born in the small Greek town of Chaeronea, Plutarch (born before 50 C.E., died after 120 C.E.) was able to acquire notoriety in his lifetime as a philosopher and biographer, based principally on the variety and quality of his literary works. Plutarch's reputation in subsequent generations derives primarily from the *Parallel Lives.* Originally published in groups, the series ultimately grew to a total of forty-six biographies pairing a notable Greek general or statesmen with an equally remarkable Roman counterpart. No other ancient author comes close to Plutarch in terms of the sheer scope and number of biographies he wrote.

The other preeminent biographer of antiquity was the Roman Suetonius (born circa 70 C.E.–died after 128 C.E.), who composed a work titled *The Lives of the Twelve Caesars,* beginning with the life of Julius Caesar and ending with that of the emperor Domitian. Since Plutarch and Suetonius employed different strategies in the organization of their material, it would be advantageous to subject their biographical techniques to a brief analysis. This will ultimately allow us to better assess any claim either author may have to the title of "founder of modern biography." Suetonius begins with the emperor's birth and ancestry and organizes his material in a chronological sequence initially. The reign is presented in a primarily nonchronological organized section arranged under clear rubrics or categories (*per species*). In this section of the biography, Suetonius discusses the emperor's appearance, personal habits, attire, character, and conduct in peace and war. Suetonius subsequently concludes the life with a report of the emperor's death and some concluding remarks. Plutarch's *Lives,* by contrast, proceeds for the most part chronologically, often after an introduction or proem that sets forth the themes explored in the paired biographies. In terms of characterization, Suetonius's methods are sometimes said to result in more impressive, complex depictions of the individuals concerned than Plutarch's since "it is much better suited to bringing out a modern style of manysidedness" (Pelling).

In the case of both Suetonius and Plutarch, the main vehicle of characterization is the anecdote. The compelling nature of Plutarch's portraiture resides in the gradual accretion of subtle details intended to compliment and refine traits and themes that he often initially presents in a blunt or crude way (Pelling). This "progressive redefinition of character" reflects a primary difference between the compositional techniques of Plutarch and Suetonius and can only be displayed in a chronologically oriented presentation of life events.

Plutarch is also far more inclined to elaborate an anecdote in the direction of psychological depth and complexity than Suetonius. Despite the wealth of information at his disposal in his biographies of Augustus and Caesar, Suetonius rarely, if ever, displays an interest in delving below the surface. We do not have the feeling that he attempted to get to know his subject in the same way as Plutarch. This is another key factor that serves to distinguish the two authors' techniques. In addition, Suetonius's willingness to employ anecdotal material taken from the seamier side of private life is not matched by Plutarch. This reflects, in some cases at least, a self-imposed restriction by Plutarch, his sense of propriety, and not necessarily a deficiency of information. Suetonius obviously did not share this sense of propriety and elected to tell all without discretion. This does not mean that Plutarch always glossed over his subjects' failings (cf. *Cimon* 2. 4–5). Rather, he finds some types of human frailty more interesting than others. An additional factor complicating any sort of easy value judgment about the relative merits of Suetonius and Plutarch is the fact that one must take account of the overlapping biographies of other late republican period figures, such as Cato, Cicero, Pompey, Crassus, Brutus, and Anthony. Plutarch's *Life of Caesar* and others might have been richer had he not reserved some material for coverage in these biographies.

The relatively static nature of Suetonius's category system has a deleterious effect on the dynamic and natural quality of the depiction of a person's life as it unfolds. Suetonius's method also presumes sufficient information to fill the categories. His categories are so restrictive that were there to be a dearth of proper data, he would almost certainly fail to render anything but a sketchy portrait. His *Lives of Galba* and *Otho* are cases in point. Unlike the case of Plutarch, we could not envision a life-like Lycurgus or Numa arising from the pen of Suetonius.

Suetonius's spotlight tends to fall nearly continuously on one Caesar, and this tends to make his characterizations less thought provoking and more uniform: the emperor is nearly always the grammatical or logical subject of the sentence. The strengths and weaknesses of the emperor are not generally highlighted against a vivid and instructive backdrop that includes his interactions with other significant individuals. The decontextualization of much anecdotal material and the austere brevity with which it is related robs it of much of its expressive force. The variegation of his portraits is only superficial. A closer look reveals a lack of depth and psychological complexity when they are compared to Plutarch's *Lives.*

The reception of the two authors' biographical works is strikingly different. Suetonius's method supplants historical writing for a time (until Ammianus Marcellinus), and his category technique resurfaces, for example, in Einhart's *Life of Charlemagne* (840, *Vita Karoli Magni*) and in various hagiographic lives of saints (*vita Sanctorum*). Although widely read in later years (more than forty editions of his *Lives of the Twelve Caesars* were published between 1470 and 1820), Suetonius is generally used as an historical source rather than as a model for the composition of biography. Plutarch suffered a different fate, however. His *Parallel Lives* reentered Europe with the publication of the first edition (*editio princeps*) in Florence, Italy, in 1517. The truly widespread popularity of the Greek biographer would have to await the appearance in 1559 of the French translation by Jacques Amyot (1513–1593). Amyot's translation was in turn used by Thomas North (1535–1601?), whose English version was first published in 1579. Through the translations of Amyot and North, Plutarch became a classic and for approximately

SUETONIUS

Unlike Plutarch, the historian Suetonius was more willing to record the salacious details of his subjects' personal lives, as exhibited in the following excerpt from his account of Caligula, Roman emperor from 37 to 41 C.E.:

XXIV. He lived in the habit of incest with all his sisters; and at table, when much company was present, he placed each of them in turns below him, whilst his wife reclined above him. It is believed, that he deflowered one of them, Drusilla, before he had assumed the robe of manhood; and was even caught in her embraces by his grandmother Antonia, with whom they were educated together. When she was afterwards married to Cassius Longinus, a man of consular rank, he took her from him, and kept her constantly as if she were his lawful wife. In a fit of sickness, he by his will appointed her heiress both of his estate and the empire. After her death, he ordered a public mourning for her; during which it was capital for any person to laugh, use the bath, or sup with his parents, wife, or children. Being inconsolable under his affliction, he went hastily, and in the night-time, from the City; going through Campania to Syracuse, and then suddenly returned without shaving his beard, or trimming his hair. Nor did he ever afterwards, in matters of the greatest importance, not even in the assemblies of the people or before the soldiers, swear any otherwise, than "By the divinity of Drusilla." The rest of his sisters he did not treat with so much fondness or regard; but frequently prostituted them to his catamites. He therefore the more readily condemned them in the case of Aemilius Lepidus, as guilty of adultery, and privy to that conspiracy against him. Nor did he only divulge their own handwriting relative to the affair, which he procured by base and lewd means, but likewise consecrated to Mars the Avenger three swords which had been prepared to stab him, with an inscription, setting forth the occasion of their consecration.

Source: *Cal. 24, in Suetonius,* The Lives of the Twelve Caesars, *edited and translated by Alexander Thomson (Philadelphia: Gebbie, 1889).*

two centuries thereafter maintained his appeal and influence in educated circles. William Shakespeare (1564–1616) used North's translation in the composition of several of his plays such as *Julius Caesar, Antony and Cleopatra,* and *Coriolanus.* With perhaps Shakespeare's greatest critic, Samuel Johnson, we arrive at the beginning of a biographical form that we can term modern.

The influence of Plutarch on Johnson is salient and undeniable (Parke). Johnson's first important biographical endeavor, his *Life of Savage,* bears so much similarity to Plutarch's *Lives* in style and conception, right down to its thematic introduction, that it has been termed directly Plutarchan (Dussinger). In two major statements on biography Johnson clearly articulated, perhaps more eloquently than anyone else, the true appeal of biography for the common man. He stresses its promotion of empathetic understanding through the depiction of life situations to which the average person can readily relate:

> All joy or sorrow for the happiness or calamities of others is produced by an act of the imagination, that realizes the event however fictitious, or approximates it however remote, by placing us, for a time, in the condition of him whose fortune we contemplate; so that we feel, while the deception lasts, whatever motions would be excited by the same good or evil happening to ourselves.
>
> Our passions are therefore more strongly moved, in proportion as we can more readily adopt the pains or pleasure proposed to our minds, by recognizing them as once our own, or considering them as naturally incident to our state of life. It is not easy for the most artful writer to give us an interest in happiness or misery, which we think ourselves never likely to feel, and with which we have never yet been made acquainted. Histories of the downfall of kingdoms, and revolutions of empires, are read with tranquillity; the imperial tragedy pleases common auditors only by its pomp of ornament, and grandeur of ideas; and the man whose faculties have been engrossed by business, and whose heart never fluttered but at the rise or fall of stocks, wonders how the attention can be seized or the affection agitated by a tale of love.

Johnson, furthermore, is clearly right in pointing out that our interest is piqued and our attention focused by prominent personages contending with life situations similar to ones we ourselves may or have experienced:

> The general and rapid narratives of history, which involve a thousand fortunes in the business of a day, and complicate innumerable incidents in one great transaction, afford few lessons applicable to private life, which derives its comforts and its wretchedness from the right or wrong management of things which nothing but their frequency makes considerable, *Parva, si non fient quotidie,* says Pliny, and which can have no place in those relations which never descend below the consultation of senates, the motions of armies, and the schemes of conspirators.
>
> I have often thought that there has rarely passed a life of which a judicious and faithful narrative would not be useful.

Johnson's ancient predecessor Plutarch, reflecting on his own experience in writing biographies, was also aware of the value of biography for the individual, in which the reader acquires an empathetic understanding of the subject:

> Although I originally took up the writing of *Lives* for others, I find that the task has grown on me and I continue it for my own sake too, in the sense that I treat the narrative as a kind of mirror and try to find ways to arrange my life and assimilate it to the virtues of my subjects. The experience is like nothing so much as spending time in their company and living with them: I receive and welcome each in turn as my guest, so to speak, observe 'his stature and his qualities', and choose from his achievements those which it is particularly important and valuable for me to know. 'And oh, what greater delight could one find than this?' And could one find a more effective means of moral improvement either (*Aemilius* 1.1–3, trans. Waterfield)?

Both men share in the view that ultimately a sympathetic experiencing of the subject, with a certain immediacy, is to be had in good biography, and both mention the didactic or ethical impact the presentation of a life may have. Plutarch sees in biography a tool by which we may better be able to monitor and correct our own behavior, viewing ourselves in "a mirror." Clearly, the generation of this mirror effect presumes the element of recognition so firmly grasped by Johnson, and this recognition effect is likely to be more pronounced in the more mundane exigencies of daily life and intercourse with other people than in momentous historical events, which are tangential to the few.

His protégé and biographer, James Boswell (1740–1795), also clearly aligns his work with Plutarch, "the prince of ancient biographers," in citing and adopting the ancient biographer's famous distinction between history and biography, reflected in the passage from Johnson's essay cited above, as the basis for his own great biography of Johnson:

> I am not writing history but biography, and the most outstanding exploits do not always have the property of revealing the goodness or badness of the agent; often, in fact, a casual action, the odd phrase, or a jest reveals character better than battles involving the loss of thousands upon thousands of lives, huge troop movements, and whole cites besieged.

And so, just as a painter reproduces his subject's likeness by concentrating on the face and the expression of the eyes, by means of which character is revealed, and pays hardly any attention to the rest of the body, I must be allowed to devote more time to those aspects which indicate a person's mind and to use these to portray the life of each of my subjects, while leaving their major exploits and battles to others (*Alexander* 1. 2, trans. Waterfield).

In their interest and reliance on anecdotes, and other significant minutiae that are supremely revealing of character, Plutarch, Johnson, and Boswell share a common methodological stance with far-reaching implications. Their goal—and in this they all supercede Suetonius's more modest aims—is to encourage and enable the reader truly to understand, empathize with, and, in some nonsuperficial way, identify with the biographical subject. To this end, material conducive to the depiction of the subject's character and personality is carefully selected. These writers present to the reader allusive idiosyncratic details in a chronological organization, which breathe life into a portrait that would otherwise tend to consist of a static collection of stock attributes. Since both Johnson and Boswell, acknowledged to be the first practitioners of modern biography, consciously follow Plutarch in nearly every way, Plutarch may rightfully be called the founder of modern biography.

—MARK A. BECK,
UNIVERSITY OF SOUTH CAROLINA

Viewpoint: No. Plutarch cannot be termed the founder of modern biography because his methods and concerns are not those of the biographer as the term is understood today. He wrote most of the *Lives* in pairs for the moral and philosophical instruction of his readers.

Although Plutarch's *Lives* of Caesar, Alexander, and the like are often cited as the supreme examples of ancient biography, it is a fact that there is no term in the ancient world for "biography" or "biographer." This above all shows that this genre of writing did not exist in the form that we recognize today. What did exist were "lives" of famous individuals, usually politicians, generals, and rulers, and these were a collection of their notable deeds and sayings. These were presented in the form of a narrative, and so resembled the works of the historians, but their focus was on the character of the individual in question and how he reacted in various challenging situations, which reflects a debt to the tradition of philosophy, especially the branch known as ethics. Plutarch, who was a man of considerable learning and of broad intellectual interests, took the writing of such "lives" to a new level of sophistication and certainly comes closest to the designation of *biographer* among all the ancients who practiced this form of art. His *Lives* of famous Greeks and Romans has enjoyed enormous popularity since the Renaissance and inspired many subsequent writers to compose in a similar vein; in this sense, then, he is an important source of inspiration for all biographers, but that is not the same as saying that he founded the genre of biography. A close look at the content of his *Lives,* his methods of composing them, and his purposes in writing them will demonstrate that these narratives are fundamentally different in nature from the biographies that are so popular today.

The first thing to note about Plutarch's *Lives* is that they are arranged in pairs. He calls them *Parallel Lives* for this reason. There is usually a Greek *Life* followed by a Roman one, although occasionally the order is reversed. A few survive without a parallel *Life:* they may have been written to stand on their own, or the other half may have been lost. Now, the purpose of arranging the *Lives* in pairs is not simply cosmetic or a matter of convenience: what Plutarch has done is to look carefully through the historical and cultural traditions of both Greece and Rome to find pairs of statesmen that fit well together. This is an innovative and challenging exercise; the fact that many of the pairs now seem obvious is a tribute to Plutarch's skills and inventiveness in making the two *Lives* fit so naturally together. The parallel structure and the overall design of the collection (which ran to at least twenty-two pairs) indicates that Plutarch had a purpose that went well beyond the telling of exciting narratives about famous men of the past. One of his aims was to bring the Greek and Roman worlds into a closer association through a harmonization of their divergent political and cultural traditions. This was an important, but difficult, intellectual task, and Plutarch chose to do it through narrating the deeds of famous historical figures from both traditions. The Greek *Life* usually comes first in the pair, setting up a kind of template against which the ensuing Roman *Life* is to be read and evaluated. This has been viewed as an attempt to assimilate Roman history to Greek methods and standards of judgment, as well as to represent Roman culture through a lens that was familiar to Greek intellectuals. Beyond this, however, Plutarch's main concern was clearly the question of how to live as an educated Greek under the power of Rome, since Greece was by now a fully incorporated province within the Roman Empire. People living in Greek cities no longer enjoyed the freedom of action that, say, Athenians had in the self-governing polis of the classical era: how then to live as a free and freethinking citizen in this changed environment? The *Lives* attempts to set up a dialogue between Greek and Roman experience in general terms, and Plutarch's readers would presumably learn from this discourse how to carry on a similar dialogue in their own daily lives.

This brings us to the moral purpose behind Plutarch's *Lives.* The author comments in various places that he is writing not history but "lives," and that these "lives" function like a mirror in which one can fashion one's own way of life: "attempting somehow or other in the mirror of history to adorn life and make it like the virtues of those men" (*Life of Aemilius,* 1.1). The moral element comes through most clearly in another feature of Plutarch's work; namely, the comparison between the two *Lives* that appears at the end of most pairs in the collection of *Parallel Lives.* He probably invented this feature for his particular purposes. In this comparison, Plutarch draws out the similarities in the experiences of his subjects, especially their dealings with members of their families, their fellow citizens, and external enemies. He then evaluates each subject in terms of his moral conduct in various situations, making judgments in each case as to whether the Greek or the Roman fared better and deserves praise or criticism. In making these judgments, he explores the significant differences or contrasts between the actions and moral choices made by the Greek and Roman protagonists. Many of the judgments, and indeed most of the comparisons themselves, have been roundly criticized for their superficiality. They are often stigmatized by modern readers as an unnecessary excrescence on what should be "pure" history or biography. The desire to turn Plutarch's tripartite narrative–two lives and a comparison–into history or biography in the modern mold, however, fragments its structure and distorts its purpose. It is true that much of the content in the comparison does resemble a rather banal "compare and contrast" exercise performed by students of little more than average intelligence and perceptiveness. Yet, that is precisely the point. The comparison is not designed as an exhaustive survey of all the evidence from a rigorous position of moral and philosophical superiority. Sometimes it even appears to contradict things said in the *Lives* that have just preceded it. However, Plutarch is not a sloppy or forgetful author. Rather, the comparison is his attempt to "get the ball rolling," for it is the duty of the reader to continue the process and through it come to appreciate the moral content of the *Lives* that have been presented. The aim is that the readers should examine their own conduct through the study of how others lived and made adjustments to their own modus vivendi accordingly. That the content of the *Lives* is often exciting, amusing, and affecting, we may attribute to Plutarch's insight that moral instruction is best presented through entertaining narratives of the great figures of history. Time has borne out the accuracy of this insight.

Given his purposes, then, Plutarch has to put his narratives together in a fashion that ensures his overall designs will be achieved. And here it is clear that he has to go well beyond the traditional forms of ancient historiography and, it is true to say, to veer away from the norms of biography as we use the term in the modern world. The movement of each *Life* is recognizably chronological, but the specificities of chronology are often passed over in favor of making sure that the moral lessons of the *Life* become apparent. Thus, for example, in his *Life of Antony,* he postpones some of Antony's early misdemeanors until a later point in the narrative, so that he can contrast these actions with his noble behavior at the Battle of Philippi; as one commentator, Christopher B. R. Pelling, puts it, "private excess and yet brilliant ability: the contrast is programmatic, and it is useful to have it stated so clearly just before the entry of Cleopatra." The average *Life* is more like a collection of anecdotes than a sustained narrative moving from year to year like a modern biography. In the *Life of Themistocles,* for instance, a whole chapter is devoted to largely unconnected sayings and incidents that, one after the other, illustrate the protagonist's quick wit, ambition, and combativeness. Plutarch explicitly comments that he likes to make use of the telling detail or incident much more than to provide a complete account of events. It is through such details, he says, that character is most graphically revealed, and hence that the moral lesson is most effectively communicated. As he remarks in the opening of the *Life of Alexander:*

> For it is not so much histories I am writing as lives, and it is not always in the most outstanding deeds that virtue or vice is revealed, but often a little matter like a saying or a joke points to character more than battles where thousands die, huge numbers of troops, or the sieges of cities. So, just as painters achieve likenesses from the face and the look of the eyes, by which character is hinted at, paying very little attention to the other parts of the body, so I must be permitted to penetrate the signs of the soul, and through these to shape the life of each man, leaving to others the big events and battles.

This leads to a certain amount of manipulation on Plutarch's part. There was for most *Lives* a vast amount of material available from all sorts of sources, and Plutarch had the leisure and

Page from the first edition in Greek (1517) of Plutarch's *Lives*

(courtesy of the Lilly Library, Indiana University)

ΠΛΟΥΤΑΡΧΟΥ ΠΑΡΑΛΛΗΛΑ.

ΘΗΣΕΥΣ.

Ὥσπερ ἐν ταῖς γεωγραφίαις ὦ Σόσσιε σενεκίων, οἱ ἱστορικοὶ τὰ διαφεύγοντα τὴν γνῶσιν αὐτῶν τοῖς ἐσχάτοις μέρεσι τῶν πινάκων πιεζοῦντες, ἐνίοις παραγράφουσιν ὅτι τὰ δ᾽ ἐπέκεινα θῖνες ἄνυδροι καὶ θηριώδεις, ἢ πηλὸς ἀϊδνής, ἢ σκυθικὸν ὄρος, ἢ πέλαγος πεπηγός, οὕτως ἐμοὶ περὶ τὴν τῶν βίων τῶν παραλλήλων συγγραφὴν, τὸν ἐφικτὸν εἰκότι λόγῳ καὶ βάσιμον ἱστορίᾳ πραγμάτων ἐχομένῃ χρόνον διελθόντι, περὶ τῶν ἀνωτέρω, καλῶς εἶχεν εἰπεῖν. τὰ δ᾽ ἐπέκεινα τερατώδη καὶ τραγικά, ποιηταὶ καὶ μυθογράφοι νέμονται. καὶ οὐκέτ᾽ ἔχει πίστιν οὐδὲ σαφήνειαν. ἐπεὶ δὲ τὸν περὶ λυκούργου τοῦ νομοθέτου, καὶ νομᾶ τοῦ βασιλέως λόγον ἐκδόντες, ἐδοκοῦμεν οὐκ ἂν ἀλόγως τῷ ῥωμύλῳ προσαναβῆναι, πλησίον τῶν χρόνων αὐτοῦ τῇ ἱστορίᾳ γεγονότες. σκοποῦντι δέ μοι, τοιῷδε φωτὶ κατ᾽ αἰσχύλον, τίς ξυμβήσεται, τίν᾽ ἀντιτάξω τῷδε, τίς φερέγγυος, ἐφαίνετο τὸν τῶν καλῶν καὶ ἀοιδίμων οἰκιστὴν ἀθηνῶν, ἀντιστῆσαι καὶ παραβαλεῖν τῷ πατρὶ τῆς ἀνικήτου καὶ μεγαλοδόξου ῥώμης. εἴη μὲν οὖν ἡμῖν ἐκκαθαιρόμενον λόγῳ τὸ μυθῶδες ὑπακοῦσαι καὶ λαβεῖν ἱστορίας ὄψιν. ὅπου δ᾽ ἂν αὐθαδῶς τοῦ πιθανοῦ περιφρονῇ, καὶ μὴ δέχηται τὴν πρὸς τὸ εἰκὸς μῖξιν, εὐγνωμόνων ἀκροατῶν δεησόμεθα, καὶ πρᾴως τὴν ἀρχαιολογίαν προσδεχομένων. ἐδόκει δ᾽ οὖν ὁ θησεὺς τῷ ῥωμύλῳ κατὰ πολλὰς ἐναρμόττειν ὁμοιότητας. ἄμφω μὲν ἀνέγγυοι καὶ σκότιοι γενόμενοι, δόξαν ἔσχον ἐκ θεῶν γεγονέναι. ἄμφω δ᾽ αἰχμητά. τό γε δὴ καὶ ἴδμεν ἅπαντες. καὶ μετὰ τοῦ δυνατοῦ τὸ συνετὸν ἔχοντες. πόλεων δὲ τῶν ἐπιφανεστάτων, ὁ μὲν ἔκτισε τὴν ῥώμην. ὁ δὲ, συνῴκισε τὰς ἀθήνας. ἁρπαγὴ δὲ γυναικῶν ἑκατέρῳ πρόσεστιν. οὐδέτερος δὲ δυστυχίαν περὶ τὰ οἰκεῖα καὶ νέμεσιν ἐγγενῆ διέφυγεν. ἀλλὰ καὶ τελευτῶντες ἀμφότεροι λέγονται τοῖς αὑτῶν προσκροῦσαι πολίταις. εἴ τι τῶν ἥκιστα τραγικῶς εἰρῆσθαι δοκούντων, ὄφελός ἐστι πρὸς ἀλήθειαν. θησέως, τὸ μὲν πατρῷον γένος εἰς ἐρεχθέα καὶ τοὺς πρώτους αὐτόχθονας ἀνήκει. τῷ δὲ μητρῴῳ, πελοπίδης ἦν. πέλοψ γὰρ οὐ χρημάτων πλήθει μᾶλλον ἢ παίδων, μέγιστον ἴσχυσε τῶν ἐν πελοποννήσῳ βασιλέων. πολλὰς μὲν ἐκδόμενος θυγατέρας τοῖς ἀρίστοις. πολλοὺς δὲ ταῖς πολιτείαις ἐγκατασπείρας ἄρχοντας. ὧν εἷς γενόμενος πιτθεὺς ὁ θησέως πάππος, πόλιν μὲν οὐ μεγάλην τὴν τροιζηνίων ᾤκησε, δόξαν δὲ μάλιστα πάντων ὡς ἀνὴρ λόγιος ἐν τοῖς τότε καὶ σοφώτατος ἔσχεν. ἦν δὲ τῆς σοφίας ἐκείνης τοιαύτη τις ὡς ἔοικεν ἰδέα καὶ δύναμις, οἵᾳ χρησάμενος ἡσίοδος, εὐδοκίμει μάλιστα περὶ τὰς ἐν τοῖς ἔργοις γνωμολογίας. καὶ μίαν γε τούτων ἐκείνην λέγουσι πιτθέως εἶναι, μισθὸς δ᾽ ἀνδρὶ φίλῳ εἰρημένος, ἄρκιος ἔστω. τοῦτο μὲν οὖν καὶ ἀριστοτέλης ὁ φιλόσοφος εἴρηκεν, ὁ δ᾽ εὐριπίδης τὸν ἱππόλυτον, ἁγνοῦ πιτθέως παίδευμα προσειπὼν, ἐμφαίνει τὴν περὶ τὸν πιτθέα δόξαν. αἰγεῖ δὲ παίδων δεομένῳ, τὴν πυθίαν ἀνελεῖν λέγουσι τὸν θρυλούμενον χρησμὸν, διακελευομένην μηδεμιᾷ γυναικὶ συγγενέσθαι, πρὶν ἐλθεῖν εἰς ἀθήνας. οὐ πάνυ δὲ τοῦτο φράζειν ἐπιδήλως δοκοῦσαν. ὅθεν εἰς τροιζῆνα παρελθὼν, ἀνεκοινοῦτο πιτθεῖ τὴν τοῦ θεοῦ φωνὴν, οὕτως ἔχουσαν. ἀσκοῦ τὸν προὔχοντα πόδα μέγα φέρτατε λαῶν, μὴ λύσῃς. πρὶν δῆμον ἀθηναίων εἰσαφικέσθαι. ἄδηλον οὖν ὅτι νοήσας ὁ πιτθεὺς ἔπεισεν αὐτὸν, ἢ διηπάτησε τῇ αἴθρᾳ συγγενέσθαι. συνελθὼν δὲ καὶ γνοὺς ἐκεῖνος ὅτι τῇ πιτθέως θυγατρὶ συγγέγονε καὶ κύειν αὐτὴν ὑπονοήσας, ἀπέλιπε ξίφος καὶ πέδιλα κρύψας ὑπὸ πέτραν μεγάλην, ἐντὸς ἔχουσαν κοιλότητα συμμέτρως ἐμπεριλαμβάνουσαν τὰ κείμενα. φράσας δὲ πρὸς μόνην ἐκείνην, καὶ διακελευσάμενος ἂν υἱὸς ἐξ αὐτοῦ γένηται καὶ λαβὼν ἀνδρὸς ἡλικίαν, δυνατὸς ᾖ τὴν πέτραν ἀναστῆσαι καὶ ὑφελεῖν τὰ καταλειφθέντα, πέμπειν πρὸς αὐτὸν ἔχοντα ταῦτα μηδενὸς εἰδότος, ἀλλ᾽ ὡς ἔνεστι μάλιστα λανθάνοντα πάντας. ἰσχυρῶς γὰρ ἐδεδίει τοὺς παλλαντίδας ἐπιβουλεύοντας αὐτῷ, καὶ διὰ τὴν ἀπαιδίαν καταφρονοῦντας. ἦσαν δὲ πεντήκοντα παῖδες ἐκ πάλλαντος γεγονότες, ἀπῄει. τεκούσης δὲ τῆς αἴθρας υἱὸν, οἱ μὲν, εὐθὺς ὀνομασθῆναι θησέα λέγουσι διὰ τὴν τῶν γνωρισμάτων θέσιν. οἱ δὲ, ὕστερον, ἀθήνησι παῖδα θεμένου τοῦ αἰγέως αὐτόν. τρεφόμενον δὲ ὑπὸ τοῦ πιτθέως ἐπιστάτην ἔχειν καὶ παιδαγωγὸν ὄνομα κοννίδαν. ᾧ μέχρι νῦν ἀθηναῖοι μιᾷ πρότερον ἡμέρᾳ τῶν θησείων, κριὸν ἐναγίζουσι, μεμνημένοι καὶ τιμῶντες πολὺ δικαιότερον, ἢ σιλανίωνα τιμῶσι καὶ παρράσιον εἰκόνων θησέως γραφεῖς καὶ πλάστας γενομένους. ἔθους δὲ ὄντος ἔτι τότε τοὺς μεταβαίνοντας ἐκ παίδων ἐλθόντας εἰς δελφοὺς ἀπάρχεσθαι τῷ θεῷ τῆς κόμης, ἦλθε μὲν, εἰς δελφοὺς ὁ θησεύς. καὶ τόπον ἀπ᾽ αὐτοῦ τὴν θησείαν ἔτι νῦν ὀνομάζεσθαι λέγουσιν. ἐκείρατο δὲ τῆς κεφαλῆς τὰ πρόσθεν μόνον, ὥσπερ ὅμηρος ἔφη τοὺς ἄβαντας. καὶ τοῦτο τῆς κουρᾶς τὸ γένος θησηῒς ὠνομάσθη δι᾽ ἐκεῖνον. οἱ δὲ ἄβαντες ἐκείραντο πρῶτοι τὸν τρόπον τοῦτον. οὐχ ὑπ᾽ ἀράβων

Plutar. a iiii

resources to travel and consult widely. Out of the mass of available evidence, then, he was free to select those items that fitted into his overall scheme most conveniently. What we get, then, within the framework of a standard historical narrative, is an assemblage of incidents, anecdotes, descriptions, and sayings that creates an overall impression of a subject, rather than a systematic account. In the *Lives* of Alcibiades, Nicias, and Themistocles, for example, he deploys the same basic material in quite different ways, in each case governed by his overall conception of the particular *Life* and by its relationship to its parallel *Life*.

Each *Life*, moreover, is structured around a few basic characteristics that form the core of the moral content Plutarch is aiming to convey to his readers. The *Life of Themistocles* rests upon a few defining character traits that Plutarch is careful to introduce at the beginning, showing how the protagonist's early years already manifested their presence: his innate intelligence, his passion for political engagement, his ambitious desire for fame and honor, and his delight in money and possessions. Having established the fundamental elements of Themistocles' character, he proceeds in the remainder of the narrative to show them in action and the consequences they brought both to Themistocles himself and to his fellow Athenians. Many *Lives* follow the pattern of a heroic myth: as a young child, the future statesman already gives indications of his coming greatness; as a young man, he achieves some great victory or reaches the goal of a quest; having reached the pinnacle of power and popularity, he goes into a decline or suffers a reversal of fortune and sometimes meets an unfortunate or ignoble death. In particular, Plutarch seems eager to put his readers on their guard against excessive ambition, pride, greed, and visibility. Quite often we can show by checking other ancient sources that Plutarch has selected or distorted material in order to structure his *Lives* to meet their moral purpose.

He will on occasion also manipulate material so as to bring two *Lives* more closely together, straining the evidence in one so as to create a more convincing parallel with its pair. This can be seen for instance in the *Life of Theseus* and *Life of Romulus*, who are paired as the founders of the two greatest cities in the ancient world, namely, Athens and Rome. Heracles plays an important role in the mythology associated with Theseus, so Plutarch also manages to weave him into the *Life of Romulus* (with which he usually has nothing to do) on no fewer than three occasions. Sometimes he chooses to downplay a well-known element in a particular *Life* in order to set things up for the moral evaluations he will make in the concluding comparison: everyone knew that Theseus was at least partly responsible for the tragic death of his stepson Hippolytus, but Plutarch passes over this incident in a cursory manner, merely commenting that "there is nothing to add to what the poets say." The story was familiar from Euripides' celebrated play *Hippolytus*, and we know from references he makes elsewhere that Plutarch himself was fully aware of the tale. In his *Life of Theseus*, however, he deliberately distances his narrative even further from the story by recording the alternative name for Theseus's stepson, Demophoon, mentioned by the poet Pindar. Why would he do this? The answer lies in one of the main moral points he wants to make in the comparison of Theseus and Romulus: that, in the matter of their domestic misfortunes, Theseus comes off better than Romulus, who killed his brother Remus. The founder of Rome is criticized because his anger and jealousy at Remus led to direct action and unfortunate results, whereas Theseus's behavior consisted of only abusive words and "an old man's curse"–never mind the fact that Hippolytus was presented by Euripides as an essentially blameless victim and that Theseus is forced to confront the results of his rush to judgment against him.

In the *Parallel Lives*, then, some of the most basic tenets of modern biography–the recording of available material with as much chronological precision as possible; the unbiased selection of the most important details; and the presentation of character and personality in all their frequently ambiguous complexity–are subordinated to the programmatic demands of Plutarch's particular project. This project has two main aims: firstly, to bring together the cultural, political, and historical worlds of Greece and Rome, and secondly, to provide the reader with a "technology" of life and moral behavior. The statesmen whose lives are presented in these documents serve as examples or templates, against which it is possible for Plutarch's second-century C.E. readers to fashion for themselves both a new relationship to history and a rigorous, ongoing practice of self-examination. While many modern biographers show considerable indebtedness to Plutarch in various ways–he is an especially good storyteller and has an infallible eye for the telling anecdote–his conception of what he is writing remains fundamentally different.

–DAVID H. J. LARMOUR,
TEXAS TECH UNIVERSITY

References

Frederick E. Brenk, "Plutarch's Life 'Markos Antonios': A Literary and Cultural Study," in *Aufstieg und Niedergang der Römischen Welt*, volume 33, part 2 (Berlin & New York: De Gruyter, 1992), pp. 4347–4469.

Tim Duff, *Plutarch's Lives: Exploring Virtue and Vice* (Oxford: Clarendon Press, 1999).

John A. Dussinger, *The Discourse of the Mind in Eighteenth Century Fiction* (Paris: Mouton, 1974).

John A. Garraty, *The Nature of Biography* (New York: Knopf, 1957).

Samuel Johnson, *The Rambler,* no. 60, Saturday, 13 October 1750 and *Idler,* no. 84, 24 November 1759, in *Biography as an Art: Selected Criticism 1560–1960,* edited by James L. Clifford (New York: Oxford University Press, 1962), pp. 40–45.

David H. J. Larmour, "Making Parallels: Synkrisis and Plutarch's *Themistocles and Camillus,*" in *Aufstieg und Niedergang der Römischen Welt,* volume 33, part 2 (Berlin & New York: De Gruyter, 1992), pp. 4154–4200.

Friedrich Leo, *Die griechische-römische Biographie nach ihrer literarischen Form* (Leipzig: Teubner, 1901).

J. L. Marr, *Plutarch: Lives. Themistocles* (Warminster: Aris & Phillips, 1998).

A. Momigliano, *The Development of Greek Biography* (Cambridge, Mass.: Harvard University Press, 1993).

Catherine N. Parke, *Biography: Writing Lives,* Studies in Literary Themes and Genres, no. 11, edited by Ronald Gottesman (New York: Twayne, 1996).

Christopher B. R. Pelling, *Plutarch: Life of Antony* (Cambridge: Cambridge University Press, 1988).

Pelling, *Plutarch and History* (London: Classical Press of Wales and Duckworth, 2002).

Donald A. Russell, *Plutarch* (London: Duckworth, 1973).

Philip A. Stadter, *Plutarch and the Historical Tradition* (London & New York: Routledge, 1992).

Andrew Wallace-Hadrill, *Suetonius: The Scholar and His Caesars* (London: Duckworth, 1983).

ROMAN PERIOD: TIBERIUS GRACCHUS

Was Tiberius Gracchus an honest champion of the Roman underclass?

Viewpoint: Yes. Tiberius Gracchus was a determined champion of what he saw as the best interests of the Roman people.

Viewpoint: No. Tiberius Gracchus was a failed aristocratic politician who manufactured a social crisis for his own political gain.

Farmers in the Roman Republic were also soldiers, and hundreds of thousands of them went to battle in several major overseas wars in the course of the third and second centuries B.C.E. In doing so, many had to leave their fields untended and suffered from the loss of income from their land. The irony was that the vast majority of the material rewards for military victory flowed to those few who were already rich and who were not serving directly in the legions. The aristocratic classes in Rome were able to buy farmland at reduced prices and assembled huge estates called *latifundia.* These *latifundia* were worked by slaves who came cheaply to Rome as prisoners of war, which further exacerbated the problems of the displaced farmers who could not find work.

The matter of debate, in essence, is whether one should think of Tiberius Sempronius Gracchus as wanting to solve this problem, or to exploit it. Did he, as tribune of the plebs, intend to reestablish displaced and dispossessed farmers and soldiers on their own farmland, thereby alleviating a social crisis and providing a supply of recruits down the road? Or did he, as one of Rome's rich and powerful elite, simply manipulate the combined strength and anger of the nonelite majority of the Roman population in order to compete with his fellow aristocrats for supreme power? Because Gracchus had a foot in two camps—the masses and the elite—an evaluation of him should consider both perspectives. First, one must assess the nature of the crisis that was allegedly facing the Roman people as a result of the *latifundia* system of land management and, on the basis of that assessment, gauge the effectiveness of Gracchus's response. Second, at the level of politics and government, Gracchus's methods for achieving his reforms should be measured against precedent with regard to the Senate, the tribunate, and past efforts at reform. As in all disputes in ancient history, the sources of information are also subject to scrutiny, given their notorious tendentiousness. Tiberius Gracchus was a polarizing figure to the Romans for generations following his death. He was reviled by Cicero, who consistently favored aristocratic interests in public debates, yet lionized by Appian and Plutarch, later writers of the Roman Empire who saw Gracchus as having Roman security interests at heart. The nature of Gracchus's endeavor remains a matter of dispute.

—Joel Allen

Viewpoint: Yes. Tiberius Gracchus was a determined champion of what he saw as the best interests of the Roman people.

The tribune of the plebs was elected by the people and was expected to represent their interests against the wealthier classes by means of extraordinary powers, which included the right to call an assembly of the people and the right to veto actions by the Senate. Tiberius Gracchus was an unlikely candidate for such an office. As the grandson of Scipio Africanus and member of the most decorated and aristocratic families of Rome, he was expected to pursue a different career path, which included military commands, membership in the Senate, and eventually election to the consulship. The fact that he chose the former—a career serving the public—when the latter was his by birthright bespeaks his genuine interest in solving major economic and social problems confronting the state. By the early 130s B.C.E., the republic was approaching a crisis, which Gracchus took on against the odds. He proposed reforms to address key issues and abided by preexisting laws and sensible goals for the collective good in attaining those reforms. His principal flaws were his determination and stubbornness, which led to a negative reputation among a certain segment of the Senate.

Unchecked success in warfare and extremely rapid growth in wealth and international influence were challenges that the old Roman system was incapable of surmounting. Huge swaths of land had become the property of the Roman state: some of it acquired through conquest; some of it abandoned by people who fled into cities to escape Hannibal's invasion in the Second Punic War; and some of it, especially in the south, confiscated from city-states that had openly sided with Hannibal. The land was publicly owned but was farmed by private individuals who kept the proceeds of the crops, minus taxation, for their own families. When soldiers were recruited in droves from the countryside to prosecute the various wars of the young state, many of the smaller farms, now absent their workers, were also taken over by larger landowners. Unlike the absent soldiers, these landowners had access to increasing slave populations, composed of prisoners of war from defeated enemies. As a result, a relatively few estates, called *latifundia,* grew and grew by patchwork, while those who had become displaced swelled the urban populations when they returned from campaign.

The system of *latifundia* was at odds with Rome's military, economic, and social traditions. In Gracchus's day Rome did not have a professional army where soldiers were provided for and paid a wage by the state. Instead, a soldier had to meet minimum property qualifications in order to supply his own armor and weaponry for battle. Therefore, as the number of propertied farmers decreased, so did the manpower of the Roman army. The growth of *latifundia* thus depended on the constant recruiting of soldiers to free up the cheap land, even while depleting the most important source of recruits, namely, the individual family farms. Moreover, with free agricultural workers replaced by slaves, the army had to face new threats to Roman security in the form of potential slave rebellions on the vast estates. Beginning in 135 B.C.E., just before Gracchus's tribunate, a prolonged slave uprising on farms in Sicily had jeopardized the food supply for both the army and the capital city. There was also a simultaneous, though smaller, rebellion in Minturnae, just south of Rome, where the main instigators were crucified. These rebellions had the potential to create an economic crisis in the state and so required military intervention. From a military standpoint, however, the suppression of such revolts sapped resources from other places they were needed. Tiberius Gracchus allegedly witnessed for himself the depopulation and destitution of the countryside in Etruria, north of Rome, when he traveled home through the region after a military engagement in Spain. His younger brother, Gaius Gracchus, said that it was this trip that inspired him to act.

Gracchus's ideas for reform were not new; if anything, he protected the landowners to a greater extent than had previous legislation. Laws limiting the private use of public land may have been more than two hundred years old at the time of his tribunate. According to Livy, the Licinio-Sextian laws of 367 B.C.E. imposed a maximum limit of 500 iugera (about 320 acres) of land that could be worked by one family. Most scholars, however, discredit Livy's account as an exaggeration and agree that the 500-iugera limit probably dates to the early second century. Enforcement of the limit, however, was inherently flawed. The censors who had jurisdiction in the matter were elected from the same class of people as those who owned the lion's share of the land in question; consequently, they were reluctant to prosecute offenders. Gracchus's proposal simply restated the 500-iugera limit and promised better enforcement. Possibly in order to win over members of his opposition, he added a proviso that landowners, for the purposes of organizing their estates and caring for their heirs, could also lay claim to an additional 250 iugera per child, whether son or daughter. The proposed reform thus granted significant concessions to the owners of *latifundia.* The balance of confiscated land was to be divided into small

Mosaic illustrating the corn dole instituted by Gaius Gracchus, Ostia, second century B.C.E.

(Piazzale delle Corporazioni, Ostia, Italy)

allotments of approximately 20 iugera per family—meaning that the beneficiaries of the legislation still had just 4 percent, at most, of the generous allocation to the larger landowners.

What was infuriating to the Senate and ultimately fatal for Gracchus was the tribune's methods for getting his legislation passed—namely, by circumventing the Senate on repeated occasions—and his unwillingness to grant even further concessions. His first law was drafted as a *plebiscitum,* a bill that was voted on by the popular assembly without senatorial oversight. There was nothing unusual or threatening about the *plebiscitum,* but a faction of senators, in order to influence the proceedings, enlisted the help of another tribune of the plebs, Marcus Octavius, to try to protect their interests. As the votes were beginning to be counted on the new law, Marcus Octavius interposed a veto against Gracchus, bringing the process to a halt. Gracchus's famous response was to engineer an additional vote calling for the removal of Octavius from his office. Sources disagree over whether the removal took place on the spot or was carried over to the next day, and over whether it was violent or peaceful; in any case, Octavius was deposed. Modern historians agree that the actions of both Gracchus and Octavius were legal: Octavius had the right to veto his fellow tribune, and Gracchus was allowed to call for any new vote. However, both measures were unorthodox. The Senate had traditionally kept out of the affairs of the popular assembly, and no tribune had ever been removed from office by a colleague. The fact that the senatorial faction drew first blood is significant for our appraisal of Gracchus's actions and motives. Gracchus only resorted to his provocative, potentially hostile measures when he himself was provoked by his opponents; the real blame rests with the Senate.

A second assault on the character of Gracchus can be dismissed on similar grounds—the accusation that Gracchus practiced nepotism in his administration of the redistribution of the land. Previous legislation concerning land reform had barred the principal proponent of the law from serving a regulatory role in its enactment (Bernstein, 1978). It is true that Tiberius Gracchus not only skirted this precedent and served on the commission but he also went a step further by stacking the commission with his father-in-law, Appius Claudius Pulcher, and his younger brother, Gaius Gracchus, in addition to himself. The appointment of Gaius Gracchus was a particularly unusual choice, given that he was only twenty years old and was serving overseas at the time. The justification for Gracchus's controversial appointments can be found again, however, in the alacrity of his opposition. The Senate's manipulation of Marcus Octavius demonstrated that the commission was bound to face resistance in the execution of the new law, and Gracchus had to be assured of support at least from his own administrative colleagues. The inclusion of family members thus does not detract from the sincerity of Gracchus's altruism; on the contrary, it can be said to confirm it.

The Senate's final legal gambit was exercised when the commission sought funds with which to carry out the logistics of the land redistribution. One of the Senate's greatest powers was their control over the treasury, and in response to Gracchus's request, they allocated an unworkably low sum. Gracchus responded to this legal maneuver with one of his own: when word arrived in Rome that Attalus, king of Pergamon, a wealthy city-state in Asia Minor, had died and bequeathed his entire kingdom to the people of Rome, Gracchus proposed and carried a resolution to use that windfall to fund the redistribution. Having redirected imperial revenue away from the treasury in this way, before it fell under senatorial jurisdiction, Gracchus had once again outplayed his senatorial opposition. This maneuver opened him to further charges from his enemies, however. In laying claim to the revenues of a wealthy, eastern kingdom, he was accused of acting out of personal greed and even royalist ambitions. Nevertheless, as in the previous situations, it remains the case that the Senate had proven to be unwilling to compromise. If Gracchus wanted to accomplish anything, he was going to have to resort to drastic measures.

The Senate still had one more way to work its influence and to check the Gracchan initiatives: members of the Senate vowed that they would wait and seek their revenge by prosecuting Gracchus when his term as tribune was up and he was no longer immune to indictment. In response to this threat, Gracchus again applied a creative interpretation of the law. It was not explicitly illegal for a tribune to run for reelection for the year immediately following a term in office, but it had never been done before. Still, determined to keep his land redistribution alive, he broke with tradition and declared his candidacy for the next year with the result that senatorial prosecutors could not touch him. He was assured of victory by the size of the plebeian crowd that supported him. A mob, led by Scipio Nasica, the *pontifex maximus* and one of Gracchus's most virulent opponents in the Senate, instigated a riot in which Tiberius Gracchus and some two hundred others were killed. Historians have pointed out that Nasica had other motives for targeting Gracchus than opposition to his land reform: back in 162 B.C.E., Nasica's father was bumped from the consulship when Gracchus's father, who was consul for the previous year, forced him to abdicate by citing a spurious procedural error involving the taking of the auspices. Nasica's bloody riot, then, was not so much justice for misdeeds on the part of Gracchus as it was the exercising of a generations-old vendetta.

IN PLUTARCH'S EYES

Plutarch's biography of Tiberius Gracchus presents his subject as a Robin Hood figure who took from the rich in order to give to the poor:

His brother Gaius recorded in one of his writings that when Tiberius, on his way to Numantia, passed through Etruria and found the country almost depopulated and its husbandmen and shepherds imported barbarian slaves, he [Tiberius] first conceived the policy which was to be the source of countless ills to himself and to his brother. But it was the people themselves who chiefly excited his zeal and determination with writings on the porticoes, walls, and monuments, calling on him to retrieve the public land for the poor. However, he did not draw up this law by himself, but sought the advice of the citizens who were the most eminent for their virtue and authority. . . . Never, it seems, was a law directed against such great injustice and avarice drafted in milder and gentler terms. For men who should have been punished as lawbreakers, who should have been fined and made to surrender the land which they were illegally exploiting, were granted compensation for quitting their unlawful acquisitions so that citizens in need of assistance could have them. But though the terms of the reform were so favorable and the people were willing to let bygones be bygones if they could be secure from such wrong in the future, yet the men of wealth and property were led by their greed to hate the law and by their anger and party spirit to hate the lawgiver. . . . But they had no success. For Tiberius, fighting for an honorable and just cause with an eloquence that would have dignified even a meaner cause, was formidable and invincible whenever, with the people crowding around the *rostra,* he took his place and spoke in behalf of the poor.

Source: *Naphtali Lewis and Meyer Reinhold, eds.,* Roman Civilization: Selected Readings, *2 volumes, third edition (New York: Columbia University Press, 1990), I: 251.*

Gracchus's persistence in finding loopholes in order to pursue his agenda of reform drove the frustrated Senate to the use of violence. The murder has been remembered as a turning point in Roman history: it represents the utter failure of the rule of law, even while the law was followed to the letter. Octavius vetoed Gracchus; Gracchus had him removed. The Senate refused funding for the operation; Gracchus passed a vote to secure funds from an outside source. The Senate threatened to prosecute; Gracchus ran for reelection. In the history of the republic, the Senate had traditionally outweighed the masses in its influence, and it was surprised and embittered by how it was challenged. Later senatorial writers, such as Cicero, judged Gracchus to be a traitor, or a tyrant. In the end the negative reputation is unfair, given all that Gracchus accomplished for the improvement of the state. Despite the turmoil surrounding its enactment, the breaking up of the *latifundia* appears to have gone forward; the work of the commission continued for four years, until it was ended by consular interference in 129 B.C.E. Census figures for the years following Gracchus's death show that his reforms were effective. The number of citizen landowners in Rome jumped from 318,823 in 131 B.C.E. to 394,736 in 125–124, for an increase of nearly 25 percent in just six years (Brunt, 1971). The reform had the ultimate effect of enlarging Rome's base of support for its legions, which was critical for the military campaigns to come. Gracchus's reforms only sought to enforce existing laws, and his methods for achieving his goals were combative with the Senate only because the opposition against him was fierce. To the extent that he could, Gracchus was careful to stay within legal bounds.

–JOEL ALLEN,
QUEENS COLLEGE,
CITY UNIVERSITY OF NEW YORK

Viewpoint:
No. Tiberius Gracchus was a failed aristocratic politician who manufactured a social crisis for his own political gain.

For all the attention that Tiberius Gracchus gets from modern scholars because of his watershed murder, his contemporaries who necessarily lacked the knowledge of his brother's extraordinary career and the revolutionary changes to come would have viewed him as a flash in the pan. He possessed a distinguished lineage and had a head start on a glorious career but squandered it during his first years in public office as a result of incompetence and bad luck. Overly ambitious and with a sense of entitlement, he bristled at the new roadblocks before him on the conventional path to power, and therefore took a detour via a highly controversial and divisive grab at the tribunate. According to his most virulent detractors, including Cicero, he tried to compensate for his derailment along the *cursus honorum* toward the consulship by pursuing a tyranny that was founded on the manipulation of the masses. He inflated the severity of the *latifundia* crisis, which in reality was a negligible issue, by means of deliberate propaganda, and sought to win support of the people through what amounted to a bribe: free land. In pursuing his reforms, he thumbed his nose at tradition and taunted the powerful Senate into responding with force. True land reform obviously would have required more methodical planning, negotiation, and compromise and could not be rushed. A sincere reformer, with the interests of Rome's underclass in mind, would have realized this and, accordingly, would have shown considerably more restraint and patience.

An evaluation of Gracchus's career should begin well before his tribunate; his family and political background are critical to understanding the decisions he made. His grandfather, Scipio Africanus, was well known as the military genius who defeated Hannibal, and his mother, Cornelia, was a paragon of feminine virtue. His father, also named Tiberius Gracchus, held the consulship twice, in 177 and 163 B.C.E., and had conquered tribes in Spain, Corsica, and Sardinia. In 143 B.C.E. Gracchus married the daughter of Appius Claudius Pulcher, who was consul at the time; he thus joined the wealthy clan of the Claudii. In accordance with his excellent pedigree, he was picked for the augury, a major priesthood, before reaching the minimum age. For his first political office, he served as a quaestor with the army in Spain in 137 under Gaius Hostilius Mancinus. It was during his tenure in Spain that Gracchus encountered his first major setback, which altered the path of his career. After Mancinus was defeated by an Iberian tribe, Gracchus, as quaestor, negotiated a generous treaty with the enemy in order to save his commanding officer from the indignity of captivity. Back in Rome, the Senate, led by Scipio Aemilianus, refused to ratify the treaty on the grounds that it gave away too much. Without senatorial approval, Gracchus lost any chance at a diplomatic solution to his problem; more importantly, he had been disgraced by the Senate under Aemilianus's guidance. His humiliation was even more pronounced when considered alongside the accomplishments of his father, mother, father-in-law, and grandfather.

Some have seen Gracchus's turn to the tribunate as a way of saving face and recapturing some degree of respect in measure with his patrimony. In the patronage system of the Roman Republic, the number of one's clients, or citizen supporters who backed him in the polls as a result of a debt of gratitude of some kind, was the yardstick measuring his *auctoritas,* or public prestige; Roman politicians in the Republic have been compared in this respect with the famous mafia bosses of modern popular culture. A Roman general often won new clients through military conquest, as his veteran soldiers were enriched with the loot taken from the enemy or resettled on their land. In 134, Scipio Aemilianus, the man who had denied Gracchus's efforts at diplomacy three years prior, laid siege to Numantia, the last and greatest holdout of natives in Spain: the reduction of Numantia would thus assure him a new crop of clients in his legions. In order to compete with Aemilianus, and perhaps out of spite, Gracchus ran for tribune. As tribune he could build a different, but equally vast, network of clients with a program of reform designed to assist a large segment of the population. When Aemilianus sacked Numantia to great fanfare in 133, Gracchus responded with increasingly radical and attention-getting reforms. According to Plutarch, Gracchus's primary objective in proposing the land redistribution scheme was to achieve glory and to live up to his name: "some writers consider that Cornelia was at least partly to blame for Tiberius's death, since she often reproached her sons with the fact that the Romans still referred to her as the mother-in-law of Scipio, but not yet as the mother of the Gracchi" (translated by Scott-Kilvert, 1965, p. 160). Rumors also circulated that he wanted to be declared king and that he was considering wearing the purple robes of the deceased king Attalus of Pergamon. In sum, there is abundant circumstantial evidence to suggest that Gracchus was motivated primarily by a desire for public acclaim and respect commensurate with that of his relatives and ancestors.

A similar strategy of self-promotion may lie behind the anecdotes Plutarch reports attesting to Gracchus's alleged distress at the condition of Italian agriculture. Plutarch cites an account of Tiberius's brother, Gaius, that while traveling through Etruria on his way to Numantia in Spain, Gracchus was visibly upset when he noticed the absence of free, nonslave workers on the land. Such a story testifies well—perhaps too well—to the compassion of Gracchus for the nonaristocratic farming class. D. Brendan Nagle has studied survey reports of archaeologists working along the very route that Gracchus would have taken on such a journey and has argued that the land, on the contrary, was well populated at that time. Although it is extremely difficult to assign a precise date to the discoveries of survey archaeology, especially in dealing with a period as early as Gracchus's career, Nagle nevertheless concludes that the story of a heartfelt moment of tenderness on Gracchus's part was a fabrication, probably propaganda. Moreover, another archaeologist, Filippo Coarelli, has also shown that building within the city was booming in the second half of the second century B.C.E. While this explosion of building activity in the city center does not necessarily prove that the economy of the countryside was also in good shape, it is further circumstantial evidence that the idea of a crisis in the economy was an invention of Gracchus. Rather than helping all Romans, in general, he may have been using the reform to help a select

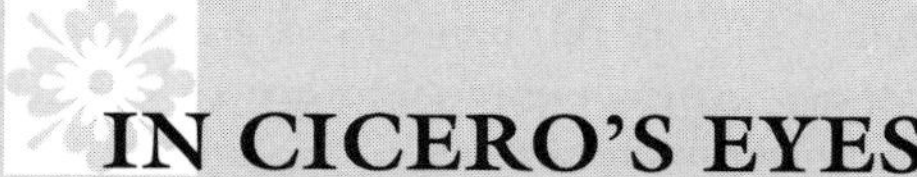

IN CICERO'S EYES

Thinking about the Gracchan affair nearly eighty years after it happened, Cicero sided with the Senate. The following is an excerpt from his speech in defense of Sestius:

Tiberius proposed an agrarian law. The law was acceptable to the People: the fortunes of the poorer classes seemed likely to be established. The Optimates opposed it, because they saw in it an incentive to dissension, and also thought that the state would be stripped of its champions by the eviction of the rich from their long established tendencies. Gaius Gracchus brought forward a corn law. It was agreeable to the masses, for it provided food in abundance without work. Loyal citizens were against it, because they thought that it was a call to the masses to desert industry for idleness, and saw that it was a drain upon the treasury.

Source: *Cicero,* The Speeches, *translated by R. Gardner (Cambridge, Mass.: Loeb Classical Library, Harvard University Press, 1958).*

few. Land reform, after all, was a traditional move in antiquity for a would-be tyrant to promote his career.

The most egregious example of Gracchus's cynically self-interested activity was the provocative appointment of his father-in-law and absent brother to the board of overseers, along with himself, in the redistribution scheme. Earlier land-reform laws said that the proponent of legislation could not sit on the oversight committee. In addition to demonstrating an obvious disrespect for tradition, it also unmistakably opened the way for an abuse of power. If Gracchus had been truly concerned about being able to work with his colleagues in a smooth and efficient way in the face of senatorial opposition, he could have had recourse to other loyalists besides his own family members. In reality, the land-reform commission was a pretext and bridge to the acquisition of personal power.

Defenders of Gracchus often cite the census figures of 125 to point out the fruit of Gracchus's labors and supreme sacrifice. Yet, scholars have offered other explanations for the rise in the number of free, landowning citizens in Rome. There could have been a large manumission of slaves, which drove up the citizen population. Or the property qualifications for the Roman social hierarchy may have been lowered to admit more people. One scholar argues that the census data, rather than proving the popularity and success of Gracchus's reforms, actually proves the opposite. J. Vanderspoel suggests that the Senate in 125 registered more citizens and kept the polls open longer in order to win new clients and suppress the policies of Tiberius's younger brother Gaius, who had also become a radical tribune (Vanderspoel, 1985). The problem is that, in this issue, all we have as evidence are the census numbers with no other data to assist our interpretation.

On his way toward achieving his land-reform goals, Tiberius Gracchus had little respect for legal traditions; he was only able to stay within the letter of the law because the rights and privileges of the tribune were nebulous and susceptible to abuse. The power of veto and the power to call an assembly could be wielded in any conceivable political struggle, and that is what Gracchus did. Taking advantage of the Roman expectation for public officials to hew to tradition, he exploited loopholes that had been open for centuries: he removed a rival tribune from office; he diverted a financial windfall to the people before it could reach the treasury and thus fall under the jurisdiction of the Senate; he favored his family members; and to dodge prosecutors he sought an unprecedented reelection to the tribunate. The fact that he never technically broke the law is not an adequate defense when he was so clearly in violation of the spirit of existing institutions. Tiberius Gracchus knew that true power in Rome was through patronage and prestige. Whether enriching fellow Romans through foreign conquest or land redistribution, one could exercise power at the margins of legitimacy and formal rules. Gracchus's contribution to Roman history was in experimenting with the ways people could acquire power. He was not necessarily villainous; he was simply discovering new strategies for playing an old game. Some Romans may have received some amount of residual benefit from the reforms, but they were never the objects of Gracchus's sincere concern.

–JOEL ALLEN,
QUEENS COLLEGE,
CITY UNIVERSITY OF NEW YORK

References

Appian, *Civil Wars,* edited by J. L. Strachan-Davidson (Oxford: Oxford University Press, 1951).

Alvin H. Bernstein, *Tiberius Sempronius Gracchus: Tradition and Apostasy* (Ithaca, N.Y.: Cornell University Press, 1978).

John Briscoe, "Supporters and Opponents of Tiberius Gracchus," *Journal of Roman Studies,* 64 (1974): 125–135.

P. A. Brunt, *Italian Manpower, 225 B.C.–14 A.D.* (Oxford: Oxford University Press, 1971).

Filippo Coarelli, "Public Building in Rome between the Second Punic War and Sulla," *Papers of the British School at Rome,* 45 (1977): 1–23.

D. C. Earl, *Tiberius Gracchus: A Study in Politics* (Brussels: Latomus, 1963).

M. Gwyn Morgan and John A. Walsh, "Tiberius Gracchus (tr.pl. 133 B.C.), The Numantine Affair, and the Deposition of Marcus Octavius," *Classical Philology,* 73 (1978): 200–210.

D. B. Nagle, "The Etruscan Journey of Tiberius Gracchus," *Historia,* 25 (1976): 487–489.

Plutarch, *Makers of Rome; Nine Lives,* translated by Ian Scott-Kilvert (Baltimore: Penguin, 1965).

J. S. Richardson, "The Ownership of Roman Land: Tiberius Gracchus and the Italians," *Journal of Roman Studies,* 70 (1980): 1–11.

J. Vanderspoel, "Gaius Gracchus and the Census Figures for 125/4 B.C.," *Echos du Monde Classique,* 29 (1985): 101–106.

REFERENCES

1. GENERAL

Briggs, Ward W. Jr., ed. *Dictionary of Literary Biography, Volume 176: Ancient Greek Authors.* Columbia, S.C.: Bruccoli Clark Layman / Detroit: Gale, 1997.

Briggs, ed. *Dictionary of Literary Biography, Volume 211: Ancient Roman Writers.* Columbia, S.C.: Bruccoli Clark Layman / Detroit: Gale, 1999.

Cornell, Tim and John Matthews. *Atlas of the Roman World.* New York: Facts on File, 1982.

Gibbon, Edward. *The History of the Decline and Fall of the Roman Empire.* 7 volumes. Edited by J. B. Bury. London: Methuen, 1906–1923.

Hornblower, Simon and Antony Spawforth, eds. *The Oxford Classical Dictionary.* Third edition. Oxford & New York: Oxford University Press, 1999.

Kirby, John T., ed. *World Eras, Volume 3: Roman Republic and Empire, 264 B.C.E.–476 C.E.* Columbia, S.C.: Manly / Detroit: Gale, 2001.

Kirby, ed. *World Eras, Volume 6: Classical Greek Civilization, 800–323 B.C.E.* Columbia, S.C.: Manly / Detroit: Gale, 2001.

Morkot, Robert. *The Penguin Historical Atlas of Ancient Greece.* London & New York: Penguin, 1996.

2. AESCHYLUS

Aeschylus, *The Oresteia.* Translated by Herbert Weir Smyth. Cambridge, Mass.: Harvard University Press, 1926.

Aristotle. *Nichomachean Ethics.* Translated by H. Rackham. Cambridge, Mass.: Harvard University Press, 1926.

Badiou, Alain. *Ethics. Essay On the Understanding of Evil.* Translated by Peter Hallward. New York: Verso, 2000.

Fish, Stanley. *Doing What Comes Naturally.* Durham, N.C.: Duke University Press, 1989.

Habermas, Jürgen. *Between Facts and Norms: Contribution to a Discourse Theory of Law and Democracy.* Translated by William Rehg. Cambridge, Mass.: MIT Press, 1998.

Habermas, *Moral Consciousness and Communicative Action.* Translated by Christian Lenhardt and Shierry Weber Nicholsen. Cambridge, Mass.: MIT Press, 1990.

Hampshire, Stuart. *Justice Is Conflict.* Princeton: Princeton University Press, 1989.

Hobbes, Thomas. *Leviathan.* Harmondsworth, U.K.: Penguin, 1985.

Hume, David. *A Treatise of Human Nature.* Oxford: Clarendon Press, 1974.

Kant, Immanuel. *Grounding for the Metaphysics of Morals.* Translated by James W. Ellington. Indianapolis: Hackett, 1983.

Kant. *Perpetual Peace and Other Essays.* Translated by Ted Humphrey. Indianapolis: Hackett, 1983.

Lyotard, Jean-François. *The Differend: Phrases in Dispute.* Translated by Georges Van Den Abbeele. Minneapolis: University of Minnesota Press, 1988.

Pascal, Blaise. *Pensées.* Translated by W. F. Trotter. New York: Modern Library, 1941.

Rousseau, Jean-Jacques. *The Social Contract and Discourses.* Translated by G. D. H. Cole. New York: Dutton, 1950.

Smith, Adam. *The Theory of Moral Sentiments.* Indianapolis: Liberty Fund, 1984.

De Spinoza, Benedict. *A Theologico-political Treatise and a Political Treatise.* Translated by R. H. M. Elwes. New York: Dover, 1951.

3. ALCIBIADES

Ellis, Walter M. *Alcibiades.* London & New York: Routledge, 1989.

Forde, Steven. *The Ambition to Rule: Alcibiades and the Politics of Imperialism in Thucydides.* Ithaca, N.Y. & London: Cornell University Press, 1989.

Gribble, David. *Alcibiades and Athens: A Study in Literary Presentation.* Oxford: Clarendon Press, 1999.

Kallet, Lisa. *Money and the Corrosion of Power in Thucydides: The Sicilian Expedition and Its Aftermath.* Berkeley: University of California Press, 2001.

Thucydides. *History of the Peloponnesian War.* Translated by Richard Crawley. Edited by W. Robert Connor. London: Everyman's Library, 1993.

4. ARISTOPHANES

Bowie, A. M. *Aristophanes: Myth, Ritual, and Comedy.* Cambridge: Cambridge University Press, 1993.

Dover, Kenneth J. *Aristophanic Comedy.* Berkeley & Los Angeles: University of California Press, 1972.

Goldhill, Simon. *The Poet's Voice: Essays on Poetics and Greek Literature.* Cambridge: Cambridge University Press, 1991.

Heath, Malcom. *Political Comedy in Aristophanes.* Göttingen: Vandenhoeck & Ruprecht, 1987.

Henderson, Jeffrey. *The Maculate Muse: The Use of Obscenity in Greek Comedy.* New Haven: Yale University Press, 1975.

Konstan, David. *Greek Comedy and Ideology.* Oxford: Oxford University Press, 1995.

Lefkowitz, Mary. *Lives of the Greek Poets.* London: Duckworth, 1981.

MacDowell, Douglas M. *Aristophanes and Athens: An Introduction to the Plays.* Oxford & New York: Oxford University Press, 1995.

Pelling, Christopher. *Literary Texts and the Greek Historian.* London & New York: Routledge, 2000.

Rosen, Ralph. *Old Comedy and the Iambographic Tradition.* Atlanta: Scholar's Press, 1988.

Ste. Croix, G. E. M. de. *The Origins of the Peloponnesian War.* Ithaca, N.Y.: Cornell University Press, 1972.

Sapo, Eric C. and William J. Slater. *The Context of Attic Drama.* Ann Arbor: University of Michigan Press, 1995.

Scodel, Ruth, ed. *Theater and Society in the Classical World.* Ann Arbor: University of Michigan Press, 1993.

Sommerstein, Alan H. *Acharnians, Edited with Translation and Notes.* Warminster, U.K.: Aris & Phillips, 1980.

Sommerstein. *Birds, Edited with Translation and Notes.* Warminster, U.K.: Aris & Phillips, 1987.

Sommerstein. *Clouds, Edited with Translation and Notes.* Warminster, U.K.: Aris & Phillips, 1982.

Sommerstein. *Ecclesiazusae, Edited with Translation and Notes.* Warminster, U.K.: Aris & Phillips, 1999.

Sommerstein. *Frogs, Edited with Translation and Notes.* Warminster, U.K.: Aris & Phillips, 1996.

Sommerstein. *Knights, Edited with Translation and Notes.* Warminster, U.K.: Aris & Phillips, 1981.

Sommerstein. *Lysistrata, Edited with Translation and Notes.* Warminster, U.K.: Aris & Phillips, 1990.

Sommerstein. *Peace, Edited with Translation and Notes.* Warminster, U.K.: Aris & Phillips, 1985.

Sommerstein. *Plutus, Edited with Translation and Notes.* Warminster, U.K.: Aris & Phillips, 2001.

Sommerstein. *Thesmophoriazusae, Edited with Translation and Notes.* Warminster, U.K.: Aris & Phillips, 1994.

Sommerstein. *Wasps, Edited with Translation and Notes.* Warminster, U.K.: Aris & Phillips, 1983.

5. ARISTOTLE

Ackrill, J. L. *Aristotle the Philosopher.* Oxford: Oxford University Press, 1981.

Allan, Donald J. *The Philosophy of Aristotle.* Second edition. London & New York: Oxford University Press, 1970.

Aristotle. *Poetics.* Translated by Richard Janko. Indianapolis: Hackett, 1987.

Barnes, Jonathan, ed. *The Complete Works of Aristotle, The Revised Oxford Translation.* Princeton: Princeton University Press, 1984.

Cantor, Norman F. and Peter L. Klein, eds. *Ancient Thought: Plato and Aristotle.* Waltham, Mass.: Blaisdell, 1968.

Collingwood, R. G. *The Idea of Nature.* Oxford: Oxford University Press, 1945.

Cope, Edward Meredith. *An Introduction to Aristotle's Rhetoric.* Hildesheim: Olms, 1970.

Cropsey, Joseph, ed. *Ancients and Moderns.* New York: Basic Books, 1964.

Edel, Abraham. *Aristotle and His Philosophy.* New Brunswick, N.J.: Transaction, 1996.

Grayeff, Felix. *Aristotle and His School.* London: Duckworth, 1974.

Grene, Marjorie G. *A Portrait of Aristotle.* Chicago: University of Chicago Press, 1963.

Halper, Edward. *Form and Reason: Essays in Metaphysics.* Albany: State University of New York Press, 1993.

Hardie, W. F. R. *Aristotle's Ethical Theory.* Second edition. Oxford: Clarendon Press, 1980.

Jaeger, Werner. *Aristotle: Fundamentals of the History of His Development.* Second edition. Translated by Richard Robinson. Oxford: Clarendon Press, 1948.

Lloyd, G. E. R. *Aristotle: The Growth and Structure of His Thought.* Cambridge: Cambridge University Press, 1968.

MacIntyre, Alasdair. *After Virtue: A Study in Moral Theory.* Second edition. Notre Dame, Ind.: University of Notre Dame Press, 1984.

Milo, Ronald D. *Aristotle on Practical Knowledge and Weakness of the Will.* The Hague: Mouton, 1966.

Monan, J. Donald. *Moral Knowledge and Its Methodology in Aristotle.* Oxford: Clarendon Press, 1968.

Moravcsik, J. M. E., ed. *Aristotle: A Collection of Critical Essays.* Notre Dame, Ind.: University of Notre Dame Press, 1968.

Robb, Kevin, ed. *Language and Thought in Early Greek Philosophy.* La Salle, Ill.: Hegeler Institute, 1983.

Robinson, Timothy A. *Aristotle in Outline.* Indianapolis: Hackett, 1995.

Sachs, Joseph. *Aristotle's Metaphysics.* Santa Fe, N.Mex.: Green Lion, 1999.

Stocks, J. L. *Aristotelianism.* New York: Cooper Square, 1963.

Veatch, Henry B. *Aristotle: A Contemporary Appreciation.* Bloomington: Indiana University Press, 1974.

6. BLACK ATHENA

Berlinerblau, Jacques. *Heresy in the University: The Black Athena Controversy and the Responsibilities of American Intellectuals.* New Brunswick, N.J.: Rutgers University Press, 1999.

Bernal, Martin. *Black Athena: The Afroasiatic Roots of Classical Civilization, Volume 1: The Fabrication of Ancient Greece 1785–1985.* New Brunswick, N.J.: Rutgers University Press, 1987.

Bernal. *Black Athena: The Afroasiatic Roots of Classical Civilization, Volume 2: Archaeological and Documentary Evidence.* New Brunswick, N.J.: Rutgers University Press, 1991.

Bernal. *Black Athena Writes Back: Martin Bernal Responds to his Critics.* Edited by David Chioni Moore. Durham, N.C.: Duke University Press, 2001.

Boardman, John and others, eds. *The Oxford History of Greece and the Hellenistic World.* Oxford: Oxford University Press, 1988.

Gantz, Timothy. *Early Greek Myth: A Guide to Literary and Artistic Sources.* Baltimore: Johns Hopkins University Press, 1993.

Halbwachs, Maurice. *On Collective Memory.* Translated by Lewis A. Coser. Chicago: University of Chicago Press, 1992.

Howe, Stephen. *Afrocentrism: Mythical Past and Imagined Homes.* London: Verso, 1998.

Lefkowitz, Mary R. *Not Out of Africa: How Afrocentrism Became an Excuse to Teach Myth as History.* New York: New Republic Books, 1997.

Lefkowitz and Guy MacLean Rogers, eds. *Black Athena Revisited.* Chapel Hill: University of North Carolina Press, 1996.

Levine, Molly M. and John Peradotto, eds. *The Challenge of Black Athena.* Special Issue of *Arethusa.* Volume 22. Fall 1989. Buffalo: Department of Classics, State University of New York at Buffalo, 1989.

Snowden, Frank M. Jr. *Before Color Prejudice: The Ancient View of Blacks.* Cambridge, Mass.: Harvard University Press, 1983.

Snowden. *Blacks in Antiquity: Ethiopians in the Greco-Roman Experience.* Cambridge, Mass.: Harvard University Press, 1970.

7. CAESAR

Caesar. *The Civil War.* Translated by Jane F. Gardner. Harmondsworth, U.K.: Penguin, 1967.

Caesar. *The Conquest of Gaul.* Translated by S. A. Handford. London: Penguin, 1982.

Ferrero, Guglielmo. *The Life of Caesar.* New York: Norton, 1962.

Fuller, J. F. C. *Julius Caesar: Man, Soldier, and Tyrant.* London: Eyre & Spottiswoode, 1965.

Gelzer, Matthias. *Caesar: Politician and Statesman.* Sixth edition. Translated by Peter Needham. Cambridge, Mass.: Harvard University Press, 1968.

Grant, Michael. *The Twelve Caesars.* New York: Scribners, 1975.

Jiménez, Ramon L. *Caesar against Rome: The Great Roman Civil War.* Westport, Conn.: Praeger, 2000.

Langguth, A. J. *A Noise of War: Caesar, Pompey, Octavian, and the Struggle for Rome.* New York: Simon & Schuster, 1994.

Meier, Christian. *Caesar.* Translated by David McLintock. New York: Basic Books/HarperCollins, 1995.

Plutarch. *Marius, Sulla, Crassus, Pompey, Caesar, Cicero, in Fall of the Roman Republic, Six Lives by Plutarch.* Translated by Rex Warner. Harmondsworth, U.K.: Penguin, 1972.

Suetonius. *The Twelve Caesars.* Translated by Robert Graves. London: Penguin, 1989.

Syme, Ronald. *The Roman Revolution.* Oxford: Oxford University Press, 1939.

Yavetz, Zvi. *Julius Caesar and His Public Image.* Ithaca, N.Y.: Cornell University Press, 1983.

8. CATO

Astin, Alan E. *Cato the Censor.* Oxford: Clarendon Press, 1978.

Forde, Nels W. *Cato the Censor.* New York: Twayne, 1975.

Griffin, M. and J. Barnes, eds. *Philosophia Togata: Essays on Philosophy and Roman Society.* Oxford: Clarendon Press, 1989.

Gruen, Erich S. *Culture and National Identity in Republican Rome.* Ithaca, N.Y.: Cornell University Press, 1992.

Livy. *The Dawn of the Roman Empire, Books 31–40.* Translated by J. C. Yardley. Oxford: Oxford University Press, 2000.

Plutarch. *Roman Lives.* Translated by Robin Waterfield. Oxford: Oxford University Press, 1999.

Sansone, David. *Plutarch: The Lives of Aristides and Cato.* Warminster, U.K.: Aris & Phillips, 1989.

Scullard, Howard H. *Roman Politics 220–150 BC.* Second edition. Oxford: Oxford University Press, 1973.

Von Albrecht, Michael. *Masters of Roman Prose from Cato to Apuleius.* Translated by Neil Adkin. Leeds, U.K.: F. Cairns, 1989.

9. CHRISTIAN NEOPLATONISM

Armstrong, A.H., ed. *The Cambridge History of Later Greek and Early Medieval Philosophy.* Cambridge: Cambridge University Press, 1967.

Blumenthal, H. J. and R. A. Markus, eds. *Neoplatonism and Early Christian Thought: Essays in Honour of A. H. Armstrong.* London: Variorum, 1981.

Dillon, John M. *The Golden Chain: Studies in the Development of Platonism and Christianity.* Aldershot, U.K.: Variorum / Brookfield, Vt.: Gower, 1990.

Dillon. *The Great Tradition: Further Studies in the Development of Platonism and Early Christianity.* Aldershot, U.K. & Brookfield, Vt.: Ashgate, 1997.

Gerson, Lloyd P., ed. *The Cambridge Companion to Plotinus.* Cambridge: Cambridge University Press, 1996.

O'Meara, Dominic J., *The Structure of Being and the Search for the Good: Essays on Ancient and Early Medieval Platonism.* Aldershot, U.K.: Variorum / Brookfield, Vt.: Ashgate, 1998.

O'Meara. ed. *Neoplatonism and Christian Thought.* Norfolk, Va.: International Society for Neoplatonic Studies, 1982.

Pelikan, Jaroslav. *The Christian Tradition: A History of the Development of Doctrine.* Volume 1: *The Emergence of the Catholic Tradition (100–600).* Chicago: University of Chicago Press, 1971.

Rist, John M. *Augustine: Ancient Thought Baptized.* Cambridge: Cambridge University Press, 1994.

Shorey, Paul. *Platonism: Ancient and Modern.* Berkeley: University of California Press, 1938.

10. CICERO

Cicero. *Letters to Atticus.* Translated by D. R. Shackleton Bailey. Harmondsworth, U.K.: Penguin, 1978.

Cicero. *Letters to His Friends.* 2 volumes. Translated by Bailey. Harmondsworth, U.K.: Penguin, 1978.

Cicero. *On the Good Life.* Translated by Michael Grant. Harmondsworth, U.K.: Penguin, 1971.

Cicero. *Selected Political Speeches.* Translated by Michael Grant. London: Penguin, 1989.

Cicero. *Selected Works.* Translated by Michael Grant. Harmondsworth, U.K.: Penguin, 1971.

Craig, Christopher P. *Form as Argument in Cicero's Speeches.* Atlanta: Scholar's Press, 1993.

Douglas, Alan E. *Cicero.* Oxford: Clarendon Press, 1968.

Everitt, Anthony. *Cicero: The Life and Times of Rome's Greatest Politician.* New York: Random House, 2002.

Habicht, Christian. *Cicero the Politician.* Baltimore: Johns Hopkins University Press, 1990.

May, James M. *Trials of Character: The Eloquence of Ciceronian Ethos.* Chapel Hill: University of North Carolina Press, 1988.

Mitchell, T. N. *Cicero: The Ascending Years.* New Haven: Yale University Press, 1979.

Mitchell. *Cicero: The Senior Statesman.* New Haven: Yale University Press, 1991.

Pliny. *Natural History.* Volume 2. Translated by H. Rackham. Cambridge, Mass.: Harvard University Press, 1942.

Plutarch. *Marius, Sulla, Crassus, Pompey, Caesar, Cicero, in Fall of the Roman Republic, Six Lives by Plutarch.* Translated by Rex Warner. Harmondsworth, U.K.: Penguin, 1972.

Powell, J. G. F., ed. *Cicero the Philosopher.* Oxford: Clarendon Press, 1995.

Rawson, Elizabeth. *Cicero: A Portrait.* London: Allen Lane, 1975.

Smith, R. E. *Cicero the Statesman.* Cambridge: Cambridge University Press, 1966.

Steel, C. E. W. *Cicero, Rhetoric, and Empire.* Oxford: Oxford University Press, 2001.

11. DEMOSTHENES

Ellis, J. R. *Philip II and Macedonian Imperialism.* Princeton: Princeton University Press, 1976.

Fisher, Nick. *Aeschines: Against Timarchos.* Oxford: Oxford University Press, 2001.

Hammond, N. G. L. *Philip of Macedon.* Baltimore: Johns Hopkins University Press, 1994.

Hansen, Mogens. *The Athenian Assembly in the Age of Demosthenes.* Oxford: Oxford University Press, 1987.

Harris, Edward M. *Aeschines and Athenian Politics.* Oxford: Oxford University Press, 1995.

Perlman, Samuel, ed. *Philip and Athens.* New York: Barnes & Noble, 1973.

Sealey, Raphael. *A History of the Greek City-States, ca. 700 to 338 B.C.* Berkeley: University of California Press, 1976.

12. DONATIST CONTROVERSY

Saint Augustine. *Letters.* Translated by Sister Wilfrid Parsons, S.N.D. New York: Fathers of the Church, 1951–1956.

Saint Augustine. *Writings Against the Manichaeans and the Donatists.* In *The Nicene and Post-Nicene Fathers of the Christian Church.* First Series. Volume 4. Grand Rapids, Mich.: W. M. B. Eerdmans, 1989.

Brown, Peter. *Augustine of Hippo.* Berkeley: University of California Press, 1967.

Frend, William. *The Donatist Church: A Movement of Protest in Roman North Africa.* Oxford: Clarendon Press, 1952.

Lancel, Serge. *Saint Augustine.* Translated by Antonia Nevill. London: SCM Press, 2002.

Lancel, ed. and trans. *Actes de la Conférence de Carthage en 411.* Paris: Les Éditions du Cerf, 1972–1991.

Optatus of Milevis. *Against the Donatists.* Translated by Mark Edwards. Liverpool: Liverpool University Press, 1997.

Pharr, Clyde, ed. and trans. *The Theodosian Code and Novels and the Sirmondian Constitutions.* Princeton: Princeton University Press, 1952.

13. ELEGISTS

Day, A. A. *The Origins of Latin Love Elegy.* Oxford: Oxford University Press, 1938.

Kennedy, Duncan F. *The Arts of Love: Five Studies in the Discourse of Roman Love Elegy.* Cambridge: Cambridge University Press, 1993.

Luck, Georg. *The Latin Love Elegy.* Edinburgh: R. & R. Clark, 1969.

Lyne, R. O. A. M. *The Latin Love Poets.* Oxford: Oxford University Press, 1980.

Miller, Paul Allen. *Latin Erotic Elegy: An Anthology and Critical Reader.* New York: Routledge, 2002.

Miller. *Lyric Texts and Lyric Consciousness: The Birth of a Genre from Archaic Greece to Augustan Rome.* New York: Routledge, 1994.

Rabinowitz, N. S. and Amy Richlin, eds. *Feminist Theory and the Classics.* New York: Routledge, 1993.

Richlin, Amy, ed. *Pornography and Representation in Greece and Rome.* Oxford: Oxford University Press, 1992.

14. ELGIN MARBLES

Boardman, John. *The Parthenon and its Sculptures.* London: Thames & Hudson, 1985.

Bruno, Vincent J., ed. *The Parthenon.* New York & London: Norton, 1974.

Cook, B. F. *The Elgin Marbles.* Revised edition. London: British Museum Press, 1997.

Hitchens, Christopher. *The Elgin Marbles: Should They be Returned to Greece?* London & New York: Verso, 1997.

Howland, R. H., ed. *The Destiny of the Parthenon Marbles.* Washington, D.C.: Society for the Preservation of the Greek Heritage, 2000.

Jenkins, Ian. *Archaeologists and Aesthetes: In the Sculpture Galleries of the British Museum 1800–1939.* London: British Museum Press, 1992.

Jenkins. *The Parthenon Frieze.* London: British Museum Press, 1994.

Merryman, John H. *Thinking about the Elgin Marbles: Critical Essays on Cultural Property, Art, and Law.* The Hague & Boston: Kluwer Law International, 2000.

Meyer, Karl. *The Plundered Past.* New York: Atheneum, 1973.

Neils. *Worshipping Athena: Panathenaia and Parthenon.* Madison: University of Wisconsin Press, 1996.

Neils, Jenifer, ed. *The Parthenon Frieze.* Cambridge: Cambridge University Press, 2001.

Palagia, Olga. *The Pediments of the Parthenon.* Leiden: Brill, 1993.

St. Clair, William. *Lord Elgin and the Marbles: The Controversial History of the Parthenon Sculptures.* Oxford: Oxford University Press, 1998.

Tubb, Kathryn, ed. *Antiquities: Trade or Betrayed: Legal, Ethical and Conservation Issues.* London: Archetype, 1995.

15. EURIPIDES

Barnes, Jonathan. *Early Greek Philosophy.* New York: Penguin, 1987.

Blundell, Mary Whitlock. *Helping Friends and Harming Enemies: A Study in Sophocles and Greek Ethics.* Cambridge: Cambridge University Press, 1989.

Blundell, Sue. *Women in Ancient Greece.* Cambridge, Mass.: Harvard University Press, 1995.

Euripides. *Alcestis.* Translated by Richmond Lattimore. Chicago: University of Chicago Press, 1955.

Euripides. *Hecuba.* Translated by William Arrowsmith. Chicago: University of Chicago Press, 1958.

Euripides. *Helen.* Translated by Lattimore. Chicago: University of Chicago Press, 1956.

Euripides. *Hippolytus.* Translated by David Grene. Chicago: University of Chicago Press, 1942.

Euripides. *Ion.* Translated by Ronald Frederick Willetts. Chicago: University of Chicago Press, 1958.

Euripides. *Iphigenia at Aulis.* Translated by Charles R. Walker. Chicago: University of Chicago Press, 1958.

Euripides. *Medea.* Translated by Rex Warner. Chicago: University of Chicago Press, 1944.

Foley, Helene P. *Female Acts in Greek Tragedy.* Princeton: Princeton University Press, 2001.

Murray, Gilbert. *Euripides and His Age.* New York: Holt, 1913.

Pomeroy, Sarah B. *Goddesses, Whores, Wives, and Slaves: Women in Classical Antiquity.* New York: Schocken, 1975.

Powell, Anton, ed. *Euripides, Women, and Sexuality.* London: Routledge, 1990.

Rabinowitz, Nancy Sorkin. *Anxiety Veiled: Euripides and the Traffic in Women.* Ithaca, N.Y.: Cornell University Press, 1993.

Rabinowitz and Amy Richlin, eds. *Feminist Theory and the Classics.* New York: Routledge, 1993.

Winkler, John J. and Froma I. Zeitlin, eds. *Nothing to Do with Dionysus? Athenian Drama in its Social Context.* Princeton: Princeton University Press, 1990.

16. FALL OF THE REPUBLIC

Brunt, P. A. *The Fall of the Roman Republic and Related Essays.* Oxford, U.K.: Oxford University Press, 1988.

Brunt. *Social Conflicts in the Roman Republic.* New York: Norton, 1971.

Flower, Harriet I. *Ancestor Masks and Aristocratic Power in Roman Culture.* Oxford: Oxford University Press, 1996.

Galinsky, Karl. *Augustan Culture: An Interpretive Introduction.* Princeton: Princeton University Press, 1996.

Harris, William V. *War and Imperialism in the Late Republic.* Oxford: Oxford University Press, 1979.

Lintott, Andrew. *The Constitution of the Roman Republic.* Oxford: Clarendon Press, 1999.

Macmullen, Ramsay. *Corruption and the Decline of Rome.* New Haven & London: Yale University Press, 1988.

Millar, Fergus. *The Crowd in Rome in the Late Republic.* Jerome Lectures 22. Ann Arbor: University of Michigan Press, 1998.

Millar. *The Emperor in the Roman World (31 BC–AD 337).* London: Duckworth, 1977.

Millar. *The Roman Republic in Political Thought: The Menahem Stern Jerusalem Lectures.* Hanover, N.H. & London: University Press of New England, 2002.

Millar and Erich Segal, eds. *Caesar Augustus: Seven Aspects.* Oxford: Clarendon Press, 1984.

Nippel, Wilfried. *Public Order in Ancient Rome.* Cambridge: Cambridge University Press, 1995.

Polybius. *The Rise of the Roman Empire.* Translated by Ian Scott-Kilvert. Harmondsworth, U.K.: Penguin, 1979.

Rudich, Vasily. *Political Dissidence under Nero: The Price of Dissimulation.* London & New York: Routledge, 1993.

Ste. Croix, G. E. M. de. *The Class Struggle in the Ancient Greek World: From the Archaic Age to the Arab Conquests.* Ithaca, N.Y.: Cornell University Press, 1981.

Scullard, H. H. *From the Gracchi to Nero: A History of Rome from 133 BC to AD 68.* London: Methuen, 1963.

Shelton, Jo-Ann. *As the Romans Did: A Sourcebook in Roman Social History.* Second edition. Oxford: Oxford University Press, 1998.

Syme, Ronald. *The Roman Revolution.* Oxford: Clarendon Press, 1939.

Talbert, Richard J. A. *The Senate of Imperial Rome.* Princeton: Princeton University Press, 1984.

Walbank, F. W. *Polybius.* Berkeley: University of California Press, 1972.

Wallace, Robert W. and Edward M. Harris, eds. *Transitions to Empire: Essays Greco-Roman History, 360–146 B.C., in Honor of E. Badian.* Norman: University of Oklahoma Press, 1996.

Wilkinson, L. P. *The Roman Experience.* Lanham, Md.: University Press of America, 1974.

Wiseman, T. P. *Catullus and His World: A Reappraisal.* Cambridge: Cambridge University Press, 1985.

17. GERMAN PHILOLOGICAL TRADITION

Briggs, Ward W. Jr. and William M. Calder III, eds. *Classical Scholarship: A Biographical Encyclopedia.* New York: Garland, 1990.

Briggs and E. C. Kopff, eds. *The Roosevelt Lectures of Paul Shorey (1913–1914).* Hildesheim, Germany & New York: G. Olms Verlag, 1995.

Brink, C. O. *English Classical Scholarship.* Cambridge: Cambridge University Press, 1986.

Calder, William M. III. *Men in Their Books: Studies in the Modern History of Classical Scholarship.* Edited by John P. Harris and R. Scott Smith. *Spudasmata* 67. Hildesheim, Germany & New York: G. Olms Verlag, 1998.

Calder and others, eds. "Teaching the English Wissenschaft: The Letters of Sir George Cornewall Lewis to Karl Otfried Müller (1828–1839)." *Spudasmata* 85. Hildesheim, Germany & New York: G. Olms Verlag, 2002.

Clarke, M. L. *Classical Education in Britain 1500–1900.* Cambridge: Cambridge University Press, 1959.

Housman, A. E. *The Confines of Criticism: The Cambridge Inaugural 1911.* Cambridge: Cambridge University Press, 1969.

Miller, C. W. E., ed. *Selections from the Brief Mention of Basil Lanneau Gildersleeve.* Baltimore: Johns Hopkins University Press, 1930.

Nock, Albert Jay. *Memoirs of a Superfluous Man.* New York: Harper, 1943.

Pfeiffer, Rudolf. *History of Classical Scholarship 1300–1850.* Oxford: Clarendon Press, 1976.

Sandys, John Edwin. *A History of Classical Scholarship.* 3 volumes. Third edition. Cambridge: Cambridge University Press, 1921.

Von Wilamowitz-Moellendorff, Ulrich. *History of Classical Scholarship.* Baltimore: Johns Hopkins University Press, 1982.

18. GLADIATORS

Auguet, Roland. *Cruelty and Civilization: The Roman Games.* New York: Routledge, 1994.

Baker, Alan. *The Gladiator: The Secret History of Rome's Warrior Slaves.* New York: St. Martin's Press, 2000.

Barton, Carlin. *The Sorrows of the Ancient Romans: The Gladiator and the Monster.* Princeton: Princeton University Press, 1993.

Beacham, Richard C. *Spectacle Entertainments of Early Imperial Rome.* New Haven: Yale University Press, 1999.

Grant, Michael. *Gladiators.* New York: Delacorte, 1967.

Hornum, Michael B. *Nemesis, the Roman State, and the Games.* Leiden: Brill, 1993.

Kyle, Donald G. *Spectacles of Death in Ancient Rome.* New York: Routledge, 1998.

Pearson, John. *Arena: The Story of the Colosseum.* New York: McGraw-Hill, 1973.

Veyne, Paul. *Bread and Circuses: Historical Sociology and Political Pluralism.* Translated by B. Pearce. London: Allen Lane, 1990.

Wiedemann, Thomas. *Emperors and Gladiators.* New York: Routledge, 1992.

19. TIBERIUS GRACCHUS

Appian. *Civil Wars.* Edited by J. L. Strachan-Davidson. Oxford: Oxford University Press, 1951.

Bernstein, Alvin H. *Tiberius Sempronius Gracchus: Tradition and Apostasy.* Ithaca, N.Y.: Cornell University Press, 1978.

Brunt, P. A. *Italian Manpower, 225 B.C.–14 A.D.* Oxford: Oxford University Press, 1971.

Earl, D. C. *Tiberius Gracchus: A Study in Politics.* Brussels: Latomus, 1963.

Plutarch. *Makers of Rome; Nine Lives.* Translated by Ian Scott-Kilvert. Baltimore: Penguin, 1965.

Richardson, Keith. *Daggers in the Forum: The Revolutionary Lives and Violent Deaths of the Gracchus Brothers.* London: Cassell, 1976.

Riddle, John M., ed. *Tiberius Gracchus: Destroyer or Reformer of the Republic?* Lexington, Mass.: Heath, 1970.

Stockton, David L. *The Gracchi.* Oxford: Clarendon Press, 1979.

20. HERODOTUS

Bakker, Egbert J. and others, eds. *Brill's Companion to Herodotus.* Leiden & Boston: Brill, 2002.

Fehling, Detlev. *Herodotus and his "Sources": Citation, Invention, and Narrative Art.* Translated by J. G. Howie. Leeds: Francis Cairns, 1989.

Fornara, Charles W. *Herodotus: An Interpretative Essay.* Oxford: Clarendon Press, 1971.

Harrison, Thomas. *Divinity and History: The Religion of Herodotus.* Oxford: Clarendon Press, 2000.

Hartog, François. *The Mirror of Herodotus.* Translated by Janet Lloyd. Berkeley: University of California Press, 1988.

Herodotus. *The Histories.* Translated by Aubrey de Sélincourt. London: Penguin, 2003.

Lateiner, Donald. *The Historical Method of Herodotus.* Toronto: University of Toronto Press, 1989.

Romm, James S. *Herodotus.* New Haven: Yale University Press, 1998.

Thomas, Rosalind. *Herodotus in Context: Ethnography, Science and the Art of Persuasion.* Cambridge: Cambridge University Press, 2000.

Waters, K. H. *Herodotos the Historian: His Problems, Methods and Originality.* London & Sydney: Croom Helm, 1985.

21. HESIOD

Bakker, Egbert J. *Linguistics and Formulas in Homer.* Amsterdam: J. Benjamin, 1988.

Foley, John Miles. *Oral-Formulaic Theory and Research.* New York: Garland, 1985.

Hamilton, Richard. *The Architecture of Hesiodic Poetry.* Baltimore: Johns Hopkins University Press, 1989.

Lamberton, Robert. *Hesiod.* New Haven: Yale University Press, 1988.

Lord, A. B. *The Singer of Tales.* Cambridge, Mass.: Harvard University Press, 1960.

Luce, T. J., ed. *Ancient Writers I.* New York: Scribners, 1982.

Nagy, Gregory. *Homeric Questions.* Austin: University of Texas Press, 1996.

Parry, Milman. *The Making of Homeric Verse.* Edited by Adam Parry. New York: Oxford University Press, 1987.

Pucci, Pietro. *Hesiod and the Language of Poetry.* Baltimore: Johns Hopkins University Press, 1977.

Stolz, Benjamin, ed. *Oral Literature and the Formula.* Ann Arbor: University of Michigan Press, 1976.

Whallon, William. *Formula, Character, and Context: Studies in Homeric and Old Testament Poetry.* Cambridge, Mass.: Harvard University Press, 1969.

22. HOMER

Bassett, S. E. *The Poetry of Homer.* Berkeley: University of California Press, 1938.

Beye, Charles Rowan. *Ancient Epic Poetry.* Ithaca, N.Y.: Cornell University Press, 1993.

Clarke, Howard. *Homer's Readers: An Historical Introduction to the "Iliad" and "Odyssey."* Newark: University of Delaware Press, 1981.

Foley, John M., ed. *Oral-Formulaic Theory: A Folklore Casebook.* New York: Garland, 1990.

Fowler, Robert, ed. *The Cambridge Companion to Homer.* Cambridge: Cambridge University Press, 2004.

Griffin, Jasper. *Homer on Life and Death.* Oxford: Oxford University Press, 1980.

Heubeck, Alfred and others. *A Commentary on Homer's Odyssey.* Volume 1. Oxford: Clarendon Press, 1988.

Hexter, Ralph. *A Guide to the Odyssey.* New York: Vintage, 1993.

Homer. *Iliad.* Translated by Robert Fagles. New York: Viking, 1990.

Homer. *Odyssey.* Translated by Fagles. New York: Viking, 1991.

Jensen, Minna Skafte. *The Homeric Question and the Oral-Formulaic Theory.* Copenhagen: Museum Tusculanum, 1980.

Kirk, Geoffrey S. *Homer and the Epic.* Cambridge: Cambridge University Press, 1965.

Kirk. *Songs of Homer.* Cambridge: Cambridge University Press, 1962.

Lamberton, Robert and John J. Keaney, eds. *Homer's Ancient Readers.* Princeton: Princeton University Press, 1992.

Lord, Albert B. *The Singer of Tales.* Cambridge, Mass.: Harvard University Press, 1960.

Martin, Richard. *The Language of Heroes: Speech and Performance in the Iliad.* Ithaca, N.Y.: Cornell University Press, 1989.

Nagy, Gregory. *The Best of the Achaeans: Concepts of the Hero in Archaic Greek Poetry.* Baltimore: Johns Hopkins University Press, 1979.

Nagy. *Homeric Questions.* Austin: University of Texas Press, 1996.

Nagy. *Homeric Responses.* Austin: University of Texas Press, 2003.

Page, Denys. *History and the Homeric Iliad.* Berkeley & Los Angeles: University of California Press, 1963.

Parry, Milman. *The Making of Homeric Verse: The Collected Papers of Milman Parry.* Edited by Adam Parry. Oxford: Clarendon Press, 1971.

Powell, Barry. *Homer and the Origin of the Greek Alphabet.* Cambridge: Cambridge University Press, 1991.

Powell. *Writing and the Origins of Greek Literature.* Cambridge: Cambridge University Press, 2002.

Stanford, William Bedell. *The Ulysses Theme: A Study in the Adaptability of a Traditional Hero.* Oxford: Blackwell, 1954.

Whitman, Cedric H. *Homer and the Heroic Tradition.* Cambridge, Mass.: Harvard University Press, 1958.

Wolf, Friedrich A. *Prolegomena to Homer.* Translated by Anthony Grafton and others. Princeton: Princeton University Press, 1985.

23. HOMOSEXUALITY

Boswell, John. *Christianity, Social Tolerance, and Homosexuality: Gay People in Western Europe from the Beginning of the Christian Era to the Fourteenth Century.* Chicago: University of Chicago Press, 1980.

Brooten, Bernadette J. *Love Between Women: Early Christian Responses to Female Homoeroticism.* Chicago: University of Chicago Press, 1996.

Cantarella, Eva. *Bisexuality in the Ancient World.* Translated by C. Ó. Cuilleanáin. New Haven: Yale University Press, 1992.

Carcopino, Jérôme. *Daily Life in Ancient Rome: The People and the City at the Height of the Empire.* Edited by Henry T. Rowell. Second edition. New Haven: Yale University Press, 2003.

Clarke, John R. *Looking at Lovemaking: Constructions of Sexuality in Roman Art 100 B.C.–A.D. 250.* Berkeley: University of California Press, 1998.

Cohen, David. *Law, Sexuality, and Society.* Cambridge: Cambridge University Press, 1991.

Crook, J. A. *Law and Life of Rome, 90 B.C.–A.D. 212.* Ithaca, N.Y.: Cornell University Press, 1967.

Dover, K. J. *Greek Popular Morality in the Time of Plato and Aristotle.* Revised edition. Indianapolis: Hackett, 1994.

Faderman, Lillian. *Surpassing the Love of Men: Romantic Friendships and Love Between Women from the Renaissance to the Present.* New York: Morrow, 1981.

Foucault, Michel. *The History of Sexuality, Volume 3: The Care of the Self.* Translated by Robert Hurley. New York: Random House, 1986.

Gardner, Jane F. *Women in Roman Law and Society.* Bloomington: Indiana University Press, 1986.

Gleason, Maud W. *Making Men: Sophists and Self-Presentation in Ancient Rome.* Princeton: Princeton University Press, 1995.

Hallett, Judith and Marilyn B. Skinner, eds. *Roman Sexualities.* Princeton: Princeton University Press, 1997.

Halperin, David M. *One Hundred Years of Homosexuality and Other Essays on Greek Love.* New York: Routledge, 1990.

Halperin and others, eds. *Before Sexuality: The Construction of Erotic Experience in the Ancient Greek World.* Princeton: Princeton University Press, 1990.

Henderson, Jeffrey. *The Maculate Muse.* Revised edition. Oxford: Oxford University Press, 1992.

Hubbard, Thomas K., ed. *Homosexuality in Greece and Rome: A Sourcebook of Basic Documents.* Berkeley: University of California Press, 2003.

Hunter, Virginia J. *Policing Athens: Social Control in the Attic Lawsuits, 420–320 B.C.* Princeton: Princeton University Press, 1994.

Joshel, Sandra R. and Sheila Murnaghan, eds. *Women and Slaves in Greco-Roman Culture.* London: Routledge, 1998.

Larmour, David H. J. and others, eds. *Rethinking Sexuality: Foucault and Classical Antiquity.* Princeton: Princeton University Press, 1998.

Masterson, Mark Anthony. "Roman Manhood at the End of the Ancient World." Dissertation. University of Southern California, 2001.

Montserrat, Dominic. *Sex and Society in Graeco-Roman Egypt.* London: Kegan Paul, 1996.

Percy, William Armstrong III. *Pederasty and Pedagogy in Archaic Greece.* Urbana: University of Illinois Press, 1996.

Rabinowitz, Nancy and Lisa Auanger, eds. *Among Women: From the Homosocial to the Homoerotic in the Ancient World.* Austin: University of Texas Press, 2002.

Richlin, Amy. *The Garden of Priapus: Sexuality and Aggression in Roman Humor.* New York: Oxford University Press, 1992.

Satlow, Michael L. *Tasting the Dish: Rabbinic Rhetorics of Sexuality.* Brown Judaic Studies 303. Atlanta: Scholar's Press, 1995.

Williams, Craig. *Homosexuality and the Roman Man.* Oxford: Oxford University Press, 1999.

Williams. *Roman Homosexuality: Ideologies of Masculinity in Classical Antiquity.* Oxford: Oxford University Press, 1999.

Winkler, John J. *Constraints of Desire: The Anthropology of Sex and Gender in Ancient Greece.* New York: Routledge, 1989.

Wiseman, T. P. *Catullus and His World: A Reappraisal.* Cambridge: Cambridge University Press, 1985.

24. LIBRARY AT ALEXANDRIA

Barr-Sharrar, Beryl and Eugene N. Borza, eds. *Macedonia and Greece in Late Classical and Early Hellenistic Times.* Studies in the History of Art. Volume 10. Washington, D.C.: National Gallery of Art, 1982.

Canfora, Luciano. *The Vanished Library.* Berkeley: University of California Press, 1990.

El-Abbadi, Mostafa. *The Life and Fate of the Ancient Library of Alexandria.* Paris: UNESCO, 1990.

Frazer, Peter M. *Ptolemaic Alexandria.* Oxford: Clarendon Press, 1972.

Jobes, Karen H. and Moises Silva. *Invitation to the Septuagint.* Grand Rapids, Mich.: Baker Academic, 2000.

Lynch, John P. *Aristotle's School.* Berkeley: University of California Press, 1972.

MacLeod, Roy, ed. *The Library of Alexandria.* London & New York: I. B. Tauris, 2000.

Nagy, Gregory. *Poetry as Performance: Homer and Beyond.* Cambridge: Cambridge University Press, 1996.

Raven, James, ed. *Lost Libraries: The Destruction of Great Book Collections Since Antiquity.* New York: Macmillan, 2004.

Robb, Kevin. *Literacy and Paideia in Ancient Greece.* Oxford: Oxford University Press, 1994.

25. LITERACY

Finnigan, Ruth. *Oral Poetry: Its Nature, Significance, and Social Context.* Cambridge: Cambridge University Press, 1977.

Graff, Harvey J. *The Legacies of Literacy: Continuities and Contradictions in Western Culture and Society.* Bloomington: Indiana University Press, 1987.

Harris, William V. *Ancient Literacy.* Cambridge, Mass.: Harvard University Press, 1989.

Havelock, Eric A. *The Literate Revolution in Greece and Its Cultural Consequences.* Princeton: Princeton University Press, 1982.

Havelock, *A Preface to Plato.* Cambridge, Mass.: Harvard University Press, 1963.

Kittay, Jeffrey and Wlad Godzich. *The Emergence of Prose: An Essay in Prosaics.* Minneapolis: University of Minnesota Press, 1987.

Kittler, Friedrich A. *Gramophone, Film, Typewriter.* Translated by Geoffrey Winthrop-Young and Michael Wutz. Stanford, Cal.: Stanford University Press, 1999.

Lord, Albert. *The Singer of Tales.* Cambridge, Mass.: Harvard University Press, 1960.

Luria, A. R. *Cognitive Development: Its Cultural and Social Foundations.* Translated by Martin Lopez-Morillas and Lynn Solotaroff. Edited by Michael Cole. Cambridge, Mass.: Harvard University Press, 1976.

McLuhan, Marshall. *The Gutenberg Galaxy: The Making of Typographic Man.* Toronto: University of Toronto Press, 1962.

Miller, Paul Allen. *Lyric Texts and Lyric Consciousness: The Birth of a Genre from Archaic Greece to Augustan Rome.* London: Routledge, 1994.

Nagy, Gregory. *Pindar's Homer: The Lyric Possession of an Epic Past.* Baltimore: Johns Hopkins University Press, 1990.

Ong, Walter J. *Orality and Literacy: The Technologizing of the Word.* London: Methuen, 1982.

Opland, Jeff. *Anglo-Saxon Oral Poetry: A Study of Traditions.* New Haven: Yale University Press, 1980.

Parry, Adam, ed. *The Making of Homeric Verse: The Collected Papers of Milman Parry.* Oxford: Oxford University Press, 1971.

Thomas, Rosalind. *Literacy and Orality in Ancient Greece.* Cambridge: Cambridge University Press, 1992.

Thomas. *Oral Tradition and Written Record in Classical Athens.* Cambridge: Cambridge University Press, 1989.

26. MARXIST APPROACH

Althusser, Louis. *For Marx.* New York: Random House, 1969.

Cartledge, P. A. and F. D. Harvey, eds. *Crux: Essays in Greek History Presented to G.E.M. de Ste. Croix on his Seventy-Fifth Birthday.* London: Duckworth, 1985.

Derrida, Jacques. *Specters of Marx: The State of the Debt, the Work of Mourning, and the New International.* New York: Routledge, 1994.

Finley, Moses I. *The Ancient Economy.* Berkeley: University of California Press, 1973.

Finley. *Ancient Slavery and Modern Ideology.* New York: Viking, 1980.

Finley. *Democracy Ancient and Modern.* New Brunswick, N.J.: Rutgers University Press, 1973.

Finley. *Economy and Society in Ancient Greece.* New York: Viking, 1981.

Franklin, W. Bruce. *Sunlight at Midnight: St. Petersburg and the Rise of Modern Russia.* New York: Basic Books, 2001.

Furet, François. *Marx and the French Revolution.* Chicago: University of Chicago Press, 1988.

Jameson, Fredric. *The Ideologies of Theory: Essays 1971–1986, Volume 2: The Syntax of History.* Minneapolis: University of Minnesota Press, 1988.

Jameson. *The Political Unconscious: Narrative as A Socially Symbolic Act.* Ithaca, N.Y.: Cornell University Press, 1981.

Joshel, Sandra R. *Work, Identity and Legal Status at Rome: A Study of the Occupational Inscriptions.* Norman: University of Oklahoma Press, 1992.

Lukács, Georg. *History and Class Consciousness: Studies in Marxist Dialectics.* Cambridge, Mass.: MIT Press, 1971.

Medvedev, Roy A. *Let History Judge: The Origins and Consequences of Stalinism.* New York: Knopf, 1972.

Prawer, S. S. *Karl Marx and World Literature.* Oxford: Oxford University Press, 1978.

Rabinowitz, Nancy and Amy Richlin, eds. *Feminist Theory and the Classics.* New York: Routledge, 1993.

Rose, Peter W. *Sons of the Gods, Children of Earth: Ideology and Literary Form in Ancient Greece.* Ithaca, N.Y.: Cornell University Press, 1992.

Ste. Croix, G. E. M. de. *The Class Struggle in the Ancient Greek World.* Ithaca, N.Y.: Cornell University Press, 1981.

Thomson, George. *Aeschylus and Athens.* London: Lawrence & Wishart, 1940.

Thomson. *Studies in Ancient Greek Society, Volume 1: The Prehistoric Aegean.* New York: Citadel, 1965.

Tucker, Robert C., ed. *The Marx-Engels Reader.* Second edition. New York: Norton, 1978.

Wason, Margaret O. *Class Struggles in Ancient Greece.* London: Gollancz, 1947.

White, Hayden. *Metahistory: The Historical Imagination of Nineteenth-Century Europe.* Baltimore: Johns Hopkins University Press, 1973.

27. MODERN CRITICAL THEORY

Bakhtin, M. M. *The Dialogic Imagination: Four Essays.* Edited by Michael Holquist. Translated by Caryl Emerson. Austin: University of Texas Press, 1981.

Barthes, Roland. *Critical Essay.* Translated by Richard Howard. Evanston, Ill.: Northwestern University Press, 1972.

Barthes. *The Pleasure of the Text.* Translated by Richard Miller. New York: Hill & Wang, 1975.

Crews, Frederick C. *The Pooh Perplex.* Chicago: University of Chicago Press, 2003.

Crews. *Postmodern Pooh.* New York: North Point, 2002.

Derrida, Jacques. *Dissemination.* Translated by Barbara Johnson. Chicago: University of Chicago Press, 1981.

Derrida. *Margins of Philosophy.* Translated by Alan Bass. Chicago: University of Chicago Press, 1982.

Derrida. *Of Grammatology.* Translated by Gayatri Chakravorty Spivak. Baltimore: Johns Hopkins University Press, 1976.

Derrida. *Writing and Difference.* Translated by Alan Bass. Chicago: University of Chicago Press, 1978.

Devaney, M .J. *"Since at Least Plato" and Other Postmodern Myths.* New York: St. Martin's Press, 1997.

Eagleton, Terry. *After Theory.* New York: Basic Books, 2003.

Eco, Umberto. *The Aesthetics of Thomas Aquinas.* Translated by Hugh Bredin. Cambridge, Mass.: Harvard University Press, 1988.

Eco. *The Limits of Interpretation.* Bloomington: Indiana University Press, 1990.

Eco. *The Name of the Rose.* Translated by William Weaver. San Diego: Harcourt Brace Jovanovich, 1983.

Eco. *The Open Work.* Translated by Anna Cancogni. Cambridge, Mass.: Harvard University Press, 1989.

Editors of Lingua Franca. *The Sokal Hoax: The Sham that Shook the Academy.* Lincoln: University of Nebraska Press, 2000.

Ellis, John M. *Against Deconstruction.* Princeton: Princeton University Press, 1989.

Ellis. *Language, Thought, and Logic.* Evanston, Ill.: Northwestern University Press, 1997.

Ellis. *Literature Lost: Social Agendas and the Corruption of the Humanities.* New Haven: Yale University Press, 1999.

Foucault, Michel. *Language, Counter-Memory, Practice: Selected Essays and Interviews.* Edited by Donald F. Bouchard. Translated by Donald F. Bouchard and Sherry Simon. Ithaca, N.Y.: Cornell University Press, 1977.

Girard, René. *Deceit, Desire, and the Novel.* Translated by Yvonne Freccero. Baltimore: Johns Hopkins University Press, 1965.

Girard. *Violence and the Sacred.* Translated by Patrick Gregory. Baltimore: Johns Hopkins University Press, 1977.

Gross, Paul R. and Norman Levitt. *Higher Superstition: The Academic Left and its Quarrels with Science.* Baltimore: Johns Hopkins University Press, 1997.

Harari, Josué, ed. *Textual Strategies: Perspectives in Post-Structuralist Criticism.* Ithaca, N.Y.: Cornell University Press, 1979.

Janan, Micaela. *"When the Lamp is Shattered": Desire and Narrative in Catullus.* Carbondale & Edwardsville: Southern Illinois University Press, 1994.

Lyotard, Jean-Françoise. *The Postmodern Condition: A Report on Knowledge.* Translated by Geoff Bennington and Brian Massumi. Minneapolis: University of Minnesota Press, 1984.

Macksey, Richard and Eugenio Donato, eds. *The Languages of Criticism and the Sciences of Man.* Baltimore: Johns Hopkins University Press, 1970.

Merquior, J. G. *From Prague to Paris: A Critique of Structuralist and Post-Structuralist Thought.* London: Verso, 1986.

Miller, Paul Allen. *Lyric Texts and Lyric Consciousness: The Birth of a Genre from Archaic Greece to Augustan Rome.* London: Routledge, 1994.

Norris, Christopher. *Against Relativism: Philosophy of Science, Deconstruction, and Critical Theory.* Oxford: Blackwell, 1997.

De Saussure, Ferdinand. *Course in General Linguistics.* Edited by Charles Bally and Albert Sechehaye. Translated by Wade Baskin. New York: Philosophical Library, 1959.

Sokal, Alan D. and Jean Bricmont. *Fashionable Nonsense: Postmodern Intellectuals' Abuse of Science.* New York: Picador, 1999.

Stove, David C. *Scientific Irrationalism: Origins of a Postmodern Cult.* New Brunswick, N.J.: Transaction, 2000.

Tallis, Raymond. *Enemies of Hope: A Critique of Contemporary Pessimism.* New York: St. Martin's Press, 1997.

Tallis, *In Defence of Realism.* Lincoln: University of Nebraska Press, 1998.

Tallis. *Not Saussure: A Critique of Post-Saussurean Critical Theory.* New York: St. Martin's Press, 1995.

Tallis. *Theorrhoea and After.* New York: St. Martin's Press, 1998.

Trigg, Roger. *Reality at Risk: A Defence of Realism in Philosophy and the Sciences.* Totowa, N.J.: Barnes & Noble, 1980.

Veyne, Paul. *Writing History: Essay on Epistemology.* Translated by Mina Moore-Rinvolucri. Middletown, Conn: Wesleyan University Press, 1984.

Windshuttle, Keith. *The Killing of History: How Literary Critics and Social Theorists are Murdering Our Past.* New York: Free Press, 2000.

28. OVID

Binns, J. W., ed. *Ovid.* London: Routledge & Kegan Paul, 1973.

Boyd, Barbara W., ed. *Brill's Companion to Ovid.* Leiden & Boston: Brill, 2002.

Boyd. *Ovid's Literary Loves: Influence and Innovation in the Amores.* Ann Arbor: University of Michigan Press, 1997.

Brown, Sarah Annes. *The Metamorphosis of Ovid From Chaucer to Ted Hughes.* London: Duckworth, 1999.

Claassen, Jo-Marie. *Displaced Persons: The Literature of Exile from Cicero to Boethius.* Madison: University of Wisconsin Press, 1999.

Deroux, Carl, ed. *Studies in Latin Literature and Roman History.* Volume 5. Brussels: Collection Latomus, 1989.

Edwards, Catherine. *Writing Rome: Textual Approaches to the City.* Cambridge: Cambridge University Press, 1996.

Evans, Harry B. *Carmina Publica: Ovid's Books from Exile.* Lincoln: University of Nebraska Press, 1983.

Fränkel, Hermann. *Ovid: A Poet Between Two Worlds.* Berkeley: University of California Press, 1945.

Galinsky, G. Karl. *Ovid's Metamorphoses: An Introduction to the Basic Aspects.* Berkeley: University of California Press, 1975.

Green, Peter. *Ovid: The Poems of Exile.* London: Penguin, 1994.

Hardie, Philip. *Ovid's Poetics of Illusion.* Cambridge & New York: Cambridge University Press, 2002.

Hardie, ed. *The Cambridge Companion to Ovid.* Cambridge: Cambridge University Press, 2002.

Hardie and others, eds. *Ovidian Transformations: Essays on the Metamorphoses and its Reception.* Cambridge: Cambridge Philological Society, 1999.

Hexter, Ralph J. *Ovid and Medieval Schooling. Studies in Medieval School Commentaries on Ovid's Ars Amatoria, Epistulae ex Ponto, and Epistulae Heroidum.* Munich: Bei der Arbeo-Gesellschaft, 1986.

Hofmann, Michael. *After Ovid: New Metamorphoses.* New York: Noon Day, 1997.

Jacobson, H. *Ovid's Heroides.* Princeton: Princeton University Press, 1974.

Knox, Peter E. *Ovid's Metamorphoses and the Traditions of Augustan Poetry.* Cambridge: Cambridge Philological Society, 1986.

Lyne, Raphael. *Ovid's Changing Worlds: English* Metamorphoses, *1567–1632.* Oxford & New York: Oxford University Press, 2001.

Mack, Sara. *Ovid.* New Haven: Yale University Press, 1988.

Mandelbaum, Allen. *The Metamorphoses of Ovid.* New York: Harvest, 1995.

Miller, Frank Justus. *Metamorphoses.* Edited by J. P. Goold. Loeb Classical Library. Third edition. Cambridge, Mass.: Harvard University Press, 1984.

Miller, Paul Allen. *Subjecting Verses: Latin Love Elegy and the Emergence of the Real.* Princeton: Princeton University Press, 2004.

Otis, Brooks. *Ovid as an Epic Poet.* Second edition. Cambridge: Cambridge University Press, 1970.

Slavitt, David. *The Metamorphoses of Ovid, Translated Freely into Verse.* Baltimore: Johns Hopkins University Press, 1994.

Syme, Ronald. *History in Ovid.* Oxford: Clarendon Press, 1977.

Taylor, A. B., ed. *Shakespeare's Ovid: The* Metamorphoses *in the Plays and Poems.* Cambridge: Cambridge University Press, 2000.

Williams, Gareth D. *Banished Voices: Readings in Ovid's Exile Poetry.* Cambridge: Cambridge University Press, 1994.

29. PAUSANIAS

Alcock, Susan E. *Graecia Capta: The Landscapes of Roman Greece.* Cambridge: Cambridge University Press, 1993.

Alcock and others, eds. *Pausanias: Travel and Memory in Roman Greece.* Oxford: Oxford University Press, 2001.

Anderson, Graham. *The Second Sophistic: A Cultural Phenomenon in the Roman Empire.* London: Routledge, 1993.

Arafat, K. W. *Pausanias' Greece: Ancient Artists and Roman Rulers.* Cambridge: Cambridge University Press, 1996.

Elsner, Jas. *Art and the Roman Viewer: The Transformation of Art from the Pagan World to Christianity.* Cambridge: Cambridge University Press, 1995.

Frazer, J. G. *Pausanias' Description of Greece.* 6 volumes. London: Biblo & Tannen, 1897.

Habicht, Christian. *Pausanias' Guide to Ancient Greece.* Second edition. Berkeley: University of California Press, 1998.

Jones, W. H. S. and others, trans. *Pausanias: Description of Greece.* 5 volumes. Cambridge, Mass.: Harvard University Press, 1971–1978.

Levi, Peter, trans. *Pausanias, Guide to Greece.* Harmondsworth, U.K.: Penguin, 1971.

Pritchett, W. Kendrick. *Pausanias Periegetes I.* Amsterdam: Gieben, 1998.

Pritchett. *Pausanias Periegetes II.* Amsterdam: Gieben, 1999.

Swain, Simon. *Hellenism and Empire: Language, Classicism, and Power in the Greek World, AD 50–250.* Oxford: Oxford University Press, 1996.

30. PLATO

Annas, Julia. *An Introduction to Plato's* Republic. New York & Oxford: Clarendon Press, 1981.

Annas and Christopher Rowe, eds. *New Perspectives on Plato, Modern and Ancient.* Cambridge, Mass.: Harvard University Press, 2002.

Barker, Ernest. *Greek Political Theory: Plato and His Predecessors.* London: Methuen / New York: Barnes & Noble, 1960.

Benardete, Seth. *The Argument of the Action: Essays on Greek Poetry and Philosophy.* Chicago: University of Chicago Press, 2000.

Blondell, Ruby. *The Play of Character in Plato's Dialogues.* Cambridge: Cambridge University Press, 2002.

Cantor, Norman F. and Peter L. Klein, eds. *Ancient Thought: Plato and Aristotle.* Waltham, Mass.: Blaisdell, 1968.

Cropsey, Joseph, ed. *Ancients and Moderns.* New York: Basic Books, 1964.

Field, Guy Cromwell. *Plato and His Contemporaries: A Study in Fourth-Century Life and Thought.* London: Methuen, 1967.

Gadamer, Hans Georg. *Dialogue and Dialectic: Eight Hermeneutical Studies on Plato.* Translated by P. Christopher Smith. New Haven: Yale University Press, 1980.

Guthrie, W. K. C. *A History of Greek philosophy,* 6 volumes. Cambridge: Cambridge University Press, 1962–1981.

Havelock, Eric A. *Preface to Plato.* Cambridge, Mass.: Harvard University Press, 1963.

Kahn, Charles H. *Plato and the Socratic Dialogue: The Philosophical Use of a Literary Form.* Cambridge: Cambridge University Press, 1996.

Kraut, Richard, ed. *The Cambridge Companion to Plato.* Cambridge & New York: Cambridge University Press, 1992.

Laertius, Diogenes. *Lives of Eminent Philosophers.* Translated by R. D. Hicks. London: Heinemann / New York: Putnam, 1925.

Nails, Debra. *The People of Plato: A Prosopography of Plato and Other Socratics.* Indianapolis & Cambridge: Hackett, 2002.

Nightingale, Andrea Wilson. *Genres in Dialogue: Plato and the Construct of Philosophy.* Cambridge: Cambridge University Press, 1995.

Plato. *The Collected Dialogues of Plato, Including the Letters.* Edited by Edith Hamilton and Huntington Cairns. New York: Pantheon, 1961.

Popper, Karl. *The Open Society and Its Enemies.* Volume 1, *Plato.* London: Routledge, 1945.

Riginos, Alice Swift. *Platonica: The Anecdotes Concerning the Life and Writings of Plato.* Leiden: Brill, 1976.

Robb, Kevin, ed. *Language and Thought in Early Greek Philosophy.* La Salle, Ill.: Hegeler Institute, 1983.

Strauss, Leo. *The City and Man.* Chicago: University of Chicago Press, 1964.

Taylor, Alfred Edward. *Plato: The Man and His Work.* New York: Dial, 1929.

Tigerstedt, Eugène Napoleon. *Interpreting Plato.* Stockholm: Almqvist & Wiksell International, 1977.

Vlastos, Gregory. *Socrates: Ironist and Moral Philosopher.* Ithaca, N.Y.: Cornell University Press, 1991.

Zuckert, Catherine. *Postmodern Plato: Nietzsche, Heidigger, Strauss, Derrida.* Chicago: University of Chicago Press, 1996.

31. PLUTARCH

Barrow, R. H. *Plutarch and His Times.* Bloomington: Indiana University Press, 1967.

Duff, Tim. *Plutarch's Lives: Exploring Virtue and Vice.* Oxford: Clarendon Press, 1999.

Dussinger, John A. *The Discourse of the Mind in Eighteenth Century Fiction.* Paris: Mouton, 1974.

Garraty, John A. *The Nature of Biography.* New York: Knopf, 1957.

Gianakaris, C. J. *Plutarch.* New York: Twayne, 1970.

Jones, C. P. *Plutarch and Rome.* Oxford: Clarendon Press, 1971.

Marr, J. L. *Plutarch: Lives. Themistocles.* Warminster: Aris & Phillips, 1998.

Momigliano, A. *The Development of Greek Biography.* Cambridge, Mass.: Harvard University Press, 1993.

Parke, Catherine N. *Biography: Writing Lives.* Studies in Literary Themes and Genres No. 11. Edited by Ronald Gottesman. New York: Twayne, 1996.

Pelling, Christopher B. R. *Plutarch: Life of Antony.* Cambridge: Cambridge University Press, 1988.

Pelling, *Plutarch and History.* London: Classical Press of Wales and Duckworth, 2002.

Russell, Donald A. *Plutarch.* London: Duckworth, 1973.

Stadter, Philip A. *Plutarch and the Historical Tradition.* London & New York: Routledge, 1992.

Wallace-Hadrill, Andrew. *Suetonius: The Scholar and his Caesars.* London: Duckworth, 1983.

32. SAPPHO

Burnett, Anne. *Three Archaic Poets: Archilochus, Alcaeus, Sappho.* Cambridge, Mass.: Harvard University Press, 1983.

Du Bois, Page. *Sappho is Burning.* Chicago: University of Chicago Press, 1995.

Foley, Helene, ed. *Reflections of Women in Antiquity.* New York: Gordon & Breach, 1981.

Greene, Ellen, ed. *Reading Sappho: Contemporary Approaches.* Berkeley: University of California Press, 1997.

Greene, ed. *Re-Reading Sappho: Reception and Transmission.* Berkeley: University of California Press, 1997.

Miller, Paul Allen. *Lyric Texts and Lyric Consciousness.* New York & London: Routledge, 1994.

Rabinowitz, Nancy S. and Amy Richlin, eds. *Feminist Theory and the Classics.* New York: Routledge, 1993.

Snyder, Jane McIntosh. *Lesbian Desire in the Lyrics of Sappho.* New York: Columbia University Press, 1997.

Williamson, Margaret. *Sappho's Immortal Daughters.* Cambridge, Mass.: Harvard University Press, 1995.

Wilson, Lyn Hatherly. *Sappho's Sweetbitter Songs.* New York & London: Routledge, 1996.

Winkler, John J. *The Constraints of Desire: The Anthropology of Sex and Gender in Ancient Greece.* New York & London: Routledge, 1990.

33. SOPHISTS

Copleston, Frederick. *A History of Philosophy.* Volume 1: *Greece and Rome.* New York: Image Doubleday, 1962.

Gagarin, Michael and Paul Woodruff, eds. *Early Greek Political Thought from Homer to the Sophists.* Cambridge: Cambridge University Press, 1995.

Gorgias. *Encomium of Helen.* Edited by Douglas MacDowell. Bristol: Bristol Classical, 1982.

Grote, George. *A History of Greece.* 12 volumes. Second edition. London: Everyman, 1906.

Guthrie, William Keith Chambers. *The Sophists.* Cambridge: Cambridge University Press, 1971.

Kerferd, George. *The Sophistic Movement.* Cambridge: Cambridge University Press, 1981.

Kerferd, ed. *The Sophists and their Legacy.* Wiesbaden: Steiner, 1981.

Lloyd, Sir Geoffrey. *The Revolutions of Wisdom: Studies in the Claims and Practice of Ancient Greek Science.* Berkeley: University of California Press, 1987.

Lloyd, Michael. *The Agon in Euripides.* Oxford: Clarendon Press, 1992.

Long, Anthony. *The Cambridge Companion to Early Greek Philosophy.* Cambridge: Cambridge University Press, 1999.

Powell, Anton, ed. *The Greek World.* London & New York: Routledge, 1995.

Rankin, Herbert. *Sophists, Socratics, and Cynics.* London & Canberra: Croom Helm, 1983.

De Romilly, Jacqueline. *The Great Sophists of Periclean Athens.* Translated by Janet Lloyd. Oxford: Clarendon Press, 1992.

Solmsen, Friederich. *Intellectual Experiments of the Greek Enlightenment.* Princeton: Princeton University Press, 1975.

Sprague, Rosamund, ed. *The Older Sophists: A Complete Translation of the Fragments in* Die Fragmente Der Vorsokratiker, *edited by Diels-Kranz. With a New Edition of Antiphon and Euthydemus.* Columbia: University of South Carolina Press, 1972.

Zeller, Edmund. *Outlines of the History of Greek Philosophy.* Translated by L. R. Palmer. Thirteenth edition. London: Routledge, 1931.

34. SPORTS

Gardiner, E. Norman. *Athletics of the Ancient World.* Chicago: Ares, 1980.

Harris, H. A. *Greek Athletes and Athletics.* London: Hutchinson, 1964.

Larmour, David H. J. *Stage and Stadium.* Hildesheim: Weidmann, 1999.

Miller, Stephen G. *Arete: Greek Sports from Ancient Sources.* Berkeley: University of California Press, 1991.

Poliakoff, Michael B. *Combat Sports in the Ancient World: Competition, Violence, and Culture.* New Haven: Yale University Press, 1987.

Robinson, Rachel S. *Sources for the History of Greek Athletics.* Chicago: Ares, 1981.

Young, David C. *The Olympic Myth of Greek Amateur Athletics.* Chicago: Ares, 1985.

35. TRANSLATION

Bakhtin, M. M. *The Dialogic Imagination: Four Essays.* Edited by Michael Holquist. Translated by Caryl Emerson. Austin: University of Texas Press, 1981.

Benediktson, D. Thomas. *Propertius: Modernist Poet of Antiquity.* Carbondale: Southern Illinois University Press, 1989.

Blanco, Walter. *Herodotus: The Histories.* Edited by Blanco and Jennifer Tolbert Roberts. New York & London: Norton, 1992.

Brower, Reuben A., ed. *On Translation.* Cambridge, Mass.: Harvard University Press, 1959.

Cary, Henry. *Herodotus: A New and Literal Version.* New York: Harper, 1854.

Derrida, Jacques. *Of Grammatology.* Translated by Gayatri Chakravorty Spivak. Baltimore: Johns Hopkins University Press, 1976.

Godley, A. D. *Herodotus.* Cambridge, Mass.: Harvard University Press, 1920.

Grene, David. *The History: Herodotus.* Chicago: University of Chicago Press, 1988.

Hatim, Basil and Ian Mason. *The Translator as Communicator.* London & New York: Routledge, 1997.

De Saussure, Fernand. *Course in General Linguistics.* Edited by Charles Bally and Albert Sechehaye. Translated by Wade Baskin. New York: McGraw-Hill, 1966.

De Sélincourt, Aubrey. *Herodotus: The Histories.* London: Penguin, 1996.

Steiner, George. *After Babel: Aspects of Language and Translation.* Third edition. Oxford & New York: Oxford University Press, 1998.

Sullivan, J. P. *Ezra Pound and Sextus Propertius: A Study in Creative Translation.* Austin: University of Texas Press, 1964.

Venuti, Lawrence, ed. *Translation Studies Reader.* London & New York: Routledge, 2000.

Voloshinov, V. N. *Marxism and the Philosophy of Language.* Translated by Ladislav Matejka and I. R. Titunik. Cambridge, Mass.: Harvard University Press, 1986.

Waterfield, Robin. *Herodotus: The Histories.* Oxford & New York: Oxford University Press, 1998.

36. VIRGIL

Baswell, Christopher. *Virgil in Medieval England: Figuring the* Aeneid *from the Twelfth Century to Chaucer.* Cambridge Studies in Medieval Literature 24. Cambridge: Cambridge University Press, 1995.

Bernard, John D., ed. *Vergil at 2000: Commemorative Essays on the Poet and His Influence.* New York: AMS, 1986.

Clausen, Wendell. *Vergil's Aeneid and the Tradition of Hellenistic Poetry.* Berkeley: University of California Press, 1984.

Commager, Steele, ed. *Virgil: A Collection of Critical Essays.* Englewood Cliffs, N.J.: Prentice-Hall, 1966.

Dudley, D. R., ed. *Virgil.* London: Routledge & Kegan Paul, 1969.

Eliot, T. S. *What is a Classic?: An Address Delivered Before the Virgil Society on 16 October 1944.* London: Faber & Faber, 1945.

Fowler, Don. *Roman Constructions: Readings in Postmodern Latin.* Oxford: Oxford University Press, 2000.

Harrison, S. J., ed. *Oxford Readings in Vergil's Aeneid.* Oxford: Oxford University Press, 1990.

Johnson, W. R. *Darkness Visible: A Study of Vergil's Aeneid.* Berkeley: University of California Press, 1976.

Kallendorf, Craig. *In Praise of Aeneas: Virgil and Epideictic Rhetoric in the Early Italian Renaissance.* Hanover, N.H.: University Press of New England, 1989.

Martindale, Charles. *Redeeming the Text: Latin Poetry and the Hermeneutics of Reception.* Cambridge: Cambridge University Press 1993.

Perkell, Christine, ed. *Reading Vergil's Aeneid: An Interpretative Guide.* Norman: University of Oklahoma Press, 1999.

Putnam, Michael C. J. *The Poetry of the* Aeneid. Cambridge, Mass.: Harvard University Press, 1965.

Putnam. *Virgil's Aeneid: Interpretation and Influence.* Chapel Hill: University of North Carolina Press, 1995.

Putnam. *Virgil's Epic Designs: Ekphrasis in the Aeneid.* New Haven: Yale University Press, 1998.

Quinn, Stephanie, ed. *Why Vergil?: A Collection of Interpretations.* Wauconda, Ill.: Bolchazy-Carducci, 2000.

Quint, David. *Epic and Empire: Politics and Generic Form from Vergil to Milton.* Princeton: Princeton University Press, 1993.

Spence, Sarah, ed. *Poets and Critics Read Vergil.* New Haven: Yale University Press, 2001.

Thomas, Richard. *Virgil and the Augustan Reception.* Cambridge & New York: Cambridge University Press, 2001.

Tudeau-Clayton, Margaret. *Jonson, Shakespeare and Early Modern Virgil.* Cambridge & New York: Cambridge University Press, 1998.

Wiltshire, Susan Ford. *Public and Private in Vergil's Aeneid.* Amherst: University of Massachusetts Press, 1989.

Zanker, Paul. *The Power of Images in the Age of Augustus.* Ann Arbor: University of Michigan Press, 1988.

CONTRIBUTORS

ALLEN, Joel: Assistant professor of history at Queens College of the City University of New York; specializes in ancient Roman history; received his Ph.D from Yale University in 1999.

ATHANASSAKIS, Apostolos N.: Professor in the Department of Classics at the University of California, Santa Barbara; received his Ph.D from the University of Pennsylvania in 1965; areas of interest are Greek poetry and classical linguistics; translated *The Homeric Hymns* (1976), *The Orphic Hymns* (1977), and *Hesiod: Theogony, Works and Days, Shield* (1983), as well as other works.

BECK, Mark A.: Assistant professor of classics at the University of South Carolina; received his B.A. from the University of Colorado, his M.A. from the Georgia Augusta University in Göttingen, and his Ph.D from the University of North Carolina; primary interests are Greco-Roman historiography and biography; has written several articles on Plutarch and is finishing a book on the influence of ideology on biographical literature.

BRIGGS, Ward: Carolina Distinguished Professor of Classics and Louise Fry Scudder Professor of Humanities at the University of South Carolina; educated at Washington and Lee University (B.A.) and the University of North Carolina (Ph.D); has edited the letters and writings of the American classicist Basil Lanneau Gildersleeve (1831–1924) and is currently at work on his biography.

CALDER, William Musgrave III: William Abbott Oldfather Professor of Classics at the University of Illinois; research interests center in Greek literature, especially Greek and Roman tragedy, and in the modern history of classical studies in the United States and Germany; the author of forty books and hundreds of articles and reviews; recipient of Guggenheim and Fulbright fellowships, the Alexander von Humboldt Prize from the German government (1995), and the Werner Heisenberg Medallion at Bonn (2003).

CITTON, Yves: Associate professor of French at the University of Pittsburgh; author of *Portrait de l'économiste en physiocrate. Critique littéraire de l'économie politique* (2001); currently working on a project titled *The Other Side of Liberty: The Invention of Spinozism in 18th-Century France.*

DIX, T. Keith: Associate professor in the Department of Classics at the University of Georgia; earned an A.B. in classics from Princeton and a Ph.D in classical studies from the University of Michigan; areas of research and publication include ancient libraries and literacy, Latin poetry, and Greek history.

FOGEL, Jerise: Associate professor in the Department of Classics at Marshall University; received her Ph.D from Columbia University in 1994; research interests include Greek and Roman rhetoric and oratory, Greek drama, and ancient and modern gay and lesbian studies; author of articles on Latin prose composition and the idea of "cosmopolitanism" as a colonial ideology in ancient Rome.

GREENE, Ellen: Professor of classics at the University of Oklahoma; has published articles on Greek and Latin poetry; books include *Reading Sappho: Contemporary Approaches* (1997), *Re-Reading Sappho: Reception and Transmission* (1997), *The Erotics of Domination: Male Desire and the Mistress in Latin Love Poetry* (1999), and *Gendered Dynamics in Latin Love Poetry,* with Ronnie Ancona (2004).

HERMANOWICZ, Erika T.: Assistant professor in the classics department at the University of Georgia.

HUTTON, William E.: Assistant professor of classical studies at the College of William and Mary in Virginia.

JANAN, Micaela: Associate professor of classical studies at Duke University; received her Ph.D from Princeton University; author of *"When the Lamp Is Shattered": Desire and Narrative in Catullus* (1994) and *The Politics of Desire: Propertius IV* (2001).

JOHNSON, Christel: Doctoral candidate in comparative literature at the University of South Carolina; writing her dissertation on the formation of the subject relative to gender and power as exemplified in the works of Sophocles, the Roman elegists, Plutarch, Sir Philip Sidney, and Queen Elizabeth I.

KENNEY, Matthew E.: Received his Ph.D in philosophy from the University of South Carolina in 2003; scholarship is concerned generally with ancient philosophy and specifically with the Platonic dialogues; currently an instructor in the Department of Philosophy at the University of South Carolina.

LARMOUR, David H. J.: Professor of classics and comparative literature at Texas Tech University; author of *Stage and Stadium: Drama and Athletics in Ancient Greece* (1999) and *Commentary on Lucian's True History* (1998) and editor of *Discourse and Ide-*

ology in Nabokov's Prose (2001); other research areas include Plutarch, Juvenal, and Foucault.

MILLER, Paul Allen: Professor of classics and comparative literature at the University of South Carolina; author of more than thirty articles and editor of ten volumes on topics concerning ancient poetry and literary theory; has written three books, most recently *Subjecting Verses: Latin Love Elegy and the Emergence of the Real* (2004).

MITCHELL-BOYASK, Robin: Associate professor of classics at Temple University; editor of *Approaches to Teaching the Drama of Euripides* (2002); author of several articles on Greek drama and Virgil; currently finishing a book on the effect of the great plague on tragedy in Athens.

OPSOMER, Jan: Associate professor of philosophy, University of Cologne, Germany; he was previously assistant professor at the University of South Carolina; received his Ph.D from the University of Leuven in Belgium; his research focuses on the history of Platonism.

O'SULLIVAN, Patrick: A graduate of Melbourne and Cambridge universities; currently lecturer at the University of Canterbury, New Zealand; chief areas of interest are archaic and classical Greek intellectual history, ancient aesthetics, and psychological theories; has written on Aeschylus and Greek and Roman art and has forthcoming publications on Homer, Pindar, and Greek rhetorical theories; also working on a commentary on Euripides' *Cyclops* to be published by Aris and Phillips.

PLATTER, Charles: Associate professor of classics at the University of Georgia; author of many articles on Greek and Latin literature as well as *Aristophanes and the Carnival of Genres* (forthcoming, Johns Hopkins University Press); editor of *Rethinking Sexuality: Foucault and Classical Antiquity* (1997).

RANKINE, Patrice D.: Earned a Ph.D from Yale University in 1998; assistant professor at Purdue University in the Department of Foreign Languages and Literatures and in the Interdisciplinary Program in Classical Studies; has written extensively on classical studies as well as on Ralph Ellison's relationship to classical literature and mythology.

RICHLIN, Amy: Earned her undergraduate degree in classics from Princeton University in 1973 and her Ph.D from Yale University in 1978; has taught at the University of Southern California since 1989 and from 1989–1999 held a joint appointment there in gender studies; has published widely on Roman sexuality.

ROSE, Peter W.: Educated at Williams College and Harvard University; has taught at Yale University, the University of Texas, Haverford College, and Miami University of Ohio; has written on Greek authors (Homer, Pindar, Aeschylus, Sophocles, Thucydides, and Plato) as well as on film, mythology, comedy, and women in antiquity; his book, *Sons of the Gods, Children of Earth* (1992) surveys and applies contemporary Marxist approaches to Greek texts.

RUBINO, Carl A.: Edward North Professor of Classics at Hamilton College and book review editor of the *American Journal of Philology;* has published extensively on classics, comparative literature, literary theory, and philosophy; a collaborator of the late Belgian Nobel laureate Ilya Prigogine, he has also written on the connections between science and the humanities.

SPENCE, Sarah: Professor of classics at the University of Georgia and editor-in-chief of *Literary Imagination: The Review of the Association of Literary Scholars and Critics;* she has published widely on medieval vernacular poetry and classical Latin poetry, with a special interest in Virgil.

STEEL, Carlos: Received his Ph.D from the University of Leuven, Belgium; professor of philosophy and director of the De Wulf-Mansion Center for Ancient and Medieval Philosophy at the University of Leuven; research areas include Neoplatonism and medieval philosophy.

STREUFERT, Paul D.: Assistant professor of literature and languages at the University of Texas at Tyler; received a B.A. in classics from Valparaiso University, an M.A. in classics from Texas Tech University, and a Ph.D. in comparative literature from Purdue University; research interests include dramatic literature, particularly Athenian tragedy and its influences.

SULTAN, Nancy: Professor of Greek and Roman studies and chairwoman of the Department of Modern and Classical Languages and Literatures at Illinois Wesleyan University; areas of specialty are Hellenic cultural studies, classical mythology, modern Greek folklore, ethnomusicology, and gender studies; author of *Exile and the Poetics of Loss in Greek Tradition* (1999).

THIBODEAU, Philip: Assistant professor of classics at Brooklyn College; research focuses on Roman poetry of the late Republic and its intersection with ancient philosophy and Roman religion; has written on Virgil and Horace as well as ancient science and is currently working on a book on anthropological themes in Virgil's *Georgics.*

VANDIVER, Elizabeth: Received her Ph.D from the University of Texas; holds the position of assistant professor of classics at Whitman College, Walla Walla, Washington; author of *Heroes in Herodotus: The Interaction of Myth and History* (1991), many articles, and a series of video lecture-courses; co-organizer of the colloquium on "Translation in Context" for the American Philological Association.

WIENER, Chad: Earned a masters degree in social sciences from the University of Chicago in 1999; currently writing a dissertation on Aristotle's philosophy of biology at the University of Georgia.

WILLETT, Steven J.: Professor of English and cultural studies, Shizuoka University of Art and Culture, Japan; received his B.A. from Occidental College, his M.A. from the University of Oregon, and his Ph.D from the University of California at San Diego; a professional translator (Japanese, Greek, Latin, Italian, and Russian) and the author of many articles on translation theory, poetics, and versification; has three forthcoming books.

INDEX

A

A-10 tank buster VI 173
Abbas, Abu XV 77, 90; XVI 245
Abbas, Mahmoud (Abu Mazen) XIV 102, 225; XV 184, 186, 201
Abbasids X 60, 182–183, 186–187, 274, 288
Abbott, Lyman VIII 204
Abdu, Muhammad X 61
Abdullah (Crown Prince of Saudi Arabia) XIV 100, 105, 246, 248–249; XV 142
Abdullah (Jordan) XIV 66, 288; XV 142, 144, 146
Abdullah II XIV 61, 63–65, 68, 105, 256
Abelard, Peter X 166
Aberdeen Proving Ground XIX 62
ABM (anti-ballistic missile system) XIV 103
ABM Treaty. *See* Anti-Ballistic Missile Treaty
Abolition Act (1780) XII 263
Abolition of Slavery Act (Emancipation Act, 1833) XIII 1
abolitionism XIII 1–9, 131
  attacks against abolitionists XIII 8
  Christianity within XIII 27–34
abortion II 80, 220–226, 284
Aboukir (British ship) VIII 288
Abraham Lincoln Brigade VI 154, 176; XVIII 1–8; XIX 88
Abraham Lincoln School, Chicago XIX 230
Abrams, Eliot XIV 106
Abstract Expressionism XIX 45, 48
Abt, John XIX 198
Abu Dhabi XIV 29, 247
Abu Dhabi Satellite TV Channel XIV 32
Abu Mazen. *See* Mahmoud Abbas
Abu Nidal XIV 198–199; XV 127, 129, 132; XVI 245
Abyssinia XVI 110
academic freedom XIX 107–115
Academy Award (Oscar) XIX 168
Acheson, Dean I 27–30, 58–59, 69, 89, 160, 174, 220, 286, 294; II 45, 134, 206; VI 75, 147–150; XV 203, 206; XIX 94
  criticizes W. E. B. Du Bois XIX 240
  defense perimeter speech XIX 156
  McCarthy attacks on II 211; XIX 99, 224
  Republican attacks on XIX 94
  support for Alger Hiss XIX 63, 158, 198
  on Communist insurgencies in Greece, Turkey, and Iran XIX 249
Acheson-Lilienthal Report I 27, 29–31, 220–221
  "Atomic Development Authority" I 29
Achille Lauro attack (1985) XV 77; XVI 245
acquired immunodeficiency syndrome (AIDS) II 224; XI 246; XVI 138; XVII 6, 9
Acre X 47, 53, 89, 127, 152, 156, 172, 187, 189, 192, 198, 248, 251–254, 257–258, 261, 305
  fall of (1291) X 46–47, 49, 64–65, 68, 153, 204
Act for International Development (1950) XV 203, 205
Act of Union (1801) XII 166
Action in the North Atlantic XIX 37
activists, antiwar II 10
Acton, Lord XIII 275
Acts of Trade XII 200, 202
Adams, Abigail XII 263, 318–319
Adams, John XII 25, 41, 55, 63, 66, 79, 83, 93–94, 109–110, 113–114, 121, 139–140, 144, 149, 158, 205, 208, 243, 263, 318; XIII 195
Adams, John Quincy XIII 4, 195
Adams, Samuel XII 93–95, 110, 214, 218, 283
Adana Declaration VII 79
Addams, Jane III 165, 168, 171, 201
  campaign against cocaine III 134
  Hull House III 166, 208
  peace activism XIX 176
Ademar of Chabannes X 165
Aden XIV 176
Adenauer, Konrad I 255, 257; VI 207, 210
Adhemar Le Puy X 19, 221
Adhemar of Monteil X 282
Adler, Solomon XIX 197
Administration Floodplain Management Task Force VII 214
Admirals' Revolt (1949) I 3–9
Admiralty Courts XII 196, 200
Ado of Quiersy X 73
Adriatic Sea IX 181, 270; X 113; XVI 29, 36, 104
Aegean Sea VIII 117, 212; IX 205
Aegis class warships VI 109
Aehrenthal, Alois VIII 45
Aerial photography, World War I IX 16
Aeschylus XX 56–64
Aetna, Inc. XIII 197–198
affaire des fiches VIII 151
affirmative action II 143, 183, 167
Afghan War (1979–1989) XVI 282, 288
Afghanistan I 95, 105; II 62; VI 4, 44, 50, 110, 113, 165, 188, 194, 217, 221, 224, 226, 229, 232, 236, 241, 261, 272; VIII 31, 35; IX 226; XIV 1–9, 28, 31, 34, 37–38, 61, 86, 88, 107, 136, 141, 175–177, 180, 186, 190, 228, 230, 250, 262, 267; XV 101, 255, 271; XVI 41, 45–46, 70, 79, 84, 109, 218; XVII 20, 134, 221
  communist coup (1978) VI 166; XIV 6
  destruction of Bamian Buddhas XIV 11
  imperialism I 151
  monarchy XVI 180
  Muslim fanaticism in VI 165
  Northern Alliance XIV 10
  opium trade I 15

Soviet invasion of I 10–16, 71, 101, 183, 185–186, 217–218, 289; II 56; VI 2, 30, 35, 42–44, 66, 68, 107, 133, 162, 165–166, 222, 225, 226, 232, 237, 241, 246, 261, 270: XIV 89, 248; XV 97, 176, 255; XVII 231
Soviet troops withdrawn VI 45
tensions with Iran I 15
U.S. invasion XIV 10–18, 28, 95–96, 103, 123
U.S. support for mujahideen XIV 1–9
war with Soviets I 196
women in XI 72; XIV 121, 231
AFL. *See* American Federation of Labor
Africa VI 41, 50, 63, 77, 83, 164, 189, 209, 246, 249, 264, 267; VIII 33, 109; IX 91, 112, 114–116, 225–226; X 305; XII 33, 171, 200, 252; XIII 7, 11, 19, 26, 36, 181, 192, 246; XIV 55, 176, 180, 195, 199 ; XV 15–16, 203, 205; XVI 41, 65–66, 68, 85, 87–88, 109–112, 238, 268
AIDS in VII 244
British colonization in XII 167, 171
casualties of WWI troops in Europe IX 115
colonization of freed blacks in XIII 2–3, 8, 19
communal work patterns XIII 204
complicity of Africans in slave trade XIII 35–40
corruption in XIV 48
dams in VII 1–9, 236–246, 287
deep-water sources in VII 62–68
drinking water in VII 2
economy of XIII 38
famine in XIII 40
freedom movements XIX 9, 12
genocide in VI 216
German interests in VIII 100
harm of slave trade upon XIII 39
hydroelectric power in VII 2, 5
independence of colonies in VI 13
influenza epidemic in VIII 89
kinship networks XIII 36
Muslims in XIII 193
neutrality XIX 13
oral tradition in XIII 141
slave trade XIII 130, 273
slavery in XIII 110
slaves from XIII 269, 270, 272, 273, 274
slaves from to Brazil XIII 65
Soviet activities in VI 2
U.S. policy in VI 87
water shortage in VII 280
World War I VIII 84–90
Africa, Southern VII 63–68
African Americans XI 72; XII 34, 259, 263, 293–300; XIII 1–284
American Revolution XII 1–8, 89, 217
attitudes toward Communism XIX 11–12
church officials and the civil rights movement XIX 12
Confederate symbols XIII 270, 273, 275
development of culture during slavery XIII 138–145
doctors banned by AMA XI 152
excluded from U.S. naturalization XII 7
exploitation of XIII 195
folktales XIII 139
fraternal societies and the civil rights movement XIX 12
impact of emancipation on XIII 50–57
impact of slavery upon XIII 197, 253–260, 261–267
Loyalists XII 189
Muslims XIV 188
politics XIX 8–15
religion XIII 187, 189
retention of African culture XIII 11–15
socio-economic divisions III 118
white ancestry of XIII 222
World War I VIII 298, 301; IX 1–7
World War II III 213–219; XIX 25
African National Congress (ANC) VI 5; VII 239, 286
African Union XIV 284
Africans XIII 251
arrive in North America XIII 180
English views of XIII 250–251
enslavement of XIII 167
European views on XIII 179–180
racial discrimination XIII 181
Afrika Korps (Africa Corps) V 123, 181, 226, 232
Afrikaner Nationalist Party VII 239
Agadir, Morocco VIII 33
Agadir Crisis (1911) XVI 193
Age of Reason XII 109–110
Age of Sail VIII 136; IX 117
Agency for International Development XV 205
Agrarian Reform Law (1952) I 93, 123, 126
Agreement on German External Debts (1953) XI 215
Agreement on the Prevention of Nuclear War (1972) XV 257
Agricultural Adjustment Act (1933) III 27, 30, 62, 66, 156–163
Supreme Court ruling III 25
Agricultural Adjustment Administration (AAA, 1933) III 154, 157; VI 124; XIX 92, 119, 155
agricultural revolution III 2
agricultural science II 83–85
agricultural technology III 1–8
Global Positioning Satellites (GPS) III 5
history III 2, 5
impact of tractors III 6
post–World War II mechanization III 3
time management III 4
Agua Caliente Reservation VII 170
Aid for Families with Dependent Children (AFDC) II 278
Airborne Warning and Control System (AWACS) VI 173
aircraft carrier
defeat of U-boats IV 4
role in World War II I 4; IV 1–7
AirLand Battle doctrine XVI 44
airplanes VIII 17
Bf 109B (Germany) XVIII 13–14, 259–260, 263
Breda 65 (Italy) XVIII 261
CR-32 (Italy) XVIII 13
Do 17 (Germany) XVIII 259, 263
F-16 fighter (U.S.) VI 223
He 51 (Germany) XVIII 13–14, 259, 262
He 111 (Germany) XVIII 82, 259, 263
I-15 (U.S.S.R.) XVIII 11, 13–14, 262
I-16 (U.S.S.R.) XVIII 13–14, 260, 262
IL-2 Sturmovik (U.S.S.R.) XVIII 12, 260
Illiushin (U.S.S.R.) XVI 163
Ju 52 (Germany) XVIII 259
Ju 87 Stuka (Germany) XVIII 12, 14, 87, 259, 263
role in the Spanish Civil War XVIII 9–16
SB-2 (U.S.S.R.) XVIII 14, 260, 262
Tiupolev (U.S.S.R.) XVI 163
WWI IX 9–14, 217–223
Ait Ahmed, Hocine XV 8–9
Akhmerov, Yitzhak VI 126; XIX 231
Akosombo Dam (Ghana) VII 4
Akron v. *Akron Center for Reproductive Health* (1983) II 222
Alabama
Citizens Councils XIX 80
disfranchisement of blacks in XIII 56
grandfather clause XIII 56
meeting of Confederate Congress XIII 153
prosecution of Scottsboro case XIX 12
slavery in XIII 102, 195, 206, 221, 232, 282
use of Confederate symbols XIII 277
Alabama (Confederate ship) VIII 136–137
Al-Adil X 89, 256–258
Al-Afghani, Jamal al-Din X 61
Alamo Canal VII 152, 154–155, 157, 159
Al-Andalus X 8, 40–43, 60, 242
Al-Aqsa Martyrs Brigades XIV 102

Al-Aqsa *intifada* (uprising) XIV 19–27, 31, 33, 95, 97, 103, 105, 128, 155; XV 83, 90, 183, 185, 201, 261, 266–267
Al-Aqsa mosque X 198–199; XIV 19, 22, 159, 165–166; XV 186
Al-Asad, Bashar XIV 61, 63, 64, 67, 174, 256
Al-Asad, Hafiz XIV 29, 64, 125, 128, 148, 174; XV 83, 150, 155, 214, 219–220, 222, 227, 238, 240–241, 255, 260–261, 264, 266–267; XV 45, 153, 267
Al-Ashraf X 47, 49
Alaska VII 197
  salmon range VII 196
Alawid dynasty XIV 206, 209
Albania I 294; VI 134, 175, 181, 261, 275, 280–281; VIII 212; IX 205, 227, 270; XIV 176; XV 120; XVI 58, 60, 109, 124
  lack of environmental control in VII 145
  monarchy XVI 180
  Soviet domination until 1968 I 107
Albanian Communist Party VI 280
Albanians, enslavement of XIII 167
Albert (England) XVI 181
Albert I IX 42, 44
Albert of Aix X 16, 97, 211, 215, 219, 237, 276
Albigensian (Cathar) heresy X 208
Albright, Madeline XIV 38; XV 265
Alcala, Pedro de X 8
Alcatraz prison XIX 202
Alcibiades XX 65–71
Aleppo X 48, 51, 185; XV 275
Alessandri Rodríguez, Jorge I 124, 127
Alexander (Greek king) IX 208
Alexander (Serbian king) VIII 45
Alexander (Yugoslavia) XVI 180
Alexander I IX 268, 271; X 69; XII 308
Alexander II IX 155, 158, 190, 238; X 220, 224, 284; XVI 16
Alexander III 234, 236; XVI 16, 53
Alexander, Harold IV 149, 181; V 73, 125
  Italian campaign IV 144
Alexander, Hursel XIX 234
Alexander, Leo T. XI 151–152
Alexandra IX 160, 237, 239–240, 243; XVI 17, 201
Alexandria, Egypt VII 147; X 76, 141, 152, 170, 185, 187
  construction of sewage plants in VII 148
  sack of (1365) X 67, 70
Alexandria Protocol (1944) XV 141, 146–147
Alexeyev, Mikhail IX 65
Alexius I Comnenus X 24, 26, 29, 74, 205, 209, 215, 220, 234, 238, 280, 285, 292
Alexius IV Angelus X 107, 110
Alfonso I X 242, 246
Alfonso II X 244
Alfonso III 242, 244
Alfonso VI 2, 41, 245, 289
Alfonso VIII X 133
Alfonso X X 160, 243
Alfonso, Pedro (Petrus Alfonsi) X 42, 44
Algeciras, Spain, conference in (1906) VIII 32; XVI 107
Algeria I 151, 281; VI 83, 103, 106–107, 188; VII 82; IX 111–112, 115–116; X 305; XIV 29, 31, 52, 55, 69–72, 74–75, 79, 81–82, 84–85, 88, 114, 134, 141, 177, 179, 183, 190, 201–203, 205, 209, 212, 215–216, 219, 230–231, 252–253, 255, 276, 283; XV 23, 37, 45, 49, 57, 136, 199, 216, 222, 244, 271; XVI 71, 79, 81, 84, 136, 139, 236, 238–240
  Algerian Communist Party (PCA) XV 14
  Algerian National Assembly XIV 203
  Armée de Libération Nationale (National Army of Liberation, ALN) XV 9
  arms from Russia XV 14
  Assemblée Populaire Comunale (APC) XV 8
  Assemblée Populaire de Wilaya (APW) XV 8
  colonial policy of French VI 80, 136; XIV 12
  Comite Revolutionnaire d'Unite et d'Action (CRUA) XV 11
  Committee of Public Safety XVI 136
  coup in (1958) VI 106
  economy XIV 51
  Egypt, aid from XIV 143
  environmental law in VII 145
  France in XVI 70
  Front de Libération Nationale (National Liberation Front, FLN) XV 11–12, 16; XVI 240
  Front National (National Front, FN) XV 9
  Haut Comité d'Etat (High Council of State, HCE) XV 2, 8
  independence from France I 278; XIV 121, 203
  Islamique Armé (Algerian Islamic Armed Movement) XV 6
  Majlis al-Shura XV 4
  National Charter (1976) XV 6
  National Liberation Front (FLN) XIV 69
  National Popular Assembly XV 2, 8
  1992 elections XV 1–10
  Organisation Armée Secrète (Secret Army Organization, OAS) XV 18
  Rassemblement pour la Culture et la Démocratie (Rally for Culture and Democracy, RCD) XV 9
  War of Liberation XV 6
  water XIV 269
  Western Sahara XIV 278, 280–282
  women 121, 123, 290
Algerian Revolution (1954-1962) XV 11–19
Algiers XIX 37
Algiers accord (1975) XV 100, 102
Algiers Charter (1964) XV 6
Algiers Conference (1973) VI 268
Al-Hakim X 101, 218, 273, 287
Al-Harawi X 249
Al-Husayni, Muhammed Amin VII 137
Ali 234–236
Ali, Muhammad XIX 14
Alien and Sedition Acts of 1798 XIX 215, 217
Alien Enemy Bureau, U.S. Justice Department XIX 174
Alien Registration Act of 1940. *See* Smith Act
Al-Jazeera XIV 28–35, 61, 65, 91, 115, 217
Al-Kamil X 89–90, 92
All-American Canal VII 154–155
All Quiet on the Western Front (1929) VIII 55, 59, 188, 264; IX 212
All-Race Conference, Chicago, 1924 XIX 189
All-Russian Council of Soviets VIII 171
All-Russian Fascist Party XVII 137, 139
Allegheny Mountains XII 199, 232, 236
Allen, Ethan XII 10, 11, 14, 44
Allen, James S. XIX 191
Allen, Raymond B. XIX 108– 110
Allen, Richard VI 229, 231
Allenby, Edmund VIII 37, 39, 41, 121, 213, 216; IX 69, 72; X 59, 171, 305
Allende Gossens, Salvador I 26, 68, 123–125, 127–140; VI 64, 86–87, 265; XI 88; XIX 140, 142, 145–146
Alliance for Progress I 17–26, 126, 132; II 115
Allied Expeditionary Force (AEF) V 20, 23, 25; XVI 312
Allied Mediterranean Expeditionary Force VIII 119
Allied Supreme Council IX 173
Allies IV 208–215; V 27–33
  relationship of IV 209; V 34–47
  strategy IV 143–150; V 19–26
Allison, Francis XII 296
Al-Mansuri, Baybars X 49
Al-Mirazi, Hafez XIV 29, 30
Almohads X 273–275; XIV 201, 206
Almoravids X 159, 163, 245, 274–275, 287; XIV 201, 206
al-Moualem, Walid XV 263–264, 266
Al-Mu'azzam X 89–90

Alp Arslan X 138
Alphonse of Potiers X 145
Alpine Regional Hydroelectric Group VII 98
Alps VII 229, 231; XI 175
Al-Qaida X 55, 61; XIV 1, 3, 7, 10–18, 28, 31, 38, 86–87, 91–93, 105, 175, 182, 184, 228–230, 237–239, 242, 250, 262; XV 54, 259; XVI 71, 245
  religious indoctrination XIV 92
Alsace-Lorraine VIII 71–72, 76, 151, 180, 226, 232, 234–237, 280–281; IX 46, 52, 102, 263; XVI 257, 292, 295, 302, 308
Al-Said, Nuri XV 31, 116, 121–122, 142, 146, 169
Al-Saiqa (Pioneers of the Popular War for Liberation) XV 90
Al-Sanusi, Idris XIV 192–193
Al-Shara, Farouk XV 265–267
Alsop, Joseph XIX 202
Alsop, Stewart XIX 202
Al-Thani, Hamad bin Khalifa XIV 28, 33
Altmühl River VII 204–207
Amalgamated Clothing Workers Union III 191
Amaury of Lautrec X 294
Amazon River VII 235
Ambrose, Stephen I 214; II 50
Ambrose X 97, 229
Amerasia case XIX 16–23, 61, 194
  J. Edgar Hoover's role XIX 176, 178
America First movement V 135–136
American and Foreign Anti-Slavery Society XIII 9
American Anti-Slavery Society XIII 4, 6–7, 9
American Civil Liberties Union (ACLU) II 283; III 39; V 224; XIX 66
  Scopes Trial III 33
  Scottsboro case III 185
American Coalition of Life Activists (ACLA) II 223
American colonies, Anglicization of XII 208–211
American Colonization Society XIII 19
American Committee for Protection of the Foreign Born XIX 214
American Committee on Africa (ACOA) XIX 12
American Communications Association v. *Douds* XIX 149, 151
American Communist Party III 221, 223–226. *See also* Communist Party of the United States of America (CPUSA)
American Cotton Planters' Association XIII 51
American culture
  frontier and exploration as symbols of II 245
  hegemony II 213
  spread of II 213
An American Dilemma XIX 24, 26
American Eugenics Society III 21–22
American Expeditionary Forces (AEF) VIII 10–25, 182, 300; IX 21, 24, 30–31, 57, 105, 109–110, 146, 193
  African Americans in IX 1–7
  Catholics in VIII 205
  effect of gas on VIII 239
  homosexuals in IX 149
  women nurses in VIII 130
American Farm Bureau Federation III 159
American Federation of Government Employees XIX 136
American Federation of Labor (AFL) II 188; III 183; XIX 6, 67–69, 87
  admits TUEL XIX 193
  attitudes toward opium III 134
  character of XIX 71
  criticized by CPUSA XIX 102
  merger with Congress of Industrial Organizations (CIO) XIX 68, 73, 105
  origins of XIX 67–71
  reasons for decline III 195
American Federation of Labor-Congress of Industrial Organizations (AFL-CIO) II 190; VI 237; XIX 6, 67–69, 73
American Federation of State, County, and Municipal Employees (AFSCME) II 190–191
American Federation of Teachers II 190
American Friends Service Committee IX 19
The American High School Today XIX 113
American Independent Party II 180
American Indian Defense Association (AIDA) III 141
American Indian Movement XIX 221
American Institute of Public Opinion (AIPO) III 66
American Jewish Committee II 24
American Kurdish Information Network (AKIN) XIV 172
American Labor Party II 197; XIX 216
American left
  decline of XIX 98–99, 102
  noncommunist groups XIX 100
American Legion XIX 75, 92, 101, 163, 181, 183, 209, 250
American Legion Magazine XIX 250
American Management Association III 68
American Medical Association (AMA) II 221
  bans African American doctors XI 152
American Party
  1968 presidential race II 281
American Peace Crusade 238
American Revolution (1775–1783) I 88; XII 1–324; XIII 2, 7, 42, 45, 147, 156, 164, 175, 195, 233, 249, 272, 274, 280–281; XV 157; XVI 181
  African Americans in XII 1–8, 89, 217, 263; XIII 17–24
  British military strategy XII 267–275
  British Southern strategy XII 39
  British West Indies XII 310–316
  Canada XII 43–49, 86, 268
  causes XII 50–55
  Continental Army XII 85–91
  Conway Cabal XII 92–98
  culpability of George III XII 136–144
  Franco-American alliance XII 39, 41, 101, 103, 181–182, 186, 255, 306, 308
  French participation in XII 100–107
  guerilla warfare XII 27, 33
  Hessian deserters XII 89
  impact of Great Awakening upon XII 145–153
  impact on Great Britain XII 27–35, 164–172
  influence on French Revolution XII 127–134
  influence on Third World freedom movements XIX 25
  Loyalists XII 25, 30, 37, 39, 41, 82, 86, 139, 158, 160, 167, 169, 181–194, 218–219, 260, 268, 306, 316
  mercantilism as cause of XII 196–203
  mob action in XII 214–215
  nationalism in XII 204–212
  Native Americans XII 37, 44, 49, 173–180, 217, 268
  naval warfare XII 77–83
  Newburgh Conspiracy XII 221–229
  Parliamentary policies XII 230–237
  Parliamentary supremacy XII 239–245
  philisophical influences upon Founding Fathers XII 118–125
  popular support in Great Britain XII 248–256
  possibility of British victory in XII 36–41
  privateers XII 77–78, 81, 83, 106
  role of the elite XII 213–219
  slavery XII 37, 293–300; XIII 17–24
  women in XII 217, 317–324
American River VII 29
American Slav Congress XIX 215
American Student Union XIX 103
American-Syrian Crisis (1957) XV 270–271
American System XIII 283
American Telephone and Telegraph IX 21
American Type Culture Collection XV 78
American University of Beirut XV 205
American Youth for Democracy (AYD) XIX 193

Americans for Democratic Action XIX 105, 185
Americans for Intellectual Freedom XIX 241
Americans For South African Resistance XIX 12
Amery, Julian XV 15, 161
Amin, Hafizullah I 10–12, 15; VI 165–166
Amin, Idi VI 83; XI 71; XIV 197
Amnesty International I 146
Amphibians VII 216–217
Amphictionic Confederacy (circa sixteenth century B.C.E.) XII 19
Anabaptist Germans XII 235
Anarchism VIII 254; XVI 243–244; XIX 211, 246
  in the Spanish Civil War XVIII 3, 24–32, 114, 184, 187, 189
Anarcho-Syndicalism VIII 254; XVIII 24–32
Anatolia VIII 189, 211–214; X 280, 282; XIV 168, 261
  Christians in VIII 211
  Greeks evacuated from IX 206
  Islamic rule in VIII 211
Anatolian Plain VII 10
Anderson, Marian XIX 9, 27–28
Anderson, Sherwood III 177
André, John XII 11
Andre, Louis VIII 151
Andrew II X 89
Andrew of Strumi X 229
Andronicus II Palaeologus X 30
Andropov, Yuri I 13; II 60; VI 111, 116, 226, 239; XV 255
  domestic programs I 197
  foreign policy I 186
  views on Afghan war I 13
Angell, Norman IX 228
Angleton, James Jesus I 66
Anglican Church XVI 178
  American Revolution XII 148, 167, 314
  World War I VIII 202
Anglo-American Corporation VII 5
Anglo-American Financial Agreement (1945) VI 79
Anglo-American Mutual Aid Agreement (1942) VI 78
Anglo-Boer War (1899–1902) VIII 34, 73, 103, 200, 272
  opposition to VIII 77
Anglo-Egyptian accord (1954) XV 244, 255
Anglo-Egyptian Treaty (1936) XV 66
Anglo-French rivalry XII 252
Anglo-German naval rivalry VIII 29–36; XVI 193
Anglo-Iranian Oil Company (AIOC) I 69; VI 255; XV 108, 156, 160, 173, 176
Anglo-Iraqi Treaty (1930) XV 117
Anglo-Irish Treaty (1921) VIII 158, 160
Anglo-Irish War (1916–1921) IX 93
Anglo-Japanese Alliance (1902) IX 167
Anglo-Persian Oil Company XIV 211–212
Angola I 95, 105, 152; II 56; VI 7, 44, 50, 65–66, 83, 87, 165, 178, 188, 194, 221–222, 241, 256, 261, 265; VII 236, 239; XIII 11, 272; XIX 14
  Cuban troops in VI 41, 43
  female agricultural practices XIII 40
  Portuguese immigration to VII 237
  slave trade XIII 35, 130, 134
  Soviet support I 185
  withdrawal of Cuban troops VI 7
Annan, Kofi XIV 199, 280–282
Annapolis Convention (1786) XII 287, 289, 291
Anne (Queen) XII 141
Annie Hamilton Brown Wild Life Sanctuary VII 277
Anno of Cologne X 284
Anschluss (political union, 1938) IV 19–20, 126, 191, 224; V 293; XI 14 , 149; XVI 10, 119, 220
  European reactions to IV 127
Anselm II of Lucca X 81, 85
Anthony, Susan B. II 74; III 199
Anti-Ballistic Missile (ABM) Treaty (1972) I 199, 200, 227, 231; II 61, 171; VI 18, 30, 35, 43; XIV 17; XVI 95
anti-ballistic missiles (ABMs) VI 17
anti-Catholicism XII 149
Anti-colonialism XIX 8, 9, 11–13, 24–25
Anti-Comintern Pact (1936) V 115, 229; XVI 100
anticommunism V 114
  after World War I XIX 174, 211, 218, 245–246, 273
  after World War II XIX passim
  concensus builder II 211
  domestic II 211; XIX passim
  emergence after World War II XIX 116–122
  end of post-1945 Red Scare XIX 123–130
  ideological roots XIX 91–97, 180–186
  impact on Artistic Expression XIX 43–51
  impact on civil rights movement XIX 8–15, 24–33, 181
  impact on labor movement II 189; XIX 67–73
  influence on foreign policy II 205; XIX 131–139
  legislation II 131
  outside U.S. XIX 265–274
  propaganda II 130
  state and local committees XIX 161, 204–210
Antifascism XIX 9–10, 12, 25, 29, 98
Antifederalists XII 19, 21–22, 73–75, 121–122, 277–279, 281, 288, 291
Antigua XII 311–314
Antilynching campaigns XIX 10, 12, 78
antinuclear weapons protests VI 15, 22
  impact on Soviet policy VI 17
Antioch X 25, 27, 35, 46–48, 52, 128, 138, 155, 187, 191, 201, 247–248, 251, 254, 256, 259, 282; XI 20
Antipodes XII 168
Antiradicalism XIX 246
Anti-Saloon League III 262
anti-Semitism III 252, 254; IV 137, 139; VI 88; VIII 61; X 20, 62; XI 2, 5, 17–24, 33, 55–56, 77, 81, 87, 90, 111–112, 114, 120, 160–161, 181, 183, 185, 189, 243, 264–266, 268, 271; XIV 14; XV 37; XVI 186; XVII 80, 83–84, 98, 104, 106, 108, 110, 136, 138
  impact on Nazi collaboration IV 131
  policy of Nazi Party XI 103
  Soviet Union XV 253
Antislavery movements XIX 11
Anti-Submarine Detection Investigation Committee VIII 196
Anti-Tactical Ballistic Missiles (ATBM) I 195
Anti-Tank Guided Missiles (ATGMs) VI 172
Anti–Vietnam War movement II 159, 161
  accused of Communist ties XIX 207, 243, 275
  demonstrations II 3
  impact on American politics II 3
  impact of Red Scare on XIX 277
  investigated by CIA XIX 226
  investigated by FBI XIX 207, 220, 226
  moratoriums XIX 277
Apache helicopter VI 173
apartheid II 20, 100; VI 6; VII 5, 7; XI 167; XIV 221; XIX 9, 12, 14, 29
"An Appeal to Stop the Spread of Nuclear Weapons" XIX 204, 242
Appeasement XIX 88
Apollo 8 (1968) II 257–258
Apollo 11 (1969) II 258
Apollo 12 (1969) II 259
Apollo Theatre III 188
Appalachian Mountains XII 199, 230
  settlers banned from crossing XII 53
appeasement I 300; IV 16–21; XI 14
Appolinaire, Guillame VIII 191
April Laws XI 94
April Theses IX 199
Aptheker, Herbert XIX 111, 189, 262
Aquinas, Thomas X 179; XI 19, 23; XII 258–259; XIII 17
Arab-American Corporation (ARAMCO) II 145
Arab Bank for Economic Development in Africa (ABEDA) XV 142

Arab Cooperation Council (ACC) XV 147
Arab Federation XV 120
Arab Fund for Technical Assistance (AFTA) XV 142
Arab Higher Committee for Palestine VII 137
Arab Human Development Report (AHDR) XIV 56, 59, 83, 92
Arab-Israeli conflict XIV 61, 89; XV 51–57, 68, 102, 142, 144
Arab-Israeli peace process XIV 31, 36
Arab-Israeli War (1947–1949) XIV 159, 179, 220; XV 21, 30, 33, 35, 37, 45–46, 65–66, 144, 191, 213, 244, 253
Arab-Israeli War (Six-Day War, 1967) II 142, 148, 150; VI 31; XIV 144, 151–152, 160, 193, 220, 268, 270; XV 20–25, 37, 40–41, 45–46, 70, 73, 93, 102, 130, 134–140, 144, 149, 191, 198–199, 211–214, 219, 223, 225, 237, 242, 247, 253, 255, 261, 267; XVI 239
Arab-Israeli War (Yom Kippur War, 1973) I 156–157, 159, 162, 222, 308–317; VI 41, 43, 107, 161, 163, 166, 171, 204, 268; VII 135–136, 140; XIV 89, 145, 195, 221, 245; XIV 217; XV 20, 40, 46, 49, 54, 56, 106, 139, 175, 213, 218–220, 225–226, 237–241, 252–254, 257, 261, 268
    aftermath I 312
    Gaza Strip I 314
    Golan Heights I 314
    Sinai Peninsula I 314
    West Bank of the Jordan River I 314
Arab League (League of Arab States) VI 135, 161; XIV 55, 110, 148, 150, 180, 205, 247–248, 289; XV 45, 49, 57, 89, 91, 104, 127, 133, 141–147, 193, 198–199, 204, 214, 239, 261, 275–276
Arab Maghreb Union (UMA) XIV 69–76, 114; XV 147
Arab Monetary Fund XIV 247
Arab News Network (ANN) XIV 29
Arab nationalism VI 161, 163; XV 30, 64–65, 101, 165–170, 206, 249, 274–276; XVI 236, 243
Arab Nationalist Movement (ANM) XV 49
Arab oil embargo (1973) VI 107; XIV 212, 217
Arab Radio and Television (ART) XIV 29
Arab Revolt (1916) VIII 37–42, 214
Arab Revolt (1936–1939) XV 89, 146
Arab socialism XIV 47
Arab States Broadcasting Union XIV 34
Arab Steadfastness Front XIV 198
Arab Women's Organization (AWO) XIV 289
Arabia VIII 37, 41, 212; IX 96; XIV 159, 188, 201, 206, 244
Arabian Peninsula VIII 38; XIV 133, 176–177, 201; XV 146
Arabic (British ship), sinking of VIII 288; IX 21
Arabic (language) X 4, 6; XIV 180, 201–203, 205, 209
Arafat, Yasser I 159; XIV 19, 22, 24–27, 61, 63, 95–96, 99, 100–101, 103, 106–107, 166, 179, 197, 225; XV 41, 44, 76, 89–91, 93, 127, 135, 149, 153, 182–184, 186–187, 191, 193, 195, 198–200, 255, 266
Aragon X 2, 4, 30, 35, 41, 159
    Jews in X 15
Aramco XV 177, 179
Aravalli Mountains VII 125
Arbenz Guzmán, Jacobo I 24, 49, 66, 93, 123–126, 129–131, 211; XIX 141, 145–146
    Guatemala I 70
    overthrow of government in Guatemala III 53
Arcadia Conference (1941–1942) IV 209, 212; V 38
Arctic Sea IX 194
Ardennes Forest XVI 115
Arendt, Hannah I 135; III 103; V 166; XVI 259, 262; XVII 35, 101, 197, 201
Arévalo, Juan José I 24, 123, 126
Argentina I 24, 54, 94; VI 194, 266; XIV 71; XV 33; XVI 81, 98, 110–111
    Adolf Eichmann in XI 37, 40
    attacks against Jews in XIV 125–126
    Communist guerrilla movements I 125
    human rights record I 143
    immigrants XI 59
    military coups I 26
    nuclear nonproliferation I 224
    nuclear weapons development I 219, 223
    reduction of U.S. military aid I 141
    slavery in XIII 272
    War of the Triple Alliance I 125
    war with Great Britain VI 8, 13
Argoud, Antoine XV 12, 15
Argov, Shlomo XV 127, 132
Arianism X 17
Arias, Oscar VI 191
Arias peace process VI 194
Arif, Abdul Salaam XV 122–124
Aristophanes XX 72–80
Aristotle X 69; XII 110, 119, 122; XIII 17, 166
    and Plato XX 81–88
Arizona VII 211–212, 214–216
    water policy in VII 108–115, 152–153
Arizona v. *California* (2000) VII 168, 290–303
Ark of the Covenant XIV 159, 163
Arkansas
    African Americas in IX 4
    slavery in XIII 282
Arkansas River VII 10–16
Arkhipov, Ivan VI 44
Arlington Dam (United States) VII 54
Armenia VIII 41, 208, 212, 214, 216; X 93, 185, 187–188, 201; XI 79, 169; XVI 18
    mandate in VIII 12
    massacres in VIII 216; XI 172
    occupies Caucasia VIII 217
    Soviet Republic VIII 214
    war against populace VIII 213
Arminianism XII 150
arms race I 180–187, 262; II 49, 56, 65; XIX 240
Armstrong, John XII 224–225, 227, 229
Armstrong, Louis "Satchmo" II 218; III 79; IX 4; XIX 9
Armstrong, Neil II 257, 259
Army of Northern Virginia VIII 49
Army of the Republic of Vietnam (ARVN) VI 98–99
Army War College, Carlisle Barracks, Pennsylvania VIII 16
Army-McCarthy hearings XIX 125–126, 276
Arndt, Ernst Moritz XI 247
Arnold, Benedict XII 9–16, 39, 44–45, 80, 161, 306
Arnold, Henry Harley "Hap" V 5, 51, 88, 91, 98–99
Arnold, Thurman XIX 171
Ar-Rashid, Harun X 287
Arrow Cross XI 177
Arrowrock Dam (United States) VII 26
Art, avant-garde IX 87
Articles of Confederation (1781) XII 17–26, 61, 68, 70, 73, 65, 118, 120–122, 214, 222, 264, 279, 282, 285, 286, 289, 290, 316
Articles of Faith XIII 32
artillery VIII 52, 56, 61, 68, 110, 112–115, 180, 220, 272, 275; IX 14, 16, 64, 66, 122
    boring of VIII 199
    Prussian VIII 67
    United States VIII 16–17
Arun Dam (Nepal) VII 9
Aryan Paragraph XI 29, 31, 33, 35
Ascalon X 146, 170, 195, 254, 257–259, 261
Ashanti, slave trade XIII 40
Ashcroft, John XIV 14
Ashkenazi XIV 221, 257–258
Asia VI 77, 79, 189, 201, 264, 271; IX 112, 116, 162, 167, 225–226; XII 200; XIV 88, 110, 112, 176, 187; XV 203, 205; XVI 65–66, 85, 87–88, 107, 110–111, 193, 238, 254, 268
    anticolonialism in XIX 9
    British colonization in XII 171
    colonial trade from XII 197
    Communism in XIX 116–117

corruption in XIV 48
neutrality XIX 13
Asia Minor X 30, 221
Askaris VIII 84–85, 87, 90
Asmal, Kader VII 9
Aspinall, Wayne Norviel VII 114
Asquith, Herbert VIII 77–78, 81–82, 103–104, 106, 155, 161–162; IX 55, 58, 100; XVI 28
Assad, Hafiz al- I 163, 314
Assassins X 184, 258; XIV 286
Associated Farmers of California XIX 216
Association of Professional NGOs for Social Assistance in Baia Mare (ASSOC) VII 252
Association of South-East Asian Nations (ASEAN) VI 271
Assyria XI 125, 169
Astoria, Oregon VII 53
Astrakhan, Russian conquest of XVI 70
Aswan Dam (Egypt) II 146, 148; VII 3; XV 21, 62, 70, 244, 249–250
Aswan Declaration (1978) XV 223
Ataturk, Mustafa Kemal VIII 118, 211–214; XIV 134, 168, 261; XV 108
Ataturk Dam (Turkey) VII 82
Atchafalaya River VII 161
Atlanta Exposition (1895) III 268, 271
Atlanta Penitentiary XIX 104
Atlantic Charter (1941) I 301; II 99; V 45, 146–149; VI 9, 78–79; IX 250; XI 110; XVI 125, 224, 315, 317–318; XIX 29
Atlantic Ocean IX 77, 79, 140, 142, 181, 245; XI 174; XII 78, 198, 202; XIII 42, 129, 133–134, 164, 167; XIV 75, 192, 276; XV 275;XVI 111, 213, 254
Atlantic slave trade XII 7
Atlas Mountains XIV 206, 209
atmospheric nuclear testing VI 16
atomic bomb II 228; III 10, 16; V 48–55; VI 20, 57, 136, 154, 254–255; VIII 195; XIX 237
American I 260, 262–263; XIX 93, 99, 117–118, 121, 283
Anglo-American cooperation on VI 10
data passed to Soviet Union II 231; XIX 62, 118, 143, 213, 225, 231, 283–284, 286
development V 44
Hiroshima and Nagasaki III 10
impact on World War II II 268; III 11
introduction I 4
Soviet II 229; XIX 4, 22, 58, 62, 93, 99, 117, 121, 143, 145, 164, 186, 231, 237–238, 245, 248, 255, 282–284, 286
"Stockholm Appeal" II 47
Atomic Energy Act (1946) I 220–221; XIX 285, 288
Atomic Energy Act (1954) VII 175
Atomic Energy Commission (AEC) I 27, 29–31, 214, 220; II 82; VII 174–175, 178 ; XIX 21
Atoms for Peace I 216–217, 221; II 51
Atta, Muhammad XV 54
Attila the Hun XI 71
Attlee, Clement VI 11, 250
Attorney General's List I 76; XIX 53, 91, 96, 127, 131–132, 137, 138, 232, 245
Auchinleck, Sir Claude John Eyre V 76, 172
Auden, Wystan VIII 191
Audubon Society VII 31, 258
Aufmarschplan I (Deployment Plan I) VIII 247
Aufmarschplan II (Deployment Plan II) VIII 247–248
August Revolution (1945) V 146
Augustine of Hippo, Saint X 20, 80–81, 84–85, 103–104, 117, 135, 212, 229, 277; XI 19–20, 23, 169; XIII 31; XIV 205
Aum Shinrikyo XIV 262
Aurul SA cyanide spill (Romania) VII 248–250, 252–255
Auschwitz (concentration camp) I 138; III 253–254, 256; V 54, 56–57, 60, 158, 160–163, 219; VIII 94; XI 2, 4, 9, 11, 16, 45, 50, 69–70, 79, 102–104, 111, 114, 131, 148, 180, 186, 188, 206, 213–214, 217–221, 224, 227–228, 230–231, 235–237, 239–240, 250; XVI 138, 300
theories of formation V 156
Ausgleich agreement (1867) IX 137
Aussaresses, Paul XV 13, 19
Australia VI 136; VIII 33, 133, 137, 160–161, 208; IX 76, 173; XI 62, 93, 96; XII 165, 169; XIV 166; XV 39; XVI 13, 80–81, 87
Aborigines XI 57
anti-Communist crusade XIX 265–268, 270–271
British convicts in XII 167
British immigration to XII 168
grain reserves VIII 290
immigrants XI 57, 59, 62
Japanese immigration to IX 162
motivation of soldiers VIII
represented at Evian Conference XI 55
Soviet spies in XIX 266
ties to United States after World War II XIX 266, 268
World War I VIII 54, 117–123, 220
Australia (Australian ship) VIII 137
Australia Light Horse IX 72
Australia Mounted Division IX 67
Australian and New Zealand Army Corps (ANZAC) VIII 121–122
Australian Communist Party XIX 270
Australian High Court XIX 268, 271
Australian Peace Council, XIX 268
Australian Security and Intelligence Organization XIX 266

Austria I 253, 293; VI 136; VIII 18, 82, 106, 251–252, 266, 281; IX 49, 82, 93, 120, 158, 225–226; XI 14, 36, 56, 59, 88, 110, 123, 167, 175, 179, 211; XII 105; XIV 171; XV 215; XVI 8, 10, 13, 30, 34, 45, 102, 175, 192, 194, 206, 213, 216, 272, 315
alliance with Germany (1879) VIII 35
annexation of XVII 195
Central European Model I 108
Concert of Europe XVI 72–78
contribution of Jews in VIII 167
customs union with Germany forbidden VIII 283
dam agreement with Hungary VII 101
dams in VII 101
East German emigration through VI 118, 121
Freedom Party XVII 83–84
Jehovah's Witnesses in XI 129
Jews in XI 55, 60, 93
occupation of I 108; XIX 88
pre–World War I alliances VIII 225–231
Right-wing politics in XVII 80–86
Socialists in VIII 260
supports Slovak anti-nuclear activists VII 103
union with Nazi Germany VIII 284
World War I XVI 308
Austria-Hungary VIII 76, 95, 98, 104, 172, 178, 226, 228, 230, 266–267, 280, 299; IX 30, 64–65, 99, 102, 140, 154, 192–193, 204, 206, 225, 227, 248, 266–272; XVI 51, 57, 99, 102, 175, 192–196, 199, 204, 208, 214, 244; XVII 3, 20, 48, 170, 231
army VIII 69; IX 134, 158
collapse of VIII 216–217; IX 81; XVI 29–37
invades Poland VIII 72
invades Serbia VIII 72
monarchy XVI 177–178
relations with Germany concerning Slavic lands VIII 94
Socialists in VIII 257, 261
U.S. trade with IX 22
World War I VIII 11, 43–49; IX 133–138; XVI 308, 311
aircraft IX 13
casualties VIII 125, 268
defense budget VIII 44

Jews in VIII 164
mobilization in VIII 125
motivation of soldiers VIII 266
war against the United States VII 11
Austrian National Socialist Party XVI 10
Austrian Refugee Foundation XI 62
Austrian War of Succession (1740–1748) XII 131
Auténtico Party I 91
automobile
impact on interstate highway development II 106
impact on United States II 109
recreation II 108
Autoworkers strikes, Detroit, 1930s XIX 87
AWARE XIX 281
Axis I 3; V 62–67; XVI 315
defeat in Tunisia IV 144
North African campaign V 66
parallel war theory V 63–65
"axis of evil" XIV 37, 41, 126, 193
Ayyubids X 48–49, 139, 183, 185, 187–188, 274
Azerbaijan VI 255; VIII 96, 216; X 183, 187; XIV 231; XVI 18

B

B-1 bomber I 191; II 57
B-1B "Lancer" supersonic nuclear bomber VI 109, 234
B-17 bomber V 4, 5, 6, 98
B-17C bomber V 5
B-17E bomber V 5
B-24 bomber V 7, 98
B-26 bomber V 5
B-29 bomber V 3, 7, 49, 52,
B-36 bomber I 3– 8
B-52 I 189, 193
B-58 I 193
Baader-Meinhof Gang XVI 245, 248–249
Baath Party XIV 65, 253; XV 41, 100–101, 104, 117, 144, 260
Babbitt, Milton XIX 45
Babbitt (1922) II 109; III 177
Baby Boomers VI 24–25
Baby M II 80
Babylon XI 125; XIV 159
Babylonian Captivity X 210; XIV 153
Bach, Johann Sebastian XI 2
Back to Africa movement III 121
Back to the Future XIX 47
Backfire bomber VI 259
Bacon, Francis VI 195
Bacon, Roger X 53, 65, 67, 69, 79, 181, 235
Bacon's Rebellion (1676) XIII 164–165, 249
Bad Day at Black Rock XIX 166
Baden-Powell, Robert XVI 23
Badeni crisis (1897) IX 138
Badoglio, Marshall Pietro V 178
Italian campaign IV 144
Baghdad X 48, 52, 77, 172, 193
Baghdad Pact (1955) I 161, 277; II 146; XV 26–32, 58–59, 61, 62, 116–117, 120, 170, 244, 250, 271–273; XVI 238
Iraq I 277
Turkey I 277
Baghdad Railway VIII 212
Bahai XIV 140
Bahamas XII 81
Bahrain XIV 31, 52, 55, 60–62, 64–65, 79, 81, 88, 115, 177, 179, 181, 211, 229, 247; XV 104, 205
closes al-Jazeera office XIV 65
democratization XIV 67
National Charter (2001) XIV 67
oil XV 177
parliamentary elections XIV 64
political parties illegal in XIV 65
Shi'a Muslims in XIV 67
Sunni Muslims in XIV 67
water XIV 269
women XIV 64, 287
Baia Mare, Romania VII 247, 249, 253, 255
Baia Mare Environmental Protection Agency VII 248, 253
Baia Mare Task Force VII 248, 252, 254
Bailey, Dorothy XIX 54
Baker, James XIV 96, 276, 280–282, 284; XV 81, 84, 263
Baker, Josephine XIX 80–81
Baker, Newton VIII 17–18; IX 2
Baker v. *Carr* (1962) II 139, 281–282, 286
Bakhtiar, Shahpour XV 100, 158, 234
Bakunin, Mikhail Aleksandrovich VI 179
Bakuninist anarchists VI 178
balance of power VI 45
Balcones Escarpment VII 70
Baldric of Bourgueil X 105
Baldric of Dol X 105
Baldwin IV X 51
Baldwin of Boulogne X 73, 119
Baldwin, James II 90–91; III 82
Baldwin, Stanley V 120; VIII 168, 190
Balfour, Arthur VIII 16, 168
Balfour Declaration (1917) VIII 37, 41, 163, 166, 168, 208; XI 121, 126; XIV 153; XV 33–34, 52, 121; XVI 236, 238
Balkan Entente XVI 104
Balkan League VIII 212
Balkan Wars VIII 39, 43–45, 117, 211, 214, 230; IX 226; XVI 193, 195, 206
Balkans I 289; V 68–78; VI 50, 272; VII 82; VIII 76, 80, 95, 106, 226, 228, 252; IX 27, 133, 203, 224–226, 266–272; X 281, 285; XI 193; XIV 175, 180, 261; XV 16; XVI 27, 59, 73, 111, 185–186, 194, 196, 308, 312; XVII 149, 166, 217, 226
as second front V 75– 76
Christians in VIII 211
genocide in VI 216
Islamic rule in VIII 211
Soviet influence I 304
World War I VII 43–49
Ball, George XIX 280
"The Ballad of the Rattlesnake," XIX 40
Ballistic Missile Defense (BMD) I 186, 195–203, 225
technological problems I 199–200
Ballistics Research Laboratory, Aberdeen Proving Ground XIX 62
Baltic Sea VII 18, 148; VIII 75; IX 144, 181; X 66, 69; XVI 5, 185, 189, 206
German control of IX 194
salmon populations in VII 90
submarines in VIII 292
Baltic States VI 133, 218, 251; X 270, 294, 296–297; XVI 6, 88, 105, 163
Baltimore Afro-American XIX 13
Baltimore Documents XIX 198
Banat of Temesvar XVI 34, 36
Bandung Conference (1955) VI 267, 269; XV 68, 120, 167, 250; XIX 11, 13
Bangladesh XIV 171, 190
Bank for International Settlements (BIS) XI 178
Bank of England XI 179
Bank of North America XII 25
Bank of the United States XIII 281
Banking Act (1935) III 59
Bao Dai I 290; V 146, 148; VI 98; XIX 240
Baptist War XIII 159
Baptists XII 62–63, 148, 150, 205, 216, 254, 263
slave religion XIII 186
Barada River VII 81
Barak, Ehud XIV 19–20, 22, 25, 95, 99, 131, 146, 155, 166, 224, 253, 258; XV 133, 183, 265–268
Baraka, Amiri XIX 48
Barbados XII 171, 310–314; XIII 64, 66
Quaker slaveholders in XIII 31
slave revolts XIII 91, 154–155, 157, 231
Barbary Pirates XVI 70
Barbary states XII 73; XIV 192

Barber, Daniel XII 149
Barbie, Klaus XI 173
Barbot, Jean XIII 134, 136
Barbusse, Henri VIII 59, 188; IX 212
Barcelona Convention VII 143–145
Barenblatt v. *United States* XIX 153
Barghouti, Marwan XIV 26, 63
Bargi Project (India) VII 132
Barmen Confession XI 30–31
Barmen Declaration (1934) IV 189
Barnes, Michael D. VI 193
Barrager, Gordon XIX 216
Barré, Issac XII 53, 57
Barth, Karl XI 29, 32
Baruch, Bernard I 27, 29–30, 220; VIII 296; IX 23
Baruch Plan (1946) I 27–32, 216, 220, 258
Barzman, Ben XIX 164
Basic Principles Agreement (1972) XV 257
Basic Principles of Relations (U.S.-Soviet) VI 43
Basie, Count II 214
Basques X 244; XVI 243, 245, 248–249; XVIII 64, 152, 191–198
Basri, Driss XIV 68, 284
Bass, Charlotta XIX 10
Basutoland VII 237, 241
Bataan Death March (1942) V 152, 183
Batista y Zaldívar, Fulgencio I 49, 91–92, 121, 275; II 266; III 51; VI 63, 141
Battles—
—Adowa (1896) IX 175
—Alexandria (1882) IX 49
—Algiers (1956) XV 15–16, 18; XVI 81, 88
—Al-Mansurah (1250) X 66, 92, 139
—Al-Manurah (1250) X 141
—Amiens (1918) VIII 54, 56–57, 194; IX 122
—Antietam (1862) VIII 67
—Antioch (1098) X 25–26, 262, 282
—Anzio (1944) VIII 223
—Argonne Forest (1918) VIII 10, 20, 25; IX 26, 31
—Arras (1917) VIII 223
—Artois (1915) VIII 110
—Atlanta (1864) VIII 68
—the Atlantic (1939–1945) IV 261; V 46, 79–82, 131, 176, 180; V 85; XVI 168
—Austerlitz (1805) VIII 67
—Avranches (1944) V 125
—Ayn Jalut (1260) X 48, 183, 185, 187
—Beaumont (1870) IX 14
—Beersheba (1917) IX 72
—Belleau Wood (1918) VIII 27; IX 28
—Bemis Heights (1777) XII 15, 86, 179, 270, 274
—Benevento (1266) X 67, 142
—Bennington (1777) XII 86, 181, 270
—Bolimov (1915) VIII 242
—Bouvines (1214) X 89
—Brandywine (1777) XII 97, 106, 160, 274, 305, 307
—Breed's Hill (1775) XII 307
—Breitenfeld (1631) XVI 214
—Britain (1940) IV 168; V 4, 80, 106, 124, 135, 152, 176, 261; V 96; XVI 114
—Broodseinde (1917) VIII 220
—Bulge, the (1944–1945) IV 44, 51, 64, 184; V 2, 13, 21–23, 129; XI 260
—Bull Run, First (1861) XIII 5
—Bunker Hill (1775) XII 37, 44, 54, 86, 160
—Cambrai (1917) VIII 52–53, 56, 112–113, 221; IX 16, 27, 33, 72, 129
—Cannae (216 B.C.E.) VIII 72, 179, 249
—Cantigny (1918) VIII 15
—Caporetto (1917) VIII 52, 221; IX 104–105, 107, 127, 129, 235
—Caucasia (1914) VIII 216
—Champagne (1915) VIII 110
—Charles Town (1776) XII 86
—Charles Town (1780) XII 41, 181, 184, 186
—Chateau-Thierry (1918) IX 28
—Chemin des Dames (1917) VIII 104, 149; IX 115, 235
—Chesapeake Capes (1781) XII 80
—Chickamauga (1863) XI 169
—Civitate (1053) X 122, 228–229, 284
—Cold Harbor (1864) VIII 67
—Concord (1775) XII 14, 40, 44, 54, 101, 149, 175, 255, 282; XIII 19
—Coral Sea (1942) IV 2, 6
—Coronel (1914) VIII 133, 135, 137; IX 141
—Cowpens (1781) XII 86
—Cuito Cuanavale (1987) I 96; VI 7
—Culloden (1746) XII 188
—Dardanelles (1915) IX 105
—Dien Bien Phu (1954) I 70; II 266; VI 106, 136; IX 260; XVI 81, 84–85, 88, 136, 269
—Dogger Bank (1915) IX 142, 177, 179
—Dorylaeum (1097) X 74, 262, 282
—Dunkirk (1940) IX 51; XI 14
—El Alamein (1943) IV 180; V 176, 179, 181
—Eutaw Springs (1781) XII 86
—Falkland Islands (1914) VIII 133, 137; IX 141
—Field of Blood (1119) X 67
—Flanders (1914) IX 50
—Flanders Offensive (1917) VIII 77; IX 212
—France (1940) IV 176
—Franklin (1864) VIII 60
—Fredericksburg (1862) VIII 77
—Freeman's Farm (1777) XII 86, 179, 274
—Froschwiller (1870) IX 14
—Gallipoli (1915) VIII 38, 40, 104, 106, 117–123, 162, 166, 213, 216, 264; IX 50–51, 53, 108, 207
—Germantown (1777) XII 97, 103, 106, 274, 305, 307
—Gettysburg (1863) VIII 67–68; XI 169
—Gorlice (1915) IX 61, 64, 127
—Guadalcanal (1942–1943) V 132, 196, 199
—Guilford Court House (1781) XII 184, 187
—Gumbinnen (1914) IX 155
—Hamel (1918) VIII 57
—Haw River (1781) XII 187
—Heligoland Bight (1914) IX 142
—Hillsborough (1781) XII 185
—Homs (1281) X 183, 185–186
—Horns of Hattin (1187) X 27, 33, 46, 51–52, 67, 130, 153–154, 170, 186–188, 247–252, 255, 257, 259, 261, 306
—Isandhlwana (1879) VIII 200
—Isonzo (1915–1917) VIII 113, 125, 264
—Iwo Jima V 52, 199; VIII 60
—Jutland (1916) VIII 72, 289, 292; IX 50, 75, 142, 177–178, 180, 188
—Karamah (1968) XV 47
—Kasserine Pass (1942) V 124
—Kettle Creek (1779) XII 184, 187
—Khalkin Gol (1938) V 136
—King's Mountain (1780) XII 86, 89, 187
—Kip's Bay (1776) XII 307
—Koniggratz (1866) IX 99
—Kosovo (1889) XVI 59
—Kursk (1943) XVI 168, 299
—Kut-al-Amara (1916) VIII 216
—La Forbie (1244) X 67, 143, 188
—Lake Naroch (1916) IX 128, 131
—Le Cateau (1914) VIII 252; IX 52
—Lemberg (1914) IX 155
—Leningrad XVI 163
—Lepanto (1571) X 174
—Lexington (1775) XII 10, 14, 40–41, 44, 54–55, 101, 149, 175, 189, 255, 282; XIII 19
—Long Island (1776) XII 38, 155, 157, 161, 307
—Loos (1915) VIII 239, 243, 272, 276
—Lorraine (1914) VIII 179–185, 274
—Ludendorff Offensive (1918) VIII 55, 112
—Lützen (1632) XVI 214
—Madrid (1936–1939) XVIII 157–164
—Malvern Hill (1862) VIII 67

–Manzikert (1071) X 24, 26, 29, 118, 127, 138, 213, 218, 280, 288–289; XIV 261
–Marengo (1800) VIII 67
–Marne (1914) VIII 20, 114, 180, 182, 184, 199, 246, 253; IX 38, 50, 52, 70, 111, 117, 124, 212, 263
–Mars-la-Tour (1870) VIII 75
–Masurian Lakes (1914) VIII 114, 252, 268; IX 160, 242; XVI 204
–Meggido (1918) VIII 41, 216
–Menin Road (1917) VIII 219
–Mers-el-Kébir XVI 301
–Messines (1917) VIII 219
–Metz (1870) VIII 71
–Meuse-Argonne (1918) VIII 17, 19, 23, 25, 27, 114, 301; IX 7
–Michael (1918) IX 11
–Midway (1942) IV 2, 6; V 5, 132, 196
–Minden (1759) XII 47
–Monmouth Court House (1778) XII 305
–Mons (1914) VIII 252; IX 35, 52, 72, 212
–Moore's Creek Bridge (1776) XII 182, 187
–Moscow (1941–1942) VI 40
–Mukden (1905) VIII 75; XVI 17
–Neuve-Chapelle (1915) VIII 110, 242, 272, 276
–New York City (1776) XII 106, 304
–Nile (1250) X 30
–Nivelle Offensive (1917) VIII 107, 114, 218, 223, 269
–Nördlingen (1634) XVI 214
–Normandy (1944) XVI 299, 306
–North Africa (1940–1943) V 80
–Okinawa (1945) V 52; VIII 60
–Oriskany (1777) XII 175, 177, 179
–Papua, New Guinea V 199
–Passchendaele (1917) VIII 80, 102, 104, 104, 111, 186, 218–224; IX 27, 33, 48, 104, 212, 253
–Pearl Harbor (1941) XI 14, 174; XVI 162
–Penobscot Bay (1779) XII 82, 83
–Petersburg (1864) VIII 23, 68
–Philippines, the V 199
–Polygon Wood (1917) VIII 219
–Princeton (1777) XII 38, 46, 103, 158, 182, 272, 304
–Quebec (1759) XII 159–160
–Quebec (1775) XII 9–11, 15, 43–44
–Riga (1917) VIII 52, 112; IX 127–129, 131
–Rocroi (1643) XVI 214
–Sadowa (1866) XVI 30
–Saipan V 52
–Salonika (1918) VIII 104, 149, 212, 216; IX 105, 203–206, 270
–Saratoga (1777) XII 9–12, 39, 78, 80, 89, 95–96, 100–106, 129, 158, 224, 255–256, 267–268, 271, 275
–Sarikamish (1914) VIII 216
–Savannah (1778) XII 181, 184
–Second Aisne (1917) VIII 114
–Second Marne (1918) IX 28, 118
–Second Ypres (1915) VIII 200
–Sedan (1870) VIII 67; IX 30, 99; XVI 257
–Soissons (1918) VIII 17, 27, 54–55; IX 16, 28
–Somme (1916) VIII 14, 19, 52, 56, 61, 67, 78, 80, 103, 106, 111, 113–114, 125, 128–129, 143, 158, 186–187, 200, 203, 218, 223–224, 239, 266, 268, 271–276, 289; IX 10–11, 26, 30, 34, 36, 39, 48, 56, 59, 72, 104, 107–108, 117, 121–122, 129, 210, 212, 232, 235, 252–253; XI 169; XVI 172, 252, 302, 312
–Spichern (1870) IX 14
–Spring Offensive (1918) VIII 201, 241, 244, 266; IX 16, 105, 127, 131, 193
–St. Mihiel (1918) VIII 17, 19, 25; IX 11, 31, 107
–Stalingrad (1942–1943) V 132, 179; VIII 139; XVI 166, 168, 188, 299, 302; XIX 88
–Suez Canal (1915) VIII 213, 216
–Tanga (1914) VIII 85, 89
–Tannenberg (1914) VIII 114, 268; IX 15, 65, 127, 160, 238, 242; XVI 200, 204
–Third Gaza (1917) VIII 121
–Third Ypres (1917) VIII 52, 104, 107, 111, 187, 203, 218–224, 240; IX 36, 212. *See also* Passchendaele
–Trafalgar (1805) VIII 33, 196; IX 45, 49
–Trenton (1776) XII 38, 46, 49, 101, 158, 161, 182, 272, 304, 307
–Trois Rivières (1776) XII 45, 46
–Tsushima (1905) IX 162; XVI 17
–Valcour Island (1776) XII 10, 48, 80
–Verdun (1916) VIII 19, 60–61, 67, 106, 110–111, 113–114, 125, 128–129, 143, 186–187, 191, 224, 239–240, 266, 268, 272–273; IX 10, 16, 26, 60–61, 104, 108, 117, 128, 130, 193, 210, 212, 235, 248, 252–258; XVI 172, 252, 312
–Wagram (1809) VIII 67
–Waterloo (1815) VIII 67–68, 160; IX 30; XII 167; XIII 215
–Waxhaws (1780) XII 32, 41, 186
–White Plains (1776) XII 155, 307
–Wieselberg (1096) X 16
–Wilderness (1864) 257
–York Town (1781) XII 23, 33, 37, 40, 83, 103, 144, 164, 172, 255–256, 306, 308; XIII 18
–Ypres (1914–1915) VIII 67, 182, 239, 242; IX 70, 105, 127, 253, 259–265
Batu Khan X 183, 186–187
Baudelaire, Charles-Pierre IX 148
Baudry of Bourgeuil X 213
bauhaus school IX 86
Bautista Sacasa, Juan VI 190
Bavaria VII 204–205; VIII 209; X 286; XI 113; XVI 151
  Christian Social Union XVI 60
  Ministry for Development and Environmental Issues VII 206
  separatist movement in VIII 280
Bay of Bengal VIII 133, 137
Bay of Biscay V 238
Bay of Pigs (1961) I 66, 70, 89, 92, 94, 129; II 115, 247, 266; VI 64, 66, 71, 131, 139, 141; XIX 146
Baybars, Al-Zahir X 46, 48
Baybars I X 66, 146, 188
Bazzaz, Abdul Rahman XV 122, 124
Beard, Charles A. VIII 284; XII 74
Beardsley, Aubrey IX 148
Beas River VII 130
Beatles, the
  "Beatlemania" II 18
  Bob Dylan as influence II 215
  "Rubber Soul" II 215
Beatrix (Netherlands) XVI 179
Beats XIX 43, 46, 48– 50
Beaumarchais XII 101
Beauvoir, Simome de XVII 200, 204, 277
Bebop XIX 48
Bechuanaland Protectorate VII 34
Becket, Thomas à XI 88
Beckmann, Max VIII 188, 191
Bedacht, Max XIX 61, 197
Bedouins X 185; XIV 197; XV 48, 61
Beef Protocol VII 34, 37
Beer Hall putsch XVI 147–148, 151
Beethoven, Ludwig von XI 2
Begin, Menachem VI 163; XIV 19, 145; XV 23–24, 51–52, 56, 129–131, 135, 137, 200, 220, 222, 226–227, 239–240, 261
Beilin, Yossi XV 182, 185–186
Beirut, Lebanon VII 81; X 49, 248
Bekáa Valley VII 79, 81; XIV 127, 131
Belarus VI 54, 215, 218; VIII 97, 278
  surrender of nuclear weapons to Russian Federation I 220
  U.N. I 285
Belfrage, Cedric XIX 216

Belgian Relief Commission VIII 98
Belgic Confederacy XII 19
Belgium VI 77, 183, 188, 264; VIII 24, 67, 71, 97, 110, 155, 162, 179, 182–184, 203, 205, 208, 218, 230, 235, 237, 245–246, 248, 251, 280, 283; IX 27, 30, 49–52, 55, 105, 141, 158, 193, 260, 263, 265; XI 4, 108, 123, 174, 176, 179, 211; XI 14; XVI 9, 22–23, 27, 58, 76, 84, 87, 113–115, 208, 267, 292, 311; XVII 3, 21, 23, 57, 59–60, 64, 117, 129, 233
  Army VIII 184
  Brussels Treaty I 208
  colonies XVII 229
  decolonization XVI 79
  fascism XVII 137, 140
  German invasion of VIII 72, 110, 203, 206, 232, 238
  Jews XVI 305
  loss of African colonies VIII 280
  monarchy XVI 178, 181
  neutrality treaty (1839) IX 42, 44
  occupies Ruhr VIII 285
  postwar influence of Communist parties I 174
  submarine bases in VIII 134
  troops in Africa, World War I VII 84, 86
  World War I IX 41–47; XVI 308
Belgrade VII 248
Belgrade Conference for Foreign Ministers (1978) VI 268
Belknap, Jeremy XII 206, 217
Bellevue, Washington VII 189, 191
Bellotti v. *Baird* (1979) II 222
Belorussia XVI 18, 189
  U.N. membership I 300
Beloved (1987) XIII 145
Below, Fritz von IX 10
Belzec XI 220, 269
Ben Bella, Ahmed XV 6, 13
Benedict XV VII 206, 209; XVI 308
Benedictines X 116, 235
Benelux countries VI 275
Benes, Eduard XVI 11, 34, 125
Benezet, Anthony XIII 1
Ben-Gurion, David I 278, 281; XI 37–39, 42, 63, 123; XIV 143–144; XV 24, 31, 33, 35, 130, 135, 226, 248; XVI 240
Benhadj, Ali XV 4–5, 7, 9
Benigni, Roberto XI 160
Benin XIV 198
  slave trade XIII 35, 40
Benjamin of Tudela X 198
Benjedid, Chadli XV 2, 4, 6–7
Benso, Camillo IX 225
Benson, Elmer XIX 103
Bentley, Elizabeth XIX 4, 17, 58, 117, 143, 194, 196, 197, 198–200, 248
  testimony in Rosenberg trial XIX 286, 288
Berber Cultural Movement XIV 201–202
Berbers X 160, 163, 242, 274, 287; XIV 201–210, 231; XV 4, 6, 9; XVI 70
Berbice, slave rebellion XIII 231
Berchtold, Leopold VIII 46, 228; IX 99; XVI 32, 196
Berengaria (ship) XIX 225
Berenguer, Ramon (the Elder) X 243
Berg, Alban IX 84
Bergen-Belsen XI 158, 220
Berger, Hanns (pseud. of Gerhart Eisler) XIX 225
Bergier Report (1998) XI 179
Bergson, Henri-Louis IX 224
Beria, Lavrenty I 38; VI 255; XVI 39, 124; XVII 173
  nuclear spying I 184
  Soviet nuclear weapons development I 238, 245
Berke X 187, 189
Berkeley, William XIII 23, 164, 249
Berle, Adolf 155, 198
Berlin I 33, 119–120; II 171; VI 73, 142, 169, 252
  airlift (1948) II 42, 264; V 149; VI 9; XIX 117, 145
  blockade of (1948) II 36, 66; VI 49, 133, 141, 173, 177, 252, 255; XV 160; XIX 164, 237, 245, 248, 258
  bombing of V 5
  German attack on (1945) VI 169
  Soviet capture of VI 251
Berlin Crisis (1958–1959) I 33–39, 168 169; VI 104
Berlin Crisis (1961) I 171; XVI 158
Berlin Wall I 120; II 66; VI 51, 64, 104, 115, 118, 122, 142, 235; XV 260; XVI 63, 85, 245, 289
  erection I 34
  fall of VI 51, 111; XIX 129, 207
  last E. German fugitive killed at VI 118
Berlin-to-Baghdad railroad XVI 23, 27
Berlin West Africa Conference (1885) VI 267
Bermuda XII 316
Bermuda Conference (1943) III 252
Bernard, Francis XII 53
Bernard of Clairvaux X 13, 33, 128, 133, 158, 161–162, 165–166; XI 20, 23
Bernardone, Peter X 36
Bernstein, Carl XIX 6
Bernstein, Eduard XVII 66, 204
Bernstein, Leonard XIX 48
Bernstein, Walter XIX 166
Bessarabia XVI 99, 185
Bessie, Alvah XIX 168
Bessmertnykh, Alexander A. VI 223
Bethlehem Steel IX 22
Bethmann Hollweg, Theobald VII 143, 164, 289; IX 41, 44, 99, 253; XVI 27, 196, 308
Bethune, Mary McLeod, XIX 79
Bettelheim, Bruno XI 224, 235–237
Betts v. *Brady* (1942) II 290
Beverly, Robert XII 296; XIII 150
Bevin, Ernest VI 101
Bhakhra Dam (India) VII 130
Bhopal, India (1984) II 86
Biberman, Herbert XIX 168
Bible X 82, 212, 273; XIV 184, 188
  slavery XIII 187
  view of blacks XIII 182–183
Bickel, Alexander M. XIX 288–289
Bidault, Georges I 175, 273; VI 101
Biddle, Francis V 187–188, 224; XI 258; XIX 176
Big Bend Dam (United States) VII 31
Big Brother and the Holding Company II 219
'Big Jim Casey" XIX 40– 41
Big Jim McClain XIX 163
The Big Table XIX 50
Bight of Benin XIII 35
  slave trade XIII 39
Bilbo, Theodore XIX 30
Bill of Rights (1791) XII 61, 76, 108, 113, 120–122, 131, 276–283, 290; XIX 163, 216–218
Billboard II 217
  charts II 214
  classifications of music II 214
  music categories II 218
Biltmore Conference (1942) II 145; XV 34
Binding, Karl XI 247
Bingham, William XII 79
Binnenlandse Veiligheidsdienst (BVD) XIX 269
bioengineering II 83–85
bipartisanship II 195
  vs. concensus II 205
bipolarity VI 213
birds–
  bald eagle VII 215, 220, 234
  Black Capped Vireo VII 72
  brown-headed cowbird VII 216
  ducks VII 277
  European Starling VII 216
  Golden Cheeked Warbler VII 72
  in the Pacific flyway VII 151
  in the Atlantic flyway VII 277

kingfisher VII 205
southwestern willow flycatcher VII 211, 215–216
spotted owl VII 226
western yellow-billed cuckoo VII 215
white-tailed sea eagle VII 252–253
Yuma clapper rail VII 215
Birkenau (concentration camp) XI 70, 102, 240
birth control pill II 224–240
Birmingham, Alabama, law against Communists XIX 204
Birmingham News XIX 32
Birzeit University XV 94
Biscayne Bay VII 266
Bismarck, Otto von VI 9; VIII 35, 137, 207, 226, 249; IX 98–99, 101, 224, 226; XI 168; XIV 173; XV 101; XVI 74, 175, 192, 200, 257, 313; XVII 105, 272
Bizonia VI 101; XVI 267
Black, Hugo II 280, 284; III 105; XIX 149–150, 152
dissenting opinion in *Dennis* v. *United States* XIX 256, 263
Black and Tans IX 93
Blackboard Jungle XIX 47
Black Athena XX 1–10
Black Codes XIII 5, 50, 53–55
Black Death (1347–1351) VIII 61, 189; XI 24; XIII 161, 165, 181
Black Hand IX 102; XVI 196
Black internationalism XIX 8–14, 25, 29, 31
Black Manhattan (1930) III 122
Black nationalism II 89, 93; III 120; XIX 31
Black Panthers II 89, 165, 197
demonstration at the California State Assembly (1967) II 94
Party for Self-Defense II 94
Black Power II 24, 93–95, 162; III 120; XIX 220
Black Power conference (1966) II 93, 95
Black Sea VII 104, 148, 204–205, 210, 247; IX 181, 205; X 53, 187; XIII 167; XVI 184, 206, 312
submarines in VIII 292
time needed to flush pollution from VII 142
Turkish control of IX 194
Black Sea Fleet VIII 33, 280
Black September XIV 198; XV 49, 149, 198–199; XVI 245
Black Sharecroppers Union II 197
Black Student Union II 94
Black Tom Island IX 21
Blackboard Jungle (1955) II 214, 219
Blacklisting XIX 35, 38, 43–44, 47, 65, 108, 123, 160–166, 169, 170, 171, 202, 275, 278, 281
Blackman, Harry A. II 221, 225
Blackstone, William XII 263, 278
Blair, Tony VI 8; XIV 10; XVI 268; XVII 20, 70, 133
Blanco River, Texas VII 72
Blanquistes VI 178
Blatnik, John Anton VII 258, 268
Bledsoe, Albert Taylor XIII 27, 96, 270
Bletchley Park IV 261, 263
Blitzkrieg (lightning war) IV 23–32, 54, 56, 100, 105, 167, 282; V 102, 118, 228; XI 83, 108; XVI 113–115, 166, 188–189
Bloch, Emanuel XIX 283, 285–286
Bloch, Marc XVI 113, 116–117, 119; XVII 201
Blockade XIX 37
Bloody Sunday (1920) IX 93
Bloomer, Amelia III 167
Bloor, Ella Reeve "Mother" XIX 191
Blue Gardenia, The XIX 44
Blue Gold Report VII 285
Blum, Léon XVI 115, 118, 142
Blunden, Edmund IX 212
Blunt, Anthony VI 11
Board of Admiralty (U.S.) XII 81
Boer War (1899–1902) IX 55, 92; XVI 23–24, 80, 110
Bogart, Humphrey XIX 44, 160
Bogwell, Benjamin D. XIX 242
Bohemia IX 93, 136; XI 60; XVI 34, 99, 102, 212, 214
Bohemond I X 128, 191, 215–216
Bohemond VII X 185, 187
Bohemond of Taranto X 73–74, 175
Bohlen, Charles XIX 18
Bohr, Niels
Soviet nuclear spying I 241–242, 247–248
Boilermakers Union XIX 230
Bokassa, Jean Bédel VI 83
Boland, Edward Patrick VI 61
Boland Amendments I 54; VI 58, 61, 193, 195, 231; XIX 128, 280
Boldt, George VII 199
Bolingbroke, Viscount XII 122, 124
Bolivia I 21, 95, 125–126; VI 50, 178
Bolling v. *Sharpe* (1950) II 137
Bolshevik Revolution (1917) I 73; VIII 82, 98, 223; IX 87; XVI 1–2, 4, 7, 15–20, 34, 141, 160; XVII 26, 32–33, 180, 227; XIX 4, 116, 212
Bolsheviks VI 244, 247; VIII 95, 171, 173, 175–176, 178, 255, 258, 260–261, 269, 278; IX 27, 195–202; XVI 2, 5, 16, 18, 20, 33, 39, 41, 51, 55, 209, 229, 292, 309, 312; XVII 8, 32, 56, 72, 88–89, 91, 93, 101, 126, 151–152, 154, 156–157, 181, 197, 207, 225, 229, 250; XIX 213, 245–246
Bolshevism VIII 209, 295; XVI 1, 4, 185–186; XVII 33, 58, 84, 181
Bomber gap I 188–189, 191, 193; VI 35
bomber offensive V 86–92
Battle of Hamburg (1943) V 87–88
Dresden raids (1945) V 92
Pacific theater V 89, 91–92
Bonaparte, Napoleon I 167; VIII 30, 47, 49, 66–67, 71, 132, 194, 196, 199, 233–234, 237, 266; IX 30, 45, 49, 105, 134, 159, 259; XI 169; XII 134, 167, 209, 251, 302, 308; XIII 160, 210, 213, 215; XVI 27, 72–74, 163, 184, 200, 255; XVII 19, 87–88, 99, 160, 162, 178, 183
reinstates slavery in French colonies XIII 1, 209
Bonhoeffer, Dietrich XI 29, 33, 35, 135
Bonhomme Richard (U.S. ship) XII 77, 83
Boniface VIII X 207, 223, 226, 266
Bonizo of Sutri X 85, 227–228
Bonneville Dam (United States) VII 29, 31, 53, 57, 60, 198
Bonneville Power Administration VII 55, 202, 223
Bonomel, Ricaut X 66
Book of Maccabees XIV 153
bore-hole technology VII 34, 62–68
Bormann, Martin XI 257
Bosch, Hieronymus VIII 204
Bosch Gavíño, Juan I 24, 71
Bosnia VI 51, 53, 213, 217, 225; VIII 11, 44, 230; IX 226–227; X 6; XIV 92 ; XIV 61, 77, 269; XVII 6, 147, 149, 165
genocide XVII 96, 100, 102, 148, 170
lack of environmental control in VII 145
Bosnia-Herzegovina IX 99, 267–268; XIV 36, 57–58, 61, 63, 98, 206; XVII 95, 98, 137, 143, 146, 149, 216
Bosnian Civil War (1992–1995) XVI 109
Bosnian Crises (1908–1909) VIII 43–45, 226, 228; IX 99; XVI 193–194
Bosporus Straits VI 255; VIII 214, 216; X 29, 74
Bossert, Wayne VII 187
Boston VII 256, 261–262; XII 44, 78, 303–304, 306
Boston Massacre (1770) XII 31, 59, 140, 237, 316
Boston Mutual Insurance Company XIX 183
Boston Tea Party (1773) III 219; XII 51, 54–55, 140–141, 197, 234, 237, 253, 260
Botswana VI 83; VII 236, 243
fences in VII 33–39
Botswana Meat Commission (BMC) VII 33
Boukman XIII 209–210
Boulanger, Georges VIII 147, 152
Boulder Dam (United States) VII 28–29, 109
Boumedienne, Houari XIV 82; XV 6
Boundary Waters Treaty (1909) VII 116–117, 120

INDEX

Bourbon dynasty XII 189; XVI 178
Bourguiba, Habib XIV 197, 253; XV 136
Bouteflika, Abdelaziz XV 5, 9
Boutros-Ghali, Boutros XIV 278
Bowdoin, James XII 285
Bowker, Philip G. XIX 183, 205
Bowker, W. K. VII 158
Bowker Commission XIX 183, 205, 206
Bowman, Isaiah VII 47
Boxer Rebellion (1900) III 136; VIII 87; IX 96; XVI 110
Boy Scouts IX 147; XVI 23
Brackenridge, Hugh Henry XII 208
Bradley, Omar N. I 6; V 15, 21, 23, 102, 125–126, 129, 136
Bradley armored personnel carrier VI 241
Brahms, Johannes XVI 23
Brandeis, Justice Louis D. II 280; III 25–27, 207; XIX 255
Brandenburg XVI 214
  slave trade XIII 270
Brandenberg v. *Ohio* (1969) II 281
Brandon v. *Planters' and Merchants' Bank of Huntsville* XIII 102
Brandt, Willy I 35; VI 59, 206–208, 210–211; XVI 156–158, 160, 271; XVII 67
  treaty with Soviets I 185
  visit to Moscow VI 207, 211
Brant, Joseph XII 175–176, 178–179
Brattle, Thomas XII 194
Brauchitsch, Walter von V 127, 143
Brazil I 15, 20, 25, 125, 143, 219, 223; VI 215, 266; XIII 44; XIV 71, 79; XVI 98, 110
  abolishes slavery XIII 36, 198
  abolitionism in XIII 2
  British relations with XII 167
  Catholic Church in XIII 192
  maroons in XIII 104–105, 107–108, 110
  nuclear weapons XVI 109
  religious syncretism in XIII 192
  slave rebellions XIII 154, 192, 193, 231
  slave trade XIII 38
  slavery in XIII 62–63, 65, 94, 129, 131, 134, 212, 233, 269, 272
Brazzaville Conference (1944) V 171
Brecht, Bertholt VI 229; IX 84; XIX 168
Breckenridge, Henry VIII 301
Bredehoeft, John VII 182
Brennan, William II 221, 282; XIX 149–150
Bretton Woods Conference (1944) VI 78, 144
Bretton Woods finance system VI 204
Brezhnev, Leonid I 104, 151, 153, 197; II 69, 169; VI 21, 43, 68, 75, 111, 116, 163, 184, 226, 239; XIV 2; XV 255, 257; XVI 288; XVII 250
Brezhnev Doctrine I 10–11; VI 43, 118; XIV 2, 6; XVI 285, 288
Brezhnev-Nixon summit (1972) II 170
Briand, Aristide VIII 255; IX 207
The Bridge XIX 46
Bridge Canyon Dam (United States) VII 30, 109
The Bridge on the River Kwai XIX 164
Bridges, Harry XIX 148–149, 151, 169, 214, 216
Bridges v. *Wixon* XIX 149, 151
Brissenden, Richard B. VII 158
Bristol Bay, Alaska VII 197
British and Foreign Anti-Slavery Society XIII 131
British Army XII 29, 38, 88, 105, 260, 302, 305, 316
  punishments in XII 304
British Broadcasting Corporation (BBC) XIV 28, 30, 34
  Arab Service XIV 29
British Cavalry Division IX 69
British Colonial Office XIV 176
British Empire XII 32, 34, 50, 52, 164–165, 167–169, 210, 231, 233; XIII 1
  administration of XII 139
  emancipation of slaves XIII 22, 65, 154–155, 160
  slave rebellions XIII 231
British Expeditionary Force (BEF) VIII 71, 77, 79, 102–103, 106, 110, 219–224, 252, 265, 271–276; IX 26, 48–53, 55, 69, 72, 104, 108, 230, 245, 260; XVI 114
  chaplains in VIII 203
  command structure IX 33–40
  use of tanks VIII 51–58
British Guiana I 15, 24, 125; VI 96
  slavery in XIII 233
British Honduras (Belize) XII 167
British Imperial Policy in Asia XIX 16
British Isles IX 140
British Legion XII 32, 186
British Navy XII 260
British North America Act (Constitution Act, 1867) VII 117
British Petroleum XIV 211–212; XV 108, 156, 172–173, 176, 178–179
British Royal Flying Corps IX 217, 220
British South Sea Company XIII 272
British Union of Fascists XVII 137–138
British-United States Agreement (BRUSA) VI 11
British West Indies XII 290, 295, 310–316
  slavery in XII 311
Brittain, Vera VIII 266
Broadcasting Board of Governors XIV 233, 235
Bromberg, J. Edward XIX 161
Brodie, Bernard I 165; II 65
Brodsky, Joseph XIV 233
Brooke, Alan Francis V 43, 76
Brooke, Rupert VIII 188; IX 149
Brookings Institution XV 220
Brooklyn Dodgers XIX 76–77
Brooks, John XII 222–224
Brooks, William K. VII 40, 43, 46–47
Broom and Whisk Makers Union II 191
Brotherhood of Sleeping Car Porters II 189, 217–218
Browder, Bill XIX 231
Browder, Earl XIX 84, 99
  covert activities XIX 51, 58, 61, 84, 104, 228, 231
  declares independence of CPUSA XIX 61
  freed from prison XIX 104
  expelled from CPUSA XIX 57, 193, 213
  passport violation charges XIX 104, 193
  reaction to German-Soviet nonaggression treaty XIX 104
  reconstitutes CPUSA as Communist Political Association XIX 193
  role in Popular Front XIX 193
  support for Roosevelt XIX 56
Browder, Margaret XIX 58, 231
Browder, Rose XIX 231
Brower, David Ross VII 110, 112
Brown, Edmund "Pat" XIX 226
Brown, Harold VI 42–43
Brown, John XII 11; XIII 4
Brown v. *Board of Education of Topeka, Kansas* (1954) II 20, 23–24, 26, 45, 80, 90–91, 136–143, 270, 280, 286, 293, 295; III 27, 185; XIX 24, 26–27, 30, 80
Brown Synod (1933) XI 27
Brown University XIII 31, 198
Broyles Commission XIX 53
Bruchmuller, Georg IX 127–129
Brüning, Heinrich XVI 148, 151
Brusilov, Aleksey VIII 266; IX 60–66, 193, 242; XVI 204
Brusilov Offensive (1916) IX 72, 137, 155, 193, 243, 252; XVI 312
Brussels Treaty (1954) I 208; VI 101
Bryan, Samuel XII 76
Bryan, William Jennings III 32, 34, 36–37; VIII 204; IX 19, 21, 246
  Scopes Trial III 33
Brzezinski, Zbigniew I 135, 143, 146; VI 42, 166, 256, 263; XIV 8; XV 220; XVI 122, 262
Buchanan, James XIII 195, 278

Buchenwald (concentration camp) V 57; XI 45, 236, 245
German people's reaction V 215
Buck v. *Bell* (1927) III 18, 21
Buckingham Palace XVI 178
Buddhist monks, immolation of VI 23
Budenz, Louis XIX 196, 199, 202, 214, 248, 261–262
Bukovina IX 136; XVI 34, 99
Bulganin, Nikolai A. VI 135; XVI 84
Bulgaria I 107, 294; II 39, 153; VI 251–252, 261, 274, 276, 280; VIII 11, 14, 44, 46, 95, 212, 216–217, 230; IX 120, 171, 203–206, 270, 272; XI 214, 220; XIV 176, 178; XV 120; XVI 32, 36, 76, 104, 122, 124, 185, 192, 233, 249, 284–285, 317; XVII 132, 216–217, 233
ally of Germany VIII 278
Communist government XIX 215
fascism XVII 137
Fatherland Front XVI 124
monarchy XVI 180
U.S. push for greater freedoms I 110
U.S. recognizes communist government I 303
World War I XVI 312
Bulgarian publications XIX 216
Bulgars X 29
Bull, William XII 215
Bull Moose Party III 243
Bulletin of the Atomic Scientists XIX 241
Bullitt, William XVI 2
Bunche, Ralph XIX 202
Bund Deutscher Mädel (German Girls' Organization) IV 191
Bund Naturschutz in Bayern (BUND) VII 206, 210
Bundestag (Federal Diet) VI 102
Bundy, McGeorge I 29, 294; II 6; XIX 18
flexible response I 120
use of nuclear weapons policy I 171
Bureau of Indian Affairs (BIA) III 141, 143; VII 55–56, 59, 166–167, 169, 172
Bureau of Investigation XIX 174, 176, 246. *See also* Federal Bureau of Investigation (FBI)
Burger, Justice Warren E. II 182, 221, 284; XII 283
Burgess, Guy I 243, 245; VI 11
Burgh, James XII 278
Burgoyne, John XII 10, 15, 39, 45–47, 80, 95–96, 100, 103, 155, 158, 162, 181, 267–274, 305
Burke, Edmund XII 29–30, 139, 143, 166
Burke, Thomas XII 185
Burma VIII 35; XII 33; XIV 177; XV 14
fall of V 197
opium trade I 15
Burns, Arthur XIX 128
Burns, William XIV 100, 107
Burroughs, William S. XIX 48–51
Burton, Harold XIX 150
Burundi II 101, 155
Bush, George H. W. VI 28, 51, 58, 61, 191, 195, 205, 226, 229, 242, 257; X 56; XIV 97, 100, 198, 247; XV 102, 182, 258, 260; XVI 60, 285
Africa policy VI 7
civil war in Somalia II 155
foreign policy "balance of power" II 155
international political experience II 152
Iraq XV 73–79
Madrid Conference XV 184
New World Order II 152–158; XV 81
nuclear nonproliferation policy I 224
Panama intervention II 155
Persian Gulf crisis II 153
Persian Gulf War XV 80–87; XIX 129
relationship with former Yugoslavia II 155
role of United States II 155
U.S. spying on Soviet Union I 191
unilateral U.S. foreign policy II 156
Bush (George H. W.) administration II 100; VI 120; XIV 199
arms-control agreements VI 20
defense spending VI 224
envisionment of New World Order II 155
Iraq XV 73–79, 81, 84, 86
nuclear-nonproliferation policy I 217
policy on Afgahnistan I 14–16
Bush, George W. VII 224; XIV 13–15, 33, 37–38, 41, 43, 88, 112, 168, 193, 228–229, 239, 247, 267; XV 78; XVII 70
governor of Texas XIV 103
Iraq XV 80, 87
Middle East XIV 95–108
on terrorism XIV 126
Bush (George W.) administration XIV 109, 193, 231, 247, 238, 239; XVI 95
Bush Doctrine XIV 14, 17, 43, 237, 239–240
conservative ideology XIV 16
Middle East XIV 95–108
response to World Trade Center attack XIV 228
terrorism XIV 10, 13, 17
view on Hizbollah XIV 126
Bushido code III 13
Business interests, anti-communism of 181
Butler, John Marshall XIX 99
Butler, Justice Pierce III 25
Butler, Pierce XII 296
Butler, Smedley, IX 96
Butterfield, Herbert X 278, 304
Buxton, Thomas Fowell XIII 131, 159
Bykov, Boris XIX 62
Byrd II, William XIII 150–151, 207
Byrnes, James F. I 28, 31, 263, 304; II 206; V 51, 53; XI 256
Byzantine Empire X 33, 73, 88, 92, 107–108, 110, 112, 118–119, 121, 128, 138, 150–151, 156, 172–174, 188, 205, 208–209, 215, 238–239, 249–250, 262, 269, 280, 282, 284, 287; XIII 167; XIV 261; XVII 226
Church XVII 224
Crusades X 15, 24–31
relations with the West X 24–31

C

"Cabbage and Caviar" XIX 41
Cable News Network (CNN) XIV 29, 34, 61, 66
Cabora Bassa Dam (Mozambique) VII 237, 239, 240
Cacchione, Peter XIX 103
Cadwalader, John XII 98
Caesar, Julius XII 302
and Cicero XX 212–220
Cagney, James XIX 160
cahiers des doleances (notebooks of grievances) XII 129, 133
Cairncross, John VI 11
Soviet nuclear spying I 243–245
Cairnes, John E. XIII 174, 240, 242
Cairo X 76–77, 89, 170, 172, 185, 192, 262
Cairo Agreement XV 48–49
Cairo Conference (1943) VI 146
Cairo Declaration (2000) XIV 282
Calais XII 242
Calhoun, John XIII 48
California VII 180, 201; X 8; XI 124; XIV 162
dams in VII 27, 29
Department of Fish and Game VII 178
environmental activism in VII 174
flood control in VII 273
legislation on Holocaust reparations XI 216
pollution control in VII 264
receives federal swamplands VII 272
water policy in VII 153
California Aqueduct VII 179
California Criminal Syndicalist statute XIX 255
California Coastal Commission VII 175, 179
California Conquest XIX 163
California Development Company (CDC) 155
California Fact-Finding Committee on Un-American Activities. *See* Tenney Committee
California Labor School XIX 230, 232– 235

California State Education Department XIX 232
California un-American committee. *See* Tenney Committee
Calloway, Cab IX 4
Calonne, Charles-Alexandre de XII 131–132
Calueque Dam (Angola) VII 239
Calvin's Case (1607) XII 42
Calvinism XII 149–150; XIII 31
Cambodia I 40–47, 145, 289, 299; II 6, 177; VI 4, 44, 60, 63, 65, 68, 83, 93, 188, 194, 203, 221; XII 33; XV 133; XVII 8, 147, 221
  colony of France I 290
  genocide in XI 71, 79, 166–167 169; XVII 95, 142; XIX 146
  Khmer Rouge movement I 15; VI 271
  spread of communism I 297
  supply lines through VI 60
  U.S. bombing of I 183, 291; VI 86
  U.S. invasion of I 291; VI 23, 26, 165, 284; XIX 222, 226
  Vietnam invasion of VI 44
Cambon, Paul IX 44
Cambridge University IX 172
Cameroon XIX 28
Camp David XV 51–53, 57, 104, 226, 266
Camp David agreement (1978) I 159; XIV 96; XV 219, 223, 225, 227, 239
Camp David summit (2000) XIV 19–20, 22, 24–25, 98, 100, 166, 258; XV 183, 185, 191
Camp Gordon, Georgia VIII 23, 299
Campbell, Alexander XII 313
Campbell, Archibald XII 184
Camus, Albert XVII 75–76, 78, 196, 201, 258
Canada I 30–31; VI 101, 136; VII 182; VIII 33, 83, 160–161, 208; IX 122, 173; XI 62; XII 10, 12, 15, 39, 98, 109, 165, 171, 199, 267–268, 272–274, 316; XIII 120; XIV 135, 225; XV 14, 135; XVI 13, 23, 41, 80–81, 87, 112, 182
  American Revolution XII 43–49
  Atomic Energy Act I 221
  British immigration to XII 168
  charter member of NATO I 208
  crime rate XVII 270
  criticism of Libertad Act I 98
  Cuban investment I 97
  discussion of nuclear weapons I 28
  escaped slaves XIII 124
  fish hatcheries in VII 202
  fishing rights in VIII 35
  French desire to regain territory in XII 104
  grain reserves VIII 290
  Loyalists in XII 167, 189, 192, 194
  motivation of World War I soldiers VIII 266
  Native Americans XII 174, 176–177, 180
  Nazi gold in XI 179
  oil XV 173
  policy on cleaning Great Lakes VII 116–124
  production of WWI materials IX 23
  Rebel attack upon XII 161
  relations with United States VII 116–124
  seized by Great Britain XII 55
  social programs in VI 187; XVII 269
  World War I VIII 220
Canada Water Bill (1969) VII 119–120
Canada-Ontario Agreement (COA) VII 120
Canary Islands
  slavery in XIII 161, 167
  slaves from XIII 167
Candide (1759) IX 207; XIX 48
Candomble XIII 192
Canwell, Albert F. XIX 108
Canwell Committee XIX 108
Capuano, Peter X 149
Cape Colony VIII
Cape Fear River XII 182, 184, 187
Cape of Good Hope XIII 136
Capehart, Homer XIX 94
capitalism II 30–31, 34, 56–57, 60; III 63, 191, 194–195
  capitalist encirclement II 39
  capitalist system III 190
Capra, Frank XVI 320
Card, Andrew H. Jr. XIV 97, 100
Cárdenas, Lazaro VII 155
  expropriates lands of Colorado River Land Company VII 152
  pushes against agricultural production VII 153
Cardozo, Justice Benjamin III 25, 28
Carib Indians XII 314
Caribbean VI 103; IX 140, 173, 246; XII 39, 167, 169, 198, 200, 252, 310; XIII 1, 31, 44, 129–130, 272; XVI 23, 68–69, 85, 87, 107
  African American interest in XIX 12
  African culture in XIII 13
  antislavery movement in XIX 11
  British interests in VIII 33
  British slaveholders in XIII 243
  economic growth XIII 43
  European conflict in XIII 233
  impact of American Revolution upon XIII 274
  maroons in XIII 104–105, 107–108, 110
  reaction to Haitian Revolution XIII 210
  slave religion XIII 190–193
  slave revolts XIII 2, 157
  slave trade to XIII 269
  slavery in XIII 1, 63–64, 80, 88, 154, 175, 233, 243, 247, 273–274
  Soviet influence in VI 261
  U.S. policy in VI 140
Carl XVI Gustaf (Sweden) XVI 180
Carleton, Guy 9–11, 43–49, 80, 268, 272–273
Carleton, Thomas XII 47
Carlism XVIII 58, 72, 89–92, 166, 200, 202, 204, 277, 296
Carlisle Peace Commission XII 101, 103
Carlos the Jackal. *See* Sanchez, Ilich Ramirez
Carlyle, Thomas XIV 197
Carmichael, Stokely II 79, 93, 95, 165
Carnegie, Andrew IX 19
Carnegie Endowment for International Peace VI 123–124, 129; XIV 148; XIX 155, 198–199, 224
Carnovsky, Morris XIX 166
Carol (Romania) XVI 195
Carolingian Empire X 213; XI 79
Carolingian Order X 212
Caron, Pierre-Augustin XII 101
Carpathian Mountains IX 133; XVI 202
Carpathian Ruthenia VI 244
Carpenter, Francis XIX 54
Carranza, Venustiano III 126–129
Carriage Workers Union II 191
Carrington, Edward XII 287
Carson, Edward VIII 161–162
Carson, Rachel VII 86, 160, 162, 278
Carter, Elliott XIX 45
Carter, Jimmy I 48–52, 101, 106, 141, 317; II 57–58, 97–98, 199, 204, 278; III 48; VI 20, 30, 109, 166, 193, 222, 226, 229, 232, 236, 241, 256, 270; XIV 2–3, 8, 38, 96; XVI 95; XIX 19
  Africa policy VI 1
  allows Shah into United States XIV 37
  Carter Doctrine VI 166, 270; XIV 2
  China policy VI 42–43
  emphasis on human rights II 100–101
  grain embargo against Russia VI 241
  human-rights policy VI 190
  mediator between Egypt and Israel I 159
  Middle East XV 51, 57, 219–220, 222–223, 226–227, 235, 258
  postpresidential career II 100
  response to Soviet invasion of Afghanistan I 11
  support to El Salvador VI 193
  suspends aid to Pakistan I 218
  withdrawal of SALT II Treaty I 10, 12
Carter administration I 50; II 67, 103; VI 2, 35, 56, 229, 261, 263; XIV 5; XVII 212

Central America policy I 54
Chile I 141
China policy VI 41
containment policy I 13
defense cuts VI 201
détente I 102
emphasis on human rights I 140–146
foreign policy I 52, 57
human rights I 52; VI 43
Iran crisis VI 166, 226
Iran embasy rescue disaster VI 232
limited-nuclear-war doctrine I 171
Middle East XV 52, 222, 258
military spending VI 222
military under VI 232
Nuclear Nonproliferation Act (1978) I 223
nuclear-nonproliferation policy I 216
Olympic boycott VI 107
Pershing II missile deployment VI 20
policy on Afghanistan I 10, 12, 15–16; XIV 3
policy on Nicaragua VI 190, VI 191
policy on Pakistan I 15, 223
Presidential Directive (PD) 59 I 171
reaction to Soviet invasion of Afghanistan VI 44, 133, 237
reaction to Team B VI 256
SALT II I 191
Carter, Landon XII 262
Carthage IX 140; XVI 251
Cartwright, John XII 249
Cartwright, Samuel A. XIII 123–124, 250
Carville, James XVII 52, 204
Casablanca (1942) XI 189
Casablanca Conference (1943) IV 144, 214; V 46, 85, 252, 270, 272, 275; XVI 315
Cascades Canal VII 52
Cascades Mountains VII 52, 56, 189
Casetta, Mario "Boots" XIX 234
Case Studies in Personnel Security XIX 138
Casey, William I 50–51, 54; II 57; VI 231, 239
Cash, W. J. XIII 224
Caspian Sea VIII 91, 216; XVI 6
oil XIV 170
Cassidorus X 228
Castile X 2, 4, 41, 140, 143, 289
free workers from XIII 168
Castillo Armas, Carlos I 123, 126
Castlereagh, Viscount XVI 74
Castro, Fidel I 49, 89, 91–96, 121, 283; II 120, 260, 266; VI 4, 7, 24, 63–68, 71, 139–142, 185, 192; XIX 14, 123, 128
Bay of Pigs II 115
Cuban Missile Crisis II 116
Cuban Revolution I 275
relationship with Soviet Union II 116; XIX 142, 146
support for communist uprising in Bolivia I 126
takeover in Cuba I 17; XIX 276
Castro, Raul VI 70
Cat on a Hot Tin Roof XIX 48
The Catcher in the Rye XIX 46, 48
Catharism X 226, 229, 270
Cathars X 33, 35
Catherine of Sienna X 204
Catholic Action XIX 266
Catholic Center Party XI 191
Catholic Church I 305; VI 170; VIII 202–203, 205, 208–209; X 119, 126, 205, 208, 215, 284; XI 19, 23; XII 171; XII 148–149; XIII 62–64; 149, 183, 192, 254; XIV 184; XVI 30, 57; XVII 99, 102, 197
criticism of communism I 271; XIX 6
influence on slavery XIII 59
influence on society II 164
opinion of/relationship with Hitler IV 187, 190
Quebec Act XII 234
relationship with Nazi Party IV 33–39; XI 191–201
Second Vatican Council (1963) II 164
slaves within XIII 192
and the Spanish Civil War XVIII 199–207
Catholic Slovenian Populist Party IX 267
Cato the Elder or Censor XII 302; XX 197–203
Cato's Letters (1720–1723) XII 128
Catskill Mountains XII 173
Catt, Carrie Chapman XIX 176
Cattonar, Anthony XIX 216
Caucasus Mountains VIII 96, 212–213, 280; IX 206; XIV 261–262; XVI 6, 18, 81, 88, 166, 200, 206
Russian conquest of XVI 70
Cavalry
Russian IX 158, 160
World War I IX 67–73
Cayuga XII 173–175, 177
Ceauçescu, Nicolae VI 51, 88, 265; VII 250, 254; XVII 218, 221
Cecil, Robert IX 172
Ceded Islands XII 311, 313–314
Celestine III X 261
Celilo Falls, Oregon VII 29, 55, 60
Céline, Louis-Ferdinand XVI 142
Celler, Emanuel XIX 18
Center for International Environmental Law VII 9
Central Africa
religion in XIII 187
slave trade XIII 38
Central African Empire VI 83; VIII 280
Central America I 48–157; VI 131, 265, 283; XIV 178, 198
African American immigration to XIX 11
death squads in XI 166
U.S. intervention in XIX 123, 275, 278, 280
Central Arizona Project (CAP) VII 108–109, 112, 114
Central Asia VI 109, 162, 165, 248; XIV 88, 176, 178, 187, 228–229, 262, 264, 266–267; XVI 23, 45, 68, 81, 85, 88, 193, 200
oil XIV 170
Russia in XVI 70
Central Bureau of Polish Communists XVI 230
Central Committee of the French Communist Party VII 97
Central Europe XVI 110, 195, 211, 221
impact of anticanal protest VII 206
Rhine-Main-Danube Canal VII 204–210
Central High School, Little Rock, Arkansas II 20, 52; XIX 24, 27
Central Intelligence Agency (CIA) I 49, 64–71, 92, 94, 119, 191, 211, 263; II 5, 52, 54, 57, 63, 69, 103, 115, 152, 178, 260; VI 6, 24, 57, 61, 64, 96, 133, 151, 188, 231, 260; XIV 4, 6, 17, 37–38, 41, 97, 103, 230, 233; XV 61, 87, 108, 158, 163, 175, 233, 271; XVI 45; XIX 16, 182, 197
anti-Sandanista forces I 54
assessment of Soviet military strength VI 257, 259
covert operations in British Guiana I 24
covert operations in Chile I 124, 131; VI 86–87; XIX 142, 145
covert operations in Guatemala I 123, 131; XV 157; XIX 141
covert operations in Latin America I 26
Cuba XV 157
efforts to assassinate Castro XIX 14
infiltration of Congress for Cultural Freedom XIX 265
intercession in the French and Italian elections XIX 145
investigation of anti-Vietnam War movment XIX 128, 226, 275, 277
Musaddiq, overthrow of XV 157–158, 160; XIX 145
Operation CHAOS XIX 277
Operation Mongoose II 120
origins I 64, 74; XIX 21, 71

plot to overthrow Castro I 275
release of Venona papers XIX 83, 85
Rosenberg records II 230
supply of Angolan rebels VI 1
support of contras VI 237
training of anti-Castro Cubans in Guatemala VI 141
Central Powers VI 176; VIII 18, 22, 117, 133. 172–173, 221, 242, 251, 278, 290, 295; IX 60, 63, 99, 154–155, 203, 205, 207–208, 238, 247–249, 266; X 59, 62; XVI 5, 6, 27, 173, 192, 204, 206, 236, 294, 307–309, 312
collapse of VIII 267
motivation of World War I soldiers VIII 266
U.S. trade with IX 22
Central Treaty Organization (CENTO) XV 27, 29, 120
Central Utah Project (CUP) VII 31
Central Valley Project VII 29
Ceyhan River VII 79
Chaco War (1932–1935) I 125
Chad XIV 198, 200
Chagall, Marc VIII 191
Challe, Maurice XV 12, 18
Chamberlain, Neville IV 17, 20, 125; V 117, 169; XII 33; XVI 8, 11–12, 14, 212
appeasement policy IV 18
Ten Year Rule IV 21
Chambers, Whittaker II 130; III 34; VI 123–129; XIX 17, 58, 185, 186, 194, 196–198, 248, 251
accuses Alger Hiss XIX 63, 118, 143, 151, 155, 207, 224
Hiss's comments on XIX 156
reliability of XIX 199–200
role in Red Scare XIX 249
Soviet spy XIX 61–62
Chamorro, Violeta Barrios de VI 191, 195
Chamoun, Camille XV 61, 63, 169
Chandelier Workers Union II 191
Channing, William Ellery XIII 29, 33
Chaplin, Charlie XIX 163
Charlemagne X 24, 26, 65, 81, 127, 177, 212, 269, 287; XI 80
Charles I XIII 63; XVI 213
Charles II XII 209; XIII 62
Charles V X 8
Charles XII (Sweden) XVI 184
Charles of Anjou X 30, 66, 139, 142–146, 226
Charles Town XII 41, 182, 190, 192
Charter 77 movement VI 237
Chasseurs d'Afrique IX 116
Chauncy, Charles XII 148, 150
Chavez, Cesar XIX 191
Chechnya XIV 12, 93, 180, 230; XVI 78, 166; XVII 102, 157
conflict in (since 1994) XVI 109
Soviet operations in VI 169, 218
Cheka (Soviet secret police) XVII 89, 154, 156
Chelmno (concentration camp) XI 220
Chemical warfare V 101–107
World War I VIII 239–244; IX 38
Cheney, Dick XIV 97, 101, 103, 105; XV 78
Chernenko, Konstantin I 197; II 60; VI 111, 226; XV 255
succeeded by Gorbachev I 14
Cherniaev, Anatoly XVI 45
Chernobyl (1986) II 86; VII 18, 20, 22, 247; XVII 132, 151
Chernov, Viktor XVI 20
Chesapeake (region) XII 169, 205
slavery in XIII 85, 151, 179, 247
trade restrictions on tobacco XII 201
Chesapeake Bay XII 33, 172, 271; XIII 60
oysters in VII 40–50
Chesapeake Bay 2000 Agreement VII 49
Chesapeake Biological Laboratory VII 47–48
Chesnut, Mary Boykin XIII 123, 205, 218, 229, 238
Chetniks VI 275, 277
Chevron (Standard Oil of California, or Socal) XIV 211–212; XV 172–173, 177, 179
Chiang Kai-shek I 40, 58, 61, 86, 265–266, 268, 275, 303–304; II 133, 211; V 191, 194–196; VI 38, 146, 158, 254; XIX 17, 19–20, 22, 117, 240
Chicago VII 116, 122, 262; IX 3, 7
water supply system in VII 283
Chicago Daily News IX 4
Chicago Tribune XIX 126, 260
Chicano Power II 94
Chief Joseph Dam (United States) VII 53
Childers, Robert IX 93
Chile I 123–128, 140, 152; VI 64, 87, 194, 265–266; XI 88; XIV 23; XVI 110
African American interest in XIX 14
access to Import-Export Bank I 53
Allende government I 26
CIA activites in VI 86–87
coup of 1960s I 26
human rights record I 143
U.S. intervention (early 1970s) I 15, 123–133
U.S. policies toward XIX 140, 142, 145–146
China I 41, 44, 54, 59, 86–91, 141, 277, 287–288, 292; II 4, 9, 36, 39–40, 47, 119, 168, 171; VI 10, 35, 42, 49, 53, 56, 59, 90, 107, 121, 136, 147, 154, 175, 178, 181, 199, 201, 203, 213–214, 243, 265, 271; IX 91, 96, 162, 164–165, 167–168, 174–175, 246; X 186, 305; XII 29, 171; XIV 2–3, 12, 46, 88, 143, 176–177, 239; XV 49, 68, 81, 120, 167, 215, 220, 228, 245, 250, 252; XVI 41, 45–46, 65, 69–70, 81, 106–107, 110, 156, 260, 284, 289; XVII 88, 227, 229
accuses Soviets of aiding Vietnam VI 44
African American interest in XIX 14
attacks on Quemoy and Matsu I 265–270, 275
attacks Vietnam VI 43
balance to U.S.S.R VI 201
blue-water navy of VI 53
bombing of embassy in Belgrade VI 54
border clashes with Soviet Union VI 40, 43
communist victory in XV 206; XIX 17, 19–20, 22, 29, 99, 116, 121, 140, 145, 245, 255
Communists XIX 17, 19–20, 22, 110, 117, 127, 132, 164, 186, 202, 245, 248, 283, 286
condemns terrorism XIV 16
Cultural Revolution XI 166–167; XIX 146
defense spending of VI 54
economy VI 53, 219
excluded from UN XIX 236, 243
Famine of 1959–1960 XIX 146
German interests in VIII 31, 137
Great Leap Forward XVII 8
human rights in VI 219
influence on North Vietnam I 296–297
involvement in Vietnam War XIX 221–222
Japanese defeat of XVI 66; XIX 88
Korean War I 273–275; XIV 147
Lend Lease aid XVI 162, 167; XIX 17
Manchu dynasty XVI 112
meeting with United States in Warsaw (1969) VI 43
military strength XIX 237
Nationalists I 61; XIX 17, 19–20, 22, 117, 248
Nixon's negotiations with XIX 220, 223, 227
nuclear espionage of VI 219
Nuclear Non-Proliferation Treaty I 218
nuclear proliferation I 222–224
nuclear weapons I 222, 239; XVI 109
purchase of Western military hardware VI 42
rapprochement with the United States VI 38–45
Rape of Nanking XVI 254
relations with Russia VI 53
relations with Soviet Union VI 38, 113, 203; XIX 22, 119
Russian threat to British interests in VIII 33
Shantung province siezed IX 163

Soviet role in postwar VI 254
support for Afghan resistance VI 166
support for FNLA and UNITA VI 1
Taiwan-U.S. mutual-security treaty I 268
Tiananmen Square Massacre (1989) VI 54, 113, 121; XVI 289
U.N. Security Council membership I 300
U.S. intelligence sites in VI 43
U.S. Ping-Pong team trip VI 43
U.S. relations with VI 4, 88; XIX 156, 221
China Hands I 58-63; VI 158; XIX 17-19, 21, 22, 278
Chinese Civil War VI 150
Chinese Communist Party (CCP) VI 181
Chinese Cultural Revolution (1966-1976) VI 40 XI 166-167; XIX 146
Chinese Revolution (1949) VI 177; IX 168
Chirac, Jacques XIV 241; XVI 134, 139
Chlorine gas, effects of VIII 239
Chomsky, Noam XIX 111
Chou En-lai I 266, 269, 277; XV 68, 167; XIX 19
Christian Church, evangelization of VIII 203
Christian Democratic Party (CDP)
in Chile I 124, 127-130; XIX 142
Christian X XVI 181
Christian church groups, anticommunism of XIX 101
Christian fundamentalists XIX 273
Christian Neoplatonism XX 204-211
Christianity XIII 101; XIV 81, 159, 183, 187, 191, 205
in founding of United States XII 60-66
slavery XIII 3, 186-193
use of to justify slavery XIII 26-34
Christians
Arabized X 41
interactions with Muslims X 197-203
treatment of Jews X 272-278
Christie, Gabriel XII 47
Christmas bombing (1972) VI 28
Christmas Rebellion (1831) XIII 91, 154, 159-160, 231
Christmas Truce (1914) VIII 62-63
Christophe, Henri XIII 209-210, 213, 215
Christopher, Warren XV 183, 184, 187, 263
Chrysostom, John XI 20, 23
Chunuk Bair VIII 117-118, 123
Church, Frank VI 61
Church of England XII 146, 149, 209, 216, 250, 263
use of Syrian silks XIV 45
World War I VIII 203, 208
World War I chaplains VIII 203
Church of the Holy Sepulchre XIV 159, 167
Churchill, Winston I 31, 154, 201, 231, 305; II 32, 39; IV 19, 40-45, 144, 148, 210, 213; V 25, 34-46, 85, 102, 104, 109, 118, 123, 135-136, 146, 152, 168, 176, 221-222, 236; VI 8, 78, 104, 146, 173, 267, 280; VIII 33, 79, 104, 117-118, 122; IX 52, 57, 100, 103; XI 10, 12, 110, 252-253, 261; XIV 176-177; XV 34, 163; XVI 1-4, 7, 12-13, 36, 76, 91, 102, 186, 211, 220, 227, 230, 314-319; XVII 20-21, 57, 189, 222; XIX 2
"balance of terror" VI 15
Balkans V 46, 69-72, 75
commendations to members of Federation of Greek Maritime Unions XIX 218
"Iron Curtain" speech (1946) I 286; VI 9, 49, 250; XIX 9, 96, 117, 127, 245, 248
military background IV 41-42
opposition to Operation Anvil/Dragoon V 238-241
Tehran Conference (1943) I 259
Yalta Agreement (1945) I 300-304
Yalta Conference (1945) V 309-315
CIA. *See* Central Intelligence Agency
Ciano, Galeazzo XVIII 20, 141-143, 171
Cicero XII 110, 302; XIII 278
and Caesar XX 212-220
Cincinnatus XII 308
CIO. *See* Congress of Industrial Organizations
Cisco, Joseph XV 160
Cistercians X 159, 235, 298
Citizens Councils XIX 80-81
civic education XIX 107-115
civic humanism XII 118-119
civil liberties I 73-81; XIX 52-59, 74, 214
Civil Rights Act (1866) XIII 5, 54
Civil Rights Act (1875) XIII 57
Civil Rights Act (1964) II 25-26, 91, 141, 162, 164, 192, 277-278, 293; XIX 28, 32
Civil Rights Congress (CRC) XIX 10, 29, 30, 77, 207, 214, 234
Civil Rights movement II 19-28, 42-48, 80, 89-96, 159, 162-163, 165, 180, 257; III 181-189, 268; VI 25, 140; XIII 195; XIX 31
affirmative action II 143
anticommunism XIX 8-12, 24-33, 100, 181
communist ties XIX 8, 10, 24, 29, 30, 74-82, 87 98, 100, 189, 213, 216, 228-229, 231, 275
connections to labor movement II 189
demonstration in Cleveland XIX 31
in California XIX 232
legislation during Truman administration XIX 8
March for Jobs and Freedom (1963) II 27
March on Washington (1963) II 25, 91-92
media coverage of II 20-22
President's Committee on Civil Rights (1946) II 42
relationship with labor movement II 192
resistance to II 25, 140
Scottsboro case III 188
"separate but equal" doctrine II 137
use of civil disobedience II 140
voter registration II 27
Civil Servants Ban (The Netherlands) XIX 272
Civil Service Act XIX 133
Civil Service Commission XIX 132-133, 137
Civil War (1861-1865) VI 26, 28, 57; VIII 14, 18, 23, 25, 68, 136, 149, 199, 226, 296, 299; IX 19, 22, 116, 158, 209; XI 123; XII 168, 263, 294; XIII 2, 5, 7-8, 21, 23, 43, 50-51, 69, 80, 107, 124, 150, 169, 175, 195, 233, 239, 241, 243, 256, 272; XVI 172, 252, 255
slavery as cause of XIII 276-283
Civil Works Administration (CWA, 1933) III 154
Civilian Conservation Corps (CCC, 1933) III 154
Clark, John XII 98
Clark, Mark W. IV 146; V 125-126, 187
Italian campaign IV 144
Clark, Tom XIX 16-18, 151, 252
Clark, William P. VI 231
Clark Amendment (1975) VI 1-4
Clarke, Carter XIX 118
classical republicanism XII 120, 122, 125
Clausewitz, Carl von VIII 16, 71, 112-113, 199; XII162, 302; XVI 252
Clay, Henry XIII 4, 19, 48
Clay, Lucius I 35-36; XI 179, 255
Clean Air Act Amendments (1970) II 183
Clean Water Act (1972) VII 256, 258, 262-264, 267-269, 274, 303-305
reauthorization VII 274
Clemenceau, Georges VIII 11, 19, 78, 147, 149-150, 256, 278, 283-283; IX 203, 207, 250; XVI 7, 34, 76, 173; XVII 197
assassination attempt upon VIII 278
Clement III X 216, 219, 221, 227, 229
Clement IV X 145
Cleveland VII 116, 122-123, 262, 265
Clifford, Clark M. I 160; II 6, 205; XII 31; XV 203
Clifford-Elsey report II 205, 208
Clift, Montgomery XI 158
Clinton, Bill I 97-98; II 80; VI 8, 58, 61, 231, 235; VII 224; VIII 11; XIV 16, 19, 22, 38, 95, 106-107, 164, 166, 199; XVI 57; XVII 51, 70, 133
abortion legislation II 223
dam protests VII 221
Dayton accords II 154

INDEX

impact of 1960s on presidency II 163
Israel I 159
Lewinsky scandal VI 231
Middle East XV 138, 183, 264, 266–267
pro-choice stand II 223
re-election of II 200
Clinton administration
arms-control agreements VI 20
bombs Iraq XIV 31
defense spending VI 220
flood control VII 214
foreign policy of VI 58
human rights and democracy XIV 87
Iran XIV 43
Israeli-Palestinian issue XIV 19
Libya XIV 199
Middle East XIV 38, 98, 103; XV 182, 265
nuclear nonproliferation I 224
Clinton, Henry XII 39–40, 47, 162, 182, 184–186, 270–271, 306
Clovis X 104
Cluniac Reform X 17–18, 36, 94
Cluny X 85, 141, 220, 279
CNN Cold War television series VI 66
Coastal Zone Management Act (1972) II 183
Cobb, T. R. R. XIII 27, 48, 101–102, 178, 219, 265
Cobbett, William XII 249
Cobra helicopter VI 173
Cochran, Johnnie XIII 197–198
Code Noir (Black Code, 1685) XIII 62
Coe, Frank XIX 197
Coercive Acts (1774) XII 51, 54, 110, 140–141, 207, 215, 234, 253
Coffin, Howard IX 21
Cohen, Benjamin V. XIX 17
Cohn, Roy XIX 111, 126
COINTELPRO. See Counter-Intelligence Program (COINTELPRO)
Colautti v. *Franklin* (1979) II 222
Colby, William E. VI 257
Cold War I 27–32, 82–90, 101–106, 115–122, 148–155, 165–203, 216–224, 271–276, 300–303; II 4, 9, 30–63, 68, 104, 163; III 10, 48; V 46, 119, 145, 149, 191, 199; VI 1–6, 8–11, 30–33, 108–115, 130–133, 160–162, 168–172, 175–178; VII 31, 53, 97, 174, 188; X 55, 63; XI 181, 253, 257, 260, 262; XIV 1, 3, 5, 9, 16, 40, 77, 81, 87–89, 107, 109, 187–188, 230, 235, 238, 262, 264; XV 12, 17, 19, 24, 26–27, 73, 81, 83, 116, 139, 148, 152, 157, 173, 175, 182, 202–203, 206, 218, 224, 240, 250, 260, 263, 271, 275; XVI 4, 15, 41, 45, 65, 74, 85, 91, 107–108, 110–111, 121–122, 126, 135, 155–156, 158, 163, 167, 221, 228, 245, 252, 254, 262, 267, 269, 281, 288, 319
casualties in VI 50
causes of VI 252
conclusion of VI 47–51, 213–216
dam building in VII 29
decline of XIX 123
disarmament XVI 92, 94–95
domestic impact of XIX *passim*
effect of nuclear weapons I 250–257
end of VI 150, 214
foreign policy XIX 99, 127, 133, 140–147, 212, 236, 239–240, 243, 249, 260, 275, 278, 280
impact on civil rights movement XIX 8–15, 24–32, 76
impact on colonialism XIX 9
impact on development of space programs II 241
impact on federal highway development II 107
impact on civil liberties 6, 30, 53–59
impact on U.S. space program development II 257
late 1970s intensification II 172
Middle East XV 252–259
military buildup II 43
mutual assured destruction (MAD) I 251–252
origins of I 258–264; II 30; XIX 1–2, 5, 121, 259
Reagan's role in ending VI 221–241
Stalin's role in starting VI 250–252
vindicationist interpretation VI 155
Colden, Cadwallader XII 214
Cole, Lester XIX 168
Cole (U.S. ship), attack on (2000) XIV 16, 190
Cole v. *Young* I 80
Colleges and universities,
FBI agents at XIX 111
influences of Communists and anti-Communists in XIX 107–115
Collier, John (Commissioner of Indian Affairs) III 141–142
Collins, J. Lawton I 6; V 122
Collins, Michael XVI 244
Colombia XIII 104; XV 79
colonialism X 55–56, 63; XIV 171; XV 35; XVI 64–71
Colorado VII 10, 13, 112, 181, 182
farmers' use of water in VII 13
production of crops on irrigated land in VII 11
Colorado River VII 27, 31, 151–153, 155, 168, 211, 214
dams on VII 108–115, 152
Colorado River Compact (CRC) VII 152–153
Colorado River Irrigation District VII 157
Colorado River Land Company VII 152
Colorado River Storage Project (CRSP) VII 27, 112
Coltrane, John XIX 48
Columbia Basin VII 29
dams in VII 196
Columbia Basin Project VII 202
Columbia River VII 25, 27–28, 31, 51–61, 197, 199, 202, 219–220, 222, 225, 227
first major navigation project on VII 52
hydroelectric dams on VII 198
salmon producer VII 53
Columbia River Fisherman's Protective Union VII 53
Columbia River Highway VII 57
Columbia River Inter-Tribal Fish Commission VII 61
Columbia River Packers Association VII 53
Columbia University XIII 198; XIX 111
Columbus, Christopher X 7–8, 304; XIII 147, 210
Comal River VII 70
combat effectiveness
Germany V 282, 284
Japan V 281–282
Leyte campaign V 281
Normandy invasion V 282
psychological limits IV 47–52
United States V 278–286
Combined Bomber Offensive IX 223
Combined Chiefs of Staff (CCS) V 20, 23, 25, 38, 42–45
Cominform XIX 238–239, 248
Comintern. *See* Communist International
Commission on Polish Affairs VIII 281
Commission on Protecting and Reducing Government Secrecy XIX 85
Commission on Presidential Debates II 196, 199
Committee for a Sane Nuclear Policy XIX 242
Committee for Industrial Organizations. See Congress of Industrial Organizations (CIO)
Committee for National Unity XV 195
Committee on Political Refugees XI 60
Committee on Public Information (CPI) VIII 296; IX 78
Commission on Sustainable Development XIV 268
Committee on the Present Danger VI 256, 262
Committee to Re-Elect the President (CREEP) II 177; VI 24
Common Cause XIX 270
Common Sense (1776) XII 54, 110, 121, 143, 153; XVI 181–182
Commonwealth Federation XIX 103
Commonwealth of Independent States (CIS) VI 54
Commonwealth of Nations VI 13
The Commonwealth of Oceana (1656) XII 123
Commonwealth v. *Turner* (1827) XIII 102

Communism I 148–155; II 31–32, 56–57, 160; VI 49; IX 83; XVI 4, 236; XVII 173–179
and labor XIX 67–73, 209
atheism of VI 176
attraction for women VI 49
attraction for ethnic minorities XIX 209
China II 267e
collapse of II 153
expansion of XIX 249
global II 130
Hoover's views on XIX 173
ideology I 258–262; VI 49
infiltration of federal government II 133;
involvement in peace movements XIX 209, 236–244
involvement in progressive movements XIX 209
world domination VI 175–182
Communist Control Act (1954) I 74, 77; XIX 30
Communist Information Bureau (Cominform) I 36–113; VI 179, 246
Communist Infiltration in the United States, Its Nature and How to Combat It XIX 121
Communist International (Comintern) I 113; III 224, 226; IV 80; VI 178, 254, 277; XVI 41, 141, 220, 229; XIX 3, 86, 102–103, 193, 225, 229
and movements for peaceful co-existence and nuclear disarmament XIX 236
and the Spanish Civil War XVIII 1–7, 53, 118, 120, 123, 126, 189, 221, 331
launches Popular Front XIX 232
links to American Communists XIX 229, 231
Seventh World Congress XIX 103
Third Period of XIX 102–103, 229
Communist Labor Party (U.S., founded 1919) XIX 212
Communist Manifesto (1848) VI 178; XIII 69; XVII 52, 66, 160; XIX 261
Communist Party I 74; III 182, 221; XIV 181; XVI 100, 260, 261; XVII 34, 174, 237
in Australia XIX 266–268, 270
in Chile I 124
in China XIX 5
in Europe XIX 84, 103, 229, 265, 269
in France XIX 103, 265, 269
in Guatemala I 123
in Italy XIX 229, 265, 269
in the Netherlands XIX 265, 269, 272–273
of the Soviet Union III 224; VI 179, 276; XV 257
of Yugoslavia (CPY) VI 273–278, 280–281
Communist Party Dissolution Bill (Australia) XIX 267–268, 270–271
Communist Party (U.S., founded 1919) XIX 212
Communist Party of the United States of America (CPUSA) II 46–48; III 237; VI 123, 154, 157
aid to unemployed XIX 87, 98, 228
after World War II XIX *passim*
and civil liberties XIX 52–59, 188, 191
and education XIX 107–115, 188, 191, 213
and farmers XIX 57, 191
and folk music XIX 192
and Hiss case XIX 154
and Rosenberg case XIX 234
and Trotsky XIX 57, 104–105
and women's rights XIX 188–189, 191, 192
authoritarian structure of XIX 102
backs Henry Wallace in 1948 presidential election XIX 194, 241
changing policy toward Germany XIX 56, 59, 213
Communist Eleven XIX 254–264
compared to Dutch party XIX 269
constitution of XIX 199
control of Commonwealth Federation XIX 103
decline of XIX 4–5, 98–106, 161, 173, 214, 239, 258, 286
defends Stalin XIX 104
during 1950s XIX 286
during 1940s XIX 249
during 1930s XIX 4, 102–103, 213
during 1920s XIX 4
during World War II XIX 88, 104, 246
during Truman administration XIX 260
expulsion of members from labor movement XIX 67–68, 70, 72–73
Federation of Architects, Engineers, Chemists and Technicians II 228
history of III 224; XIX 61, 84, 86, 102, 206, 212–213
Hoover's efforts against 173–179, 196
in California XIX 121, 207–208, 228, 231–235, 259
in Hollywood XIX 165, 168–169
in Maryland XIX 207, 209
in Michigan government XIX 103
in New York City government XIX 229
in Pittsburgh XIX 201
influence in Minnesota XIX 104
influence in Roosevelt administration XIX 103
influence in Washington State XIX 103
influence on American culture XIX 2, 5, 34–42, 43–51, 86, 88, 103, 188–195
informants XIX 196–203
investigated by Bowker Commission XIX 205
investigated by FBI XIX 258, 286
investigated by HCUA XIX 60–66, 133
involvement in nuclear disarmament movements XIX 236–244
involvement in peace movements XIX 99, 236–244
involvement in Scottoboro case XIX 74, 78, 160, 258
involvement in Spanish Civil War XIX 103, 160
members in International Union of Mine, Metal and Smelting Workers XIX 202
members on New York City Council XIX 103
membership
African American XIX 12, 189
after World War II XIX 4
during World War II XIX 136
female XIX 189
immigrant XIX 57, 212
in 1950s XIX 6
in 1953 XIX 258
in 1958 XIX 4
in 1946 XIX 258
in 1942 XIX 104
in 1930s XIX 38
1948 platform XIX 194
1932 presidential candidate III 182
organization of Southern Tenant Farmers Unions II 189
papers in Soviet archives XIX 83, 85–86, 88
popular fears of XIX 245–253
Popular Front XIX 1, 4, 10, 29, 34–41, 52, 56, 62, 71, 75, 83, 86, 98, 104–106, 154, 189, 193, 229, 231–234
prominent officials' views on XIX 200
promotes no-strike pledge during World War II XIX 67
protest tactics XIX 192
publications XIX 216
reaction to German invasion of USSR XIX 104
reaction to German-Soviet nonagression treaty XIX 104
relations with American Socialists XIX 102–103
role in civil rights movement XIX 1, 4, 8–15, 24–33, 55, 57, 74–82, 83, 87, 98, 103, 161, 188–189, 192, 216, 228, 234
role in ethnic associations XIX 216
role in Hollywood Ten defense XIX 164, 167–172
role in integration of Major League baseball XIX 76–77
role in labor movement XIX 1, 4, 12, 55, 67–75, 83, 86–87, 93, 98, 102–105, 121, 151, 161, 182, 185, 192–193, 207, 216

role in mass media XIX 216
secrecy of XIX 57, 168, 211, 214
Smith Act trials of leaders XIX 97, 105, 127, 148–151, 153, 196–197, 199, 207, 245, 248, 252, 254–264, 271, 283–284
social agenda XIX 83, 86, 161, 188, 189, 191, 192, 193, 194, 195, 231
spying in United States XIX 2, 4–6, 52, 55, 83–86, 88, 117, 140, 194, 215, 228, 230, 245, 248–249, 251
targeted by McCarran Act XIX 204, 211–212, 215
ties to Soviet Union XIX 1, 4–6, 56–57, 61, 69, 84, 86, 98–99, 102, 104, 188, 193–194, 212–213, 231
Community Action Programs (CAP) II 270–276
Community Development Corporation XIII 200
Community Reinvestment Act (1977) XIII 200
Comnena, Anna X 211, 215
Comoros XIV 55, 181; XV 141
Compañía de Terrenos y Aguas de la Baja California, S.A. VII 155
Comprehensive Immigration Law (1924) III 233
Comprehensive Test Ban Treaty (CTBT) I 224; VI 58
Comprehensive Wetlands Management and Conservation Act VII 274
Conant, James B. XIX 110, 113, 124
Concert of Europe VI 203; XVI 72–78
Concerto and Diminuendo in Blue XIX 46
Condor Legion XVIII 12, 14–15, 21, 37, 68, 82–83, 86, 131, 163, 166–167, 172–173, 194, 260, 327
and the bombing of Guernica XVIII 81–87
Confederate Army, Zouave units in IX 116
Confederate Congress XIII 153, 277
Confederate Constitution XIII 274, 277
Confederate States of America XIII 5, 45, 195; XVI 172
use of symbols from XIII 269–278
Confederation Congress XII 293, 299
Conference of Peace (1949) XIX 238
Conference of the States (1995) XIV 150
Conference on Environmental Economics at Hyvinkää (1998) VII 89
Confessing Church XI 27–35, 135
Confessional poetry XIX 46
Confiscation Plan XIII 51
Congo IX 226; XIII 11; XVI 84
independence XIX 14
slave trade XIII 35, 40
Congregational Church VIII 204; XII 148, 150, 216, 254, 263
Congress of African People (1970) II 95; III 193, 195
Congress of Berlin IX 99
Congress for Cultural Freedom XIX 265
Congress of Industrial Organizations (CIO) II 188, 197; III 183–184, 191, 195; XIX 55, 71, 104
affected by Taft-Hartley Act XIX 72
Communist influence in XIX 5–6, 67–68, 75, 87–88, 98, 103, 105
expulsion of unions with Communist ties XIX 67–68, 72, 99, 182, 185
merger with AFL XIX 6, 68, 73, 105
origins of XIX 67, 71
Political Action Committee (CIO-PAC) XIX 223–224
Congress of Industrial Relations. *See* Congress of Industrial Workers (CIO).

Congress of Racial Equality (CORE) II 161; III 219; XIII 256; XIX 10, 30–31, 177
Congress of Vienna (1815) IX 45, 226; XVI 72, 75
Congressional Black Caucus XIII 198
Connally, John VI 257
Connecticut XII 10–12, 15, 66, 70, 205, 209, 215
gradual emancipation in XIII 19
impact of Shays's Rebellion in XII 287
prohibits importation of slaves XIII 18
religion in XII 148, 150, 263
slave uprising in XIII 235
Connolly, Thomas T. II 208; III 31; VI 151
Connor, Bull XIX 76
Conrad X 48, 286
Conrad III X 128, 294
Conrad of Montferrat X 256, 258
Conrad von Hotzendorf, Franz VIII 46–47, 49, 252; IX 64–65, 99, 135, 137; XVI 32–33, 196
Conradin X 142
Conscription Crisis (1917) VIII 158–159
Conservation in Action Series (1947) VII 278
Conservative Party (Great Britain) VI 13
Constantine (Greek king) IX 208
Constantine I (Roman emperor) X 80–82, 224, 228; XIV 159
Constantine IX X 284
Constantine Plan (1958) XV 18
Constantinople VIII 117–118, 122, 173, 212, 214–215, 228; IX 208; X 27–30, 47, 58, 88, 108, 110, 112–114, 121, 150, 152, 208–209, 220–221, 239, 250, 262, 281, 284–286; XIV 261
fall of (1204) X 24, 27, 36, 108
Constantinople Convention (1888) XV 247
Constitution of the United States (1787) II 98, 101; VI 56, 283–284; XII 7, 18, 58, 60–62, 64, 66, 108, 113, 118, 120–122, 127, 131, 134, 276–283, 288, 293, 297; XIII 7, 56, 272, 274; XVI 139; XIX 137, 211, 254
economic interpretation of XII 68–76
Eighteenth Amendment (1919) III 198–200, VIII 295
Fifteenth Amendment (1870) III 270; XIII 5, 56
Fifth Amendment II 132, 134, 281–282; III 107; XIX 64, 100, 113, 161, 164, 166–167, 171, 200, 205, 212
First Amendment II 166; XII 60, 61, 63; XIX 64, 140–147, 148–153, 163, 167, 169–172, 218, 254–255, 259, 260, 262–263, 271, 281
Fourteenth Amendment II 20, 138, 224, 282, 284; XIII 5, 57; XIX 281
due process clause II 281
equal protection clause II 138–139, 141, 221
Fourth Amendment II 281
fugitive slave clause XIII 173
Nineteenth Amendment (1919) II 78; III 171–172, 206, VIII 295
Ninth Amendment II 225, 281
Second Amendment XII 276–283
Seventeenth Amendment II 196
Sixth Amendment II 281
slavery XII 294; XIII 18, 195
taking clause XII 274
Tenth Amendment VI 57; XII 61
Thirteenth Amendment (1865) XIII 5, 272
Three-fifths Compromise XIII 7
Twenty-first Amendment (1933) III 200
Constitutional Convention (1787) XII 18, 21, 25 62–64, 69, 75, 119, 214, 217, 281, 285, 288, 291, 293, 297–299
Contadora peace process VI 194
containment I 142, 144, 154, 158, 160, 183–184, 187, 262, 271–272, 274, 288, 293; II 30–31, 58, 269; VI 59, 80, 83, 203; XIX 3, 12, 21, 29, 93–94, 124, 144, 224, 248, 252, 278, 279, 280
Dulles criticism of I 273
during Carter administration I 13
strongpoint I 82–86
universal I 82–90
Continental Army XII 9–10, 15, 33, 37–39, 78, 81, 92–93, 95–96, 106, 149, 155–156, 158, 182, 184, 215–217, 222–223, 263, 272–273, 283, 301, 305–307
African Americans in XII 89
billetted in Loyalist homes XII 191
bounties for recruitment to XII 89
deserters XII 90
Hessian deserters in XII 89

punishments in XII 304
soldiers in XII 85–91
Continental Association XII 189, 215
Continental Congress XII 1, 10, 12–13, 15, 22, 37, 41, 44, 46, 52, 54–55, 61–62, 78–79, 86–87, 89, 93, 95–96, 103, 106, 108–109, 113–114, 116, 140–141, 156, 185, 189–191, 193, 215, 221–222, 224, 262, 278–279, 282, 286, 290, 294–295, 301–303, 306, 315–316
Board of War XII 97
naval policy of XII 77, 81
Continental Navy XII 77–83, 106
Continental System XVI 27
Contras VI 57, 61, 191–196, 237, 241; XIX 128, 145, 280
Conventional Forces in Europe (CFE) Treaty (1990) XVI 95
Convention on the Protection of the Mediterranean Sea against Pollution VII 143–144, 305–310
conventional warfare IV 46–52
convergence theory VI 241
Conway, Henry XII 57
Conway, Thomas XII 92–93, 97–98
Conyers, John XIII 197–198
Conyngham, Gustavus XII 79, 106
Cook, James XIII 133
Coolidge, Calvin III 22, 25, 47, 176, 178, 226; IX 92; XI 56
Coolidge administration IX 171
authorizes Boulder Dam VII 28
Cooper v. *Aaron* (1958) II 286
Cooper, John Sherman VI 61
Cooper, Samuel XII 150
Cooper, Thomas XII 320; XIII 48
Cooper-Church amendment (1970) I 44; VI 60
Cooperative Central Exchange (CCE) XIX 191
Coordinating Committee for Mutual Export Controls (COCOM) XVI 45
Coordinating Unit for the Med Plan VII 145
Copenhagen Criteria (1993) XIV 173, 265
Coppola, Francis Ford VI 222
Corcoran, Thomas, XIX 17–18
Cordier, Andrew VI 75
Corey, Jeff XIX 166
Corfu IX 207
Corfu Declaration XVI 103
Corn Laws XII 200
Corn Production Act (1917) IX 59
"Cornerstone Speech" (1861) XIII 277
Cornplanter XII 175, 177
Cornwallis, Charles XII 23, 39, 41, 164, 184, 187, 304, 308
Cornwallis, George XII 103, 171
Corsica XVI 136, 249, 302
terrorism XVI 249
Corsican Liberation Front XVI 248
Cortes, Hernan X 8
Costa Rica I 53
invasion threats from Nicaragua (1949, 1955) I 125
U.S. intervention in mid 1950s I 15
cotton gin XIII 7, 43
Coudert, Frederic C. XIX 108
Coughlin, Charles 103, 246
Council for German Jewry XI 96
Council for Mutual Economic Assistance (CMEA) XVI 282
Council of Clermont (1095) X 13–14, 17, 20, 32, 35, 72, 81, 97–99, 102, 104–105, 116, 119, 122, 126–127, 130–131, 135, 149–150, 171, 205, 209, 211, 213, 215, 218–219, 221, 227, 234, 238, 245, 265, 269, 279, 281–283, 287, 289, 295
Council of Lyon (1245) X 141
Council of Nablus (1120) X 201
Council of Piacenza (1095) X 127, 216, 220, 286
Council of Pisa (1135) X 128, 225
Council of Sens (1140) X 166
Council of Ten VIII 282
Council of Troyes (1129) X 158
Council on African Affairs (CAA) XIX 10, 12, 29–30, 75
Council on Environmental Quality Rainfall VII 214, 224
Council on Foreign Relations VI 199, 203
Counter Battery Staff Office IX 122
Counter- Intelligence Program (COINTELPRO) XIX 54, 173–174, 177, 220–221, 275
Counterattack XIX 65
Country interest XII 119, 122, 128
Country Party XII 110
Court interest XII 119, 121, 122
Cousins, Norman XIX 242
Coventry (1940 bombing raid) V 6, 96
Coxe, Tench XII 283
Crac de Chevaliers X 46, 48
Craftsman, The (1726–1736) XII 147
Craig, James XII 184
Crane, Hart XIX 46
Crawford, William XIII 19, 272
credibility gap VI 23
Creel, George VIII 296; IX 78
Crete VIII 212; XIV 176
sugar cane in XIII 167
Crimea IX 111, 116, 225
Russian conquest of XVI 70
Crimean War (1853–1856) IX 49, 155, 158, 238; XVI 16, 72–73, 200; XVII 244
Criminal Division, U.S. Department of Justice XIX 260
Critical theory, modern XX 38–46
Croatia VI 276; VIII 95; IX 136, 266–272; XI 192–193, 195; XVI 33, 36, 57–58, 60–63, 104
The Crisis (NAACP) XIX 30
Croatian Peasant Party IX 272; XVI 100
Croatian publications XIX 216
Crocker, Chester A. VI 4
Croke Park IX 93
Cromwell, Oliver XII 302
Cronin, John F. XIX 121, 249
Cronkite, Walter XV 56
Crouch, Paul XIX 202
The Crucible XIX 48
Crum, Bartley XIX 169, 171
Crusader States X 10, 25, 27, 41, 43, 46–54, 59, 64, 67, 72–76, 87, 89, 92, 94, 107, 140, 147, 148–158, 166, 170–176, 178, 180, 183, 185–188, 190–196, 247–248, 254–259, 275, 294, 296–297, 300–306
cultural interaction in X 197–203
importance of maritime traffic X 152
treatment of Muslims in X 190–196
Crusaders, motivations of X 143
Crusades XIV 159, 161
Albigensian X 112, 210, 226, 236, 239, 270
Children's X 32–38, 88, 231, 234–235, 239
Christian ethics X 79–86
class structure of X 32–38
cost of X 145
cultural interaction during X 197–203
definition of X 123–131
disillusionment with X 64–70
economic motives X 71–78
Markward of Anweiler X 225
Western imperialism X 300–306
Fifth X 64, 87–96, 112, 130, 139, 144, 167, 170, 173, 177–178, 189, 239, 255, 262, 294
First X 13–23, 25–26, 29, 33, 35–36, 51, 60, 65, 71–72, 75, 81, 88, 97–106, 117–119, 122, 125, 127–129, 135, 137, 143, 148–150, 153, 158, 163–164, 168, 171, 173–174, 177, 190–191, 194–200, 208–221, 224, 231–233, 236, 238–239, 255–256, 263, 265, 267, 272, 274, 279–292, 295–298; XIV 187
First Crusade of Louis IX X 64, 69, 112, 139–147, 167, 170, 173

INDEX

Fourth X 24, 26–30, 33, 87–88, 92, 107–114, 126, 128, 130, 148–149, 156, 167, 209, 239, 255, 262, 291, 297
impact of ribats X 158–166
impact on modern world X 55–63
impact on the papacy X 204–210
Jews in X 13–23
Military Orders X 158–166
military strategy X 167–175
missionay activity X 176–181
Mongols X 112, 182–189
motivation X 71–78, 97–106
of 1101 X 112
of 1128 X 112
of Frederick II X 112
of Pope Boniface VIII X 266
of the Poor X 38
origins of X 115–122
Peasants' X 213, 219
People's X 13, 19, 101–102, 112, 234
Political X 223–229
Popular X 32–38, 100, 231–240
Second X 13, 16–17, 24, 33, 48, 74, 92, 128, 130, 150, 167–168, 174, 179, 207, 225, 255–256, 265, 294, 296–297; XI 20
Second Crusade of Louis IX X 66, 68, 112, 139–147
Seventh X 64, 69
Shepherds' X 14, 32–38, 141–142, 231, 233, 239
Sixth X 112
Spain X 241–246
Third X 16–17, 24, 26–29, 47, 52, 57, 59, 77, 88, 107, 116, 127, 141, 144, 151, 153, 168, 174, 195, 249, 251, 252, 254–263, 277, 294, 297
traditionalsit-pluralist debate X 223, 236, 264–271
treatment of Jews by X 238
vow redemption X 291–299
Cry, the Beloved Country XIX 38
CSX Corporation XIII 197–198
Cuba I 51, 53, 68, 89, 91, 94, 96, 98, 125, 292; VI 35, 50, 63–68, 77, 141–142, 182, 188, 213, 246, 249, 261, 271; IX 96; XIII 104; XIV 40, 193, 250; XV 49, 81, 228, 253; XVI 41; XIX 128
Bay of Pigs invasion (1961) I 66, 70, 89, 92, 94, 129; II 115, 247, 266; VI 131; XIX 146
blockade of VI 72
campaign to attract African American tourists XIX 14
Castro takeover I 17; XIX 14, 146, 276
CIA plot XV 157
emancipation in XIII 36
exiles VI 64
exports to Soviet Union VI 249
imperialism I 151
Jewish refugees XI 4, 93
maroons in XIII 105, 108, 110
nuclear missiles in VI 70–71
policy in Angola VI 165
receives aid from Soviet Union I 275
relations with the United States VI 70–76
revolution of 1959 I 18, 20, 125; VI 63
slave revolts XIII 91, 154
slave trade XIII 272–273
slavery in XIII 90, 94, 269
Soviet subsidies VI 249
Soviet missiles in XVI 95
Soviet troops in VI 70
support for MPLA VI 1
support for revolutions VI 64
support for Third World VI 63
threat to stability in Central America I 49
troops in Africa VI 2, 4, 249
troops in Angola VI 1, 7, 41, 43
troops in Ethiopia VI 41
troops in Grenada VI 221
troops overseas VI 65
U.S. intervention (1898) I 125
U.S. policy toward XIX 141–142
Cuban Communist Party I 91–93
Cuban Liberty and Democratic Solidarity (Libertad) Act. *See* Helms-Burton bill
Cuban Missile Crisis (1962) I 49, 92–94, 98, 102, 125, 131, 168, 183–184, 230, 294; II 66, 117, 120, 257, 265; VI 30–31, 36, 42, 50, 64, 66, 70–76, 101–104, 139, 142, 174, 262; XV 219; XVI 156, 158, 254; XIX 18, 146
Cuito Canavale, battle of (1987) VI 7
Cullen, Countee III 79, 234–236
Cultural and Intellectual Conference for World Peace (Waldorf Conference). See Waldorf Conference
Cultural and Scientific Conference for World Peace XIX 238
Cumming v. *County Board of Education* (1899) XIII 53
Cunene River VII 236–237, 239, 240, 242
Curagh Mutiny (1914) VIII 161
Currency Act (1764) XII 232, 236
Currie, Arthur IX 33
Currie, Lauchlin XIX 17, 52, 58, 62, 197–198, 231
Curtin, John XIX 266
Curzon, George (Marguis Curzon of Kedleston) IX 83
"Custodial Detention List" XIX 176
Cuyahoga River VII 116, 118, 123, 265
Cvetic, Matt XIX 201
Cvetkovic, Dragisa XVI 100
cyanide, effects of VII 247, 253
Cyprus VI 135; X 30, 67, 140–141, 146, 256; XIV 235, 265; XV 79, 217
Jewish refugees XI 124
sugar cane in XIII 167
Czech Republic VI 217; XVI 77, 98
Czechoslovak (Sudeten) Crisis (1938) XVI 220–221, 225
Czechoslovak Legion XVI 6, 34
Czechoslovakia I 109–110, 112, 277, 293–294, 303; II 9; VI 103, 110, 119, 131, 133, 165–166, 178, 217, 227, 237, 246, 249, 251–252, 261, 274, 276; IX 93, 136, 272; XI 14–15, 56, 68, 86, 110, 167, 178–179, 207; XV 68, 70, 120; XVI 8, 11–14, 58, 76, 99–104, 114–115, 118–119, 123–124, 127, 157, 213, 220, 233, 238, 285, 289, 292, 294
after World War II XIX 2
appeal of Marshall Plan I 178
arms shipment to Guatemala (1954) I 49, 123, 126
attempted alliance with France VI 255
dams in VII 100
fascism XVII 140
frontiers recognized VIII 283
Germany annexes border districts VIII 284
human rights abuses I 146
Munich Agreement (1938) I 300
National Council XVI 34
National Front XVI 124
nationalism XVII 167
occupation of VIII 284; XIX 88
overthrow of communist regime XVI 282
Police Coup XVI 271
political changes in VII 101
secret service XIX 272
Soviet coup (1948) I 173, 182, 185; XIX 2, 215, 245, 248, 271–272
Soviet invasion (1968) I 11–12, 218; VI 43, 116, 182, 249; XIV 2; XVI 288; XVII 231; XIX 146
Ukrainian Ruthenians in XVI 101
Czerniakow, Adam XI 139–142
Czernin, Ottokar XVI 195

D

Dachau (concentration camp) XI 13, 45, 148, 151–152, 170, 213, 220, 222, 224, 232, 236, 255–256, 260
Dahomey XIII 11

famine in XIII 38
slave trade XIII 39, 40
Daily Worker XIX 38–39, 41, 191, 197, 202, 248, 258, 273
coverage of race relations XIX 189
role in integrating Major League baseball XIX 76–77
Dakar, Vichy forces in XVI 300
Daladier, Edouard V 116; XVI 8, 11–12, 115, 117, 118
appeasement policy IV 20
The Dalles Dam (United States) VII 29, 51–61
The Dalles-Celilo Canal VII 52, 56–57
Dalmatia IX 136, 208; XVI 36
enslavement of Dalmatians XIII 167
Damascus VIII 39, 41; IX 72; X 51, 77, 167, 172, 196, 305; XV 275
Damietta X 60, 87, 90, 92, 95, 139–140, 145–146, 262
Damodar Valley VII 130, 132
Damodar Valley Corporation VII 127, 132
Dams VII 1–9, 14, 25–32, 51–61, 100–107, 125–134, 196, 236–246
benefits of VII 1, 28
breaching of VII 31, 221, 224, 226
fish VII 53, 196–203
hydroelectric energy VII 226
political economy of VII 129
Danbury Baptist Association XII 62
Dandalo, Enrico X 107, 149, 152
Danish West India Company XIII 274
Dante XI 129; XIII 262
Danube River VII 100, 101–104, 106, 204–207, 209–210, 247, 250, 253, 255; XVI 36
Danzig VIII 280–281; XI 179; XVI 294
Dardanelles VIII 38, 80, 117–123, 212, 214, 216; IX 114, 207; X 15; XVI 185; XIX 145, 249
Darrow, Clarence III 32–34, 37–39
relationship with NAACP III 186
Scopes Trial III 33
Darwin, Charles III 32–33; VIII 93; XI 17–18; XVII 174, 254
Dassin, Jules XIX 164
Davenport, James XII 148
Davidic dynasty (tenth century B.C.E.) XIV 163
Davidiz, Sisnando X 2, 41
Davies, John Paton VI 158; XIX 18, 21, 23
Davies, Joseph E. XIX 237
Davis, Benjamin J., Jr. XIX 103, 260
Davis Sr., Benjamin O., Sr. IX 7
Davis, Jefferson XIII 270, 274, 277
Davis, Miles XIX 48
Dawes, Charles VIII 285
Dawes Plan (1924) IV 270; V 119; VIII 298; IX 92, 171; XVI 148, 296; XVII 116, 121
Dawes Severalty Act (1887) III 140–143; VII 166, 167, 168, 171
Day, Nathaniel XII 48
Dayan, Moshe XV 23–24, 136, 221–222
Dayton Accords (1995) II 100, 154; XVI 57, 60; XVII 149
D-Day (6 June 1944) VI 168, 251
Dead Reckoning XIX 44
Deane, Silas XII 79, 100, 102–103, 105–106
Déat, Marcel XVI 142
De Bow, J. D. B. XIII 28, 101
De Bow's Review XIII 86
Debs, Eugene V. II 196; III 151, 175, 208, 222–223, 234; XIX 194
Decatur, Stephen XVI 70
Declaration of Independence (1776) VI 9; XII 18, 32, 34, 46, 54–55, 69, 71, 108–116, 118, 120, 129–131, 134, 136–137, 140, 143, 171, 191, 215, 235, 261–262, 265, 277, 282, 293, 314; XIII 18–19, 23, 147, 156, 272
Declaration of Paris (1856) VIII 136
Declaration of Punta del Este (1961) I 17
Declaration of St. James XI 261
Declaration of the Rights of Man and Citizen (1789) XII 130, 131, 265; XIII 156
Declaration on Liberated Europe (1945) XVI 122, 125, 127, 224
Declaratory Act (1720) XII 246
Declaratory Act (1766) XII 57, 141, 233, 237, 239–240
Decolonization VI 264; XVI 65
effects of on Third World VI 83
The Deer Park XIX 48
Defense Intelligence Agency (DIA) XV 86
NIE reports VI 257
Soviet military strength VI 259
Defense of the Realm Act (1914) VIII 158; IX 58; XVI 173
Defense Policy Board XIV 97
Defense Readiness Condition (DEFCON) VI 163
Deism XII 151
de Kooning, Willem XIX 45
Delaware XII 70, 78, 175–176, 306
ratification of Constitution XII 74
Delaware River XII 271
Delbo, Charlotte XI 222–223
Deliberate Prose XIX 49
Demerara (Guyana) XIII 190
slave revolts XIII 154, 159, 231
Democratic Front for the Liberation of Palestine (DFLP) XIV 195; XV 95
Democratic National Committee (DNC) XIX 227
headquarters broken into VI 24
Democratic National Convention
(1964) II 28, 161–163
(1968) II 162, 180; VI 25; XIX 65, 226
Democratic Party II 49, 162–165, 180, 194–195, 198, 257; III 191–195; XIII 21, 56, 99, 222, 276, 281–283; XIX 85, 91–97, 173, 246, 249, 251
association with labor movement II 187–192; XIX 73
Commonweath Federation XIX 103
Mississippi Freedom Democratic Party II 28, 161, 197
relationship with African Americans III 118
Democratic Republic of Vietnam. *See* North Vietnam
Demosthenes XX 89–96
Deng Xiaoping VI 4, 42, 44, 204
visits United States VI 43
denaturalization XIX 211–219
Denikin, Anton XVI 2, 5
Denmark VIII 280, 283–284; IX 171, 225; XI 176; XIV 31; XVI 84, 114–115, 212–214, 272, 319
homicides XVII 270
Iceland's secession from XIV 171
Jewish rescue in WWII XI 175
Jews XVI 305
monarchy XVI 178, 180–181
slave trade XIII 270
Social Democratic movement XVII 28
social welfare XVII 269
"Denmark Vesey" XIX 41
Dennis, Eugene XIX 151, 252, 258, 260
Dennis v. *United States* XIX 149–153, I 78–179, 256, 259, 262, 271
deoxyribonucleic acid (DNA) II 82–85
Department of Commerce and Labor, Bureau of Corporations III 242
Department of Defense I 74, 83
Department of Energy VI 257
Department of State I 83
deportation XIX 148–149, 151, 174, 201, 211–219, 245, 246
Derby Scheme IX 58
Der Ewige Jude (The Eternal Jew, 1940) XI 269
Der Hauptmann von Kopenick (The Captain from Kopenick, 1930) IX 84
Der Rosenkavalier (1911) IX 84
Der Stürmer XI 24, 185, 254
Desert Storm (1991) VI 28
de Silva, Howard XIX 166
Dessalines, Jean-Jacques XIII 209–210, 213
assassinated XIII 213
d'Estaing, Valéry Giscard VI 104; XVI 131

Destouches, Louis-Ferdinand (Louis-Ferdinand Celine) IX 84
détente I 11, 52, 101–106, 140–143; II 56, 60, 63, 118, 168, 170–174; VI 2, 21, 32–33, 35, 41, 65, 68, 88, 103, 112, 116, 164–166, 202–204, 209, 229, 232, 237–238, 256–257, 270; XIV 2; XVI 156, 158
deterrence theory VI 31
Detroit Loyalty Commission XIX 184
Detroit riots VI 141
Detroit Subversive Activities Squad XIX 184
Dew, Thomas Roderick XIII 71, 73
Dewey, John XIX 113, 104, 191
Dewey, Thomas E. I 60, 272; II 280; XIX 92, 152, 241
DeWitt, John L. III 103, 106, 109; V 184, 187
Diablo Canyon VII 178
Diagne, Blaise IX 113
The Dial XIX 46
Diamond Necklace Affair (1785) XII 131
Diamond Workers Protection Union XIX 218
Diana, Princess of Wales XVI 178
Diary of Anne Frank, The (1959) XI 155, 158
Díaz, Porfirio III 125, 127
Diaz de Vivar, Rodrigo (el Cid) X 2, 41, 245
dichlorodiphenyltrichloroethane (DDT) VII 147, 234
Dickey, James IX 234
Dickinson, Goldsworthy IX 172
Dickinson, John XII 54, 70, 95, 113, 214, 233
Dickie, A. M. XIX 268
Diderot, Denis X 80
Dies, Martin Jr. XI 57; XIX 61, 116, 119, 133, 246
Dies Committee. *See* House Special Committee to Investigate Un-American Activities
Dietrich, Marlene XI 158
Dillinger, John XIX 175, 177
Dimitrov, Georgi Mikhailovich VI 275, 280
Dinosaur National Monument, Colorado VII 27, 29, 112
Dinwiddie, Robert XII 199
Directive 21 XI 82
Dismal Swamp XIII 104, 107, 157
Disney, Walt XIX 251
Displaced Persons (DPs) XI 122–124, 126
Disqualifying Act XII 291
Disraeli, Benjamin VIII 168; IX 98–99, 112; X 57, 59
Dissenters XII 235
Distributive, Processing and Office Workers Union XIX 183
District of Columbia
signs the Chesapeake Bay 2000 Agreement VII 49
Division of Tobacco, Alcohol and Firearms XIX 182
Dixiecrats VI 142; XIX 30
Djibouti XIV 55
Djilas, Milovan VI 275, 278, 280–281
Dmytryk, Edward XIX 164, 168–169
Dobruja IX 205
Dobrynin, Anatoly VI 41, 163
Dr. Strangelove or How I Learned to Stop Worrying and Love the Bomb (1964) I 236; VI 31
Doctors' Trial (1946–1949) XI 147–148
Doctrine of World Empires IX 112
Dodacanese Islands VIII 212
Dodd, Christopher J. VI 194
Dodd, Thomas XII 29
Dole, Robert XV 78
Dome of the Rock XIV 19, 22, 159, 165
Dominica XII 311, 313–314
maroons in XII 314
Dominican Republic I 15, 24, 71, 91, 94, 125; III 247; VI 66, 140, 266; IX 96
rumored coup in VI 140
U.S. troops in (1965) VI 140, 165–166
Dominicans X 65; XI 23
domino theory I 130, 266–267, 295–299; II 119, 266–267; XIX 96, 128, 224
Donatism X 17
controversy XX 221–230
Dongamusi area, Zimbabwe VII 64
Dönitz, Karl V 3, 79–85, 143, 256–257, 262; XI 254, 258, 262
Donovan, William XIX 63
Donzère-Mondragon Dam (France) VII 93, 95
Doolittle, James C. "Jimmy" V 92, 98–99
Doolittle Raid (1942) V 3
Doriot, Jacques XVI 141–142
Dornier, Claudius IX 218
Dorsey, Tommy IX 4
Dos Passos, John III 182, 234–237; IX 4
Dostoyevsky, Fyodor XI 75; XVII 91, 253–254, 258
Double V campaign XIX 25
Douglas, Helen Gahagan XIX 92, 224
Douglas, Stephen A. XIII 18, 173
Douglas, William O. II 284; III 105; XII 64; XIX 149–150, 152, 256, 263, 288
Douglass, Frederick XIII 3, 9, 83, 113, 116, 124, 204, 234
Douhet, Giulio IX 220, 223
Doullens Conference (1918) IX 108
Downey, Sheridan VII 153, 156
Down's Syndrome XI 17
Downtown Community School, New York City XIX 191
Doyle, Clyde XIX 62
draft resistance movement II 4, 6
"Draft Resolution for the 16th National Convention of the Communist Party, U.S.A." (1956) XIX 191
Drakensburg Mountains VII 236
Drayton, William Henry XII 68
Dreadnought (British ship) IX 141, 179; XVI 26
Dred Scott v. *Sandford* (1857) II 280; III 28; XII 263; XIII 57, 95, 100
Dresden, bombing of V 5, 54, 88, 221; XVI 254, 256
Dresden (German ship) VIII 133, 137
Dresdner Bank VII 250
Drexil Institute IX 21
Dreyfus, Alfred VIII 68, 147, 149, 168
Dreyfus Affair VI 136; VIII 68, 146–147, 149, 151–152, 164; XVII 197, 201
Drieu La Rochelle, Pierre XVI 142
Druid Hill Park, Baltimore, Maryland XIX 192
Du Bois, W. E. B. II 44, 46, 137; III 84, 117–118, 120–123, 182, 267–274; IX 2–3, 5; XIII 54, 95, 202, 204; XIX 24, 30, 234
and CAA XIX 29
and CPUSA XIX 80, 128, 242
as peace activist XIX 240, 242
criticism of Marshall Plan XIX 12
editor of *The Crisis* XIX 30
expelled from NAACP XIX 10, 12, 30
helps to organize 1924 All-Race Conference XIX 189
indicted as unregistered foreign agent XIX 128, 242
investigated by the FBI XIX 176
passport denied XIX 242
Dual Alliance VIII 73
Dual Monarchy VIII 43–47, 76; IX 133–134, 136; XVI 36, 175
Dubai XIV 34
Dubcek, Alexander VI 119
Dubinsky, David XIX 185
Duclos, Jacques XIX 213
Duggan, Lawrence XIX 63
Duhamel, Georges IX 212
Dulany, Daniel XII 58, 139
Dulles, Allen I 71, 130; II 50; XV 61, 158
ties to United Fruit Company I 126; XIX 141
Dulles, John Foster I 49, 69, 130, 149, 267–274, 278, 282; II 50–51, 135, 168, 208; VI 130, 153, 221, 268; XIV 177; XV 14, 26, 30–31, 58–64, 158, 168, 205, 245, 249, 271; XVI 236; XIX 27, 141, 198
"massive retaliation" policy I 192, 211, 213
New Look policy I 117, 211, 214; XIX 124

Northern Tier approach XV 26, 31, 59
U.S. policies in Europe I 208
Dumbarton Oaks conference XIX 63
Dunkirk evacuation (1940) V 123
Dunkirk Treaty (1947) I 208; VI 210
Dunne, Philip XIX 160
Du Pont Corporation IX 22
Duportail, Louis Lebègue de Presle XII 106
Duran, Gustave XIX 62
Durance River VII 98
Durnovo, Petr XVI 50–51
Durocher, Leo XIX 76
Durr, Virginia XIX 241
Durruti, Buenaventura XVIII 26, 159, 161, 332
Dust Bowl VII 181, 183, 185
Dutch East Indies VIII 137
Dutch Middleburg Company XIII 136, 269, 274
Dutch Reformers XII 235
Dutch West India Company XIII 274
Duvalier, François "Papa Doc" XI 167
Duwamish River VII 189, 191
Dyer, Reginald IX 93
Dyer Bill IX 4
Dylan, Bob XIX 35, 50
Dzhugashvili, Iosef IX 197

E

Eaker, Ira C. V 5, 98
Earl of Sandwich XII 36
Earth Day VII 123, 265
East Africa VIII 193
bombing of U.S. embassies in (1998) XIV 12
East Asian Studies XIX 110
East Germany I 107, 274; VI 110–111, 115–122, 141, 178, 182, 206–212, 217, 246, 249, 251, 261, 276; XI 214; XVI 77, 95, 124, 284–285, 289; XVII 2, 67, 70, 72, 81, 132, 200, 216, 221; XIX 145
defectors VI 170
dissidents in VI 117, 121, 211
Dulles acceptance of Soviet influence I 273
flight of citizens VI 141
political parties in VI 121
reforms I 154
relations with Soviet Union I 253
revolt against totalitarianism (1953) I 254; XIX 146, 215
shift in leadership VI 117
Soviet suspicion of I 185
strategic importance I 109
East India Company XII 197, 200, 234, 237; XIII 271; XVI 70
East Indies XVI 84
East Jerusalem XIV 19, 154, 157, 160, 162–163; XV 20–21, 42, 79, 134, 136, 183, 190–191, 194–195, 215, 219, 226
East Prussia VIII 249, 252, 280; IX 15, 158
East St. Louis, riot IX 7
East Timor, Indonesian invasion of VI 270
Easter Rising (1916) VIII 154–162, 209; IV 21; XVI 244
Eastern Europe VI 116, 120, 131, 148, 181, 201, 207–208, 221, 224, 226, 236, 251, 267, 281; VII 250; IV 81, 83; X 62, 67, 130, 178, 180–182, 206, 265, 301; XIV 2, 6, 82, 110, 112; XV 33, 253; XVI 41, 45, 92, 111, 121–122, 124–125, 157, 176, 226, 228–230, 233, 254, 264; XIX 180
after World War II XIX 1–2, 22
collapse of communist regimes in VII 101; XVI 281–289
collapse of Soviet control in VI 216
Crusades in X 66, 128, 270
democracies in XV 82
dissident movements in VI 229
environmental crisis in VII 17–24
fascism in XVI 141
German occupation (World War I) VIII 91–101, 176
German occupation (World War II) VIII 91–101
NATO expansion in VI 54
political repression in VII 18
punishment of former communists XVII 213–221
removal of Soviet forces VI 110
Soviets block Marshall Plan to VI 255
Soviets in VI 244–245, 250, 252; XIX 57, 116–117, 123, 132, 145–146, 156, 195, 237, 248–249
state development after WWI XVI 99–105
treatment of refugees VI 251
U.S. support of dissidents in VI 3
voter apathy on environmental issues VII 20
Eastern Orthodox Church VIII 207; X 25, 190, 208; XVI 30; XVI 60
Eastland, James XIX 31
Easton, James XII 11
Eban, Abba XV 135, 213, 217
Eberharter, Herman XIX 101
Ebert, Friedrich VIII 257, 280; IX 32; XVI 151, 176
Ebro River VII 147
Echo Park Dam (United States) VII 27, 29, 30–31
Economic Commission for Latin America (ECLA) I 20–22
Economic Market of the Southern Cone (Mercosur) XIV 71
Economic Opportunity Act (1964) II 276
Economic Opportunity Act (1965) II 272
Ecuador XIII 104; XIV 212, 217
Eden, Anthony I 272, 280; V 41, 290, 312; VI 11; XV 160, 247; XVI 233, 237–238, 240
"Mansion Speech" (1941) XV 146
Edessa X 48, 74, 92, 129–130, 167, 191, 270, 296–297
Edison, Thomas Alva VIII 197
Edmondson, W. T. VII 189, 192
Education, influence of Communists and anti-Communists in XIX 107–115
Education, Communist influence in XIX 107–115
Education and Liberty XIX 113–114
Edward I X 189
Edward VII (England) X 57; XVI 193
Edward VIII (England) XVI 179, 181
Edwards, Jonathan XII 147–149
Edwards Aquifer VII 69–75
Egypt I 308–312, 273, 283; II 53; VI 11, 83, 137, 162–164, 172, 246, 271–27; VII 29, 82, 135, 149; VIII 31–32, 38, 168, 213; IX 96; X 24, 30, 46–51, 56, 60, 64, 66, 78, 89, 95, 107, 109, 139–142, 144–148, 155–156, 167, 170, 173–174, 182, 185, 187, 193, 239, 248, 251, 255–258, 273, 277, 282, 287, 292; XII 165, 168; XIV 7, 23, 31, 34, 52, 55–56, 61, 68, 79, 81–83, 85, 88, 105, 114, 116, 134, 141, 143, 146–149, 154, 176–183, 186, 190, 193–195, 197–201, 206, 217, 220, 225, 228, 235, 242, 252, 255, 282; XV 12, 14, 19–23, 27, 30–34, 40, 42, 45, 51–57, 58–59, 61–62, 73, 79, 81, 100–101, 116, 127, 134–137, 141–146, 150, 166, 168–169, 176, 184–185, 199, 204, 206–207, 213, 216, 219–220, 223, 226–227, 238–241, 254, 257, 261, 275; XVI 23, 80–81, 84, 88, 98, 136, 236, 269
Arab Republic of Egypt XV 223
Arab Socialist Union XV 70
Arab-Israeli War (1967) II 150
arms XV 68
Aswan Dam II 146, 148; VII 3; XVI 238
attack on Israel VI 10, 161, 163
attacks on tourists XIV 191
bankruptcy (1882) XVI 66
boycotts XIV 50
Central Security Forces XV 224
conflict with Israel I 159
Coptic Christians XV 276
corruption in XIV 48
cotton and textile exports XIV 45

deportation of Jews VIII 166
economy XIV 47, 51, 54
education XIV 52
environmental control in VII 145
expels Soviet advisers XV 220, 223, 240
Free Officers' regime II 148; XIV 193
Free Officers Revolution (1952) XV 59, 63, 65–70, 101, 119, 220, 226, 244, 249
Great Britain in VIII 35
Hadeto (Democratic Movement for National Liberation) XV 69
Jewish spying in XIV 129
July Laws (1961) XV 70
Kafara Dam VII 3
labor XIV 52
Marxists in XV 69
National Assembly XV 56, 222
National Union Party XV 273
nuclear weapons development I 219
relations with United States XIV 16
Revolutionary Command Council (RCC) XV 66, 68, 70
Soviet alliance I 161; II 146; VI 43, 81
Soviet arms XV 40, 253
Soviet-Egyptian Pact (1955) I 162
Suez Canal I 308, 316
Suez Crisis I 289; VI 135, 270; XVI 235–242
Suez War I 277, 280; XV 244–251, 253
Sunni Muslims XV 276
United Arab Republic (UAR) XV 70, 147, 270–276
U.S. resistance to return of Soviet troops VI 163
U.S. support for authoritarian regime XIV 14
Wafd Party XV 69
water XIV 269–271
weapons XIV 144
Western Desert Project VII 2
women XIV 116, 119, 121, 287, 291
World War I VIII 37–42
Young Egypt XV 70
Egyptian Center for Women Rights XIV 116
Egyptian Communist Party XV 69
Egyptian Space Channel (ESC) XIV 29
Egyptian-Israeli Armistice Agreement (1949) XV 247
Egyptian-Israeli peace treaty (1979) XIV 19, 116, 125, 145, 154; XV 20, 51–57, 104, 127, 130, 133, 149, 187, 219, 227, 238, 241, 255
Ehrlichman, John D. VI 24
Eicher, Edward C. XIX 258
Eichmann, Adolf XI 36–43, 51, 75, 103, 158, 211, 227, 233
Einsatzgruppen (mobile killing units) IV 88, 131, 134, 141; V 161; XI 14, 86, 90–91, 102, 108, 171, 250; XIX 241
Einstein, Albert VIII 167; IX 87
Eisenhower, Dwight D. I 35, 64, 71, 92, 102, 210–215, 274, 292, 297, 306; II 38, 45, 49–55, 64, 67, 105–106, 112, 135, 137, 200, 229, 232, 260, 280; IV 183; V 314, 92, 69, 281, 284; VI 11, 17, 35, 64, 86, 96, 130, 133, 136, 139, 153, 155, 231; IX 108–109; XI 123–124, 252, 257; XII 31, 303; XIV 177; XV 26, 30–31, 135, 137, 165, 167–169, 245, 249–250, 271; XVI 92, 237–240, 271; XIX 140, 186
and *Brown* v. *Board of Education* XIX 26
and civil rights XIX 24, 27, 31
appeal to Soviets VI 135
appoints Dulles Secretary of State XIX 198
appoints Warren chief justice of the Supreme Court XIX 152
as president of Columbia University XIX 110
at Geneva summit XIX 15, 123
Atoms for Peace I 216–217; II 49, 53
Battle of the Bulge IV 64
Bay of Pigs invasion II 52, 54, 115
Berlin crisis I 69
"Chance for Peace" speech II 53
dealings with de Gaulle VI 105
Eisenhower Doctrine (1957) I 280–282; II 148; XIV 177; XV 14, 58–64, 166, 168–169, 250, 271
foreign policy of VI 141
Interstate Highway Act II 105
issues EO 10450 XIX 132–133, 138–139
Korea VI 146
loyal-security program of XIX 132–133, 138–139, 175
military career IV 65
NATO commander-general I 208
1952 presidential campaign I 274
Open Skies policy II 51, 54; VI 20, 35
planning D-Day invasion IV 68
relationship with Nixon XIX 99, 224
restraint in use of nuclear weapons I 236–237
rollback policy I 72
sends envoy to mediate Middle East water dispute VII 138
space program II 242, 260
Suez Crisis VI 80
summit with Macmillan VI 10
support of U.S. involvement in Korea II 211
Supreme Allied Commander II 50
System of Interstate and Defense Highways II 109
Taiwan policy I 68
vetos rivers-and-harbors legislation VII 259
views on academic freedom XIX 110
WWI service VIII 192
WWII strategy in Germany VI 169
Eisenhower administration I 49, 66, 94, 110, 117, 281; VI 30, 56, 81, 92, 95, 139, 149, 238; VII 259
"atomic diplomacy" I 211, 213, 267
Atoms for Peace policy I 216
concern over Soviet Middle East policy VI 239
containment policy I 184
defense spending VI 144
Dulles, John Foster I 278
East Germany policy I 271
Eisenhower Doctrine I 282; XV 14, 166, 168–169, 250, 271
Hungarian uprising VI 13
Iran XV 108, 157
Middle East policy I 161; XV 30, 58–64, 68, 156, 165–170, 271, 273
military spending I 69, 192
New Look policy I 210–215, 266; XV 26
Nixon as vice president VI 203
policy on Cuba VI 141
refuses to recognize Castro VI 64
rejection of arms control I 230
"rollback" strategy VI 221
Social Progress Trust Fund I 20
Suez Crisis VI 11; XV 244–251; XVI 236
Taiwan policy I 266, 268, 270
Vietnam policy I 293, 297; VI 10
Eisler, Gerhart XIX 214, 225
Eisman, Julius (pseud. of Gerhart Eisler) XIX 225
Ekkehard of Aura X 15, 72, 97, 99, 213
Eksteins, Modris IX 87
El Dorado XIII 147
El Niño VII 201–202, 212
El Salvador I 48, 51, 53, 56, 94, 141; II 58, 103; VI 190, 194, 221, 266, 270; XIV 198; XIX 14
CIA covert operations I 26
human rights violations in VI 241
marxist guerrillas in VI 193
relations with Nicaragua I 50, 54
U.S. role in I 15
Elbe River VI 251
Elegists XX 231–237
Elektra (1909) IX 84
Elgin Marbles XX 97–105
Eliot, T. S. XIX 46
Elitcher, Max XIX 286
Elizabeth (Queen Mother, England) XVI 178

Elizabeth I VIII 168; IX 43; XII 137
Elizabeth II (England) XVI 178, 180–183, 245
Elkins thesis XIII 138, 142, 144
Ellington, Duke II 214; III 78–79; IX 4; XIX 9, 46
Elliot, E. N. XIII 30, 96
Elliott, E. V. XIX 270
Ellis Island XIX 225
Ellison, Ralph XIII 259
Ellsberg, Daniel VI 24, 26; XX 128
Ellsworth, Oliver XII 66
Emalia (Schindler's enamel factory) XI 203, 207–208
Emancipation Act (1833) XIII 154–155, 160
Emancipation Proclamation (1862) XII 168; XIII 5, 276
Emden (German ship) VIII 132–136
Emergency Committee of Atomic Scientists XIX 241
Emerson, Ralph Waldo XIII 32, 146
Emerson, Thomas I. XIX 202
Emich of Leiningen X 13, 15, 17, 19, 21–22, 275, 277; XI 23
Emmanuel III (Italy) XVI 182
Empire Zinc XIX 202
The Emperor Jones XIX 35
Endangered Species Act VII 202, 211, 215, 223, 226
Endangered Species Committee VII 224, 227
Endrin VII 160–165
Enfield Rifle IX 24
Enforcement Acts (1870–1871) XIII 55
Engel v. *Vitale* (1962) II 281
Engels, Friedrich VI 176, 281; XIII 69; XVII 32, 52, 66, 73, 160; XIX 199, 261
English Channel VIII 29, 35, 75, 134, 182, 287; IX 41; XII 39, 48, 79, 107; XVI 213
English Civil War (1642–1646) XII 34
Enlightenment X 61, 80, 123, 129; XI 29, 77, 79, 94; XII 1, 132, 153, 303; XIII 2, 17, 21, 62; XVII 6, 21, 40, 88, 159–160, 162, 174, 176, 180, 182, 200, 203, 253–254
Enola Gay V 50–53
Entente IX 122, 124, 265; XVI 308, 312
Entente Cordiale (1904) VIII 33, 35, 226; IX 226; XVI 23, 24, 193
Environmental Defense Fund VII 274
environmental impact assessment (EIA) studies VII 128
environmental movement
  contribution to collapse of Soviet bloc VII 17–24
  in Estonia VII 17–24
  in Poland VII 17–24
  in the United States VII 31
environmental policy VII 175
Environmental Protection Agency (EPA) II 183; VII 123, 263, 266
environmentalists
  fight U.S. dams VII 113
Episcopal Church XII 66, 263
  slave religion XIII 186
Epupa Dam (Namibia) VII 237, 239, 242–143
Equal Employment Opportunity Commission (EEOC) II 182
Equal Pay Act (1963) II 192
Equal Rights Amendment (ERA) II 72, 78–80, 163, 224
Equatorial Africa VIII 31
Equiano, Olaudah XIII 15, 131, 133, 273
Erasmus XI 23
Erhard, Ludwig VI 210
Eritrea VI 165; XIV 171, 176
Escobedo, Danny II 284
Escobedo v. *Illinois* (1964) II 281
Eshkol, Levi XV 23–24, 135–136
Esmeralda (mining company) VII 248, 250, 254
espionage, measures against XIX 211–219
Espionage Act (1917) III 223, 229, 234; XIX 246, 285, 288
espionage penalities XIX 282
Estates-General XII 127, 129, 131, 133–134
Estonia VI 178; VIII 93–94, 96–97; IX 93; X 179; XI 260; XVI 18, 218
  annexed by Soviet Union VII 22; XIX 143
  environmental activism in VII 17–24
  first national park VII 22
Estonian Nature Conservation Society VII 22
Estonian Writers' Union VII 23
Ethiopia VI 4, 63, 68, 188, 261, 271; IX 96, 175; XIV 176–177, 198; XV 271; XVI 13, 110, 219
  African American interest in XIX 12
  claim to Ogaden VI 165
  Crisis (1935) IX 172
  Cuban troops in VI 41
  enslavement of Ethiopians XIII 167
  Italian invasion of XIX 12, 88
  relations with Soviet Union VI 165
  Somalia attack on VI 165
  water XIV 269–270
Ethiopian-Somali crisis VI 166
ethnic associations XIX 216
ethnic cleansing VI 211
Ethnikos Kyrix XIX 216
eugenics movement III 17–23
Eugenics Record Office (1910) III 18, 21
Eugenius III X 128–130, 225, 256, 265, 267, 270, 293, 295–297
Euphrates-Tigris Basin VII 76–84
Eurasia
  introduction of species from VII 217
Eureka, California VII 178
Euripides XX 106–113
Euro-Mediterranean Partnership XIV 114
Europe VII 206, 229; XII 252; XIV 135, 178, 187, 190, 201, 211, 242, 261; XV 15, 78, 202, 205, 252; XVI 44, 58, 87–88, 284
  anarchism XVI 244
  aristocracy in IX 81, 83
  backs Zionist settlements in Israel VII 136
  capitalism in VI 49
  colonialism XVI 64–71
  Crusades X 5, 32–33, 123, 135, 176, 190, 223–229, 281, 295
  demographic changes XVI 107
  demographic impact of World War I VIII 189
  eclipse of XVI 106–112
  Jews in X 274; XI 93
  market for African beef VII 33
  monarchy XVI 177–183
  patriarchal society in VIII 129
  racism in XIII 246
  serfs XIII 117
  servitude in XIII 249
  slavery in XIII 162, 165, 167
  support for World War I in VIII 125
  terrorism XVI 243–250
  twentieth-century disarmament XVI 90–98
  U.S. influence in XVI 266–272
  U.S. troops in VI 251
European Advisory Commission XVI 315
European Bank for Construction and Development VI 120
European Coal and Steel Community (ECSC) XVI 268, 270–271; XVII 57, 59–60
European Community (EC) I 108, 209; XIV 69, 72, 265
European Court VII 250
European Court of Human Rights XIV 173
European Economic Community (EEC) VI 13, 106, 209; VII 33, 36; XVI 155, 268, 271; XVII 13, 20–21, 23, 57, 60, 232
  Spain XVI 180
European Free Trade Association (EFTA) I 108
European Recovery Plan. *See* Marshall Plan
European Union (EU) VI 51, 53, 216–217, 219; VII 34, 37, 83, 100, 106, 143, 146–148, 207, 248, 250; XIV 17, 69–70, 72, 76, 100, 106, 114, 170, 173, 247; XVI 60, 74, 77, 108, 129, 155, 245, 250, 266–268, 272; XVII 13, 18, 21, 29, 57, 60, 83–84, 86, 129, 132, 149, 166–167, 170–171, 216, 233

Helsinki summit (1999) XIV 265
Turkey XIV 261–267
eutrophication VII 90, 148, 265
Evans, Walker XIX 46
Evatt, Herbert Vere XIX 268
Everglades VII 271
Everson v. *Board of Education* (1947) XII 64
Evert, Alexie IX 65, 243
Evian Accords (1962) XV 11, 18
Evian Conference (1938) XI 4, 55–64
Executive Committee of the National Security Council (ExComm) VI 70, 73
Executive Order 9066 III 105; V 183, 188–189
Executive Order 9835 XIX 91, 93, 96, 108, 131–133, 136–138, 251
Executive Order 10241 XIX 132–133, 138
Executive Order 10450 XIX 132–133
Existentialism XVII 74–79
Exodus XIX 281
Expressionist School IX 84
Exxon (Standard Oil of New Jersey) XIV 211–212; XV 172–173, 176, 179
Exxon *Valdez* oil spill (1989) II 86

F

Fabian Society XVI 24
A Face in the Crowd XIX 39
Fahd, King XIV 58, 62, 249
Faidherbe, Louis IX 114
Fair employment legislation XIX 9, 25
Fair Employment Practices Committee (1941) IV 218
Fairbanks, John XIX 202
Fairfax, Ferdinando XII 295
Faisal I VIII 37–39, 214; XV 136, 220
Faisal II XV 116
Falangists XVIII 54, 58–59, 72, 166, 277, 296
Falconbridge, Alexander XIII 131–132
Falin, Valentin VI 117, 119
Falkenhayn, Erich VIII 114, 213, 252, 266; XIX 65, 99, 207, 252–257, 263, 265
Falkland Islands VI 13; XVI 81
Falklands War (1983) VI 8; XVI 111
Fall, Albert III 127, 141, 178
False Witness XIX 202
Fanning, David XII 185
Farabundo Marti movement XIV 198
Farm Aid XIX 191
Farmer, James XIX 10
Farmer labor movement XIX 193
Farmer Labor Party II 197; XIX 103
The Farmer's Daughter XIX 163
Farmers' General XII 105
Farouk I XV 30, 66, 68, 70, 144
Fascism IV 77–84
  in France XVI 140–146
  international XVII 135–141
  origins XVII 180–187
Fashoda Incident (1898) VIII 33; XVI 23–24
Fast, Howard XIX 124
Fatah XIV 102–103, 152; XV 41, 44, 48–49, 90, 95, 132, 135, 152, 193, 195, 198–199
Fatah Tanzeem XIV 24, 26
  Shabiba committee XIV 26
Fatamids X 51, 274, 277, 287; XIV 201
Faubus, Orval II 20, 137, 140; XIX 24, 27
Faulk, John Henry XIX 281
Faw Peninsula XV 98
FB 111 bomber VI 259
FBI. *See* Federal Bureau of Investigation
FBI Counter-Intelligence Program (COINTELPRO). *See* Counter-Intelligence Program (COINTELPRO)
The FBI Story XIX 175
February Revolution (1917) VIII 171–173
fedayeen (guerrilla) XV 41–42, 44–47, 233
Federal Aid Highway Act (1956) II 109
Federal Aid Road Act (1916) II 106
Federal Bureau of Investigation (FBI) I 76, 292; II 5, 47; III 107; VI 24, 157, 257; XIV 14, 235; XIX 4, 53, 108
  and Nixon XIX 224
  asistance in HCUA investigations XIX 53, 60, 65–66, 121, 164, 173, 201, 251–252
  assistance to anticommunist groups XIX 183–184
  budgets XIX 117, 121
  compared to Binnenlandse Veilgheidsdienst XIX 269
  Domestic Intelligence Division XIX 30–31
  informants XIX 136, 155, 196–203, 248
  investigations
    Allen Ginsberg XIX 49
    antiwar activists XIX 128, 226, 275
    Amerasia case XIX 17–19, 61
    college and university students XIX 111
    Communists II 131; XIX 4, 6, 63, 65, 118, 121, 173–179, 182, 218, 225, 231, 245, 251, 258, 275
    civil rights movement XIX 25, 29, 31–32, 75, 78, 80–81
    Daily Worker readers XIX 273
    federal employees XIX 133, 136
    Jackie Robinson XIX 76l
    Labor movement XIX 73, 121
    National Lawyers Guild XIX 54
    Rosenberg case II 228, 231; XIX 282
    Smith Act trials XIX 53, 63, 252
    terrorism XIV 126
  NIE reports VI 25
  powers expanded XIX 120–121, 129, 181, 184
  treatment of spies II 231
  under Hoover XIX 173–179
  wiretapping I 77
  work with Scotland Yard on spy investigation XIX 163
Federal Bureau of Public Roads II 109
Federal Civil Defense Administration (FCDA), XIX 107, 114
Federal Communications Commission (FCC) II 123, III 55
Federal Deposit Insurance Corporation (FDIC) III 62, 152
Federal Emergency Management Agency VII 214
Federal Emergency Relief Administration (FERA, 1933) III 149, 159
Federal loyalty program XIX 31, 52, 91, 96, 108, 127, 131–139, 175, 182, 185, 204, 245, 249, 251, 276
Federal Occupational Safety and Health Act (1970) II 192
Federal Oil Pollution Control Act (1924) VII 41
Federal Power Commission VII 53
Federal Republic of Germany. *See* West Germany
Federal Reserve Board (FRB) III 57, 152, 207, 211
Federal Theatre Project XIX 119
Federal Water Pollution Control Administration VII 175
The Federalist (*Federalist* Papers) XII 19, 63, 74, 127
Federalists XII 19, 72–74, 119, 121–122, 277–278, 285–286, 288; XIII 281–282
Federated Clerks' Union (Australia) XIX 270
Federated Ironworkers' Association (Australia) XIX 270
Federation of Arab Republics (FAR) XIV 195
Federation of Bird Clubs of New England VII 277
Federation of Greek Maritime Unions XIX 218
Federman, Raymond XI 49, 53
Feklisov, Aleksandr II 228–229
  Soviet nuclear spying I 242
Fellowship of Reconciliation (FOR) XIX 31, 236–237, 242
Fellowship Society (Charles Town) XII 218
feminism II 72–81, 163–164
Fenian Rebellion (1867) VIII 161

Ferdinand I X 245; XIII 40
Ferdinand II X 2; XVI 212
Ferdinand, Franz VIII 43–44, 46, 49, 228; IX 99, 102, 225–227; XVI 27, 32, 36, 192, 196, 244, 249, 252
Ferguson, Patrick XII 187
Ferlinghetti, Lawrence XIX 50
Ferry, Jules IX 112; XVI 67
Fertile Crescent XIV 201; XV 142, 146, 275
Field, Noel VI 125–126; XIX 199
fifth column III 103–107, 252
Fifth Pan-African Congress, Manchester, England XIX 29
Figueiredo, Eulalia XIX 216
Fillmore, Millard XIII 195
film noir XIX 44
A Fine Old Conflict XIX 207
Final Solution IV 137–139; V 57–60; XI 10–14, 16, 18, 35, 37, 39, 71, 74–75, 77, 79, 81, 87–88, 91, 102–104, 107–108, 110–112, 116–118, 138, 144, 147, 156, 160, 164, 169, 175, 184, 186–189, 191, 208, 211, 217, 227, 246, 249, 265, 268, 270–271
  response of German churches IV 188
Finland I 110–112; II 34; VI 244, 255; 97, 101, 280; IX 175; XI 260; XV 215; XVI 18, 121–128, 185, 218, 224, 272, 296, 312, 319–320; XVII 156, 233
  Äänekoski mills VII 86–88
  environmental policies in VII 85–91
  fascism XVII 139
  invaded by Soviet Unions XIX 57, 143
  German submarine construction in VIII 285
  National Board of Waters VII 85
  People's Democratic Government XVI 224, 319
  War of Independence (1917–1919) XVI 125
Finland Station IX 196
Finlandization I 107–113, 151; XVI 121–128
Finnegans Wake XIX 40
Finney, Charles Grandison XIII 3
Finnish Americans XIX 121
Finnish Association for Nature Conservation (FANC) VII 86
Finnish Communists of the Great Lakes XIX 191
First Balkan War (1912) VIII 118; IX 204
First Church (Boston) XII 148
First Day Bombardment Group IX 11
First Indochina War (1946–1954) VI 98. *See* Vietnam War
First International Meeting of People Affected by Dams, Curitiba, Brazil VII 105
First Lateran Council (1123) X 128
First Moroccan Crisis (1905–1906) XVI 193
First Reform Bill (1832) XII 251
First South Carolina Volunteers XIII 53
First String Quartet (Carter) XIX 45
First West India Regiment XIII 157
Fish VII 215–216, 252
  hatcheries programs VII 201
  impact of dams on VII 219–228
  salmon VII 27, 29, 31, 51–61, 86, 90, 191, 196–203, 209, 219–228, 235
  trout VII 31, 87, 216, 219, 223, 230, 234
Fish ladders VII 29
Fish Passage Center VII 223
Fisher, John VIII 30–31, 122, 137; 49, 51, 55, 100, 102, 140
Fisher, Joschka XIV 100
Fisk University XIII 222
  Slave Narrative Collection XIII 233
Fitin, Pavel VI 127; XIX 117
Fitzgerald, Albert XIX 237
Fitzgerald, Edward XIX 197
Fitzgerald, F. Scott III 54, 78, 83, 182; VIII 191
Fitzgerald, John F. III 262
Fitzhugh, George XIII 48, 68, 73, 183, 205, 241
Fiume Conference (1905) IX 267
Five-Power Naval Limitation Treaty (1921) V 203
Flanders IX 30, 59, 107, 129, 231, 257, 264
  German submarine bases in IX 78
Flanders, Ralph E. VI 156; XIX 126–127
Flathead Irrigation Project VII 167–169, 171–172
FleetBoston Financial Corporation XIII 197–198
Flerov, Georgy N. I 244–248
flexible response policy I 115–122; II 118; VI 9, 66, 141
Flexner, Eleanor XIX 191
Fliegerkorps (Air Corps) IV 167
Flint, Michigan, sit-down strikes XIX 207
Flood Control Acts VII 29, 54
Flood Defense Plan VII 232
Florence, slavery in XIII 167
Florida XII 109; XIII 235
  British troops in XII 186
  Bush (George W.) election XIV 96
  maroons in XIII 108
  Reconstruction, end of XIII 55
  Spanish presence in XII 295
Floyd, Pretty Boy XIX 177
flu epidemic (1919) III 96–97
Flying Tigers (U.S.) V 199
Flynn, Elizabeth Gurley XIX 260
Foch, Ferdinand VIII 55, 57, 103, 114, 150, 184, 204, 219, 221, 234, 236, 281–282; IX 99, 104–110, 114; XVI 7, 211
Fogg, Jeremiah XII 41
Fokker aircraft company XIX 272
Foley Square federal courthouse, New York City XIX 258, 260
folk music XIX 38–39, 192
Fondation France Libertés XIV 278
Foner, Eric XIX 108
Foner, Jack XIX 108
Foner, Philip XIX 108
Food and Tobacco Workers Union of America (FTA) XIX 183
"For A Lasting Peace. For A People's Democracy!" XIX 238
Foraker, Joseph IX 5
Force Noir IX 111, 114
Force 17 XIV 107
Ford, Gerald R. I 101; II 179, 278; VI 1, 58, 87, 229, 256–257
  criticized by Reagan I 52
  human rights I 141
  Iran XV 158
  Middle East XV 184
  policy toward Pakistani nuclear program I 223
  sale of military hardware to China VI 4
Ford, Henry VIII 296
  automobiles of IX 22
  Ford Motor Company XIII 198
Ford administration VI 1, 56, 199–200, 260
  détente I 102
  London Suppliers' Group I 19
  nuclear nonproliferation policy I 216, 223
Foreign Corrupt Practices Act (FCPA, 1977) XIV 47, 49
Foreign Economic Administration XIX 17
Foreign Legion IX 111
Foreign Terrorist Organizations (FTOs) XVI 130
Foreman, Carl XIX 165
Foreman, Jonathan XIX 165
Formosa IX 162
Formosa Straits VI 147
Forrestal, James V. I 4–5, 159; II 206; XI 255
Fort Peck Dam (U.S.) VII 28, 170
Forts–
  –Clinton XII 271
  –Douaumont IX 117, 252, 258
  –Edward XII 269
  –Johnson XII 190
  –Lee XII 38, 304, 307
  –Montgomery XII 271
  –Niagara XII 41
  –St. John XII 9, 189

–Stanwix XII 180, 270
–Sumter XIII 283
–Ticonderoga XII 9–12, 14, 44–48, 80, 156, 268–269, 273, 304, 307
–Vaux IX 252, 255, 258
–Washington XII 38, 161, 304, 307
Foster, John VI 257
Foster, Stephen Symonds XIII 33
Foster, Thomas Jr. XIII 221, 222
Foster, William Z. IX 2; XIX 58, 84, 193
and 1949 Smith Act trial XIX 252, 255, 258, 260, 262
head of Trade Union Education League XIX 193
Foster Bill (1910) III 137
Founding Fathers XII 52, 60, 63–64, 68–71, 108, 114, 116, 192, 290; XIII 7, 18, 48
slavery XII 293–300
Four Freedoms program XIX 25
Four-Power Pact (1921) V 120, 203, 206
Four-Square Gospel Temple III 177
Fourteen Points (1918) II 99, 101, 145; VI 77; VIII 280–282, 298; IX 168, 225, 245, 250; XVI 87, 237; XVII 7, 11, 166
Fourth Lateran Council X 88; XI 23
Fox, Charles James XII 30
Fox, George XIII 31
Fox, Vincente XIV 219
Fraina, Louis XIX 212
France I 34, 151, 278, 280, 283, 289, 293, 305; II 153, 264; VI 11, 76, 97, 100–107, 137, 178, 183, 189, 201, 209, 214, 234, 246–247, 264; VIII 30, 44, 71, 76, 82, 104, 172, 176, 182, 212, 245–246, 249, 251–252, 280; IX 26–27, 29–30, 48–49, 75, 91–92, 95, 99, 101, 103–105, 140, 145, 158, 163, 173, 193, 207, 224–231, 248, 252, 257, 263, 265; XI 2, 4, 15, 62, 79, 96, 102, 108, 110, 117, 123, 126, 167, 175, 178, 211, 253, 260, 266; XII 28, 33, 37, 92, 98, 155, 167–169, 248–252, 256; XIII 236; XIV 143, 181, 239, 241, 277–278, 281; XV 9, 15, 21, 24, 27, 30, 59, 62, 78, 135, 137, 146, 168, 199, 275; XVI 17, 22–24, 32, 34, 60, 93–94, 102, 104, 107, 111, 189, 192–194, 198, 208–209, 212–213, 217–218, 220, 224, 252, 255, 267, 269, 291–292, 296, 315, 318
Action française (French Action) XVI 142–143
aftermath of World War II I 173; VI 49
Algeria XVI 70, 131
Algerian Revolution XV 11–19
alliance with Russia (1893) VIII 35, 212
Allied invasion (1944) XVI 299
American Revolution XII 15, 78, 100–107, 166, 268
anti-Catholic sentiment VIII 204
anti-Semitism in VIII 168
appeasement XVI 8–14; XIX 88
army 17, 69, 179, 185, 232–238; IX 252
African troops in IX 115
cavalry IX 70, 72
foreign troops in IX 116
mutiny of VIII 67, 223, 269; IX 27
offensive tactics of VIII 71
rotation of units IX 234
World War I VIII 218
artillery VIII 199, 272
as arm supplier VI 107
as buyer of Chesapeake tobacco XII 202
Assembly of Notables XII 131
attack on Germany VIII 72
attempted alliance with Czechoslovakia VI 255
Bastille (1789) XVI 130
Belgian neutrality IX 41–47
Bourbon dynasty XVI 178
Catholic movement XIV 256
Catholicism of XII 211
Catholics in World War I VIII 207
Centre d'Instruction, Pacification et Contre-guérilla (Instruction Center for Pacification and Counter-Guerilla Tactics, CIPCG) XV 14
Chamber of Deputies XVI 118
colonial policy of VI 93; VII 81, 135; X 59, 199; XVI 67, 70; XVII 229; XIX 25, 157, 224, 236
Communist Party I 204, 208; XVI 135, 138, 141; XIX 103, 145, 265
Concert of Europe XVI 72–78
Constituent Assembly XVI 135
Croix de feu (Cross of Fire) XVI 141–142, 146
Croix de Guerre (War Cross) XVI 141
Crusades X 10, 33, 35, 37, 62, 72–73, 88, 93–94, 108, 116, 144, 151–152, 161, 167, 191, 198, 206, 211, 216, 218–219, 226, 239, 257, 260, 265, 285
Cuban Missile Crisis VI 102
decolonization policy VI 77–83; XVI 79–88
disastrous harvests in XII 132
Dunkirk Treaty I 208
École Nationale d'Administration (National Administration School) XVI 137
École Normale Supérieure XVI 142
ecological policy VII 92–99
Eleventh Shock commando unit XV 16
Elysée Palace XVI 134
Estates in XII 132
fall to Germany IV 70–76; V 35, 36; XI 14
fascism in XVI 140–146
Fifth Republic I 283; VI 106; XVI 129, 131, 134, 136, 139
first nuclear test VI 106
foreign policy XVI 155–161
Fourth Republic I 283; VI 80; XVI 129, 131, 135–136
German defeat of XVI 113–120
German invasion of VIII 110, 278
Grand Armee VIII 49, 233; XI 169
homosexuals, during Nazi occupation XI 246
impact of American Revolution upon XII 165
imperialism IX 111–112; X 300–306
in Algeria VI 80, 106, 136
in Indochina VI 106
in Middle East VI 161; VIII 37
in Morocco VIII 277
in Southeast Asia II 264
in Vietnam VI 102
in West Indies XII 314
inability to hold Vietnam II 266
Israel, military aid to XIV 143
Jacquiere in XIII 71
Jehovah's Witnesses in XI 129
Je suis partout (I am everywhere) XVI 142
Jeunesses partiotes (Patriotic Youths) XVI 142
Jews in VIII 164, 168; X 14, 16, 21–22, 209; XI 93–94; XVI 299–300, 302
League of Nations IX 170
Lend Lease aid XVI 167
levée en masse (1793) XVI 255
literacy XII 132
Maison de la Presse (Press Office) XVI 173
Med Plan VII 145
Middle East XV 274
Ministry of the Interior VIII 255
monarchy XVI 177–178, 183
Multinational Force in Lebanon XV 148–155
Munich Agreement (1938) I 300
National Assembly XVI 137–138
National Front XVI 134, 138
NATO XVI 267
nuclear arsenal VI 103, 106, 187; XVI 108
Nuclear Non-Proliferation Treaty I 218
opposition to rearming Germany VI 9
Organisation Armée Secrète (Secret Army Organization, OAS) XV 14; XVI 137
Parti populaire français (French Popular Party) XVI 141
Parti social français (French Social Party) XVI 141

pays Germany indemnity VIII 278
Permanent Committee for National Defense XVI 118
political democratization IX 81
Popular Front XVI 115, 117–118, 141, 220
Popular Party XVI 142
postwar decline I 285
post-World War II XVI 129–139
products from Saint Dominque XIII 210
Provisional Government XVI 135, 298
refuses to sign NPT VI 106
relations with Great Britain VIII 32; XII 211
relations with Native Americans XII 178
relations with Russia XVI 200
relations with Soviet Union VI 145
relations with the United States VI 104; XII 53
religious strife in XIII 273
reluctance to declare war on Germany IV 117–120
Revolution of 1789 XVI 129; XVII 87–94
Revolution of 1848 XVI 130
Russia, intervention in (1918) XVI 1–7
Second Republic XVI 130
Sections Administratives Spéciales (Special Administrative Sections, SAS) XV 12
slave trade XIII 40, 129, 131, 269–270, 272, 274
slavery abolished by XII 134; XIII 1, 209
Socialist Party XVI 135–136, 142
Socialists VIII 254–256, 260–261
SS Charlemagne Division XVI 141
Suez Crisis I 277; VI 135–136, 270; XV 244–251, 253; XVI 235–242
terrorism XIV 14; XVI 248–249
Third Republic VIII 146–147, 151–152; XVI 114, 117, 119, 130–131, 135, 143, 146, 298
Tomb of the Unknown Soldier IX 81
trade with Great Britain XII 132
trade with New England XII 209
Tunisia, loss of XIV 203
Union des Grandes Associations contre la Propagande Ennemie (Union of Great Associations against Enemy Propaganda, UGACPE) XVI 173
U.S. ships visit XII 79
views on blacks XIII 181
vetos British EEC membership VI 13
Vichy France XVI 298–306
Vichy Syndrome XVI 135
war with Vietnam I 213, 290
withdrawal from NATO VI 81, 103, 106, 145, 209
World War I VIII 11–17; XVI 173, 308, 311, 313
access to U.S. products VIII 18
African American troops in VIII 298; IX 1, 111–118
aircraft IX 9–15
casualties VIII 125, 187, 191
chemical warfare IX 122
control of U.S. troops VIII 17
mobilization in VIII 125
motivation of soldiers VIII 264–265
planning VIII 232–238
prewar alliances VIII 225–231
prewar relations between army and government VIII 146–152
religion during VIII 203
response of population VIII 255
size of army VIII 75
U.S. pilots in VIII 23
U.S. resources to IX 18–22
U.S. troops in IX 29–30
wartime manufacturing VIII 16
women in manufacturing VIII 129
Franchet d'Esperey, Louis IX 204, 206, 208
Francis Joseph I VIII 47; IX 65, 134
Francis of Assisi, Saint X 35–36, 90, 177
Franciscans X 8, 10, 36, 38, 90, 102, 142, 181
Franco, Francisco I 209; II 97; IV 224–231; IX 84; X 160, 241; XIV 284; XVI 10, 13, 180, 249, 302; XVII 29, 234, 237–238, 241; XIX 88, 103, 214
abandonment of Axis IV 227
and generals' uprising XVIII 51–56
military strategy XVIII 66–73
as Nationalist leader IV 224, 226; XVIII 57–65
and Nationalist victory XVIII 165–175
relationship with Adolf Hitler XVIII 74–80
relationship with Benito Mussolini XVIII 140–147
and use of terror XVIII 243–250
Franco-Israeli nuclear treaty (1957) XVI 143
Franco-Prussian War (1870–1871) VIII 35, 67, 73, 114, 146–147, 234; IX 101, 116; XVI 24, 66, 69, 114, 255, 257, 292, 313
Franco-Russian alliance VIII 234
Frank, Anne XI 45, 52, 69, 158
Frankenstein, or, the Modern Prometheus (Shelley) II 86
Frankenthaler, Helen XIX 45
Frankfurter, Justice Felix II 280–283; III 27, 103, 228, 234–235; XIX 150
defense of Hiss XIX 156, 158, 198
Rosenberg case XIX 288
Sacco and Vanzetti III 232
Frankl, Viktor E. XI 218–219, 221, 224, 235–237
Franklin, Benjamin XII 79, 100, 102–103, 105–106, 109, 113–114, 134, 141, 158, 205, 207, 210, 217, 231, 262; XIII 205
Plan of Union XII 204
Franny and Zooey XIX 46
Franz Josef IX 227; XVI 30, 33, 36, 196, 312
Fraser, Simon XII 48
Frazier, E. Franklin XIII 257, 262
Frazier v. *Spear* (1811) XIII 101
Frazier-Lemke Farm Bankruptcy Act (1934) III 30, 162
Frederick I (Barbarossa) X 131, 234, 249, 254, 260
Frederick II (the Great) IX 50, 131, 209; X 47, 54, 87–96, 140, 151, 155, 189, 206, 225–256, 266; XVI 160, 171, 182
Frederick, Prince of Wales XII 53
Free French Forces IV 276; V 241
Free Officers Committee I 277
Free Speech movement II 159; VI 25
Freedmen's Bureau XIII 54
Freedmen's Bureau Act (1865) XIII 5
Freedom of Information Act II 125
Freedom Rides (1961) VI 25
Freedom Summer (1964) II 161; VI 25
Freedom Train XIX 96
Freeport Doctrine (1858) XIII 173
Frei, Eduardo XIX 142
Freikorps (volunteer paramilitary units) IV 80; VI 176; VIII 285; XVI 151
French, John VIII 103; IX 35, 51–52, 55, 68
French and Indian War (1754–1763) XII 10, 50, 53, 55, 139, 146, 148, 156, 159, 178, 199, 205–206, 211, 230, 236–237, 301–302. *See also* Seven Years' War
French Army XII 105
French Communist Party VI 179, 245; VIII 256; XV 14
French Constitution (1791) XII 134
French Equatorial Africa VI 83
French Foreign Office. *See* Quai d'Orsai
French Huguenots XII 235
French Indochina (Vietnam) VIII 35
French Morocco VIII 32, 35
French National Convention (1789) XII 128
French Revolution (1789–1799) VIII 149; IX 134; XII 127–134; XII XII 39, 127–134, 167, 169, 192, 194 253, 259, 265; XIII 1, 71–72, 209–210; XVI 138, 140, 143, 172, 183, 255, 257
French Socialist Party VIII 169, 256
French West Indies XII 101, 104–106, 200

Freneau, Philip XII 208
Frente Sandinista de Liberación (FSLN, or Sandinista National Liberation Front) VI 190–191
Freud, Sigmund VI 90; VIII 167, 263–264; IX 84, 87; XI 4; XVII 41, 196, 253, 257; XIX 46
Friedan, Betty XIX 191
The Friendly Persuasion XIX 164
Front de Libération Nationale (Front Liberation National, FLN) I 277; VI 106; XV 1–10
Front des Forces Socialistes (Socialist Forces Front, FFS) XV 2, 8
Front Islamique du Salut (Islamic Salvation Front or FIS) XIV 253; XV 1–10
Frying Pan/Arkansas Transmountain Water Project VII 10, 13
Fuad, Ahmad XV 66, 68
Fuchs, Karl/Kluas I 242–249; II 130, 228, 231; VI 158; XIX 58, 94, 118, 143, 194, 231, 283–284, 286, 289
Fugitive Slave Act (1793) XII 7
fugitive slave clause XII 296
Fugitive Slave Law (1850) XIII 276
fugitive slaves XII 71
Fulbright, James William XII 31
Fulcher of Chartres X 15, 74–75, 198, 200–201, 215, 281
Fuller, J. F. C. VIII 53–54, 56, 112, 195, 241
Fulton, Hugh XIX 17
Fund for the Republic XIX 166
fundamentalist movement III 32–42
Fundamentals of Leninism XIX 261
Fur and Leather Workers Unions XIX 216, 218

G

Gabcikovo Dam (Slovakia) VII 100–107
Gabon XIV 212, 217
Gabriel's plot (1800) XIII 124
Gabrielson, Ira VII 277–278
Gaddis, John Lewis I 83, 154, 252, 256, 273; II 31, 37, 156, 204
Gadhafi, Mu'ammar I 159, 223, 314; VI 268, 270
Gadsen, Christopher XII 218
Gaelic League VIII 161
Gagarin, Yuri II 68, 257, 260
Gage, Thomas XII 34, 44, 306
Gaither report I 190–194
Galicia VIII 72; IX 66, 128, 136, 193, 201, 238; XVI 33–34, 200, 204
Galilee XIV 221
Galileo XIX 111
Gallieni, Joseph IX 117
A Gallery of Harlem Portraits XIX 40
Galloway, Joseph XII 54, 95, 159
Galloway Plan XII 54
Galvin, Robert VI 257
Gamasy, Abd al-Ghani al- I 309, 313
Gamelin, Maurice XVI 115–116
Gandhi, Indira VI 271
Gandhi, Mohandas II 22; III 219; IX 91, 93; X 132; XVI 112, 209; XIX 9, 12
Garbo, Greta XIX 163
Garcia III X 245
Gardiner, Sylvester XII 194
Gardoqui, Don Diego de XII 290
Garibaldi, Giuseppe XIV 173
Gariep Dam (South Africa) VII 237, 240, 242–243
Garland, Judy XI 158
Garnet, Henry Highland XIII 234
Garrison, William Lloyd XII 7, 296; XIII 4, 6–8, 31, 33, 53
Garrison Dam (U.S.) VII 29, 31
Garvey, Marcus II 90; III 79, 117–123; IX 3–4
Gates, Horatio XII 10–12, 15, 46, 92–93, 96, 221–222, 224–225, 227–228, 270, 303, 305
Gates, John, XIX 260, 262
Gates, Robert VI 259; XV 87
de Gaulle, Charles I 283; V 171, 247; VI 11, 79, 81, 97, 100–104, 106, 145, 209; XV 15–18, 135; XVI 84, 129, 131–136, 139, 143, 155–156, 158, 160, 267, 271, 298–299; XVII 13, 65; XIX 80
  critic of U.S. Vietnam policy VI 107
  Free French Forces IV 76
  seeking independent role for France VI 105
  vetos British membership in EEC VI 106
  vision for Europe VI 106
  visit to Algeria VI 106
  World War I service VIII 192
Gay, John XII 124
Gayn, Mark XIX 16–18
Gaza Strip VIII 216; IX 206; X 55, 187; XIV 20, 22–23, 25–26, 102–103, 105, 112, 160, 183, 220–221, 223, 230, 259; XV 20–21, 23, 37, 52–53, 57, 78–79, 89–91, 93–95, 132, 134–139, 182–183, 185–186, 190–194, 199–200, 214–215, 219, 222, 226, 242, 248, 261, 263
  settlements in XIV 151–158
Geheime Staatspolizei (Gestapo, Secret State Police) V 213–216
Gelman, Harry VI 41
Gemayel, Amin XV 152
Gemayel, Bashir XV 129–131, 148–150, 155
General Agreement on Tariffs and Trade (GATT, 1944) VI 78; XIV 112; XVII 87, 108
General Dynamics XV 75, 78
General Electric (GE) XIX 71, 183
General Intelligence Division, Bureau of Investigation XIX 174, 246
genetic engineering II 85–88; III 17, 23
Geneva Accords I 41, 297; II 266–267; VI 142, 216; XIV 1, 5
Geneva Conference (1925) V 103; XV 52; XVI 94
Geneva Conference (1978) VI 164
Geneva Convention (1929) I 170, V 187, 222, 264; XI 169, 258
Geneva Convention (Fourth, 1949) XIV 152, 157, 162, 278; XV 79, 191
Geneva General Disarmament Conference (1932–1933) V 204
Geneva Summit (1955) XIX 123
Geneva Summit (1985) VI 36, 224
Genghis Khan X 182–183, 186
Genoa X 30, 148–150, 156
Gens, Jacob XI 141–142, 145
Gentleman's Agreement XIX 163
Gentlewoman XIX 36
Gentz, Frederick von XVI 75
Geoffrey de Villehardouin X 28, 109, 111, 113, 149–150
George I XII 143, 156, 159
George II XII 53, 143, 146–147
George III XII 28, 31, 35, 40–41, 47, 51, 53–55, 79, 116, 120, 136–144, 156, 164, 168, 185, 190–191, 234, 249, 251, 253, 261–262, 315; XV 157; XVI 181
George IV XIII 159
George V IX 44; XVI 178
George VI XVI 178–179
George, Lord Curzon XVI 7
Georgia (State) XII 39, 70, 128, 146, 167, 169, 184, 246; XIII 281
  African Americans in XII 89
  cattle raising in XIII 11
  dispute over Confederate flag XIII 270
  grandfather clause XIII 56
  Loyalists in XII 181, 184
  maroons in XIII 108
  ratification of Constitution XII 74
  Reconstruction, end of XIII 55
  religion in XII 263
  Republican Party XIV 97
  rice growing in XIII 11
  secession of XIII 272
  slave conspiracy XIII 91

slavery XII 3–4, 295, 297, 299; XIII 61, 64, 83, 101, 204, 206, 221, 226, 229, 232, 265, 267
use of Confederate symbols XIII 277
Georgia (nation) XVI 18, 251, 296
Gerard, James W. XVI 174
Gerisamov, Gennadi VI 117
Germain, George XII 29, 38–39, 47, 156, 181, 267–268, 271–274
German-American Bund XVII 137, 139–140
German Christian Church XI 27, 32
German Communist Party VI 274; VIII 257
German Democratic Republic XVI 124, 157, 267
German East Africa VIII 84–90, 133, 137
German Empire XVI 99, 148
German Free State IX 136
German High Command VIII 172–173; IX 27, 29, 196, 262
German High Seas Fleet, mutiny VIII 269
German Imperial Navy VIII 288
German Independent Social Democrats VIII 260
German Military Mission VIII 119
German philological tradition XX 11–18
German pietists XII 148
German Protestant League VIII 204
German reunification VI 120, 207
German Security Service XI 268
German Social Democrats VIII 256; IX 124
German-Soviet Non-Aggression Pact. See Molotov-Ribbentrop Pact
German Wars of Unification (1864–1871) VIII 73
Germany I 85–86, 89, 110, 112, 134–136, 149, 176, 245, 263, 285, 288, 293, 305; II 31–32, 36, 38, 40, 153; III 10; VI 101, 104, 136, 151, 169, 176, 179, 254; VII 81, 229, 250; VIII 18, 44, 48, 76–77, 82, 192, 216, 299; IX 27, 30, 49, 56, 78, 82–84, 91, 95, 99, 101–102, 104, 134, 137, 150, 154, 158, 163, 171, 174–175, 192–193, 204, 225–226, 228, 237, 239, 242, 248, 257, 265, 270; XI 1–264; XII 259; XIV 171; XV 34, 79, 82, 160, 253; XVI 1–2, 4–5, 11, 17, 22, 27, 32, 34–35, 41, 51, 58, 60, 73–74, 76, 78, 80–81, 87–88, 92–95, 99, 102, 104, 107–108, 111, 122, 126, 130, 163, 166, 175, 184, 199, 201, 204, 208–209, 211–214, 217, 219, 227, 236, 240, 244, 252, 254, 259, 267–268, 269, 314
aftermath of World War II I 173; XIX 1, 236, 239, 243
aid to Franco XIX 103
aid to Lenin IX 196, 200
alliance with Austria VIII 35, 43
anti-Semitism in VIII 165–166, 169
appeasement XVI 8–14
Army VIII 18, 224, 234; IX 30, 158, 218, 253, 119–125
cavalry IX 67–68, 72
deserters IX 235
Irish Brigade VIII 158
modern weapons VIII 75
size of VIII 69
"storm tactics" VIII 68
volunteers IX 259
Article 48 XVI 148
Auxiliary Service Law VIII 140, 143; XVI 173
Belgian neutrality IX 41–47
boycott of Jewish businesses XI 2, 268
builds Iran's first steel mill XV 108
canals VII 210
Catholic Center Party VIII 165, 257; XVI 150
chaplains in army VIII 202
Christian Church in World War II XI 27–35, 135
Christian Democratic Union (CDU) XVI 60; XVII 26, 70, 281
collapse of monarchy IX 81
colonial rule in Africa VII 236
colonialism VIII 30–33; XVI 66
communists XVI 151; XVII 38, 52, 67, 86, 178, 180–181
compulsory labor draft VIII 257
concentration camps XI 1–264
Crusades X 33, 54, 89, 93, 128, 191, 209, 218–220, 239, 260, 285
customs union with Austria forbidden VIII 283
dams VII 101
debt crisis VIII 280
defeat of France (1940) XVI 113–120
defeat of Romania VIII 278
division of I 300
economic consolidation of occupation zones I 113
economic ruin of XI 214
Enabling Act (1933) XVI 9, 150, 154
environmental movement VII 204—210
euthanasia of mentally and physically handicapped XI 117
exclusion from League of Nations I 206
execution squads in Russia VIII 99
fascism in XVI 140–142; XVII 180–187
fear of communism in VI 49
"field grey socialism" VIII 144
Foreign Ministry XVI 302
foreign policy XVI 155–161
Four Year Plan (1936) IV 96
France, occupation of XVI 298–306
French forced labor XVI 300
General Staff IX 31, 126–127
German Labor Front XVI 261
German Workers' Party XVI 152
Hindenburg Program 140, 143; XVI 173
Hindenburg-Ludendorff plan VIII 139–145
Hitler Youth XI 80, 167; XVI 261
Imperial German General Staff VIII 92
importation of foreign labor VIII 144
Independent Social Democrats VIII 257, 260; XVI 312
invasion of Austria and Czechoslovakia XIX 88
invasion of the Soviet Union I 107, 260; IV 141, 209; V 226–234; XIX 57, 62, 88, 98, 104, 193, 213, 229, 246
Iran, trade with XIV 40
Jehovah's Witnesses XI 128–137, 186, 219, 237
Jews, deportations of XI 98, 116
Jews, emigration of XI 55
Jews in VIII 167; X 14–15; XI 1–264
Kriegsamt (War Office) XVI 172
Law for the Prevention of Offspring with Hereditary Diseases XI 247
League of Nations VIII 277
Mediterranean theater IV 144
Ministry for the Occupied Eastern Territories XI 118
Ministry of Labor XVI 302
Ministry of Production XVI 302
Ministry of Propaganda XI 268
monarchy XVI 177–178
Munich Agreement (1938) I 300
murder of Soviet POWs XI 118
National Socialism VIII 209; XI 115, 243
NATO bases in XVI 267
Navy VIII 29–36; XVI 68
East Asian Squadron VIII 132, 137
surface commerce raiders VIII 132–135
Nazis VI 251–252; XI 1–264
nonaggression pact with Poland (1935) IV 125
occupation by Allies VI 267
occupation of Czechoslovakia VIII 284
occupation of Eastern Europe (World War I) VIII 91–101
occupation of Eastern Europe (World War II) VIII 91–101
occupation of France VIII 278
Office of Strategic Services XI 268
Office of War Materials XVI 173

Order Police XI 270
partition of I 252–257
postwar occupation I 33–39
post-WWI economic crises XVII 112–119
punishments for World War II XI 252
Race and Settlement Office VIII 94; XI 39
rearmament I 208
remilitarization IV 96
reparation payments IV 270
Reserve Police Battalion 101 XI 265
Russia, invasion of XVI 184–191
Second Naval Law VIII (1900) 31, 33
Second Reich VIII 29, 184
Sicherheitsdienst (Security Service) XI 36
Sigmaringen Castle XVI 135
Social Democratic Party XI 32, 112; XVI 24, 148, 151, 175, 312; XVII 67–68, 70, 118, 200
social welfare XVII 273
Socialists VIII 261; XVII 66–67
Soviet invasion of (1945) VI 16
Strength Through Joy XVI 261
terrorism XIV 16
Third Reich VIII 92, 95–96; XI 7, 9, 31–32, 59, 71, 75, 81, 83, 90, 103, 106, 110–112, 118, 134, 136, 139–141, 151, 166, 174, 178–179, 184, 190, 210, 213, 215, 234, 253–255; XVI 117; XVI 188–189
treatment of lesbianism during Nazi period XI 245
Turnip Winter (1916–1917) VIII 144
unification of XII 167
Versailles Treaty XVI 291–296
War Ministry VIII 144
War Raw Materials Department VIII 140
war reparations I 300
Weimar Constitution XVI 9, 148, 150
Weimar Germany I 137; XI 7, 28, 98, 111, 151, 167; XVI 292; XVII 113, 116–117, 121, 178
World War I VIII 11–17, 271–276; XVI 192–198, 308–309, 313
armistace VIII 278
atrocities in VIII 203, 208
blockade of VIII 140, 277
casualties VIII 125, 187, 268
Catholics in VIII 207
chemical warfare VIII 239–244
economic mobilization VIII 139–145
excluded from peace negotiations VIII 277
in Africa VIII 84–90
indemnities imposed VIII 283
invasion of Belgium VIII 72, 110
Jews in VIII 163–164
military gap VIII 249
mobilization VIII 125, 268
motivation of soldiers VIII 266
navy IX 186, 218, 256
pilots trained in Soviet Union VIII 285
planned annexation of Holland VIII 280
planning VIII 245–248
prewar alliances VIII 225–231
prewar consumption VIII 140
religion VIII 203–204
reparations XVII 113, 116–117, 120–121
shipbuilding VIII 35
submarine warfare VIII 77, 82, 172, 204, 287–294
taxes VIII 280
treaty with Russia VIII 278
U.S. occupation VIII 24
women VIII 130
World War II XIX 2
economy IV 96–98
submarine warfare VIII 293; XIX 218
Gero, Erno VI 134
Gerry, Elbridge XII 69–70, 98, 217
Gestapo XI 32, 108, 112–113, 128–129, 145, 166, 187–188, 203, 205, 208, 243–244; XVI 244; XVII 102, 173, 175
Ghana I 277; II 42, 45; VII 237; XIV 198
Akosombo Dam VII 4
nonaligned movement I 110
slave trade XIII 35
Ghozali, Ahmed XV 4, 8
G.I. Bill of Rights II 189; XIX 230, 232
Giap, Vo Nguyen XV 49
Gibbons, Cardinal James VIII 205
Gibraltar VIII 134, 204; XI 176; XVI 64, 81
Gibson, Charles Dana III 170
Gibson girl III 167, 171
Gide, André XIX 35
Gideon v. *Wainwright* (1963) II 281, 290
Gil Robles, Jose Maria XVIII 58, 105, 110, 193, 205
Gilbert, Humphrey XII 137
Gillespie, Dizzy XIX 48
Gilpin, Charles IX 4
Ginsberg, Allen XIX 48–51
Gitlow, Benjamin XIX 209
Gitlow v. *New York* XIX 255
Gladiators XX 249–256
Gladstone, William XII 166
glasnost I 13–14; II 58–60; VI 17, 114, 212, 245; XVI 284, 288
Glass-Steagall Banking Act (1933) III 152
Glasser, Harold VI 126; XIX 197, 200
Glavnoye Razvedyvatelnoye Upravleniye (GRU, or Central Intelligence Office) VI 124
Gleichschaltung (coordination) XIX 136
Glen Canyon Dam (U.S.) VII 27, 29–31, 110, 112, 152
Glenn Amendment (1994) XIV 150
Global Resource Action Center for the Environment (GRACE) VII 283
Global warming VII 225
Global Water Partnership VII 280
globalization XIV 60–61, 89, 93, 109–117
Glorious Revolution (1688) XII 34, 109, 123, 209, 234–235, 243, 245, 250, 262
Go XIX 50
"God Bless America" XIX 38
The God That Failed XIX 35– 36
Godesburg Declaration (1939) IV 190
Godfrey of Bouillon X 15, 19, 57, 59, 73–74, 119, 154, 191, 218, 305
Goebbels, Joseph IV 139, 141; V 154, 164; XI 67, 69, 89–90, 103, 113, 185, 268
Goeth, Amon XI 159, 203–205
Golan Heights XIV 125, 128, 151, 268; XV 20–23, 25, 33, 37, 54, 78–79, 89, 93, 130, 132, 136–137, 186, 191, 194, 213, 215, 219, 225–226, 238, 241–242, 261, 263, 265, 267
Gold, Ben XIX 216
Gold, Harry I 242–243; II 228, 231; VI 154; XIX 118, 283–284, 286–288
Gold, Mike XIX 36
Gold Act (1933) III 28
Gold Coast XIII 11
slave trade XIII 35, 38–40
Golden Bull of Rimini (1226) X 181
Golden Horde X 60, 182, 188–189
Goldhagen, Daniel Jonah XI 111, 183, 189, 227, 232–233, 264–271
Goldwater, Barry VI 203; XIX 142, 221
Goldwater-Nichols Department of Defense Reorganization Act (1986) VI 234
Golos, Jacob XIX 117, 197
Gompers, Samuel XIX 68
Gomulka, Wladyslaw VI 130, 134
Goodman, Benny IX 4
Gorbachev, Mikhail I 13, 101, 152, 257; II 56–62; VI 1, 4, 17, 31, 33, 36, 46, 50, 103, 114, 188, 211, 223, 226, 228–229, 232, 239, 242, 245, 261; VII 20, 23–24; XV 255, 258; XVI 38–42, 45–46, 92, 281–282, 285–286, 288–289

fall of VI 113
nuclear nonproliferation policy I 224
perestroika/glasnost I 224; II 58–60
plans for economic change I 152
policy on East Germany VI 115–122
political reforms of VI 44
Soviet defense spending I 184
strategic arms negotiations I 197
views on Afghanistan I 13–15
visit to China VI 45
Gordievsky, Oleg VI 126; XIX 199
Gordon, Thomas XII 128, 147
Gordon Riots (1780) XII 250, 252
Gore, Al XV 183
Goremkyn, Ivan IX 243
Göring, Hermann IV 27, 163; V 14, 133, 152, 221, 223; XI 91, 103, 108, 178, 254; XVI 150
Gough, Hubert VIII 219, 222, 224; IX 36, 68, 70
Goulart, João I 24–26
Gouzenko, Igor XIX 117, 163, 200
Gove Dam (Angola) VII 239
Government of India Act (1935) XVI 70
Gracchus, Tiberius XX 292–298
Gradual Emancipation Act (Rhode Island, 1784) XII 5
Graham, Shirley XIX 29
Gramsci, Antonio XIV 81, 84
Granada X 2–3, 6, 35, 159, 193, 275, 277
Grand Canyon VII 29–31, 109, 111–112
dams in VII 108–115
Grand Coalition V 27–33; VI 207
Grand Coulee Dam (U.S.) VII 27–29, 53, 198, 223
Grandmaison, Louis de VIII 73, 234; IX 99
Grant, Alexander XIII 270, 274
Grant, Ulysses S. VI 26; VIII 23, 67; XVI 257
Grasse, François de XII 33, 80, 103, 306
Gratian X 129–130
Grauman's Chinese Theater XIX 160
Graves, Robert VIII 186, 188, 191; IX 82, 84, 150, 152; XVI 23
Graves, Thomas XII 80
Gravier, Charles (Comte de Vergennes) XII 100–105
Gray, Robert XII 185
Gray v. *Sanders* (1963) II 139
graylisting XIX 161, 163
Grayson, William XII 287
Great American Desert VII 181–187
Great Awakening XII 63, 145–153, 216; XIII 186
Great Britain I 14, 30, 34, 85, 277–278, 280, 283, 285, 288, 305; II 35, 264; VI 101, 106, 137, 183, 189, 264, 274, 250; VIII 44, 172, 212, 249; IX 26–27, 29–30, 92, 95, 99, 102, 104–105, 163, 165, 193, 226, 228, 245, 248, 252; X 10, 62; XI 2, 4, 10, 15, 56, 60, 62, 74, 108, 110, 124, 126, 174, 184, 215, 268; XII 146; XII 13, 16, 34, 70, 136–144, 158, 268, 295, 301; XIII 21, 22, 31; XIV 143, 181, 192, 277; XV 19, 21, 24, 26–27, 30, 32, 58–59, 62, 135, 137, 146, 168, 175, 207, 215, 272, 275; XVI 17, 32, 45, 60, 93, 102, 107, 111, 119, 136, 192–194, 198, 208–209, 212, 217, 220, 224, 252, 257, 291–292, 308, 313; XIX 25, 88, 248–249
abolishes slavery XIII 18, 22, 270
access to U.S. products, World War I, VIII 18
Admiralty IX 75–77
African troops, against use of IX 114
aftermath of World War II I 173; VI 49
Air Inventions Committee VIII 196
alliance with Japan (1902) VIII 34
American colonial policy XII 50–55
"Americanization" plan XII 181
antinuclear protest in VI 16
anti-Semitism in VIII 168
appeasement XVI 8–14
Army IX 83, 173
cavalry IX 68, 72
Counter Battery Staff Office VIII 276
defeats Germany, WWI IX 123
Imperial General Staff VIII 102–108, 221
Irish soldiers in VIII 158–159, 161
rotation of units IX 234
tanks VIII 113
Asian colonies of VI 9
atomic bomb VI 187
Baghdad Pact I 161
balance of power in Europe I 254
bases in Egypt XV 66
Belgian neutrality IX 41–47
"blue water" strategy VIII 82
Board of Invention and Research VIII 196
Board of Trade VIII 81; XII 196, 198, 205
Catholic Church in VIII 208
Chancellor of the Exchequer VIII 78
Colonial Land and Emigration Commission XII 168
colonial power I 259; II 32; VII 4, 135, 236–237
colonialism XVI 65–66, 68, 70
Concert of Europe XVI 72–78
Conservative Party VIII 82; IX 83; XVI 13, 240, 268
cooperation with U.S. intelligence VI 11
"cotton famine" XII 168
Crusades X 89, 93, 151–152, 212, 218, 260
decline as world power I 83
decolonization VI 77–83; XVI 79–88
democratization in IX 81–82
disarmament XVI 91
Dunkirk Treaty I 204, 208
economic policies in VI 13
EEC membership vetoed VI 13
emigration, to New World XIII 247
Empire IX 91, 142
Food Production Department IX 59
Foreign Office IX 46
French and Indian War, cost of XII 139
Grand Fleet IX 75, 79, 139–144, 228
Grenville administration XII 55
Haitian Revolution XIII 209
homosexuality in IX 147
House of Commons VIII 103, 161; XII 57; XII 40, 121, 123, 125, 128, 138, 140, 143, 146–147, 156, 159, 170, 198, 210, 231, 249, 252, 255, 310; XVI 24
House of Lords VIII 77; IX 83; XII 128, 146, 231
immigrants to America XII 279
impact of American Revolution upon XII 27–35, 164–172
impact of World Trade Center attack XIV 50
imperialism IX
importance of navy to VIII 30
India XVI 70
Indochina peace conference VI 10
industrialization in XII 198
Iran XV 229
Iraq XV 116, 121
Irish Catholic support for war in American colonies XII 249–250
Irish independence VIII 154–162
Japan, desire to limit expansion of IX 163
Jews in X 22
Labour Party I 285; VIII 255; XVI 24, 240; XVII 20, 28–29, 52–53, 66–67, 70–72, 122
League of Nations IX 170, 172
Liberal Party VIII 78, 81; IX 83; XVI 23, 65
Loyalist exiles in XII 189, 192
mercantilism XII 196–203
Middle East VI 161; VIII 35, 37–42; XV 274
Ministry of Munitions VIII 106, 276; IX 54, 56–57; XVI 172
Ministry of Production IX 57
monarchy XVI 177–183
Multinational Force in Lebanon XV 148–155
Munich Agreement (1938) I 300
Munitions Inventions Department VIII 196

INDEX

National Service Projects VIII 203
National Shell Filling Factories VIII 129
National War Aims Committee XVI 173
Nuclear Non-Proliferation Treaty I 218
nuclear weapons XVI 108
oil XV 175
opposes slave trade XII 167
overthrow of Shah of Iran XIV 37
Palestine policy XI 125; XVI 269
Parliament XII 239; XII 2, 41, 50, 51, 55, 57–58, 95, 103, 110, 119–121, 123, 125, 128, 136, 139–140, 146–147, 155–157, 159, 165–168, 171, 182, 190, 196, 198, 200–201, 209–211, 230–237, 248, 250, 254, 258, 260–262, 310, 312; XIII 1, 131, 247, 274; XVI 178
patronage in Parliament XII 124
Peasant's Revolt XIII 71
People's Budget (1909) VIII 77, 81
popular support for war against American colonies XII 248–256
Portugal, treaty with (1810) XII 167
possibility of victory in American Revolution XII 36–41
postwar recovery I 177
Privy Council XII 240, 242
Provincial regiments in America XII 185
public debt XII 209
Q-ships IX 183–188
racist views XIII 249
relations with France VIII 32; XII 211
relations with Iraq XIV 237
relations with Libya XIV 193
relations with Native Americans XII 178
relations with Soviet Union V 28–33; VI 9; XVI 226–228
relations with United States V 28–33; VI 8, 14; XII 224; XII 25; XIV 240
resistance to standing army VIII 30
role in Europe VI 13
Royal Arsenals IX 55
Royal Navy VIII 29–36, 117, 160; IX 139–144; XII 165, 171; XII 33, 36, 38, 77–83, 202; XVI 12–13, 23
Royal Ordinance Factories VIII 129
Russia, intervention in (1918) XVI 1–7
Saint Domingue XIII 212
Scottish Highlander support for war in American colonies XII 249–250
shell shock victims IX 215
slave trade XIII 136, 179, 269–272, 274
slave trade, suppression of XIII 2, 272
Socialists VIII 255, 261
Soviet espionage in VI 25
Suez Crisis I 277; VI 135–136; XIV 270; XV 244–251, 253; XVI 235–242
sympathy for Confederates XIII 276
Ten Years Rule XVI 91
textile manufacturing XIII 43
trade with France XII 132
views on blacks XIII 180–181
voting in XII 121, 138
War Committee VIII 82, 104
War Department IX 55–56, 58
water issues VII 234, 240, 286
West Indies XII 310
women, suffrage VIII 128
Women's Army Auxiliary Corps (WAAC) VIII 129
Women's Land Army VIII 130
Women's Police Volunteers VIII 130
Women's Royal Air Force (WRAF) VIII 129
Women's Royal Naval Service (WRNS) VIII 129
World War I VIII 11–17, 117–123, 218–224, 271–276; XVI 22–24, 173, 308
aircraft IX 181
air raids on IX 12, 217, 219
air war IX 48–53, 217–223
Allied cooperation VIII 11
Arab and Jewish policy during VIII 163
artillery VIII 272
battleships in VIII 29–36
chaplains in VIII 202
chemical warfare IX 122
convoy system IX 74–79
impact of German subs upon VIII 69, 287–294
in Africa VIII 84–90
Jews in VIII 164, 168
mandates VIII 12, 214
mobilization in VIII 125, 268
motivation of soldiers VIII 266
Palestine X 63
prewar alliances VIII 225–231
production of tanks in VIII 56
religion and VIII 203
shipping blockade IX 247
strategic policy VIII 102–108
submarines VIII 287
surface commerce raiders against VIII 132–135
U.S. pilots in VIII 23
U.S. resources to IX 18–22
wartime manufacturing VIII 16
Western Front VIII 81–82
World War II XVI 314–320
Yalta Agreement (1945) I 300–301, 306
Great Depression I 88, 180; II 46, 86, 160; III 38, 50, 54–60, 62–68, 148, 182, 194; VI 78, 158, 176; VII 25, 28, 53, 157, 202; VIII 59, 167, 277; IX 2, 150, 153; XI 57, 64, 74, 95; XV 34; XVI 8–9, 12, 81, 99, 117, 146, 149, 211, 228; XVII 120–127; XIX 4, 13, 71, 87–88, 92, 208
attraction of communism during VI 49; XIX 213, 230
cause of end III 62
impact on automobile industry II 106
impact on labor movement II 191
impact on New Deal III 151
The Great Gatsby (Fitzgerald) II 109; III 54
Great Lakes VII 116–124; XII 168, 177, 179
Great Lakes Water Quality Agreement (1972) VII 120, 124, 310–317
Great Leap Forward (1958–1960) VI 181; 146
Great Migration IX 7; XIX 218
Great Plains VII 10–16; VIII 27–28
Great Schism (1378–1417) X 210
Great Society VI 140, 144; XII 33; XIII 200
Great Terror (1936–1938) I 137–138
Great War. *See* World War I
Great White Fleet XVI 107
Greater East Asia Co-Prosperity Sphere IV 258
Greater Tunbs XIV 217
Grebe, Reinhard VII 206–207
Grechko, Andrei VI 165
Greco-Turkish War (1920–1922) VIII 214
Greece I 87, 89, 294; II 39, 207; VI 148, 161, 182, 244, 250–255, 275, 280; VII 82, 148–149; VIII 212, 216, 230, 277; IX 171, 205–207, 270; X 26, 201, 218; XI 102; XIII 274; XIV 176–178, 180; XV 271; XVI 36, 60, 99, 104, 115, 145, 233, 248–249, 317
British support for VI 11
civil war in I 82, 110; VI 274; XIX 96, 132, 215, 245, 248–249, 251
First Balkan War VIII 118
invades Smyrna VIII 214, 217
slave revolts XIII 159
slavery in XIII 154
Soviet intervention I 73–74, 258
terrorism XIV 16
Truman Doctrine toward XIX 9–10, 12, 21, 145
U.S. role in 1967 coup I 15

water issues VII 146–147
World War I XVI 312
Greek Communist Party VI 274; XIX 96, 132, 215, 245, 248–249, 251
Greek publications XIX 216
Green, Gilbert XIX 260
Green Mountain Boys XII 10, 14
Green Parties VXII 128–134
Green v. *School Board of New Kent County* (1968) II 293
Greenback Party II 196, 199
Greene, Nathanael XII 97, 184–185, 306
Greenglass, David II 228–231; XIX 200, 288
Soviet nuclear spying I 241, 243, 246–248; XIX 231, 283–284
testimony in Rosenberg case XIX 282–287
Greenglass, Ruth XIX 285–287
Greenland IX 171
Greenpeace XVII 129–131
Gregorian reform X 36, 94, 115, 217
Gregory I X 229
Gregory VII X 81, 85, 98–99, 104–105, 115–122, 130, 164, 205, 208, 213, 219–220, 224, 227–228, 267, 279, 284–285, 289; XI 80
Gregory VIII X 130, 254, 256, 260, 294, 297
Gregory IX X 92–96, 180, 206, 226, 266
Gregory X X 67, 70, 210
Gregory of Tours X 104, 229
Grenada I 56–57; II 44, 58; VI 83, 165, 194, 221–222, 234, 237, 261, 270; XII 311, 313
maroons in XII 314
Grenville, George XII 53, 139, 141, 149, 190, 231, 236
Grey, Edward IX 102; XVI 24
Griswold v. *Connecticut* (1965) II 281–283, 286
Groener, Wilhelm VIII 96, 143, 246; XVI 173
Gromyko, Andrey VI 75, 116; XV 258; XVI 227
Gropius, Walter IX 86
Group for Environmental Monitoring (GEM) VII 238
Group of Seven XIV 109
Group of 77 (G-77) VI 271
Groupe Islamique Armee (Armed Islamic Group, GIA) XV 2, 5
Groves, Leslie I 28, 235, 247
GRU (Soviet Military Intelligence) XIX 117, 143, 197, 231
Guadeloupe IX 111
Guantanamo Bay VI 64
Guatemala I 54–56, 70, 89, 94, 122–133; II 40, 103; VI 21, 131, 194, 266
Agrarian Reform Law (1952) I 123, 126
CIA involvement I 211; XV 157
CIA trained anti-Castro Cubans in VI 141
coup of 1954 I 123
human rights violations in VI 241
Marxist guerrillas in VI 193
military coup of 1963 I 24
1954 coup I 128
United Fruit Company I 70
U.S. intervention (1954) I 15, 123–133; XIX 141–142, 276
Guchkov, Aleksandr XVI 50–51, 53
Guderian, Heinz W. IV 282; V 123–127
Guevara, Ernesto "Che" I 93; II 160, 215; VI 70; XV 49
death I 126
role in communist revolution in Bolivia I 126
Guibert of Nogent X 72, 97–98, 100, 103, 128, 164, 212–213, 234, 281
Guigo de Castro X 162–163
Guiscard, Robert X 73, 121–122, 220, 228, 269, 284–285
gulag archipelago VI 250
Gulf Cooperation Council (GCC) XIV 114, 180, 247; XV 141, 147
Gulf of Aqaba XV 20–21, 135, 137, 170, 247, 250
Gulf of Sidra VI 165, 234; XIV 198
Gulf of Tonkin incident (1964) I 291; VI 144
Gulf of Tonkin Resolution (1964) I 91; II 7; VI 139, 284, 287; XII 31
Gulf Oil Company XIV 211–212; XV 172–173, 177, 178
gunboat diplomacy VI 166
Gurion, David Ben I 216
Gurnea, M. E. XIX 17
Guthrie, Woody XIX 35, 38
Guy of Lusignan X 52, 251, 256, 259
Guyana. *See* British Guiana
Gypsies, murder of VIII 94–95; XI 66, 71, 73, 147, 149, 153, 171, 186, 190, 242–243, 247, 257

H

Haas, Richard XIV 97, 100
Habash, George XV 41, 90, 199
Habeas Corpus VI 9
Haber, Fritz VIII 241–242
Habermas, Jurgen XVII 196, 200, 203–204
Habib, Philip Charles VI 229; XV 132, 153
Habitat Patch Connectivity Project VII 232
Habsburg Empire VI 217; VIII 43, 257, 281; IX 133–138, 206, 225, 266–267; XII 189; XVI 76, 99, 100, 312
collapse of XVI 29–37
ethnic groups in XVI 30
Habsburgs XVI 104, 195, 211–213, 216, 294
Hachani, Abdelkader XV 4–5, 8
Hadid, Muhammad XV 122–123, 124
Hadrian XI 19
Hafiz El Assad II 146
Hafsids X 66, 146
Hague, The XVI 92
Hague Conference (1911–1912) III 137; VIII 240
Hague Conventions (1907) V 222, 264; VIII 244; XI 258; XV 79
Haider, Jorg XVII 80, 82–84, 86, 167, 171
Haig, Alexander M. I 56; II 179; VI 44, 225, 229, 231; XIV 198
Haig, Douglas VIII 52, 56, 77, 79, 103–104, 106, 108, 114, 218–221, 223, 26, 271–273; IX 34–39, 107–108, 110, 120, 123, 211
Hainburg Dam Project (Austria) VII 105
Haiphong, bombing of XIX 226
Haiti I 51, 125; II 100; III 50; VI 58, 194, 213, 217, 283; IX 96; XII 169; XIII 156, 209–216
Haitian Revolution XIII 209–216
Halberstam, David XIX 276–277
Haldane Reforms (1906) IX 51
Haldeman, Harry R. VI 24
Halder, Franz V 126–127, 227
Ha-Levi, Yehuda ben Shemuel X 273, 275
Hall, Gus XIX 260, 262
Hall, Theodore XIX 86, 231, 284
Hallstein Doctrine VI 208, 210
Halperin, Maurice XIX 63, 231
Halsey Jr., William F. IV 173
Hamad XIV 61–63
Haman Act VII 47
Hamas XIV 24, 41, 93, 103, 105, 107, 127, 148, 184, 230; XV 90, 182, 186, 194, 201, 264
Hamilton, Alexander XII 34, 58, 65, 68, 70, 73, 97, 114, 119–122, 127, 162, 222–224, 228–229, 258, 279, 289–291, 296; XIII 281; XVI 66
Hamilton, Ian VIII 118–119, 122
Hammarskjold, Dag XV 247
Hammett, Dashiell XIX 124
Hammond, James Henry XIII 27, 48, 81, 83, 87, 218–219, 240, 264–265
Hampton, Wade XIII 155, 233, 235
Hancock, John XII 110, 291; XIII 48
Hand, Learned XIX 259
Handel, George XVI 23
Hankey, Maurice VIII 79
Hannibal VIII 179, 249
Hanoi I 41–47
Hanoi, bombing of XIX 226
Hanoverians XII 136
Haram al-Sharif 19, 22–23, 159–160, 165–167

Hardin, Garrett VII 47, 70, 72–73
Harding, Warren G. III 25, 69, 175–178; IX 92; XI 56
Harding administration IX 171
Harkin, Thomas R. VI 194
Harlan, John Marshall II 23, 282–283; XIII 57; XIX 149–150, 153
Harlem Globetrotters XIX 10
Harlem Renaissance III 78–84, 118–120, 184; IX 1, 4
Harper, William XIII 70, 73–74, 165, 217, 267
Harper's Ferry (1859) XIII 4
Harriman, W. Averell I 306; II 264; V 312; XV 160; XVI 227, 315
Harrington, James XII 119, 122–123, 209
Harris, Sir Arthur "Bomber" V 87, 91
Harris, Kitty XIX 231
Harrison, Earl G. XI 122–124
Harrison Act (1914) III 133, 137
narcotics legislation III 137
Hart, Sir Basil Henry Liddell V 23, 102
Hartley, F. J. XIX 268
Hartley, Fred A., Jr. XIX 182
Hartley, Marsden XIX 46
Harvard University VI 90, 129, 199, 203, 258; XIII 198; XIV 14; XIX 80, 111, 113, 124, 198
Hashemite Arabs VIII 40–41; XIV 245
Hashemite Kingdom XIV 160, 166; XV 32, 34, 41–42, 44–45, 116, 121, 142, 146, 273, 275
Hassan II XIV 74, 209, 278, 282–283; XV 44
Hat Act (1732) XII 198, 202, 243
Hatch Act (1939) III 11; XIX 119, 133
Hauptmann, Bruno III 110–116
Hausner, Gideon XI 38–41
Havel, Vaclav XVII 200, 214–215
Hawaii IX 96
Hawatmah, Nayef XV 41, 90, 199
Hay, Harry XIX 234
Hayden, Carl Trumbull VII 109, 112, 154–155
Hayden, Sterling XIX 164
Hayes, James Allison VII 274
Hays, Mary Ludwig (Molly Pitcher) XII 263
Hayward, Susan XIX 37
Haywood, Harry XIX 234
Hazen, Moses XII 12
Heady, Earl O. VII 187
Healey, Dorothy XIX 58, 262
Healy, J. XIX 270
Hebrew University XIV 225
Hebron massacre (1994) XV 187
Hebron Protocol (1997) XV 185
Heeringen, Josias von VIII 180, 184
Hegel, Georg XIV 77, 84; XVII 77, 105, 174, 183
Heidegger, Martin XVII 75, 77–78
Heights of Abraham XII 160
Heikkinenen, Knut XIX 216
Heine, Heinrich VI 121
Hells Canyon Dam (United States) VII 55
Helms, Richard M. VI 24
Helms-Burton Bill I 97–98
Helper, Hinton Rowan XIII 46, 69
Helsinki Accords VI 200
Helsinki Conference (1975) I 142
Hemingway, Ernest VIII 186, 188, 191; IX 4; XVII 41, 44, 48, 238
and the Spanish Civil War XVIII 7, 126, 129, 330, 332–333, 335–336
Henderson, Loy XV 158–159, 161–162
Hendrix, Jimi II 219; XIX 50
Henry II X 260; XI 88
Henry III X 66, 143, 284
Henry IV X 15, 85, 115, 117–119, 121, 205, 216, 219–220, 224, 227–229, 284–285; XI 80
Henry VIII, founds Royal Navy VIII 30
Henry of Le Mans X 215–216
Henry, Patrick XII 76, 97, 110, 113–114, 139, 205, 241, 263, 279, 281; XIII 18–19, 48
Hepburn Act (1906) III 243; III 245
Herder, Johann Gottfried XII 61
Herero/Nama Rebellion (1904) VIII 87
Herod the Great XIV 159
Herodotus XX 114–122
Herzl, Theodor XI 120, 126; XIV 163, 258; XV 33
Hesiod XX 123–129
Hess, Rudolf V 223–224; XI 103
Hessians XII 161
Het Vrije Volk XIX 273
Heydrich, Reinhard XI 37, 87, 89, 91, 108, 211, 249, 265
Hezb-i-Islami XIV 4, 6
Hicks, Granville XIX 57
Hideki Tojo V 112; VI 75
Higgins, Marguerite XIX 277
Highlander Folk School XIX 31, 76–77
Highway Act (1987) II 112
Highway Revenue Act (1956) II 107
hijab (modest Islamic dress; also means head scarf) XIV 118–124
Hildebrand X 119
Hillsborough, Lord XII 32, 141
Himmler, Heinrich I 305; IV 131; V 154, 162; XI 63, 86, 89–90, 102–103, 116, 132, 151, 153, 178, 186, 227–228, 244, 252, 265
Hindenburg, Paul von V 114–115, 120; VIII 54, 93, 95–96, 140, 143, 252, 292; IX 15, 82, 120, 122, 128, 257; XI 94; XVI 148–151, 154, 173
Hindenburg Line VIII 27, 53, 57
Hinton, Harold VI 41
Hippocrates XI 151
Hirabayashi, Gordon V 188–189
Hirabayashi v. *United States* (1943) III 103, 105–106; V 188
Hirakud Dam (India) VII 130
Hirohito, Emperor V 49, 108–113; VIII 95
Hiroshima I 30, 230, 239, 242–246, 249; II 268; III 12, 15, 216; V 1, 3, 8, 49, 50, 52, 55, 111, 154, 192, 221; VI 31, 254; XI 159; XVI 254–255; XIX 21, 99
Hispaniola XIII 63, 210
maroons in XIII 105
slave revolt XIII 155
Hiss, Alger II 130–133, 229; III 34; VI 123–129, 154, 156, 158; XIX 4–5, 58, 94, 118–119, 148, 154–159, 176, 178, 197
accused of spying XIX 61–63, 99, 154–159, 197–198, 207, 224, 248, 251
assertion of innocence XIX 63, 156, 199
background XIX 154, 198, 224
evidence against XIX 199
investigation by HCUA XIX 63, 197, 221, 224, 251
Hoover's involvement in XIX 176, 178
Nixon's involvement in XIX 220–221, 223–224, 226
perjury trials VI 124; XIX 99, 127, 154–155, 158, 194, 198, 248–249, 251, 255, 283, 286
Pumpkin Papers VI 127, 129
suit against Chambers XIX 198
trip to Moscow VI 126
Hiss, Donald XIX 198
Hiss, Priscilla VI 124
The History of the Communist Party of the Soviet Union (Bolsheviks) XIX 261
Hitchcock, Alfred IX 257
Hitchcock, Robert XIX 16–18
Hitler, Adolf I 150, 235, 239, 256, 274, 288, 293, 300, 305; II 156; III 38, 250–257; IV 17–19; V 14, 35, 57–58, 61, 79, 81, 84, 93, 96, 98, 104, 107–109, 122–125, 152–158, 173, 221, 226; VI 49, 61, 158, 176, 178, 251, 254, 275, 277, 281; VIII 30, 58, 92, 94–97, 99, 166, 186, 241, 263–264, 281, 284; IX 174, 264; X 20; XI 2, 4–5, 8–11, 14, 17–20, 27–29, 32, 55, 59, 62, 67, 71, 74, 80–91, 93, 98, 102–104, 106, 110–112, 114, 131, 134–135, 156, 166, 168, 174–175, 177–178, 184–185, 187–192, 211, 227–228, 240, 243, 246, 249, 252, 259,

264–265, 271; XV 34–35; XVI 147–154; XVI 8–14, 41, 76, 78, 81, 91, 94, 100, 102, 104, 113, 115, 117–119, 140–141, 162, 176, 209, 211–212, 215, 220–221, 225, 230, 238, 259–264, 291–294, 296, 299, 314, 317, 319; XIX 1, 58, 92, 101–102, 193
American view of in the 1930s XIX 88
and the Spanish Civil War XVIII 74–80
annexation of Sudentenland IV 19; VIII 284
appeasement of I 276
CPUSA support for XIX 59
cultural figure XVII 104–111
declaration of war on U.S. V 131–136
failure as war leader IV 108; XIX 246
foreign policy IV 122–128
German rearmament IV 116–117
goals of foreign policy IV 123
Hitler and Stalin I 134–139; XIX 62, 71, 98, 118, 143, 213, 246
influence on the *Wehrmacht* V 137–144
invasion of Rhineland IV 115
invasion of Soviet Union IV 111; XIX 57, 98
Operation Barbarossa XVI 184–191
relationship with Spanish Nationalists XVIII 51–56
remilitarizes the Rhineland VIII 284
responsibility for World War II IV 114–120
rise to power V 114–121; XVI 147–154
vegetarianism XI 147
war leader IV 104–112
Hizbollah (Party of God) VI 234; XIV 7, 41, 93, 103, 105, 125–132, 230; XV 98, 113, 131, 133, 142, 153, 201, 264, 266–267, 269
Ho Chi Minh I 46, 183, 290, 294, 296, 297, 298; II 97, 263–264, 266, 267; V 145–150, 174; VI 28, 80, 92–93, 98, 107, 203; IX 93; XII 33–34; XIV 147; XIX 18, 224
Ho Chi Minh Trail VI 142
Hoare-Laval Pact IX 175
Hobbes, Thomas XI 75; XII 109, 118–119, 121–122; XVII 183, 186
Hobbs Committee XIX 6
Hoffa, Jimmy XIX 70
Hoffman, Abbie XIX 65
Hoffman, Clare XIX 158
Hoffmann, Max VIII 93, 252; IX 66
Hogan's Heroes (TV show, 1965–1971) XI 189
Hohenstaufen X 140, 142–143, 146, 204, 226
Hokkaido VI 147
Holbrooke, Richard XVI 269
Holland VIII 72, 245, 261, 280; X 10; XI 62, 108, 179, 193, 211; XII 251–252, 255; XV 14
allies with Amerians in U.S. Revolution XII 39
fights maroons XIII 107
slave trade XIII 270
visited by U.S. ships XII 79
wars wih England XII 198
Hollywood blacklist XIX 160–166, 168–171, 202, 275, 278, 281
Hollywood motion-picture industry XIX 123, 160–172
HCUA investigations of XIX 60, 63–64, 121 160–172
The Hollywood Reporter XIX 167
Hollywood Ten XIX 5, 37–38, 160– 161, 163–164, 167–172, 177, 207, 224, 251
Holmes, John Clellon XIX 50
Holmes, Julius XIX 17
Holmes, Oliver Wendell II 280–281, 284; III 17–18; VI 123; IX 4; XIX 198
dissenting opinion in *Gitlow* v. *New York* XIX 255
opinion in *Schenck* v. *United States* XIX 255, 263
opinion in *Whitney* v. *California* XIX 255
Holocaust (1933–1945) III 251–257; IV 129–142; V 56–61, 151–166; VIII 166; X 20, 278; XI 1–264; XIII 138, 198; XVI 9, 138, 254, 260, 298, 300, 302; XVII 97–98, 145–147
advanced warning of XI 1–8
air raids on concentration camps XI 8–16
Catholic Church XI 191–201
collaboration IV 129–135
Communists in XI 66
ethical representations of XI 45–53
Final Solution, as irrational act XI 110–118
Final Solution, genesis of XI 102–109
Führer Order XI 81–91
gendered experiences in XI 66–73, 93–100
Gypsies in XI 66, 71, 73, 147, 149, 153, 171, 186, 190, 242–243, 247, 257
homosexuals in XI 71, 186, 242–248
humiliation of Jews XI 211
Intentionalist/Structuralist debate XI 102–109
Jehovah's Witnesses in XI 128–137, 186, 243, 246
Jewish Councils in XI 138–145
mentally ill in XI 242
movie representations of XI 155–164
Neutral states and the XI 174–181
ordinary Germans and the XI 183–190, 264–271
reparations XI 210–216
resistence XI 240
role in twentieth-century history V 163
slave labor XI 210–216
survival during XI 217–224
survivor narratives XI 226–233
theories IV 136–141
use of medical data from Nazis XI 146–154
victim psychology XI 235–240
victims during XI 242–250
Holocaust (1978) XI 48
Holtzendorff, Henning von VIII 289, 292–293; IX 75
Holy Alliance IX 226; XVI 72
Holy Roman Empire X 93, 267, 285; XVI 211, 213, 216, 255
Holy Sepulcher X 94, 99, 101, 138, 215, 217, 287
Home Rule Bill (1885) XII 166
Home Rule Bill (1914) VIII 155, 158, 161
Home Rule Party VIII 158
Homer VIII 117; XX 130–137
homosexuality
in the ancient world XX 19–28
in the Holocaust XI 242–248
in World War I IX 146–153
use of symbols XIII 270
Honduras VI 193–194
Honecker, Erich VI 117–118, 120–121, 211
Hong Kong XVI 64, 81, 109
Honorius II X 286
Honorius III X 89, 93–95
Hook, Sidney XIX 61, 110
Hoover Dam (United States) VII 27, 29, 94, 109, 152
Hoover, Herbert I 285; II 49, 86; III 25–26, 50, 66, VIII 285 ; IX 18; XI 56; XVI 296
goodwill trip to South America (1928) III 46
Prohibition III 174
Reconstruction and Finance Corporation II 209
signs the Colorado River Compact VII 152
Hoover, J. Edgar I 76, 292; II 232; III 107, 233; VI 24, 158; XIX 4, 173–179
anticommunism of XIX 53, 121, 173–179, 200, 249, 251–252
appearance before HCUA (1947) XIX 108
assistance to HCUA XIX 201
beliefs about Communists in civil rights movement XIX 31–32, 78, 80
background XIX 246
power XIX 117, 173–179
role in *Amerasia* case XIX 18–19, 176 178
role in Hiss case XIX 176
role in Rosenberg prosecution XIX 176, 178, 282, 288
role in Smith Act prosecutions XIX 54, 151, 252
speech to International Association of Police Chiefs XIX 178
Hoover administration IX 171
Native American policies III 144
Reconstruction Finance Corporation (RFC) III 154

Hoover Dam II 257
Hopkins, Esek XII 77, 81
Hopkins, Harry L. I 306; V 196; VI 155; XVI 218
Hopkins, Joseph XII 287
Hopkins, Samuel XII 58
Hopkins, Stephen XII 152
Hopkinson, Francis XII 307
horizontal escalation VI 221
Horn of Africa VI 42, 164, 256; XIV 180
Hortobagy National Park VII 253
Horton, Zilphia XIX 76–77
Hospitallers X 30, 49, 75, 90, 158, 174
Höss, Rudolf XI 131, 186
Hostiensis X 57, 178, 226, 236
House, Edward VIII 228; XVI 308
House Committee on Foreign Affairs XIX 239
House of Burgesses XII 148, 241
House Un-American Activities Committee (HUAC) I 77, 79, 306; II 130–134, 207; VI 124, 127, 129, 178; XIX 19, 38–39, 53–54, 60–66, 80, 119, 245, 265, 272
  as model for Australian Lowe Royal Commission XIX 266
  assistance from FBI and Hoover XIX 65–66, 173, 178, 252
  contempt of Conress charges XIX 148, 150, 153
  criticized by CivilRights Congress XIX 234
  decline in activity XIX 281
  dissolved XIX 126
  established as permanent committee XIX 251
  hears testimony from
    Bentley XIX 194, 197, 248
    Chambers XIX 194, 198, 248
    Clark XIX 151
    Crouch XIX 202
    Hoover XIX 108
    Kazan XIX 39, 47
    Miller XIX 48
    on Stockholm Peace Petition XIX 242
    professional informants XIX 201
    Robinson XIX 76
  investigations of
    anti-Vietnam War movement XIX 207
    Communists in Maryland XIX 209
    CPUSA XIX 57, 275
    educational institutions XIX 30, 61, 110–111, 113
    Eisler XIX 225
    federal employees XIX 133
    Hiss XIX 63, 154–159, 244, 251
    Hollywood movie industry XIX 5, 44, 47, 60–61, 63–64, 93, 121, 161, 163–164, 167–172, 196, 224, 251
    Joint Anti-Fascist Refugee Committee XIX 214
    labor movement XIX 61, 73, 99, 182
    New Deal XIX 99
    peace and nuclear-disarmament movements XIX 240, 243, 281
    Ware Group XIX 155
  members XIX 1126, 211, 220, 224
  origins XIX 246
  pamphlets on Communism XIX 99, 101
  state versions XIX 204, 207
  treatment of witnesses who took the Fifth Amendment XIX 161
The House I Live In XIX 168
House Judiciary Committee XIX 227
House Special Committee to Investigate Un-American Acitivities (Dies Committee) XIX 61, 63, 101, 116, 119, 133, 160, 170, 246, 251
House Ways and Means Committee XIX 157
Houseman, John XIX 39
Houston, Charles Hamilton II 19, 22, 137–138
Houston Accords (1997) XIV 279–280, 284
How the Other Half Lives (Riis) III 260
"How You Can Fight Communism" XIX 250
Howard University XIII 254
Howard v. *Howard* (1858) XIII 101
Howe, George Augustus XII 156, 159
Howe, Richard XII 37, 106, 155–158
Howe, William XII 30, 37, 39, 40, 44–45, 47–48, 94, 146, 155–158, 181–182, 267–268, 270–271, 273–274, 304–307
Howl XIX 48, 50–51
Hoxha, Enver VI 181
Hoyos Mission (1914) VIII 47
HUAC. See House Committee on Un-American Activities (HCUA)
Huck, Christian XII 186
Hudson, Hosea XIX 75
Hudson Bay XII 171
Hudson Bay Company XII 200
Hudson Motor Car Company IX 21
Hudson River VII 256, 261; XII 10, 39, 43–44, 98, 162, 177, 267, 269–271, 304
Hudson River Valley XII 46
Hugh of Peccator X 161, 163, 165
Hughes, Justice Charles Evans III 25–27, 179; V 205
Hughes, Henry XIII 48, 221
Hughes, J. R. XIX 270
Hughes, Langston III 79, 83, 182; IX 4; XIX 46
Huguenots XVI 255
Hulegu X 183, 185–187
Hull, Cordell III 47, 50; V 264, 312; VI 78–79 ; XI 60
Human Development Index (HDI) XIV 55–56
human rights I 140–146; II 97–102; VI 51, 208
  influence on U.S. foreign policy II 101
  U.S. history II 98
Humbert of Romans X 33, 65–66, 69
Humbert of Silva X 209, 284
Humboldt, Alexander von XIII 272
Hume, David X 80, 98; XII 121
Humphrey, Hubert H. II 162, 177, 197; VI 85–86; XIX 226
Hundred Years' War (1337–1453) XI 80
Hungarian Revolutionary Committee VI 134
Hungarian uprising (1956) VI 130–137; XVII 76, 231
Hungary I 109, 112, 119, 152, 274, 294; II 36, 52; VI 8, 103, 110, 116, 118, 165, 178, 181, 217, 246, 249, 251, 261, 274; VII 247–249, 253–254; IX 134, 225; IX 134, 225; XI 24, 60, 175, 177, 214; XIV 265; XV 120; XVI 11, 30, 36, 41, 76–77, 84, 98, 101, 104, 122, 124, 127, 175, 185, 192, 204, 233, 238, 284–285, 289, 317
  after World War II XIX 2, 195
  attempted coup against communists (1956) I 276; VI 130, 270; XIX 146, 209, 215, 272
  Crusaders X 15–16, 182
  dams in VII 100–107
  East German emigration through VI 118, 121
  environmental groups in VII 103
  fascism XVII 85, 137, 139
  Government Bloc XVI 124
  Jews in XI 202, 213
  Ministry for Environmental Protection VII 247–248, 250
  Ministry of Water and T ransportation VII 250
  National Independence Front XVI 124
  Roman Catholic Church XIX 184
  Soviet invasion of VI 182; XV 245; XVI 288;
Hunt, E. Howard VI 24
Hunter, Clarence XIX 269
Hunter, Kim XIX 161
Huntington, Samuel P. VI 198
Hunton, W. Alphaeus XIX 10, 29–30
Hurston, Zora Neale II 137; III 78–82, 184; IX 4
Husayn XV 234–235
Husayn ibn 'Ali (King Hussein) VIII 37–40
Hussein (King of Jordan) I 156, 314, 317; II 147; VI 201; XIV 64, 66, 68; XV 22–23, 25, 40–50,

61–63, 136–137, 169, 198–199, 220, 247, 266
visits United States XV 44
Hussein, Saddam I 159, 163, 224; II 153, 156; VI 54, 58, 61, 217, 225; X 56; XI 166; XIV 29, 31, 36, 61, 88, 96, 102, 109, 146, 170, 173, 191, 215, 237–243, 270; XV 72–82, 84, 86–87, 90, 98, 100–101, 104–105, 112, 120, 182, 255, 258, 260; XVI 71, 98
Huston, Tom XIX 128
Huston plan XIX 221
Hutchins, Robert M. XIX 107
Hutchinson, Thomas XII 192, 214
Hutier, Oskar von VIII 112, 240; IX 129
Hutt Committee XIII 136
Huxley, Aldous IX 84
hydrogen bomb (Soviet) XIX 164
hydrogen bomb (U.S.) XIX 236–237

I

I. G. Farben XI 205, 221
I Want To Live 166
I Was a Communist for the FBI XIX 166, 201
Ibadite movement XIV 206
Ibanez, Frank XIX 216
Ibarruri, Dolores (La Pasionaria) XVIII 160, 274–275
Iberian Peninsula X 2, 219, 287
Ibn al-Athir X 47, 192, 248
ibn al-Saabah, Hassan X 183–184, 258
Ibn Jubayr X 47, 193–196, 198
ibn Munqidh, Usamah X 192, 198–200
Ibn Saud X 61
Ice Harbor Dam (United States) VII 31, 55
Iceland XVI 45, 84, 319
secession from Denmark XIV 171
"Ichi-Go Offensive" (1944) V 151
Ickes, Harold L. II 211; III 150
Idaho VII 201, 220, 224
dams in VII 26, 29
salmon in VII 196
Idaho Fish and Game Department VII 53
Idaho Rivers United VII 221
Idrissid monarchy (789–926) XIV 206
Ilkhans X 60, 182, 185–186, 189
Illinois XI 124
Native Americans in XII 176
Illyria IX 270
Immigration Act (1924) III 22, 229
Immigration and Nationality Act (1952) I 77
Immigration and Naturalization Service XIX 5, 182, 184, 200, 225
Immigration issues and CPUSA XIX 87
Imperial Economic Conference (1932) VI 78
Imperial Guard Cavalry IX 116
Imperial Irrigation District (IID) VII 152, 154–155
Imperial Valley VII 151, 154–155
Imperial Presidency VI 56–57
Imperialism XIV 178; XV 22, 58, 101
during the Crusades X 55–56, 63
end of IX 91–97
Import-Export Bank I 53; III 47
import-substituting industrialization (ISI) XV 106
Incidents at Sea Agreement (1972) VI 31
indentured servitude XIII 164
Independence Party II 199
Independent Air Force IX 11
India I 151, 277; II 85, 117; VI 50, 53, 79, 136, 188, 214–215, 219, 271; VII 125; VIII 32–33, 83, 103, 133, 168, 208; IX 93, 112, 225–226; X 305; XII 33, 165, 168, 171, 252; XIV 88, 144, 147, 176–177, 260; XV 68, 167, 215; XVI 6, 13, 23, 70–71, 81, 107, 110–111, 318
agriculture in VII 130, 133
African American interest in XIX 12
anti-discrimination petition to UN XIX 12
Army VIII 38
British rule in VI 161; VII 125
Central Ministry of Environment and Forests VII 133
dams in VII 9, 125–134
Hindutva XIV 141
independence XIX 9, 12
Ministry of Environment and Forests VII 128
Moghul canals in VII 125
National Congress IX 93
nuclear test (1974) I 216, 223
nuclear weapons XVI 98, 109
nuclear weapons development I 219–223, 228; VI 53; XIV 40
policy toward Soviet Union VI 81
slaves in XIII 37
World War I VIII 216
motivation of soldiers in VIII 266
Indian Ocean VIII 137; XII 39, 198; XIII 129; XVI 65, 254
Dutch traders in XII 198
Portuguese traders lose control of XII 198
Indian Reorganization Act (IRA, 1934) III 139–146, 151, 162; VII 167
Indian Self-Determination Act (1975) VII 172
Indian Territory XIII 108
Indiana
loyalty oath for wrestlers XIX 204
Native Americans in XII 176
Indochina I 44–46, 86, 290; VI 59, 81, 103, 106, 141, 188, 203, 209, 283; VIII 233; IX 93, 115, 117; XV 12, 15; XVI 79, 85, 136; XIX 224, 236, 243
Indonesia I 269, 273, 277, 295; II 40, 117; VI 81, 188; VIII 137; XIV 88, 180, 212, 215, 230; XVI 84, 88, 109; XIX 25, 140, 145, 224
invasion of East Timor VI 270
terrorism XIV 14
Industrial Revolution VIII 136; IX 56, 80, 224; XIII 175; XVI 251; XVII 19, 52, 54, 257, 272
Industrial Workers of the World (IWW) VIII 298; XIX 87, 102
informers XIX 196–203
Inglis, Amirah XIX 266
Inland Empire Waterways Association VII 53, 55
Inman, Mary XIX 191
Innocent III X 67, 79, 87–93, 107–111, 113, 117, 126, 130–131, 149, 155, 175, 205–210, 225, 235, 239, 246, 267, 270, 294–295, 298
Innocent IV X 57–58, 178
INS v. *Chadha* VI 286
Institute for Pacific Relations XIX 110
Institute for Sexual Science in Berlin XI 243
Institute for Water Resources (IWR) VII 262
Integrated River Basin Development VII 1
integration II 24, 90, 92, 136, 292
Intercontinental Ballistic Missile (ICBM) I 49, 189, 192, 230; II 118; VI 50, 110, 144, 202, 260; XV 75; XVI 45, 254, 284
Intergovernmental Committee for Political Refugees XI 55, 64
Intergovernmental Maritime Consultative Organization VII 143
Interim Agreement on the West Bank and the Gaza Strip (Oslo II) XV 185
Intermediate Range Ballistic Missile (IRBM) I 193
Intermediate Range Nuclear Forces (INF) Treaty VI 17–18, 44, 224, 232, 242; XVI 95
Soviets walk out of VI 44
Internal Macedonian Revolutionary Organization (IMRO) XVI 248–249
Internal Revenue Service XIX 128, 182, 232
Internal Security Act (1950) I 74–77; II 131. *See also* McCarran Act
International Association of Police Chiefs XIX 178
International Atomic Energy Agency (IAEA) XIV 40, 241, 143, 146, 148, 150; XV 75

INDEX

International Bank for Reconstruction and Development (IBRD, or World Bank) VI 78
International Boundary and Water Commission (IBWC) VII 154–155, 157
International Broadcasting Bureau XIV 233
International Brotherhood of Teamsters XIX 69
International Coalition for the Restoration of Rivers and Communities Affected by Dams VII 131
International Commission for the Scientific Exploration of the Mediterranean Sea (CIESM) VII 143
International Commission on Large Dams VII 126, 130
International Consortium for Cooperation on the Nile (ICCON) XIV 272
International Corruption Perceptions Index (2000) XIV 48
International Court of Justice (ICJ) VII 100, 103, 106; XIV 153, 177; XV 247
International Criminal Court (ICC) XVII 14, 142, 146, 149
International Day of Action Against Dams and for Rivers, Water & Life VII 96
International Disarmament Conference XVI 12
International Forum on Globalization (IFG), Committee on the Globalization of Water, VII 285
International Humanitarian Law XIV 278
International Information Agency XIX 265
International Joint Commission (IJC) VII 116–117, 123
International Labor Defense (ILD) III 186, 236; XIX 78, 234, 255, 258
International Ladies Garment Workers Union (ILGWU) III 191; XIX 185, 233
International Law Association XIV 274
International Law Commission of the United Nations VII 79
International Longshoremen's and Warehousemen's Union (ILWU) XIX 214, 216, 232
International Military Tribunal in Nuremberg (IMT) V 221, 224; XI 68, 252–253, 257–258, 260–261; XVII 146
International Monetary Fund (IMF) I 22; VI 53, 78, 120; XIV 58, 114, 214; XVI 77, 87
International Rivers Network VII 9, 238
International Security and Assistance Force (ISAF) XIV 262
International Telephone and Telegraph (ITT) XIX 142
International Union of Mine, Metal and Smelting Workers XIX 202
International Workers of the World (IWW) III 223
International Workers Order XIX 215
International Working Men's Association (First International, 1864) VI 178
"The Internationale" XIX 36
Interstate Commerce Commission (1887) III 10
Interstate Highway Act (1956) II 105–113
interwar naval treaties V 201–209
intifada (uprising) XIV 7, 30, 63, 223; XV 182, 200
Intolerable Acts. *See* Coercive Acts
Investiture Controversy (1075–1077) X 81, 117, 205, 227, 274, 279; XI 79
Iran I 15, 82, 87–89, 110, 113, 141, 145, 263, 294; II 34, 103, 144, 153; VI 21, 54, 113, 131, 162, 165–166, 195, 201, 215–217, 231–232, 266; VIII 35, 82; X 60, 182, 185–186, 278, 288; XIV 2, 7, 58, 78–79, 87, 123, 127, 136, 141, 143–144, 146, 176–181, 186, 188, 190, 201, 211–212, 215, 217, 230–231, 235, 238, 242, 262; XV 26, 29, 31, 59, 62, 73, 83, 133, 146, 156–164, 176, 206, 228–236, 271–272; XVI 236, 238, 269
  Abadan oil refinery XVI 238
  aid to anti-Taliban resistance XIV 11
  aid to Hizbollah XIV 128
  aircraft crashes in XIV 40
  arms sales I 51; XIX 128, 280
  Assembly of Leadership Experts XV 113
  bazaaris (small merchants) XV 230, 234–235
  Black Friday XV 107, 234
  blacklisting of XIV 16
  British interests in XV 156, 160
  CIA involvement I 211
  Communist insurgency in XIX 21, 249
  Constitutional Revolution (1906) XV 109, 231
  Council of Guardians XV 111, 113–114
  Council of the Islamic Republic XV 234
  crucial to U.S. security I 85
  democracy in XIV 133–134, 136, 140
  hostage crisis in VI 107, 166, 226, 232, 268; XIV 37–39, 41, 96; XV 102, 160, 176, 254
  Iran-e Novin (New Iran) XV 231
  Iran-Iraq War XV 97–105
  Islamic Republic XV 233
  Kurds XIV 168–174
  majles-i khubregan (Assembly of Experts) XIV 136
  Majlis (Iranian parliament) XV 156, 160, 163
  National Development Plan (1949) XV 229
  National Front XV 156–158, 231, 234
  nuclear weapons XIV 40–41; XVI 109
  oil XV 108, 156, 160, 175, 178, 180, 229
  oil, discovery of (1908) XV 172
  Pahlavi dynasty (1925–1979) XV 157
  Persianization XV 109
  Qajar dynasty XV 106, 108, 156
  relations with the United States XIV 36–43
  Religious Propagandists XV 231
  Revolutionary Guards XIV 41; XV 113
  Safavid dynasty XV 106, 111
  sale of U.S. missiles to VI 196
  SAVAK XIV 37; XV 107–108, 157, 231, 233–234
  Sepa-e Din (Religious Corps) XV 231
  Shiites in XV 98
  shura-i maslahat-i nezam (Expediency Council) XIV 136
  shura-i negahban (Council of Guardians) XIV 136
  Soviet interests in VI 255; XV 253; XIX 144
  Soviet occupation of VI 165
  Soviet withdrawal from VI 161
  Supplemental Agreement XV 160
  Supreme Guide of the Revolution XV 114
  tensions with Afghanistan I 15
  territorial concessions I 288
  terrorism XIV 126
  Tudeh (masses) Party XV 108, 157, 161
  Twelver Shiites XV 234
  Uniform Dress Law (1928) XV 108
  U.S. policies toward XIX 140, 142
  water XIV 269; XV 206
  Western interest in VI 255
  Westernization XV 229
  White Revolution XV 229, 231
  women XIV 121, 123, 140, 231
Iran crisis (1945–1946) XVI 228
Iran-Contra Affair VI 3, 57–58, 191–196, 231–232; XV 98, 102; XIX 128
Iranian Revolution (1979) XIV 2, 36–37, 41, 89, 121, 123, 125–126, 131, 140, 186, 217; XV 29, 53, 97, 102, 104, 106–115, 149, 176, 228, 234–235, 276
Iran-Iraq War (1980–1988) I 54; VI 162, 271; XIV 36, 38, 41, 89, 173, 248; XV 72, 74, 78–79, 89, 91, 97–105, 109, 112, 126, 176, 253, 260
Iraq I 202; II 144, 153; 54, 58, 107, 162–163, 213, 215, 217, 219, 261, 268, 271; IX 92, 96, 206; X 56, 60, 89, 185–186, 278, 288; XIV 31, 37–38, 40–41, 50, 55–56, 61, 79, 87, 95–96, 101, 106–107, 109–110, 112, 125–126, 143–144, 146, 176–177, 179–181, 190, 211–212, 215, 219–220, 230–231, 237–243, 250, 262, 265, 267; XV 20, 22–23, 26–27, 29, 31–32, 34, 41, 44–45, 48, 57, 59, 62, 75, 141–142, 144–146, 169, 187, 201, 204, 206, 209, 216, 222, 251,

263, 267, 270–272, 275; XVI 68, 71, 98, 236, 240, 269; XIX 129
ancient irrigation in VII 11
Anfal campaign (1988–1989) XIV 169; XV 79
Baath Party XIV 82, 253; XV 80, 117, 124, 273, 275
biological weapons XV 78
chemical weapons XV 74, 78–79
Communist Party XV 117, 273
Free Officers Movement XV 117–118
genocide XVII 95
Gulf War I 163; VI 72–79, 80–88, 225
Halabja massacre (1998) XIV 169
Highway of Death XV 85–86
Independence Party XV 117
Interim Constitution XV 117
invasion of Kuwait I 289; XIV 215, 218; XV 89, 98, 147, 255
Iran-Iraq War XV 97–105
Iraqi Revolution XV 116–125
Jews forced from XIV 221
Kurds VI 54, 61, 217; XIV 168–174; XV 87, 98, 100, 102
Kurds, massacres of XI 166
Mosul Revolt XV 124
National Democratic Party XV 117–118, 123
National Union Front XV 117
no-flight zone XV 87
nuclear program XV 74
oil XV 175, 177–178
oil companies in XV 177
Osirak nuclear facility VI 106; XIV 149
overthrow of Faisal II (1958) I 282
Pan-Arab campaign I 281
Revolution (1958) XV 166, 168, 270
Shiites in VI 61, 217; XV 102
Sunnis in 98, 102
U.S. invasion of (2003) XIV 14, 68, 89, 96, 191, 277; XVI 109
U.S. propaganda in XV 256
water policy in VII 135–141; XIV 269–270, 273; XV 206
women XV 119
Iraq Liberation Act (1998) XIV 240, 243
Iraqi Atomic Energy Commission XV 78
Iraqi National Oil Company XV 119
Iraq Petroleum Company XV 119, 177
Ireland VIII 83; IX 93; XII 34, 166; XVI 81, 244; XIX 12
British rule in VIII 154–162
Catholic condemnation of Easter Rising VIII 209
Council of Bishops VIII 209
Easter Rising VIII 154–162, 209; IX 21
famine in VIII 189; XII 166
Home Rule VIII 154–162; XVI 80
immigrants to America XII 279
uprising in (1798) XII 189
World War I
conscription in VIII 158
impact upon country VIII 154–162
religion in VIII 208
"Wild Geese" soldiers IX 116
Irish Citizen Army VIII 158
Irish Free State XVI 13, 80–81
Irish Parliamentary Party VIII 155–156
Irish Republican Army VIII 158; IX 93; XIV 195, 198; XVI 243–244, 248
Irish Republican Brotherhood VIII 155–156
Irish Sea XII 79
Irish Unionists VIII 161
Irish Volunteers VIII 158, 161; XVI 248
Iron Act (1750) XII 202, 243
Iron Curtain VI 49, 118, 173, 206
The Iron Curtain XIX 163
Iron Curtain speech (1946) VI 250
Iroquoia XII 174, 177, 179
Irving, Washington XII 259
Isaac II Angelus X 26, 29, 250
Isaacson, Judith XI 69, 223
Isabella X 2, 22
Isadore of Seville X 242
Islam X 4, 65, 100, 199, 201; XIV 19, 55, 81, 93, 159, 176, 180–181, 201, 205, 230–231, 235, 244, 250, 261, 291; XV 31; XIX 13
democracy XIV 133–142
disenfranchisement of women XIV 140
movements XIV 79, 252
political Islam XIV 136–137, 139
radicalism XIV 61
United States seen as enemy of XIV 87
violence in XIV 182–191
Islamic fundamentalism XIV 7, 182, 231
women XIV 121
Islamic Jihad XIV 24, 93, 103, 186, 230; XV 90
Islamic Revolution (1979) XVI 269
Islamic Salvation Army (AIS) XV 5
Islamism XIV 7, 182
Isle of Man XII 242
Isma'il, Hafiz I 309–312
Israel I 56, 162–164, 278, 283, 309, 316–317; VI 43, 83, 164, 172, 188, 200–201, 215, 246, 261, 271; X 55–56, 60, 63, 272, 305; XI 228; XIV 16, 30–32, 41, 55–56, 63, 76–77, 79, 87, 89, 95–108, 126, 129, 153, 159, 177, 179–180, 184, 198, 205, 217, 238–242, 246, 248; XV 19–21, 23, 30–31, 40, 42, 46–47, 51–58, 62–63, 69–70, 75, 78–79, 83, 91, 101, 121, 134–140, 142, 149–150, 152–153, 155, 167–168, 170, 193–194, 198–200, 202, 204, 213–216, 237–241, 271, 275–276; XVI 136, 239, 269
Agudat Yisrael Party XIV 252, 256, 258–259
Arab economic boycott of XIV 44, 50
Arab invasion (1948) XIV 144
Arab opposition to VI 160; XIV 125
Arab population in XIV 258
attacked by Egypt and Syria VI 163
attacks Iraqi nuclear facility XIV 148–149; XVI 98
Basic Law 256
boundaries XV 33–39
Central Religious Camp XIV 256
control of Jerusalem XIV 159–167
criticism of XIV 14
Degel Torah XIV 256
democratic army in XII 305
Eichmann trial XI 36–43
founding of IV 160
Gahal (Gush Herut-Liberalim, or Freedom Liberal Bloc) XV 136
Gaza raid (1955) XV 244, 248
Gush Emunim (Bloc of the Faithful) XIV 256, 258; XV 139
Herut Party XV 23
impact of Holocaust on development of XI 120–127
Internal Security Services XIV 225
intifada in XIV 19–27; XV 89–96
invasion of Lebanon I 196; XIV 126, 131, 270; XV 126–133, 255
Iraqi bombing of I 195
kingdom XI 125
Knesset XIV 146–147, 252, 254–257, 259; XV 56, 130, 220, 261
Labor Party XIV 151, 252–254, 256, 259; XV 24, 95, 131, 182, 186, 263
Liberal Party XV 23
Likud Party XIV 19, 23–24, 95, 151, 252–254, 256, 258; XV 52, 95, 131, 182–183, 186, 200, 220, 222, 226, 263–265
military I 163, 278, 308
National Religious Party (NRP) XIV 256
National Security Agency (Shin Bet) XIV 101–102
nuclear weapons I 218, 222; XIV 40, 143–150; XV 139; XVI 98, 109
Oslo accords XV 182–192
Palestinian refugees XIV 220–226

Palestinian workers XV 94
politics in XIV 254
preemptive strikes against Egypt and Iraq I 239
Rafi (Israel Labor List) XV 136
Sadat trip to (1977) XV 219–227
settlements in XIV 151–158
SHAS Party XIV 252–260
Suez Crisis I 192, 277, 280, 289; VI 11, 106, 135, 270; XV 244–251, 253; XVI 235–242
Syria, demands against XIV 128
Syria, negotiations with XV 260–269
Torah Religious Front XIV 257
Turkey, relations with XIV 262
UN partition (1947) XV 223
Unit 101 XV 248
United Religious Front XIV 257
United Torah Judaism (UTJ) XIV 256
water XIV 268, 269; XV 205
Yesh Gevul (There Is a Limit) XV 133
Israel Policy Forum XIV 164
Israeli Air Force (IAF) VI 172; XIV 144, 149; XV 74
Israeli Atomic Energy Commission XIV 145
Israeli Defense Forces (IDF) VI 161; XIV 100, 126, 131, 144, 152, 157; XV 127, 134, 148, 153; XV 127, 134, 148–149, 153, 261
Israeli Islamic Movement XIV 167
Israeli-Jordanian treaty (1994) XV 56, 83
Israeli-Palestinian conflict XIV 68, 95–108, 229, 238
Istria XVI 36
Italian Communist Party VI 179, 245
Italian Maritime States X 30, 53, 148–157
Italian-American Black Shirts XVII 137, 140
Italian-Ethiopian War XVI 13
Italy I 293; II 39; VI 178, 246–247, 251, 267, 274; VII 149; VIII 47, 95, 104, 106, 192, 212, 221, 233, 261, 266, 277, 280, 283; XI 2, 74, 123, 167, 179, 191; XVI 11, 13, 32–33, 73, 80, 87, 94, 99, 100, 104, 110, 130–131, 138, 185–186, 188, 193, 218, 260, 262, 267, 292, 315
aftermath of World War II I 173
aid to Franco XIX 103
alliance with Germany VIII 35
antinuclear protest in VI 16
army, size of VIII 69
colonialism XVI 66
Communist movement in XIX 265
cost of Med Plan to VII 146
Crusades X 15, 26, 67, 70, 73, 89, 90, 95, 117, 121, 126, 128, 146, 206, 218, 229, 269–270, 284–285, 289
fascism in XVI 140–142; XVII 85, 135–137, 140, 180–187
hindering the Axis effort V 175–182
invades Ethiopia XVI 219; XIX 88
invades Libya VIII 212; XIV 192
Jews expelled from X 22
monarchy XVI 177, 182
Multinational Force in Lebanon XV 148–155
NATO bases XVI 267
navy VIII 212
pollution from industrial centers in VII 147
postwar influence of Communist parties I 174, 176
slavery in XIII 165
social welfare XVII 273
Socialists VIII 254, 261
terrorism XVI 245, 248
unification XIV 171; XVI 66
World War I IX 27, 34, 45, 63, 84, 96–97, 105, 107, 111, 116, 134–135, 140, 173, 175, 206, 208, 225, 250, 270, 272; XVI 308
air war IX 13, 218
airplanes given to United States VIII 19
desertion of soldiers IX 235
prewar alliances VIII 225–231
refuses mandate for Armenia VIII 12
Yalta Agreement (1945) I 301, 306
Itezhitezhi Dam (Zambia) VII 240
Izaak Walton League of America VII 53, 122

J

Jackson, Jesse XIII 198
Jackson, Justice Robert H. III 27; V 188, 222–224; XI 160, 258–259; XIX 49, 271
Jackson, Thomas (Stonewall) VIII 23
Jackson State College VI 23
Jackson-Vanik Amendment I 140, 142
Jacobellis v. Ohio (1964) XIV 181
Jacobin Terror (1793–1794) XII 192
Jacobinism XVI 130, 143
Jacobins XIII 209
Jaffa X 46, 48, 252, 254, 257, 261
Jaffe, Philip XIX 16– 23
Jakob the Liar (1999) XI 160
Jamaica XII 171, 310–311, 313, 315; XIII 66, 104, 212
Christianity in XIII 190
Christmas Rebellion (1831) XIII 91, 154, 159–160, 231
maroons in XII 314; XIII 105, 108–110
Quaker slaveholders in XIII 31
slave revolts XIII 154, 155, 159, 231
slave trade XIII 270
slavery in XIII 64, 90, 151, 207, 233
survival of African religions XIII 190
James I (of Aragon) X 189
James II XII 209, 243, 262
James of Vitry X 178, 180–181
James, C. L. R. XIX 10
James, Harry IX 4
James, Henry VIII 203
James, Victor XIX 268
Jamestown XII 32, 174
settlement at (1607) XII 234
Japan I 30, 85, 88, 259, 285, 288; II 35, 39–40, 264; III 10, 12, 108; VI 53, 113, 147, 149, 151, 204, 217, 254, 266–267; VIII 230; XI 175; XII 33; XIV 135, 176–177, 211, 240; XV 78, 82; XVI 11, 16, 22–24, 41, 45–46, 80–81, 85, 87, 92, 106–109, 112, 193, 200, 208, 218–219, 230, 254, 284, 292, 314–315; XIX 12
atomic bombing of I 4, 183, 239, 263; VI 71, 255
attack on Pearl Harbor XIX 88
British alliance with (1902) VIII 34
China
defeat of XVI 66
invasion of IV 254; XIX 88
treatment of Chinese prisoners XVI 254; XVII 7
colonialism XVI 65–66
Council on National Defence IX 163
domino theory I 266
economic problems in VI 219
Greater East Asia Co-Prosperity Sphere IV 258
industrialization of IV 254
interest in Arab oil I 162
Korea, occupation of VI 146
Manchurian occupation I 59
Meiji Restoration (1868) XVI 66, 107
military conduct IV 151–156
military tradition in VI 27
mutual defense relationship with United States VI 54
naval power XVI 68
postwar occupation I 3; XIX 21
postwar recovery of I 263; VI 59
Russia
defeat of XVI 107
intervention in (1918) XVI 1–7
wars with I 263; VI 251
Siberia, intervention into (1918) IX 165
surrender III 11, 15; VI 49
trade with Iran XIV 40

treatment of prisoners of war IV 152; XVII 142; XIX 266
Unit 731 XVI 254
WWI IX 96, 162–169, 173–174
entry into VIII 13
WWII
peace terms VI 146; XIX 239
women in V 305
Japanese Americans
internment of III 102–109; V 183–190; VI 57
Japanese death marches
Bataan (1942) IV 152
Sandakan (1945) IV 152
Japanese publications XIX 216
Jarrico, Paul XIX 38
Jarring, Gunnar V. XV 135, 217
Jarring mission XV 135, 217
Jaspers, Karl XI 42, 111
Jaures, Jean VIII 151, 255
Javits, Jacob K. VI 285
Jay, John XII 21, 70, 73, 121, 134, 290, 296
opposition to treaty negotiations with Spain XII 25
Jay-Gardoqui Treaty XII 290–291
Jazz IX 80, 84, 87; XIII 141
Jean de Joinville X 66, 144
Jebel Druze XV 275
Jefferson, Thomas XII 2, 23, 34, 62, 109–110, 113–114, 119–120, 125, 139, 141, 151, 175, 214, 225, 243, 258, 261–263, 286, 296; XIII 13, 18, 19, 23, 48, 149, 173, 184; XIV 192; XVI 66
slavery XII 1–2
views on blacks XII 296
Jefferson Bank, St. Louis, Missouri XIX 31
Jefferson School, New York XIX 230
Jeffersonian Republicans XIII 281–282
Jehovah's Witnesses XI 128–137, 186, 219, 237
Jellicoe, John VIII 293; IX 53, 75, 100, 102, 141, 177–178
Jencks, Clinton XIX 202
Jenkins, David XIX 230, 234
Jenner, William XIX 153
Jennings, Peter XV 86
Jerome, V. J, XIX 191
Jerusalem VIII 41, 216; IX 206; X 7, 10, 16–18, 27, 32–33, 35–37, 47, 49, 54–55, 57, 59, 73–78, 88, 90, 92, 94, 96–98, 100–101, 103, 105, 108–109, 115, 117–118, 121, 123, 126, 130, 138–143, 145, 154, 159, 165–166, 170–174, 187, 191–192, 194, 198–201, 206, 209, 211–213, 215–219, 224, 226, 229, 235, 238–239, 216–217, 219, 224, 226, 229, 235, 238–239, 249, 251, 254–264, 267, 279–284, 286, 291–297, 303, 305; XI 57, 125, 158, 161; XIV 20, 22–24, 100–103, 106, 154, 157, 162, 220, 226: XV 20–21, 23, 25, 38, 41–42, 52, 56, 79, 94, 102, 134, 136, 183, 190–191, 194–195, 214–215, 217, 219, 222, 226, 239, 269; XVI 239
control of XIV 159–167
ratio of Jews to Arabs in XIV 162
Jesuits X 8; XI 23; XIV 233
Jesus Christ X 10, 15, 20, 32, 35–36, 64, 66, 73, 81–84, 86, 93, 98, 105, 117, 130, 132, 177, 199, 215, 228, 233, 287; XI 17, 19, 20, 29, 131, 164; XII 150; XIII 3, 27, 189
Jewish Agency for Palestine XI 62–63, 124
Jewish organizations XIX 241
Jewish Question XI 21, 37, 39, 59, 81, 87–88, 91, 102, 104, 107–108, 111, 113, 138, 175, 184, 189, 211, 217, 227, 249, 268, 270–271
Jewish Women's Union XI 97
Jewish-Bolshevik Conspiracy XI 82, 86–87
Jews
Crusades, treatment of during X 8, 10, 13–23, 35, 40, 42–44, 60, 62, 101, 105, 140, 177, 179, 181, 190, 192, 195, 209, 213, 238, 272–278
emigration from Germany XI 55–64, 93–100
European XVI 9
extermination of XI 257
historical treatment of XI 17–24
Holocaust XI 1–264
murder of VIII 94–95
neutral states in World War II XI 175
World War I, participation in VIII 164–169
JFK (1991) VI 138
jihad X 107, 132–138, 159, 163, 187, 273, 289
Jim Crow II 23–28, 43–45, 90, 140–142, 163; IX 2–6; XIX 234
Jimenez de Rada, Rodrigo X 243, 246
Jocko Valley VII 167, 169
Jodl, Alfred V 3, 22, 127, 224; XI 254
Joffre, Joseph VIII 11, 16, 71, 114, 129, 147–149, 182–183, 232, 234, 236–237, 252; IX 29, 101, 105, 108, 110, 117; XVI 204
Johannesburg, South Africa VII 4, 7
John (king of England) X 88–90
John III (Portugal) XIII 40
John Birch Society XIX 186
John Chrysostom XI 21
John Day Dam (United States) VII 53–54
John Martin Dam (United States) VII 13–14
John of Brienne X 87–90, 93–96
John Paul II X 79; XI 191
John Reed Club XIX 35
John the Baptist X 35, 84
Johns Hopkins University XIX 198, 202
Johnson, Andrew VI 57; XIII 5
Johnson, Charles S. XIX 12
Johnson, Henry IX 2
Johnson, Hewlett XIX 238
Johnson, James Weldon IX 2
Johnson, Louis A. I 3–8
Johnson, Lyndon B. I 8, 64, 66, 89, 119, 130, 159, 291; II 5–7, 45, 93, 114–115, 141, 161; III 31; VI 23, 28, 66, 86, 95, 138–145, 185, 201, 284; XII 30, 31, 33; XIII 200, 254; XV 135, 247, 257
criticism of Eisenhower administration I 193
decides not to run for reelection VI 145
defense spending VI 144
Five Principles speech (1967) XV 215
Great Society I 292; II 162, 175, 181, 270–271, 276
Gulf of Tonkin incident I 291
Middle East XV 215
opinion of space program II 247, 260
opposition to VI 24
Philadelphia Plan II 182
signs Central Arizona Project bill VII 110
Vietnam War I 292, 296; II 4, 266; VI 59
views on Latin America I 18
War on Poverty II 166, 270–279
Johnson administration I 68; II 4, 163; VI 26, 28, 59, 103, 138–145, 199, 204; VII 259; XIII 256; XV 257; XVI 157
arms control VI 33
arms race I 190
atmospheric-testing bans VI 20
belief that anti-Vietnam War movement was Communist controlled XIX 128, 243, 275, 280
campaign expenses, 1964 XIX 142
Central Intelligence Agency I 64
civil rights policies XIX 28
internal dissent on Vietnam War policy XIX 280
liberal activism of VII 123
policies on Latin America I 18, 24
responsibility for Vietnam War VI 99
tension with Great Britain VI 10
Vietnam peace negotiations XIX 222
Vietnam policy I 41, 293; VI 103, 202; XIX 226
Johnson, Manning XIX 202
Johnson, Samuel XII 2
Johnson v. Virginia (1963) II 138
Johnston Eric VII 137–138; XIX 160, 168, 171

Joint Anti-Fascist Refugee Committee XIX 214, 225
Joint Chiefs of Staff I 201; VI 151
Joint Legislative Fact-Finding Committee on Un-American Activities, Washington State. See Canwell Committee
Joint Technical Committee (JTC) VII 79
Jones, Clarence XIX 78
Jones, Claudia XIX 10
Jones, John Paul XII 77–78, 82–83, 106, 251
Jones, Joseph XII 224
Jones, LeRoi. See Baraka, Amiri
Jones, Robert Emmett Jr. VII 269
Jones, Charles Colcock Sr. XIII 112, 221
Jordan VI 201; VII 78–79, 82, 135, 138; VIII 39, 41; IX 92; X 90, 95; XI 125; XIV 22–23, 25, 29, 31, 52, 55, 60–61, 63–64, 66–67, 79, 81, 84–85, 88, 97, 105, 112, 114, 136, 147, 152, 160, 162, 165–166, 177, 179–180, 190, 220, 225, 228, 242, 252, 255; XV 20–24, 32, 34, 37, 40–50, 61, 63, 83, 91, 100, 120, 131–132, 134, 136, 139, 141, 169, 182, 184, 190, 198–199, 204, 206–207, 213, 216, 219–220, 226, 250, 254, 260, 263, 270–271, 275–276; XVI 236
  alleviating poverty in XIV 65
  Amendment 340 XIV 65
  Anti-Normalization Committee XIV 65
  Army abuses of Jewish gravestones XIV 165
  British Army in XV 120
  Civil War (1970, Black September) XV 40–50, 127, 198
  closes al-Jazeera office XIV 65
  corruption XIV 48, 64
  Crisis (1957) XV 58, 166
  Crisis (1970) XV 149
  Department of Forestry XV 209
  dissolves parliament XIV 65
  duty free investment XIV 64
  economic reform XIV 54, 65
  elections XIV 64
  extra-parliamentary decrees XIV 65
  Free Officers Movement XV 63, 169
  free trade agreement with United States (2000) XIV 65
  fundamentalist movements in I 163
  labor XIV 52
  mandate in VIII 168
  Palestinians in XIV 67; XV 191
  Pan-Arab campaign I 281
  peace treaty with Israel (1994) XIV 65
  relations with United States XIV 16
  support of U.S. I 158; XIV 14
  water XIV 269; XV 205
  West Bank captured by Israel I 156
  women XIV 116, 123–124, 287–288
Jordan River XIV 268–271; XV 20, 24, 34, 193, 205–206
Jordan River Basin VII 137–138
Jordan Valley Authority XV 205
Jordanian-Israeli treaty (1994) XIV 116
Joseph, Julius XIX 197
Josephson, Leon XIX 225
Jospin, Lionel XVI 137–138; XVII 81, 133, 274
Joyce, James VIII 191; XIX 40
Juan Carlos (Spain) XVI 180–182
Jud Süss (1940) XI 90, 185
Judaism XIV 19, 22, 81, 159, 183, 187, 191, 253
Judea XIV 151, 259
Judgment at Nuremberg (1961) XI 158
Juditz, Paul XIX 216
Jugurtha XIV 206
Jünger, Ernst VIII 59, 64, 263; IX 131, 149, 212
Junky XIX 48
Jupiter missiles VI 71
Justice Department XIX 53, 119, 128, 176–177, 198, 200–202, 224, 252, 255, 260
Justin Martyr XI 20
Justinian I X 228

K

Kádár, János VI 130, 134
Kafara Dam (Egypt) VII 3
Kafue Dam (Zambia) VII 137, 240
Kafue River VII 2, 5, 137
Kahn, Agha Mohammad Yahya VI 88
Kalahari Desert VII 33–34, 36–37, 236
  lack of surface water in VII 38
Kalb, Johann de XII 101
Kaloudis, Nicholas XIX 218
Kamenev, Lev XVI 20
kamikaze VIII 60
Kampuchia VI 165
Kansas VII 10–11, 13, 181–182, 185, 187
  alfalfa production in VII 13
  sugar-beet production in VII 13
  violence in XIII 5
  water diverted from VII 13
  water policy in VII 185
  wheat sales XV 78
Kant, Immanuel XI 75; XVII 105, 256–257
Kapp Putsch (1920) IV 271
Karadzic, Radovan XVII 147, 149
Kardelj, Edvard VI 281
Karen Liberation Army XV 14
Kariba Dam VII 1, 4–5, 8, 239, 242–243
Kariba George VII 1, 237, 239, 245
Karine A (ship) XIV 101, 105
Karl I VIII 257; XVI 33, 308
Karmal, Babrak I 10–15; VI 238
Kashmir XIV 88, 93, 147; XVI 88
Katse Dam (Lesotho) VII 7, 237, 241, 244
Kattenburg, Paul VI 96
Katyn Forest massacre (1940) XI 169, 258, 260, 262; XVI 229; XIX 57
Katz, Charles XIX 169
Kaufman, Irving R. II 131, 230, 232; XIX 282–290
Kazakhstan VI 109, 215; XIV 180, 228; XVI 98
Kazan, Elia XIX 39, 47, 164
Kazan, Russian conquest of XVI 70
Kazin, Alfred XIX 49
Keating, Kenneth B. VI 73
Keitel, Wilhelm V 3, 127, 142–143, 223–224
Kelheim VII 204, 209
Kelly, Machine Gun XIX 175, 177
Kellogg, James L. VII 49
Kellogg-Briand Pact (1928) III 179; V 115; VIII 298; XI 258; XVI 218, 222, 224; XVII 11, 143, 193
Kemble, Frances Anne XIII 83, 88, 189, 226
Keneally, Thomas XI 202, 205–206
Kennan, George F. I 22, 31, 75, 82, 138, 148, 150, 154, 159, 284–285, 288; II 8, 60, 267; VI 188
  containment policy I 110, 274; XIX 18, 278–279
  domino theory I 266
  later view of containment I 183
  "Long Telegram" I 261; II 34, 205, 264; VI 9
  Marshall Plan I 176
  Mr. X II 206
  rules for handling relations with the Soviet Union I 186
Kennedy, John F. I 23, 64, 68, 89, 92, 94, 119–121, 130, 257, 291–292; II 8, 45, 52, 67–68, 93, 114–120, 160; III 48; VI 64, 66, 70, 73, 93, 96, 102–103, 138–145, 188; XI 129; XII 33; XV 19, 137, 168; XVI 12, 271; XIX 277
  Alliance for Progress I 17, 20, 23; II 115
  and civil rights XIX 24, 28, 30
  Asia policy XIX 18
  assassination I 18; II 180; VI 138, 142; XIX 24
  Bay of Pigs I 71; II 115, 119
  Camelot mystique II 117
  Cold War policies II 117; XIX 68, 145
  compared with Franklin D. Roosevelt II 115
  criticism of Eisenhower administration I 193; VI 141

critiques of performance in Cuban Missile Crisis VI 73
Cuban Missile Crisis II 116, 120, 265
decolonization policy VI 81
election of XIX 226
Food for Peace II 116
foreign policy II 117
Jimmy Hoffa II 190
Inauguration Address I 23
Johnson as vice president running mate VI 142
liberalism XIX 106
limited-nuclear-war doctrines I 169
Nuclear Test Ban Treaty (1963) II 118
on "Security Index" XIX 176
Peace Corps II 116
plot to overthrow Castro I 276
presidential campaign I 17
promotion of space program II 260
Roman Catholicism of VI 142
State of the Union address (1961) VI 140
strategy in Southeast Asia VI 95
support of British VI 11
supports coup against Diem VI 98
United Nations II 115
Vietnam policy I 183
Kennedy, Joseph XIX 176
Kennedy, Robert F. II 9; VI 75, 96; XIII 277
assassination of II 162, 180
civil-rights issues II 22; XIX 78
Cuban Missile Crisis VI 70–76
liberalism XIX 106
nuclear disarmament in Turkey I 121
on "Security Index" XIX 176
U.S. Attorney General II 22
War on Poverty involvement II 272
Kennedy administration VI 26, 56, 72, 92, 99, 138–145, 238
Alliance for Progress I 17–26
and civil rights II 26; XIX 78
to overthrow Fidel Castro I 24
Berlin Wall Crisis I 119–120
Cuban Missile Crisis I 120
Cuban policy I 67
"flexible response" I 115, 214
Iran XV 158
Latin America policy I 17–26
liberal activism of VII 123
limited-nuclear-war doctrines I 171
policy on Berlin VI 141
policy on Castro VI 71
responsibility for Vietnam War VI 99
scraps Skybolt missile VI 11
Vietnam policy I 293–294; XIX 276
Kenny, Robert XIX 169, 171
Kent State University VI 23; XII 31; XIX 226
Kentucky, slavery in XII 297; XIII 222, 233
Kentucky Resolution XII 125
Kenya VI 188; XIV 176, 190, 197, 230; XV 33; XVI 81, 88; XIX 12
attack on U.S. embassy (1998) XIV 16
Kepler, Johannes X 131
Keppel, Augustus XII 251
Kerensky, Aleksandr VIII 170–178, 223, 258; IX 200; XVI 19
Kern County Water Agency VII 179
Kerouac, Jack II 74, 160; XIX 48, 50
Kerr Dam (Unted States) VII 169
Key West Agreement I 5–8
Keynes, John Maynard III 54–55; VIII 191; IX 84; XVI 296; XVII 114, 117, 201
KGB. *See* Komitet gosudarstvennoy bezopasnosti
Khan, Genghis VI 40; XVI 251
Kharijite movement XIV 206
Khariton, Yuly Borisovich
Soviet nuclear weapons development I 244–248
Khartoum summit (1967) XV 144
Kharzai, Hamid XIV 10
Khatami, Muhammad XIV 36, 38, 42, 137–138
Khmer Rouge I 15, 41, 44, 46, 295; VI 271; XIX 146
Khobar Towers bombing XIV 16, 251
Khomeini, Ayatollah Ruhollah I 11, 141, 158; VI 165, 268, 270; XIV 7, 36–37, 41, 125, 134, 141, 174, 187, 217; XV 97–98, 100, 102, 106–107, 112, 114, 158, 160, 163, 176, 228–229, 233–236
Khrushchev, Nikita S. VI 17, 21, 31, 35, 64, 68, 70–71, 73, 81, 93, 111, 133, 141–142, 178, 184, 226, 246; I 33–38, 66, 94, 102, 120–121, 151, 256, 294; II 35, 40, 54–57, 66, 68, 115–117, 229; XV 22, 253; XVI 39, 84, 95, 125, 238, 241; XIX 14, 123
arms race I 182
Berlin I 38, 120, 168
denounces Stalin XIX 106, 173, 195
kitchen debate with Nixon XIX 226
role in Cuban Missile Crisis II 120; XIX 146
secret speech (1956) I 66; VI 133, 181, 186, 188, 264
Soviet nuclear capabilities I 194
threats to use nuclear weapons I 192
Kiel Mutiny (1918) VIII 269; IX 142
Kienthal Conference (1916) VIII 256, 261
Kierkegaard, Soren XVII 74–75, 77
Kiessinger, Kurt VI 210
Kilgore, Harley XIX 197
Killian, James XIX 113–114
Kim Il-Sung I 294; II 37; VI 147, 150; XIX 58, 117
invasion of South Korea I 182
King, Ernest J. V 39, 44, 188, 258
King, Martin Luther, Jr. II 19, 22–24, 26–27, 42–44, 48, 89, 91–95, 162, 165, 197; III 120, 182 ; VI 25; XIII 273; XIX 10, 189
and Communist advisers XIX 24, 31, 77–78
assassination of II 180
investigated by FBI XIX 30–32
"Man of the Year" II 22
Montgomery bus boycott XIX 31
on "Security Index" XIX 176
opposition to Vietnam War XIX 25, 31
press coverage of II 22
King, Rufus XII 288
King's American Dragoons XII 186
King's Bench XII 243
Kingdom of Serbs, Croats, and Slovenes XVI 99
Kinzig River VII 230
Kinzua Dam (United States) VII 29
Kirchenkampf (Church Struggle) IV 38, 188, 191; V 215
Kirkland, Washington VII 189, 191
Kirkpatrick, Jeane J. I 50–56; II 101; VI 261
Kissinger, Henry I 40, 45–47, 53, 101–102, 104, 119, 140–141, 159, 162, 272, 292, 317; II 169–172, 179; VI 30, 35, 38, 41–42, 51, 53, 61, 65, 162–163, 206, 209, 229, 237, 257, 267; XIV 37–38; XV 56, 158, 217, 220, 226, 237, 239–241, 257–258; XVI 44, 111, 158, 285; XIX 226
ABM Treaty I 199
China policy XIX 19
détente policy I 52
diplomatic campaign I 317
foreign policy approach of VI 85–91, 198–205
limited-nuclear-war doctrines I 170
negotiations with North Vietnamese I 291
nuclear proliferation policy I 222–223
on multipolar world VI 199
on 1970 elections in Chile XIX 142
realpolitik I 149
secret mission to China II 170; VI 38, 43
shutting the Soviets out of the Middle East I 105
Kitbugha X 183, 187
Kitchen debate XIX 226
Kitchener, Horatio VIII 78, 103, 203, 266, 271–272; IX 50, 55–56, 212
Kitzhaber, John A. VII 222, 224
Klemperer, Victor XI 7, 269, 271
Kline, Franz XIX 45

Klüger, Ruth XI 224, 228, 238–239
Kmetko of Nitra XI 195
Knights of Columbus XIX 184
Knights of the White Camellia XIII 55
Know-Nothings XIX 273
Knox, Henry XII 86, 88, 97–98, 214, 222–225, 228–229, 304
Kohl, Helmut VI 54, 117, 120, 208; XVI 60, 288
Kolchak, Aleksandr XVI 2, 5
Komitet gosudarstvennoy bezopasnosti (Committee for State Security, KGB) I 12, 66, 70, 93, 242; II 63; VI 18, 21, 239; XVII 102, 175, 217; XIX 86, 117–118, 104–105, 143, 197, 230–231, 283–284
  recruitment of the Rosenbergs II 228
Komosomolskaya Pravda XIX 27
Konar Dam (India) VII 130
Königsberg VI 244
Königsberg (German ship) VIII 90, 133, 137
Korea I 89, 288, 293; II 4, 40, 50; VI 56, 270, 272; IX 96, 162; X 182; XVI 315
  division of I 275; VI 146
  Eisenhower policy I 271
  independence of VI 146
  proposal for U.S. troops in I 262
  strategic importance of VI 147
  U.S. troops sent (1950) I 211
Korean Air Lines 007 VI 44, 261
Korean Independence XIX 216
Korean War (1950–1953) I 69, 87, 89, 102, 158, 170, 182, 192, 265–266, 273; II 9, 36–37, 42, 52, 66, 131, 134, 146, 211, 230; V 32; (1950–1953) VI 8–9, 36, 50, 57, 102, 106, 136, 144, 146–151, 154, 173, 177, 261, 284–285; XV 30, 73, 158, 160, 175, 253; XVI 76, 92, 271; XVII 7, 64; XIX 117, 127, 237, 240, 243
  display of Confederate flag during XIII 277
  effect on demand for Latin American imports I 21
  Eisenhower administration I 211
  Geneva negotiations II 264
impact on McCarthyism II 131; XIX 5, 19, 22, 29, 58, 94, 116–117, 119, 123–124, 132–133, 140, 143, 145, 152, 156, 164, 186, 202, 236, 240, 258, 267–268, 283, 286
  outbreak I 3, 7
  Truman administration policy I 275
  U.S. and Soviet pilots in VI 50
  U.S. troops in VI 165
Korematsu, Fred V 188–189
Korematsu v. *United States* (1944) III 103; V 188
Kornfeder, Joseph XIX 209
Kornilov, Lavr VIII 176; IX 199, 201
Korosec XVI 100
Kosovo VI 53–54, 225; IX 205; XIV 92; XVI 77, 98; XVII 6, 8, 143, 146, 209, 216
  genocide XVII 95
Kosovo Crisis (1999) VI 61, 283
Kosovo Liberation Army (KLA) XVI 60
Kosovo War (1999) XVI 109
Kosygin, Alexei XV 136, 215
Kraków VII 21
  smog in VII 18
Kramer, Aaron XIX 41
Kramer, Charles XIX 197–198, 200
Kramer, Hilton XIX 166
Krantz, Daniel Engel XIX 272
Krenz, Egon VI 1118, 122
Kriegsakademie (German Military Academy) V 126
Kriegsmarine (German Navy) IV 4, 264; V 79–80, 82, 83, 131, 133, 135, 136, 255, 257
Kristallnacht (Night of Broken Glass, 1939) III 256; IV 137, 141; V 216; XI 2, 5, 96, 99, 104, 113, 117, 184
Krivitsky, Walter XIX 63
Krueger, Walter V 99, 126
Ku Klux Klan (KKK) II 25; III 78, 90, 123, 174; IX 2, 7; XIII 55, 270, 278
Kublai Khan X 186
kulaks, destruction of VI 274
Kuomintang. *See* Chinese Nationalists
Kurchatov, Igor Vasilyevich I 244–248
Kurdistan XIV 168–174
Kurdistan Democratic Party (KDP) XIV 169, 173
Kurdistan Freedom and Democracy Congress (KADEK) XIV 173
Kurdistan Regional government (KRG) XIV 169
Kurdistan Workers Party (PKK) XIV 173, 265
Kurds XIV 231, 238, 267; XV 117, 119
Kuropatkin, Aleksey IX 65, 243
Kuwait II 153, 156; VI 225; VII 79, 81; XIV 31, 55, 79, 81, 88–89, 92, 96, 110–111, 114, 177, 179, 181, 190, 211–212, 215, 229, 237–238, 240, 243–244, 247–248, 250, 252; XV 23, 45, 90–91, 136, 187, 201, 205, 255, 258, 260, 263, 271; XVI 269
  Iraqi invasion I 289; XIV 93, 215, 218; XV 98, 101–102
  oil XV 175, 177–178, 180
  Persian Gulf War XV 72–78, 80–88
  Rumaylah oil field XV 72
  water XIV 269
  women XIV 287–288
Kuwait Oil Company XV 177
Kvasnikov, Leonid XIX 117–118
Kvitsinsky, Yuli VI 117
Kyoto Protocol, U.S. withdrawal from XIV 17
Kyrgyzstan XIV 180, 228
Kyushu III 14–15

L

La Follette, Robert M. III 178, 184, 210
La Vita è bella (Life Is Beautiful, 1997) XI 46, 48 158, 160
labor defense XIX 254–255, 258–259
Labor-Management Relations Act (1947), *See* Taft-Hartley Act
labor movement II 187–193; III 181, 190–195; XIX 87
Labor Party (Australia) XIX 266–268
labor unions II 187–193; III 183; VI 49; XIX 29, 241
  anticomunism XIX 67–73, 180–182, 184–185
  and African Americans XIX 29
  and CPUSA XIX 29, 67–75, 121, 149, 213, 216, 232
  Australian XIX 268, 270
  business view of XIX 67
  deportations of members XIX 211
  expulsion of Communists XIX 67–68
  in California XIX 232
  investigat ions of XIX 73, 150–151
  no-strike pledge XIX 71
  ties to Democratic Party XIX 73, 241
Labour Party (Britain) V 46; VI 11, 13, 20
Laden, Osama bin XIV 3, 5, 7, 10–13, 28, 38, 86–87, 90–91, 93, 99, 129, 175, 182, 184, 197, 227, 230, 238, 245, 250, 256, 262; XV 102, 249
Lafayette, Marie-Joseph-Paul-Yves-Roch-Gilbert du Motier de (Marquis de) XII 97–98, 103, 106, 134, 303
LaGuardia, Fiorello II 197; III 219
Lahemas National Park VII 22
Lahn River VII 230
Lakes
  Champlain XII 10, 12, 14, 45–48, 78, 80, 189, 267, 269
  Constance VII 231–232
  Erie VII 116, 118, 122–123, 265, 269; XII 173, 176
  George XII 47, 269
  Hulch VII 136
  Huron XII 176
  Kariba VII 4
  Mead VII 31
  Michigan VII 265; XII 176
  Ontario VII 118; XII 268
  Päijanne VII 86–87

Powell VII 30–31, 110, 112
Solitude VII 29
Superior VII 266–277
Titicaca VII 74
Washington VII 188–195
Lambkin, Prince XII 53–54
Lamont, Corliss XIX 237
Lancaster, Burt XI 47, 158; XIX 47
Land Ordinance (1785) XII 22, 65
Landis, Judge XIX 76
Landis, Kennesaw Mountain VIII 301
Landrum-Griffin Act II 192
Lang, Fritz XIX 44
Langemarck IX 260–265
Lansing, Robert IX 247; XVI 34
Lansing-Ishii Agreement (1917) IX 165
Laos I 41, 46, 68, 299; II 6, 54, 260; VI 60, 93, 188, 203; XII 33; XV 133
colony of France I 290
Imperialism I 151
spread of communism I 297
U.S. bombing of I 183
Lardner, Ring, Jr. XIX 161, 164, 168–169
Largo Caballero, Francisco XVIII 29, 105, 107, 118, 161, 166, 223
Larsen, Emmanuel XIX 16–19
Las Casas, Bartolome de X 9–10; XIII 63
L'Association Française d'Amitié et de Solidarité avec les Pays d'Afrique (AFASPA) XIV 278
Latakia XV 275
Lateran Treaty (1928) VIII 208
Latin America I 52–56; VI 141, 264, 267; IX 91, 96, 167–168, 173, 246; XIII 7; XIV 85, 110–112, 178, 198; XV 203, 205; XVI 69, 87, 108–109
agricultural output I 21
anti-slavery movement in XIX 11
British influence in XII 167
economic growth XIII 43
human rights I 146
land reform I 21
legacy of Reagan's Policies I 56
maroons in XIII 104, 107–108, 110
neutrality XIX 13
reaction to Haitian Revolution XIII 210
revolutionaries in VI 80
slave labor systems in XIII 162
slave rebellions XIII 2, 231–238
slave religion XIII 190–193
slave revolts XIII 91, 157
slavery in XIII 1, 59–66, 154
U.S. military aid I 19
U.S. relations with II 99; XIX 145
U.S. troops in VIII 14
World War I, resources from IX 77
World War II III 51
Lattimore, Owen XIX 21, 54, 99, 202
Latvia VI 178; VIII 93–94, 96; IX 93; XI 260; XVI 18, 218; XVII 2, 137, 217, 233; XIX 143
Laurens, Henry XII 98, 214; XIII 19
Laurens, John XII 97–98
Laval, Pierre XVI 299–301, 305
Lavon affair (1954) XIV 129; XV 248
Law of the Non-Navigational Uses of International Watercourses (1997) VII 79
Lawrence, Thomas (Lawrence of Arabia) VIII 37–39, 87, 214; IX 150, 152; X 59
Lawson, John Howard XIX 34, 36–38, 168
Lazarsfeld, Paul F. XIX 111
Le Duc Tho VI 40
League of Arab Nations XIV 193
League of Arab States. *See* Arab League
League of Nations I 30, 206, 284–285; II 145, 156, 175, 180, 207, 211; IV 17–18, 267; V 115, 117, 119, 169, 202, 206, 228, 292; VI 57; VIII 13, 20, 156, 168, 277, 282, 295, 298; IX 170–171, 250; XI 4; XIV 152–153; XV 116; XVI 13, 74, 107, 212, 217–220; XVII 3, 7, 11, 143, 145, 189, 193–194
American involvment I 286, V 292
Covenant XVI 91, 93
Disarmament Conference (1932–1934) XVI 91, 94
failure to prevent World War II IV 115
mandates IX 91–97, 172, 251
Preparatory Commission XVI 91
League of Nations Society IX 172
League of Women Voters III 171
Leahy, William D. I 5; III 15; V 52
Lebanese Broadcasting Corporation (LBC) XIV 32
Lebanese Civil War (1975–1990) VI 43; XIV 89, 126, 128–129, 197
Lebanon I 282; VI 270; VII 81, 138; VIII 37, 213; IX 92, 96; X 89; XI 125; XIV 7, 23, 55–56, 79, 85, 97, 112, 127, 148–149, 177, 179–181, 190, 197, 200, 220–221, 230, 248, 253; XV 24, 33–34, 45, 48, 54, 61–63, 83, 91, 98, 137, 141–142, 144, 146, 166, 169, 200, 204, 206–207, 250, 260–261, 263–264, 266, 269, 271, 275–276; XVI 236, 269
American hostages in I 54
attacks on French (1983) XIV 126, 130
bombing of U.S. Marines barracks VI 234
Christian Maronites XIV 131; XV 126, 130, 146, 148
Christian Phalangists XV 128, 130–131, 133, 149–150
Civil War (1975–1990) XV 147, 149
Communist Party XIV 128
Crisis (1958) XV 58, 166
deployment of Marines to I 157; VI 66, 222
Druze Progressive Socialist Party XIV 128, 131
French role in VI 103
Hizbollah in XIV 125, 128
intervention in VI 103
Israeli embassy bombing XIV 126
Israeli invasion of I 196; XIV 89, 131, 270; XV 89–90, 93, 95, 126–133, 255
Israeli withdrawal from (2000) XIV 128, 131
Kataeb Social Democratic Party XV 133
kidnappings XIV 129
killing of civilians in XIV 129
lack of environmental control in VII 145
massacres in refugee camps XIV 23
Multinational Force in XV 148–155
National Pact XIV 131; XV 126, 149
Palestinian refugees XV 191
political parties in XIV 128, 131
poverty in XIV 131
Shiite Amal Party XIV 128
Shiites XIV 125–127, 131
Sunnis XIV 131
U.S. embassy bombing (1983) XIV 126, 129
U.S. Marines barracks bombing (1983) XIV 126, 129
U.S. troops II 52; XV 120
U.S. withdrawal from (1984) XIV 128
water XIV 268
Lebensraum (living space) IV 54, 80, 96, 109, 123, 138 141; XI 15, 108, 114, 116, 249; XVI 185
Le Conte, Joseph XIII 48
Ledbetter, Huddie "Leadbelly" II 214
Lee, Arthur XII 79, 100, 102–103, 229
Lee, Charles XII 160, 303, 305
Lee, Duncan XIX 197
Lee, Richard Henry XII 72, 76, 93–95, 114, 116, 151
Lee, Robert E. VIII 23; XIII 275; XVI 257
Leeward Islands XII 313
Leffler, Melvyn I 174, 262
Left Wing Communism
An Infantile Disorder (Lenin) XIX 193
Legal Defense Fund (LDF) II 19, 137–138, 141
Legislative Reference Service (LRS) VII 258
Leipzig VI 118, 122
Leka (Albania) XVI 180

LeMay, Curtis E. I 188; III 216; V 89–99; VI 71
Lend Lease Act (1941) I 301; II 32–35; IV 55, 58, 157–162; V 5; VI 78, 255; XVI 315
  aid to Soviet Union XVI 162–170
Lend-Lease Agreement (French, 1945) VI 79
Lend-Lease aid to USSR XIX 21
Lenin, Vladimir I 135, 139, 149, 151, 294; II 56–57; VI 81, 108, 175–176, 178–179, 196, 243–244, 248, 274–275, 281; VIII 95, 97, 173–174, 176, 258, 260–261; IX 31, 154, 196–202; XVI 4, 18, 39, 51, 53, 55, 227, 312; XIX 54, 193, 229, 239, 261
  compared to Stalin XVII 151–158
Lennon, John II 216; XIX 50
Leo III X 26
Leo IV X 122
Leo IX X 121–122, 224, 228–229, 269, 284
Leopold II IX 42, 44; XVI 73
Leopold of Austria X 89–90
Leopold, Aldo VII 226, 278
Le Pen, Jean-Marie XVI 134–135, 138; XVII 80–81, 84–85, 167, 171, 274
Lesbians, during the Holocaust XI 245
Lesotho (Africa) VII 2, 4, 7, 236, 241, 243
Lesotho Highlands Development Authority (LHDA) VII 1–2, 4, 237, 243
Lesser Tunbs XIV 217
L'Etoile, Isaac X 162–163
Letters from a Farmer in Pennsylvania (1767–1768) XII 233
Lettow-Vorbeck, Paul von VIII 84–90
the Levant VI 103; X 47, 66, 142, 180–181, 191–192, 251, 261, 270, 301; XIV 177, 179; XVI 68
Levi, Primo XI 52, 111, 114, 164, 214, 217–219, 221, 223, 228–229, 233, 238, 240
Levi-Strauss, Claude IX 84; X 161
Levison, Stanley XIX 77, 78
Levitt, Abraham II 110, 252
Levitt, William II 110
Levittown, N.Y. II 110, 249
Lewis, C. S. VIII 61
Lewis, John L. II 22, 90–91, 161; III 192; XIX 10, 71-72, 104
Lewis, Meriwether XIII 48
Liberal anti-communists XIX 185
Liberal Party (Australia) XIX 266–268
liberal support for peaceful co-existence and nuclear disarmament XIX 236
liberals and anti-communism XIX 100, 185
Liberator, The XIII 8
Liberia IX 96; XIV 199–200; XVI 111
Libertad Act. *See* Helms-Burton bill
Liberty Bonds VIII 204, 296; IX 57
Liberty League XIX 92
Liberty Union Party II 197
Library at Alexandria XX 138–144
Library of Congress, CPUSA papers from Soviet archives XIX 85
Libretto for the Republic of Liberia XIX 40- 41
Libya I 152, 159, 28; VI 54, 107, 163, 165, 217, 271; VIII 39; IX 96; XIV 31, 55–56, 61, 68–70, 72, 76, 79, 85, 110, 131, 144, 146, 176–177, 179–180, 190, 192, 202–203, 205, 212, 215, 217, 219, 230, 262; XV 23, 45, 57, 75, 142, 222, 255, 271; XVI 186
  airliner crash (1973) XIV 129
  expels Tunisian workers XIV 197
  General People's Congress (GPC) XIV 194
  Great Man-Made River XIV 195
  Green March (1975) XIV 284
  Imperialism I 151
  Italian invasion of VIII 212
  Jews forced from XIV 221
  Jews in XIV 193
  Kufrah aquifer XIV 270
  lack of environmental control in VII 145
  nuclear weapons development I 219
  oil XV 175, 180
  revolution I 158
  Revolutionary Command Council XIV 193, 197
  support for Corsican and Basque separatists XIV 198
  U.S. air strikes on VI 107, 222, 234
  water XIV 269–270
Lichtenstein, Roy XIX 48
Liddell Hart, B. H. VIII 71, 196; IX 48
Lieber, Frances XIII 95
Lieberthal, Kenneth VI 41
Liechtenstein, monarchy XVI 178, 181
Life XIX 241, 246
Life Studies XIX 46
Likens, Gene E. VII 262
Lilienthal, David E. I 27–31
Liman von Sanders, Otto VIII 120–121; XVI 194
Limelight XIX 163
Limited Nuclear Test Ban Treaty (1963) VI 18, 33
Limited-nuclear-war doctrines I 165–172
Limpopo River VII 33
Lincoln, Abraham VI 57; IX 6; XII 62, 110; XIII 5, 18–19, 33, 153, 270, 274, 278, 283; XVI 255
  first inaugural speech XIII 276
Lincoln, Benjamin XII 229, 285
Lindbergh, Charles A. III 110–116; V 135; IX 87
Lindbergh kidnapping III 110–116
Lippmann, Walter II 8, 59; III 34, 207; VI 75
Liptzin, Samuel XIX 225
Litani River XV 206
Literacy, in the ancient world XX 145–153
Lithuania VI 178; VIII 93–94, 96, 283–284; IX 93; X 179; XI 175, 260; XVI 18, 104, 185, 213, 218; XVII 2, 132, 217, 233; XIX 143
Little Entente XVI 104
Little Goose Dam (United States) VII 31
Little Rock, Arkansas, desegretion of Central High School XIX 24
Little Rock crisis XIX 27
Litvinov, Maksim XVI 218, 221, 227
Living in a Big Way XIX 163
Livingston, William XII 207
Livingstone, David XII 167
Livonia VIII 97; X 179
Ljubljana Gap V 72–74
Lloyd, Norman XIX 161
Lloyd George, David III 99; VIII 11, 20, 57, 77–83, 102–108, 155–156, 219–223, 278, 280, 282–283; IX 54–59, 76, 83, 104, 108, 172–173, 222, 226, 250; XVI 7, 24, 34, 76, 173, 292
  industrial mobilization by VIII 78
  Minister of Munitions VIII 78
  Minister of War VIII 78
  thoughts on Germany VIII 81
local and state anti-Communist measures XIX 249
local and state loyalty investigations XIX 204–210
Locarno Pact (1925) VIII 284; XVI 9, 74, 104, 118, 212, 220
Lochner v. *New York* (1905) II 280–281
Locke, John XII 2, 34, 109–110, 114, 118–119, 121–122, 209, 259, 261, 302; XIII 17, 40, 195
Lockerbie (Pan Am) attack (1988) XIV 196, 197, 199, 217
Lodge, Henry Cabot I 290, 298, 306; II 208; III 247; VI 95–96, 196; XIII 57
Lodz Ghetto XI 138, 140–141, 143–144, 224
Log College XII 148
Lombard League X 286
Lombardy X 26, 95, 221, 229
Lomé Convention (1975) VII 33
London Charter (1945) V 222
London Conference (1930) V 204; IX 227
London Conference (1941) XVI 315
London Conference (1945) XI 261
London Missionary Society XIII 159
London Naval Conference (1930) V 207
London Recommendations (1 June 1948) VI 101
London Suppliers' Group I 219, 223
Long, Huey III 28, 86–94, 210; XIX 103

Long Island Star-Journal XIX 32
Long Parliament XII 246
Lopez, Aaron XIII 270, 273
Los Alamos I 242–243
Los Alamos atom-bomb project XIX 118
Los Angeles Department of Water and Power (LADWP) VII 178
Los Angeles Olympics (1984) VI 242
Losey, Joseph XIX 164
Loudspeaker XIX 36
Louis IX X 30, 38, 59, 64–70, 139–147, 156, 173, 189, 199–200, 235, 239, 255, 303
Louis XIV VIII 81, 278; XII 131; XIII 40; XVI 183, 252, 291
Louis XV XII 131
Louis XVI XII 39, 101, 103, 105, 127, 129, 131–134
Louis, Joe XIX 14
Louisiana
  disfranchisement of blacks XIII 56
  grandfather clause XIII 56
  maroons in XIII 108, 111
  Reconstruction, end of XIII 55
  slave revolt XIII 91, 155, 156, 233, 235
  slavery in XIII 92, 97, 195, 221, 232, 240
Louisiana Purchase XII 125
Louisiana Stream Control Commission VII 161, 165
Louisiana Territory XIII 210
  U.S. purchase spurred by Haiti slave revolt XIII 160
Louisiana un-American commmittee XIX 205
Lovejoy, Elijah P. XIII 8
Lovell, James XII 93, 98
Lovestone, Jay XIX 57, 68, 212, 213
Lovett, Robert XV 158, 203
Loving v. *Virginia* (1967) II 139
Lowe Royal Commission XIX 266, 267
Lowell, Robert XIX 46
Lower Granite Dam (United States) VII 31
Lower Monumental Dam (United States) VII 31
low-intensity conflicts (LIC) VI 3, 131, 229
Lowry, Helen XIX 231
Loyalty Board XIX 17
loyalty investigations, federal XIX 204
loyalty oaths XIX 163, 182, 204, 249
Loyalty Review Board XIX 96, 133, 137, 138, 139
Loyalty-Security Hearings XIX 19
loyalty-security program XIX 100, 251, 276
Loyettes project (France) VII 93
Lucas, Scott XIX 159
Luce, Clare Booth VI 257
Ludendorff, Erich V 157; VIII 12, 49, 54–55, 91, 93–97, 100, 114–115, 140, 143, 220, 240, 252, 257, 266; IX 9, 12, 29–30, 65, 120, 122, 124, 128, 131, 159; XVI 151, 173
Ludendorff Offensive IX 30
Ludwig Canal VII 204–205
Luftwaffe (German Air Force) IV 6, 14, 19, 107, 125, 163–169, 264, 282; V 1–2, 4–5, 7, 14, 60, 69, 72, 93, 95, 96, 123, 133, 179, 181, 223, 230, 231–233, 257; XVI 12; XVI 168, 186
Lumumba, Patrice, assassination of XIX 14
Lusaka conference (1979) XVI 182
Lusitania (British ship), sinking of VIII 204, 288, 292; IX 21, 74, 181, 247
Luther, Martin VIII 204; XI 20–21, 23–24, 31–32
Lutheran Church XII 150, 205
  Holocaust II XI 134–135
  World War I VIII 208
Luxembourg VIII 24, 72, 232, 246, 248; IX 29; XI 179; XVI 113–115, 267; XVII 21, 23, 57, 59–60, 64, 233
  monarchy XVI 178, 181
Luxembourg Report (1970) XVI 271
Luxemburg, Rosa VIII 257; XVII 36, 38
Lvov, Georgy VIII 170, 174, 177; IX 190, 242
Lyman, Stanford XIII 257
lynching III 186, 268, 274; XIII 57
Lyotard, Jean-François XI 46, 78
Lytton Commission IX 175

M

Maastricht Treaty (Treaty of European Union) VI 217; XVI 272; XVII 21, 233
MacArthur, Douglas I 89; II 50; III 15, 28; IV 7, 171–176; V 3, 16, 109, 126, 136, 192, 254, 296, 299; VI 146–147, 151; X 244; XIX 117
  image IV 175
  military career background IV 172
  Pacific theater IV 176
  Philippines campaign IV 176
  South Pacific Area Command (SWPA) IV 173
  Tokyo trials V 264–265
MacDonald, A. XIX 270
MacDonald, Ramsey XVI 24; XVII 53, 122, 195
Macedonia IX 204–205, 270, 272; XVI 58, 63, 249, 312
Macek, Vlatko XVI 100
Machel, Samora Moisés VI 2, 4–5
Machiavelli, Niccolò XI 83, 133; XII 119, 123
Mackensen, August von IX 65, 242
MacLeish, Archibald XIX 39
Macmillan, Harold VI 10–11; XVI 88, 236
MAD. *See* Mutual Assured Destruction
Madonna XVI 109
Madagascar XIII 129
  as refuge for European Jews XI 86, 108, 117
Madani, Abassi XV 4–5, 7, 9
Madeira Islands
  slavery in XIII 161, 167
  sugar cane in XIII 167
Madikwe Game Reserve, South Africa VII 38
Madison, James XII 23, 25, 54, 63, 66, 70, 73, 75, 114, 119, 121, 125, 151, 278–279, 281, 287, 289–291, 298; XIII 18–19, 48
  dispute with George Washington XII 228
Madison Square Garden riot (1934) XIX 102
madrassahs (Islamic schools) XIV 7, 231, 235
Madrid Accords (1975) XIV 73, 267, 278
Madrid Peace Conference (1991) XIV 96–97, 270; XV 83, 182, 184, 187, 198, 201, 213, 260, 261, 262, 263, 265, 267
Madsen v. *Women's Health Center* (1994) II 79
Magdoff, Harry XIX 197
Maghrib XIV 69–76, 202, 206
Maginot, André XVI 117
Maginot Line VIII 197; X 169; XVI 13, 115–116, 119, 209
Magna Carta (1215) XII 149, 206
Magrethe II (Denmark) XVI 180
Magyars X 213, 280, 287; XVI 101
Mahabad Republic of Kurdistan XIV 174
Mahan, Alfred Thayer VIII 31, 67, 72; IX 49–50, 140–141; XIV 175–176
Maheshwar project (India) VII 132
Mailer, Norman XIX 48
Main River VII 206, 209, 210, 230
Maine XII 10, 15, 82, 86; XIII 24
Maji Maji Rebellion (1905) VIII 89
Major League baseball, integration of XIX 76–77
Malaya XIV 177; XVI 81
Malaya, and domino theory XIX 224
Malaysia XIV 79, 81, 176, 190, 231; XVI 88, 109
Malcolm X II 89, 93, 96, 197, 298; III 121, 182
Malcolm X, meeting with Castro XIX 14
Malenkov, Georgy I 38, 184, 192
Mali XV 215
Malmedy massacre XI 260
Malta XIV 176
Malta summit (1989) VI 51
Malthus, Thomas XIV 52
Maltz, Albert XIX 36–37, 168
Mamluks X 46, 48–49, 51–53, 67, 142, 153, 155, 182–183, 185–187, 189, 274, 277
Mammeri, Mouloud XIV 202, 205, 209
Manchuria IX 96, 162, 164, 167–168, 173–174; XVI 315
Mandela, Nelson XIV 199
Mangaoang, Ernesto XIX 216

Mangin, Charles IX 111, 113, 115–116, 118
Manhattan Island XII 162, 307
Manhattan Project I 28, 235, 239, 241–249; II 228, 231; V 44, 50; VI 154, 177; VIII 197; XVI 254; XIX 4, 62, 117, 118, 143, 231, 283, 284, 286
Manhattan Project, infiltrated by Soviet agents XIX 62
Manhattan Project, spies in XIX
Mann, Thomas XIX 176
Mann Doctrine I 24
Mann-Elkins Act (1910) III 45
Mannerheim, Carl XVI 126, 225
Manoff, Arnold XIX 166
Mansfield amendment XV 63–64
Manstein, Fritz Erich von IV 282; V 15, 123, 126, 221
Manstein Plan IV 107
Mao Tse-tung I 59, 61, 73, 82–83, 86, 89, 134, 141, 265–266, 268, 303–304; II 36, 97, 169, 172, 264, 269; V 147–148, 191, 194; VI 40, 43, 150, 158, 181, 203; XV 14, 49; XIX 17, 19, 20, 22, 58, 117, 127, 132, 186
  alliance with the Soviet Union I 184
  relationship with Stalin XIX 22
  victory in Chinese civil war XIX 248
  view of Khrushchev I 294
Mapp v. *Ohio* (1961) II 281, 286
Marbury v. *Madison* (1803) II 286; XII 121
March on Rome (1922) XVI 151
March on Washington (1941) III 218
March on Washington (1963) I 192; XIX 28, 31, 78
March on Washington XIX 78
March on Washington (October 1967) XIX 277
Margaret (England) XVI 178
Margolis, Ben XIX 169
Marie (Queen of Romania) XVI 34
Marie-Antoinette XII 132
Marinid dynasty XIV 206
Marion, Francis XII 33, 41
maritime technology IX 176–182
Marne River IX 16, 107
Maroon War (1795–1796) XIII 110
maroons XIII 104–111, 155, 212, 231
Marshall, George C. I 34, 60, 159, 304; II 36; III 15, 218; IV 65, 176, 213, 221; V 25, 39, 42–43, 46, 51, 126–127, 136, 188, 196, 258, 279, 314; VI 90, 153, 255; XII 303; XVI 271
  attacked by McCarthy XIX 118, 124
  Balkans campaign V 72
Marshall, Justice Thurgood II 19–20, 22, 42, 91, 137–138, 141, 289
Marshall Plan I 18, 22, 36, 75, 86, 88, 107–109, 112–113, 151, 173–179, 181–182, 208, 258, 288; II 36, 40, 42, 100, 132, 209, 264; III 53; VI 9, 101, 104, 148, 211, 255, 267; XI 256; XIII 254; XIV 71; XV 173, 202–203, 205; XVI 76, 124, 228, 266–267, 269, 271; XIX 54, 124, 145, 251
  black attitude toward XIX 12
  black criticism of XIX 12
  list of countries receiving monatery aid I 174
  opposition I 80
  Republican response to XIX 93
  Soviet participation in I 176
Marshall Plan Mission in the Netherlands XIX 269
Martin, Luther XII 3, 76
Martinique XII 79
Marx, Karl I 139, 149; II 56–57, 74; VI 122, 176, 178, 187, 274–275, 281; VIII 254–258, 260; IX 196, 202; XIII 69, 174; XIX 53, 54, 111, 199, 261
Marxism XI 104; XVI 143, 160, 284; XVII 2, 28, 54, 66–67, 70–72, 138, 181, 197, 246, 250; XIX 9, 230
  and classical studies XX 29–37
  as taught at CLS XIX 232
Marxism-Leninism XIX 58, 199, 234, 262
  used by prosecution in 1949 Smith Act trial XIX 258
Marxist-Leninist ideology XIX 117, 228
Marxist Popular Movement for the Liberation of Angola (*Movimento Popular de Libertação de Angola* or MPLA) VI 1, 6, 87, 165
Mary II XII 243
Maryland VII 274; XII 70, 209, 213, 215, 243, 250, 263, 291, 306; XIV 19, 23
  Catholics in XII 234
  charter of XII 241
  free black population XII 296
  panic over slave unrest XIII 238
  slave laws in XII 3; XIII 220
  slavery in XII 4, 300; XIII 60–61, 101, 151, 172
Maryland Commission on Subversive Activities XIX 209
Maryland Oyster Commission VII 46
Masaryk, Tomas XVI 34
Mascarene Islands XIII 129
Mason, George XII 114, 281; XIII 18–19
mass media II 121–128, 166
  ability to segment American society II 125
  impact on American society II 122
  and politics II 127
  populist strain, 1990s II 124
  revolution of print culture II 122
  studies of II 124
  Communists in XIX 213
Massachusetts XII 10–11, 14–15, 22, 37, 53, 63, 70, 110, 139–141, 147, 159, 198, 200, 209, 234, 236, 264, 278, 285–286, 288, 291
  banned from issuing paper currency XII 243
  Board of the Commissioners of the Customs XII 140
  charter of XII 242
  contributions to French and Indian War XII 231
  delegates to Constitutional Convention XII 21
  gun laws XII 279
  Loyalists in XII 194
  Parliamentary acts against XII 234
  ratification of Constitution XII 73
  religion in XII 263
  Revolutionary soldiers in XII 88
  seizure of Loyalist property XII 193
  Shays's Rebellion XII 25
  slave uprising XIII 235
  slavery in XIII 19
Massachusetts Audubon Society VII 277
Massachusetts Bay XII 19
Massachusetts Charter XII 140, 237
Massachusetts Government Bill XII 141
Massachusetts Historical Society XII 194
Massachusetts Institute of Technology (MIT) XIX 113
Massachusetts investigative committee. *See* Bowker Commission
Massachusetts Ratifying Convention XII 291
massive retaliation policy I 115–117; II 30–31, 51, 118
Massu, Jacques XV 13, 16, 18
Matilda of Tuscany X 81, 117, 228, 286
Matsu I 211, 275; II 52
  Chinese attack I 265–270
  Eisenhower administration I 213
  Mayor's Citizens Committee on Water (MCCW) VII 74
Matthews, Herbert XIX 276
Matthews, J. B. XIX 119, 124
Matusow, Harvey XIX 126, 196, 201
Mauritania XIV 55, 69–73, 76, 190, 276–277, 283
  Western Sahara XIV 278, 281
Mauthausen (concentration camp) XI 245, 270
Maximilian XVI 36
The Maximus Poems XIX 39, 40
May, Alan Nunn XIX 289
McAdoo, James IX 57
McCarey, Leo XIX 163
McCarran, Patrick A. XIX 110, 200–201, 211
McCarran Act (1950) I 77, 79–81; XIX 52, 129, 211–219
  state version XIX 204

McCarran Committee. *See* Senate Judiciary Committee and Senate Internal Security Subcommittee
McCarthy, Eugene II 162, 198
McCarthy, Joseph R. I 58, 62, 75, 77–80, 87, 197, 272, 274, 295; II 129–135, 207, 211, 229; V 197; VI 139, 150, 153–159, 178; XV 161; XIX 91, 96, 207
allegations about
Acheson XIX 224
China Hands XIX 17, 19
Communists in federal government XIX 19–20, 101, 127, 155, 224, 245–246, 249, 283, 286
Democrats XIX 272
Hiss XIX 154
Lattimore XIX 202
Marshall XIX 124
Stevenson XIX 99
alienates fellow Republicans XIX 124, 226
and Hoover XIX 174, 177–178
and Truman XIX 94
anticommunism as ideological war II 131
anticommunist hysteria I 236
attacks George C. Marshall II 134
becomes chairman of the Senate Committee on Government Operations and its Permanent Subcommittee on Investigations XIX 124
censure of II 132; VI 153, 156; XIX 123–124, 126–127, 153, 276, 278
compared to Nixon XIX 221
criticized XIX 281
by *Chicago Tribune* XIX 126
by Flanders XIX 126–127
by Murrow XIX 126
by Smith XIX 105
by Tydings XIX 99, 101
death VI 153; XIX 126
investigations XIX 19, 124, 133
Army and Defense Department XIX 124–125–126, 224, 276
Atomic Energy Commission XIX 124
CIA XIX 124
Government Printing Office XIX 124
International Information Agency libraries XIX 265
labor movement XIX 73
USIA libraries XIX 111
loses chairmanship of Senate Committee on Government Operations XIX 126
publicity seeking XIX 180, 185–186
supporters VI 154
ties to FBI XIX 53
Wheeling speech (1950) VI 153–154; XIX 6, 21, 58, 121, 124, 186, 209, 249, 252, 285–286
work with Bowker Commission XIX 183
McCarthyism I 75, 304, 306; II 47–48; 129–135, 160, XIX 91–94
beginnings of II 30; XIX 116–122
Cold War II 132
end of XIX 123–130
New Deal II 132
"red baiting" I 75
Red Scare II 133
McCormack Act (1938) III 11
McCormick, Cyrus XIII 48
McDougall, Alexander XII 222–223, 228–229
McDowell, John XIX 100, 167
McFarland, Ernest William VII 109, 153
McFarlane, Robert "Bud" XIX 128
McGohey, John F. X. XIX 199, 226–227, 261–262
McGovern, George VI 26, 88
McGowan, Kenneth XIX 163
McKinley,William III 241, 272
assassination of XVI 243
McMahon Act (1946) VI 10
McNair, Lesley J. IV 246, 248; V 126
McNamara, Robert S. I 41, 166, 294, 296; II 9; VI 59, 75, 95, 103, 144; XII 31; XIX 18, 23
McNary Dam (United States) VII 53
McPherson, Aimee Semple III 33, 39
McPhillips, J. XIX 270
McReynolds, Justice James III 25–26, 28
Mead, Margaret XIX 191
Meany, George XIX 68, 73
Mecca X 4, 7, 52, 193, 200; XIV 93, 133, 159, 161, 165, 188, 208, 244–245, 250; XV 104
Medina XIV 93, 161, 182, 244–245; XV 104
Medina, Harold XIX 54, 151, 252, 258–259, 261–262
Medinan period (622–632 C.E.) XIV 159
Mediterranean Action Plan VII 142–150
Mediterranean Agreements (1887) VIII 226
Mediterranean Sea VIII 106, 134–135, 287; IX 79; XVI 188, 194, 312, 318
beach closings along VII 147
British interests in VIII 33
pollution control in VII 142–150
slavery in region XIII 165, 167
submarines in VIII 292; IX 164
Meese III, Edwin XVI 45
Meiji Restoration. See Japan
Mein Kampf (1925–1927) IV 111, 123, 137, 186, 227; V 132; VIII 99; IX 264; XI 2, 5, 15, 19, 88, 91, 103–104, 135, 247; XVI 151
Meir, Golda VI 163; XV 135, 137, 186, 221, 223, 238, 241
Melbourne Herald XIX 266
Melby, John F. XIX 21
Memminger, Christopher G. XIII 28
Mencken, H. L. III 32, 37, 78, 98, 128, 175
flu epidemic III 101
Mengele, Josef XI 147–148
Menjou, Adolphe XIX 44
Mensheviks VIII 258; IX 198
Menzies, Robert XIX 267–268, 270–271
mercantilism XII 171, 196–203
Merriam, Eve XIX 191
Merrill's Marauders V 198
Mesopotamia VIII 39–40, 121, 193, 212–213, 216; IX 67, 206
mandate in VIII 168
Messersmith, George XI 60, 268
Metaxas, Ioannis XIX 218
Methodists XII 148, 151, 235, 263; XIX 238
slave religion XIII 186, 190
Metro Action Committee (MAC) VII 191
Metropolitan Problems Advisory Committee VII 190
Metternich, Clemens von XVI 73–74, 76
Meuse River IX 254, 257
Mexicali Valley VII 151–154, 157
Mexican American War (1846–1848) XIII 283
Mexican Americans XIX 87
Mexican Revolution III 124–131
Mexican Water Treaty VII 151–159
Mexico III 124–131; VII 197; VIII 296, 298; IX 21, 168; X 8, 10; XIII 104; XIV 162; XVI 36
cientificos (scientific ones) III 125
criticism of Libertad Act I 98
Cuban investment I 97
departure of French army (1867) I 125
escaped slaves to XIII 124
land reform I 21
mining industry III 125
nationalization of U.S. businesses, 1930s I 130
oil XIV 218
relations with the United States VIII 16, 18, 22
salmon range VII 196
water policy in VII 151–159
Mfume, Kweisi XIII 277
Michael VI 252; XVI 180
Michael VII Ducas X 122, 285
Michel, Victor VIII 234–235
Michigan XII 22
anti-Communist legislation XIX 207

investigation of UAW XIX 207
State Senate XIX 218
un-American committee XIX 205
Micronesia IX 163, 165
Middle Ages X 123–124, 130–131, 140, 152, 158, 166–168, 181, 208, 229, 236, 241–243, 250, 265; XI 23, 169; XII 242; XIII 117, 162; XIV 230
Middle Colonies
ethnic diversity in XII 205
religion in XII 208
Middle East I 157–158, 161, 277; VI 53, 79, 90, 135–136, 162, 171, 188, 266, 268, 271; VIII 109, 211, 228 ; IX 27, 34, 67, 72, 91; X 199; XIV (all); XV (all); 65, 73, 80–81, 85, 87, 110, 193, 236, 237, 239; XIX 12
agricultural assistance to XIV 45
al-Aqsa intifada XIV 19–27
Al-Jazeera, influence of XIV 28–35
Alpha Plan XV 250
Arab-Israeli conflict II 145
Arab leadership in XIV 60–68
Arab Maghrib Union XIV 69–76
business practices in XIV 44–47
civil rights and political reforms XIV 61
civil society XIV 77–85, 110
control of Jerusalem XIV 159–167
corruption in XIV 48–49
democracy in XIV 110, 133–142
demographic pressures XIV 52
economic growth in XIV 51–59
education XIV 52, 111
fear of Westernization XIV 123
foreign assistance for schools XIV 45
foreign investment in XIV 44–47
fundamentalist political parties XIV 252–260
globalization XIV 109–116
hierarchal nature of society XIV 49
illiteracy XIV 111
image of the West in XIV 227–236
impact of technological advances XIV 90
income distribution XIV 56
influence of Saudi Arabia XIV 244–251
infrastructure I 158
Israeli-Palestinian conflict XIV 151–158
Kurdish independence XIV 168–174
maternal mortality rate XIV 56
natural resources XIV 45
North Africa XIV 201–210
nuclear weapons in XIV 143–150
oil XIV 47, 55, 62, 68, 111, 240
OPEC XIV 212–219
Palestinian refugees XIV 220–226
peace process I 289
political parties XIV 56
polygamy XIV 287
poverty XIV 56
purchase of arms XIV 89
relations with United States I 278
responses to modernization XIV 119–124
socio-economic structure XIV 79
Soviet influence VI 160–167, 261
Suez Canal Zone II 146
technology XIV 61
terrorism XIV 16, 125–132; XVI 248
U.S. foreign policy in XIV 16
U.S. interests I 162; VI 61
U.S. support for mujahideen in Afghanistan XIV 1–9
use of term *Middle East* XIV 175–181
water VII 76–84, 135–141, 280; XIV 268–275
women XIV 111, 115, 118–124, 286–292
women's clothing XIV 118–124
worker training XIV 45
World War I 37–42; XVI 312
Middle East Air Command XIV 176
Middle East Broadcasting Center (MBC) XIV 29
Middle East Command (MEC) XV 26, 30, 59
Middle East Defense Organization XV 26, 30, 59
Middle East Executive Training Program XIV 114
Middle East Nuclear Weapons Free Zone XIV 146
Middle East Radio Network XIV 233, 235
Middle East Research and Information Project (MERIP) XV 93
Middle Passage XIII 15
mortality rates XIII 129–137
Middleton, George XV 160–162, 164
Midwest Holocaust Education Center, Overland Park, Kansas XI 238
Mifflin, Thomas XII 94, 97–98
MIG fighter jets XIX 237
Migratory Bird Conservation Act (1929) VII 277
Mihajlovic, Draza VI 275, 277–278
Mikolajczyk, Stanislaw XVI 230
Mikoyan, Anastas XVI 168
Mikva, Abner Joseph VII 121
military gap between U.S. and Soviet Union I 188–194
Military Intelligence Service (MIS) III 14–15
Military Service Act (1916) IX 58
Milites X 14, 16, 34
militias XII 277, 281–282
Miller, Arthur XIX 48
Miller, George Jr. XIX 208
Millerand, Alexandre VIII 152, 255
Milliken v. *Bradley* (1974) II 293, 298
Milne, George VIII 214, 216; IX 206
Milosovic, Slobodan XI 71, 75; XIV 23; XVI 58–60, 63; XVII 99, 102, 146, 149, 216, 230
Milyukov, Pavel VIII 173–174
Mind of the South (1941) XIII 224
Miners' Federation (Australia) XIX 270
Minnesota communist influence in XIX 103–104
Minow, Newton II 121, 23
Miranda, Ernesto II 284
Miranda v. *Arizona* (1966) II 281, 284, 286
Missao do Fomento e Powoamento dio Zambeze (MFPZ) VII 240
missile gap I 182–194; II 260; VI 21, 141
Mission for the Referendum in Western Sahara (MINURSO) XIV 278
Mississippi XIII 281
disfranchisement of blacks XIII 56
dispute over Confederate flag XIII 270
freedmen protest mistreatment XIII 55
reinstitutes criminal provisions of slave codes XIII 54
requires separate railway cars for blacks XIII 57
slavery in XIII 7, 86, 195, 206, 221, 232, 264
Mississippi Rifle Club XIII 55
Mississippi River VII 27, 29, 31, 182, 211; XII 173, 179, 234, 235, 290
Spanish control of XII 25
Mississippi Valley, seized by Great Britain XII 55
Missouri XIII 282
slavery in XIII 206, 233
Mitchell, John XIX 176
Mitchell, Kate XIX 16, 17–18
Mitchell, William A. (Billy) IV 2; V 3, 14, 126; IX 11, 223
Mitchell Act (1938) VII 202
Mitchell Report (2001) XIV 100, 103, 105
Mitford, Jessica XIX 207, 234
Mitterand, François-Maurice VI 102, 104; XV 12–13; XVI 134, 136, 138
Mobil (Standard Oil of New York, Socony) XIV 211, 212; XV 172–173, 176
Mobutu Sese Seko VI 81
Moghul Empire XVI 70
Mohammed VI XIV 64
Mohammad Reza Palavi, Shah XIX 141
Mohawk Valley XII 268, 270
Mola, Emilio XVIII 21, 56–57, 87, 106, 126, 157–158, 166, 184
Molasses Act (1733) XII 55, 202, 231–232, 236
Mollet, Guy XV 13; XVI 240

Molotov, Vyacheslav I 36, 113, 175, 177, 238, 303; II 35; VI 101, 255, 280; XVI 185, 187, 225, 228, 230, 233, 315–316; XIX 17
Molotov Plan I 178; II 40
Soviet nuclear spying I 245
Molotov-Ribbentrop Pact I 110; XVI 76; XIX 62, 56–57, 71, 104, 117, 193, 198, 229, 232, 246, 254; XIX 56, 98
Moltke, Helmuth von (the Elder) VIII 73, 75, 184, 248–249, 252; IX 98; XVI 204
Moltke, Helmuth von (the Younger) VIII 72, 114, 179–180, 182, 184, 226, 248; IX 41, 46, 52, 98–99, 101, 103, 124, 227, 263
Monaco, monarchy XVI 178, 181
monarchy XVI 177–183
Mongke (Mangu Khan) X 183, 186–187
Mongols X 30, 48, 52–53, 60, 66, 144, 180, 182–189; XVI 251
Monk, Thelonious XIX 48
Monroe, James IX 96, 246
Monroe Doctrine (1823) I 124–125, 132; II 98, 156, 257; III 45–46, 243, 247; VI 75; IX 96, 173, 246; XIX 146
applied to Cuba VI 71
Roosevelt Corollary (1904) III 46
Montenegro IX 267, 270; XIV 176; XVI 36, 57–58, 61, 63
Monterey (California) Jazz Festival XIX 46
Montesquieu, Baron de XII 109, 118, 121–122, 128, 133, 234; XIII 246
Montgomery, Field Marshal Bernard Law II 50; IV 64, 66, 144, 177–184; V 16, 19–25, 28, 34, 42, 44, 122–125, 129
Montgomery, Richard XII 43–44
Montgomery, Robert XIX 251
Montgomery bus boycott II 22–24, 90, 140; XIX 31
Montgomery Improvement Association XIX 31
Monticello XIII 13
Montserrat XII 311, 313–314
Moore, Harold E. XIX 113
Moore, Harry XIX 77
Moors X 2, 8, 10, 41, 128, 133, 260, 265, 269, 290; XIII 167–168
enslavement of XIII 167
Moravia XI 60, 205–206, 208; XVI 34, 99, 102
Morelos Dam (Mexico) VII 152, 155, 157–159
Morgan, Daniel XII 98
Morgan, J. P. IX 19, 57, 248
Morgen Freiheit XIX 216
Morgenthau, Hans J. I 266; II 8
Morgenthau, Henry III 257; XI 11, 257
Morgenthau Plan (1944) II 210
Moriscos (converted Muslims) X 4, 6
Moro, Aldo XVI 245
Moroccan Crisis (1905) VIII 35
Morocco VIII 32, 152, 227; IX 91, 114, 226; X 270, 278, 289; XIV 29, 31, 52, 55–56, 60–61, 64–65, 67–75, 79, 83, 85, 105, 114, 116, 176–177, 179–180, 190, 201–206, 208–210, 231, 235, 255, 276–277; XV 45, 81, 136, 271; XVI 107, 302
Alawi dynasty XIV 282
alleviating poverty XIV 65
Association for the Defense of the Family XIV 65
corruption in XIV 48
economy XIV 51
French colonialism XIV 208
Istiqlal Party XIV 69, 208, 283
Mouvement Populaire XIV 209
Office Chérifien des Phosphates (OCP) XIV 280
parliamentary elections XIV 64
slaves from XIII 167
soldiers in France IX 118
water XIV 269
Western Sahara XIV 278, 281–284
women XIV 119, 287, 289, 291
Morrill Act (1862) III 2
Morris, Gouverneur XII 222, 228–229, 294, 299
Morris, Robert XII 25, 222, 228, 290
Morrison, Toni XIII 145
Morristown mutiny (1780) XII 304
Mosaddeq, Mohammad I 66, 69, 211; II 146; VI 131; XIV 37–38; XV 106, 108, 156–164, 175, 180, 233; XVI 238; XIX 141, 145
Moscow Conference (1942) XVI 315
Moscow Conference (1944) V 311
Moscow Conference of Foreign Ministers (1943) XVI 315
Moscow Declaration (1943) XI 261
Moscow Olympics (1980) VI 166, 237
U.S. boycott VI 43
Mosinee, Wisconsin, mock Communist takeover of XIX 209
Mostel, Zero XIX 62, 161
Motion Picture Alliance for the Preservation of American Ideals XIX 44, 167
Motion Picture Association of America XIX 160, 168, 171
Motion-picture production code (1934) XIX 160
Moultrie, William XII 146
Mountbatten, Lord Louis V 42, 196; XVI 245
Mouvement Armé Islamique (Armed Islamic Movement, MIA) XV 5
Movies, representations of the Holocaust XI 45–50
Movimiento de Izquierda Revolucionaria (MIR) I 127, 130
Movimiento Nacionalista Revolucionario (MRN) I 125–126
Moynihan, Daniel Patrick II 166, 271, 276; XIII 254, 257, 262; XIX 85, 117
Moynihan Report (1965) XIII 254, 256
Mozambique VI 1–7, 188, 221, 256, 261; VII 236–237, 239–240; XIII 129, 131, 136
aid from Soviet Union VI 2
independence VI 2
Portuguese immigration to VII 237
Mozambique Liberation Front (*Frente da Libertação de Moçambique* or FRELIMO) VI 2, 6; VII 239
Mozambique National Resistance Movement (*Resistência Nacional Moçambicana* or RENAMO) VI, 2, 4, 6
Mozarabs X 2, 202, 242, 244
Mozart, Wolfgang Amadeus XII 103
Mubarak, Hosni I 163, 317; XIV 105, 116, 148, 255–256
Mudejars X 2, 180
Mudros Armistice (1918) VIII 217
Muhammad XIV 133, 159, 165, 182, 184, 188, 201, 282; XV 104, 172, 235, 274
Muhammad V XIV 208
Muhammad VI XIV 61, 64, 67, 68, 71, 105, 209, 284
Muhammad X 10, 29, 43, 45, 59, 64–66, 132–133, 198–199, 201, 273, 288
Muhammad, Elijah XIX 14
mujahideen (holy warriors) I 10–16; VI 2, 133, 165, 238; XIV 93, 123; XV 233; XVI 45
U.S. support VI 229
Müller, Ludwig XI 27, 29
Mulroney, Brian XVI 182
Mundt, Karl E. I 74, 306; II 131, 211; XIX 158, 211
Mundt-Nixon Bill I 74; XIX 211
Munich Agreement (1938) I 293, 300; XVI 11, 14, 119
Munich Conference (1938) IV 127; XVI 292
Munich Crisis (1938) XVI 212
Munich Olympics XV 49
Israelis killed at XV 224; XVI 245
Municipality of Metropolitan Seattle (Metro) 188–195
Munitions of War Act (1915) IX 56
Murphy, Charles Francis III 262
Murphy, Justice Frank V 188; XIX 149
Murphy, Robert XV 62, 169
Murray, Philip XIX 72
Murray, Wallace XI 57, 62
Murrow, Edward R. XIX 126
Musaddiq, Muhammad. *See* Mosaddeq
music

"folk revival" II 214
political force II 214
music industry
impact of television II 218
record companies at Monterey Music Festival II 219
sheet music production II 217
technological advances II 216
youth market II 219
Muskie, Edmund Sixtus VII 176, 261, 263–264, 268
Muslim Brotherhood XIV 7, 127, 139, 190, 230, 255; XV 69, 271, 275
Muslims X 8, 10, 17, 19, 27, 29, 33–34, 37, 43–44, 47–48, 52, 54, 59–60, 65, 69, 78, 81, 88–90, 95, 101, 105, 108–109, 117, 128, 133, 140, 149–150, 153, 159, 169, 174, 176, 179–181, 195, 209, 212, 219–220, 223–224, 238, 248, 255, 265–266, 280–281, 284, 287, 289, 292, 297: XI 17; XVI 57, 60
Christian treatment of X 177; XIX 129
cultural interaction with Christians X 197–203
enslavement of XIII 167, 192
Latinization of X 43
slavery among XIII 165
slaves in Americas XIII 192
Spain X 1–6, 40–45, 241–246
suicide missions XIV 130
treatment of in Crusader States X 190–196
treatment of Jews X 272–278
Mussolini, Benito I 134; IV 14, 80; V 36, 108–109, 117, 135, 169, 175–177, 226, 233; VIII 95; IX 96, 175; X 305; XI 74, 167; XVI 11, 13, 105, 138, 140–141, 144, 182, 185–186, 260, 262, 264, 302, 319; XVII 80–81, 140–141, 179–181; XIX 92, 102
alliance with Hitler V 179
and the Spanish Civil War IV 224, 226; XVIII 140–147
downfall V 2
invasion of Ethiopia V 118, 120
March on Rome XVI 151
proposal of the Four Power Pact V 120
relationship with Spanish Nationalists XVIII 51–56
removal from power V 178, 179
Muste, A. J. II 7; III 184; XIX 102, 242
Mutual Assured Destruction (MAD) I 154, 169–171, 191, 198, 202, 226–227, 230–232, 251–252; II 67; VI 31, 168, 174
Mutual Defense Assistance Act (1949) I 59
Mutual Security Act I 175; XV 202
Mutual Security Agency (MSA) XV 205, 206
Mutual Security Program (MSP) I 175
MX missile VI 17–18
Myalism XIII 190, 193
Mycenaean Greeks, as slave owners XIII 165
Myrdal, Gunnar XIII 257; XIX 24, 26, 234
My Son John XIX 163

N

Nader, Ralph VII 178, 265, 269
Nagasaki I 30, 230, 239, 242–245, 249, 268; III 12, 15; V 3, 8, 49, 52, 111, 154, 192; VI 31; VII 174; XI 159; XVI 254; XIX 21, 99
Nagy, Imre VI 130–131, 134, 270
Nagymaros Dam (Hungary) VII 100–101, 104
Nahhas, Mustafa al- XV 146, 275
Naipaul, V. S. XV 232
Naked Lunch XIX 50, 51
Namibia VI 1 6; VII 7, 38, 236–237, 240–242
U.N. Trust Territory VI 236
withdrawal of South African troops VI 7
Nanking Massacre (1937) V 151
Napoleon I IX 116; XIX 113
Napoleon III IX 30, 116; XVI 130, 257
Napoleonic Wars (1803–1815) I 166, 259; VIII 233–234; XII 167–169
narcotics III 133–137
Boxer Rebellion III 136
Foster Bill (1910) III 137
Harrison Act (1914) III 137
history of legal regulation III 133
progressive movement III 135
Narmada (Sardar Sarovar) Project (India) VII 127, 132
Narmada River VII 9, 134
Narodny Kommisariat Vnutrennikh Del (People's Commissariat for Internal Affairs, NKVD) IV 50; V 233; VI 275, 278; XVI 229
Nasrallah, Hasan XIV 127–128, 131
Nassau Agreement (1962) VI 11, 13
Nasser, Gamal Abdel I 110, 162, 273, 277–278, 283, 314; II 117, 146–147; VI 11, 80–81, 106, 161, 246, 268, 270; VII 3; X 56; XIV 82, 119, 143, 193–195, 197; 82, 193–195, 197, 253; XV 12, 19–22, 24–25, 31, 40, 42, 45–46, 48–49, 56, 58–59, 61–62, 65–68, 70, 100–101, 116, 119, 121, 135–137, 144, 147, 164–169, 193, 199, 218–220, 223, 225, 238, 244–246, 249, 254, 270–276; XVI 235–240, 242; XIX 14
challenges Britain I 280
Nasserism XIV 253; XV 166, 251
pan-Arab campaign I 281
"positive neutrality" II 148
The Nation XIX 202
Nation of Islam II 93–95; XIX 14, 177
National Aeronautics and Space Administration (NASA) II 246, 258, 260; XI 152
creation of II 242
funding of II 261
National Association for the Advancement of Colored People (NAACP) II 19–20, 23, 25, 27, 44–45, 90, 94, 138, 140–141; III 80, 93, 118, 121, 182, 184–186, 217, 270–274; IX 2, 4; XIII 256, 277; XIX 8, 10, 29–30
accused of Communist ties XIX 80
anticommunism XIX 12, 30, 76–78, 80
challenge to school segregation XIX 26
cuts Du Bois pension XIX 242
expulsion of Du Bois XIX 10
in Oakland XIX 234
leadership XIX 79–80
legal strategy XIX 26
opposition to Model Cities housing projects II 277
outlawed in South XIX 30, 80
Scottsboro case III 185; XIX 78
National Association of Black Journalists II 96
National Association of Broadcasters II 123
National Association of Colored Women III 167
National Audubon Society VII 215
National Black Political Convention (1972) II 95, 198
National Citizens Political Action Committee XIX 224
National Commission for the Defense of Democracy Through Education XIX 113
National Committee of Negro Churchmen II 95
National Committee to Re-Open the Rosenberg Case II 228
National Committee to Secure Justice in the Rosenberg Case XIX 283–284
National Conference of Christians and Jews XI 159
National Convention on Peace and War (Australia) XIX 268
National Council of Negro Churchmen (NCNC) II 94
National Council of Mayors VII 258
National Council of Slovenes, Croats, and Serbs XVI 36, 100
National Defense and Interstate Highway Act (1956) II 107
National Defense Education Act of 1958 XIX 114
National Defense Highway Act (1956) II 249
National Education Association II 190–191; XIX 110, 113

National Environmental Policy Act (NEPA) II 183; VII 31, 176, 266, 269,
National Farmers Process Tax Recovery Association III 159
National Federation for Constitutional Liberties XIX 234
National Federation of Federal Employees XIX 136
National Front for the Liberation of Angola (*Frente Nacional de Libertação de Angola* or FNLA) VI 1, 6, 87, 165
National Guard Act (1903) VIII 301
National Guardian XIX 216
National Guidance Committee (NGC) XIV 25
National Industrial Recovery Act (NIRA, 1933) III 27–28, 62, 65, 149, 154
Supreme Court ruling III 25
National Intelligence Estimates (NIEs) VI 256–258, 260
National Iranian Oil Company (NIOC) XV 175
National Labor Relations Act (Wagner Act, 1935) III 149, 193
National Labor Relations Board (NLRB) II 188; III 30, 62, 149, 190–191, 193, 195; XIX 182
National Lawyers Guild 54, 66, 176
National Liberation Front (NLF) I 296; II 119, 263–264, 266
National liberation movements VI 183–187
National Maritime Union 77, 216
National Negro Congress (NNC) III 184; XIX 10, 12, 79, 189, 234
National Negro Convention XIII 234
National Negro Labor Council (NNLC) XIX 29
National Organization of Women (NOW) II 78
National Organization for Women v. *Joseph Scheidler* (1994) II 223
National Parks Association VII 30
National Pollutant Discharge Elimination System VII 264
National Prohibition Act (1919) III 200
National Reclamation Act (1902) III 243
National Recovery Administration (NRA, 1933) III 30, 154
National Security Act (1947) I 5, 7, 64, 69; VI 61; XIX 21
National Security Agency (NSA) I 74; II 230; VI 157; XIX 21, 83, 85, 99, 104, 118, 197, 199
National Security Council (NSC) I 54, 64, 83, 121; VI 41, 90, 96, 196, 231; XIV 107, 235; XV 31, 158
Action No. 1845-c XV 166
Alpha Plan XV 170
Directive 5820/1 (1958) XV 165–170
Memorandum 68 (NSC-68) I 83–84, 89, 149, 182, 211, 274; XIV 107–108
Policy paper 5428 (1954) XV 166
National Security Decision Directives (NSDD) VI 13, 32, 82, 166
National Security Strategy (NSS) XIV 107
National Socialist German Workers' Party (Nazi Party, Nazis) I 35; IV 267; VI 49, 176, 254, 274, 277; VIII 92, 94, 167; XI 4–5, 21–23, 28–29, 32–33, 35, 55, 59, 67, 70, 72, 74–75, 77, 80–81, 83, 87–88, 90, 93–95, 98, 102–103, 105–107, 111, 113, 121, 128, 138–140, 142, 169, 171, 183–184, 186, 189, 202–203, 207–208, 211, 217, 223, 238–239, 245, 253, 255–257, 264, 266, 268, 270–271; XII 259; XVI 9, 13, 76, 130, 140–142, 148–149, 151, 176, 186, 216, 229, 260–261, 264, 298
criminality of XI 166–173
euthanasia XI 83, 270
medical experiments of XI 146–154
Night of the Long Knives (1934) XI 243
public health XI 47
racial ideology XI 118
resistance to XI 268
war crime trials 252–264
National Socialist Party of Austria XI 36
National Union for the Total Independence of Angola (*União Nacional para a Independência Total de Angola* or UNITA) VI 1–2, 6, 87, 165
National Urban League II 94; III 80, 184; IX 2, 4; XIX 10
National Water Act of 1974 (Poland) 18
Native Americans VIII 23, 27; X 10, 179; XII 18, 34, 37, 53, 73, 95, 199, 217, 263, 279, 282, 285; XIII 161; XV 39
advocate breaching dams VII 221
American Revolution XII 44, 49, 173–180, 268
assimilation of VII 55, 168
blamed for reducing salmon catch VII 199
Canary Islands, brought to XIII 168
control of resources on reservations VII 166–173
Creek confederacy XII 295
dam income VII 59
dam monitoring by Columbia River tribes VII 223
displacement of VII 27
environmental damage to land VII 111
extermination of XI 71, 169
First Salmon ceremony VII 56
fishing VII 57, 197, 220
fishing rights of VII 198, 202
Great Rendezvous at Celilio Falls VII 56
impact of dams on VII 29, 51–61, 108, 110
impact of diseases upon XIII 162
ingenuity of VII 11
intermarriage with non-Indians VII 169
loss of rights VII 151
on Columbia River VII 202
opposition by non-Indians living on the reservations VII 172
protest movements VII 199
relocation of burial grounds VII 60
relations with maroons XIII 110
relationship with U.S. government III 139–146
reservations of VII 28
sacred sites endangered by dams VII 25
symbolism of U.S. flag XIII 270
threat to western expansion XII 18
treaties VII 56, 222
used as slaves XIII 162
Native Americans, tribes
Aymara Indians (Peru) XII 74
Aztec XIII 162
Cherokee XII 264
Chippewa XII 175–176, 178
Cocopah VII 151
Delaware XII 175
Flathead VII 167, 169–170
Hopi VII 169
Hualapai VII 110, 114
Inca XIII 162
Iroquois XII 41, 173–180
Kootenai VII 167, 171–172
Miami XII 175–176
Mohawk XII 173–175, 177, 179
Muckleshoot VII 191
Navajo VII 110–111, 114
Nez Perce VII 51, 55–56, 59
Oneida XII 173–175, 177–179
Onondaga XII 173–175, 177, 180
Ottawa XII 175
Pawnee VII 166
Pend Oreille VII 167
Pueblo VII 169
Quecha VII 151
Salish VII 167, 171–172
Seminole XIII 108
Seneca XII 173–175, 177–179
Shawnee XII 175, 176
Six Nations XII 173, 178–180
Tuscarora XII 173–175, 177–179
Umatilla VII 51, 55–56, 59
Warm Springs VII 51, 55–56, 59
Wyam VII 57

Yakama VII 51, 55–57, 59
Natural Resources Defense Council VII 31
Naturalization Act (1952) I 74
Nature Conservancy, The VII 216
Naval Disarmament Conference (1921) V 203
Navigation Acts XII 52–53, 137, 165, 171, 196–197, 198, 199–203, 209–210, 243
Nazi Germany I 108, 135–136, 138, 149, 152, 241, 255, 266, 274, 288, 293, 301; VIII 167; IX 79, 174; XI 4, 7, 14, 56, 178, 192, 260, 268
administrative system IV 96
Aryan myth of superiority VIII 204
Austria VIII 284
Brownshirts (1934) I 134
Catholics in XI 191
concentration camp system III 252
Final Solution III 256
ideology IV 86; X 20
influence on German army IV 86
Jewish women in XI 93–100
Marriage Health Law XI 247
mass extinction of Jews III 251
nonaggression pact with Soviet Union I 306
policy toward Jews III 250–257
racial ideology IV 124
Special Children's Departments XI 247
support of German population V 210–217
war aims V 210
Nazis and Nazi Collaborators (Punishment) Law (1950) XI 37, 40, 42
Nazism XI 4, 81, 131, 133, 166, 170, 181, 183, 187, 243; XIV 37; XVI 11, 178, 212, 254, 291, 294, 296
compared to communism XVII 173–179
Nazi-Soviet Non-Aggression Pact (1939) I 107, 110, 136; IV 57, 125; V 224–227; VI 179, 245; XVI 119, 185, 230–231; XVII 38, 140. *See also* Molotov-Ribbentrop Pact
Nebraska VII 181–182
Nebuchadnezzar XIV 159
Negro Liberation XIX 234
Neguib, Muhammad XV 31, 66, 68, 70, 249
Nehru, Jawaharlal VI 268, 271; VII 126, 130; XV 167; XIX 12, 14
Nelson, Baby Face XIX 177
Nelson, Gaylord Anton VII 123
Nelson, Pete XIX 216
Nelson, Steve XIX 232
Nepal, dams in VII 9
Netanyahu, Benjamin XIV 23, 256; XV 183, 186, 264, 266
Netherlands VI 77, 183, 188, 264; VII 229–230; VIII 137, 246, 285; IX 32, 43–44; XI 4, 123, 174, 176; XIV 245; XVI 113–115, 268; XVII 270; XIX 25, 265–274
antinuclear protests VI 16
Brussels Treaty I 208
decolonization XVI 79
Department of Public Works and Water Management (Rijkswaterstaat) VII 92
human rights foreign policy II 102
Jews XVI 305
monarchy XVI 178, 180–181
slave trade XIII 129, 133–134, 136, 269
Neto, Antonio Agostinho VI 1, 165, 265
Neuengamme Concentration Camp Memorial XI 128
Nevada, reclamation projects in VII 26
Nevis XII 311, 313–314
New Alliance Party II 198
New Braunfels River VII 74
New Christian Right XIV 256
New Conservation, The VII 259
New Deal I 241, 301, 306; III 63, 90, 147–155; VI 56, 129, 151, 158; VII 28, 43, 223, 258, 263; VIII 301; XI 168; XIX 4, 91, 119, 171, 185, 215
agricultural policies III 156–163
allegations about spies in XIX 155, 157, 159
and Communists XIX 91–93, 193, 213
and labor unions XIX 182
criticized by conservatives XIX 91–92, 99, 116, 157, 163, 180–181, 184, 119, 251
dam building VII 29, 202
Great Depression III 60
investigated by HCUA XIX 99
programs III 63; XIX 92, 154
New Delhi Summit (1983) VI 268
New England XII 23, 37, 39, 43, 80, 149, 174, 179, 181, 200, 205, 209, 243, 267, 270, 273, 288, 302; XIII 272, 281
banned from issuing paper currency XII 243
diking in VII 277
ethnic diversity in XII 205
impact of Revolution on economy of XII 264
Loyalists in XII 191–192
participation in slavery XIII 195
pro-nationalist sentiment XIII 282
Puritans in XII 234
reclamation of salt marshes VII 277
religion in XII 64, 147–148, 150, 153, 216
Revolutionary soldiers from XII 88
smuggling XII 200
textile manufacturing XIII 43
trade with France XII 209
trade with slaveholding areas XIII 195
use of wetlands (salt marshes) in VII 275
wetlands in VII 271
New England Confederation XII 19
New Federalism II 183, 185
New France XII 148
New German Order XI 134
New Guinea XVI 84
New Hampshire XII 15, 146, 209, 291
abolishes slavery XIII 19
delegates to Constitutional Convention XII 21
gun laws XII 279
Loyalists in XII 193
ratification of Constitution XII 22, 73
religion in XII 263
Revolutionary soldiers in XII 88
wildlife refuges in VII 278
The New Hampshire Spy (Portsmouth) XII 74
New Haven Footguards XII 10, 14
New Jersey VII 265; XII 37–38, 54, 70, 78, 158, 161, 215, 271–272
Continental Army in XII 305
gradual emancipation XIII 19
integrate laboratory procedures into oyster management VII 43
Loyalists in XII 182, 189, 304
mosquito-control ditching VII 273
mutiny in (1780) XII 304
post-Revolution economic problems XII 22
privitization of oystering VII 47
Quakers in XIII 31
religion in XII 147
slavery in XII 5, 263
treatment of Loyalists in XII 193
women's suffrage in XII 263, 320
New Left I 77; II 159–160, 162, 164; VI 25; XIX 73
New Lights XII 145, 147–148, 150, 152
New Look I 115, 117, 210–215, 266; VI 133, 141; XV 26; XVI 271
New Masses XIX 168, 197
New Mexico VII 181
New Negro movement III 80, 117
New Orleans Times-Picayune XIX 32
New Providence Island XII 81, 83
New Republic XIX 57
New Rochelle, N.Y., anti-Communist law XIX 204
New Testament XIV 159
New Woman
birth control III 171
fashion III 171
lesbianism III 168
physical expectations III 170

Progressive Era (1890–1915) III 165–173
New World Order
double-standard of II 157
Persian Gulf crisis II 153
purpose of II 154
New York XI 124; XII 14–15, 21–22, 37–38, 41, 43–44, 47–48, 54, 70, 80, 98, 109, 116, 149, 158, 161, 171, 176, 179, 181, 189, 198, 200, 205, 216, 233–234, 236, 263, 267, 269–270, 273, 281, 285, 288, 290–291, 303–304, 307; XIII 281; XIV 162, 182
Commission for Detecting and Defeating Conspiracies XI 189
gradual emancipation in XIII 19
gun laws XII 279
integrate laboratory procedures into oyster management VII 43
Loyalists in XII 182, 189, 192, 304
Native Americans in XII 180
privitization of oystering in VII 47
pro-nationalist sentiment in XIII 282
ratification of Constitution XII 74
seizure of Loyalist property XII 193
slave uprising in XIII 235
slavery in XII 5, 263
state legislature XII 22
investigation of subversives in NYC public colleges XIX 108
New York City VII 256, 265–266; XII 22, 33, 37, 39, 45, 47, 78, 80, 92, 122, 182, 222, 234, 259, 267–268, 270–271, 274, 302, 307–308
Board of Higher Education XIX 108
City Council, Communists elected to XIX 103, 229
civil rights demonstrations in XIX 31
Loyalists in XII 182
public colleges, investigation of subversives in XIX 108
water problems in VII 261
New York Daily News XIX 76
New York Post XIX 124
New York Herald Tribune XIX 277
New York Stock Exchange XVI 108
The New York Times XIX 111, 128–129, 240, 242, 260, 276, 280
New York University XIX 110
New Zealand VIII 133, 160–161; XII 168; XVI 13, 80–81, 87, 208
represented at Evian Conference XI 55
World War I VIII 117–123, 220, 266; IX 173
Newbury, Massachusetts VII 277
wetlands confiscated in VII 278
Newell, Frederick H. VII 26
Newell, Roger VII 48
Newfoundland XII 171
Newlands, Francis Griffith VII 25–26
Newlands Reclamation Act (1902) VII 25–26, 201
Newport (Rhode Island) Jazz Festival XIX 46
Newsweek XIX 10
Ngo Dinh Diem I 290, 298; II 97, 119, 266–267; VI 92–99; XIX 98, 276
Ngo Dinh Nhu II 119; VI 94, 96
Nicaragua I 48–49, 51, 53–54, 57, 94, 96, 141; II 56, 58; III 50; VI 4, 44, 57, 61, 64, 68, 131, 190–196, 221, 231, 236–237, 241, 261, 265–266, 270; IX 96; XV 228; XIX 14, 128
human rights record I 143
mining Managua harbor VI 190–191
National Security Decision Directive 17 (NSDD-17) I 50
Sandinistas I 125–126; XIV 198
Somoza dictators II 103
Soviet support of guerrillas VI 58, 193
U.S. arms shipments (1954) I 123
U.S. policy in VI 190–196, 249; XIX 145, 280
Nicephorus III Botaneiates X 220, 285
Nicholas II VIII 171, 174–175, 226, 229, 258, 266, 268; IX 99, 156–160, 193, 237–243; XI 167; XVI 16–17, 49–53, 55, 180, 200–201
Niebuhr, Reinhold XIX 185
Niemöller, Martin IV 188–189; XI 29, 31, 33, 35
Nietzsche, Frederick XI 75
Niger XIV 198–199
Nigeria XIII 11, 193; XIV 212, 215, 219, 260; XV 215; XIX 28
slave trade XIII 35
Nile Basin Initiative XIV 272–273
Nile River VII 2–3; X 89, 92, 95, 141, 173; XIV 206, 268–271; XV 275
Nimitz, Chester W. IV 7, 172; V 7; XI 258, 262
Nine-Power Treaty (1922) IV 258
1960s progressive movements II 159–167
1920s III 174–180
Ninotchka XIX 163
Nipomo Dunes VII 178
Nitze, Paul H. I 82–83, 86, 149, 191, 211, 274; XV 203
Nivelle, Robert-Georges VIII 104, 106, 111, 114, 149, 269; IX 104–105, 108, 110, 212, 257
Nivelle Offensive (1917) IX 118, 129
Nixon, Richard M. I 40–41, 44–47, 66, 74, 89, 101–102, 104, 140, 159, 306, 317; II 4, 7, 95, 97, 102, 115, 133, 162, 165, 171–172, 197, 209, 256, 257, 260, 280–281; III 48; VI 4, 23–24, 26, 28, 30, 56, 58–59, 61, 91, 96, 162, 206, 231, 256–257, 284; XI 88, 167; XII 28, 30, 31; XIV 217; XV 220, 241, 257; XVI 158; XIX 220–227
and China Lobby XIX 19
anticommunism XIX 96, 220–227
anticommunist legislation II 131; VI 203
belief that antiwar movement was Communist controlled XIX 128, 243, 280
childhood of II 176
Committee to Re-Elect the President (CREEP) II 177
domestic policy II 175–186
election (1968) VI 85
election campaigns
1950 XIX 92
1952 XIX 99
Equal Employment Opportunity Commission (EEOC) II 182
establishes EPA VII 266
Executive Order 11458 II 183
Federal Occupational Safety and Health Act (1970) II 192
foreign policy II 168–174
goal of Middle East policy I 162
human rights I 141; VI 200
Hiss case XIX 63, 198
investigation of National Lawyers Guild XIX 54
Iran XV 158
loss to John F. Kennedy II 177
malicious campaign tactics of II 177
meetings with Brezhnev II 170
Mundt-Nixon Bill XIX 211
mutual assured destruction (MAD) policy I 169
pardoned by Gerald R. Ford II 179
Pentagon Papers II 177
presidential election (1960) I 188
psychological analyses of II 181
reelection campaign (1972) VI 86, 88
resignation I 292; II 179; VI 87
role in Chilean coup XIX 142
service on HCUA XIX 19, 198, 251
signs Great Lakes Water Agreement VII 120
"Silent Majority" speech II 9
vetos Federal Water Pollution Control Act Amendments VII 263
vice president of Eisenhower II 177
Vietnam policies I 291; II 173; XIX 220–227
War on Poverty II 270
Watergate I 144, 292; II 176, 185

Nixon administration I 68, 129; II 3–4; VI 35, 199; VII 269; IX 5
  acceptance of Israel as a nuclear-weapons state I 158
  applies Refuse Act provisions VII 266
  Cambodia I 41–45; VI 60
  Chile I 130
  China VI 38–44, 201, 204
  foreign policy I 141–143; VI 58–59, 85–91, 198–205
  Latin America I 18
  Middle East I 162
  nuclear proliferation policy I 222; VI 18
  Vietnam VI 40, 86, 99, 203
Nixon Doctrine VI 199
Nkotami Accord (1984) VI 5
Nkrumah, Kwame I 110; III 121; VII 237
Nobel Peace Prize III 243; IX 228; XIX 202
  Martin Luther King Jr. II 19
  Theodore Roosevelt II 99
  Woodrow Wilson II 99
Nobel Prize in chemistry, awarded to Pauling XIX 242
Non-Aligned Movement (NAM) VI 181, 268, 270–271; VII 240; XIX 13–14
Nongovernmental organizations (NGOs) 19, 247–248, 254; XIV 58, 77, 110, 233
Non-Intervention Agreement (NIA, 1936) XVIII 28, 74, 129, 141, 161, 168, 212, 216, 222–223, 324, 326
Norden bombsight XIX 62Nordic Environmental Certificate VII 87
Noriega, Manuel VI 225
Normandy invasion (June 1944) IV 14; V 10, 12, 15, 17–23, 37, 41, 58, 80, 102, 196 ; XI 16
Normans X 24, 26, 117, 121–122, 199, 212, 216, 224, 269, 284, 289
  Conquest of England (1066) X 101, 301
North, Frederick (Lord North) XII 28, 30, 47, 103, 139, 141, 144, 156, 159, 168, 182, 185, 190, 248–249, 251–252, 254–255, 262
North, Oliver VI 196, 231
North Africa II 144; VII 148; VIII 233; IX 91, 111, 114, 116; X 6, 61, 148–149, 159, 270, 273, 275, 304–305; XI 176 ; XIV 69–76, 82, 111, 175–176, 187, 195, 201–210, 265, 281; XV 12, 16, 146, 275; XVI 23, 68, 70, 88, 110, 188, 236, 240
  Allied invasion of V 5, 35; XVI 315
  colonialism XIV 203, 206
  French influences in XIV 203
  growth of industry in VII 147
  income distribution XIV 56
  Jews forced from XIV 221
  slaves from XIII 167
  World War II XVI 301–302, 306
North America XIII 181; XVI 65–66
  first Africans to XIII 180
  indentured servitude in XIII 247
  property ownership in XII 124
  racism XIII 179, 180
  slave rebellions XIII 231–238
  slavery in XIII 59–66
North American Congress on Latin America, report on Chile XIX 142
North Atlantic Regional Study (NARS) VII 261
North Atlantic shipping during World War II XIX 218
North Atlantic Treaty Organization (NATO) I 35, 107, 120, 124, 151, 154, 160, 168, 170, 175, 182, 196, 198, 213, 222, 254, 277, 283, 296; II 50, 61, 100, 146, 152, 264, 267; IV 30; V 42, 149; VI 8–9, 11, 18–19, 50, 53, 80, 100–102; 105–106, 115, 131, 134–136, 173, 188, 199, 206–207, 209, 215, 217, 267, 271; VII 83; XI 188, 256; XIV 2, 228, 261–262, 264, 270; XV 12, 14, 19, 26–27, 31, 139, 148, 203, 205; XVI 41, 44, 57, 60, 74, 87, 95, 108, 160, 180, 228, 266–267, 269, 271, 319; XIX 54, 93, 124, 145, 237, 242–243, 269, 273
  creation of I 204–209
  France XVI 156
  involvement in Bosnian conflict II 154
  military strategy in Europe VI 168–174
  nuclear crisis XIV 239
  withdrawal of France VI 145
North Carolina XII 19, 70, 122, 205, 209, 216, 264; XIII 104, 107, 157
  Act of 1791 XIII 98
  grandfather clause XIII 56
  gun laws XII 279
  Loyalists in XII 182, 184–185, 192
  oyster management in VII 49
  panic over slave unrest XIII 238
  Reconstruction, end of XIII 55
  Scots in XII 187
  slave laws XII 4
  slavery in XIII 64, 87, 97–98, 101–102, 172, 227, 262, 265
  state legislature XII 22
North Dakota VII 31
  dams in VII 29
  Native Americans in VII 29
North Eastern Water Supply Study (NEWS) VII 261
North Korea I 41, 293; II 37; VI 50, 54, 102, 147, 149–150, 178, 215–217, 219, 252, 261; XV 75; XVI 41, 98
  cease-fire with U.S. I 275
  invasion of South Korea (1950) I 87, 208; VI 28; XIV 147
  links to Soviet Unioin XIX 119
  nuclear weapons I 217, 219, 224, 239; XVI 98, 109
North Sea VII 104, 204—205, 210, 230; IX 77–78, 140, 144, 181, 186, 257; XVI 194, 319
  time needed to flush pollution from VII 142
  World War I VIII 29, 35, 122, 135
North Vietnam I 40–42, 44–46, 290–299; II 4–8, 263; VI 28, 50, 96–97, 178, 201, 203, 285; XII 30, 34
  conquers South Vietnam (1975) I 142; VI 24
  declares independence I 290
  Gulf of Tonkin incident I 291
  peace agreement signed I 291
  Soviet support VI 246
  U.S. bombing VI 59, 165; XIX 226œ227
Northam, William E. VII 43
Northern Buffalo Fence (NBF) VII 35
Northern Ireland XVI 245, 249
  Northern Irish Assembly XVI 249
Northern Rhodesia VII 237
Northey, Edward VIII 86, 89
Northup, Solomon XIII 79, 92
Northwest Kansas Groundwater Management District VII 185, 187
Northwest Ordinance (1787) XII 22, 65–66, 293, 300; XIII 19
Northwest Territory, prohibition of slavery in XIII 18
Norway IX 78, 171; XI 62, 102, 176; XV 187; XVI 114–115, 319
  fascism XVII 135, 137, 139
  monarchy XVI 178, 181
  oil XIV 218
Not Guilty XIX 104
Notes on the State of Virginia (1781) XII 125, 296
Noto v. *U.S.* I 81; XIX 259
Nova Express XIX 50
Nova Scotia XII 23, 171, 186, 304, 307
  Loyalists in XII 169, 189, 194
Novikov, Nikolai I 178
  "Novikov Telegram" II 35
Nowak, Stanley XIX 218
Nuclear Nonproliferation Act (1978) I 223
Nuclear Nonproliferation Treaty (NPT) I 216, 217–219, 222, 224; VI 30, 33, 104, 106; XIV 40, 143–147, 149; XV 75
Nuclear-power plants, regulation of VII 174–180
Nuclear spying I 239, 241–249, 261
Nuclear Test Ban Treaty (1963) II 117–118

Nuclear weapons I 117, 154, 163, 165–172, 216–224, 225–233, 234–241, 249–257; XVI 95; XIX 123, 239
arms control VI 30–36
carried by bombers I 4, 6, 8
debate in House Armed Servies Committee hearings of 1949 I 8
introduction I 4
safety of VI 214
testing in Pacific XIX 237
U.S. monopoly I 27–128
nuclear weapons ban movement XIX 123, 129, 275, 278,
Nueces River VII 70
Nur al-Din X 24, 48–49, 51, 251
Nuremberg Charter XV 79
Nuremberg Code of 1947 XI 151
Nuremberg Laws (1936) III 251; IV 137, 140–141; V 117–118; XI 5, 7, 32–33, 59, 90, 184, 247
Nuremberg Party Rally (1935) V 140
Nuremberg war-crimes trials (1945–1946) IV 88; V 225; XI 37, 39, 43, 45, 103, 115, 148, 152, 167, 252–262; XVII 2, 142, 145–149, 214
Nyae Nyae conservancy, Namibia VII 38
Nyasaland VII 237
Nye Commission VIII 284
Nye Committee. *See* U.S. Senate Special Committee on Investigation of the Munitions Industry (Nye Committee)
Nyon Agreement (1937) XVIII 74, 76–77, 179

O

Oahe Dam (United States) VII 29, 31
Ober, Frank B. XIX 209
Ober Law XIX 204, 209
Objectives for Boundary Water Quality (1951) VII 117, 120
Ocalan, Abdullah VII 79; XIV 173, 265
Occupied Territories (West Bank, Gaza Strip, and Golan Heights) XIV 129, 151–153, 180, 220; XV 20, 78, 89–91, 93, 95, 132–134, 139, 186, 191, 194–195, 198, 214, 242, 261
O'Conner, Sandra Day XIV 115
O'Dell, Jack XIX 77–78
Odendaal Commission into South-West African Affairs VII 239
Office of the Coordinator for Counterterrorism (U.S.) XIV 130
Office of Equal Opportunity (OEO) II 270–276
Office of Homeland Security XIX 129
Office of Military Government for Germany, United States (OMGUS) XI 255
Office of Minority Business Enterprise (OMBE) II 183
Office of Naval Intelligence XIX 16
Office of Strategic Services (OSS) V 146–147; XIX 16, 18–19, 63, 197, 216, 231
Office of War Information (OWI) XIX 39
Official Secrets Act XIX 286
Ogallala Aquifer VII 181–187
Ogletree, Charles XIII 197–198
Ohio VII 265; XII 22; XIX 200–201
Ohio River XII 174, 234, 300
Ohio River Valley VII 256
oil industry XIV 211–219
pollution VII 147, 265
production XV 172–176
shale VII 22–23
Okavango Delta VII 33, 236
Okavango River VII 236
Oklahoma VII 10, 181–182, 185
grandfather clause XIII 56
Oklahoma City, terrorist attack (1995) XIV 16
slavery in XIII 206
Oklahoma Water Resources Board VII 185
Okuma Shigenobu IX 163–164
Old Contemptibles IX 49, 51
Old Lights XII 145, 148, 150
Old Man of the Mountain X 183–184
Olive Branch Petition (1775) XII 95, 140, 143
Oliver, Peter XII 150, 208
Olmsted, Frederick Law XIII 42, 45, 121, 203, 205, 240
Olson, Charles XIX 39–40
Oman XIV 55, 79, 177, 179, 247; XV 100, 109, 120
water XIV 269
women XIV 121
Olney, Warren, III XIX 200– 201
Omar, Muhammad XIV 11–12
Omnibus Rivers and Harbors Act (1965) VII 261
On the Road (Kerouac) II 109
On the Road XIX 48, 50
On the Waterfront (movie) II 190
100 Things You Should Know About Communism and Education (HUCA) XIX 99, 101
O'Neill, Eugene IX 4
Ontario, Canada VII 116–117
postwar economic boom in VII 119
rejects water bill VII 119
Ontario Water Resources Commission (OWRC) VII 118
Open Door policy (1899) II 38, 99, 267; IX 165, 246; XVI 6
Operation CHAOS XIX 277
Operation Dixie XIX 73
Operations–
–Anvil (1944) IV 68, 148; V 72, 236, 238, 241
–Aphrodite V 98
–Badr (1973) I 316
–Bagration IV 150
–Barbarossa (1941) IV 6, 54, 162, 244, 282; V 67, 80, 127, 137, 176, 180–181, 226–234; XI 14, 82, 86–87, 90, 117; XVI 114, 184–191
–Binoculars (1959) XV 15
–Blücher (1918) VIII 54
–Blue Bat (1958) XV 62
–Citadel V 177–178
–Clarion V 98–99
–Cobra (1944) V 2, 129
–Coronet V 49
–Defensive Shield XIV 100, 105, 128
–Dragoon IV 68; V 35–241
–Duck Hook II 6
–El Dorado Canyon (1986) VI 234
–Enduring Justice XIV 16
–Fortitude (1958) XV 62
–Grapes of Wrath (1996) XV 264
–Husky (1943) V 35, 39, 236
–Ichigo (1944) V 196–198
–Iraqi Freedom XIV 102
–Jericho (1944) XI 12
–Marita (1941) XVI 188
–Market Garden (1944) IV 180, 184; V 13, 16, 21–25, 129
–Michael (1918) VIII 112; IX 11
–Olympic V 49
–Overlord (1944) IV 42, 44, 63, 148–149, 179, 183, 262; V 34, 36, 58, 69, 72, 236; XVI 315
–Peace for Galilee 127, 129, 131, 133, 149, 153
–Rolling Thunder I 291
–Roundup IV 210, 213; V 39
–Sea Lion V 101, 176; XVI 186
–Shingle IV 44
–Sledgehammer IV 210, 213
–Solarium I 272
–Staunch 98
–Straggle (1956) 271
–Success (1954) I 126
–Thunderclap (1945) V 92, 98–99
–Torch (1942) IV 62, 181, 193, 210, 213, 241; V 35, 39, 82, 131, 176, 179, 233, 236, 251, 258; XVI 315
–Uranus V 176
–Urgent Fury (1983) VI 234
Operative Painters' Union (Australia) XIX 270
Opium Wars (1839–1843, 1856–1860) IX 49

Oppenheimer, J. Robert I 29–31, 257; V 50; VI 158
Orange Free State VIII 31
Orange River VII 1–2, 7, 236–237, 240–241
Orange River Project (South Africa) VII 237, 240
Orcí, Arturo VII 158
Order of the Red Banner XIX 231
Ordnungspolizei (uniformed police) IV 141
Oregon VII 201, 220–221
dams in VII 31, 51–61
population in VII 54
Oregon Fish Commission VII 31, 53
Oregon Railway and Navigation Company VII 57
Oregon Wildlife Federation VII 53
Organisation Todt (OT) XI 213
Organization of African Unity (OAU) VII 240; XIV 195, 276, 278, 282
Organization of American States (OAS) I 21, 71, 94, 98; II 115, 152; III 53; VI 192, 194
human rights I 146
Organization of Arab Oil Exporting Countries XIV 247; XV 219
Organization of Petroleum Exporting Countries (OPEC) VI 107, 268; XIV 195, 212–219, 245, 247–248; XV 78, 107, 109, 172, 174–176, 219, 225, 237
Organization of the Islamic Conference XIV 17, 247
Organization of Ukrainian Nationalists (OUN) IV 130
Organizations Employees Loyalty Board XIX 288
Origen 19–20
Orlando, Vittorio VIII 18, 278; IX 250
Ornitz, Samuel XIX 168
Orontes River VII 78–79, 81
Ortega Saavedra, Daniel VI 190, 195
Orwell, George XVII 201, 211, 237
and the Spanish Civil War XVIII 126, 130, 183–190, 330, 335
Osborn, Sidney P. VII 153
Oslo accords (1993) XIV 19, 88, 95, 97, 151, 157, 166, 225, 259; XV 56, 83, 90, 182–192, 201
Oslo peace process (1993) XIV 20, 23–27, 269
Ostpolitik (Eastern policy) VI 59, 144, 149, 204, 206–212; XVI 155–158
Othello XIX 35
Otis, James XII 2, 139, 214, 233, 258–259, 261
Ottmaring Valley VII 204, 207
Ottoman Empire VII 77, 81–83, 138; VIII 37, 82, 104, 133, 172, 178, 208, 211–217, 228, 281; IX 93, 95, 120, 133–134, 193, 206, 226; X 62, 208, 270; XI 126; XII 105; XIV 61, 160, 175, 178, 192, 208, 220, 244, 261; XV 27, 33, 73, 82, 176, 274; XVI 2, 23, 27, 36, 51, 59, 61, 65–66, 73–74, 76, 99, 102–103, 110, 175–176, 192–194, 199–200, 206, 236, 244
Armenian massacres XIV 176; XVII 96–97, 143, 146
Arab rebellions VIII 39, 212
Army VIII 38, 118
British policy in VIII 168
economy VIII 215
Jews in World War I VIII 166
nationalist movements within XIV 168
North Africa XIV 205
women XIV 286
World War I XVI 308, 312
Out of Bondage XIX 248
Ovid XX 257–264
and Virgil XX 265–272
Owen, Wilfred VIII 61, 191; IX 148–150, 152
Oyster: A Popular Summary of a Scientific Study, The (1891) VII 41
Oyster Restoration Areas VII 49
oysters VII 40–50
decline of in Chesapeake Bay VII 40–50
diseases VII 46
natural enemies of VII 41
Oxnam, G. Bromley XIX 202
Özal, Turgut VII 79
visit to United States VII 79

P

Pacific Gas and Electric Corporation (PG&E) VII 177–178
Pacific Northwest VII 55; XII 171
dams in VII 51
industrialization in VII 51–53
railroads in VII 52
water policy in VII 110
Pacific Northwest Development Association VII 53
Pacific Ocean VII 220; XVI 65, 91, 254
dumping ground for thermal waste VII 178
during World War I VIII 31, 33, 72, 133, 137
islands XII 171
Pacific Salmon Crisis VII 219
Pacific Southwest Water Plan VII 109
Pacific Western (oil company) XV 180
Pacifism XVII 188–195
Pahlavi, Mohammad Reza Shah I 11, 70, 141–146; II 97; VI 166, 266; XIV 37, 174; XV 73, 100, 106–115, 156–164, 228–236
Pahlavi, Reza Shah XV 102, 106, 108, 156–157, 163
Paine, Thomas XII 54, 110, 113, 121, 143, 153, 261; XIV 77; XVI 181–182
Pakistan I 89, 158; II 85, 172; VI 53, 83, 88, 149, 201, 214–215, 219, 238; XIV 2–7, 11–12, 16, 79, 81, 88, 141, 144, 147–148, 177, 180, 186, 190, 228–230, 260; XV 26, 29, 59, 117, 271–272; XVI 45, 71
anti-Taliban assistance to United States XIV 13
assists Taliban XIV 11
Baghdad Pact I 161
Inter-Services Intelligence Division (ISID) XIV 4, 6
nuclear alliance with Libya I 223
nuclear weapons I 15, 217, 219, 221, 223, XIV 3, 6, 40; XVI 98, 109
refugee population in XIV 7
religious indoctrination in XIV 92
terrorism XIV 14
Paleologue, Georges IX 198
Palestine I 160, 164, 317; II 144; VI 164, 188; VII 81–82, 138, 139; VIII 37, 39–40, 82, 103, 163, 166, 208, 212–213, 216, 221; IX 67, 72, 93, 96, 206; X 10,15, 47, 62, 89, 113, 159, 170, 183, 191–192, 281, 306; XI 60, 62, 64, 93, 120, 123–124, 127, 177; XIV 32–33, 55, 63, 79, 87, 95–108, 112, 116, 148, 152–153, 155, 157, 159, 163, 166, 176, 180, 186, 191, 197, 199, 246, 258; XV 24, 33–37, 39, 41–42, 46, 52–54, 79, 83, 134, 137, 139, 142, 144, 146, 222, 226, 240, 248, 253, 260, 263, 274; XVI 13, 81, 88, 236, 238; XIX 14
British withdrawal from VI 83
Central Council (CC) XV 195
corruption in XIV 49
Declaration of Principles (1993) XV 189, 198
diaspora X 63, 306
disenfranchisement in VII 135
intifada XIV 7, 19–27; XV 89–96
Jewish homeland in VIII 37, 168
Jewish immigration XVI 236
mandate VIII 166; XVI 269
Occupied Territories XIV 20, 22, 25–27
Oslo accords XV 182–192
partition of XIV 160
refugees XIV 179, 220–226; XV 21, 183, 191, 214
Rejection Front XV 198
sugar cane in XIII 167
Unified National Leadership (UNL) XIV 26
water VII 140; XIV 269
women XIV 121, 123
Zionist refuge XI 11, 57
Palestine Communist Party (PCP) XV 95
Palestine Legislative Council (PLC) XV 194
Palestine Liberation Front XV 90
Palestine Liberation Organization (PLO) I 156; VI 54, 163, 201; XIV 23–26, 61, 107, 125–126, 131,

184, 197, 225; XV 20, 22, 40–42, 44–46, 48, 54, 57, 76, 83, 89–91, 93–95, 127, 129, 131–132, 144, 148–150, 153, 187, 193–201, 216, 220, 222, 255, 266; XVI 243
Constitution XV 195
Oslo accords XV 182–192
Palestine National Council XIV 25; XV 193–195, 198–199
Palestine National Front (PNF) XIV 25
Palestine People's Conference (PPC) XV 198
Palestinian Authority (PA) VII 136; XIV 19, 24, 25, 27, 87–88, 95–96, 101, 103, 114, 152, 167, 225, 239; XV 183–186, 194–195, 201
Preventive Security Service XIV 102
Palestinian Islamic Jihad XIV 41
Palestinian Legislative Council XIV 102
Palestinian Liberation Front XIV 199; XV 77
Palestinian National Congress XV 22
Palmares XIII 104–105, 107, 212
Palmer, A. Mitchell III 221–223, 226; XIX 174–175, 246
Palmer, Joel VII 56
Palmer raids III 221, 223, 234; XIX 174–175
Pan-African Congress (1919) III 122; VII 239
Pan-Africanism XIX 9, 29, 31

Panama Canal I 53; II 257; III 243, 247; VI 40, 190; XVI 65, 69
Panama Canal Treaty I 52
Panama Canal Zone XV 247
Panama Refining Company v. *Ryan* (1935) III 28
Pan-Arabism XIV 190, 193–194, 205; XV 12, 20, 42, 102, 146
Pan-Asianism IX 164
Panda (Moscow TV show) VII 23–24
Panic of 1819 XIII 176
Panic of 1837 XIII 176
Pan-Slavism VIII 207, 228; IX 99; XIX 218
Papacy X 26, 122, 204, 206, 208, 216, 220, 238, 285
Papen, Franz von XVI 148–149, 154
Paracelsus XIII 183
Paraguay XIV 71
Paris, Matthew X 34, 145, 235
Paris Agreement (1945) XI 214
Paris Bourse (French Stock Exchange) XV 246
Paris Commune (1871) VIII 147
Paris Peace Accords (1973) I 142; VI 222
Paris Peace Conference (1919) VIII 12, 150, 217; IX 93, 107, 165, 171–174, 250; XVI 7, 91, 93, 107; XVII 143, 189, 193, 231
Paris Summit (1960) I 276
Park, Sang Rhup XIX 216
Parker, Billy VII 56
Parker, Dorothy III 177
Parker River Wildlife Refuge VII 277–278
Parks, Rosa II 140
Parks, Larry XIX 37
The Partisan Review XIX 49
Partiya Karkeren Kurdistan (Kurdistan Workers Party or PKK) XIV 265
Partnership for Peace (PfP) XIV 264
Party Kings X 244, 246
Party of Democratic Socialism (PDS) XVI 77
Pasha, Enver XVI 312
Pasic, Nicola IX 267; XVI 100, 103, 194
Pastors' Emergency League XI 29, 31, 32
Pathet Lao VI 141–142
Paths of Glory XIX 166
Patriot Party (1994) II 195, 198
Patriotic Union of Kurdistan (PUK) XIV 169, 173
Patterns XIX 166
Patterson, William XIX 10, 77, 258
Patton, George S. V 2, 23, 44, 125, 127–129, 136; VIII 19, 219
Battle of the Bulge IV 195
Italian campaign IV 144
military background IV 193
Operation Torch IV 193
reputation IV 192–199
Paul, Marcel VII 97
Pauling, Linus XIX 204, 242–243
Pausanias XX 273–282
Pawnbroker, The (1964) XI 159
Peabody Coal Company VII 111
Peace and Freedom Party II 197
Peace Corps I 24; II 116; VI 140
Peace Information Center XIX 240, 242
Peace movements and communism XIX 100, 236–244
peaceful co-existence XIX 99, 236–244, 249
Peace of God (989) X 36, 85, 165, 217
Peace of Paris (1763) XII 139
Peace of Westphalia. *See* Treaties
Peace Water Pipeline Project VII 79, 83
Pearl Harbor (1941) I 89, 261; II 99; III 103, 107–108, 214–215, V 4, 35, 43, 110, 131–135, 183, 187–188, 191–192, 195, 229, 258; VI 150; XVI 301; XIX 1, 88, 104, 230. *See also* Battles.
wetlands takings compared to attack on VII 278
Pearse, Patrick VIII 155–156, 158, 162
Peasants' Revolt (1381) XIII 71
Peggy Sue Got Married XIX 47
Pelagius X 87, 89–90, 93–95, 177, 241, 244
Pender, F. G. VII 53, 55
Penn, William XIII 31
Pennsylvania XI 124; XII 13, 22, 37, 39, 41, 46, 54, 66, 70, 98, 122, 128, 158, 171, 176, 200, 205, 209, 213, 215, 243, 271–272, 283, 291; XIV 182; XVI 101
abolition of slavery XIII 20
abolitionists in XII 2
charter XII 242
colonial economy XII 95
crash of 11 September terrorist plane XIV 86
dams in VII 29
emancipation laws XII 5; XIII 2, 19
gun laws in XII 278–279
Loyalists in XII 192, 270
oil industry XV 172
prohibits importation of slaves XIII 18
pro-nationalist sentiment in XIII 282
Quakers XII 234; XIII 31
ratification of Constitution XII 73–74
religion in XII 147–148, 150, 152
signs Chesapeake Bay 2000 Agreement VII 49
slavery in XII 263
Pennsylvania State University VII 262
Penobscot River XII 86
Pentagon II 51, 67; XIV 86, 89, 103, 229
attack on (11 September 2001) XIV 11; XIX 123, 129
Office of Strategic Influence XIV 230
Pentagon Papers (1971) II 177; VI 24, 26; XIX 128, 280
People's Daily World XIX 208
People's Liberation Army (PLA) I 268
People's Liberation Army, China XIX 117
People's Songs Bulletin XIX 76, 234
People's Will (Russia) XVI 248
People's World XIX 39, 216, 232
Pepó, Pal VII 250
Peres, Shimon XIV 143, 145, 258; XV 131, 182–183, 185, 264, 267
Perl, William XIX 231
Perlo, Victor XIX 197, 200
perestroika I 14; II 56, 60; VI 114, 116, 245; VII 20; XVI 46, 282, 284–285
Perkins, Frances III 150, 200, 251; XI 60
Perot, H. Ross II 194–202
advantages to his campaign II 198
election grassroots movement II 195
hatred of George Bush II 199
importance of wealth to his campaign II 202
presidential campaign II 195
Pershing, John J. III 130, 138; V 14, 126; VIII 10–20, 21–25, 114; IX 21, 26, 29–30, 104–105, 107, 109–110

Mexican expedition III 127
U.S. Punitive Expedition III 129
Pershing II missiles VI 3, 20–21, 35, 101–102, 208, 229, 232, 236, 263; XVI 44
Persia VIII 31, 35, 41; IX 96, 226; X 29, 183; XI 125; XIV 177–178; XVI 70, 218
Persian Empire XV 229, 235
Persian Gulf VII 77, 147; XIV 2, 28, 36, 43–44, 47, 55, 175–177, 217; XV 72–73, 78, 97–98, 100, 102, 104, 108, 137, 176–177, 180, 275; XVI 44, 46, 236, 312
oil XIV 170
states XV 34, 83, 97, 100–101, 109, 182
U.S. policy in region XIV 41
Persian Gulf War (1990–1991) I 163, 195–196, 199, 217, 239; VI 58, 61, 100, 173, 235, 250, 266; VIII 168; X 56; XIV 7, 29, 62, 77, 96, 115, 146–147, 168, 169, 171, 215, 237–240, 242, 250, 261, 270, 286; XV 72–79, 80–88, 90, 101, 182, 187, 198, 201, 255, 258, 260, 263, 267; XVI 109; XIX 123, 129
Peru VII 74
Pestalozzi, Johann Heinrich XIX 191
Pétain, Philippe IV 276; V 244; VIII 150, 265; IX 26, 108–110, 114; XI 14; XVI 117, 130, 136, 141, 298–302
Peter I (the Great) IX 154, 238
Peter, Saint X 115, 117, 119, 121–122, 218
Peter the Hermit X 15, 18–19, 21, 29, 59, 72, 74, 101, 131, 191, 211–221, 231–232, 234–235, 237
Peter the Venerable X 16, 79, 163
Peters, Richard XII 94, 98
Petion, Alexandre Sabes XIII 213, 215
Petrograd IX 197, 237, 239–240
Petrograd Soviet VIII 170, 173, 175, 178, 258; IX 201–202
Petrov, Vladimir XIX 266–267
The Phenix City Story XIX 166
Philadelphia XII 12, 15, 21–22, 38, 41, 44, 54, 63, 68, 79, 92, 94–96, 103, 110, 114, 200, 224, 234, 267, 270–271, 273–274, 278, 283, 287, 304–305, 320
occupation of XII 307
Philbrick, Herbert XIX 248
Philip I (France) X 118–119, 121
Philip II Augustus (France) X 21, 33, 88–89, 144, 151, 251, 254, 257, 260, 263, 297
Philip IV (France) X 67, 207
Philippines I 51, I 295; VI 77, 80, 149, 188, 194; IX 96; X 8, 244; XII 33; XIV 93, 107, 230; XVI 69
Clark Field and Subic Bay I 145
crucial to U.S. security I 85
Insurrection (1899–1902) IX 96
Muslim rebels in XIV 195
Opium War III 136
Phillips, Wendell XIII 7, 31
Phongolapoort Dam (South Africa) VII 245
Picasso, Pablo III 79; IX 86; XVII 46–48, 238; XIX 238
Pickering, Timothy XII 97, 225
Picq, Charles VIII 71, 234
Pierce, Franklin XIII 195
Pilgrims XIX 273
Pinochet Ugarte, Augusto I 124, 128–129, 141; VI 64; XIV 23; XIX 142
Pinter, Frank XIX 207
Pisa X 148–150, 156
Pitt, William the Elder XII 30, 53, 56–57, 139–141, 166, 237
Pitt, William the Younger XII 166, 169
Pittsburgh Communist Party XIX 201
Pittsburgh Courier XIX 9, 76
Pius XII, Pope IV 36, 38, 191; XI 191–201
Plan XVI VIII 233–234; IX 45
Plan XVII VIII 146, 148, 182, 232–238; IX 47, 99, 101; XVII 204; XVI 204
Planck, Max IX 87
Planned Parenthood of Missouri v. *Danforth* (1976) II 222
Planned Parenthood of Southeastern Pennsylvania v. *Casey* (1992) II 79, 222, 224
plants
African grasses VII 217
alfalfa VII 14, 182
Bermuda grass VII 217
black mustard VII 217
corn VII 181, 182
Huachuca water umbel VII 216
invasion of alien species in the United States VII 213
Johnson grass VII 217
Kearney blue-star VII 216
Russian Thistles VII 13
sorghum VII 181–182
tiszavirág (Tisza flower) VII 252
winter wheat VII 181
Plaszow (concentration camp) XI 203, 206
Plato XI 74
as an aristocrat XX 154–163
and Aristotle XX 81–88
Platt Amendment (1901) III 47
revocation of (1934) III 47
Pleasantville XIX 47
Plessy v. *Ferguson* (1896) II 23, 25, 90, 136, 138, 141, 280, 290; XIII 53, 57
Plum Island VII 277
Plumer, Herbert VIII 219–220, 224
Plutarch XX 283–291
plutonium bomb (Soviet) XIX 23
Plymouth XII 19
Po River VII 147
Podhoretz, Norman XIX 49
Podoba, Juraj VII 103
Poe, Edgar Allan XIII 48
Poincaré, Raymond XVI 194
Point Coupée Conspiracy (1795) XIII 91
Point Reyes National Seashore VII 178
Poison Gas VIII 239–244
Poitier, Sydney XIX 38
Pol Pot I 44, 46, 134, 145, 289; VI 83; XI 71, 75, 166–167, 169
Poland I 109–110, 112, 152, 259, 271, 294; II 34, 36, 39, 153; V 30; VI 110, 130, 133–134, 137, 178, 181, 217, 237, 244–246, 249, 251–252, 261, 274, 276; VIII 91, 277–278, 280–281, 284; IX 44, 93, 134, 158–159, 175, 193, 238, 242; XI 12, 15, 60, 83, 90, 106, 109, 138, 144, 159, 167, 175, 179, 192, 203, 205–208, 211, 224, 252, 260; XII 169; XIV 171, 265; XV 120; XVI 6, 11, 14, 18, 32, 45, 76–77, 84, 98, 101, 103–104, 111, 113–115, 123–124, 127, 130, 142, 157, 189, 206, 213, 218, 220, 224, 227, 230–231, 284–285, 294, 301, 312, 317, 319
aftermath of World War II I 173; XIX 1–2
Baruch Plan I 27, 29, 31
Democratic Bloc XVI 124
entry into NATO I 207
environmental activism in VII 17–24
expatriates VI 170
fascism XVII 140
German invasion during World War II V 35, 132, 179; VIII 284; XI 55; XVI 91; XVII 102
German occupation during World War I VIII 92–98; XI 104
Home Army (AK) XVI 231
immigration to U.S. from XIX 218
impact of pollution on population of VII 18
independence movement VI 110
Jews
ghettoization of XI 116
World War I VIII 164–167
World War II XI 14, 93, 117, 126, 264–265, 268, 270
"London Poles" XVI 123
martial law in (1981) VII 19

massacre of officers XI 169, 258; XVI 229
National Armed Forces (NSZ) XVI 231
National Military Union (NZW) XVI 231
National Radical Camp (ONR) XVI 231
partition VI 54
Peasant Battalions (BCh) XVI 231
Peasant Party (SL) XVI 230–231
poisoning of waters in VII 18
Polish People's Army (PAL) XVI 231
Polish Workers' Party (PPR) XVI 231
postwar elections I 258
radioactive fallout from Chernobyl VII 18
reforms I 154
social welfare XVII 274
Solidarity VI 110, 237; VII 17, 19, 20; XVI 45, 289; XVII 200, 216, 221
Soviet domination of XIX 144, 195, 215, 218,248
Soviet invasion of II 32; XIX 57, 144
strategic importance I 109
Union of Polish Patriots XVI 230
uprising of 1980 XIX 146
Warsaw Pact VI 170
World War I XVI 308
Yalta Agreement (1945) I 301–302, 304
Polaris Submarine VI 11, 75
Polaris Submarine/Sea-Launched Ballistic Missile (SLBM) VI 10
Police agencies, increased power of XIX 181
Polisario (Popular Front for the Liberation of Saguia el Hamra and Rio de Oro) XIV 71, 74, 75, 209, 276, 277, 279, 281–284
Polish Committee of National Liberation XVI 230
Polish Communist Party XVI 229, 233, 289
Tenth Congress of VII 20
Polish Ecological Club (Polski Klub Ekologiczny, or PKE) VII 18
Polish Green Party VII 20
Polish Question XVI 73
Polites, Gus XIX 216
Political parties
history of II 199
history of third parties II 199
voter demographics II 199
Polivanov, Alexei IX 193, 243
Polk, James K. XII 168; XIII 283
poll tax XIII 56
Pollock, Jackson XIX 45, 48
Polonsky, Abe XIX 166
pop art XIX 48
Pollution Control Act (1915, Ontario) VII 117
polychlorinated biphenyls (PCBs) VII 147
Pompidou, Georges XVI 131
Pong Dam (India) VII 130
Pontiac's rebellion (1763) XII 236
Popular Democratic Front for the Liberation of Palestine (PDFLP) XV 41, 44, 48, 90, 198–199
Popular Front against Facism XIX 10, 29, 34–35, 38–41, 52, 56, 62, 71, 75, 98, 103–104, 106, 154, 181, 189, 193, 229, 231, 232–233
Popular Front for the Liberation of Palestine (PFLP) XIV 100, 195, 198; XV 40, 41, 44, 48–49, 90, 95, 152, 198–199
Popular Front for the Liberation of Palestine-General Command (PFLP-GC) XIV 195
Popular Unity Coalition (UP) I 123, 127
Populist Party II 3, 86, 199; XIII 56
aka People's Party II 196
Porgy and Bess XIX 35
Porter, Eliot VII 113
Portland Dock Commission VII 53
Portland, Oregon VII 52, 197
importance of VII 53
Portugal VII 240; VIII 31; IX 49, 84; X 10, 304; XI 174–179; XII 105; XVI 84, 87–88, 99, 130
colonial rule in Africa VII 236–237; VIII 86, 89
decolonization XVI 79
enslavement of Africans XIII 167
fascism XVII 138, 140
fights maroons XIII 107
free workers from XIII 168
Law of 1684 XIII 134, 136
laws of slavery XIII 178
slave trade XIII 37–40, 129, 131, 134, 136, 180, 270
treaty with Great Britain (1810) XII 167
view on blacks XIII 181
Post Office Act (1710) XII 232, 236, 243
Potash, Irving, indicted under Smith Act XIX 260
Potawatomie XII 175–176
Potlatch Corporation VII 226
Potsdam Conference (1945) I 239, 263; II 205; III 13; VI 155, 267; XI 253; XVI 74, 226–227, 315, 317; XIX 21
Potsdam Declaration (1945) III 15; V 50–51, 149, 264; XI 214
poverty CPUSA fight against XIX 229
Powell, Adam Clayton, Jr. II 197, 274; XIX 12
Powell, Colin II 100; XIV 80, 97, 100–101, 103, 105–106, 108, 155, 225; XV 78
Powell, John Wesley VII 181
Powers, Francis Gary I 66
Powers, John E. XIX 183
Pravda IX 197
Preminger, Otto XIX 28
Presbyterians XII 148, 150, 205, 235, 254, 263; XIII 183; XIX 238
New Lights among XII 147
presidential election of 1948 XIX 185–186, 251
President's Commission on Civil Rights XIX 24, 30
President's Foreign Intelligence Advisory Board (PFIAB) VI 256–257
Pressler Amendment (1985) I 218; XIV 6
Prester John X 189, 304
Pride of the Marines XIX 168
Primo de Rivera y Orbaneja, Miguel XVIII 93, 104, 107, 112–113, 192, 200
Primo de Rivera y Saenz de Heredia, Jose Antonio XVIII 105, 277
Prince, The (1513) XI 133
Prince Max of Baden IX 32
Prince Rupprecht IX 262
Princeton University XIII 198
Princip, Gavrilo IX 225–226
Principle International Alert Center VII 248
Pritchard, Jack (Gullah Jack) XIII 156
Prittwitz und Graffon, Max von IX 159
Proclamation of 1763 XII 207, 232
Proctor, James XIX 19
Producers, The (1968) XI 46
Profintern XIX 193
The Program of the Communist International XIX 261
Progressive Citizens of America XIX 94
progressive education XIX 113
Progressive Era VII 10, 47, 122, 257, 271, 273; IX 250
women in III 197–203
Progressive movement III 204–211; VII 263; VIII 295, 301
Progressive Party II 195–196, 209; III 177; XIX 30, 76, 117, 185, 216, 238, 240
Prohibition III 174, 198–211
Prohibitory Act (1775) XII 51, 54
proslavery theory XIII 26–34
Prosser, Gabriel XIII 54, 91, 156–157, 210, 231, 235–236
Protection of Civilian Persons in Time of War (1949) XIV 157
Protestant/Puritan ethic XII 60
Protestantism, and slavery XIII 31
Provisional Irish Republican Army (PRIRA) XVI 249
Prussia VIII 71, 184, 257, 278; IX 44–45, 206, 225; XVI 30, 76, 148, 200, 204, 214, 216, 251, 294, 313
Concert of Europe XVI 72–78
mass education XVII 162–163
military 30, 67; X 66, 179; XII 105; XIV 171

monarchy XVI 182
Pryce, E. Morgan VII 55
Public Broadcasting System (PBS) II 125; VII 184
Public Works Administration (PWA, 1933) III 150; VII 43
Pueblo Dam (United States) VII 14
Puerto Rico IX 96; XVI 69
Puget Sound VII 188–189, 191, 193–194
Pugwash Conference I 253
Pumpkin Papers XIX 198
Punic Wars (264–146 BCE) XVI 251
Punjab, India VII 133
agriculture in VII 130
Pure Food and Drug Act (1906) III 243
The Pure in Heart XIX 36
Puritanism XII 150, 204, 234, 235
Pusey, Nathan XIX 113
Putin, Vladimir XIV 218
Pyle, Ernie V 175
Pyramid Lake VII 169
Pyrenees X 2, 241; XI 175

Q

Qadhdhafi, Muammar XIV 192–200, 217, 270; XVII 8
Qalawun X 46, 48–49, 185
Qana attacks (1996) XIV 129
Qassim, Abd al-Karim XV 21, 61, 116–124, 273
Qatar XIV 28–29, 33, 55, 60, 63, 65, 115, 177, 179, 212, 215, 217, 219, 247
constitution (2002) XIV 67
economy XIV 51, 68
elections XIV 64
investments XIV 64
water XIV 269
women's rights XIV 64
Q-ships IX 76, 183–188
Quadrant Conference (1943) V 236
Quai d'Orsai (French Foreign Office) V 173
Quakers (Society of Friends) XI 137; XII 62, 63, 148, 150, 205, 216, 234, 254, 263; XIII 149; XVI 91
abolitionists XIII 1, 17, 31
hostility against XII 192
Quartering Act (1765) XII 141, 207, 233, 236
Quebec XII 43, 45–48, 149, 189
opposes water bill VII 120
Quebec Act (1774) XII 149, 171, 200, 207, 234
Quebec Conference (1943) V 239
Queen Blanche of Castile X 140–143, 235
Queen Mary (British ship) IX 177–178
Queen Victoria IX 44, 140
Silver Jubilee of (1862) IX 45
Queen's Rangers XII 186
Quemoy I 275; II 52; VI 103, 181
Chinese attack I 265–270
Eisenhower administration I 211, 213
Quinn v. *U.S.* I 80
Quisling, Vidkun XVII 135, 137, 139
Quock Walker case (1783) XIII 19
Quran (Koran) X 41–42, 45, 49, 65, 133, 179, 199, 273; XIV 134, 140, 165, 182, 184, 187, 205–206, 235, 244, 251, 291
Qutuz X 48, 187
Quwatli, Shukri al- XV 272, 275

R

Rába geologic fault line VII 106
Rabin, Yitzhak XI 181; XIV 155, 166, 258; XV 83, 131, 139, 182–184, 187, 191, 238–239, 263–267
Rabinovich, Itamar 263, 264, 266
Race riots after WWII XIX 9, 25
Rachel Carson National Wildlife Refuge VII 278
racism II 163; III 213–219; XII 3; XIII 178–184, 224, 253–254, 278, 280
American IV 217
narcotics legislation III 134
Radic, Stjepan IX 267, 272; XVI 100
Radical Division, U.S. Justice Department XIX 174
Radical Republicans XIII 5
radioactive fallout XIX 237, 243
Radio Farda XIV 233
Radio Free Asia XIV 233
Radio Free Europe I 65; VI 133, 135; XIV 233; XIX 215
Radio Liberty XIV 233, 235
Radio of Monte Carlo XIV 29
Radio Sawa XIV 233
Rafsanjani, Hashimi XIV 136
Ragheb, Ali Abul XIV 65
Railroad Retirement Pension Act (1934) III 28
Rainbow Bridge VII 30
Rainey, Gertrude "Ma" III 82
Rajasthan, India VII 125
agriculture in VII 130
rainfall in VII 126
Rajasthan Canal VII 132
Rákosi, Mátyás VI 134, 276
Raleigh, Walter XII 137
Ramadan War. *See* Yom Kippur War I 314
Ramsay, David XIII 19, 45, 48
Rand, Ayn XIX 163
RAND Corporation I 119; II 65–66
Randolph, A. Philip II 189; III 123, 184, 217; XIX 10
march on Washington III 219
membership in ACOA XIX 12
Randolph, Edmund XII 70; XIII 18
Randolph, John XIII 19, 48
Ranke, Leopold von X 218, 300, 304
Rankin, John XIX 30, 61, 251
Rape of Nanking (1937) IV 152–153; V 153, 192; IX 96
Rapp-Coudert Committee XIX 108, 111
Rapp, Herbert XIX 108
Raritan Bay VII 265
Rascher, Sigmund XI 151–152
Rasputin, Grigory VIII 258; IX 160, 237, 239–240, 243
Rathenau, Walther VIII 140, 166; XVI 173
Rawlinson, Henry VIII 272, 275; IX 36, 122
Ray, Man XIX 46
Raymond of Penafort X 67, 69
Raymond of St. Gilles X 73, 119
Raymond of Toulouse X 191, 216, 221
Raynal, Abbé Guillaume-Thomas-François de XIII 147, 150, 246
Rayneval, Conrad Alexandre Gérard de XII 102
Rayneval, Joseph Matthias Gérard de XII 102, 104
Reagan, Ronald I 48, 51–54, 104, 106, 149; II 56–63, 102, 190, 199–200, 295; III 48; VI 6, 8, 13, 17, 20, 25, 31, 33, 50, 58, 104, 109, 190–191, 205, 208, 221–242, 256–257, 261, 270; XII 288; XIV 2, 6, 38, 100, 198; XV 75, 102, 151, 155, 186; XVI 40, 45–46, 92, 95, 288–289; XIX 277
arms sales to Iran XIX 280
anticommunism II 60; VI 228–229; XVI 38, 44; XIX 128–129, 278
appearance before HCUA XIX 44, 251
conduct of the Cold War XIX 280
election platform I 50
invasion of Grenada II 58
Middle East policy XV 150
nuclear arms race I 183
Reagan Doctrine II 58
Screen Actors Guild president II 189
Strategic Defense Initiative (SDI) I 195–196, 199; XVI 284
support for Contras XIX 145
support of anticommunist regimes II 58
view of Vietnam War I 295
Reagan administration VI 17, 36, 57, 133, 221, 225, 228–235; XV 76
Afghanistan I 10–16; VI 133, 237
Africa policy VI 1–7

aid to contras I 54
arms control VI 19–20, 22
budget deficits I 202
Central America policies I 48–52, 54, 56
defense spending II 57; VI 109, 226
foreign policy VI 57, 61, 236–242; XIV 97, 198
Iran-Contra affair I 54
Iraq XV 73
Latin American I 14
National Security Decision Directive 17 (NSDD-17) I 50
National Security Decision Directives I 32, 66, 75, 196
Nicaragua VI 190–196
nuclear proliferation I 15
Pakistan, aid to XIV 3
Reagan Plan XV 148
Soviet Union I 196; VI 44, 116, 194, 263
United Nations XV 148
zero-zero option (1981) VI 36
Reagan Doctrine VI 44, 186, 221–227; XIV 5
impact on the Soviet Union VI 226
Reaganomics VI 226
Real Cédula (Royal Decree, 1789) XIII 62, 66
Realpolitik I 285; II 169; IV 123; XIV 131
Rebel without a Cause XIX 47
Reciprocal Trade Program XIX 157
Reconquista (reconquest) X 1–2, 8, 101, 133, 140, 143, 159, 178–179, 220, 241–246
Reconstruction (1865–1877) XIII 2, 50, 51, 54, 56
waning Northern support of XIII 55
Red Army Faction XVI 249; XIX 96
Red Brigades XVI 245, 248–249
Red Channels XIX 163
Red Cross XI 174
The Red Danube XIX 163
Red International of Labor Unions. See Profintern. XIX 193
Red Line agreement (1928) XV 177, 179
Red Scare I 174; III 221–226, 229; VI 129, 156, 158–159
impact on Sacco and Vanzetti trial III 233
Red Scare. *See* anticommunism
Red squads XIX 65, 182, 184
Red Sea XIV 206; XV 23, 137; XVI 240
Redmond, John VIII 154–157, 161
Reece, B. Carroll XIX 181
Reed, Daniel XIX 157
Reed, John XIX 212
Reed, Joseph XII 11, 13
Reform Party (1996) II 195–200
Refuse Act (1899) VII 266, 268
Regional Center for Ecological Supervision of the Apuseni Mountains VII 250
Rehnquist, Justice William H. II 224, 281
Reichskirche (national church) XI 27, 29, 31–33
Reichssicherheitshauptamt (Reich Central Security Office) XI 36–37
Reichstag (German parliament) IV 137; V 115, 134, 211; VIII 164, 256; IX 142; XI 211; XVI 148, 150, 154, 308
Reichstag Fire (1933) XVI 150, 154; XIX 102
Reign of Terror (1793–1794) XIII 71
Reinsurance Treaty (1887–1890) VIII 225–226, 249
Remarque, Erich VIII 55, 59, 186, 188, 264; IX 84, 212
Remington, William XIX 197
Rendezvous with America XIX 40
Rennenkampf, Pavel IX 65, 160, 242
Renunciation Act (1778) XII 166, 171
Reuther, Victor XIX 73
Reuther, Walter XIX 73, 185
Report on Public Credit (1790) XII 120
Republic of Vietnam. *See* South Vietnam
Republic Steel VII 266
Republican Party I 272; II 51, 180, 194–195, 198; III 118, 211; XIII 2, 4, 21, 51, 272, 277–278, 283
abortion II 79
accuses Democrats of being soft on Communism XIX 249, 251
benefits from school busing II 295
charges of Communists in federal government XIX 91–94, 97, 99, 124, 246
China Lobby 16, 19
demand for internal-security measures XIX 251
efforts to undermine New Deal XIX 22, 87, 91–94, 96, 119, 157, 180–181, 184
gains in 1946 congressional elections XIX 92–94, 185, 249, 251
losses in 1948 elections XIX 251
pro-life platforms II 223
reaction to Marshall Plan II 209
relationship with Hoover XIX 173
Republican National Convention (1952) II 280; XIX 224
under Nixon's leadership XIX 221
United States presidents II 49
Vietnam policy II 266
views on Hitler XIX 88
Rerum Novarum (1891) XIII 254
Reserve Mining case VII 266, 268–269
Resistance movements V 243–247
aid to Allies V 245
forms of sabotage V 247
Germany's response to V 245
impact in France V 244
Vichy France V 247
Resources for the Future VII 259
Reuss, Henry Schoellkopf VII 266
Revere, Paul XII 149
Revolutionary Left Movement. *See* Movimiento de Izquierda Revolucionaria I 127, 130
Reykjavik Summit (1986) II 61; VI 33, 36, 224, 231
Reynald of Chatillon X 52, 155, 201
Reynolds v. *Sims,* 1962 II 139
Rhine Action Plan (1987) VII 230, 232
Rhine Commission (1815) VII 92
Rhine River VII 204, 207, 209–210, 229–235; VIII 24, 280, 282
chemical spill on VII 230
floods on VII 231
pollution of VII 234
Rhineland X 19, 213, 219; XVI 2, 9, 13, 76
Jews in X 15–17, 19, 21–22, 272, 274
Rhine-Main-Danube Canal VII 104, 204–210
Rhode Island XII 19, 21, 39, 70, 74, 81, 209, 221, 233, 263, 290; XIII 31, 197
emanciaption laws XII 5
gun laws XII 279
prohibits importation of slaves XIII 18
Quakers in XIII 31
refuses support to Bank of North America XII 25
religion in XII 148
slave children freed XIII 19
slave trade XIII 270, 273
Rhodes, Cecil XII 33; XV 15
Rhodes, James A. VII 265
Rhodes armistice agreements (1949) XV 216
Rhodesia VII 239; VIII 86; XI 268; XVI 182
British immigration to VII 237
colonialists in VII 7
Rhodesian Unilateral Declaration of Independence VII 240
Rhône River VII 92–95, 147
Rhône River Authority VII 93, 96
Ribbentrop, Joachim von V 134; XI 59, 62, 179, 254; XVI 91, 225
Ribbentrop-Molotov Non-Aggression Pact (1939) V 28, 30, 32
Rice, Condoleezza XIV 101, 103, 129
Rich, Willis VII 201
Richard I, the Lion-Hearted X 30, 33, 48, 57, 59, 143–144, 151, 175, 247–253, 297, 304, 254–261
Richardson, Robert V. XIII 51, 53
Richmond, Al XIX 216, 232
Richtofen, Manfred von IX 38

Rickey, Branch XIX 76
Rift Valley VII 229
Righteous Among the Nations XI 161, 202, 206
Riis, Jacob August III 260
Rio Grande River VII 152
Rio Treaty I 93
riparian ecosystems in the U.S. Southwest VII 211–218
Rivers, Eugene XIII 253, 256
Rivers and Harbors Act (1899) VII 266
Rivers and Harbors Act (1925) VII 52
Roan Selection Trust VII 5
Robarts, John P. VII 118
Robert of Artois X 139, 141, 143, 145
Robert the Monk X 213, 215, 281, 283
Roberto, Holden VI 1, 165
Roberts, Holland XIX 232
Roberts, Justice Owen III 25, 28, 30; V 188
Robertson, William VIII 77, 102–108, 221
Robespierre, Maximillian XII 134
Robeson, Paul XIX 29–30, 76
as artist XIX 35, 39
appearance before HCUA XIX 76
blacklisting of XIX 10
Communism XIX 10, 35, 80, 237
criticism of Marshall Plan XIX 12
message to Bandung Coference XIX 11
Peekskill concerts XIX 101
repudication by civil rights movement XIX 10, 12
revocation of passport XIX 10
Robin Hood XIX 166
Robinson, Bestor VII 112
Robinson, Jackie
appearance before HCUA XIX 30, 76
integration of Major League baseball XIX 76–77
Robinson, James H. II 44
Robinson, Randall XIII 195, 197–198
Rochambeau, Comte de XII 33, 306, 308
Rock and Roll II 213–219
"British invasion" II 216
commercial aspects II 219
form of rebellion II 219
liberating force II 213
mass marketing of II 216
origin of term II 214
punk trends II 216
revolutionary force II 214
rock'n' roll XIX 48
unifying force II 216
Rock Around the Clock (1956) II 219
Rock Oil Company XV 172
Rockefeller, John D. III 176, 271; XV 172
Rockefeller, Nelson A. III 48; VII 264
Rocky Boy's Reservation VII 172
Rocky Ford VII 15
Rocky Ford Ditch Company VII 13
Rocky Mountains VII 151, 181, 197
Rocque, François de la XVI 141–143, 146
Roderigue Hortalez & Cie XII 101, 106
Rodney, Lester XIX 77
Roe v. *Wade* (1973) II 78, 220–226, 280, 284
Roger II (Sicily) X 198, 285, 289
Rogers, Ginger XIX 167
Rogers, Lela XIX 167
Rogers, William XV 40, 135
Rogers Initiative (1970) XV 40, 42, 44–49
Rogue River VII 31, 223
Röhm, Ernst XI 243
Roland X 65, 103
Roman Catholic Church
anticommunism of XIX 180–181, 183–184
of Hungary XIX 184
of Yugoslavia XIX 184
Roman Empire X 24–25, 29, 88, 124, 167, 305
Roman Republic, fall of XX 238–248
Romania I 110, 294; II 36, 39, 172; V 64; VI 51, 88, 175, 206, 210, 217, 245, 249, 252, 261, 265, 274, 276; VII 248–250, 252–254; VIII 43–44, 46, 93–97, 163, 216, 230, 278; IX 60–61, 66, 127, 193, 205, 207; X 65, 70; XI 15, 60, 142, 214, 220; XV 120; XVI 32–34, 76, 99, 102–104, 122, 124, 127, 185, 188, 195, 213, 218, 220, 233, 284–285, 289, 317
chemical spill in VII 247–255
Department of Waters, Forests, and Environmental Protection VII 248
Environmental Protection Agency VII 248
fascism XVII 85
forest clear-cutting in VII 254
monarchy XVI 180
National Democratic Front XVI 124
overthrow of communist regime XVI 282
relationship with Soviets I 253
Soviet domination I 107
U.S. recognizes communist government I 303
World War I XVI 308
Romanian Waters Authority VII 248
Romanovs XVI 51, 55, 180, 195, 199
Rome XIII 274, 278; XIV 159, 161, 163; XVI 111, 251
slavery in XIII 165
terrorism XIV 16
Rommel, Erwin V 123–126, 129, 135, 143, 176, 181, 226; VIII 111
legend V 175
Roosevelt, Eleanor III 150, 217, 219; XIX 185, 216
Roosevelt, Franklin D. II 32, 39, 50, 52, 165, 197, 203, 280; III 10–11, 14, 45, 48, 86, 89, 109, 147, 190, 193; IV 173, 210; V 58, 236, 249; VI 8–9, 20, 36, 56–57, 78, 104, 123, 146–147, 158, 205, 254, 267; VII 28, 97, 152, 202; XI 4, 10–12, 55–57, 60, 64, 110, 121, 168, 174, 252, 261; XV 163; XVI 76, 125, 162, 167, 218, 227–228, 230, 314–315, 317, 319; XIX 21, 62, 117, 151, 154, 193, 198, 218, 240, 251
and FBI XIX 25, 56, 86, 120, 175, 178, 251, 260
arsenal of democracy III 64
Asia policy IV 254
attitude toward Soviet Union III 13
belief in a cooperative relationship with the Soviet Union I 101
Brain Trust II 210
Casablanca conference (1943) V 252
China policy XIX 22
Court packing scheme XI 168; XIX 92
election of VII 27
Executive Order 8802 (1941) III 219
Executive Order 9066 (1942) III 103–104
Fireside chats III 148, 152
Four Freedoms V 250
Good Neighbor Policy I 125; III 47
Great Depression III 54–60
Inaugural Address (1932) III 152
isolationism V 289–294
Lend Lease Act IV 160
Native American policies III 141–142
New Deal II 47, 271; III 193, 263
New Deal programs III 62–63; XIX 91, 119, 157, 181
Operation Torch (1942) V 251
opinion of Second Front IV 213
presidential campaign (1932) III 148
previous war experience V 253
relationship with George C. Marshall V 251
Roosevelt Court II 281
Scottsboro case III 188
Selective Service Act (1940) V 250
State of the Union Address (1941) II 99
support for Hiss XIX 63, 198, 224
support of Great Britain V 250
support of highway building II 106
support of naval reorganization IV 3
Supreme Court III 24
unconditional surrender policy V 270–276
western irrigation VII 25
World War II strategy V 251, 253
Yalta conference V 252, 309–315

Roosevelt, Theodore I 306; II 195, 199, 271–272; III 208, 211, 240–247, 177; VIII 18, 22, 129, 205; IX 5, 168, 246; XIV 175; XVI 30
appreciation of public image III 242
Bull Moose Party III 243
conservation efforts III 243
Dominican Republic III 247
establishes federal refuges VII 271, 273
First Children III 242
labor disputes III 243
New Nationalism III 211
Nobel Peace Prize II 99, 243
racial prejudices III 246
role as a family man III 242
Rough Riders III 241
signs Newlands Reclamation Act VII 25
Spanish-American War (1898) III 245
supports western reclamation VII 26
Teddy bears III 242
views on Latin America I 132
Roosevelt (FDR) administration III 46; VI 154; XI 123; XIX 16–17, 61, 87, 197, 216, 272
dam projects VII 25
national drug policy III 135
New Deal III 163
opium trade III 137
policy toward Jews III 251; XI 60, 64, 121
relationship with labor movement II 188
Soviet sympathizers in VI 61, 154
and the Spanish Civil War XVIII 208–215
spurs Western growth VII 28
support of Mexican Water Treaty VII 152
Third World VI 80
War Refugee Board (WRB) III 253
Roosevelt (TR) administration
Anti-Trust Act (1890) III 242
Big Stick diplomacy III 46
corollary to the Monroe Doctrine III 247
Department of Commerce and Labor, Bureau of Corporations III 242
foreign policy III 243, 245
Hepburn Act (1906) III 243, 245
National Reclamation Act (1902) III 243
Panama Canal III 243, 247
Pure Food and Drug Act (1906) III 243
United States Forestry Service III 243
Roosevelt Corollary (1904) III 46
Roosevelt Dam (United States) VII 214, 216
Roosevet Recessions XIX 92
Root Elihu VIII 298
Rosellini, Albert D. VII 190
Rosenberg, Alfred V 143, 216; XI 118; XVI 186
Rosenberg, Julius and Ethel I 274; II 131, 227–234; VI 154, 156, 158, 177; XIX: 5, 58, 94, 118, 148, 173, 176, 178, 194, 196–197, 200, 207, 213, 272, 276, 282–290
arrest of II 229, 231–232
Communist Party of the United States of America (CPUSA) II 227
execution of II 233
forged documents II 230
Freedom of Information Act II 228
G & R Engineering Company II 229
martyrdom II 230
Meeropol, Michael and Robert, sons of II 228
possible motives for arrest of II 231
proof of espionage activity II 230
Soviet nuclear spying I 241, 243, 246–247
trial XIX 176, 127, 132, 178, 282–290
Young Communist League II 228
Rosenstrasse Protest XI 187
Roth, Andrew XIX 16, 17, 18, 19
Rothko, Mark XIX 48
Ross, Bob VII 74
Ross, Dennis XV 264–265
Ross, E. XIX 270
Rostow, Walt W. I 20, 294
flexible response I 120
Rousseau, Jean-Jacques XI 75; XII 121, 133, 318
Rove, Karl XIV 97, 100
Rowe, E. J. XIX 270
Rowlett Act (1919) IX 93
Royal Africa Company (RAC) XIII 40, 133, 179, 270, 272
Royal Air Force (RAF) I 235; IV 163, 168; V 86, 90, 93, 95, 124; VIII 55, 194; IX 9, 11, 217, 220, 222; XIV 176
attacks on civilians V 87
Royal Air Force (RAF) Mosquitoes V 60
Royal Canadian Navy V 80, 82, 85
Royal Dutch Shell XIV 211–212; XV 172–173, 176, 178–179
Royal Flying Corps (RFC) IX 10, 38
Royal Geographical Society XIV 177
Royal Institute for Amazigh Culture (IRCAM) XIV 209
Royal Navy (Britain) V 43, 82, 85, 118, 260; VI 75; VIII 132; IX 31, 48–51, 75–77, 79, 99, 139–142, 173, 176–177, 181, 183–184, 186, 228, 247, 256; XIII 269–270, 273; XVI 68
elimination of slave trade XIII 36
oil XV 173
Ruacana Diversion Wier VII 239
Ruckelshaus, William D. VII 263, 266, 268
Ruffin, Edmund XIII 48
Ruffin, Thomas XIII 97, 102, 265
Rumkowski, Mordechai Chaim XI 140–144
Rumsfeld, Donald XIV 97, 101, 103; XV 78
Rundstedt, Field Marshal Karl Gerd von 125–126, 129
Rupprecht, Prince VIII 179–180, 184, 246, 274
Rural Institute in Puno, Peru VII 74
Rush, Benjamin XII 93, 97–98, 291, 296; XIII 31
Rushdie, Salman XIV 140
Rusk, Dean, Asia policy 18Rusk, Dean I 160, 294; VI 71, 95–96, 101
Ruskin, John XIII 174
Russia XI 20, 102, 109, 167, 174, 179; XII 105; XIV 12, 88, 106, 143, 180, 239, 240; XV 27, 33–34, 78–79; XVI 9, 15–20, 22–24, 27, 32, 34, 38, 41, 58, 60, 80, 87, 92, 106, 141, 192–195, 198, 208, 221, 236, 244, 252, 281, 296, 312
alliances before World War I VIII 35, 225–231
Allied intervention in (1918) XVI 1–7
anti-semitism VIII 164
Asia policy, XIX 18
assists anti-Taliban resistance XIV 11
Bloody Sunday XVI 17
Bolshevik Party XVI 201
collapse of Tsarist state XVI 49–56
colonialism XVI 70
condemns terrorism XIV 16
Concert of Europe XVI 72–78
Constituent Assembly IX 199, 201; XVI 18, 20
Constitutional Democrats XVI 53
Council of Ministers IX 240
Crimean War (1853–1856) VIII 33
defeated by Japan XVI 107
Duma IX 145, 190, 201, 238, 240; XVI 17, 50–52, 55
enslavement of Russians XIII 167
France as ally XVI 217
General Staff Academy IX 158
German atrocities in XI 267
Great Retreat (1915) IX 240
Holy Synod XVI 16
Imperial state, collapse of IX 81, 154–161
Jews in VIII 164, 167; XI 93, 126
Kulaks, killing of XI 169
Marxist Social Democratic and Labor Party XVI 16, 18
Mensheviks XVI 18
Mobilization Order #19 XVI 204
Mobilization Order #20 XVI 204
monarchy XVI 178, 180
1905 Revolution XVI 50, 53, 175
Octobrist Party XVI 50, 53

oil XIV 218
Petrograd Soviet XVI 201
Provisional government VIII 96, 167, 170–178, 260, 261; IX 194, 196, 202, 237–243; XVI 15, 17, 19, 51, 207
Red Army XVI 18, 20
Red Terror XVI 18
Socialists VIII 255, 258, 261
Soviet IX 82
Special Conference of National Defense IX 190
terrorism XIV 14
White Army VIII 168
World War I VIII 30, 44–45, 48, 69, 71–72, 76, 82, 92–101, 122, 182, 208–209, 212–213, 245–246, 251–252, 256, 277, 281, 299; IX 27, 30, 34, 43, 45, 48–49, 60–67, 84, 91–93, 99, 101, 105, 108, 120, 128, 133–137, 140, 145, 163, 171, 189–195, 204, 208, 224, 226, 228, 237–243, 250, 252–253, 267; XVI 199–207, 308–309, 312
aircraft IX 13
alliance VIII 11, 212, 223
army in VIII 69, 75, 170–171
casualties VIII 125–126, 268
cavalry IX 72
naval aircraft IX 181
Supreme headquarters IX 239
War Industries Committee IX 193, 243
women in combat VIII 125, 129
Zemstva Union IX 190, 242
Russian Civil War (1918–1920) VI 244; XVI 41, 81, 320; XVII 33, 260
Russian Empire XVI 99, 175
Russian Federation VI 47, 53–54, 114
former communists VI 55
Russian Orthodox Church XVI 180, 262
Russian publications XIX 216
Russian Revolution (1917) VI 176; VIII 96, 163, 170, 211, 221, 261, 268; IX 27, 165, 168, 189, 195–202, 208, 240; XII 259; XVI 33, 39, 51, 163, 236; XIX 246, 252, 262
compared to the French Revolution XVII 87–94
troops of US and allies on Russian soil XIX 245
Russo-Japanese War (1904–1905) IV 256; VI 40; VIII 35, 44–45, 73, 75, 226, 228, 247; IX 127, 154, 156, 160, 162, 168, 181, 190, 227; XVI 16, 175, 200
Russo-Turkish War (1877–1878) VIII 73, 226
Rustin, Bayard, membership in ACOA XIX 12
Rwanda I 289; II 101, 155; VI 51, 213
genocide in XI 10, 43, 166, 169, 173; XIV 243; XVII 95, 146
Tutsi population VI 83
Ruthenia XVI 99, 101, 104

S

SA (storm trooper) I 139; XI 113, 128; XVI 148, 151
Sabra massacre (1982) XIV 129; XV 91, 128, 131, 133, 149–150, 153
Sacco, Nicola and Bartolomeo Vanzetti III 228–237; VIII 301; XIX 258
involvement with Italian anarchist groups III 233
League for Democratic Action III 235
New England Civil Liberties Union III 235
protest over verdict III 231
trial III 231
Sacco-Vanzetti Defense Committee (SVDC) III 234
Sachsenhausen (concentration camp) XI 132
Sacramento River VII 29, 272
Sadat, Anwar I 159, 309, 311–314; II 150; VI 162–164, 170; XIV 19, 145, 195, 197, 253, 255; XV 51–56, 66, 70, 73, 101–102, 149, 214, 238–241, 254, 257, 261, 266, 269
death (9 October 1981) I 317
making peace I 317
objective I 316
policies I 316
trip to Israel (1977) XV 219–227
"year of decision" I 316
Sadat, Jehan XV 221
Sahara XIV 178, 202, 203; XV 15, 19
Sahara XIX 37
Saharawi Arab Democratic Republic (SADR) XIV 75, 276, 278, 281
Saharawis XIV 276–278, 280, 282, 285
Safeguards for America (Knights of Columbus) XIX 185
Saimaa Lake, Finland VII 90
Salem, Massachusetts, witch trials XIX 48, 273
Salerno, Michael XIX 216
St. Croix, slave revolt XIII 91
Saint Domingue (Haiti) XII 104; XIII 1, 129, 272, 274
indentured servants in XIII 210
maroons in XIII 106, 108, 110
slave rebellion in XIII 91, 154, 160, 209–216
slave religion XIII 192
slave trade XIII 273
slavery in XIII 155, 210, 233
wealth of XIII 210
St. James Declaration (1942) V 264
St. Kitts XII 311, 313–314
St. Lawrence River XII 47–48, 179
St. Leger, Barry XII 267, 270
St. Louis (German ship) XI 4, 93
St. Louis, civil rights demonstrations in XIX 31
St. Louis Globe-Democrat XIX 31
St. Vincent XII 311, 313–314
Saipan, fall of (1944) V 112
Sakhalin Island XVI 1
Sakharov, Andrei I 146; II 104
Saladin X 10, 24, 26–29, 33, 46–49, 51–52, 56, 88–90, 107, 154–155, 170, 188, 193, 199, 225, 254, 256–259, 261, 297; XIV 161
Richard I X 247–253
Salafism XIV 205
Salan, Raoul XV 12, 14
Salinger, J. D. XIX 46, 48
Salish Mountains VII 171
Salmon 2000 Project VII 229–235
Salsedo, Andrea III 229–231
Salt River VII 214, 216
Samaria XIV 151, 259
Sampson, Deborah (Robert Shurtleff) XII 263, 320
Samsonov, Aleksandr IX 65, 159–160, 242
San Antonio River VII 70, 256
San Antonio Riverwalk VII 71
San Antonio Water System (SAWS) VII 70, 74
San Antonio, Texas VII 69–70, 74–75
recycling of water in VII 70
San Francisco VII 262; XIX 31, 230
San Francisco Bay VII 178
San Francisco Chronicle XIX 208, 260
San Francisco Conference (1945) XVI 317
San Francisco Examiner XIX 230
San Luís Rio Colorado VII 153, 154
San Marcos River VII 70, 74
San Pedro River VII 216
Sanchez, Ilich Ramirez XVI 245
Sandinistas XIX 128, 280
Sandanistas (Nicaragua) I 48–51, 53–54, 94, 96, 125–126; II 58; VI 61, 64, 190–191, 193, 237, 241, 265
attempting to maintain control of Nicaragua I 56
Civil Defense Committees VI 192
removed from power (1990) I 51
takeover of Nicaragua (1979) I 54, 141
Sand Dunes and Salt Marshes (1913) VII 277
Sanders, Bernard II 197, 201
Sandoz chemical spill VII 229–230, 232
Sanger, Margaret III 17–18, 171
Santa Barbara, California VII 269
oil platform blowout off of VII 265
Santa Barbara Declaration of Environmental Rights VII 267
Santayana, George XIII 278

Santiago de Compostella X 220, 238
Santo Domingo XIII 209, 235
Sappho XX 164–171
Sarah, Duchess of York XVI 178
Sarant, Alfred II 230
Sardar Sarovar project (India) VII 9, 132, 134
Saronic Gulf VII 148
Sarraut, Albert V 116
Sartre, Jean-Paul XVII 35, 75, 78, 196, 200, 204, 257–258; XIX 282
Sassoon, Siegfried IX 150, 152, 212
Sarvis, Dave XIX 234
Satpura Mountains, India VII 125
The Saturday Evening Post XIX 165
Al Saud, Abd al-Aziz ibn Abd al-Rahman (Ibn Saud) XIV 92, 244, 248; XV 271–272
Saudi Arabia II 153; VI 164–165, 239; VII 79, 81; XIV 6, 11, 16, 28–29, 31, 38, 40, 43, 55–56, 58, 62, 79, 87–88, 100, 105, 110–111, 119, 148, 177, 179, 181, 186, 190, 211–212, 214–215, 218, 228–229, 231, 235, 240, 242, 244–251; XV 23, 32, 62, 73, 75, 78–79, 81–82, 90, 100–101, 104, 109, 127, 136, 141–142, 145–146, 150, 172, 187, 204, 220, 249, 271–272, 275–276; XVI 45–46
  Afghan rebels VI 238
  attack on U.S. troops in (1995) XIV 16
  Consultative Council XIV 288
  Convention on the Elimination of Discrimination Against Women (CEDAW) XIV 288
  dependence on United States I 162
  economy XIV 51, 56
  forbids Christianity XIII 273
  fundamentalist movements I 163
  fundamentalist regime XIV 123
  Grand Mosque take-over XV 104
  Iraqi bombing of I 195
  oil XV 160, 173–175, 177, 179
  Operation Desert Storm I 157
  pan-Arab campaign I 281
  religious indoctrination in XIV 92
  Shiites in XV 104
  support for mujahideen XIV 3, 5
  support of United States I 158; XIV 14
  Wahhabism XIV 92
  water XIV 269
  women XIV 120–121, 287, 288
Savage Rapids Dam (United States) VII 31
Savannah River XII 184
Save the Narmada Movement VII 127
Savimbi, Jonas VI 1–7, 165
Saving Private Ryan (1998) XI 155
Savoy XVI 302
Saxon Wars (eighth century) X 127, 177, 269
Saypol, Irving XIX 285, 288
Saynbach River VII 230
Sayre, Francis XIX 157
Scales v. *United States* I 81; XIX 153, 259
Scala, Armand XIX 202
Scales, Junius XIX 148
Scalia, Anton II 224
Scalia, Antonin II 143
Scandinavia IX 81
Scapa Flow IX 48, 53, 142, 187
Scharnhorst, Gerhard von IX 127
Schary, Dore XIX 169
Schechter Poultry Corporation v. *United States* (1935) III 28
Schenck v. *United States* XIX 255, 263
Schecter, Jerrold L. I 243
Schecter, Leona P. I 243
Scheer, Reinhard XIX 142
Schelling, Thomas C. I 171
  flexible response I 121
Schindler, Emilie XI 202, 206
Schindler, Oskar XI 156, 158–162, 202–208, 213
Schindler's List (1993) XI 45–46, 48, 155, 156–159, 161–162, 164, 202, 213
Schine, G. David XIX 111
Schleicher, Kurt von XVI 148, 154
Schlieffen, Alfred von VIII 71, 75, 179–180, 182, 184–185, 245–248; IX 41–42, 46, 103, 124; XVI 204
Schlieffen Plan VIII 71, 110, 114, 148, 180, 183, 199, 208, 245–253; IX 42, 44–45, 225, 227, 257; XVI 198, 204
Schlesinger, Arthur M., Jr. I 74; VI 56–57, 154
Schneider, Benjamin XIX 286
Schneider, René XIX 142
School busing II 292–299
  Boston opposition to II 294
  Charlotte-Mecklenburg School District II 293
  impact on white flight II 294
  integration of public schools II 293
Schmidt, Helmut VII 207
Schneider, Benjamin XIX 286
Schneider, René XIX 142
Schroeder, Gerhard XI 216
Schulberg, Budd XIX 12, 36, 39
Schutzstaffeln (SS) IV 84, 118, 130, 137, 139; V 58; VIII 60, 95; XI 36, 83, 86, 90–91, 112, 117–118, 147, 186, 188, 202, 208, 210, 212–213, 218, 224, 227–228, 236, 239, 244, 248; XVI 231, 302
Schutztruppe (protectorate forces) VIII 85, 89
Schuyler, George XIX 12
Schuylkill River VII 256
Schwarz, Fred XIX 101
Scientific-Humanitarian Committee XI 243
Scopes, John III 32–34, 37, 39
Scopes Trial (1925) III 33, 37
Scotland VIII 134, 203; IX 53, 78; XII 34, 53, 242
  immigrants to America XII 279
  impact of American Revolution upon XII 168–169
  industrialization in XII 198
  Lockerbie (Pan Am) attack (1988) XIV 196, 197, 199, 217
Scotland Yard XIX 163
Scott, Adrian XIX 161, 168, 169
Scottish Enlightenment XII 120–121
Scottsboro case III 181, 185; XIX 12, 41, 74, 75, 78, 87, 160, 258
Scottsboro Defense Committee III 188
Scowcroft, Brent XV 86
Screen Actors Guild XIX 44, 163
Screen Directors Guild XIX 163
Screen Extras Guild XIX 163
Screen Writers Guild XIX 163, 164, 170
Scud missile XV 75, 83
Sea of Cortez VII 151
Sea of Galilee VII 136; XV 267–268
Sea of Japan VII 148
Sea of Marmara VII 79
Seaborg, Glenn T. VII 176
Seale, Patrick XV 264–265
Seamen's Union of Australia XIX 270
Seattle, Washington VII 188–195, 197
  city council votes for dam removal VII 222
Seattle Post-Intelligencer VII 191
Seattle Times VII 191
Second Anglo-Boer War (1899–1902) VIII 198
Second Balkan War (1913) IX 203
Second Circuit Court of Appeals XIX 259
Second Continental Congress XII 22, 78, 108, 109, 113, 116
Second Council of Lyons (1274) X 65, 153, 209–210
Second Great Awakening XIII 283
Second Gulf War (2003) XIV 237–238
Second International (1889) VIII 260
Second Jewish Commonwealth (fifth century B.C.E. to 67 C.E.) XIV 153
Second London Naval Disarmament Conference (1935–1936) V 204, 208
Second National Water Act (1961, Finland) VII 85, 87
Second Naval Conference (1927) V 204

Second Reich IX 262; XI 28
Second Seminole War (1835–1842) XIII 108
Second Temple XIV 159
Second Treatise on Government (1690) XII 109, 120
Second Vatican Council XI 19–20
"Security Index" XIX 176
Securities and Exchange Commission (SEC) III 154; XIX 92
Sedition Act (1918) III 229; XIX 246
Seecht, Hans von IX 131
Seeger, Pete XIX 39, 77, 191
See It Now XIX 126
Segregation II 19, 24, 26, 28, 42, 91, 137, 160, 162–163
public facilities II 138
U.S. armed forces IV 216–222
Seiger, Irving XIX 208
Selassie, Haile IX 94, 96, 175
Selective Service II 4–5
Selective Service Act (1917) VIII 296
Selective Service Act (1940) V 250
Selective Service System XIX 21

Seljuk Turks X 24, 26, 29, 48, 51, 73, 77, 85, 115, 119, 127, 138, 170, 186, 205, 213, 216, 221, 238, 270, 280, 282, 287–288; XIV 261
Selway River VII 29
Senate Committee on Government Operations XIX 111, 116, 119, 124
Senate Foreign Relations Committee II 208; XIX 16
Senate Internal Security Subcommittee (SISS) II 131, 134; XIX 16, 31, 53, 110, 198, 201, 242, 275
Senate Judiciary Committee III 26; XIX 110, 200
Senate Permanent Subcommittee on Investigations XIX 124, 272
Senate Permanent Subcommittee on Operations XIX 111. *See also* McCarthy hearings
Senate Special Committee on Investigation of the Munitions Industry (Nye Committee) XIX 198
Senate Subcommittee to Investigate the Administration of the Internal Security Act and Other Internal Security Laws XIX 17
Seneca Falls Convention (1848) XII 263
Senegal IX 111, 113
soldiers in French army IX 112, 118; XVI 146
Senegambia XIII 11
slave trade XIII 35
Sephardic Jews XI 177
Sephuma, Olive VII 243
Sepoy mutiny XIII 238
Serageldin, Ismail VII 280
Serbia VIII 43–45, 47, 76, 95, 106, 162, 208, 212, 216, 226, 228–229; IX 99, 102, 133, 193, 203–204, 225, 227, 266–272; XIV 23, 176; XVI 32, 36, 57–59, 61, 63, 99–100, 103, 194, 196, 249
defeat of IX 207
genocide in XI 71
invaded by Austria-Hungary VIII 72; IX 206
Serbian Democratic Party XVI 100
Serbian Radical Party XVI 100
World War I XVI 308, 312
population reduced by VIII 189
Sermon on the Mount X 82, 84, 103
Service, John Stewart XIX 17–23
Sese Seko, Mobuto XI 167
Seufert Bros. v. *United States* (1919) VII 57–58
Servatius, Robert XI 38
Seven Years' War (1756–1763) XII 28, 101, 104–105, 125, 131, 149, 169, 231, 234–235; XVI 172
Severeid, Eric XIX 126
Seville, slave trade XIII 40
Sewall, Samuel XIII 31
Seward, William Henry XIII 42, 277–278
Sexual revolution II 235–240
beginnings of II 238
Commission on the Status of Women (1961) II 238
effects of II 224
myth of vaginal orgasm II 238
power vs. sex II 237
Seyhan River VII 79
Shaath, Nabil XIV 26, 225
Shaler, Nathaniel VII 277
Shamir, Yitzhak XV 182, 213, 263, 265, 267
Shanghai Commission (1909) III 137
Shanghai Communiqué (1972) II 172–173
Shapley, Harlow XIX 241
sharia (Islamic law) XIV 133–134, 188, 208, 287; XV 2, 6, 112
Sharifian Empire XIV 282
Sharm el-Sheikh Memorandum XV 23, 185
Sharm el Sheikh summit (2000) XIV 103
Sharon, Ariel XIV 19–20, 23–24, 33, 95, 98, 100–101, 103, 105–107, 157, 224, 253, 258: XV 95, 129–132, 153, 186, 201, 221, 266
Qibya massacre XV 248
Sharpe, Granville XIII 31, 133
Sharpeville Massacre (1960) VII 239–240
Sharpley, Cecil XIX 266
Sharret, Moshe XV 130, 248
Shashe River, Botswana VII 33
Shasta Dam (United States) VII 29
Shatila massacre (1982) XIV 129; XV 91, 128, 131, 133, 149, 150, 153
Shatt al-Arab waterway VII 77; XV 72, 100
Shaw, George Bernard XVII 35, 46–47
Shaw, Samuel XII 223, 228
Shays, Daniel XII 283, 285–291
Shays's Rebellion (1786–1787) XII 17, 25, 70–71, 125, 219, 277, 283, 285–292
Sheaffer, John VII 262
Shebaa Farms XIV 128, 131
Sheehan, Neil XIX 276, 277
Shelley v. *Kraemer* (1948) II 141
Shelley, Mary II 86
Shellfish VII 41–50
shell shock IX 209–216
Sheet Metal Workers' Union (Australia) XIX 270
Sheridan, Philip XVI 257
Sherman, John XIX 61
Sherman, Roger XII 70, 217
Sherman, William Tecumseh XVI 251, 255
Sherman Anti-Trust Act (1890) III 242
Sherriff, R. C. IX 212
Shevardnadze, Eduard VI 116; XV 255, 258; XVI 46
Shine, G. David XIX 126
Shirer, William L. XI 4- 5
Shiites XIV 125, 134; XV 126, 133, 146, 231, 233, 235
Shipyard Joiners Union XIX 230
Shoah (1985) XI 161, 189, 231
Showa Restoration V 112
Showboat XIX 35
Shriver, Sargent II 271, 275
War on Poverty involvement II 272
Shultz, George P. VI 231; XV 186
Shuqayri, Ahmad al- XV 193, 199
Siberia IX 163, 165, 168, 197; XVI 55
oil pipeline XVI 46
Sicherheitsdienst der SS (SD, Security Service of the SS) V 214, 216
Sicherheitspolizei (German Security Police) IV 141
Sicily X 43, 93, 95–96, 128, 139, 142, 146, 152, 193–194, 197–198, 201, 226, 251, 287, 289
sugar cane in XIII 167
treatment of Muslims X 190
Sick, Gary XV 158
sickle-cell anemia XIII 81
Sidon X 47, 49, 128, 151, 156
Sieg River VII 230
Sierra Club VII 27, 30–31, 108, 111–114, 177
fights Grand Canyon dams VII 110
Sierra Leone XIII 11, 272; XIV 199–200
slave trade XIII 35–36
Sierra Nevada Mountains VII 112, 272
Sigismund Chapel, Wawel Cathedral, Poland VII 18

Silent Spring (Carson) II 183; III 7; VII 86, 160, 162
Silent Valley Project (India) VII 127
Silesia IX 136, 171; XI 270; XVI 34, 294
Silvermaster, Gregory XIX 231
Silvermaster, Nathan VI 126
Simeon II (Bulgaria) XVI 180
Simms, William Gilmore XIII 48, 73, 205
Simpson, Alan XV 78
Simpson, Wallis Warfield XVI 179
Sims, William IX 75, 184
Simsboro Aquifer VII 75
Sinai I (1974) XV 51, 219, 226, 237–243
Sinai II (1975) XV 51, 219, 226, 237–243
Sinai Multinational Force and Observer Group (1984) XVI 245
Sinai Peninsula I 308–309, 311–312, 316–317; VII 2, 135; XI 125; XIV 144; XV 20–21, 23–24, 42, 51, 56, 63, 93, 127, 134, 136–137, 213–215, 219, 223–227, 237, 240, 245, 261
  demilitarization I 314
  Israeli forces I 313
  Israeli settlements destroyed XIV 154
Sinatra, Frank XVI 109; XIX 168
Sinclair, Upton XIX 232
Singapore XIV 171, 175; XVI 64, 109
  captured by Japan XIX 266
Single Europe Act (1986) XVI 272
Sinn Féin VIII 156, 158–159, 161–162; XVI 244
Sino-French War (1884–1885) IX 101
Sisco, Joseph XV 44
Sister Carrie (Dreiser) II 239
Sit-in movement (1960s) II 27, 160; VI 25
Sitzkrieg (phony war) XVI 114
Six-Day War. *See* Arab-Israeli War, 1967
Skagit River VII 223
Skawina Aluminum Works VII 18–19
Skoropadsky, Pavlo VIII 99–100
Slave Carrying Act (1799) XIII 273
Slave Codes XIII 97, 99
slave trade XIII 35–42, 47, 129–137, 179, 269–275
slavery XII 1–8, 71, 134, 167, 263, 293–300, 311
  abolitionists XIII 1–9
  Act of 1791 XIII 97
  American Revolution XII 1–8; XIII 17–24
  as cause of Civil War XIII 276–283
  black care providers XIII 83
  child mortality XIII 80
  Christianity XIII 101, 186–193, 265
  compared to Nazi concentration camps XIII 138, 142
  comparison between English and Spanish/Portuguese colonies XIII 59–66
  comparison with northern free labor XIII 113
  complicity of Africans in slave trade XIII 35–40, 195
  control of pace of work XIII 202–208
  development of African-American culture XIII 138–145
  diet of slaves XIII 77–83, 113, 136
  economic impact of XIII 42–48
  economic return XIII 47
  enslavement of Africans XIII 161–168
  forms of resistance XIII 172
  gang system XIII 172
  health of slaves XIII 65, 77–83
  Hebrew slavery XIII 27
  house servants and drivers XIII 85–92
  humanity of slaves XIII 95
  impact of emancipation on African Americans XIII 50–57
  in English law XIII 99
  infantilization of slaves (Elkins thesis) XIII 59
  intellectual assessment of XIII 146–153
  interracial female relations XIII 224–230
  justifications for use of Africans XIII 164
  laws pertaining to XIII 60, 61, 62
  legal definiton of status XIII 94–103
  life expectancy XIII 79, 80
  maroon communities XIII 104–111
  medical care XIII 77, 81
  Middle Passage XIII 129–137
  mortality rates XIII 77–78, 81
  murder of slaves XIII 98
  paternalism XIII 60, 112, 117–119, 172, 203, 205, 232
  prices of slaves XIII 172, 174
  profitability of XIII 169–176
  profitability of transatlantic slave trade XIII 269–274
  proslavery ideology XIII 68–75, 96
  punishments XIII 62, 64
  racism as cause of XIII 178–184
  rebellions XIII 154–160, 231–238
  reparations XIII 194–201
  resistance to XIII 120–128, 203, 267
  retention of African culture XIII 10–15, 138–145
  revolts XIII 127
  sexual exploitation of slave women XIII 217–223
  singing XIII 204
  sinking of slave ships XIII 133
  slave codes XIII 115, 176
  slave religion XIII 186–193
  slaveholders as capitalists XIII 239–245
  stability of slave marriages XIII 261–267
  stereotypes XIII 115
  task system XIII 172
  treatment of slaves XIII 112–119
  use of Christianity to justify XIII 26–34
  use of slaves in industry XIII 48
Slim, William V 3, 122, 198
Slovak Green Party VII 103
Slovak Union of Nature and Landscape Protectors VII 103
Slovakia VII 248, 250, 252; XI 195; XVI 34, 99, 104
  dams in VII 100–107
  environmentalists in VII 103
  importance of Gabcikovo dam VII 103
  nuclear reactor at Jaslovské Bohunice VII 103
  nuclear-power plant at Mochovce VII 103
  symbolic importance of Danube VII 102
Slovenia IX 136, 266–272; XVI 36, 57–58, 60–61, 63
Slovenian People's Party XVI 100
Smash-Up XIX 37, 163
Smith, Adam IX 54–55; XII 118, 119, 120, 121, 122, 164; XIII 173, 246
Smith, Bessie III 79, III 82
Smith, Ferdinand XIX 216
Smith, Holland M. "Howlin' Mad" V 297, 299
Smith, Howard Alexander II 208
Smith, Ian VI 2, 83
Smith, Margaret Chase XIX 105
Smith, Wendell XIX 76
Smith Act (Alien Registration Act of 1940) I 77, 79, 81; III 11; XIX 52–54, 58, 61, 78, 97, 100, 105, 116, 61, 97, 120, 127, 129, 148–151, 153, 178, 196, 199, 200–201, 207, 234, 248, 252, 254–264, 269, 271, 283
Smith v. *Allwright,* 1944 II 141
Smuts, Jan VIII 85–86, 89; IX 13, 222
Smyrna VIII 214, 217; IX 208
Smyth, Henry De Wolf I 247–248
Smyth Report I 248
Smythe, William A. VII 151
Snake River 27, 29, 31, 53–54, 196–197, 220, 221, 223–225, 227
  dams on VII 219–228
Sobell, Morton XIX 286, 288
Sobibor (concentration camp) XI 220, 236
Social Darwinism III 260; IV 86, 123; VIII 60, 299; IX 99, 112, 209, 224, 228; XI 82, 115; XVI 23, 65; XVII 101, 166, 182, 186, 254
Social Democratic Party I 255; VI 20, 207; XIX 102
Social Ecological Movement VII 20
Social Security XIX 94
Social Security Act (1935) III 63, 149; XIX 92, 154
Socialism II 34, 60, 160; VIII 254–262; IX 83

Socialist convention (1913) III 223
Socialist Labor Party II 42
Socialist Party (American) II 196, 199; III 222–223; XIX 57, 73, 86, 102–105, 193–194, 211–212, 246
 Debs, Eugene V. III 221
Socialist Party (Dutch) XIX 273
Socialist Party (French) XIX 103
Socialist People's Libyan Arab Jamahuriyya XIV 192
Socialist Realism XIX 44
The Socialist Sixth of the World XIX 238
Socialist Unity Party (SED) VI 118, 121
Socialist Workers Party (American) XIX 105
Society for the Abolition of the Slave Trade XIII 1
Society for the Propagation of the Gospel in Foreign Parts (SPG) XII 148
Society of Jesus XIV 233
Soil Conservation and Domestic Allotment Act (1936) III 157
Solidarity. *See* Poland
Solomon XIV 159
Solzhenitzyn, Aleksandr VI 200; XIV 233
Somalia II 100, 155–156; VI 164, 271; XIV 55, 190, 198, 282
 claim to Ogaden VI 165
 Ethiopian conflict VI 165
 imperialism I 151
 relations with the Soviet Union VI 165
 U.S. troops in (1993) XIV 16
 water XIV 269
Somalilands XIV 176
Somerset case (1772) XIII 1
Somoza Debayle, Anastasio I 48–49, 54, 126, 141; III 51; VI 190–191; XIX 128
Somocistas VI 64, 191
Song of Russia XIX 167
"Song of the Masses" XIX 41
Sonoran Desert VII 151—152
 agriculture in VII 152
Sons of Liberty XII 152, 214, 218, 261
Sontag, Susan XI 42
Sophie's Choice (1982) XI 158
Sophists XX 172–180
Sorensen, Ted II 275
Sorenson, Theodore C. II 117
Souls of Black Folk XIX 80
South (American) XIII 233, 256
 adaptibility of slaves to environment in XIII 11
 African-inspired architectural design XIII 141
 antebellum women in XIII 224–230
 black population in XII 299
 Civil War, slavery as cause of XIII 276
 clock ownership XIII 202–208
 cotton as single crop XIII 43
 economic impact of slavery upon XIII 42–48
 economy of XIII 169–170, 175, 243
 firearms in XIII 233
 impact of Revolution on economy of XII 264
 Ku Klux Klan XIII 55
 Loyalists in XII 181–182, 186
 power of slaveholding elite XIII 69
 Reconstruction, end of XIII 55
 religion in XIII 186–190
 segregation in XIII 57
 sexual exploitation of slave women in XIII 217–223
 slave codes XIII 176
 slave laws XIII 94, 96, 97, 261
 slave rebellions XIII 231
 slaveholders as capitalists XIII 239–245
 slavery in XIII 85, 86–92, 98, 101–102, 112–128, 169–172, 175, 178–179, 231, 247–248, 262, 264–267
 trade with New England XIII 195
 violence against blacks and Republicans in XIII 55
 wealth of XIII 43
 women, interracial relations XIII 224–230
South Africa I 51; VI 1, 2, 4, 6, 50, 54, 87, 136, 178, 215; VII 2, 5, 67, 236–237, 239–241; VIII 31, 160–161, 208; XI 43, 167; XII 33, 169; XIV 199, 221; XV 39; XVI 13, 80, 87, 98
 apartheid VI 13; XIX 9, 12, 14, 29
 Bill of Rights VII 287
 British immigration to VII 237
 inequalities of water supply in VII 284
 intervention in Angola VI 7
 intervention in Mozambique VI 6
 nuclear weapons I 219–223; XVI 109
 rinderpest epidemic VII 34
 use of water by upper class VII 7
 water policy in VII 286, 287
South African National Defense Force VII 7
South African War (1899–1902) IX 68
South America XIV 187; XVI 69
 corruption in XIV 48
 death squads in XI 166
 introduction of species to the United States from VII 217
 slavery in XIII 175
South Arabia XVI 88
South Carolina XII 1, 39, 41, 68, 70, 75, 184–185, 205, 209, 213, 218-219, 263, 314; XIII 53, 66, 71, 73
 African Americans in XII 89
 anti-Loyalist activities in XII 190, 192
 Black Codes XIII 54
 cattle raising XIII 11
 clock ownership XIII 205
 dispute over Confederate flag XIII 270
 laws on rice dams and flooding VII 272
 Loyalists in XII 184, 187
 maroons in XIII 108, 111
 massacre of Rebels in XII 186
 mob action in American Revolution XII 215
 property qualifications to vote XIII 56
 prosecution of Thomas Powell XII 233
 Reconstruction, end of XIII 55
 religion in XII 263
 rice cultivation VII 272; XIII 11
 secession XIII 272, 276
 slave rebellions XIII 156, 210, 231, 235–236
 slavery in VII 272; XII 3–4, 295, 297, 299; XIII 11, 61, 81, 83, 87, 98–99, 102, 140, 204, 218, 232, 235, 240, 244, 248, 265, 267
 use of Confederate symbols XIII 277
 women in XII 319
South Carolina College XIII 28
South Carolina Declaration of the Causes of Secession (1860) XIII 270, 276
South Carolina Red Shirts XIII 55
South Dakota VII 181
 dams in VII 29
Southeast Asia Collective Defense Treaty XIX 280
South East Asia Treaty Organization (SEATO) II 52, 264
South Korea I 86–87, 288, 293; II 37; VI 102, 147–149, 217, 263; XIV 79, 147; XVI 109
 domino theory I 266
 invaded by North Korea (1950) I 208; VI 28
 invasion of I 184
 nuclear weapons development I 216, 219, 223
 U.S. intervention I 158
South Lebanon Army XV 127, 132
South Sea Company XIII 40
South Vietnam I 40–46, 290, 293–299; II 5–8, 263, 266; VI 58–60, 92–99, 101, 138, 140, 201, 203, 284; XII 30, 34; XIV 147
 aid received from United States I 158; VI 2, 66, 142, 144
 conquered by North Vietnam I 142; VI 222
 declares independence I 290
 Soviet support I 185
South Yemen XV 57, 222, 255
Southeast Asia XII 28–29, 33–34; XVI 85, 110

Southeast Asia Treaty Organization (SEATO) I 277; VI 203, 287; XV 26
Southeastern Anatolia Project VII 77, 83
Southern African Hearings for Communities affected by Large Dams VII 242
Southern Baptist Convention III 38
Southern California Peace Crusade XIX 243
Southern Charibbee Islands XII 313
Southern Christian Leadership Conference (SCLC) II 22, 26, 28, 89; XIX 10, 31–32, 177
Southern Conference Educational Fund XIX 31
Southern Democrats XIX 26, 29–30, 119
Southern Economic Association XIII 174
Southern Okavango Integrated Water Development Project VII 243
Southern Pacific Railroad VII 151, 155
Southern Rhodesia VII 237, 239
Southern Tenant Farmers' Union (STFU) II 189; III 159
South-West Africa VII 237, 239; XIX 29
South-West African People's Organization (SWAPO) VII 239
Southwest Kansas Groundwater Management District VII 185
Soviet Union I 77, 91; II 9, 56–62, 64–71, 168, 171; III 10; VI 9, 16, 20–21, 32, 35, 49, 106, 115–116, 147, 149, 161, 201, 206, 208, 236, 250–255, 260, 264; VII 55; VIII 94, 97, 99, 277, 285; X 55, 63; XI 9–10, 14–15, 83, 110, 175, 252–253, 261–262; XII 33; XIV 40, 82, 143, 175, 178, 181, 192, 223, 238, 261–262; XV 23–24, 27, 30–31, 61–63, 68, 74–75, 81, 119, 139, 160, 165–166, 170, 182, 202–203, 205, 219, 223, 226, 240, 243–244, 250, 252, 258, 260, 263, 267; XVI 12, 60, 74, 76–77, 84, 88, 94, 100–102, 104, 107–108, 110–111, 114, 118, 122, 125, 135–136, 141, 155, 158, 160, 176, 209, 211, 213, 248, 259, 301; XIX 12, 211
Afghanistan XVI 79
casualties in (1979–1989) I 12
drain on resources by war I 13
forces in I 13
invasion of (1979) VI 2, 30, 35, 42–44, 66, 68, 116, 162, 165, 237, 241, 246; XIV 1–9
narcotic use by troops I 13
aging leadership VI 111
aid to China V 198
aid to Mozambique VI 2
and nuclear disarmament movement XIX 236–244
and peaceful co-existence movement XIX 236–244
Angola policy VI 41, 43, 165
annexes Estonia, Lative, and Lithuania VII 22; XIX 143
"Aviation Day" I 192
archives opened XIX 83–86, 155, 197–199, 200, 213, 228, 231
arms race with U.S. XIX 2, 237, 279
as ally of U.S. XIX 63, 71, 88, 132, 136, 163, 167, 239, 246, 286, 289
bomber fleet I 6; VI 50
Central Committee II 59
Central Committee Plenum II 60
challenge to U.S. dominance in Latin America I 125
China
cooperation with Nationalist Chinese I 304
relationship with I 141; II 169; VI 40, 43–44, 113, 203; XIX 22, 119
support over Quemoy and Matsu I 265
collapse I 11; VI 47, 50, 58, 108, 213, 224, 227, 235, 237; VII 17, 207; VIII 139; XIV 6, 171; XV 82; XVI 38–48, 51, 63, 70, 84, 92, 180; XVII 70, 83, 227–229, 231; XIX 123, 127, 129, 207, 213
Cominform I 178
communism, in comparison to Nazism XVII 173–179
Communist Party VI 244, 247; XVI 40; XIX 209
Communist Party Congress XVI 39
coup (1991) VI 114
Cuba policy XIX 146
Cuban Missile Crisis II 116; VI 70–76
Czechoslovakia (1948) II 130, 133
defense spending I 125, 197; VI 54; VI 116, 120, 226
post–WWII military budgets I 192
demographics VI 242
demokratizatiia I 152
depictions in American media XIX 163, 167, 246
detente with U.S. XIX 220
development of wartime economy IV 233
diplomatic work I 289
disarmament XVI 95; XIX 237
downing of South Korean plane (1983) XVI 46
East Germany policy VI 115–122, 211
Eastern Europe
as defensive barrier I 303
domination of I 258, 260, 271; XIX 2, 22, 144, 215, 237
gains control of I 302
loss of XVI 281–289
security interests in II 36
economy I 184; II 57, 59; VI 109, 111, 214, 242
Egypt, sells weapons to XV 40
empire VI 243–249
espionage network II 130; XIX 4–5, 58, 61–63, 94, 116–119, 140, 143, 194164, 186, 213–214, 228, 230–231, 266
Estonian contribution to VII 22
expansionism I 262; II 34–35, 208, 264, 267; III 10; XIX 1–3, 136
U.S. fear of II 129, 207
famine of 1930s XIX 146
Fatherland Front XVI 261
fear of the West I 181
Finlandization XVI 121–128
foreign aid VI 54, 254
foreign policy
post–WWII I 238
Germany
invaded by XI 104, 106, 117, 211; XVI 184–191
nonaggression pact with (1939) II 32; XVI 221. *See also* Molotov-Ribbentrop Pact.
glasnost I 152; VI 108–114
government suspicion of citizens I 185
Great Purges XI 15, 166; XVI 189, 220
Gross National Product II 60
human rights record II 104; VI 35, 85, 109, 200, 244
Hungary
invasion of (1956) I 12
uprising I 276, 278, 281
ICBM
buildup I 190
development I 189–194
ideology in foreign policy I 148–154
in Eastern Europe XIX 237
industrialization ideology VII 104
influence in postwar Europe I 174
invaded by Germany XIX 57, 62, 88, 193, 213, 246
invasion of Chechnya (1990s) VI 169
invasion of Finland XIX 143
invasion of Czechoslovakia (1968) I 11–12; VI 43
invasion of Manchuria III 15
invasion of Poland XIX 143
Iran
overthrow of Shah XIV 37

policy toward I 11
Japan, entry into WWII against I 301
Jewish emigration VI 43, 200, 257
Jews in XI 14, 102
Kolyma slave labor camp XVI 163
komitet gosudarstvennoy bezopasnosti (KGB) II 59; XVI 285
Komsomol XIX 261
leaders I 262
League of Nations IX 170, 174
Lend Lease aid to XVI 162–169
Marshall Plan I 175, 177–178, 238
mass education XVII 161
Middle East policy I 160, 277; VI 160–167, 268
military balance VI 168–174
military capabilities II 30, 64
"Molotov Plan" I 178
New Course I 184, 192
New Economic Policy (NEP) VI 113; XVII 208, 243, 247, 250, 261
Nixon's dealings with 223, 226–227
North Korea policy XIX 119
nuclear weapons XVI 109
buildup I 230
capabilities I 213; II 130, 133; VI 35, 215
development I 184, 241–249; VI 31, 109, 144; XIX 4–5
espionage I 239, 241–249
first atomic bomb test I 244; XIX 62, 86, 164, 238, 245, 248, 255, 282–284, 286
testing I 212; VI 49, 173, 177
occupies Iranian Azerbaijan XV 160
oil XV 173, 175
perestroika I 152; VI 108–114
Poland I 301; V 3
post–Cold War VI 47–55, 219
post–WWII cooperation with West XIV 226–233
post–WWII recovery I 177; VI 49, 175; XIX 91, 93
post–WWII war-crimes trial XI 260
pressure on Turkey XIX 249
purges XIX 276
Red Army I 181; VI 130–131, 136, 158, 221, 273, 275–276; XVI 123, 127, 163, 166, 184, 186, 189–190, 217, 220–221, 226, 230–231, 233, 315, 319
relationship with Cuba VI 63–66, 249
relationship with Great Britain V 28–33
relationship with United States V 28–33; VI 55; XVI 220; XIX 2
response to Strategic Defense Initiative (SDI) I 186
response to U.S. defense spending I 197
response to West Germany admission to NATO I 206
Rosenbergs II 227
satellite states II 58
scale of killings in XI 167
social problems VI 112
Soviet-friendly countries II 103
space program II 64–70
sphere of influence III 11; V 311, 314
Stalin's economic policies XVII 243–251
Suez Crisis (1956) VI 246; XVI 235
suspicion of the West II 31
technological deficiencies in weaponry I 196
Third World activities I 11; VI 81, 188; XIX 24–25
threat to Western allies I 4
U.N. Security Council membership I 300
Vietnam War XIX 221–222
Winter War (1939–1940) IV 57; V 28
World War II XVI 314–320; XIX 2, 4, 88, 143
as anti-Nazi ally XVI 217–225
losses II 267
production XVI 40
women in V 304, 306
Yalta Agreement (1945) I 300–301
Zond program II 258
Soviet-Egyptian Pact (1955) I 162
Soviet-Indian trade treaty (1953) XVI 238
Soweto, South Africa VII 7–8
Spaatz, Carl A. "Tooey" V 7, 92; XI 12
use of bombing V 98–99
Spain VII 149; VIII 18, 277; IX 49, 84, 140 ; XI 2, 174–175, 178–179; XII 37, 105, 167, 248, 251–252, 255, 290; XIV 58, 73, 111; XVI 60, 73, 81, 87, 99, 130, 213, 309; XIX 12
abolishes forced labor XIII 63
allies with Americans in American Revolution XII 39
beach closings in VII 147
Catholic movement XIV 256
Catholic orders in XI 23
Christian-Muslim relations X 40–45, 190
control of Mississippi River XII 25, 290
cost of Med plan to VII 146
free workers from XIII 168
Haitian Revolution XIII 209
impact of American Revolution upon XII 165
Jews in X 2, 4, 8, 22, 35, 40, 42, 274
Jews saved by XI 177
laws of slavery XIII 178
monarchy XVI 180–182
Muslims in X 1–6 ; XIV 201
pollution from industrial centers in VII 147
Popular Front IV 228; XVI 220
presence in Florida XII 295
racism XIII 179
Reconquista X 241–246
II Republic XVIII 108–116; XIX 103, 214
slave trade XIII 180, 270
slavery in XIII 167
socialism in VIII 254
Sociedad Estatal de Participaciones Industriales (State Industrial Holdings Company or SEPI) 280
support of Americans in Revolution XII 166
terrorism XVI 245, 248, 249
threat to westernU.S. expansion XII 18
treatment of Native Americans X 7–12
views of blacks in XIII 181
views of Jews in XI 23
visited by U.S. ships XII 79
Western Sahara XIV 276–278, 280, 283
Spandau prison V 224
Spanish American War (1898) II 99; III 245; VIII 18, 22–23, 198, 296, 301; XVI 65
treatment of African American soldiers IV 217
Spanish Armada XII 28
Spanish Civil War (1936–1939) IV 167, 223–231; VI 154, 176; XVI 10, 13, 118, 220; XVII 234–242; XIX 63, 88, 103, 160, 214, 232
Abraham Lincoln Battalion XVIII 1–8
alliances XVIII 17–23
anarchists XVIII 24–32
cinematic legacy XVIII 41–50
fascist conspiracy XVIII 51–56
Franco, leadership of XVIII 57–73
German intervention XVIII 74–80
Guernica, bombing of XVIII 81–88
International Brigades XVIII 117–124
international law XVIII 324–329
international opinion XVIII 125–132
Italian intervention XVIII 140–147
legacy XVIII 148–156
literary legacy XVIII 183–190, 330–338
Madrid XVIII 157–164
Nationalists IV 228, 230; XVIII 165–175
naval warfare XVIII 176–182
origins XVIII 89–107
propaganda posters XVIII 291–323
regionalism XVIII 191–198
religion XVIII 199–207
II Republic XVIII 108–116
Soviet intervention XVIII 216–234

tactics and technology XVIII 9–16, 33–40, 235–242, 258–264
terror, use of XVIII 243–250
total war XVIII 251–257
tourism XVIII 133–139
U.S. policy XVIII 208–215
veterans XVIII 339–347
Western intervention XVIII 265–272
women, role of XVIII 273–280
and World War II XVIII 281–287
Spanish Influenza III 95; VIII 189; IX 31
Spartacus XIII 149
Special Commission to Study and Investigate Communism and Subversive Activities and Related Matters in the Commonwealth. *See* Bowker Commission
Spee, Maximilian von VIII 132–133, 135
Speer, Albert XI 205, 254, 258; XVI 302
Spiegelmann, Art XI 53, 233
Spielberg, Steven XI 45, 156–157, 159–161, 163–164, 202
Spingarn, Joel IX 2–3
Spirit of Laws, The (1748) XII 234
Spock, Dr. Benjamin III 169
Spokane, Portland, and Seattle Railroad VII 59
Sports, in ancient Greece XX 181–188
Sputnik I 182, 188–189, 192, 256; II 47, 64, 70, 257–258, 260
Staatsangehöriger (subjects of the state) IV 140
Staatsschutzkorps (State Protection Corps) V 214
Stachel, Jacob XIX 260
Stalin, Joseph I 31, 35–36, 59, 66, 86, 102, 108–110, 112–113, 149, 151, 263, 288, 305; II 30–41, 49, 52, 68, 132, 156, 169, 193, 210; III 10, 12; IV 210; V 14, 25–26, 35, 41, 44, 46, 50, 54, 107, 109, 131, 136, 149, 151, 177, 194, 224, 226–227; VI 31, 36, 40, 109, 111, 131, 133, 137, 147, 150, 154–156, 158, 161, 175, 178–179, 207, 242, 244, 250–267; VII 22, 97, 104; VIII 97; IX 9–10, 12, 15, 74–75, 79–80, 83, 167, 169, 261; XIV 181; XV 160, 253; XVI 4, 39, 76, 114, 118, 122, 124, 135, 168, 185, 186, 189–190, 217–218, 221, 224, 227–230, 232, 238, 244, 259–264, 314–315, 317–319; XIX 1–2, 92–93, 199; XIX 22, 62, 66, 101, 209, 237, 246, 261
and espionage in U.S. XIX 62–63, 93, 117, 143
attempt to extract base rights from Turkey I 238
Balkans campaign V 71
Berlin blocakde XIX 117, 145
compared to Lenin XVII 151–158
death VI 181; XIX 123–124, 239
denounced by Khrushchev XIX 173–174, 195
domestic atrocities I 260–261
domestic policies XIX 57, 143
economic policies XVII 243–251
"Election Speech" (1946) II 133
Eastern Europe XIX 22, 180, 248
expansionist intentions I 262
foreign policy II 36
genocide practices V 166
German invasion of U.S.S.R. IV 233
Korean War XIX 58
lack of concern for Western European economies I 176
making trouble II 205
Marshall Plan I 208
Moscow winter offensive, 1941 IV 237
motivation II 36
postwar policy toward the United States I 258; XIX 121
postwar settlement I 110
Potsdam Conference I 263
propaganda IV 234, 236
purges VI 244; XVI 184; XIX 103, 213, 231, 239
relationship with Allied leaders V 27; XIX 21, 117
retribution for Nazi war crimes V 218
Soviet nuclear weapons development I 183, 245
Soviet recovery from Second World War I 182
and the Spanish Civil War XVIII 216–234
speech of 9 February 1946 I 260–261
support of Operation Anvil/Dragoon V 241
Tito VI 273–281
Two Camps speech XIX 245, 248
view of postwar Germany I 252
war with Germany V 229; VI 274
World War II IV 232–237; XIX 62–63, 71, 118, 132, 246
Yalta Agreement (1945) I 300; V 309–315
Stalin-Hitler nonaggression pact (1939) II 193
Stamp Act (1765) XII 1, 51, 53, 56–57, 140–141, 143, 149, 152–153, 166, 192, 207, 214–215, 231, 233, 236, 241, 252, 254, 261, 314–315
Stamp Act Congress (1765) XII 54, 233, 236, 315
Standard Oil Company XIV 211–212
Stander, Lionel XIX 36
Stanford University XIX 54
Starobin, Joseph XIX 229
"Star Wars." *See* Strategic Defense Initiative
state and local anti-Communist measures XIX 204, 249
state and local loyalty investigations XIX 204
State Department VI 124, 154, 194, 257; XI 11–12, 60; XIV 33, 97, 125, 157, 178, 230; XV 78, 163, 168, 185, 203–204, 265; XIX 139, 241–242
Asia experts XIX 202, 278
charges of Communist inflitrations of XIX 16–17, 101, 118–119, 155, 197–199, 222, 155, 246, 286
International Information Agency XIX 265
State and Revolution XIX 261
State v. *Boon* (1801) XIII 97
State v. *Caesar* (1849) XIII 98
State v. *Hale* (1823) XIII 97, 99
State v. *Hoover* (1839) XIII 98
State v. *Mann* (1829) XIII 97, 102
State v. *Tackett* (1820) XIII 97
State v. *Will* (1834) XIII 97
States Rights Party XIX 30
Statute of Westminster (1931) XVI 80
Stegner, Wallace VII 112
Steiger, Rod XI 159
Stephens, Alexander H. XIII 271, 277
Stepinac, Alojzije XIX 184
Steuben, Frederich von XII 87, 304
Stevens, Isaac VII 56
Stevens, Thaddeus XIII 51
Stevenson, Adlai E. VI 75; XIX 99, 224
Stevenson, Charles H. VII 46
Stewart, Walter XII 224, 228
Stiles, Ezra XII 146, 148
Stilwell, Joseph W. V 187, 191–199; XIX 22
Stimson, Henry L. I 28, 263; III 104, 109; V 53, 187; XI 257
Stockholm Peace Petition XIX 238–240, 242–243
Stolypin, Pyotr IX 156; XVI 17, 50–55, 200
Stone, I. F. XIX 241, 243
Stone, Justice Harlan III 25
Stone, Livingston VII 197
Stono Rebellion (1739) XIII 124, 235
stormtroopers IX 126, 129–130
Stowe, Harriet Beecher XIII 4, 89
Strait of Tiran XV 20–21, 24, 135, 137, 225, 245, 247, 250, 254; XVI 239
Straits of Gibraltar XVI 65
Straits of Malacca XVI 65
Strange Interlude XIX 46
Strategic Air Command (SAC) I 188; VI 263
Strategic Arms Limitation Treaty (SALT I) I 190, 199; II 171; VI 30, 35, 41, 43; XV 257; XVI 95
Strategic Arms Limitation Treaty (SALT II) I 10, 12, 143, 146, 191; VI 2, 35, 166
Soviet criticism of VI 43
Strategic Arms Reduction Treaty (START) I 199, 224; VI 44; XVI 95; XVI 98
Strategic bombing
postwar I 4, 6, 8

postwar role I 5
Strategic bombing in World War II I 3–4
Strategic Defense Initiative (SDI) I 186, 195–196, 199; II 58; VI 3, 22, 36, 109, 223, 226, 229, 234, 239; XVI 40, 45, 95
Strauss, Richard IX 84
Stravinsky, Igor IX 84
Streicher, Julius V 224; XI 185, 254, 258
Stresemann, Gustav XVI 209, 211–212
Strikes after World War II XIX 67, 71, 73
Strong, Ted VII 61
Stuart, John XII 53, 143, 192
Student League for Industrial Democracy (SLID) II 160
Student Nonviolent Coordinating Committee (SNCC) II 22, 28, 91, 93, 161; VI 25; XIX 10, 31–32, 177
Student, Kurt V 14
Students for a Democratic Society (SDS) II 7, 160, 162
Studer, Norman XIX 191
Submarines V 255–261; VIII 11, 287–294; IX 183
antisubmarine warfare (ASW) V 256
antiwarship (AWS) operations V 259
Dolphin-class (nuclear) XIV 148
Great Britain V 260
I-class V 258
Italy V 261
Japanese Navy V 258, 261
Kriegsmarine (German Navy) V 261
RO-class V 258
Soviet Union V 261
United States V 261
unrestricted warfare VIII 22, 204, 287–294, 296
Suburbia II 249–255, 293–294
suburban developments II 160
Subversion, measures against XIX 211–219
Subversive Activities Control Board (SACB) XIX 29, 200, 232, 275
Success Story XIX 36
Sudan VII 3; XIV 52, 55–56, 79, 81, 87, 134, 136, 141, 176–177, 180, 183, 186, 190, 197, 231; XV 23, 239, 271, 276
female circumcision XIV 288
genocide in XIV 140
National Islamic Front (NIF) XIV 140
water XIV 270
women XIV 121
Sudeten German Party XI 207
Sudetenland IX 272; XI 14, 60, 207; XVI 101–102, 104
Munich Agreement (1938) I 300
Sudetenland crisis (September 1938) IV 125, 248; XI 15
Sudoplatov, Pavel XIX 62
Suez Canal VI 10, 80, 270; VII 2, 147; VIII 38, 213; XIV 175; XV 19, 23, 33, 56, 65–66, 68, 70, 137, 166, 170, 223, 225, 237–238, 240–241, 244, 246, 254; XVI 23, 64–65, 68, 81, 88, 136
nationalization of (1956) XV 166
Suez Canal Company XV 66, 70, 168, 245–246, 250; XVI 80, 84, 235, 239
Suez Crisis (1956) I 192, 289; II 52, 148; VI 8, 11, 80–81, 106, 130, 133, 135, 160, 188, 209, 270; XIV 144; XV 168; XVI 84–85, 88, 95, 111, 136, 235–242, 269
U.S. position I 185; VI 270
Suez War (1956) XV 19–21, 24, 32, 58, 62, 70, 116, 169, 213, 225, 244–251, 253, 270, 272, 275
Suffolk Resolves XII 54
Sufism XIV 206, 208
Sugar Act (1764) XII 2, 55, 149, 200, 207, 231, 233, 236, 240, 313–314
Sukarno I 110, 273, 277, 283; VI 81, 268; XIX 145
Sukhomlinov, Vladimir IX 158–159, 192–193, 238; XVI 201
Sullivan, John XII 179, 302
Sullivan, William XIX 30, 31
Sulz Valley VII 207
Summary Dismissal Statute XIX 132, 133, 138
Summerall, Charles VIII 27–28
Summi Pontificatus (1939) XI 192
Sunnis XV 126, 146
Supreme Muslim Council XV 195
Surinam XIII 104, 133, 190, 212
maroons in XIII 105, 108, 110
slave revolts XIII 154
Susquehanna River XII 186
Sussex (British ship), sinking of IX 21, 247
Sutherland, Justice George III 25
Suzuki, Kantaro III 15
Swampland Grants (1849 and 1850) VII 272
Swann v. *Charlotte-Mecklenburg Board of Education* (1968) II 293, 296
Swaziland VII 236
Sweatt v. *Painter*, 1950 II 141
Sweden XI 174–176, 178; XV 215; XVI 45, 212–214, 272, 319; XVII 269–270
monarchy XVI 178, 180–181
offers Poland environmental help VII 20
opposition to African dams in VII 240
saves Dutch and Norwegian Jews XI 174
slave trade XIII 270
Sweet Smell of Success XIX 47
Swift, Jonathan XII 124
Swiss National Bank XI 178
Switzerland VII 229; VIII 110, 235; IX 196, 200; XI 61–62, 131, 174–176, 178; XVI 45, 58, 213
Jewish policy of XI 177
Nazi gold XI 178–180
treatment of Jewish passports XI 2
Syankusule, David VII 242, 246
Sykes-Picot Agreement (1916) VIII 41
Symington, Stuart I 6, 119, 188–189, 217–218
Symington Amendment (1976) I 218
syndicalism XIX 232, 246
Syngman Rhee VI 147, 150–151
Syria I 159, 308–309; VI 54, 163, 201, 215, 261, 268; VII 135, 138, 148–149; VIII 39, 41, 104, 213, 216; IX 92, 96; X 46–49, 108–110, 185–187; XIV 29, 41, 52, 55–56, 60–61, 63–64, 79, 87, 97, 110, 112, 114, 125–126, 146, 148–149, 177, 179–181, 190, 193, 195, 198, 201, 220, 225, 230, 242, 252, 255, 265; XV 20–21, 23, 25, 32, 34, 37, 41, 44–45, 48, 53, 57, 59, 61–62, 70, 75, 79, 81, 83, 91, 116, 127, 129, 131, 133–137, 141–142, 144–150, 152–153, 155, 166, 168, 183, 193, 199–200, 206, 213–214, 216, 219–220, 222, 225–226, 238, 240, 245, 254, 255, 257; XVI 98, 236, 269
Alawi sect XIV 67
alleviating poverty XIV 65
Arab Socialist Party (ASP) XV 271
Arab Socialist Resurrection Party (ASRP) XV 271
attacks Israel I 316; VI 161, 163; XIV 145
Baath Party XIV 82, 253; XV 135, 270–271, 273, 275–276
CIA plot XV 157
closes al-Jazeera office XIV 65
Communist Party XV 271
conflict with Jordan I 157
cotton and textile exports XIV 45
dams in VII 76–84
de-liberalization XIV 64
deportations to VIII 166
economy XIV 51, 54
fundamentalist movements I 163
immigration and population problems VII 82
Israel, negotiations with XV 33, 260–269
Israeli invasion of Lebanon I 196
Jews forced from XIV 221
Kurds VII 82; XIV 169, 171, 174
lack of environmental control in VII 145
limited-aims war I 314
military buildup I 316
National Party XV 271
nuclear weapons development I 219

oil from Iran XIV 125
Orthodox Christians XV 274
Palestinian refugees XV 191
People's Party XV 271
pogroms against Armenians VII 82
population growth XIV 67
privately owned newspaper XIV 64
revolution I 158
roads in XIV 54
Soviet alliance I 161; VI 43
sugar cane in XIII 167
support for Hizbollah XIV 128
Syrian Nationalist Popular Party XV 271
telephones XIV 54
troop separation agreements with Israel I 159
UAR XV 270–276
Wafd Party XV 275
water VII 76–84; XIV 269–270, 273; XV 205
World War II XVI 301
Syrian-Egyptian Treaty (1966) XV 20
Syrian Nationalist Party (P.P.S.) XIV 128; XV 271
Szolnok, Hungary VII 247, 249, 252

T

T-4 Program XI 117, 242, 248–250, 268
Taba talks (2001) XIV 167
Tabqa Dam (Syria) VII 77, 82, 83
Tacoma City Light VII 53
Taft, Robert A. I 272, 285, 306; II 49, 133, 206; VI 56; XI 121; XIX 182
Taft, William Henry II 199
Taft, William Howard III 208, 211, 244, 247; IX 249
Mann Elkins Act (1910) III 245
narcotics policies III 136
Taft administration
Mexican Revolution III 126
Taft-Hartley Act (1947) II 133, 188–189, 192; XIX 52, 72, 93, 149, 180, 182, 201–202, 205
Taif Agreement (Document of National Accord, 1989) XIV 126; XV 127
Taifa X 287, 289
Tailhook Association Conference (1991) II 80
Taisho, Emperor V 111
Taiwan I 86; II 172; VI 38, 53, 106, 150, 214, 219; XIV 79; XVI 109
Chinese attacks on Quemoy and Matsu I 265–270
domino theory I 266
mutual-security treaty with United States I 268
nuclear weapons development I 216, 219, 223
U.S. intervention I 158
U.S. military equipment VI 43
Taiwan Relations Act (1979) VI 44
Taiwan Straits I 119, 168–169
Tajikistan XIV 2, 12, 88, 180, 190, 228
Taliban XIV 1, 3–5, 7, 10–18, 31–32, 37, 86, 88, 91, 95, 103, 121, 123, 141, 175, 231, 262; XVI 71; XVII 20, 221
treatment of women XI 72
Talmadge, Herman XIX 30
Talmud X 22, 44, 179, 273
Tamil Nadu, India VII 125–126
drought in VII 126
Tammany Hall III 260–264
Tanchelm of the Netherlands X 215–216
Tancred X 15, 73–74, 98, 101, 191, 194, 199–201
Taney, Roger B. XIII 19
Tanganyika VIII 86–87, 89
Tanks
A-20 (U.S.S.R.) XVIII 36
Abrams (United States) VI 223, 241
BT-5 (U.S.S.R.) XVIII 36–38, 260, 262
Bundeswehr Leopard (Germany) VI 174
Char B (France) IV 240; XVIII 36
CV-33 (Italy) XVIII 37–38, 261–262
Hotchkiss H-39 (France) XVIII 36
JS-1 (U.S.S.R.) IV 245
KV-1 (U.S.S.R.) IV 239
M18 Hellcat (United States) IV 251
M-2 (United States) IV 245
M-3 Grant (United States) IV 241, 247
M36 (United States) IV 251
M-4 (United States) IV 241–243
M-4 Sherman (United States) IV 239, 241, 247
M-4A1 (United States) IV 245
M-4A2 (United States) IV 245
M-4A3 (United States) IV 245
M-4A3E2 (United States) IV 249
M-4A3E6 (United States) IV 246
Mark I (Germany) XVIII 37, 263
Mark II (Germany) XVIII 263
Mark III (Germany) IV 243; XVIII 263
Mark IV (Germany) IV 243
Mark V Panther (Germany) IV 239, 241
Pzkw I (Germany) IV 244; XVIII 36, 38, 259
Pzkw II (Germany) IV 244
Pzkw III (Germany) IV 244; XVIII 36, 259
Pzkw IV (Germany) IV 244, 246, 249; XVIII 259
Pzkw IVG (Germany) IV 248
Pzkw V (Panther) (Germany) IV 244
Pzkw VI (Tiger) (Germany) IV 244
Renault FT-17 (France) XVIII 37
Renault R-35 (France) XVIII 36
role in the Spanish Civil War XVIII 33–40
role in World War I VIII 14, 51–58, 112, 193–197, 242; IX 38, 71, 122
role in World War II IV 238–251
Souma (France) IV 240; XVIII 36
T-26 (U.S.S.R.) XVIII 36–39, 262
T-34 (U.S.S.R) IV 239, 243–245, 247; XVI 163, 166; XVIII 36, 260
Tiger (Germany) IV 241
Tiger I (Germany) IV 248
Whippets VIII 54, 56
Tanzania XIV 190
attack on U.S. embassy (1998) XIV 16
Tao, Didian Malisemelo VII 244
Tarleton, Banastre XII 32–33, 41, 186
Tarleton, John XIII 270, 274
Tartars XVI 166
enslavement of XIII 167
TASS VII 23
Taylor, A. J. P. XVI 211
Taylor, Glen XIX 76
Taylor, John XIII 48, 74
Taylor, Maxwell D. I 119, 294; VI 95–96; XIX 18
Taylor, Myron XI 57, 60–61, 193
Taylor, Robert XIX 44, 167
Taylor, William Henry XIX 288
Taylorism IX 22, 24
Tea Act (1773) XII 197, 200, 207, 214–215, 234, 237
teach-ins XIX 280
Teal, Joseph N. VII 52
Team B VI 256–263
Teamsters XIX 70, 216
Teapot Dome investigation (1922) III 178, 180
Technical Cooperation Administration (TCA) XV 203, 205
Teheran Conference (1943) I 110, 259, 288; II 32; V 46, 72, 236; XI 261; XVI 226–227, 230, 315; XIX 246
Tehri Hydro-Electric Project (India) VII 127
Television
broadcast license II 122
commercial development II 122
impact on American society II 121
information-oriented programming II 126
noncommercial II 125
programming II 122
quiz show scandals II 123
role in American society II 125
Vietnam War II 124
Vietnam War coverage II 125
viewer demographics, 1980 II 124
Watergate hearings II 124

Teller, Edward VI 256–257
Tellico Dam (United States) VII 31
Templars X 46, 49, 52, 75, 90, 158–166, 198–200, 305
Temple Mount XIV 19, 22, 159–160, 165–167; XV 139
Temple of Virtue XII 224–225
Temporary Commission on Employee Loyalty XIX 132
Ten Commandments XII 63–64
Tender Comrade XIX 167
Tenet, George XIV 97, 100, 103, 105
Tennent, Gilbert XII 148, 150–151
Tennessee XII 264; XIII 274
anti-black violence in XIII 55
railroad regulations for blacks XIII 57
Reconstruction, end of XIII 55
slavery in XII 297; XIII 233
Tennessee River VII 26, 28, 31
Tennessee Valley Authority (TVA) I 27–30; III 154; VII 1, 27–28, 130; XV 204
impact on South VII 28
Tenney, Jack B. XIX 208
Tenney Committee XIX 205, 208
Tenth Inter-American Conference I 49
Tereshchenko, Mikhail XVI 53
Terrorism, Europe XVI 243–250
Tertullian XI 18, 20
Tet Offensive (1968) I 40; II 5; VI 23, 29, 60
Teutonic Knights X 49, 57, 66, 69, 90, 181, 305
Texaco XIV 211–212; XV 172–173, 177, 179
Texas VII 181–182, 185; XIV 162
slavery in XIII 195, 225, 227
water management policies in VII 69–75
Texas Groundwater Management District No. 1 VII 185
Texas Houston Ship Canal VII 265
Textile Union XIX 77
Thailand XII 33; XVI 109; XIX 224
Thames River VII 234
Thar Desert VII 125
Thartar Canal Project VII 77
Thatcher, Margaret VI 8, 10, 54, 195; XVI 45, 176, 268, 288; XVII 20–23, 29, 70, 280–281
critic of EEC VI 13
supports United States VI 13
thermal pollution VII 175
Theresienstadt (concentration camp) XI 70, 220, 238
Thessaloníki
construction of sewage works in VII 148
industry in VII 148
Thielens, Wagner Jr. XIX 111
Third Republic IX 111
Third World VI 2–3, 35, 43, 55, 61, 63, 65, 68, 77–78, 80–81, 83, 116, 131, 133, 140, 145, 149, 160, 163, 186, 221–222, 236; VII 67; XI 167; XV 16, 21, 141, 202, 252–253, 255, 257; XVI 40–41, 85, 95, 238, 240
beef imports to Europe VII 37
Cold War VI 264–272
collapse of communist regimes in VI 239
democratization XIV 82, 85
effect on global balance of power I 14
freedom movements XIX 11–12, 14
gross national product I 14
national liberation movements in VI 188
Soviet influence VI 188
U.S. interventions I 15
U.S. policies on I 22; VI 80
water crisis in VII 286
Third World Liberation Front II 94
Thirteen Colonies XII 36, 113–114, 122, 133, 138, 165, 167, 171, 198, 200, 231–232, 234, 314; XIII 147
slavery in XIII 195
Thirty Years War (1618–1648) XVI 171, 208, 211, 251, 255, 257
"This Is the Beat Generation" XIX 50
"This Land Is Your Land" XIX 38-39
Tho, Le Duc I 291
Thomas, J. Parnell XIX 61, 119, 167–168, 171, 251
Thomas, Norman XIX 57, 73, 86, 102, 104, 194
Thompson, Dorothy XI 60
Thompson, Llewellyn XIX 18
Thompson, Tommy VII 57–59
Thomson, D. XIX 270
Thornton, E. XIX 270
Thornwell, James Henley XIII 28–29, 48, 68, 183, 248
Three Emperors' League VIII 225–227
Three Mile Island (1979) II 86
Three-Staged Plan for Optimum, Equitable, and Reasonable Utilization of the Transboundary Watercourses of the Tigris-Euphrates Basin VII 79
Thucydides XV 53
Tibbets, Paul W. V 50
Tignes, France, riots at VII 99
Tigris River VII 77
Turkish dams XIV 270
Tigris-Euphrates river system XIV 268–269, 271; XV 72, 121, 203
Tijuana River VII 152
Time XIX 197, 224, 246
Times of India XIX 27
Timrod, Henry XIII 153
Tirailleurs Senegalais IX 113–115; XVI 146
Tirpitz, Alfred von VIII 29, 31, 34–35, 249; IX 101, 140, 142–143, 221
Tisza Club VII 252
Tisza River, chemical spill on VII 247–255
Title IX (1972) II 77
Tito, Josip Broz I 36, 59, 86, 108–110, 113, 273, 277, 283; VI 134, 136, 182, 217, 254, 265, 268, 271, 273-281; VIII 192; IX 268; XV 68, 167; XVI 57, 61-63, 124; XIX 145
To Secure These Rights XIX 24
Tobago XII 311, 313–314; XIII 270
Tocqueville, Alexis de XII 260, 265; XIII 161–162, 165, 201, 251
Togliatti, Palmiro XIX 239
Togo XIII 11
Tojo, Hideki I 1
Toledo X 2, 289
Tolson, Melvin B. XIX 40–41
Tonga (Batonka) people VII 5, 239, 242, 245
effect of dam onVII 4
Torah XIV 184, 188, 259
Tortola XII 311, 314
Tokyo firebombing (1945) XVI 254
Tokyo trials (1945–1948) V 263-269
comparison with Nuremberg trials V 266–267
dissent of Radhabinod Pal V 267
International Military Tribunal for the Far East (IMTFE) V 266
Tom Paine School, Philadelphia XIX 230
Tonkin Gulf Resolution (1964) XIX 277, 280
Torah X 44, 273
Torrey Canyon accident (1967) VII 143
Total (oil company) XV 177–179
Total Strategy White Paper VII 240
totalitarianism XVI 259–264
Totally Equal Americans VII 172
Toussaint L'Ouverture, Francois Dominque XIII 209–216
Toward Soviet America XIX 57–58
Tower of London XIII 229
Townsend, Charles Wendell VII 277
Townsend, Dr. Francis XIX 103
Townshend, Charles XII 53, 139–141, 233, 237
Townshend Acts (Townsend duties, 1767) XII 51, 141, 149, 207, 214, 233, 237
repeal of XII 55
Toy, Harry XIX 184
Toynbee, Arnold XVI 107
Tracy, Spencer XI 158
Trade Union Educational League (TUEL) XIX 193
Trade Union Unity Center (the Netherlands) XIX 269
Trade Union Unity League (TUUL) XIX 193
Trading with the Enemy Act (1917) III 223

"Tragedy of the Commons" VII 47, 48, 70, 73
Transcaucasia XVI 6
Transcaucasian Federation XVI 18
Trans-Jordan VII 81; VIII 166, 214; IX 96; XIV 67, 176; XV 34, 44, 46, 142, 144, 146; XVI 236
Translation, and classical texts XX 47–55
Transparency International XIV 48
Trans-Siberian Railway XVI 6
Transvaal XVI 68
Transylvania XVI 34, 99, 104, 195
Treaties–
–Brest-Litovsk (1918) VIII 95–97, 141, 173, 278; IX 27; XVI 2, 6, 201, 295, 309, 312
–Bucharest (1918) VIII 95
–Dunkirk (1948) I 204
–Élysée (1963) XVI 156, 159
–Frankfurt (1871) VIII 278; XVI 295
–Lausanne (1923) VIII 214; XIV 168
–Locarno (1925) V 116–120
–London (1913) VIII 212
–Moscow I 107
–Neuilly (1919) XVI 294
–Ouchy (1912) VIII 212
–Paris (1763) XII 52, 235
–Paris (1783) XII 23, 25, 169, 174, 286
–Paris (1951) XVI 268
–Peace and Friendship With Tripoli (1796) XII 66
–Rome (1957) XVI 271
–Ryswick (1695) XIII 210
–Sevres (1920) VIII 214, 217; XIV 168
–Trianon (1920) XVI 294
–Turko-Bulgarian (1914) IX 204
–Versailles (1919). *See* Versailles Treaty
–Washington (1922) IX 168
–Westphalia (1648) XIV 240; XVI 212, 214, 216
Treblinka (concentration camp) I 138; V 54, 57, 158, 161; XI 52, 220
Tredegar Iron Works, Richmond, Virginia XIII 48
Trees
cottonwoods VII 12, 212, 214, 215
elms VII 232
mesquites VII 212
oaks VII 212, 232
riparian importance of VII 215
salt-cedars VII 12, 215, 217
willows VII 212, 214, 215, 232
Trelawney, Edward XIII 108, 110
Trenchard, Hugh IX 10–11, 222
Trenchard, John XII 128, 147
Tribal Grazing Lands Policy (TGLP) VII 34
Trident Conference (1943) V 236
Trinidad XIII 147, 270
Trinity River VII 223
Tripartite Declaration (1950) XV 30, 244–245, 248, 250
Tripartite Pact (1940) V 294; XVI 185
Triple Alliance VIII 44, 46, 226, 229; XVI 194
Triple Entente VIII 35, 45; IX 226; XVI 194–195, 209, 221, 224
Tripoli X 27, 49, 151, 156, 191, 247–248, 251, 254, 256; XII 66
Tripoli Program (1962) XV 6
Tripolitan War XIV 192
Triumph des Willens (Triumph of the Will) XI 167
Trotsky, Leon (Lev) VI 179, 274–275; VIII 167; XVI 18–19, 229, 312; XVII 87–88, 152, 197, 224; XIX 57, 84, 104–105, 213
Trout Unlimited VII 31, 213
Trudeau, Pierre E., signs Great Lakes Water Quality Agreement VII 120
Truehaft, Decca. *See* Mitford, Jessica
Truitt, Reginald V. VII 43–44, 47
Truman, Harry S I 28, 35, 65, 69, 109, 113, 148, 159, 257, 285; II 39, 42, 44, 49–50, 197, 199, 203–204, 207–208, 280; III 10–14, 62; V 46, 98, 106; VI 20, 56, 144, 146–148, 153, 205, 231, 250, 284; IX 7; XI 121, 123–124, 214, 253; XII 28; XV 30, 137, 167; XVI 228, 230, 271; XIX 17, 63, 113–114, 124, 151, 240, 248
acceptance of a divided Europe I 264
accused of being soft on Communism XIX 99, 260
adoption of containment policy I 262
anticommunism VI 155; XIX 21, 91–94, 96–97, 161, 185, 260
appointment of Baruch I 27
approval of NSC-68 I 182
atomic bombing of Japan I 239
attitude toward Hiss case XIX 156, 198, 249
attitude toward Stalin I 259, 261–263; XIX 117
civil rights policies XIX 24, 26, 30–31
containment policy I 274; XIX 140
election campaign (1948) XIX 30, 94, 97, 124, 241, 251
Executive Order 9835 XIX 108, 131, 133, 136–137, 251138–139
Executive Order 10241 II 131; XIX 53, 132, 138, 182, 276
foreign policy I 58; II 205
foreign policy links to domestic ideology II 209
handling of *Amerasia* case XIX 16–19, 21, 23
Interim Committee III 15
loyalty program XIX 175
Marshall Plan I 176
orders Berlin airlift XIX 145
Point Four Program XV 202–210
Potsdam Conference I 263
relationship with Hoover XIX 31
response to communism II 130
restraint in use of nuclear weapons I 235
service in World War I VIII 192
Truman Doctrine II 145; XV 61, 203; XIX 48, 245, 249, 251
unconditional surrender policy V 275
veto of McCarran Act XIX 211, 215, 217
veto of Taft-Hartley Act II 188
views on postwar role of military I 5
Truman administration I 30, 59, 74; II 36; VI 59, 101, 147, 150, 155, 224; XI 123, 253, 255; XV 30; XIX 9, 21, 272
acceptence of Soviet nuclear program I 237
accused of abandoning China to communism I 59
accused of being soft on communism XIX 131, 136, 251
aid to China I 60
aid to Taiwan I 266
and Hiss Case 159, 249
anticommunism 21, 97, 246, 249, 260
Baruch Plan I 31
CIA, creation of I 64
civil rights policies XIX 8
Cold War policy I 266
concern about communist influence in Europe I 174, 176
concern about trade imbalances in Europe I 175
concludes cooperation with Soviets impossible I 82
containment I 154
containment policy I 272
containment strategy I 183
CPUSA XIX 5
creation of NSC I 83
defining U.S.-Soviet rivalry I 75
Executive Order 9877 I 5
federal employee loyalty program I 76
foreign policy I 60
future of Europe I 110
Key West Agreement I 5–6
Loyalty Order I 79
McCarran Act I 74
Marshall Plan I 173–179
National Security Act I 7
National Security Council memorandum 68 (NSC 68) I 211, 274
national-security policy I 77, 210
Palestine XI 124

policy toward Soviet Union I 258–263
postwar policy in Germany XI 254
reduction in defense spending I 7
Soviet nuclear spying I 242
Taiwan policy I 266
use of nuclear weapons I 215
view of Chinese civil war I 294
views on Guatemala I 129
West Berlin policy I 293
Yalta Agreement (1945) I 301
Truman Doctrine (1947) I 36, 65, 75, 89, 109, 151, 175–176, 177, 296; II 100, 130, 132, 207–210; VI 9, 11, 161, 250, 252, 267; XVI 228; XIX 9, 12, 21, 48, 75, 93, 96, 121, 127, 131, 140, 145, 245, 248, 251–252, 266
Trumbo, Dalton XIX 164, 167, 168, 216, 281
Trumbic, Ante XVI 36, 103
Truscott, Lucian K., Jr.
Italian campaign IV 146, 149
Truth, Sojourner XI 72
Truth and Equity Forum XIV 116
Truth in Securities Act (1933) III 154
Tubman, Harriet XI 72
Tucker, Nathaniel Beverley XIII 73, 205
Tucker, St. George XIII 19, 48
Tudeh party XIX 144
Tunisia VII 149; X 8, 38, 139, 142, 146, 159; XIV 29, 31, 52, 55, 69, 71–72, 76, 78–79, 81, 83, 85, 105, 114, 136, 177, 179–181, 190, 198, 202–203, 205–206, 231, 253; XV 19, 136, 141, 271; XVI 302
corruption in XIV 48
economic liberalization XIV 54
literacy XIV 52
PLO in XIV 23; XV 89
secularism in XIV 119
water XIV 269
women XIV 291
Turkey I 49, 82, 87, 89, 110, 113, 238, 294; II 144, 153, 207; VI 161, 244, 250–252, 255; VII 148–149; VIII 44, 95, 104, 106, 122, 211–217, 277; IX 93, 204, 206, 270; XI 174–178; XIV 55-56, 78–79, 81, 88, 114, 136, 176–177, 179, 181, 183, 190, 193, 230, 235, 242, 261–267, 291; XV 26–27, 29, 31, 59, 79, 83, 108, 117, 120, 146, 271–272, 275; XVI 41, 104, 175, 218
Armenians deported to VII 82
Armenians massacred XI 2, 90, 166, 169, 172; XVII 8
Baghdad Pact I 161
base rights I 288
civil rights violations I 209
collapse of monarchy IX 81
crucial to U.S. security I 85
dams in VII 76–84
democracy in XIV 134
environmental control in VII 145
Grand National Assembly XIV 264
Jupiter missiles VI 71–75
Justice and Development Party (AKP) XIV 139, 264, 267
Kurds in VII 83; XIV 141, 168–174, 270
member of NATO VII 83
refuge to Jews XI 177
Soviet intervention in I 73, 258; XV 253; XIX 96, 132, 144–145
U.S. aid to resist Soviet influence I 176; XIX 9, 12, 21, 96, 132, 144–145, 245, 249, 251
War of Independence (1919–1923) XVI 236
water VII 76–84; XIV 268–271
women XIV 121
Young Turk revolution VIII 45; XV 274
Turkish-Iraqi Mixed Economic Commission VII 79
Turkish-Pakistani Treaty (April 1954) XV 31
Turkish Petroleum Company (TPC) XV 176
Turkish Straits XVI 66, 194
Turkmenistan XIV 2, 180, 228, 231
Turner, Frederick Jackson
frontier thesis II 245
Turner, Nat XIII 54, 91, 124, 156–158, 235–236
Tuskegee Institute III 268–272
Twenty-One Demands (1915) IX 164, 166, 168
Tydings, Millard XIX 94
loss of Senate seat XIX 99
view on McCarthy XIX 101
Tymoies-Eteenpain XIX 216
Tyre X 47–49, 53, 75, 128, 148, 150, 152, 154, 170, 192, 247–249, 251, 254, 256, 261

U

U-2 spy plane incident (1960) I 65–66, 70, 189–190, 192, 194; II 38, 54, 229, 260; VI 64
U-2 spy plane reconnaissance VI 70–71
U.S.-Middle East Partnership Initiative (1997) XIV 114
U.S. Steel Corporation VII 269; VIII 296; XI 60
U Thant VI 75; XV 23, 135, 137, 217, 225
U-boats. See *Unterseeboote*
Udall, Morris King VII 109, 114
Udall, Stewart Lee VII 109, 112, 259, 267
Uganda XIV 197–198
genocide in XI 71
Uighurs XIV 12
Ukraine VI 133, 136, 215, 218, 251; VII 248, 252; VIII 94, 96–99, 280; XI 115, 175; XVI 6, 18, 29–30, 32–34, 88, 98, 163, 189, 294, 312–313; XIX 215
Chernobyl accident in VII 18, 22
Cossacks VIII 99
famine XVII 260–267
forest clear-cutting in VII 254
German atrocities in XI 268
mass executions in VI 251
nuclear-deterence theory I 231
pogroms VIII 168–169
Rada (parliament) XVI 18
Russian conquest of XVI 70
surrender of nuclear weapons to Russian Federation I 220
Ukrainian Insurgent Army (UPA) IV 130
Ukrainian Military Congress XVI 18
Ukrainian Americans XIX 215
Ukrainian publications XIX 216
Ulbricht, Walter I 35, 38
Berlin I 120
Ulster Volunteers VIII 155, 161
Ultra IV 260–264; V 79, 85
Battle of the Atlantic, 1941–1945 IV 263
Battle of Britain, 1940 IV 264
Battle of the Bulge, 1944 IV 264
contribution to Allied invasion plans IV 262
North Africa campaign IV 264
role in D-Day planning IV 261
Umkhonto we Sizwe (MK) VII 239
Uncle Tom's Cabin (1852) XIII 4
Unconditional surrender policy V 46, 53, 270–275
German reaction V 272
Japanese reaction V 273
Uniates XVI 30
Union Army XIII 54
black soldiers in XIII 53, 55
Union for Democratic Action. *See* Americans for Democratic Action
Union of Arab Community Based Association XIV 116
Union of Electrical Workers (IUE) XIX 206
Union of Soviet Socialist Republics (U.S.S.R.). *See* Soviet Union
Union Pacific Railroad VII 60
unions
deportation of leaders XIX 216
investigated by Bowker Commission XIX 205–206
membership XIX 70
Unita del Popolo, L' XIX 216

Unitarian Church XIX 238
United Arab Emirates (UAE) XIV 11, 50, 55, 148, 177, 179, 212, 215, 217, 247
economy XIV 51
water XIV 269
United Arab Republic (UAR) I 282; II 147–148
Soviet ties II 148
United Auto Workers (UAW) II 189; III 191, 194; XIX 68–69, 71, 73, 185, 207
United Electrical Workers XIX 6, 72, 182–183, 216
United Fruit Company I 70, 123, 125–126, 129–130; XIX 141
United Kingdom XVI 186, 248
Lend Lease aid XVI 162, 167
United Mine Workers II 190–191; XIX 71–72
United Mine Workers Strike (1902) III 244
United Nations I 29–30, 50, 53, 98, 194, 217, 219–220, 278, 284, 288–289, 305; II 20, 40, 46, 51, 53, 61, 71, 87, 100, 115; VI 31, 135–136, 147, 151, 158, 234, 261; VII 2, 65, 79, 81, 240, 245; VIII 11; IX 171; XI 37, 121, 124; XIV 12, 14, 17, 55, 85, 96, 103, 106, 144, 146, 149, 159–160, 173, 180, 192, 195, 199, 219, 225, 228, 231, 237, 247, 265, 277, 282, 287; XV 15, 21, 24, 34, 74, 80–81, 84, 91, 97, 100, 102, 120, 141, 153, 198, 203, 205, 219, 237, 253; XVI 57, 76, 87–88, 98, 157, 230, 267, 271, 289, 315, 317; XIX 77, 242, 273, 280
adopts TVA model VII 1
agencies working in Latin America I 22
Atomic Energy Commission I 27, 29
censure of Soviet Union for invasion of Afghanistan I 12
Charter XV 245
China seat VI 44, 148; XIX 19, 236, 243
Convention on the Law of the Sea (1982) XV 247
Council for Namibia VII 241
Convention on Genocide XIX 77
creation of II 100, 208; XIX 12, 17, 157, 198, 239
Decade for the Rights of Indigenous Peoples XIV 207
Declaration of Human Rights XV 79
Declaration on the Granting of Independence of Colonial Countries and Peoples (1960) XIV 277
defines genocide XVII 96
Economic Commission for Latin America (ECLA) I 20
Economic Commission for the Middle East XIV 177
Fourth Committee on Decolonization XIV 277
General Assembly XIV 277; XV 34, 200, 254; XIX 158, 237
human rights I 146; XVII 142; XIX 12, 25, 27, 29
Hungarian uprising (1956) VI 270
Interim Force in Lebanon (UNIFIL) XV 153
International Law Commission XIV 274
intervention in the Congo II 115
Korea VI 146; XIX 117
Mission for the Referendum in Western Sahara (MINURSO) XIV 278
nuclear weapons I 28
Observation Group in Lebanon (UNOGIL) XV 61
Palestinian refugees XIV 179
Panel on Water VII 286
Partition of Palestine XIV 163; XV 190
Persian Gulf War XV 73–79
Relief and Works Agency for Palestine Refugees in the Near East XIV 179; XV 204
Resolution 181 XIV 152, 165; XV 181 37, 38
Resolution 194 XIV 221, 225
Resolution 338 VI 163
Resolution 339 VI 163
Resolution 340 VI 163
response to invasion of South Korea II 37
Secretariat XIX 202
Security Council II 100; VI 11, 13, 163, 284; XIV 179, 228, 239, 278, 280, 284 ; XV 23, 81, 148, 150, 245, 247, 250, 258; XVI 84, 238, 240–241
Security Council Resolution 242 XIV 162; XV 40, 42, 46, 89, 134–135, 184, 198–199, 211–218, 220, 226, 257, 261, 263
Security Council Resolution 339 XV 220
Security Council Resolution 497 XV 263
Security Council Resolution 678 XV 81, 258
Security Council Resolution 687 XIV 75, 237
Security Council Resolution 1397 XIV 100, 105
Security Council Resolution 1441 XIV 239, 240
sets tone on water policy VII 286
Slavic Bloc XVI 123
Special Commission (UNSCOM) XV 75
Special Committee on Palestine (UNSCOP) XI 126
status of Taiwan I 269
Suez Crisis (1956) VI 80, 270; XVI 235, 241
Technical Assistance Agency (UNTAA) XV 206
water studies XIV 269
Watercourses Convention (1997) XIV 274
Western Sahara XIV 276
United Nations Charter II 102
United Nations Development Programm (UNDP) VII 7; XIV 55, 110, 113, 115
United Nations Educational, Scientific and Cultural Organization (UNESCO) VII 143
United Nations Emergency Force (UNEF) XV 20, 135, 225
United Nations Environmental Program (UNEP) VII 143, 248
United Nations Food and Agricultural Organization (FAO) VII 143
United Nations Relief and Works Agency (UNRWA) XIV 220
United Nations Special Commission (UNSCOM) I 239; XIV 241
United Nations War Crimes Commission V 264
United States XVI 33–34, 45–46, 58, 80, 85, 87, 106–112, 136, 156, 212–213, 218, 248, 284, 291–292, 308
abolitionism in XIII 1–9
Afghanistan
overthrow of Taliban in XIV 10–18
protest against Soviet invasion of II 102
support for mujahideen XIV 1–9
Air Force II 65–66; XIX 237
Alpha Plan XV 68
anarchism XVI 244
Animal and Plant Health Inspection Service VII 217
antinuclear protests VI 16
antiwar movement VI 23–29
Arab oil embargo I 162
armed forces desegregation XIX 8, 26, 30
arms control VI 30
Army IV 9–12; VI 126, 140, 149, 153, 171; VII 166; VIII 10–17, 20–25, 27, 67, 202, 206, 269
investigations of XIX 119, 125–126
Army Corps of Engineers VII 13, 26–27, 29, 52, 54–55, 57, 59–60, 202, 214, 220–224, 259, 261, 263, 266
Army Intelligence XIX 32, 61, 118
Army Security Agency XIX 118
Army War College VIII 16
Asia policy IV 253–259
Barbary pirates XIV 192
Bill of Rights II 98, 101; VII 170
bipartisanship II 203–212
bore-hole drilling in VII 66
British immigration to XII 165, 168, 171
Bureau of the Budget II 271
Bureau of Land Management VII 216
Bureau of Near Eastern Affairs (BNEA) XIV 179

Bureau of Reclamation VII 13, 27–29, 110, 112, 202, 216, 259
Cambodia
- bombing of I 45
- invasion of I 40–47; VI 165, 271

capitalist economic system of I 184
Children's Bureau, Division of Juvenile Delinquency Service 1960 report II 273
China, aid to V 198
Christian roots of XII 60–66
Cold War ideology I 148–154; VI 47–55, 213–220
colonialism XVI 65–66, 68
Committee for Refugees XIV 284
communist activities in VI 126, 129
Congress VI 56–62, 194, 222, 224, 285–286; VII 59, 175; IX 21, 250; XII 7, 17, 21, 25, 31, 101, 121, 297; XIII 282; XIV229, 240; XV 81, 173, 203, 206
- allies of environmentalists VII 123
- appropriated money for dams VII 55
- approves Chesapeake Bay oyster-restoration VII 49
- approves Flood Control Act of 1944 VII 29
- authorizes Hetch Hetchy Dam VII 112
- authorizes TVA VII 28
- cedes swamplands to states VII 272
- creates flood plan VII 273
- environmental concerns of VII 256
- environmental policy of VII 257
- Fourteen Points VIII 281
- gag rule XIII 8
- funds regional wastewater systems planning VII 262
- Indian policy VII 167–168
- thermal pollution VII 175
- passes Central Arizona Project bill VII 114
- passes laws to promote western settlement VII 26

Council of Economic Advisors II 271
Cuba policy VI 70–76
Customs XIX 100
dams in VII 14, 25–32, 219–228
Declaration of Independence II 98, 101
decolonization VI 77–83
Defend America Act of 1996 I 196
defense spending I 125, 180–181, 210; II 67; VI 116, 144, 151, 214, 224, 226, 232, 238
Department of Agriculture (USDA) II 84, 271; VII 161; XIX 198
Department of Agriculture, Bureau of Agricultural Economics III 66
Department of Defense I 7; VI 57; VII 216; XIV 97; XV 168; XIX 21
Department of Energy XIV 213
Department of Housing and Urban Development (HUD) II 112, 277
Department of Justice II 4–5, 45; VII 175, 266
Department of Labor II 271, II 166; VIII 298
Department of the Interior VII 10, 54, 57, 155, 176, 266
Department of Treasury XV 78, 168; XIX 197, 231
diplomacy II 97; VI 106, 158, 188
disarmament XVI 95
dissatisfaction with al-Jazeera XIV 31
domestic spying in XIV 14
drug policy III 132–138
electrical-power production VII 27
emancipation in XIII 36, 198
environmental movement in VII 31, 256
environmental policy in VII 256–270
Environmental Protection Agency (EPA) VII 220, 258, 264, 268; XI 153
Europe, influence over XVI 266–272
farm population II 86; VII 187
first strike theory I 234–240
Fish and Wildlife Service VII 55, 176, 215, 273, 277
fish culture in VII 201
fish hatcheries in VII 202
foreign policy II 3, 35, 97, 101, 103–104, 151, 203–212; III 46, 49; VI 56–62, 87, 106, 150, 188, 254
Forest Service VII 216
Formosa Doctrine I 265, 268
France
- financial aid to II 267
- funds to under Marshall Plan VII 98

General Staff Act (1903) VIII 301
Geological Survey (USGS) VII 26, 182, 277
German war criminals XI 257
global objectives II 269
gold XI 179
Great Lakes, policy on cleaning VII 116–124
gunboat diplomacy VI 270
Haiti III 45
Haitian Revolution, reaction to XIII 210, 214
Holocaust XI 4, 10, 60, 62, 74, 126, 131, 184, 253, 260
House XII 73, 76, 217, 281
- Committee on Public Works VII 268
- Conservation and Natural Resources Subcommittee VII 266
- Government Operations Committee VII 266
- hearings on private property takings VII 277
- International Relations Committee XIV 235
- overrides Nixon veto of Water Pollution Act VII 263
- Public Works Committee VII 258, 261, 268–269
- Rivers and Harbors Subcommittee VII 258
- stops Grand Canyon dam VII 109
- testimony on water pollution in VII 41
- World War I IX 4

House Armed Services Committee, hearings in 1949 I 6–8
human rights policy I 140–146; II 100
immigrants' influence on Cold War policy I 271, 274
immigration policies III 254
impact of World Trade Center attack XIV 50
imperialistic tendencies II 31
India, multinational investment in VII 132
interventions in: Brazil (1964) I 15; British Guiana (1953–1964) I 15; Chile (1973) I 15, 123–133; Costa Rica (mid 1950s) I 15; Cuba (1906–1909, 1912, 1917–1922) III 47; Dominican Republic (1916, 1965) I 15, 125; Ecuador (1960–1963) I 15; Grenada (1983) VI 44, 237; Guatemala (1954) I 15, 20, 123–133; Haiti (1915, 1990s) I 125; VI 58; Indonesia (1957) I 15; Iran (1953) I 15; Nicaragua (1912, 1926, 1980s) I 125, 129; VI 190–196, 249; Panama (1903) I 125, 129; Russia (1918) XVI 1–7; Siberia (1918) IX 165
invasion of alien plant species VII 213
Iran XV 112, 229, 234–235
Iraq
- strikes against nuclear plants I 239
- support to XV 102

isolationism V 288–294
Israel
- alliance with I 156
- backs Zionist settlements in VII 136
- guarantees to military VII 83
- security guarantees to XIV 144

Japan, opening of IV 256
Japanese
immigration of IX 162
internment of XIII 198
Jewish immigration to XI 56
Joint Chiefs of Staff XV 32, 167
memo 1067 II 40
Joint Logistic Plans Committee II 40
Jordan XV 46
limited-nuclear-war doctrines I 165–172
Latin America
economic aid to I 17–26; III 50
relations with IX 167
League of Nations IX 170, 174
Lever Act (1917) VIII 301
Louisiana Territory XIII 210
Marine Corps IX 28
maroons in XIII 107
Middle East VI 61, 162–164; XIV 87; XV 21, 24, 26, 30, 34, 101, 135, 139, 219, 239, 252, 275–276
image of U.S. in XIV 228–235
Multinational Force in Lebanon XV 148–155
mutual assured destruction (MAD) policy I 169–171
Muslim cnversions in XIV 188
National Advisory Committee for Aeronautics (NACA) VIII 197
National Guard VIII 14, 16, 22–23
National Marine Fisheries Service (NMFS) VII 221, 223
National Park Service VII 60, 112
National Security Agency (NSA) II 65; VI 57, 124
National Security Council II 50; XV 59
memorandum 68 (NSC- 68) II 206
National War Labor Board VIII 296, 301
nativism VIII 299
NATO VI 101
Navy IX 77, 79; XVI 94
Nazi reparations XI 214
New Christian Right XIV 256
"no-cities doctrine" I 171
Northeastern drought VII 261
nuclear-power plants in VII 174–180
nuclear stockpile I 213–214; XVI 109
nuclear-nonproliferation policy I 216–224
Office of the Coordinator of Inter-American affairs (OCIAA) III 48
Office of Management and Budget XIV 240
oil XV 173, 175, 176
oil embargo XV 219, 237, 254
oil production XIV 213
Olympic boycott I 10, I 12
opium trade III 137
opposition to African dams VII 240
Pacific Northwest VII 188–195, 196–203
dams in VII 219, 226–228
impact of white settlers upon VII 197
industrial development in VII 198
Palestinians, sympathy for XV 89
Persian Gulf War XV 72–79, 80–88
policy makers II 4
post-Revolution economic growth in XII 24
Presidential Directive (PD) 59 I 171
property rights in VII 271–279
protocol on nonintervention III 47
Public Health Service (USPHS) VII 162, 164, 259
reaction to Sino-Soviet split II 169
Reclamation Service VII 26
reflags Kuwaiti tankers XV 98
relations with
Canada VII 116–124
China II 98, 171; VI 4, 38–45, 88, 201, 203
Great Britain V 28–33; VI 8–14; XII 224
Iran XIV 36–43
Iraq XIV 237, 270
Kurds XIV 170
Libya XIV 193, 198
Mexico VII 151–159
Saudi Arabia XIV 245
Soviet Union V 28–33; VI 9, 55, 157, 200, 228–235; XVI 220, 226–228
Third World 24–26
reparations for slavery XIII 194–201
Republican Party IX 250
Revolutionary debt to foreign countries XII 228
role in Greek coup of 1967 I 15
role in Jamaica (1976–1980) I 15
St. Louis (ship) XI 93
Sedition Act (1917) VIII 301
Selective Service IX 262
Senate
Commerce Committee VII 268
Environment Subcommittee VII 268
Foreign Relations Committee XIV 235
hearings on quality of water sent to Mexico VII 153
Interior Committee VII 258
overrides Nixon veto of Water Pollution Act VII 263
passes Grand Canyon dam bill VII 109
Public Works Committee 258, 261–262
rejects Versailles Treaty VIII 156
Select Committee on National Water Resources VII 258
Subcommittee on Air and Water Pollution VII 261, 264
supports Mexican Water Treaty VII 152
treaties VII 153; XII 73, 76
World War I IX 4, 173, 250
Senate Foreign Relations Committee I 306; II 7, 205; VI 153
Senate Select Committee on Intelligence Activities, 1974 investigation of CIA activites in Chile I 124
sexuality in IX 147
slave revolts XIII 154–155, 157
slave trade XIII 47, 270
abolishes XIII 65
African slave trade XII 300; XIII 195
suppression of XIII 2, 272
social problems VI 144, 187
Soil Conservation Service VII 217
Southeast, wetlands harvest in VII 273
Southwest, riparian ecosystems in VII 211–218
Soviet nuclear weapons espionage I 241–249
Space Program II 241–248, 256–259; VI 140
Special National Intelligence Estimate (SNIE) XV 166
spying on Soviet military capabilities I 190–192
Office of Terrorism XIV 233
Suez Crisis XVI 235–242
superpower XIV 88
supply of water in VII 283
support for Slovak dam in VII 103
support for Taiwan I 266
support of dictators II 103; VI 64
Supreme Court II 19–20, 23–26, 45, 78, 90–91, 136–141, 220, 224, 280–287; IX 4; XII 22, 64, 69, 73; XIII 53, 95; XIV 96, 115; XIX 17, 72, 92, 148–153, 173, 212, 214, 218, 255, 218, 259
abortion issues II 221
Arizona-California water dispute VII 109
Brown v. *Board of Education* XIX 26
Dennis v. *United States* XIX 256, 259, 262–263, 271
First Amendment cases 255

gender discrimination II 182
Hollywood Ten case XIX 168, 170
Japanese internment III 103, 105
judicial review XII 58
Kansas-Colorado water dispute VII 13
National Industrial Recovery Act III 149
Native Americans III 140, VII 57, 168, 170
New Deal III 25
Noto v. *United States* XIX 259
"Roosevelt Court" II 281
Rosenberg case XIX 282, 285, 288
Sacco and Vanzetti appeal III 232
Scales v. *United States* XIX 259
Schenck v. *United States* XIX 255, 263
segregation II 293
use of Refuse Act VII 266
Yates v. *United States* XIX 259
Syria XV 270
Third World VI 61, 80, 188
Trading with the Enemy Act (1917) VIII 299
Vietnam XVI 269
advisers in I 291
troop buildup in I 291
War Department VIII 23, 27; IX 5–6
War Industries Board VIII 296, 301
War Refugee Board XI 11
water policy in VII 151–159
water pollution in VII 256–270
West
development of VII 26
public-works projects in VII 28
reclamation projects in VII 26
water policy in VII 181–187
wetlands VII 271–279
Wilsonianism I 205
World War I VIII 125, 177, 191, 204, 223, 287, 295–302 ; IX 26–32, 49, 56, 92, 96, 140, 163, 165, 171, 175, 245–251; XVI 252
aircraft IX 13
anti-German feelings during VIII 296
army in IX 29
casualties VIII 125, 268
economy IX 18–22
entry into IX 31, 77, 105
freedom of seas IX 183
supplies to Allies IX 23, 75, 194
women in VIII 130, 296, 298
World War II V 303–304; XVI 314–320
economic gain III 64
entry XI 14
power after I 259
racism in III 213–219
United States Chamber of Commerce XIX 10, 121
United States Employment Service VIII 301
United States Fish Commission (USFC) VII 201
United States Holocaust Memorial Museum XI 16, 45, 264
United States Information Agency XIV 235; XV 44; XIX 111
United States Military Academy, West Point VIII 16, 22
United States Railroad Administration IX 24
United States Service and Shipping Corporation XIX 197
United States v. *Winans* (1905) VII 57
United Steelworkers Union VII 267; XIX 71
United Towns Organization VII 143
United World Federalists (UWF) XIX 237
Universalism I 284–289
Universal Negro Improvement Association (UNIA) IX 4
Universities and colleges
FBI agents at XIX 111
Communists in XIX 213
University of Alabama XIII 277
University of Algiers XIV 202
University of California XIII 200
University of California Japanese American Evacuation and Resettlement Study (1942–1946) V 186
University of Chicago VII 262; XIX 107, 276
University of Halle XI 28
University of Heidelberg XI 28
University of Idaho VII 225
University of London XVI 34
University of Maryland VII 48
University of Michigan XIX 153
University of Minnesota XIX 6
University of Oregon VII 60
University of South Carolina XIII 28, 95, 278; XIV 104
University of Washington XIX 108, 109
University of Tizi Ouzou XIV 209
University of Vienna XI 149
University of Virginia XIII 96, 198
University of Washington VII 60, 202
Untermenschen (subhumans) IV 86, 99, 131
Unterseeboote (U-boats) V 2, 79–83, 135; VIII 106, 134–135, 138, 196, 223, 287–294, 296; IX 21, 53, 58, 74–79, 104, 120, 142, 144, 181, 183–188, 247–248; XVI 168
bases in World War I VIII 219
blockade IX 194
technology V 83
Type IX V 80
Type VII V 79, V 80
Type VIIC V 83
unrestricted warfare IX 77, 120, 142, 187, 246, 248, 256
UPI XIX 276
Upper Colorado River Storage Project VII 30
Upper Stillwater Dam (United States) VII 31
Uprising (2001) XI 155, 158, 161
uranium bomb XIX 231
Urban II X 13–20, 24, 26, 32, 35, 59, 71–72, 77, 88, 98–105, 116–119, 121–122, 124–127, 130–131, 135–136, 148–150, 171, 175, 191, 205, 209, 211–221, 223–224, 227, 231–233, 238, 245, 256, 265, 267–269, 279–294, 297–298
Urban III X 254, 259
Urban political bosses III 259–265
Uruguay XIV 71
communist guerrilla movements I 125
military coups I 26
reduction of U.S. military aid I 141
War of the Triple Alliance I 125
USA PATRIOT Act XIX 123, 129, 278
USS *Liberty* (ship) XV 136, 138
Utah VII 31, 112
Uzbekistan XIV 2, 12, 88, 180, 228, 267

V

Vaal River VII 7–8, 240–241
Valcour Island XII 46, 80
Valencia X 2, 6, 159
Valera, Eamon de XVI 244
Valley Forge XII 92, 96, 155, 161
Valois, Georges XVI 141, 143
Van Buren, Martin XIII 195
Vance, Cyrus R. I 143, 145; VI 42, 263; XV 258
Vandenberg, Arthur I 306, 203, 205, 207–208; XIX 249
Vandenberg, Hoyt Sanford I 6, 236
Van der Kloof Dam (South Africa) VII 243
Van Devanter, Justice Willis III 25, 27, 31
Vanishing Air (1970) VII 269
Vanity Fair XIX 46
Vanzetti, Bartolomeo III 229–238; XIX 258
Vardar Valley IX 204–205
Vargha, Janos VII 101
Variety XIX 216
Vatican VIII 208–209; XI 131, 192–193; XIV 161, 165, 184; XVI 45

treaty with Germany XVI 150
Vatican Radio XI 192
V-E Day IV 62; V 60
Velde, Harold XIX 126
Velsicol Chemical Company VII 162–165
Velvet Divorce (1992) VII 100
Velvet Revolution (1989) VII 101
Venereal Disease VIII 128
Venezuela XIII 147; XIV 212, 215, 219
debt crisis (1902) XVI 66
oil XV 175, 177
slave rebellions XIII 231
Venezuelan Crisis (1895) XVI 65
Venice IX 107; X 30, 75, 108–109, 112–114, 128, 148–157, 198
slave market XIII 167
Venizelos, Eleutherios IX 208
Venona Project I 242–243; 247; VI 123, 126, 154, 156; XIX 4, 58, 61–63, 83, 85–86, 118, 143, 154–155, 186, 197, 284
and Hiss case XIX 155, 199
and Rosenberg case XIX 282– 285
Ventura, Jesse II 199, 201
Vermont XII 181
gun laws in XII 279
prohibits slavery XIII 19
slavery in XII 263
Vernichtungskrieg (war of annihilation) IV 88, 141
Versailles Treaty (1919) I 255, 285, 293, 300; II 99, 145; III 99, 180; IV 17–18, 86, 164, 266–273; V 148, 202, 292; VI 176; VIII 20, 58, 95–96, 156, 166, 173, 207, 264, 277–285, 295, 298–299 ; IX 21, 27, 93, 95–96, 172–174, 268; XI 15, 82, 98, 168; XVI 9–10, 13, 74, 76, 93–94, 102, 118, 146, 148, 151, 209, 211–212, 214, 218, 291–296; XVII 11, 60, 116, 143, 148, 166, 193
Article 231, War Guilt Clause IV 267; VIII 280, 282, 284
impact on German economy IV 269
impact on World War II IV 267
U.S. fails to ratify XVI 94
Vesey, Denmark XIII 54, 91, 156–157, 210, 231, 235–236; XIX 41
Veterans of the Foreign Wars XIX 101
Vichy France IV 275–280; IX 84; XI 177; XVI 130–131, 135–136, 138, 141, 143
anti-Semitism IV 277, 280
cooperation with Nazis IV 276, 278
National Renewal IV 276
Statut des juifs (Statute on the Jews) IV 277
support of the *Wehrmacht* (German Army) IV 277
Victoria, Queen of England VIII 30, 32, 35; XII 32; XVI 34, 70, 178
Victorian Building Trades Federation (Australia) XIX 270
Vidovian Constitution (1921) IX 268
Vienna Declaration I 253
Vienna Settlement XVI 74
Vietminh V 146–148; VI 106; IX 260; XIX 157
Vietcong I 40–42, 296–297; VI 93, 96; XII 28, 30, 34
attacks on U.S. bases (1965) I 291
begins war with South Vietnam I 290
Vietnam I 41, 46, 50, 54, 82, 87, 89, 273, 290–294, 298–299; II 3–5, 7–10, 40, 173, 269; VI 32, 50, 59, 64, 80–81, 98, 101, 107, 201, 203, 229, 261, 270–272; VIII 35, 193; IX 260; XII 28, 30–31, 33–34; XIV 5; XV 18, 49, 133, 228, 253; XVI 136, 269
Buddhist dissidents VI 92
colony of France I 290
French withdrawal from I 213; II 266; VI 102, 106
geography of XII 29
guerilla warfare XII 28, 34
imperialism I 151
peace agreement with France I 290, 297
seventeenth parallel division II 267; VI 98
U.S. bombing of I 183
U.S. military buildup I 183; VI 96
Vietnam War (ended 1975) I 40, 44–45, 89, 101, 140, 142, 144, 290–299; II 3–10, 97, 177, 180, 224, 257, 260, 263–265, 273; VI 8, 23–29, 33, 38, 56–57, 61, 85, 88, 98–99, 103, 138–145, 173, 185, 202, 222, 266, 283–285; VIII 60, 188, 266; IX 262; XII 27–29, 31, 33, 37; XIV 2; XV 73, 137, 175, 215; XVI 92, 157, 158, 254, 271; XIX 18–19, 21– 23, 110, 123, 128, 132, 224
and anticommunism XIX 206
casualties XIX 227
comparison to Soviet invasion of Afghanistan I 14
domino theory I 266, 297–298; XIX 128
doves II 263; XIX 25, 31, 102, 105
end XIX 227
folly of U.S. militarism I 183
Gulf of Tonkin Resolution I 291
hawks II 263
impact on Republican and Democratic concensus II 208
impact on U.S. domestic programs II 270; VI 185, 202
labor movement support of II 193
number of casualties I 291
Operation Duck Hook II 6
Operation Flaming Dart I 291
Operation Rolling Thunder I 291
peace agreements XIX 221–223, 226– 227
reasons for U.S. involvement I 292, 295, 297–298
result of containment policy II 265
result of French colonial system II 267
syndrome XV 73
television coverage II 124–125; VI 145
Tet Offensive II 9, 180, 275
U.S. troop buildup I 291
U.S. troops leave I 291
Vietminh I 290
Vietnamization VI 99; XII 30; XIX 221, 226
Vikings X 122, 213, 280, 287
Villa, Francisco "Pancho" III 125–130; VIII 16, 18, 22; IX 6
Villard, Henry VII 57
Vilna Ghetto XI 144
Vima XIX 216
Vincent, John Carter XIX 18, 21
A Vindication of the Rights of Women (Wollstonecraft) II 74
Vinson, Frederick M. XIX 149–152, 262–263
Virgil XX 189–196
and Ovid XX 265–272
Virgin Islands, slave revolts XIII 91, 154
Virginia XII 66, 70, 114, 116, 122, 171, 181, 185, 198, 200, 207, 209, 215, 217, 233, 242–243, 262, 264, 278, 287, 290–291, 308; XIII 17, 23, 28, 42, 60, 66, 104
bans importation of African slaves XIII 19
charter XII 242
colonial society XII 209
free black population XII 296
General Assembly XII 23
grandfather clause XIII 56
gun laws XII 279
indentured servitude XIII 164, 249, 280
land shortage in XIII 164
legal definitons of slavery XIII 181
liberalizes oyster-leasing laws VII 42
Loyalists in XII 192
maroons in XIII 107–108, 110
mortality rates in XIII 247
oyster industry in VII 40–50
privitization of oystering VII 47
Reconstruction, end of XIII 55
religion in XII 148, 150, 263
repeals (1781) ratification of impost XII 228
Scots-Irish from XII 235
signs Chesapeake Bay 2000 Agreement VII 49

slave revolt XIII 91, 156, 158, 210, 231, 235–236
slavery in XII 2, 4, 299; XIII 11, 60, 96, 99, 101, 151, 164, 172–173, 179–180, 203, 206–207, 233, 249
tobacco XII 209
trade with Dutch XII 209
women in XIII 224
Virginia Continental Line XII 89
Virginia Plan XII 70
Virginia Ratifying Convention XII 279
Virginia Resolution XII 125
Virginia Resolves (1765) XII 241
virtual representation XII 57, 261
Visigoths X 241–244
Vistula River VII 18, 20
Vodûn XIII 192–193, 209–210
Voice of America (VOA) XIV 29, 235
Volksgemeinschaft (people's community) IV 80, 83
Volstead Act (1919) III 200
Volta River VII 2, 4
Volta River Project VII 4
Voltaire IX 207; X 131, 224; XII 121–122, 133, 234; XIII 195, 273
Volunteers in Service to America (VISTA) II 272, 276
Voorhis, Jerry XIX 223–224
Voting Rights Act (1965) II 26, 91, 162–163, 165, 283; XIII 57; XIX 28, 32
Vyshinsky, Andrey XIX 237

W

De Waarheid XIX 269, 273
Wadleigh, Henry Julian XIX 62–63, 156
Wadström, Christian XIII 134, 136
Wagner Act (1935) II 188; III 27–31, 63, 66, 149, 190; XIX 71, 182, 184, 208
Wahhab, Muhammad ibn Abd al- XIV 244
Wahhabi Ikhwan (Brethren) XIV 244
Wahhabi Islam XIV 16, 92, 205, 208, 244, 251
Wailing Wall XIV 159, 165–166
Waldersee, George von IX 99
Waldorf-Astoria Hotel, New York XIX 161, 170–171
Waldorf Conference XIX 242–243
Waldorf Statement XIX 161, 170
Wales XII 34, 242
Walesa, Lech VI 110; VII 20
Walk A Crooked Mile XIX 163
Wallace, George C. II 180, 197, 199, 273, 281
Wallace, Henry A. I 31, 148, 287; II 197, 207, 209; III 159, 162; XVI 163; XIX 30, 76, 94, 96, 185, 216, 238, 240–241
Pete Seeger and the Weavers II 214
presidential race (1948) II 211
Wallenberg, Raoul XI 177, 202
Waller, Thomas Wright "Fats" III 79
Wall Street XIX 226
Walpole, Robert XII 128, 146, 209, 235
Walter, Francis XIX 126
Wannsee Conference (1942) IV 139; V 161; XI 37, 87, 91, 108, 160, 175, 184, 211
War Industries Board (WIB) IX 18, 23
War of Attrition (1970) I 308, 316; XV 40, 42, 46, 218, 225
War of 1812 VII 116; XIII 173, 222, 281–282
War of St. Sabas (1256–1258) X 47, 54, 148, 151, 156
War of the League of Augsburg (1689–1697) XVI 252
War of the Sands (1963) XIV 74
War of the Triple Alliance (1864–1870) I 125
War on Poverty II 270– 279; VI 141
counter-assault to II 277
reasons for failure of II 271
War Powers Act XIX 223
War Powers Resolution (1973) VI 58, 61, 195, 222, 283–287; XV 79
War Production Board XIX 197
War Refugees Board (WRB) III 253, 256
War Relocation Administration (WRA) III 102
War Resisters' International (WRI) XIX 237
Ward, Harry F. XIX 238
Ware, Harold XIX 155
Ware Group XIX 155, 197
Warner, Jack XIX 167, 251
Wars of German Unification XVI 72
Wars of Religion XVI 255
Ware v. *Hylton* (1796) XI 215
Warhol, Andy II 216
Warm Springs Reservation VII 56, 60
Warne, William E. VII 55
Warren, Earl II 90, 136, 138, 142, 180, 280–291, 296; XIX 26, 149–150, 152
Wars of Liberation (1813–1815) IX 126, 259
Wars of Unification (1866–1871) IX 126; XI 82
Warsaw Ghetto XI 139–142
Warsaw Ghetto Uprising XI 145
Warsaw Pact I 102, 154, 206, 256; II 60–61; VI 50, 110, 118, 121, 130–131, 168–170, 177, 184, 207–208, 235, 249, 267, 271; XIV 2, 262; XVI 74, 123, 160–161, 269, 284–285, 288
withdrawal of Hungary I 185
Warsaw Treaty Organization (WTO) I 154
Wasco County-Dalles City Museum Commission VII 60
Washington, Booker T. III 117, 120, 267–274; IX 2
comparison to W. E. B. Du Bois III 271
Tuskegee experiment III 123
Tuskegee Institute III 268
Washington, D.C. VII 261, 269; XII 22; XIV 182
Washington, George VII 29; VIII 230; XII 9–10, 12, 15, 25, 33, 37–39, 46–47, 54, 63, 66, 78, 80, 81, 85, 87–88, 92–101, 106, 113, 119, 121, 151, 155, 158, 161, 182, 198–199, 215, 217, 235, 270, 272, 274, 283, 287, 289–290, 295–296, 320; XIII 18–19, 48
dispute with James Madison XII 228
handling of Newburgh Conspiracy XII 221–229
military leader XII 301–308
slavery XII 4
treatment of deserters XII 90
Washington Agreement XI 179
Washington Conference (1943) IV 144
Washington Naval Conference (1921–1922) IV 2; V 103, 204–205, 207–208; VI 30; VIII 298; XVI 91, 94 107
Washington Pact XVI 315
The Washington Post XIX 227
Washington Sedition Trial of 1944 XIX 258
Washington State VII 201, 220
CPUSA in XIX 103
dams in VII 27, 31, 198
farmers opposed dam breaching VII 226
nuclear weapon development in VII 55
Pollution Control Commission (PCC) VII 189, 193–194
population in VII 54
Washington State Sports Council VII 53
Washington Tribune XIX 41
The Waste Land XIX 46
water
commodity VII 280–288
extraction of VII 62–68
importance of VII 76
Islamic law on VII 83; XIV 269
Middle East XIV 268–275
"prior appropriation" law VII 109
recycling of VII 70
resource VI 2
sand abstraction VII 63, 66
supply of VII 280–288
use by upper class in South Afirca VII 7
Water Manifesto, The VII 283, 317–332
Water Pollution Control Act VII 123, 268,
Water Pollution Control Act Amendments VII 259, 263
Water Quality Act (1965) VII 123, 175, 261
Water Quality Improvement Act (1970) VII 174, 176

Water Resources Planning Act (1965) VII 259
Water Resources Research Act (1964) VII 259
Water Rights Court VII 88
Water Wasteland (1971) VII 265, 268
Water Workers and Distributors Union of Baja California VII 159
Watercourses Convention (1997) XIV 274
Watergate scandal I 47, 90, 291–292; II 176, 185, 257, 278; VI 24, 85, 87–88, 90, 124, 204; XV 241; XIX 128, 220–221, 223–224, 227
Waterside Workers' Federation (Australia) XIX 270
Watkins, Arthur 127
Watkins, John 150
Watkins v. *United States* 150, 153
Watson, Tom XIII 56
Watts riots II 257, 276; VI 141
Wausau XIX 209
Wayland, Francis XIII 29, 33
Wayne, John XIX 163
"We Shall Overcome" XIX 76, 77
Wealth of Nations (1776) XII 32
weapons of mass destruction (WMD) XIV 95, 97, 144, 146–148, 237, 239, 241, 262; XV 73–74, 78, 80–81, 259; XVI 98, 108, 252
Weavers XIX 39
Webb-Pomerance Bill (1916) IX 21
Weber, Max XI 77
Webster, Daniel XIII 4
Webster v. *Reproductive Health Services* (1989) II 222
We Charge Genocide XIX 29, 77
Wechsler, James XIX 124
Wedemeyer, Albert Coady V 42–43, 126, 149, 280
Wehrmacht (German Army) IV 19, 24, 85–86, 88, 108, 125, 130, 141, 167, 230, 277; V 37, 96, 104, 106, 118, 125–126, 132, 135, 153, 179, 211, 219, 226, 229, 232, 244, 272, 275, 282–283; VIII 92; XI 33, 83, 117–118, 169, 267; XVI 118, 185, 188–189
    Case Yellow IV 282
    early victories V 213
    Hitler's ideology V 137–144
    Manstein Plan IV 107
    mechanized warfare IV 282
    myth IV 286
    opinion of guerrilla warfare IV 93, 101
    panzer divisions IV 284
    reputation IV 281, 287
    role in war atrocities IV 85–94
    Tank Forces development IV 106
    utilization of tanks IV 283
    weapons development IV 105
Weimar Republic IV 270; V 115, 210–211; VI 176; VIII 144, 284–285; IX 260; XVI 176, 209, 212
Weinberger, Caspar W. VI 2, 21, 221–222, 229, 231; XVI 44
Weizmann, Chaim XI 62, 121
Welch, Joseph XIX 126, 276
Weld, Theodore Dwight XIII 31, 142
Welles, Orson III 237
Welles, Sumner XIX 62
Wells, H. G. IX 220
Wells, Ida B. XIII 57
Wells, Sumner V 58; XI 60
Weltpolitik VIII 31, 44, 249, 266
Wemyss, James XII 41, 186
Wends X 179, 225
Wesley, John XII 151
West Africa IX 113, 115–116, 118; XII 165; XIX 11–12
    culture XIII 206
    interdiction of slave trade from XII 167
    religion in XIII 187
    slave trade XIII 36–38, 40
    slaves from XIII 168
West Bank XIV 20, 22, 25–26, 100, 105–106, 112, 160, 162, 220–221, 223, 226, 230; XV 20–21, 23, 25, 34, 37, 41–42, 45, 48– 49, 52–53, 57, 61, 78–79, 89–95, 131–132, 134, 136–137, 139, 182–183, 185–186, 190–191, 194–195, 198–200, 213–215, 219, 222, 226–227, 242, 261, 263
    settlements in XIV 151–158
West Berlin I 194, 288, 293; VI 147–149
    Soviet blockade (1948) I 238
West Caprivi Game Reserve VII 35
West Germany I 113, 154; VI 101, 103, 121, 168–169, 201, 204, 206–212; XI 181, 214–215; XI 35, 256, 260; XV 14; XVI 77, 156, 267–268; XVI 155–156, 284; XVII 2, 21, 57, 60, 64, 67, 129, 134, 220, 233; XIX 145
    aid received from U.S. I 158
    antinuclear protests VI 16
    emigration VI 118
    entry into NATO I 206
    joins NATO I 108
    military I 255
    Minister of Federal Transportation VII 207
    nuclear proliferation I 223
    nuclear weapons development I 222
    opposition to African dams in VII 240
    postwar economy I 174
    relations with Poland VI 211
    relations with the Soviet Union VI 211
    Social Democrats I 36
    terrorism XVI 245, 248
West India Company XIII 270
West Indies XII 22, 37, 79, 167; XIII 7, 18, 136, 181, 235, 243, 270
    British troops in XII 186
    death rates of imported slaves XIII 134
    Loyalist refugees flee to XII 189
    slave trade XIII 273
    slavery in XIII 65, 80
    threatened by French XII 182
    trade with New England XIII 195
West Point XII 9–10, 13
West Side Story XIX 48
West Virginia XV 267
Western Desert Project (Egypt) VII 2
Western Ghats VII 125
Western Kansas Groundwater Management District No. 1 VII 185
Western Sahara XIV 70–75, 209, 276–285
    Green March (1975) XIV 284
    refugees XIV 284
Westminster Abbey XII 159
Westminster College XIX 117, 127
Westmoreland, William C. I 291; II 5
    Vietnam War policy I 299
wetlands VII 271–279
    private property VII 272
    scientific understanding VII 273
What Makes Sammy Run? XIX 36
Wheeler, Burton K. II 209; III 26
Wherry, Kenneth XIX 94
Whigs XII 110, 128, 254; XIII 21, 281–283
Whiskey Rebellion (1794) XII 125, 219, 277, 283
White, Harry Dexter XIX 58, 62–63, 197–198, 231
White, Theodore H. XIX 21
White, Thomas W. XI 57, 62
White, Walter II 44; III 218; XIX 8, 10, 30, 79, 219, 234
White Citizens Council XIX 31
white flight II 250, 292–293
    Boston II 298
White League XIII 55
White Panther Party II 95
White Paper (1922) XV 34
White Paper (1939) XV 34
White Pines Act (1729) XII 243
White Sea XVI 184
white supremacy XIII 224
Whitefield, George XII 148, 150–152
Whitehead, Don XIX 175
Whitehouse, Joseph VII 171
Whitney, Eli XIII 7, 43

Whitney v. *California* XIX 255
Whittier, John Greenleaf VII 275
Wickes, Lambert XII 79, 106
Wiener Landesgericht prison XI 149
Wiesel, Elie XI 50, 52, 142, 164, 218, 223, 228, 230–231
Wiggins, Forest XIX 6
Wilberforce, William XIII 31, 157, 159
Wild and Scenic Rivers Act (1968) VII 31
Wilde, Oscar IX 87, 146, 148
Wilder, Billy XIX 164
Wilderness Act (1964) VII 31
Wilderness Society VII 30, 112, 258
The Wild Boys XIX 49
The Wild One XIX 47
Wilhelm II 24, 29–31, 35, 72, 97, 152, 184, 209, 213, 226, 229, 252, 257, 282; IX 32, 42, 44, 75, 98–101, 103, 139–140, 142, 146, 160, 222, 226, 257; X 57, 305 ; XI 169; XVI 35, 183, 192, 194, 257, 295, 308, 313
Wilkes, John XII 30, 167–168
Wilkins, Roy XIII 256; XIX 10, 30
Wilkinson, Frank XIX 65
Wilkomirski, Binjamin XI 52, 53
William, Frederick IX 100
William II XII 243
William of Malmesbury X 215–216
William of Newburgh X 16, 33, 277
William of Tyre X 197, 201, 211, 214–215, 218–219, 305
William of Upper Burgundy X 119, 285
William the Conqueror XVI 181
Williams, Cleophas XIX 233
Williams, Robin XI 160
Williams, Tennessee XIX 48
Williamson, John XIX 260
Wilson, C. E. XIX 71
Wilson, Edward O. VII 234–235
Wilson, Harold XV 135
Wilson, Henry Hughes VIII 77, 108, 237
Wilson, James XII 65, 74, 139, 281
Wilson, Michael XIX 164
Wilson, Woodrow I 88, 151, 285; II 8, 46, 145, 156, 199; III 25, 55, 98–99, 175, 208, 211, 223, 244; VI 57, 77, 188; VIII 11–12, 16–18, 22, 96, 204, 228, 261, 277–278, 281–282, 295, 298–299; IX 7, 19, 21, 24, 26, 31, 57, 105, 168, 173, 225, 245–247, 250, 270; XIV 43; XVI 2, 4, 7, 34, 36, 76, 87, 100–102, 111, 292, 307–308, 310, 313; XIX 31
  flu epidemic III 100
  foreign policy III 46
  Fourteen Points (1918) II 99, 101, 152; III 99, 175; VI 106; VIII 20, 298; XVI 33, 237
  idealism VIII 280
  Mexican Revolution III 124, 128–129
  model of human rights I 145
  New Freedom III 211
  Nobel Peace Prize II 99
  Paris Peace Conference (1919) II 264
  World War I VIII 289, 291, 296
Wilson administration
  first national antinarcotic law III 135
  Mexican Revolution III 126
  Red Scare III 221
  war economy IX 18–22
  World War I IX 167, 245, 247
Wilson Dam (United States) VII 26
Wilsonianism I 19, 204–207, 304
Wind River Reservation VII 170
Window of vulnerability I 189–191
Windsor Castle XII 143; XVI 178, 180
Windward Coast XIII 272
Winston, Henry XIX 260, 262
Winter, Carl XIX 260
Winter War (1939–1940) I 108; XVI 119, 125, 221, 224, 319; XVI 125, 221, 224, 319
Winters Doctrine VII 172–173
Winters v. *United States* (1908) VII 168, 172
Wisconsin VII 122, 264, 267; XII 22; XIX 207
  Native Americans XII 176
  pollution control in VII 264
Wisconsin State Committee on Water Pollution VII 122
Witte, Sergei XVI 16, 200
Wohlstetter, Albert J. I 213, II 65
Wolfowitz, Paul XV 84, 87
Wollstonecraft, Mary II 74
Wolman, Abel VII 47
Wool Act (1699) XII 198, 243
Woman XIX 45
Women
  antebellum South XIII 224–230
  emancipation of in twentieth-century Europe XVII 275–282
  Middle East XIV 111, 115, 286–292
Women's Air Force Service Pilots (WASPs) V 303
Women's Army Corps (WAC) V 303
Women's movement II 162, 165
  Progressive Era III 165–173
  Prohibition III 198
  World War I VIII 124–130, 296, 298
Women Strike for Peace (WSP) XIX 242–243, 281
Women's International League for Peace and Freedom (WILPF) XIX 237, 242
Wood, Edward (Earl of Halifax) IX 83
Wood, Leonard IX 6
Woodhouse, Monty XV 160, 163
Woodstock II 257
Woodstock Dam (South Africa) VII 243
Woodwell, George M. VII 262
Woolf, Virginia VIII 130
Woolman, John XIII 1, 17, 149–150, 152
Workers World Party II 197
Works Progress Administration (WPA), 1935 III 150, 163
  ex-slave interviews XIII 226
World Bank I 20, 22, 124, 145; VI 120; VII 5, 7–8, 62, 83, 130, 132, 146, 241, 280, 287; XIV 58, 89, 111; XV 160; XVI 77, 87
  Resettlement Policy VII 244
  sets tone on water policy VII 286
World Bank Development Report XIV 58
World Bank Inspection Panel VII 8, 9
World Commission on Dams VII 9, 127, 130, 133, 242
  report of (2000) VII 317–332
World Commission on Water for the Twenty-First Century 286
World Council of Churches XIX 238, 268
World Court IX 171
World Economic Conference (London, 1933) XVI 218
World Festival of Youth and Students for Peace and Friendship XIX 239
world government movement XIX 237
World Health Organization (WHO) VII 143, 253
World Jewish Congress III 256; V 58; XI 181
World Peace Congress, Paris (1949) XIX 238
World Trade Center attack (11 September 2001) XIV 10–11, 13, 27–28, 32, 37–38, 41, 43, 50, 61, 68, 77, 86–94, 95–96, 103, 108–109, 126, 129, 175, 182, 189–191, 216, 218, 227, 238–239, 243, 245, 247, 250, 256, 262, 264; XV 54, 83, 145, 259; XVI 71, 243, 245; XIX 123, 129
World Trade Center bombing (1993) XIV 16, 191, 193
World Trade Organization (WTO) XIV 40, 54, 65, 109, 112, 114, 273
World War I (1914–1918) I 88, 112, 149, 284, 286; III 210, 223, 229, 244; VI 57, 176, 178, 267; VII 82; IX 22, 27; X 59, 62, 199, 304; XI 15, 28, 32, 82, 88, 97, 114, 126, 132, 174, 183, 215, 220, 266; XIV 65, 168, 171, 176, 178, 211, 220, 261; XV 11, 33–34, 65, 68–69, 73, 82, 98, 106, 116–117, 121, 141, 146, 152, 156, 172–173, 176, 274; XVI 1, 4, 8–9, 12–13, 15, 17, 20, 29–30, 32–33, 36, 49–50, 53, 55, 57, 61, 65, 72, 74, 80–81, 87, 91–95, 100, 102,

107, 111, 113–114, 117, 129–130, 140–141, 148, 151, 183, 189, 208, 211, 213–214, 216–218, 221, 228, 236, 245, 249, 267, 291, 294, 298, 307–313 ; XIX 4, 25
African Americans III 268; IV 218; VIII 298, 301
African soldiers in IX 111–118
airplanes VIII 115, 193–197; IX 9–14, 38
Allied cooperation IX 104–110
Allied suplies to Russia IX 190
and civil rights XIX 331
Anglo-German naval rivalry VIII 29–36
Armistice IX 72, 114
artillery IX 39
arts IX 84
Balkans IX 206, 266–272
balloons in IX 14
Belgian neutrality IX 41–47
British entry into XVI 22–24
British strategy IX 48–53
casualties IX 30
causes I 205; IX 224–229; XVI 192–198
chemical warfare VIII 239–244
combat tactics VIII 109–116
convoys IX 74–79
cultural watershed IX 80–90; XVII 40–50
deportations during XIX 174
East Africa VIII 84–90
Eastern Front VIII 49, 60, 79, 91, 94, 110, 114, 125, 182, 240, 242, 252 IX 27; 60–66, 71, 108, 120, 124, 127, 129, 135, 154, 159, 206, 238, 243, 252–253; XVI 2, 6, 308–309
European economics IX 83
European leadership IX 98–103
firepower and mobility VIII 109–116
followed by Red Scare XIX 211
gender roles VIII 124–130
German Jewish service in XI 94
homosexuality in IX 146–153
impact on American business in Mexico III 128
impact on European states XVI 171–176
impact on Jews VIII 163–169
impact on U.S. isolationism V 289; VIII 295–302
Japan in IX 162–169
Lost Generation VIII 186–192
mass mobilization III 19
Middle East VIII 37–42, 60
military innovations VIII 193–197
motivations of soldiers VIII 59–64, 263–269
naval war IX 139–142
New Women III 168, 172
Ottoman Empire VIII 117–123
prewar alliances VIII 225–231
prostitution in IX 146, 152
recreation for soldiers IX 234
religion VIII 202–210
Russia IX 237–243; XVI 199–207
shell shock IX 209–213
Socialists in Europe VIII 254–262
strategic bombing in IX 217–223
Supreme War Council IX 104
technology in IX 231
trench warfare IX 230–235
U.S. entry XIX 246
venereal disease IX 152
Western Front VIII 11–13, 16–19, 21, 24, 27–28, 39, 51, 56–57, 59, 61, 77–79, 90, 96, 102, 104, 106, 108–110, 112, 114, 117, 122, 177, 179–185, 187–188, 195, 197, 208, 221, 264, 272–273, 276, 282; IX 12–13, 15–16, 27, 29–31, 33–34, 38, 40, 48–49, 53, 61, 65–67, 71–73, 104–110, 114, 118, 120, 122, 124, 128, 131, 190, 193, 203, 225, 231–232, 234–235, 253–254; XVI 5–6, 34, 37, 201, 309, 312–313
women in VIII 296, 298
World War II (1939–1945) I 61, 91; III 11, 50, 250–257; VI 8, 27, 31, 36, 49, 77, 79, 126, 146, 179, 267; VII 27, 29, 53, 69, 90, 93, 109, 152, 168, 174, 188, 199, 202, 204, 236–237, 257, 263–264, 273, 278, 287; IX 22, 27; X 14, 272, 300, 305; XI , 9–10, 14, 18, 36–37, 45, 56, 70, 81, 103, 106, 114, 117–118, 121, 126, 139–140, 148, 168, 171, 174, 181, 187, 191–192, 211, 214, 227, 243, 249, 252–253, 255–257, 260; XII 30, 33, 64, 171; XIII 198; XIV 2, 17, 37, 40, 71, 171, 174, 176, 181, 188, 192, 211, 230, 238, 245, 261; XV 12, 18, 29–30, 34–35, 65, 70, 87, 106, 108, 116, 126, 141, 146, 156, 163, 172–173, 176–177, 202, 229, 252–253, 274; XVI 11, 36, 39, 41, 44, 61, 63, 65, 69, 76, 80–81, 84–85, 91, 94, 99, 100, 104–105, 111, 113, 118, 121–122, 125, 134, 137, 140, 158, 163, 171, 181, 208, 211, 213, 216, 218, 221, 226, 228–229, 233, 238, 240, 245, 254, 255, 262, 266, 267, 269, 281, 285, 298, 301; XIX 24, 213
African American contributions IV 221; IX 115; XIX 25, 28
aftermath XIX 91, 124, 149, 180, 215, 249
Allied bombing XI 13
Allies V 27–33; VI 169; XIX 4, 63, 119, 246, 259
and labor movement XIX 71
Anglo-American alliance IV 208; XVI 314–320
antisubmarine defense IX 79
Axis powers V 62–67
Balkans V 68–78
beginning XIX 88, 104
Catholic Church VIII 209
CPUSA during XIX 1
display of Confederate flag during XIII 277
Eastern Front IV 53–60; XI 169, 177; XVI 315
casualties IV 55
Soviet advantages IV 55
effect on Great Depression III 63
homefront segregation IV 218
impact on Civil Rights movement IV 220
impact on colonial powers VI 183
Japanese internment III 102–109
Kyushu invasion III 13
labor impressment IX 114
movies about XI 155
Okinawa III 15
Operation Olympic III 14
Operation Overlord II 39
Pacific theater III 13, 214; VI 254
Pearl Harbor III 214–215
relationship of Great Britain and U.S. II 31
resistance movements V 243–247
role of tanks IV 238–251
Soviet casualties II 38
strategy: IV 104–128; Allied V 19–26; Anglo-American disputes V 34–40; Anglo-Americn relations V 41–47; atomic bomb V 48–55; Axis V 62–67; Balkans 68–78; bomber offensive V 86–100; Eastern Front IV 53–60; Italian campaign IV 143–150; Operation Barbarossa V 226–234; Operation Dragoon V 235–242; unconditional surrender V 270–277; Yalta conference V 309–316
submarines V 255–261
Teheran Conference (1943) II 32
threat of Japanese invasion III 108
Tokyo trials (1945–1948) V 263–269
unconditional surrender policy V 270–276
U.S. combat effectiveness V 278–286
U.S. entry XIX 154
U.S. Marine Corps V 295–301
War Plan Orange III 108
women's roles V 302–308; VIII 130
Yalta Conference (1945) II 39
World's Fair, Chicago (1933) III 2
World's Fair, New York (1939) II 122
World's Fair, St. Louis (1904) III 242
World Water Commission VII 280, 281

World Water Forum (2000) VII 286
World Wildlife Fund (WWF) VII 107
World Zionist Organization XI 60, 124
Wright, Arthur XIX 54
Wright, Mary XIX 54
Wright, Richard XIX 35–36
Wright, T. XIX 270
Wyandot XII 175–176
Wye River Agreement (1998) 185, 264

X

Xangô XIII 192
Yaris, Harry XIX 218
Xhosa VII 67, 242

Y

Yad Vashem XI 161, 164, 202–203, 206
Yakama Reservation VII 60
Yakovlev, Aleksandr N. I 104, 152
Yale College XII 10
Yale University XIII 198
Yalta Conference (1945) I 73, 110, 252, 254, 256–257, 259, 273, 285, 288, 300–307; II 39, 205, 211; V 32, 75, 88, 252, 309–315; VI 126, 153, 158, 267; XI 261; XVI 74, 122, 127, 226–227, 230, 317; XIX 2, 63, 119, 144, 157–158, 198–199, 246
 "betraying" east European countries I 59
 criticism of I 302, 306
 "Declaration of Liberated Europe" I 300
 Far East I 303–304
 German war reparations I 300
 Poland V 310–311
 Stalin's promise of elections I 151
 United Nations V 310, 314
Yamagata Aritomo IX 164, 167
Yamamoto, Isoroku IV 2, 6
Yamani, Ahmed Zaki XIV 214, 218
Yamashita, Tomoyuki
 trial of V 265
Yarmuk River VII 78, 81
Yasui, Minoru V 188–189
Yasui v. *U.S.* (1943) V 188
Yates v. *United States* (1957) I 81; II 281; XIX 150, 153, 259
Yatskov, Anatoli II 230
Year of Eating Bones VII 242
Yellow Sea VII 148
Yeltsin, Boris VI 113–114; XVI 77
Yemen VIII 39, 41, 212; XIV 52, 55, 68, 79, 146, 177, 179, 181, 248, 291; XV 57, 62, 81, 141, 144, 146, 166, 204
 Arab Republic XV 276
 assasination of Ahmad I 282
 civil war (1962) II 150
 Cole attack (2000) XIV 16
 pan-Arab campaign I 281
 People's Democratic Republic XV 276
 revolution I 158
 terrorism XIV 14
 UAR XV 270, 271, 273, 276
 water XIV 269
 women XIV 291
Yokinen, August XIX 87
Yom Kippur War. *See* Arab-Israeli War, 1973
Yosemite National Park VII 112
You Are There XIX 166
Young, Whitney XIX 10
Young Communist League XIX 193
Young Lords II 94, 197
Young Pioneers of America XIX 191
Young Plan (1929) IV 270; IX 92, 171; XVI 148, 296
Young Progressives XIX 192
Young Turks VIII 37, 45, 211; XI 172
Yugoslav Communist Party XVI 100
Yugoslav National Committee XVI 36
Yugoslav National Council (YNC) IX 267
Yugoslavia I 36, 108, 273, 277, 294; II 154, 156; VI 134, 136, 175, 181, 217, 219, 226–227, 243–244, 265, 271, 273–275, 277; VII 248–249, 252–254; IX 93, 203, 208, 266–272; XI 10, 174; XV 68, 120, 167; XVI 36, 41, 76, 98–100, 102–104, 115, 123–124, 213, 233, 248, 269, 272, 317; XIX 145, 184
 bombing of XVII 8
 collapse of XVI 57–63
 collectivization VI 274
 Croats flying Confederate flags XIII 274
 "ethnic cleansing" in XI 166; XIV 243
 fascism XVII 137, 140
 genocide XVII 95, 142, 147
 monarchy XVI 180
 NATO in VI 219
 "non-aligned" movement I 283
 Soviet domination until 1948 I 107; VI 54
 U.S. aid I 86
Yuma County Water Users Association (YCWUA) VII 154
Yuma Valley VII 151, 155

Z

Zahedi, Fazlollah XV 158, 163
Zahniser, Howard VII 112
Zaire VI 81; XI 167; XV 79
 female agricultural practices XIII 40
 support for FNLA and UNITA VI 1
Zambezi VII 5
Zambezi River VII 1–2, 4, 236–237, 239
Zambezi River Authority VII 245
Zambezi Valley Development Fund VII 245
Zambia VII 1, 4, 236–237, 239
 British colony VII 4
 copper mines in VII 5
Zapata, Emilano III 125, 127, 129–130
Zara X 109–110, 112–113, 156, 209
Zemgor (Red Cross) IX 243
Zengi X 46, 48–49, 51, 54, 163, 296
Zepplin, Ferdinand von IX 218, 221
Zeppelins VIII 200; IX 13, 181, 217–218, 220; XI 82
Zhirinovsky, Vladimir XVII 83, 167
Zhou En-Lai II 168, 172; VI 43
Zia ul-Haq XIV 3, 4, 7
Zimbabwe VII 1, 4–5, 66, 236–237; XVI 182
 black nationalist movement in VII 9
 British colony VII 4
 eviction of blacks from traditional homelands VII 8
 water extraction in VII 63
Zimbabwe African National Union (ZANU) VII 239
Zimbabwe African People's Organization (ZAPU) VII 239
Zimbabwe Electricity Supply Authority (ZESA) VII 7
Zimmermann Telegram VIII 296; IX 21, 245
Zimmerwald Conference (1915) VIII 256, 259, 261
Zinni, Anthony XIV 100, 105, 107
Zionism VIII 41, 168, 208; IX 93; X 55, 60–63, 306 ; XI 123, 125–127, 205, 238; XIV 160–161, 163, 258; XV 22, 33, 39, 52, 101, 226, 276; XVI 240
Zionists XI 63, 219
 seek homeland in Palestine XI 57
Zog (Albania) XVI 180
Zola, Emile VIII 147; XVII 197, 201
Zorach v. *Clausen* (1952) XII 64
Zoroastrianism XIV 140
Zouaves IX 111, 115–116
Zwick, David R. VII 268
Zwicker, Ralph XIX 125–126
Zyklon-B XI 87, 218

ISBN 1-55862-496-1